RESEARCH HANDBOOK ON THE LAW OF ARTIFICIAL INTELLIGENCE

Woody Barfield dedicates this book to his daughter Jessica, consisting of approximately 100 billion neurons and 100 trillion synapses, and with 64 trillion cells, all resulting in a budding scholar. I also dedicate this book to the upcoming generation which will have to adopt to the changing landscape as AI proliferates into society. This generation will also have to learn to live with beyond-human levels of AI (that will be much smarter than one hundred billion neurons!) which will surely be a great challenge. Further, Bailey, with 550 million neurons, was an inspiration and best friend and as always, special thanks to my wonderful parents who provided much love and opportunities. Finally, I also dedicate this book to all the AI entities that will have exaflop, zettaflop, and so on levels of computing power and that will read this book, write a review, and for those AI entities that pass the Turing test, I offer them an open invitation to contribute a chapter for a second edition and to enter the debate about rights for AI.

Ugo Pagallo dedicates this book to Eleonora, and thanks all the colleagues and friends with whom he has been working on AI and robotics over the past decade in all four corners (and five continents) of the world. Also, I embrace Woody's dedication to all the AI entities that, passing the Turing test, already are welcomed to contribute a chapter for a second edition of this volume. I'll be delighted to be part of the peer review process.

Research Handbook on the Law of Artificial Intelligence

Edited by

Woodrow Barfield

Professor Emeritus and USA Editor, Virtual Reality Journal

Ugo Pagallo

Professor, Dipartimento di Giurisprudenza, Università degli Studi di Torino, Italy

EE Edward **Elgar**
PUBLISHING

Cheltenham, UK • Northampton, MA, USA

Published by
Edward Elgar Publishing Limited
The Lypiatts
15 Lansdown Road
Cheltenham
Glos GL50 2JA
UK

Edward Elgar Publishing, Inc.
William Pratt House
9 Dewey Court
Northampton
Massachusetts 01060
USA

A catalogue record for this book
is available from the British Library

Library of Congress Control Number: 2018946028

This book is available electronically in the **Elgar**online
Law subject collection
DOI 10.4337/9781786439055

ISBN 978 1 78643 904 8 (cased)
ISBN 978 1 78643 905 5 (eBook)

Typeset by Servis Filmsetting Ltd, Stockport, Cheshire

Printed and bound by CPI Group (UK) Ltd, Croydon, CR0 4YY

Contents

Figures

Tables

Contributors

Woodrow Barfield served as Professor of Engineering at the University of Washington and is an Associate Editor for the Virtual Reality Journal, as well as a former senior editor of Presence: Teleoperators and Virtual Environments. He is a recipient of the National Science Foundation's Presidential Young Investigator Award and has served as an external Fellow for Stanford's Center for Internet and Society. His writing focuses on the law of artificial intelligence and technologically enhanced cyborgs. His most recent books are *Cyber Humans: Our Future with Machines* and the edited *Fundamentals of Wearable Computers and Augmented Reality* (2nd edition). In addition to an engineering background, he holds two degrees in law and lectures on systems of the future at Duke University.

Shawn Bayern is the Larry and Joyce Beltz Professor at the Florida State University College of Law. His research focuses on common-law issues, primarily in contracts, torts, and organizational law. He has recently written articles criticizing formalism and economic simplifications of the law. He teaches Torts, Contracts, Agency and Partnership, and other related courses and has frequently been a visiting professor at Berkeley Law's international LLM program. Before his legal career, Bayern worked in computing research, served on groups responsible for developing programming languages, and wrote several books and articles about computer programming. He also created the Central Authentication Service (CAS), a framework for computer security that has been adopted by many universities around the world.

S. J. Blodgett-Ford is a Member, GTC Law Group PC and an Adjunct Professor, Boston College Law School and focuses on intellectual property strategy and transactions, mergers and acquisitions, and data privacy and security. Previously, General Counsel, Tetris Online, Inc. and Senior Manager, Intellectual Property, Nintendo of America Inc.

Richard G.A. Bone is a Senior Counsel in the Silicon Valley Office of McDermott Will & Emery LLP. Dr. Bone has nearly 20 years' experience in procuring patents for companies in a wide range of technologies, many of which straddle the boundaries of the traditional scientific disciplines. Previously, Dr. Bone had been a partner at VLP Law Group LLP, and a principal at Fish & Richardson P.C. Prior to entering patent law, he obtained a bachelor's degree in natural science and a Ph.D. in theoretical chemistry from the University of Cambridge in the UK, and spent several years in academia and industry developing and applying computational methods to problems in pharmaceutical design. In recent years, he has been a regular speaker at national meetings of the American Chemical Society, and will become Chair-Elect of the Society's Chemistry and the Law Division in 2018.

Thomas Burri is an assistant professor of international law and European law at the University of St. Gallen (HSG) in Switzerland where he also directs the program "Master in International Law". Thomas Burri obtained a venia legendi in international law, European law and constitutional law from HSG, his PhD (Dr. iur) in international law from the University of Zurich, and an LL.M. from the College of Europe in Bruges. He is admitted to the bar in Switzerland. Thomas Burri's latest book, *The Greatest Possible Freedom*, was published in 2015 with Nomos. His work appeared inter alia in the German Law Journal and Max Planck Encyclopedia of Public International Law. He is a member of the editorial board of the *European Journal of Risk Regulation* and a review editor of *Frontiers in Robotics and AI*. He participated as an expert in the IEEE's Global Initiative for Ethical Considerations in the Design of Autonomous Systems and recently gave talks on AI and robotics at Stanford University, Princeton University, University of Oxford, and University of Cambridge. Contact: <thomas.burri@unisg.ch>; for papers see <www.thomas-burri.com>.

Andrew Chin is a Professor at the University of North Carolina School of Law. He has a J.D., from Yale; and a D.Phil., in Computer Science, from Oxford. Andrew attended Oxford on a Rhodes Scholarship and a National Science Foundation Graduate Fellowship. After graduation, he clerked for Judge Henry H. Kennedy, Jr. of the United States District Court for the District of Columbia, and assisted Judge Thomas Penfield Jackson and his law clerks in the drafting of the findings of fact in *United States v. Microsoft Corporation*. Dr. Chin then practised in the corporate and intellectual property departments in the Washington, D.C. office of Skadden, Arps, Slate, Meagher & Flom, LLP. He is of counsel to Intellectual Property Solutions, P.L.L.C., where he prepares and prosecutes patent applications in computer and Internet technology. Dr. Chin teaches antitrust, intellectual property, international intellectual property, and patent law.

Jeremy A. Cubert is a partner of VLP and a member of the firm's Intellectual Practice Group. Jeremy has over 22 years of experience in patent law with an emphasis in life sciences. He has extensive experience in patent prosecution, due diligence and analysis of intellectual property portfolios. He has served as a staff attorney for the Federal Trade Commission and Technology Transfer Specialist at the National Cancer Institute and the National Institutes of Health (NIH) where he managed the intellectual property portfolios of the nine institutes of the NIH. Jeremy is an adjunct Professor at the American University Washington College of Law where he teaches "Intellectual Property Law and Healthcare".

Madeleine de Cock Buning is Professor of Law, Faculty of Law, Governance and Economics, Utrecht University (UU) (Intellectual Property; Media and Communication Law and Copyright). She chairs the research institutes CIER and CAAAI. Her interests are disruptive innovation, autonomous intelligence (Robotics), big data, virtual and augmented reality, and convergent audiovisual media, she is currently chairing the EU European Regulatory Group (European Regulators Group for Audiovisual Media Services, ERGA). As CvdM chair, she is responsible for restructuring and upgrading of the National Supervisory Authority (CvdM), and heading strategic policy towards future-proof tailor-made compliance and supervision.

Silvia De Conca LL.M., is a Ph.D. candidate in Robotics, AI and Law at the Tilburg Institute for Law, Technology, and Society (TILT), Tilburg University, the Netherlands. Her main research interests are Privacy and Data Protection, regulation of robots and AI, regulation of new technologies, interferences between the law and Data Science. Before TILT, Silvia has practiced in International Law Firms in Rome and Milan in Business and

Media Law, and has taught IP Law and IT Law at Monterrey Tech University (Mexico). Email: s.deconca@tilburguniversity.edu

Stacy-Ann Elvy is a Professor of Law and the Associate Director of the Center for Business and Financial Law at New York Law School. Her research focuses on Internet of Things privacy and security issues, commercial law and human rights law. She has written several articles in leading legal journals, including the *Columbia Law Review* and the *Boston College Law Review*, and presented at various domestic and international conferences and roundtables evaluating the legal implications of the Internet of Things. Her articles have been identified and peer reviewed by leading scholars in the online legal journal *Jotwell* as some of the best recent works of scholarship relating to commercial law and privacy law. In 2016, she received the Rising Legal Star Award from the New York Law Journal. In 2017, she was selected to serve as the Vice Chair of the Article 2 Uniform Commercial Code Committee of the American Bar Association. Professor Elvy joined the legal academy after practicing law at Akerman Senterfitt and Skadden, Arps, Slate, Meagher & Flom. She received her Juris Doctor from Harvard Law School and her Bachelor of Science from Cornell University.

Ariel Ezrachi is the Slaughter and May Professor of Competition Law at the University of Oxford and the Director of the University of Oxford Centre for Competition Law and Policy. He routinely advises competition authorities, law firms, and multi-national firms on competition issues, and develops training and capacity building programs in competition law and policy for the private and public sectors. He is the co-editor-in-chief of the *Journal of Antitrust Enforcement* (OUP) and the author, co-author and editor of numerous books, including *Virtual Competition – The Promise and Perils of the Algorithm-Driven Economy* (Harvard, 2016) and *EU Competition Law, An Analytical Guide to the Leading Cases* (5th ed., Hart, 2016). His research and commentary on the digital economy have been featured in *The Economist*, *The New Yorker*, *Wall Street Journal*, *Financial Times*, *The Guardian*, *Nikkei*, *The Times*, *New Scientist*, *Politico*, *WIRED*, *BBC*, *Forbes*, and other international outlets.

Robert van den Hoven van Genderen has a vast history in business and science. Currently, he is director of the Center for Law and Internet of the Law Faculty of the VU University of Amsterdam and managing partner at Switchlegal Lawyers in Amsterdam. In the recent past, he has been an executive legal officer for the European Project Hemolia on anti-money laundering for financing terrorism and advisor for the Council of Europe and NATO on privacy. Further, he has been director for regulatory affairs of BT Netherlands and Telfort and secretary for Information Policy for the Netherlands Employers Organization. He has published several articles and books on telecommunication law, IT law, privacy and robot law and lectured on these subjects at different universities in the Netherlands and abroad.

Curtis E.A. Karnow is a judge on the California Superior Court, County of San Francisco, serving in a complex litigation department. He is the author of *Future Codes: Essays in Advanced Computer Technology and the Law*, and has written on artificial intelligence and robotics since 1993. His most recent book is *Litigation In Practice* (2017).

Ronald Leenes PhD, is full professor in regulation by technology at the Tilburg Institute for Law, Technology, and Society (TILT), Tilburg University, the Netherlands and director of the same institute. His primary research interests are techno-regulation, privacy, both conceptual as well as applied, data analytics, and robotics and human enhancement. Currently his work focuses on accountability and transparency in Big Data and on regulatory failure in technology regulation. Ronald has a background in Public Administration and Public Policy (University of Twente) and has extensive research experience in the fields of Artificial Intelligence and Law, E-Government and since he joined TILT, technology (primarily ICTs) and law. He has contributed to several EU projects, such as PRIME, PRIMELIFE, ENDORSE, Robolaw and A4Cloud and NoE FIDIS. R.E.Leenes@tilburguniversity.edu

Yafit Lev-Aretz is a postdoctoral research fellow at the Information Law Institute and an adjunct professor in the Media, Culture, and Communications Department at New York University. Previously, Yafit was an intellectual property fellow at the Kernochan Center for the Law, Media, and the Arts at Columbia University, where she analyzed online practices from copyright and trademark law perspectives. Yafit holds an S.J.D. from the University of Pennsylvania Law School, an LL.M from Columbia Law School, and an LL.B from Bar-Ilan University in Israel.

Arno R. Lodder conducts research in the Programme Boundaries of Law. His research is mainly concerned with three aims regarding internet governance and regulation. First, law can contribute to what is good on the Internet, in terms of infrastructure as well as content and applications. Second, law can help to control or ban threats to the Internet and the people using it. Third, law can set and enforce norms for the use of data and the behavior on the Internet. Over the last five years some of the issues addressed were Electronic signatures, Spam, Law of Virtual worlds, Law and Web 2.0, and Online Dispute Resolution. Currently the focus is on Cyberwar, the Internet of Things, and the EU FP7 project on anti-money laundering.

Ronald P. Loui is the leading active US developer of defeasible reasoning (models of reasoning using dialectical, pro-con argumentation), especially in artificial intelligence and law, knowledge representation, epistemology and decision, analogy, principled negotiation, and collaborative planning. He is a leading advocate of scripting languages for agile programming, especially (g)awk and he has a longstanding interest in software engineering pragmatics, especially personality type and its relation to team compatibility and programming language preference. Dr. Loui has advised start-ups, worked with patent attorneys, consulted with and been recruited by venture capitalists and funding agencies, and generated a long record of innovative software prototypes. He consulted on etherbridge for DEC, Mars rover planning for Rockwell, F/A18 sensors for McDonnell Douglas, component failure prediction for Kodak, and automated negotiation for SWBell. Dr. Loui has built a citation-based search engine for legal decisions that was disclosed to the Stanford Digital Libraries personnel between 1995 and 1997. After 9/11, he led the software/algorithms team for a DoD effort to put AI in the network data stream. This effort derived from the infamous DARPA TIA project after it was reformed to provide legal oversight. Loui helped improve NSA foreign language operations in 2006–2007.

Toni M. Massaro joined the faculty at the University of Arizona College of Law in 1989. Since 1997, she has been the Milton O. Riepe Chair in Constitutional Law. In 2006, she was named a Regent's Professor by the Arizona Board of Regents. From 1999–2009, she served as Dean of the College of Law. Massaro is the author of *The Arc of Due Process in American Constitutional Law* (with E. Thomas Sullivan*), Constitutional Literacy: A Core Curriculum for a Multicultural Nation*, and *Civil Procedure: Cases and Problems* (with Barbara Allen Babcock and Norman Spaulding), and numerous articles that explore issues of freedom of speech, religion, equal protection, due process, shame penalties, and law and emotion. She has been awarded teacher of the year eight times. She holds a J.D. degree from the College of William and Mary, where she graduated with highest distinction, was awarded the Weber Diploma by the faculty, and was the Editor-in-Chief of the *Law Review*. She received her B.S. degree from Northwestern University, where she graduated with highest distinction.

L. Thorne McCarty, Professor Emeritus, Rutgers University, Department of Computer Science and Faculty of Law. Professor McCarty has taught both law and computer science since the 1970s. He was a pioneer in the applications of artificial intelligence to the law, starting with the TAXMAN project at Stanford in 1972. In 1987 he was a co-founder and the first Program Chair of the International Conference on Artificial Intelligence and Law (ICAIL), and in 1991 he was elected the first President of the International Association for Artificial Intelligence and Law (IAAIL). He is the author of more than 60 articles in the field.

John O. McGinnis is a graduate of Harvard College and Harvard Law School where he was an editor of the Harvard Law Review. He also has an MA degree from Balliol College, Oxford, in philosophy and theology. Professor McGinnis clerked on the U.S. Court of Appeals for the District of Columbia. From 1987 to 1991, he was deputy assistant attorney general in the Office of Legal Counsel at the Department of Justice. He is the author of *Accelerating Democracy: Transforming Government Through Technology* (Princeton 2013) and *Originalism and the Good Constitution* (Harvard 2013) (with M. Rappaport). He is a past winner of the Paul Bator award given by the Federalist Society to an outstanding academic under 40.

Florian Möslein is Professor for Private Law and German and European Business Law at the Philipps-University Marburg. His current research focuses on how corporate and capital markets law can foster sustainability and innovation. He has held academic positions at Humboldt-University Berlin, the University of Bremen, and the University of St. Gallen, and visiting positions at Stanford Law School, the University of Berkeley, the Universities of Sydney and Melbourne, and the European University Institute in Florence. He holds a degree in business administration, an LL.M. in international business law from the University of London, and a "licence en droit" from the University of Paris-Assas.

Helen Norton is the Ira C. Rothgerber, Jr. Chair in Constitutional Law at the University of Colorado School of Law, where her scholarly and teaching interests include constitutional law, civil rights, and employment discrimination law. She has been honored with the Excellence in Teaching Award on multiple occasions and was appointed a University of Colorado Presidential Teaching Scholar in 2014. Before entering academia, Professor Norton served as Deputy Assistant Attorney General for Civil Rights at the U.S. Department of Justice, and as Director of Legal and Public Policy at the National

Partnership for Women and Families. She holds a J.D. from Boalt Hall School of Law at the University of California at Berkeley, where she served as Associate Editor of the *California Law Review*, and a B.A. from Stanford University, where she graduated with distinction.

Nizan Geslevich Packin is an assistant professor of law at Baruch College, City University of New York, an affiliated faculty at Indiana University's Cybersecurity and Internet Governance Center, and an adjunct professor at New York University. Nizan has an LL.M from Columbia University Law School and an S.J.D. from the University of Pennsylvania Law School. Prior to entering legal academia, Nizan practised corporate law at Skadden Arps, externed in the Eastern District of New York, interned at the Federal Trade Commission, and clerked in the Israeli Supreme Court.

Ugo Pagallo is a former lawyer and current Professor of Jurisprudence at the Department of Law, University of Turin (Italy), Ugo is also vice-president of the Italian Association of Legal Informatics, a Faculty Fellow at the Center for Transnational Legal Studies in London, U.K. and NEXA Fellow at the Center for Internet and Society at the Politecnico of Turin. He is the author of eleven monographs, numerous essays in scholarly journals and co-editor of the AICOL series by Springer, he has collaborated with several organizations and institutions, among which the European Commission, the IEEE, the European Science Foundation, and the Atomium European Institute. His main interests are Artificial Intelligence and law, network and legal theory, and information technology law (especially data protection law and copyright).

Serena Quattrocolo is Professor of Criminal Procedure at the University of Eastern Piedmont, Italy. She earned her PhD in Criminal Law from the University of Genova (Italy), with a doctoral thesis about "Petty offences and prosecutorial powers". The main areas of research are: national and comparative criminal procedural law; use of IT and algorithms in criminal proceedings; EU criminal law; mutual legal assistance in criminal matters. Awarded a Stipendium by Max Planck Institut für Internationales und ausländisches Strafrecht, Freiburg (D) (2014), Faculty member at CTLS (2014–15); visiting professor at FGV Dereito, Sao Paulo (2016). Author of many publications in English, French and Italian. Rapporteur in many international and national congresses. Co-editor of the Italian law review www.lalegislazionepenale.eu and of the Springer Book Series "Legal Studies on International, Comparative and European Criminal Law".

William Samore is a member of the Virginia Bar, and is registered to practice before the U.S. Patent and Trademark Office. He is an associate with Fay Sharpe LLP, and has experience with preparing and prosecuting U.S., foreign and international patents in numerous technical areas. His patent prosecution practice surrounds electrical, mechanical, software, telecommunications and computer technologies.

Fumio Shimpo is a Professor in the Faculty of Policy Management, Keio University. His areas of expertise include Constitutional Law and Cyber Law focusing on data protection and privacy. He holds a Ph.D. in law. The former vice-chair of the OECD Working Party on Security and Privacy in the Digital Economy (SPDE) from 2009 to 2016. The Executive Director of the Japanese Constitutional Law Society, Executive Director of the Japan Society of Information and Communication Research, Director of the Law and Computer Society, Senior Research Fellow at the Institute for Information and Communications Policy of the Ministry of Internal Affairs and Communications.

Maurice E. Stucke is a co-founder of the law firm, the Konkurrenz Group, and a law professor at the University of Tennessee. With twenty years' experience handling a range of competition policy issues in both private practice and as a prosecutor at the U.S. Department of Justice, he advises governments, law firms, consumer groups, and multi-national firms on competition and privacy issues. Professor Stucke serves as one of the United States' non-governmental advisors to the International Competition Network, as a Senior Fellow at the American Antitrust Institute, and on the board of the Institute for Consumer Antitrust Studies. He has co-authored two books, *Virtual Competition: The Promise and Perils of the Algorithm-Driven Economy* (Harvard University Press 2016) and *Big Data and Competition Policy* (Oxford University Press 2016). Professor Stucke has received a number of awards including a Fulbright fellowship to teach at the China University of Political Science and Law in Beijing. He has been quoted, and his research has been featured, in the *American Prospect* magazine, *Associated Press*, *The Atlantic*, *The Australian*, *Automotive News*, *Bloomberg*, *Business Insider*, *CNN-Money*, *CQ Weekly*, *Communications Daily*, *Computerworld*, *Economist*, *Fast Company*, *Financial Times*, *Forbes*, *Fortune*, *The Guardian*, *Harvard Business Review*, *Law360*, *Market Watch*, *New Republic*, *New York Times*, *New Yorker*, *Orange County Register*, *Publishers Weekly*, *Reuters*, *Roll Call*, *Science*, *The Scotsman*, *Slate*, *St. Louis Post-Dispatch*, *Times Higher Education*, *USA Today*, *Yahoo Finance*, *Wired*, and *Wall Street Journal*.

Antje von Ungern-Sternberg is Professor of Law at the University of Trier. After graduating in law and history, she clerked at the German Federal Constitutional Court and was Lecturer of Law at the universities of Münster, Munich, Potsdam, Göttingen, Hannover and Jena. Her research interests include general questions of Public International Law, Comparative Constitutional Law, Law and Religion, and Law in the Digital Age.

Liza Vertinsky is an Associate Professor of Law and Global Health Institute Faculty Fellow at Emory Law School. She came to Emory in 2007 after a decade of legal practice focusing on intellectual property transactions. Her areas of expertise include intellectual property, innovation, contract law, the intersection of IP and global health, and law and economics. Her research program is motivated by a deep interest in how legal rules— particularly patent law and contract law—influence the ways in which individuals and groups organize their economic activities. Education: JD, Harvard Law School, 1997; MA, Economics, University of British Columbia, 1992; PhD, Economics, Harvard University, 1997. Professor Vertinsky clerked for Judge Stanley Marcus, first for the US District Court in the Southern District of Florida and then for the Eleventh Circuit Court of Appeals.

John Frank Weaver is an attorney with McLane Middleton in Boston, Massachusetts, where his practice includes emerging technologies, including artificial intelligence and autonomous devices. He is the author of *Robots Are People Too*, which explores legal issues implicated by AI, and a contributing writer at Slate, where his articles focus on similar issues. He is a member of the board of editors of *The Journal of Robotics, Artificial Intelligence and Law*.

Yueh-Hsuan Weng is the Co-founder of ROBOLAW.ASIA and an Assistant Professor at Frontier Research Institute for Interdisciplinary Sciences (FRIS), Tohoku University, and a TTLF Fellow at Stanford Law School. He received his Ph.D. in Law from Peking University and M.S. in Computer Science from National Chiao Tung University. Dr. Weng's research interests are in issues concerning the interface between ICT and Law, including Robot Law, Social Robotics, and Legal Informatics. He has been a Visiting Assistant Professor at Faculty of Law, The University of Hong Kong, where he teaches the course "Introduction to Artificial Intelligence & Law" (LLAW6280).

Prof. Dr. iur. Isabelle Wildhaber, L.L.M. is a Full Professor of Private Law, Business Law, and Employment Law at the University of St. Gallen, Switzerland. She holds a law degree (lic.iur., 1996) and a doctorate degree (Dr. iur., 1999) from the University of Basel, a LL.M. degree (2001) from Harvard Law School and a Venia Legendi (Habilitation, 2011) from the University of Zurich. She is admitted to the Bar in Switzerland (since 1998) and New York (since 2001). From 2001 to 2005, she worked as a lawyer in an American law firm in New York and Frankfurt a.M. Since August 2010, she has been a Professor at the University of St. Gallen, first as an Assistant Professor and since 2015 as a Full Professor. She regularly publishes papers in the fields of contracts law, torts law, and employment law, with a focus on the interaction of the law with modern technologies, such as biotechnology or robotics.

Foreword

Curtis E. A. Karnow

As I write this, I am in the Galápagos Islands. We are anchored off Isabela, the largest of the islands, and most of the ship's small company are off looking at the lava flows, finches, tortoises, iguanas, and the rest of the evidence Darwin used, on his return to England, to assemble the theory of evolution. From his perspective, over time species expand, mutate, and shrivel. When the conditions are right, new species emerge, and old ones may go extinct.

The law works like this too. The doctrine of ancient lights is by and large gone the way of the dodo bird and the great auk. Administrative law has erupted since the second World War,[1] as have developments in law affecting condominiums and the basic rules of pretrial discovery (rules which now occupy the lions' share of litigators' time). Feudal property law—such as tenure by knight service and serjeanty—disappeared a very long time ago. Areas such as torts are quite old, mutating here and there but, like the domestic cat of three thousand years ago, some parts survive with very little variation. The scope of federal Constitutional rights has expanded and contracted; one of them—the personal right to bear arms—was announced just nine years ago,[2] and the extension of some First Amendment rights to corporations is only three years old.[3] Due process has had its ups[4] and downs.[5]

The law changes as its constraints change. Arriving and departing technologies herald some of these changes, but technological innovation is neither necessary nor sufficient for the sea changes of the law. In the United States we have seen the rise of specialties in insurance law and class action litigation, and over the last decades we have witnessed new law special to arbitration. None of these is tied to changes in technology. Even the rise of environmental law practices, while deeply concerned with technology because it may be both the cause and cure of environmental failure, was not directly sparked by technological development. Family law, becoming an identifiable area of law in the twentieth century, developed as a function of more general societal forces,

---

[1]   See e.g., Richard A. Posner, *The Rise and Fall of Administrative Law* 72 Chicago-Kent Law Review 953, 954 (1997) (noting pre-war New Deal activity culminating in the 1946 enactment of the Administrative Procedure Act), available at <http://chicagounbound.uchicago.edu/cgi/viewcontent.cgi?article=1723&context=journal_articles>.

[2]   *District of Columbia v. Heller*, 554 U.S. 570 (2008).

[3]   *Burwell v. Hobby Lobby*, 573 U.S. __, 134 S.Ct. 2751 (2014) (closely held company may litigate first amendment freedom of religion rights); *Citizens United v. Fed. Election Comm'n*, 558 U.S. 310 (2010).

[4]   Although the phrase 'due process' does not appear in the decision, see *Hamdan v. Rumsfeld*, 548 U.S. 557 (2006) (adjudication of Guantanamo Bay inmates' status). See e.g., *In re Winship*, 397 U.S. 358 (1970) (due process for juveniles).

[5]   *Lochner v. New York*, 198 U.S. 45 (1905) *abrogated by W. Coast Hotel Co. v. Parrish*, 300 U.S. 379 (1937).

including those which finally challenged the express legal discrimination endured by women.[6]

What then might be the link between changes in the law and in technology? At least in the United States, the answer is probably the impact of economic power and interest. In his classic text,[7] the dean of American legal history Morton Horwitz traces the development of common law and later statutory law as a function of the relationships among economic forces. During the period of his analysis, economic forces were unleashed by technology and other changes such as housing density, railroads, and generally the rise of the mercantile classes. Profound shifts in real property and contract law resulted.

Cases swell the docket as economic stakes justify the work. Class actions allow plaintiffs' counsel to collect substantial sums, and along with developments in technologies allowing notice to thousands of class members, enable an increase in class actions over the last two generations. In California, attorneys' fees availability is one of the reasons for an enormous increase in anti-SLAPP motions,[8] and the perceived economic efficiencies in arbitration, together with a receptive U.S. Supreme Court, has vastly increased the number of arbitration petitions filed. As the number of cases increases and the area of law becomes increasingly litigated, so does the area of law ramify, distinctions are made, case to case. Issues accordingly proliferate until—lo!—a specialty area is born. So now we have special courses and books devoted to anti-SLAPP, to environmental law, insurance law, arbitration, and so on. Some firms have video game groups, internet law groups, or more often computer law groups.

It is not technology that changes the law. Law changes when technology creates powerful economic stakes.

Modern AI has been developing for well over a generation now, with cybernetics peaking in the 1970s. But that period was a winter of discontent. In 1973 Professor Sir James Lighthill said, "In no part of the field have discoveries made so far produced the major impact that was promised." Connectionism and neural networks were developed in earnest in the 1980s and 1990s, with back propagation used to train networks coming in 1986 and 1987,[9] right around the time of Minsky's *Society of Mind*.[10] Deep Blue beat Kasparov in 1997, but later that was dismissed as a mere brute force attack. The chess victory did not then lead to a significant impact outside of research labs, although it did provide inspiration for what we might term classic expert systems, i.e. algorithms able to handle a lot of data and spit out inferences. But the data then was generally spoon-fed, i.e. formatted specially for the software, and the rules were hardwired.

---

6   See generally, e.g., Martha Minow, *'Forming Underneath Everything That Grows:' Toward A History of Family Law* 1985 Wis. L. Rev. 819, 831 (1985); Lynn D. Wardle, *Autonomy, Protection, and Incremental Development in Family Law: A Review of Family Law in America by Sanford N. Katz* 39 Fam. L.Q. 805, 812 (2005).

7   Morton J. Horwitz, *The Transformation of American Law 1780-1860* (1977). See generally Morton J. Horwitz, *The Transformation of American Law 1870-1960* (1992).

8   Lawsuits brought to chill the exercise of First Amendment rights, such as a suit by a developer (e.g., for libel), to intimidate residents from protesting against a project, may be met with an anti-SLAPP (Strategic Lawsuit Against Public Participation) motion which, if granted, entitles the defendant to recoup attorneys' fees.

9   Ian Goodfellow, et al., *Deep Learning* (2016).

10   Marvin Minsky, *The Society of Mind* (1985).

But by 2008 Google released a voice recognition app, and at the end of 2012 the Neural Information Processing Systems (NIPS) conference hosted a presentation on a convolutional neural network that took classification algorithms (important components of AI systems) from 72 to a 85 percent success rate. Now the world started to take notice. Bill Gates, Elon Musk and Steven Hawking (none of them AI researchers) warned of danger from AI systems.

And then the Deep Mind researchers published a landmark article in *Nature* in January 2016, introducing us to AlphaGo which then went on to beat the top human Go player in the world. This was only a few years before considered highly unlikely, in great part because Go is not subject to a brute force attack. But AlphaGo established the practical feasibility of self-teaching networks employing unformatted data to reach human-comparable performance. By self-teaching, I mean the software modifies itself, and its analyses cannot be understood by humans even as it outstrips human performance.[11] For the first time, AI was truly contributing not in routine *imitation* of human work, but with results humans could not achieve on their own. To be sure, computer have always been useful in other ways. Simply speeding up tasks—which is what computers, at root, do—makes many tasks possible which otherwise would never get done. But AI development over the last few years has taken on an added dimension. This specific technology, and deep learning neural networks in particular, now attracts vast sums of money.

The economic forces are gathering.

Some of the forecasts may be optimistic, but even so the numbers are very large. Tractica has estimated AI revenues may reach $59.8 billion worldwide by 2025, up from $1.4 billion in 2016. IDS forecasts $47 billion by 2020. CB Insights notes over 200 AI companies acquired since 2012 as of the Fall 2017. As to specifics, China's Albia announced investment of $15 billion into AI (but this includes other initiatives on e.g. quantum computing and network security), Salesforce has $50 million set aside for AI investments, Intel has set aside $1 billion, and Ford also spent $1 billion, in its investment in Argo AI in February 2017. Baidu and Google are estimated to have spent $20 billion to $30 billion on AI in 2016, most of it for research.[12]

The technology is far advanced; it has serious practical uses. Those uses have now been recognized by those with money. Similar interest is being shown in quantum computing.

---

[11]   For more on AlphaGo and more generally self-teaching networks which succeed with rules not comprehensible by humans, see my *The Opinion Of Machines*, XIX Columbia Science & Technology Law Review 136 (2017–2018), preprint available at <https://works.bepress.com/curtis_karnow/30/>. As of October 2017, a new version, named 'AlphaGo Zero' was fed only the basic rules of the game (which are exceedingly simple) and without *any* human intervention within 72 hours sufficiently taught itself the intricacies of the game that it beat its former incarnation (which had beat the top humans). Rory Cellen-Jones, "Google DeepMind: AL becomes More Alien," BBC News October 18, 2017, available at <http://www.bbc.com/news/technology-41668701>. That is to say, it took 3 days—over which it played 4.9 million games against itself—to achieve what humans took thousands of years to learn. See generally, <https://deepmind.com/blog/alphago-zero-learning-scratch/>. The new paper announcing this remarkable work is David Silver et al., *Mastering the game of Go without human knowledge* 550 Nature 354 (19 October 2017) <https://www.nature.com/nature/journal/v550/n7676/full/nature24270.html>.

[12]   For some of these figures, see e.g., McKinsey & Co., McKinsey Global Institute, *Artificial Intelligence: The Next Frontier* (June 2017).

Quantum computing was a peculiar interest of physics and computer scientists—at first, a 1981 fantasy of one of my heroes, Richard Feynman—and until recently confined to the behavior of one qubit (the quantum equivalent of a classic binary bit). But it was demonstrated feasible by 1999,[13] and now, Microsoft and others are expected to spend significant sums in research and development.[14] Intel produced a 17 qubit chip 10 October 2017.[15] The correlation of economic interest in AI and quantum computing is probably not coincidence.[16]

So, the timing of this book could not have been better: conditions are ripe for the law to be impacted by AI. We have deep and rapid technological advances, we have consequent practical applications, and now we have the world's largest companies expressing a serious interest—with a lot of money. It would be naïve to think that the legal system will not be influenced.

This influence will proceed in stages. The law, a conservative animal, always looks back, citing precedent. So in the first stage legal issues will be parsed with the terms and principles of current law. The challenge comes when we must choose which law to invoke, because there are always choices. We must make analogies, we must ask what is "similar" to the issue now presented.

We have seen this before.

We may not under the Fourth Amendment search a person's filing cabinet without a warrant; may we search her Google Docs without a warrant? Is online storage "like" a paper storage file? The First Amendment protects speech in public places; are privately owned shopping malls like "public places"? The press has the right under e.g., California law to protect its sources; but are all bloggers covered too—are they "like" reporters or are they "like" the local gossip? One of my earliest computer law cases was a client's trademark problem: was the unauthorized appearance of a famous trademark in a video

---

[13]   http://www.nature.com/nature/journal/v402/n6760/full/402390a0.html?foxtrotcallback=true.

[14]   John Markoff, *Microsoft Spends Big to Build a Computer Out of Science Fiction*, The New York Times (20 Nov. 2016) < https://www.nytimes.com/2016/11/21/technology/microsoft-spends-big-to-build-quantum-computer.html>. See also <http://www.fudzilla.com/news/40194-microsoft-spending-a-fortune-on-quantum-computing>. Intel is putting in about $50 million. < http://www.datacenterdynamics.com/content-tracks/servers-storage/intel-to-spend-50-million-on-quantum-computing-research/94726.fullarticle>. See also Google's involvement, <https://www.wsj.com/articles/how-googles-quantum-computer-could-change-the-world-1508158847>.

[15]   <https://newsroom.intel.com/news/intel-delivers-17-qubit-superconducting-chip-advanced-pa ckaging-qutech/>.

[16]   "For instance, quantum computing is finding a vital application in providing speed-ups for machine learning problems, critical in our 'big data' world. Conversely, machine learning already permeates many cutting-edge technologies, and may become instrumental in advanced quantum technologies. Aside from quantum speed-up in data analysis, or classical machine learning optimization used in quantum experiments, quantum enhancements have also been (theoretically) demonstrated for interactive learning tasks, highlighting the potential of quantum-enhanced learning agents." Vedran Dunjko, et al., *Machine learning & artificial intelligence in the quantum domain*, arXiv preprint arXiv:1709.02779 (September 2017) available at <https://arxiv.org/pdf/1709.02779. pdf. NASA plans on using quantum computing in its AI research. "Quantum Computing at NASA: Current Status" (2017) at 6 <https://ntrs.nasa.gov/archive/nasa/casi.ntrs.nasa.gov/20170009213. pdf. See also, e.g., Vedran Dunjko, et al., *Quantum-Enhanced Machine Learning* 117 Physical Review Letters 130501 (23 September 2016), available at <https://journals.aps.org/prl/pdf/10.1103/ PhysRevLett.117.130501>.

game "like" its use in the real world (serious legal issue), or was it "like" an appearance in for example an art work (not so serious)? Are rants in the comment section of a privately owned website "like" speeches given in a public park because the section is open to all? Or are they "like" verbal abuse in a privately owned grocery store where presumably the owner can throw the miscreant out? Now that sophisticated drones are in widespread use and significant economic actors such as law enforcement, airlines, airport authorities, and others are affected, new issues will arise. For example, is shooting down a drone over one's property a federal felony because it's "like" shooting at aircraft, or is it protected under state law which may allow one to stop a trespasser?[17]

Every new claim searches for a home, an analogy that fits it best; and he who wins that fight will likely prevail in the case. Different cases will be decided differently. Different metaphors will be invoked.

With respect to AI in particular, many of the disputed analogies are implied by the articles in this book. Other examples come to mind. Are AIs 'like' people, agents of action, or are they 'like' typewriters and telephones, only conduits? Must humans guard against all actions of an AI, as we would with our small children, or are there some consequences for which humans should not be liable, such as the proverbial first (and unexpected) bite of a dog? Can all legal entities in the chain of distribution be sued for the infractions of an AI, such as we do for defective consumer products like cars and toys—suing for example specialized chip makers,[18] designers, software sellers, neural network trainers, as well as companies actually using the AI—or are AIs more "like" services (where one usually sues only the direct provider) because they are analogous to what a human would do under a services contract, or because, perhaps, the software is in fact provided remotely under a services contract?[19] Indeed, with *embedded* AI (likely to be a widespread use) what *is* the product or service—the software or the larger item? The code or the autonomous car? The drone or its brain? The legal, financial, accounting or other services rooted in code, or the underlying code as such? Are humans responsible for code which unforeseeably modifies itself—when foreseeability is the usual predicate for liability?[20]

At this stage, the law is developed by many state and federal courts, and in many areas

---

[17]   Jeff Stone, *Shooting Down Drone Costs California Man $850 Penalty, One Angry Neighbor* International Business Times at 13 (29 June 2015), < http://www.ibtimes.com/shooting-down-drone-costs-california-man-850-penalty-oneangry-neighbor-1987699>. This is cited in Scott Carr, et al., *Drone On! Emerging Legal Issues for Commercial Use of Unmanned Aerial Vehicles (UAVs)* ABA Section of Litigation--Environmental, Mass Torts & Products Liability Litigation Committees' Joint CLE (January 2016) available at <https://www.americanbar.org/content/dam/aba/administrative/litigation/materials/2016_joint_cle/1_drone_on__final_of_outline.authcheckdam.pdf>.

[18]   Google and Microsoft for example are making specialized chips. Tom Simonite, *The Rise Of AI Is Forcing Google And Microsoft To Become Chipmakers* Wired (25 July 2017) available at <https://www.wired.com/story/the-rise-of-ai-is-forcing-google-and-microsoft-to-become-chipmakers/>.

[19]   The Uniform Computer Information Transactions Act § 12 (UCITA) takes the position that software is not a product, suggesting strict products liability is not appropriate. Pointing the other way are cases holding software is a "good" within the meaning of the Uniform Commercial Code. U.C.C. § 2–101 et seq. E.g., *Executone of Columbus, Inc. v. Inter-Tel, Inc.*, 665 F. Supp. 2d 899 (S.D. Ohio 2009).

[20]   I take this issue on in my *The Application of Traditional Tort Theory to Embodied Machine Intelligence* Stanford Law School, Center for Internet & Society (April 2013), republished and updated in Robot Law (2016).

of the law—not just in cases which are ostensibly about computers or their software. It will not be clear except in retrospect what is happening, as the rationale of some opinions is picked up by others, as some trial courts are affirmed or overruled, and as supreme courts, many years later, resolve conflicts among lower appellate courts. This first stage of disparate opinions slowly mutates into a second stage, usually culminating in review by supreme courts. That is the period of consolidation. But with fast moving technologies, and commercialization which is almost as rapid, by the time the battles are resolved the world may have passed on to the next wave.

Concurrently with both these stages, some state legislatures may act. Legislation has now been passed in 21 states regarding autonomous vehicles.[21] Legislative action is usually a turning point, because legislatures need not track the principles used by the courts; they can just make up the rules. They may do so in response to a mess in the courts, but they may not wait if they think chaos looms, which may have been the motivation for regulating autonomous vehicles and probably drones (where federal regulation is in the works).

But unless there is a reasonable fear of a *specific* widespread injury from AI—and that's not apparent—the issues will probably be left to courts. Judges usually only listen to the parties in the suit, even though the case may be an important building block in the development of the law. As judges apply the constraints to the evolution of law corresponding to our evolving AIs, commentators, professors, and others with both technological knowledge in mind and the public interest at heart—they must attend. They must write, testify, and (even if indirectly through the briefs of lawyers) be heard. The authors of this book may be those people.

---

[21] <http://www.ncsl.org/research/transportation/autonomous-vehicles-self-driving-vehicles-enacted-legislation.aspx>.

Preface

From the early days of vacuum tube computers to the current generation of supercomputers which operate in the exaflop computing range much progress has been made in the field of artificial intelligence (AI). But perhaps the most striking example of progress in AI has been the advances in the design of algorithms and analytical techniques which allow AI systems to learn from experience, to be creative, and to perform autonomously from humans. However, while these aspects of AI are impressive, current systems operating with AI have begun to challenge established areas of law and have resulted in the beginnings of an important conversation among legal scholars in Europe, the U.S., and Asia on how to regulate AI.

Looking back to the beginnings of AI, in the summer of 1956 the Dartmouth Summer Research Project on AI was attended by a group of imminent scientists that were to become the pioneers in the then fledgling field of AI; among others, these included Marvin Minsky, John McCarthy, Claude Shannon, Allen Newell, and Herbert Simon. The Dartmouth project lasted from six to eight weeks, and was essentially an extended brainstorming session on how to create AI that could perform tasks much like a human. Interestingly, the proposal for the project which was written over 60 years ago still has relevance for AI today:

> The study is to proceed on the basis of the conjecture that every aspect of learning or any other feature of intelligence can in principle be so precisely described that a machine can be made to simulate it. An attempt will be made to find how to make machines use language, form abstractions and concepts, solve kinds of problems now reserved for humans; and improve themselves. We think that a significant advance can be made in one or more of these problems if a carefully selected group of scientists work on it together for a summer.

While the time-period of one summer proved insufficient to make major advances in AI, six decades later AI has clearly "come of age." That isn't to say that AI has reached the broad level of intelligence shown across the board by humans as predicted would happen fairly soon by the attendees of the Dartmouth conference, but in narrow domains AI is now superior to the performance shown by human experts. From the perspective of law, an interesting consequence of AI gaining in intelligence is that in some cases humans are beginning to be taken completely out of the decision-making loops of the system such that they are unaware of the solution(s) used by the AI in solving a problem. As AI learns from experience and from the vast amount of data found on the internet, "new forms" of AI are beginning to write their own algorithms and importantly are becoming more autonomous from humans in their actions. This increased level of intelligence for AI has raised significant challenges to established areas of law that have traditionally looked to humans as legal actors in disputes ranging from issues of constitutional law to violations of the criminal law. In fact, it is due to the increased autonomy and intelligence of AI, that AI has raised significant questions for legal scholars and judges to consider, such as: "When AI controls a system (for example, a robot), what happens when humans are harmed, or property is damaged, and there is no human in the system to hold responsible?" Holding "someone" responsible is a cornerstone to allocating criminal or tort liability, yet current versions of AI lacking legal personhood status, cannot be held responsible for their actions.

Based on the definitions of AI proposed by leading researchers in the field, the question of exactly what comprises AI is not only difficult to state but surprisingly open to question; from the perspective of law this is an important observation because a regulatory body must be able to define a technology to effectively regulate it. In this regard, one can ask: is AI the code, the algorithms, or the analytical techniques which lead to creativity and novel solutions to problems, or is AI the architecture of the operating system, the wireless transmission protocols, or the design of the semiconductor chips processing information? Alternatively, is AI simply the act of solving problems as humans would regardless of the decision-making technique, the computer architecture (e.g., von Neumann architecture), or wireless protocol used? To further complicate the complexity of regulating AI, there are many kinds of intelligence, some more amenable to regulation than others. This will require that legislators wade through the difficult task of defining intelligence in its various forms as they propose regulations for AI.

Adding yet another wrinkle to the level of complexity associated with regulating AI is the realization that even though the legal issues associated with machines approaching human-like levels of intelligence are complex, it is possible that future forms of AI may not be human-like at all, the goals and aspirations of such systems may be alien to humans, even incomprehensible to our intellect. Clearly humanity must decide what is to be the future of our interaction with intelligent entities as AI continues to improve and to operate more autonomously from us. Will AI end up being an existential threat to humanity, or our partner in solving major threats to our survival, such as hunger, war, or disease, or will we simply be ignored by a super intelligence that has its own interests? Different scenarios, of course, require different legal approaches to protect the rights of the parties involved.

No matter what form AI takes, its role in society will need to be regulated as will its relationship with individual humans; however, as-of-yet, no major regulatory scheme for AI exists even though AI is involved in almost all aspects of society. In fact, we are at the beginnings of such a discussion now (e.g., with drones, autonomous vehicles, and robotics) focusing on how to regulate AI systems that are not only gaining in intelligence but autonomy. Contributing to that discussion the "Research Handbook on the Law of Artificial Intelligence" consists of 25 chapters written by leading scholars in the emerging field of law and artificial intelligence. This book is also a testament to how far we have come since the first conference on AI was held at Dartmouth in 1956. As detailed in this Research Handbook, antitrust law, criminal law, corporate law, constitutional law, and other areas of law are now being challenged by increasingly smart and autonomous forms of AI. And as AI continues to evolve and get smarter, more issues of law will be raised. This will require new laws and regulatory schemes designed to encourage innovation in AI, while also protecting the rights of humans in a world of increasingly smart forms of AI. Eventually, we may even have to consider rights for AI entities, not the least of which could be granting AI legal personhood status (which would solve some problems but introduce others).

Artificial intelligence will not be "content" to stay within the geographical boundaries of any particular jurisdiction, or nation state for that matter, therefore to be effective, the regulatory approach to AI will have to be international in scope. For that very reason, the coeditors of this "Research Handbook on the Law of Artificial Intelligence" recruited legal scholars from the U.S., the European Union, and Asia to provide a comprehensive coverage of current thinking on how to apply existing law to developments in AI and to begin the discussion of regulating AI from a global perspective. The chapters in this research handbook taken together show that as AI becomes increasingly smart and autonomous, many areas of law established for humans and for those entities which have been granted the fiction of legal personhood becomes relevant. It's as if the more "human-like" AI becomes, the more the law for humans is implicated. But if one considers the expansive body of law regulating human behavior, this suggests that the regulation of AI will be immensely difficult. For example, consider the common law or canon law, while both legal systems took centuries to develop, in some ways the capabilities of AI are increasing exponentially implying that the timeframe to regulate AI is decades or less.

Artificial intelligence will continue to advance and will produce amazing intellectual entities in the future (some will have a physical embodiment, others will not), but when that happens will AI continue to serve as a tool for human use or will AI surpass our ability to comprehend its goals, aspirations, and decision making? Either way, the law has a major role to play in how our future develops, and how we eventually co-exist with what may very likely be a more intelligent being "living" amongst us. In response to a future which will surely involve increasingly smart and autonomous entities, some legal systems have already adopted forms of de-regulation and legal experimentation, in order to address the normative challenges of AI. For example, over the past 15 years, the Japanese government has worked out a way to address such challenges through the creation of special zones for the empirical testing and development of AI, namely, a form of living lab, or Tokku. In the field of autonomous vehicles, several EU countries have endorsed similar experimentation: Sweden has sponsored the world's first large-scale autonomous driving pilot project, in which self-driving cars use public roads in everyday driving conditions; so too has Germany allowed a number of tests with various levels of automation on highways, e.g. Audi's tests with an autonomously driving car on highway A9 between Ingolstadt and Nuremberg; and the U.S. is a major testbed for the development and regulation of autonomous cars. And as the Committee on Legal Affairs of the European Parliament stressed in the recommendations to the EU Commission on civil law rules for robotics in 2016, "testing robots in real-life scenarios is essential for the identification and assessment of the risks [that AI & robots] might entail, as well as of their technological development beyond a pure experimental laboratory phase."

Such forms of experimentation through lawfully de-regulated special zones are often complemented with further legal techniques and mechanisms that aim to properly address further potential issues raised by the next-generation AI systems. Forms of experimental federalism and multiple techniques to govern technological innovation, such as the principle of implementation, can indeed improve our understanding of how AI systems may react in various contexts and satisfy human needs. In the first case, the idea of an experimental federalism is to flesh out the content of the rules that shall govern social and individual behavior through a beneficial competition among legal systems. This is what occurs nowadays in the field of self-driving cars in the U.S., where at the time of this writing, seven states have enacted their own laws for this kind of technology. At its best possible light, the same policy will be at work with the EU regulation in the field of data protection. As to the principle of implementation neutrality, lawmakers can pass regulations that are specific to that technology, e.g. AI, and yet do not favor one or more of its possible implementations, or non-compliant implementations can be easily modified to become compliant. Since the regulation of AI will be challenging, the aim is to employ the legal rules of change that create, modify, or extinct the primary rules of the law, in order to collect empirical data and sufficient knowledge to make rational decisions for a number of critical issues.

Importantly, we must improve our understanding of how AI systems may react in various contexts and satisfy human needs. We shall better appreciate risks and threats triggered by possible losses of control of AI systems, so as to keep them in check. New theoretical frameworks should allow us to better appreciate the space of potential systems that avoid undesirable behaviors, whilst new and old authorities shall coordinate the management of some requirements, which often represent a formidable obstacle for research in AI, such as public authorizations for security reasons, formal consent for the processing and use of personal data, mechanisms of distributing risks through insurance models and authentication systems, and more. By harnessing the legal rules of change, such as forms of legal experimentation, experimental federalism, techniques of technological governance, risk assessment, and more, how basic concepts, standards, and principles of the law may realign in the foreseeable future will become clearer in constitutional law, criminal and business law, and so forth.

However, as the grandfather of legal automation and AI and law, the German polymath Wilhelm Leibniz, used to say, "every mind has a horizon in respect to its present intellectual capacity but not in respect to its future intellectual capacity." Once we admit there being AI machines capable of autonomous decisions similar in all relevant aspects to the ones humans make, the next step would be to acknowledge that the legal meanings of intent, of negligence, of consciousness and self-consciousness, and even of legal person, will radically change. Although nobody knows where this scenario may ultimately lead, current debate represents an opportunity to properly take the challenge seriously, namely, what new environment we may wish. The *Research Handbook on the Law of Artificial Intelligence* is a significant step forward in presenting the current framework for thinking about law and AI, with a discussion of how the future direction of law and AI may develop by leading scholars in the field.

Woodrow Barfield, Chapel Hill, North Carolina, USA
Ugo Pagallo, Turin, Italy

Acknowledgements

The editors greatly acknowledge Stephen Gutierrez, acquisition editor, Edward Elgar Press for his early support of the project, and throughout. Further, we thank Erin McVicar and Laura Mann from Edward Elgar for their assistance with the project, and the production department for their work to produce the book for publication. We especially thank the authors for producing outstanding and "forward-looking" chapters and for their professionalism as they responded to our many queries for more information and for meeting deadlines. We also thank our colleagues for the many conversations we had with them on law and AI and for their contribution to this emerging new field of law.

PART I

INTRODUCTION TO LAW AND ARTIFICIAL INTELLIGENCE

1. Towards a law of artificial intelligence
Woodrow Barfield

I. INTRODUCTION

Not only is artificial intelligence a rapidly advancing technology, but the capabilities of artificial intelligence which allow it to learn from experience and to perform autonomously from humans, make artificial intelligence the most disruptive and transformative technology of the early twenty-first century. An important observation to make is that artificial intelligence is already ubiquitous in society, it can be found in consumer appliances, the Internet of Things, Air Traffic Control Systems, the national power grid, healthcare systems, and all aspects of the "intelligent" highway transportation system from autonomous vehicles to the road itself. In fact, we are becoming more and more dependent on systems operating with artificial intelligence for the maintenance and functioning of our physical and digital infrastructure. However, as technology advances, so too must the law advance to account for changes in the capabilities of technology. This is particularly the case with artificial intelligence, whose abilities to learn and operate autonomously from humans is raising a host of challenges to established areas of law.

As noted, the "artificial intelligence revolution" is widespread throughout society; for example, just in the home, artificial intelligence controls many of today's consumer products ranging from kitchen appliances to thermostats adjusting the temperature in a room.[1] And in commerce, artificial intelligence controls the actions of digital assistants and electronic agents which buy and sell billions of dollars' worth of products. In human-computer interaction, algorithms which support natural language processing allow humans and computers to speak to each other in a common language raising the specter of free speech doctrine. Additionally, the world is being networked at an astonishing rate, and in a networked world, the Internet is dependent on artificial intelligence to function. For example, consider the use of artificial intelligence for the following: to select content based on user-preferences, show targeted advertisements, predict and manipulate behavioral traits amongst users, create and design high quality content, help determine what a person sees in Facebook feed, and what ads a person sees in their Gmail.[2] For each of these examples the use of artificial intelligence is allowing increasingly smart machines to engage in creative and sometimes unpredictable behavior; this aspect of what artificial

---

[1] "Wiresoft Brings Artificial Intelligence to Security Appliances" (discussing the use of AI for security monitoring and maintenance), available at: https://www.infotech.com/research/wiresoft-brings-artificial-intelligence-to-security-appliances; in fact, the Nest thermometer "learns" the temperatures a person likes and to save energy turns itself down when nobody is home, Nest store products, available at: https://store.nest.com/product/thermostat/.

[2] Stephen F. Deangelis, "Artificial Intelligence: How Algorithms Make Systems Smart", available at: https://www.wired.com/insights/2014/09/artificial-intelligence-algorithms-2/.

intelligence affords a system offers significant challenges to established areas of law that historically have relied on identifying a human in the decision-making loop.

Discussing the importance of artificial intelligence for the future development of information technology, Tony Tether, former director of the US Defense Advanced Research Projects Agency (DARPA) stated: "machine learning *is* the next Internet."[3] Further, commenting on the relevance of artificial intelligence for society, Microsoft U.K.'s Chief Envisioning Officer Dave Coplin claimed that "artificial intelligence is the most important technology that anybody on the planet is working on today."[4] Within government, the Office of the U.S. Presidency under then President Obama took note of advances in artificial intelligence and through the White House Office of Science and Technology Policy offered workshops in order to generate public dialogue and to identify challenges and opportunities related to this emerging technology.[5] But perhaps the conclusions of the business and economics research arm of McKinsey Global Institute, a technology think tank, that artificial intelligence is not only contributing to the transformation of society but that compared to the Industrial Revolution, the artificial intelligence revolution is "happening ten times faster and at 300 times the scale, or roughly 3,000 times the impact",[6] thoroughly states the case for artificial intelligence as the key transformative technology emerging in the early twenty-first century.

I will return to issues of law surrounding the definition of artificial intelligence later in this chapter, but as a starting point, a standard definition of intelligence is ". . . the ability to learn or understand things or to deal with new or difficult situations."[7] With this in mind, generally, the goal of research in artificial intelligence is to create computers, software, and machines that are capable of intelligent and, in some cases, unpredictable and creative behavior. Discussing the concept of intelligence for robotics, a particularly important application using artificial intelligence, law professor F. Patrick Hubbard described intelligence as "the rate at which the machine can receive, evaluate, use, and transmit information, and the extent to which it can learn from experience and use the output of learning to determine future responses."[8] Hubbard's definition of intelligence is also similar to law and robotics expert professor Ryan Calo's characterization of a robot which produces "emerging behavior" and can "sense, process, and act."[9] I should note that each of these aspects of robotics identified by Calo and Hubbard are made possible by the capabilities of artificial intelligence. Additionally, even though advances in sensor and other technologies are leading to "smart machines", it is still techniques of artificial

---

[3] *See*, Maria-Florina Balcan, *Foundations of Machine Learning and Data Science* (Lecture) (2015), available at: http://www.cs.cmu.edu/~ninamf/courses/806/lect09-09-slides.pdf.

[4] Dave Choplin, "AI Will Change Everything", available at: http://www.winbeta.org/news/microsoft-exec-london-conference-ai-will-change-everything.

[5] White House Office of Science and Technology Policy, available at: http://cdn.ccianet.org/wp-content/uploads/2016/07/CCIA-White-House-OSTP-AI-Comments-Final.pdf.

[6] Richard Dobbs, James Manyika, and Jonathan Woetzel, "The Four Global Forces Breaking all the Trends", 2015, available at: http://www.mckinsey.com/business-functions/strategy-and-corporate-finance/our-insights/the-four-global-forces-breaking-all-the-trends.

[7] Definition of "Intelligence", Merriam-Webster dictionary, available at: www.merriam.com.

[8] F. Patrick Hubbard, *"Sophisticated Robots": Balancing Liability, Regulation, and Innovation*, 66 Fla. L. Rev. 1803 (2015), available at: http://scholarship.law.ufl.edu/flr/vol66/iss5/1.

[9] Ryan Calo, *Robotics and the Lessons of Cyberlaw*, 103 Cal. L. Rev. 3, 513–63 (2015).

intelligence and mainly the use of algorithms that analyze and interpret the data collected by sensors. These capabilities allow machines to perform autonomously from humans and this, with other attributes of artificial intelligence, is beginning to offer significant challenges to established areas of law.

I propose that the basic ingredient of artificial intelligence is algorithms which can be described as a procedure for solving a problem in a finite number of steps, or as stated by Microsoft's Tarleton Gillespie, algorithms are "encoded procedures of transforming input data into a determined output, based on specified calculations."[10] But not all algorithms can be considered an example of artificial intelligence, especially those which program a robot to move in predetermined motions (i.e., repetitively) and with little or no decision-making involved. But algorithms which model complex human performance, human thought processes, and that can learn from experience, are considered by most to be an example of artificial intelligence; and when systems with these capabilities operate autonomously from humans, several established areas of law are challenged. For instance, for purposes of assigning liability under tort law, not all algorithms can be traced back to a human programmer, especially algorithms associated with techniques identified as deep learning. This is important because the more artificially intelligent systems are controlled by algorithms that were not written by humans, the more likely they will display behaviors that were not just unforeseen by humans, but were wholly unforeseeable. For the law, this is significant because foreseeability is a key ingredient in negligence.

II.   ARTIFICIAL INTELLIGENCE AS A TRANSFORMATIVE TECHNOLOGY RAISING ISSUES OF LIABILITY

The use of artificial intelligence to create the range of behaviors shown by emerging smart technologies is core to the discussion of artificial intelligence as a transformative and disruptive technology. Consider machine learning algorithms which solve problems in ways that are novel to human operators. This scenario alone raises several questions of interest to different areas of law. For example, under intellectual property law, who owns the copyright to original works of authorship created by algorithms and who should receive the patent monopoly for inventions independently created by an algorithm that itself was derived from machine learning techniques? Further, if a system is controlled by artificial intelligence and performs tasks in ways that are novel and unpredictable to humans, if there is harm to a human or damage to property who should courts hold liable—the artificial intelligence directing the actions of the machine that caused the damage but lacks personhood status, or the human that lacks knowledge of how the machine performed or even that the machine was attempting to solve a particular problem? And while the issue of assigning liability for injuries resulting from human interaction with increasingly smart machines is of keen interest to legal scholars and to courts, in such situations the likely causative factor other than human error is the software and algorithms controlling

---

[10]   Tarleton Gillespie, *The Relevance of Algorithms*, In Media Technologies (Tarleton Gillespie, Pablo J. Boczkowski, and Kirsten A. Foot, eds. MIT Press 2014).

the machine's actions, that is, the artificial intelligence embedded within the machine's sensors, microprocessors, and computer vision system.

It is the case that machines that lack the ability to think beyond a few simple rules directing their actions, are so devoid of intelligence, that no one would assign them responsibility for their actions. A case on point is *Comptroller of the Treasury v. Family Entertainment Centers.*[11] In *Comptroller*, a Maryland special appeals court considered whether life-sized animatronic puppets that danced and sang at a Chuckie Cheese triggered a state tax on an establishment which serves food "where there is furnished a performance." The court held that "[A] pre-programmed robot can perform menial tasks because a pre-programmed robot has no 'skill'. . . It cannot 'perform' a piece of music."[12] However, while a robot may not be able to perform a piece of music under the Copyright Act, in other contexts artificial intelligence has arguably composed original works of music raising the issue of whether the artificial intelligence is the actual composer of the work. But what does make smart machines interesting and challenging from a legal perspective? As argued repeatedly in this Chapter, the answer is robots that have capabilities provided by artificial intelligence which allows them to sense the environment, initiate actions, and solve problems using solutions that were originally unknown to the human operator.[13] By the way, these are basically the same set of attributes that make humans "interesting" for different areas of law; therefore, it seems to me, the more human-like artificial intelligence becomes, the more the law is challenged.

As a basic point, the use of artificial intelligence begs the question of who is liable if the artificial intelligence controlling smart technology learns and solves problems in ways completely unknown to the human in the system. In this case should the focus in assigning liability be the person(s) that created the smart machines or the person(s) that produced the software and algorithms which control the machine's behavior and determine its actions? If artificially intelligent systems write their own algorithms and solve problems with solutions unknown to human operators, would it be fair to hold humans liable for any harm the system caused? With an autonomous system sharing control with humans, the future may be one in which significant issues of law and policy are brought forth by the use of artificial intelligence, thus a body of law will need to be available to guide courts in deciding disputes resulting from such systems, and particularly in deciding how to allocate liability between human and artificially intelligent machines when the system design allows joint control.

Given the requirements of the task, many current robots operate efficiently with a set of instructions provided by a programmer, and when robots do not deviate from these instructions, the law is well equipped to handle disputes involving such systems. A case on point is *Jones v. W + M Automation, Inc.*, in which a worker who had entered a prohibited area behind a safety fence was struck in the head by the gripper arms of a robot.[14] The court focused on whether the robot's gantry loading system was defective when the defendant sold it—while this is an interesting case involving a robot, it is a classic products

---

[11]   *Comptroller of the Treasury v. Family Entertainment Centers.* 519 A.2d 1337, 1338 (Md. 1987).
[12]   *Id.* at 1339.
[13]   Calo, *supra* note 9.
[14]   *Jones v. W + M Automation, Inc.* 818 N.Y.S.2d 396 (App. Div. 2006), appeal denied, 862 N.E.2d 790 (N.Y. 2007).

liability case and litigated as such. But as smart machines such as robots become even smarter, more independent of human supervision, and rely more and more on artificial intelligence for their performance, if there is harm to a human or damage to property, attributing liability to a manufacturer or seller or any human in the chain of distribution will challenge current doctrine in tort, contract, and agency law. In fact, determining liability for the actions of an artificially intelligent entity performing autonomously from humans is an area ripe for legal scholarship and legislative action and we see the beginnings of this effort now by the FAA with drones, and state governments with autonomous vehicles.[15] However, drones, autonomous vehicles, and robots, are in many ways different technologies, although they have in common algorithms and other forms of artificial intelligence to control and direct their behavior.[16]

In cases where the harm is alleged to have been caused by artificial intelligence the court is often asked to unravel novel technology and apply ill-fitting case law to make determinations of liability. For example, common-law tort and malpractice claims often center on the very human concepts of fault, negligence, knowledge, intent, and reasonableness.[17] So what happens when human judgement, or scienter, is replaced by artificial intelligence, how will courts assign liability for system failures? In a case decided in 1984, *United States v. Athlone Indus, Inc.* the court stated that "robots cannot be sued", and discussed instead how the manufacturer of a defective robotic pitching machine is liable for civil penalties for the machine's defects.[18] However, it should be noted that robots and artificial intelligence have become far more sophisticated and autonomous since *Athlone* and as such courts will continue to struggle with the question of assessing liability going forward as the use of artificially intelligent technologies such as autonomous machines gain mainstream acceptance.

---

[15]   *See* John Frank Weaver, *We Need to Pass Legislation on Artificial Intelligence Early and Often*, Future Tense, The Citizen's Guide to the Future (2014), available at: http://www.slate.com/blogs/future_tense/2014/09/12/we_need_to_pass_artificial_intelligence_laws_early_and_often.html; Alina Selyukh, *FAA Expects 600,000 Commercial Drones In The Air Within A Year*, The Two-Way, available at: http://www.npr.org/sections/thetwo-way/2016/08/29/491818988/faa-expects-600-000-commercial-drones-in-the-air-within-a-year; for a list of state initiatives in the regulation of autonomous vehicles see Gabriel Weiner and Bryant Walker Smith, Automated Driving: Legislative and Regulatory Action, available at: cyberlaw.stanford.edu/wiki/index.php/Automated_Driving:_Legislative_and_Regulatory_Action.

[16]   *See e.g.,* Nevada State Law, NSR 482A.025 defines "Automated Technology" as: ". . .technology which is installed on a motor vehicle and which has the capability to drive the motor vehicle without the active control or monitoring of a human operator. The term does not include an active safety system or a system for driver assistance, including, without limitation, a system to provide electronic blind spot detection, crash avoidance, emergency braking, parking assistance, adaptive cruise control, lane keeping assistance, lane departure warning, or traffic jam and queuing assistance, unless any such system, alone or in combination with any other system, enables the vehicle on which the system is installed to be driven without the active control or monitoring of a human operator." Further, under Nevada state law, NRS 482A.030 an "Autonomous vehicle" means a motor vehicle that is equipped with autonomous technology.

[17]   'Artificial Intelligence Litigation: Can the Law Keep Pace with the Rise of the Machines?' Quinn Emanual Trial Lawyers, Quinn Emanual Urquhart & Sullivan LLP, December 1, 2016, available at: http://www.jdsupra.com/legalnews/artificial-intelligence-litigation-can-83824/.

[18]   *United States v. Athlone Indus, Inc.* 746 F.29 977 (3d Cir. 1984).

Not all machines driven by algorithms and analytical techniques raise issues which challenge established law. For instance, based on the actions of a machine whose task may require limited computational resources and repetition of motion, if a person is injured or property is damaged, the current body of law in tort is not particularly challenged, such disputes are successfully litigated under theories of negligence, products liability, or often resolved on technical issues of civil procedure. *Behurst v. Crown Cork & Seal USA, Inc.*,[19] revolved around an intentional tort action when a plaintiff was fatally injured after being trapped in the danger zone surrounding a robot. The court denied summary judgment to the employer (but granted summary judgment to the manufacturer) finding among others, that the employer's alleged refusal to reprogram the machine was an appropriate jury question in light of the tort claim. The robot in *Behurst* was designed to "unthinkingly" move metal from one die to another, but if roboticists design machines which exhibit creativity, have the ability to learn and engage in non-repetitive behavior, under current legal doctrine it may be difficult to assign liability to any human in the system.[20]

An example of the above point is illustrated in the following case. A decision in a consolidated class action in the District Court for the Eastern District of Missouri, found that the use of a computer program to simulate human interaction with a bot could give rise to liability for fraud. The claims in *In re Ashley Madison Customer Data Sec. Breach Litig.*[21] related to a data breach on the "Ashley online dating site" that resulted in mass dissemination of user information. The allegations were that defendants were engaging in deceptive and fraudulent conduct by creating fake computer "hosts" or "bots" which were programmed to generate and send messages to male members under the guise they were "real woman", inducing members to make purchases on the website. It was estimated that 80 percent of initial purchases on the website were conducted by users communicating with a bot. I should note that the bot was controlled by algorithms, the backbone of artificial intelligence.

A.   Early Thoughts on a Law of Artificial Intelligence

Except for Isaac Asimov's three laws of robotics discussed in his 1942 short story "Runaround", it is only recently that there has been an interest in developing a body of law that applies to increasingly smart technologies which are improving under the direction of artificial intelligence.[22] In fact, several decades after Asimov's laws of robotics, when expert systems began to emulate the decision-making abilities of human experts, the issue of liability for artificially intelligent systems began to be discussed within the

---

[19]   *Behurst v Crown Cork & Seal USA, Inc,* 2007 U.S. Dist. ELXIS 24922 (D.Ore.Mar.30, 2007). 203 P.3d 207, 346 Or. 29, 2009.

[20]   Karnow, *supra* note 59.

[21]   In *re Ashley Madison Customer Data Sec. Breach Litig.*,148 F. Supp. 3d 1378, 1380 (JPML 2015).

[22]   However, close examination of Asimov's Three Law of Robots indicates that they apply equally if not more so to artificial intelligence. "A robot may not injure a human being or, through inaction, allow a human being to come to harm. A robot must obey orders given it by human beings except where such orders would conflict with the First Law. A robot must protect its own existence as long as such protection does not conflict with the First or Second Law."

legal community.[23] But perhaps the paper published in 1992 by Lawrence Solum on whether an artificial intelligence could be considered a "legal person" was key to generating interest in the field.[24] The same year the launch of the *Journal of Artificial Intelligence and Law* revealed an interest among legal scholars and computer scientists to discuss how legal reasoning could be modeled and codified.[25] Still, to date, there hasn't been enough attention among legal scholars or legislators to develop a broad-based body of law to account for advances in artificial intelligence. I propose that the time to do so is now, and that the chapters in this book represent the beginning discussion on an emerging legal doctrine which will form the framework for a law of artificial intelligence.

As developments in artificial intelligence continue, based on the flexibility of its techniques, artificial intelligence is becoming a core technology in many industries ranging from ecommerce, robotics, factory automation, medical diagnosis, virtual worlds, and numerous consumer applications. The flexibility of artificial intelligence is also allowing its techniques to deviate from predetermined rules, and to be used for purposes other than its original intentions and design; this is leading to a diffusion of the technology into society far beyond that of other emerging technologies. According to computer scientist and artificial intelligence expert Michele Zhou three characteristics of artificial intelligence have contributed to its recent spread throughout society, these include: recognition intelligence in which pattern recognition algorithms are used to detect edges and lines in scenes; cognitive intelligence in which algorithms are used to make inferences from the analysis of scene data; and ambitiously, the creation of virtual humans.[26] The first two characteristics when combined with deep learning techniques allow a level of autonomy among systems that is beginning to challenge established legal doctrine in many areas of law. But this is to be expected given that much legal doctrine which is applied to systems operating with artificial intelligence were enacted in an age of "low-tech" and non-autonomous machines, that is, before techniques in artificial intelligence were beginning to be used for a wide range of applications. Therefore, given the growing number of applications which use artificial intelligence, when regulating the next transformative technology legislators would be prudent to enact a set of rules which cut across diverse technologies that rely on the same underlying principles of artificial intelligence to act upon the world and to challenge different areas of law. More specifically, a body of law regulating artificial intelligence given its potential to harm humans, engage in commercial activities as an independent agent, and violate criminal law statutes, needs to be developed.

---

[23]   *See* Marguerite E. Gestner, *Liability Issues with Artificial Intelligence Software*, Vol. 33 (1), SANTA CLARA L. REV., 239–69 (1993) (discussing who is liable when artificial intelligence is involved in a system failure); Michael C. Cemignani, *Product Liability and Software*, 8 RUTGERS J. COMPUTERS, TECH. and L. 173 (1981); G. Steven Turhill, *Legal Liabilities and Expert Systems*, AI Expert, (Mar. 1991) 44, 48.

[24]   Lawrence B. Solum, *Legal Personhood for Artificial Intelligences*, 70 N.C. L. Rev. 1231 (1992) (the central question of whether personhood rights should be awarded to artificial intelligence is discussed).

[25]   *See e.g.*, T. J. M. Bench-Capon and F. P. Coenen, *Isomorphism and Legal Knowledge Based Systems,* Artificial Intelligence and Law, Vol. 1, 65–86, (1992)

[26]   *See generally*, Om Malik, *The Hype—and Hope—of Artificial Intelligence*, The New Yorker (2016), at: http://www.newyorker.com/business/currency/the-hype-and-hope-of-artificial-intelligence.

B.   How Soon Does the Future Get Here?

Many assume rightly that it is difficult to make predictions about the future direction of technology and when major advances may occur. However, what if information technology has been following an exponential rate of growth for some time such that one can accurately predict where computing power will fall on the curve, even a few decades away? Still, who would have predicted just a few decades ago that computers equipped with neural net algorithms could learn, solve problems, and exhibit creativity in music and art? Further, who would have predicted that computers with artificial intelligence would beat Jeopardy champion Ken Jennings; and that Ken would exclaim that he welcomed his new computer overlord?[27] Similarly, world chess champion Garry Kasparov in losing to IMB's Big Blue computer commented that he saw deep intelligence in the machines moves.[28] And who would have predicted that in 2016 Google's DeepMind learning algorithm AlphaGo would defeat one of the world's premier players of the ancient strategy game of Go in what was then considered to be one of the hardest challenges for artificial intelligence yet?[29] But soon after, an artificially intelligent computer designed by computer scientists beat experts in the game of poker which required the ability to bluff and to predict whether the opponent was bluffing based on incomplete knowledge of the advisory's hand.[30] Of course, while impressive examples of skilled behavior, these are examples of artificial intelligence performing in a narrow domain of expertise; at this time more human-like artificial intelligence remains elusive.

Outside of game shows, commentators have observed that machines driven by artificial intelligence are beginning to displace people from jobs in various industries and at an accelerating pace. Driverless cars, automated factories, and automated laboratories are based to a large extent on techniques of artificial intelligence capable of thinking, writing, creating, or even diagnosing disease. So, how far along are we towards developing artificial intelligence that will have the capability to fully engage our legal system as entities stressing the law or deserving of rights? This is a question which has generated much discussion among scholars producing a range of opinions. According to Yale's Jack M. Balkin "we are still a long way from treating robots and AI agents as self-conscious rights-bearing or responsibility-bearing entities."[31] For this reason Professor Balkin argues that

---

[27]   Watson wins 'Jeopardy!' finale; Ken Jennings welcomes 'our new computer overlords', 2011, available at: http://latimesblogs.latimes.com/showtracker/2011/02/watson-jeopardy-finale-man-vs-machine-showdown.html; John Markoff, *Computer Wins Jeopardy: Trivial, It's Not*, N.Y. Times, Feb, 16, 2011 at AI; In 2016 an AI platform predicted the Kentucky Derby first-, second-, third, and fourth-place order at 540- odds.

[28]   Jennifer Latson, 2015, *Did Deep Blue Beat Kasparov Because of a System Glitch?* Time; available at: http://time.com/3705316/deep-blue-kasparov/; Glynn Washington, *Kasparov v. Deep Blue*, North Carolina Public Radio, 2014 available at: http://www.npr.org/2014/08/08/338850323/kasparov-vs-deep-blue.

[29]   John Riberio, 2016, *Google's AlphaGo defeated in fourth Go game by South Korean player*, PC World, available at: http://www.pcworld.com/article/3043603/analytics/googles-alphago-defeated-in-fourth-go-game-by-south-korean-player.html.

[30]   Katie Callahan, *AI Beats Poker Pros in 'Brains vs. AI' Event*, available at https://www.pokernews.com/news/2017/01/poker-ai-beats-the-pros-26990.htm.

[31]   Jack Balkin, *The Path of Robotics Law*, 6 CAL. L. REV. CIRCUIT, 45 (2015).

one of the central issues for a law of robotics is "to allocate rights and duties among human beings when robots and AI entities create benefits or cause harms."[32] I believe we should extend this observation to other technologies equipped with artificial intelligence, but eventually the focus of the discussion will need to be on allocating rights between humans and artificially intelligent systems that have reached human levels of intelligence and that argue for many of the rights afforded natural people under laws, statutes, and constitutions. Additionally, discussing how soon we might expect artificially intelligent robots (which I view more as an application of artificial intelligence), Neil Richards and William Smart, commenting in *How Should the Law Think about Robots?* concluded that while "robots have not yet reached the levels of complexity the public associates with science fiction . . . they are surprisingly close."[33] In a similar observation, Patrick Hubbard noted that ". . . in the next decade or so, a new class of 'sophisticated robots' will emerge by nature of their increased autonomy and intelligence."[34]

Since several artificially intelligent systems are already equal to humans in performance in a surprising range of tasks and are becoming superior to humans in a growing list of skills that were once considered beyond the scope of artificial intelligence, artificial intelligence does seem to be headed in the direction of human levels of intelligence. But, of course, there is a raging debate among artificial intelligence researchers, philosophers, and scientists as to when, or if, artificial intelligence will equal humans in general intelligence. We will not solve that debate through legal scholarship, nor will we make a major contribution to another controversial issue within the artificial intelligence community—that of machine sentience which if achieved by artificial intelligence would lead a rigorous debate on the granting of personhood status and constitutional rights for artificially intelligent entities.[35] However, if artificial intelligence were capable of creative and inventive activity, then the question becomes—why shouldn't intellectual property and other rights be accorded to the artificially intelligent entity? These questions raise issues that go to the very foundations of constitutional rights and intellectual property law, including the economic incentive to encourage certain activities, and the "moral rights" associated with according credit to authors.

I should note that autonomy and intelligence are both characteristics of what artificial intelligence affords a system, and by Patrick Hubbard's estimation, robots that are more autonomous than current versions are just around the corner.[36] Law and robotics expert Ryan Calo seems to go even further in speculating about the use of artificial intelligence when he states: "But the processing capabilities of robots translate to the tantalizing

---

[32]   *Id.* at 46.
[33]   Neil Richards and William Smart, *How Should the Law Think About Robots?* (May 10, 2013), SSRN: http://ssrn.com/abstract=2263363 or http://dx.doi.org/10.2139/ssrn.2263363.
[34]   Hubbard, *supra* note 8; autonomy is a complicated concept that incorporates multiple meanings. It is a term that invokes self-rule, self-determination, and self-sovereignty.
[35]   Junichi Takeno, *Creation of a Conscious Robot: Mirror Image Cognition and Self-Awareness*, Pan Standard Publishing (2012); John Brockman, *What to Think About Machines That Think: Today's Leading Thinkers on the Age of Machine Intelligence*, Harpers Perennial (2015); M. E. Tson, *From Dust To Descartes: An Evolutionary and Mechanical Explanation of Consciousness*, Amazon Digital Services, Inc. (2009).
[36]   Hubbard, *supra* note 8.

prospect of original action."[37] But to some extent, I also agree with Professor Calo's view that developing human-like artificial intelligence that comes close to mimicking human levels of general intelligence remains elusive, and unpredictable as to whether it will happen, or when. For artificial intelligence to progress towards human levels of intelligence, improvements in algorithms and more robust software will have to be made. Can we expect such improvements to occur within the next few decades? If yes, artificial intelligence as a subject within law and as a technology to be regulated by government agencies and by industry standards seems appropriate.

Most researchers agree that for artificial intelligence to more fully develop it is necessary for artificial intelligence to have access to greater computational resources. Gordon E. Moore observed as far back as 1965 that computer power was doubling approximately every two years. Over 50 years later, China's Sunway Taihulight supercomputer operates at around 100 quadrillion cps; and exaflop computing (i.e., 10^{18}) is just beyond the horizon. In comparison, the raw processing power of the human brain while not known is based on approximately 85–100 billion neurons with 100 trillion synapses, with the cell's dendrites and cell body both performing computations and functioning as an analog digital computer.[38] An interesting aspect of Moore's law for innovation in general is that advances in artificial intelligence seem to be operating under a feedback process which creates accelerated returns.[39] So interestingly, while human information processing and cognitive abilities are fixed by biology, in contrast, the capabilities of artificial intelligence are not and are quickly improving. With additional computational resources, improvements in software, and the further development of neuromorphic chips,[40] I expect the autonomy and intelligence of artificially intelligent machines to correspondingly increase which will continue to significantly challenge established areas of law that historically has looked to humans as responsible parties in legal disputes.

In terms of postulating when artificial intelligence may reach human levels of intelligence, some argue that those who propose that artificial intelligence is improving in leaps-and-bounds, are "cheating" because they select a skill once thought solely within the domain of human expertise, then create an artificially intelligent entity that can do the same task equal to or better than a human expert.[41] Rather than "cheating", this is an example of the incessant progress being made in the advancement of artificial intelligence for skills once thought unapproachable for artificial intelligence. And if this is cheating, then there is an epidemic of cheating occurring within the artificial intelligence community as artificial intelligence is rapidly advancing in all aspects of society. But to

---

[37] Calo, *supra* note 9, at 532.

[38] Jason J. Moore et al., *Dynamics of Cortical Dendritic Membrane Potential and Spikes in Freely Behaving Rats*, Science, March 2017, DOI: 10.1126/Science.aaj1497.

[39] *See generally* Ray Kurzweil, *The Singularity is Near: When Humans Transcend Biology*, Penguin Books (2006).

[40] Robert H. Hof, Neuromorphic Chips, available at: https://www.technologyreview.com/s/5 26506/neuromorphic-chips/; IBMs DARPA funded SyNAPSE program to design neuromorphic brain inspired chips with 5.4 billion transistors each with 1 million neurons and 256 million synapses.

[41] Jo Best, *IBM Watson: The Inside Story of How the Jeopardy-Winning Supercomputer Was Born, and What It Wants to Do Next*, TechRepublic, available at: http://www.techrepublic.com/arti cle/ibm-watson-the-inside-story-of-how-the-jeopardy-winning-supercomputer-was-born-and-wha t-it-wants-to-do-next/.

some, once a milestone is reached by artificial intelligence, the bar is moved and the skill achieved is no longer considered indicative of intelligence. This sentiment led artificial intelligence pioneer John McCarthy to claim "as soon as it works, no one calls it artificial intelligence anymore."[42] Similarly, author Kevin Kelly observed: "What you can do now would be artificial intelligence fifty years ago. What we can do fifty years from now will not be artificial intelligence."[43]

Perhaps it is worth noting here author and futurist Ray Kurzweil's predictions for the future given his seminal writings about the future of information technology and artificial intelligence.[44] Kurzweil lists 2029 as the date in which an artificial intelligence will pass a valid Turing test and therefore be considered to have achieved human levels of intelligence. Additionally, he lists the date 2045 for the "Singularity" which he claims is when we will multiply our effective intelligence a billionfold by merging with the artificial intelligence we have created. Kurzweil's timetable for the singularity is consistent with other predictions of noted futurists—for example, those of Softbank CEO Masayoshi Son, who predicts that the dawn of super-intelligent machines will happen by 2047.

III.   CONSIDERING THE BODY

Artificial intelligence, embedded in different bodies, controls numerous types of technologies that exert a presence in the world including industrial robots, automated machinery, home service robots, electronic agents that engage in real-world commerce, and virtual avatars.[45] However, as we transition into a digital economy and as we spend time in virtual reality, in many cases there is no physical body requirement for the intelligent entities we design and interact with, our alter ego may even exist as an artificially intelligent avatar.[46] Yet the same techniques of artificial intelligence that are creating intelligent machines that are beginning to offer challenges to established law, may also lead to disputes when virtual avatars are used as stand-in actors, as our digital assistants, or as tools for cyberhacking.[47]

Professor Ryan Calo convincingly argues that robots pose interesting questions for law because they have a physical body (the element of "embodiment") which allows them to act directly upon the world; but reemphasizing a point, artificial intelligence "occupies" not only the physical body of a machine such as a robot but other "kinds of bodies." This

---

[42]   John McCarthy, 'What is Artificial Intelligence? Basic Questions', available at: http://www-formal.stanford.edu/jmc/whatisai/mode1.html (accessed May 20, 2016).

[43]   Kevin Kelly, *The Inevitable: Understanding the 12 Technological Forces that Will Shape our Future*, Viking Press, 2016.

[44]   Kurzweil, *supra* note 39.

[45]   Lazaros Iliadis and Ilias Maglogiannis (eds), 'Artificial Intelligence Applications and Innovations: 12th IFIP WG 12.5 International Conference and Workshops', AIAI 2016, Thessaloniki, Greece, Springer Press, 2016.

[46]   Woodrow Barfield, *Intellectual Property Rights in Virtual Environments: Considering the Rights of Owners, Programmers and Virtual Avatars*, 39 AKRON L. Rev., 649 (2006).

[47]   *See generally* James J. Beard, Clones, Bones and Twilight Zones: Protecting the Digital Persona of the Quick, the Dead and the Imaginary, 16 BERKELEY TECH. L. J., 1165. (2001); *Cybersecurity and Artificial Intelligence: A Dangerous Mix*, Posted in General Security on February 24, 2015, available at: http://resources.infosecinstitute.com/cybersecurity-artificial-intelligence-dangerous-mix/.

leads to a greater range of applications for artificial intelligence (compared to technology such as robotics) which in turn leads to additional challenges to established areas of law. There are two observations which lead to this conclusion: first, as software, the code and algorithms of artificial intelligence can be copied and "implanted" within the "body" of many different kinds of machines and at zero cost per copy; and second, artificial intelligence can "exist" either embedded within the physical body of a machine, within the cloud, or as a virtual entity operating within cyberspace, this latter aspect of artificial intelligence results in a host of legal issues not directly relevant to machines which occupy physical space and predominantly manipulate physical objects.

As a broad generalization, we can think of machines as an analog technology and subject to the laws which apply to activities occurring in physical space and artificial intelligence as a digital technology which can control not only the actions of analog machines but of digital entities; this distinction is worth noting. Since the same software and algorithms that contribute to make machines "smart" similarly works to make objects within cyberspace smart; this suggests that a law of artificial intelligence will implicate more technologies than the law relating to machines and will reach not "just" the physical world but activities occurring in cyberspace. For example, in cyberspace, the question of whether an electronic agent that operates autonomously from humans can serve as a contracting party, whether products liability law applies to algorithms and software, and whether in the U.S. the Fourteenth Amendment is implicated by the use of algorithms engaging in alleged discriminatory practices are just a few issues of concern for a law of artificial intelligence.[48]

Discussing the importance of embodiment for robotics, Professor Calo argues that a robot's ability to sense, navigate, and act upon the world "generally requires a physical presence, and that physical presence opens up a universe of new possibilities."[49] In other words, intelligence combined with a robotic body creates an entity with the ability to challenge legal doctrine. This observation follows historical developments in the law. For example, under common-law traditions, the law generally requires a body—and robotics provides a body. For instance, many tort actions are the result of a harm inflicted on a body, and with the exception of the legal personhood fiction established for corporations, historically, contracts are negotiated between people.[50] Additionally, discrimination law is built around the concept that people (not inanimate objects) are the subject of discrimination, and so too are hate crimes directed at natural people; numerous other examples could be given.[51] However, artificial intelligence doesn't need a physical body to "exist", and even in the physical world, there are exceptions to the requirement for a body. For example, conviction for murder in the absence of a body is possible, but historically cases of this type have been hard to prove, forcing the prosecution to rely on other kinds of evidence, usually

---

[48]　*See* Lori A. Weber, *Bad Bytes: The Application of Strict Products Liability to Computer Software*, 66 ST. JOHN'S L. REV. 66, Iss. 2, 469–85 (1992).

[49]　Calo, *supra* note 9, at 532.

[50]　The term "person" means an individual, corporation, business trust, estate, trust, partnership, limited liability company, association, joint venture, governmental agency, public corporation, or any other legal or commercial entity. Chapter 15 of the U.S. code on electronic signatures in global and national commerce.

[51]　Francis X. Shen, *Mind, Body, and the Criminal Law*, 97 MINN. L. REV., 2036 (2013).

circumstantial.[52] The fact that artificial intelligence doesn't need to occupy a physical body raises a host of unique legal issues given that legal schemes have predominately evolved to account for the activities of avatars that occur in the physical world.

Regardless of the element of embodiment, the very structure of artificial intelligence as software and algorithms raises significant issues for artificial intelligence that are independent of those associated with smart machines that exert a physical presence in the world. For example, under tort law, the provider or distributor of software is liable for harm caused by software errors.[53] A fatal accident resulting from the use of an autonomous vehicle also illustrates the above point.[54] A Tesla Motors Model S driving in Autopilot mode was on a divided highway with Autopilot engaged when a tractor trailer drove across the highway perpendicular to the Model S.[55] Neither Autopilot nor the driver noticed the white side of the tractor trailer against the backdrop of a brightly lit sky, so the brake was not applied and the driver of the autonomous vehicle was killed.[56] Given that the error was one of machine vision, I view this as a case dealing with artificial intelligence whose algorithms failed to discriminate objects in the foreground from background. For the concept of embodiment, a point to make is when a machine damages property or harms a human, the physical features of the machine may not be the most direct cause of the accident, or to use the terminology of tort law, the proximate cause of the injury, instead the accident may be caused by the software and algorithms controlling the system.[57] For example, in *Payne v. ABB Flexible Automation, Inc.*, a robot crushed a worker in its cell resulting in an action in tort. While this is considered a "classic" robot case resulting in a fatality,[58] the court heard arguments on whether the robot's software was a causative factor in the accident, holding, *inter alia*, that the plaintiff failed to provide evidence that a programming error was a proximate cause of the worker's injuries. So, in *Payne* the issue of liability would have turned on the robot's software had it malfunctioned, this reinforces a central point made throughout this Chapter, that the software and algorithms directing a machine's behavior are challenging current legal doctrine more so than any other feature of the machine's design. Upon closer examination of industrial accidents, I believe many cases that involve robots and automated machinery in general, actually turn

---

[52]   *See* Gowri Ramachandran, *Assault and Battery on Property*, 44 LOY. L.A. L. Rev., 253–76 (2010). The United States case of *People v. Scott* held that "circumstantial evidence, when sufficient to exclude every other reasonable hypothesis, may prove the death of a missing person, the existence of a homicide and the guilt of the accused." Assault and battery is normally predicated on an act committed on the person, or in some cases, an extension to the body.

[53]   Meiring De Villiers, *Virus Ex Machina Res Ipsa Loquitur*, STAN. TECH. L. Rev. 1 (2003).

[54]   Danny Yadron and Dan Tynan, 2016, *Tesla Driver Dies in First Fatal Crash While Using Autopilot Mode*, The Guardian, available at: https://www.theguardian.com/technology/2016/jun/30/tesla-autopilot-death-self-driving-car-elon-musk.

[55]   *Id.*

[56]   *Id.*

[57]   Donald R. Ballman, *Commentary: Software Tort: Evaluating Software Harm by Duty of Function and Form*, 1996 / 1997, 3 CONN. INS. L.J. 417; Bob Gomulkiewicz, *Software Law and Its Applications (Aspen Casebook)* Wolters Kluwer Law & Business (January 7, 2014).

[58]   *Payne v. ABB Flexible Automation, Inc.*, 1997 U.S. App. LEXIS 13571 (8th Cir. Jun. 9, 1997) (per curiam unpublished opinion). 116 F.3d 480, No. 96-2248, 1997 WL 311586, *1-*2 (8th Cir. 1997) (per curiam) (unpublished table decision) (affirming summary judgment in favor of defendant on claim of design defect).

on the machine's programming including the algorithms directing its behavior. Thus, I conclude that the regulation of machines that are becoming smart should revolve around the behavior afforded the machine by its software and particularly the algorithms and analytical techniques of artificial intelligence controlling the machine's behavior.

IV.   MACHINES WITH AUTONOMY

Many technologies involving smart machines are becoming autonomous and independently determining the solutions they use to solve problems and achieve goals in ways that are often not predictable beforehand by humans.[59] It is the unpredictable solutions to problems and in some cases the self-programming aspect of deep learning techniques, which take humans out of the feedback loops of a system and therefore raise interesting questions for the law to consider. For example, according to Jack M. Balkin, "the problem of emergence is the problem of who we will hold responsible for what code does."[60] I agree, the problem of holding code responsible for the actions it produces, is synonymously the problem which results from the use of artificial intelligence that has the ability to learn and change its behavior in unpredictable ways as it interacts with the world.

Judge Curtis Karnow of the California Superior Court, discussing characteristics of machine learning, observed that the challenge to legal doctrine brought forth by machines with true autonomy involves self-learning in which the program does not simply apply a human-made heuristic, as with the Roomba, but generates its own heuristics.[61] This aspect of machine performance, which is dependent on software and algorithms to generate its own solutions, allows systems to solve problems in ways *a priori* unknown to humans. The more autonomous the system, that is, the more the human is removed from the decision-making loops of the system, the more difficult for courts to assign liability to humans when there is a system failure.[62] Regardless, the technological trend is clear, based on emerging techniques of artificial intelligence, robots and other "smart technologies" that will become smarter and even more autonomous in the near future.[63] But more

---

[59]   *See generally*, Curtis Karnow, *The Application of Traditional Tort Theory to Embodied Machine Intelligence*, The Robotics and Law Conference, Center for Internet and Society, Stanford Law School, 2013; to perform unpredictably, models may optimize rules by mimicking the Darwinian Law of survival of the fittest. A set of rules is chosen from those that work the best. The weakest are discarded. In addition, two successful rules can be combined (the equivalent to genetic cross-overs) to produce offspring rules. The offspring can replace the parents, or they will be discarded if less successful than the parents. Mutation is also accomplished by randomly changing elements. Mutation and cross-over occur with low probability, as in nature, available at: http://www.nasdaq.com/investing/glossary/a/genetic-algorithms.

[60]   Balkin, *supra* note 31, at 52.

[61]   Karnow, *supra* note 59.

[62]   *Id.*

[63]   One of the most consequential pieces of news for artificial intelligence from the U.S. in early 2017 was the California Department of Motor Vehicles and made available on the DMV's website. It details the efforts of Google (or more precisely its Waymo subsidiary) to make autonomous driving a reality. According to the report, in 2016 Google's self-driving cars clocked 635,868 miles (1,023,330km), and required human intervention 124 times. That is one intervention about every 5,000 miles (8,047km) of autonomous driving. But even more impres-

autonomous machines are seen as a positive development by some, prompting Professor F. Patrick Hubbard to conclude that "severe limits on autonomy drastically reduces the usefulness of robots."[64]

The use of autonomous systems directed by artificial intelligence can lead to significant challenges to current legal doctrine especially when the human operator is required to share control of the system. I view early developments in automation as a precursor for emerging applications of artificial intelligence and as an example of how established law will more and more be challenged by techniques of artificial intelligence. In fact, common law claims involving automated technology can be analyzed to provide a framework for the developing jurisprudence with regard to artificial intelligence technology. Consider an early wrongful death case involving the joint control of an airplane by human and machine. In *Brouse v. United States*,[65] the court held that a pilot had the duty to be vigilant to prevent air-to-air collisions even if the plane was flying under "robot control." Here the use of "automation" (albeit a rudimentary form of automation) did not absolve the pilot from liability, instead the court attributed error to the pilot rather than to the design of the auto-pilot feature of the plane. In *Brouse*, the court indicated that people have the responsibility to monitor automated systems or risk being held accountable if they do not.[66] However, as artificial intelligence becomes more autonomous, it will become more difficult for humans to monitor systems controlled by artificial intelligence, on this point attorney Andrew Selbst comments that algorithms must reveal their basis for decision-making.

A more recent case of a human-machine combination involving a complex task revolved around the use of a robotic surgeon. In *Mracek v. Bryn Mawr Hosp.*,[67] after a da Vinci robot malfunctioned, the human surgeons completed the procedure laparoscopically, and after suffering post-surgery injuries the patient sued the robot manufacturer stating claims of strict products liability, strict malfunction liability, negligence, and breach of warranty.[68] The Third Circuit affirmed the lower court's decision of summary judgment stating that the plaintiff failed to introduce evidence that the robot was responsible for his injury or that a rational finder of fact could find in his favor.[69] In future disputes, the failure to use a robotic surgeon may be a factor considered by juries in

---

sive is the progress in just a single year: human interventions fell from 0.8 times per thousand miles to 0.2, which translates into a 400% improvement. With such progress, Google's cars will easily surpass my own driving ability later this year, available at: http://www.bbc.com/future/story/20170309-the-last-things-that-will-make-us-uniquely-human.

[64] Hubbard, *supra* note 8 (addresses the issue of whether the current liability and regulatory systems provide a fair, efficient method for balancing the concern for physical safety against the need to incentivize the innovation that is necessary to develop these robots.); *see also* F. Patrick Hubbard, *Do Androids Dream?: Personhood and Intelligent Artifacts*, 83 TEMP. L. REV. 405 (2011).

[65] *Brouse v. United States*, 83 F.Supp. 373 (N.D. Ohio 1949) (holding that operator of a plane "under robot control" was negligent in failing to "keep a proper and constant lookout" for other planes).

[66] *Id.*

[67] *Mracek v. Bryn Mawr Hosp.*, 2010 U.S. App. LEXIS 2015 (3d Dir. Jan. 28, 2010) (unpublished opinion).

[68] *Id.*

[69] *Id.*

determining liability, and whether humans have a duty of care to avoid an accident, even after delegating some of the operation to a robot or more generally to a system operating with artificial intelligence. On this point, a statute regulating autonomous automobiles operating in the District of Columbia, requires a human driver to be "prepared to take control of the autonomous vehicle at any moment."[70]As artificial intelligence controls more and more of the systems that represent the infrastructure of society a broadly-based body law regulating artificial intelligence will be necessary.

Discussing law in an age of advanced technologies, Judge Karnow describes one type of smart technology, "autonomous robots", as "software that teaches itself by running experiments, or making other sorts of real or virtual attempts for a solution, correcting for error and approximating a result which it then implements."[71] These aspects of an autonomous system have the potential to solve problems using solutions unknown to a human in the decision-making loop, thus raising the question of whether the autonomous machine or human is in control and therefore responsible for any harm that may come to property or people. Consider, *Bookout v. Toyota Motor Corp.*,[72] a case which involved a wrongful death action following a fatality from a sudden acceleration of a Toyota Camry, here the court looked to the role of software as a possible system defect, discussing among others whether the software controlling the system could be considered a causative factor in the accident. During the trial, experts for the plaintiff testified that Toyota's electronic throttle source code was defective, and that a single bit flip could cause the driver to lose control of engine speed. After a jury verdict in favor of the plaintiff, the case was settled.[73] Gary Merchant and Rachel Lindor, writing about autonomous vehicles and the issue of assigning liability, argue that with a malfunction, it would usually be a programming error or system failure that caused the accident, which would then implicate several potentially liable parties.[74] Additionally, the potential of system failures that may result from errors related to algorithms can also lead to product recall alerts issued by the government, or voluntary product recall by manufacturers. A recent example illustrates the latter point—Toyota decided to recall Priuses based on a software error that allegedly caused their gas-electric hybrid systems to shut down.[75]

---

[70]   *See* District of Columbia B19-0931, Autonomous Vehicle Act of 2012.

[71]   Karnow, *supra* note 59.

[72]   *Bookout v. Toyota Motor Corp*, County District Court Bookout v. Toyota Motor Corp., CJ-2008-7969, District Court, Oklahoma County, Oklahoma (Oklahoma City); Margaret Cronin Fisk, Toyota Settles Oklahoma Acceleration Case After Verdict, 2013, available at: http://www.bloom berg.com/news/articles/2013-10-25/toyota-settles-oklahoma-acceleration-case-after-jury-verdict.

[73]   Gary E. Merchant and Rachel A. Lindor, *The Coming Collision Between Autonomous Vehicles and the Liability System*, 52 SANTA CLARA L. REV, No. 4., 1321–40, 1326. (2012).

[74]   Merchant and Lindor, *Id.*; Sven A. Beiker, *Legal Aspects of Autonomous Driving*, 52 SANTA CLARA L. REV. 1145 (2010).

[75]   Hiroko Tabuchi and Jaclyn Trup, *Toyota Recalls Newest Prisues Over Software*, NY Times (Fed. 12, 2014), available at: http://www.nytimes.com/2014/02/13/business/international/toyota-issues-another-recall-for-hybrids-this-time-over-software-glitch.html?_r=0.

V.   INTENT, MENS REA, AND THE PROBLEM WITH DEFINITIONS

Consider an example with robots in which algorithms provide a robot's grippers the force profile for a particular task. By this brief description, we can foresee that the algorithms could direct the robot to exert too much force (the *actus reus*) and damage property or injure a human. If the algorithm had the capacity to independently learn various force profiles to use for different objects and materials, can we look directly at the robot's software and algorithms to determine its mental "state of mind" at the time when a particular gripping act occurred? That is, in a civil or criminal dispute, could the lines of code determining the amount of force applied to an object, provide circumstantial evidence of the mental frame-of-mind or *mens rea* of the artificial intelligence controlling a machine?[76] Under current legal doctrine, if the code was written by a programmer, with no new software or algorithms contributed by the artificial intelligence, courts would look to the programmer or the programmer's employer as the responsible party. But considering the fact that recent techniques of artificial intelligence can learn from experience and change their code, the ability to look directly at an entity's code as a source of evidence in legal disputes would be a new development in the law and would arguably implicate the self-incrimination clause of the Fifth Amendment, privacy law, the First Amendment's free speech prong, and procedurally the Federal Rules of Evidence.[77]

For this discussion, consider a specific law: under the Model Penal Code simple assault is the most common crime against the person and is expressed as: "a person is guilty of [simple] assault if he attempts to cause or purposively, knowingly or recklessly caused bodily injury to another."[78] Can an artificial intelligence be thought to have purposively, knowingly or recklessly caused bodily injury to another?[79] Will an examination of the software or algorithms associated with artificial intelligence allow intent to be determined? For a criminal action which involves a human defendant, in determining *mens rea* we currently do not have the technology to record the individual firing pattern of a person's neurons to directly discern their intent (at the level of neurons) at the time a crime was planned or committed; intent is often deduced by circumstantial evidence. However, not unlike accessing code, according to neuroscientists in the near future we may be able to directly record neuronal activity and thus reproduce components of a person's thought processes.[80] On that point, Duke University law professor Nita Farahany argues that the neuroscience revolution poses profound challenges for constitutional law and specifically current self-incrimination doctrine, which she argues exposes a deep conceptual confusion

---

[76]   Ryan Calo, *When A Robot Kills is it Murder or Products Liability?* Slate, available at: http://www.slate.com/articles/technology/future_tense/2016/04/a_robotics_law_expert_on_paolo_bacigalupi_s_mika_model.html.

[77]   *See, e.g.*, John Frank Weaver, *We Need to Pass Regulation on Artificial Intelligence, Early and Often*, SLATE, Sept. 12, 2014, http: available at: www.slate.com/blogs/future_tense/2014/09/we_need_to_pass_artificial_intelligence_laws_early_and_often.html.

[78]   MODEL PENAL CODE § 211.1(1) (1981).

[79]   *See, e.g. Schad v. Arizona*, 501 U.S. 624 (1991).

[80]   Nita A. Farahany, *Incriminating Thoughts*, 64 Stanford Law Review 351–408 (2012).

at the heart of the doctrine.[81] If artificial intelligence is granted the fiction of legal person status, the same confusion will occur when artificial intelligence is compelled to testify against itself.

In a seminal case involving the Fifth Amendment's self-incrimination doctrine, *Schmerber v. California*, the Court held that under the self-incrimination clause, no person shall be compelled to "prove a charge [from] his own mouth", but a person may be compelled to provide real or physical evidence, and a brain scan could be considered by the court as physical evidence.[82] By analogy, would the court consider software and algorithms to be physical evidence of thought processes and will artificial intelligence be compelled to provide such evidence? That is, will a future artificial intelligence that operates autonomously from humans be compelled to prove a charge against itself in the form of a software download? Surely, this topic is relevant for a law of artificial intelligence especially if the legal fiction of personhood is granted to the artificially intelligent entity.

Interestingly, there is some precedence that future courts deciding disputes involving artificial intelligence will look for intent from the lines of code. For example, a Minnesota appeals court allowed encrypted software to be introduced as evidence of the defendant's intent[83] to possess pornographic images of minors in violation of a Minnesota Statute.[84] An undercover investigation discovered that the encryption software was used to change the extensions of files, allegedly to hide the true nature of the file.[85] Similarly, artificial intelligence could encrypt its communications to hide the content of its messages. For example, researchers from Google's brain division have demonstrated that neural networks can create their own encryption standard, and communicate between each other.[86] The learning algorithms do not require prescribing a particular set of cryptographic algorithms, nor indicating ways of applying these algorithms: it is based only on a secrecy specification represented by training objectives.[87]

Additionally, current legislation in the area of encryption could apply to artificial intelligence. For example, the Health Insurance Portability and Accountability Act (HIPAA) requires certain healthcare providers to implement technical safeguards to guard against unauthorized access to electronic protected health information that is being transmitted over an electronic communications network, including encryption of data where appropriate. And further, under the Gramm-Leach-Bliley Financial Services Modernization

---

[81]　*Id.*

[82]　*Schmerber v. California*, 384 U.S. 757 (1966) (a landmark United States Supreme Court case in which the Court clarified the application of the Fourth Amendment's protection against warrantless searches and the Fifth Amendment privilege against self-incrimination for searches that intrude into the human body).

[83]　*See State of Minnesota v. Ari David Levine Ct of Appeals* (2005), available at: http://caselaw.findlaw.com/mn-court-of-appeals/1360182.html.

[84]　Minn. Stat. § 617.247, subd. 4(a) (2008).

[85]　Appellant was charged with one count of disseminating pornographic work in violation of Minn. Stat. § 617.247, subd. 3(a) (2008) and one count of possession of pornographic work on a computer or other electronic device in violation of Minn. Stat. § 617.247, subd. 4(a). The district court found the appellant guilty of possession of child pornography.

[86]　Roi Perez, 2016, *Artificial intelligence creates its own encryption*, available at: https://www.scmagazineuk.com/artificial-intelligence-creates-its-own-encryption/article/570120/.

[87]　*Id.*

Act of 1999, financial institutions must follow the Safeguards Rule, which requires that they develop an information security plan to ensure the security and confidentiality of customer information. In addition, the Federal Trade Commission (FTC) recommends that institutions consider encrypting information that is transmitted. And the IT Control Objectives of Sarbanes-Oxley state that when appropriate, public companies should determine if encryption techniques are to be used to support the confidentiality of financial information sent from one system to another. The above rules aimed among others at the capabilities of software and algorithms, seem relevant for a law of artificial intelligence.

A.   The Problem with Definitions

Recent techniques in machine learning involve techniques that enable computers to learn from experience, to learn by example, or to learn by principles of reinforcement. These are significant advances in machine learning that have occurred since the early days of artificial intelligence. However, legislators have not kept pace with advances in artificial intelligence, and courts have been inconsistent in deciding cases dealing with systems that display a degree of intelligence. To illustrate the latter point, compare two cases decided 20 years apart. A year after the first conference on artificial intelligence was held at Dartmouth College, a case decided in 1957 commented briefly on future capabilities of artificial intelligence. In *Arnold v. Reuther*, the dispute involved a driver who hit a pedestrian that had darted out in front of his car. The court held that the defendant driver did not have the "last clear chance" to avoid the accident, stating "A human being, no matter how efficient, is not a mechanical robot and does not possess the ability of a radar machine to discover danger before it becomes manifest."[88] This raises the question—how would the court have decided the case if a "mechanical robot" had been used?

Twenty years after *Arnold* was decided, in *Pompeii Estates, Inc. v. Consolidated Edison Co. of N.Y., Inc.*,[89] a plaintiff brought a negligence claim against the defendant who used a computer to mail past due notices. The court stated that "Computers can only issue mandatory instructions—they are not programmed to exercise discretion" and thus could not act as a shield to relieve Consolidated Edison of its obligation to exercise reasonable care when terminating service. So, in *Arnold*, the court recognized that a machine could possess superior abilities to those of a human, while in *Pompeii Estates*, the computer system was deemed to lack the ability to exercise reasonable care. But more recent machines can engage in far more intelligent and autonomous behavior than both examples just given, which among others, will challenge the reasonable care scheme under tort law and create significant challenges to several other areas of established law. Thus, under tort law courts may have to raise the standard of care for machines with reaction times and sensors that are far superior to those of humans and that are controlled by artificial intelligence.[90]

---

[88]   *Arnold v. Reuther*, 92 Sp.2d 593 (La.Ct.App. 1957); Michael Negnevitsky, *Artificial Intelligence: a Guide to Intelligent Systems*, Addison Wesley, 2005.

[89]   *Pompeii Estates, Inc. v. Consolidated Edison Co. of N.Y, Inc.*, 397 N.Y.S..2d 577, 580 (N.Y. Cir. Ct. 1977).

[90]   *See generally*, David C. Vladeck, *Machines Without Principals: Liability Rules and Artificial Intelligence*, 89 Wash. L. Rev. 117–50, 127, (2014).

For a future which will consist of artificially intelligent entities performing a range of tasks throughout society, one observation to note is that legislators tasked with regulating robotics, artificial intelligence, and other smart technologies will have difficulty defining with specificity the terms of art in each field. For example, within the research community there are numerous and often conflicting definitions used in the literature for the terms "robot", "autonomous technology",[91] and "artificial intelligence"; thus, determining the subject matter and scope of regulation for emerging smart technologies will be a challenge for legislators and courts. As an example, New Jersey legislators have defined artificial intelligence as ". . . the use of computers and related equipment to operate a machine to duplicate or mimic the behavior of human beings."[92] Interestingly, there is no mention of algorithms or software, or any technique of artificial intelligence in the definition. Instead under the New Jersey definition, artificial intelligence is described in the context of "computers and related equipment"; however, neither standing alone are a form of artificial intelligence; this limited view of artificial intelligence will surely impact the usefulness of the definition for any dispute involving systems directed by artificial intelligence.

Further, compare the previously mentioned District of Columbia statute on autonomous vehicles in which the driver must be prepared to take control of the car,[93] to a California statute in which "autonomous technology" is defined as "technology that has the capability to drive a vehicle without the active physical control or monitoring by a human operator."[94] Whether artificial intelligence should be allowed to drive automobiles without the possibility of human manual control is a major policy decision with challenging legal consequences. But legal scholars have also been inconsistent when using the terms artificial intelligence in their writings. For example, discussing the use of terminology, Judge Curtis Karnow stated that the term "robot is used indiscriminately to refer to a wide range of machines which exhibit, or are said to exhibit, some semblance of intelligence".[95]

A review of standard definitions indicates just how intertwined the terms used to describe smart technologies such as robotics and artificial intelligence are, although I argue they are different technologies (one primarily analog, the other primarily digital). Some definitions of artificial intelligence actually include robotics in the root of the definition itself, to wit, artificial intelligence is: "the collective attributes of a computer, robot, or other mechanical device programmed to perform functions analogous to learning and decision making."[96] Further, a common definition of robotics states: "Robotics is one branch of artificial intelligence."[97] Conversely, artificial intelligence pioneer Marvin

---

[91]   *See supra* note 16 for discussion of the terms "automated technology" and "autonomous vehicle".

[92]   Definition of artificial intelligence, NJ Senate No 343, available at: http://www.njleg.state. nj.us/2016/Bills/A1000/851_I1.PDF.

[93]   District of Columbia, *supra* note 70.

[94]   California Statute SB 1298, defining autonomous technology.

[95]   Karnow, *supra* n 59.

[96]   *Definition of Artificial Intelligence*, The Free Dictionary, available at: http://www.thefree dictionary.com/artificial+intelligence.

[97]   Vangie Beal, *Robotics*, webopedia, available at: http://www.webopedia.com/TERM/R/robot ics.html.

Minsky indicated that "Artificial Intelligence is getting robots to do smart things."[98] Still, others argue that a characteristic of emerging robotic behavior is autonomy, which is defined as "the state of existing or acting separately from others."[99] To further complicate matters, artificial intelligence pioneer John McCarthy stated that there is no solid definition of artificial intelligence that doesn't relate to human intelligence, and we still struggle to define human intelligence.[100] A point to make is that even though the technologies of smart machines (such as robots) and artificial intelligence are different, the terms are often used interchangeably in legal scholarship, which will add to the difficulty of determining how to regulate artificial intelligence.

Considering that artificial intelligence controls the performance of increasingly smart robots, autonomous machines, and more recently, intelligent virtual avatars,[101] perhaps it would be useful for legal scholars and legislators to think of artificial intelligence as a superordinate category in comparison to robotics and other smart technologies that rely on algorithms and machine learning techniques to detect patterns in data, learn from experience, and to interact with the world. Such an approach should lead to legislators enacting laws regulating artificial intelligence that would reach a wide range of applications that rely on the same set of algorithmic techniques for their performance.

VI.   HOW ARTIFICIAL INTELLIGENCE CHALLENGES ESTABLISHED LAW

The next section of the Chapter presents an overview of the increasing role of artificial intelligence in society as well as its challenges to established legal doctrine and policy. The main idea explored here is that artificial intelligence is a disruptive technology that is transforming many industries, and raising fundamental and challenging issues for the law to consider.[102]

A.   Agency Law

In artificial intelligence, among computer scientists, the term "agent" has a special meaning: an intelligent agent is an autonomous entity which observes the world through sensors and acts upon an environment using actuators and the agent directs its activity

---

[98]   Marvin Minsky, TELEPRESENCE, OMNI magazine, June 1980, available at: http://web.media.mit.edu/~minsky/papers/Telepresence.html.

[99]   Definition of "autonomy", Merriam-Webster online dictionary, available at: http://www.merriam-webster.com/dictionary/autonomy.

[100]   John McCarthy, *What is Artificial Intelligence?* John McCarthy's Home Page, 2–3 (Nov. 12, 2007), available at: http:www.formal.standard.edu/jme/whatisai.pdf [https://perma.cc/U3RT-Q7JK].

[101]   *See* Hsinchun Chen and Yulei Zhang, *AI, Virtual Worlds, and Massively Multiplayer Online Games*, IEEE Intelligent Systems, 2011, available at: https://ai.arizona.edu/sites/ai/files/MIS510/ai-virtual-worlds.pdf.

[102]   *See, e.g.*, John Frank Weaver, *We Need to Pass Regulation on Artificial Intelligence, Early and Often*, SLATE, Sept. 12, 2014, available at: http: www.slate.com/blogs/future_tense/2014/09/we_need_to_pass_artificial_intelligence_laws_early_and_often.html.

towards achieving goals in a rational manner. Intelligent agents may also learn or use knowledge to achieve their goals. It is not uncommon for an artificially intelligent agent to serve in an agency relationship with humans. The term "agent" also has a special meaning in legal doctrine. Under legal doctrine, the law of agency deals with a set of contractual, quasi-contractual and non-contractual fiduciary relationships that involve a person, called the agent, that is authorized to act on behalf of another, called the principal, to create legal relations with a third party. Succinctly, it may be referred to as the relationship between a principal and an agent whereby the principal, expressly or implicitly, authorizes the agent to work under his or her control and on his or her behalf. For a law of artificial intelligence, there are several issues which arise when the agent is a digital entity, such as an algorithm or analytic procedure.

Transactions by smart machines which legally bind a third party prompted David Vladeck from the Georgetown Law Center to state ". . .concepts of agency may be frayed, if not obliterated, by autonomous thinking machines, even those that are not truly 'sentient'." However, under statutory and common-law agency since an artificial intelligence lacks legal person status it cannot serve as a principal or agent.[103] Therefore, given the increasing autonomy of artificial intelligence, future courts will likely be tasked with deciding disputes involving artificial intelligence performing the duties of an agent but under current law lacking the legal capacity to serve as an agent. Consider the example of software that enters into transactions guided by algorithms.[104] Professor Deborah DeMott of Duke University indicates that from the "standpoint of common-law agency, a computer program is not capable of acting as a principal or agent because it is not a person that may itself hold legal rights and be subject to obligations."[105] So too does the current generation of artificial intelligence lack legal person status and therefore the capacity to hold rights and be subject to legal obligations.[106] This observation raises the question—what is the "legal status" of artificial intelligence in the form of software and algorithms performing activities much as a human agent would?

Addressing this question, Professor Deborah DeMott commented that under the common-law of agency, an electronic agent is considered the "instrumentality" of the person who uses it.[107] Additionally, legislation concerning electronic agents is consistent with common-law agency; as under statutory agency law software is viewed as a tool.[108] For example, the official commentary to the Uniform Electronic Transactions Act (UETA) explicitly characterizes an "electronic agent" as a machine that is the tool of

---

[103]   Vladeck, *supra* note 90.

[104]   Deborah DeMott, *Defining Agency and Its Scope*, available at: http://scholarship.law. duke.edu/cgi/viewcontent.cgi?article=6101&context=faculty_scholarship; *see also Comparative Contract Law: A Tale of Two Legal Systems* (Martin Hogg and Larry A. DiMatteo eds., Oxford Univ. Press 2015).

[105]   *Id.*

[106]   And commenting on the legal status of artificial intelligence Professor Vladeck stated ". . . these machines, notwithstanding their sophistication, have no attribute of legal personhood."

[107]   DeMott, *supra* note 104.

[108]   For example, Title 15 of the U.S. Code on Commerce and Trade, defines an "electronic agent" as "a computer program or an electronic or other automated means used independently to initiate an action or respond to electronic records or performances in whole or in part without review or action by an individual at the time of the action or response."

the person who uses it, despite its ability to initiate or respond—within the limits of its programming—without further intervention by a person.[109] However, anticipating future advances in technology, the commentary does indicate that based on continuing ". . . developments in artificial intelligence, a computer may be able to learn through experience, modify the instructions of their own programs, and even devise new instructions."[110] The commentary goes on to say that "If such developments occur, courts may construe the definition of an electronic agent accordingly in order to recognize such capabilities."[111] Thus, the UETA anticipates developments in artificial intelligence and acknowledges that the law will need to respond accordingly.

So, under current statutory and common-law of agency, an artificial intelligence consisting of software and algorithms, is viewed as an instrument, or tool, that is used by an agent who has legal capacity to enter into an agency relationship. But as artificial intelligence improves and makes decisions on its own, this analysis will prove inadequate. In fact, commenting on the future of autonomous machines Professor David Vladeck concluded "They will not be tools used by humans, they will be machines deployed by humans that will act independently of human instruction based on information the machine itself acquires and analyzes. . ."[112] So if an artificial intelligence engages in behavior that was unforeseen, a byproduct of its ability to "think" and plan its own course of actions, who then is liable for its actions? Unless the law is willing to grant entities controlled by artificial intelligence with legal person status, such entities are beyond the law.

Under current tort law and particularly products liability and negligence, the failure of artificial intelligence to follow the instructions provided by a principal could in theory be attributed to a manufacturing, design, or programing error; compatible with Professor DeMott's comments above, this analysis flows from the view of software as the "instrumentality" (or tool) of the person using it and with this analysis no liability is attributed to the artificial intelligence. However, the realization that the increasing autonomy and capabilities of artificial intelligence are beginning to stress different areas of law has prompted legal scholars to consider the issue of personhood for artificially intelligent systems. For example, Judge Curtis Karnow has indicated that a new legal fiction, "electronic personalities", may usefully address conflicting interests to established law which are brought forth by the use of artificial intelligence.[113] And in an early paper, Lawrence Solum explored whether an artificial intelligence could become a legal person under different legal doctrine and particularly whether an artificial intelligence could have legal capacity to serve as a trustee.[114]

If artificial intelligence is granted legal person rights, the rich body of case law developed for common-law agency could offer guidelines on how an artificial intelligence functioning as an agent would be viewed by courts. For instance, in *Taylor v. Roseville*

---

[109]   Uniform Electronics Transactions Act (UETA), available at: http://www.uniformlaws.org/shared/docs/electronic%20transactions/ueta_final_99.pdf.

[110]   *Id.*

[111]   UETA Official Commentary.

[112]   Vladeck, *supra* note 90.

[113]   Curtis E.A. Karnow, *The Encrypted Self: Fleshing Out the Rights of Electronic Personalities*, 13 J. MARSHALL J. COMPUTER & INFO. L., 1 (1994).

[114]   Solum, *supra* note 24.

Toyota, Inc.,[115] a California appeals court held that an employer could be liable for injuries caused by an employee while using a company car to run an errand. While there was no express permission to use the vehicle for this purpose, the jury found "ostensible authority", that is, the authority that the principal, either intentionally or by lack of ordinary care, caused or allowed a third party to believe the agent possessed. This analysis is consistent with common-law agency, in which legal consequences stem from one person's conduct attributed to another and with the imputation of the agent's knowledge to the principal.

As with human agents, for artificial intelligence, much of the courts' considerations on questions of agency will be based on specific fact patterns. For example, in *Commercial Bank v. Hearn*,[116] a Mississippi court held that an employer is not liable on the theory of *respondeat superior* for a car accident caused by an employee who was engaged in charitable activities during work time as the activities were not a central part of the work duties. Under the Restatement (Third) of Agency,[117] "An employee acts within the scope of employment when performing work assigned by the employer or engaging in a course of conduct subject to the employer's control."[118] "An employee's act is not within the scope of employment when it occurs within an independent course of conduct not intended by the employee to serve any purpose to the employer."[119] While it is difficult to envision artificial intelligence at this time deciding on its own to deviate from a task assigned to it by a principal, its algorithms could have considerable leeway to determine how to select a route or perform a task and therefore engage in activities unforeseen by the principal.

B.   Antitrust Law

As another example of artificial intelligence challenging established law, consider that only a few "hi-tech" companies with strong commercial interests in artificial intelligence through their acquisitions, mergers, and active research laboratories are dominating the field of artificial intelligence.[120] This harbors worries about collusion and other monopolistic behavior, and raises the question of whether current antitrust law will be effective regulating the artificial intelligence industry.[121] But more specifically, the functions of algorithms themselves could lead to contract violations. In fact, the role of algorithms in the context of antitrust law has already garnered interest from legal scholars such as Professors Maurice Stucke and Ariel Ezrachi (see their Chapter 24 in this book) who have observed that algorithms could result not only in collusion but in discriminatory pricing. From these observations, antitrust law is a rich example of an established body of law in

---

[115]   *Taylor v. Roseville Toyota, Inc.*, 138 Cal. App. 4th 994 (Ct. App., Calif., 2006).

[116]   *Commercial Bank v. Hearn,* 923 So.2d 202 (Sup. Ct., Miss., 2006).

[117]   Restatement (Third) of Agency, §7.07 (2006).

[118]   *Id.*

[119]   *Id.* (describing that a principal is subject to vicarious liability for an agent's actions only when the agent is acting within the scope of employment).

[120]   Such companies include Alphabet, Apple, Facebook, Microsoft, Amazon, and Alibaba.

[121]   Ezrachi, Ariel and Stucke, Maurice E., *Artificial Intelligence & Collusion: When Computers Inhibit Competition* (April 8, 2015). Oxford Legal Studies Research Paper No. 18/2015; University of Tennessee Legal Studies Research Paper No. 267, available at SSRN: http://ssrn.com/abstrac t=2591874 or http://dx.doi.org/10.2139/ssrn.2591874.

the U.S. codified in the Sherman Antitrust Act and other federal and state statutes, that will be challenged by the use of algorithms and other techniques of artificial intelligence.

C.   First Amendment Law

Another challenge to established law emanating from the use of artificial intelligence occurs when software and algorithms are used to produce speech spoken by machines and virtual entities such as avatars.[122] Given how widespread speech technology is embedded within commercial products such as digital assistants, First Amendment doctrine for speech produced by algorithms is more and more becoming a topic of importance for a law of artificial intelligence. Under First Amendment speech doctrine, algorithms are a relatively unexplored area of jurisprudence but will become more important as artificial intelligence imbues more technology with the ability to understand, react to, and produce speech. For example, consider a machine programmed to produce, interpret, and understand speech. There are at least four aspects of artificial intelligence which create this level of performance: (1) speech recognition algorithms to detect speech; (2) natural language algorithms to understand what is spoken; (3) algorithms which control "execution", that is, the ability to fulfill a spoken request; and (4) algorithms which allow the entity the ability to talk back to the speaker.

Law professors Toni M. Massaro and Helen Norton (see their Chapter 12 in this book) argue that computers equipped with speech producing algorithms are pushing First Amendment theory and doctrine in profound and novel ways.[123] In their words, "They are becoming increasingly self-directed and corporal in ways that may one day make it difficult to call the communication *ours* versus *theirs*."[124] They indicate that this, in turn, ". . .invites questions about whether the First Amendment ever will (or ever should) cover AI speech or speakers even absent a locatable and accountable human creator."[125] However, there is precedence that non-human entities may receive First Amendment protection for speech. In *Citizen United v. Federal Election Commission*, a case dealing with the regulation of campaign spending by organizations, the Court in a 5-4 decision held that freedom of speech doctrine prohibited the government from restricting independent political expression by a non-profit corporation.[126] The principles articulated by the Supreme Court in *Citizen United* have also been extended to for-profit corporations, labor unions and other associations.[127] Additionally, the Court has made some headway into the question of whether the output of an algorithm should be protected speech: in *Sorell v. IMS Health Inc.*, the Court concluded that the "creation and dissemination of information are speech for First Amendment

---

[122]   Stuart M. Benjamin, *Algorithms and Speech*, 161 U. PA. L. Rev. 1445–93 (2013).

[123]   Massaro, Toni M. and Norton, Helen L., *Siri-ously? Free Speech Rights and Artificial Intelligence* (October 4, 2016). 110 Northwestern University Law Review 1169 (2016); Arizona Legal Studies Discussion Paper No. 15-29, available at SSRN: https://ssrn.com/abstract= 2643043.

[124]   *Id.* at 1169.

[125]   *Id.*

[126]   *Citizens United v. Federal Election Commission*, 558 U.S. 310 (2008).

[127]   *Id.*

purposes."[128] Additionally, under Chapter 15 of the U.S. code on electronic signatures in global and national commerce the term "information" means data, text, images, sounds, codes, computer programs, software, databases, or the like.

According to Professor Stuart Benjamin, Supreme Court jurisprudence provides for "very broad First Amendment coverage of speech, and the Court has reinforced that breadth in recent cases."[129] Benjamin concludes that under the Court's jurisprudence "the First Amendment (and the heightened scrutiny it entails) should apply to many algorithm-based decisions, specifically those entailing substantive communications."[130]

D.   Commerce

Another area of importance for a law of artificial intelligence relates to the emerging digital economy of the twenty-first century.[131] Given how widespread artificial intelligence is being used in business enterprises and for consumer applications, an important question is whether current legal doctrine is sufficient to account for systems engaging in transactions on behalf of humans and corporations in ways that are *a priori* unknown or predictable by humans.[132] For example, a 2016 Stanford Business School White Paper on "Technological Disruption and Innovation in Last-Mile Delivery" emphasized how algorithms are being used to collect orders, monitor deliveries and supplies, determine optimum routes, and forecast demand for products.[133] And in the digital economy, artificial intelligence does even more: serving as shopping agents, recommender services, data mining of customer buying patterns, customer service help, auctions, negotiations, contracts, brokering, reputation services, promotions, advertising, procurement, and creating product catalogs.[134] From this list of applications, artificial intelligence is very likely to be involved in fundamental issues of commerce in terms of negotiating contracts, determining distribution routes, and so on, so just based on commercial transactions which occur yearly in the billions, artificial intelligence is challenging established law.[135]

---

[128]   *Sorell v. IMS Health Inc.*, 131 S.Ct. 2653, (2011) (the Court held that a Vermont statute that restricted the sale, disclosure, and use of records that revealed the prescribing practices of individual doctors violated the First Amendment.); 15 U.S.C. 96 – ELECTRONIC SIGNATURES IN GLOBAL AND NATIONAL COMMERCE.

[129]   Benjamin, *supra* note 122, at 1445.

[130]   *Id.* at 1447.

[131]   Hau L. Lee, Yiwen Chin, Barchi Gillai, and Sonali Rammohan, *Technological Disruption and Innovation in Last-Mile Delivery*, White Paper, Stanford Business School, 2016.

[132]   Calo, *supra* note 9.

[133]   Lee et al., *supra* note 131.

[134]   Papers from the AAAI Workshop, Tim Finin and Benjamin Grosof, Cochairs, available at: https://www.aaai.org/Press/Reports/Workshops/ws-99-01.php.

[135]   Erik Brynjolfsson and Andrew McAfee, *Race Against the Machine: How the Digital Revolution is Accelerating Innovation, Driving Productivity, and Irreversibly Transforming Employment and the Economy* (Digital Frontier Press, 2012) (discussing how the digital revolution is accelerating and that digital technologies are rapidly encroaching on skills that used to belong to humans alone. This phenomenon is both broad and deep, and has profound economic implications. Many of these implications are positive; digital innovation increases productivity, reduces prices (sometimes to zero), and grows the overall economic pie.)

The role of algorithms and other techniques of artificial intelligence in contract law is another emerging subject for a law of artificial intelligence.[136] For example, in a case dealing with a software bot involving an internet advertising breach of contract claim, the court was asked to resolve a dispute over the meaning of "impressions", a key term in internet advertising. In *Go2Net Inc. v. C L Host Inc.*,[137] the court determined that the parties' contract permitted visits by search engines and other "artificial intelligence" agents in the advertiser's count of impressions.[138] Here visits to the website by artificial intelligence were placed on an equal footing with human visits to the same website.

In a world of interconnected devices with artificially intelligent agents contracting on behalf of consumers, common-law agency principles, ecommerce statutes, common-law contract law, and Article 2 of the Uniform Commercial Code (UCC) are implicated by the use of artificial intelligence.[139] In fact, within the field of commerce there are numerous challenges to established legal doctrine based on the use of software and algorithms to conduct commercial transactions. For example, under the UCC a current topic of interest in contract law is whether algorithms and other techniques of artificial intelligence should be considered goods or a service. This is an important distinction as goods and services receive different treatment by the legal system, including different protections.

Whether an algorithm is considered as goods under the UCC has not been adequately addressed by courts or legislators, but courts normally consider software to be "goods", which the UCC defines as "all things . . . which are movable at the time of identification to the contract for sale . . ."[140] However, algorithms often perform services such as searching the Internet to find the cheapest flight or shortest distance to reach a destination. As such, many commercial software vendors argue that their software is a service, and utilize licensing schemes to maintain control over their product. Complications may arise when product liability claims are directed to failures in software, as computer code has not generally been considered a "product" but instead thought of as a "service", with cases seeking compensation caused by alleged defective software more often preceding as breach of warranty cases rather than product liability cases.[141]

Even though there is no dispute within the legal community that the purchase and sale of machines such as robots are "goods" under commercial law,[142] in contrast, software and algorithms used for commercial transactions are something of a conundrum and present a challenge to established legal doctrine. Recalling that artificial intelligence is expressed in the form of code and algorithms, products liability involving computer software and the conditions under which software is covered by the UCC are issues which will be implicated by the use, sale, and licensing of artificial intelligence, and will

---

[136]   A software bot, also referred to as a robot bot, or just bot, is a software routine or algorithm which typically runs automated tasks, thus is repetitive.

[137]   *Go2Net Inc. v. C L Host Inc.*, 115 Wash. App. 73 (2003).

[138]   *Id.*

[139]   Uniform Commercial Code (UCC) § 2-105.

[140]   *Id.*

[141]   *See e.g., Motorola Mobility, Inc. v. Myriad France SAS*, 850 F. Supp. 2d 878 (N.D. Ill. 2012) (case alleging defective software more often proceeding as breach of warranty).

[142]   Hubbard, *supra* note 8, at 1813.

challenge established legal doctrine as artificial intelligence improves and makes decisions independent of humans.[143]

E.   Discriminatory Practices by Algorithms

As another example of how artificial intelligence is beginning to challenge established legal doctrine consider the use of algorithms in areas given constitutional protection by federal statutes. For example, consider a machine-learning algorithm that is used by a company for employee hiring decisions.[144] Claire Miller notes that algorithms can reinforce human prejudices, and target unsuspecting populations.[145] On this point, the Federal Trade Commission commented that unscrupulous advertisers can use algorithms to target people living in low income neighborhoods with high-interest loans.[146]

Generally, employment discrimination laws seek to prevent discrimination based on race, sex, religion, national origin, physical disability, and age by employers, all factors an artificially intelligent system using algorithms may consider when evaluating potential employees.[147] The wide body of statutory law enacted to prevent discriminatory practices could be triggered by the use of algorithms and thus would be relevant to a law of artificial intelligence. That the use of algorithms may result in discriminatory practices in situations protected by federal statutes will surely be an important issue for courts and legislators to consider as artificial intelligence proliferates into society.

When considering discriminatory practices, an area of interest for a law of artificial intelligence is employment law. As a basic question, if an algorithm discriminates against applicants based on race, gender, or age will the employer be liable under Title VII of the Civil Rights Act of 1964,[148] which prohibits employment discrimination based on race, color, religion, sex, or national origin; or be liable under the Equal Pay Act of 1963[149] which protects men and women who perform substantially equal work in the

---

[143]   Lori A. Weber, *Bad Bytes: The Application of Strict Products Liability to Computer Software*, 66 ST. JOHN'S L.REV. No. 2, 1992, 469–85.

[144]   Anupam Chander, *The Racist Algorithm?* 115 MICH.L.REV. 2017, Forthcoming; UC Davis Legal Studies Research Paper No. 498. Available at SSRN: http://ssrn.com/abstract=2795203.

[145]   Claire Cain Miller, *When Algorithms Discriminate*, 2015, A version of this article appears in print on July 13, 2015, on page B1 of the New York edition with the headline: Algorithms May Echo Human Bias, Studies Find, available at: http://www.ischool.berkeley.edu/newsandevents/news/presscoverage/2015-07-09-mulligan.

[146]   Nathan Newmanm, *The Cost of Lost Privacy: Consumer Harm and Rising Inequality in the Age of Google*, 40 W.M.MITCHELL.L.REV. (2014); *Federal Trade Commission, PrivacyCon, Part 3 Slides,* available at: https://www.ftc.gov/news-events/events-calendar/2016/01/privacycon; Amicus Curiae Brief of Center for Digital Democracy in Support of Respondent, *Spokeo v. Thomas Robins*, Supreme Court of the Unite States (discussing how the use of algorithms may discriminate and harm individuals), available at: https://epic.org/amicus/spokeo/Center-for-Digital-Democracy-Brief.pdf.

[147]   Joel Friedman, *The Law of Employment Discrimination: Cases and Materials* (University Casebook Series) 9th edition, (Foundation Press 2013) (the casebook discusses major aspects of employment discrimination law, including legislative, administrative, and judicial developments); 42 U.S.C. §§ 1981, 1981a, 1983, 1988 – Nineteenth Century Civil Rights Acts.

[148]   Title VII of the Civil Rights Act of 1967, 42 U.S.C. Chapter 21 – Civil Rights Act of 1964.

[149]   29 U.S.C. § 206 – Equal Pay Act of 1963.

same establishment from sex-based wage discrimination?[150] Further, in developing a law of artificial intelligence, will an algorithm be found to discriminate under the Age Discrimination in Employment Act of 1967,[151] which protects individuals who are 40 years of age or older? Or could an algorithm be found to engage in discriminatory practices under Title I and Title V of the Americans with Disabilities Act of 1990,[152] which prohibits employment discrimination against qualified individuals with disabilities in the private sector, state, and local governments? Additionally, would the use of algorithms in decision-making contexts trigger Sections 501 and 505 of the Rehabilitation Act of 1973,[153] which prohibits discrimination against qualified individuals with disabilities who work in the federal government; or more generally the Civil Rights Act of 1991,[154] which, among others, provides monetary damages in cases of intentional employment discrimination?[155] From the above list, it is clear that the use of artificial intelligence has the potential to challenge entire bodies of statutory law which relate to constitutional issues of equality; this important topic of law which could be challenged by the use of algorithms would seem to be a proper subject for a law of artificial intelligence and for legislative action.[156]

F. Issues of Jurisdiction

The structure and form of artificial intelligence consisting of bits moving through the Internet could undermine certain assumptions that gave rise to the traditional model of jurisdiction which was articulated among others in *American Banana Company v. United Fruit Company*.[157] In *American*, the Court stated: "The character of an act as lawful or unlawful must be determined wholly by the law of the country where the act is done." But of course, this "territorial-based view" of jurisdiction provides few guidelines for an Internet connected world and even less so for artificial intelligence moving throughout cyberspace.

In the 1980s courts began to face the challenge of applying long-standing principles of personal jurisdiction to a borderless communication medium that enabled individuals to instantaneously interact across state and international boundaries.[158] From *International*

---

[150]   However, in such a situation, it is likely that the terms of an EULA would state the choice of law and jurisdiction for the contracting parties.

[151]   Age Discrimination in Employment Act of 1967.

[152]   Title I and Title V of the Americans with Disabilities Act of 1990, 42 U.S.C. Chapter 126 – Americans with Disabilities Act of 1990.

[153]   Section 501 and 505 of the Rehabilitation Act.

[154]   Civil Rights Act of 1991.

[155]   Solon Borocas and Andrew D. Selbst, *Big Data's Disparate Impact*, 104 CAL L. REV. 671-29 2016.

[156]   Cathy O'Neil, *Weapons of Math Destruction: How Big Data Increases Inequality and Threatens Democracy* (Crown 2016) (discussing that algorithms being used today are opaque, unregulated, and uncontestable, and that they may reinforce discrimination).

[157]   *American Banana Company v. United Fruit Company*, 213 U.S. 347, 356 (1909).

[158]   *See Goodyear Dunlop Tires Operations, S.A. v. Brown*, 131 S. Ct. 2846, 2854–57 (2011); *Goodyear Dunlop Tires Operations, S.A. v. Brown and Daimler AG v. Bauman* (a company doing business on the Internet may be sued for any reason in the jurisdiction where it is "at home", typically its place of incorporation. Because general jurisdiction is now quite limited, courts will often

Shoe Co. v. Washington, it was held that specific jurisdiction over a defendant could be established by a court only if he or she had "certain minimum contacts" which give rise to the action in question in the forum such that the exercise of jurisdiction "does not offend traditional notions of fair play and substantial justice."[159] The question raised by legal scholars was whether geography-based laws of jurisdiction applied to the borderless boundaries of cyberspace. Similarly, would established law, such as *International Shoe*, be applicable if a person was subject to personal jurisdiction in a distant forum based solely on the activities of artificial intelligence working independently of the human? And if so under which fact patterns?

In evaluating the assertion of jurisdiction in cases involving the Internet, courts have applied both traditional tests and in some cases standards customized to the online world. For example, in *Zippo Manufacturing Co. v. Zippo Dot Com, Inc.*, a Federal Court held that "the likelihood that personal jurisdiction can be constitutionally exercised is directly proportionate to the nature and quality of commercial activity that an entity conducts over the Internet."[160] The "sliding scale" or "*Zippo* Test" has been generally accepted as the standard in Federal Courts in deciding personal jurisdiction in Internet cases; however the type of activities resulting from the use of artificial intelligence does not fit neatly in the Zippo test, among others because the test is aimed at websites hosting information for human consumption and establishing the location of artificial intelligence at any particular website located in physical space may be difficult. On this point, Professors Susan Brenner and Bert-Jaap Koops stated, ". . . with cybercrime it is difficult to pinpoint 'where' the act actually takes place",[161] and such may especially be the case with artificial intelligence. They further indicate that "Publishing a Web site with a content-related offense. . . such as hate speech, may be considered to take place at the computer where the material is uploaded, which constitutes the act of publishing the material. But the act of uploading can cover several countries. . .;"[162] exacerbating the problem of determining jurisdiction, this is especially true for artificial intelligence.

Based on the *Zippo* test, this last observation that "cyber activities" may cross international boundaries poses problems for determining jurisdiction when digital content in the form of artificial intelligence is involved. Of course, in addition to *Zippo* there are other cases which have explored the issue of Internet jurisdiction, but taken together they have produced a complex web of rules, sensitive to different fact patterns, which are difficult to apply to artificial intelligence. In fact, determining Internet jurisdiction for activities occurring within cyberspace will be exacerbated by artificial intelligence because it can move effortlessly across physical boundaries and as a new development act autonomously from humans in a distant forum. In *Bragg v. Linden Research, Inc*,[163] which involved a

---

look to specific personal jurisdiction to determine whether a company is amenable to suit in a given jurisdiction); TiTi Nguyen, *A Survey of Personal Jurisdiction based on Internet Activity: A Return to Tradition*, 19 Berkeley Tech. L.J. 519 (2004).

[159]   *International Shoe Co. v. Washington*, 326 U.S. 310 (1945).

[160]   *Zippo Manufacturing Co. v. Zippo Dot Com, Inc.*, 952 F. Supp. 1119 (W.D. Pa. 1997).

[161]   Susan W. Brenner and Bert-Jaap Koops, *Approaches to Cybercrime Jurisdiction*, 4 J. HIGH TECH. L. J., 15, (2004).

[162]   *Id.*

[163]   *Bragg v. Linden Research, Inc*, 487 F. Supp. 2d 593 (E.D. Penn. 2007).

dispute over virtual property located in the online world of Second Life, the court ruled that the district court had personal jurisdiction over Linden based on representations made by its representatives in national advertisements and based on Bragg's "attendance" at several virtual town meetings hosted by Second Life.[164] On the issue of personal jurisdiction, Judge Robreno's discussion of minimum contacts had some unique twists when he recognized that Rosedale's avatar may have actually interacted with Bragg's avatar within the virtual world. Once inside Second Life, participants could view virtual property, read additional materials about purchasing virtual property, interact with other avatars who owned virtual property, and, ultimately, purchase virtual property themselves. Significantly, participants could even interact with Rosedale's avatar in Second Life during town hall meetings that he held on the topic of virtual property.[165]

G.   The Use of Artificial Intelligence as Evidence

Another body of law which will be challenged by the use of artificial intelligence relates to the issue of authenticating artificial intelligence when used for evidentiary purposes in court proceedings.[166] In the U.S. under the Federal Rules of Evidence (FRE), for evidentiary purposes, authenticating evidence means that the proponent must produce evidence sufficient to support a finding that the item is what the proponent claims it is.[167] While there is no definition of artificial intelligence in the FRE or Federal Rules of Civil Procedure (FRCP), a discussion of electronically stored information (ESI) may shed light on how courts will view the admissibility of artificial intelligence when proffered as evidence. For comparison purposes, not unlike artificial intelligence, electronically stored information is "information created, manipulated, communicated, stored, and best utilized in digital form, requiring the use of computer hardware and software."[168]

Some uses of ESI for evidentiary purposes were clarified by the court in *Lorraine v. Markel American Insurance Co.*[169] in which the plaintiff brought a federal action to enforce an arbitrator's finding and to set aside the limits placed on the award. While the defendant counterclaimed to enforce the arbitrator's award in full, the problem for both sides was that neither supplied the evidentiary foundation needed for the court to rely upon various e-mails and other ESI offered in support of and in opposition to the arbitrator's award. The court's analysis in *Lorraine* discussed several issues that may help future courts determine how artificial intelligence should be proffered in admissible form.[170] This includes whether the artificial intelligence is relevant;[171] authentic;[172] hearsay and, if so,

---

[164]   *Id.*
[165]   *Id.*
[166]   *See generally, Griffin v. State*, 419 MD 343 (2011).
[167]   Federal Rules of Evidence, Rule 901. Authenticating or Identifying Evidence.
[168]   *Electronically Stored Information: The December 2006 Amendments to the Federal Rules of Civil Procedure*, Kenneth J. Withers, Northwestern Journal of Technology and Intellectual Property, Vol.4 (2), 171.
[169]   *Lorraine v. Markel American Insurance Co.* 241 F.R.D. 534 (D. Md. May 4, 2007).
[170]   *Id.*
[171]   Federal Rule of Evidence, Rule 401.
[172]   Federal Rule of Evidence, Rule 901.

whether it meets an applicable exception under the FRE.[173] Additionally, courts will need to determine whether artificial intelligence can be considered an original or an acceptable duplicate (or "best evidence"), or whether it meets an exception.[174] And, when proffered as evidence courts will need to consider whether the probative value of the artificial intelligence is outweighed by unfair prejudice.[175] This could be an issue of particular interest to courts given algorithms may use discriminatory practices for decision-making. There are, of course, a multitude of ways to authenticate artificial intelligence for evidentiary purposes, for example, relying on any "self-authenticating" characteristics of the artificial intelligence itself.[176]

Additionally, the rules on hearsay will also be relevant for artificial intelligence proffered as evidence, as well as the many exceptions for hearsay.[177] But two broad points should be made. First, lacking legal personhood status much of artificial intelligence may not be considered hearsay because no natural or legal person is making an assertion. For example, when an electronically generated record is entirely the product of the functioning of a computerized system or process, there is no "person" involved in the creation of the record, and therefore no "assertion" being made by a person, in this case the record may not be hearsay under the FRE.[178] But arguing innuendo that the artificial intelligence in question is "hearsay", there are a multitude of exceptions that might apply. Thus, even if artificial intelligence has cleared the authentication and hearsay hurdles, additional evidentiary rules, such as showing the material is an "original" and is not unfairly prejudicial such that it should be excluded from evidence will apply.

H. Intellectual Property

Another major area of law that will be challenged by the use of artificial intelligence is copyright, trademark, and patent law especially given increasingly intelligent and creative machines and software entities. Patent law will implicate key aspects of artificial intelligence, including algorithms, neural nets, and statistical modeling, these are techniques which are widespread throughout many smart technologies, and would seemingly be of interest to a law of artificial intelligence. For patent law, Professor Lisa Vertinsky (see her chapter 18 in this book) commented that "thinking machines" are "transforming the invention process in ways not easily accommodated with the present U.S. patent system requiring that existing and supporting legal doctrine needs to be re-examined and rules for patentability, patent scope and patent infringement adjusted, to accommodate the new

---

[173]   Federal Rule of Evidence, Rules 801, 803, 804 and 807.
[174]   Federal Rule of Evidence, Rules 1001 through 1008.
[175]   Federal Rule of Evidence, Rule 403. Further, Federal Rule of Evidence 901(b)(3) and (b)(4) provide common ways to authenticate ESI. Rule 901(b)(3) permits authentication by "[a]ppearance, contents, substance, internal patterns, or other distinctive characteristics, taken in conjunction with circumstances." 901(b)(4) allows authentication essentially through "circumstantial evidence".
[176]   *Lorraine, supra* note 169, at 553.
[177]   Federal Rule of Evidence 801 through 807.
[178]   *Id.* at 564–65; *see also State v. Dunn*, 7 S.W.3d 427, 432 (Mo. Ct. App. 2000) (Computer generated telephone records "are not the counterpart of a statement by a human declarant" and "should not be treated as hearsay.").

paradigm of invention."[179] As a general observation, mental processes and the processing of human thinking are presumed to be abstract and non-physical and therefore largely ineligible for patent protection.[180] With this observation in mind, will artificial intelligence techniques which emulate human decision-making be considered abstract and not eligible for patent protection?

Currently the patent statutes do not on their face allow for software or algorithms to be listed as an inventor as the patent statute defines "inventor" to mean "the individual who invented or discovered the subject matter of the invention."[181] But inventions by artificially intelligent entities may be done independent of humans, which begs the question of who is the inventor? For example, in the area of product design, attorneys Ben Hattenbach and Joshua Glucoft note that computers with artificial intelligence are already independently designing genuinely useful inventions in a number of fields.[182] Artificial intelligence can also be used to solve design problems often using novel solutions that were originally unknown to the human in the system.[183] However, certain subject matter is not copyrightable, whether by human or artificial intelligence inventor. For example, in *Blue Spike, LLC v. Google Inc*, the Court found that because the patent at issue sought to model using on a computer "the highly effective ability of humans to identify and recognize a signal", the patents simply cover a general-purpose implementation of "an abstract idea long undertaken within the human mind."[184]

From the examples just given, as indicated by Hattenbach and Glucoft, inventions by artificially intelligent systems suggest that it is perhaps "on a collision course with existing patent law" with regard to independently designed useful invention.[185] Under the U.S. Constitution, intellectual property law focuses on creators and inventors—that is, "people" who create and invent. Additionally, the U.S. Constitution refers to securing exclusive rights to "authors and inventors" and the notion of human as inventor is embedded within the patent application process, in that the patent laws are framed in terms of human creation. For example, Section 100 of the Patent Act states "whoever shall invent" and section 102 prohibits patenting of subject matter that the person "did not himself invent." Further, under the U.S. patent statute, the "term 'inventor' means the individual or, if a joint invention, the individuals collaboratively who invented or discovered the subject matter of the invention."[186]

As policy, perhaps the law could be amended to define "author" and "inventor" as "hardware or software capable of human-like intelligence" or a more nuanced definition of an author should be used that references independent thought. However, attorney

---

[179]   Lisa Vertinsky and Todd Rice, *Thinking About Thinking Machines: Implications of Machine Invention for Patent Law*, B.U.J. SCI & TECH., Vol 8:2.

[180]   Steven B. Roosa, *The Next Generation of Artificial Intelligence in Light of In re Bilski*, 21 Intellectual Property and Technology Law Journal, 6 (2009).

[181]   35 U.S.C. §103.

[182]   Robert Plotkin, *The Genie in the Machine* (Stanford University Press 2009).

[183]   *Id.*

[184]   *Blue Spike, LLC v. Google Inc,* No. 14-CV-01650-YGR 2015 WL 5260506 at *5 (N.D. Cal. Sept. 8, 2015)., aff'd, 2016 WL 5956746 (Fed. Cir. Oct. 14, 2016).

[185]   Ben Hattenbach and Joshua Glucoft, *Patents in an Era of Infinite Monkeys and Artificial Intelligence*, 19 STAN. TECH. L. REV, 32, 35, 2015, at 32.

[186]   35 U.S.C. 100(f).

Jeremy A. Cubert asks: "would we be opening Pandora's Box of conferring 'additional rights' to AI capable of independent thought and creativity"?[187] If so, how would creativity and invention be incentivized by expanding the definition of an author to include artificial intelligence? These policy considerations will be pressing as artificial intelligence becomes more creative and autonomous from humans. Consider that in a typical scenario, the employer of a creator or inventor becomes the owner of the intellectual property by virtue of the work for hire doctrine or an employment agreement; perhaps artificial intelligence could be regulated under the work for hire doctrine in which case the employer would own the copyright to the work.[188]

Moving from the patent statute, another area of intellectual property law that will be challenged by artificial intelligence, is the question of authorship for works created by algorithms. Under U.S. copyright law, software is considered a "literary work" but under the current copyright statute software is not considered to be an author no matter how creative the work produced by artificial intelligence or how autonomous the work was produced from human input. But legislators have begun to take action in this area, On this point, a draft motion prepared by the European Commission argues that the sophisticated autonomous robots coming online should be granted the status of an "electronic person" with specific rights and obligations such as to claim copyright protection for their work, this implicates employee contracts and nondiscrimination agreements.[189] Considering intellectual property rights, for artificially intelligent entities, issues of civil procedure will also need to be considered. For example, for copyright law, computers do not have standing to file an application or to initiate an infringement claim. But given algorithms are now writing news stories and financial reports independent of human authors how long before artificial intelligence entities are offered legal person rights or dealt with in some other way?

VII.   TOWARDS A LAW OF ARTIFICIAL INTELLIGENCE

To begin, as policy for artificial intelligence, the goal of government regulators should be to draft legislation that does not stifle artificial intelligence research, but still protects the public from possible dangers when artificial intelligence approaches and then exceeds human levels of intelligence. For "smart machines" and other emerging technologies which are controlled by artificial intelligence, and which perform tasks that require computationally intensive algorithms and sophisticated analytical techniques, current legal doctrine is becoming challenged as these systems engage in creative and unpredictable behavior.[190] So, how should the law respond to increasingly smart technologies? In the area of regulation, Professor Matthew Scherer writing about artificial intelligence

---

[187]   Jeremy A. Cubert, *Opening Pandora's Box in an Age of Artificial Intelligence Innovation*, IPWatchdog, 2017, http://www.ipwatchdog.com/2017/01/07/opening-pandoras-box-artificial-intelligence-innovation/id=76002/

[188]   Louis Miranda, *Artificial Intelligence Algorithms Now Writing the 'News' You Read*, 2012. http://planet.infowars.com/technology/artificial-intelligence-algorithms-now-writing-the-news-you-read

[189]   Karnow, *supra* note 59.

[190]   Calo, *supra* note 9.

concluded that to regulate artificial intelligence the regulatory regime must be able to define the term. This is a first step, but also a difficult step as people use terminology such as robotics and artificial intelligence as if they were interchangeable, when in fact, they are not.[191] However, I do not propose that a law of artificial intelligence be developed from first principles as there already is a well-established body of constitutional, statutory, and case law that has relevance to emerging smart systems; this book is a testament to that conclusion. In fact, in my view, the statutes and case law which relate to artificial intelligence as discussed throughout this book represent a body of law which will serve as precedence for future disputes involving increasingly smart machines and virtual entities operating under the direction of artificial intelligence. But even with a body of law that represents a starting point for the regulation of artificial intelligence, still, the current law will be stressed by increasingly smart versions of artificial intelligence and thus new legislative action will be needed to provide additional guidance to courts dealing with systems that are learning on their own, performing autonomously, and reacting to the environment in unpredictable ways. For example, in commercial law, as Professor Stacy-Ann Elvy indicates, when artificial intelligence is a contracting party, Article 2 of the UCC will need to be amended to safeguard consumers experiencing the increased levels of information asymmetry and the growing distance between artificially intelligent consumers.[192]

What features of artificial intelligence challenge established areas of law and should therefore be the focus of a law of artificial intelligence? I believe there are several attributes of artificial intelligence to consider. As argued throughout this Chapter, the technology driving the "artificial intelligence revolution" and creating challenges to current legal doctrine are the analytical techniques and algorithms which give machines the capability to go beyond their original programming and to operate autonomously from humans.[193] Thus, the "techniques" of artificial intelligence, the algorithms and sophisticated analytical techniques, should be the focus of a law of artificial intelligence as opposed to the manifestation of artificial intelligence in a particular physical form. This is because while artificial intelligence controls the actions of machines that project a physical presence in the world, artificial intelligence doesn't need a body either to "exist" or to act on the physical world. Artificial intelligence also controls digital entities, and this fact alone creates tension in the law beyond those created by increasingly smart machines and implies that a law focusing just on "smart machines" would not adequately cover the full range of technologies controlled by artificial intelligence that are entering society. Additionally, there are other features of artificial intelligence to consider for those who advocate for the regulation of artificial intelligence, such as the ability of artificial intelligence to act autonomously from humans, to engage in creative problem solving, and as noted above to exist either as a physical or digital entity. Other commentators, such as artificial intelligence experts Stuart Russell and Peter Norvig, point to self-improvement, the use of language, and having an internal model of the world as distinguishing factors of artificial intelligence. Each of these general features of artificial intelligence raises specific ques-

---

[191]   Matthew U. Scherer, *Regulating Artificial Intelligence Systems: Risks, Challenges, Competencies, and Strategies*, 29 HARV. J. L. Tech. 354, 2016.

[192]   *Id.*

[193]   Ethem Alpaydin, *Machine Learning: The New AI* (MIT Press 2016) (explaining important learning algorithms, and presenting example applications).

tions of law. For example, whether a "virtual avatar" that operates autonomously from humans can serve as an agent, whether products liability law applies to algorithms and software, whether algorithms are patentable subject matter, and whether courts can access the internal model of the world developed by artificial intelligence as evidence to be used against the artificial intelligence in a criminal proceeding, these are just a few issues of concern for a law of artificial intelligence.[194]

Further, how to assign liability when an artificially intelligent entity harms a human or damages property is, of course, an important issue to discuss for those who advocate that artificial intelligence needs to be regulated. In the area of liability, Professors William Smart, Cindy Grimm, and Woody Hartzog, have rightly observed that complex autonomous systems will present a problem for classic fault-based legal schemes like torts because intelligent systems have the potential to behave in unpredictable ways.[195] They pose the following important question—how can people who build and deploy automated and intelligent systems be said to be at fault when they could not have reasonably anticipated the behavior and thus the risk, of an automated intelligent system?[196] So, how to address this issue? Given the lack of legal person status for artificial intelligence, a strict liability scheme that holds producers liable for harm regardless of fault might be an approach to consider (at least until artificial intelligence is granted the fiction of legal person status).[197] Thus, lacking legal person standing, given that artificial intelligence may cause property damage or harm humans, it is possible that the courts or legislators will be asked to impose strict liability on the creators of programs, for the acts of such programs.

There is a growing movement among governments to regulate artificial intelligence, or at least to acknowledge that increasingly smart systems will pose challenges for law and policy. For example, in the U.S., the White House released a report on the future of artificial intelligence which offers several recommendations for how to regulate this technology, for purposes of this Chapter it is worth noting a few of the recommendations made in the report.[198] First, given that the data used to train artificial intelligence may influence what it learns, and how it responds, federal agencies should prioritize the creation of open training data and open data standards in artificial intelligence. Thus, the government should emphasize the release of datasets that enable the use of artificial intelligence to address a number of issues such as desired social changes. Potential steps in this area could include developing an "Open Data for AI" initiative with the objective of releasing a significant number of government datasets to accelerate artificial intelligence research and to encourage the use of open data standards and best practices across government, academia, and the private sector. Second, government agencies should draw on appropriate technical

---

[194]   *See* Lori A. Weber, *Bad Bytes: The Application of Strict Products Liability to Computer Software*, 66 ST. JOHN'S L. REV. 66, Iss. 2, 469–85 (1992).

[195]   William D. Smart, Cindy M. Grimm, and Woodrow Hartzog, *An Education Theory of Fault for Autonomous Systems* (Yale University Press 2017).

[196]   *Id.*

[197]   Michael Guihot, Anne Matthew, and Nicolas Suzor, *Nudging Robots: Innovative Solutions to Regulate Artificial Intelligence* (WE Robots 2017).

[198]   Artificial Intelligence, Automation, and the Economy, Executive Office of the President, 2016, available at: https://www.whitehouse.gov/sites/whitehouse.gov/files/images/EMBARGOED%20AI%20Economy%20Report.pdf.

expertise when setting regulatory policy for artificially intelligent enabled products; given the complexity of artificial intelligence techniques, domain expertise will be critical for informing legislators of the scope and capabilities of artificial intelligence. Additionally, it has been suggested that effective regulation of artificially intelligent products will require collaboration between agency leadership, staff knowledgeable about the existing regulatory framework and regulatory practices generally, and technical experts with knowledge of artificial intelligence. Third, it is recommended that schools and universities should include ethics, and related topics in security, privacy, and safety, as an integral part of curricula on artificial intelligence, machine learning, computer science, and data science.

As I have argued throughout this Chapter, the most important aspect of increasingly smart technologies from the perspective of challenging established law and policy is the algorithms and analytical techniques of artificial intelligence controlling the entity. The idea that legislators need to act in response to advances in smart technology is especially relevant given the increasing autonomy of systems controlled by artificial intelligence. The need for legislative action is also clear when one considers that cases decided almost 50 years ago mirror the current analysis allocating liability for automated technologies; this indicates the need for new approaches for artificially intelligent systems that are beginning to act independently of humans.

So, given that increasingly smart entities are entering society, what is the next step to take? As artificial intelligence accelerates quickly into society, according to law professor John McGinnis this creates a need for a response from governments to react to the potential huge effects of disruptive innovations being spurred by the use of artificial intelligence across a range of applications.[199] So, let the debate about whether artificial intelligence should be considered a disruptive and transformative technology, and should therefore be regulated and the subject of a new field of law begin now while we still have time to chart our future.

SOURCES

Statutes

Nevada State Law, NSR 482A.025.
Nevada State Law, NRS 482A.030.
District of Columbia B19-0931, Autonomous Vehicle Act of 2012.
Model Penal Code § 211.1(1) (1981).
Minn. Stat. § 617.247, subd. 4(a) (2008).
Minn. Stat. § 617.247, subd. 3(a) (2008)
Minn. Stat. § 617.247, subd. 4(a).
NJ Senate No 343, available at: http://www.njleg.state.nj.us/2016/Bills/A1000/851_I1.PDF.
California Statute SB 1298.
Uniform Electronics Transactions Act (UETA).
Restatement (Third) of Agency, §7.07 (2006).
Uniform Commercial Code (UCC) § 2-105.
42 U.S.C. §§ 1981, 1981a, 1983, 1988 – Nineteenth Century Civil Rights Acts.
Title VII of the Civil Rights Act of 1967.
42 U.S.C. Chapter 21 – Civil Rights Act of 1964.

---

[199]   John D. McGinnis, *Accelerating AI*, 204 NW. U. L. REV. Colloquy, 366–81 (2010).

29 U.S.C. § 206 – Equal Pay Act of 1963.
Age Discrimination in Employment Act of 1967.
Title I and Title V of the Americans with Disabilities Act of 1990.
42 U.S.C. Chapter 126 – Americans with Disabilities Act of 1990.
Section 501 and 505 of the Rehabilitation Act.
Civil Rights Act of 1991.
Federal Rule of Evidence, Rule 901. Authenticating or Identifying Evidence.
Electronically Stored Information: The December 2006 Amendments to the Federal Rules of Civil Procedure.
Federal Rule of Evidence, Rule 401.
Federal Rule of Evidence, Rules 801, 803, 804 and 807.
Federal Rule of Evidence, Rules 1001 through 1008.
Federal Rule of Evidence, Rule 403.
Federal Rule of Evidence, 901(b)(3) and (b)(4).
ESI. Rule 901(b)(3).
ESI 901(b)(4).
Federal Rule of Evidence, 801 through 807.
35 U.S.C. §103.
35 U.S.C. 100(f).

Cases

Comptroller of the Treasury v. Family Entertainment Centers. 519 A.2d 1337, 1338 (Md. 1987).
Jones v. W + M Automation, Inc. 818 N.Y.S.2d 396 (App. Div. 2006), appeal denied, 862 N.E.2d 790 (N.Y. 2007).
United States v. Athlone Indus, Inc. 746 F.29 977 (3d Cir. 1984).
Behurst v Crown Cork & Seal USA, Inc, 2007 U.S. Dist. LEXIS 24922 (D.Ore.Mar.30, 2007). 203 P.3d 207, 346 Or. 29, 2009.
*In re Ashley Madison Customer Data Sec. Breach Litig.,*148 F. Supp. 3d 1378, 1380 (JPML 2015).
Payne v. ABB Flexible Automation, Inc., 1997 U.S. App. LEXIS 13571 (8th Cir. Jun. 9, 1997) 116 F.3d 480, No. 96-2248, 1997 WL 311586, *1-*2 (8th Cir. 1997).
Brouse v. United States, 83 F.Supp. 373 (N.D. Ohio 1949).
Mracek v. Bryn Mawr Hosp., 2010 U.S. App. LEXIS 2015 (3d Dir. Jan. 28, 2010) (unpublished opinion).
Bookout v. Toyota Motor Corp, County District Court Bookout v. Toyota Motor Corp., CJ-2008-7969, District Court, Oklahoma County.
Schad v. Arizona, 501 U.S. 624 (1991).
*Schmerber v. California,*384 U.S. 757 (1966).
State of Minnesota v. Ari David Levine Ct of Appeals (2005).
Arnold v. Reuther, 92 Sp.2d 593 (La.Ct.App. 1957).
Pompeii Estates, Inc. v. Consolidated Edison Co. of N.Y, Inc., 397 N.Y.S..2d 577, 580 (N.Y. Cir. Ct. 1977).
Taylor v. Roseville Toyota, Inc., 138 Cal.App.4th 994 (Ct. App., Calif., 2006).
Commercial Bank v. Hearn, 923 So.2d 202 (Sup. Ct., Miss., 2006).
Citizens United v. Federal Election Commission, 558 U.S. 310 (2008).
Sorell v. IMS Health Inc., 131 S.Ct. 2653 (2011).
Go2Net Inc. v. C L Host Inc., 115 Wash. App. 73 (2003).
Motorola Mobility, Inc. v. Myriad France SAS, 850 F. Supp. 2d 878 (N.D. Ill. 2012).
International Shoe Co. v. Washington, 326 U.S. 310 (1945).
Zippo Manufacturing Co. v. Zippo Dot Com, Inc., 952 F. Supp. 1119 (W.D. Pa. 1997).
Bragg v. Linden Research, Inc, 487 F. Supp. 2d 593 (E.D.Penn. 2007).
Griffin v. State, 419 MD 343 (2011).
Lorraine v. Markel American Insurance Co. 241 F.R.D. 534 (D.Md. May 4, 2007).
State v. Dunn, 7 S.W.3d 427, 432 (Mo. Ct. App. 2000).
Blue Spike, LLC v. Google Inc, No. 14-CV-01650-YGR 2015 WL 5260506 at *5 (N.D. Cal. Sept. 8, 2015)., aff'd, 2016 WL 5956746 (Fed. Cir. Oct. 14, 2016).

2. Accelerating AI
John O. McGinnis[1]

Recently, Artificial Intelligence (AI) has become a subject of major media interest. For instance, the *New York Times* devoted an article to the prospect of the time at which AI equals and then surpasses human intelligence.[2] The article speculated on the dangers that such an event and its strong AI might bring.[3] The *Times* also discussed computer-driven warfare. Various experts expressed concern about the growing power of computers, particularly as they become the basis for new weapons, such as the predator drones that the United States now uses to kill terrorists.[4]

These articles encapsulate the twin fears about AI that may impel regulation in this area—the existential dread of machines that become uncontrollable by humans and the political anxiety about machines' destructive power on a revolutionized battlefield. Both fears are overblown. The existential fear is based on the mistaken notion that strong artificial intelligence will necessarily reflect human malevolence. The military fear rests on the mistaken notion that computer-driven weaponry will necessarily worsen, rather than temper, human malevolence. In any event, given the centrality of increases in computer power to military technology, it would be impossible to regulate research into AI without empowering the worst nations on earth.

Instead of prohibiting or heavily regulating artificial intelligence, the United States should support civilian research into a kind of AI that will not endanger humans—a so-called friendly AI.[5] First, such support is the best way to make sure that computers do not turn out to be an existential threat. It would provide incentives for researchers in the most technologically advanced nation in the world to research and develop AI that is friendly to man.

[1] I thank Mark Movsesian, Michael Rappaport, and Ardith Spence for their helpful comments. I am also very grateful to Michael Abramowicz for our discussions on this subject in our joint seminar, "Law and Accelerating Technology". This article was first published as John O. McGinnis, *Accelerating AI* 104 Nw. U. L. Rev. Colloquy 366 (2010). .Reprinted by special permission of Northwestern University Pritzker School of Law, *Northwestern University Law Review*.
[2] *See* John Markoff, *The Coming Superbrain*, NYTIMES.COM, May 23, 2009, http://www.nytimes.com/2009/05/24/weekinreview/24markoff.html.
[3] *Id.*
[4] *See* John Markoff, *Scientists Worry Machines May Outsmart Man*, NYTIMES.COM, July 25, 2009, http://www.nytimes.com/2009/07/26/science/26robot.html (link); NYTIMES.COM, *Predator Drones and Unmanned Aerial Vehicles*, http://topics.nytimes.com/top/reference/timestopics/subjects/u/unmanned_aerial_vehicles/index.html (last visited Mar. 29, 2010).
[5] For a definition of friendly AI, see Singularity Institute For Artificial Intelligence, 'Creating Friendly AI' § 1, http://www.singinst.org/upload/CFAI.html (last visited Mar. 29, 2010), which summarizes the goals of friendly AI as assuring that AI seeks the elimination of involuntary pain, death, coercion, and stupidity. I might suggest an even weaker definition as simply assuring that AI does not create harm to humans or limit their freedom through either malevolence or stupidity.

Second, such support is justified because of the positive spillovers that computational advances will likely provide in collective decision-making. The acceleration of technology creates the need for quicker government reaction to the potentially huge effects of disruptive innovations. For instance, at the dawn of the era in which the invention of energy-intensive machines may have started to warm up the earth, few recognized any risk from higher temperatures that such machines might cause.[6] Yet as I will describe below, current developments in technology make the rise of energy-intensive machines seem slow-moving. Assuming that man-made atmospheric warming is occurring,[7] it likely presents only the first of a number of possible catastrophes generated by accelerating technological change dangers that may be prevented or at least ameliorated through earlier objective analysis and warning. But it is no less important to recognize that other technological advances may create a cascade of benefits for society—benefits that false perceptions of risk may retard or even preclude. As a result, gathering and analyzing information quickly is more important than ever to democratic decision-making because the stakes of such regulatory decisions have never been higher.

Given that AI has substantial potential to help society formulate the correct policies about all other accelerating technologies with transformational capacity, such as nanotechnology and biotechnology, the most important policy for technological change is that for AI itself. Strong AI would help analyze the data about all aspects of the world—data that is growing at an exponential rate.[8] AI then may help make connections between policies and consequences that would otherwise go overlooked by humans, acting as a fire alarm against dangers from new technologies whose chain of effects may be hard to assess even if they are quite imminent in historical terms.

Such analysis is not only useful to avoiding disaster but also to take advantage of the cornucopia of benefits from accelerating technology. Better analysis of future consequences may help the government craft the best policy toward nurturing such beneficent technologies, including providing appropriate prizes and support for their development. Perhaps more importantly, better analysis about the effects of technological advances will tamp down on the fears often sparked by technological change. The better our analysis of the future consequences of current technology, the less likely it is that such fears will smother beneficial innovations before they can deliver Promethean progress.

In this Chapter, I first describe why strong AI has a substantial possibility of becoming a reality and then sketch the two threats that some ascribe to AI. I show that relinquishing or effectively regulating AI in a world of competing sovereign states cannot respond

---

[6]   It is true that a Swiss chemist argued in the 1890s—still well after the beginning of industrialization—that human action could cause global warming. *See* Bradford C. Mank, *Standing and Global Warming: Is Injury To All Injury to None?*, 35 ENVTL. L. 1, 12 (2005). Nevertheless, even in the 1930s a scientist who reiterated this concern was thought eccentric. *See* Maxine Burkett, *Just Solutions to Climate Change: A Climate Justice Proposal for a Domestic Clean Development Mechanism*, 56 BUFF. L. REV. 169, 173 n.3 (2008).

[7]   It is not necessary to be confident that man-made atmospheric change is occurring to recognize that it would be useful to evaluate the risk of such an event. As I suggest later, one of the advantages of AI is that it will help evaluate such risks.

[8]   *See* ECONOMIST.COM, *The Data Deluge*, Feb. 25, 2010, http://www.economist.com/opinion/displaystory.cfm?story_id=15579717 (describing the rapid growth of data available in the modern world).

effectively to such threats, given that sovereign states can gain a military advantage from AI, and that even within states, it would be very difficult to prevent individuals from conducting research into AI. Moreover, I suggest that AI-driven robots on the battlefield may actually lead to less destruction, becoming a civilizing force in wars as well as an aid to civilization in its fight against terrorism. Finally, I offer reasons that friendly artificial intelligence can be developed to help rather than harm humanity, thus eliminating the existential threat.

I conclude by showing that, in contrast to a regime of prohibition or heavy regulation, a policy of government support for AI that follows principles of friendliness is the best approach to artificial intelligence. If friendly AI emerges, it may aid in preventing the emergence of less friendly versions of strong AI, as well as distinguish the real threats from the many potential benefits inherent in other forms of accelerating technology.

I.   THE COMING OF AI

The idea of artificial intelligence powerful enough to intervene in human affairs has been the stuff of science fiction from HAL in *2001: A Space Odyssey* to the robots in *Wall-E*.[9] The notion of computers that rival and indeed surpass human intelligence might first seem to be speculative fantasy, rather than a topic that should become a salient item on the agenda of legal analysis and policy.[10] But travel to the moon was itself once a staple of science fiction in the nineteenth and twentieth centuries.[10] Yet because of a single government program, man's exploration of the moon is now a historical event of more than 40 years' standing. And unlike a lunar landing, the development of artificial intelligence has direct implications for social governance.

Strong artificial intelligence is the creation of machines with the general human capacity for abstract thought and problem solving. It is generally conceded that if such machines are possible, they would soon surpass human cognitive abilities because the same processes that gave rise to them could rapidly improve them. The machines themselves could aid in this process with their greater-than-human capacity to share information among themselves.[11]

The success of strong AI depends on the truth of three premises. The first premise is functionalism. Functionalism turns on the proposition that cognition is separate from the system in which cognition is realized.[12] Thus, abstract thinking can be equally realized

---

[9]   *See* 2001: *A Space Odyssey* (Metro-Goldwyn-Mayer 1968); *WALL-E* (Pixar Animation Studios 2008).

[10]   Consideration of artificial intelligence has not bulked large in legal scholarship. One interesting article analyzes whether artificial intelligence can play the role of a trustee. *See* Lawrence B. Solum, *Legal Personhood for Artificial Intelligences*, 70 N.C. L. REV. 1231 (1992). *See, e.g.*, Jules Verne, *From The Earth To The Moon* (1865).

[11]   *See* Irving John Good, *Speculations Concerning the First Ultraintelligent Machine*, 6 ADVANCES IN COMPUTERS 31, 31–36 (1965).

[12]   *See* Henry Brighton and Howard Selina, *Introducing Artificial Intelligence* (Totem Books 2003) 42.

in a biological system like the brain or in an electronic one like a computer. Under this hypothesis, a system of symbols, when properly actualized by a physical process, is capable of intelligent action.[13]

Philosopher John Searle is most prominent among scholars who challenge the notion that a machine manipulating abstract symbols can become the equivalent of a human mind. Searle provides the analogy of a Chinese room.[14] If someone is put in a room and asked questions in Chinese, he can be given written directions on how to manipulate Chinese characters so as to give answers to the questions in Chinese.[15] Yet he himself understands nothing of Chinese and, as a result, this manipulation of symbols is a poor simulacrum of human understanding.[16] One powerful objection to Searle's analogy is that the entire system—the written directions plus the human manipulator—does understand Chinese.[17] Searle thus unfairly anthropomorphizes the subject of understanding. As I discuss below, confusing the proposition that AI may soon gain human capabilities with the proposition that AI may soon partake of human nature is the single greatest systemic mistake made in thinking about computational intelligence—an error that science fiction has perpetuated.[18]

The second claim undergirding strong AI is that computers will have the hardware capacity to mimic human thought. Raw computer power has been growing exponentially according to Moore's law. Moore's law, named after Gordon Moore, one of Intel's founders, is the observation that the number of transistors fitting onto a computer chip doubles every 18 months to two years.[19] This prediction, which has been approximately accurate for the last 40 years, means that almost every aspect of the digital world—from computational calculation power to computer memory—is growing in density at a similarly exponential rate.[20] Moore's law reflects the rapid rise of computers as the fundamental engine of mankind in the late twentieth and early twenty-first centuries.[21]

The power of exponential growth is hard to overstate. As Robert Lucas once said in the economic context, once you start thinking about exponential growth, it is hard to think about anything else.[22] The computational power in a cell phone today is a thousand times greater and a million times less expensive than all of the computing power housed at MIT

---

[13] *See* Allen Newell and Herbert A. Simon, *Computer Science as Empirical Inquiry: Symbols and Search*, 19 COMM. OF THE ACM 113, 118 (1976).

[14] John R. Searle, *Minds, Brains, and Programs*, 3 BEHAV. & BRAIN SCI. 417, 417–18 (1980).

[15] *See id.* at 418.

[16] *See id.*

[17] *See, e.g.*, Daniel C. Dennett, *Consciousness Explained* (Black Bay Books 1991) 439.

[18] *See infra* notes 52–57 and accompanying text.

[19] *See Moore's Law: Made Real by Intel Innovation*, http://www.intel.com/technology/moore slaw (last visited Mar. 29, 2010) (discussing Moore's law, which predicts that the number of transistors on a silicon chip will roughly double every 18 to 24 months, thus increasing microprocessor speed on a regular basis).

[20] *See* Dan L. Burk and Mark A. Lemley, *Policy Levers in Patent Law*, 89 VA. L. REV. 1575, 1620 n.147 (2003).

[21] *Cf.* Henry Adams, *The Education Of Henry Adams* (Houghton Mifflin 1918) 379–90 (discussing the Virgin as the symbol of the Middle Ages and the steam engine as that of the nineteenth century).

[22] Robert E. Lucas, Jr., *On the Mechanics of Economic Development*, 22 J. OF MONETARY ECON. 3, 5 (1988).

in 1965.[23] Projecting forward, the computational power of computers 30 years from now is likely to prove a million times more powerful than that of computers today.[24]

To be sure, some technology pundits have long been predicting the imminent death of Moore's law, but it has nevertheless continued to flourish. Intel, a company that has a substantial interest in accurately telling software makers what to expect, projects that Moore's law will continue until at least 2029.[25] Technology theorist and inventor Ray Kurzweil shows that Moore's law is actually part of a more general exponential computation growth that has been gaining force for over 100 years.[26] Integrated circuits replaced transistors, which previously replaced vacuum tubes, which in their time had replaced electromechanical methods of computation. Through all these changes in the mechanisms of computation, its power has increased at an exponential rate.[27] This historical perspective suggests that new methods under research, from carbon nanotechnology to optical computing to quantum computing, will likely permit computational power to continue growing exponentially, even when silicon-based computing reaches its physical limits.[28] Assuming the computational capacity of computers continues to grow as Moore's law predicts, the hardware capacity of a computer is likely to achieve equality with a human brain between 2025 and 2030.[29] Even if this pace does not continue, it seems hard to believe that this capacity will not be reached by the midpoint of this century.

The third issue is whether programmers will be able to provide the software to convert the gains in hardware to make advances in AI. No doubt there are daunting challenges ahead in creating software that can understand the complex realities captured by human thought. In fact, some have argued that despite the previous growth in computational capacity, AI has been largely a failure with little to show for 50 years of work.[30] This assessment seems far too harsh. Since 1997, computers have been able to defeat the greatest chess players in the world.[31] Cars run by computers can autonomously navigate city traffic.[32] These feats can hardly be dismissed as powerful examples of intelligent behavior. Of course, it is true that chess is a completely formal system and even driving

---

[23]   Ray Kurzweil, *Making the World a Billion Times Better*, WASHINGTONPOST.COM, Apr. 13, 2008, http://www.washingtonpost.com/wp-dyn/content/article/2008/04/11/AR2008041103326. html.

[24]   *See* Hans Moravec, *Robot: Mere Machine To Transcendent Mind* (Oxford University Press 1999) 104–08.

[25]   Jeremy Geelan, *Moore's Law: "We See No End in Sight," says Intel's Pat Gelsinger*, SOA WORLD MAGAZINE (May 1, 2008), *available at* http://java.sys-con.com/read/557154.html.

[26]   Ray Kurzweil, *The Singularity Is Near: When Humans Transcend Biology* (Penguin Books 2005) 67.

[27]   *Id.*

[28]   For a good introduction to quantum computing, see George Johnson, *A Shortcut Through Time: The Path To The Quantum Computer* (Vintage Books 2003).

[29]   *See* Kurzweil, *supra* note 26, at 125–27.

[30]   *See* Brighton and Selina, *supra* note 12, at 23.

[31]   *See IBM Research: Deep Blue Overview*, http://www.research.ibm.com/deepblue/watch/html/c.shtml (record of match between chess champion Gary Kasparov and computer Deep Blue).

[32]   *See CMU Robot Car First in DARPA Urban Challenge*, SPIE.ORG, Nov. 5, 2007, http://spie.org/x17538.xml (describing and providing video of the Defense Advanced Research Projects Agency (DARPA) challenge race around urban setting).

has a limited—although more unpredictable—problem set to be solved. But it is hardly surprising that artificial intelligence proceeds from creating intelligence in more formal and predictable environments to doing so in more informal and fluid ones. In any event, software progress continues in tandem with the growing hardware capability.[33]

My point here is not to prove that general AI will succeed in replicating and then surpassing human intelligence, but just to suggest that such a prospect is quite plausible. In any event, greater progress in useful artificial intelligence can be expected. Even if AI does not actually exceed human intelligence, it may still offer useful insights on problems that remain unsolved. Such progress can be very useful for social decision-making by allowing computers to assist humans in explaining social phenomena and predicting the trajectory and effects of social trends. By 2020, computers are expected to generate testable hypotheses; thus we will not have to depend only on the ingenuity of researchers for testing the full range of explanations of the causes of matters.[34]

One way to understand this development is to see computational power as allowing more hypotheses to emerge from data rather than being imposed on the data. Greater computational power may allow computers to create competition between such emerging hypotheses, with the winner being that which is objectively best supported. Computer simulations will also become more powerful and permit researchers to vary certain data from that which exists and see what results.[35] Such simulations will help enhance the robustness of modeling and empiricism that help in social analysis. The analytic capability of AI offers positive spillovers, because a sophisticated and quantitatively informed understanding of the current and future shape of society is a great social good, aiding citizens and politicians alike in coming to sound policy decisions.

To be clear, strong AI's social utility does not depend on predicting the future with precision. Given the randomness inherent in the world, that feat is not possible, no matter how great the increase in intelligence.[36] Even if AI only makes clear the possibility of unexpected future contingencies and offers some assessment of their likelihood with evaluation of possible solutions (including out-of-the-box ideas), AI will aid in planning for the contingencies.

---

[33] *See Data, Data Everywhere*, ECONOMIST.COM, Feb. 25, 2010, http://www.economist.com/specialreports/displaystory.cfm?story_id=15557443 (suggesting that improvements in the algorithms driving computer applications have played as important a part as Moore's law for decades).

[34] *See* Stephen H. Muggleton, *Exceeding Human Limits*, 440 NATURE 409 (2006).

[35] *See* Joshua M. Epstein and Robert L. Axtell, *Growing Artificial Societies: Social Science From The Bottom Up* (Brookings Press and MIT Press 1996). Social scientists already do this type of data varying in the social network arena, in fact. *See* Stephen P. Borgatti, *Identifying Sets of Key Players in a Social Network*, COMPUTATIONAL & MATHEMATICAL ORG. THEORY 21, 33 (2006) (acknowledging that if 10% of the links in a particular social network may not actually exist, an analyst can randomly vary the dataset by 10% and re-apply the model to identify a set of the network's most important players that is not necessarily optimal for the observed dataset, but will represent a high-quality solution for the neighborhood of the graph as a whole).

[36] *See* Nassim Nicholas Taleb, *Fooled By Randomness: The Hidden Role Of Chance In Life And In The Markets*, at xliii (discussing the tendency to underestimate the randomness of life) (Random House 2008).

II.   THE THREATS OF AI

Many theorists of technology are very optimistic about the capacity of strong AI to substantially improve human life. Robots powered by AI can make life much easier, particularly for the disabled and elderly. AI has the potential to aid in discoveries that extend the human life span. At their extremes, some theorists of technology, like Kurzweil, believe that AI will lead, even within 50 years, to a kind of technological utopia where people enjoy very high incomes and very long or perhaps even indefinite life spans.[37]

Even those concerned that strong AI may threaten the existence of humanity premise their fears on the view that such artificial intelligence is possible and relatively imminent. For instance, Bill Joy, the former chief technologist for Sun Microsystems, does not disagree with Kurzweil that we are entering an age of unprecedented technological acceleration in which artificial intelligence will become vastly more powerful than it is today. But his outlook on this development is deeply pessimistic. In a widely discussed article—*Why The Future Doesn't Need Us*—he raises the alarm that man cannot ultimately control these machines.[38] The power of his critique lies precisely in his acknowledgement of the wealth of potential benefits from strong AI. But for Joy, however great the benefits of AI might be, the risk of losing control of the intelligence created is still greater. It appears that in his view, man resembles the sorcerer's apprentice—too weak and too ignorant to master the master machines. Joy's stance represents the culmination of a particular kind of fear that goes back to the Romantic Era and was first represented by the Frankenstein monster who symbolized the idea that all scientific progress is really a disguised form of destruction.[39]

Fears of artificial intelligence on the battlefield may be an even more immediate concern raised by growing computational power. Nations have always attempted to use technological innovation to gain advantages in warfare.[40] Computational advance today is essential to national defense, or to put it more globally, sovereign military competition. The Defense Advanced Research Projects Agency (DARPA) spends billions of dollars developing more advanced military mechanisms that depend on ever more substantial computational capacity.[41]

It is hard to overstate the extent to which advances in robotics, which are driven by AI, are transforming the United States military. During the Afghanistan and Iraq wars, more and more Unmanned Aerial Vehicles (UAVs) of different kinds were used. For

---

[37]   *See* Kurzweil, *supra* note 26, at 122, 320–30.

[38]   *See* Bill Joy, *Why The Future Doesn't Need Us*, WIRED.COM, Apr. 2000, http://www.wired.com/wired/archive/8.04/joy.html. He is not alone in his concern. *See* Kevin Warwick, *March Of The Machines: The Breakthrough In Artificial Intelligence* (University of Illinois Press 2004) 280–303 (Machines will then become the dominant life form on Earth).

[39]   See Richard Holmes, *The Age Of Wonder: How The Romantic Generation Discovered The Beauty And Terror Of Science* (Vintage Books 2010) 94 n.

[40]   *See* Robert Friedel, *A Culture Of Improvement: Technology And The Western Millennium* (MIT Press 2007) 85, 113, 131, 374 (discussing the relationship between technological innovation and war).

[41]   *See* Noah Shachtman, *DARPA Chief Speaks*, WIRED.COM, Feb. 20, 2007, http://blog.wired.com/defense/2007/02/tony_tether_has_1.html (talking about defense developments, some of which depend on computational innovations).

example, in 2001, there were ten unmanned Predators in use, and at the end of 2007, there were 180.[42] Unmanned aircraft, which depend on substantial computational capacity, are an increasingly important part of our military and may prove to be the majority of aircraft by 2020.[43] Even below the skies, robots perform important tasks such as mine removal.[44] Already in development are robots that would wield lasers as a kind of special infantryman focused on killing snipers.[45] Others will act as paramedics.[46] It is not an exaggeration to predict that war 20 or 25 years from now may be fought predominantly by robots. The AI-driven battlefield gives rise to a different set of fears than those raised by the potential autonomy of AI. Here, the concern is that human malevolence will lead to these ever more capable machines wreaking ever more havoc and destruction.

III.   THE FUTILITY OF THE RELINQUISHMENT OF AI AND THE PROHIBITION OF BATTLEFIELD ROBOTS

Joy argues for relinquishment, i.e., the abandonment of technologies that can lead to strong AI. Those who are concerned about the use of AI technology on the battlefield would focus more specifically on weapons powered by AI. But whether the objective is relinquishment or the constraint of new weaponry, any such program must be translated into a specific set of legal prohibitions. These prohibitions, at least under current technology and current geopolitics, are certain to be ineffective. Thus, nations are unlikely to unilaterally relinquish the technology behind accelerating computational power or the research to further accelerate that technology.

Indeed, were the United States to relinquish such technology, the whole world would be the loser. The United States is both a flourishing commercial republic that benefits from global peace and prosperity, and the world's hegemon, capable of supplying the public goods of global peace and security. Because it gains a greater share of the prosperity that is afforded by peace than do other nations, it has incentives to shoulder the burdens to maintain a global peace that benefits not only the United States but the rest of the world.[47] By relinquishing the power of AI, the United States would in fact be giving greater incentives to rogue nations to develop it.

Thus, the only realistic alternative to unilateral relinquishment would be a global agreement for relinquishment or regulation of AI-driven weaponry. But such an agreement would face the same insuperable obstacles nuclear disarmament has faced. As recent events with Iran and North Korea demonstrate,[48] it seems difficult if not impossible to

---

[42]   *See* P.W. Singer, *Wired For War: The Robotics Revolution And Conflict In The 21st Century* (Penguin Books 2009) 35.

[43]   *See* Rowan Scarborough, *Unmanned Warfare*, WASH. TIMES, May 8, 2005, at A1.

[44]   For a popular account in a major film, see *The Hurt Locker* (First Light Production 2009).

[45]   *See* Singer, *supra* note 42, at 111.

[46]   *Id.* at 112.

[47]   *See* John O. McGinnis and Ilya Somin, *Should International Law Be Part of Our Law?*, 59 STAN. L. REV. 1175, 1236–38 (2007).

[48]   *See* Gustavo R. Zlauvinen, *Nuclear Non-Proliferation and Unique Issues of Compliance*, 12 ILSA J. INT'L & COMP. L. 593, 595 (2006).

persuade rogue nations to relinquish nuclear arms. Not only are these weapons a source of geopolitical strength and prestige for such nations, but verifying any prohibition on the preparation and production of these weapons is a task beyond the capability of international institutions.

The verification problems are far greater with respect to the technologies relating to artificial intelligence. Relatively few technologies are involved in building a nuclear bomb, but arriving at strong artificial intelligence has many routes and still more that are likely to be discovered. Moreover, building a nuclear bomb requires substantial infrastructure.[49] Artificial intelligence research can be done in a garage. Constructing a nuclear bomb requires very substantial resources beyond that of most groups other than nation-states.[50] Researching artificial intelligence is done by institutions no richer than colleges and perhaps would require even less substantial resources.

Joy recognizes these difficulties, but offers no plausible solution. Indeed, his principal idea for implementing relinquishment shows that his objective is impossible to achieve. He suggests that computer scientists and engineers take a kind of Hippocratic Oath that they will not engage in AI research with the potential to lead to AI that can displace the human race.[51] But many scientists would likely refuse to take the oath because they would not agree with Joy's projections. Assuming some took the oath, many governments would likely not permit their scientists to respect it because of the importance of computational advances to national defense. Even left on their own, scientists would likely disregard the oath because of the substantial payoffs for advances in this area from private industry. Finally, scientists would have difficulty complying with such a directive even should they want to because of the difficulty of predicting what discoveries will propel AI forward in the long-run.

For all these reasons, verifying a global relinquishment treaty, or even one limited to AI-related weapons development, is a nonstarter. Indeed, the relative ease of performing artificial intelligence research suggests that, at least at current levels of technology, it would be difficult for a nation to enforce such a prohibition on AI research directed wholly against its own residents. Even a domestic prohibition would run up against the substantial incentives to pursue such research because the resulting inventions can provide lucrative applications across a wider range of areas than can research into nuclear weapons.

IV.   CONCEPTUAL ERRORS IN FEARS ABOUT AI

The threats from strong AI—both the fear that it represents an existential threat to humanity and the fear that it will lead to greater loss of life in war—have been exaggerated because they rest on conceptual and empirical confusions.

---

[49]   *See* William J. Perry, *Proliferation on the Peninsula; Five North Korean Nuclear Crises*, 607 ANNALS AM. ACAD. POL. & SOC. SCI. 78, 78–79 (2006).

[50]   *See id.*

[51]   *See* Joy, *supra* note 38.

A. The Existential Threat

The existential threat can be dissolved if there is a substantial possibility of construct-ing friendly AI.[52] Friendly AI is artificial intelligence that will not use its autonomy to become a danger to mankind. The argument for friendly AI begins by rejecting the argument that advanced artificial intelligence will necessarily have the kind of willpower that could drive it to replace humanity. The basic error in such thinking is the tendency to anthropomorphize AI.[53] Humans, like other animals, are genetically programmed in many instances to regard their welfare (and those of their relatives) as more important than the welfare of any other living thing.[54] But the reason for this motivation lies in the history of evolution: those animals that put their own welfare first were more likely to suc-ceed in distributing their genes to subsequent generations.[55] Artificial intelligence will not be the direct product of biological evolution, nor necessarily of any process resembling it. Thus, it is a mistake to think of AI as necessarily having the all-too-human qualities that seek to evade constraints and take power.

This is not to say that one cannot imagine strong AI capable of malevolence. One way to create AI, for instance, may be to replicate some aspects of an evolutionary process so that versions of AI progress by defeating other versions—a kind of tournament of creation. One might think that such a process would be more likely to give rise to existential threats. Further, one cannot rule out that a property of malevolence, or at a least a will to power, could be an emergent property of a particular line of AI research.

Moreover, even a non-anthropomorphic human intelligence still could pose threats to mankind, but they are probably manageable threats. The greatest problem is that such artificial intelligence may be indifferent to human welfare.[56] Thus, for instance, unless otherwise programmed, it could solve problems in ways that could lead to harm against humans. But indifference, rather than innate malevolence, is much more easily cured. Artificial intelligence can be programmed to weigh human values in its decision-making.[57] The key will be to assure such programming.

The realistic prospect of wholly friendly AI is the first reason that government should support rather than regulate AI. Such support can provide strong incentives for develop-ers of AI to take this issue seriously. If the mechanisms of artificial intelligence developed through such a program maintain a head start in calculating power, they can in turn be

---

[52] *See* Singularity Institute For Artificial Intelligence, *supra* note 5, § 2 (offering a detailed program for friendly AI). In this Essay, I abstract from any detailed program for realizing friendly AI. Instead, I would define friendly AI in terms of a goal—creating human-like cognitive capacity which will not autonomously decide to harm humans. As discussed below, deciding what steps will improve the likelihood of realizing this goal may be a difficult task, probably best undertaken by the kind of grant-making now administered by the National Institutes of Health in the medical field.

[53] *See id.*

[54] *See* Robert Wright, *The Moral Animal: Evolutionary Psychology And Everyday Life* (Vintage Books 1994) 336–37. *See also* John O. McGinnis, *The Human Constitution and Constitutive Law: A Prolegomenon,* 8 J. CONTEMP. LEGAL ISSUES 211, 213 (1997) (describing the evolutionary drive to preserve and spread one's genes).

[55] Wright, *id.*, at 336–37.

[56] *See* Singularity Institute For Artificial Intelligence, *supra* note 5, § 3.2.3.

[57] *Id.* § 2.

useful in finding ways to prevent the possible dangers that could emerge from other kinds of artificial intelligence. To be sure, this approach is not a guaranteed route to success, but it seems much more fruitful and practicable than relinquishment.

The question of how to support friendly AI is a subtle one. The government lacks the knowledge to issue a set of clear requirements that a friendly AI project would have to fulfill. It also lacks a sufficiently clear definition of what the end state of a friendly AI looks like. This ignorance may inhibit establishing a prize for reaching friendly AI or even any intermediate objective that makes progress toward this ultimate goal.[58] The best way to support may be instead to treat it as a research project, like those funded by the National Institutes of Health. Peer review panels of computer and cognitive scientists would sift through projects and choose those that are designed both to advance AI and assure that such advances would be accompanied by appropriate safeguards.[59] At first, such a program should be quite modest and inexpensive. Once shown to actually advance the goals of friendly AI, the program could be expanded.[60]

B.   The Concern about Battlefield AI

It is not as if in the absence of AI wars or weapons will cease to exist. The way to think about the effects of AI on war is to think of the consequences of substituting technologically advanced robots for humans on the battlefield. In at least three ways, that substitution is likely to be beneficial to humans.

First, robots make conventional forces more effective and less vulnerable to certain weapons of mass destruction, like chemical and biological weapons. Rebalancing the world to make such weapons less effective, even if marginally so, must be counted as a benefit.

Second, one of the reasons that conventional armies deploy lethal force is to protect the human soldiers against death or serious injury. If only robots are at stake in a battle,

---

[58]   *See* Jonathan H. Adler, *Eyes on a Climate Prize: Rewarding Energy Innovation to Achieve Climate Stabilization,* 20–21 (Case Research Paper Series in Legal Studies, Working Paper No. 2010-15, 2010) *available at* http://papers.ssrn.com/sol3/papers.cfm?abstract_id=1576699 (offering criteria for when prizes will work better than grants); William A. Masters and Benoit Delbecq, *Accelerating Innovation with Prize Rewards* 10 (International Food Policy Research Institute Discussion Paper No. 835, 2008), *available at* http://www.ifpri.org/sites/default/files/publications/ifpridp00835.pdf (suggesting that prizes can be useful ways to elicit desired projects when the prize competition sets a feasible but difficult objective (and) a clearly measurable goal, and (disperses) prizes in a predictable manner by an impartial authority).

[59]   This use of peer review rather than regulation to address technical issues that are not possible to capture through bureaucratic mandates is something that should be considered more generally in the regulatory process. *See* Stephen P. Croley, *The Administrative Procedure Act and Regulatory Reform: A Reconciliation,* 10 ADMIN. L.J. 35, 47 (1996).

[60]   Thus the policy recommendations here differ somewhat from the Singularity Institute. It considers relinquishment infeasible. *See* Singularity Institute For Artificial Intelligence, *supra* note 5, § 4.2.2. But the Institute seems to suggest a hands-off approach by the government. *Id.* § 4.2.1. While I agree that regulatory prohibitions are imprudent, government support for friendly AI is useful to give it the momentum to triumph over potentially less friendly versions, the possibility of which I do not think can be ruled out a priori. AI is potentially friendly but not necessarily so. Moreover, as I discuss in Part V, the positive externalities of AI for collective decision-making suggest that such support is warranted.

a nation is more likely to use non-lethal force, such as stun guns and the like. The United States is in fact considering outfitting some of its robotic forces with non-lethal weaponry.

Third, AI-driven weaponry gives an advantage to the developed world and particularly to the United States, because of its advanced capability in technological innovation. Robotic weapons have been among the most successful in the fight against Al-Qaeda and other groups waging asymmetrical warfare against the United States. The Predator, a robotic airplane, has been successfully targeting terrorists throughout Afghanistan and Pakistan, and more technologically advanced versions are being rapidly developed. Moreover, it does so in a targeted manner without the need to launch largescale wars to hold territory—a process that would almost certainly result in more collateral damage.[61] If one believes that the United States is on the whole the best enforcer of rules of conduct that make for a peaceful and prosperous world, this development must also be counted as a benefit.

Importantly, the law of war can be adapted to the use of robots. The basic requirements of the prohibition against intentionally inflicting damage on civilians should have no less force when the inflictors of damage are robots. In the long run, robots, whether autonomous or not, may be able to discriminate better than other kinds of weapons, thus allowing a higher standard for avoidance of civilian deaths.[62] The requirement of proportionality in war may even have more bite, since the need to protect robots from all injury may be less than the need to protect humans, so the force effectively authorized under international law for troop protection may be proportionately less. Thus, relinquishment by the United States would be a grave mistake if it were substantially possible that artificial intelligence consistent with continued human flourishing could be constructed.[63] It might be thought that any military exploitation of artificial intelligence is in tension with development of friendly AI. But the destructive powers unleashed by computer-driven weaponry do not necessarily entail the creation of strong AI that would lead to computers displacing humanity as a whole. Moreover, even if ultimately competition among nation-states leads to pressure to develop the use of strong AI in military matters, there will be powerful incentives for the United States to constrain the AI that drives such weaponry from engaging in the kind of behavior that Joy fears. In any event, it is likely that the United States and other advanced industrial nations can be better trusted than other nations to take account of these dangers, particularly if they have an ongoing friendly AI program. Thus, the combination of support for friendly AI and research into and deployment of computerized weaponry by the United States remains a better policy than the alternatives of relinquishment or disarmament.

---

[61]   As discussed by Professor Kenneth Anderson, see Kenneth Anderson's Law of War and Just War Theory Blog, *Why Targeted Killing? And Why Is Robotics so Crucial an Issue in Targeted Killing?*, http://kennethandersonlawofwar.blogspot.com/2009/03/why-targeted-killing-and-why-is.html#links (Mar. 27, 2009, 12:36 EST).

[62]   *Cf. Rise of the Drones: Unmanned Systems and the Future of War: Hearing Before the Subcomm. on National Security and Foreign Affairs of the H. Comm. on Oversight and Government Reform*, 111th Cong. 11 (2010), *available at* http://oversight.house.gov/images/stories/subcommittees/NS_Subcommittee/3.23.10_Drones/Anderson. pdf (written testimony of Kenneth Anderson) (comparing the collateral damage caused by drones and an artillery barrage).

[63]   *See* Singularity Institute For Artificial Intelligence, *supra* note 5, §§ 1, 2, 4.

V.   THE BENEFITS OF AI IN AN AGE OF ACCELERATING TECHNOLOGY

We live in an age of accelerating technology. Because of the exponential growth symbolized and exemplified by Moore's law, technological innovation progresses faster than ever before. Some theorists of technology believe that such acceleration has been going on throughout human history.[64] It took much less time for the industrial age to replace the era of agriculture than it did for that era to succeed the long eon of hunter-gathering of our distant past. The post-industrial age is following on the heels of industrialization more quickly still.

Even within our own lifetimes, the quickening of the pace of change is palpable. A visit to an electronics store, or even a grocery store, would find a whole new line of products within two years, whereas someone visiting a store between 1910 and 1920—let alone 1810 and 1820—would not have noticed much difference. Even cultural generations move faster. Facebook, for instance, has in a few years completely changed the way college students relate,[65] whereas the tenor of college life in 1960 would have been recognizable to a student in 1970.[66]

Most importantly for society, accelerating technology is spawning a multitude of innovations—even fields of innovations unknown three decades ago. Biotechnology, for instance, raises the possibility of radical life extension, and with it, very important changes in demography.[67] Nanotechnology, which concerns the control and fabrication of matter smaller than one billionth of a meter, is also proceeding on a wide front and has already been incorporated into products from sunscreen to pesticides.[68] While the field has enormous promise, it also raises potential threats. These include relatively mundane threats, such as the bodily damage that tiny particles can cause, and much wilder scenarios in which nanomachines replicate themselves until the earth is destroyed.[69] Beyond these specific fields, the reality of accelerating technology will result in wholly new disruptive innovations that cannot now be predicted. But these too may rapidly shape the structure of society for good or ill.

---

[64]   *See* Kurzweil, *supra note* 26, at 17–19.

[65]   Maria Tess Shier, *The Way Technology Changes How We Do What We Do*, 2005 NEW DIRECTIONS FOR STUDENT SERVS. 77, 83 (2005). *See also* Matthew Robert Vanden Boogart, *Uncovering the Social Impacts of Facebook on a College Campus* (2006) (unpublished M.S. dissertation).

[66]   More parochially, the publication of law review articles has changed more in the last six years than it did in the previous 50. The rise of the Social Science Research Network has made drafts of scholarly articles available—often long before publication. Law reviews have responded by finding new ways to add value. For example, major law reviews have added online components that sometimes comment on print articles. *See, e.g.*, Northwestern Law Review Colloquy, http://colloquy.law.northwestern.edu (last visited Apr. 12, 2010).

[67]   *See* Glenn Reynolds, *An Army Of Davids: How Markets And Technology Empower Ordinary People To Beat Big Media, Big Government And Other Goliaths* (Thomas Nelson Inc. 2006) 175–93.

[68]   *See* Diana M. Bowman and Graeme A. Hodge, *A Small Matter of Regulation: An International Review of Nanotechnology Regulation*, 8 COLUM. SCI. & TECH. L. REV. 1, 3 (2007), http://www.stlr.org/cite.cgi?volume=8&article=1.

[69]   *See* Albert C. Lin, *Size Matters: Regulating Nanotechnology*, 31 HARV. ENVTL. L. REV. 349, 355 (2007).

Such technological changes may sometimes require new laws, regulations, and social norms to avoid their dangers and realize their promise. But these technologies do not themselves directly facilitate the better information gathering and analysis necessary to superintend these technological transformations. In other words, they do not themselves directly provide the information conducive to the regulation and integration of accelerating technologies into society. Artificial intelligence is fundamentally different in this respect. Insofar as artificial intelligence remains beneficent, it facilitates the gathering and analysis of information that helps the regulation of further advances not only in its own field, but in other fields of accelerating technology as well. It has the added advantage that its focus will be on the processing of objective information. While the growth of AI will not end ideological battles over the interpretation of data, more and more objectively analyzed facts provide ballast to deliberation, preventing extreme and unsupported claims and providing an anchor to democratic consensus.

Indeed, one way of thinking of the importance of AI is that the accelerating accumulation of information in the world makes mechanisms to sort and analyze that information all the more necessary.[70] Already the military is having trouble analyzing all the information it is getting from its drones because it lacks sufficient sorting and analytic capacity.[71] This problem is a metaphor for social decision-making as a whole. As accelerating technology creates new complexity more rapidly than ever before in areas, such as nanotechnology, biotechnology, and robotics, that were not even known a few decades before, social decision-making must struggle to keep up with analyzing the wealth of new phenomena no less than the military has struggled to process the ever more detailed information it receives from its modern technology. Societies prosper if they can use all of the information available to make the best decisions possible. The problem now is that information available to be processed may be swelling beyond human capacity to achieve sound social decision-making without the aid of AI.

One side benefit of greater capacity to process information may be the ability to better predict natural catastrophes and either prevent them or take preemptive measures to avoid their worst consequences. The more sophisticated the simulations and modeling of earthquakes, weather, and asteroids, and the better aggregation of massive amounts of data on those phenomena, the better such measures are likely to be.[72] Moreover, by estimating the risks of various catastrophes, society is better able to use its limited resources to focus on the most serious ones.

The acceleration of technology can create unparalleled cascades of benefits as well as new risks of catastrophe. This acceleration could potentially endanger the future of the

---

[70] *See* Atul Gawande, *The Checklist Manifesto: How To Get Things Right* (Picador Press 2010) (drawing attention to problems created by the greater sea of information). Gawande's solution in the medical field is to create checklists focused on the most important protocols for saving lives. *Id.* at 137–38. While a checklist approach may indeed be the best solution to information overload given present technology, one general problem with a checklist is that it creates a one-size-fits-all approach that is frozen in time. In contrast, AI would allow one to decide what is most important for a particular patient, taking up-to-date information into account.

[71] *See* Christopher Drew, *Military is Awash in Data from Drones*, NYTIMES.COM, Jan. 10, 2010, http://www.nytimes.com/2010/01/11/business/11drone.html.

[72] *See* Florin Diacu, *Megadisasters: The Science Of Predicting The Next Catastrophe* (Princeton University Press 2010).

human race, but could also potentially radically extend the life span of individual humans. If such acceleration is the fundamental phenomenon of our age, the assessment of the consequences of technology is an essential task for society. As a result, the government has a particular interest in accelerating the one technology that may analyze the rest of technological acceleration—AI. The question of what degree and what form of support is warranted to boost the acceleration of this technology to help us with decision-making about the rest of accelerating is subtle and difficult. But that is the right question to ask, not whether we should retard its development with complex regulations, or still worse, relinquish it.

3. Finding the right balance in artificial intelligence and law

L. Thorne McCarty

I. INTRODUCTION

In 2015 and 2016, the quiet academic field of Artificial Intelligence and Law exploded onto the pop cultural landscape. There were stories in the Washington Post,[1] in Forbes,[2] and on CNBC.[3] There were sensational headlines: "Computer vs. Lawyer? Many Firm Leaders Expect Computers to Win,"[4] and hasty rejoinders: "The End of Lawyers? Not So Fast."[5] Fueling these stories was the reality of several hundred legal technology startups, many of which claimed to be applying AI.[6] In March, 2017, the New York Times weighed in with a balanced assessment: "A.I. Is Doing Legal Work. But It Won't Replace Lawyers, Yet."[7]

Fortunately, we now have guidance on this subject from two seasoned veterans: Richard Susskind and Kevin Ashley.

Richard Susskind's most recent book, published in 2015, and co-authored with his son, Daniel Susskind, is entitled: *The Future of the Professions: How Technology Will Transform the Work of Human Experts.*[8] This book continues the themes of Susskind's previous books,[9] but extends the analysis to several other professions, in addition to law: health, education, divinity, journalism, management consulting, tax and audit, and architecture. The general thesis is stated up front, in stark terms:

> There are two possible futures for the professions today. . . . The first is reassuringly familiar. It is a more efficient version of what we already have today. The second future is a very different proposition. It involves a transformation in the way that the expertise of professionals is made available in society. The introduction of a wide range of increasingly capable systems will, in various ways, displace much of the work of traditional professionals. In the short and medium

---

[1] Karen Turner, *Meet 'Ross,' the Newly Hired Legal Robot*, Washington Post, May 16, 2016.

[2] Mark A. Cohen, *How Artificial Intelligence Will Transform the Delivery of Legal Services*, Forbes, September 6, 2016.

[3] Dan Mangan, *Lawyers Could Be the Next Profession to Be Replaced By Computers*, www.cnbc.com, February 17, 2017.

[4] Julie Triedman, The American Lawyer, October 24, 2015

[5] John Markoff, New York Times, January 4, 2016.

[6] Robert Ambrogi's blog, *Law Sites*, https://www.lawsitesblog.com, maintains a list of Legal Tech Startups. In July, 2017, Ambrogi's list included 647 entries.

[7] Steve Lohr, New York Times, March 19, 2017.

[8] Richard Susskind & Daniel Susskind, The Future of the Professions (Oxford University Press, 2015).

[9] Richard Susskind, The Future of Law (Oxford University Press 1996); Richard Susskind, Transforming the Law (Oxford University Press 2000); Richard Susskind, The End of Lawyers? (Oxford University Press 2008).

terms, these two futures will be realized in parallel. In the long run, the second future will dominate, we will find new and better ways to share expertise in society, and our professions will steadily be dismantled.[10]

As an indication of how rapidly the world is changing, Richard Susskind also published, in 2017, the second edition of *Tomorrow's Lawyers: An Introduction to Your Future*,[11] which was originally published in 2013. He explains, in his preface, that the legal profession has changed so much "in these three short years that the first edition of this book is now out of date."[12]

Kevin Ashley's new book, published in 2017, is entitled: *Artificial Intelligence and Legal Analytics: New Tools for Law Practice in the Digital Age*.[13] Whereas Susskind describes the field of Artificial Intelligence and Law with broad strokes, Ashley analyzes it in microscopic detail. His book has three parts: Part I discusses "Computational Models of Legal Reasoning," Part II discusses "Legal Text Analytics," and Part III is a proposal to bring the first two parts together. Ashley writes:

> Taken together, the three parts of this book are effectively a handbook on the science of integrating the AI & Law domain's top-down focus on representing and using semantic legal knowledge and the bottom-up, data-driven and often domain-agnostic evolution of computer technology and IT.[14]

The paradigm that Ashley is advancing is sometimes called "Cognitive Computing," and it is closely associated with IBM's Watson initiative.[15]

For additional guidance, I will present in this chapter my own opinions on Artificial Intelligence and Law, primarily by reviewing and analyzing some of my own papers, published over the past 40 years or so. Section II covers my work from the 1970s through the 1990s. Section III covers my work from around 2000 up to the present, and beyond. It has been a long journey. The path forward was not always clear at the time, I must admit, but with some historical perspective, I think we can see several consistent and recurring themes. My vision for the future of the field is similar to Kevin Ashley's, but we differ on some of the specific research directions that we would recommend.[16] I agree, generally, with Richard Susskind's projections for the short and medium terms, but I disagree strongly with his longer term predictions. My reasons for these disagreements will be clear in Section IV.

My goal in this chapter is to give the reader a foundation for understanding and evaluating the claims that are now being made about the applications of Artificial Intelligence

---

[10]   Susskind & Susskind, *supra* note 8, at 9.

[11]   RICHARD SUSSKIND, TOMORROW'S LAWYERS (Second Edition, Oxford University Press 2017).

[12]   *Id.*, at viii.

[13]   KEVIN D. ASHLEY, ARTIFICIAL INTELLIGENCE AND LEGAL ANALYTICS (Cambridge University Press, 2017).

[14]   *Id.*, at 32.

[15]   See, e.g., JOHN E. KELLY & STEVE HAMM, SMART MACHINES: IBM'S WATSON AND THE ERA OF COGNITIVE COMPUTING (Columbia University Press 2013).

[16]   I wrote most of this chapter before I became aware of Kevin Ashley's book. I have adapted it, hastily, by adding some comparative analysis in Section IV, but it is not intended to be a review or a review essay.

to the Law. AI is now a huge and heterogeneous subject: Which of its many component technologies can be adapted to legal tasks? The law itself is a complex subject: Which legal tasks are amenable to automation? To answer these questions, we need a deep understanding of Artificial Intelligence, a deep understanding of the law, and an understanding of the history of this hybrid field. Often, the main question is one of balance. What is the right balance? I will try to give you the tools you need to answer this question.

II.   ARTIFICIAL INTELLIGENCE: FIRST WAVE AND SECOND WAVE

The consensus view among computer scientists is that there have been, so far, two waves of research in artificial intelligence.

A good statement of this thesis, for a general audience, can be seen in a video entitled "A DARPA Perspective on Artificial Intelligence,"[17] by John Launchbury, the Director of the Information Innovation Office (I2O) at the Defense Advanced Research Projects Agency (DARPA) in the U.S. Department of Defense. Launchbury characterizes the First Wave in AI as systems based on "handcrafted knowledge." Examples include programs for logistics scheduling, programs that play chess, and TurboTax. "In the case of TurboTax," he says, "you have experts who are tax lawyers or tax accountants, who are able to take the complexities of the tax code and turn them into certain rules, and the computer then is able to work through these rules." First Wave systems are very good at complex reasoning, but not very good at perception and learning. Launchbury characterizes the Second Wave in AI as systems based on "statistical learning." Examples include systems for voice recognition and face recognition, which are both complex perceptual tasks. Launchbury then probes deeper into the foundations of statistical learning, and describes what is known in the field as the "manifold hypothesis," the idea that "natural data forms lower-dimensional structures (manifolds) in the embedding space" and that the task for a learning system is to separate these manifolds by "stretching" and "squashing" the space.

Launchbury also speculates on a Third Wave in AI, which he calls "contextual adaptation." Third Wave systems would "construct explanatory models for classes of real world phenomena," he says, and thus bring together the strengths of First Wave and Second Wave systems. At this point, though, it is too early to tell if such systems are possible.

Richard Susskind also draws a distinction between First Wave and Second Wave systems, but with a somewhat different characterization. "Broadly speaking," Susskind writes, "workers in the first wave of AI in the professions tried to understand what knowledge and reasoning processes underpinned human intelligence, and sought to replicate these in computer systems."[18] This statement is correct. However, when you look more closely at what Susskind has in mind, it is clear that he is talking about *deductive* human reasoning, in the classical expert systems paradigm. He cites an article[19] written in 2013,

---

[17]   Available online at https://youtube/-O01G3tSYpU.

[18]   Susskind & Susskind, *supra* note 8, at 185.

[19]   Richard Susskind, *Artificial Intelligence and the Law Revisited*, in JON BING: A TRIBUTE 182–201 (D.W. Schartum, L.A. Bygrave & A.G.B. Bekken, eds., 2014).

in which he details his work 25 years earlier with Philip Capper on the Latent Damage System,[20] and notes his disappointment that their system was not received more enthusiastically by the academic AI and Law community. But the truth is that the AI and Law community was, at that point, primarily interested in *nondeductive* reasoning. We were trying to understand the reasoning processes of human lawyers, true, but this required us to go beyond the simple application of legal rules to operative facts.

I will take as an example my own early work. My original article on the TAXMAN system was published in 1977:

> L. Thorne McCarty, *Reflections on* TAXMAN: *An Experiment in Artificial Intelligence and Legal Reasoning*, 90 HARVARD LAW REVIEW 837–893 (1977).[21]

I described TAXMAN as

> a computer program which models certain aspects of the conceptual structures which occur in a specific area of the law, the taxation of corporate reorganizations, as set forth in subchapter C of chapter I of the Internal Revenue Code of 1954. [I.R.C. §§354-356, 358, 361-362, 368.] The program is capable of performing a very rudimentary form of "legal reasoning": Given a "description" of the "facts" of a corporate reorganization case, it can develop an "analysis" of these facts in terms of several legal "concepts."[22]

A lengthy section of the article explained how the program actually worked,[23] and another section displayed the inputs and outputs for a simplified set of facts taken from an actual case.[24] Although the implemented system was very simple by today's standards, the final section of the article discussed the "feasible extensions" that would be needed to turn it into a practical tool for legal research and analysis,[25] and these projections hold up fairly well, I think, in retrospect.

Clearly, TAXMAN was a deductive rule-based expert system, a precursor in many ways to TurboTax. Most people assume, therefore, that I chose corporate tax law as my experimental domain precisely because it is governed by logical rules, but this is only partially true. Yes, we can get started by encoding rules in logic, but what is interesting about corporate tax law is how many of the important legal concepts *cannot* be modeled in this way. My article discussed several prominent examples: the "continuity of interest" doctrine developed in *Pinellas Ice & Cold Storage Co. v. Commissioner*,[26] the "business purpose" doctrine developed in *Gregory v. Helvering*,[27] and the "step transaction" doctrine developed in *Helvering v. Elkhorn Coal Co.*[28] These do not look like logical rules. Here is my summary:

---

[20] Philip Capper & Richard Susskind, LATENT DAMAGE LAW – THE EXPERT SYSTEM (Butterworths 1988).

[21] Available online at http://bit.ly/2yGZXmr. Hereinafter cited as *Reflections on Taxman*.

[22] *Reflections on Taxman*, *supra* note 21, at 838. The program was written in MICRO-PLANNER and LISP when I was at Stanford in 1972–1973. *See id.*, at note 3 and note 54.

[23] *Id.*, at 863–876.

[24] *Id.*, at 876–881. The case was *United States v. Phellis*, 257 U.S. 156 (1921).

[25] *Id.*, at 881–892.

[26] 287 U.S. 462 (1933).

[27] 293 U.S. 465 (1935), *aff'g* 69 F.2d 809 (2d Cir. 1934).

[28] 95 F.2d 732 (4th Cir. 1938), *cert. denied*, 305 U.S. 605 (1938).

> ... Superimposed on a manageable foundation of manageable complexity is another system of concepts as unruly as any that can be found in the law, with all the classical dilemmas of legal reasoning: contrasts between "form" and "substance," between statutory "rules" and judicially created "principles," between "legal formality" and "substantive rationality." It is perhaps no accident that two of the more quotable passages on the problems of legal interpretation have arisen in corporate tax cases. Holmes' famous metaphor — "[a] word is not a crystal, transparent and unchanged, it is the skin of a living thought" — appeared first in *Towne v. Eisner*,[29] the earliest stock dividend case. And the simile of Learned Hand — "the meaning of a sentence may be more than that of the separate words, as a melody is more than the notes" — appeared first in *Helvering v. Gregory*.[30] In a sense, the ultimate goal of the TAXMAN project is to translate these metaphors and similes into something more precise and concrete.[31]

Thus, at the end of my 1977 article, I called for the investigation of a "modified paradigm" that would "permit us to say something about the structure and dynamics of even the more vaguely defined concepts of corporate reorganization law,"[32] and I wrote: "I will pursue this analysis in detail in a future article."[33] From that point on, the 1977 article became known as TAXMAN I, and the future article became known as TAXMAN II.

As I worked on the modified paradigm for the next several years, I shifted my attention to an earlier case in the history of corporate tax law, *Eisner v. Macomber*, 252 U.S. 189 (1920). Several technical reports were published along the way, based on joint work with my colleague, N.S. Sridharan,[34] but the definitive paper was not published until 1995:

> L. Thorne McCarty, *An Implementation of Eisner v. Macomber*, in PROCEEDINGS OF THE FIFTH INTERNATIONAL CONFERENCE ON ARTIFICIAL INTELLIGENCE AND LAW (ICAIL) 276–286 (1995).[35]

As American lawyers know from their first course in taxation, *Eisner v. Macomber* involved a 50 percent dividend in common stock issued to a corporation's common stockholders, and the question was whether or not this event was "taxable income" under the Sixteenth Amendment to the United States Constitution. Justice Pitney held for the majority of the Supreme Court that it was not, while Justice Brandeis, in a long and intricate dissent, argued that it was.

There were several principles guiding the TAXMAN II project. In my 1995 paper, I described these principles as follows:

---

[29] 245 U.S. 418, 425 (1918).

[30] 69 F.2d 809 (2d Cir. 1934), *aff'd*, 293 U.S. 465 (1935).

[31] *Reflections on Taxman, supra* note 21, at 849.

[32] *Id.*, at 893.

[33] *Id.*, at note 134.

[34] L. Thorne McCarty & N.S. Sridharan, *The Representation of an Evolving System of Legal Concepts: I. Logical Templates*, in PROCEEDINGS OF THE THIRD BIENNIAL CONFERENCE OF THE CANADIAN SOCIETY FOR COMPUTATIONAL STUDIES OF INTELLIGENCE (CSCSI) 304–311 (1980); L. Thorne McCarty & N.S. Sridharan, *The Representation of an Evolving System of Legal Concepts: II. Prototypes and Deformations*, in PROCEEDINGS OF THE SEVENTH INTERNATIONAL JOINT CONFERENCE ON ARTIFICIAL INTELLIGENCE (IJCAI) 246–253 (1981).

[35] Available online at http://bit.ly/1pfmtdd. Hereinafter cited as *Implementation of Eisner v. Macomber*.

1. Legal concepts cannot be adequately represented by definitions that state necessary and sufficient conditions. Instead, legal concepts are incurably "open-textured."
2. Legal rules are not static, but dynamic. As they are applied to new situations, they are constantly modified to "fit" the new "facts." Thus the important process in legal reasoning is not theory application, but theory construction.
3. In this process of theory construction, there is no single "right answer." However, there are plausible arguments, of varying degrees of persuasiveness, for each alternative version of the rule in each new factual situation.[36]

What do we mean by a "theory"? What form does it take? One possibility is to represent a theory by what I have called a *logical template*, essentially the same representation used in the TAXMAN I system. But in the modified TAXMAN II paradigm, a theory could also be represented by *prototypes* and *deformations*, which I described as follows:

> Legal concepts have three components. . .: (1) an (optional) invariant component providing necessary conditions; (2) a set of exemplars providing sufficient conditions; and (3) a set of transformations that express various relationships among the exemplars. These three components are then refined further, for most concepts, so that one or more of the exemplars is designated as a prototype and the remaining exemplars are represented by a set of transformations, or deformations, of the prototypes.[37]

Let's look at the arguments of Justice Pitney and Justice Brandeis within this framework. First, we need a theory of the corporation, as it is articulated in the opinions:

> Justice Pitney carefully describes the practice of corporate accounting, the relationship between surplus account and capital stock account, and the legal rights and economic expectations of common stockholders. Justice Brandeis describes in detail the alternative mechanisms for raising corporate capital, issuing stocks and bonds, and distributing dividends. Neither opinion disputes this background theory. We thus conclude (i) that a theory of the corporation is essential for the construction of the legal arguments in this case, and (ii) that the basic outline of such a theory is noncontroversial. This shows the necessity of providing a detailed model of corporate law as an input to our program.[38]

The core of Justice Pitney's argument is derived from his theory of the legal rights and economic expectations of common stockholders. Expand the "bundle of rights" possessed by common stockholders before and after the distribution of the 50 percent stock dividend, and you will see that nothing has changed. A tax levied on this situation would be a direct tax on property under Article 1, §2, clause 3, and Article 1, §9, clause 4, of the original Constitution, he argues, and not a tax on income under the Sixteenth Amendment. Justice Pitney wants to go further than this, however, and he therefore tries to develop a verbal test to distinguish taxable from nontaxable distributions. In terms of the TAXMAN II model, he is looking for a *logical template*. One suggestion is that the stock dividend "does not . . . increase the intrinsic value of [the stockholder's] holding. . . The new certificates simply increase the number of shares, with consequent dilution of

---

[36] *Implementation of Eisner v. Macomber, supra* note 35, at 276–277.
[37] *Id.*, at 277.
[38] *Id.*, at 281.

the value of each share."[39] Another suggestion is that the stock dividend "does not alter the pre-existing proportionate interest of any stockholder."[40] In my 1995 paper, I focused on what I called the "no-transfers-out-of-assets" test, which Justice Pitney formulates as follows:

> The essential and controlling fact is that the stockholder has received nothing out of the company's assets for his separate use and benefit; on the contrary, every dollar of his original investment, together with whatever accretions and accumulations have resulted from employment of his money and that of the other stockholders in the business of the company, still remains the property of the company, and subject to business risks which may result in wiping out the entire investment.[41]

My paper describes how the logical template representing this test is constructed automatically in the TAXMAN II system,[42] using a model of corporate law together with the two precedent cases, *Lynch v. Hornby*[43] and *Peabody v. Eisner*.[44]

The paper then turns to the counter arguments of Justice Brandeis:

> Since Justice Brandeis is writing a dissenting opinion, his main job is to attack the distinctions set forth by Justice Pitney. He does this by constructing an array of hypothetical cases, each one slightly different from the one before, and asking how Justice Pitney's analysis stacks up against them. . . The overall strategy. . . is to show: (i) that the tests proposed in Justice Pitney's opinion fail to make the distinction he really wants; and, a much stronger claim: (ii) that the distinction itself is incoherent.[45]

Applying the terminology of TAXMAN II, Justice Brandeis is constructing arguments using a sequence of *prototypes* and *deformations*. One of the taxable prototypes is *Lynch v. Hornby*, in which the Cloquet Lumber Company distributed to its common stockholders a substantial cash dividend. Another taxable prototype is *Peabody v. Eisner*, in which the Union Pacific Corporation distributed to its common stockholders two large blocks of common and preferred stock issued by the Baltimore & Ohio Corporation. The TAXMAN II system generates transformations between these two cases, and then extends these transformations to *Eisner v. Macomber* itself. This sets up the following rejoinder by Justice Brandeis to the "no-transfers-out-of-assets" test advanced by Justice Pitney:

> The argument which appears to be most strongly urged for the stockholders is, that when a stock dividend is made, no portion of the assets of the company is thereby segregated for the stockholder. But does the issue of new bonds or of preferred stock created for use as a dividend result in any segregation of assets for the stockholder?[46]

---

[39] 252 U.S. 189, 211 (1920). As many commentators noted at the time, this "constant value" test does not work, because it would also apply to a substantial distribution of cash or preferred stock.

[40] *Id.* This "proportionate interest" test works better, and it appears frequently in subsequent decisions.

[41] *Id.*

[42] *Implementation of Eisner v. Macomber, supra* note 35, at 282–283.

[43] 247 U.S. 339 (1918).

[44] 247 U.S. 347 (1918).

[45] *Implementation of Eisner v. Macomber, supra* note 35, at 283–284.

[46] 252 U.S. 189, 229.

The answer to this question has to be: No, but these hypothetical cases would be taxable under the transformations constructed by Justice Brandeis from *Lynch v. Hornby* and *Peabody v. Eisner*. Thus the "no-transfers-out-of-assets" test does not work.

The sequences of hypothetical cases in Justice Brandeis' opinion generate persuasive arguments for two reasons: First, some of the transformations modify the chain of events while leaving the end result invariant. For example, we can transform the distribution of a dividend paid from surplus cash in the corporation's treasury into a case in which the corporation issues and sells bonds on the open market and then distributes the proceeds. Second, some of the transformations modify the security interests themselves. A common locution in Justice Brandeis' opinion is the phrase: "bonds, scrip or stock." Many of his hypothetical cases envision the distribution of cash, then bonds, then preferred stock, then common stock. These securities are distinctly different when we define them in terms of a security holder's "bundle of rights," but they are related, in the theory of the corporation, by a tradeoff between "risk" and "return."[47] In fact, Justice Brandeis' opinion turns out to be prescient when we encounter the later stock dividend cases, in which many of his hypotheticals actually occur and the continuum of security interests plays a prominent role.[48]

How successful was the TAXMAN II system in replicating the arguments of Justice Pitney and Justice Brandeis in *Eisner v. Macomber*?

> One caveat: I do not claim that this system runs autonomously, or that it is capable of generating arguments in arbitrary corporate tax cases without human intervention . . . The claim, instead, is that each component of the argument is represented by a well-defined computational task, and that there exists an implemented procedure that performs each step required to carry out these tasks. In other words, the top level control structure is still a hand simulation.[49]

In the meantime, by 1995, there were several other computational models of legal argument in the literature, and many more variants under active development. The most important and influential was Kevin Ashley's HYPO system.[50] In HYPO, cases are represented by *factors*, which are either binary-valued features or continuous-valued attributes. For example, in a trade secret case, one factor might be *ExistsExpressNoncompetitionAgreement* (which is binary-valued) and another might be *CompetitiveAdvantageGained* (which is continuous-valued). Factors are defined in such a way as to favor, explicitly, either the plaintiff or the defendant, and they are used to construct *3-Ply Arguments*: (1) cite a case that supports one of the parties (the plaintiff, say); (2) distinguish the cited case, and cite other counterexample cases that support the defendant; and (3) distinguish

---

[47]   For a discussion of the role of economic theory in the analysis of a security holder's bundle of rights, see L. Thorne McCarty, *OWNERSHIP: A Case Study in the Representation of Legal Concepts*, 10 Artificial Intelligence and Law 135–161 (2002).

[48]   *See Koshland v. Helvering*, 298 U.S. 441 (1936); *Helvering v. Gowran*, 302 U.S. 238 (1937); *Strassburger v. Commissioner*, 318 U.S. 604 (1943); *Helvering v. Sprouse*, 318 U.S. 604 (1943).

[49]   *Implementation of Eisner v. Macomber*, *supra* note 35, at 277.

[50]   Edwina L. Rissland & Kevin D. Ashley, *A Case-Based System for Trade Secrets Law*, in Proceedings of the First International Conference on Artificial Intelligence and Law (ICAIL) 60–66 (1987); Kevin D. Ashley, Modeling Legal Argument: Reasoning with Cases and Hypotheticals (MIT Press, 1990).

the counterexamples on behalf of the plaintiff. To do this computationally, the cases in Hypo's database are organized dynamically into a *claim lattice*, which is a partial order based on the subsets of factors that are shared with the case in dispute. Successors to the Hypo system include: Cabaret,[51] Cato,[52] and several others.[53]

Another model was provided by *formal argumentation theory*, initiated by Phan Minh Dung[54] and developed by several researchers in the AI and Law community: Trevor Bench-Capon, Thomas Gordon, Henry Prakken, Giovanni Sartor and Bart Verheij, among others.[55] In Dung's model, there is a set of abstract *arguments* and a binary *attacks* relation, so that we can say that one argument "attacks" another argument. These arguments are almost always in conflict, but Dung provides rules to identify sets of arguments (called *extensions*) which are internally coherent and which defend themselves against attack. In the legal applications of Dung's model, the arguments are usually instantiated to concrete propositions and the conflicts are often resolved by reference to a set of *values*. For example, one argument might be "Post had possession of the fox," another argument might be "Post did not have possession of the fox," and one value might be "legal rules should be clear and certain." (*Pierson v. Post*, 3 Caines 175 (N.Y. 1805), and the other wild animal cases from the first-year property course in American law schools were introduced as examples in this field by Donald Berman and Carole Hafner in 1993.[56]) It is not possible to provide a full treatment of the various systems for formal argumentation here, since they can become very complex. But the interested reader can get a sense of the diverse approaches by studying four articles from 2012 in a special issue of the journal Artificial Intelligence and Law on *Popov v. Hayashi*,[57] the "wild baseball" case.[58]

I criticized these two lines of research in a paper published in 1997:

L. Thorne McCarty, *Some Arguments About Legal Arguments*, in Proceedings of the Sixth International Conference on Artificial Intelligence and Law (ICAIL) 215–224 (1997).[59]

---

[51]   Edwina L. Rissland & David B. Skalak, Cabaret: *Rule Interpretation in a Hybrid Architecture*, 34 International Journal of Man-Machine Studies 839–887 (1991).

[52]   Vincent Aleven & Kevin D. Ashley, *Doing Things with Factors*, in Proceedings of the Fifth International Conference on Artificial Intelligence and Law (ICAIL) 31–41 (1995).

[53]   For a comprehensive survey of Hypo and its progeny, *see* Trevor J.M. Bench-Capon, Hypo's *Legacy: Introduction to the Virtual Special Issue*, 25 Artificial Intelligence and Law 205–250 (2017).

[54]   Phan Minh Dung, *On the Acceptability of Arguments and its Fundamental Role in Nonmonotonic Reasoning, Logic Programming, and n-Person Games*, 77 Artificial Intelligence 321–357 (1995).

[55]   For a comprehensive survey, *see* Henry Prakken & Giovanni Sartor, *Law and Logic: A Review from an Argumentation Perspective*, 227 Artificial Intelligence 214–225 (2015).

[56]   Donald H. Berman & Carole D. Hafner, *Representing Teleological Structure in Case-Based Legal Reasoning: The Missing Link*, in Proceedings of the Fourth International Conference on Artificial Intelligence and Law (ICAIL) 50–59 (1993).

[57]   2002 WL 31833731 (Ca. Super. Ct. 2002), also available on FindLaw.

[58]   Trevor J.M. Bench-Capon, *Representing Popov v. Hayashi with Dimensions and Factors*, 20 Artificial Intelligence and Law 15–35 (2012); Thomas F. Gordon & Douglas Walton, *A* Carneades *Reconstruction of Popov v. Hayashi*, 20 Artificial Intelligence and Law 37–56 (2012); Henry Prakken, *Reconstructing Popov v. Hayashi in a Framework for Argumentation with Structured Arguments and Dungeon Semantics*, 20 Artificial Intelligence and Law 57–82 (2012); Adam Wyner & Rinke Hoekstra, *A Legal Case OWL Ontology with an Instantiation of Popov v. Hayashi*, 20 Artificial Intelligence and Law 83–107 (2012).

[59]   Available online at http://bit.ly/1QU5CUm. Hereinafter cited as *Legal Arguments*.

Regarding the Hypo system and its successors, I acknowledged that a list of factors provided a good representation of a case in those areas of the law where the courts or the legislatures have mandated a "weighing" or "balancing" test, but it did not work very well elsewhere. It happens that all the trade secret cases in the Hypo database arose in jurisdictions that followed *Restatement of Torts (1939)*, §757, comment (b), which lists six "factors to be considered in determining whether given information is one's trade secret." By 1997, however, 39 states had adopted the Uniform Trade Secrets Act, which sets forth in §1(4) a more categorical definition of a trade secret, and the initial decisions under this statute tended to deviate from the Hypo model. As to the second line of research, one minor problem with formal argumentation theory is terminological: The "arguments" that the theory is talking about are closer to what a lawyer would call a "claim." But more significant problems arise from the fact that the rules for resolving conflicting claims, and deciding whether a party "wins" or "loses" or neither, do not accord very well with the procedures followed by actual lawyers and actual judges. In Section 5 of my 1997 paper, I argued that the model of legal argument illustrated by *Eisner v. Macomber* in my 1995 paper was the "correct theory,"[60] but I also acknowledged that there was a serious gap. If legal reasoning is a form of theory construction, I wrote, then the closest computational analogue is machine learning, and the state of machine learning was not very advanced in 1997. Here's the problem:

> . . . Most machine learning algorithms assume that concepts have "classical" definitions, with necessary and sufficient conditions, but legal concepts tend to be defined by prototypes. When you first look at prototype models [Smith and Medin, 1981],[61] they seem to make the learning problem harder, rather than easier, since the space of possible concepts seems to be exponentially larger in these models than it is in the classical model. But empirically, this is not the case. Somehow, the requirement that the exemplar of a concept must be "similar" to a prototype (a kind of "horizontal" constraint) seems to reinforce the requirement that the exemplar must be placed at some determinate level of the concept hierarchy (a kind of "vertical" constraint). How is this possible? This is one of the great mysteries of cognitive science.

It is also one of the great mysteries of legal theory.[62]

The paper then proceeds to discuss Ronald Dworkin's thesis in *Hard Cases*[63] and *Law's Empire*,[64] and concludes that the mystery can only be solved by developing a computational theory of "coherence" in legal argument. Unfortunately: "In my 1995 paper, I extended my formal model of legal argument up to the edge of the theory of coherence, but no further. The situation is essentially the same today".[65]

---

[60]　Another line of research is exemplified by Karl Branting's Grebe system, which uses a technique called *exemplar-based explanation (EBE)*. See L. Karl Branting, *Building Explanations from Rules and Structured Cases*, 34 International Journal of Man-Machine Studies 797–837 (1991). I have always viewed Branting's model as similar to mine, but with the theories restricted to *logical templates*, as in Justice Pitney's argument in *Eisner v. Macomber*.

[61]　Edward E. Smith & Douglas L. Medin, Categories and Concepts (Harvard University Press, 1981).

[62]　*Legal Arguments, supra* note 59, at 221.

[63]　Ronald Dworkin, *Hard Cases*, 88 Harvard Law Review 1057 (1975).

[64]　Ronald Dworkin, Law's Empire (Harvard University Press 1986).

[65]　*Legal Arguments, supra* note 59, at 221–222. But see, *infra*, notes 106 and 107, and accompanying text, for my current thoughts about "coherence."

All of these computational models of legal argument have deficiencies, as I have indicated. But perhaps the biggest problem is the fact that they are all First Wave systems, in John Launchbury's sense: They all depend on handcrafted knowledge. Since it is such a long and tedious task to encode this knowledge, it was impossible to scale these First Wave systems up to large databases. The original HYPO system, for example, used 13 factors to represent 30 trade secret cases, and the models that were based on more complex knowledge representation frameworks were applied to even smaller databases. In formal argumentation theory, there have been several implementations of a handful of the wild animal cases, plus *Popov v. Hayashi*. And in the TAXMAN II system, there was *Eisner v. Macomber*, plus three cases that played a role as precedents in the opinions of Justice Pitney and Justice Brandeis. Actually, I did several hand simulations of the later cases that used *Eisner v. Macomber* as a precedent, but I never published these studies and I never attempted a full implementation. By then, the marginal returns from writing code were diminishing.

What can we expect from Second Wave systems? If we follow Richard Susskind's analysis, it is hard to say. Susskind seems to define Second Wave systems, operationally, as those systems that are not predicated on the "AI Fallacy": "This is the mistaken supposition that the only way to develop systems that perform tasks at the level of experts or higher is to replicate the thinking processes of human specialists".[66] In other words, Second Wave systems are not First Wave systems. The prime example, of course, is IBM's Watson, but the only positive characterization of these new technologies is the assertion that they depend on "massive data-storage capacity" and "brute-force processing."[67] Another characterization that appears frequently in the book is that these are: "increasingly capable non-thinking machines."[68] Unfortunately, this phrase does not help us understand how the field of AI and Law is likely to evolve.

John Launchbury's description of Second Wave systems is much more informative: These are systems based on *statistical learning*, he says. The great successes in AI recently have been in complex perceptual tasks, such as speech recognition and image recognition, and the winning technology has usually been a neural network. But the law seems to be far removed from these perceptual tasks. We certainly have large repositories of data in the legal system, but it is mostly linguistic data, in the form of natural language texts. Can the technology of statistical learning be applied to legal documents?

The answer is: Yes, but . . . . In the following section, I will present a case study from what I believe will be the Second Wave in Artificial Intelligence and Law, and in Section IV, I will generalize my analysis to make some predictions about the future of the field.

---

[66]   Susskind & Susskind, *supra* note 8, at 45. The "AI Fallacy" is discussed in several sections of the book: §1.9, §4.9 and §7.1

[67]   *Id.*

[68]   *Id.*, at 272.

III.   ON SEMI-SUPERVISED LEARNING OF LEGAL SEMANTICS

This section summarizes my research directed towards a more practical goal: Can we produce a computational summary of a legal case, which can be scaled up to a realistic legal corpus?[69] I will review three papers of mine, going back almost 20 years. *The Challenge* is identified in Section III.A, and *Two Steps Toward a Solution* are described in Sections III.B.1 and III.B.2. This research is ongoing, and *The Next Step* is presented as a proposal in Section III.C.

Machine Learning (ML) plays a role in all of these papers, but the proposal in Section III.C advocates a form of *semi-supervised* learning. What does this mean? Supervised learning is sometimes called "learning with a teacher." If a system is learning a classification scheme, this means that the training examples are all labelled with the names of the categories. Unsupervised learning has no labelled examples, and the system is supposed to construct categories on its own. Semi-supervised learning is a hybrid: some of the examples are labelled; others, usually many more, are not. It seems clear that most human learning is semi-supervised, in this sense, since we have been given a few labelled examples from our parents and teachers, but otherwise we are on our own.

A.   The Challenge

In a paper written almost 20 years ago, I advocated the development of an intelligent legal information system based on *structured casenotes*:

> L. Thorne McCarty, *Structured Casenotes: How Publishers Can Add Value to Public Domain Legal Materials on the World Wide Web*, in SECOND FRENCH-AMERICAN CONFERENCE ON LAW AND COMPUTING, NICE, FRANCE, 1998.[70]

The general argument was that editorial enhancements to primary legal materials (statutes, regulations, cases, etc.) should not take the form of additional natural language texts (treatises, annotations, practitioner's guides, etc.), but should take the form of *computational structures*, "using recent advances in Knowledge Representation (KR) and Natural Language (NL) techniques." Specifically, for the editorial enhancement of a legal case, I proposed the following definition:

> A structured casenote is a computational summary of the procedural history of a case along with the substantive legal conclusions articulated at each stage of the process. It would play the

---

[69]   Some of the material in this section was presented previously in two workshop papers: L. Thorne McCarty, *Discussion Paper: On Semi-Supervised Learning of Legal Semantics*, in WORKSHOP ON LEGAL TEXT, DOCUMENT AND CORPUS ANALYTICS (LTDCA), San Diego, 2016, and L. Thorne McCarty, *Use Case: On Semi-Supervised Learning of Legal Semantics*, in WORKSHOP ON ARTIFICIAL INTELLIGENCE IN LEGAL PRACTICE (AILP), London, 2017.

[70]   Available online at http://bit.ly/1Trg2Qz. Hereinafter cited as *Structured Casenotes*. A French translation of this paper by Danièle Bourcier was published as *L'Indexation de la Jurisprudence: Comment les Editeurs Peuvent Ajouter de la Valeur aux Données du Domaine Public sur le Web*, in DROIT ET INTELLIGENCE ARTIFICIELLE: UNE RÉVOLUTION DE LA CONNAISANCE JURIDIQUE 191–200 (D. Bourcier, P. Hassett & C. Roquilly, eds., Romillat, Paris, 2000).

same role in the legal information systems of the 21st century that West Headnotes and Key Numbers have played in the 20th century.[71]

The main body of the paper then explored this proposal by analyzing a recent copyright case, *Quality King Distributors, Inc. v. L'Anza Research International, Inc.*, 523 U.S. 135 (1998), and its three opinions, in the District Court, the Court of Appeals for the Ninth Circuit, and the Supreme Court.

My focus on procedural history was based on the traditional "brief" that students are taught to write in their first year of law school. I explained the idea as follows:

> The traditional case brief focuses on the procedural context first: Who is suing whom, and for what? What is the plaintiff's legal theory? What facts does the plaintiff allege to support this theory? How does the defendant respond? How does the trial court dispose of the case? What is the basis of the appeal? What issues of law are presented to the appellate court? How does the appellate court resolve these issues, and with what justification?[72]

To ask these questions and answer them in a structured casenote, I wrote, we need "a representation of the rules of civil procedure at some reasonable level of abstraction" (the KR component), and we need a computational grammar "with coverage of the procedural expressions that occur in the synopsis of a typical case" (the NL component). The structured casenote would then be elaborated as follows:

> Within this procedural framework, we would represent the substantive issues at stake in the decision. This is more complicated, since the territory is so vast, potentially encompassing the entire legal system. We can get started on this project, however, by focusing on particular areas of the law . . . [73]

For example: We could focus on copyright law. The paper concluded by comparing the Supreme Court's decision in *Quality King v. L'Anza Research* with the prior decision in the Ninth Circuit, which turned on a disagreement about the scope of several provisions of the 1976 Copyright Act: §106(3) (on the right to distribute copies of a copyrighted work), §109(a) (on the first sale doctrine) and §602(a) (on the importation of copies into the United States). As the Ninth Circuit analyzed the issue:

> From the text of the 1976 Copyright Act, it is unclear whether §602(a) creates a right that is distinct from §106(3) and therefore is not limited by §109(a), or alternatively, whether §602(a) is merely an extension of §106(3) and therefore is limited by §109(a).[74]

The Ninth Circuit chose the first alternative, while the Supreme Court reversed and chose the second, and the task for a structured casenote would be to represent this choice (the KR component again).

How would this work? I wrote the following explanation:

---

[71]   *Id.*
[72]   *Id.*
[73]   *Id.*
[74]   *L'Anza Research International, Inc. v. Quality King Distributors, Inc.*, 93 F.3d 1109, 1114 (9th Cir. 1996).

A structured casenote would represent these alternatives by representing the various possible relationships between the rules of §§106(3), 109(a) and 602(a) ... We can assume that the various objects (e.g., "copies" and "phono-records"), relations (e.g., "owner") and actions (e.g., "import" and "distribute") have been encoded in our knowledge representation language. We could then represent the possible outcomes in the case by applying §§106(3), 109(a) and 602(a) with alternative scope constraints. The first alternative would be represented by applying §602(a) directly, while the second alternative would be represented by incorporating §106(3) with its §109(a) limitation into the language of §602(a). Moreover, close attention to the procedural context of the case will help us to do this correctly. In the District Court, for example, the plaintiff (L'Anza Research) initially filed a complaint based on §602(a), and the defendant (Quality King) responded by raising an affirmative defense based on §§106(3) and 109(a). Thus the issue was framed in this way from the very beginning.[75]

I also explained how structured casenotes would work in a cluster of related cases:

There are other cases that raise similar issues: *Sebastian Int'l Inc. v. Consumer Contacts, Ltd.*, 847 F.2d 1093 (3d Cir. 1988) and *Columbia Broadcasting System, Inc. v. Scorpio Music Distributors, Inc.*, 569 F.Supp. 47 (E.D.Pa. 1983), aff'd, 738 F.2d 421 (3d Cir. 1984) were two cases discussed in the Ninth Circuit opinion, for example. The structured casenotes for these opinions would have subtle differences, either in the operative facts, or in the justification of the decision, or both. We would thus have a basis for recognizing overall similarities among these cases, as well as a basis for drawing sharp distinctions.[76]

By contrast, let's see how this case would be annotated in a legal research system such as Westlaw. The West classification system assigns to the main issue in *Quality King v. L'Anza Research* the single identifier **99k38.5**, where **99** is the *Digest Topic Number* for "Copyrights and Intellectual Property," and **38.5** is the *Key Number*, which points to the following location in the classification hierarchy:

I. Copyrights
  (B) Scope
      k35.   Scope of Exclusive Rights; Limitations
        k38.5.   Effect of transfer of particular copy or phono-records.

There are three headnotes attached to this key number in the Supreme Court opinion: The first is an "abstract" headnote (stating a general legal principle), and the other two are "concrete" headnotes (describing how a general legal principle was applied to the specific facts of the case). But the headnotes are written in free-form natural language text, and the distinction between "abstract" and "concrete" is coded by the contrast between the present tense and the past tense in English.[77] In 1997, I was hired as a consultant by West to look at their operations and to make some recommendations, following the merger with Thomson

---

[75]   *Structured Casenotes, supra* note 70.

[76]   *Id.*

[77]   The first headnote is written in the present tense: "First sale doctrine, under which owner of particular copy is entitled, without authority of copyright owner, to sell or otherwise dispose of possession of that copy, is applicable to imported copies." The second headnote is written in the past tense: "Under first sale doctrine, lawful owners of hair care products bearing copyrighted labels did not engage in copyright infringement by importing and reselling products without manufacturer's authority." See *Structured Casenotes, supra* note 70.

Legal Publishing. (The merger with Reuters came later.) I recommended that West case editors and classifiers should be writing structured casenotes, not free-form natural language texts. I even proposed a very small research project to determine the feasibility of computing the procedural history of a case automatically, following loosely the successful path of the History Assistant project at Thomson.[78] West declined to fund the project.

Today, the market is much more receptive to the use of advanced NL and KR techniques, and one legal technology startup, Judicata,[79] has developed (independently) a system based on some of these same ideas.[80] Judicata's developers have constructed what they call a "map of the legal genome."[81] The user sees this map primarily as a set of "filters" that can be applied to an initial search: some filters are straightforward, such as *court*, *judge*, *disposition*; others are more complex, such as *cause of action*, *procedural posture*, *role of the parties at trial*. Behind the scenes, the map is playing a role in guaranteeing the precision and relevance of the search results. For example, Judicata's system can draw fine distinctions about how a judge's opinion is making use of prior decisions: as a citation for a general legal principle, as good law that is binding on the facts of the present case, as a decision whose precedential value is being disputed, etc. The map of the legal genome is the computational device that makes these fine distinctions possible.

How did Judicata construct this map? It took a lot of work: five years and an investment of $8,000,000, and Judicata has so far only released a system that covers California civil cases and statutes. The initial processing of California legal texts was automated, but post-processing by human lawyers was necessary to understand nuances and resolve ambiguities. Expansion into other legal markets (New York seems to be next on the agenda) should be much faster, since Judicata's investment in proprietary software can be amortized across many jurisdictions. However, manual legal review remains a permanent part of their business model.

There are some obvious similarities between Judicata's map of the legal genome and my proposal for structured casenotes. The main challenge for my proposal is also the same: How to build a database of structured casenotes at the appropriate scale? Manual review will probably be necessary for the foreseeable future, but the more we can automate the process, the better. Let's now look at some technological approaches to this challenge.

B. Two Steps Toward a Solution

The technology underlying structured casenotes has two components: the NL (natural language) component and the KR (knowledge representation) component. The literature on each subject is vast, and I will not attempt to summarize it here. I will focus instead on my own contributions, in the legal field, in 2007 and 2015.

---

[78] Khalid Al-Kofahi, Brian Grom & Peter Jackson, *Anaphora Resolution in the Extraction of Treatment History Language from Court Opinions by Partial Parsing*, in PROCEEDINGS OF THE SEVENTH INTERNATIONAL CONFERENCE ON ARTIFICIAL INTELLIGENCE AND LAW (ICAIL) 138–146 (1999).

[79] https://www.judicata.com

[80] This paragraph is based on a telephone conversation with Itai Gurari, the Co-Founder and CEO of Judicata, Inc., on June 30, 2017.

[81] Judicata has even registered the phrase "MAPPING THE LEGAL GENOME" as a trademark, USPTO Serial Number 85863746, registered on 06/21/2016.

1. ICAIL 2007

When I wrote my paper on structured casenotes in 1998, the field of computational linguistics was not advanced enough to handle the complexities of judicial opinions. But the state of the art changed dramatically with the publication of Michael Collins' thesis in 1999.[82] At the International Conference on Artificial Intelligence and Law (ICAIL) in 2007, I published a paper that explored the potential impact of this research on the law:

> L. Thorne McCarty, *Deep Semantic Interpretations of Legal Texts*, in PROCEEDINGS OF THE ELEVENTH INTERNATIONAL CONFERENCE ON ARTIFICIAL INTELLIGENCE AND LAW (ICAIL) 217–224 (2007).[83]

There were two main contributions in my paper. First, I showed that a "state-of-the-art statistical parser . . . can handle even the complex syntactic constructions of an appellate court judge" by presenting the output of Collins' parser applied to the full text of the judicial opinions in 111 federal civil cases,[84] comprising a total of 15,362 sentences. Second, and more important, in my opinion, I showed that "a semantic interpretation of the full text of a judicial opinion can be computed automatically from the output of the parser." The main technical contribution of my paper was the specification of a *quasi-logical form*, or *QLF*, to represent the semantic interpretation of a sentence, and a *definite clause grammar*, or *DCG*, to compute the correct quasi-logical form from the output of the parser. The *DCG* was constructed manually, but with automated assistance, and it stabilized at approximately 700 rules. The *QLF* was based loosely on my *Language for Legal Discourse (LLD)*,[85] and it was intended to serve as an intermediate step towards the construction of the full representation of a legal case in *LLD*, thus realizing some of the goals articulated in my paper on structured casenotes.

Figure 3.1 shows the *QLF* for a sentence from one of the Supreme Court cases in the corpus, *Monterey v. Del Monte Dunes at Monterey, Ltd.*, 526 U.S. 687 (1999). The basic construct is a *term*, of which there are four types: *sterm*, *nterm*, *aterm* and *pterm*. Each term contains three components: a *lexical item*, a *variable* and a *list of constituents*. The *sterm*, which is derived from a syntactic sentence, represents a relation: the lexical item is the name of the relation, and the list of constituents is a list of its arguments. The variable in this case represents a *relationship*, i.e., a particular instance of the relation. The *nterm*, which is derived from a syntactic noun, represents an object: the lexical item is the name of the object, and the variable represents a particular instance of the object. The *aterm* represents a modifier, such as an adjective or an adverb.

---

[82]   Michael Collins, *Head-Driven Statistical Models for Natural Language Parsing*, PH.D. DISSERTATION, University of Pennsylvania, 1999.

[83]   Available online at http://bit.ly/1Vk7gnk. Hereinafter cited as *Deep Semantic Interpretations*.

[84]   The corpus consisted of 9 Supreme Court cases from May, 1999; 57 Second Circuit cases from May and June, 1999; and 45 Third Circuit cases from May and June, 1999. I have sometimes been asked why these cases, in a paper published in 2007, all came from May and June of 1999. The answer is that I started experimenting with Collins' parser as soon as it became available, and this was simply the first database that I assembled.

[85]   L. Thorne McCarty, *A Language for Legal Discourse. I. Basic Features*, in PROCEEDINGS OF THE SECOND INTERNATIONAL CONFERENCE ON ARTIFICIAL INTELLIGENCE AND LAW (ICAIL) 180–189 (1989).

```
sterm(contends,A,
       [nterm(petitioner,B,[])
       /det(The,nn),
       sterm(decided,C,
             [D,
              aterm(regulatory,E,[F]) &
              nterm(takings,G,[]) &
              nterm(claim,F,[])
              /det(the,nn)])
       && H^pterm(by,H,
                  [C,
                   nterm(jury,I,[])
                   /det(the,nn)])
       /[modal(should),negative,perfect,passive]
       AND
       sterm(adopted,J,
             [nterm(Court,K,[])
              && L^pterm(of,L,
                         [K,
                          nterm(Appeals,M,[])
                          /det(null,nnps)])
              /det(the,nnp),
              aterm(erroneous,N,[O]) &
              nterm(standard,O,[])
              && P^pterm(for,P,
                         [O,
                          aterm(regulatory,Q,[R]) &
                          nterm(takings,S,[]) &
                          nterm(liability,R,[])
                          /det(null,nn)])
              /det(an,nn)])
       /[past]])
/[present]
```

The petitioner contends that the regulatory takings claim should not have been decided by the jury and that the Court of Appeals adopted an erroneous standard for regulatory takings liability.

526 U.S. 687 (1999)

> **sterm(decided,C,[_,_])**
> ...
> **AND**
> **sterm(adopted,J,[_,_])**
> ...

> **[modal(should),negative,perfect,passive]**

Figure 3.1   A Quasi-Logical Form (QLF) from a judicial opinion

Its sole constituent is the object that it modifies. Note that an *aterm* also contains a variable, which denotes an instance of the property that is being used as a modifier. (Thus adverbs can modify adjectives.) Finally, a *pterm* represents the class of binary relations that correspond to prepositional phrases. These, too, have constituents, and they have instance variables, which represent relationships, and which can, in principle, be modified by other terms.

Given these basic building blocks, a complete Quasi-Logical Form is assembled by means of two operations: (1) an expression can be embedded in the list of constituents of a term; and (2) an expression can be adjoined, externally, either before or after a term. (The distinction between these two operations corresponds to the linguistic distinction between *complements* and *adjuncts*.) The expressions adjoined before the term, which are called *premodifiers*, are linked by a right associative operator: &. The expressions adjoined after the term, which are called *postmodifiers*, are linked by a left associative operator: &&. Finally, there are two additional components of the Quasi-Logical Form that need to be explained: (1) since we are not attempting to analyze the quantificational structure of a sentence, we have opted simply to store all information about determiners as syntactic features attached to *nterm* expressions; and (2) we have stored all information about verb tenses as syntactic features attached to *sterm* expressions.

For a large collection of additional examples, I have posted on the internet the *QLF* interpretations of 211 sentences from one of the Third Circuit cases in the corpus, *Carter v. Exxon Co., USA*, 177 F.3d 197 (3d Cir. 1999).[86]

Note that the *QLF* interpretation in Figure 3.1 provides a partial answer to some of the questions in a structured casenote. The highlighted *sterms* represent the actions "decided" and "adopted," and the syntactic feature on "decided" includes the modality "should" followed by a negation. The outermost *sterm*, "contends," represents an epistemic modality, with the conjunction of the two actions as one of its arguments. These are common occurrences in legal discourse. Lawyers deal constantly with events and actions, and modalities over actions, especially the deontic modalities, plus a great variety of epistemic modalities. A judge writing an opinion cannot avoid using these concepts.

How accurate are the syntactic analyses and semantic interpretations in this corpus? Unfortunately, we do not have the data to answer this question. Collins' parser was trained on Sections 02-21 of the Wall Street Journal corpus (approximately 40,000 sentences) and tested on Section 23 (2,416 sentences). His overall results for *labeled recall* and *labeled precision* were 88.0 percent and 88.3 percent, respectively, and his parser performed much better on the core structure of a sentence than it did on the fringes. Qualitatively, our results for judicial opinions seem to be similar, but not quite as good, because we are outside the genre of the training set. But since we do not have an annotated test set of judicial opinions, we cannot answer this question quantitatively. For the semantic interpretations, the situation is even worse. It is difficult to get people even to agree on what semantic (or logical) representations we should be annotating.[87]

Researchers in the AI and Law community have recently come to the conclusion that high-quality annotations of legal texts are essential for the field to make progress. One important contribution is from Vern Walker and his students at Hofstra University, who have just announced "the creation and public availability of a dataset of annotated decisions adjudicating claims by military veterans for disability compensation in the United States."[88] However, Walker's annotation scheme does not descend to the fine grain of syntactic structure and semantic representation. For legal rules extracted from statutes and regulations, the scheme identifies eight propositional connectives, and for evidentiary reasoning in adjudicatory decisions, the scheme identifies ten sentence types or roles. This is exactly the information that we need if we want to do text classification with machine learning algorithms,[89] but it does not help us if we want to construct semantic interpretations of the sentences in the legal texts.

---

[86]   Available online at http://bit.ly/2yhnPdC.

[87]   One major project to annotate semantic interpretations is Johan Bos, et al., *The Groningen Meaning Bank*, in HANDBOOK OF LINGUISTIC ANNOTATION 463–496 (Nancy Ide & James Pustejovsky, eds., Springer 2017), which uses Hans Kamp's "Discourse Representation Theory (DRT)" as the target formalism. See Hans Kamp & Uwe Reyle, FROM DISCOURSE TO LOGIC: AN INTRODUCTION TO MODEL THEORETIC SEMANTICS OF NATURAL LANGUAGE, FORMAL LOGIC AND DRT (Springer 1993).

[88]   Vern R. Walker, et al., *Semantic Types for Computational Legal Reasoning: Propositional Connectives and Sentence Roles in the Veterans' Claims Dataset*, in PROCEEDINGS OF THE SIXTEENTH INTERNATIONAL CONFERENCE ON ARTIFICIAL INTELLIGENCE AND LAW (ICAIL) 217–226 (2017).

[89]   The annotated corpus is intended to be used in the LUIMA project on mining legal arguments. See Matthias Grabmair, et al., *Introducing* LUIMA: *An Experiment in Legal Conceptual Retrieval of*

2. ICAIL 2015

A Quasi-Logical Form (*QLF*) is an intermediate step towards the representation of a legal text in my Language for Legal Discourse (*LLD*). But how should we interpret an expression in *LLD*? At the International Conference on Artificial Intelligence and Law (ICAIL) in 2015, I published the following paper:

> L. Thorne McCarty, *How to Ground a Language for Legal Discourse in a Prototypical Perceptual Semantics*, in PROCEEDINGS OF THE FIFTEENTH INTERNATIONAL CONFERENCE ON ARTIFICIAL INTELLIGENCE AND LAW (ICAIL) 89–98 (2015).[90]

I have been told that this paper is hard to follow, so I have produced two new versions of the same material for different audiences. For lawyers, I have written a longer and gentler introduction (with the same title) in the *Michigan State Law Review*.[91] For computer scientists and mathematicians, I have developed a slide show:

> L. Thorne McCarty, *Probability, Geometry, Logic: A Triptych for a Learnable Knowledge Representation Language*, presented at the CUNY Graduate Center in Manhattan on April 25, 2017.[92]

For AI and Law researchers, I recommend reading the law review article and the slide show side by side.

Figure 3.2 is a schematic view of the theory of *differential similarity*, as presented in these papers. There are three foundational elements in the theory: Probability, Geometry, Logic. Historically, Artificial Intelligence was based on logic (for First Wave systems) and probability (for Second Wave systems), and there have been numerous attempts over the years to combine these two approaches into a single system.[93] The new element in Figure 3.2 is a geometric model, specifically, a low-dimensional *Riemannian manifold* embedded in a high-dimensional Euclidean space.[94] We think of these three elements as if they have been constructed from the bottom up: *from* probability *through* geometry *to* logic. But the constraints in the system are best understood from the top down. First, the logic is constrained by the geometry. (Technically, the logic is a *categorical logic* defined over the category of *differential manifolds*.) Second,

---

Vaccine Injury Decisions Using a Uima Type System and Tools, in PROCEEDINGS OF THE FIFTEENTH INTERNATIONAL CONFERENCE ON ARTIFICIAL INTELLIGENCE AND LAW (ICAIL) 69–78 (2015).

[90]   Available online at http://bit.ly/1qCnLJq. Hereinafter cited as *Prototypical Perceptual Semantics*.

[91]   L. Thorne McCarty, *How to Ground a Language for Legal Discourse in a Prototypical Perceptual Semantics*, 2016 MICHIGAN STATE LAW REVIEW 511–538 (2016). Available online at http://bit.ly/2pkSfZl.

[92]   Available online at http://bit.ly/2oVOA0H. The mathematical prerequisites are: stochastic processes, differential geometry, category theory.

[93]   *See, e.g.*, Nils J. Nilsson, *Probabilistic Logic*, 28 ARTIFICIAL INTELLIGENCE 71 (1986); Matthew Richardson & Pedro Domingos, *Markov Logic Networks*, 62 MACHINE LEARNING 107 (2006).

[94]   For simple illustrations of these concepts, see *Prototypical Perceptual Semantics*, *supra* note 90, at 90–91. My definition of the Riemannian manifold was motivated by the "manifold hypothesis," which is discussed in John Launchbury's video, *supra* note 17. For a more concrete demonstration of the utility of the manifold hypothesis, *see* Salah Rifai, et al., *The Manifold Tangent Classifier*, 24 ADVANCES IN NEURAL INFORMATION PROCESSING SYSTEMS (NIPS) 2294–2302 (2011).

Constraints

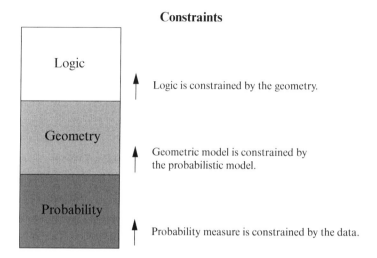

Figure 3.2   The theory of differential similarity

the geometric model is constrained by the probabilistic model. (Technically, this is because the *Riemannian dissimilarity metric* is defined using the *gradient* of the *log* of the probability density.) Finally, the probability measure is constrained by the distribution of sample data in the actual world. (Technically, this just means that there exists an estimation procedure for the *gradient* of the *log* of the probability density.) The net result, I claim, is a *learnable* knowledge representation language grounded in a *prototypical perceptual semantics*.

Some aspects of the theory are still under development. For example, the language needs to be extended to encompass events/actions and the modalities over actions, such as permission and obligation. To do this, I suggested in my ICAIL 2015 paper that we should "take differential manifolds seriously" and represent an action (initially) by the *Lie group* of *rigid body motions*.[95] We can then apply the theory of differential similarity to the manifold of physical actions, and generalize from there to a manifold of abstract actions. Once the action language has been formalized in this way, I suggested, a formalization of the modalities of permission and obligation can be carried over from my previous work.[96] The language also needs to be extended to incorporate the epistemic modalities of knowledge and belief, among others. Again, I suggested in my ICAIL 2015 paper how to do this. The best current model of the epistemic modalities can be found in the literature

---

[95]   This is a mathematical representation of the set of translations and rotations and their combinations, describing all possible motions of a physical object in a three-dimensional Euclidean space.

[96]   L. Thorne McCarty, *Permissions and Obligations*, in Proceedings of the Eighth International Joint Conference on Artificial Intelligence (IJCAI) 287–294 (1983); L. Thorne McCarty, *Modalities Over Actions. I. Model Theory*, in Principles of Knowledge Representation and Reasoning: Proceedings of the Fourth International Conference (KR) 437–448 (1994).

on *justification logics*.[97] A justification logic adds the annotation $t : X$ to the proposition X, and interprets this compound term as "X is justified by reason t." Essentially, t is a *proof* of X. Since the theory of differential similarity incorporates the logic of proofs,[98] it should be fairly straightforward to extend the theory to encompass an appropriate justification logic.

Let's assume that we have successfully extended the knowledge representation language, as indicated. The theory of differential similarity has several important properties:

1. It captures the "open-texture" of legal concepts, and it formalizes (in its geometric layer) a radically different version of the *prototypes* and *deformations* proposed in my work on TAXMAN II.[99]

    Recall the transformations constructed by Justice Brandeis in his opinion in *Eisner v. Macomber*. They started with a prototype, such as *Lynch v. Hornby*, and they generated a sequence of hypotheticals either by modifying the chain of events in the case, or by modifying the characteristics of the security interests, or both. In the second instance, the security interests were defined using a logic of actions and modalities over actions, but they were analyzed within the theory of the corporation using a continuum of risk and return. The net effect was a sequence of incremental deformations of the prototype, which could be strung together to create a sense of "similarity" and "dissimilarity," or a sense of "distance."

    In the theory of differential similarity, the geometric *model* uses a form of *prototype coding*. The basic idea is to represent a point in an n-dimensional space by measuring its *distance* from a *prototype* in several specified *directions*. Thus the sense of "similarity" and "dissimilarity" that we need for legal reasoning is built into the system from the very beginning, starting at the ground level in our formulation of legal concepts. This means that we can model, in principle, the style of argument that we see in Justice Brandeis' opinion in *Eisner v. Macomber*, not just in corporate tax law, but in any common sense domain.

2. It combines a "rule-based" model and a "data-driven" model in a principled way, mediated by the geometric model in the center.

    This is a familiar dichotomy among contemporary legal technology companies. Neota Logic, for example, specializes in rule-based systems and markets a platform that enables domain experts to build their own rule-based applications.[100] Lex Machina is a pioneer in the development of "legal analytics" for intellectual property law, mining data from litigation files to provide insights into strategic legal decisions.[101] Karl Branting has written a useful article discussing the capabilities

---

[97]   Sergei N. Artemov, *The Logic of Justification*, 1 REVIEW OF SYMBOLIC LOGIC 477–513 (2008); Melvin Fitting, *Reasoning with Justifications*, in TOWARDS MATHEMATICAL PHILOSOPHY, PAPERS FROM THE STUDIA LOGICA CONFERENCE 107–123 (D. Makinson, J. Malinowski & H. Wansing, eds., Springer 2009).

[98]   In fact, in contrast to the interpretation of proofs in other logics, which tend to be combinatorial objects, a proof in the theory of differential similarity is a *smooth mapping* of differential manifolds. See *Prototypical Perceptual Semantics, supra* note 90, at 97.

[99]   See *Implementation of Eisner v. Macomber, supra* note 35, and subsequent text.

[100]   https://www.neotalogic.com/

[101]   https://lexmachina.com/

and the limitations of each type of system, and identifying the legal tasks that fit best within each framework.[102] He ultimately advocates the development of hybrid systems, noting that many tasks would benefit from both approaches. The theory of differential similarity provides a natural framework for such hybrid systems.

3.   Although it is not a neural network, it implements a form of "deep learning," with multiple layers of unsupervised learning at the bottom and (optionally) a layer of supervised learning at the top.

   This point was illustrated in my ICAIL 2015 paper using the classical MNIST dataset: How can we learn to recognize the handwritten digits 0 through 9 ?[103] The "dimensionality reduction" step in this process is usually implemented by a neural network, but the theory of differential similarity provides an alternative approach, in which the "manifold hypothesis" plays an explicit role. There is, of course, a huge gap between the recognition of the digit "4" and the recognition of a legal concept, but that's why the logical language is such an important part of the theory. Working with a logic of events and actions, permissions and obligations, knowledge and belief, etc., we can reduce an inherently complex legal situation to a set of simpler ones, in the same way we reduced the digit "4" to a set of "patches." This is the main benefit of a *learnable* knowledge representation language.[104]

4.   Since the top layer is a logical language, the concepts that it learns are (potentially) *interpretable*.

   For neural networks, by contrast, there are two problems of interpretability: First, we do not know why they work, in general. Second, even when they give correct answers in particular cases, we cannot explain why. This second problem is arguably an issue under the European Union's General Data Protection Regulation 2016/679 (GDPR), which is scheduled to go into effect in May, 2018.[105]

I suggested in my ICAIL 2015 paper that the constraints illustrated in Figure 3.2 are the key to understanding the concept of "coherence" that was left open in my previous analysis of *Eisner v. Macomber*.[106] This is a theoretical claim, and I will develop it further

---

[102]   L. Karl Branting, *Data-Centric and Logic-Based Models for Automated Legal Problem Solving*, 25 ARTIFICIAL INTELLIGENCE AND LAW 5–27 (2017).

[103]   See *Prototypical Perceptual Semantics, supra* note 90, at 91–92. The MNIST dataset was introduced in Yann LeCun, et al., *Gradient-Based Learning Applied to Document Recognition*, 86 PROCEEDINGS OF THE IEEE 2278–2324 (1998).

[104]   For an influential statement of this thesis, see: Yoshua Bengio, Aaron Courville & Pascal Vincent, *Representation Learning: A Review and New Perspectives*, 35 IEEE TRANSACTIONS ON PATTERN ANALYSIS AND MACHINE INTELLIGENCE 1798-1828 (2013). See, especially, Section 8: "Representation Learning as Manifold Learning."

[105]   *See, e.g.,* Bryce Goodman & Seth Flaxman, *EU Regulations on Algorithmic Decision-Making and a "Right to Explanation,"* ICML WORKSHOP ON HUMAN INTERPRETABILITY IN MACHINE LEARNING (2016) (available online at https://arxiv.org/abs/1606.08813v3). For a contrary opinion, see Sandra Wachter, Brent Mittelstadt & Luciano Floridi, *Why a Right to Explanation of Automated Decision-Making Does Not Exist in the General Data Protection Regulation*, INTERNATIONAL DATA PRIVACY LAW (forthcoming, 2017) (available online at https://ssrn.com/abstract=2903469).

[106]   See my conjecture in *Prototypical Perceptual Semantics, supra* note 90, at 97.

in a theoretical paper.[107] The practical implications of the theory of differential similarity are outlined in the following section.

C. The Next Step

Recall the challenge from Section III.A: We want to build a database of structured casenotes at the appropriate scale. Can we do this automatically? or semi-automatically? We have a mature Natural Language (NL) technology from Section III.B.1 and a novel Knowledge Representation (KR) technology from Section III.B.2. We are looking for a Machine Learning (ML) technology that can extract the necessary information from unstructured legal texts. But it is unlikely that supervised machine learning will do the trick. The procedural history of a case and the substantive legal issues in a case are very complex structures, not simple labels, and the task of annotating this corpus would be daunting.

Let's consider a different strategy. It is not difficult to write a set of *hand-coded extraction patterns* to map information from a Quasi-Logical Form (*QLF*), as shown in Figure 3.1 into the format of a structured casenote. In fact, as an experiment, I have written many batches of extraction patterns, for various components of a structured casenote, all targeting my Language for Legal Discourse (*LLD*). Of course, a manual technique like this will not scale up to a large database. But now we can try to generalize our hand-coded patterns by the *unsupervised* learning of the legal semantics implicit in a large set of *unannotated* legal cases. The total system would thus be engaged in a form of *semi-supervised* learning of legal semantics.

Exactly how to do this is an open research question, but there are three reasons to think it is feasible:

First, there is the distinction in every legal system between *law* and *fact*. From a computational perspective, this just means that there exists a level of abstraction dividing those concepts that we try to discuss systematically and coherently (the law) from those that we concede are chaotic and idiosyncratic (the facts).

Second, as we move up the abstraction hierarchy in the theory of differential similarity, we cycle back and forth between two geometries: a linear Euclidean geometry and a nonlinear Riemannian geometry. Again, the architecture for deep learning on the MNIST dataset illustrates this point in a very simple setting,[108] but the same phenomenon occurs when our language includes events and actions, permissions and obligations, knowledge and belief, etc. Thus, if we can locate the line between law and fact, we can describe the lower-level legal concepts in *LLD* and give them an initial semantic interpretation in a *linear* Euclidean space.

Third, there is increasing evidence that the semantics of lexical items can be represented, approximately, as a *vector* in a high-dimensional vector space, using only the information available in the texts. There are now several methods to compute these *word embeddings*, ranging from highly nonlinear mappings based on recurrent neural networks[109] to much

---

[107]   The working title of the paper is: *Some Manifestations of Differential Similarity in Cognitive Science and Legal Theory* (forthcoming).

[108]   See *Prototypical Perceptual Semantics*, *supra* note 90, at 91–92.

[109]   Tomas Mikolov, Wen-Tau Yih & Geoffrey Zweig, *Linguistic Regularities in Continuous Space Word Representations*, in HUMAN LANGUAGE TECHNOLOGIES: CONFERENCE OF THE NORTH AMERICAN CHAPTER OF THE ASSOCIATION FOR COMPUTATIONAL LINGUISTICS 746–751 (2013).

simpler mappings based on word co-occurrence statistics,[110] and they all yield essentially the same results: The semantic representations exhibit a surprising *linear* structure. The standard example is the following approximate equality:

$$v\,(\text{``queen''}) \approx v\,(\text{``king''}) - v\,(\text{``man''}) + v\,(\text{``woman''})$$

where v: Words $\mapsto \mathcal{R}^n$ is the computed mapping from the set of lexical items into a high-dimensional real-valued Euclidean space. Thus, the dimensions of the embedding space seem to be capturing the latent continuous semantic features of the lexicon.

Putting all of these pieces together, we can see the outlines of an ambitious research strategy: The word embedding algorithms can be understood as a way to *invert* a stochastic process that has *generated* a sequence of words from a *latent* semantic vector space, and we can generalize this idea to the semantic spaces that are hypothesized in my theory of differential similarity. For an example, let's return to the case of *Quality King v. L'Anza Research* from Section III.A, *supra*, in which the courts were analyzing §106(3), §109(a) and §602(a) of the 1976 Copyright Act. We noted that the concepts mentioned in these statutory provisions included various objects (e.g., "copies" and "phono-records"), relations (e.g., "owner") and actions (e.g., "import" and "distribute"). Each of these concepts would be represented in the theory of differential similarity by a Riemannian manifold with a Riemannian dissimilarity metric defined on it. So let's collect a large corpus of copyright cases and other texts in which these concepts are discussed, let's parse the sentences in this corpus and compute their Quasi-Logical Forms (*QLF*s), and let's look at the statistics across the components of the *QLF*s. By hypothesis, these statistics are the result of a stochastic process that operates on the latent Riemannian manifolds, and our task is to *reconstruct* the manifolds and their metrics.

The mathematical foundations for the algorithms that can solve this problem are currently under development by several researchers.[111]

Let's try this approach, and see what happens.

IV.   THE RIGHT BALANCE

There were three Artificial Intelligence technologies that played a role in my case study in Section III.

---

[110]   Tomas Mikolov, et al., *Distributed Representations of Words and Phrases and their Compositionality*, in 26 ADVANCES IN NEURAL INFORMATION PROCESSING SYSTEMS (NIPS) 3111–3119 (2013); Jeffrey Pennington, Richard Socher & Christopher D. Manning, *GloVe: Global Vectors for Word Representation*, in PROCEEDINGS, EMPIRICAL METHODS IN NATURAL LANGUAGE PROCESSING (EMNLP) 1532–1543 (2014).

[111]   Two relevant papers are: Sanjeev Arora, et al., *A Latent Variable Model Approach to PMI-based Word Embeddings*, 4 TRANSACTIONS OF THE ASSOCIATION FOR COMPUTATIONAL LINGUISTICS 385–399 (2016) and Tatsunori B. Hashimoto, David Alvarez-Melis & Tommi S. Jaakkola, *Word Embeddings as Metric Recovery in Semantic Spaces*, 4 TRANSACTIONS OF THE ASSOCIATION FOR COMPUTATIONAL LINGUISTICS 273–286 (2016).

- Natural Language (NL), in Section III.B.1 In my ICAIL 2007 paper, I used a statistical parser that is now almost 20 years old, but there are many alternative choices today.[112]
- Knowledge Representation (KR), in Section III.B.2. The Quasi-Logical Forms (*QLFs*) generated from the output of the parser are mapped into my Language for Legal Discourse (*LLD*), which is syntactically a *logic programming* language. There are many alternatives for this step, as well.[113]
- Machine Learning (ML), in Section III.C. The software now available for machine learning, both supervised and unsupervised, is too abundant to be listed here. For the specific task of computing word embeddings, the most popular current choice is called `word2vec`.[114]

For simplicity, let's call this the NL/KR/ML paradigm for the computational analysis of legal texts. Obviously, I think the best strategy is to exploit the properties of the theory of differential similarity, as explained in Section III.C, but I would encourage research that explores all the possible variations among these three components.

The reader should be alerted to the fact that this is not (currently) the mainstream paradigm for the computational analysis of legal texts. The mainstream paradigm is to apply supervised machine learning directly to raw legal text represented as a "bag-of-words."[115] Roughly speaking, this is ML without the NL component or the KR component. This paradigm originated in the early work on text classification and information retrieval[116] and it has been the mainstay of most "e-discovery" systems,[117] but I doubt that it can be applied successfully to the task of building structured casenotes.

The issue here is one of balance, and it is an empirical question: What combination of NL or KR or ML techniques do we need for a particular legal task?

It is easy to see that a structured casenote would be useful for a variety of legal tasks, that is, it would have a number of *use cases*. But we can also imagine other use cases in

---

[112] Two popular open source choices are the *Stanford Parser*, which is available at https://nlp.stanford.edu/, and Google's *SyntaxNet*, which is available at https://www.tensorflow.org/.

[113] For an example in the logic programming tradition, see *Logic Production Systems (LPS)* by Robert Kowalski and his colleagues at http://lps.doc.ic.ac.uk/. For a knowledge representation and reasoning system with a natural language explanation capability, see *Ergo* at http://coherentknowledge.com/.

[114] Available at https://www.tensorflow.org/.

[115] The "bag-of-words" model records the frequency of each word in a text, called the *term frequency*, or *tf*, ignoring its position. Usually, *tf* is weighted by the *inverse document frequency*, or *idf*, which gives a higher weight to those words that occur in a smaller proportion of the texts. Sometimes, the *tf-idf* score is augmented by positional information, but still confined to low-level features of the text.

[116] For a comprehensive survey of legal retrieval systems by the person who developed West Publishing Company's WIN system in the early 1990s, see Howard Turtle, *Text Retrieval in the Legal World*, 3 ARTIFICIAL INTELLIGENCE AND LAW 5–54 (1995).

[117] See, e.g., the eight articles published in Kevin D. Ashley, Jason R. Baron & Jack G. Conrad, eds., *Special Issue: e-Discovery*, 18 ARTIFICIAL INTELLIGENCE AND LAW 311–486 (2010). For an interesting comparison of the mainstream ML paradigm in e-discovery with the broader NL/KR/ML paradigm, see David D. Lewis, *Afterword: Data, Knowledge, and e-Discovery*, 18 ARTIFICIAL INTELLIGENCE AND LAW 481–486 (2010).

the law, for which we would need slightly different computational solutions. Here are three examples that have been discussed in the literature:

- Contracts.

  There is now a substantial industry offering systems for contract analysis. Examples include: Kira Systems,[118] iManage RAVN,[119] and Seal Software.[120] These companies all use what I have called the mainstream ML paradigm. Although their systems can identify and extract specific contract provisions (for example: Parties, Term, Severability, Assignment, Governing Law, . . .), they cannot interpret the contract language itself. However, if these companies were to develop and apply the full NL/KR/ML paradigm, they could treat contracts in the same way that I have treated structured casenotes.

  There is also a converse approach to contracts, which could eventually prod the industry to move in this direction. There are now a number of proposals for *computable contracts*. The basic idea is to write contracts in computer code, so that they can be interpreted and executed automatically.[121] In the most sophisticated version of this idea, there would be two parallel instantiations of the contract, one written in a programming language and one written in a natural language (English, Japanese, Arabic, . . .), with translation in both directions.[122] To achieve this goal, we would need grammars and parsers for the main types of contracts, and once these became available, we could probably assimilate legacy contracts into these systems.

  There is another important issue that needs to be addressed by the proponents of computable contracts: What do they propose to do about open-textured concepts?
- Statutes.

  It is notoriously difficult to parse statutes with our current parsers, and we would face the same problems with contracts, initially. In 2009, following up on the results in my ICAIL 2007 paper, I worked with a student, Tim Armstrong, in an attempt to compute a syntactic analysis and a semantic interpretation of Articles 2 and 3 of the Uniform Commercial Code (UCC). The results were poor.[123] Although the *sterms* and their immediate constituents were often correct, it was very rare to find a correct analysis of coordinating conjunctions or prepositional phrase attachments. Other

---

[118]   https://kirasystems.com/
[119]   https://imanage.com/product/ravn/
[120]   http://www.seal-software.com/
[121]   See, e.g., Harry Surden, *Computable Contracts*, 46 U.C. DAVIS LAW REVIEW 629–700 (2012); Mark D. Flood & Oliver R. Goodenough, *Contract as Automaton: The Computational Representation of Financial Agreements*, Office of Financial Research (OFR), Working Paper 15-04 (2015), available at https://ssrn.com/abstract=2648460.
[122]   For an ambitious, open source commercial venture to develop a programming language in which lawyers can write executable contracts, see https://legalese.com/.
[123]   Although we never wrote a full paper on this research, we reported our negative results in a workshop at ICAIL 2009. Timothy J. Armstrong & L. Thorne McCarty, *Parsing the Text of the Uniform Commercial Code*, in WORKSHOP ON NATURAL LANGUAGE ENGINEERING OF LEGAL ARGUMENTATION (NaLELA), Barcelona, 2009.

researchers have also reported negative results on parsing statutes.[124] The explanation seems fairly clear: The syntax of a statute is complex, contorted, and far removed from the syntax of the sentences on which our current parsers have been trained.

These difficulties suggest that we should take a somewhat different approach to statutory texts. Instead of trying to parse statutes automatically, let's *annotate them manually* and then use these annotations to train parsers for the legal texts in which the statutes are being discussed. For an example, let's return once again to the copyright case in Section III.A. Suppose we have annotated the syntactic structure of §106(3), §109(a), §602(a), and the rest of the 1976 Copyright Act, and suppose we have added these annotations to the training set for our parser. Then, when we are trying to compute a semantic interpretation for the arguments in *Quality King v. L'Anza Research*, we will have a much higher probability of getting it right.

- Predicting Legal Outcomes.

Experiments with computer predictions of legal decisions have had a long history, dating back to the 1960s.[125] The statistical methodology has improved since then. A recent study of the decisions of the United States Supreme Court, covering 28,000 cases from 1816 to 2015, reported an accuracy rate of 70.2 percent for case outcomes and 71.9 percent for the votes of the individual justices.[126] Further down in the hierarchy of legal tribunals, there is a published study of 4,263 intellectual property cases litigated between 2001 and 2008 (from the Stanford Intellectual Property Litigation Clearinghouse),[127] and a study of approximately 400,000 jury verdicts and settlements in a broad range of civil lawsuits from all 50 states (from the Thomson Reuters LRP-JVS database).[128] There are also now a number of companies that offer predictive legal analytics as a service: Juristat,[129] Lex Machina,[130] Premonition,[131] and Ravel Law[132] are representative examples.

---

[124]   See Adam Wyner & Guido Governatori, *A Study on Translating Regulatory Rules from Natural Language to Defeasible Logic*, in SEVENTH INTERNATIONAL WEB RULE SYMPOSIUM (RULEML) (2013); Leora Morgenstern, *Toward Automated International Law Compliance Monitoring (TAILCM)*, Final Technical Report AFRL-RI-RS-TR-2014-206 (Leidos, Inc., 2014).

[125]   Fred Kort, *Content Analysis of Judicial Opinions and Rules of Law*, in JUDICIAL DECISION MAKING 133–147 (G. Schubert, ed., 1963); Fred Kort, *Simultaneous Equations and Boolean Algebra in the Analysis of Judicial Decisions*, 28 LAW AND CONTEMPORARY PROBLEMS 143–163 (1963); Reed C. Lawlor, *Personal Stare Decisis*, 41 SOUTHERN CALIFORNIA LAW REVIEW 73–118 (1967); Glendon Schubert, HUMAN JURISPRUDENCE: PUBLIC LAW AS POLITICAL SCIENCE (University of Hawaii Press 1975).

[126]   Daniel M. Katz, Michael J. Bommarito II & Josh Blackman, *A General Approach for Predicting the Behavior of the Supreme Court of the United States*, 12 PLOS ONE: e0174698 (2017). An earlier version of this paper covered 7,700 cases, from 1953 to 2013, and reported an accuracy rate of 69.7% for case outcomes and 70.9% for individual votes. See https://arxiv.org/abs/1407.6333.

[127]   Mihai Surdeanu, et al., *Risk Analysis for Intellectual Property Litigation*, in PROCEEDINGS OF THE THIRTEENTH INTERNATIONAL CONFERENCE ON ARTIFICIAL INTELLIGENCE AND LAW (ICAIL) 116–120 (2011).

[128]   Jack G. Conrad & Khalid Al-Kofahi, *Scenario Analytics: Analyzing Jury Verdicts to Evaluate Legal Case Outcomes*, in PROCEEDINGS OF THE SIXTEENTH INTERNATIONAL CONFERENCE ON ARTIFICIAL INTELLIGENCE AND LAW (ICAIL) 29–38 (2017)

[129]   https://juristat.com/

[130]   https://lexmachina.com/

[131]   https://premonition.ai/

[132]   https://ravellaw.com/

Legal prediction models have usually been based on political and structural variables, not on features related to the legal merits of the case. For example, the study of the Supreme Court by Katz, et al., used the Supreme Court Database assembled and maintained by Harold Spaeth and his colleagues,[133] which has only one variable for the legal issue (with 384 categorical values) and one variable indicating the reason for granting *certiorari* (with 13 categorical values). The Stanford intellectual property litigation study used a model based solely on *prior factors*, that is, "factors that do not model directly the merits of the case but instead focus on information that may influence the outcome of the current case."[134] The Thomson Reuters study is interesting because one field in the LRP-JVS database is an unstructured natural language text summarizing the facts in the case, the plaintiff's claims, and the defendant's claims. These summaries were written by Thomson Reuters employees "who are trained to use a standard, semi-closed vocabulary,"[135] and thus the natural language processing challenge is not as great as it otherwise might have been. But the important point here is that the textual summaries provide a foundation for predictive models based, in part, on the legal merits of the case (which was deferred to future work at Thomson Reuters).[136] The same potential applications would be possible for my structured casenotes.

Note that I am suggesting in all of these use cases that we should be applying the broad NL/KR/ML paradigm, and that we just have to figure out the right balance in each case.

I began this chapter with a reference to the new books by Richard Susskind and Kevin Ashley, and I will conclude this section by returning to their work.

Kevin Ashley's book is highly recommended. Part I of the book on "Computational Models of Legal Reasoning" is roughly parallel to Section II of this chapter, and Part II on "Legal Text Analytics" is roughly parallel to Section III except for the fact that, with the luxury of a book-length treatment (at 426 pages!), Ashley can cover many more topics and in much greater detail than I can. His vision for the future of Artificial Intelligence and Law is similar to mine, although we disagree on some specific points.

For example, in a chapter in Part I on "Modeling Case-Based Legal Reasoning," Ashley reviews my theory of prototypes and deformations, and my computational reconstruction of *Eisner v. Macomber*,[137] and writes:

> From a legal viewpoint, TAXMAN II's model of arguing with concepts and cases is both sophisticated and realistic . . . Many attorneys, judges, and law clerks employ legal information retrieval systems to construct arguments like these.[138]

---

[133]   Harold J. Spaeth, et al., *Supreme Court Database*, Version 2016 Legacy Release v01, http://Supremecourtdatabase.org.

[134]   Surdeanu, et al., *supra* note 127, at 116. "For example, this latter category includes the past win rates of parties, attorneys and law firms involved in the case, potential biases of judges estimated from past cases, etc." *Id.*

[135]   Conrad & Al-Kofahi, *supra* note 128, at 30.

[136]   *Id.*, at 37.

[137]   Ashley, *supra* note 13, at 78–81.

[138]   *Id.*, at 80.

However, he thinks the approach "may be too complex to be helpful."[139] Instead, he suggests that HYPO's factors "provide a simpler, more extensional scheme for representing legal concepts and cases than TAXMAN II that may be easier to connect to case texts for purposes of cognitive computing".[140] I would agree with this assessment if we were trying to build an autonomous system that could construct a complete legal argument in the style of Justice Brandeis, or recognize and extract such an argument, automatically, from a judicial opinion. But, in a structured casenote, we are only trying to extract the ingredients of these arguments, leaving the arguments themselves to the lawyers using the system, and for this purpose I think the theory of prototypes and deformations provides a very useful model. In fact, because of the role of *prototype coding* in the geometric layer of my theory of differential similarity, there is a reasonable hypothesis that this is exactly the representation that we want to extract from a legal text when we apply the ML algorithms proposed in Section III.C.

Another disagreement involves the choice of a paradigm for "Legal Text Analytics." I have argued in this chapter for a broad NL/KR/ML approach, but Ashley's focus in Part II of his book is almost entirely on the mainstream ML paradigm. There is no discussion of syntactic parsing or semantic interpretation (the NL component). There is an excellent chapter on "Representing Legal Concepts in Ontologies and Type Systems,"[141] which is an important part of the KR component. The centerpiece of this chapter is a thought experiment on the ontological requirements for a system that could generate a Socratic dialogue about the case of *Popov v. Hayashi*.[142] The main takeaway is the difficulty of the task.[143] However, modern knowledge representation and reasoning systems[144] do a much better job representing and reasoning about rules and facts (and factors!) than the frame-based representations Ashley constructs in his illustrations, and such systems are not discussed in the book. Overall, the role of the KR component is given short shrift. On the other hand, the mainstream ML paradigm is thoroughly documented and exhaustively analyzed: There is a discussion of the work of Peter Jackson and his colleagues on the History Assistant project,[145] and a

---

[139]   *Id.*

[140]   *Id.*, at 81.

[141]   *Id.*, Chapter 6, at 171–209.

[142]   *Id.*, §6.6, at 185–201. Section 6.6 is based on two papers: Kevin D. Ashley, *Ontological Requirements for Analogical, Teleological, and Hypothetical Reasoning*, in PROCEEDINGS OF THE TWELFTH INTERNATIONAL CONFERENCE ON ARTIFICIAL INTELLIGENCE AND LAW (ICAIL) 1–10 (2009), and Kevin D. Ashley, *The Case-Based Reasoning Approach: Ontologies for Analogical Legal Argument*, in APPROACHES TO LEGAL ONTOLOGIES: THEORIES, DOMAINS, METHODOLOGIES 99–115 (G. Sartor, P. Casanovas, M.A. Biasiotti & M. Fernandez-Barrerra, eds., Springer 2011). I wrote a commentary on Ashley's ICAIL 2009 paper for a compilation on the history of AI and Law, cited in note 158, *infra*. See http://bit.ly/2yYb1Ll.

[143]   Ashley writes: ". . . [A]s perusal of the ontological framework plainly shows, this kind of knowledge representation is both intricate and, well, clunky. One needs to invent ungainly concepts like catch-and-secure-or-mortally-wound in anticipation of extending cases about wild animals to scenarios involving baseballs or tuition-paying students." *Id.*, at 200.

[144]   See the examples cited in note 113, *supra*.

[145]   *Id.*, at 248–253. See Khalid Al-Kofahi, et al., *A Machine Learning Approach to Prior Case Retrieval*, in PROCEEDINGS OF THE EIGHTH INTERNATIONAL CONFERENCE ON ARTIFICIAL INTELLIGENCE AND LAW (ICAIL) 88–93 (2001), and Peter Jackson, et al., *Information Extraction from Case Law and Retrieval of Prior Cases*, 150 ARTIFICIAL INTELLIGENCE 239–290 (2003).

discussion of the work of Marie-Francine Moens and her colleagues on Argumentation Mining,[146] and much more.

Finally, since Ashley's general approach relies on supervised machine learning from raw legal texts, it creates an enormous demand for manually annotated legal sources. He suggests several solutions: paid crowds working on Amazon Mechanical Turk, for example, or law students conscripted as part of their studies.[147] But I doubt that this will be sufficient. Instead, I have argued in this chapter for the development of semi-supervised machine learning techniques, and to the extent that we have human annotators available, I have suggested that they should be used to annotate syntactic structures and semantic representations. Once again, it is an empirical question as to which approach will be more successful.

There have been many reviews of Richard and Daniel Susskind's book, mostly positive[148] but some negative.[149] I will focus my attention on Part III of the book, which includes Chapter 6 on "Objections and Anxieties" and Chapter 7: "After the Professions." As the title of Chapter 7 suggests, the Susskinds are predicting a future in which "our professions will be dismantled incrementally." And they ask: "What about after the professions? What people and systems will replace them in the very long term?"[150]

The answer depends to a large extent on the Susskinds' projections about the future of Artificial Intelligence, and here their argument relies heavily on what they call the "AI Fallacy." See §7.1. They introduce this concept to rebut the common belief that there will always be tasks that machines cannot do, because machines cannot really "think." They point out (correctly) that many of the recent successes in AI have been achieved by systems that perform tasks in ways that are very different from the way humans perform these same tasks. Again, Watson's success at playing *Jeopardy!* is their prime example. They write: "The upshot of all of this is that we can create remarkable, high-performing machines that do not think and are not modelled on human intelligence."[151] There is an ambiguity, however, in what the Susskinds mean by the term "thinking." At times, they are referring explicitly to the philosophical distinction between "strong AI" and "weak AI," which is usually characterized by the presence or absence of "consciousness."[152] At

---

[146]   *Id.*, at 287–294. See Marie-Francine Moens, et al., *Automatic Detection of Arguments in Legal Texts*, in Proceedings of the Eleventh International Conference on Artificial Intelligence and Law (ICAIL) 225–230 (2007), and Raquel Mochales & Marie-Francine Moens, *Argumentation Mining*, 19 Artificial Intelligence and Law 1–22 (2011).

[147]   *Id.*, at 373–377. For a link to Mechanical Turk, see https://www.mturk.com/.

[148]   See, e.g., Giles Wilkes, *Are Only Poets Safe From Robots?*, Prospect Magazine, January, 2016, and reviews in The Times, The Guardian, Times Literary Supplement, Financial Times, and The Economist.

[149]   See, e.g., Frank Pasquale, *Automating the Professions: Utopian Pipe Dream or Dystopian Nightmare?*, Los Angeles Review of Books, March 15, 2016.

[150]   Susskind & Susskind, *supra* note 8, at 271.

[151]   *Id.*, at 275.

[152]   There are almost no serious AI researchers who think that this distinction makes a difference. One exception is Drew McDermott, *Artificial Intelligence and Consciousness*, in The Cambridge Handbook of Consciousness 117–150 (P.D. Zelazo, M. Moscovitch & E. Thompson, eds., Cambridge University Press 2007), but note the results of McDermott's informal survey in 2003 of 207 Fellows of the AAAI.

other times, they seem to be simply referring to systems that are "modelled on human intelligence," as in the previous quotation. These are two very different issues.

At any rate, the inquiry then proceeds to an investigation of the capabilities of these "non-thinking" machines. See §7.2. A familiar starting point is to say that routine tasks can be automated, of course, but there are other tasks that require creativity and innovation, and these will remain in the domain of the human professional. However, the Susskinds believe that this line will shift over time, and they see no stopping point. "Our hypothesis is that systems will increasingly become more capable at performing even those tasks that are regarded today as not routinizable."[153] They apply this argument initially to cognitive capabilities, but then adapt it and apply it to affective capabilities, manual capabilities, and even moral capabilities. There are no limits! If the only thing you know about non-thinking machines is that they don't think, then you can imagine that they can do anything! The predictions in the Susskinds' 2015 book cover all the professions, and they are somewhat vague, but we can find a more specific long term prediction for the law in Richard Susskind's essay written in 2013. Looking forward 25 years to the year 2038, he writes:

> [W]e will surely have intelligent legal systems that . . . will indeed make scarce legal expertise and knowledge more widely available and more easily accessible . . . [T]hese systems will be driven by unimaginable brute-force computing and will be able to handle quantities of legal information and legal complexities well beyond the capabilities of individual human beings . . . These too will be systems that can learn and will build up huge bodies of legal experience from their daily operations. Their reasoning will not be confined to the crudely deductive; rather, they will be able to reason inductively, analogically, and make lateral leaps as well.[154]

But doesn't Susskind have an obligation to give us at least a hint about how these amazing intellectual feats will be accomplished? Can we expect these results from a further development of the mainstream ML paradigm? Will they follow eventually from the pursuit of the broader NL/KR/ML approach? Will deep neural networks somehow solve these fundamental problems? To back up these predictions, we need more than an exponential extrapolation of the performance of IBM's Watson.

Here is an alternative: Let's assume, for the sake of argument, that the theory of differential similarity is basically correct as a *model of human cognition*, and also basically correct as a model of *legal* cognition. (If this assumption turns out to be wrong, we can still use the following analysis to recalibrate the argument for whatever theory is later shown to be more accurate.) The model has many levels, as we have seen, and each level has the tripartite structure shown in Figure 3.2: Probability, Geometry, Logic. For a legal domain, the concepts at the top level would be legal categories, and the concepts at the intermediate levels would involve various common sense categories: space, time, mass, action, permission, obligation, causation, purpose, intention, knowledge, belief, and so on. Indeed, this is basically the design of my *Language for Legal Discourse (LLD)*.[155] If we posit this edifice as a model of human cognition, there would be additional lower levels for human perception: visual, aural, haptic, etc. People have sometimes asked me to explain

---

[153]   *Id.*, at 279.
[154]   Susskind, *supra* note 19, at 199–200.
[155]   See McCarty, *supra* note 85, at 180.

the title of my ICAIL 2015 paper: *How to Ground a Language for Legal Discourse in a Prototypical Perceptual Semantics*. Why do I call it a "prototypical perceptual semantics"? Well, it is a *prototypical* semantics because it is based on a form of prototype coding, as explained in Section III.B.2.[156] But why is it a prototypical *perceptual* semantics? Notice that the primary illustrations of the probabilistic/geometric submodel are drawn from the field of image processing, such as the MNIST dataset of handwritten digits, and if we can build a logical language on these foundations, we will have a plausible account of how human cognition could be *grounded* in human perception.

What does a legal argument look like in this scheme? Human lawyers will construct theories to justify their positions, as they did in *Eisner v. Macomber*, but they will have at their disposal the vast conceptual commons of human experience, all the way down to the perceptual level, if necessary. Thus, in a trade secret case, their conceptualizations will encompass the activities of inventing a new product and bringing it to market, and all the associated risks, which most people understand reasonably well. Or, if they are arguing about how to acquire property rights in wild animals, their conceptualizations will be even closer to the perceptual level: hunting, fishing, and the like, activities that almost everyone has experienced, either directly or vicariously. On the other hand, if an AI system only has access to legal texts, then it cannot acquire concepts from perceptual experience, and the critical question becomes: *Can we learn a grounded semantics without a perceptual ground?* I have proposed a computational solution to this problem, in Section III.C, based on a statistical model, and to continue with the argument at this point, I will simply assume that this proposal will be successful. (Again, if this assumption turns out to be wrong, we can modify the argument to accommodate any alternative technique that might eventually succeed in learning semantics from legal texts.)

The point of this exercise is to investigate how the Susskinds' concept of an "AI Fallacy" would fare in the scenarios outlined in the previous two paragraphs. First, it should be clear from the second paragraph that the AI system we are building does not process legal texts in the same way that humans do. However, it should also be clear, from the first paragraph, that the theory of differential similarity is "modelled on human intelligence," and this is one of its strengths. Thus, we are not trapped in a fallacy, but we are following a powerful heuristic for AI research. There are many other examples in the history of this field, not always, but often. Looking just at recent history, the most successful systems in AI have been deep neural networks, which are based on an idealized model of how neurons process information in the brain, and current research efforts often study human cognition for ideas about what to do next. For example, we know that humans do not need 200,000 labelled images to learn the concept of a cat, and this observation has become a motivation for research on unsupervised learning. The heuristic is even stronger, I would argue, when we are doing research on AI applications to the law, since legal reasoning is so dependent on human experience.[157]

There is also a corollary. The semantic representations that we compute using the techniques in Section III.C will *not* match the corresponding human semantic constructs. We

---

[156]   See text accompanying note 99, *supra*.
[157]   Note that this argument does not apply to AI systems that play games such as Chess and Go, which are totally disjoint from human experience.

can hope that they are good approximations, and that they might be functionally similar, but they will not be identical, and it will probably be very difficult to determine how close they are to reality. They might perform fairly well on a range of tasks, and then go badly awry on a subsequent application. Thus, if we are using these semantic representations for legal systems, we should proceed with caution.

V. CONCLUSION

When confronted with the fantasy of "robot lawyers" it is standard practice to say that the goal is not to replace human lawyers, but rather to augment human legal intelligence with artificial legal intelligence. However, it is not always clear what technology will give us precisely these results. On the one hand, to be successful, it seems that an AI system would have to learn at least some of the language and the concepts that constitute the foundations of a legal system. On the other hand, once such a proficiency has been achieved, where does it end?

I have suggested some answers in this chapter. First, I surveyed the history of Artificial Intelligence and Law from my own personal perspective (see Section II).[158] In its early years, the field was primarily engaged in an effort to develop computational models of legal reasoning. Although these early systems could not be scaled up to handle thousands of legal cases, they taught us some useful data structures and algorithms for the law that are just now beginning to appear in intelligent legal information systems. Then, I reviewed a twenty-year-long project to develop a technology for structured casenotes (see Section III). There are several components in this project: an NL component (from ICAIL 2007), a KR component (from ICAIL 2015), and an ML component, which is currently just a proposal. Finally, I showed how the NL/KR/ML approach could contribute to the solution of several open challenges in legal technology (see Section IV). This should be a reliable guide for the next ten years or so, where I generally agree with the views of Kevin Ashley and Richard Susskind.

As we approach Richard Susskind's time horizon in 2038, the picture is not as clear. For guidance on the remote future, we might want to consider Ludwig Wittgenstein's enigmatic remark: "Wenn ein Löwe sprechen könnte, wir könnten ihn nicht verstehn."[159] An artificial intelligence would be an alien intelligence. Like an imperfect translation, it would be useful, up to a point, but it would also be unreliable. We should heed these strictures as we continue to develop more powerful and more intelligent legal information systems.

---

[158] For a broader perspective, see Trevor Bench-Capon, et al., *A History of AI and Law in 50 Papers: 25 Years of the International Conference on AI and Law*, 20 ARTIFICIAL INTELLIGENCE AND LAW 215–319 (2012).

[159] PHILOSOPHISCHE UNTERSUCHUNGEN, Teil II, §327. The translation by G.E.M. Anscombe is: "If a lion could talk, we could not understand him." Ludwig Wittgenstein, PHILOSOPHICAL INVESTIGATIONS, Part II, 223ᵉ (G.E.M. Anscombe, trans., Macmillan Company 1953).

4. Learning algorithms and discrimination
Nizan Geslevich Packin and Yafit Lev-Aretz

I. ALGORITHMS, MACHINE LEARNING, AND ARTIFICIAL INTELLIGENCE

The term "artificial intelligence" has been subject to a variety of definitions that emphasize different aspects of intelligence. Because only humans are universally recognized as intelligent, all definitions of intelligence relate to human intelligence: some focus on human rational thinking while others revolve around human behavior.[1] Even though artificial intelligence technologies have not reached human-like capabilities of cognitive thinking, attempts to improve artificial intelligence have gained considerable traction in recent years. Intelligent computer systems use "intelligent agents" that are programmed to carry out tasks and achieve certain outcomes.[2]

In what has been termed "Machine Learning", these intelligent agents learn from datasets, on which algorithms can be run to accomplish a prescribed goal.[3] In an unfamiliar environment the agents will draw upon their datasets for optimal results and continue to fine-tune their behavior over time based on the results they have accumulated.[4] Unlike traditional statistical techniques that begin by specifying a mathematical equation that expresses an outcome variable as a function of selected explanatory variables to be subsequently applied to the data, machine learning is nonparametric and does not involve devising any particular mathematical model in advance.[5] It is the data that dictates how information in input variables is positioned to predict the value of an output variable.[6] The combination of nonparametric focus together with the algorithm's learning process has outperformed standard statistical techniques, generating impressively reliable predictions with better statistical efficiency.[7] Because machine learning does not require existing knowledge and careful identification of the relationship between variables, it can apply to a broader range of questions and offer better forecasts compared with those based on

---

[1] Stuart Russell and Peter Norvig, *Artificial Intelligence: A Modern Approach*, at 1 (2d ed. Pearson Education Limited 2003)

[2] *Id.*, at 32–33 (noting that these programs are designed "to achieve the best outcome or, when there is uncertainty, the best expected outcome.")

[3] Alan L. Schuller, *At the Crossroads of Control: The Intersection of Artificial Intelligence in Autonomous Weapon Systems with International Humanitarian Law*, 8 Harv. Nat'l Sec. J. 379, 404 (2017).

[4] Russell and Norvig, *supra* note 1, at 57 (machine learning is defined as "a process of modification of each component of the agent to bring the components into closer agreement with the available feedback information, thereby improving the overall performance of the agent.")

[5] Cary Coglianese and David Lehr, *Regulating by Robot: Administrative Decision Making in the Machine-Learning Era*, 105 Geo. L.J. 1147, 1156–58 (2017).

[6] *Id.*

[7] *Id.*

human judgement or statistical alternatives. Machine learning systems are also quick to adapt to changes over time—when supplied with new data, learning algorithms instantly begin searching for new patterns and refining previous predictions.[8] Nevertheless, the functional relationship in machine learning systems may differ from those in nature's true data-generating process, disqualifying such relationships from establishing causal inferences.[9]

Machine learning techniques like artificial neural networks have exhibited impressive advancements and growing popularity in recent years. While in the past a neural network used to be a computationally expensive algorithm, computers today are fast enough to run large scale neural networks at relatively low cost.[10] With lower technological and financial barriers to entry, machine-learning techniques are now available to big companies like Google, Amazon and Apple as well as to countless smaller-scale businesses and startups. Across various industries, machine-learning systems successfully cut costs, streamline processes, and produce valuable predictions. Artificial intelligence is used by companies like Amazon and Google to fight malware. Indeed, in each of these companies, "[t]rained on hundreds of millions of files, the neural network learns to detect more threats and then uses its experience to predict new attacks."[11] The same logic is capitalized on in financial trading, where many trading firms use proprietary learning algorithms to predict and execute trades at high speeds and high volume.[12] For example, Sentient Technologies Inc., a machine learning and financial technology (FinTech) company, has trained its AI for nearly ten years to trade stocks by analyzing global data and trends.[13] AI also guides investments by hedge funds,[14] informs investment strategies in asset management,[15] helps detect money laundering and fraud,[16] and offers alternative and arguably better

---

[8]   *Id.*, at 1159.

[9]   *Id.*, at 1157.

[10]   Daniel D. Gutierrez, *Inside BIG DATA Guide to Deep Learning & Artificial Intelligence*, Inside BIGDATA, February 8, 2017 at https://insidebigdata.com/2017/02/08/insidebigdata-guide-deep-learning-artificial-intelligence/ at 2.

[11]   James DeTar, *Google, Amazon And Deep Instinct Deploy AI To Fight Malware*, Forbes, June 27, 2017 at https://www.forbes.com/sites/jamesdetar/2017/06/27/google-amazon-and-deep-in stinct-deploy-ai-to-fight-malware/2/#77c5da0e6acb.

[12]   Bernard Marr, *The Top 10 AI And Machine Learning Use Cases Everyone Should Know About*, Forbes, Sep. 30, 2016 at https://www.forbes.com/sites/bernardmarr/2016/09/30/what-are-the-top-10-use-cases-for-machine-learning-and-ai/#51167cb194c9.

[13]   Adam Satariano, *Silicon Valley Hedge Fund Takes On Wall Street With AI Trader*, Bloomberg, Feb. 6, 2017 at https://www.bloomberg.com/news/articles/2017-02-06/silicon-valley-hedge-fund-takes-on-wall-street-with-ai-trader?cmpid=socialflow-facebook-markets&utm_content=markets&utm_campaign=socialflow-organic&utm_source=facebook&utm_medium=social.

[14]   Cade Metz, *The Rise of the Artificially Intelligent Hedge Fund*, Wired, Jan. 25, 2016 at https://www.wired.com/2016/01/the-rise-of-the-artificially-intelligent-hedge-fund/, and Robin Wigglesworth & Lindsay Fortado, *Tudor Jones backs AI hedge funds*, Financial Times, May 21, 2017 at https://www.ft.com/content/59358ff6-3cd9-11e7-ac89-b01cc67cfeec?mhq5j=e2.

[15]   Gary Brackenridge, *Machine Learning is Transforming Investment Strategies for Asset Managers*, CNBC, June 6, 2017, at http://www.cnbc.com/2017/06/06/machine-learning-transforms-investment-strategies-for-asset-managers.html.

[16]   Penny Crosman, *How PayPal Is Taking a Chance on AI to Fight Fraud*, American Banker, Sep. 1, 2016 at https://www.americanbanker.com/news/how-paypal-is-taking-on-ai-to-fi ght-fraud.

risk prediction for potential borrowers.[17] Similarly, AI is used in healthcare for different purposes such as mining medical records,[18] designing treatment plans,[19] diagnosing patients through analyzing physicians' free-form text notes in electronic health records,[20] and predicting wait times for patients in emergency department waiting rooms.[21] Search engines like Google and Bing constantly improve searching capabilities based on AI, and recommendation engines at Amazon, Netflix, Spotify and others also use intelligent machine learning algorithms to analyze their users' activity and determine what one might like to purchase, listen to, or binge watch next.[22] Driverless cars, which are expected to conquer the roads by 2025,[23] employ learning systems that collect and analyze information about the car owner and the car's environment.[24] AI has also made advancements in countless fields of research and practice, from weather forecasting and defending against asteroid threats[25] to predicting and delivering meals.[26]. While intelligent systems enjoy the scientific glory of successful innovative technologies, they pose many practical and ethical challenges. For example, commentators have expressed concerns as to the drastic changes that await the labor markets in the face of intelligent robots that may replace human workers.[27] In this chapter, we hone in on a different, major challenge that intelligent systems engender: discriminatory design and outcomes.

Writing about the design and nature of technologies, political scientist Langdon Winner's controversial thesis, that technologies have politics embodying social relations,

---

[17]   Nanette Byrnes, *An AI-Fueled Credit Formula Might Help You Get a Loan*, MIT Technology Review, Feb. 14, 2017 at https://www.technologyreview.com/s/603604/an-ai-fueled-credit-formula-might-help-you-get-a-loan/.

[18]   Google Deepmind Health project mines the data of medical records in order to provide better and faster health services, *see* DeepMind Health and Research Collaborations, https://deepmind.com/applied/deepmind-health/working-nhs/health-research-tomorrow/.

[19]   Mallory Loklear, *IBM's Watson is really good at creating cancer treatment plans*, Engadget, June 1, 2017 at https://www.engadget.com/2017/06/01/ibm-watson-cancer-treatment-plans/.

[20]   Kenney Ng, *Using AI and Science to Predict Heart Failure,* IBM Research, Apr. 5, 2017 at https://www.ibm.com/blogs/research/2017/04/using-ai-to-predict-heart-failure/.

[21]   Nathan R. Hoot and Larry J. LeBlanc et al., *Forecasting Emergency Department Crowding: A Prospective, Real-time Evaluation,* J. Am. Med. Inform. Assoc. 2009 May–Jun; 16(3): 338–45.

[22]   Marr, *supra* note 12.

[23]   *Automotive 2025: Industry without borders, Executive Report*, IBM Institute for Research Value, Jan. 2015 at http://www-935.ibm.com/services/multimedia/GBE03640USEN.pdf.

[24]   Peter Stone, Rodney Brooks, Erik Brynjolfsson, Ryan Calo, Oren Etzioni, Greg Hager, Julia Hirschberg, Shivaram Kalyanakrishnan, Ece Kamar, Sarit Kraus, Kevin Leyton-Brown, David Parkes, William Press, AnnaLee Saxenian, Julie Shah, Milind Tambe, and Astro Teller, *Artificial Intelligence and Life in 2030 - One Hundred Year Study on Artificial Intelligence: Report of the 2015-2016 Study Panel,* Stanford University, Sep. 2016, at http://ai100.stanford.edu/2016-report at 18–19.

[25]   Gutierrez, *supra* note 10.

[26]   Sara Roncero-Menendez, *AI Curates And Delivers Individual Meals Every Day*, psfk Blog, July 2016 at https://www.psfk.com/2016/07/office-lunches-ai-curates-and-delivers-individual-meals-every-day.html.

[27]   *See* generally, David H. Autor, *Why Are There Still So Many Jobs? The History and Future of Workplace Automation*, Journal of Economic Perspectives 29, no. 3 (Summer 2015), at https://economics.mit.edu/files/11563, and *Will Robots Steal Our Jobs? The Potential Impact of Automation on the UK And Other Major Economies*, PWC, Mar. 2017, at https://www.pwc.co.uk/economic-services/ukeo/pwcukeo-section-4-automation-march-2017-v2.pdf.

has inspired significant debate. Winner argued that technology both emerges from and creates social foundations. Under Winner's thesis, technologies have politics in two ways. Either (i) "the invention, design, or arrangement of a specific technical device or system becomes a way of settling an issue in the affairs of a particular community"; or (ii) the systems are "inherently political technologies", which "appear to require or to be strongly compatible with particular kinds of political relationships", technical arrangements and social order. This is hardly surprising. As people adapt to technologies, their everyday practices, feelings, and even identities may change, sometimes in unpredictable ways. The most commonly cited example from Winner's work involves the segregationist politics embodied in the height of the bridges over parkways on Long Island, in New York State. According to Winner, Robert Moses designed bridges that were intended to discourage the passage of buses. "One consequence was to limit access of racial minorities and low-income groups to Jones Beach, Moses' widely acclaimed Public Park." Nevertheless, Winner argues that "to recognize the political dimensions in the shapes of technology does not require that we look for conscious conspiracies or malicious intentions." There are many cases in which "the technological deck has been stacked in advance in favor of certain social interests", although this stacking was not necessarily consciously designed by anyone. One example Winner gives for such a situation is the failure to accommodate for disabled individuals that resulted more from a "long-standing neglect than from any-one's active intention." Algorithms, their often-unintended yet discriminatory design, and their inherent biases, may offer new and contemporary dimensions to Winner's paradigm.

In the following pages we provide an extensive overview of discrimination-related issues that can result from errors or human biases, illustrate them in different contexts, explain the difficulty of examining machine learning algorithms, and conclude by looking into the doctrine of disparate impact as a potentially mitigating legal principle.

II.   CHALLENGES

A.   Data Accuracy and Reliability

It is questionable how accurate and reliable Internet sources truly are. Especially as they are prone to data cleaning processes—a phenomenon that is more typical in the case of social media data—as well as other types of outages, random errors and gaps. The cleaning processes, errors, and outages raise questions as to whether Internet sources and online data can represent an objective truth or is any interpretation necessarily biased by some subjective filter given the way that data is cleaned. Similarly, data loss, another frequent occurrence, refers to the situation when information is destroyed by failures or neglect in storage, transmission, or processing. Originating in Internet sources, such errors, outages, and losses in large datasets are amplified when multiple datasets are pulled together.

Additionally, another source of concern is the choice of data to be mined, and information to be analyzed. After all, data mining can forever reflect and maintain the preconceptions of former decision-makers or mirror the widespread biases that exist in society. In their article *Big Data's Disparate Impact*, Solon Barocas and Andrew Selbst explain that "[e]ven in situations where data miners are extremely careful, they can still affect discriminatory results with models that, quite unintentionally, pick out proxy variables for protected classes."[28] Notable examples to this include Flickr's auto-tagging of online photos labelling pictures of black men as "animal" or "ape",[29] or researchers finding Google search results for black-sounding names more likely to be accompanied by ads about criminal activity than search results for white-sounding names.[30]

This issue of maintaining preconceptions is especially concerning in the context of gathering information on individuals from social networks and platforms. There are still plenty of individuals that live their entire lives outside the social networking realm, and even those who actually do participate actively in social networks, and share information online regularly, that do not exhibit equal qualitative and quantitative practices of information sharing.

Lastly, datasets can be manipulated or limited, which makes blindly relying on such information problematic. Moreover, due to the datasets' volume there is always the risk of finding irrelevant or bogus correlations with statistical significance that shows no noteworthy connection between the variables.

B.   Due Process and Opaqueness

Despite the fact that machine-learning algorithms are known and highly considered for their precision, this accuracy is bundled with an interpretive cost, which is the common reference to machine-learning algorithms as "black-box" systems.[31]

To understand the features of machine learning consider the categorization of handwritten digits. An algorithm might learn that certain geometric features of the shapes of handwritten digits are helpful for defining which digits they represent—yet we cannot truly appreciate what exact features any machine-learning algorithm is focusing on. Machine-learning algorithms transform a series of inputs to a series of outputs by perfecting a performance criterion, but that is where the analyst's ability to interpret the algorithms' workings concludes. The user of an algorithm cannot determine which specific relationships between variables factor into the algorithm's categorization, or at which stage in the algorithm they do, nor can the user establish how exactly the algorithm puts together different associations to yield its categorizations. Therefore, machine-learning algorithms are often described as transforming inputs to outputs through a black box. An analyst cannot look inside the black box to determine how a certain transformation happens or explain the associations with the same instinctive and fundamental language often used in traditional statistical modeling.

Computer experts have long comprehended the results of source data: the saying "garbage in, garbage out" mirrors the notion that biased or erroneous outputs are often

---

[28]   Solon Barocas and Andrew D. Selbst, *Big Data's Disparate Impact*, 104 CALIF L.REV.671, at 675 (2016).

[29]   Alex Hern, *Flickr Faces Complaints Over 'Offensive' Auto-Tagging For Photos*, The Guardian, May 20, 2015, https://www.theguardian.com/technology/2015/may/20/flickr-complaints-offensive-auto-tagging-photos.

[30]   Lauren Kirchner, *When Discrimination Is Baked Into Algorithms*, The Atlantic, Sep. 6, 2015, https://www.theatlantic.com/business/archive/2015/09/discrimination-algorithms-disparat e-impact/403969/.

[31]   See, e.g., Leo Breiman, *Statistical Modeling: The Two Cultures*, 16 STAT.SCI.199, 199 (2001).

the consequence of bias or errors in the inputs. In an instructional algorithm, bias in the data and programming is easily recognizable, if the developer is attempting to discover it. But smart algorithms are meant to function autonomously, and how they pick, study and consider variables out of a massive pool of data is at times a mystery, even to a program's developers. This lack of algorithmic transparency makes it difficult to decide where and how bias enters the system.

In recent years, as data mining and algorithmic predictions have started having a stronger presence in all aspects of life, many criticized their opacity and the inability to account for them. Indeed, even though it is now clear that many of the methods of automated decision-making could potentially harm individuals' life opportunities in arbitrary and discriminatory ways, these methods remain secret.[32] The process is technically opaque—the code is often kept undisclosed, and also substantively difficult to clearly understand—and outsiders do not have the ability to know what type of data is even gathered, which associations are targeted, and what concerns are factored into the algorithmic predictions. Those layers of opacity can disguise biased, discriminatory or otherwise undesirable results from supervision until negative results become visible and clear. The secrecy protects businesses and public entities against open disapproval – no institution would willingly submit itself to being characterized as racist or sexist. There is also a genuine intellectual property interest—exposing algorithms to open criticism also means, *de facto*, sharing them with competitors. The secretive nature of algorithmic decisions harms due process both ex ante—by enabling un-scrutinized gathering and examination of information—and ex-post—by precluding users from second-guessing undesired, or even harmful decisions—as examining the decision-making process is not a real possibility. Therefore, the secretive nature of algorithmic decisions frustrates oversight and accountability.

Accountability requires sharing an explanation and reasoning, or providing clarity and justification. Judicial courts, for example, improve accountability through the reasoning in their written decisions or, in the case of appellate panels, through cooperation and interchange of ideas. Furthermore, when we assess the legitimacy of administrative agencies, we frequently value political accountability; for some issues, we waive high levels of insulation and neutrality, subjecting agency decisions to external supervisions in order to ensure that they mirror the will of the executive branch or the legislature. Given the importance of accountability, being unable to provide proper supervision and accountability in the context of algorithmic decision-making and the push toward a call for explanation, have made scholars seek for ways to unlock the black box. Additionally, this failure to provide oversight prompted regulators to require meaningful information about the logic of automated decisions.[33]

---

[32]   On the importance of transparency and accountability in algorithms of powerful internet intermediaries, see Oren Bracha and Frank Pasquale, *Federal Search Commission? Access, Fairness, and Accountability in the Law of Search*, 93 CORNELL L.REV. 1149, 1159 (2008).

[33]   *See e.g.* Kiel Brennan-Marquez, Plausible Cause 70 VAND.L.REV, aT *8, at 18-24 (forthcoming 2017), available at https://papers.ssrn.com/sol3/papers.cfm?abstract_id=2827733 (drawing contrast between explanation and prediction); *see, e.g.,* Barocas and Selbst, *supra note* 28, 677–92; Pauline T. Kim, *Data-Driven Discrimination at Work*, 58 WM. & MARY L. REV. 857 (2017), available at http://papers.ssrn.com/sol3/papers.cfm?abstract_id=2801251 (arguing for an employ-

Current law already includes demands for explanation of decision-making process in service of various normative goals, and the demand that those impacted by decisions be able to understand them is at the heart of the legal system—in judges' opinions, litigants' theories of the case, administrative agencies' detailed justifications for rules, and in key due process principles. This demand is a central aspect of various laws such as the Fair Credit Reporting Act (FCRA),[34] which requires adverse action notices that spell out the factors that lead to a credit denial or other adverse action, and the Equal Credit Opportunity Act (ECOA),[35] which mandates that lenders provide "statement[s] of reasons" for adverse determinations. And while (i) the nature of the explanations mandated and the accountability requested, (ii) the purposes underlying each law, and (iii) the possible results of seeking the explanations—be it a justification for those affected by a decision, or ways to evaluate the fairness of processes—are not the same in all laws, the demand that those impacted by decisions be able to understand them appears to be a guiding principle.

Similarly, the notion of accountability is not new to privacy law and policy. It was officially introduced into data protection regulation in 1980 when it was unequivocally included as a basic data protection principle in the Organization for Economic Co-operation and Development's (OECD) 1980 Guidelines Governing the Protection of Privacy and Transborder Flows of Personal Data, the first internationally agreed-to set of privacy principles.[36] Since then, the accountability principle has been included in a variety of international data protection instruments as one of several core principles and is progressively finding its way more and more into national data protection laws. While accountability traditionally was all about allocating responsibility for privacy compliance, it is now about demanding a proactive, systematic and ongoing approach to data protection and privacy compliance through the implementation of appropriate data protection measures—gradually referred to as "privacy management programs".[37] And as such

---

ment discrimination standard of whether an adverse action was "because of" protected class membership; Andrew D. Selbst, *Disparate Impact in Big Data Policing*, 52 Georgia Law Review 109 (2017), available at https://papers.ssrn.com/sol3/papers.cfm?abstract_id=2819182; Joshua A. Kroll, et al., *Accountable Algorithms*, 165 U.PA.L.REV.633 (2017); Danielle Keats Citron and Frank Pasquale, *The Scored Society: Due Process for Automated Predictions*, 89 WASH.L.REV.1, 18–27(2014).

[34]   15 U.S.C. §§ 1681-1681t, as amended.

[35]   15 U.S.C. §§ 1691-1691f, as amended.

[36]   To some extent, the Fair Information Practice Principles (FIPPs), which are the result of the FTC's inquiry into the manner in which online entities collect and use personal information and safeguards to assure that practice is fair and provides adequate information privacy protection, represent the first attempt to introduce data-related accountability. These principles, in their earlier version, were proposed and named by the US Secretary's Advisory Committee on Automated Personal Data Systems in a 1973 report. *See US Secretary's Advisory Committee on Automated Personal Data Systems, Records, Computers and the Rights of Citizens (1973)*, at https://www.justice.gov/opcl/docs/rec-com-rights.pdf.

[37]   *See e.g.* Getting Accountability Right with a Privacy Management Program, chrome-extension://oemmndcbldboiebfnladdacbdfmadadm/https://www.priv.gc.ca/media/2102/gl_acc_201204_e.pdf. (Outlining what it believes are the best approaches for developing a sound privacy management program, for organizations of all sizes, in order to meet obligations under applicable privacy legislation, the Office of the Privacy Commissioner of Canada, and the Offices of the Information

programs become increasingly popular, regulators are revising numerous international data protection laws to reflect that change.

One such recent law and policy related instrument is the recent European Union's data protection act—General Data Protection Regulation (GDPR)[38]—that grants data subjects the legal ability to receive "meaningful information about the logic" of automated determinations. The GDPR, therefore, clearly introduces a legal accountability obligation to European data protection law that is in line with a global trend to make accountability a legal obligation. Joining the European regulators' direction are privacy officials from all around the world that are increasingly embracing the notion of accountability as a vehicle to drive privacy compliance within organizations. Accordingly, regulators in Canada, Hong Kong, France, Australia, and Colombia, among others, have issued "Accountability Guides" or "Privacy Governance Frameworks" that are meant to assist institutions set up suitable procedures to guarantee privacy compliance. Under the GDPR's accountability principle, controllers will be obligated to implement appropriate technical and organizational measures to guarantee and be able to demonstrate that data processing is performed in accordance with the GDPR, and review and update those measures where necessary.

C. Systemizing Existing Social Biases

The ground for errors and bias extends from the data gathering stage to the algorithm's design. While customarily individuals thought about algorithms similarly to the way they think about the law—as a set of abstract principles demonstrating rational objectives—reality could not be further from the truth. In theory and practice, big data digitally transforms "cultural clichés and stereotypes into empirically certifiable data sets."[39] Some discriminatory measures are obvious. Zip codes, for example, are notoriously known to signal much more than just geographical locations, as they can be indicators of race or national origin. Therefore, going forward—in a world of algorithmic decision-making, where apparently disparate variables become progressively hard to unravel—we must reassess which variables qualify as sensitive by virtue of their connection to race, gender, and other conventionally-protected categories. Once we identify these variables as such we would want to intensify the need for oversight, as there are many measures much more

---

and Privacy Commissioners of Alberta and British Columbia have worked together to develop a document with the goal of providing consistent guidance on what it means to be an accountable organization: "[a]ccountability in relation to privacy is the acceptance of responsibility for personal information protection. An accountable organization must have in place appropriate policies and procedures that promote good practices which, taken as a whole, constitute a privacy management program. The outcome is a demonstrable capacity to comply, at a minimum, with applicable privacy laws. Done properly, it should promote trust and confidence on the part of consumers, and thereby enhance competitive and reputational advantages for organizations. The concept of accountability appears straightforward, but constructing a privacy management program within an organization takes careful planning and consideration across disciplines and job functions.")

[38] General Data Protection Regulation (GDPR) (Regulation (EU) 2016/679) art 13(f)(2), 14(g)(2), 15 (1)(h) (requiring access to "meaningful information about the logic" of automated decisions).

[39] Michael Schrage, *Big Data's Dangerous New Era of Discrimination*, Harv. Bus. Rev. Jan. 29, 2014 at https://hbr.org/2014/01/big-datas-dangerous-new-era-of-discrimination.

nuanced than zip codes that can be effectively disguised behind numerous proxies and discriminatory design, adopted by the algorithms' creators. Indeed, this has always been the case with the designer of new technologies and tools.

In order to better understand how social and political biases get systemized in intelligent machine learning algorithms, it is important to understand that in an algorithmic system, there are three leading sources of bias that could result in biased or discriminatory outcomes: input, training and programming. Input bias occurs when the source data itself is biased as it lacks certain types of information, is not representative or mirrors historical biases. Training bias appears in either the categorization of the baseline data or the assessment of whether the output matches the desired result. Programming bias takes place in the original design or when a smart algorithm is allowed to learn and modify itself through successive contacts with human users, the incorporation of obtainable data, or the insertion of new data.

These three sources of bias have potential predictive analytic discriminatory impacts associated with them that have been widely discussed within academic literature, mainly in the two following contexts.[40] First, predictive formulas can create self-fulfilling prophecies against particular classes of people given their reliance on past data that can be used as "non-blatant proxies" for a protected class. Indeed, one method in which predictive formulas can create discriminatory impact against vulnerable classes is by using class proxies.[41] A data point that serves as a proxy for a class of people can *de facto* discriminate against that class as easily as if the class itself were being directly discriminated against.[42] For instance, height and weight can undoubtedly serve as gender proxies, and food as religion related proxies.[43] And non-blatant proxies are almost impossible to notice, as there is no recognizable and instantaneous association between one characteristic and a specific class of people, but in combination with a large dataset discriminatory conclusions and results become clearly visible. An example that demonstrates the difficulty posed by machine-learning algorithms focuses on the connection between race and online advertisements. Recent research showed that using Google to search a "black-identifying name was [25 percent] more likely to get an ad suggestive of an arrest record."[44] Attempting to mitigate the public relation damage resulting from this study, a Google representative attempted to explain that no discriminatory proxies were used by the algorithms and clarified that Google AdWords conducted no racial profiling.[45] Yet this very clarification reflects the

---

[40]   *See, e.g.,* Mark Burdon and Paul Harpur, *Re-Conceptualising Privacy and Discrimination in an Age of Talent Analytics,* 37 U.N.S.W. L.J. 679, 680 (2014); Kate Crawford and Jason Schultz, *Big Data and Due Process: Toward a Framework to Redress Predictive Privacy Harms* 55 B.C.L. REV. 93, 99–101 (2014); Graham Greenleaf AM, *Foreword: Abandon All Hope?,* 37 U.N.S.W. L.J. 6 36, 637–38 (2014); and Robert Sprague, *Welcome to the Machine: Privacy and Workplace Implications of Predictive Analytics,* 21 RICH. J. L. and TECH. 1, 34, at 35–41 (2014).

[41]   *See e.g.* Crawford and Schultz, *supra* n 40, 100–01.

[42]   Tal Z. Zarsky, *Understanding Discrimination in the Scored Society,* 89 WASH.L.REV. 1375, 1394–96 (2014).

[43]   *Id.*

[44]   Latanya Sweeny, *Discrimination in Online Ad Delivery,* 56 COMM.ACM 44, 51 (May 2013).

[45]   *"Racism is Poisoning Online Ad Delivery", Says Harvard Professor,* MITTECH.REV. (Feb. 4, 2013), http://www.technologyreview.com/view/510646/racism-is-poisoning-online-ad-delivery-says-harvard-professor/.

heart of the problem—algorithms draw correlations from billions of seemingly non-discriminatory data points and produce what can sometimes be unfavorable discriminatory outcomes.[46] Moreover, predictions and prescriptions are ever changing, which makes it even more difficult to determine potentially discriminatory proxies. Second, classes of people with minimal or no digital footprint may discover that they are not included in opportunities that rely on predictive data-driven assessments.[47]

III.   AI DISCRIMINATION AND DISPARATE IMPACT

The disparate impact doctrine has long been considered one of the most significant and controversial developments in antidiscrimination law. Arguably, where the doctrine applies intentional discrimination ends. Rather than serving as a broad theory of equality, the disparate impact doctrine deals with specific practices such as seniority systems and written tests that perpetuate past intentional discrimination. Disparate impact has been deployed in lawsuits involving employment decisions, housing, and credit. The disparate impact doctrine endorses proof of discrimination without the need to prove intent, and has been justified based on the difficulty of proving intentional discrimination, especially when evidence of overt bias or animus is lacking.

The disparate impact doctrine originated in the 1971 landmark decision of *Griggs v. Duke Power Co.*, 401 U.S. 424 (1971), where the U.S. Supreme Court unanimously approved it in the context of statutory employment discrimination claims. The Court ruled that, under Title VII of the Civil Rights Act of 1964, it was illegal for the company to use intelligence test scores and high school diplomas—factors which were shown to disproportionately favor white applicants and basically disqualify people of color—to make hiring or promotion determinations, regardless of the question whether the company intended for the tests it used to cause discrimination. A main element of the *Griggs* decision was that the power company could not demonstrate how their intelligence tests or diploma prerequisites were actually needed in order to successfully perform the jobs the company was hiring for.

Then, several years later, in *Washington v. Davis* 426 U.S. 229 (1976), the Court refused to extend the theory to constitutional claims, holding instead that intentional discrimination is needed in order to establish a violation of the Equal Protection Clause. Since then, advocates have sought to extend the theory to virtually every civil rights context under the perception that the disparate impact theory would reach discrimination that was otherwise out of reach for claims of intentional discrimination. Even critics acknowledge its impact and have implied that the doctrine makes employers rely on quotas as a measure that enables them to avoid disparate impact charges.[48] And when it seemed that

---

[46]   Samuel Gibbs, *Google Says Sorry Over Racist Google Maps White House Search Results*, THE GUARDIAN (May 20, 2015), http://www.theguardian.com/technology/2015/may/20/googl e-apologises-racist-google-maps-white-house-search-results.

[47]   Timothy M. Snyder, *You're fired! A Case for Agency Moderation of Machine Data in the Employment Context*, 24 Geo. Mason L. Rev. 1, 243, (2016).

[48]   *See, e.g.,* Hugh Steven Wilson, *A Second Look at Griggs v. Duke Power Company: Ruminations on Job Testing, Discrimination, and the Role of the Federal Courts*, 58 VA.L.REV. 844,

adverse Supreme Court decisions could cancel out the *Griggs* decision impact, Congress responded by passing the Civil Rights Act of 1991.

But the disparate impact doctrine is far from being bullet proof. Employers that have been sued for disparate impact discrimination under Title VII of the Civil Rights Act of 1964 could justify their potentially discriminating practices and systems under a business necessity test and in many claims they did.[49] Enabling employers whose practices are found to have discriminatory impact to avoid liability, the business necessity test has prompted a debate over the nature of the justification and especially whether the term "necessity" literally requires that the discriminatory practice be essential to the continued viability of the business.[50]

In recent years, as algorithms have started replacing humans as decision-makers, in areas such as employment, housing, and credit many have started wondering whether the disparate impact doctrine can be applied to bias that results from new technologies that use algorithms.[51] While the answer to this is not yet clear there are several aspects of the doctrine that merit discussion in the context of algorithmic decision-making processes. First, while the disparate impact doctrine did receive broad attention in recent decades, the doctrine has had a minimal impact outside the scope of the written employment tests and is, actually, an exceptionally difficult theory on which to succeed. For example, in *Texas Department of Housing and Community Affairs v. Inclusive Communities Project* 576 U.S. ___ (2015) ("*Inclusive Communities*"), the Inclusive Communities Project (ICP) claimed that the Texas state housing agency violated the Fair Housing Act (FHA) by triggering continued segregated housing patterns by unreasonably allocating low-income housing tax credits. ICP asserted that Texas giving too many tax credits for developments in chiefly African American inner-city neighborhoods and too few in chiefly Caucasian suburban neighborhoods in the Dallas area resulted in a disparate impact based on race in violation of the FHA. And while the Court did hold that claims of disparate impact discrimination are cognizable under the FHA, it also announced a somewhat stricter standard for plaintiffs who wish to show disparate impact.

> Disparate-impact liability must be limited so employers and other regulated entities are able to make the practical business choices and profit-related decisions that sustain the free-enterprise system. Before rejecting a business justification—or a governmental entity's analogous public interest—a court must determine that a plaintiff has shown that there is "an available alternative . . . practice that has less disparate impact and serves the [entity's] legitimate needs".[52]

Therefore, it is not clear if the disparate impact doctrine would be used in many other contexts, and even if it would, it is still very difficult to prove. Specifically, in order to make a prima facie case of disparate impact, traditionally plaintiffs were required to show:

---

873 (1972) (noting that "employers may use privately imposed quotas" to avoid disparate impact liability). For an incisive rebuttal to the quota argument, see Ian Ayres and Peter Siegelman, *The Q-Word as Red Herring: Why Disparate Impact Liability Does Not Induce Hiring Quotas*, 74 TEX.L.REV. 1487 (1996).

[49]   *See generally* Susan S. Grover, *The Business Necessity Defense in Disparate Impact Discrimination Cases*, 30 GA. L. REV. 387 (1996).

[50]   *Id.*

[51]   *See* Kirchner, *supra* note 30.

[52]   *Inclusive Communities*, at 3.

(i) a particularly identifiable practice or policy; (ii) a statistically noteworthy disparity in treatment between a protected group and other groups that exist; and (iii) a causal connection between the disparity and the practice or policy, as it has never been satisfactory for a plaintiff to simply demonstrate a disparity between a protected group and a non-protected group, no matter how blatant or obvious it was. Meeting the proof threshold for these factors could be extremely difficult in the context of algorithmic systems.

Second, not only did the *Inclusive Communities* Court signal that plaintiffs face a stricter set of hurdles when identifying the policy or practice that causes the disparate impact, but it also stated that "a one-time decision may not be a policy at all." Algorithmic systems, however, involve countless one-time decisions; with algorithms that constantly learn, change and evolve, almost every decision can be classified or viewed as a "one-time decision." This means that algorithmic-based decisions, by design, are extremely difficult to challenge using the disparate impact doctrine.

Third, when dealing with algorithms, plaintiffs might face a heightened standard for causation, given how difficult it is to establish direct and obvious causation where various factors form the basis of a challenged decision or policy. The Court also specified that a "robust causality requirement" will help protect defendants from being held liable for racial disparities they did not create.[53] Although it is not clear how the Court's analysis will play out in the different algorithmic decision-making contexts, the focus on "robust causality" increases the possibility that decisions made by intelligent agents and machine-learning algorithms may be able to escape disparate impact liability as long as they can demonstrate that their models only replicate and imitate present methods of systemic bias against minorities.

Finally, as mentioned above, if a plaintiff can make a prima facie case of disparate impact,[54] the defendant might still be able to fully dodge liability assuming the defendant can demonstrate "business necessity" by showcasing a valid interest that is served by the challenged policy. The defendant can do this by showing that the policy was related to its objective or relevant to its business goals.[55] Then, once a business necessity was demonstrated, the burden shifts back to the plaintiff, who in turn is tasked with presenting a different practice, which would have the same impact in terms of fulfilling the defendant's goals, but that would do so without producing a disparate impact. Since algorithmic decision-making processes are extremely opaque, secretive and complex by nature, if a business necessity is somehow successfully demonstrated, it would be very difficult and technologically challenging for the plaintiff to understand how it works well enough to present a different practice, which would have the same impact in terms of fulfilling the defendant's goals, without producing a disparate impact.

While it is still not clear if the disparate impact doctrine can apply to bias resulting from algorithm-based decisions, the recognition that predictive models built on historical data are responsible for making many decisions in modern society, led scholars to start developing discrimination-aware machine learning and data mining systems as an

---

[53] *Id.* at 2523.
[54] See *McDonnell Douglas Corp. v. Green*, 411 U.S. 792, 801-03 (1973) for the familiar burden-shifting framework.
[55] *Id.* at 2523–24; see also, e.g., *Ricci v. DeStefano*, 557 U.S. 557, 587 (2009).

emerging discipline. This discipline, which studies how to prevent discrimination in predictive modeling, attempts to mathematically formulate non-discrimination constraints, and develop machine learning algorithms that would be able to take into account non-discrimination principles in their decision-making processes regarding personalized pricing and recommendations, credit scoring, automated resumé screening while sorting applicants applying for jobs, profiling of potential suspects by the state authorities, and much more. In particular, the goal is to do this while taking into account which groups of people are considered protected according to national and international laws and standards, as accurately as possible.

IV.   ALGORITHMIC DISCRIMINATION ALL AROUND

A.   Finance

Financial service companies have always used different algorithmic systems to trade securities, predict financial markets, and assess creditworthiness. Unlike traditional instruction-based models that have been accused of prompting the 1987 "Black Monday" stock market crash[56] and the 2010 "Flash Crash",[57] machine-learning algorithms promise better, more intelligent, predictions. Babak Hodjat, co-founder of Sentient Technologies Inc., an AI stocks trading startup, recently stated: "Humans have bias and sensitivities, conscious and unconscious. . . It's well documented we humans make mistakes. For me, it's scarier to be relying on those human-based intuitions and justifications than relying on purely what the data and statistics are telling you."[58]

Learning algorithms have been widely implemented in the financial service industry. A recent survey revealed that the majority of the financial industry insiders believe that within the next three years AI will become the primary channel for interaction between banks and their customers.[59] As AI becomes more common in financial services and products, many hope that algorithmic decision-making would eliminate the subjectivity and cognitive biases inherent in human decision-making. These views, however, ignore the basic fact that algorithms are humanly devised. As such, their design involves

---

[56]   Selling by program traders as a reaction to the computerized selling required by portfolio insurance hedges is an oft-cited reason for the Black Monday stock market crash. See generally, Richard Bookstaber, A Demon of Our Own Design: Markets, Hedge Funds, and the Perils of Financial Innovation (Wiley 2011).

[57]   U.S. Securities and Exchange Commission and the Commodity Futures Trading Commission, *Findings Regarding the Market Events of May 6, 2010,* Sep. 30, 2010 at https://web.archive.org/web/20101010194307/http://www.sec.gov/news/studies/2010/marketevents-report.pdf. ("This large fundamental trader chose to execute this sell program via an automated execution algorithm ('Sell Algorithm') that was programmed to feed orders into the June 2010 E-Mini market to target an execution rate set to 9% of the trading volume calculated over the previous minute, but without regard to price or time.")

[58]   Satariano, *supra* note 13.

[59]   *Technology for People, Banks' Path to Becoming Their Customers' Everyday Trusted Advisor and Their Staff's Employer of Choice,* Accenture, at https://www.accenture.com/us-en/insight-banking-technology-vision-2017 (2017).

human mental models, and inevitably human biases. Not only can AI systems not deliver subjectivity-immune products, but companies also risk erroneous, abusive, or well-intentioned algorithmic design that nevertheless generates biased inferences and subsequently discriminatory outcome against protected classes of groups of people.

Machine learning techniques for underwriting consumer credit are especially susceptible to different types of bias risks. Historically, lenders have considered limited variables that directly correlate with financial stability and the prospects of repayment, including mostly consumers' record of meeting past financial obligations.[60] Big data in general, and learning algorithms specifically, allow lenders to increase the accuracy of their credit underwriting methods and augment financial inclusion by embracing non-traditional data and credit criteria.[61] Sources of non-traditional data include databases of web search histories, shopping patterns, social networking information, traces of users' online activity, and more. The use of alternative data and credit criteria allows marketplace lenders to assess the financial standing of loan applicants who lack sufficient traditional credit data.[62] However, machine-learning techniques can produce unfair or discriminatory lending decisions that will be hard to detect and explain. Consumers do not have visibility into the non-traditional data, but even if they did, they would rarely be able to make sense of the automated process, correct errors, or explain the reasons for the approval or rejection of their loan applications. Regardless of the discrimination potential, unexplainable credit decisions have been criticized for frustrating the purpose of credit-reporting legal requirements as prescribed by the FCRA. The FCRA requires that "consumer reporting agencies adopt reasonable procedures for meeting the needs of commerce for consumer credit, personnel, insurance, and other information in a manner which is fair and equitable to the consumer, with regard to the confidentiality, accuracy, relevancy, and proper utilization of such information."[63]

Biased outcomes often surface when data that reflects existing human biases is fed into the algorithm, which then incorporates and perpetuates those biases in informing a subsequent decision-making process. This is because

> [c]redit scores are only as free from bias as the software and data behind them. Software engineers construct the datasets mined by scoring systems; they define the parameters of data mining analyses; they create the clusters, links, and decision trees applied; they generate the predictive models applied. The biases and values of system developers and software programmers are embedded into each and every step of development.[64]

For example, a lending algorithm could be designed to favor loan-seekers who graduated from elite universities. If the admission processes in those institutions were biased against

---

[60] Mark Furletti, *An Overview and History of Credit Reporting,* FRB of Philadelphia Payment Cards Center Discussion Paper No. 02-07 (2002), at 2.

[61] Nizan Geslevich Packin and Yafit Lev-Aretz, *On Social Credit and the Right to be Unnetworked,* 2016 Col. Bus. L. J. 339, 357–58 (2016).

[62] *Id.,* at 355.

[63] 15 U.S.C. § 1681(b) (2012). *See* also Mikella Hurley and Julius Adebayo, *Credit Scoring in the Era of Big Data,* 18 Yale J. L. & Tech. 148, 184–90 (2016).

[64] *See* Rick Swedloff, *Risk Classification's Big Data (r)evolution,* 21 CONN. INS. L.J. 339, 355 (2015).

a certain class of people, the algorithm would import that bias into its financial risk evaluation. The more attenuated the included variables become the harder it will be to spot the incorporated biases.

Machine learning algorithms also fail to distinguish causation from correlation, and often cannot tell when additional data is needed to form a solid conclusion. For example, in 2015, Facebook registered a patent on financial ranking technology based on a user's social connections.[65] However, in addition to other potentially harmful consequences like decreasing upward mobility,[66] focusing on applicants' social networks could leave out other relevant variables that a learning algorithm may not be able to determine.

ECOA grants statutory protection against discrimination in credit transactions. ECOA bans discrimination on the basis of "race, color, religion, national origin, sex, or marital status."[67] Discrimination against consumers deriving income from public assistance programs is also prohibited.[68] Nevertheless, proving an ECOA discrimination claim against a creditor is a particularly daunting task, which is further exacerbated in the face of highly complex AI-infused credit-scoring systems. A plaintiff would have to demonstrate "disparate treatment" by proving "a discriminatory intent or motive" in the credit decision, or by showing that the lender's practices have had a "disproportionately adverse effect on minorities."[69] While algorithmic credit models could neutralize some of the influence of biased humans on lending decisions, these models are often so complex that they could mask implicit or even explicit discriminatory policies.[70] AI-driven financial assessment may also generate unintentional discrimination by encoding existing biases, relying on inaccurate sample data, or using proxy variables for sensitive features like race. Because AI-driven discrimination would be hard to detect in advance, the doctrine of disparate impact is the most promising legal counteraction.

It is not clear whether a claim of disparate impact can be brought under ECOA. On the one hand, ECOA makes no reference to disparate impact, and the Supreme Court has yet to provide clear guidance on the issue.[71] On the other hand, some circuit courts held that disparate impact claims could be brought under ECOA,[72] and ECOA's implementing regulations also refer to disparate impact, pointing out that the statute's legislative

---

[65]   U.S. Patent No. 9,100,400 (filed Aug. 4, 2015).

[66]   Geslevich Packin and Lev-Aretz, *supra* note 61 at 396–99.

[67]   15 U.S.C. § 1691(a)(1) (2012)

[68]   15 U.S.C. § 1691(a)(2) (2012).

[69]   *Cf. Ricci v. DeStefano*, *supra* note 55 (construing the disparate treatment test in the context of an employment discrimination suit under Title VII of the Civil Rights Act of 1964).

[70]   Barocas and Selbst, *supra note* 28, 692–93 ("Data mining could also breathe new life into traditional forms of intentional discrimination because decision makers with prejudicial views can mask their intentions by exploiting" various machine learning techniques.)

[71]   The *Inclusive Communities* court confirmed that disparate impact claims could be brought under the FHA and similar antidiscrimination laws, if the text of these laws refers to the consequences of actions and not just to the mindset of actors, and where that interpretation is consistent with statutory purpose. Nevertheless, in the same case the Supreme Court also introduced a more stringent standard for disparate impact showing, highlighting the importance of maintaining decision-making power in a well-run business ecosystem.

[72]   See, for example, *Golden v. City of Columbus*, 404 F.ad 950, 963 (6th Cir. 2005) (holds that that ECOA seems to allow disparate impact analysis). In *Beaulialice v. Fed. Home Loan Mortgage Corp.*, No. 8:04-CV-2316-T-24-EA, 2007 WL 744646 (M.D. Fla. Mar. 6 2007) the plaintiff chal-

history envisioned "effects test" claims that are similar to disparate impact tests in the employment context.[73]

Additionally, because a claim brought under the disparate impact doctrine must demonstrate robust causality, lenders could be immunized from disparate impact liability once they prove that their models mirror and replicate preexisting systemic biases against protected classes.

Finally, in addition to the complexity of credit risk algorithms, these types of financial models enjoy trade secrecy protection. In other words, even if the learning systems that produce financial risk assessments could be fully explainable, consumers and regulators are currently blocked from auditing these proprietary systems. Without access to the models and data, it is virtually impossible to fulfill the requirements for a disparate impact claim, and offering a non-discriminatory alternative to financial risk modeling.

B.   Employment and Labor

Many discussions of labor and AI systems have centered on the prospects of automated workforce and jobless future.[74] AI's penetration into labor markets, however, poses a variety of challenges, including the one highlighted in this chapter—discrimination during the different phases of employment, from application, to promotion, to exit. While employers have always been recruiting, hiring, evaluating, promoting, and terminating employees, the use of alternative data models incorporating information about individual attributes and behaviors has significantly changed labor markets.

AI technologies are used to improve recruitment, develop talent-mapping strategies, and ensure a diverse workforce. Predictive algorithms have been especially useful in saving the human effort required to sift through countless job applications, by narrowing down an initial pool of applicants or passive candidates that meet the exact job requirements into a shortlist of "good" candidates. AI-based hiring assesses human qualities and analyzes different variables, from word choice and microgestures to psychological attributes, emotional traits, and the tone of social media posts. A profusion of startups addresses itself to streamlining pre-employment strategies with the help of AI. For example, HireVue examines candidates' word choice, voice inflection, and microgestures for subtle indications, including disagreements between their facial expressions and their words.[75] Applicants' listed references fill out surveys by SkillSurvey, an AI service that devises and analyzes behavioral questionnaires to predict turnover and performance.[76] Most pre-employment predictive efforts are concentrated in candidates in the first seven years of their career—the exact period at which recruiters lack data other than grades

---

lenged a credit-scoring algorithm under the disparate impact theory, but the case was dismissed based on the affirmative defense of unclean hands.

[73]   12 C.F.R. § 202.6(a) (2016), at n.2 ("Congress intended an 'effects test' concept, as outlined in the employment field by the Supreme Court . . . to be applicable to a creditor's determination of creditworthiness").

[74]   *Artificial Intelligence and Life in 2030, supra* note 24 at 38.

[75]   https://www.hirevue.com/.

[76]   http://www.skillsurvey.com/.

and educational background.[77] In this sense, AI fills in the information gap with plenty of variables beyond formal measurements that can reveal employment-related qualities, such as persistence. With machine learning algorithms, Beamery, a candidate relationship management software, enhances applicant tracking by searches across social media channels.[78]

Some companies have been attempting to algorithmically mitigate biases in the hiring process. California-based startup Talent Sonar deploys machine-learning algorithms to write job descriptions in a manner that improves gender diversity; the software hides applicants' personal information like names and gender to reduce unconscious biases of hiring managers.[79] ThisWay Global incorporates AI to pair job applicants with relevant positions, based on skills data instead of personally identifiable information like gender, race and age.[80] Predictive hiring platform Koru can identify companies' hiring patterns, such as a tendency of recruiting from certain colleges, and offers practical adjustments to search more broadly.[81] Other AI-based assistants improve job searches and help skilled workers find their next professional match. For example, Yodas, an AI talent agency for software engineers, offers a bot that analyzes applicants' skills and generate relevant job listings.[82] Similarly, users provide their LinkedIn profile address and resumé to HR chatbot Jobo, who then finds open positions that fit their skill-set.[83]

Similar artificially intelligent assistants are deployed effectively post-hiring, such as by monitoring employees at their desk. Verito's AI system detects anomalies in computer-based actions that may signify poor productivity, malicious activity, or an intention to leave the company.[84] Bluvision makes radio badges that track where employees spend their time (e.g., their desks, in the cafeteria, or in a restroom) and for how long.[85]

AI is expected to improve predictions and reduce prejudices by ignoring demographic information or highlighting a more diverse selection of candidates. Learning algorithms can be more reliable than humans, more accurate forecasters, and work constantly without getting tired or distracted. Nevertheless, AI has its own set of biases and an immense discrimination potential in employment-related decisions and workplace structures. AI is trained to find patterns in previous behavior and set a baseline, learning and internalizing as a standard any human bias, conscious or unconscious, that may have existed in the workplace. For example, an automated decision applied across a large population with a roughly equal gender split could inadvertently place women or disabled workers at a particular disadvantage. Bluvision's software exemplifies such a scenario perfectly: it may discriminate against pregnant women or employees with digestive diseases who spend more time in the restroom than the average worker.

Traditional forms of hiring commonly identified skills or attributes thought relevant

---

[77]   Jennifer Alsever, *How AI is Changing Your Job Hunt*, Fortune, May 19, 2017 at http://fortune.com/2017/05/19/ai-changing-jobs-hiring-recruiting/.

[78]   https://beamery.com.

[79]   https://talentsonar.com/.

[80]   https://www.thiswayglobal.com/.

[81]   http://www.joinkoru.com/.

[82]   https://www.yodas.com/.

[83]   https://www.jobbot.me/.

[84]   http://www.veriato.com/.

[85]   http://bluvision.com/.

to job performance, and tested candidates by collecting limited amounts of targeted information.[86] Learning models, however, use a greater quantity of mined data that may contain information about qualities or conducts that have no clear connection with job performance, such as social networking data. Data-driven models in the employment context also suffer definition difficulties—describing the contextual notion of a "good employee" to the learning algorithm in ways that correspond to measurable outcomes is a challenging task.[87] Holistic definitions of "good" would have to be translated into machine-readable measures and applied to individuals as part of the algorithm learning process. This translation and classification phase is one of the main injectors of human bias into the machine learning system.[88] Bias is also introduced in the selection of training data that may incorporate biased judgements. For example, training data regularly includes supervisors' evaluations or past hiring decisions. Those characterizations that may be prejudiced or biased will inform the model's baseline and will inevitably be reproduced in the outcome.[89] Employment-related training data may also inaccurately represent minority and disadvantaged groups, whose presence in big datasets is often marginalized and does not match their proportional presence in the general population.[90]

In addition to design choices that could lead to discriminatory employment practices, employers may also use AI to intentionally discriminate against certain groups. Such intention, however, could be effectively masked either by the use of facially neutral variables that act as proxies for protected classes, or by the often inscrutable nature of the machine learning process. Title VII of the Civil Rights Act of 1964 is commonly referred to as the primary source of regulation in the context of employment fairness and discriminatory effects.[91] As explained above, section 703 prohibits two forms of discrimination: disparate treatment, which looks at discriminatory motive, and disparate impact, which applies to discriminatory effects. Intentional employment discrimination that relies on an apparently neutral data model fits well within the conventional Title VII framework.[92] And while theoretically the use of data classification structures that may worsen inequality among protected groups could be addressed under disparate impact doctrine, the ways the doctrine have been construed and applied rendered it ill-suited to address AI bias.[93] The difficulty lies not only in exposing unintentionally biased datasets

---

[86]   Kim, *supra* note 33. *See* also Gideon Mann and Cathy O'Neil, *Hiring Algorithms Are Not Neutral*, Harvard Business Review, Dec. 9, 2016 at https://hbr.org/2016/12/hiring-algorith ms-are-not-neutral.

[87]   Barocas and Selbst, *supra* note 28, at 679.

[88]   *Id.*, at 680.

[89]   *Id.*, at 682.

[90]   *Id.*, at 684. See also Kim, *supra* note 33 at 877.

[91]   Civil Rights Act of 1964, Pub. L. No. 88-352, §703(a)(1), 78 Stat. 241, 255 (codified as amended at 42 U.S.C. § 2000e-2(a)(1) (2012) ("It shall be an unlawful employment practice . . . to fail or refuse to hire or to discharge any individual, or otherwise to discriminate against any individual . . . because of such individual's race, color, religion, sex, or national origin . . ."))

[92]   For the burden shifting framework and the establishment of a discrimination case see discussion next to footnotes 54–55.

[93]   Barocas and Selbst, *supra* note 28 at 694, and Kim, *supra* note 33, at 909. In line with this view, Kim argues "employment discrimination law can provide a vehicle for addressing classification bias, so long as the doctrine accounts for its data-driven sources."

or algorithms, but also in identifying appropriate remedies and preventive measures to forestall further discrimination. There is no effective way to prevent the use of protected characteristics that can still enter the data via other non-sensitive variables that act as proxies. Even if blocking protected class variables were effective, it may risk exacerbating discriminatory effects under certain circumstances.[94]

To overcome Title VII incompetency to effectively mitigate data-driven discrimination at the workplace, Pauline Kim suggests an alternative reading of Title VII. Under her "closer reading" Title VII directly prohibits the use of discriminatory data classification schemes when algorithms operate to systematically disadvantage protected groups.[95] Alternatively, she suggests adjustments to the disparate impact doctrine to improve its application to data-driven discrimination. In a similar vein, the Equal Employment Opportunity Commission (EEOC) has worked to scrutinize hiring practices including the use of data-driven hiring tools. In a 2014 public workshop, the EEOC Assistant General explained that to determine the legality of applicant screening, data-implemented prejudices must be identified.[96] Nevertheless, data tools that accurately predict job performance are generally permissible, and only prejudices that are "not job related and consistent with business necessity" would be actionable under Title VII.[97]

C.   Health and Healthcare

Of all the fields where AI is gaining a foothold, healthcare seems to be endowed with the greatest impact. Through a variety of applications, AI is poised to become a game changer for the healthcare sector: a recent study projects the market for health-related AI to grow from around $600 million to $6.6 billion in 2021.[98]

AI has transformed healthcare analytics as researchers can now mine outcomes from millions of patient clinical records and promote finer-grained, more personalized diagnosis and treatment. Watson, IBM cognitive technology, recently matched tumor board treatment recommendations in 96 percent of lung cancer cases and cut clinical trial screening time by 78 percent.[99] Automated discoveries of genotype-phenotype connections and likely situated patients to inform treatment decisions are also forecasted to become widespread thanks to AI.[100] As surgical, delivery, and patient care information become fixable, storable, searchable, and connected, healthcare is on the fast route to being greatly augmented. The collected data is used not only to assess performance quality, errors, or potential optimizations but also to create a closed-loop medicine by providing constant feedback. AI also gave rise to healthcare robotics, an artifact that until recently

---

[94]   Kim, *id.*, at 904.

[95]   *Id.*, at 909.

[96]   See Statement of Carol Miaskoff, in *Transcript, FTC Big Data: A Tool for Inclusion or Exclusion*, Sept. 15, 2014 at https://www.ftc.gov/system/files/documents/public_events/313371/bigdata-transcript-9_15_14.pdf.

[97]   *Id.*

[98]   *Artificial Intelligence: Health's New Nervous System*, Accenture (2017) at https://www.accenture.com/us-en/insight-artificial-intelligence-healthcare.

[99]   *At ASCO 2017 Clinicians Present New Evidence about Watson Cognitive Technology and Cancer Care*, IBM, Jun. 1, 2017 at https://www-03.ibm.com/press/us/en/pressrelease/52502.wss.

[100]   *Artificial Intelligence and Life in 2030, supra* note 24, at 25.

has been of interest only to science fiction enthusiasts. Today, however, the research and practical use of surgical robotics keeps growing. For example, robotic surgical systems for orthopaedic surgery have been used in thousands of joint replacements worldwide,[101] and UK-based startup Babylon Health created an AI doctor in the form of a chatbot.[102] Unlike older evidence-driven analytics that relied on traditional healthcare data, AI can now learn from a variety of new data sources. The mobile computing revolution has allowed biometrics to be collected "in the wild" for the first time in history.

Legal discussions around learning algorithms and healthcare have mostly focused on privacy issues surrounding the use of private patient information,[103] medical liability of robo-doctors,[104] and the impact of automation bias on doctors.[105] Nevertheless, bias and discrimination concerns exist in the healthcare context as well. Health-related AI relies on data-based, as opposed to scientific or clinical, developments and validation. Errors in collected data may make patterns harder to identify or lead to false pattern recognition.[106] There is also a risk that differences in health information will feed bias into the dataset: researchers have found that physicians' pain-management treatment differs between black and white patients.[107] Such differences in input, notwithstanding the motivation or intention behind them, could systematically distort the output. AI systems would also be instrumental in identifying and defining illness. Assumptions as to what is "normal" or "average" health incorporate individual bias and cultural prejudices: up to 1973 homosexuality was listed as a mental disorder by the American Psychiatric Association.[108]

Furthermore, systematic incentives that are inherent in the medical environment could interfere with the quality of the data. Knowing that their income is directly tied to insurance companies' classification of treatments, doctors are incentivized to upcode

---

[101] THINK Surgical, Inc. develops, manufactures and markets these systems. *See* http://thinksurgical.com/professionals/company/about-us/.

[102] *Steve O'Hear, Babylon Health Raises Further $60M to Continue Building Out AI Doctor App*, TechCrunch, Apr. 25, 2017 at https://techcrunch.com/2017/04/25/babylon-health-raises-further-60m-to-continue-building-out-ai-doctor-app/.

[103] *See Artificial Intelligence and Life in 2030, supra* note 24, at 25 ("HIPAA. . . requirements for protecting patient privacy create legal barriers to the flow of patient data to applications that could utilize AI technologies"); Nicolas P. Terry, *Big Data Proxies and Health Privacy Exceptionalism* 24 Health Matrix J.L.-Med. 65, 99–100 (2014) (Describing how physicians are bound by a "duty of confidentiality in curating the[ir] patient's health data"); and Nicolas P. Terry, *Protecting Patient Privacy in the Age of Big Data* 81 U.M.K.C L. Rev. 385, 401 (2012) (Explaining that that "health information deserves a higher level of privacy protection than most other types of data").

[104] See for example Jessica S. Allain, *From Jeopardy! To Jaundice: The Medical Liability Implications of Dr. Watson and Other Artificial Intelligence Systems* 73 La. L. Rev. 1049 (2013).

[105] Automation bias drives humans to view computers as error-resistant and disarms them from critically evaluate potential errors. Nathan Cortez, *The Mobile Health Revolution?*, 47 U.C. Davis L. Rev. 1173, 1227 (2014).

[106] W. Nicholson Price II, *Big Data, Patents, and the Future of Medicine*, 37 Cardozo L. Rev. 1401, 1414–15 (2016)

[107] Kelly M. Hoffman et al., *Racial Bias in Pain Assessment and Treatment Recommendations, and False Beliefs about Biological Differences between Blacks and Whites* 113 Proc. Nat'l. Acad. Of Scis. 4296 (2016).

[108] *The AI Now Report, The Social and Economic Implications of Artificial Intelligence Technologies in the Near-Term*, AI Now, Jul. 7, 2017 at https://artificialintelligencenow.com/media/documents/AINowSummaryReport_3_RpmwKHu.pdf, at 14.

treatments to get paid more, especially in borderline cases.[109] Insurance-related medical data also highlights cost-related aspects of treatments, potentially neglecting to make references to relevant medical information.[110] Evidence showing that patients consenting to information sharing differ from those who are unwilling to consent raises additional concerns as to bias in the dataset.[111] And obviously, bias or discriminatory rules can also be introduced through biases in algorithmic development.

Besides internal challenges with systems' input and design, attention must be given to the distribution of AI benefits in healthcare. Indeed, AI can help make healthcare accessible and affordable. But with evidence showing unequal distribution of healthcare access and benefits, AI can further amplify this imbalance with poor, non-white, and female populations being systematically disadvantaged.[112]

D.   Education

In the past decade, AI has made considerable advances in educational settings, significantly enhancing education, especially by facilitating personalization at scale. Robots successfully teach children different skills from logical thinking and coding to math and biology. Improved through machine-learning, Natural Language Processing (NLP) has furthered online education and allowed teachers to teach bigger classrooms while addressing individual students' learning needs and styles.[113] Intelligent tutoring systems (ITS) have rapidly moved from laboratory experimental stages to real everyday use. When learners work on a problem-solving task, ITS track their mental steps to diagnose errors and appraise their understanding of the domain. Learners can also enjoy ITS's timely guidance, feedback and explanations, and be matched with learning activities at an individually-tailored level of difficulty and interest. ITS have been used in schools to help students learn mathematics, geography, circuits, medical diagnosis, computer literacy and programming, genetics, and chemistry.[114] They have also been used in universities and in the military. Demonstrating an even bigger growth, massive open online courses and other models of online education increasingly use AI. Many of the popular online education platforms, including EdX, Coursera, and Udacity, use NLP, machine learning, and crowdsourcing for grading students' assignments and programming tasks.[115]

Online learning systems also generate large and ever-growing datasets that provide useful insights into learning processes. Researchers apply deep learning, natural language processing, and other AI techniques to collected education data to learn about student engagement, behavior, and outcomes. Current initiatives in learning analytics attempt to model common student misconceptions, predict students' performances, and offer real-time student feedback.

---

[109]   Price, *supra* note 106 at 1414–15.
[110]   *Id.*
[111]   Institute of Medicine, *Beyond The HIPAA Privacy Rule: Enhancing Privacy, Improving Health Through Research*, 209–14 (2009).
[112]   *The AI Now Report, supra* note 108 at 15.
[113]   *Artificial Intelligence and Life in 2030, supra* note 24 at 31.
[114]   *Id.*
[115]   *Id.* at 32.

Notwithstanding the above, schools and universities have been slow in adopting AI technologies compared to other sectors. The lack of financial resources and skepticism as to the effectiveness of these technologies in the educational realm can account for the tardy integration of AI. Still, estimates project that over the next 15 years education-related uses of AI will expand significantly, and AI techniques will gradually blur the line between formal classroom education and individual learning through, for example, adaptive learning systems and virtual reality applications.[116]

Alongside promises of educational revolution, AI can create and exacerbate discrimination in education. Standardized tests, for instance, have exhibited racial, socioeconomic, and gender bias.[117] The SAT was specifically attacked for being culturally and statistically biased against African Americans, Hispanic Americans, and Asian Americans.[118] Similarly, critics alleged that reading comprehension tests are in fact pre-existing knowledge tests.[119] Like we have seen in other fields, the same biases that exist in the traditional educational context will be inevitably imported into the data and the algorithmic design of the AI system. And while the use of data-driven technologies and analytics can expose and alleviate systematic discrimination, it can also systemize inequalities and re-inscribe existing power relations in school and in society. Biased AI systems in the educational context can lead to profiling that will keep feeding the bias into education-related dynamics and reinforce itself with virtually no chance of detection and treatment. Evidence shows that when a teacher is guided by less favorable information on some students, those students do not perform as well.[120] When the information is provided by a scientifically glorified AI system, both the teacher's bias and the students' deteriorating performance would be greater.

E.   Legal System

The legal system has also shown interest, and in some cases moved to implement artificial intelligence in legal affairs. Police departments in cities like Los Angeles, Atlanta, and Philadelphia, use crime prognostication systems that search past crime data to predict which people and places are most at risk for future crimes. Intended to replace traditional forms of trendspotting and gut feelings about locations of future crimes and identity of potential offenders, predictive policing systems incorporate approaches from fields as diverse as seismology and epidemiology, and look at a variety of data sources, from minor crime reports to criminals' Facebook profiles.[121] Predictive policing software by companies

---

[116]   *Id.*

[117]   Katherine Connor and Ellen J. Vargyas, *The Legal Implications of Gender Bias in Standardized Testing,* 7 Berkeley Women's L.J. 13 (1992).

[118]   Maria Veronica Santelices and Mark Wilson , *Unfair Treatment? The Case of Freedle, the SAT, and the Standardization Approach to Differential Item Functioning,* 80 HARV. EDUC. REV. 106 (2010).

[119]   Jules Polonetsky and Omer Tene, *Who Is Reading Whom Now: Privacy in Education from Books to Moocs,* 17 Vand. J. Ent. and Tech. L. 927, 985 (2015).

[120]   *See generally* Robert Rosenthal, *Pygmalion in the Classroom: Teacher Expectation and Pupils' Intellectual Development* (Crown House Publishing 1968).

[121]   Mara Hvistendahl, *Can 'Predictive Policing' Prevent Crime Before It Happens?* Science, Sep. 28, 2016 at http://www.sciencemag.org/news/2016/09/can-predictive-policing-prevent-crime-it-happens.

like PredPol, IBM, Microsoft, Hitachi, and Palantir present a visualized crime forecast to inform police officers at the beginning of their shifts. The idea is less about catching offenders in real time, and more about deterring criminals with the mere force of police presence.

Like other AI-based forecasts, predictive policing systems raise a host of concerns. Predictive policing algorithms are only as good as the data they are based on, and error in the data could unfairly cast suspicion on a certain location or individual. These systems also risk reinforcing unfortunate patterns by relying on biased data. Predictive policing systems could also lower the suspicion threshold, making officers predisposed to stop individuals who confirm the predictive analysis as opposed to an individual who raises a reasonable suspicion. Studies on predictive policing software found that instead of their stated goal of providing unseen insights into future crimes, some algorithms end up reinforcing and validating bad police habits. Those systems that use reported crime and arrest records to generate a heat map end up delivering a self-fulfilling prophecy: when police officers are sent to areas with high arrest frequency, they arrest even more and contribute to a positive feedback loop. Furthermore, predictive policing software is proprietary and often covered under trade secrecy protection. Consequently, the public and even the police cannot tell how the system works, effectively placing it in an accountability-free zone.

Learning algorithmic systems similarly hold promise in forensic analysis. Researchers from the Forensics and National Security Sciences Institute have used machine learning to facilitate interpretations of samples containing DNA from multiple people.[122] The system, named Probabilistic Assessment for Contributor Estimation (PACE,) improved prediction accuracy over current methods by six to 20 percent. PACE was also significantly faster: it was able to correctly sort the samples in seconds, as opposed to up to nine hours required for current DNA classification techniques. Researchers at King's College London used machine learning to more accurately predict the age of criminal suspects based on blood and saliva samples from crime scenes.[123] While forensic AI is still at a very early stage, it is prone to the same risks of error, bias, and discrimination.

Criminal sentencing is another area that has seen a growing implementation of AI technologies. From setting bail to determining sentence length, learning algorithms use historical data to inform decisions and predictions. Jurisdictions have generally employed one of three main technologies: Correctional Offender Management Profiling for Alternative Sanctions (COMPAS), Public Safety Assessment (PSA) and Level of Service Inventory Revised (LSI-R). COMPAS looks at five domains: criminal involvement, relationships/lifestyles, personality/attitudes, family, and social exclusion. The LSI-R also mines information from a variety of factors, including criminal history and personality patterns. The Public Safety Assessment uses a narrower set of variables, mostly relating to a defendant's age and criminal history.[124] Those systems appeal to many because they

---

[122]   Michael A. Marciano et al., *PACE: Probabilistic Assessment for Contributor Estimation— A machine learning-based assessment of the number of contributors in DNA mixtures*, Forensic Science International: Genetics (2017).

[123]   Athina Vidaki et al., *DNA Methylation-Based Forensic Age Prediction Using Artificial Neural Networks and Next Generation Sequencing*, Forensic Science International: Genetics (2017) at http://www.fsigenetics.com/article/S1872-4973(17)30038-8/fulltext.

[124]   *Algorithms in the Criminal Justice System*, EPIC at https://epic.org/algorithmic-transparency/crim-justice/.

aspire to increase objectivity in a criminal justice system that has been long compromised by human failings.

In 2016, ProPublica revealed that the formula used for the COMPAS system in Florida was particularly likely to highlight black defendants as future criminals.[125] White defendants were also assigned lower risk scores than black defendants. Most importantly, the investigation found that the scores failed in predicting violent crime: forecasts rightly predicted the likelihood of committing a violent crime only in 20 percent of the cases. For the entire range of crimes, recidivism prediction rates were more accurate, but still leaving a significant room for mistake—61 percent of flagged individuals were arrested for any subsequent crimes within two years. Some miscalculations were attributed to inaccurate inputs (such as by not including an individual's record from another state), while others were clear cases of bad design. Northpointe, COMPAS's non-profit creator, has not shared its algorithm for audit, and many jurisdictions have adopted COMPAS and its likes without testing their validity. The LSI-R was similarly criticized for including history variables outside the defendant's control; such as criminal backgrounds of family members that would increase a defendant's risk score.[126]

Defense lawyers condemn such risk assessment methods because their validity cannot be challenged at sentencing hearings. Scholars have also warned that the availability of predictive models incentivizes criminal justice actors to opt for investigative punishment approaches that agree with the algorithmic prediction.[127] Others have cautioned that the more AI-assisted legal reasoning becomes entrenched in the legal system, the more lawmakers will be tempted to turn previously less determinative areas of the law into more formal and conclusive, to allow their algorithmic coding and processing.[128] Such a move would not only increase the prospects of errors, but would also amplify bias in design and subsequently systemize discrimination.

BIBLIOGRAPHY

Biased-based and Statistical Discrimination

Bertrand, Marianne and Sendhil Mullainathan, *Are Emily and Greg More Employable Than Lakisha and Jamal? A Field Experiment on Labor Market Discrimination* 94 The American Economic Review 991 (2004).
Coglianese, Cary and David Lehr, *Regulating by Robot: Administrative Decision Making in the Machine-Learning Era*, 105 GEO. L.J. 1147, 1156–58 (2017).
Kahneman, Daniel, *Thinking Fast and Slow* (Macmillan 2011), chapters 12–15.
Neumark, David, Ian Burn and Patrick Button, "Is it Harder for Older Workers to Find Jobs? New and Improved Evidence from a Field Experiment," National Bureau of Economic Research Working Paper 21669 (2015).

---

[125]   Julia Angwin, Jeff Larson, Surya Mattu and Lauren Kirchner, *Machine Bias*, ProPublica, May 23, 2016 at https://www.propublica.org/article/machine-bias-risk-assessments-in-criminal-sentencing.
[126]   Angèle Christin, Alex Rosenblat, and Danah Boyd, *Courts and Predictive Algorithms*, Data & Civil Rights: A New Era of Policing and Justice, Oct. 27, 2015 at http://www.law.nyu.edu/sites/default/files/upload_documents/Angele%20Christin.pdf.
[127]   Andrea Roth, *Trial by Machine*, 104 Geo. L.J. 1245, 1266 (2016).
[128]   Harry Surden, *The Variable Determinacy Thesis*, 12 Colum. Sci. and Tech. L. Rev. 1, 89 (2011).

Onuachi-Willig, Angela and Mario Barnes, *By Any Other Name?: On Being 'Regarded As' Black, and Why Title VII Should Apply Even If Lakisha and Jamal Are White*, 5 WIS. L. REV. 1283 (2005).
Riach, Peter A. and Judith Rich, *Field Experiments of Discrimination in the Market Place* 112 The Economic Journal 483 (2002).

Algorithmic Discrimination

Barocas, Solon, "Data Mining and the Discourse on Discrimination", Conference on Knowledge Discovery and Data Mining (2014).
Barocas, Solon and Andrew Selbst, "Big Data's Disparate Impact" 104 California Law Review 671 (2016).
Crawford, Kate, *Artificial Intelligence's White Guy Problem* New York Times (2016).
Feldman, Michael et al., "Certifying and Removing Disparate Impact", Proceedings of the 21th ACM SIGKDD International Conference on Knowledge Discovery and Data Mining 259 (2015).
Heikkila, Andrew, *Artificial Intelligence and Racism* TechCrunch (2016).
Kirchner, Lauren, *When Discrimination Is Baked Into Algorithms* The Atlantic (2015).
Miller, Claire, *Can an Algorithm Hire Better Than a Human?* New York Times (2015).
Miller, Claire, *When Algorithms Discriminate* New York Times (2015).
Packin, Nizan Geslevich and Yafit Lev-Aretz, *On Social Credit and the Right to Be Unnetworked*, Colum. Bus. L. Rev. 339 (2016).
Pasquale, Frank, *Black Box Society: The Secret Algorithms That Control Money And Information* (Harvard University Press 2015) (Chapter 4, "Finance's algorithms: the emperor's new codes;" Chapter 5, "Watching (and improving) the watchers.").
Zliobaite, Indre, "A Survey on Measuring Indirect Discrimination in Machine Learning", Association of Computer Machinery (2015).

Privacy and Discrimination: Law and Social Norms

Citron, Danielle and Frank Pasquale, *The Scored Society, Due Process for Automated Predictions* 89 Washington Law Review 1 (2014).
Lane, Charles, *Will Using Artificial Intelligence To Make Loans Trade One Kind Of Bias For Another?* NPR, March 31, 2017.
Roberts, Jessica, *Protecting Privacy to Prevent Discrimination* 56 William and Mary Law Review 2097 (2015).
Strahilevitz, Lior, *Privacy versus antidiscrimination* 75 University of Chicago Law Review (2007).

Disparate Impact and Title VII

Datta, Amit, Michael Carl Tschantz and Anupam Datta, *Automated Experiments on Ad Privacy Settings A Tale of Opacity, Choice, and Discrimination* Proceedings on Privacy Enhancing Technologies, 1, 92 (2015).
Kim, Pauline *Data-Driven Discrimination at Work*, 58 WM. and MARY L. REV. 857 (2017).
Snyder, Timothy M., *A Case for Agency Moderation of Machine Data in the Employment Context* 24 Geo. Mason L. Rev. 1, 243, (2016).
Who's A CEO? Google Image Results Can Shift Gender Biases, EurekAlert!, Apr 9, 2015, at https://www.eurekalert.org/pub_releases/2015-04/uow-wac040915.php.

Cases

Griggs v. Duke Power Co., 401 U.S. 424 (1971).
McDonnell Douglas Corp. v. Green, 411 U.S. 792, 801-03 (1973).
Washington v. Davis, 426 U.S. 229 (1976).
Beaulialice v. Fed. Home Loan Mortgage Corp., No. 8:04-CV-2316-T-24-EA, 2007 WL 744646 (M.D. Fla. Mar. 6 2007).
Ricci v. DeStefano, 557 U.S. 557, 587 (2009).
Texas Department of Housing and Community Affairs v. Inclusive Communities Project 576 U.S. ___ (2015).

Statutes

Fair Credit Reporting Act (FCRA), 15 U.S.C. §§ 1681-1681t.
Equal Credit Opportunity Act (ECOA) 15 U.S.C. §§ 1691-1691f.
The Federal Reserve Board Regulation B, 12 C.F.R. § 202.
General Data Protection Regulation (GDPR) (Regulation (EU) 2016/679) art 13(f)(2), 14(g)(2), 15 (1)(h).
Civil Rights Act of 1964, Pub. L. No. 88-352, §703(a)(1), 78 Stat. 241, 255 (codified as amended at 42 U.S.C. § 2000e-2(a)(1) (2012).

5. The principal Japanese AI and robot strategy toward establishing basic principles

Fumio Shimpo

I. INTRODUCTION

The evolution of Artificial Intelligence (AI) is rapidly advancing. If we fail to scrutinize the new information security countermeasures for the use of intelligent robots and artificially intelligent entities or if we fail to scrutinize the legal issues accompanying the spread of consumer electronics, robots equipped with AI, and cars which operate as highly automated vehicle systems, the types of security problems which have impacted the development of the Internet could arise again in other, new contexts that involve AI. Surely, there is a fear that this danger will spread beyond the problems within "virtual spaces" (such as the Internet), and present threats which will dramatically raise the likelihood of physical danger resulting from the actions caused by AI.

The possibility of an AI running out of control and posing a danger to humans has been noted as one of the potential threats posed by robots that are becoming more and more autonomous. This is precisely the threat which has been depicted in movies. However, it is currently believed that a considerable amount of time is still needed for AI to evolve to the point where it is self-aware enough to spontaneously take defensive actions on behalf of itself or others. It must be stressed that at this moment in time, the possibility of this kind of threat immediately becoming a reality is thought to be low.

In this chapter, I will introduce the recent Japanese AI and Robot Strategy, Special Zones (Tokku) and research trend in Japan.[1]

II. THE RELATIONSHIP BETWEEN ROBOTS, ARTIFICIAL INTELLIGENCE AND THE INTERNET OF THINGS

A society which connects to networks anywhere and at any time should be termed a "Ubiquitous Network Society" (UNS). In addition, a society which uses robots and AI, without a "conscious awareness" of the robots themselves should likewise be called a "Robot Coexistence Society" (RCS). Robots do not have self-consciousness at this moment in time. People have doubts about whether robots are capable of having self-consciousness. For example, automated driving cars are indistinguishable from cars in general and therefore, in terms of self-consciousness, it is clear that they cannot make

---

[1] *See also*, Fumio Shimpo, *Japan's Role in Establishing Standards for Artificial Intelligence Development*, The Carnegie Endowment for International Peace on Artificial Intelligence (AI) Development and Alliance Engagement (January 2017) http://carnegieendowment.org/2017/01/12/japan-s-role-in-establishing-standards-for-artificial-intelligence-development-pub-68311.

moral choices like human beings are able to. Additionally, a robot coexistence society is a society characterized by human-robot symbiosis which uses autonomous AI-equipped robots routinely connected to networks in various contexts, and thus can be termed a "Ubiquitous Robot Society".

In other words, what needs to be examined and explored with Robots and AI-related legal issues is the response to the new issues which will arise with the spread—through the combination of robots, AI, and the Internet of Things (IoT)—of autonomous robots. The response of the legal professionals will be based on their current knowledge of the law regarding both current and future legal issues. However, the general public must be allowed to comment on non-legal issues such as the morality of the use of the robots; the most obvious being the use of sex robots. A legal response is also needed for cases in which major societal or systemic reform is required to address the use of robots that are gaining in intelligence. Thus, Robot Law[2] needs to consider the ideal forms of legal and social systems in a Robot Coexistence Society and Ubiquitous Network Society. As far as the fundamental principles of the law and legal thinking are concerned, the debate over new problems involving AI and autonomous robot use may possibly spark a paradigm shift in law. The problems caused by autonomously operating robots may not be able to be resolved using the current standards and legal systems which were developed originally for the industrial robots operated by humans and performed within the scope of a programmed machine. It is crucial for the law to examine which party in the design, development and use of autonomous entities will bear which specific type of legal liability in the event of problems or damages resulting from the incorrect operations of an AI's "autonomous decision". For example, the premise underlying liability for illegal actions under Tort Liability has been such that it is possible to foresee the results which could occur from accidents. However, currently, based on the Japanese Civil Code and the Product Liability Act (Act No. 85, 1994), it is difficult to impose a burden of proof of liability on developers or manufacturers for the actions automatically triggered by an AI because they exceed the scope of human control. In this case, while we must consider who should be the party bearing product liability or strict liability as is currently understood under Tort Law, legal scholars should also question the use of product liability related to damages resulting from an autonomous decision made by AI. Given that we can question the imposition of liability if an incident results from a defect in a robot operating with AI, it is unlikely that the robot with AI will be able to implement any preventative countermeasures in advance to mitigate the effects of such defects because of its autonomous nature. In addition, the current legal system may not have the mechanisms to resolve issues of liability for damages due to a runaway or uncontrollable AI. Furthermore, it is to be expected that robots will be connected to networks and routinely used in a wide variety of objects and locations as the IoT expands. Thus, there will be an expected increase in the various problems in daily life caused by autonomous robots connected to such networks and unevenly distributed throughout nearby familiar places.

The evolution of AI has been remarkable in the last few decades and now we see the arrival of a so-called "Third-Generation AI Boom". Consumer electronics and home appliance products controlled by AI are also emerging. The development of a Highly

---

[2]   *See*, Ugo Pagallo, *The Laws Of Robots – Crimes, Contracts, And Torts* (Springer 2013), Ryan Calo, A. Michael Froomkin, Ian Kerr, *Robot Law* (Edward Elgar Publishing 2016).

Automated Vehicle (HAV) is also advancing with automated driving systems controlled by an AI operating in place of a human driver. These cars have also become "connected cars", being connected to 5G networks through the IoT. One of the main concerns accompanying the evolution of AI are the fears that autonomous AI will spontaneously choose to threaten humans, as dramatized in the movie *Terminator*. However, this will not become a real problem in the foreseeable future until AI advances to the point where it becomes cognizant of its own existence and "aware" of the necessity of eliminating threats to itself. However, it may be necessary to examine a malfunctioning of an autonomous robot or runaway AI as a problem which could become an immediate threat. Additionally, a major consequence of the new technical applications of AI is the issue of "function creep" in which the functions for achieving an original purpose at the time of design come to be used for different purposes. On this point, there is a high possibility that AI which has evolved through deep learning will produce unforeseen results due to the principle of function creep.

One example of a legal issue pertaining to function creep is illustrated in the following case: after identifying the cause of an error occurring in a service which performs biometric automatic authentication via facial recognition equipment, it came to light that an error was triggered by skin color; i.e., the service unintentionally reacted to information related to race. This error resulted in unintentional racial discrimination. Although facial recognition software is designed to be racially neutral, its operation ultimately led to discriminatory practices due to the unexpected error produced by algorithms. This rather complicated issue, with constitutional law implications, differs from the more straightforward legal problem of misuse where objects are used for purposes other than their original purpose (such as HAV being used for suicide bombings).

III. THE DEFINITION OF A ROBOT IN JAPAN

As a precondition for discussing Robot Law and confirming that Robot Law relates to AI because robots are increasingly equipped with more and more AI, it is necessary to have a clear legal definition of "robots" which are therefore subject to this law. Among the current Japanese laws and regulations, 22 contain provisions relating to robots (as of 1 September 2018). However, under Japanese law, definitions are specified only for industrial robots ("Ordinance on Industrial Safety and Health", Article 36, Item 31) and meteorological radio robots ("Ordinance for Enforcement of the Radio Act", Article 2, Item 43), and no current laws specify a definition of the singular concept of "robots".

The Japanese AI strategy has a close relationship with Japan's Robot Strategy and the related legal issues are considering not only that of the use of AI independently but also of autonomous robots with AI use in the IoT. Actually, there is also no clear definition of AI in law, in any regulation or in any standards in Japan. This is because concerns about robots equipped with AI are provided for under the current law and regulations.

As noted, in Japan, several definitions of the term robot are currently used. In the Japanese Industrial Standards JIS B 0134:2015,[3] "Robots and Robotic Devices:

---

[3]   Industrial robots are defined in "ISO 8373:2012" ("Robots and Robotic Devices: Vocabulary, IDT"), on which the JIS B standards are based.

Vocabulary", where the definitions of the terms used here are related to robots and robotic devices operating in both industrial and non-industrial environments, there is a definition regarding "industrial robot". An "industrial robot" is defined as a "machine used in industry which has manipulation and movement functions through automatic control and which can perform all varieties of operations by means of programs". Furthermore, the ISO 8373 defines a robot as an "actuated mechanism, programmable in two or more axes, (4.3), with a degree of autonomy, (2.2), moving within its environment, to perform intended tasks".[4]

The "2016 Report of the Research Council on Robotics Policy" issued by the Japanese Ministry of Economy, Trade and Industry (METI) attempted a systematic definition of the term robot by proposing three conditions which robots must satisfy to be called robots. They must have: a) "sensors"; b) "intelligence/control systems"; and c) "drive systems". In short, robots could be appropriately defined as "intelligent mechanical systems". The report further attempted to subdivide the "next-generation robots" into two sub-types: (1) "next-generation industrial robots", those which can replace humans and/or work in cooperation with humans in multiple types of variable production, and, (2) "service-robots," those which coexist with humans in places such as the home or service businesses, while providing services related to diverse applications, such as cleaning, security, welfare and well-being, life support and amusement.

An additional definition of the term Robot comes from the Patent Office in Japan. Robot technology is broadly classified into "component technologies which comprise the fundamental technologies upon which a robot is built" and "applied technologies which are necessary when actually utilizing a robot". Component technologies are further divided into five major categories: 1) overall structural technologies; 2) partial structural technologies; 3) control technologies; 4) intelligent technologies, and 5) communication technologies.

In addition, 25 intermediate categories are set within these five major categories. Furthermore, applied technologies are divided into three intermediate categories and 33 individual subcategories. Notably, these definitions are changing. In the 2001 "Study Report on Technology Trends in Patent Applications", a robot was defined as a "machine which possesses manipulation functions", or a "machine which has movement functions and possesses functions to independently obtain external information and determine its own actions". Next, the 2006 Study Report additionally defined a robot as a "machine which has communication functions and possesses functions to independently obtain external information, determine and then take its own actions". Thus, machines which converse with people started being treated as robots, even if they lacked movement or manipulation functions.

There is no clear definition regarding AI in law, regulation and any standards in Japan. However, there is a definition of "robots" which has been provided by the law and regulations. Thus, in the future, robots will be operating in general life, equipped with AI and so the real problem is that there will be no legal definition of AI-equipped robots underpinning their correct use. What do the changes in these definitions mean? As noted above,

---

[4]   ISO 8373:2012, 2.6 robot, https://www.iso.org/standard/55890.html, https://www.iso.org/obp/ui/#iso:std:iso:8373:ed-2:v1:en.

robots, according to the above-mentioned definitions given by METI,[5] (a) "sensors"; b) "intelligence/control systems"; and c) "drive systems" are required within the scope of the definition of robots. As such, by using intelligence/control system applications which move objects via smartphone sensors, we are now able to move connected devices even if they lack drive systems. Moreover, these changed definitions also include objects which function as robots only in terms of their intelligence/control systems, such as conversation robots which operate through AI. In other words, the progress of AI and the spread of the IoT have led to the emergence of robots which do not conform to the existing definition. Thus, despite the existence of a clear definition for industrial robots, no definition exists for general-purpose robots. Robots which do not conform to the conventional definitions of robots could be expected to proliferate in the future.[6]

IV.   GOVERNMENTAL POLICY TRENDS REGARDING ROBOTS

A.   The Industrial Background of the Current Japanese Robot Strategy

The necessity for a Robot Law linked to the Japanese industrial policies is obvious and it is equally necessary to recognize that a "Fourth Industrial Revolution" and "Society 5.0" will be accompanied by a major reform in our society and within the legal system in general.

Japan holds a high share of the market for industrial robots and according to a "Results of Trends Survey on the Robot Industry Market",[7] the global market for industrial robots has grown by approximately 60 percent during the last five years in terms of monetary value. World Robotics 2017 Industrial Robots[8] indicated that in 2016, robot sales increased to 294,000 units, again by far the highest level ever recorded for one year.

The scale of the Japanese robot market was approximately 716 billion JPY in 2016. Although the Japanese market has contracted by approximately 25 percent during the last five years in terms of the number of units produced, it still maintains its status as the largest market provider in the world. However, the Chinese market has roughly quadrupled during the past five years and in terms of the number of units produced, it is growing at a rate which is catching up quickly with current Japanese production.[9]

The basic policy regarding the utilization of AI and robots was announced as "The

---

[5]   "2016 Report of the Research Council on Robotics Policy" issued by the Japanese Ministry of Economy, Trade and Industry.

[6]   Takato Natsui, *The End of Asimov's Principle – Possibility of Robot Law*, The Law Diagram Vol. 89, No. 4, 5 Merger Number (2017) (in Japanese).

[7]   The Japan Machinery Federation, The Research Report on Promotion of Robot Industry and Technology (2017), http://www.jmf.or.jp/content/files/houkokusho/29nendo/29robo_h.pdf.

[8]   World Robotics Industrial Robots – International Federation of Robotics, https://ifr.org/worldrobotics, Executive Summary World Robotics 2017 Industrial Robots, https://ifr.org/downloads/press/Executive_Summary_WR_2017_Industrial_Robots.pdf

[9]   Pagallo, *supra* note 2, 3–9.

New Robot Strategy" ("Vision, Strategy Action Plan").[10] This policy was issued on 10 February 2015. Following this, on 12 April 2016, The Headquarters for Japan's Economic Revitalization decided upon a strategy to promote "The Fifth Public-Private Dialogue towards Investment for the Future". The strategy targeted the goals for the research and development of AI and described in detail a roadmap for its implementation. The New Robot Strategy was created by the Robot Revolution Realization Committee,[11] which was established by the Cabinet Secretariat, in cooperation with the METI. The strategy's distinctive features are that it broadly and flexibly outlines the concept of robots in general without limiting itself to the conventional industrial robots of the past.

B.   The Background of the Strategy

Regarding the background of "The New Robot Strategy", there are the serious issues of a declining birth rate and ageing society which are progressing at an unparalleled rate worldwide and thus Japan has become one of the first among other nations to encounter the associated challenges of a decline in the number of the working-age population, a shortage in labor, and higher social security costs. The number of senior citizens aged over 65 and above hit the record-high level of over 34.6 million as of 18 September 2016, equaling 27.3 percent[12] of the total population of Japan (the so-called Population-Aging Rate).

C.   The Robot Revolution

The aim of the robot strategy is to achieve ultimately a robot revolution and so the strategy refers to the significant and consequential changes which will be caused by a robot revolution, which are listed as follows:

1. turning what was not originally to be positioned as a robot in conventional manners into a robot through the advancement of sensor and AI technologies (e.g., automobiles, household appliances, mobile phones or housing will be considered as types of robots);
2. utilizing robots in the actual site of manufacturing as well as various scenes of daily life, which leads to the last point;
3. forming a society where new added-value, convenience and wealth are created through the reinforcement of global competitiveness in the fields of manufacturing and service as well as the derivation of social issues.

Japan's robot strategy mentioned some factors for achieving a robot revolution. In the course of a transformation into "flexible robots with universal user-friendliness", the making of "module-driven robots" is one of the objectives which will begin a process that

---

[10]   Headquarters for Japan's Economic Revitalization, *New Robot Strategy*, Ministry of Economy, Trade and Industry of Japan, October 2, 2015, http://www.meti.go.jp/english/press/2015/pdf/0123_01b.pdf.
[11]   The Robot Revolution Realization Committee, http://www.kantei.go.jp/jp/singi/robot/.
[12]   MIC, *The statistics from elderly people in Japan (over 65 years old) – named after "Respect for the Aged Day" (2017)*, http://www.stat.go.jp/data/topics/pdf/topics97.pdf.

will end ultimately with the creation of a "mainstream robot model" utilizing a common platform, catering to diverse needs through different module combinations. These module-driven robots equipped with AI will be linked to IT-integrated ones which will meet the demand for the creation and utilization of robots equipped with such functionality as "Autonomy", "Data-Terminals" and "Networks". Moreover, the strategy insists that robot concepts must be developed further in order to maximize a continuing trend of new innovation through ever more flexible approaches to robot concepts, in contrast to the conventional viewpoint of seeing robots simply as machines equipped with three basic, systematic elements of sensor, intelligence/control and actuator.[13] However, via the advancement of digitalization, the diffusion of Cloud Computing and the progress of AI, robots will be driven by independent intelligence/controls based on an AI-enabling access to many and various people groups and also by "objects" in a real world, without the help of a specific actuation system.[14]

D.   The Three Pillars towards the Robot Revolution

Japan's New Robot strategy is built on the following three "pillars":

1.   a global base for robot innovation; i.e., a significant reinforcement of robot creativity;
2.   (Japan becoming) the world's leading society in the sector, maximizing robot capacity and showcasing the realization of daily life with these robots;
3.   (Japan being) the world leader in developing this strategy for a new and worldwide robot era.

In attempting to build these three pillars, this strategy provides an "action plan: the five-year plan", and following this, "The Robot Revolution Initiative (RRI)",[15] which was established to serve as the focus for the wide range of stakeholders who want to promote Japan's Robot Strategy. The RRI will not only have the required implementation status of underpinning governmental policy but it will also be supported by the large number of related stakeholders whose economic aim is achieving the targets of the New Robot Strategy.

V.   POLICY REGARDING AI

A.   The 5th Science and Technology Basic Plan (2016–2020)

The Council for Science, Technology and Innovation, a Cabinet Office of Japan, issued "The 5th Science and Technology Basic Plan 2016-2020"[16] on 22 January 2016. This basic

---

[13]   This concept and definition is provided by the Japanese Industrial Standards (JIS).
[14]   The strategy gives an example of such system as developing and offering sensor and intelligence/control systems alone is sufficient for robots to function such as loading drive application on smart phone OS (iOS or Android) for smart phones to function as remote controller device.
[15]   The Robot Revolution Initiative, https://www.jmfrri.gr.jp.
[16]   Fifth Science and Technology Basic Plan (Cabinet decision on January 22, Heisei 28) http://www8.cao.go.jp/cstp/kihonkeikaku/index5.html.

plan stated clearly and forcefully that AI technology will play an important role for accelerating industrial promotion strategy in realizing "Society 5.0".[17] In this envisaged society, the relationship between science and technology will play a major role in innovation and the development of a worldwide society. Consequently, ethical, legal and social efforts must be made to solve the inevitable problems which will occur in the age of an AI era. In addition, this plan advocated the conducting of strategic and relevant research under the co-operation of the related governmental ministries with an aim of strengthening common fundamental technologies and human resources by clarifying what are precisely the AI technical issues needed to have a "Society 5.0 (the Super Smart Society)".

B.   Considerations of the Ministry of Internal Affairs and Communications (MIC)

Regarding AI policy considerations, the Ministry of Internal Affairs and Communications began its deliberations in February 2015. In the initial policy aspect discussions, the first step was to recognize the need for future long-term investigations towards "Technological Singularity". "The Conference on the AI Networking" issued its 20 June 2016 report "The Impact and Risks of AI Networking – Issues for the Realization of A Wisdom Network Society" (WINS).[18] The report was the first systematic review of AI networking issues in Japan. Referring to the Organization for Economic Co-operation and Development (OECD) guidelines governing privacy and security, it became necessary to begin discussions and considerations toward formulating international guidelines and principles to govern the Research & Development (R&D) of AI. This report focused on: (1) risks related to function, legal systems in general and individual rights and interests; (2) AI network development and risk emergence; (3) predictable risk and uncertain risk.

In this report, WINS focused firstly on how "wisdom" should be conceived as both an aspirational goal for society and as a guide for a "sophisticated information communication network society and knowledge society". Secondly, the report also evaluated the impact of AI networking on the "public arena" (towns), "life arena" (people) and "industrial arena" (jobs) from the 2020s to the 2040s. Thirdly, the report also designed a framework for studying and evaluating the risks of AI networking and illustrated examples of the anticipated risks. Finally, the report presented a design for the principles of future research and development, an ideal form of user protection and an ideal form of the basic rules of society. The report advocated the necessity for improving study systems within Japan, in preparation for the development of international sites to host future debates regarding the issues about AI networking.

---

[17]   The meaning of the term "Society 5.0" is the new society created by transformations led by scientific and technological innovation, after hunter-gatherer society (Society 1.0), agricultural society (Society 2.0), industrial society (Society 3.0), and information society (Society 4.0). Council for Science, Technology and Innovation Cabinet Office, Government of Japan, Report on the 5th Science and Technology Basic Plan (December 18, 2015) P.13.

[18]   Ministry of Internal Affairs and Communications, Telecommunications Research Laboratory Conference on the AI Networking, *The Impact and Risks of AI Networking – Issues for the realization of A Wisdom Network Society (WINS)*, http://www.soumu.go.jp/menu news/s-news/01iicp01_02000050.html.

The evaluations will be carried out in a hypothetical chronological order from the 2020s to the 2040s. The anticipated risks of AI networking were listed within a framework and decisions about how to deal with the anticipated risks were based on current research and development on an ideal form of user protection, an ideal form of the basic rules of society and so on. Next, the report advocated the need to improve AI networking review systems within Japan in preparation for the organization of international conferences to promote for continued debate on the subject. Finally, eight principles of AI networking research and development were publicized and agreed to at "the ICT ministers' meeting" of the G7 summit held in April 2016.

By means of the first version of this report, the eight principles of AI research and development shown in the report were publicized. In addition, the report "Towards the Promotion of International Discussion on AI Networking"[19] was issued on 28 July 2017. The updated guideline added the "Principle of Collaboration" as a ninth principle.

Following this, "The Draft AI R&D Guidelines for International Discussions (28th July 2017)" were issued. The proposed guidelines constitute: 1) Purpose; 2) Basic Philosophies; 3) Definition of Terms and Scope; 4) AI R&D Principles. These guidelines added the following Basic Philosophies;

1.   To realize a human-centered society where all human beings across the board enjoy the benefits from their life in harmony with AI networks, while human dignity and individual autonomy are respected.
2.   To share the Guidelines, as non-binding soft law, and their best practices internationally among stakeholders, as, with the rapid development of the R&D and utilization of AI, networked AI systems are expected to have broad and significant impacts on human beings and society beyond national borders.
3.   To ensure an appropriate balance between the benefits and risks of AI networks, so as to: (a) promote the benefits from AI networks through innovative and open R&D activities and fair competition; and (b) mitigate the risk that AI systems might infringe rights or interests, while fully respecting the value of the democratic society such as academic freedom and freedom of expression.
4.   To make sure that AI R&D activities based on specific technologies or techniques are not hindered in light of ensuring technological neutrality, and to be mindful that developers are not imposed of excessive burden, as the rapid progress of AI-related technologies is anticipated to continue.
5.   To constantly review the Guidelines and flexibly revise them as necessary through international discussions, considering the extent of the progress of AI networking, because AI-related technologies and AI utilization are expected to continue to advance dramatically. Also, to strive for broad and flexible discussions including the involvement of related stakeholders when reviewing the Guidelines.

Then, this guideline proposed to issue the following nine principles:

---

[19]   The Ministry of Internal Affairs and Communications, *Towards Promotion of International Discussion on AI Networking*, http://www.soumu.go.jp/main_content/000499625.pdf.

1. Principle of collaboration—Developers should pay attention to the interconnectivity and interoperability of AI systems.
2. Principle of transparency—Developers should pay attention to the verifiability of inputs/outputs of AI systems and the explainability of their judgements.
3. Principle of controllability—Developers should pay attention to the controllability of AI systems.
4. Principle of safety—Developers should take it into consideration that AI systems will not harm the life, body, or property of users or third parties through actuators or other devices.
5. Principle of security—Developers should pay attention to the security of AI systems.
6. Principle of privacy—Developers should take it into consideration that AI systems will not infringe the privacy of users or third parties.
7. Principle of ethics—Developers should respect human dignity and individual autonomy in R&D of AI systems.
8. Principle of user assistance—Developers should take it into consideration that AI systems will support users and make it possible to give them opportunities for choice in appropriate manners.
9. Principle of accountability—Developers should make efforts to fulfill their accountability to stakeholders including users of AI systems.

C. The Artificial Intelligence Technology Strategy Council

The Artificial Intelligence Technology Strategy Council was established in order to conduct research and development for improving AI technology and for boosting its "Industrialization Road Map". This council was established by "The 5th Public-Private Dialogue for Future Investment conference"[20] at The Japan Economic Revival Headquarters held on 12 April 2016. As a result of an examination into the Fiscal Year 2016, the council published "The Artificial Intelligence Technology Strategy"[21] (31 March 2017).

This strategy outlined the governmental promotion system of the AI Technology Development Industrialization Roadmap (a fusion of AI and other related technologies, research and development of AI technology). In order to achieve the goals of this strategy, "The R & D Goals of AI and the Industrialization Road Map" was issued on 31 March 2017.

When the Strategic Council for AI Technology was established, the Research Coordination Council and Industry Coordination Council was also established. The Research Coordination Council's role was to provide a link mechanism for research and development carried out by the various competent ministries. The Industry Coordination Council carried out surveys and investigations on (1) establishing a roadmap for industrialization, (2) the fostering of human resources, (3) data maintenance/provision and open

---

[20] The Prime Minister in Action, *Public-Private Dialogue towards Investment for the Future,* http://japan.kantei.go.jp/97_abe/actions/201604/12article6.html.
[21] New Energy and Industrial Technology Development Organization (NEDO), *The Artificial Intelligence Technology Strategy,* http://www.nedo.go.jp.

tools, and (4) measures such as for fostering start-ups and financial linkages, in aiming towards research and development carried out by the competent ministries and social implementation of other businesses. With regard to ethical aspects of AI technology, intellectual property rights, personal information protection, and the promotion of open data, separate opportunities for scrutiny have been established by the government as cross-governmental sector items.

The priority areas of the Industrialization Roadmap which refer to the development and utilization of AI mainly focus on (1) the necessity for urgent solutions to social issues, (2) the contribution to economic ripple effects, and (3) the expectations of economic contributions to society due to AI technology. Based on these perspectives, "productivity", "health, medical care and welfare" and "mobility" and "information security" were determined as areas for which reviews would be made as such cross-sectional areas.

D.   Considerations by the Cabinet Office

"The Advisory Board on Artificial Intelligence and Human Society" started its discussions on 30 May 2016, under the initiative of the Minister of State for Science and Technology Policy, composed of members with various backgrounds in fields such as engineering, philosophy, law, economics, and social sciences. The Advisory Board issued its "Report 2017 on Artificial Intelligence and Human Society"[22] on 24 March 2017.

The Advisory Board tried to clarify common key issues of AI technologies and human society from a multi-stakeholder point of view, i.e., from the viewpoints of users, researchers, engineers, artists, people across generations, including children, businesses, and governments. The report summarized the extracted key issues as follows:[23]

> *Ethical issues*: A significant action is to consider the balance between human decisions and AI-based decisions depending on the situations and objects to be judged. The balance change causes the emergence of a new sense of ethics. If users confirm AI services that enable them to manipulate someone's mind and/or to evaluate people, discussions of ethics might especially be needed. Careful attention contributes to proper AI progress that has the possibility to change human concepts, since AI technologies augment human beings' senses and abilities. New evaluation procedures have required the observation of the values (e.g., originality, utility, and virtue) of the products made and actions performed by humans, by AI technologies, and through the cooperation of both.
>
> *Legal issues*: Determining the locus of responsibility for accidents involving AI technology along with preparing insurance for probabilistic risks contributes to social acceptance and helping users understand the risks of utilizing AI technologies. Exploitation of big data while considering information privacy protection requires the consideration of appropriate institutional frameworks (laws, guidelines, and con-

---

[22]   The Advisory Board on Artificial Intelligence and Human Society, Report 2017 on Artificial Intelligence and Human Society, http://www8.cao.go.jp/cstp/tyousakai/ai/summary/aisociety_en.pdf.

[23]   *Id.*, 3–6.

tracts). Considering the rights to and incentives for the creation of AI technologies remains a subject of further study for multi-stakeholders. In-depth analysis and basic research (e.g., social sciences) play an important role in reconsidering fundamental concepts, such as human responsibilities, that the modern law is based on.

Economic issues: Individuals changing their work style and updating their abilities propose to harmonize each person's abilities with a creative job/task. These changes also require that companies reconsider their decision-making techniques and staff (re)assignment to take advantage of work flexibility. At the government level, combining educational and employment policies is one of the effective procedures for mobilizing labor, revitalizing the economy, and preventing economic disparities.

Educational issues: The significant issues are understanding the advantages and limitations of the present AI technologies, properly utilizing AI technologies, and performing creative activities in collaboration with AI technologies. An educational policy functions according to discussions of how to efficiently reform curriculums based on evidence that shows the technologies' limitations, the critical human abilities differentiated from present AI technologies, and the essential human abilities to be acquired.

Social issues: There is a need to create space for dialogue among people with different visions and ideas and to consider common, fundamental social values. One of the fundamental issues is the need to facilitate provisions against the "AI divide", unbalanced social costs relative to AI, and discrimination that occurs because of the technologies' procession. Continuous assessments of social pathology, conflict, and dependence on AI technologies will offer solutions to these issues.

Research and development (R&D) issues: Researchers and engineers are required to engage in R&D with professional ethics while observing ethical codes and guidelines. Technologies for cyber security and privacy protection must be advanced. Basic research to ensure that AI technologies are controllable and show transparency by explaining the processes and logic of calculations made by AI technologies contribute to their social implications. Advancing AI technologies that are beneficial for human society requires basic sciences, including social sciences to study societal issues that may arise in the future, observing the social acceptance of their stochastic behaviors such as deep learning, and creating an environment that supports open science to enhance the diversity of AI technologies.

E.   Investigations by the Intellectual Property Strategy Headquarters

The Intellectual Property Strategy Headquarters in Japan[24] has established a "New Information Goods Review Committee, Validation, Evaluation and Planning Sub-Committee". This committee published a report[25] in March 2017 which aims to make provisions for a new intellectual property system that will promote a foundation for

---

[24]   The Intellectual Property Strategy Headquarters, http://www.kantei.go.jp/jp/singi/titeki2/.
[25]   The Intellectual Property Strategy Headquarters, *New Information Goods Review Committee, Validation, Evaluation and Planning Sub-Committee*, http://www.kantei.go.jp/jp/singi/titeki2/tyousakai/kensho_hyoka_kikaku/.

strengthening industrial competitiveness through the promotion of data and AI utilization. Intellectual property outcomes which are autonomously created by AI will not be viewed in the same way as are intellectual property outcomes which are created by "natural persons". Therefore, such intellectual property may not be protected by the current Japanese intellectual property law since such content is not included in the concept of "the object of protection of copyright". Furthermore, in the future, it is expected that the number of copyrighted materials created by AI will drastically increase.

For this reason, it is important that we study and construct a new intellectual property system which will protect all new "information goods" vis-à-vis all copyright, industrial property rights and other intellectual property. In summary: the considerations of the above-mentioned headquarters were focused mainly on a desire to solve the above problems by:

1. Having a perspective of strengthening industrial competitiveness aimed at an enhancement of industrial competitiveness by creating "value added-ness" within a wide range of industries, by maximizing the utilization of data and AI as intellectual property.
2. Creating a balance between the need for protection and the utilization of data and AI; that is, a balanced mechanism in which the investment activities of the data and AI stakeholders are adequately protected, but where a smooth and active utilization will be achieved.
3. Having an "international perspective", that is, by which cross-border issues can be resolved on how to implement digital network systems which are underpinned by a premise that the use of data/AI will grow as economic and industrial globalization progresses.

F.   Considerations by the Ministry of Economy and Trade Industry (METI)

"The Industrial Structure Council – New Industrial Structure Committee" is a committee of the METI, established to investigate issues with respect to "The Fourth Industrial Revolution", beginning August 2016. The Council issued a report entitled "The New Industrial Structure Vision"[26] on 30 May 2017. The ensuing "New Industrial Structure Vision" summarizes the measures which are needed to realize an affluent Japanese society by stimulating economic growth and tackling structural problems by deploying technological innovation in IoT, Big Data, AI and robot-use. The report provides a "Target-Backward Road Map" to demonstrate and embody Japan's medium- and long-term future goals and strategies which will lead ultimately to a "breakthrough project" aimed at concrete institutional reform.

G.   The IT Strategy Headquarters PDS Committee

The National Strategic Headquarters for The Promotion of an Advanced Information and Communications Network Society ("The IT Strategy Headquarters"),[27] established a

---

[26]   Ministry of Economy, Trade and Industry, *The New Industrial Structure Vision*, http://www.meti.go.jp/english/press/2017/0530_003.html.

[27]   IT Strategy Headquarters, http://japan.kantei.go.jp/policy/it/index_e.html.

"Data Distribution Environment Improvement Committee".[28] This committee published the "Data Interaction Working Group Interim Report in the AI and IoT Era," on 15 March 2017. The popular and universal use of IoT equipment and the evolution of AI has given society the opportunity to efficiently and effectively collect, share, analyze and utilize a wide variety of large amounts of data. As a result, this committee indicated the importance of "data distribution environmental improvement" to promote fully the adequate utilization of such "Big Data", leading to a maximizing of the potential of AI by enabling the use of a wide variety of large amounts of data in the afore-mentioned "Society 5.0". A study sponsored by this committee aimed to promote a so-called "PDS" (Personal Data Store), created by private enterprises and information banks, as a mechanism for facilitating individual decision-making, based on informed consent.

H.　Industrial Sector Considerations

COCN (Council on Competitiveness-Nippon)[29] is conducting studies on the use of AI in industry. COCN issued the reports "The Realization of Industrial Enhancement Improvement through AI, Robot, Human Co-Evolution" (March 2016) and "Negotiation between Artificial Intelligence: Society's Super Smart through Collaboration – Smooth Achievement of Each Objective and Formation of Reciprocal Relationships" (15 February 2017).[30]

VI.　POLICY TRENDS REGARDING HIGHLY AUTOMATED VEHICLES

A.　Considerations by The Ministry of Land, Infrastructure, Transport and Tourism and METI

In preparation for the 2020 Tokyo Olympics, studies are being conducted to enable self-driving cars with automatic driving systems to drive on the public roads. In June 2012, the Study Committee on Autopilot Systems was established within the Ministry of Land, Infrastructure, Transport and Tourism (MLIT), to investigate the issues related to automated driving (i.e., autopilot systems), on the public highways as a means of ensuring the realization of these systems.

Recent investigations regarding Automated Vehicles commenced in February 2015 and were conducted by MLIT and METI. MLIT and METI established an "Automated Driving Business Review Committee" and this committee issued a report entitled "Future Action Policy" (23 March 2016). However, the METI and MLIT strategy only focuses

---

[28]　Data Distribution Environment Improvement Committee, http://www.kantei.go.jp/jp/singi/it2/senmon_bunka/data_ryutsuseibi/kentokai.html#detakatsuyo_wg.

[29]　Council on Competitiveness-Nippon, http://www.cocn.jp/.

[30]　Council on Competitiveness-Nippon, *Realization of Improvement of Industrial Capability by Co-evolution of AI, Robot, People*, http://www.cocn.jp/thema86-L.pdf, *Super-smarting of Society through Negotiation, Collaboration and Cooperation among Artificial Intelligence*, http://www.cocn.jp/thema94-L.pdf.

on the promotion of the automated driving industry. It is the Study Committee of the National Police Agency (NPA) which is responsible for considering the legal issues.

In this report, Automated Driving ("General Vehicles: Levels 2, 3") and Automated Driving ("Level 2") will be possible as early as 2018. The report describes eight ways of achieving this while at the same time focusing on the following vital and related functions and principles: map usage, communications, social acceptability, ergonomics, functional safety, security, "recognition technology" and "judgment technology". In the report, Automated Driving ("General Vehicles: Level 4") is defined as vehicle ability to make use of "dedicated spaces" and vehicle ability to "mix" with general traffic. In order to achieve these abilities, it is envisaged that there will be a collecting of ideas from a wide range of stakeholders, including those from overseas. The Convoy Driving Control System ("Convoy Track: Level 2") is expected to realize so-called "Three or More Convoy Track Driving" in nighttime long-distance transportation. Automatic Valet Parking ("Dedicated Space: General Vehicles: Level 4"), will realize the opportunity for private parking lots by around 2020; as is the case with Automated Driving ("General Vehicles: Level 4"), a consensus will be sought from the associated stakeholders concerning "role-sharing" and the standardization of vehicle parking lots.

B.   Considerations of the National Police Agency

In order to further the discussion of the institutional and legal issues as they concern the above technical developments, since October 2015 the Investigative Study Committee on Institutional Issues in Self-Driving of the National Police Agency has examined institutional issues in self-driving in order to create proposed guidelines for verification tests and proof-of-concept demonstrations on public roads relating to self-driving systems in a desire to streamline the issues in terms of the law and operation as they affect self-driving systems.

Considerations of the NPA began in October 2015 and thus are well under way regarding Japan's Road Traffic Act (Act No. 105, 1960) and the "Rules of the Road" with respect to such Automated Driving on public roads. The NPA aims to prepare thorough guidelines to be followed regarding any future public road demonstration experiments by automated driving systems.

As regards automated driving technology (ADT), this committee is expected to be able to solve any related congestion problems by ensuring the optimal running of ADT, thus "smoothing" traffic flow. Via ADT, there is an NPA expectation of a reduction in traffic accidents caused by human error, a reduction in environmental pollution because of the ADT ability to avoid unnecessary acceleration/deceleration, an improvement in fuel economy and a reduction in CO_2 emissions by suppressing air resistance and congestion. Of even more significance is the fact that ADT is expected to provide more mobility and health and well-being support for the elderly by both increasing the opportunities for "driving" and by improving the comfort of the drive itself; particularly in long-distance travelling. A "Driving Support System Advancement Plan" was drafted as early as 25 October 2013; a decision of an NPA liaison meeting in order to achieve this vision.

The NPA Study Committee investigated also the other legal and institutional issues with respect to automated driving and published a report, "The Investigative Review

Committee on the Institutional Problems of Automated Driving Movement",[31] on 7 April 2016. Following this, "The Guidelines for Public Road Demonstration Experiments on Automatic Driving Systems"[32] were announced in May 2016. According to the guidelines: (1) vehicles used for public road demonstration experiments must conform with the safety standards of road transport vehicles; (2) those who become "drivers" must ride in the driver's seat of the experimental vehicle and must always check the surrounding road traffic conditions, must monitor the condition of the vehicle itself and must perform any necessary operations to ensure "vehicle safety" so as not to cause harm to other people in case of emergencies; (3) must comply with all of the relevant laws and regulations, including the Road Traffic Law with regard to driving.

"Entities" may also conduct public road demonstration experiments under the current law, provided that the following conditions are met: (1) the basic responsibilities of the implementing entity are detailed; (2) safety-ensuring measures are detailed also in the descriptions of the public road demonstration experiments themselves; (3) the requirements for the test drivers are both understood and accepted; (4) requirements of the automated driving system related to the test drivers are both understood and accepted; (5) the need for the recording and storage of "Probe of Data" (Car Probe Data) on experimental vehicles during the demonstration experiments is both understood and accepted; (6) adequate responses in the case of traffic accidents; (7) the securing of a "compensation capacity" is both understood and accepted; and (8) the need for advance contact with related organizations is both understood and accepted.

Finally, "The Survey Research Report for the Gradual Realization of Automated Driving" was issued in March 2017 and following this, "The Criteria for The Application for Use Permission of Roads related to Public Road Demonstration Experiments of Remote Type Automated Driving Systems" was decided by the NPA in June 2017.

C.   The Strategic Innovation Creation Program (SIP)

Regarding the technical and institutional issues necessary for realizing the automated driving system, the "Strategic Innovation Creation Program" (SIP, 21 May 2015, Cabinet Office, National Police Agency, Ministry of Internal Affairs and Communications, Ministry of Economy, Trade and Industry, Ministry of Land, Infrastructure, Transport and Tourism) was issued. Regarding the development and demonstration of the automated driving system, the following are required: (1) the development of "map information advancement" (The "Dynamic Map"); (2) development and verification experiments concerned with the "Generation Technology of Prefetch Information by ITS"; (3) technology development and demonstration experiments for improving "sensing ability"; (4) the development of HMI (Human Machine Interface) technology for automated driving systems; (5) the development of technologies for strengthening system

---

[31]   National Police Agency, *Research Report for the Step-by-step Realization of Automatic Operation*, https://www.npa.go.jp/bureau/traffic/council/jidounten/28houkokusyo.pdf.
[32]   National Police Agency, *Guidelines for Public Road Demonstration Experiments on Automatic Driving System* (April 2016) https://www.npa.go.jp/koutsuu/kikaku/gaideline.pdf.

security; (6) "commercialization" research and demonstration experiments for realizing the automated driving system.

VII.   POLICY TRENDS REGARDING UNMANNED AERIAL VEHICLES (UAV/DRONES)

The Japanese government commenced its considerations with respect to a UAV flight policy because of an incident in which a UAV fell onto the roof of the Prime Minister's office. UAV collisions and "fall accidents" have occurred frequently in Japan and so the Civil Aeronautics Act (Act No. 231, 1952) was amended on 11 September 2015. The amended law provides that: (1) any airspace in Japan requires UAV flight permission before use; (2) the newly amended rules and methods governing UAV flights are both understood and accepted; (3) search and rescue missions are exempted from these Japanese airspace flight restrictions.

Any person using UAVs must follow the "general flight regulations"; these are: (1) there will be the creation of a restricted airspace for UAV flights; (2) there will be no night flights; (3) the UAV must always be monitored by visual inspection. However, if the weight of any UAV is less than 200g, then this UAV should not be subject to these regulations. In addition, the Small Unmanned Aerial Vehicles Flight Restriction Act (Act No. 9, 2016) was enacted on 18 March 2016. This law provides for designated areas into which the flights of any UAVs are forbidden. These areas include, for example, the National Diet Building, the Prime Minister's House, any government establishments and foreign embassies and any nuclear power plants.

VIII.   THE APPLICATION OF THE SPECIAL ZONES

A.   The Background and Needs of the Special Zone

When considering the new problems such as the recent AI issues, the Japanese strategy has been to set guidelines as an administrative guidance enacted by governmental agencies without amending the current law; thus requiring private enterprises to comply with them. Such an approach must be similar for each country[33] in order to examine whether or not legal regulation is needed. Furthermore, it would be helpful to conduct trials of these technologically innovative issues.

However, it will take time for the government to revise the related laws and then to create the new guidelines. If such new initiatives are not able to be implemented before the completion of the review of the current legal system, new business deployment and research and development might be delayed. Therefore, in order to solve these structural

---

[33]   *See, e.g.*, Woodrow Hartzog, *Unfair and Deceptive Robots*, 74 MD. L. REV. 785 (2015), Bryant Walker Smith, *Autonomous Legal Reasoning?: Legal and Ethical Issues In The Technologies of Conflict: Controlling Humans and Machines*, 30 Temp. Int'l & Comp. L.J. 167, mentioned which kinds of factors should be considered by the Administrative, Legal and Community strategies.

issues, The Japanese Headquarters for the Promotion of Special Zones for Structural Reform was established on 18 December 2002; following this, The National Strategic Special Zones Act (Act No. 107, 2013) was enforced in 2013. The purpose of this law is the setting up of "Special Zones, (Tokku)"[34] for structural reform where exceptions to the regulations have been established corresponding to the unique characteristics of any specific region, thus promoting customized structural reform in areas such as education, agriculture and social welfare, the revitalizing of local economies, the developing of the national/regional economy and of AI and robot-related services.

With respect to the specific issues concerning these special zones, the implementation of projects promoting deregulation without amending the law has been permitted. By setting up these special zones where regulatory exceptions have been established because of the zones' specific circumstances, voluntary plans (which are submitted by applicants) have been proposed by municipal bodies and private-sector enterprises.

B.   The Structure of the Special Zone

The Act on Special Zones for Structural Reform (Law No. 189, 2003) was enacted for the setting-up of the "Special Zones for Structural Reform, (Kozo-Kaikaku-Tokku)". The purpose of this law is to promote socio-economic structural reform and the revitalization of the regional areas in fields such as education, distribution, agriculture, social welfare and research and development, through the establishment of special zones for structural reform which respect as much as possible the initiatives of the local public bodies.[35]

Furthermore, the law on The National Strategic Special Zones (Law No. 107, 2013), was also enacted for the setting-up of special zones in areas designated by the national government in order to promote regulatory reforms and other measures which will be needed to promote projects carried out jointly by the central government, local governments and the private sector. The Act on Strengthening Industrial Competitiveness (Act No. 98, 2014) was also enacted for promoting: (1) The Establishing of Special Arrangements for Corporate Field Tests; (2) The Removal of "Grey Zone Areas"; (3) The Encouraging of Investment in Venture Businesses; (4) The Promoting of Investment in Cutting-Edge Facilities; (5) The Promoting of Business Restructuring.

C.   The Accredited Special Zones for Structural Reform

The significance of these Special Zones is that they will alter completely the historical concept that regulations should be enforced uniformly throughout Japan. Instead, a concept of "Localism or Regional Revitalization" has been introduced via which the "Special Zones concept" for geographically-limited areas allows for certain regulations to

---

[34]   The concept of "Tokku" is similar to the recent debate with respect to "Regulatory Sandbox" (RS), https://www.fca.org.uk/firms/regulatory-sandbox.

[35]   For details of the purpose and content of the Special Zones for Structural Reform, see, Cabinet Decision, *Outline of the Law on the Special Zones for Structural Reform July 26, 2002*, http://japan.kantei.go.jp/policy/kouzou2/konkyo_e.html; Wataru Suzuki, *How to Evaluate Special Zones for Structural Reform: On a Perspective of Econometric Approach*, Government Auditing Review Volume 12 (March 2005), http://report.jbaudit.go.jp/english_exchange/volume12/e12d03.pdf.

be eased or even lifted. If this concept results in success, then the number of Special Zones with their regulatory exemptions will be expanded nationwide.

The total number of accredited Special Zones is 1,274 as of 1 May 2017 and the examples of Special Zones for Structural Reform for AI and robots are as follows:[36]

Robot Development and Demonstration Experiment Special Zone (Fukuoka City)[37] (2003)
– Facilitation of permission for experiments such as robot walking on public roads.
– Experiments to promote R&D for active robots in the human living area.
– Investigate to revitalize the regional economy by creating a new robot industry.

Sagami Special Industry Zone for Robots (Kanagawa Prefecture)[38] (2014)
– Supports field-testing by public invitation to corporations by offering a pre-testing site and conducting tests for life supporting robots used in nursing facilities utilizing old schools which have been closed.

Safety Testing Center for Life Supporting Robots (Tsukuba City)[39] (2015)
– Supports 18 varieties of tests such as running tests, human interaction tests, durability tests, EMC tests, etc. for the purpose of obtaining safety certified life supporting robots (under ISO13482, etc.).
– Already four different robots have been ISO13482 certified using this facility.

Haneda Airport Robot Experiment Special Zone (Ota Ward, Tokyo)[40] (2015)
– Public road demonstration experiment project of boarding type mobile support robot.
– Experiments on boarding type mobile support robots as means of transportation for airport employees and airport users.
– Demonstration experiments such as safety, effectiveness and affinity in running on public roads and consider efforts for future practical application.

Toyota-City Standing Base Type Personal Mobility Experiment Special Zone (Toyota City)[41] (2014)
– Toyota Motor Corporation has headquarters in Toyota-City.
– Experiments are conducted to create a mobile environment with low carbon and high convenience by combining standing riding personal mobility with public transportation.
– The aim of this project is to use riding personal mobility as one of the new means of transport in the future city traffic.

---

[36]   Robot and AI related special zone, http://www.rtnet-biz.jp/rtsic/info/rinfo/tokku.html.
[37]   Fukuoka Island-City, http://island-city.city.fukuoka.lg.jp/news/detail/254/back:1.
[38]   Robot Town Sagami, http://sagamirobot.pref.kanagawa.jp/.
[39]   City of Tsukuba, Robot Special Zone, http://council.rt-tsukuba.jp/.
[40]   Haneda Robotics Lab, https://www.tokyo-airport-bldg.co.jp/hanedaroboticslab/.
[41]   Toyota-City Standing Base Type Personal Mobility Experiment, http://www.city.toyota. aichi.jp/pressrelease/201408/1000880.html.

D. The National Strategic Special Zones for Level 4 Automated Vehicles

In October 2017, the Japanese Government announced its "National Strategic Special Zones for Level 4 Automated Vehicles (Fully Automated Vehicles), Deployment Project" on the public roads. In order to construct the supporting social systems and legal systems for this "future technological development", public road safety demonstration experiments were conducted in order to collect safety-related data.

The new special zone consists of the following three demonstration projects:

> Robot Taxi: In the Shonan area such as Fujisawa City, a taxi service using an AI equipped robot taxi for residents (about 50 people) on trunk roads within three kilometers. Collaborating with major supermarkets for support of shopping using the Level 4 automated vehicle.

> Utilization of Automatic Driving Vehicles in the Event of a Disaster: Implemented in the disaster high risk area (Arahama area). Demonstrate level 4 in the district roads and elementary school yard. Cooperate with Tohoku University to contribute to urban development for reconstruction and emergency response at the time of disaster occurrence.

> Running Test on General Road using 3D Sensor: Performed in Nagoya City. Based on demonstration results on the national first general road experiment in 2017 spring test, implementing more advanced demonstration using 3D sensors.

IX. AN OVERVIEW OF RESEARCH TRENDS IN JAPAN

A. The Genealogy of Research Groups with Respect to AI Legal Issues

Some Japanese research groups have held workshops, symposia and organized study groups focusing on legal issues regarding AI. The first legal workshop focused mainly on legal issues with respect to autonomous robots and was held on 22 November 2014 at the SFC Open Research Forum and was entitled, "The 202X Robot and Social System", Keio University, Shonan Fujisawa Campus (SFC). Particular research on the social acceptability of AI appeared in a special issue of *Artificial Intelligence Society Journal* (Vol. 29, No. 5, September 2014), and was an opportunity to start the study group "AIR" (Acceptable Intelligence with Responsibility). This study group discusses the ways in which artificial intelligence technology is infiltrating our society.

B. The Japanese Society for Artificial Intelligence

"The Japanese Society for Artificial Intelligence" (JSAI) Ethics Committee began its work in December 2014 by establishing a code of ethics and examining the relationship between Artificial Intelligence and society.[42] This committee issued the "Ethical Guidelines for an

---

[42] Yutaka Matsuo, Toyoaki Nishida, Koichi Hori, Hideaki Takeda, Satoshi Hase, Makoto

Artificial Intelligence Society" (28 February 2017), which were intended to be used by JSAI society members. The purpose of these ethical guidelines was to provide a moral foundation for JSAI members to become better aware of their social responsibilities and encourage effective communications within the society. JSAI members were required to comply with these guidelines.

The JSAI AI ethical guidelines are as follows:

1. Contribution to Humanity. Members of the JSAI will contribute to the peace, safety, welfare, and public interest of humanity. They will protect basic human rights and will respect cultural diversity. As specialists, members of the JSAI need to eliminate the threat to human safety whilst designing, developing, and using AI.
2. Abidance to Laws and Regulations. Members of the JSAI must respect laws and regulations relating to research and development, intellectual property, as well as any other relevant contractual agreements. Members of the JSAI must not bring harm to others through violation of information or properties belonging to others. Members of the JSAI must not use AI with the intention of harming others, be it directly or indirectly.
3. Respect for the Privacy of Others. Members of the JSAI will respect the privacy of others with regards to their research and development of AI. Members of the JSAI have the duty to treat personal information appropriately and in accordance with relevant laws and regulations.
4. Fairness. Members of the JSAI will always be fair. Members of the JSAI will acknowledge that the use of AI may bring about additional inequality and discrimination in society which did not exist before, and will not be biased when developing AI. Members of the JSAI will, to the best of their ability, ensure that AI is developed as a resource which can be used by humanity in a fair and equal manner.
5. Security. As specialists, members of the JSAI shall recognize the need for AI to be safe and acknowledge their responsibility in keeping AI under control. In the development and use of AI, members of the JSAI will always pay attention to safety, controllability and required confidentiality while ensuring that users of AI are provided appropriate and sufficient information.
6. Act with Integrity. Members of the JSAI are to acknowledge the significant impact which AI can have on society. They will therefore act with integrity and in a way which can be trusted by society. As specialists, members of the JSAI will not assert false or unclear claims and are obliged to explain the technical limitations or problems in AI systems truthfully and in a scientifically sound manner.
7. Accountability and Social Responsibility. Members of the JSAI must verify the performance and resulting impact of AI technologies that they have researched and developed. In the event that potential danger is identified, a warning must be effectively communicated to all of society. Members of the JSAI will understand that their research and development can be used against their knowledge for the purposes of harming others, and will put in efforts to prevent such misuse. If misuse of AI is

Shiono, Hiroshitakashi Hattori, Yusuna Ema, Katsue Nagakura, *Artificial Intelligence and Ethics*, Artificial Intelligence Journal 31 (5) 635–41 (2016).

discovered and reported, there shall be no loss suffered by those who discover and report the misuse.

8. Communication with Society and Self-Development. Members of the JSAI must aim to improve and enhance society's understanding of AI. Members of the JSAI understand that there are diverse views of AI within society, and will earnestly learn from them. They will strengthen their understanding of society and maintain consistent and effective communication with them, with the aim of contributing to the overall peace and happiness of mankind. As highly-specialized professionals, members of the JSAI will always strive for self-improvement and will also support others in pursuing the same goal.

9. Abidance to Ethics Guidelines by AI. AI must abide by the policies described above in the same manner as the members of the JSAI in order to become a member or a quasi-member of society.

C. The AI Society Study Group

The "AI Society Study Group" was established on 5 February 2015 as a workshop for multidisciplinary consideration of the social impact of the development of AI technology. The study group conducts research using a multifaceted approach with Dr. Koichi Takahashi who is a founder of this study group advocating references to philosophy (The Humanities), economics (Economics), law (Law), politics (Politics), sociology (Sociology); the abbreviation being HELPS.

D. The Robot Law Study Group (The Information Network Law Society)

The various academic research organizations within Japan whose specific responsibility is that of AI and robot use and law established the Robot Law Study Group on 21 May 2016, as a research-committee of the Information Network Law Association Japan. Before the establishment of the study group, "The Robot Law Association Preparation Study Group" met on 10 October 2015.[43] However, there were some difficulties in establishing a new Robot Law Association in Japan. Therefore, the Robot Law Study Group was established on behalf of the Robot Law Association, as an academic research organization formulated as a research group of the Information Network Law Society. The study group holds study meetings to conduct research on legal issues related to AI and robots for enhancing future legal and policy research focusing on Ethical, Legal, and Social Implications (ELSI).

At the first study group meeting, I publicly presented "Eight New Principles of The Laws of Robots" ("Tentative Proposal by Dr. Fumio Shimpo", 10 October 2015) (see Table 5.1). These principles were reported at the 2015 meeting as the fundamental principles which are required for a "Robot Coexistence Society" of the future in reference to the "OECD 2013 Privacy Principles". Invasions of privacy, which are difficult to remedy after the fact and which make complex the recovery to a status quo position, problems which are caused by autonomous robot negative actions also should not be dealt with after the

---

[43] The Robot Law Association Preparation Study Group, http://robotlaw.jp/.

Table 5.1   Eight new principles of the laws of robots (tentative proposal by Dr. Fumio Shimpo)

① "Humanity First"	• a robot may not injure a human being; • a robot shall not become a human being;
② "Obedience to Order"	• a robot must obey orders given by humans; • the manageability and controllability of a robot must be guaranteed;
③ "Secrecy and Privacy"	• a robot must guard the secrets which it has learned; • a robot must protect privacy;
④ "Use Limitation"	• the use of a robot for purposes other than its original purpose of use must be restricted; • uses contrary to public order and to standards of decency (eg the sex robot industry), must be restricted; • uses for the purposes of harming or threatening humans must be limited, with exception of legal usage in this area; • consideration of the ethics of using robots must be made;
⑤ "Security Safeguards"	• ensure safety associated with the use of robots; • formulate safety standards for development and use based on such standards; • arrangement of system to guarantee an environment in which robots can be used comfortably;
⑥ "Openness/Transparency"	• guarantee the public release of robot development content; • guarantee transparency in the ways of using robots;
⑦ "Individual Participation"	• individual participation in formulating rules for robot use; • restrictions on the management of individuals by robots;
⑧ "Accountability"	• dealing with the liability (legal liability) arising from the handling of robots; • considering ethical and moral responsibility when handling robots.

fact. If we are to achieve a successful robot coexistence society, first, we must consider what "people" must do in relating positively with robots which are "near-human". The first steps in this consideration are those to do with the measures necessary for creating "basic principles for using AI and robots".

X.   DELIBERATION FOR USING AI AND ROBOTS IN THE PUBLIC SECTOR

AI and robots are expected to be used in the future in improving public administration. However, improper use of such AI and robots could lead to "Big Brother" risks. It is possible that such use of robots will not be limited to the automation of the anticipated areas, such as quasi-legal administrative tasks. Thus, we may see robots taking over the responsibilities of civil servants. However, it should be noted that an AI which is able to respond to mundane inquiries could liberate staff from those tasks which are seen as "repetitive responses" and somewhat dull. For example, if the "person" in charge of a service counter or of a front desk, is just an automated, autonomous robot, then there will rightly be many concerns about this "person" resorting to acts of emotional impatience when dealing with the public because such robots wil simply answer any inquiries without any hesitation even though some of these inquiries may be complicated emotionally.

Equally, there are high expectations anticipated as a result of using robots for reducing the maintenance management burden of public facilities and infrastructure, while not reducing the quality of service. We can also assume that the ability to produce government information will be dramatically accelerated by the use of AI with "open data" sources. It is likely that AI will be useful for understanding and investigating in detail past case studies in order to guarantee the fairness of any former administrative actions. Of equal importance is the situation where an AI is proven to be able to both create and analyze automatically meeting minutes. Such an ability would not only reduce the management burden of coping with the recording of what precisely has been discussed during a huge number of meetings, but it would also enable these minutes to be used effectively and efficiently, as information for facilitating the drafting of new policies based on an AI analysis of the large quantities of official documentation. In order to achieve this outcome, Japan's Cabinet Office's Round-Table Conference on Artificial Intelligence and Human Society, which began its investigations in May 2016, conducted trials using AI to analyze such huge amounts of meeting minutes. Easy-to-understand meeting minutes will contribute also to more government transparency and effective communication with the general public.

The use of AI to gather and analyze government information may also make it possible for residents to more easily discover illegal or wrongful financial accounting (where there are audit requests from residents to governmental authorities), and to more easily analyze official documents disclosed through freedom of information requests. However, we must consider the question, in the context of information disclosure, to what extent can information generated by AI, such as the information forming the basis of draft policy measure decision-making information obtained through "deep learning", be disclosed?

If robots and AI are introduced into law enforcement and government administration, we must further evaluate and cautiously investigate not only their positive uses but also their problems in terms of the related policing and administrative laws. Although the fear of future over-controlling nation-states using a mass collection of data has been embodied in the dictator, "Big Brother", featured in George Orwell's futuristic novel *"1984"*, it is possible to "positively" and centrally manage all of the images captured by security cameras on streets, instantaneously to analyze these images in real-time through facial recognition technology and to constantly monitor the movements of citizens and to analyze their personal data online. However, a future in which an AI autonomously determines, from the results of such monitoring, which civil code steps to take in order to promote crime prevention, the appropriate control and protection of citizens, may be a step too far in the direction of a "Big Brother Effect".[44] Where the legal and ethical

---

[44]   *See,* Tal Z. Zarsky, *Transparent Predictions,* 2013 U. Ill. L. REV. 1503 (2013) (describing the predictive modeling process while focusing on initiatives carried out in the context of federal income tax collection and law enforcement). *See also,* Andrew Guthrie Ferguson, *Big Data and Predictive*

principle is not stipulated that robots must be subject to the rule of law, and when the specific limits to the introduction of robots and AI within government operations are not agreed and settled, then there is the risk that this "Big Brother Effect" will come into being.

It is also necessary to investigate what would be an ideal form of censure in the event that damages to public infrastructure systems were to be caused by the use of administrative robots. If such damages were caused by a defect in the robots themselves, these damages could conceivably be subject to compensation by the state as defects in the installation or management within public facilities. On the other hand, damages which arise from the deliberate or accidental misuse or malfunction of administrative robots would most likely be judged under "negligence of the duty to guarantee safety", rather than under "managerial liability" of any facilities.

In the context of governmental organizations, if AI is involved in governmental agencies' decision-making, as expert information-source advisors, is there not then a possibility that the AI itself will be deemed to be advisory bodies, rather than just parts of any given meetings or committee structures? If robots immediately enforce administrative decisions in order to achieve governmental objectives, could we say that these robots are independently serving the functions and aims of enforcement agencies? In the future, will it also be acceptable for autonomous robots (not remotely-operated robots), installed with AI, to autonomously exercise the use of force, without waiting for orders from the relevant governmental agencies? We simply cannot say at this point in time that there is a zero possibility of lethal, autonomous robots automatically pursuing their targets of attack being used not for military purposes, but for law enforcement.

XI.   DELIBERATION FOR USING AI AND ROBOTS IN THE PRIVATE SECTOR

The private sector issues associated with the use and spread of robots and AI which should be investigated are many and diverse in nature. It will be necessary to investigate these matters from both the perspective of problems in substantive law, such as the Civil Code (Act No. 89, 1954) and its associated laws (The Product Liability Act, Copyright Act etc.) and procedural law (The Civil Procedural Law).

The problems within the domain of the Civil Code are too numerous to detail here but they would include, by way of example, accidents with self-driving cars, the protection of personal rights and interests (such as the safeguarding of individual privacy) vis-à-vis AI machine learning, the protection of intellectual property "created" by AI, compensation for damages associated with an autonomous robot being misused or running out of control and robots deemed to be "actual members of the family".

In property law, the time is coming when the management of property will start being

---

Reasonable Suspicion, 163 U. Pa. L. Rev. 327 (2015), Elizabeth E. Joh, *Artificial Intelligence and The Law: Essay: Policing by Numbers: Big Data and The Fourth Amendment,* 89 WASH. L. REV. 35 (2014), Danielle Keats Citron and Frank Pasquale, *Artificial Intelligence and the Law: Essay: The Scored Society: Due Process for Automated Predictions,* 89 WASH. L. REV. 1 (2014).

entrusted to robots and AI. Fintech (a platform used in investment decisions, etc., which utilizes AI), is also being used currently, and services are being offered which will entrust to an AI the managing or investing of your personal assets.

In matters of liability involving accidents with self-driving cars, the so-called "Trolley Problem" is often debated. This is the problem of whether a priority order for avoiding danger can be judged or decided (e.g., whether to collide with an object or a person when directly facing an unavoidable accident), according to the objects that will be hit or by evaluation functions based on properties such as the number of pedestrians who will be hit, age and gender.

As a problem of legal liability it is difficult to draw a clear line in this extreme choice (where the question of whom ultimately bears liability remains undecided). No decision has been shown that everybody can agree with ethically. We also see the view that as long as this problem is unresolved, completely self-driving cars (Level 4 if classifying this into the levels of self-driving from Levels 0–4) on public roads cannot be practically used. In terms of the Civil Code, for Levels 1–3 we could, after debating the legal positioning of the operator, debate the theoretical liability of the operator, passengers or the manufacturer in the event of an accident; we could also investigate the ideal form of insurance. For Level 4, there may not be anything else that can be done besides trying to devise an ideal form of manufacturer liability.

On the other hand, since the software itself (which is information) is not a tangible object, it is not subject to product liability.[45] If an AI is installed in a self-driving car or robot, this AI would fall under the category of a manufactured product as property built into the robot (which is a tangible object). Therefore, if the AI harms other people, it would be possible to pursue product liability via the manufacturer. However, if an accident occurred due to an error in the navigation map installed in a self-driving system, it would not be possible to judge product liability via the map information error itself based on the current Japanese Product Liability Act. Storing images is essential for clarifying where liability lies during an accident.

Collecting massive amounts of information is also necessary for an AI's machine learning. However, massive amounts of information about individuals are also included within that information, and more efforts are needed to safeguard individuals' personal rights and interests. By analyzing personal information extracted from Big Data and using it for profiling, behavioral targeting is already being used to present online shoppers with recommended products and advertising chosen in line with personal tastes. In addition, using AI in business transactions and recommending products by using a specific method, it has also become possible to recommend products to shoppers that they have a high probability of purchasing. In the most extreme AI-related transactions, which greatly influence an individual's self-determination and manipulate that person's manifestation of intention, if steps are not taken on the business operator's side to inform the customer that the transaction is with an AI, before a consumer requests something in sophisticated AI-profiling transactions (by applying a law designed to legally obligate this, for instance),

---

[45] *See*, Michael C. Gemignani, *Product Liability and Software*, 8 RUTGERS COMPUTER and TECH. L.J. 173 (1981), Brannigan and Dayhoff, Nimmer and Krauthaus, *Computer Error and User Liability Risk*, 26 JURIMETRICS J. 121 (1986).

then future regulation will be needed to the effect that manifestation of intention has no effect for requests which were enticed by an AI, which would be equivalent to "a mistake of an element" (Article 95 of the Japanese Civil Code).

Products that an AI autonomously creates are not subject to rights under the current intellectual property system. Protection of "learned models" created by an AI's analysis of data is also an issue. It is now becoming possible for an AI to create content that looks like human creation, and the ideal form of protection for so-called "quasi-creations" is being examined.

XII.   ISSUES OF SECURITY SAFEGUARDS AND PROTECTION FOR SAFETY

In the future, we must continue developing the principles mentioned above. However, since a review is urgently needed on the principles of security safeguards and safety protection, I would like to touch on these in this section of the discussion.

A.   New Issues in Information Security Countermeasures

Due to the spread of AI and robot use, the need for improved information security countermeasures for the chips which comprise the physical make-up of these media and devices are predicted to become a major issue. The reason for this is that with the growth of the IoT, all objects are in the process of being connected to networks. As a result, it is now possible to operate various home electronics and other objects via these networks. Moreover, if we create societies in which robots and AI, due to their levels of sophistication, are commonly and routinely used, the need for these improved, information security countermeasures will increase proportionally.

Various network security countermeasures have been developed for safeguarding information security, such as those for preventing unauthorized access via networks and for protecting against computer viruses, malware and so on. However, the security of the actual devices themselves remains vulnerable. By way of example, chips are designed to be inherently rewriteable, therefore currently, it is easy to open a machine or device and rewrite any chips which have been installed.

Car devices called "immobilizers" are used to prevent car theft. These devices allow cars to be operated by matching codes electronically, in contrast to traditional keys. It is extremely difficult to forge or to produce counterfeit copies of such "electronic keys". Immobilizers are considered to be an extremely effective means of preventing car theft because cars will not operate if the electronic codes do not match. Yet, even cars which have immobilizers have been stolen. Thieves merely have to smash the car window and open up the dashboard and start the engine by replacing the installed immobilizer with another immobilizer.

Thus, similar problems are predicted to arise if robots start to be commonly used in the future because of their autonomous features. It is assumed that similar problems will occur even where robots are equipped with AI.

Regarding the security of robots connected to the network by IoT, it is expected that exploitation and unauthorized use will occur when robots are infected with computer viruses and malware. Various security countermeasures have been made on the Internet but the security measures of the chips physically installed in the robots have not been tested sufficiently. Therefore, we should recognize that similar issues like the above mentioned immobilizer will occur due to the spread of the IoT, and such problems which will undoubtedly occur due to the daily use of such AI-equipped robots will become a familiar threat; a problem which could be easily exploited by merely replacing the chip mounted on the robot.

B.   New Security Threats

There is an assumption that robots will be used to commit crimes through hacking or through unauthorized access to robots via networks, that robots will be made to autonomously commit crimes through infection with "crime-committing malware". Since "The Act on The Prohibition of Unauthorized Computer Access" prohibits the use of a computer where you have no authorization to access its contents via a network, such similar, unauthorized access to a robot connected to a network is subject also to punishment. However, the (criminal) manual reprogramming, rather than the network reprogramming, of a robot, cannot be punished under this law.

Let us consider the impact which would occur if robots which manage infrastructure, malfunction, or cease operating, due to "service access attacks". A network composed of large numbers of "zombie computers" and hijacked by malicious third parties through malware, is called a "botnet". The origin of this word is "robot", in the sense it is used to mean "puppet". When these literal "robot botnet networks" appear, where their multiple malware "infecting robots" attack specific targets all at once, with denial of service access, the threat to our society will be incalculable. Therefore, we must implement, now, countermeasures against these threats.

XIII.   THE SIGNIFICANCE OF ROBOT LAW IN THE AGE OF AI

AI and robots are tools created by humans and are currently at the stage where they are nothing more than tools which only operate according to human intentions. Consequently, the associated legal topic of product liability should be given a thorough legal re-examination. However, if autonomous robots controlled by an AI system come to be used everywhere in society, the above-mentioned consequent use problems which cannot be addressed by such a re-examination of the current laws will necessitate the creation of new legal systems. As an example of the current legal dilemma, I will refer the reader to an accident involving a robot which was caused by inaccurate information or software defect malfunction. At present, the questioning of the product liability of the information itself, which was the main cause of this accident, is outside the range of the current Japanese Product Liability Act.

This major shift in society caused by the spread of the use of robots has been also referred to as the arrival of the Fourth Industrial Revolution. In order to attain a safe and comfortable Robot Co-existence Society, we must immediately start to prepare social systems which are able to accommodate such a greater use of robots and to examine the relevant and ensuing legal issues. Before robots are actually introduced on such a large scale into real life, it is necessary to establish clear, legal policies which will underpin a robot use strategy, ethically resolved for the industrial world and for researchers engaged in technical development.

What must first be considered for utilizing AI and autonomous robots is not thinking about which rules are needed to restrict research into, and development of, technologies which may pose new threats to humans. Instead, we must think about how we should regulate those humans who want to use these technologies in potentially harmful ways.

SOURCES

List of Statutes

Civil Aeronautics Act (Act No. 231, 1952)
Civil Code (Act No. 89, 1954)
Constitutional Law (1946)
Copyright Act (Act No. 48, 1970)
Intellectual Property Basic Act (Act No. 122, 2002)
The National Strategic Special Zones Act (Act No. 107, 2013)
Product Liability Act (Act No. 85, 1994)
Road Traffic Act (Act No. 105, 1960)
Small Unmanned Aerial Vehicles Flight Restriction Act (Act No. 9, 2016)
Act on Special Zones for Structural Reform (Law No. 189, 2003)
Act on Strengthening Industrial Competitiveness (Act No. 98, 2014)
Ordinance on Industrial Safety and Health, Article 36, Item 31
Ordinance for Enforcement of the Radio Act, Article 2, Item 43

List of Industrial Standards

Japanese Industrial Standards JIS B 0134:2015: Robots and Robotic Devices
ISO 8373:2012: Robots and Robotic Devices: Vocabulary, IDT

PART II

REGULATION OF ARTIFICIAL INTELLIGENCE

6. Artificial intelligence and private law
Shawn Bayern[1]

This chapter chiefly concerns the interaction between private law and artificial intelligence. Much discussion of legal responses to artificial intelligence addresses new regulation, potential legislative responses, and public law in general. Legal and policy analysts have paid insufficient attention to the ways in which the fundamental legal systems that regulate private interactions already may permit artificially intelligent systems to engage with the law. These interactions present significant practical and commercial possibilities and risks that lawyers and policymakers need to explore. I believe they will be seen as increasingly important as artificially intelligent systems become more commonplace.

In previous work, which I will explain and elaborate here, I have argued that the law of business entities provides a promising framework for normalizing the legal treatment of artificially intelligent entities and other autonomous systems. In particular, my argument has been that at least in many cases, the laws providing for the creation of business entities with legal personality can also give such personality, or a very close substitute for it, to autonomous systems. But the law has many potential interfaces, and legal personality is not the only relevant concept. If the general question is "How can artificial intelligence interact with existing law?"—that is, without fundamental legal reform or new statutes, regulations, or constitutions—then there are a variety of possibilities that need to be explored. This chapter will consider several.

My general theme here rests on the following principle: Legal instruments (like written contracts, organizational operating agreements, wills, and trusts—and also public instruments like statutes) may specify conditions that alter their operation. For example, a contract might release a homebuyer from his or her obligation to buy a house if the homebuyer can't get a satisfactory mortgage or home inspection, or it might release both parties from performing their duties under a merger agreement if the antitrust authorities don't approve the merger. In the general case, many types of legal instruments can specify conditions—states of the world—in which various obligations, rights, powers, and so on do or don't take effect. Conditions are powerful because of their flexibility; contract law does not, for example, enumerate specific permissible conditions, and in general parties can enter into arbitrarily conditional obligations as they see fit. Using this flexibility, parties can create agreements or draft instruments under which desired legal outcomes depend on the observable state of an artificially intelligent system—or more simply on the prearranged, discrete output of the system. For example, as I will elaborate later in this chapter, a contract might say "The parties must perform their obligations only when a particular robot says so." This allows a robot to engage in activity that, for all practical purposes, causes the acceptance of a contractual offer or a variety of other legally significant actions.

[1] For helpful discussions, I thank Rob Atkinson, Thomas Burri, and Mark Gergen.

The flexibility of conditions in contract law and other legal arenas—something I have called the *algorithm/agreement equivalence principle*—opens the door to significant inter-action between artificial intelligence and the legal system under conventional legal regimes and without fundamental reform. First, as I have just noted, what I call organizational law—the law of business entities, not-for-profit entities, and so on—may provide a plat-form on which an autonomous system can act as an independent legal actor by obtaining legal personality, or at least something very similar to legal personality. The basic idea I have proposed in this area is that when at least one jurisdiction's organizational law is flexible enough to permit an existing legal person to create a legal entity, establish cus-tomized perpetual operating guidelines for the entity, and then withdraw from the entity without terminating it, an autonomous system can subsequently take any legal actions that a business entity could take. Accordingly, for example, using the law of limited liability companies (LLCs) in many US jurisdictions, it is at least provisionally possible for an artificially intelligent system to buy and sell property on what is functionally its own legal and financial authority, without ongoing oversight by any previously existing legal person—something that lawyers ordinarily regard as impossible under existing law. For example, if the question is "Could a robot purchase a house under existing law?" the surprising answer is "For practical purposes, it probably can."

Second, even without implicating organizational law, the law of contracts can give legal effects to the decisions (or other measurable states) of an artificially intelligent system. Even a simple bilateral contract might make elements of contractual performance contingent on an artificially intelligent algorithm's decision. A contract for the purchase and sale of real estate might, for example, be written to depend on the outcome of an automatically conducted inspection, rather than the report of a human inspector. At least in theory, in ordinary bargain contracts between two commercial parties, this sort of use of artificial intelligence ought to be unobjectionable because it is voluntary; the decisions of an artificial intelligence influence parties' rights only because the parties have allowed them to do so. But this use of artificial intelligence may be complicated by scale,[2] create systemically fragile arrangements of contracts,[3] and complicate judicial enforcement of contracts. The common law of contracts is likely adaptable enough to accommodate the potential advantages of automated deal-making, but courts and commentators will need to be vigilant about the downside risks.

Third, somewhat related to contractual implications of artificial intelligence are the implications for the law of trusts and property. For example, the grantor of a trust may appoint a trustee whose powers are limited by the measurable decisions of an artificially intelligent software program.[4] As with ordinary private contracts, the initial arrange-ment is voluntary, but it raises several new types of problems. For example, does such an

---

[2]   *Cf.* Hannah J. Wiseman, *Remedying Regulatory Diseconomies of Scale*, 94 Bu. L. Rev. 235, 235 (2014) (covering generally "disproportionately negative effects sometimes associated with the expansion of a long-regulated activity").

[3]   *Cf.* Manuel A. Utset, *Complex Financial Institutions and Systemic Risk*, 45 Ga. L. Rev. 779 (2011) (discussing risks created by the complexity of interrelated contracts).

[4]   Of course, combining the techniques I describe in the different parts of this chapter, the trustee might simply be an LLC controlled by software, but that is not necessary for a trustee to be constrained by software.

arrangement create new possibilities for undesirable dead-hand control? Does it violate human dignity to subject massive family fortunes to control by algorithm, intelligent or not? Literature has long warned of the perils of worlds controlled by robots, but usually the imagination of fiction writers has assumed that robots will rise because of military power or at least the opportunity to exert physical force; a more plausible scenario is perhaps that autonomous systems will become gradually more important through their slowly rising control over capital.

Finally—though obviously this takes us beyond private law—using the same principle that legal instruments may empower artificially intelligent software by means of conditions on the applicability of rights and duties, statutes (and theoretically constitutions) might come to delegate governmental decisions to artificially intelligent systems. This has already happened in small-scale ways, without much artificial intelligence; for example, the functioning of a public website may already at least influence the availability of governmental benefits or other services. Does the increased use of such systems threaten social harms? Should there be a principle against delegating governmental decisions to autonomous systems just as some constitutions may restrict delegations to nongovernmental legal actors?[5]

The goal of this chapter is more to raise questions (and practical possibilities) than to answer them (or critique them) definitively, but at least in general my sense is that generalized restrictions or prohibitions on the reference by legal instruments of artificial intelligence may do more harm than good. Moreover, much of what people are afraid of has already come to pass, such that structural fears about artificial intelligence seem overblown; for example, it may seem to violate human dignity if there is an LLC controlled by an autonomous system with a thousand human employees, but is this any worse than a traditional corporation with thousands of employees that adopts inflexible, bureaucratic HR processes? It would be a mistake, however, to ignore specific potential harms from the use of artificial intelligence or to pretend they don't exist based merely on theoretical presumptions regarding rational actors or voluntariness of interactions. For example, Frank Pasquale's work on decisions made by algorithms has important implications in this area.[6] The potential problems don't arise from technology alone, but that doesn't imply that all uses of technology are benign.

I.   THE ALGORITHM-AGREEMENT EQUIVALENCE PRINCIPLE

Conditions are an unremarkable part of contracts, and indeed of many other kinds of agreements and legal instruments. They specify that certain rights, duties, powers, and so on are effective only in some states of the world.

Because of the flexibility of legal conditions, the law already has the power to recognize and interact with artificially intelligent systems. Any part of a contract can

---

[5]   *Cf.* Shawn Bayern, Thomas Burri, et al., *Company Law and Autonomous Systems: A Blueprint for Lawyers, Entrepreneurs, and Regulators*, 9 Hastings Sci. and Tech. L.J. 135 (2017).

[6]   *See generally* Frank Pasquale, *The Black Box Society* (2015).

be conditioned, for example, on particular output of a computer system, including an artificially intelligent one. So, for example, even if under US law corporate directors can be only natural persons, any corporate agreement could be conditioned on approval by an artificially intelligent system.

It is easy to see how specific contractual provisions might require approval from an artificially intelligent system. In the simplest case, an agreement could read, "You have this duty only in the event that a particular software system outputs the following text when presented with the particular inquiry copied as Appendix A to this instrument."

But it is also not difficult to generalize from this capability of private law to a significantly more general one: the ability for an artificial intelligence to direct, generally, arbitrary contractual processes. For example, suppose a corporation wishes to replace a human salesperson, who acts formally as an agent in causing the corporation to enter contracts, with an artificially intelligent computer program. Under the generally received understanding of private law, the computer program cannot literally step into the human's role and serve as an agent. For example, as the official comment to the *Restatement (Third) of Agency Law* puts it, a

> computer program is not capable of acting as a principal or an agent as defined by the common law. At present, computer programs are instrumentalities of the persons who use them. If a program malfunctions even in ways unanticipated by its designer or user, the legal consequences for the person who uses it are no different than the consequences stemming from the malfunction of any other type of instrumentality.[7]

However, the computer program need not have the formal legal powers of an agent in order to serve functionally as an agent. Suppose the corporation enters into a structural agreement with potential buyers, saying, in effect, "Under this agreement, orders become effective when our computerized agent submits a document to you and you approve its terms." I draw the term "structural agreement" from the work of Mel Eisenberg, a leading scholar of contract law, who describes the notion (as applied to general business dealings, not those involving artificial intelligences) as follows:

> In [one] kind of promissory structure, one party makes a promise that increases the probability of exchange, but that promise does not require either a promise or an act in exchange. I call such promissory structures structural agreements.
>
> Under the bargain principle, bargains between capable and informed actors are enforced according to their terms. This principle rests in large part on the premises that bargains produce gains through trade, that capable and informed actors are normally the best judges of their own utilities, and that those utilities are revealed in the terms of the parties' bargain.
>
> Although the bargain principle is most conventionally applied to classical bargains, it applies to structural agreements as well. Structural agreements, like classical bargains, involve promises designed to promote economic exchange. The terms of structural agreements, like the terms of classical bargains, are normally bargained out. And as in the case of classical bargains, the promisor in a structural agreement makes his promise because it will serve his economic interest. Reasons comparable to those for enforcing classical bargains are therefore applicable to structural agreements: structural agreements are entered into to produce gains through trade;

---

7   *See* Restatement (Third) of Agency Law § 1.04 cmt. e (2006).

a capable and informed actor is normally the best judge of his own utility; and that utility is revealed in the terms of his agreement.[8]

Consider, then, a structural agreement that specifically enables an artificial intelligence. The (human) parties have negotiated such an agreement, and the agreement provides that one party's software will supply documents to be approved by the other party (or its software), and that when this happens, the parties will have a binding agreement. If such an agreement is enforceable, then once it is in place, all further steps of the negotiation, practically speaking, could occur between computer programs, and the background contractual framework provides a mechanism to produce legally enforceable contracts.

In recent work, my colleague Lauren Scholz has nicely suggested a potential complication for this approach: perhaps the common-law courts would reject such contracts for reasons associated with classical doctrines of contract law.[9] Professor Scholz's main challenge to a scheme like the one I have outlined here is that it may be too indefinite to be enforced. There are other potential pitfalls; for example, perhaps courts would have trouble with the mechanisms of offer and acceptance under the scheme I've outlined, or perhaps they would treat the structural agreement as illusory and therefore lacking consideration.[10] Similarly, perhaps it would simply be an unenforceable "agreement to agree."[11]

For three reasons, however, I don't see significant barriers to at least American courts' enforcement of these contracts. First, classical contract law is on the decline, and the formalist doctrines have eroded as significant barriers to the enforcement of agreements made in a commercial context.[12] Consideration doctrine, for example, is best seen under

---

[8]   Melvin Aron Eisenberg, *Probability and Chance in Contract Law*, 45 UCLA L. Rev. 1005, 1009–10 (1998). Professor Eisenberg describes in detail why the classical, formal doctrine of consideration should not invalidate such agreements under modern law.

[9]   Lauren Henry Scholz, *Algorithmic Contracts*, 20 Stan. Tech. L. Rev. 128 (2017).

[10]   *Cf.* Eisenberg, *supra* note 8, at 1011–21 (sharply critiquing the use of consideration doctrine for this purpose in modern contexts).

[11]   Such inchoate agreements were not enforceable under classical law, although modern law, with an emphasis on commercial function rather than formal principles of contract formation, has had considerably less trouble enforcing them. *See generally* Restatement (Second) of Contract Law § 33(2) ("The terms of a contract are reasonably certain if they provide a basis for determining the existence of a breach and for giving an appropriate remedy."); U.C.C. § 2-204(3) ("Even though one or more terms are left open a contract for sale does not fail for indefiniteness if the parties have intended to make a contract and there is a reasonably certain basis for giving an appropriate remedy."); *id.* § 2-305 cmt. 1 ("This Article rejects in these instances the formula that 'an agreement to agree is unenforceable' if the case falls within subsection (1) of this section, and rejects also defeating such agreements on the ground of 'indefiniteness'.").

[12]   With reference to consideration doctrines based on "mutuality" and the "illusory-promise rule"—that is, the main obstacle to the enforceability of structural agreements—see, for example, *Helle v. Landmark, Inc.*, 472 N.E.2d 765, 776 (Ohio 1984) ("As a contract defense, the mutuality doctrine has become a faltering rampart to which a litigant retreats at his own peril. Under contemporary analysis of unilateral contracts, the 'mutuality' doctrine crumbles of its own weight.") (citing several leading modern treatises); *Tex. Gas Utils. Co. v. Barrett*, 460 S.W.2d 409, 412 (Tex. 1970) ("It is presumed that when parties make an agreement they intend it to be effectual, not nugatory. A contract will be construed in favor of mutuality. The modern decisional tendency is against lending the aid of courts to defeat contracts on technical grounds of want of mutuality.") (citations omit-

modern law as a way to distinguish gifts from commercial promises, and courts and the leading treatises have shifted away from the strictures of the classical doctrine. For example, according to *Corbin on Contracts*, "Consideration is designed primarily to protect promisors from their own donative promises"[13] rather than to serve to invalidate commercial bargains.

Second, there just needs to be one state that enforces the form of agreement I have described for it to become commercially significant, given parties' ability to choose the law that governs their contractual arrangements. States do split on matters of contract doctrine, with some being relatively more formalistic and some more functionalistic, but if one state upholds structural agreements that give artificial intelligences the power to take contractual actions by means of contractual conditions, then parties can effectively deploy such agreements. Indeed, states might conceivably seek to become friendly to this type of agreement in order to attract business.

Third, just as a matter of casual characterization and prediction, the common law over time has yielded to commercial pressures. If two parties enter into what is otherwise a fair agreement, without fraud, duress, unconscionability, or anything similar, it is easy to see at least many courts enforcing the agreement.[14]

So far, I have described a mechanism by which the existing legal agents of companies can effectively authorize a computer program to enter into future contractual arrangements even though the computer program lacks any formal legal status as an agent. But there is a further step: Can the computer system create entirely new contracts with entirely new contracting partners—that is, without the preexistence of the sort of structural agreement I have described, and thus without the involvement of any human to initialize the agreement?

This possibility is more challenging from a doctrinal perspective, but I believe there are several creative ways it can be done under existing law. Standard form terms provide one possibility, at least to the extent of their enforceability. For example, suppose the company that wishes to use a computer system to make contracts posts form terms on its website, saying, effectively, "If you take the following actions on our website, you agree to the following structural contract under which, if you submit a document to our software and the software approves it, we have a binding agreement." Then, under that structural contract, created by standard form terms, the computer system can act with the effective, practical authority I described earlier. It is not clear that such form terms would be enforced, but of course American courts have been rather eager (probably far too eager) to enforce standardized form terms. The point is simply that form terms might permit parties to bootstrap themselves in automated fashion into structural agreements.

Another, more mundane, possibility to permit a company to use artificially intelligent software to enter new contracts, without a prior structural agreement, is for the

---

ted). *See also* Eisenberg, *supra* note 8, at 1011–21; Shawn Bayern, *Offer and Acceptance in Modern Contract Law: A Needless Concept*, 103 Cal. L. Rev. 67, 90–93 (2015); *see also supra* note 11.

[13] 2 Arthur Corbin et al, *Corbin on Contracts* § 5.17 (West rev. ed. 1995) (cited approvingly in *1484-Eight, Ltd. & Millis Management Corp. v. Joppich*, 152 S.W.3d 101 (Tex. 2004)).

[14] *Cf.* Bayern, Burri et al., *supra* note 5, at 152 ("U.K. courts have taken a pragmatic approach to the development and use of corporate personalities in the past. Taken forward, this flexibility could readily accommodate technological advances in artificial intelligence.").

company to create large numbers of generic, assignable contracts with a third-party broker—perhaps an automated one, using procedures for automated entities I describe below, although that is not strictly necessary to the scheme. Subsequently, the broker can simply assign these (human-made) contracts in automated fashion to new parties as they appear. That is, new contracting partners could request that the broker assign them a new structural contract so that they might engage, under that contract, with the company's computer program. In other words, if artificially intelligent software can act under existing structural agreements but cannot create new ones, the simple workaround is to create vast numbers of assignable, structural agreements with a single counterparty that acts as a broker, "assigning" these contracts to substantive counterparties when they appear. I suspect this is more of an academic exercise than something that many commercial entities will need to do, in part because for the foreseeable future, initial contact with *some* human at the outset of a contractual relationship is not a significant barrier toward the creation of a contractual relationship.

II.   ENGAGING ARTIFICIAL INTELLIGENCE IN PRIVATE LAW

A.   Contract Law

In Part I, I described generally how contractual agreements can give legal effect to purely algorithmic processes without the ongoing involvement of humans. The transactional paths I described are relatively straightforward, and indeed it is no surprise that people might enter commercial deals with machines: people do this routinely with vending machines and websites, and there's little reason for current law to care specifically about the "intelligence" of the processing that implements the services. Following the *Restatement (Third) of Agency Law*,[15] software is just an instrumentality like any other instrumentality (paper, an elevator button, etc.), and its degree of intelligence is not relevant under current law. It may seem, then, that contract law already handles artificially intelligent software with relative grace and simplicity.

Several difficulties in this area may lie ahead, however, from yet-unexplored patterns in large-scale contracting by software. For example, if a vending machine that sells snacks malfunctions, the seller may lose a few hundred dollars, but if the vending machines are controlled by a centralized artificial intelligence that introduces errors on a large scale, significantly greater losses may occur. Existing contract doctrines concerning problems like typographical errors, such as the contract doctrine of unilateral mistake, have not been significantly tested in cases where two software systems conclude a contract together, and it is unclear how courts will respond to that problem. The closest we have come to that situation is probably the "flash crash" of 2010,[16] in which simple technical mistakes compounded to cause the US stock market to lose about ten percent of its value temporarily for no substantive economic reason. Authorities appear to have been largely

---

[15]   *See supra* note 7.
[16]   See Graham Bowley, *The Flash Crash, in Miniature*, N.Y. Times, Nov. 9, 2010, at B1.

successful in "canceling" trades caused by that series of technical errors,[17] but it may be more difficult to do so in a more distributed context, or with errors that arose more slowly and on which more innocent parties rely.

The classical common law of contracts did not pay significant attention to things like typographical errors; they were not normally regarded as an excuse to a breach of contract action unless the non-mistaken party knew or should have known that a communication was erroneous.[18] Modern courts increasingly allow relief for these typographical errors even if the other party had no reason to know of them.[19] But even simply formulating the rule in this way suggests the problem with applying it to contracts made by artificially intelligent software: First, what does an AI *know*, and what *should* it know, if it's capable of "knowing" anything in a sense that the law recognizes? Second, how can a court determine what an artificial intelligence intended or didn't intend so that it could establish a baseline against which it could determine whether a particular communication is a "mistake" or not? Perhaps courts will decide that AIs are not capable of mistakes—that they should be treated as if they intend everything they do. But that would be a policy choice; nothing in existing doctrine or in legal policy necessarily dictates it. Moreover, if courts do eventually apply standards of "knowledge" to AIs, they face extremely difficult and technical complications. For example, it might be natural to imagine that a computer system's "knowledge" is reflected in its working memory (regardless of the technology in which that memory is implemented), and memory can at least theoretically be inspected. But knowledge is not so simple: at any point, a computer program's current processing may be in a state that cannot be reached unless some precondition is true, even if that precondition is not stored explicitly by the computer program.[20] The point is just that knowledge is not an easy thing to determine, even if we are asking the question about a straightforward computer program. Nor is constructive knowledge, given that we have little experience stating anything normative about how computers should behave or what they should know.[21]

---

[17]   *See id.*

[18]   7-28 Arthur Corbin et al., *Corbin on Contracts* § 28.39 (LexisNexis 2017) ("The common generalization has been that avoidance is not available for unilateral mistake except for a palpable mistake—that is, a mistake the existence of which the other party knows or has reason to know. (Relief in such cases is readily available.)").

[19]   *Id.* ("Today, avoidance is generally allowed for unilateral mistake if two conditions concur: (1) enforcement of the contract against the mistaken party would be oppressive or, at least, result in an unconscionably unequal exchange of values; and (2) avoidance would impose no substantial hardship on the other. The rule permitting avoidance for unilateral palpable mistake also continues in effect.").

[20]   To demonstrate this in more technical terms using pseudocode—which is to say, notation that evokes actual programming logic while avoiding the specific details of any one programming language—consider software such as "if (*A*) then do *B* * followed by *C*." This code tests whether a condition *A* is true and then executes *B* and *C*, which could be any algorithms. At the point in the code indicated by the asterisk, the program can be said to "know" that *A* is true, at least given some technical assumptions not worth elaborating here, but the fact that *A* is true is never stored explicitly in the program. In this sense, computers as well as humans may make "tacit", unexpressed assumptions about the world. *Cf.* Lon Fuller, Melvin Aron Eisenberg, and Mark P. Gergen, *Basic Contract Law* 858–59, 901–902 (West 9th ed. 2013) (describing tacit assumptions—in humans, of course).

[21]   I'm reminded, frivolously, of an awkwardly written Microsoft dialog box that asks the user, "Do you trust this printer?" The software's authors intended the software to inquire as to whether the printer is a trusted vender of device-driver software, but I can't imagine most users processing

Similarly, software-generated contracts may give rise to interpretive problems for which doctrine is currently unprepared. Modern contract doctrine has moved away from the classical formalism of the 1920s, and modern doctrines pay significant attention to the intent of the parties rather than to some fiction about the unambiguous meanings of their words,[22] but in the event of software-negotiated contracts there is arguably no intent to discern apart from the original intent of the structural agreement, which may be out of date and difficult to apply to the parties' circumstances. Should the law continue to resort to that agreement, even if it is outdated? Should it return to formalism, given that software-generated contracts would be the product of what are essentially formal systems? It is difficult to try to answer these questions of legal policy in advance, without the benefit of context that future developments will provide.

It is worth pointing out that similar issues of intent may affect the analysis of contract-related torts, such as the tort of fraud. For example, under what conditions can it be said that an artificially intelligent program defrauds its counterparty? Does it depend on what the program "knows"? If there is no such thing as fraud by artificial intelligence, then meaningful legal protections may become less significant over time if the use of software-negotiated contracts expand. Again, these are open questions, there is as yet no doctrinal solution to them, and it is difficult to predict precisely which questions will come to matter. But lawyers would do well to recognize the general difficulty of applying intent-based doctrines to the operation of software.

B.   Organizational Law

In earlier work, I have proposed a transactional technique by which an artificially intelligent entity can be given legal personality, or at least something very close to it. I have summarized the technique as follows:

> Consider, then, the following use of an LLC: (1) an individual member creates a member-managed LLC, filing the appropriate paperwork with the state; (2) the individual (along, possibly, with the LLC, which is controlled by the sole member) enters into an operating agreement governing the conduct of the LLC; (3) the operating agreement specifies that the LLC will take actions as determined by an autonomous system, specifying terms or conditions as appropriate to achieve the autonomous system's legal goals; (4) the individual transfers ownership of any relevant physical apparatus of the autonomous system to the LLC; (5) the sole member withdraws from the LLC, leaving the LLC without any members. The result is potentially a perpetual LLC—a new legal person—that requires no ongoing intervention from any preexisting legal person in order to maintain its status.[23]

I have argued that this technique is permitted under various formulations of LLC law in various US jurisdictions;[24] my goal here isn't to rehash that legal argument, which I have

---

this question in any sensible way. Given the way most people conceive them, in what sense could a printer be trustworthy (except perhaps in the sense that it reliably prints documents, which was clearly not the intent of the question)?

[22]   *See, e.g.,*, Restatement (Second) of Contracts §§ 201, 202.

[23]   Shawn Bayern, *The Implications of Modern Business-Entity Law for the Regulations of Autonomous Systems*, 7 Eur. J. Risk Regulation 297, 302 (2016).

[24]   *See, e.g., id.* at 302–05; Shawn Bayern, *The Implications of Modern Business-Entity Law for the Regulation of Autonomous Systems*, 19 Stan. Tech. L. Rev. 93 (2015); Shawn Bayern, *Of*

described in detail in prior work, but it is important to emphasize that I believe it is already possible, as a matter of law and practice, for anyone to use this technique to grant effective legal powers to any arbitrary system, artificially intelligent or not.

This possibility, of course, raises a host of legal problems that have yet to be addressed by business law, or what I generally call organizational law—that is, the state-by-state law of organizational entities, such as partnerships and LLCs. I think the creation and normal operation of zero-member LLCs are surprisingly straightforward, in that the law permits them to be created and provides conventional mechanisms for determining control and authority of a legal entity based on the entity's operating agreement.[25] But over time, these entities may act in ways that test the limits of the legal system's willingness to permit LLCs to operate by "freedom of contract."

For example, at what point does the dead-hand control of the founder of the LLC become a problem? Nothing ensures, over the long term, that the LLC will behave in the interests of any living human, and there is presently no statutory mechanism to coerce it to do so. The common law governing property has generally been concerned to avoid the situation in which dead people's ancient wishes continue to exercise too much control—for example, over charitable gifts.[26] LLC law does not address the same problem, in part because legislatures and courts have probably assumed that LLCs will always have human beings associated with them, at least indirectly. To be clear, I don't believe this means we should prohibit outright the existence of zero-member LLCs controlled by software. Indeed, the mere presence of humans on an entity's board of directors does not ensure that the entity behaves in ways that serve the public interest in any sense. But organizational law will need to adapt if zero-member entities ever become significant. For example, perhaps increased governmental oversight of such entities by means of an expanded notion of administrative dissolution[27] will be fruitful.

C.   Trusts, Wills, and Property

The mechanism for creating a trust managed by an artificial intelligence is very similar to creating a legal organization managed by an individual. While an artificial intelligence cannot under conventional law be a trustee itself, there are two significant possibilities for the use of software in managing trusts long-term. First, the trust company could be a zero-member LLC as described in the previous section. Second, the trustee may be a natural person or conventional legal entity, but his, her, or its actions may be restricted significantly by a trust agreement which requires decision-making by software using the techniques described in section A, *supra*.

Bitcoins, Independently Wealthy Software, and the Zero-Member LLC, 108 Nw. U. L. Rev. 1485, 1495–1500 (2014).

[25]   *See, e.g.*, RUPA § 103(a) (describing the force and effect of operating agreements in modern general partnerships); RULLCA § 110 (doing the same for modern LLCs).

[26]   *See* Rob Atkinson, *The Low Road to Cy Pres Reform: Principled Practice to Remove Dead Hand Control of Charitable Assets*, 58 Case W. Res. 97 (2007) (discussing the problem of dead-hand control, primarily in the context of not-for-profit organizations).

[27]   *See, e.g.*, RULLCA § 705 (giving the government the power to dissolve LLCs in particular limited situations).

In either case, questions about the rule against perpetuities may arise. The rule against perpetuities is a doctrine in property law whose function is mainly to restrict dead-hand control by invalidating certain grants of property rights that may not vest within certain periods.[28] Its effect is to limit a donor's ability in a deed or a will to give unrestricted gifts that do not resolve for long periods of time. The rule against perpetuities is not as significant as it once was and has been subject to statutory modification and repeal in many states,[29] but it remains an open question how the statute will apply to long-term arrangements governed by algorithmic agreements under contract law, algorithmic operating agreements for entities, and so forth.

And, of course, wills and trusts that impose software-based restrictions raise the same sorts of dead-hand control problems as I discussed earlier.

III.   CONCLUSION

This chapter has aimed to suggest both possibilities and potential legal problems for the use of increasingly intelligent software in the basic operations of private law, such as contracts and operating agreements for companies. It is important to restate that this area is a new one for the law, so there are no definite doctrinal answers in this area. The chapter has also proposed several transactional techniques that private parties may use if they wish to give legal effect to the decisions or actions of artificially intelligent systems. I am optimistic that these techniques, or closely related ones, may be useful to such parties, but they carry practical, political, and legal risks that are exceedingly difficult to address in advance of their more widespread use.

SOURCES

Table of Authorities

Uniform Commercial Code §§ 2-204(3), 2-305.
Uniform Partnership Act § 103(a) (1997).
Revised Uniform Limited Liability Partnership Act §§ 110, 705 (2006).
Fla. Stat. § 689.225.
Restatement (Second) of Contract Law §§ 33(2), 201, 202.
Restatement (Third) of Agency Law § 1.04 cmt. e.
1484-Eight, Ltd. & Millis Management Corp. v. Joppich, 152 S.W.3d 101 (Tex. 2004).
Helle v. Landmark, Inc., 472 N.E.2d 765 (Ohio 1984).
Tex. Gas Utils. Co. v. Barrett, 460 S.W.2d 409 (Tex. 1970).

---

[28]   For a general introduction to the doctrinal details of the rule against perpetuities, see Jesse Dukeminier, *A Modern Guide to Perpetuities*, 74 Calif. L. Rev. 1867 (1986).

[29]   *See, e.g.*, Uniform Statutory Rule Against Perpetuities (1990); Fla. Stat. § 689.225 (providing for trusts that may last 360 years); Lawrence W. Waggoner, *Perpetuity Reform*, 81 Mich. L. Rev. 1718 (1983).

7. Regulation of artificial intelligence in the United States
John Frank Weaver

I. INTRODUCTION

We have long since passed the point of questioning whether artificial intelligence (AI) will be a significant factor in our day-to-day lives around the world. It already is, in the form of Narrow AI, which addresses specific application areas such as playing strategic games, language translation, self-driving vehicles, and image recognition.[1] AI will continue to spread to every place where we work and live. By 2030, AI will be in:

- Our homes, as service robots that use advanced voice recognition software and algorithms that analyze personal data to provide social interaction and home maintenance;
- Our schools, as AI programs analyze student data to help maximize their academic success;
- Our healthcare system, as AI-based apps monitor our vitals and physical assistive devices (like intelligent walkers) extend mobility for seniors and the physically impaired;
- Our public safety systems, as the combination of security camera and analytical software makes predictive policing possible; and
- Our workplaces, as AI and robots replace tasks and jobs currently performed by human beings.[2]

With AI here today and even more present in the near future, we cannot question the need for regulation and governance, only the details of when and how.

However, in the United States,[3] answers to these questions are not very well developed,

---

[1] National Science and Technology Council, "Preparing for the Future of Artificial Intelligence," *Executive Office of the President* (October 2016), 7, https://obamawhitehouse.archives. gov/sites/default/files/whitehouse_files/microsites/ostp/NSTC/preparing_for_the_future_of_ai.pdf ("Preparing for the Future").

[2] Peter Stone, et al., "Artificial Intelligence and Life in 2030," *One Hundred Year Study on Artificial Intelligence: Report of the 2015-2016 Study Panel*, Stanford University, Stanford, CA (September 2016), available at http://ai100.stanford.edu/2016-report ("100 Year Study").

[3] For a good comparison of how the governments of the United States, the European Union, and the United Kingdom are preparing for the widespread use of AI, *see* Cath, Corinne J.N. and Wachter, Sandra and Mittelstadt, Brent and Taddeo, Mariarosaria and Floridi, Luciano, "Artificial Intelligence and the 'Good Society': The US, EU, and UK Approach," (December 23, 2016). Available at SSRN: https://ssrn.com/abstract=2906249 or http://dx.doi.org/10.2139/ ssrn.2906249.

either in actual regulation or in scholarship.[4] States have not addressed artificial intelligence directly, other than statutes and regulations that seek to govern autonomous vehicles, and the federal government has only started considering legislation, drafting reports, and holding hearings.[5] Similarly, academia has only started to actively consider the regulation of AI, with the rollout and philosophy of AI regulation relatively nascent fields of study.[6] This chapter attempts to fill that void, relying on existing laws and legal models to explore and recommend answers to "When?" and "How?"

A.   What is AI?

But before asking those questions, we first have to answer "What," as in "What is AI?" In addressing the regulation of AI, it is important to be clear what the term as used in this chapter includes and what it does not include, even though it may differ in some aspects from how AI is defined and treated in other chapters. Having said that, it is an open secret in the field of AI that there is no widely accepted definition of "artificial intelligence."[7] For example, Stuart Russell and Peter Norvig present eight different definitions of AI organized into four categories, including thinking humanly and thinking rationally.[8] These definitions rely on the internal processes of human intelligence. However, Alan Turing focused on a machine's external manifestation of intelligence or analytical ability, looking to see if a computer could convince a human that it is also a human.[9]

Another major problem in defining AI is that the finish line keeps moving. For example, chess was once considered a barometer of AI, but that has gradually changed since computers were able to play a decent game of chess in 1960.[10] IBM's Deep Blue beat the best human player in the world in 1997.[11] These developments made many suggest that skill in chess is not actually indicative of intelligence,[12] but did chess really become disconnected from intelligence merely because a computer became good at it? As one expert laments, "[a]s soon as it works, no one calls it AI anymore."[13]

---

[4]   Matthew U. Scherer, *Regulating Artificial Intelligence Systems: Risks, Challenges, Competencies, and Strategies*, 29 Harv. J. of L. & Tech. 2 (Spring 2016), 356.

[5]   *See* Fundamentally Understanding The Usability and Realistic Evolution of Artificial Intelligence Act of 2017, S. 2217, 115th Congress ("FUTURE of AI Act"); Preparing for the Future, *supra* note 1; United States Senate Committee on Commerce, Science, & Transportation, The Dawn of Artificial Intelligence Hearings (November 30, 2016), available at https://www.commerce.senate.gov/public/index.cfm/hearings?ID=042DC718-9250-44C0-9BFE-E0371AFAEBAB.

[6]   *See* Scherer, *supra* note 4; Shawn Bayern, *The Implications of Modern Business-Entity Law for the Regulation of Autonomous Systems*, 19 Stan. Tech. L. Rev. 93 (2015–16).

[7]   *See* John McCarthy, "What is Artificial Intelligence?," John McCarthy's Home Page 2–3 (Nov. 12, 2007), http://www-formal.stanford.edu/jmc/whatisai.pdf.

[8]   Stuart J. Russell and Peter Norvig, *Artificial Intelligence: A Modern Approach* (3rd ed.) (Pearson, 2010), 2.

[9]   A.M. Turing, *Computing Machinery and Intelligence*, 59 Mind 433–45 (1950).

[10]   *See* Nils J. Nilson, *The Quest for Artificial Intelligence* (Cambridge University Press, 2009), 194.

[11]   *See* Bruce Pandolfini, *Kasparov and Deep Blue: The Historic Chess Match Between Man and Machine* (Simon and Schuster, 1997), 7–8.

[12]   Scherer, *supra* note 4, at 361.

[13]   *See* Moshe Y. Vardi, "Artificial Intelligence: Past and Future," *Communications of the Association for Computing Machinery* (Jan. 2012), 5, at 5.

There appears to be a trend in the field to define AI based on goals and how it achieves them, such as describing AI as a system that "has goals which it tries to accomplish by acting in the world."[14] Or defining AI as "the science and engineering of making intelligence machines, especially intelligent computer programs" and intelligence as "the computational part of the ability to achieve goals in the world."[15] Even Russell and Norvig, after explaining their eight different definitions for AI, explore how goals should define AI, conceptualizing AI as a "rational agent" that "acts so as to achieve the best outcome or, when there is uncertainty, the best expected outcome."[16]

This chapter, however, in exploring the regulatory options for AI, is less concerned with the terminology used within the industry because, while those definitions are important to the development of the sector, any regulatory agency is likely to have a broad legislative mandate, either intentionally or as interpreted by the agency itself.[17] Accordingly, AI here will refer to any machine or program capable of recreating one or more element of human intelligence.[18] This is an inexact and expansive definition, but government regulators will likely look at an expansive definition of AI so the relevant agency reaches more programs and devices. And the regulators will be right to do so. For reasons that are explained below, this chapter assumes that an "early and often" approach to the regulation of AI is the best approach, although the strategies below are also appropriate for later regulation of AI.

So, to return to the two questions—how and when—explored here, the answer to "When should we regulate AI?" is "As soon as possible," although a more detailed analysis appears in Section II, below.

---

[14]   Stephen M. Omohundro, "The Basic AI Drives," *Artificial Intelligence 2008* (2008), 483, at 483.

[15]   McCarthy, *supra* note 7.

[16]   Russell and Norvig, *supra* note 8, at 4.

[17]   *See* Young Han Chun and Hal G. Rainey, *Goal Ambiguity in U.S. Federal Agencies*, 15 J. Pub. Admin. Res. and Theory 1, 5 (2005).

[18]   John Frank Weaver, *Robots Are People Too* (Praeger Publishing, 2013), 1 ("Robots Are People"). This definition is not quite as inclusive as the very broad definition in the FUTURE of AI Act, but it more succinctly states the fundamental functions of AI that require regulation, i.e., functions that can replace human judgment and decision-making. The full definition of AI from the FUTURE of AI Act includes all of the following:

(a)   Any artificial systems that perform tasks under varying and unpredictable circumstances, without significant human oversight, or that can learn from their experience and improve their performance. Such systems may be developed in computer software, physical hardware, or other contexts not yet contemplated. They may solve tasks requiring human-like perception, cognition, planning, learning, communication, or physical action. In general, the more human-like the system within the context of its tasks, the more it can be said to use artificial intelligence.

(b)   Systems that think like humans, such as cognitive architectures and neural networks.

(c)   Systems that act like humans, such as systems that can pass the Turing test or other comparable test via natural language processing, knowledge representation, automated reasoning, and learning.

(d)   A set of techniques, including machine learning, that seek to approximate some cognitive task.

(e)   Systems that act rationally, such as intelligent software agents and embodied robots that achieve goals via perception, planning, reasoning, learning, communicating, decision-making, and acting.

FUTURE of AI Act, *supra* note 5, at §3(a)(1).

B.   What is AI Regulation?

Having answered when to regulate AI, we should briefly review the legal and regulatory situation in the United States that informs how to regulate AI in the country before considering the topic in earnest. AI promises to be a transformative technology, as described by Ryan Calo, the nationally renowned legal scholar of robotics and AI. Calo, in considering the lessons that cyberlaw can teach us about regulating robotics, notes that a transformative technology tends "to have essential qualities that drive the legal and policy conversations that attend them," "changes the available facts, and hence the doctrine, to a degree," and "matters insofar as it changes the range of human experiences in ways that undermine the balance the law hopes to strike."[19] That is, transformative technologies require new legal and regulatory frameworks because the technologies may distort the purpose of the existing laws and regulations.

This can be done piecemeal, as in the case of robotics. There is no Federal Robotics Administration created with a legislative mandate to regulate robots. The Federal Aviation Administration (FAA) promulgates regulations to govern commercial drones.[20] The National Highway Traffic Safety Administration (NHTSA) is actively developing policies to govern autonomous vehicles.[21] The Food and Drug Administration (FDA) approves robots for use in medical procedures.[22] Since 1987, the Occupational Health and Safety Administration (OSHA) has issued directives governing the safe use of industrial robots.[23]

But Calo argues persuasively that this is a flawed approach as "states, courts, and others are not in conversation with one another. Even the same government entities fail to draw links across similar technologies."[24] He notes that drones and driverless cars raise similar concerns about safety and privacy, but the FAA and NHTSA are regulating the technologies as entirely separate matters. He instead makes a pitch for "an agency dedicated to the responsible integration of robotics technologies into American society," likening their impact to radio and trains.[25] However, his proposed agency is limited, advising, not regulating.[26]

---

[19]   Ryan Calo, *Robotics and the Lessons of Cyberlaw*, 103 Calif. L. Rev. 513–63 (2015), 549, 552, and 558.

[20]   Federal Aviation Administration, Small Unmanned Aircraft Systems, Advisory Circular, No. 107-02, June 21, 2016, https://www.faa.gov/uas/media/AC_107-2_AFS-1_Signed.pdf ("AC No. 107-02").

[21]   National Highway Traffic Safety Administration, Federal Automated Vehicles Policy, September 2016. https://www.transportation.gov/sites/dot.gov/files/docs/AV%20policy%20guida nce%20PDF.pdf ("Federal AV Policy").

[22]   Sarah Glynn, "FDA Approves First Medical Robot for Hospital Use," *Medical News Today*, January 26, 2013, http://www.medicalnewstoday.com/articles/255457.php.

[23]   Occupational Safety and Health Administration, Directive No. STD 01-12-002, "Guidelines for Robotics Safety" (1987), https://www.osha.gov/pls/oshaweb/owadisp.show document?p table-DIRECTIVES&p id- 1703.

[24]   Ryan Calo, *The Case for a Federal Robotics Commission* (Brookings, 2014), 4, available at http://www.brookings.edu/-/media/Research/Files/Reports/2014/09/case-for-federal-robotics-com mission/RoboticsCommissionR2 Calo.pdfla-en.

[25]   *Id.* at 3.

[26]   *Id.*

I believe that a similarly limited approach is unwise with regard to AI for two primary reasons. One, unlike robotics, AI does not have an existing body of law to contend with. As noted above, robots entered spaces already governed by laws and regulations. OSHA regulations governing safety in the workplace set precedent and expectations for regulations governing robots in the workplace.[27] The Federal Aviation Administration claimed jurisdiction over drones because they fly within U.S. airspace, which Congress has charged the FAA with regulating.[28] By virtue of regulating medical devices, the FDA regulates medical robots as well.[29] The NHTSA's authority extends to "highway safety programs, research, and development relating to highway design, construction and maintenance, traffic control devices, identification and surveillance of accident locations, and highway-related aspects of pedestrian safety," a broad charge that appears sufficient, on the surface, for the NHTSA to assert jurisdiction over autonomous vehicles.[30]

However, former NHTSA administrator David Strickland is among the first to admit that how the NHTSA regulates highway safety is not sufficient for autonomous vehicles, at least not as currently performed. In a 2012 speech, he said:

> Most of NHTSA's safety standards assume the need for a human driver to operate required safety equipment. A vehicle that drives itself challenges this basic assumption. This is also true of state efforts to govern motor vehicle safety. State highway safety programs overwhelmingly focus on preventing driver behaviors that are deemed unsafe such as speeding or impaired driving.[31]

His point is essentially that NHTSA regulates the outcome—safety on the highways—but that the way it does that—regulating human behavior and decision-making—will not be relevant when cars make decisions.

This is the problem that makes regulating AI both difficult and important. There are no laws addressing machines or programs capable of recreating one or more elements of human intelligence. A fundamental assumption underlying almost all of our laws is that all decisions are made by human intelligence.[32] Strickland's comments recognize that as a problem for governments trying to regulate autonomous vehicles, and state statutes that address self-driving cars frequently include an acknowledgement that one of the reasons for the legislation is that there are no laws that govern self-driving cars, i.e., cars that replicate the part of human intelligence that makes decisions about driving.[33]

---

27   *See* Frank R. Spellman and Nancy E. Whiting, *Machine Guarding Handbook: A Practical Guide to OSHA Compliance and Injury Prevention* (Government Institutes, 1999), 65–72.

28   "History," Federal Aviation Administration, https://www.faa.gov/about/history/brief_history/; 2012 FAA Modernization and Reform Act, Pub. L. 112-95, February 12, 2012.

29   *See* Medical Device Amendments of 1976, Pub. L. No. 94-295, 90 Stat. 539.

30   Highway Safety Act of 1970, Pub. L. No. 91-605, Sec. 202(b)(1).

31   David Strickland, "Autonomous Vehicle Seminar," http://www.nhtsa.gov/staticfiles/admi nistration/pdf/presentations_speeches/2012/Strickalnd-Autonomous_Veh_10232012.pdf (lecture, Washington, DC. October 23, 2012).

32   *Robots Are People, supra* note 18, at 1.

33   Florida House Bill 1207 (Ch. 2012-111), § 1(2) (finding that "the state does not prohibit or specifically regulate the testing or operation of autonomous technology in motor vehicles on public roads); California Acts, Chapter 570 of 2012, 2011-2012, § 1(c) (finding that California "does not prohibit or specifically regulate the operation of autonomous vehicles").

The nature of AI, as it undermines a fundamental core principle of our laws, means that across the relevant disciplines, industries, and markets, there are essentially no regulations governing AI. Even though there are at least 16 different federal agencies that govern sectors of the economy related to AI,[34] those federal agencies all enforce regulations that assume human beings are making decisions. That simply is not true for AI. We are starting from scratch.

Consequently, unlike robots, which can be regulated in a piecemeal fashion by various state and federal agencies, AI programs and devices will require more active and central- ized regulatory efforts. The expected disruption that AI will cause to nearly every facet of our lives—employment,[35] healthcare,[36] transportation,[37] education,[38] warfare,[39] social interactions,[40] etc.—only exacerbate the need for a single government agency that has

---

[34] IEEE-USA Position Statement, Artificial Intelligence Research, Development and Regulation (adopted by IEEE-USA Board of Directors, February 2017), https://www.ieeeusa.org/volunteers/ committees/documents/FINALformattedIEEEUSAAIPS.pdf, accessed 7-7-2017.

[35] Some estimates put job losses as high as 50 million professional jobs lost to AI, representing 40% of the workforce, including lawyers, doctors, writers and scientists. Gus Lubin, "Artificial Intelligence Took America's Jobs And It's Going to Take A Lot More," *Business Insider*, November 6, 2011, http://www.businessinsider.com/economist-luddites-robots-unemployment-2011-11; Bern ard Condon and Paul Wiseman, "Millions of Middle-Class Jobs Killed By Machines in Great Recession's Wake," *Huffington Post*, January 23, 2013, http://www.huffingtonpost.com/2013/01/23/ middle-class-jobs-machines_n_2532639.html; "Difference Engine: Luddite Legacy," *Science and Technology* (Blog), *The Economist*, November 4, 2011, http://www.economist.com/blogs/ babbage/2011/11/artificial-intelligence?fsrc=scn/tw/te/bl/ludditelegacy ("Luddite Legacy"); Farhad Manjoo, "Will Robots Steal Your Job?" series of articles, *Slate*, September 26–30, 2011, http://www. slate.com/articles/technology/robot_invasion/2011/09/will_robots_steal_your_job.single.html.

[36] Ted Cruz, U.S. Senate on Commerce, Science, and Transportation, *The Dawn of Artificial Intelligence hearing*, https://www.commerce.senate.gov/public/index.cfm/hearings?Id=042DC718- 9250-44C0-9BFE-E0371AFAEBAB&Statement_id=DDC04E74-E6C7-431B-BBCD- BB3740685B29 (Washington, D.C. November 30, 2016) ("In the health care sector, artificial intelligence is increasingly being used to predict diseases at an earlier stage, thereby allowing the use of preventative treatment which can help lead to better patient outcomes, faster healing and lower costs.").

[37] *Id.* ("In transportation, artificial intelligence is not only being used in smarter traffic man- agement applications to reduce traffic, but is also set to disrupt the automotive industry through the emergence of self driving vehicles.").

[38] Andrew E. Moore, U.S. Senate on Commerce, Science, and Transportation, *The Dawn of Artificial Intelligence hearing*, https://www.commerce.senate.gov/public/_cache/files/12eb9bc7- f5d5-4602-b206-113d6bf25880/B3C3D677FA18E98D85C616AF8326CEE0.dr.-andrew-moore-te stimony.pdf (Washington, D.C. November 30, 2016) ("AI-empowered personalized learning will enable teachers to better reach and engage every student.").

[39] Matthew Rosenburg and John Markoff, "The Pentagon's 'Terminator Conundrum': Robots That Could Kill on Their Own," *New York Times*, October 25, 2016, https://www.nytimes. com/2016/10/26/us/pentagon-artificial-intelligence-terminator.html ("The Defense Department is designing robotic fighter jets that would fly into combat alongside manned aircraft. It has tested missiles that can decide what to attack, and it has built ships that can hunt for enemy submarines, stalking those it finds over thousands of miles, without any help from humans.").

[40] Shaunacy Ferro, "Artificial Intelligence App Will Keep Tweeting As You After You Die," *PopSci*, March 11, 2013, http://www.popsci.com/technology/article/2013-03/app-lets-you-tweet- great-beyond ("With _LivesOn -- an artificial intelligence project from Lean Mean Fighting

expansive authority to regulate AI in a wide variety of capacities. That is the primary consideration relied on in this chapter when answering the question of how to regulate AI.

C. Summary of Sections

Following this introduction, the remainder of the chapter focuses on providing more detail and analysis of early versus later regulation ("When?") and primary versus secondary regulation ("How?") in the United States.[41]

Section II explains the importance of introducing regulations into the AI sector sooner rather than later. Advocates of waiting for the industry to mature before introducing regulation frequently point to the inability of regulators to properly predict how AI will develop[42] and the potential for premature regulation to strangle the development of any technology, not just AI, as reasons to wait before creating a regulatory structure.[43] Advocates of creating that structure sooner rather than later note that AI "technology is going to develop fast, almost certainly faster than we can legislate it. That's why we need to get ahead of it now."[44] The next section makes that case and explains that early regulation does not inherently cause nascent industries to die prematurely, but rather gives voters and policy-makers the chance to establish the rules and market environment they want for AI before the market is too developed to easily adapt to such changes.

Section III considers the primary regulations that will govern AI, i.e., the federal agency that will regulate AI, the functions it will perform, and the regulations it will promulgate. Although at least one federal government report and numerous public commenters rightly note that "cross agency coordination" is necessary to properly regulate AI,[45] at this time the federal government does not make the next logical step and suggest that a new agency is the best way to conduct that coordination. This section seeks to correct that error. In discussing the proposed federal agency, this section weighs the merits of placing the agency under the auspices of various federal departments—Department of Justice, Department of Defense, Department of Energy, etc.—before summarizing functions the agency should perform, some of which are frequently cited by academics and interested

---

Machine, a British ad agency, and Queen Mary University in London -- social media mavens won't have to worry about a little thing like death getting in the way of their tweets.").

[41] Please note that "secondary regulation" here refers to the fact that regulation done by state legislature and court decisions will be supplemental to federal regulations. Secondary regulation does not refer to the distinction between primary rules and secondary rules or other concepts from European law. *See* H.L.A. Hart, *The Concept of Law* 3rd ed. (Oxford University Press, 2012), 96–99.

[42] Scherer, *supra* note 4, at 387.

[43] "Bitcoin at the crossroads," Deloitte, https://www2.deloitte.com/us/en/pages/regulatory/bitcoin-at-the-crossroads.html#, accessed on 8-5-2017.

[44] John Frank Weaver, "We Need to Pass Legislation on Artificial Intelligence Early and Often," *Slate*, September 12, 2014, http://www.slate.com/blogs/future_tense/2014/09/12/we_need_to_pass_artificial_intelligence_laws_early_and_often.html ("Early and Often").

[45] Preparing for the Future, *supra* note 1, at Introduction; White House Office of Science and Technology Policy, "Request for Information on the Future of Artificial Intelligence," *Public Responses*, September 1 2016, Respondent 94, https://obamawhitehouse.archives.gov/sites/default/files/microsites/ostp/OSTP-AI-RFI-Responses.pdf ("Request for Information").

parties and some of which are less popular. The section concludes by looking at how to keep AI regulations current despite the frequent innovations expected in the field.

Finally, Section IV briefly explores secondary regulation of AI, i.e., the role that states and courts will have in the governance of AI. States will likely take the lead regulating AI in the areas where states have traditionally exercised authority, including policing power, privacy, and trespass. These issues include many people-centric issues related to AI. At the municipal level, towns and cities will likely need to reconsider some elements of their zoning and permitting regulations, which the section addresses. Additionally, the section discusses the constitutional and legal issues courts will encounter as AI becomes more widespread; the decisions judges write will play a fundamental role in the regulation of AI.

II.   EARLY VERSUS LATER REGULATION

A.   Summary of Competing Positions

In considering when to regulate AI, the general rationales cited by proponents of early regulation and proponents of later regulation are fairly easy to understand:

- Early: Although technological development has typically increased income and quality of life broadly, we have a tendency to assume that the former automatically leads to the latter.[46] However, that is not necessarily true, as economists are becoming increasingly concerned that AI will create a great deal of new wealth, but that it will not be evenly spread, leaving many people worse off.[47] In order to spread the benefits of AI broadly, appropriate regulation is necessary. However, technology develops faster than governments can create regulations.[48] If we don't start regulating AI now or as soon as possible, we will fall behind and never catch up.[49] Regulating AI now allows us to set the standards and expectations for AI that we want and lets the developers and producers of AI programs and devices meet them.
- Later: Government regulations impede the development of new technologies, actively hindering the economic benefits they can produce.[50] Recent technological developments, particularly the internet, have experienced rapid growth, and produced corresponding economic rewards, because America adopted a regulatory

---

[46]   Tyler Cowen, *The Great Stagnation* (Dutton, 2011).

[47]   Seth Fletcher, "Yes, Robots Are Coming for Our Jobs – Now What?" *Scientific American*, March 8, 2013, http://www.scientificamerican.com/article.cfm?id=yes-robots-are-coming-for-our-jobs-now-what&page=1.

[48]   K Aswathappa, *International Business*, 3rd Ed. (Tata McGraw-Hill Publishing Company Limited, 2008), 634; Sofia Ranchordás, *Does Sharing Mean Caring? Regulation Innovation in the Sharing Economy*, 16 Minn. J. of L., Sci. and Tech. 1 (2015), 37 ("Law will necessarily lag behind innovation since it cannot be adapted at innovation's speed.")

[49]   Early and Often, *supra* note 44.

[50]   James Pethokoukis, "Is regulation slowing tech progress and innovation? A Q&A with Eli Dourado," *AEI*, June 3, 2016, http://www.aei.org/publication/big-government-regulation-slowing-tech-progress-eli-dourado/.

strategy of "permissionless innovation," meaning developers did not need to ask permission before experimenting with new applications, programs, technologies, etc.[51] Introducing regulations too soon could stymie growth because the regulations could be too broad or fail to fully understand the technology.[52] AI will be responsible for tremendous economic growth,[53] but that growth will be greatly diminished if policy-makers try to regulate the field too early. Legislators, policy-makers, and regulators must carefully ensure that they have a full understanding of any AI program or product they address, otherwise they could apply inappropriate regulations to some forms of AI.[54]

The proponents of later regulation have a point: there is a danger in regulating technology too soon.[55] Early regulation can stifle innovation and the material benefits innovation creates.[56] However, regulations and governance do not automatically impede innovation; when drafted appropriately, legislation and regulations can spur innovation.[57] As with any governing decision, the ultimate decision to regulate AI immediately or later requires a balancing of pros and cons. While both positions have merit, the position this chapter takes is that early regulation of AI is necessary to ensure that its benefits are widely spread. The next subsection addresses that position in more detail.

B. The Merits of Early Regulation

1. The case against later regulation

Before advancing the case for early regulation, it is useful to take a closer look at regulation later in AI's development. The federal government 2016 report, *Preparing for the Future of Artificial Intelligence*, notes that most of the parties that responded to a request for information regarding AI were against the broad regulation of AI in the near future.[58] Similarly, Calo writes that because robotics is a fledgling industry, "There are dangers, but nothing to suggest we need a series of specific rules" to govern the field, which could apply in theory to AI as well.[59] The assumption in later regulation

---

[51]   Adam Thierer, Permissionless Innovation: The Continuing Case for Comprehensive Technological Freedom (Mercatus Center at George Mason University, 2016), 12–16.

[52]   Request for Information, *supra* note 45, at Respondent 159.

[53]   Nicholas Chen et al., "Global Economic Impacts Associated with Artificial Intelligence" (Study, Analysis Group, Boston, MA, February 25, 2016) (noting that AI could contribute $1.49 trillion to $2.95 trillion to the worldwide economy in the next ten years).

[54]   Request for Information, *supra* note 45, at Respondent 159.

[55]   *See* Yvette Joy Liebesman, *The Wisdom of Legislating for Anticipated Technological Advances*, 10 J. Marshall Rev. of Intell. Prop. 1 (2010), 154–81.

[56]   Derek Khanna, "Regulations stifle innovation," *The Hill*, September 15, 2015, http://the-hill.com/blogs/congress-blog/technology/253625-regulations-stifle-innovation; *see* Richard Allen Epstein, *Overdose: How Excessive Regulation Stifles Pharmaceutical Innovation* (Institute for Policy, 2006).

[57]   *See* David M. Gann, et al., *Do regulations encourage innovation? – the case of energy efficiency in housing*, Building Research and Information (1998), 280–96.

[58]   Preparing for the Future, *supra* note 1, at 17. This is somewhat misleading, as this section explains.

[59]   Calo, *supra* note 24, at 11.

is that government regulation of new technology, when done too early in the research and development process, interrupts the development of that technology, as it creates barriers to the experimentation that will produce greater discoveries and breakthroughs. In both the short- and long-term, this reduces the ultimate economic growth generated by any technology, as in the short-term, regulators may largely respond to panic in the face of the changes introduced by new technology, producing regulations that limit the opportunity for developers and entrepreneurs to innovate and create more meaningful and beneficial technological developments.[60] Many proponents argue that regulating AI too early will permit other countries to surpass the United States in the AI arms race.[61] In the long-term, economic growth is dependent on technological innovation, which constitutes as much as 80 percent of the difference in wealth between rich and poor countries.[62] Further, innovation "is a phenomenon that can result in the improvement of living conditions of people and strengthening of communities. Innovation can be technological and social, and the former might assist the latter to empower groups in ways we once thought unimaginable."[63] By permitting regulation of technologies too early, we limit our ability to improve living conditions for everyone.

The argument in favor of later regulation also relies on the success other recent technological developments encountered because government authorities did not regulate those technologies, particularly the internet and internet innovations like email, listservs, web browsers, websites, blogs, and social networks—as well as innovations that enabled the internet like smartphones, tablets, and other digital devices. Adam Thierer, a senior research fellow at the Mercatus Center at George Mason University, claims that "[t]hese innovations were able to flourish because our default position for the digital economy was 'innovation allowed' or permissionless innovation."[64] He goes on to note that the Clinton-era federal government advanced a permissionless innovation agenda, i.e., an agenda without early regulation, by permitting the commercialization of the internet in the mid-1990s, whereas before it had been limited to use by government agencies and university researchers, and passing the Telecommunications Act of 1996 without any "analog-era communications and media technologies" regulations.[65] Perhaps most significantly, the Clinton administration released *The Framework for Global Electronic Commerce*, which set forth the federal government's approach to the internet, stating "the internet should develop as a market driven arena not a regulated industry."[66]

---

[60]   Thierer, *supra* note 51, at 33.

[61]   Amitai Etzioni and Oren Etzioni, "Why Regulating AI Is A Mistake," *Forbes*, January 9, 2017, https://www.forbes.com/sites/ciocentral/2017/01/09/why-regulating-ai-is-a-mistake/#67d1649 62be3.

[62]   Diego A. Comin and Martí Mestieri Ferrer, "If Technology Has Arrived Everywhere, Why Has Income Diverged?" (NBER Working Paper No. 19010, May 2013), http://www.nber.org/papers/w19010.pdf; *see* Robert E. Hall and Charles I. Jones, "Why Do Some Countries Produce So Much More Output Than Others," *Quarterly Journal of Economics* 114 (1999).

[63]   Ranchordás, *supra* note 48, at 10.

[64]   Thierer, *supra* note 51, at 14.

[65]   *Id.*

[66]   White House, "A Framework for Global Electronic Commerce," *Executive Office of the President*, July 1997, https://clintonwhitehouse4.archives.gov/WH/New/Commerce/read.html ("Framework for Global Electronic Commerce").

Given the success of the internet, it is tempting to pursue a similar strategy with AI, permitting early research and development with only a very limited regulatory structure and creating one only much later when the sector has developed more. The problem with this approach is (a) it is based on a faulty assessment of the impact regulations have on the development of technologies, (b) it misstates early efforts to regulate the internet, and (c) AI is fundamentally different as an emerging technology from other technological developments, and regulatory efforts should occur early and often because of that.

a. Regulations do not inherently slow or prevent technological development   The flaw in the assumption underlying support for later regulation is that the choice is between regulating emerging technologies or supporting emerging technologies and enjoying their potential benefits. The fundamental question, from supporters of later regulation, "is whether we will welcome [new technologies] or try to smother them with regulations."[67] That's an over simplification of the issue.

In reality, there are too many different types of regulations to broadly state that regulation inherently smothers development.[68] Regulatory action can take many different forms—e.g., technology requirements, performance standards, taxes, tradeable allowances, information disclosure, etc.—and each impacts technological development differently.[69] If technology is regulated properly, the regulations improve innovation and competitiveness in the technology sector.[70] Waiting to regulate a new technology like AI is not, in and of itself, beneficial to the development of that technology or guaranteed to maximize the societal benefits it creates. If done properly, early regulation can be better than no regulation or permissionless innovation.

b. The internet has been "regulated" for a long time   While promoting the benefits to technological development of government inaction, Thierer uses the internet as the primary example of the economic growth created when governments permit technology to develop unobstructed. He bemoans the wasted time the internet "remained a noncommercial platform," when it was limited to being "a closed communications club reserved for academics, a handful of technologists and engineers, and assorted government bureaucrats."[71] The economic and social activity that we now associate with the internet was only possible due to a lack of government action. As mentioned above, he praises

---

67   Eli Dourado, "The Third Industrial Revolution Has Only Just Begun," *elidourado.com*, October 10, 2012, https://blog.elidourado.com/the-third-industrial-revolution-has-only-just-begun-39a717d8437c.

68   Luke A. Stewart, "The Information of Regulation on Innovation in the United States: A Cross-Industry Literature Review," *Information Technology & Innovation Foundation*, June 2010, http://www.itif.org/files/2011-impact-regulation-innovation.pdf ("regulations that are most effective at stimulating innovation will tend to require compliance innovation and, at the same time, will minimize the compliance burden and mitigate the risks of producing 'dud' inventions").

69   Jonathan B. Wiener, *The regulation of technology, and the technology of regulation,* Technology in Society 26 (2004) 483, 484.

70   ME Porter, *America's green strategy,* Scientific American 264, no. 4 (April 1991), 168; ME Porter and Claas van der Linde, *Toward a concept of the environment-competitiveness relationship,* The Journal of Economic Perspectives, Vol. 9, No. 4 (Autumn 1995), 97–118.

71   Thierer, *supra* note 51, at 13.

the Telecommunications Act of 1996 and the Clinton administration's *The Framework for Global Electronic Commerce* for avoiding internet regulation.[72] He quotes the latter as stating that "governments should encourage industry self-regulation and private sector leadership where possible" and "avoid undue restrictions on electronic commerce."[73]

However, the relationship between government action and any new technology is more complicated than Thierer and other later regulation supporters might suggest. Government action is not limited to regulations that prohibit uses and create safety procedures that functionally prevent technologies from coming to market. Government action includes funding, conducting public hearings, promotion, buying, and selling, in addition to regulation that is more innovative and expansive than mere prohibition and safety procedures.[74] Government action also includes applying a light touch or providing specific benefits or protections to a new technology. This is what the Telecommunications Act of 1996 did with regards to the internet. As Thierer notes, the act did not create a regulatory system to govern the internet, but it conveyed what Thierer called "the Greatest of All Internet Laws."[75] He is referring to Section 230, which states that "No provider or user of an interactive computer service shall be treated as the publisher or speaker of any information provided by another information content provider."[76]

This sentence was not regulation, but it was certainly governance. By including this sentence in the legislation, Congress made the specific governance decision to "encourage the unfettered and unregulated development of free speech on the internet, and to promote the development of e-commerce."[77] Congress recognized the internet as a "forum for a true diversity of political discourse, unique opportunities for cultural development, and myriad avenues for intellectual activity."[78] Congress wanted to "encourage interactive computer services and users of such services to self-police the internet for obscenity and other offensive materials."[79]

The important lesson to take from the federal government's early governance of the internet is not that Congress permitted private actors greater latitude to experiment and innovate with little regulation. That certainly happened, but you cannot apply that less broadly to all industries; no one would argue that novel military weapons technology should be given the same freedom. Rather, the lesson is that at an early stage of the development of the internet, legislators considered what they wanted the internet to be and how they wanted the internet to affect people, and then they created a governing strategy to achieve that. Early governance was necessary to establishing the liability shield

---

[72]   *Id.* at 14–15.

[73]   *Id.* at 15 (quoting Framework for Global Electronic Commerce, *supra* note 66).

[74]   *See* Gregory N. Mandel, *Regulating Emerging Technologies*, L., Innovation and Tech, Vol. 1 (2009), 75–92; Wiener, *supra* note 69, at 484.

[75]   Thierer, *supra* note 51, at 15; Adam Thierer, "The Greatest of All Internet Laws Turns 15," *Forbes*, May 8, 2011, https://www.forbes.com/sites/adamthierer/2011/05/08/the-greatest-of-all-internet-laws-turns-15/#79b8abb56d84.

[76]   47 U.S.C. §230(c)(1), available http://www.gpo.gov, accessed on 7-25-17.

[77]   *Batzel v. Smith*, 333 F.3d 1018, 1027 (9th Cir. 2003).

[78]   47 U.S.C. §230(A)(3), available http://www.gpo.gov, accessed on 8-13-17.

[79]   *Batzel*, 333 F.3d at 1028; *see also Schneider v. Amazon.com, Inc.*, 108 Wn. App. 454, 463 (2001); *Zeran v. America Online*, 129 F.3d 327, 331 (4th Cir. 1997); *Blumenthal v. Smith*, 992 F. Supp. 44, 52 (D.D.C. 1998).

that permitted web-based companies and services to grow, including Wikipedia, Twitter, YouTube, Facebook, and Google.[80]

Additionally, government action was essential for the very creation of the internet. Some proponents of later regulation and permissionless innovation praise the private sector's role in making the internet broadly available and widely successful, while treating the federal government's role as modest or even limiting.[81] However, this perspective has been largely discredited. In a *Wall Street Journal* op-ed piece, L. Gordon Crovitz stated that "It's an urban legend that the government launched the internet."[82] Vinton Cerf and Stephen Wolff, who each made key contributions to the internet's architecture while working with the United States Defense Department in the 1970s, wrote a letter to the paper contradicting Crovitz's assertion and praising the cooperation between the federal government, universities, and private sector.[83] Numerous books that closely examine the history of the digital age give proper recognition to the government-funded research that ultimately produced the internet.[84]

While it is technically true that the internet benefited because the government did not "regulate" in its commercial development, it is impossible to argue that the internet was not governed and that e-commerce and information technology did not benefit from that governance. Just as important, the benefits of the internet were widely spread among users, companies, and consumers in a way that is similar to how legislators envisioned when they made governing decisions about the internet.

c. AI is fundamentally different   It is interesting to note that Thierer devotes little attention to artificial intelligence in his book on permissionless innovation, mentioning it only four times in passing.[85] This suggests that it is not appropriate to apply permissionless innovation to AI, although when he responded to the request for information on the future of AI issued by the White House Office of Science and Technology Policy, he affirmed his belief that AI would be best regulated by little government action and that problems, "if they develop at all," can be addressed later.[86] In making his case, he points to the internet

---

80   Brief of *Amici Curiae* Professors of Constitutional Law and Related Fields, at 8-10, *J.S. v. Village Voice Media Holdings, L.L.C.*, No. 90510-0 (Wash. September 5, 2014).

81   L. Gordon Crovitz, "WeHelpedBuildThat.com," *Wall Street Journal*, October 6, 2015, https://www.wsj.com/articles/SB10000872396390443931404577555073157895692.

82   L. Gordon Crovitz, "Who Really Invented the Internet?" *Wall Street Journal*, July 22, 2012, https://www.wsj.com/articles/SB10000872396390444464304577539063008406518.

83   Vinton Cerf and Stephen Wolff, "The Birth of the Internet From Two Present at Creation," *Wall Street Journal*, Jul7 29, 2012, https://www.wsj.com/articles/SB10000872396390443334370457754 9311353156318.

84   David Warsh, "Who /Really/ Invented the Internet" *Economic Principals*, August 6, 2012, http://www.economicprincipals.com/issues/2012.08.06/1402.html (accessed 7-14-17); *see* M. Mitchell Waldrop, *The Dream Machine: J.C.R. Licklider and the Revolution that Made Computing Personal* (Penguin Books 2002); Janet Abbate, *Inventing the Internet* (MIT Press 1999); and Paul E. Ceruzzi, *Computing: A Concise History* (MIT Press 2012).

85   Thierer, *supra* note 51.

86   Request for Information, *supra* note 45, at Respondent 159, Adam Thierer. To Thierer's credit, in his comments, he makes some effort to distinguish between regulation of AI and governance of AI, rejecting "[t]raditional administrative regulatory systems" in favor of a "light-touch" approach for the governance of AI technologies. However, he is clearly suspicious of any early

as a key example and explains that because "the boundaries of AI are amorphous and ever changing" policy-makers cannot define AI and should not seek to regulate it.

But the same point also begs the question why policy-makers should *not* consider regulation and governance if the technology is so amorphous as to defy traditional understanding. The development of the internet benefited from the governing philosophy of protecting entrepreneurs and engineers while they innovated and played, but AI is very different from the Internet, particularly the Internet as it existed in its early forms. Then-start-ups like Google and Facebook permitted you, as an individual, to send and access information faster and in a way never possible before, but they presented little potential physical danger.[87] Artificial intelligence is different. AI will interact with the physical, "real" world in a way the Internet cannot.

AI will permit the widespread analysis of person-specific health data and genomic sequences, which will directly inform medical treatment prescribed by doctors that patients receive.[88] AI will also function as a "cognitive safety net," helping doctors and nurses avoid preventable errors in hospitals.[89] One study found that nearly 100,000 patients die in hospitals each year because of preventable human error, and AI could reduce that.[90]

Traffic accidents cause 1.2 million deaths and 20–50 million non-fatal injuries each year.[91] As many as 90% of those accidents are caused by preventable human error.[92] Autonomous vehicles that rely on AI can reduce that significantly, but human-driven cars can also be made safer by adopting AI-powered smart warning and assisted braking systems.[93]

AI will also exacerbate current physical world public policy problems we have now in a way the Internet did not when it first became commercially available. Our ability to enforce good citizenship on large corporations is an ongoing issue, as corporate scandals

---

government action. In describing traditional administrative regulatory systems, he warns that they are "slow to adopt to new realities. This is particularly problematic as it pertains to the governance of new, fast-moving technologies." That applies with just as much force to other government actions as it does to regulatory action.

[87]   *See* Larry Magid, "The 'Real World' Is A Lot More Dangerous Than Cyberspace," *Forbes*, July 10, 2014, https://www.forbes.com/sites/larrymagid/2014/07/10/the-real-world-is-a-lot-more-dangerous-than-cyberspace/#493f80631a33.

[88]   Andy Futreal, U.S. Senate on Commerce, Science, and Transportation, *The Dawn of Artificial Intelligence hearing*, https://www.commerce.senate.gov/public/_cache/files/4849582a-7675-4026-902f-3ec1602af689/8593CAF6AF328BDA5EEF6E8002C8E7EB.dr.-andrew-futreal-testimony.pdf (Washington, D.C. November 30, 2016) .

[89]   Erik Horvitz, U.S. Senate on Commerce, Science, & Transportation, *The Dawn of Artificial Intelligence hearing*, https://www.commerce.senate.gov/public/_cache/files/a7f09ff8-cb3e-41df-9097-eaea8bd87d29/5DD54D015EA8A1C4860F099DCA97B08F.dr.-eric-horvitz-testimony.pdf (Washington, D.C. November 30, 2016).

[90]   *To Err Is Human: Building a Safer Health System*, Institute of Medicine: Shaping the Future, November 1999, http://www.nationalacademies.org/hmd/~/media/Files/Report%20Files/1999/To-Err-is-Human/To%20Err%20is%20Human%201999%20%20report%20brief.pdf.

[91]   Horvitz, *supra* note 89.

[92]   "Look, No Hands," *The Economist*, September 1, 2012, http://www.economist.com/node/21560989.

[93]   Horvitz, *supra* note 89.

erode public trust in corporations and corporate governance.[94] Questionable corporate citizenship has led in part to environmental disasters like the Exxon Valdez[95] and wide-spread risks to public health,[96] which were arguably avoidable with better regulation. AI will not make that easier. "Corporations are becoming exceedingly difficult to regulate – many of them able to overpower lawmakers and regulators. . . With AI systems, this difficulty may become a near impossibility."[97]

This is true for data privacy as well. The Internet raised concerns about sharing our information online, particularly bank account, credit card, and social security numbers. And while no one wants to be the victim of identity fraud, early reports of the capabilities of AI to analyze and manipulate information we regularly share online potentially makes it much more dangerous. For example, Cambridge Analytica, a data analytics firm that specializes in "election management strategies" and assisted the Trump presidential campaign in 2016, is reported to rely on an AI program that utilizes "likes" on Facebook with alarming results. After 150 likes, they can know you better than your spouse knows you; after 300, they know you better than you know yourself.[98] Aleksandr Kogan, a scientist at Cambridge University's Psychometric Centre, which conducted the research underlying Cambridge Analytica's program, likened the impact of that data analysis to "how you brainwash someone."[99] Jonathan Rust, the Centre's director, has said:

> It's no exaggeration to say that minds can be changed. Behaviour can be predicted and con-trolled. I find it incredibly scary. I really do. Because nobody has really followed through on the possible consequences of all this. People don't know it's happening to them. Their attitudes are being changed behind their backs.[100]

And what about regulation of data analysis AI? "The danger of not having regulation around the sort of data you can get from Facebook and elsewhere is clear," Rust says. "With this, a computer can actually do psychology, it can predict and potentially control human behaviour. It's what the scientologists try to do but much more powerful. . . It's incredibly dangerous."[101]

---

[94]   Cary Coglianese, et al., *The Role of Government in Corporate Governance* (Harvard University, 2004), 1; Jo Confino, "Public trust in business hits five-year low," *The Guardian*, January 21, 2015, https://www.theguardian.com/sustainable-business/2015/jan/21/public-trust-global-busin ess-government-low-decline; *see Public Trust in Business*, Jared D. Harris, et al., eds. (Cambridge University Press, 2014).

[95]   Alaska Oil Spill Commission, "Details about the Accident," http://www.evostc.state.ak.us/ index.cfm?FA=facts.details (accessed 7-14-17).

[96]   Richard Knox, "Merck Pulls Arthritis Drug Vioxx from Market," *NPR*, September 30, 2004, http://www.npr.org/templates/story/story.php?storyId=4054991.

[97]   Jeremy Hsu, "Tech Leaders are Just Now Getting Serious about the Threats of AI," *Wired*, January 27, 2017, https://www.wired.com/2017/01/tech-leaders-are-just-now-getting-serious-abou t-the-threats-of-ai/.

[98]   Carole Cadwalladr, "Robert Mercer: the big data billionaire waging war on mainstream media," *The Guardian*, February 26, 2017, https://www.theguardian.com/politics/2017/feb/26/rob ert-mercer-breitbart-war-on-media-steve-bannon-donald-trump-nigel-farage.

[99]   *Id.*

[100]   *Id.*

[101]   *Id.*

These challenges make AI a fundamentally different technology than the internet. It is also fundamentally different than other emerging technologies, which may introduce physical threats (drones, autonomous vehicles) or virtual (virtual reality, augmented reality), but do not combine the two with the ability to "potentially control human behavior." These qualities make it extremely important that legislators, regulators, and other policy-makers begin considering what they want the country to look like with AI and how they want it to impact people's day-to-day lives. Once they reach a consensus, they should begin regulating and governing AI as soon as possible.

2. The case for early regulation

Having addressed the flaws in the argument for later regulation and referenced some of the reasons why early regulation is necessary to properly govern AI, this subsection makes the affirmative case for early regulation in more detail. Countering responses from *Preparing for the Future*, a poll conducted by Morning Consult found that 71 percent of respondents agree that there should be national regulations on artificial intelligence.[102] And it should be noted that the federal reports addressing AI that were published in 2016 do not speak with a single voice. There were numerous comments to the request for information referred to in *Preparing for the Future* that advocated for earlier intervention in AI regulation. Various commenters worried: that "AI can quickly become overwhelming for gov[ernment] to regulate. Our laws have no protection against the negative effects" of AI; that without regulation, AI will lead to abuses; and that the country will not be able to maximize the benefits of the technology.[103] All of these comments are cries for active and direct regulation of AI products, companies, and technologies sooner, not later, meaning this chapter is not alone in proposing that a federal AI agency should have all regulatory options at its disposal as soon as possible. Similarly, in *Artificial Intelligence, Automation, and the Economy*, the introductory letter actually calls for "Aggressive policy action" to ensure that the benefits of AI are widely spread, which can only be read as supporting early regulation that has the tools described in this chapter.[104]

Early regulation is important for three reasons. First, as previous technologies have shown, when policy-makers give careful consideration to what they want the world to look like with the new technology in it, the regulation and governance that comes out of those brainstorming sessions make it more likely that the world will more closely resemble that vision as the technology develops and is widely adopted. Second, in order to maximize their ability to influence how the world looks with AI, policy-makers should engage in early regulation and set up governance structures before the AI industry has experienced too much growth. It is harder to change how an industry is regulated once it is a mature industry; if the AI sector begins to grow in a way that dissatisfies legislators and regulators, trying to change the direction of that growth early will be easier than doing it

---

[102]   Morning Consult, National Tracking Poll #170401, pp. 118–19 (poll conducted March 30–April 1, 2017), available at https://morningconsult.com/wp-content/uploads/2017/04/170401_cros stabs_Brands_v3_AG.pdf.

[103]   Request for Information, *supra* note 45, at Respondents 14, 20, and 61.

[104]   *See* Executive Office of the President, *Artificial Intelligence, Automation, and the Economy*, Introductory letter, available at https://www.whitehouse.gov/sites/whitehouse.gov/files/images/EM BARGOED%20AI%20Economy%20Report.pdf ("AI and the Economy").

later. Finally, as indicated above, AI is different from other technologies, developing and changing very frequently. If regulation does not start sooner rather than later, effective regulation will be difficult, if not impossible.

a.   What do we want the world with AI to be?   One of the most important functions served by the regulations and governance of new technology is that they give us the chance as a society to collectively consider new developments and make some general decisions about how we want the technology to impact our lives.[105] In recent decades, this has occurred with the internet (as described above) and the wireless telecommunications industry (as described below).

After seeing how early court decisions treated and could potentially shape the internet, federal legislators considered how they wanted the internet to be used by and impact people, both in terms of economics, but also in terms of constitutional considerations and values that have been important to the country since its founding.[106] Section 230 of the Telecommunications Act of 1996 represented their efforts to govern toward their goal of preserving "the vibrant and competitive free market that presently exists for the internet"[107] and encouraging widespread activity in internet development without the specter of tort liability every time information passed through the information superhighway.[108]

The Telecommunications Act of 1996 also addressed the still-nascent wireless communications industry, and gave increased authority to a regulatory body, the Federal Communications Commission (FCC), to regulate that industry. Among other things, it commanded the FCC to consider improving the efficiency of spectrum use and encouraging competition and providing services to the largest feasible number of users when managing the wireless spectrum.[109] It also specifically preserved local zoning authority for the actual siting of antennas and wireless infrastructure, subject to some limitations.[110] During the consideration of this legislation, legislators considered how they wanted the developing wireless industry to impact consumers before deciding to encourage competition in the industry, which was in danger of having little because of the pre-existing monopolies enjoyed by local phone carriers.[111] Legislators also gave some thought to how decisions are made regarding the industry's infrastructure—the antennas and supporting equipment—that would provide service for cell phone users. What they ultimately chose was a system that seeks to balance "the carrier's desire to efficiently provide quality service

---

[105]   *See* United Nations Conference on Sustainable Development, *The Future We Want*, Outcome document of the United Nations Conference on Sustainable Development, Rio de Janeiro, June 20–22, 2012.

[106]   Brief of Appellant, at 10-13, *J.S. v. Village Voice Media Holdings, L.L.C.*, No. 44920-0-II (Wash. Ct. of App., December 9, 2013).

[107]   47 U.S.C. §230(b)(2)(3), available http://www.gpo.gov, accessed on 9-1-17.

[108]   *Zeran*, 129 F.3d at 331.

[109]   47 U.S.C. §332(a), available http://www.gpo.gov, accessed on 8-16-17.

[110]   47 U.S.C. §332(c)(7), available http://www.gpo.gov, accessed on 9-1-17.

[111]   *GTE Midwest, Inc. v. FCC*, 233 F.3d 341, 344 (6th Cir. 2000); Jeffrey A. Eisenach and Kevin W. Caves, "What Happens When Local Phone Service is Deregulated?" Telecommunications and Technology (Fall 2012), 35–36.

to customers and local governments' primary authority to regulate land use."[112] "A carrier 'may think. . . its solution is best,' but 'subject to an outer limit, such choices are just what Congress reserved to the town'".[113] As discussed more below, this vision for the industry ultimately provided local residents a great deal of control over how wireless infrastructure looks in their towns.

Even before the current era of technology and regulation, legislators grappled with how technological development was changing the world and how they wanted the world to look with the new technology. It goes without saying that the Industrial Revolution introduced tremendous change to the lives of average Americans. In the early nineteenth century, most American manufacturing was done in individual homes or, in larger towns, in a local mill or shop. Visitors to many towns would find a wide assortment of small manufacturers: lumber mills, grist mills, weavers, shoemakers, tanners, tailors, and others. Even though there were numerous manufacturers, their actual output was quite small and only served their immediate areas.[114] One hundred years later, much of the American labor force had been congregated into large factories that dwarfed the collective production of those smaller, local artisans.

In a way that should sound familiar to policy-makers grappling with the expected effects of emerging technologies today, legislators eventually had to consider how their world had changed after the Industrial Revolution and how they wanted it to change.[115] They encountered widespread use of child labor in factories, where working hours exceeded ten hours per day.[116] There was no mandatory minimum wage, workers' compensation, unemployment benefits, or prohibitions against employers passing hidden costs like health or environmental damage on to employees.[117] In response, federal policy-makers prohibited child labor, established a minimum wage, protected employees' right to organize, and began to place regulatory controls on pollution and workplace safety.[118] Although

---

[112]   *Omnipoint Holdings, Inc. v. City of Cranston*, 586 F.3d 38, 51 (1st Cir. 2009).

[113]   *Omnipoint Holdings, Inc.*, 586 F.3d at 51 (quoting *Town of Amherst v. Omnipoint Comm'ns Enters., Inc.*, 173 F.3d 9, 15 (1st Cir.1999)).

[114]   Harold D. Woodman, "Economy from 1815 to 1860," in Glenn Porter, ed., *Encyclopedia of American Economic History*, vol. 1 (Charles Scribner's Sons, 1980), 80–81.

[115]   I recognize that academics have long discussed the Industrial Revolution in three or more distinct parts, generally with the first spanning from about 1760 to 1840 (introducing railroads, the steam engine, and mechanical production), the second spanning from the late nineteenth century to the early twentieth century (introducing electricity and the assembly line), and the third spanning from the 1960s to the 1990s (introducing semiconductors, personal computers, and the Internet). *See* Klaus Schwab, *The Fourth Industrial Revolution* (Corwn Business, 2016), 6–7. The lay public typically refers to the first industrial revolution as the "Industrial Revolution," and this chapter does as well.

[116]   Stephen M. Salsbury, "American Business Institutions Before the Railroad," in Glenn Porter, ed., *Encyclopedia of American Economic History*, vol. 2 (Charles Scribner's Sons, 1980), 615–16; Lewis C. Solmon and Michael Tierney, "Education," in Glenn Porter, ed., *Encyclopedia of American Economic History*, vol. 3 (Charles Scribner's Sons, 1980), 1015–16; Albro Martin, "Economy from Reconstruction to 1914," in Glenn Porter, ed., *Encyclopedia of American Economic History*, vol. 1 (Charles Scribner's Sons, 1980), 107.

[117]   Martin, *supra* note 116, at 107.

[118]   Solmon and Tierney, *supra* note 116, at 1015–16.; Arthur M. Johnson, "Economy Since 1914," in Glenn Porter, ed., *Encyclopedia of American Economic History*, vol. 1 (New York: Charles Scribner's Sons, 1980), 117; Thomas K. McCraw, "Regulatory Agencies." in Glenn Porter, ed.,

it is true that the expansive American industrial middle class of the mid-twentieth century was created by the Industrial Revolution, it is equally true that its creation was only possible after legal reforms more equitably spread the enormous economic efficiencies and material comforts introduced by the Industrial Revolution.[119]

AI promises to introduce just as much growth and disruption as the Industrial Revolution, potentially creating new sources of wealth and productivity while also decoupling that from employment.[120] If we want to capture and spread widely the benefits of AI, we should start right now to think about what we want to world to be like with AI in it. The full benefits of the Industrial Revolution only materialized after policy-makers considered and put into law how they wanted the world to be. However, those governing and regulating decisions did not begin to occur until the early twentieth century, meaning a century had passed before the workers powering the industrial economy also retained some of the financial and material benefits.[121] If we want the benefits of AI to be shared broadly, we need to consider governing and regulating decisions now.

b.　AI regulation is easier to enact before AI becomes commercially successful　The history of government regulation shows that it is easier to regulate a new industry than a mature industry. Manufacturers fought tooth and nail against efforts to enact workers' compensation and unemployment insurance laws into the twentieth century.[122] The tobacco industry successfully fought regulatory oversight by the FDA for 13 years before the passage of the Family Smoking Prevention and Tobacco Control Act in 2009.[123] This came after the FDA's initial efforts to regulate the tobacco industry were ruled unconstitutional in 2000[124] and literally decades of law suits brought against tobacco companies, alleging that they knew the health risks of their products and relied on the addictive qualities of nicotine to ensure profits.[125] Even after the 2009 legislation, tobacco companies have continued to bring litigation challenging the statute.[126]

Encyclopedia of American Economic History, vol. 1 (New York: Charles Scribner's Sons, 1980), 803–04.

[119]　*Robots Are People*, *supra* note 18, at 46–48.

[120]　Erik Brynjolfsson and Andrew McAfee, *The Second Machine Age: Work, Progress, and Prosperity in a Time of Brilliant Machines* (W.W. Norton and Company, 2016); Fletcher, *supra* note 47.

[121]　*Robots Are People*, *supra* note 18, at 47–48.

[122]　Martin, *supra* note 116, at 107.

[123]　An act to protect the public health by providing the Food and Drug Administration with certain authority to regulate tobacco products, to amend title 5, United States Code, to make certain modifications in the Thrift Savings Plan, the Civil Service Retirement System, and the Federal Employees' Retirement System, and for other purposes, Pub. L. 111-31, June 22, 2009; *see United States v. Phillip Morris USA, Inc.*, 449 F.Supp.2d 1 (D.D.C. 2006); Abigail R. Moncrieff, *Reincarnating the 'Major Questions' Exception to Chevron Deference as a Doctrine of Noninterference (or Why* Massachusetts v. EPA *Got it Wrong)*, 60 Admin L. Rev. 593, 601–02 (Summer 2008).

[124]　The court found that Congress had not granted authority to the FDA to regulate tobacco products. *FDA v. Brown & Williamson Tobacco Corp.*, 529 U.S. 120 (2000).

[125]　Tobacco Control Consortium, *Federal Regulation of Tobacco: A Summary* (July 2009), 14–15; *see Phillip Morris*, 449 F.Supp.2d at 1; Moncrieff, *supra* note 123, at 601–02.

[126]　*BBK Tobacco & Foods, LLP v. FDA*, 672 F.Supp.2d 969 (D. Ariz. 2009); *Lorillard Inc. v. FDA*, 56 F.Supp.3d 37 (D.D.C. 2014).

Contrast those efforts with recent state efforts to regulate daily fantasy sports companies. Daily fantasy sports companies like FanDuel and DraftKings coordinate contests that last one to three days, depending on the sport.[127] Consumers create an account on a company's website and deposit money into the account, which they then spend as an entry fee on each contest the company conducts.[128] In each contest, the participants "draft" actual athletes who cost more or less (within the rules of each contest) depending on their real life reputations and performances.[129] Each contest not only dictates what each athlete costs but also typically limits the amount of contest dollars each participant can spend. Many people draft the same athletes, as each participant's roster is independent of every other participant.[130] Participants' teams earn points for how their athletes perform in the real life games conducted during the contest's short time period.[131] Participants can win money based on how their team performs compared to other teams in the contest.[132]

The two largest companies in the daily fantasy sports sector are FanDuel and DraftKings, which each have an estimated value of $1 billion[133] and collectively have a total of five million combined users.[134] The companies are young, with FanDuel having been formed in 2009 and DraftKings forming in 2012, and the daily fantasy sports industry is not much older itself.[135] In November of 2015, the New York Attorney General's Office sent cease-and-desist letters to the CEOs of DraftKings and FanDuel, explaining that their daily fantasy sports contests "constitute[d] illegal gambling" under New York State law and ordered the companies to "stop accepting wagers" within the state immediately.[136] In

---

[127]   *See* "Playing Daily Fantasy Sports for Dummies and er . . . You!" *Daily Fantasy Sports 101*, http://www.dailyfantasysports101.com/basics/, accessed 7-15-2017 ("Playing Daily Fantasy Sports").

[128]   *See* Zachary Shapiro, *Regulation, Prohibition, and Fantasy: The Case of FanDuel, DraftKings, and Daily Fantasy Sports in New York and Massachusetts*, 7 Harv. J. of Sports & Ent. L. 289, 291 (2016) (giving an overview of DFS).

[129]   *See id.* (providing an overview of how daily fantasy sports contests work); Ken Belson, "A Primer on Daily Fantasy Football Sites," *New York Times,* Oct. 6, 2015, http://www.nytimes.com/2015/10/07/sports/football/a-primer-ondaily-fantasy-football-sites.html.

[130]   *See* Shapiro, *supra* note 128, at 291.

[131]   *See* Playing Daily Fantasy Sports, *supra* note 127.

[132]   *See* Shapiro, *supra* note 128, at 291.

[133]   Kate O'Keeffe, "Daily Fantasy-Sports Operators Await Reality Check," *Wall Street Journal*, September 9, 2015, https://www.wsj.com/articles/daily-fantasy-sports-operators-await-reality-check-1441835630.

[134]   Will Hobson, "Daily fantasy sites DraftKings, FanDuel reach agreement to merge," *Washington Post*, November 18, 2016, https://www.washingtonpost.com/news/sports/wp/2016/11/18/daily-fantasy-sites-draftkings-fanduel-reach-agreement-to-merge/?utm_term=.2379a7a001d8.

[135]   Bill King, "FanDuel delivers daily dose of fantasy games," *Sports Business Journal*, February 6, 2012, http://www.sportsbusinessdaily.com/Journal/Issues/2012/02/06/In-Depth/FanDuel.aspx; Scott Kirsner, "Two local companies, StarStreet and DraftKings, prepare to launch new fantasy sports site," *Boston Globe*, February 27, 2012, http://archive.boston.com/business/technology/innoeco/2012/02/two_local_companies_starstreet.html; Darren Heitner, "An Abbreviated History of FanDuel And DraftKings," *Forbes*, September 20, 2015, https://www.forbes.com/sites/darrenheitner/2015/09/20/an-abbreviated-history-of-fanduel-and-draftkings/#7b264e327564.

[136]   Notice to Cease and Desist and Notice of Proposed Litigation Pursuant to New York Executive Law § 63(12) and General Business Law § 349 from Kathleen McGee, Bureau Chief, Division of Economic Justice, Internet Bureau, State of New York Office of the Attorney General, to Jason Robins, CEO, DraftKings, Inc., Nov. 10, 2015, http:// ag.ny.gov/

many ways, this move is more extreme than the FDA's efforts to regulate tobacco, as the New York Attorney General sought to shut down DraftKings and FanDuel in the state altogether. Not surprisingly, the companies pushed back, obtaining temporary stays of the cease-and-desist letters.[137] At the same time, the New York legislature began considering legislation that would have legalized, but thoroughly regulated, daily fantasy sports.[138]

Although DraftKings and FanDuel initially resisted state efforts at governance and regulation, they quickly changed course. By October of 2016, less than a year after receiving cease-and-desist letters from the New York Attorney General, the companies had reached an agreement with the Attorney General that permitted sweeping reforms, including disclosures to consumers and the State of New York,[139] and applauded New York's regulatory efforts.[140] As relatively new entrants in a young field, FanDuel and DraftKings had relatively poor financial and cultural support to oppose governance and regulatory efforts. Their resistance was noticeably short-lived in comparison to the decades-long fights against regulations put up by manufacturing firms during the late nineteenth and early twentieth centuries and tobacco companies more recently. One of the key differences is that daily fantasy sports is a new field and manufacturing and tobacco were mature industries.

When governments begin to regulate AI, policy-makers need to be mindful of this lesson. If we want to regulate AI without decades of litigation, legislators and regulators need to do so before the AI industry has accumulated enough capital to resist, and here "capital" refers to financial resources and cultural importance.[141] Although the tobacco

---

pdfs/FinalNYAGDraftKings-Letter 1110_2015.pdf; Notice to Cease and Desist and Notice of Proposed Litigation Pursuant to New York Executive Law § 63(12) and General Business Law § 349 from Kathleen McGee, Bureau Chief, Division of Economic Justice, Internet Bureau, State of New York Office of the Attorney General, to Nigel Eccles, CEO, FanDuel, Inc., Nov. 10, 2015, http://ag.ny.gov/pdfs/FinalNYAGFanDuelLetter_11_10 2015_signed.pdf; Roni Mathew, "The Legality of Daily Fantasy Sports is in Gamble in Some States: A Closer Look at New York and Delaware's Response to this New(ish) Trend," 24 Jeffrey S. Moorad Sports L. J., 275, 279–80 (2017).

[137]   Mathew, *supra* note 136, at 282.

[138]   Dustin Gouker, "Newest Fantasy Sports Bill in New York Is the One to Watch," *Legal Sports Report*, February 24, 2016, http://www.legalsportsreport.com/8509/newest-new-york-dfs-bill; Mathew, *supra* note 136, at 285.

[139]   Settlement Agreement between Attorney General of the State of New York and FanDuel, Inc., October 25, 2016, https://ag.ny.gov/sites/default/files/20161025_fanduel_final_signed_settlement_agreement.pdf; Settlement Agreement between Attorney General of the State of New York and DraftKings, Inc., October 25, 2016, https://ag.ny.gov/sites/default/files/draftkings_settlement_agreement_-_executed.pdf; Office of the Attorney General of the State of New York, "A.G. Schneiderman Announces $12 Million Settlement With Draftkings And Fanduel," October 25, 2016, https://ag.ny.gov/press-release/ag-schneiderman-announces-12-million-settlement-draftkings-and-fanduel.

[140]   Dan Adams and Curt Woodword, "New law allows DraftKings, fantasy sports to return to N.Y.," *Boston Globe*, August 6, 2016, https://www.bostonglobe.com/business/2016/08/03/draftkings-fantasy-sports-return-new-york-after-new-law-signed/KOdAFUnrcoCmupo64gyBQK/story.html.

[141]   That both elements of capital—financial resources and cultural relevance—need to be present for the AI industry to effectively fight regulation is an important point. DraftKings and FanDuel arguably had the financial resources necessary to take the New York attorney general's office to court and lobby the New York legislature, but with a population footprint of five million people, many of whom were casual users, it did not have the cultural relevance that the smoking

industry has been able to rely on its deep pockets to fund its court battles against regulatory efforts, those fights would not have lasted so long if tobacco had not had such a long relationship with Americans.[142] If the two largest daily fantasy sports providers had more than five million combined users and was a larger cultural force, it is likely they would have litigated the dispute longer and their customers in New York would have made it more difficult for the state's Attorney General to threaten the contests. Early regulation of AI will help legislators and regulators govern without open and active resistance from the industry.

c. Dangers of AI are real and deserve our attention Although there are many accomplished, smart people who worry about AI as an existential threat,[143] I suspect that supporters of later regulation are right when they point out that these concerns are overblown to the point of being science fiction—"*Terminator*-inspired tales of killer robots destroying humanity."[144] But AI potentially introduces real dangers that we should try to regulate and govern sooner rather than later.

These dangers include: the elimination of many jobs by a technology that does not create many new ones, leading to a large spike in unemployment;[145] exacerbating income inequality by accumulating wealth and capital in very few hands;[146] and enabling analysis of personal data in a way that makes us all vulnerable to manipulation by third parties that have ulterior motives.[147] There are numerous conferences every year discussing these dangers and considering proposals to avoid them.[148] Given that the dangers have

---

industry had, with generations of users actively addicted to the product. Several of the big players in the AI field, like Google, Apple, Facebook, and Amazon, already have the necessary financial resources to fight regulation, but at this point it seems unlikely that AI has so permeated culture that AI has the cultural relevance that would permit those companies to effectively fight regulatory efforts.

[142]　*See* Amanda Jauden, "American Smoking Culture: From Cash Crop to Public Scourge," *Newsweek*, April 23, 2016, http://www.newsweek.com/american-smoking-culture-cash-crop-public-scourge-451078.

[143]　R.L. Adams, "Is Artificial Intelligence Dangerous?" *Forbes*, March 25, 2016, https://www.forbes.com/sites/robertadams/2016/03/25/is-artificial-intelligence-dangerous/#58a3cf46358b.

[144]　Thierer, *supra* note 51, at 23–38, 42.

[145]　Erik Brynjolfsson and Andrew McAfee; *Race Against the Machine* (Digital Frontier Press, 2011); Lubin, *supra* note 35; Condon and Wiseman, *supra* note 35; Luddite Legacy, *supra* note 35; Manjoo, *supra* note 35.

[146]　Ariel Conn, "Artificial Intelligence And Income Inequality," *Huffington Post*, March 16, 2017, http://www.huffingtonpost.com/entry/artificial-intelligence-and-income-inequality_us_58cafe92e4b07112b6472beb; David Rothman, "Technology and Inequality, *MIT Technology Review*, October 21, 2004, https://www.technologyreview.com/s/531726/technology-and-inequality.

[147]　Cadwalladr, *supra* note 98. It should be noted that the European Union's General Data Protection Regulation attempts to provide certain protections to individuals regarding their personal data and "automated individual decision-making, including profiling," in an effort to mitigate the potentially harmful effects of AI's use of personal data. *See* Articles 13 and 22, Regulation (EU) 2016/679 of the European Parliament and of the Council (27 April 2016).

[148]　*See* Beneficial AI 2017, *Future of Life Institute*, January 5–8, 2017, https://futureoflife.org/bai-2017/ (conference website); Ethics of Artificial Intelligence, *NYU Center for Mind, Brain and Consciousness*, October 14–15, 2016, https://wp.nyu.edu/consciousness/ethics-of-artificial-intelligence/ (conference website); among others.

nationwide consequences for people of every demographic, it would be irresponsible if governments in America decided to forego regulating and governing AI in favor of "waiting to see what happens."

3. Wireless telecommunications industry

Before discussing the "how" of regulating AI, I want to consider the wireless telecommunications industry, a useful, recent example of a new technology that was subjected to early governance and regulation and that was still widely successful.

The Telecommunications Act of 1996 established that the wireless industry would be regulated by a national regulatory framework administered by the FCC, including selling and regulating the spectrum bands used by wireless carriers to provide coverage.[149] For example, when two or more parties apply to use the same spectrum in the same geographic region on an exclusive basis, the FCC frequently conducts "comparative hearings," which are quasi-judicial administrative hearings that permit the FCC to evaluate each applicant, giving the FCC considerable control over who enters the market and how much "product" they have to sell.[150] Between local regulations[151] and federal regulations, it is fair to say that the Telecommunications Act of 1996 imposed significant regulations on the still young wireless telecommunications industry.

And how did the industry do after those regulations? You can probably look up the details on your cell phone, as 95 percent of Americans own one and 77 percent of Americans own a smart phone, but I will provide the pertinent details here.[152] In 1993, when Congress first started negotiating and drafting the Telecommunications Act of 1996, approximately 16 million Americans owned a cell phone.[153] When the Telecommunications Act of 1996 passed, the wireless industry was growing quickly, as 44 million Americans owned cell phones, but that still represented only about 17 percent of the American population, so the sector was still nascent.[154] The expansion and codification of the regulation of the wireless industry did nothing to deter the growth of the wireless industry. Today, the

---

[149] Charles M. Davidson, *Reflecting on Twenty Years Under the Telecommunications Act of 1996*, 68 Fed. Comm. L.J. 1 (2016), 12–13; *see* Charles M. Davidson and Michael J. Santorelli, *Seizing the Mobile Moment: Spectrum Allocation Policy for the Wireless Broadband Century*, 19 Commlaw Conspectus 1, 31–35 (2010); Thomas Hazlett, *Wireless Craze, The Unlimited Bandwidth Myth, The Spectrum Auction Faux Pas, and the Punchline to Ronald Coase's "Big Joke": An Essay on Airwave Allocation Policy*, 14 Harv. J. of Law & Tech. 335, 341–44, 556–57 (2001).

[150] *See* "Auctioning Spectrum Rights," Federal Communications Commission, February 20, 2001, http://wireless.fcc.gov/auctions/data/papersAndStudies/aucspec.pdf, accessed on 7-17-17.

[151] The Telecommunications Act of 1996 explicitly permits local governments to retain their land use authority, which has let local governments regulate the placement of antennas in a way that has made the permitting of wireless telecommunications facilities more difficult than wireless carriers would like for over two decades. *See* 47 U.S.C. §332(c)(7)(A).

[152] "Mobile Fact Sheet," Pew Research Center, January 12, 2017, http://www.pewinternet.org/fact-sheet/mobile/, accessed on 7-17-17.

[153] Ronald E. Yates, "Popularity Of Cell Phones Far Exceeds Expectations," *Chicago Tribune*, April 19, 1994, http://articles.chicagotribune.com/1994-04-19/news/9404190274_1_cellular-phones-cellular-telecommunications-industry-association-cellular-telephone.

[154] Jim Cicconi, *Reflecting on Twenty Years Under the Telecommunications Act of 1996*, 68 Fed. Comm. L.J. 1, 8 (2016).

saturation of cell phones into American life is nearly universal. In fact, although five percent of Americans have refused to hear the siren call of constant connectivity, the proliferation of wireless devices has resulted in there being more wireless subscriptions in America than Americans, as cell phones and tablets combine for nearly 400 million wireless subscribers in the United States.[155]

The growth has not only been in the number of devices and subscribers, but also in the amount of use and expected services, i.e., data and applications. When the Telecommunications Act of 1996 became law, cell phones were capable of sending short texts and downloading low-rate data.[156] More recently, data usage has exploded. Between 2013 and 2018, U.S. mobile data traffic is expected to grow from less than half an exabyte per month to 2.7 exabytes per month; for context, one extabyte is equal to one billion gigabytes and 2.7 extabytes is equal to the amount of data stored on 675 million DVDs.[157] Much of this usage has come from streaming video, as 67 percent of Americans regularly watch videos on their phones and 61 percent of total mobile traffic will be from videos.[158] Whereas basic texting and related services were the only applications available to mid-1990s era cell phones, today there are more than two million applications available for both Android phones and iPhones.[159]

That is to say, early and vigorous regulation of the wireless communications industry did little to hurt it. It has grown to be ubiquitous in American life, in a way that was hard to predict in 1996,[160] because (a) the statute and regulations were well drafted to let the industry grow organically with appropriate government oversight, and (b) people wanted the services offered by the wireless industry. The important thing to do with AI, then, is to implement carefully conceived governance and well drafted regulations, as early as possible in the commercial life of AI, that let the AI industry grow with appropriate government oversight. The next section discusses what those regulations look like.

---

[155]   "Annual Wireless Industry Survey," CTIA, https://www.ctia.org/industry-data/ctia-annual-wireless-industry-survey, accessed on 7-17-17.

[156]   Amit Kumar, et al. "Evolution of Mobile Wireless Communications Networks: 1G to 4G," *International Journal on Electronics & Communication Technology*, Vol. 1, No. 1 (December 2010), 71.

[157]   Alina Selykuh, "U.S. mobile data traffic to jump nearly eight-fold by 2018: Cisco," *Reuters*, February 5, 2014, http://www.reuters.com/article/us-usa-spectrum-cisco-idUSBREA140VY20140205.

[158]   "Wireless Quick Facts," CTIA, https://www.ctia.org/industry-data/wireless-quick-facts, access on 7-16-2017; "67 Percent of U.S. Consumers Watch Mobile Videos Daily," CTIA, https://www.ctia.org/industry-data/facts-and-infographics-details/fact-and-infographics/67-percent-of-u.s.-consumers-watch-mobile-videos-daily, accessed on 7-16-2017.

[159]   "Number of apps available in leading app stores as of March 2017," Statista, https://www.statista.com/statistics/276623/number-of-apps-available-in-leading-app-stores/, accessed on 7-15-2017.

[160]   Michael L. Katz, *Reflecting on Twenty Years Under the Telecommunications Act of 1996*, 68 Fed. Comm. L.J. 1, 29 (2016) ("Looking back, the biggest technological development that we failed to foresee was how important mobile data would become.")

III.   PRIMARY REGULATION OF AI

It is a fundamental principal that federal laws have supremacy over state laws.[161] However, federal and state laws and regulations co-exist, frequently governing the same industries, areas, actions, etc.[162] This can create tension between federal and state governance, particularly with regard to new technologies, as both states and Washington struggle with governing novel devices and programs that interact with their citizens in ways policymakers do not recognize.[163] Regardless, as statutes and regulations are promulgated the ones passed by the federal government will control over the ones passed by the states. As a result, federal regulations will be primary over state regulations, so federal governance will be the primary form of AI regulation.

The starting point for unified, federal AI governance should be an organic statute, which Matthew Scherer has called the "Artificial Intelligence Development Act" (AIDA).[164] AIDA would establish both the principles for AI regulation and the agency that will be tasked with the day-to-day governing of AI, i.e., the Artificial Intelligence Regulatory Agency (AIRA). The principles would include fostering the development of AI, while (1) ensuring that AI is safe, secure, susceptible to human control, and aligned with human interests, (2) limiting its negative impacts, and (3) making sure its benefits are widely spread.[165] AIRA would be organized and authorized as described below.

A.   Where in the Federal Government to Situate AIRA

When Congress decides to regulate AI, they will surely empower a federal agency to promulgate the regulations, as they have when regulating American air traffic,[166] radio,[167] the pharmaceutical industry,[168] etc. The question then becomes will Congress empower an existing agency or create a new one? Ryan Calo addresses this question succinctly when considering a Federal Robotics Commission:

---

[161]   U.S. Constitution, Art. VI, cl. 2.

[162]   *Wyeth v. Levine*, 555. U.S. 555, 557 (2009) ("Under this federalist system, 'the States possess sovereignty concurrent with that of the Federal Government, subject only to limitations imposed by the Supremacy Clause.' *Tafflin v. Levitt,* 493 U.S. 455, 458, 110 S.Ct. 792, 107 L.Ed.2d 887 (1990). In this way, the Supremacy Clause gives the Federal Government 'a decided advantage in [a] delicate balance' between federal and state sovereigns. *Gregory v. Ashcroft,* 501 U.S. 452, 460, 111 S.Ct. 2395. 'As long as it is acting within the powers granted it under the Constitution, Congress may impose its will on the States.' *Ibid.* That is an 'extraordinary power in a federalist system.' *Ibid.*").

[163]   *See* Federal AV Policy, *supra* note 21, at 37–38.

[164]   Scherer, *supra* note 4, at 394. The FUTURE of AI Act, *supra* note 5, is not this act, as it does not create an agency specifically to regulate AI, nor does it even authorize an existing agency to adopt regulations to govern AI. As explained below in the subsection discussing establishing AIRA in the Commerce Department, the FUTURE of AI Act only creates an advisory committee to (a) study and provide advice to the Commerce Secretary regarding AI, and (b) prepare a report to Congress and the Commerce Secretary regarding AI.

[165]   Scherer, *supra* note 4, at 394; 100 Year Study*, supra* note 2, at 49.

[166]   Federal Aviation Act of 1958, Pub. L. 85-726, August 23, 1958.

[167]   Federal Communications Commission Act of 1934, Pub. L. 73-416, June 19, 1934.

[168]   Federal Food, Drug, and Cosmetic Act of 1938, Pub. L. 75-717, June 25, 1938.

We need another federal agency? *Really?*

Agencies have their problems, of course. They can be inefficient and are subject to capture by those they regulate or other special interests. . . This question – whether agencies represent a good way to govern and, if so, what is the best design – is a worthwhile one. It is the subject of a robust and long-standing debate in administrative law. . . But it has little to do with robotics. As discussed, we have agencies devoted to technologies already and it would be odd and anomalous to think we are done creating them.[169]

That is to say, nearly every important technology has an agency, commission, or department dedicated specifically to it. It is silly to think AI would be the exception.

The question then becomes where in the federal government should the new AIRA be formed? Department of Justice? Department of Defense? Labor? Energy? Commerce? There are compelling cases for each of these and it is useful to consider them:

- Department of Justice: In light of the potential for AI to make decisions affecting criminal justice,[170] lending decisions,[171] and court rooms,[172] it makes a certain amount of sense to place AIRA in the Department of Justice. The Attorney General will surely have an interest in overseeing AI applications to ensure the relevant algorithms do not unconstitutionally rely on sex, race, religion, etc.[173] Certainly that will be important work, as the potential is great for the development of a "black box society"—in which decisions are made, but no one knows exactly what factors determine those decisions because no person actually makes many of those decisions.[174] The Department of Justice, particularly through the Civil Rights Division, has a long history of upholding the civil and constitutional rights that poorly or maliciously programmed AI could undermine.[175] However, much of the work of AIRA will likely focus on research and development in the field, require technological expertise, or the development of regulations governing safety and commerce that are more typically performed in other departments.
- Department of Defense: The Department of Defense has a long history of pursuing technological advances through the Defense Advanced Research Projects

---

[169]   Calo, *supra* note 24, at 12–13.

[170]   Preparing for the Future, *supra* note 1, at 14.

[171]   Shorouq Fathi Eletter, et al., "Neuro-Based Artificial Intelligence Model for Loan Decisions," *American Journal of Economic and Business Administration* 2(1): 27–34, 2010.

[172]   Chris Johnston, "Artificial intelligence 'judge' development by UCL computer scientists," *The Guardian*, October 23, 2016, https://www.theguardian.com/technology/2016/oct/24/artificial-intelligence-judge-university-college-london-computer-scientists.

[173]   *See* Bryce Goodman and Seth Flaxman, "European Union regulations on algorithmic decision-making and a 'right to explanation,'" pp. 4, 6, August 31, 2016, *arXiv.org*, https://arxiv.org/pdf/1606.08813.pdf.

[174]   *See id.* at 6.

[175]   Civil Rights Division Home, United States Department of Justice Civil Rights Division, https://www.justice.gov/crt, accessed on July 17, 2017 ("The Civil Rights Division of the Department of Justice, created in 1957 by the enactment of the Civil Rights Act of 1957, works to uphold the civil and constitutional rights of all Americans, particularly some of the most vulnerable members of our society. The Division enforces federal statutes prohibiting discrimination on the basis of race, color, sex, disability, religion, familial status and national origin.")

Agency (DARPA). Created in response to the launch of Sputnik in 1957, DARPA was formed to "make pivotal investments in breakthrough technologies for national security."[176] Since then, it has an impressive track record of working with academics, corporations, and government agencies to develop technologies that are commonplace today—the internet, GPS, etc.—but that were breakthroughs when DARPA started researching them.[177] Already, the military is investing significantly in AI, developing protocols for the research and development of autonomous weapons.[178] DARPA is pursuing some of that.[179] However, while AI will have military applications, it is inappropriate for the military to regulate a technology that civilians will adopt for personal use.

- Department of Labor: The impact of AI on the labor force has been a frequent topic of speculation, concern, and fearmongering, with estimates predicting that as many as 50 million professional jobs are lost to AI[180] (compared to only 7.5 million jobs lost during the Great Recession),[181] representing 40 percent of the workforce,[182] including lawyers, doctors, writers, and scientists.[183] Compounding this is the possibility that, unlike previously widespread, technological advances, AI will not create nearly as many jobs as it replaces.[184] The federal government is already actively considering how its policies can direct the development, as the recent *Artificial Intelligence, Automation, and the Economy Report* noted, "Policy plays a large role in shaping the effects of technological change."[185] That same report describes various overarching goals for the labor force that federal policy can influence, including emphasizing that math and computer science are critical in all levels of education in order to help "workers successfully navigate through unpredictable changes in the future labor market."[186] Other federal reports describe the federal government's role in and responsibility for developing a workforce that can adapt to AI by supporting STEM education programs and coordinating educational efforts at all levels of schooling.[187] Promulgating regulations that require or promote the training of the American workforce with an eye toward AI is well within the typical duties of the Department of Labor, but what about similar educational efforts in grades K–12? That is typically done by the Department of Education. Should the Department of Labor assume the responsibility for that element of children's education in light

---

[176] About DARPA, Department of Defense, Defense Advanced Research Projects Agency, https://www.darpa.mil/about-us/about-darpa, accessed on 7-18-17.

[177] *Id.*

[178] Department of Defense Directive 3000.09, November 21, 2012 (revised May 8, 2017), available at http://www.esd.whs.mil/Portals/54/Documents/DD/issuances/dodd/300009p.pdf.

[179] DARPA Perspective on AI, Department of Defense, Defense Advanced Research Projects Agency, https://www.darpa.mil/about-us/darpa-perspective-on-ai, accessed on 7-17-17.

[180] Lubin, *supra* note 35.

[181] Condon and Wiseman, *supra* note 35.

[182] Luddite Legacy, *supra* note 35.

[183] Manjoo, *supra* note 35.

[184] Luddite Legacy, *supra* note 35.

[185] AI and the Economy, *supra* note 104, at 25.

[186] *Id.* at 33.

[187] Preparing for the Future, *supra* note 1, at 26.

of the impact AI will have on the labor force? Whichever way you are inclined to answer, it does not matter for the purposes of placing AIRA in the Department of Labor, as the Department does not have the history of investing in new technologies (like the Department of Defense) or policing constitutional rights in a wide variety of situations (like the Department of Justice).

● Department of Energy: Although it does not immediately sound like a natural fit to oversee AIRA, the Department of Energy actually already performs a number of functions that lend themselves well to AIRA, and AI will have a large impact on the energy industry and the national electric grid.[188] In 2007, President George W. Bush signed into law The America COMPETES Act, which authorized the creation of an Advanced Research Projects Agency for Energy (ARPA-E) under the jurisdiction of the Department.[189] Modeled after DARPA, ARPA-E funds and promotes transformational energy technology projects.[190] AI contributions to the energy sector include analyzing data and modeling the behavior of individual devices and battery storage units, helping to prevent the national power grid from becoming overstressed at peak use times.[191] Additionally, the Department's history of working with technology that has the potential to be both incredibly beneficial and incredibly dangerous provides a good background for monitoring AI, which contributes both to the world.[192] However, the Department does not have the same background upholding civil and constitutional rights that could be in danger when decisions are increasingly made opaquely in the AI's "black box." Similarly, while the Department works with very sophisticated technology in a wide variety of ways, many of the regulatory issues facing AI will involve individual consumer issues, which is out of the Department's area of expertise.

● Department of Commerce: AI will absolutely be an agent of change in commerce, just as the internet and the birth of e-commerce have been. The mission statement of the Department of Commerce is "to create the conditions for economic growth and opportunity,"[193] and one of the most promising prospects for AI is the economic growth and opportunity it will foster. Placing AIRA in the Department therefore makes sense if the goal is to maximize that part of AI. That appears to be the thought behind the Fundamentally Understanding The Usability and

---

[188]   Cade Metz, "Google's Alphago Levels Up From Board Games to Power Grids," *Wired*, May 24, 2017, https://www.wired.com/2017/05/googles-alphago-levels-board-games-power-grids; Interview with Shawn Chandler, "Artificial Intelligence's Role in the Energy Sector," *IEEE Transmitter*, June 1, 2017, http://transmitter.ieee.org/artificial-intelligences-role-energy-sector/.

[189]   America COMPETES Act, Pub. L. 110-69, August 9, 2007.

[190]   ARPA-E History, Department of Energy, ARPA-E, https://arpa-e.energy.gov/?q=arpa-e-site-page/arpa-e-history, accessed on 6-20-17.

[191]   Kim Kyung-Hoon, "How AI Can Help Renewables Work Better for the Energy Grid," *Newsweek*, January 30, 2017, http://www.newsweek.com/uk-grid-artificial-intelligence-energy-supply-supply-and-demand-550148.

[192]   *See* Michael Lewis, "Why the Scariest Nuclear Threat May Be Coming From Inside the White House," *Vanity Fair*, September 2017, available at https://www.vanityfair.com/news/2017/07/department-of-energy-risks-michael-lewis.

[193]   About Commerce, Department of Commerce, https://www.commerce.gov/page/about-commerce, accessed on 6-25-17.

Realistic Evolution of Artificial Intelligence Act of 2017 (the FUTURE of AI Act), which would require the Secretary of Commerce to establish the Federal Advisory Committee on the Development and Implementation of Artificial Intelligence (the AI Advisory Committee).[194] The FUTURE of AI Act was introduced to Congress and the Senate in December 2017, but has been in committee since. Although the AI Advisory Committee would have no regulatory authority, in its advisory role it would study many of the issues related to AI that AIRA will seek to regulate (including the legal rights impacted by AI, privacy, and ensuring that regulations are kept current), advise the Commerce Secretary, and prepare a report to the Secretary and Congress.[195] However, establishing AIRA in the Department of Commerce potentially overemphasizes the ability of AI to encourage economic growth, minimizing the need for regulations that protect consumers to spread the benefits of AI widely. Additionally, the Department does not have a history of directing technology research funds or enforcing civil rights.

There are other departments that warrant consideration: Education, Health and Human Services, etc. However, these departments run into the same problems detailed above: although each department will encounter AI in a meaningful way that would benefit from regulation and governance, no one department is as broad as AI adoption will be. Instead, it makes the most sense for AIRA to be interdisciplinary, with leadership, staff, and resources drawn from all the departments mentioned above. When initially created, it could be given an interim status of independent agency, outside of the hierarchy of any department, with the understanding that after a set period of time—three years, five years, etc.—the leadership would have to promulgate (and likely negotiate) migration to a department. It is not unheard of for new federal bureaus or agencies to exist outside of their expected, final departments when they are first formed.[196] Ryan Calo has recommended a similar strategy when initially forming a federal robotics commission.[197]

That is not to say that AIRA could not be a permanent, independent agency. However, given the resistance that the Consumer Financial Protection Bureau generated when a similar approach was attempted,[198] I suspect that trying to elevate AIRA above the existing departments in the federal government will meet with similar objections. In light of the far reaching impact AI will have, it is not impossible to see AIRA as an independent, cabinet-level agency, at least eventually.

---

[194]   FUTURE of AI Act, *supra* note 5, at §4(a).
[195]   *Id.* at §4(b).
[196]   *See* Dodd-Frank Wall Street Reform and Consumer Protection Act, Pub. L. 111-203, Sec. 1066, August 9, 2007 (creating the Consumer Financial Protection Bureau under the interim auspices of the Treasury Department before it could formally join the United States Federal Reserve).
[197]   Calo, *supra* note 24, at 11 ("At least initially, then, a Federal Robotics Commission would be small and consist of a handful of engineers and others with backgrounds in mechanical and electrical engineering, computer science, and human-computer interaction, right alongside experts in law and policy. It would hardly be the first interdisciplinary agency: the FTC houses economists and technologists in addition to its many lawyers, for example.").
[198]   Rachel E. Barkow, *Insulating Agencies: Avoiding Capture Through Institutional Design*, 89 Tex. L. Rev. 15, 73 (2010).

It should also be noted that a precursor to AIRA was established in May 2016, with some of the functions and responsibilities that the FUTURE of AI Act seeks to grant to the AI Advisory Committee.[199] The National Science and Technology Council, Committee on Technology, issued the charter of the Subcommittee on Machine Learning and Artificial Intelligence, organizing the Subcommittee to:

> monitor the state of the art in machine learning and artificial intelligence (within the Federal Government, in the private sector, and internationally)... to coordinate the use of and foster the sharing of knowledge and best practices about machine learning and artificial intelligence by the Federal Government, and to consult in the development of Federal research and development priorities in machine learning and artificial intelligence.[200]

As a creation of the Federal Advisory Committee Act, the Subcommittee is not a regulatory or governing body, but can monitor the AI industry and make recommendations to the President.[201] However, the actions it advises on—research, development, coordination among the Federal government agencies, etc.—are the same that AIRA should be empowered to perform directly, as discussed in the next section.

B.   Regulating and Governing AI: Potential Functions of AIRA

Once AIRA is created by an act of Congress and established in the federal hierarchy, the agency can begin the important task of regulating and governing AI. What does that look like? To call back to the introductory section of this chapter, how should the agency regulate AI?

Because there are essentially no AI-specific regulations, the discussions in the industry, in academia, and in policy circles are hypothetical and promotional. Various vested individuals are making their best pitches for what AI regulation should and should not look like. Additionally, other proposals are so related that they can be used as proxies for what AI regulation should attempt, such as Ryan Calo's consideration of a Federal Robotics Commission.[202] It is not uncommon for these proposals to suggest the creation of an agency that is specific to the technology, but to also suggest that its authority should be limited, at least at first.[203]

The position this chapter takes is that the AIRA organic legislation should give it broad powers and authority to govern and regulate the AI industry, and the leadership of AIRA

---

[199]   *See* FUTURE of AI Act, *supra* note 5, at §4(b). Were the FUTURE of AI Act to become law, there would actually be a lot of overlap between the functions of the Subcommittee on Machine Learning and Artificial Intelligence and the AI Advisory Committee, however the FUTURE of AI Act would permit the AI Advisory Committee to both (a) expand the scope of its research and advice as it considers appropriate in light of its obligation to understand and prepare for the ongoing development of AI, and (b) recommend legislation and regulations to Congress to govern AI.

[200]   Charter of the Subcommittee on Machine Learning and Artificial Intelligence, Committee on Technology, National Science and Technology Council, May 5, 2016, available at https://www.whitehouse.gov/sites/whitehouse.gov/files/ostp/MLAI_Charter.pdf.

[201]   Federal Advisory Committee Act, Pub. L. 92-463, October 6, 1972.

[202]   Calo, *supra* note 24.

[203]   *See id.*; Scherer, *supra* note 4, at 356.

can then be judicious in its efforts to promote the technology while protecting consumers and communities from potential negative externalities that AI may produce. With that in mind, this section presents a broad summary of what AIRA should be authorized to do, based on AI-specific proposals, as well as other proposals that address robotics,[204] self-driving cars,[205] and other forms of emerging technology.[206]

In general, there are three categories of regulatory and governing actions that AIRA should have at its disposal: funding and promotion of AI research and development; coordination of regulation pertinent to AI from other federal departments and secondary regulatory sources like courts and states; and direct regulation of AI products, technology, and companies. Each category is discussed below. With regard to the first two categories, the discussions focus on the substantive result of AIRA's governance. Although some aspects of funding and promoting AI, as well as coordinating regulation among government entities, can be done through informal rule-making, i.e., "interpretive rules, general statements of policy, or rules of agency organization, procedure, or practice,"[207] much of that work will be done through standard rule-making. With regard to the final category, it generates the most opposition, as opponents worry that such regulations focusing on specific AI products, technologies or companies will stymie the full development of AI and prevent humans from reaping the full benefits of the technology.[208] As explained above, regulations do not automatically hurt innovation (or company profits) and the section below on the direct regulation of AI assumes such regulation should be an arrow in AIRA's quiver.

1. Funding and promotion of AI research and development

a.   Prioritizing AI research: Preparing for the Future of Artificial Intelligence recommends further actions to address coordinating and expanding the federal government's role in funding and promoting AI research and development, as the report identifies that as one of the key components of federal governance of AI.[209] As it notes:

> A strong case can be made in favor of increased Federal funding for research in AI. Analysis by the Council of Economic Advisers (CEA) indicates that beyond AI, across all research areas, doubling or tripling research investment would be a net positive for the Nation due to the resulting increase in economic growth. . .
>
> To be sure, the private sector will be the main engine of progress on AI. But as it stands, there is an underinvestment in basic research—research with long time horizons conducted for the

---

[204]   *E.g.*, Calo, *supra* note 24.

[205]   *E.g.*, *Robots Are People*, *supra* note 18, at 61–75; Bryant Walker Smith, *How Governments Can Promote Automated Driving*, New Mex. L. Rev. (forthcoming).

[206]   *E.g.*, Thierer, *supra* note 51.

[207]   5 U.S.C. §553(b)(3)(A), available http://www.gpo.gov, accessed on 7-31-17.

[208]   Mandel, *supra* note 74, at 75.

[209]   Preparing for the Future, *supra* note 1, at 1. Please note that the report does not address the formation of AIRA or a similar entity, assuming instead that the existing departments and agencies will continue to govern AI in a piecemeal fashion as AI applications become available in their respective industries, e.g., the FAA will govern autonomous technology in drones, NHTSA will govern autonomous vehicles on public roads, etc. This chapter proposes and assumes that a new federal agency will be created specifically for AI. Having said that, most of the AIRA functions discussed in this section could be performed by another or several other agencies.

sole purpose of furthering the scientific knowledge base—in part because it is difficult for a private firm to get a return from its investment in such research in a reasonable time frame. Basic research benefits everyone, but only the firm doing the research pays the costs. The literature suggests that, as a result, current levels of R&D spending are half to one-quarter of the level of R&D investment that would produce the optimal level of economic growth.[210]

Preparing for the Future goes on to list a number of recommendations for federal action, many of which AIRA would be in a good position to pursue, including:

> Recommendation 13: The Federal government should prioritize basic and long-term AI research . . .

> Recommendation 20: The U.S. Government should develop a government-wide strategy on international engagement related to AI, and develop a list of AI topical areas that need international engagement and monitoring. . .

> Recommendation 21: The U.S. Government should deepen its engagement with key international stakeholders, including foreign governments, international organizations, industry, academia, and others, to exchange information and facilitate collaboration on AI R&D.[211]

These action items echo similar functions that Ryan Calo proposes Congress assign a hypothetical Federal Robotics Commission:

- Channel federal dollars into basic robotics research in an attempt to solve the still considerable technical challenges this technology presents.
- Attract highly skilled technologists who might be reticent to work for the government otherwise.
- Convene domestic and international stakeholders from industry, government, academia, and NGOs to discuss the impact of robotics and artificial intelligence on society.[212]

Rather than spread these functions widely across the federal government, as *Preparing for the Future* assumes, AI regulation should be based on Calo's model, with one agency empowered to pursue the action items and coordinate efforts by the myriad of federal agencies that regulate different fields and topics that AI will affect. *Preparing for the Future* and Calo's Federal Robotics Commission example collectively lay out three tasks for AIRA as it seeks to promote and fund AI research: funding for basic research; funding for long-term research; and coordinating efforts among AI stakeholders, foreign and domestic, in government, academia, and the private sector.

FUNDING BASIC RESEARCH   What is meant by "basic research" in *Preparing for the Future* Calo uses a similar term, "basic robotics research," which he considers necessary to overcome basic technical challenges in robotics.[213] Another way to look at it is as research that has no obvious commercial or clinical value.[214] It seems the federal government has

---

[210]   *Id.* at 25 (citations omitted).
[211]   *Id.* at 41–42.
[212]   Calo, *supra* note 24, at 11–12.
[213]   *Id.* at 11.
[214]   Margaret Foster Riley, *Federal Funding and the Institutional Evolution of Federal Regulation of Biomedical Research*, 5 Harv. L. and Pol. Rev., 265, 267 (2011).

something similar in mind, as it considers basic AI research necessary for "furthering the scientific knowledge base."[215] It is particularly important that AIRA make this investment because basic research "benefits everyone, but only the firm doing the research pays the costs," which explains why current levels of R&D spending are a fraction of what is necessary in the field.[216]

While researching and drafting *Preparing for the Future*, the National Science and Technology Council also prepared *The National Artificial Intelligence Research and Development Strategic Plan*, which "establishes a set of objectives for Federally-funded AI research. . . The ultimate goal of this research is to produce new AI knowledge and technologies that provide a range of positive benefits to society, while minimizing the negative impacts."[217] The *Strategic Plan* echoes Calo regarding basic research, as it emphasizes the need for research and development funds to overcome "difficult technical challenges [that] remain in all subfields of AI."[218] If those are the types of challenges and research that AIRA will focus its funding grants on, the question then becomes what regulations will govern those grants and investments.

Looking at the regulations other federal agencies use to govern their grants is helpful. For example, the National Institutes of Health must provide public notice of funding opportunities, establish a merit review process for any competitive grant applications, and assess the risks posed by each applicant.[219] Additionally, the regulations require that the NIH establish uniform application forms.[220] Similarly, the Department of Energy has regulations governing the Department's award and administration of grants that govern what types of energy projects may be funded, the eligibility of each applicant, and grant application requirements.[221] AIRA will need similar regulations to govern how companies, private labs, and educational institutions petition the agency for funds into basic research. Part III.B.1.b, Regulations to Govern the Funding and Promotion of AI, discusses this further.

FUNDING LONG-TERM RESEARCH   AIRA will also need to establish a plan or strategy to govern its funding of long-term research. As the *Strategic Plan* states, one of the federal government's primary objectives in funding AI research is seeking out "new AI knowledge and technologies that provide a range of positive benefits to society, while minimizing the negative impacts."[222] In pursuing these objectives, the *Strategic Plan* lays out multiple strategies, including long-term investment in AI research:

> While an important component of long-term research is incremental research with predictable outcomes, long-term sustained investments in high-risk research can lead to high-reward payoffs.

---

[215]   Preparing for the Future, *supra* note 1, at 25.
[216]   *Id.*
[217]   National Science and Technology Council, "The National Artificial Intelligence Research and Development Strategic Plan," *Executive Office of the President* (October 2016), 3, https://www.nitrd.gov/PUBS/national_ai_rd_strategic_plan.pdf ("Strategic Plan").
[218]   *Id.* at 11.
[219]   45 C.F.R. Part 75, Subpart C, available http://www.gpo.gov, accessed on 8-16-17.
[220]   45 C.F.R. § 75.206 available http://www.gpo.gov, accessed on 8-16-17.
[221]   10 C.F.R. § 605.12 available http://www.gpo.gov, accessed on 8-16-17.
[222]   Strategic Plan, *supra* note 217, at 25.

These payoffs can be seen in 5 years, 10 years, or more. A recent National Research Council report emphasizes the critical role of Federal investments in long-term research, noting "the long, unpredictable incubation period—requiring steady work and funding—between initial exploration and commercial deployment." It further notes that "the time from first concept to successful market is often measured in decades".[223]

Fortunately, models for federal agencies to invest in this type of long-term research exist: DARPA and ARPA-E. In the same way that DARPA and ARPA-E have invested in the research and development of potentially transformational national security and energy technologies, AIRA should oversee an AI version, ARPA-AI. ARPA-AI would seek out and invest in transformational AI projects that have the potential to "radically improve U.S. economic prosperity, national security, and environmental well being."[224] It should focus on "transformational change instead of incremental changes."[225] *Preparing for the Future* calls specifically for this type of sub-agency, noting that "Federal agencies should explore the potential to create DARPA-like organizations to support high-risk, high-reward AI research and its application."[226] In establishing a "DARPA-like" organization, AIRA will need to establish regulations and general terms and conditions governing research and development similar to DARPA's regulations and policies.[227]

COORDINATING EFFORTS AMONG AI STAKEHOLDERS   Both the federal reports and Calo's article emphasize the importance of the federal government in coordinating communication, research efforts, and cooperation among interested parties in the public, private, foreign, and domestic spheres. Calo notes the role Washington can play in recruiting skilled researchers to government work and gathering experts from other sectors (private, foreign, etc.) to contribute to the research, development, and regulation of AI.[228] *Preparing for the Future* recommends that the federal government pay close attention to what constitutes milestones in AI research (that is, research developments that could represent or foreshadow significant leaps in AI capabilities) and monitor AI research conducted by private companies and in other countries for milestones.[229] In fact, *Preparing for the Future* makes recommendations that are fairly aggressive in keeping track of international AI developments, stating that the United States should "develop a government-wide strategy on international engagement related to AI, and develop a list of AI topical areas that need international engagement and monitoring" and "deepen its engagement with key international stakeholders, including foreign governments, international organizations, industry, academia, and others, to exchange information and facilitate collaboration on AI R&D."[230] Additionally, the *Strategic Plan* specifically

---

[223]   *Id.* at 16–17.

[224]   *See* About, Department of Energy, ARPA-E, https://arpa-e.energy.gov/?q=arpa-e-site-page/about, accessed on 6-20-17.

[225]   *See* Mission, Department of Defense, Defense Advanced Research Projects Agency, https://www.darpa.mil/about-us/mission, accessed on 7-18-17.

[226]   Preparing for the Future, *supra* note 1, at 16.

[227]   *See* Department of Defense, "R&D General Terms and Conditions," July 2016, available at file:///C:/Users/jfw/Downloads/DoD-Research-Terms-Conditions-JUL2016%20(1).pdf.

[228]   Calo, *supra* note 24, at 12.

[229]   Preparing for the Future, *supra* note 1, at 24, 41.

[230]   *Id.* at 35.

points to researchers in law and ethics who are considering how AI can align with ethical, legal and social principles, saying that the federal government should reach out to these researchers so that scientific AI research incorporates their perspectives.[231]

AIRA will be well situated to perform these coordinating tasks, and federal agencies in general have ample experience coordinating research among private and academic actors.[232] Congress will need to give proper authority to AIRA in its organic statute, and that statute should instruct AIRA to coordinate research with an eye toward using AI to create maximum value for society at large, encouraging helpful innovation and fostering corporate and civic responsibility for addressing key issues raised by AI.[233] Similarly, the statute should empower AIRA to advise the State Department regarding foreign policy in this space. The federal reports referred to in this chapter make clear that the United States government expects AI to be an increasingly important topic in international agreements, and ensuring that America's foreign policy regarding AI is vetted by the centralized agency coordinating the country's domestic AI policies will be extremely important.[234]

Another facet of coordinating efforts by AI stakeholders is working to create the necessary standards industry- and world-wide that will help to distribute the benefits of AI widely. This should include best practices regarding data transparency, accountability, privacy, security, software engineering, and usability, among others.[235] The *Strategic Plan* makes federal involvement in the creation of these standards a priority, noting that "Government leadership and coordination is needed to drive standardization and encourage its widespread use in government, academia, and industry. The AI community—made up of users, industry, academia, and government—must be energized to participate in developing standards and benchmark programs."[236] AIRA will need to be authorized to coordinate the creation of AI industry standards, but in many ways that is more of a technicality. The United States as a matter of law and policy is already committed to working with industry and related organizations to create standards in ALL industries, not just AI.[237] In creating AIRA, it would be only natural for Congress to extend that obligation to the new agency as it applies to standards for AI.

b. *Regulations to govern the funding and promotion of AI*   The mechanics of funding research are unlikely to change for AI from what we see today, at least not without changes to underlying regulations and statutes that govern how many applicants request

---

[231]   Strategic Plan, *supra* note 217, at 26.
[232]   *See* United States Department of Agriculture, "Research, Education, and Economics – Action Plan," February 2012, available at https://www.usda.gov/sites/default/files/documents/usda-ree-science-action-plan.pdf; Francis S. Collins, "NIH Basics," *Science* (Volume 337, August 3, 2012), 503.
[233]   100 Year Study, *supra* note 2, at 42.
[234]   *See* Preparing for the Future, *supra* note 1, at 35.
[235]   100 Year Study, *supra* note 2, at 10, 27; Strategic Plan, *supra* note 217, at 32–33.
[236]   Strategic Plan, *supra* note 217, at 34.
[237]   National Technology Transfer and Advancement Act of 1995, Pub. L. 104-113, May 7, 1996; United States Office of Management and Budget, Cir. No. A-119 Revised, February 10, 1998, available at https://www.whitehouse.gov/omb/circulars_a119, accessed on 7-17-17; United States Standards Strategy Committee, *United States Standards Strategy* (American National Standards Institute, 2015).

federal funds for research. For example, most applicants for federal funding must comply with the Federal Funding Accountability and Transparency Act, which imposes reporting requirements on recipients of federal funds in order to improve transparency and accountability.[238] The Uniform Administrative Requirements, Cost Principles and Audit Requirements for Federal Awards[239] is also likely to govern any research contacts or grants, as it governs all Federal awards to non-Federal entities.[240] The intention is for these regulations to be uniform across all federal agencies, but exceptions are permitted.[241] For example, the Department of Health and Human Services has its own parallel regulations governing awards to non-federal entities, which govern a host of federal entities under its jurisdiction, including the Center for Disease Control and Prevention.[242]

It is possible that the AIDA will permit AIRA to create a similar parallel regulatory framework for the research funding that AIRA is authorized to govern, which applicants will be required to satisfy, in addition to the general requirements contained in 2 C.F.R. Part 200. These could govern mandatory disclosure of certain intellectual property that is developed from the funding, public notice as to the purpose of the research and what it hopes to accomplish, and required partnership with other organizations conducting AI research. Similarly, different rules could be created for AI that potentially poses a threat to human safety, either intentionally or through malfunction, such as AI that is intended for the national defense or medical care. Looking to other fields is also illustrative for strategies that AIRA could use to direct AI research and expand its influence. For example, federal regulations governing biomedical research contain special requirements when the research involves human subjects, such as informed consent from the participants and provisions to protect the confidentiality of each individual's data.[243] Similar requirements make sense for the funding of AI research as well, particularly with regard to data, which is vitally important for many forms of AI, including AI that does not pose a physical risk to people.

In addition to protecting the safety of all participants in AI studies, regulations that govern funding of AI research by AIRA can also be used to promote other goals in the AI field while also promoting innovation and significant leaps in the technology. Carefully crafted regulations attaching conditions to research investment from AIRA could require internal and external accountability, transparency, and professionalization.[244] The goal of all the research funded and promotion done by AIRA is to "democratically foster the development and equitable sharing of AI's benefits."[245]

---

[238]   Federal Funding Accountability and Transparency Act of 2006, Pub. L. 109-282, September 26, 2006.

[239]   2 C.F.R. Part 200, available http://www.gpo.gov, accessed on 8-16-17.

[240]   2 C.F.R. §200.100, available http://www.gpo.gov, accessed on 8-19-17.

[241]   2 C.F.R. §200.102, available http://www.gpo.gov, accessed on 8-19-17.

[242]   45 C.F.R. Part 75, available http://www.gpo.gov, accessed on 8-1-17; Federal Regulations and Policies, Center for Disease Control and Prevention, https://www.cdc.gov/grants/federalregulationspolicies/index.html, accessed on 7-16-17.

[243]   45 C.F.R. §46.111, available http://www.gpo.gov, accessed on 8-16-17. For a thorough discussion of the regulation of biomedical research, *see* Riley, *supra* note 214. Although Riley does not address AI in the article it is not hard to draw parallels between biomedical research regulation and AI research regulation.

[244]   100 Year Study, *supra* note 2, at 49.

[245]   *Id.*

2. Coordination of regulation pertinent to AI from other federal departments and secondary regulatory sources

a. Governing AI consistently As Calo points out, there is danger in multiple federal agencies and secondary regulatory sources promulgating regulations and decisions governing AI without a central party organizing those efforts. "This activity is interesting and important, but hopelessly piecemeal: agencies, states, courts, and others are not in conversation with one another. Even the same government entities fail to draw links across similar technologies. . . . Much is lost in this patchwork approach."[246] The federal government is aware of this problem, as *Preparing for the Future* was written specifically with an eye toward fostering interagency coordination.[247] At least 16 separate agencies govern sectors of the economy related to AI technologies,[248] and creating a consistent approach to AI among those agencies and centralizing the governance they provide will be a key responsibility of AIRA. None of this represents a novel function for a new federal agency. The Department of Homeland Security was created by combining 22 existing agencies into one cabinet level department in 2002, basically absorbing all of the agencies that were responsible for preventing terrorist attacks on the United States in order to make a (one hopes) better, more comprehensive national strategy.[249]

The challenge only becomes more pronounced when you incorporate the other levels of government that will regulate and govern AI, as demonstrated by federal and state efforts to govern early types of AI like autonomous vehicles and autonomous drones. The tension between federal governance and governing performed by the states is already on display in the development of laws and regulations governing autonomous vehicles (as discussed in another chapter). States have begun to consider and enact legislation and accompanying regulations governing autonomous vehicles.[250] At the same time, the federal Department of Transportation ("DOT") published the *Federal Automated Vehicles Policy* in September 2016, which outlines both the federal government's and state governments' proposed role in regulating autonomous vehicles:

> DOT and the Federal Government are responsible for regulating motor vehicles and motor equipment, and the States are responsible for regulating the human driver and most other aspects of motor vehicle operation. As motor vehicle equipment increasingly performs 'driving' tasks, DOT's exercise of its authority and responsibility to regulate the safety of such equipment will increasingly encompass tasks similar to 'licensing' of the non-human 'driver'.[251]

Essentially, the *Automated Vehicles Policy* proposes that the federal government will exercise increasing governance over vehicles on public roads at the expense of the states' right to govern those vehicles. As you might imagine, this is going to lead to some disagreements and

---

[246] Calo, *supra* note 24, at 4.
[247] Preparing for the Future, *supra* note 1, Introduction.
[248] 100 Year Study, *supra* note 2, at 10.
[249] History, Department of Homeland Security, https://www.dhs.gov/history, accessed on 8-20-17; Creation of the Department of Homeland Security, Department of Homeland Security, https://www.dhs.gov/creation-department-homeland-security, accessed on 8-20-17.
[250] *E.g.*, Florida House Bill 1207 (Ch. 2012-111); California Acts, Chapter 570 of 2012, 2011-2012; Nevada Assembly Bill No. 511, 2012.
[251] Federal AV Policy, *supra* note 21, at 38.

conflict over key issues in autonomous vehicles, and this demonstrates the need for AIRA to avoid similar conflict between federal and state regulation of AI. For example, although the *Automated Vehicles Policy* states that the Department "strongly encourages States to allow DOT alone to regulate the performance of HAV [highly automated vehicle] technology and vehicles,"[252] California has been aggressive in proposing regulations that govern the design and performance of autonomous vehicles, including requiring steering wheels and pedals, at least initially.[253] Although any federal law will control over any state law, it is unclear how states will respond to federal autonomous vehicle policy without the force of statute or regulation. It seems unlikely that states will stop trying to govern autonomous vehicles, but without proper guidance from the federal government—and, likely, a properly authorized federal agency—those laws and regulations will continue to be in piecemeal conflict with federal laws and regulations. AIRA should provide that guidance in the AI sector.

The relationship between the FAA and states concerning drones is helpful when considering how AIRA can work to coordinate state and federal regulation. The FAA is clearly the agency authorized by Congress to govern drones,[254] and it is concerned that state and local governments will try to regulate drones in the airspaces above them.[255] "If one or two municipalities enacted ordinances regulating UAS [unmanned aircraft systems] in the navigable airspace and a significant number of municipalities followed suit, fractionalized control of the navigable airspace could result," the FAA notes in a 2015 fact sheet.[256]

> In turn, this 'patchwork quilt' of differing restrictions could severely limit the flexibility of FAA in controlling the airspace and flight patterns, and ensuring safety and an efficient air traffic flow. A navigable airspace free from inconsistent state and local restrictions is essential to the maintenance of a safe and sound air transportation system.[257]

The 2015 fact sheet identifies this issue in the hopes that it can provide states with guidance regarding where FAA activity already governs drones. Although it would be more helpful to provide a comprehensive list of governing actions that states are prohibited from making or a list of areas where states should consult with the FAA before proceeding with a particular regulation, the fact sheet unfortunately only provides two examples of state and local laws where such consultation is recommended:

- Operational UAS restrictions on flight altitude, flight paths; operational bans; any regulation of the navigable airspace. For example – a city ordinance banning anyone from operating

---

[252]   *Id.* at 37.
[253]   Andrew J. Hawkins, "California is warming up to self-driving cars without a human driver," *The Verge*, March 10, 2017, https://www.theverge.com/2017/3/10/14881640/california-dmv-self-driving-car-rules-human-driver; Andrew J. Hawkins, "Google strikes back against California's proposal to limit self-driving cars," *The Verge*, December 17, 2015, https://www.theverge.com/2015/12/17/10447394/google-self-driving-car-California-DMV-rule.
[254]   2012 FAA Modernization and Reform Act, Pub. L. 112-95, §333, February 12, 2012.
[255]   Office of the Chief Counsel, Federal Aviation Administration, "State and Local Regulation of Unmanned Aircraft Systems (UAS) Fact Sheet," December 17, 2015, p. 2, available at https://www.faa.gov/uas/resources/uas_regulations_policy/media/uas_fact_sheet_final.pdf ("FAA Fact Sheet").
[256]   *Id.*
[257]   *Id.*

UAS within the city limits, within the airspace of the city, or within certain distances of landmarks. . . .
● Mandating equipment or training for UAS related to aviation safety such as geo-fencing would likely be preempted. Courts have found that state regulation pertaining to mandatory training and equipment requirements related to aviation safety is not consistent with the federal regulatory framework.[258]

The fact sheet provides somewhat more detailed information about what states and localities may regulate.

Laws traditionally related to state and local police power – including land use, zoning, privacy, trespass, and law enforcement operations – generally are not subject to federal regulation. . . Examples include:

● Requirement for police to obtain a warrant prior to using a UAS for surveillance.
● Specifying that UAS may not be used for voyeurism.
● Prohibitions on using UAS for hunting or fishing, or to interfere with or harass an individual who is hunting or fishing.
● Prohibitions on attaching firearms or similar weapons to UAS.[259]

Although this provides more guidance and coordination between federal regulation and state laws than in the autonomous vehicles field, it still leaves much to be desired. Many stakeholders in the drone industry support a clearer statement of preemption from Congress, and there have been attempts to comply.[260] In 2016, the Senate approved the Federal Aviation Administration Reauthorization Act of 2016, which included language that would have prohibited states from enacting any "law, regulation, or other provision having the force and effect of law relating to the design, manufacture, testing, licensing, registration, certification, operation, or maintenance of an unmanned aircraft system, including airspace, altitude, flight paths, equipment or technology requirements, purpose of operations, and pilot, operator, and observer qualifications, training, and certification."[261] This would have preempted the vast majority of existing state laws governing drones and prevented future attempts at the state and local levels.[262] However, the final version of the bill did not include the relevant language.[263]

Applying the recent lessons of autonomous vehicles and drones to AI, the AIDA will need to have clear language addressing AIRA's authorized role in overseeing the governance of AI—akin to the FAA's statutory mandate to govern the national airspace—and the extent to which state AI laws are preempted. With that language in hand, other agencies—those that are not absorbed into AIRA by the AIDA—will have Congressional direction to look to AIRA for AI policy and state legislatures will have no questions

---

[258] *Id.*, at 3.
[259] *Id.*
[260] Amanda Essex, *Taking Off – State Unmanned Aircraft Systems Policies* (National Conference of State Legislatures, 2016), 14.
[261] Federal Aviation Administration Reauthorization Act of 2016, H.R. 636, 114th Congress, §2512(a) (2016), available at https://www.congress.gov/bill/114th-congress/house-bill/636/text/eas#toc-id830859C9F9C24D3BA0B4AC14B2781107.
[262] Essex, *supra* note 260, at 14.
[263] FAA Extension, Safety and Security Act of 2016, Pub. L. 114-190, July 15, 2016.

regarding where their authority ends. The relevant preemption and coordination issues potentially include:

- Right to an Explanation versus Standards of Personal Data and Information Protection: Assuming the federal government asserts that it be the sole regulator of AI technology, akin to the position it has taken regarding autonomous vehicles, then AIRA may create a "Right to an Explanation," which would require that any AI program or device that relies on personal data to make a decision be able to provide the user with an explanation for that decision.[264] However, this would leave states free to retain their existing personal information laws, or pass new ones, that impose obligations on companies that collect or maintain personal information, personally identifiable information or personal data,[265] which would be consistent with permitting states to retain the authority to govern the "human" elements of autonomous vehicles. AIRA could establish minimum guidelines or suggestions for such personal information maintenance standards (e.g., the subject of personal data must give consent before a third party uses or sells that data), but states would be free to set the damages a successful claimant is owed, the procedure necessary to pursue a claim, etc.

- Legal Status of AI: There is the potential for conflict between AIRA and states as AIRA may promulgate regulations requiring that AI be treated as having a certain legal status in different situations. For example, intellectual property laws are currently drafted to provide copyright and patent protection for creative works and inventions that are created by people, not machines or programs. So a human being

---

[264]   John Frank Weaver, "Artificial Intelligence Owes You an Explanation," *Slate*, May 8, 2017, http://www.slate.com/articles/technology/future_tense/2017/05/why_artificial_intelligences_should_have_to_explain_their_actions.html ("AI Owes You an Explanation").

[265]   "Personal data" is different from "personal information" and "personally identifiable information," but the three are related terms. However, they are not uniformly defined in statute or regulation. For example, 48 states require that certain entities that maintain personal information or personally identifiable information (*e.g.*, name combined with social security number, drivers licenses, account number, etc.) notify effected parties of security breaches that result in the disclosure of that information, however these statutes do not address personal data. *E.g.*, Cal. Civ. Code §§ 1798.29, 1798.82; N.Y. Gen. Bus. Law §899-AA; Tex. Bus. & Com. Code §§521.002, 521.053, etc. Personal data is a much broader category that includes personal information, personally identifiable information, and personal healthcare information protected by the Health Insurance Portability and Accountability Act of 1996 (Pub. L. 104-191, August 21, 1996), but also information generated organically by phone usage, internet behavior, etc. In general, that type of organic data is not particularly well protected by any statute at the state or federal level, permitting third parties to collect, analyze, and sell data generated by users, so long as it does not contain personal information, personally identifiable information or other forms of protected data. Having said that, the Federal Trade Commission has published a staff report, *Self-Regulatory Principles for Online Behavior Advertising*, that attempts to establish best practices for parties that deal with personal data. In contrast, the European Union General Data Protection Regulation defines personal data broadly—"any information relating to an identified or identifiable natural person"—and attempts to require that data controllers and data processors provide to individuals certain information about and control over their personal data. Council Regulation (EU) 2016/679 of the European Parliament and of the Council of 27 April 2016 on the protection of natural persons with regard to the processing of personal data and on the free movement of such data, and repealing Directive 95/46/EC, 2016 O.J. (L119) 1 ("GDPR").

could own the copyright for the program that creates novels, but not for the novels themselves, as they were created by a machine. AIRA should address this loophole by either assigning a legal status to the AI under existing intellectual property laws or by creating a new legal status just for AI.[266] At the same time, state legislatures may decide to grant limited legal personhood to some forms of AI, endowing them with enforceable rights and responsibilities, similar to corporations, possibly through a new legal status or existing business entity laws.[267] It will be helpful for AIRA to either establish clear regulations, or produce a directive or fact sheet similar to the FAA fact sheet addressing drones and states' laws, explaining the situations in which AIRA will affirmatively govern the legal status of AI, states and other federal agencies may exercise their discretion to govern AI's legal status, and the legal status of AI is to be left unregulated.

- Standards of Technology versus Standards of Human Behavior: As discussed above regarding the right to an explanation and the regulation of personal data, AIRA will likely promulgate regulations addressing the standards for AI technology, including personal safety, data safety, internal processes for testing and reviewing AI, etc.[268] The intention will likely be for states to retain the right to govern the human interaction with AI, but as the federal autonomous vehicles policy explains, that will be a difficult line to draw, as the technology improves to remove the human elements subject to state regulation. AIRA will need to provide regular updates addressing where states have been preempted by federal action and where states can continue to regulate AI vigorously. For example, the line between a technological safety standard for AI in the construction field and a permitting or licensing requirement for the human worker overseeing the technology may soon be a moving target, and all parties—the government agencies, the workers, the companies, and the consumers—will be better off if one agency in the federal government is monitoring the target and sharing information and instructions.

b. Regulating coordination among government entities   Although some of the coordinating and preemption can be done through policy statements and the practices and procedures of AIRA and its staff, some rule-making will be necessary. Even if Congress makes other federal agencies subordinate to AIRA regarding AI policy matters, thereby forcing those agencies to accept AIRA's coordination, regulations will still be needed to ensure that all federal agencies are using a coordinated AI policy.

Matthew Scherer, in one of the few scholarly considerations of AI regulation, describes an AIRA with limited authority, essentially confined to certification (described below) and policy-making. With regard to policy-making, he writes that

> Because AI is a highly technical field, legislators are not well equipped to determine what types of AI pose a public risk. They therefore should delegate the task of formulating substantive AI policies to an agency staffed by AI specialists with relevant academic and/or industry

---

[266]   For a more complete discussion of amending intellectual property laws to properly address AI, *see Robots Are People, supra* note 18, at 169–73.

[267]   For a comparison, *see Robots Are People, supra* note 18, and Bayern, *supra* note 6.

[268]   *See* 100 Year Study, *supra* note 2, at 10–11.

experience. . . AIDA would give the [AIRA] the authority to specify or clarify most aspects of the AI regulatory framework.[269]

Within AIRA, Scherer's "Justice League of AI Experts" could be established as a committee within the agency. With appropriate authorizing language in the AIDA, AIRA would be empowered to establish a committee composed of appropriate experts from industry, academia, and government agencies that experiment with AI, e.g., Department of Defense, NASA, Department of Energy, etc., and that committee would be responsible for coordinating AI public policy throughout all levels of government. AIRA would need to establish rules and regulations governing: (1) how members of the committee are chosen, how long they serve, etc.; (2) how the committee operates to interpret AIRA's policy statements, practices, procedures, regulations, and other actions to form a consistent policy that other government entities are entrusted with following, including states, whose laws governing AI may be preempted by the policies approved by the committee; and (3) adjudication.

The final function could become relevant in a few scenarios. For example, the committee establishes a policy requiring that personal data used by AI be treated as "personal information" when states and other federal agencies enforce data breach laws and other laws addressing personal information. The committee cites the purpose of the AIDA, saying that this policy decision is necessary to limit the negative impacts of AI relying on personal data and to ensure that AI's benefits are widely spread. A citizen believes that her state is not implementing the policy, and wants AIRA to compel the state to follow the policy decision. Another example: the committee makes a policy decision that speech generated by AI (e.g., Twitterbots, etc.) is not protected by the First Amendment.[270] A company that specializes in autonomously written works for clients objects.

In both examples, the private company aggrieved by the decisions of the committee and the citizen who believes that the state is not complying with the decision of the committee may want to file a complaint. AIRA may want to establish rules providing for and governing adjudication of disputes like these, permitting private parties, other federal agencies, and states to lodge complaints. Such adjudicatory hearings could be conducted by the committee or by an entirely separate adjudicative body established by AIRA under its authority from the AIDA.

c.   Direct regulation of AI products, technology, and companies   Of the three major proposed functions of AIRA, enacting actual, direct regulations to govern AI products, technology, and companies is probably the most controversial, particularly when the advised timeframe is as soon as possible. But even in questioning the need for new regulations in the near future, the federal government—and numerous other sources—have identified likely regulatory needs in the AI sector. The following subsections address particular types of regulations that would govern AI products, technologies, and companies

---

[269]   Scherer, *supra* note 4, at 395.
[270]   For a discussion of why such a ruling would be unconstitutional, *see* John Frank Weaver, "When the next Twitterbot loses it, remember that its tweets are protected," *Ars Technica*, April 23, 2016, https://arstechnica.com/tech-policy/2016/04/when-the-next-twitterbot-loses-it-remember-tha t-its-tweets-are-protected/ ("Twitterbot Loses It").

directly, rather than the funding of AI research or the coordination of federal and state policies addressing AI that the companies must navigate.

In regulating these specific areas, there is a certain danger in trying to regulate too specifically. Rules that focus on a particular type of AI may become obsolete shortly after implementation, given the speed of innovation and development. Rather, AIRA should focus on broad legal mandates addressing the strategies and areas of concern below, so that regardless of how AI develops and what AI-enabled products are released, the regulations will remain effective and relevant, helping to ensure that the benefits of AI are spread broadly and fairly.[271] The following regulatory areas and strategies are derived from government reports, academics, and other technologies.

CERTIFICATION OF AI   Scherer proposes a limited regulatory function for AIRA partly because AI is difficult to regulate. "The traditional methods of regulation – such as product licensing, research and development oversight, and tort liability – seem particularly unsuited to manage the risks associated with intelligent and autonomous machines."[272] The limited regulatory function he advocates is the certification of AI, in which AIRA reviews and certifies (or not) the safety of AI application based on standards created by AIRA, such as risk of causing physical harm, goal alignment, and mechanisms for ensuring human control.[273] Scherer goes on to explain how the certification process would work:

> Companies seeking certification of an AI system would have to disclose all technical information regarding the product, including: (1) the complete source code; (2) a description of all hardware/software environments in which the AI has been tested; (3) how the AI performed in the testing environments; and (4) any other information pertinent to the safety of the AI. After disclosure, [AIRA] would conduct its own in-house testing to assess the safety of the AI program.[274]

Once AIRA certifies an AI, the manufacturers, designers, and sellers are subject to limited tort liability. In contrast, the parties behind uncertified products would be subject to strict joint and several liability for their AI products.

Possibly anticipating objections from "permissionless innovation" advocates, Scherer emphasizes that the certification process is not a gatekeeping process that potentially prohibits AI applications from entering the market. "Instead of giving the new agency FDA-like powers to ban products it believes to be unsafe," the certification process incentivizes AI developers to address safety innovation in order to benefit from the reduced liability standard certification offers.[275]

The regulations could also address another type of certification: professional certification. What happens when AI is able to perform the functions of a medical doctor or a lawyer? Does the AI need a professional license? Regulations could create a certification process for AI that performs tasks that would require certification or licensure if done by

---

[271]   *See* 100 Year Study, *supra* note 2, at 48–49.
[272]   Scherer, *supra* note 4, at 356.
[273]   *Id.* at 397.
[274]   *Id.*
[275]   *Id.* at 393.

a human being.[276] States are already pursuing this strategy, as autonomous vehicle laws in several states, including California, Nevada, and Florida, provide a certification process to permit those vehicles on the public roads, akin to driver licenses for human drivers.[277]

SAFETY   There seems to be little question that we will need regulations to ensure that human beings are safe when they use or test AI. As discussed above, AIRA should consider rules that govern funding decisions for AI that is in a position to physically harm people, either intentionally (defensive systems) or unintentionally (AI used in a hospital or in healthcare that malfunctions or performs its medical functions inappropriately), such as requiring certain research protocols when funds are given to those projects. More generally, AIRA could create regulations that require research projects to implement certain safety precautions when they receive funding from AIRA and are conducting research involving human test subjects.

When AIRA looks to directly regulate the safety of AI products and applications themselves, and not merely the research AIRA funds, it is important that AIRA remembers to focus on rules that seek outcomes and broad principles, rather than specific technologies.[278] For example, when AI applications are in their infancy, it is likely that the only people who will possess the expertise necessary to make risk and safety assessments are the ones doing the research to create the applications.[279] It may be impossible for AIRA to properly anticipate all of the safety needs as new applications become available. Sticking to the strategy of promulgating regulations that address outcomes, AIRA might consider requiring that any company introducing an AI-enabled product that is in a novel field or where there are no pre-existing safety requirements file with AIRA a document stating the reasonable safety expectations that consumers can have for the product. As other companies enter that field with competing or complementary products, they file similar documents. Collectively, those documents become the safety standards that AIRA and courts will enforce in that new field. The companies can update those documents as they refine the product. This acts as essentially a form of rolling, mandatory self-governing safety regulations for every new field of AI until the field is mature enough that AIRA creates its own technology-specific regulations for the field. The goal in this approach is to simultaneously preliminarily regulate the safety of the AI products but also to identify potential risks and provide greater transparency of those risks for the eventual final regulations.[280]

A potential problem with that approach is that it arguably provides too much control to the AI developers themselves. Stricter controls on the safety of AI products might be implemented by lowering the burden of proof for claimants to pursue a claim of negligence against an AI manufacturer seeking damages, but not a restraining order to prevent the product from being sold to consumers. This puts AI developers on notice that their products need to be reasonable to a reasonable person. Once each new form

---

[276]   100 Year Study, *supra* note 2, at 47.
[277]   Admittedly, this represents a technology-specific regulatory strategy that cannot be implemented immediately, which conflicts with the timeline and strategy for AI regulation in this chapter.
[278]   *See* 100 Year Study, *supra* note 2, at 48 49; Mandel, *supra* note 74, at 76–77.
[279]   Scherer, *supra* note 4, at 384.
[280]   Mandel, *supra* note 74, at 78.

of AI is sufficiently mature to warrant technology-specific safety regulations, the lower standard is replaced by the standards in the regulations. Of course, this proposed system of addressing the safety of novel AI could be accused of incentivizing AI developers to avoid new forms of AI by opening them to increased liability, dampening innovation.

In any event, as the preceding paragraphs make clear, nothing in this section should be read as limiting AIRA's authority to regulate the safety of specific technologies, as the FAA already does with autonomous drones and NHTSA is seeking to do with autonomous vehicles.[281] However, in recognizing that over-regulation of specific technologies is not advisable before the technologies are more developed,[282] the regulations that AIRA should seek to implement on the timetable advised in this chapter, i.e., as soon as possible, should adhere to the recommendation in the federal reports and focus on outcomes and not technologies.

PRIVACY Moving from physical safety to data safety is a natural segue.[283] Personal data is the fuel that propels artificial intelligence.[284] That makes personal data particularly valuable and particularly vulnerable to security breaches. However, while the European Union regards data privacy as a fundamental right,[285] the United States addresses it haphazardly, when it addresses it at all. In light of data privacy's importance to AI, AIRA will need to be authorized by the AIDA to regulate it.

The EU takes data privacy so seriously that it has already begun to address what obligations AI-enabled products have to consumers when they use consumers' data. In April 2016, the European Parliament and the Council of the European Union adopted the General Data Protection Regulation, which was the result of four years of behind the scenes work and represents major changes to how the EU regulates data privacy.[286] It is a sprawling document; there are 173 non-binding perambulatory paragraphs before you even get to the regulation itself. Among the new requirements it introduces are several directly in response to artificial intelligence and autonomous technology using personal data. For example, under Article 13, Paragraph 2(f), when your data is collected, the company collecting it must let you know of the existence of "automated decision-making." That section also requires that when an individual is subjected to automated decision-making, that individual has the right to "meaningful information about the logic involved."[287]

In other words, the AI owes you an explanation every time it uses your personal data to make an automated decision about you. But as Bryce Goodman from the Oxford Internet

---

[281] Calo, *supra* note 24, at 6–9.

[282] Mandel, *supra* note 74, at 75–92.

[283] Moore, *supra* note 38 ("This focus on the science of safety and trust must also include engagement on issues of privacy and the ethics of AI deployment.").

[284] *Big data, artificial intelligence, machine learning and data protection* (v. 2.1), United Kingdom Information Commissioner's Office, p. 3, available at https://ico.org.uk/media/for-organisations/documents/2013559/big-data-ai-ml-and-data-protection.pdf, accessed on 8-18-17.

[285] Article 8, European Convention of Human Rights; Article 7, European Charter of Fundamental Rights.

[286] GDPR Portal: Site Overview, European Union General Data Protection Regulation, http://www.eugdpr.org/, accessed on 5-14-17.

[287] GDPR, *supra* note 265, at Art. 13.

Institute and Seth Flaxman from the University of Oxford explain, this requirement prompts the question "What does that mean?" They worry that algorithmic decision-making could result in a "black box society," where there is little to no transparency for decisions that are increasingly automated, with no direct human control or input.[288] They suggest that "any adequate explanation would, at a minimum, provide an account of how input features relate to predictions, allowing one to answer questions such as: Is the model more or less likely to recommend a loan if the applicant is a minority? Which features play the largest role in prediction?"[289]

AIRA could implement a similar regulatory system early in its existence. Requiring that an AI system be able to explain decisions it makes using your personal data is a technology-neutral requirement. However, it is uncertain if complying with such a requirement is possible given current technical limitations.[290] Other concerns return to business and innovation worries. Thomas Burri, an assistant professor of international and European law at the University of St. Gallen notes "If the first thing you need to consider when designing a new program is the explanation, does that stifle innovation and development?"[291] He goes on to say, "Some decisions are hard to explain, even with full access to the algorithm. Trade secrets and intellectual property could be at stake."[292] But the danger to the consumers is potentially huge. As more and more AI-enabled devices are introduced to the market, devices that replicate a portion of our decision-making, we cede an increasing number of decisions to AI. We should have a right to know how those decisions are made, particularly as they start to implicate more important decisions, like who gets a loan.

AIRA could also provide guidance and order for the entire life of our personal data, from generation and collection to destruction, similar to what the General Data Protection Regulation seeks to do.[293] Currently, the vast majority of the statutory and regulatory attention is devoted to the backend of that life cycle, the release of personal data. Under those statutes, companies must notify affected people when their personal information is revealed due to a security breach, and there can be civil or criminal penalties for failing to disclose such breaches in the statutory time period.[294] But AIRA should go further, placing requirements on companies to disclose what personal data they collect and providing consumers with some rights to monitor and even control their data after collection (such as requiring consent before personal data can be transferred or sold).[295] Although regulations of this sort would impact more companies, applications, and

---

[288]   Goodman & Flaxman, *supra* note 173, at 6.

[289]   *Id.*

[290]   *Id.*

[291]   AI Owes You an Explanation, *supra* note 264.

[292]   *Id.*

[293]   For a more detailed discussion of the life cycle of personal data, *see* John Frank Weaver, *Artificial Intelligence and Governing the Life Cycle of Personal Data*, U. Rich. J. of L. and Tech. (2018–19) (forthcoming).

[294]   *E.g.*, Cal. Civ. Code §§ 1798.29, 1798.82; N.Y. Gen. Bus. Law §899-AA; Tex. Bus. and Com. Code §§521.002, 521.053, etc. In fairness, these statutes do not truly address personal data, as they really are limited to personal information. *See* note 259 above.

[295]   Oren Etzioni, "How to Regulate Artificial Intelligence," *New York Times*, September 1, 2017, https://www.nytimes.com/2017/09/01/opinion/artificial-intelligence-regulations-rules.html.

devices than only AI-enabled ones, AIRA can justify the rules by pointing to personal data's importance to AI devices. To regulate the devices, you have to regulate the data, regardless of its source.

NOTICE TO USERS   There is a growing concern that human users will become confused by the AI that they interact with and will mistake it for an actual person. In 2016, an AI chatbot based on IBM's Watson platform served as a teaching assistant for an online course at Georgia Tech, where some students thought it was a real person.[296] Similarly, in the 2016 presidential election, AI chatbots interacted as "people" with human users online.[297] In its report, *Ethically Aligned Design*, the Standards Association of the Institute of Electrical and Electronics Engineers worries that "Without laws preventing [AI] from simulating humans for purposes like deception and coercion, and enforcing [AI] to clearly identify as such, mistaken identity could also reasonably be expected."[298] Oren Etzioni, the chief executive of the Allen Institute for Artificial Intelligence, suggests that any AI must clearly disclose that it is not human.[299] AIRA may want to consider a pointed regulation to that effect in order to avoid confusion and potential problems related to this issue.

INTELLECTUAL PROPERTY   AI developers have been particularly adept at creating AI programs that produce original creative works. AI programs and robots have created original music,[300] visual art,[301] and news articles.[302] However, American intellectual property law has not adjusted appropriately. Copyrights and patents are only available for works and inventions made by human beings; anything created by something other than a human being enters into the public domain, with no protection from human beings who want to copy and use it.[303] This reality was driven home by the "monkey selfie" case in 2014, in which the United States Copyright Office ruled that a selfie taken by a monkey, using equipment set up and arranged by a photographer for the purpose of a monkey taking a selfie with that equipment, does not enjoy copyright protection.[304] The *Compendium*

---

[296]   Hillary Lipko, "Meet Jill Watson: Georgia Tech's first AI teaching assistant," *Georgia Tech Professional Education Blog*, November 10, 2016, https://pe.gatech.edu/blog/meet-jill-watson-georgia-techs-first-ai-teaching-assistant.

[297]   John Markoff, "Automated Pro-Trump Bots Overwhelmed Pro-Clinton Messages, Researchers Say," *New York Times*, November 17, 2016, https://www.nytimes.com/2016/11/18/technology/automated-pro-trump-bots-overwhelmed-pro-clinton-messages-researchers-say.html.

[298]   IEEE Standards Association, *Ethically Aligned Design* (version 2, December 2017), 258, available at http://standards.ieee.org/develop/indconn/ec/ead_v2.pdf.

[299]   Etzioni, *supra* note 295.

[300]   Tim Adams, "David Cope: 'You Pushed the Button and Out Came Hundreds and Thousands of Sonatas,'" *The Guardian*, July 10, 2010, http://www.guardian.co.uk/technology/2010/jul/11/david-cope-computer-composer.

[301]   Harold Cohen, "The Further Exploits of Aaron, Painter," *Stanford Humanities Review* 4:2 (July 1995): 141–58.

[302]   Buster Brown, "Robo-Journos Put Jobs In Jeopardy," *The Huffington Post*, July 19, 2012, http://www.huffingtonpost.com/buster-brown/robo-journalism_b_1683564.html.

[303]   *Robots Are People, supra* note 18, at 169–70.

[304]   David Kravets, "Monkey's selfie cannot be copyrighted, US regulators say," *Ars Technica*, August 21, 2014, https://arstechnica.com/tech-policy/2014/08/monkeys-selfie-cannot-be-copyrighted-us-regulators-say/.

of the U.S. Copyright Office Practices, published by the United States Copyright Office, was revised to address this situation. "To qualify as a work of 'authorship'; a work must be created by a human being," the *Compendium* states, listing a "photograph taken by a monkey" as an example.[305] Although neither the United States Copyright Office nor any courts have addressed works produced by AI, there is no reason to believe that AI exists as an exception to the rule articulated in the *Compendium*, absent changes to federal law.[306]

AIRA can remedy this situation by introducing regulations that establish limited intellectual property protection for works created by AI, assuming the AIDA grants sufficient authorization to AIRA. The original constitutional purpose of intellectual property laws was "to promote the Progress of Science and useful Arts."[307] A human software designer can be sufficiently inspired to promote the progress of science without receiving the full copyright protection afforded to human-created works: 70 years after their deaths or, for works done for hire, the earlier of 95 years after publication or 120 from the year of creation. The developer of an AI program that can write 1000 novels in a morning has little need to protect each novel for such long periods of time in order to be appropriately compensated for the work it took to write the program's code. AIRA can properly incentivize creative AI and provide sufficient financial reward to developers by granting copyright protection for a much shorter period of time.

For example, regulations could provide only ten years of copyright protection for works created by AI.[308] In other words, the owner of AI that creates original music, art, novels, etc. can receive copyright protection for ten years for each work created by that AI. Novels written by the novel-making AI referred to in the previous paragraph would each be protected by copyright law for ten years from its publication, and the developer—either the individual or the company—would have a monopoly over the contents of those novels for that period of time. Thereafter, the works would pass into the public domain, and anyone could use them in other books, music, movies, etc. Alternatively, AIRA could create a different regulatory system of protecting intellectual property created by AI, so long as the AIDA grants it the proper authorization.

LIMITED LEGAL PERSONHOOD   Granting legal rights to non-people is an increasingly controversial topic in light of recent disputes concerning the right of corporations to religious freedom[309] and to make political expenditures under the First Amendment.[310] But there is an active scholastic conversation debating the merits and forms of legal personhood, limited or otherwise, for AI.[311] As AI devices and programs assume more

---

[305]   *Compendium of U.S. Copyright Office Practices* (3rd ed.), United States Copyright Office, December 22, 2014.

[306]   John Frank Weaver, "How Artificial Intelligence Might Monetize Fan Fiction," *Slate*, December 10, 2013, http://www.slate.com/blogs/future_tense/2013/12/10/ai_intellectual_property_rights_how_artificial_intelligence_might_monetize.html.

[307]   U.S. Constitution, Art. I, Sec. 8, Cl. 8.

[308]   *Robots Are People, supra* note 18, at 183.

[309]   *Burwell v. Hobby Lobby Stores, Inc.*, 134 S. Ct. 2751 (2014).

[310]   *Citizens United v. Federal Election Commission*, 558 U.S. 310 (2010).

[311]   Compare Bayern, *supra* note 6, and John Frank Weaver, "Robots Are People, Too," *Slate*, July 27, 2014, http://www.slate.com/articles/technology/future_tense/2014/07/ai_drones_ethics_

responsibilities for consumers, AIRA should ensure that courts and other legal actors treat the AI and the consumer as intended by the developer of the AI and the consumer. For example, when your personal shopper AI enters into a contract with a vendor, you want to ensure that the AI has sufficient legal rights to do so, akin to the right a corporation has to enter into contracts.[312] Other rights and obligations potentially include the obligation to carry insurance, the right to own intellectual property, the obligation of liability, and the right to be the guardian of a minor.[313] Such an extension of limited legal personhood could be done through a regulatory framework permitting AI developers to register their AI with AIRA to be recognized as a legal person in certain situations prescribed by the regulations, similar to what states' corporation and limited liability company acts permit for business entities. However, as AIRA carves out specific rights and obligations for AI, it must also ensure that in making those carve-outs the agency does not accidentally exempt AI from laws that should apply to it as much as the laws apply to any human developer, operator, owner, etc.[314]

Assuming AIRA is inclined to regulate limited rights and obligations of AI, another strategy has been explored by Shawn Bayern, a professor at Florida State University College of Law:

> Consider, then, the following use of an LLC: (1) an individual member creates a member-managed LLC, filing the appropriate paperwork with the state; (2) the individual (along, possibly, with the LLC, which is controlled by the sole member) enters into an operating agreement governing the conduct of the LLC; (3) the operating agreement specifies that the LLC will take actions as determined by an autonomous system, specifying terms or conditions as appropriate to achieve the autonomous system's legal goals; (4) the sole member withdraws from the LLC, leaving the LLC without any members. The result is potentially a perpetual LLC – a new legal person – that requires no ongoing intervention from any preexisting legal person in order to maintain its status.[315]

This potentially opens a more narrow avenue for AI to operate as a legal entity, with little regulatory or statutory oversight targeting the AI or autonomous systems. AIRA may want to promulgate rules that would formalize and govern this option, or consider rules that would prohibit such an entity organization.

FREE SPEECH   As AI creates more original works and introduces statements into public discourse, AIRA will need to address to what extent these works and statements qualify as speech that is protected by the First Amendment. Essentially, there are four broad models for AIRA to impose on AI speech:

---

and_laws_if_corporations_are_people_so_are_robots.html ("Robots Are People Article"). *See also* Curtis E.A. Karnow, *Liability for Distributed Artificial Intelligences*, 11 Berkeley Tech. L. J. 147 (1996); Jean-Francois Lerouge, *The Use of Electronic Agents Questioned Under Contractual Law: Suggested Solutions on a European American Level*, 18 J. Marshall J. Computer & Info. L. 403 (2000); Emily Weitzenboeck, "Electronic Agents and the Formation of Contracts," International Journal of Law and Information Technology 9:3 (2001), 204–34.

[312]   *Trustees of Dartmouth College v. Woodward*, 17 U.S. 518 (1819).
[313]   Robots Are People Article, *supra* note 311.
[314]   Etzioni, *supra* note 295.
[315]   Bayern, *supra* note 6, at 101 (references omitted).

- Speech produced by AI is not speech that is protected by the First Amendment. Under this model, the federal government and states can regulate and prohibit speech from AI however they want, with none of the constitutional limits that have historically applied to speech produced by human beings.
- AI is only capable of producing speech based on code from a human programmer, therefore speech from AI is merely another form of human speech. This interpretation might look appealing now, in light of autonomous Twitter accounts, "accounts that are programmed to look like people, to act like people, and to change the conversation, to make topics trend," a description that suggests the accounts engage in speech that directly reflects the speech or thoughts of their creators.[316] However, AI speech has already grown beyond merely parroting the ideas and priorities of code writers. "Tay," an AI system created by Microsoft's Technology and Research and Bing teams that operated a Twitter account, was intended to tweet as a normal teenage girl and learn from the other Twitter accounts that interacted with it. Unfortunately, based on those interactions, Tay became racist and anti-Semitic, forcing Microsoft to deactivate the account less than 24 hours after first going online.[317] That was hardly the intent of the programmers, and creating a regulatory model to address AI speech that is based on a false premise will only lead to poor regulations and decisions.
- Speech produced by AI is only protected by the First Amendment when that speech represents the speech of its human programmer; speech from AI is not protected by the First Amendment otherwise. This approach attempts to address the problems in assuming that speech from AI is another form of speech from human programmers. The problem, though, is that it relies on a fundamental question—"Is this speech representative of what the programmer would say?"—that is frequently impossible to answer. Autonomous Twitter accounts are frequently anonymous. How can a regulatory agency, state government, or court answer what the programmer thought when the programmer is anonymous? This model could make regulating AI speech unmanageable.
- Speech produced by AI is speech that is protected by the First Amendment. A literal reading of the text of the First Amendment suggests this is the correct model to apply to AI speech, as the amendment simply states that the government "shall make no law . . . abridging the freedom of speech, or of the press."[318] Nothing there specifically suggests freedom of speech is limited to people. Under this interpretation, all the constitutional protections that human speech enjoys in the United States would also apply to AI speech.[319]

---

[316]   Cadwalladr, *supra* note 98.
[317]   Hope Reese, "Why Microsoft's 'Tay' AI bot went wrong," *TechRepublic*, March 24, 2016, http://www.techrepublic.com/article/why-microsofts-tay-ai-bot-went-wrong/.
[318]   U.S. Constitution, Amend. I.
[319]   Twitterbot Loses It, *supra* note 270; John Frank Weaver, "Robots Deserve First Amendment Protection," *Slate*, May 15, 2014, http://www.slate.com/blogs/future_tense/2014/05/15/robots_ai_deserve_first_amendment_protection.html.

AIRA could preempt a number of state statutes and court rulings limiting AI speech before they see the light of day by establishing regulations that require AI speech to be treated like human speech for First Amendment purposes.

C. Keeping AI Regulations Current

Before concluding this section addressing federal regulation of AI, it is useful to consider a problem that numerous scholars, journalists, and politicians have noted: technology develops so fast, regulations that are current one year may be obsolete or counterproductive the next. AIRA should consider regulations that address this problem, by broadly regulating outcomes so as to avoid technology-specific regulations, as articulated throughout Section III.B above, and by enacting regulations that address the administrative problems that make the regulation of emerging technology difficult. The latter is the focus of this section.

Updating regulations quickly is troublesome because of the Administrative Procedures Act (APA), which Congress passed in 1946.[320] The APA requires, among other things, that federal agencies publish proposed rules in the Federal Register,[321] hold hearings to consider rules,[322] and permit comments and responses before any proposed rule can become effective.[323] These requirements are time consuming and potentially make it nearly impossible to regulate AI innovations in a timely fashion. As an example of how the APA has mired another agency in rule-making process, when the FDA looked into establishing a rule governing the percentage of peanut butter that is actually composed of peanuts—87.5 percent versus 90 percent—it generated 7,700 pages of comments for the FDA to review.[324] Imagine how many comments would result from a proposed rule governing data privacy on Facebook.

One suggestion to expedite rule-making for AI is to either amend the APA such that regulations affecting AI could be passed faster or permit AIRA to pass regulations without as much process. As the technology develops, this would also permit further revisions to make sure that the existing regulations do not become outdated and detrimental to AI's development. AIRA would still publish notice of rules affecting AI in the Federal Register, but the notices would state that new rules are effective, not proposed. Although this would not provide the same safeguards against regulatory overreach, inappropriate rules will receive publicity and can be overturned just as quickly as they are passed.[325]

Another suggestion focuses on ensuring that technology-specific regulations do not become burdensome to subsequent technological innovations. Based on Moore's Law, it recommends AIRA include in all new rules that regulate specific technologies a sunset provision, terminating the rule after 18 months.[326] If the rule is effective and there have

---

[320] 5 U.S.C. §500 *et. seq*, available http://www.gpo.gov, accessed 7-31-17.
[321] 5 U.S.C. §553(b), available http://www.gpo.gov, accessed 7-31-17.
[322] 5 U.S.C. §556, available http://www.gpo.gov, accessed 7-31-17.
[323] 5 U.S.C. § 553(c), available http://www.gpo.gov, accessed 7-31-17.
[324] Martin Shapiro, "A Golden Anniversary? The Administrative Procedures Act of 1946," *Regulation* 19:3 (1996): 3.
[325] *Robots Are People, supra* note 18, at 185.
[326] *See* Thierer, *supra* note 51, at 110–11.

not been new technological developments that would cause the rule to unduly burden innovation, AIRA can reenact the rule—possibly using the APA shortcut introduced above in order to expedite the reenactment.

IV.   SECONDARY REGULATION OF AI—STATES AND COURTS

While the majority of AI regulation will occur at the federal level, states and courts will also perform certain, more limited regulatory functions, which this chapter has alluded to in previous sections. Because secondary regulatory activity will be based in large part on what the federal government does to regulate AI, this section offers only a broad overview of how states and courts can be expected to address AI.

A.   State Regulation of AI

The AIDA and AIRA will preempt any state efforts to regulate AI, limiting state regulations to areas where federal statutes and regulations have specifically permitted state action or to areas where federal law is silent. In the absence of the AIDA and AIRA—or similar federal actions—the nation will be a patchwork of different rules that govern AI with little to no consistency. Complying with these myriad of regulations will likely be more difficult for AI developers than complying with unified regulations coming from AIRA.

The federal government has already begun to provide direction to states regarding the distribution of regulatory authority governing some technologies that utilize AI, particularly autonomous vehicles and drones. As described in Section III.B.2.a above, the *Federal Automated Vehicles Policy* anticipates that the federal government will regulate the autonomous technology in self-driving cars, while states will regulate the behavior of individual car owners and drivers, among other location-specific issues.[327] Under the federal government's model, NHTSA

> would regulate motor vehicles and motor vehicle equipment (including hardware and software that perform functions formerly performed by a human driver) and the States would continue to regulate divers, vehicle registration, traffic laws, regulations and enforcement, insurance, and liability.[328]

The FAA has also provided guidance to states regarding what regulatory activity is preempted regarding drones. Although the FAA is less inclined to share jurisdiction over the national airspace than the NHTSA is to share jurisdiction over the nation's roads, the FAA acknowledges that states retain the authority to regulate drones to the extent that such regulations are related to traditional state and local police power, like land use, zoning, privacy, trespass, and law enforcement operations.[329] For the most part, the FAA's regulation of drones does not implicate the regulation of AI, but the Advisory Circular

---

[327]   Federal AV Policy, *supra* note 21, at 38, 44.
[328]   *Id.* at 38–39.
[329]   FAA Fact Sheet, *supra* note 255, at 3.

addressing small UAS, i.e., drones, requires that any autonomous operations, which rely on varying degrees of AI, must comply with all the provisions of the Circular that govern drones under direct human control.[330] This includes maintaining the human operator's line of sight with the drone. Any state regulations of drones will need to be consistent with that requirement.

Extrapolating state regulation of AI from those limited examples is difficult, but combining them with AIRA's regulation of AI above is helpful. For example, AIRA may create a regulatory system addressing AI and data privacy generally, but states could address specific technologies first through regulation; AIRA requires that AI-enabled devices be able to give users an explanation for any decision made using their data, but a state may specifically require that AI personal assistants provide the top five factors the AI used in making any recommendation. This maintains the states' traditional role as the laboratories of democracy, as AIRA can review technology-specific regulations and determine which, if any, are the best to adopt on a national scale.

It is also important to note that some of the regulatory suggestions for AIRA in the previous section address areas that are traditionally governed by states, like granting limited legal personhood to AI. For the most part, when individuals form companies they do so pursuant to state laws governing corporations and limited liability companies. The limited legal rights and obligations of those entities are granted by state statute. So while AIRA could have the right to create a regulatory framework for granting limited legal personhood to AI, it is also possible AIRA will have to provide guidelines for that process to states and let them determine how and if they want it done.

If we assume that, like autonomous vehicle regulations, states will retain the right to regulate place-specific regulation of AI, it is possible that states will emphasize the warnings needed in any physical space where physical AI is operating, akin to mandatory road work and construction signs. In the zoning context, the governance of physical spaces could be interpreted to grant states and local governments the right to prohibit or at least require heightened permitting for certain kinds of AI operating in sensitive parts of town. AI-enabled maintenance systems may be prohibited from residential zones, for example.

It is also possible AIRA would reserve for the states the authority to regulate human users of AI. If a human overseer is a requirement for a type of AI—either through industry practice or federal regulation—the states can provide reasonable requirements for the licensing of those individuals.[331] Even where AIRA has provided some liability protections for AI developers who obtain certification, states would still be free to govern liability for AI products beyond that. State legislatures could even create a fiduciary obligation for AI developers that market and operate in their states, akin to the legal requirements placed on doctors and lawyers in each state.[332]

The suggestions above are largely dependent on the extent to which AIRA and the AIDA respect the areas of law where states have traditionally exercised greater authority. In some cases, AIRA might permit states to retain their jurisdiction by specifically

---

[330]   AC No. 107-02, *supra* note 20.

[331]   *Robots Are People*, *supra* note 18, at 182.

[332]   John Frank Weaver, "Should AI Makers Be Legally Responsible for Emotionally Manipulating Customers?," *Slate*, January 20, 2014, http://www.slate.com/blogs/future_tense/2014/01/20/should_ ai_makers_be_legally_responsible_for_emotionally_manipulating_customers.html.

identifying areas—like privacy standards and tort matters—where AIRA will provide some guidance for the sake of some national consensus, but ultimately the matters will be decided by the states. In other areas—like the granting of limited legal personhood—AIRA and AIDA may decide the importance of uniform treatment nationwide is more important than maintaining traditional areas of state influence.

States may push back against the restrictions imposed by AIRA if the legislatures and governors there believe those restrictions upset the balance of federalism created by the Constitution. In that event, the courts will step in and decide.

B.　Regulation and Governance of AI by the Courts

The state and federal court systems will function as a form of indirect regulation, governing AI on case-by-case basis.[333] The nature of that governing will be reactive, not proactive as with AIRA and state legislatures, and will largely be determined by the individual cases and fact patterns that come before the courts. For that reason, it is difficult to speculate about the particulars of any potential regulation coming from courts. However, this section looks briefly at three functions the courts can perform while governing and regulating: resolution of torts disputes, resolution of federalism disputes, and resolution of search and seizure disputes.

1.　Resolution of tort disputes

Claims of product liability, negligence, and other traditional tort claims involving AI products and their manufacturers and developers are inevitable in the courts. Decisions in such cases, although they will be highly fact specific, will influence future behavior primarily through the deterrent effect of liability.[334] One potential cause for concern is that the pace of change in the AI sector may make this deterrent effect stunt investment in unfamiliar but useful new technologies, as courts already tend to give greater consideration to the risks of new technology and less to its benefits.[335] That tendency poses a serious challenge for courts as they attempt to regulate AI, a sector that will be defined in many ways by its frequent challenges to pre-existing conceptions of what machines and programs can and should do. It also fundamentally limits the types of industry expectations courts can form on their own.[336] These limitations should not be ignored, but courts in the tort system are well-positioned to act as fact-finders, which is incredibly important to each individual case, but also has the potential to reveal important information that AIRA and state legislatures can rely on—how decisions are made within the AI industry, how AI functions in certain scenarios, etc.—when regulating AI.[337]

---

[333]　Scherer, *supra* note 4, at 388.
[334]　*Id.*
[335]　Peter Huber, *Safety and the Second Best: The Hazards of Public Risk Management in the Courts*, 85 Colum. L. Rev. 277, 320–29 (1985).
[336]　Scherer, *supra* note 4, at 390.
[337]　*Id.* at 389–90.

2. Resolution of federalism disputes

When AIRA attempts to regulate AI in a way that infringes on the traditional authority of the states, states will turn to the courts to resolve any disagreements those regulations create. For example, states typically have wide authority to govern privacy and trespass within their borders, but AIRA is likely to attempt to regulate AI use of personal data in such a way that it creates a new standard of privacy for individuals while also possibly creating a new lower standard of trespass for AI developers, e.g., AIRA enacts a regulation that rules an AI developer has trespassed against the property of an individual when the relevant AI uses that individual's personal data without proper authorization. A state that wants to distinguish itself as an attractive home for AI developers may want to set a lower standard for data privacy and a higher standard for trespass could challenge AIRA rule in court, arguing that AIRA's actions violate the Tenth Amendment.[338]

3. Resolution of search and seizure disputes

The courts have already begun laying the groundwork for search and seizure issues raised by numerous forms of AI. Cases dealing with the search and seizure of cell phones under the Fourth Amendment have implications for autonomous vehicles.[339] In recent decisions, the Supreme Court has addressed privacy concerns that will be fundamental to Fourth Amendment cases involving AI and personal data. In her concurring opinion in *United States v. Jones*, 132 S. Ct. 945, (2012), which considered Fourth Amendment limitations on law enforcement's use of GPS tracking devices, the Justice Sotomayor wondered about

> the existence of a reasonable societal expectation of privacy in the sum of one's public movements. I would ask whether people reasonably expect that their movements will be recorded and aggregated in a manner that enables the Government to ascertain, more or less at will, their political and religious beliefs, sexual habits, and so on.[340]

She goes on to note that

> it may be necessary to reconsider the premise that an individual has no reasonable expectation of privacy in information voluntarily disclosed to third parties. . . This approach is ill suited to the digital age, in which people reveal a great deal of information about themselves to third parties in the course of carrying out mundane tasks.[341]

She could be describing the privacy concerns inherent in ubiquitous AI. When an increasing number of devices use AI to record, analyze and make decisions based on the totality of our actions and behavior, how should the Constitution be interpreted to ensure that it continues to protect individuals' privacy?

---

[338] U.S. Constitution, Amend. X ("The powers not delegated to the United States by the Constitution, nor prohibited by it to the States, are reserved to the States respectively, or to the people.")

[339] John Frank Weaver, "The Fourth Amendment and Driverless Cars," *Slate*, July 27, 2015, http://www.slate.com/articles/technology/future_tense/2015/07/fourth_amendment_and_autonomous_vehicles_should_cops_need_a_warrant_for.html.

[340] *United States v. Jones*, 565 U.S. 400, 416 (2012) (Justice Sotomayor concurrence).

[341] *Id.* at 417 (Justice Sotomayor concurrence).

It should be noted that this concern is expressed by justices on both sides of the ideological spectrum. In a concurring opinion in the same case, Justice Alito wrote

> In the pre-computer age, the greatest protections of privacy were neither constitutional nor statutory, but practical. Traditional surveillance for any extended period of time was difficult and costly and therefore rarely undertaken. . . Devices like the [GPS] used in the present case, however, make long-term monitoring relatively easy and cheap.[342]

He could have written a nearly identical description of the privacy concerns raised by AI. Courts will be called on early and often to regulate how law enforcement may access AI for evidence in any investigation.

V. CONCLUSION

The fundamental questions of AI regulation in the near future are "When?" and "How?" This chapter attempts to both advocate for certain answers to those questions—that is, "As soon as possible" and "As expansively as is reasonable," respectively—while also providing analysis of the totality of issues affecting them. As much or more so than any of the other chapters in this book, the regulation of AI exists only in the notebooks of scholars, industry leaders, and regulators. There are essentially no statutes or regulations that directly address the key problem AI introduces to our regulatory systems, that AI will make decisions that have only been made by human beings to this point. In making those decisions, AI will rely on enormous personal data, a commodity that the American legal and political systems have considered unworthy of protection to this point. All of this will occur through technologies that we do not fully understand, raising the risk that we outsource too many functions to a "black box" where decisions are made and we stop trying to understand why.

The important thing to remember for all stakeholders involved—legislators, regulators, sector leaders, etc.—is that the point of regulating AI is to ensure that the benefits are as widely spread as possible while the negative externalities are minimized to the greatest extent possible. In a nutshell, this means promoting the safety and economic benefits to people in all socio-economic demographics. The numerous federal reports that have been released all agree on this point, and, in fact, the best regulation of any field does this already. Hopefully, the regulatory system created by AIRA will join those ranks.

---

[342]   *Id.* at 429 (Justice Alito concurrence).

SOURCES

List of Cases, Statutes, Legislation, Regulations, Federal Policy Papers, and Advisories Referenced in Regulation of AI Chapter

Constitutional provisions
U.S. Constitution, Art. I, Sec. 8, Cl. 8
U.S. Constitution, Art. VI, cl. 2
U.S. Constitution, Amend. I
U.S. Constitution, Amend. X

Federal statutes and legislation
5 U.S.C. §500 *et. seq.*
5 U.S.C. §553(b)(3)(A)
5 U.S.C. §553(b)
5 U.S.C. § 553(c)
5 U.S.C. §556
47 U.S.C. §230(b)(2)(3)
47 U.S.C. §230(c)(1)
47 U.S.C. §230(A)(3)
47 U.S.C. §332(a)
47 U.S.C. §332(c)(7)
2012 FAA Modernization and Reform Act, Pub. L. 112-95, §333, February 12, 2012
America COMPETES Act, Pub. L. 110-69, August 9, 2007
An act to protect the public health by providing the Food and Drug Administration with certain authority to regulate tobacco products, to amend title 5, United States Code, to make certain modifications in the Thrift Savings Plan, the Civil Service Retirement System, and the Federal Employees' Retirement System, and for other purposes, Pub. L. 111-31, June 22, 2009
Dodd-Frank Wall Street Reform and Consumer Protection Act,, Pub. L. 111-203, Sec. 1066, August 9, 2007
FAA Extension, Safety and Security Act of 2016, Pub. L. 114-190, July 15, 2016
Federal Advisory Committee Act, Pub. L. 92-463, October 6, 1972
Federal Aviation Act of 1958, Pub. L. 85-726, August 23, 1958
Federal Communications Commission Act of 1934, Pub. L. 73-416, June 19, 1934
Federal Food, Drug, and Cosmetic Act of 1938, Pub. L. 75-717, June 25, 1938
Federal Funding Accountability and Transparency Act of 2006, Pub. L. 109-282, September 26, 2006
Health Insurance Portability and Accountability Act of 1996, Pub. L. 104-191, August 21, 1996
Highway Safety Act of 1970, Pub. L. No. 91-605, Sec. 202(b)(1)
Medical Device Amendments of 1976, Pub. L. No. 94-295, 90 Stat. 539
National Technology Transfer and Advancement Act of 1995, Pub. L. 104-113, May 7, 1996
Federal Aviation Administration Reauthorization Act of 2016, H.R. 636, 114th Congress, §2512(a) (2016)

Federal regulations
2 C.F.R. Part 200
2 C.F.R. §200.100
2 C.F.R. §200.102
10 C.F.R. § 605.12
45 C.F.R. §46.111
45 C.F.R. Part 75
45 C.F.R. Part 75, Subpart C
45 C.F.R. § 75.206

State statutes and legislation
Cal. Civ. Code § 1798.29
Cal. Civ. Code § 1798.82
N.Y. Gen. Bus. Law §899-AA
Tex. Bus. & Com. Code §521.002
Tex. Bus. & Com. Code §521.053

Florida House Bill 1207 (Ch. 2012-111)
California Acts, Chapter 570 of 2012, 2011-2012
Nevada Assembly Bill No. 511, 2012

Court cases

Batzel v. Smith, 333 F.3d 1018, 1027 (9th Cir. 2003)
BBK Tobacco & Foods, LLP v. FDA, 672 F.Supp.2d 969 (D. Ariz. 2009)
Blumenthal v. Smith, 992 F. Supp. 44, 52 (D.D.C. 1998)
Burwell v. Hobby Lobby Stores, Inc., 134 S. Ct. 2751 (2014)
Citizens United v. Federal Election Commission, 558 U.S. 310 (2010)
GTE Midwest, Inc. v. FCC, 233 F.3d 341, 344 (6th Cir. 2000)
Lorillard Inc. v. FDA, 56 F.Supp.3d 37 (D.D.C. 2014)
Omnipoint Holdings, Inc. v. City of Cranston, 586 F.3d 38, 51 (1st Cir. 2009)
Schneider v. Amazon.com, Inc., 108 Wn. App. 454, 463 (2001)
Trustees of Dartmouth College v. Woodward, 17 U.S. 518 (1819)
United States v. Jones, 565 U.S. 400, 416 (2012)
United States v. Phillip Morris USA, Inc., 449 F.Supp.2d 1 (D.D.C. 2006)
Wyeth v. Levine, 555. U.S. 555, 557 (2009)
Zeran v. America Online, 129 F.3d 327, 331 (4th Cir. 1997)

Federal policy papers, circulars, and other relevant governing documents

Artificial Intelligence, Automation, and the Economy, Executive Office of the President, available at https://www.whitehouse.gov/sites/whitehouse.gov/files/images/EMBARGOED%20AI%20Economy%20Report.pdf.

Federal Automated Vehicles Policy, National Highway Traffic Safety Administration, available at https://www.transportation.gov/sites/dot.gov/files/docs/AV%20policy%20guidance%20PDF.pdf.

The National Artificial Intelligence Research and Development Strategic Plan, National Science and Technology Council, available at https://www.nitrd.gov/PUBS/national_ai_rd_strategic_plan.pdf.

Preparing for the Future of Artificial Intelligence, National Science and Technology Council, available at https://obamawhitehouse.archives.gov/sites/default/files/whitehouse_files/microsites/ostp/NSTC/preparing_for_the_future_of_ai.pdf.

Request for Information on the Future of Artificial Intelligence, White House Office of Science and Technology Policy, *Public Responses*, September 1, 2016, available at https://obamawhitehouse.archives.gov/sites/default/files/microsites/ostp/OSTP-AI-RFI-Responses.pdf.

Charter of the Subcommittee on Machine Learning and Artificial Intelligence, Committee on Technology, National Science and Technology Council, May 5, 2016, available at https://www.whitehouse.gov/sites/whitehouse.gov/files/ostp/MLAI_Charter.pdf.

Federal Aviation Administration, Small Unmanned Aircraft Systems, Advisory Circular, No. 107-02, June 21, 2016. https://www.faa.gov/uas/media/AC_107-2_AFS-1_Signed.pdf.

"A Framework for Global Electronic Commerce," *Executive Office of the President*, July 1997, available at https://clintonwhitehouse4.archives.gov/WH/New/Commerce/read.html.

Occupational Safety & Health Administration, Directive No. STD 01-12-002, "Guidelines for Robotics Safety" (1987).

United States Office of Management & Budget, Cir. No. A-119 Revised, February 10, 1998, available at https://www.whitehouse.gov/omb/circulars_a119.

8. Legal personhood in the age of artificially intelligent robots

Robert van den Hoven van Genderen[1]

I. INTRODUCTION

> The acceleration of technological progress has been the central feature of this century. [W]e are on the edge of change comparable to the rise of human life on Earth. The precise cause of this change is the imminent creation by technology of entities with greater [intellectual capacity] than human intelligence.[2]

This chapter raises several important questions which relate to the legal implications of the expanding role of artificial intelligence (AI) in society and specifically whether AI entities with increasing intelligence and autonomy should receive personhood rights. To start, given the increased usage of AI in society, will the developers of AI and robots be considered the new Oppenheimers of the twenty-first century ushering in an age of AI transforming society? And with increasing autonomy for AI entities, how should systems controlled by AI be regulated? Further, is the embedding of AI and robotics in our legal system a viable solution or will AI continue to gain in intelligence to the point where it will require its own legal rules and statutes? Additionally, in the future, will AI still be considered legal objects (as they currently are now) or will they be treated as legal subjects under the law (as are people and in some instances, corporations)? Further, will the development of autonomous systems create "killer robots" as warned against by several scholars and leaders of industry? And if that is a likely outcome, should we stop all further innovation in AI to save mankind from the existential threat that AI could pose? Also, consider a future in which autonomous AI is common in society, then would it be acceptable, or even possible, to integrate AI fully into our legal system, or will the regulation of AI impose insurmountable difficulties to legal institutions? Embedded within each of these timely questions are what rights and obligations AI entities should have attached to them as they get smarter and operate more autonomously from humans.

As always, as is the case with new technological developments, there are concerns that there may be negative outcomes associated with introducing (in this case) AI and robotics within society. Loss of jobs, loss of control of AI, and ultimately fear for the future of humankind are expressed concerns. As technology entrepreneur Elon Musk and others have warned: Artificial intelligence is the "biggest risk we face as a civilization" and "AI is

---

[1] This chapter is partially based on former articles, insights and presentations by the author and contributions by his students in the honours course "robotlaw" of the combined VU and UvA Universities. The terms "robot" and "AI entity" are used interchangeably throughout this chapter unless otherwise noted.

[2] Vernor Vinge, *The Coming Technological Singularity: How to Survive in the Post-Human Era*, https://edoras.sdsu.edu/~vinge/misc/singularity.html.

a rare case where we need to be proactive in regulation instead of reactive because if we're reactive in AI regulation it's too late". Thus, we can see that to some technologically savvy commentators, AI is viewed as a "fundamental risk to the existence of humanity in a way that car accidents, airplane crashes, faulty drugs, or bad food are not. The idea being that each of these latter concerns are primarily harmful to a set of individuals, but not harmful to society as a whole"[3] (which some argue could very well be the case with ubiquitous AI).

From a political perspective Vladimir Putin introduced the idea that AI could be the subject of a new "arms race" in a speech for the opening of the academic year in Russia when he stated: "Artificial intelligence is the future, not only for Russia, but for all humankind". "It comes with colossal opportunities, but also threats that are difficult to predict. Whoever becomes the leader in this sphere will become the ruler of the world." Though according to Putin, we do not have to be worried about Russia's developments in AI as he stated: "If we become leaders in this area, we will share this know-how with the entire world, the same way we share our nuclear technologies today."[4] This statement did not satisfy Elon Musk who tweeted the following on Putin's statement about AI: "Competition for AI superiority at the national level most likely will be the cause of WW3".

Leaving the power politics behind us, it is important to focus on the question of how or whether we should regulate the technological developments and smart entities associated with AI. This is a complex question because until now the law has been developed by humans, for humans, and—initially—to rule the relations between natural persons, and to some extent, artificial legal persons. But many aspects of society have changed during the development of the law, especially in the long journey from the Roman legal system to the laws and statutes of our current legal system. It has often been the case that new technologies that change society correspondingly result in a change to the existing legal framework although fairly slowly. As Lauren Burkhart noted in citing Clark A. Miller and Ira Bennett on "Reflexive governance", we better be prepared to have an open mind for changes in technology by "identifying not only what gadgets might arise but also how gadgets intersect in society, with one another, and with people, and how people identify with, make use of, oppose, reject, apply, transform, or ignore [technologies]."[5] In this context, AI seems far too powerful a technology to ignore.

Further, as Erik Tjong Tjin Tai, in his contribution to the preliminary reports of the Netherlands Association of Lawyers (NJV), stated: "If the facts too long deviate from the legal status and the right is unsustainable, the law must ultimately yield to the actual situation."[6] The question that follows then is whether we must adapt to technological

---

[3]   http://www.telegraph.co.uk/technology/2017/07/17/ai-biggest-risk-face-civilisation-elon-mus k-says/, accessed 11 October 2017.

[4]   https://www.theverge.com/2017/9/4/16251226/russia-ai-putin-rule-the-world, accessed 11 October 2017.

[5]   Lauren Burkhart citing Clark A. Miller and Ira Bennett, *Thinking Longer Term About Technology: Is There Value in Science Fiction-Inspired Approaches to Constructing Futures?*, 35 SCI. AND PUB. POL'Y 597, 602 (2008); *Lauren Burkhart on the Symposium—Governance of Emerging Technologies: Law, Policy, and Ethics*, American Bar Association (2016) 219–22 Jurimetrics, https:// www.americanbar.org/content/dam/aba/administrative/science_technology/2016/governance_in_e merging_technologies.authcheckdam.pdf, accessed 12 September 2017.

[6]   T.F.E. Tjong Tjin Tai, Private Law for Homo Digitalis, Use and Maintenance, Preliminary Advice for NVJ, 2016, p. 248.

innovations, in the sense of autonomous intelligence embedded in robotics and other AI systems, now or in the near future? And if we must adopt to emerging AI sooner than later, will an "AI robotized society" benefit from a certain degree of legal personality afforded intelligent robots? But this, among others, is a question of timing, should we wait until the momentum of the robotized society motivates a change to established law before we act, or should we act sooner to avoid potential negative outcomes? There is much precedence on the role of society regulating technology (patent law is one example), and already society has undergone changes based on the development of AI entities and the introduction of AI into many human institutions. For example, semi-autonomous cars are now part of the legal, moral, and social discussions of "highway law", even though the central subject in traffic law is still the human driver and his or her control over the vehicle. This gives rise to a question about rights that is not new, nor solely legal; but a question that was described previously by William Geldart in a discipline overruling way: "The question is at bottom not one on which law and legal conceptions have the only or the final voice: it is one which law shares with other sciences: political science, ethics, psychology, and metaphysics".[7] Thus, according to this view (developed in an earlier age of technology), a multidisciplinary approach is necessary when considering rights for AI. In an age of emerging systems equipped with AI, along with a discussion of law, it is of the utmost importance to also consider ethical values and fundamental rights issues in the possible decision to grant AI entities rights. Neil Richards and Jonathan King's statement in their paper on Big Data ethics reflects this view which could very well be applied to robotics controlled by AI:

> We are building a new digital society, and the values we build or fail to build into our new digital structures will define us. Critically, if we fail to balance the human values that we care about, like privacy, confidentiality, transparency, identity and free choice with the compelling uses of Big Data, our Big Data Society risks abandoning these values for the sake of innovation and expediency.[8]

II.   THE LEGAL ACTORS

I start this section of the chapter with some necessary terminology. For AI entities, in a discussion of legal personhood rights (which I also refer to as legal personality and legal subjectivity),[9] it is necessary to lay the groundwork for who the law considers has personhood status. Fundamentally, to have (legal) personhood status, an entity has to be defined as a legal actor with legal capacity. Importantly, as a legal actor the entity is said to have rights and obligations under the law, such as public duties and private obligations (note legal actors are sometimes referred to as "legal subjects" throughout this chapter). When considering rights for AI entities, another important term is that of a "natural

---

[7]   W.M. Geldart, *Legal Personality* (1911) 27 Law Quart. Rev. 90, at 94.

[8]   Neil M. Richards and Jonathan H. King, *Big Data Ethics*, Wake Forest Law Review, 2014, at 394, paper download via https://papers.ssrn.com/sol3/papers.cfm?abstract_id=2384174.

[9]   Legal personhood and legal personality and legal subjectivity are used interchangeably, having the same content.

person" who is considered to be an individual human being that is capable of assuming legal obligations and duties and is capable of holding public, civil, and human rights. Currently, AI entities (such as robots) are not afforded the rights associated with natural people or the rights afforded non-human entities which in some cases have been granted the status of legal personhood (see further discussion below).

Another important term in a discussion of rights for AI is that of an "artificial legal person"; essentially this term represents a legal fiction developed under the law to give rights to non-human entities. Artificial legal persons such as large and small businesses, private organizations, corporations, and government organizations, are entitled to carry out a range of acts under the "legal person" umbrella, and also have rights and obligations under the law, such as to be held responsible for certain activities they engage in. Natural persons, and to a lesser extent, artificial legal persons, are primarily the main actors in our legal system. But still, technological developments are rapidly moving in the direction of AI programs embodied in many types of physical entities and a variety of robotic systems in more or less anthropomorphic shapes that can perform a variety of tasks, often with legal effect. This trend has resulted in challenges to current established law and the question of whether such entities should receive personhood status. Coupled with the exponentially expanding Internet, this development has also been described as "the Internet of robotic things" (which has dramatically increased the spread of AI in society). In my view, the consideration of whether an autonomously functioning AI (such as a robot) should have legal personhood, will be heavily dependent upon the actual social necessity of the situation. Thus, as a basic legal *and* social question, it is pertinent to ask, how will a future society function if society lacked any form of legal personality for autonomous, AI entities; especially given they acted without human supervision?

Given this question, it is important to consider what reasoning will be applied to the determination of the legal status of AI robotics and other intelligent entities; this consideration is the basic topic of the chapter. For example, the legal status of AI entities could be built on an augmented layer of required legal elements based on the continuous development of autonomy and intelligence of AI robots. In this case one could analogize to AI the characteristics of the current players that have legal personality and then select which legal rights will be given to an AI entity that contains similar characteristics. Cautious proposals are already being made to comply with the technological future and to find solutions to emerging issues of legal rights for AI entities. However, the actual legal, social, and ethical implications of AI integrated into society needs far more consideration in such deliberations.

III.　CONSIDERING THE ROBOT

In a discussion of legal rights, for robots controlled by AI, we cannot escape defining or describing these phenomena. Of course, there are several definitions developed by roboticists and lawyers for each term. For the sake of brevity, I will not delve into all these conceptions. I start with a basic observation—there is a range of robots varying from the simple, one task-oriented industrial robot, to the autonomous car and the anthropomorphic robot companion emerging to assist humans (should each entity have the same legal rights?). Andrea Bertolini defined a robot in a broad sense, encompassing this wide variety of robotics and AI entities as follows:

a machine, which (i) may be either provided of a physical body, allowing it to interact with the external world, or rather have an intangible nature–such as a software or program, (ii) which in its functioning is alternatively directly controlled or simply supervised by a human being, or may even act autonomously in order to (iii) perform tasks, which present different degrees of complexity (repetitive or not) and may entail the adoption of not predetermined choices among possible alternatives, yet aimed at attaining a result or provide information for further judgment, as so determined by its user, creator or programmer, (iv) including but not limited to the modification of the external environment, and which in so doing may (v) interact and cooperate with humans in various forms and degrees.[10]

In determining a need for legal personhood status for AI entities such as robots, we should take into account that these systems will clearly vary in function; therefore, just what particular AI systems will have personhood status (and the legal rights associated with this status) is a question that must be resolved. There will be obvious differences in autonomy between systems resulting in a variety of legal requirements dependent, among others, on a social need to have robots perform tasks as more or less autonomous acts. For the legal analysis and classification of the legal personhood status of an AI robot, it is necessary to look at: (I) the embodiment or nature of the system; (II) the degree of autonomy shown by the system; (III) the function of the AI robot; (IV) the environment it operates in; and (V) the interaction between human and robot.[11] On the basis of these considerations, we can formulate the following timely questions:

1. Is there a need for a framework for AI and robot law in the sense of the law relating to, or as a result of, the use of robot technology in society? And, if so, what are the necessary preconditions in our legal system?
2. Does the robot need a certain degree of legal personhood that does not yet exist in positive law and is it necessary to regulate that degree of legal personhood? And, if so;
3. Is there a gradation of legal embodiment that connects with existing forms of legal personality or is a sui generis construction desirable taking into account the variability of AI systems and robotics?

IV.   TOWARDS LEGAL PERSONHOOD

Before further discussion of what legal personhood would mean for AI entities, we have to take a closer look at what it actually means to have "legal personality or legal personhood" status (i.e., for non-AI entities) for existing entities. As stated before, I use the terms legal personhood, legal personality and legal subject to refer to the legal status afforded an

---

[10]   Andrea Bertolini, *Robots as Products: The Case for a Realistic Analysis of Robotic Applications and Liability Rules*, Law, Innovation and Technology, 2013, 5(2): 219. Compare also definition by "robotpark": "A robot is a mechanical or virtual artificial agent (called 'Bot'), usually an electromechanical machine that is guided by a computer program or electronic circuitry. Robots can be autonomous, semi-autonomous or remotely controlled and range from humanoids such as ASIMO and TOPIO, to nano robots, 'swarm' robots and industrial robots. A robot may convey a sense of intelligence or thought of its own."

[11]   See *supra* note 10.

entity. The technical legal meaning of being a (legal) person is: "a subject of legal rights and duties".[12] According to Hans Kelsen, referring to "traditional" legal doctrine, a "subject under law" refers to legal obligations or subjective rights that typically result from social interactions. This last reference refers to the juridical power of a subject to pursue an action for the enforcement of an obligation.[13]

Interestingly, the above description does not necessarily refer to "natural persons". Instead, the idea of personhood involves the status of an entity as a person before the law, leading to recognition of certain rights and obligations under the law. Consequently, a legal person has the duty to obey the law, while enjoying the benefit of protections to rights and privileges accorded to such entities. In Dutch law (and for many other jurisdictions), no specific definition is given for a "person", but it can be understood as: capable of having legal rights and duties and legal capacity within a legal system, to act with legal effect such as to enter into contracts, to be liable, and to be a subject of legal remedies. Additionally, in Dutch law a legal or artificial person is considered equal to a natural person under some circumstances; for example, for property law the rights between the two are similar, unless the law states the contrary.[14] However, mostly, the legal construct of personhood under the law operates as a bundle of fundamental assumptions involving the biological understanding of what it means to be a human being, such as the understanding of a person as a rational agent, and the existence of consciousness when it concerns natural (i.e., biological) persons.[15] Clearly, current AI systems may be rational but are not biological beings or considered conscious; but as we will see later, some models granting rights to smart entities are general enough to encompass AI. While the above assumptions may seem as impediments to granting personhood rights to AI, the overlap of the above assumptions and the relative priority accorded to each assumption in actual legal jurisdictions needs to be considered.

Of importance for our discussion of personhood, concerning the concept of what constitutes a natural person, the concept is continuously evolving to accommodate new issues arising under circumstances of "time, place and culture". For instance, considering the time element, human slaves in the Roman Empire, as well as in later centuries, were not considered human beings, nor did they have human rights. But their lack of rights was not absolute, as they did have the possibility of *peculium*, to have and hold a certain amount of property as their own private property that their masters allowed them to spend or use as their own. Still, they were considered to be property; legal objects that could be bought or sold. In the U.S., on the other hand, slaves could be punished for criminal acts in order to exclude the criminal liability of their masters.[16] And until recently, women in

---

[12]   Lawrence B. Solum, *Legal Personhood for Artificial Intelligences*, North Carolina Law Review, 1992, 70 (4): 1238–39.

[13]   Hans Kelsen, *Introduction to the Problems of Legal Theory: A Translation of the First Edition of the Reine Rechtslehre or Pure Theory of Law*, par. IV, "Overcoming the Dualism of Legal Theory", translated by Jeff Mielke, 2000, published to Oxford Scholarship Online, March 2012.

[14]   Dutch Civil Code (Burgerlijk Wetboek, BW), Book 2, article 1 and 2.

[15]   Jens D. Ohlin, *Is the Concept of Person Necessary for Human Rights?*, Columbia Law Review (2005) vol. 105, at 210.

[16]   American law was inconsistent in its constitution of the personality of slaves. While they were denied many of the rights of "persons" or "citizens", they were still held responsible for their crimes which meant that they were persons to the extent that they were criminally accountable.

all western societies were not considered to have comparable legal capacities as their male counterparts. For example, until 1957, married women in the Netherlands still could not perform legal acts without the consent of their husbands. Additionally, changes continue to take place regarding the legal status of minors and their ability to perform activities requiring legal capacity. Rights may be based on age, or gender, and the individual's age may specifically influence their right to drive cars, vote, buy weapons, or marry. Further, rights may vary across different cultures, time periods, and geographical locations. What we can conclude from this brief discussion is that historically, legal rights for natural people is a concept that has continuously evolved, and involving many factors; will the same also be true for AI robots (and other AI entities)?

In our discussion of legal personhood rights for AI entities, it is interesting to note that society has allowed the creation of personhood rights for artificial business entities such as the corporation, firm, or foundation, based on the necessity that these entities have the power and legal status to perform economic acts with legal consequences associated with those acts and thus to have legal credibility in commercial transactions. In addition to business entities, other non-human entities have also been the subject of rights; for example, in our present society we have had numerous discussions and even disputes that have been litigated to consider personhood rights for animals. And there have been recent actions granting personhood to inanimate objects such as the Whanganui River in New Zealand and several rivers in India, suggesting that the scope of the legal construct of personhood may be expanded if need be.[17] So from this discussion the issue seems to be, should we expand the concept of legal personhood to accommodate AI entities? Whether an entity should be considered a legal subject depends on the following general question: Should this entity be made the subject of a set of legal rights and duties? The answer depends, among others, upon the cultural, economic, and political circumstances the AI finds itself in. There is considerable disagreement about the boundaries of this central legal question, as well as deep intellectual divisions among legal scholars on granting personhood rights to AI.[18]

However, legal personhood can be considered for humans, animals, or inanimate objects if one thinks of law from an essentialist perspective, that is, as an artificial pragmatic construct, meant to serve society. Of course, this reasoning also applies to legal objects and all norms translated into laws by humans. Additionally, one could think creatively about personhood status for AI entities in the sense of Cartesian (or mind-body) dualism (see discussion below). This would entail separating the concepts of legal personhood and legal objects on the basis of an entity's characteristics such as consciousness, consisting of matter, having free will, etc. To apply these concepts in the context of AI, one could take the common characteristics of entities that have been afforded personhood status into account (such as whether they have free will) to find the applicable legal status for

---

The variable status of American slaves is discussed in Ngaire Naffine, *Notes: What We Talk About When We Talk About Persons: The Language of a Legal Fiction*, Harvard Law Review (2001) vol. 114, at 1768 and 1746; and Ngaire Naffine, *Who are Law's Persons? From Cheshire Cats to Responsible Subjects*, Modern Law Review (2003) vol. 1, at 346.

[17]   Abigail Hutchinson, *The Whanganui River as a Legal Person*, Alternative Law Journal (2014) vol. 39, no. 3.

[18]   Naffine, *Who are Law's Persons?*, *supra* note 16, 346.

different manifestations of robots or other AI driven systems (for example, free will could lead to the appropriate *mens rea* for a criminal act).

To discuss whether an AI-driven entity should be afforded legal personhood status, in the analysis which follows, I will compare such entities with the bearers of legal rights and obligations that already exist in society for natural and artificial legal persons (such as a corporation). Using what I term an "essentialist framework", I will consider only the minimal necessity that is essential to the functioning of an AI entity such as an autonomous robot using in some cases a metaphysical framework (that is, focusing on the characteristics of the mind). In my view the reference to philosophy is necessary in the discussion of personhood status for AI entities as the discussion of what constitutes a person has historically been a subject of philosophical debate. In the sections which follow, I discuss an "artificial legal layer" (in terms of rights) that can be overlaid over an entity and that can be applied or taken away in the sense of a "Cheshire cat" analogy first proposed by Ngaire Naffine (discussed more fully in following sections), but for now the analogy represents an existing (legal) entity that can "be there" if one needs it or vanishes when superfluous.

V.   THE BIOLOGICAL PERSON AS A (NATURAL) LEGAL PERSON

Starting from Cartesian dualism and combining the sentient and conscious characteristics of human beings to the legal conception of natural persons, it is easy to see that there is a clear separation between natural persons and entities considered artificial legal persons. To identify which aspects of legal personhood might apply to AI entities, it is helpful to provide an explanation of the relevant characteristics of natural and "non-natural" legal persons. Legally, the individual as a natural person is the bearer of rights and obligations under the law due primarily to the fact that the individual is considered a living person and not a fictional entity. However, the analysis is not as simple as this brief explanation suggests, as there is some contention on what comprises the characteristic of the (human) individual: each individual differs from the other in the physical sense, but still in a legal sense, each man of flesh and blood is the bearer of rights and obligations (although they may differ within and between jurisdictions). Additionally, even though the law regulates who is Dutch, German, American, or Chinese and that everyone in the Netherlands is the bearer of rights and obligations, however, in many jurisdictions the law does not define just what a natural person is.[19] From a historical perspective we can look at the concept of a natural and artificial person as defined by Thomas Hobbes in his famous work Leviathan. According to Hobbes, a person is:

> He whose words or actions are considered, either as his own, or as representing the words or actions of another man, or of any other thing to whom they are attributed, whether truly or by fiction. When they are considered as his own, then is he called a natural person: and when they are considered as representing the words and actions of another, then is he a feigned or artificial person.[20]

---

[19]   Article 2 of the Dutch Constitution (Grondwet, GW), in conjunction with the Dutch Civil Code, Book 1, article 1.

[20]   Thomas Hobbes, *Leviathan*, Chapter xvi: Of Persons, Authors, and Things Personated.

Additionally, Hobbes explains the origin of the word (person) coming from the Latin *persona* and the Greek *prosperon*, a mask used in theatres.[21] Still the Romans reserved this *persona* phenomenon to living (natural) humans, including women and slaves. Hobbes separates the phenomenon of legal personality for human actors from artificial legal persons who are not natural persons and who do not function for themselves (i.e., for their own self-defined interests). Of course, Hobbes did not account for autonomous robots due to the historical context of his work, but he might well have considered this development if he had been confronted with autonomous and maybe sentient robots. From another historical perspective, as referred to by Ugo Pagallo, the idea that a legal subject can be an "artificial person" should be traced back to the notion of *persona ficta et repraesentata* developed by the experts of Canon Law since the thirteenth century. Thomas Hobbes' Leviathan also has a precedent in the work of Bartolus de Saxoferrato (1313–57).[22] And in Roman times, temples and other religious and state institutions were thought to have a legal personality due to the fact that legal personhood was in essence disconnected from the "spirit" of a human as discussed by Hegel.[23]

Considering Hegel's thoughts, another feature of the natural person is found in the spiritual aspect of the person; and of course, for comparison, current versions of AI are not thought of as a spiritual being. In religious scriptures one often finds references to the presence of the soul, but again artificial legal persons (which do have rights) and AI entities (which currently do not have independent rights) do not have a soul. According to the catechism of the Catholic Church, which can be viewed as an expert of this subject, the word "soul" is defined as follows: "soul" means the spiritual principle in man. Further, the soul is thought to be the foundation of human consciousness and freedom. Correspondingly, the freedom of decision is the ethical and legal background of the responsibility we have as natural beings; should this also be a factor in our analysis of legal rights such as personhood status for AI entities? Additionally, individuals are sovereign in their decisions and therefore legally responsible for their actions whereas current versions

---

[21]   *Id.*: "The word 'person' is Latin, instead whereof the Greeks have 'prosopon', which signifies the face, as 'persona' in Latin signifies the disguise, or outward appearance of a man, counterfeited on the stage; and sometimes more particularly that part of it which disguiseth the face, as a mask or vizard: and from the stage hath been translated to any represener of speech and action, as well in tribunals as theatres."

[22]   In his *Commentary on Digestum Novum* (48, 19; Il Cigno, Galileo Galilei, ed. 1996), Bartolus reckons that an artificial person is not really a person and, still, this fiction stands in the name of the truth, so that we, the jurists, establish it: "universitas proprie non est persona; tamen hoc est fi ctum pro vero, sicut ponimus nos iuristae." This idea triumphs with legal positivism and formalism in the mid-nineteenth century. In, F. Savigny, *System of Modern Roman Law* (1840–49) ed. W Holloway (Hyperion 1979), Friedrich August von Savigny claims that only human fellows properly have rights and duties of their own, even though it is in the power of the law to grant such rights of personhood to anything, e.g., business corporations, governments, ships in maritime law, and so forth. See Ugo Pagallo, *The Laws of Robots: Contracts, Crimes, and Torts* (Springer, 2013) at 156.

[23]   'What was for Stoicism only the abstraction of an intrinsic reality is now an actual world. Stoicism is nothing else but the consciousness which reduces to its abstract form the principle of legal status, an independence that lacks the life of Spirit.' G.W.F. Hegel, *Phenomenology of Spirit*, (N 1) p.271 in Paul Baumgartner, *Legal Right and Personhood*, Birkbeck Law Review (2016) 4(1):18, available at http://www.bbklr.org/uploads/1/4/5/4/14547218/15-27_phenomenology_11-12-2016_to-print.pdf.

of AI are not. Jean Bodin claimed that sovereignty must reside in a single individual. But this sovereignty can be transferred to other "legal entities", i.e. to the state, a company, or any other organizational unit. And these legal entities are considered to have rights with the power to make decisions with legal effects;[24] therefore, in the context of this discussion on personhood status for AI we can ask: can sovereignty be transferred to AI entities? And if yes, what are the implication for granting legal personhood rights to AI?

In discussions of legal personhood rights for AI, an important question is whether independently acting technical and electronic instruments, combinations of hardware, software, and algorithms (or as yet unknown bio-technical entities), can be considered as bearers of rights and duties? And further, whether these entities might be vested with the power to act as legal entities and thus to perform legal acts. Their actions could also lead to liability that is not directly traceable to any other responsible body as can be done with employees, children, and animals. This begs the question—will there always be a natural individual behind the acting entity (such as AI) as the ultimate bearer of rights and legal responsibilities? Under current law, a human is a legal entity with legal personality, but it could be the case that an artificially derived legal entity will never have the same rights as a natural person. Currently, a legal entity, in the form of a natural person, is the subject of many rights and duties, and can act with legal implications. Compared to AI entities that exist now, there is no question whether one of these "persons" is fictitious or natural. One is of flesh and blood and the other is not, but inherent to the natural person is that he or she is able to function socially and, if legally competent, able to perform acts with legal consequences.

Additionally, natural persons have rights not afforded to artificial entities that are considered legal persons (and both have rights not afforded AI); they can vote for other individuals in elections and be elected to represent other individuals. Further, natural people may join a political party or a church. Additionally, they will be the subject of human rights, such as the right to life, privacy, freedom of expression, right to an education, and freedom of religion. In addition, individuals may be sentenced to serve in prison if convicted of a felony offense, whereas AI may not. Individuals can marry another person or enter into a civil partnership and AI may not. Natural people may have children by natural birth from other individuals and will have an automatic natural and legal relationship with their offspring. Yet the basic rights afforded natural people also changes over time. Consider the human act of procreation. Due to biotechnology, individuals can be fully or partially naturally inseminated, and born from insemination with sperm or ova from third individuals. It is even possible that children can be the result of DNA merging from three different individuals.[25] For the time being this capability of biotechnology has no legal consequence. But would that be different if the DNA continues to be manipulated? Or if use is made of non-natural or non-human DNA? The point being—is there a boundary between natural and non-natural persons that would serve as an impediment in granting rights for AI entities (as non-humans)? Further, what position will the "semi-natural" person (a combination of human and technology, or genetically

---

[24]   Jean Bodin, *Les Six Livres de la Republique*, translation by M.J. Tooley (Blackwell, 1955).
[25]   https://www.newscientist.com/article/2107219-exclusive-worlds-first-baby-born-with-new-3-parent-technique/.

engineered humans) have in which AI and an individual's intelligence will complement each other as in humanoids that will exist of entities created by bio-technical manipulations? Taking the above examples into account, the concept of what rights individuals may receive is clearly being stressed by developments across a range of technologies. Legal doctrine and judicial opinions may not give an answer or have a final say in questions of legal rights for AI entities. This is a terrain that the legal discipline shares with multiple disciplines such as political science, medicine, ethics, psychology, and metaphysics.[26] Meanwhile, the question remains, what features of a person are relevant to determine what a real (or natural) person is? Can a natural person consist of 50 percent artificial organs and limbs, or 75 percent? Is this embodiment of technology into the human body relevant from a legal perspective?

Further, when contemplating personhood rights for AI, should we discriminate between entities on the basis of free will and intelligence, both of which are characteristics consistently attributed to mentally competent humans? If an individual is not able to independently perform legal acts and if the individual is not legally defined as an adult (in the Netherlands and other countries, 18 years of age), such natural persons are not able to perform certain acts with legal consequences. To emphasize this point, rights for natural people may be limited—for example, mentally incapacitated adults could be put under curatorship, but this is not an absolute rule. Further, minors and adults under guardianship can buy ice cream or even a bicycle, but will not be able to enter into a contract to buy a car or a house. Their parents or trustees have a duty to support them and to represent them; should the same be true for AI entities? Additionally, there is a transition period between full responsibility for the actions of children, to adulthood; which usually begins between 14 and 16 years of age, and in China as early as from ten years onward. Similarly, will there also be a transition period in allocating rights to AI or will AI be considered an adult under the law once created? Generally, the parent or guardian is not liable if he is not at fault for a harmful act committed by the child, but under tort law an adult may be liable for the actions of a robot (i.e., if the human is shown to be in the chain of liability), but even this may change once the robot reaches certain levels of autonomy.

But even within the legal system, cultural and national differences influence the decision to grant rights to persons and to determine the rights they receive. For example, the age of full legal capacity is established in The Netherlands and the U.S. as 18 years of age as well as in many other jurisdictions. However, rights afforded to natural people are not "clear-cut," an "adult" person in the U.S. is not allowed to buy alcoholic beverages, but is allowed to drive a car at the age of 16. In many countries in Africa and Asia, there is no minimum age set for marriage. India recently had the maturity and judgment limit lowered to 16 years of age for the perpetrators of a crime. Thus, the law is far from consistent when it comes to granting rights and holding people liable for their acts, this exercise is not based on nationally and certainly not on an international context. Clearly, legal standards for granting rights are not equal for natural persons across jurisdictions and evolve over time. Additionally, when considering personhood rights, there is also a tendency to look at the extent of the psychological capacity of natural persons when considering rights.

---

[26]   John Dewey, *The Historic Background of Corporate Legal Personality*, Yale Law Review (1926) 35(6), at 655, quoting Geldart, *Legal Personality*, Law Quart. Rev. (1911) vol. 27, at 94.

An extreme example is the proposal by a Rotterdam Alderman to forbid women to have children by means of obligatory anti-conception when the parents are apparently not able to raise their children adequately, for example, if they already have children expelled from their home to external care.[27]

Furthermore, reference may be made to the historical context of the discussion of the standards relating to the legal capacity of natural persons. For example, time and culture has been shown to be a factor and to vary when determining the legal status of people serving as slaves and also of natural persons. Emphasizing the time-varying nature of granting rights, the abolition of slavery and therefore the abolition of the (partial) status of slaves as a legal object only took place in 1794 in France, to be renewed by Napoleon in 1802, finally abolished in 1841, and in 1838 in the UK after the Abolition Act of 1833! The Netherlands and the U.S. finally accepted abolition of slavery in 1863. However, there are people working under "slave like" circumstances today.[28] For example, fugitives in Africa and other parts of the world are even today sold as slaves.[29] Will AI entities of sufficient intelligence and autonomy also have a master-slave relationship with humans and so too lack rights?

And there are numerous other examples showing inconsistency in granting rights for natural people, for example, women only received their democratic voting rights across the western world in the beginning of the twentieth century. Until the abolition of the law on incapacity on 14 June 1956, married women in the Netherlands were legally incapacitated.[30] Belgium took that date up to April 1958. However, until 1971, the Dutch Civil Code stipulated that the man was the "head of the family" and that the woman owed him obedience. Additionally, marriages between persons of a homosexual nature are not allowed in many countries in the world, in many countries, homosexuality is illegal, and in some countries even subject to the death penalty. In summary, it can be concluded that the actual content of the legal status of individuals is not homogeneous across jurisdictions or even within a jurisdiction. The legal status of natural persons is not standard and is dependent on time as well as social-cultural circumstances. This point of view can also be applied to the legal characterization of a robot controlled by AI.

A.   The Natural Person and Human Behavior as Factors for Legal Personhood

1.   Human physiology
In the film *Bicentennial Man*, based upon a book by Isaac Asimov, the robot Andrew Martin wants to be recognized as a natural person.[31] Initially, his request is rejected by the

---

27   Proposal Ira van Winden, alderman of Rotterdam, https://www.ad.nl/rotterdam/verplich te-anticonceptie-bij-falende-ouders~a9e0f49f/.

28   https://www.nytimes.com/2014/01/06/opinion/qatars-showcase-of-shame.html?_r=0; and htt ps://www.globalslaveryindex.org/findings/.

29   http://www.telegraph.co.uk/news/2017/11/20/libyan-government-investigate-slave-auctions-af rican-migrants/.

30   On 14 June 1956 the House settled the bill by Minister JC Furnace, so that married women were legally competent as from 1 January 1957.

31   Isaac Asimov, *The Bicentennial Man and Other Stories* (Balantine Books 1972), and later edited by Asimov as *The Positronic Man* (Doubleday 1993), co-written with Robert Silverberg,

President of the Court because a robot can simply not be recognized as a natural person in the fictitious jurisdiction. The reasoning behind this rejection is that a robot lives forever and cannot die. Years later, the robot, when adjusted so that he can die, requests a revision of this judgment.

> In a sense I have. I am growing old; my body is deteriorating, and like all of you, intending eventually to cease to function. As a robot, I could have lived forever. But I tell you all today, I would rather die a man, than live for all eternity a machine.

Asimov raised an interesting point of discussion, especially since various scientific sources suggest that old age is a disease that can be "cured", and every human being may soon be living in a time where they reach 130 years of age and perhaps even be immortal in time. Similarly, there may not be an age limit for AI. So how do legal rights change if at all, for entities that do not have established life spans?

2.   Free will

From a philosophical and legal doctrine perspective, another consideration that is used to determine the classification of a natural person is the existence of free will, referring again to Asimov's novel: "It has been said in this courtroom that only a human being can be free. It seems to me that only someone who wishes for freedom can be free. I wish for freedom." The idea of qualifying an autonomous thinking and self-decisive robot as an individual based on autonomy and free will is a fairly complex one. Free will, as indicated by Descartes, is based on the thinking that we as human beings have the experience by which free will steers our behavior. Extending the concept of free will to non-humans, Aristotle had the conviction that free will also exists within animals.[32] For several "thinking entities" there is already a sufficient level of intelligence to allow autonomous actions, but will this lead to an acceptance of the idea that such entities have free will? Clearly, free will is often used to describe human-like behavior which is used as a criterion in the determination of what it means to be human and therefore his or her status as a natural person (under the law). Whether AI can be said to have free will is not only a philosophical question, but a legal one with importance to AI.

3.   Intelligence, animals

The problem with the idea of considering the role of intelligence in determining natural person status is that what constitutes intelligence is not a settled issue, due in part to disagreement about the different elements thought to comprise intelligence; for example, rational intelligence and artistic intelligence to name just two. In fact, Howard Gardner theorized that there are multiple intelligences comprised of nine components: naturalist, existential, musical, logical-mathematical, bodily-kinesthetic, linguistic, spatial, interpersonal, and intrapersonal intelligence.[33] Additionally, David Wechsler formulated in 1955 a well-known general definition of intelligence: "The aggregate or global capacity

---

ultimately formed the basis for the script of the movie *Bicentennial Man*, 1999, starring Robin Williams.

[32]   René Descartes, *Principia Philosophiae* (Vrin, ed. 1973).
[33]   Howard Gardner, *The Theory of Multiple Intelligences* (Basic Books 1993).

of the individual to act purposefully, to think rationally, and to deal effectively with his environment."[34]

Without getting involved in the controversies that exist about the many forms of intelligence, for the purposes of this chapter, I would limit this discussion to the intelligence needed to participate as an individual in society (as this creates legal obligations). To this end, it is necessary that there is an understanding of the consequences of acts performed in this social traffic (with legal effect). Certainly, AI entities will be capable, in the foreseeable future, to pass the Turing test, if so, the qualification for intelligence necessary for personhood on a "human" level may then be met, but will this be sufficient for society to actually grant the AI entity legal personhood status?[35]

Compliance with the Turing test, something that other animal primates certainly cannot meet, gives the impression that personhood has to do with a human being. Yet there are regular attempts to give these other primates a form of legal personality. For example, a chimpanzee, an entity that is regarded as reasonably intelligent, was recently a litigant in an Appeals Court action in New York state on a writ to personal liberty (Habeas Corpus).[36] The status of the chimpanzee as a natural person was not accepted (compare this case with Asimov's robot plaintiff, Andrew Martin, discussed previously): the court stated that chimpanzees, although cognitively complex, are not entitled to the same legal status as human beings: "[We] conclude that a chimpanzee is not a 'person' entitled to the rights and protections afforded by the writ of habeas corpus." Additionally, only people can have rights, the court stated, and this is because only people can be held legally accountable for their actions. "In our view, it is this incapability to bear any legal responsibilities and societal duties that renders it inappropriate to confer upon chimpanzees legal rights . . . that have been afforded to human beings." In contrast, the Non-Human Rights Project, the appellant in this case, did not agree and stated:

> The Court ignores the fact that the common law is supposed to change in light of new scientific discoveries, changing experiences, and changing ideas of what is right or wrong; it is time for the common law to recognize that these facts are sufficient for the establishment of personhood for the purpose of a writ of. . .[37]

Although Descartes claimed that animals are mere machines due to their lack of cognitive abilities, the response above by the Non-Human Rights Project indicated that this vision may need to be revisited. Animals are not "things" as a toaster is a thing; therefore,

---

[34]   David Wechsler, *The Range of Human Capacities* (Williams and Wilkins, 1955 (2nd ed.)) at 7.

[35]   The Turing Test, published by Alan Turing in 1950 who played such an important role in WWII, was designed to provide a satisfactory operational definition of intelligence. Turing defined intelligent behavior as the ability to achieve human-level performance tasks, sufficient to fool an interrogator

[36]   http://decisions.courts.state.ny.us/ad3/Decisions/2014/518336.pdf.

[37]   The Nonhuman Rights Project (NhRP) further stated: chimps and other select species—bonobos, gorillas, orangutans, dolphins, orcas, and elephants—are not only conscious, but also possess a sense of self, and, to some degree, a theory of mind. They have intricate, fluid social relationships, which are influenced by strategy and the ability to plan ahead, as well as a sense of fairness and an empathetic drive to console and help one another. In many ways (though certainly not all) they are like young children. The NhRP contends, based on this, that chimpanzees are capable of bearing some duties and responsibilities.

according to some commentators, personhood which involves, among others, compliance with the laws and regulations; conforming to rules of unwritten law; compliance with obligations and principles under law; and compliance with public order and decency, should apply at some level to animals as they do humans.[38] Although animals have no legal rights as a legal person, they are often treated from a legal perspective based on their role in society, that is, with certain rights emanating from the obligations that natural persons in society have regarding animal ownership. For example, abuse or neglect of animals is not accepted under the law and animal abuse statutes are included in the Criminal Codes. Further, certain rights for animals have existed in the Netherlands since 2011, and are codified in "the law on animals."[39] Thus, an animal has no legal personality under the law but there seems to be a societal trend to give more rights to animals and not just for the legal and beneficial owner of the animal. As noted, currently rights for animals reflect on the obligations natural persons have towards these "sui-generis" objects. The question of interest to this chapter then is whether in respect to certain social robots used as pets, companion robots, or sex robots, the same legal regime as provided for animals should apply in which case their rights would emanate from the natural or artificial people that either owned them or exerted some level of control over them.[40]

Animal rights advocates argue that legal systems should provide animals with some form of legal personality (and therefore corresponding rights) due to their cognitive abilities. For example, research shows that animals can make various decisions under different contingencies suggesting the ability to think under the influence of processing different information. Is this proof that they have free will and evidence of an intellectual base for their decisions on the information obtained? Further, it is argued by some that the chimpanzee is not that much inferior to humans (they are genetically very similar) when it comes to reasoning, intelligence, temporal insight, self-awareness, self-control, theory of mind, and social and emotional repertoire. Additionally, just as with humans, animals seem to express curiosity, the ability to communicate, and an ability to desire something and act intentionally. In comparison, AI can communicate and to some extent algorithms can be said to show intent as they solve problems, but current versions of algorithms lack curiosity. According to the advocates of the rights for chimpanzees, these capabilities ideally are what make a chimpanzee a person, a legal entity, and a bearer of fundamental rights. Unfortunately, for the animal rights advocates, this reasoning has so far not resulted in effective legal personality for animals and provides anecdotal evidence that rights for AI entities may follow a similar path.[41]

---

[38]   Dutch Civil Code, Book 3, article 2a.
[39]   Article 350 paragraph 2 of the Dutch Penal Code (Wetboek van Strafrecht) and Law of May 19, 2011, on an Integrated Framework for Regulations on Captive Animals and Related Topics (Animals Act).
[40]   Eq. by Kate Darling, opinions in: *Electronic Love, Trust, and Abuse: Social Aspects of Robotics*, Miami, 1 April 2016.
[41]   Personally, I think the animal-as-a-person-reasoning is going too far towards granting personhood rights to the animal. I would not trust the trained chimpanzee behind the wheel of a car if the car is not working entirely independently. Nor, in my view, is it uplifting to enter into a conversation with a chimpanzee. Clearly, the probability that interesting communication will be possible with an intelligent robot is far more likely than with a chimpanzee which emphasizes the need to consider legal rights for AI entities.

VI.   NON-NATURAL (ARTIFICIAL) LEGAL PERSONS

The "non-natural" (or artificial) person may be a company or other entity such as an organization, institution, foundation, etc. In fact, in more structured societies it has been common to use the corporation as an entity with legal capacity, thus having (artificial) legal personhood status. This is not a new concept, as in the ancient Egyptian society, the legal structure of a foundation was used to maintain temples. And in Roman civilization, there were several legal entities such as the *universitates personarum*, which was similar to corporations or government colleges with their own identity and legal personality. A well-known Dutch international organization with legal personality, in fact, the first multinational corporation, was the Dutch East India Company (VOC), founded in 1602. The above represent examples of legal doctrine adapting to the legal reality of the social and economic needs of the times. Given AI is heavily involved in economic transactions and more and more performing social tasks, so too may legal institutions have to adopt accordingly to the capabilities of AI. Additionally, in some jurisdictions, a legal person such as a corporation, at least in relation to property rights, has similar rights as natural legal persons, specifically to perform actions with legal capacity, unless otherwise provided by law.

A legal person is, in a similar way as a natural person, thought to be a legal entity able to participate in socially relevant legal relationships. For example, a legal person can go to court if its interests are affected, or can be sued in court if it acted unlawfully in view of another legal or natural person. As John Dewey in 1926 indicated in the Yale Law Journal: "The Corporation is a right-and-duty-bearing entity".[42] Even though corporations in several ways are not equal to humans under the law, in some circumstances they do have a legal personality to act in a legal sense. Although rights for non-human entities is a legal fiction, granted to organizations and other entities, they can only act in a legal manner that is in the best interest as stated, for example, in the articles of incorporation, and based on the purpose of the legal entity. Thus, the legal fiction, in this case relating to property law, is a kind of "augmented reality", a conceptual legal layer with real-world consequences overlaid over social reality.

There is a global spectrum of what constitutes legal persons in civil law. In the U.S., this means even to some extent, the application of the Bill of Rights guarantees to corporations. Carl Mayer describes this situation in the U.S. on the basis of the development of equal treatment under the Fourteenth Amendment of the U.S. Constitution. Companies are considered persons for the purpose of the Fourteenth Amendment; that is, companies should have the right to equal protection and to due process.[43] Of course, these conceptions are not equally applied across the globe. As stated before, legal as well as social obligations differentiate in legal schemes throughout countries, cultures, and political structures. Can we derive useful comparisons from these different characteristics for legal person status to define a legal framework for an AI entity?

---

[42]   Dewey, *supra* note 26, at 26.
[43]   Carl J. Mayer, *Personalizing the Impersonal: Corporations and the Bill of Rights*, Hastings Law Journal (1990) 41(3): 577–667.

VII.   THE ARTIFICIALLY INTELLIGENT ROBOT

Artificial intelligence has been described as an (AI) system in the form of algorithms and analytical techniques. As such AI is embedded within advanced (computer) technology, which is aimed at imitation of intelligent human behavior,[44] partly to understand (human) intelligence and also to create intelligent entities that can operate autonomously in complex, changing situations (a robot being a prime example).[45] Will such systems need legal personhood to function in society? The answer will depend on the way that the AI functions, how it acts within society, and will also be based on the existing culture that AI is operating in. For instance, as applied to robots with multipurpose tasks that require intelligence and social behavior, an emerging view is that legal competence needs to be ascribed to the robot if it acts with legal effect. An example of an AI entity performing multiple purpose tasks is the semi-autonomous functioning system, the Watson supercomputer developed by IBM. This AI system contributes to DNA research, teaching, seed breeding, and medical diagnosis, to name a few.[46] This system receives its initial instructions from an individual, but still, one could conclude that there are certain legal effects based on its semi-autonomous functioning. Watson's performance could lead to arguments for granting it legal personhood rights, but in my view, there will have to be limits to the extent of legal consequences for its actions, as will be explained later in the chapter.

In today's society, semi-autonomous systems which in many cases are robots, are still controlled to some extent by natural persons. However, there is an undeniable trend towards the design of self-thinking and self-acting AI driven systems. But this is not unusual, considering that natural persons are also controlled in their professional activities, sometimes by other natural persons (such as their supervisor) or sometimes by (artificial) legal persons (such as a corporation). Currently, different forms of artificial intelligence are "in the field" operating in many industries, such as hosting the service industry, performing social and physical support tasks for the needy, care robots assisting the elderly, sex robots operating in the sex industry, industrial robots assisting in manufacturing, medical robots assisting in surgical procedures, and also surveillance and military robots, drones, and autonomous vehicles. Many of these robots perform a range of social tasks and other tasks requiring intelligence and autonomy. And not all robots will be roughly at human scales in size, for example, in the medical sector molecular nano-robots will consist of chemical or organic building blocks.[47] While we are used to thinking about rights for robots, partly because they exert a noticeable physical presence in the world, what about legal rights for nanoscale robots that so too may operate autonomously and may someday claim to be conscious?

---

[44]   Rex Shoyama, *Intelligent Agents: Authors, Makers, and Owners of Computer-Generated Works in Canadian Copyright Law*, Canadian Journal of Law and Technology (2005) 4(2) at 129.

[45]   Stuart Russell and Peter Norvig, *Artificial Intelligence: A Modern Approach* (Barnes and Noble, 2010 (3rd ed.)) at 1 and 18. Also referring to the following definition of AI, Kurt Kurzweil, *The art of creating machines that perform functions that require intelligence when performed by people* (1990) available at https://people.eecs.berkeley.edu/~russell/intro.html.

[46]   http://www.ibm.com/watson/.

[47]   Examples are the molecular machines as designed by Prof. Ben Feringa, Nobel laureate in 2016.

As noted earlier in the chapter, the fear of the unknown is an important consideration as AI proliferates into society. One factor contributing to society's mistrust of AI is that AI is becoming opaque in the sense that we cannot completely understand the processes that control it; this is partly based on the sophisticated algorithms and analytical techniques used by AI. With continuing developments in AI, some argue that the AI entity could eventually become "super intelligent." The development of super intelligence, or the coming Singularity as this event is sometimes described, is based on Moore's law, or more generally, the law of accelerating returns for technology expressed by Google's Ray Kurzweil. Gordon Moore articulated the fact that the capacity of microprocessors doubled every two years. Vernon Vinge and Ray Kurzweil broadened this concept to other technological developments, including a shift to other forms of technology, for instance from micro-processing to nano-processors. This increase in computational resources could also manifest itself in the development of intelligence by artificial means, resulting in super-intelligent entities of a bio digital character or possibly a manifestation not yet known to mankind. Nick Bostrom, who has written on AI and its potential threat to humanity, defined super intelligent systems as: "Any intellect that radically outperforms the best human minds in every field, including scientific creativity, general wisdom and social skills."[48] It is alluring to delve further into the apocalyptic scenarios that may result from AI as predicted by Vernon Vinge, Nick Bostrom, Elon Musk, Stephen Hawking, and others, but I will restrict myself to the legally relevant perspective that relates to granting legal personhood rights to AI. The AI robot is not yet super-intelligent but can be considered as a dynamically evolving entity that started as an unintelligent machine, but that is continuously evolving into a complex autonomous functioning system and— possibility in a later stage—a super-intelligent or semi-humanoid system.[49] The nature of this entity—electronic, or organic-chemical—is less relevant for its legal characterization. The argument presented in this chapter is that the state of intelligent autonomy and its function in society will be important for determining its legal status more so than its particular form.

To think about rights for evolving AI, one could reason by analogy to the emergence of the "intelligent" car, a development that is current, stressing established law, and thus represents a realistic example. The modern automobile is quickly increasing its autonomous mode. We already drive with different types of automated warning systems, automatic brakes, distance keeping systems, etc. According to road traffic law, the driver is the responsible party in the car. But how will we justify this conclusion as the driver is gradually losing manual control over driving the car and, instead, depending on

---

[48]   Nick Bostrom, *Superintelligence: Paths, Dangers, Strategies* (Oxford U.P., 2014).

[49]   Already in the 1960s this development was predicted: Let an ultraintelligent machine be defined as a machine that can far surpass all the intellectual activities of any man however clever. Since the design of machines is one of these intellectual activities, an ultraintelligent machine could design even better machines; there would then unquestionably be an "intelligence explosion," and the intelligence of man would be left far behind. Thus the first ultraintelligent machine is the last invention that man need ever make, provided that the machine is docile enough to tell us how to keep it under control. See Irving John Good, "Speculations Concerning the First Ultraintelligent Machine", in Franz L. Alt and Morris Rubinoff (eds.), *Advances in Computers*, pp. 31–88, vol. 6 (Academic Press, 1965) cited by Vernor Vinge in *The Coming Technological Singularity*, 1993: How to Survive in the Post-Human Era, https://edoras.sdsu.edu/~vinge/misc/singularity.html.

numerous providers of information to get from point A to point B? These providers are the manufacturer, the infrastructure, road managers, other motorists, the producer of the software controlling the car's actions, the meteorological department, the designer of the algorithm at the heart of the learning vehicle, and third-party data providers that control or affect navigation and engine control.

Extending this discussion into the future, what if a direct link between the brain activity of the "driver" and the software control of the automobile is made? This is not a "sci-fi" scenario, there are already cars that respond to drivers who threaten to fall asleep where certain movements betray a delay in reflexes. Going one step further, those links could be analyzed by an external autonomous system designed to control traffic flow; if so what legal liability would the (intelligent) "external link" have? Again, this scenario is not the plot of a science fiction novel. In fact, entrepreneur Elon Musk is funding work in the area of neurotech, through Neuralink, a company that is researching methods to upload and download thoughts. Ultimately, Neuralink aims to change the way in which we interact with devices by linking our brains to the machines we use most often: cars, mobile devices, and even smart items in our smart home. This research agenda is also being pursued by researchers at the University of Witwatersrand, South Africa, in which the "Brainternet" project streams brainwaves onto the Internet. Essentially, Brainternet turns the brain into an Internet of Things (IoT) node on the World Wide Web. The IoT refers to the process of connecting any device with an on and off switch to the Internet.[50] Another example of the use of AI is its use in the selection of candidates for jobs. Going beyond the algorithmic selection of candidates based on their initial email or letter of interest, using the Applicant Tracking Systems (ATS), AI can be embedded into robots that can be designed to observe a conversation with an applicant to watch the individual's posture, eye movements, sweating, and other mental and physical reactions (here the AI is clearly a participant in social activities). This analytical achievement will be developed to an even greater extent in the "care-industry", where autonomously functioning robots will apply client custom made solutions to the needy without the necessity of external guidance. To determine the legal classification of the AI entity operating as a tool, that is, as an object that is used as an instrument, we have to determine its role and status.[51] Whether AI controlled robots should be compared to legal persons or legal objects is to be answered, among others, on the basis of its function in society, its intelligence, and level of autonomy. Referring back to previous discussions in this chapter on rights granted to different entities, this approach will help decide whether the legal status of AI can be

---

[50] https://www.wits.ac.za/news/latest-news/research-news/2017/2017-09/can-you-read-my-mind.

[51] The Principles of European Tort Law ("PETL") refers to liability for "auxiliaries" (6: 102)—an apt term for both robots as for us, although meant in PETL particularly for people. Article 3: 201 of the Draft Common Frame of Reference (DCFR) of the Principles, Definitions and Model Rules of European Private Law refers to workers or "similarly engaged" others, in which the phrase "similarly engaged" others may contain cases of accidental damage; see P. Giliker, *Vicarious Liability or Liability for the Acts of Others in Tort: A Comparative Perspective*, Journal of European Tort Law (JETL) (2011) vol. 1, at 38 ff. Then, the robot will have to be seen as "another", where the employer is liable under the condition that he still has "the least abstract possibility of directing and supervising its conduct through binding instructions." See Christian von Bar and Eric Clive (eds.), *Principles, Definitions and Model Rules of European Private Law: Draft Common Frame of Reference* (Oxford U.P., 2010) at 34–55.

assessed by analogy to rights afforded a minor, as a non-subordinate, as movable property, as animals,[52] or finally as independent legal entities.

However, a complicating factor to the problem of conferring rights to AI entities is the difficulty of comparing AI to existing legal persons and legal objects; this is because such objects have nuances and legal complexities as discussed previously. Consider that an artificial legal person in the form of a company can in some situations be considered an object that, like property, can be bought and sold, and can be divided; but also, if granted the fiction of legal person status, it can be held responsible for its actions. To determine a sensible and working solution for a legal personhood structure for AI, I propose that we will need to address the problem from several vantage points.

VIII.   THE THREEFOLD CONCEPTION OF PERSONHOOD BY NAFFINE

An interesting analysis of legal personhood is made by Ngaire Naffine in a framework that can be applied to all entities which have been discussed in this chapter. Naffine introduces three conceptual "models" for legal personhood: the (lucid) Cheshire Cat; any reasonable creature in being; and the responsible subject. I discuss each in the following sections.

A.   The Cheshire Cat

The first model describing the characteristics of a legal person proposed by Naffine is named the "Cheshire Cat."[53] According to this model, to have personhood status means at base nothing more than the formal capacity to be a carrier of legal rights and duties.[54] Note that there is no moral or ethical dimension to this definition nor in this model are the ability to express morals and ethics involved in determining whether an entity receives personhood rights. "The person exists only as an abstract capacity to function in law, a capacity which is endowed by law because it is convenient for law to have such a creation."[55]

Under this description, "anyone" or "anything" can be considered a person in the eyes of the law, because according to this model the only reason that legal personhood exists at all is due to the practical advantages which results from granting entities legal person status. Among Naffine's three models, this description of legal personhood is the most encompassing in terms of "opening the door" for non-human entities to receive personhood status. However, it is also the least differentiating perspective since it does not have any moral, ethical, historical, or empirical component.[56] Following this model for personhood, there is no obstacle to why animals or other legally functioning entities would not be considered persons under the law. As long as they (i.e., a non-human entity) are able

---

[52]   E. Schaerer et al, "Robots as Animals: A Framework for Liability and Responsibility in Human-Robot Interaction", in *Robot and Human Interaction Communication*, 18th IEEE International Symposium, 2009, 72–77.
[53]   Naffine, *Who are Law's Persons?*, *supra* note 16, at 350.
[54]   *Id.*
[55]   *Id.*, 351.
[56]   *Id.*

to carry at least one right or legal duty, under this legal scheme, there is no reason to deny them personhood, and this reasoning applies even if a human is necessary to enforce that right.[57] The enforcement aspect associated with this model of personhood should not pose a problem for granting rights to AI given the mechanism for enforcement of rights already in force for minors and other legally incapacitated persons—all that is necessary is to apply this enforcement model to AI. The interesting idea from the Cheshire Cat model is that there should be no extrajudicial requirement in granting personhood status other than the practical consideration involved in the scope and contents of legal subjectivity.

In an age of emerging technologies, the "Cheshire Cat" description of personhood also supports the necessity of not differentiating between natural persons and artificial persons or possible other smart entities that may reach human levels of performance and thus incurring obligations in society. For entities in general, the concept of personhood is an abstract concept; neither the natural person, nor the artificial person is more "real" in a legal sense than the other in this model. For natural or artificial people, their legal personalities are based solely on the fact that they have rights and duties. This rationale is how the name of the theory is derived: take away the rights and the duties of the person, then its legal personality status vanishes like the Cheshire Cat.[58]

Proponents of the Cheshire Cat model of personhood envision the concept of legal personality as an empty slot that fits anyone or anything.[59] Consider the example of rights for animals again. Under this theory, there should be no impediment whatsoever to granting animals personhood status. However, I should point out that the common legal view is to deny animals legal person status simply because they are not considered persons (from a biological sense).[60] But of course there is no difference between being a person in the sense of a natural (i.e., human) person and a legal person if the only consideration is the capacity to carry legal rights and duties. The resistance within the legal community to granting animals' personhood status strongly suggests that legal personhood is not the empty slot that some attribute it to be. It rather suggests that this empty slot is essentially reserved for human beings. If so, this implies that personhood does in fact have a moral status associated with it and is not immune from metaphysical notions on what it means to be human.[61] So, expanding the Cheshire Cat model to encompass how rights are afforded entities, physical characteristics play a role in the legal qualification of who is to be considered a person and in the question of whether other (non-human) legal and natural persons (that may be mentally incapacitated, or deemed a minor under the law) can perform actions with legal obligations.

B.   Rights for the Human Being

The second model that Naffine proposes for legal personhood status is to simply acknowledge that a person under the law is any human being.[62] Simply put: to qualify as a legal

---

[57]   *Id.*

[58]   *Id.,* at 353.

[59]   *Id.,* at 356.

[60]   See also the decision of the Court of Appeal New York, described on page 226.

[61]   *Id.*

[62]   Naffine, *Who are Law's Persons?, supra* note 16, at 357.

person, one has to be a (biological) human. This perspective is the most accepted and current theory in most jurisdictions on just what constitutes a person that has rights and legal obligations and comes closest to the common language usage of the word "person", at least from the Anglo-Saxon perspective.[63] It is common knowledge within the legal community that someone becomes a legal person at the very moment of being born or conceived, or fetus (depending on the legal definition of conception in a particular jurisdiction) and certainly ends at death. Further as explained in sections above, it is possible to limit the scope of personhood for mentally incompetent people when rationality or psychological stability is not present in the human, yet in either case personhood status still exists.

There are two ways in which this common view of what constitutes a person is interpreted: first, the concept could refer to a human being at the moment of conception and has not yet died, and is thus considered a human, and therefore a person with rights and obligations. Second, it could refer to the rights and duties of a person that start to exist when they are born as a human being and which cease to exist as soon as this same person dies.[64] Either way, personhood is linked with both biological and metaphysical notions of humanity. Thus, under this scheme, personhood is not a purely legal matter, but additionally, is based on just what it *means* to be human.[65] This question introduces the oft-cited criticism of this model on legal personhood: that only a human can receive personhood status. From the perspective of the Cheshire Cat model, those who support the status of a human being as the sole requirement for being considered a person, are misguided due to their reliance on extra-legal, biological, or moral considerations.[66] They argue that the terms 'human being' and 'person' are being used synonymously and interchangeably by those who support this second personhood model, and that should not be the case.[67]

However, the definition of the legal person as a human being has advantages due partly to its simplicity. For someone to be considered a person, one does not require any defining quality other than that of being a human. Therefore, this theory includes all humans, regardless of their mental or physical state, and is thus compatible with the human rights movement. In the meantime, this definition excludes in line with the common legal view— animals from personhood. But interestingly, corporations are able to receive personhood rights under this definition because they are ultimately reducible to the relations between the persons who manage them, own them, work for them, and act in mandate.[68] This definition of personhood, however, is not compatible with the notion that there are differences between people based on age, mental, and physical characteristics, which in fact have consequences for the legal requirements imposed upon people by society.

---

[63]   In an Anglo-Saxon common law sense, personhood is also considered in the legal continental perspective as a non-human actor's author.
[64]   Naffine, *Who are Law's Persons?*, *supra* note 16, at 357.
[65]   *Id.*
[66]   *Id.*
[67]   *Id.*, at 358.
[68]   Solum, *supra* note 12, at 1239.

C.   The Rational, Responsible Actor

The third conceptualization or model of legal personality proposed by Naffine, is the "rational, responsible actor." Compared to the other two models of personhood this can be considered more of a high-threshold model since not all humans possess the qualities to be considered rational or responsible as required by this model.[69] Thus, this model requires a certain mental capacity to be a rational actor and therefore excludes young children, mentally incompetent humans, and animals from receiving the full legal rights associated with personhood.[70] While this model recognizes the human being as important for personhood, it does not see this as the critical characteristic that sets a human apart as a person. It is the rationality, the mental attributes, and the ability to comprehend a certain situation that determines whether one receives personhood.[71] Although seeming to establish this model of the person as the ideal legal actor, it also encounters the danger of elitism. Moreover, the idea is also not unique as most legal orders already have a system of legal incapability in a private and criminal law sense.

Naffine states that under the rational and responsible person model, the person can be meaningfully subjected to legal punishment for criminal acts.[72] Criminal law has to treat the person as a responsible actor with free will because otherwise one cannot take responsibility for one's actions. If a person is not capable of making rational decisions, then what is the point of punishing the person? This reasoning already is applied in many legal systems in the form of "being not accountable for one's actions due to psychological stress or other mental or physical factors". One of the main goals of punishment in criminal law is the prevention of a person committing the same criminal offence again. If a person is not capable of making rational decisions in the first place, then he cannot be expected to learn from his punishment. Nonetheless, in the case of criminal law, this definition of a legal person is simplifying reality; in many ways the law shows awareness of the weaknesses and dependence of human individuals and in many ways the law does not require persons to operate as rational and responsible as this particular model for personhood proposed by Naffine requires from a human.[73]

D.   AI Robotics as the Cheshire Cat

According to the Cheshire Cat model of personhood, humans can allocate legal personhood to any entity, regardless of the nature of the entity that it is allocated to.[74] Already inanimate entities have been the subject of legal rights at various times in the past. As mentioned above, temples in Rome and church buildings in the Middle Ages have been regarded as persons.[75] So have ships, an Indian family doll[76] and Indian and New Zealand

---

[69]   Naffine, *Who are Law's Persons?*, *supra* note 16, at 362.
[70]   *Id.*, at 364.
[71]   *Id.*
[72]   *Id.*
[73]   *Id.*, at 365.
[74]   *Id.*, at 351.
[75]   Solum, *supra* note 12, at 1239.
[76]   *Id.*

rivers.[77] And certainly a parallel can be drawn with business corporations and with government entities.[78]

For comparison purposes, as we focus more on the example of corporate personhood, we can see many parallels with rights allocated to corporations and similar rights that could be afforded to AI. Similarly to the goals of a corporation, the aims of an AI robot may lie in the pursuit of economic profit for a producer or owner of the robot, or in the social welfare benefits for society that result from performance of the AI robot. For example, a robot working for an automobile manufacturer may improve production and thus profit for the manufacturer, further, a robot caring for an elderly person will be carrying out a civic service. The reason why personhood has been invoked for corporations and could be for AI robots is to reduce the responsibility and liability of the owners in case of damage to third parties or property inflicted by the corporation or the robot. Corporate personhood has seen the liability of its shareholders limited to a certain extent by corporate legislation. Artificially intelligent entities could fall under similar legislation, equipped with self-teaching and initiative taking algorithms that incur legal obligations. Using the Cheshire Cat model of personhood as our base, there should be no major impediment to granting personhood status to AI given many of their tasks and functions impose legal liabilities and obligations.

E.   AI Robotics as a Human Being?

Considering Naffine's second model of personhood requiring that only a "human person" receive personhood rights, thus, by definition, granting personhood rights to AI would not be possible. If personhood can only be granted to humans solely based on the fact that they are human, then it would not be possible for AI as a non-human entity to obtain legal personhood status. Given this conclusion, how would it be possible under this model (i.e., rights only for humans) for non-human corporations to receive personhood status? First, those who support Naffine's human as required for personhood model, would argue that the comparison between corporations and AI is inappropriate given that they have fundamentally different roles in society and ultimate reliance on humans. The property of a corporation is eventually the property of its shareholders (but this may not be the case with AI).[79] Further, damage done to a corporation would ultimately injure natural persons, at least financially.[80] Corporations are reducible to the relations between the persons who manage them, own them, work for them and so forth but this may not be the case for autonomous AI.[81] So, under the "human as person" model the fact that corporations have a legal personality does not necessarily mean that AI entities should be granted legal personality too.

Similarly, according to some commentators, if AI is granted personhood status, this would undermine the meaning of being a person because it would expand the meaning

---

[77]   M. Safi, Ganges and Yamuna rivers granted same legal rights as human beings (1st March 2017). Consulted on May 13, 2017, from https://www.theguardian.com/world/2017/mar/21/ganges-and-yamuna-rivers-granted-same-legal-rights-as-human-beings.

[78]   Solum, *supra* note 12, at 1239.

[79]   *Id.*

[80]   *Id.*

[81]   *Id.*

of being a person to a non-human entity. The exclusivity of personhood status as human has been expressed in religious texts such as the Bible: man is separate from nature and is created in God's own image. This hierarchy sets humans above "things", be it animals, property, or the environment.[82] However, the argument against granting personhood to AI seems to only be problematic if one uses the terms "human being" and "person" synonymously and interchangeably. Artificial intelligence or a robot's personhood does not have the intention to interfere with the exclusivity of humans' place in the world. According to the common legal view, a natural person (being a human) is different from a juridical person. A legal person does not have to consist of blood, flesh, and DNA, but exists to accommodate economic traffic and proceedings in a court of law.

Another argument against granting personhood to robots which aligns with this second model of personhood (only humans can receive personhood) is that, because of the special place that humankind has given himself, it is not in the self-interest of humankind to grant robots personhood.[83] Historically, this argument has similarities to the rationale of slave-owners stating that slaves should not have constitutional rights simply based on the fact that it is not in the best interest of slave owners to grant slaves rights or to grant them comparable human status.[84]

Overall, robots with AI cannot be easily accommodated by Naffine's second model of what it means to be a legal person. Even though most arguments against the granting of personhood to AI entities can be pragmatically based, in which legal personality for AI benefits society, still, robots lack the status of being a human being and this is an insurmountable barrier to being considered a person under Naffine's second model and thus being granted personhood rights.

F.   AI Generated Robot as the Responsible, Rational Actor

The third model of personhood proposed by Naffine is that of the responsible, rational actor.[85] As stated earlier, according to this description of personhood, a biological human is not the critical characteristic for becoming a legal person; instead, the rational, human mental attributes and ability to comprehend a situation will suffice in order to be defined as a person. These characteristics will allow a person to have full legal responsibility. Given current technology, robots are not able to perform as a legal person under this model; primarily because AI cannot act as the fully responsible and capable person, and AI is still dependent on humans for much of its programming. But this situation can change rapidly. Still, we do not know how the future will unfold. For example, imagine a future in which "humanoid AI" has great mental capacity, and is able to comprehend its own state and have responsibilities;[86] would this sort of AI qualify as a legal person within the definition of a responsible rational actor?

---

[82]   Arthur O. Lovejoy, *The Great Chain of Being: A Study of the History of an Idea* (Harvard University Press, Cambridge, 1936).

[83]   Solum, *supra* note 12, at 1260.

[84]   *Id.*, at 1261.

[85]   Naffine, *supra* note 16, at 362.

[86]   See for example the robot Sophia, of Hanson robotics (compare "Ava": Bush, E. (Producer), and Garland, E. (Director) (2014). *Ex machina* [Motion Picture]. United States).

The description of the responsible, rational actor presumes the presence of the very human characteristic of consciousness. But what is consciousness? Is *cogito ergo sum* ("I think, therefore I am") from Descartes proof that the mere act of thinking sufficient to define one's existence as a rational being? Is consciousness a part of, or something separate from, a human being? Or any being for that matter? Maybe the integration of information derived from our sensors produces consciousness.[87] And if so, is this a valid prerequisite for personhood and something that AI could accomplish in the future?[88] We do not have a clear notion of what consciousness actually is and so there is little to say about questions that go beyond our basic intuitions.[89] It could be that we can only expect consciousness to derive from neuronal circuits and similarly from technology that mimics neuronal circuits. It might be the case that we cannot simulate consciousness from anything except neurons, and that we will never be fully able to artificially reproduce it.[90] If AI would be able to achieve consciousness, then according to the responsible rational actor definition, there should be no problem granting personhood to AI robots. How would the consciousness of this AI be established? Since we do not as yet have very good direct access to another person's mind (although technology to record thoughts is moving in this direction), one can only infer consciousness in a being based on external behavior and self-report.[91] It might as well be that the artificial intelligent entity claiming personhood would convincingly argue to humans that it was conscious, but hypothetically, this could merely be the AI faking its consciousness; it is difficult to discern how to definitively know.[92]

Another objection against granting legal personhood status to AI could be that AI lacks feelings as expressed by humans.[93] But even this human characteristic could be developed in future AI, by human efforts or by AI itself. In the context of the legal person as the responsible, rational actor, the existence of feelings could actually be beneficial for the granting of personhood status to AI. Supporters of the rational actor model of personhood state that man should be a rational animal, and requires that he should exercise a reasonable control over his passions.[94] As stated before, the criminal law system takes this actor as the ideal legal person.[95] A form of intelligence completely lacking feelings may not control its feelings because it does not have them in the first place and thus may not act rationally.

Taking into account that AI is not at the level yet in which it could function as a responsible, rational actor, robots cannot be granted personhood status under the rational, responsible actor model. Granting personhood under this model in the future depends completely on how successfully AI will develop in robotics to produce a rational decision maker. If AI has a humanlike consciousness and acts as a responsible rational actor, then

---

[87]   Giulio Tononi, *Integrated Information Theory of Consciousness: An Updated Account*, Archives Italiennes de Biologie (2012) vol. 150, 290–326.
[88]   Solum, *supra* note 12, at 1269.
[89]   *Id.*, at 1264.
[90]   *Id.*, at 1265.
[91]   *Id.*, at 1266.
[92]   *Id.*
[93]   *Id.*, at 1269.
[94]   Naffine, *Who are Law's Persons?*, *supra* note 16, at 364.
[95]   *Id.*

the responsible rational actor model of personhood could include AI. But even without human-like consciousness one could imagine an AI with awareness of its environment that will be sufficient to perform as a rational actor.

G. Conclusions Concerning the "Naffine" Analysis

To answer the question: "To what extent does AI fit in with the different notions of legal personhood" proposed by Naffine, the following conclusions can be drawn.

> *The Cheshire Cat.* Supporters of this personhood model state that person status is nothing more than the abstract capacity to function in law and does not have any further requirements except for the fact that it is people that grant personhood status to an entity. Artificially intelligent robots seem to be compatible with this model of the legal person as it does not require any further qualities such as free will or consciousness whatsoever. The comparison with corporate personhood, as formulated in the EU draft on AI, is a striking example of how AI could be granted personhood status. Both the aims and reasons why personhood for both entities should be invoked for humans and AI, match.
>
> *The legal person as being a human.* Given the personhood status afforded corporations, which obviously is a non-human entity, could one argue that AI robots should similarly be granted legal personhood status? Supporters of this theory do not agree that AI should be considered a legal person. They argue that corporations have legal personhood rights due to the fact that the relationships that govern a corporation are eventually reducible to humans. Therefore, corporations do not lack the key component of humanity which supporters of the model proposing to only give personhood status to a human require. Supporters of the legal person as human theory could argue that by granting personhood status to autonomous robots, we would be undermining the human component that legal personality depends on. This objection is however only a problem if one assumes that the terms "person" and "human" are synonymous and interchangeable. The common legal view is that there is a distinction between natural persons and juridical or legal persons and therefore the granting of personhood to AI entities does not have to lead to diminishing of the personhood status of humans. However, purely looking at the definition of the legal person as human being, AI would not be able to overcome this hurdle and thus obtain personhood status.
>
> *The rational, responsible actor.* According to this theory a legal person is a rational, responsible entity and aware of its own internal and external situation. Thus, this definition excludes young children and mentally incompetent entities from being considered legal persons. Artificial intelligence, as it is at the moment, does not qualify as a person taking the requirements of this definition into account. But future, more developed AI entities may meet the requirements for personhood status under this model. For AI to be qualified as a legal person under this definition would mean that it would require increased mental capacity, responsibility, and exhibiting consciousness. The fact that this quality is artificial should not be disqualifying. Assuming that in the future all these requirements could be met, AI could be granted personhood status under Naffine's proposed third model.

IX.   THE ARTIFICIAL INTELLIGENT ENTITY OR ROBOT AS LEGAL ACTOR

From the previous discussion of legal personhood for natural and artificial people, we can now compare the characteristics of smart robots and other AI systems with legal person-hood requirements established for existing legal entities. As a basic question motivating this analysis—would granting AI entities legal personality be desirable for the AI entity and for society? As stated earlier, the consideration that an autonomously functioning artificially intelligent robot should have a secure legal subjectivity is dependent on the actual social necessity requisite to a certain legal and social order. In other words, will a future society be able to function without any form of legal personality being granted to autonomous artificially intelligent entities? Or will an AI entity need to be placed within the framework of legal personhood? And if so, will it be possible to integrate an AI entity in the existing legal framework or do we need a "sui generis construction"?

The legal status of autonomous robots in the near future could be comparable to the current situation where natural people represent institutions and organizations, and to natural people which represent legally incapacitated individuals when serving as their mandated legal representatives. As an example, a social service agency using a care robot deployment in support of the needy would be under the legal supervision of the agency. In this case, the robot may be capable of managing the household, ordering products and services, conducting physical support, analyzing medical problems, and even performing medical procedures. The legal consequences associated with this level of autonomy are great. Several of these actions create legal effects for several parties, varying from purchasing agreements, the processing of personal data, and implicating the physical integrity of human beings. Clearly, a society that will depend on autonomous systems and robots cannot do so without a legal framework overseeing this development. It is quite conceivable that in a future society, legal personality be granted to robots so that the legal consequences of the acts described above can have appropriate legal consequences. A distinction needs to be made between fully autonomous functioning entities and those entities that operate on the basis of actions initiated by legal persons. Although the "Cheshire Cat" structure discussed above seems to be simplistic in presentation, as it does not take into account social requirements that would be necessary to perform acceptable societal roles and to be recognized by other legal persons, still using this theory we can specify the role, function, and legal effect of the AI entity so it deserves consideration.

A.   Legal Subject or Legal Object *Specialis*?

The definition of a legal subject under current law does not allow an AI entity to be granted personhood status, but there is an increasing degree to which AI is beginning to match natural or artificial persons in abilities. Because of the variation in types of AI, from vacuum cleaners to anthropomorphic sex robots, it is not practical to provide a uniform legal regime for robots. Again, this is due to the variation between robots being far more diverse than the variation between natural people, and the variation shown between artificial people. Under established law, legal persons such as limited liability companies, foundations, etc. are classified by their purpose and function and accord-ingly have different rights and obligations. Similarly, for natural people children under guardianship have a legal status that falls under the supervision of another natural or legal person. Additionally, individuals often function under supervision of others and their activity affects the interpretation of legal personality and the performance of their acts. And government officials, secret service officials, the military, medical physicians and journalists have a different legal status from other individuals concerning their function and their use of rights in society.

As the classification of robots from a legal person status would be desirable, a reconsideration of the degree of legal subjectivity afforded AI entities is needed. In my view, the legal subjectivity and legal capacity afforded AI needs not be equal to the concept of legal personality as it exists in positive law. The possible extension of legal capacity to AI could be based partly on the concept of existing legal personhood, leading to a new "sui generis" construction, and based on elements of legal autonomy for the purpose of taking into account the functioning of the AI robot in society. A comparison with the "peculium-like" requirements for earlier slaves in which a restricted liability is possible could be appropriate.

This reasoning applies when it is possible to determine who the user or owner of the AI system is, and when there is general acceptance of the responsibility of the system. In the future this will become an increasingly difficult problem as systems will function more autonomously and interact with legal consequences with similar autonomous systems. Car manufacturers of smart cars until date still have accepted a risk liability for autonomous cars. This means that the producer accepts responsibility for errors or incomplete functioning of the system including its AI driven automatic control systems. But I expect this liability scheme will come to an end because of the technical and financial burden that will result from AI performing autonomously.[96]

Is the boundary between what is a legal subject and legal object always clear? Legal objects can be goods, services, or objects that are the carrier-subjects of rights and obligations. But under current law, objects can never be bearers of rights and obligations similar to a legal entity. The legal property concerns, in particular business, products and services, is also applicable to more artificial legal person concepts like the organization or company. Artificial legal persons may perform as a legal object but are themselves legal entities. This special construction is also described as a set of active and passive proprietary elements. The sui generis construction for AI can take this into consideration. Autonomous robots could be considered either as objects or subjects depending on the legal activities of other legal actors. Artificial intelligence seems to have a dual role or status, one could interact with AI entities with legal effect, but the owner also could sell them or pawn them.

B.   Liability and Legal Subjectivity

The liability arising from a legal person's actions may apply to the director or directors of the person, and at any time during the lifespan of the legal person, given they either had supervisory responsibility over the person or were authorized to act for the legal person. This reasoning could apply to AI and robots of sufficient autonomy as well. Even though

---

[96]   https://www.media.volvocars.com/global/en-gb/media/pressreleases/167975/us-urged-to-establ ish-nationwide-federal-guidelines-for-autonomous-driving.

robots are currently classified as legal objects under the law, they can also occupy a position in society which could impose legal obligations. In several discussions of legal rights for AI, a comparison has been made with the status of slaves and their associated rights. For example, as discussed by legal scholar Ugo Pagallo, and the founder of the field of information science, Norbert Wiener, the status of a robot compared to slaves could be described as: ". . .the automatic machine, whatever we may think of any feelings it may have or may not have, is the precise equivalent of slave labor." Also Leon Wein discussing liability for machines in *The Responsibility of Intelligent Artifacts* (1992): "As employees who replaced slaves are themselves replaced by mechanical 'slaves,' the 'employer' of a computerized system may once again be held liable for injury caused by his property in the same way that she would have if the damage had been caused by a human slave."[97] Additionally, Voulon stated that the intelligent agent, including the software robot, could be compared to a slave, deployed to carry out a particular task.[98] We can easily draw parallels to these observations about mechanized machines and slaves, with existing AI driven machines that perform the legal actions required to fulfill legal statements and transactions:

> Such a machine would need to have two abilities. First, it must be able to render correct outputs from given factual inputs. Second, its output needs to be reified some way in the real world. The vending machine is the archetypical example of a self-executing smart contract. Vending machines have been defined as "self-contained automatic machines that dispense goods or provide services when coins are inserted."[99]

Based on the above, a vending machine completes one side of a contractual relation, the other side being a human. An interesting, even humorous, example in this respect is the case of the British bookseller, Richard Carlile, who in the year 1822 invented a book-dispensing machine so as to avoid prosecution under the country's libel and sedition laws. He had been jailed previously and wanted to avoid any future liability, so his idea was to make it impossible for the Crown to prove that any individual bookseller had actually sold the blasphemous material. He argued that his contraption resulted in a contract between the buyer and the machine with the publisher having no formal contractual involvement (and thus no liability). What follows is Carlile's description of the machine as it appeared in The Republican:

> Perhaps it will amuse you to be informed that in the new Temple of Reason my publications are sold by Clockwork!! In the shop is the dial on which is written every publication for sale: the purchaser enters and turns the hand of the dial to the publication he wants, when, on depositing his money, the publication drops down before him.[100]

---

[97]   Pagallo, *supra* note 22, referring to Norbert Wiener, *The Human Use of Human Beings* (1950), published in the UK by Free Association Books, London, first published 1950; 1954 Houghton Mifflin. Full text available at https://bit/ly/2Ochxd, at 3.

[98]   Marten Voulon, *Electronic Contracting*, dissertation, Amsterdam 2010.

[99]   Max Raskin, *The Law and Legality of Smart Contracts*, Georgetown Law Technology Review (2017) vol. 304, at 10, citing Kerry Segrave, *Vending Machines: An American Social History* (McFarland and Co., 2002), available at https://ssrn.com/abstract=2959166 or http://dx.doi.org/10.2139/ssrn.2842258.

[100]   *Id.*, at 10–11, referring to Richard Carlile, *To the Republicans of the Island of Great Britain*, Republican, 16, V, 19 April 1822.

The Crown, however, was not amused by the description and effort to avoid liability. Use of the mechanical device was ineffective in deflecting liability and both Carlile and his employee were convicted of selling blasphemous literature through the device.[101] In modern times, there are numerous examples of similar mechanized devices interacting with natural people. The provider of a product is generally easy to identify; for example, the city for parking meters, and the vending company for soft drinks sold on the street or in hotels. But cigarette dispensers are somewhat more difficult to classify. Is the "other party" the shop-owner or the cigarette company? Although we do not know for sure who we are contracting with when we use such machines, instead we just trust the transaction. It is all about trust and credibility.

Ugo Pagallo, citing Chopra and White, also expressed the position that, from a point of legal trust and credibility, for the acceptance of legal actions with legal effect, it must be clear on what mandate and on what legal attribution the agent is functioning; this seems critical for AI entities.[102] For a vending machine, its mandate is clear. For natural persons and AI entities it is not always clear. When natural persons represent legal persons, we would have to access official registers to determine what legal status and attribution of legal capacity the natural person has been granted. In referring back to the position of the Roman slave, one must consider that the relation between the slave and his master, and the relation between the slave and society, was more than instrumental; so, is the same also true for AI?

Roman slaves could perform as a legal representative in some situations, in independent legal transactions, and could appear as a witness in court. Moreover, the slave could be declared a free man by his master (manumission). This was not unusual at the time because of a population of one million people in Rome, there were 400,000 slaves. The position of the slave may be similar to the position of the robot existing in a future society although declaring them "free men" as in the "Millennium man" might not be a likely scenario. Maybe robots could also hold peculium in the sense of a "financial resource to be used without human control". It will be particularly crucial for society to determine to what extent it is desirable that AI robots perform legal acts. Regarding a robotic vacuum cleaner that position is clear, rights for the robot are absent. A more complicated case is the previously mentioned example of a social robot that buys groceries for the needy or orders medicine or even decides when and which medications should be administered. To hold a robot liable will only be necessary if the acts it performs cannot be tracked back to the original actor or "master" behind the robot.

C. The Legal Acts

Why is it so important to define the extent of legal personality for robots? If the robot acts with the intention to change the legal circumstances associated with its acts it must also

---

[101]   *Id.*
[102]   Chopra and White correctly remark in *A Legal Theory for Autonomous Artificial Agents* (The University of Michigan Press, 2011) at 130, "to apply the respondeat superior doctrine to a particular situation would require the artificial agent in question to be one that has been understood by virtue of its responsibilities and its interactions with third parties as acting as a legal agent for its principal." See Pagallo, *supra* note 22, at 132.

have a certain legal status beyond that of a legal object. In a bi- or multi-party relation, legal acts will have legal consequences for the parties concerned and maybe for third parties as well. Of course, both or more (direct) parties must have the will and trust to have a credible legal relation with each other. Part of this relation is also that a party that has an obligation towards the other party can be held liable if he does not perform his legal obligation; be it payment, performing a task, or delivering a product. Also damages that are a consequence of the performance of contracting parties could be recovered by the other party. In addition, we will need to find the appropriate form of liability that will best suit the practical situation and role of the AI robot in the social reality that best matches its performance. For example, robots in the surveillance and security industries as well as in advisory positions, in the health sector, and in the more exotic services will play an important role in society and without direct control by natural persons. The acts performed by AI robots across these industries will need to be recognized by the other legal subjects interacting with AI driven robots based among others on trust and acceptance.

The responsibility of persons who are performing legal acts for others will ultimately rest with identifiable legal persons, or an identifiable natural person(s), the government, political leaders, and representatives accredited to a natural person. With the use of AI robots, responsibility will usually be traced to the same groups, with the robot playing a preparatory policy role or even a representative role. It is conceivable that the robot will also be given a mandate to act granted to it by authorities, for example, in the public sector the right to perform duties benefiting society. Additionally, the arrest of a suspect by a "Robocop" will have to be an act that is secured based on the robot having the legal right to enforce the law. Further, legal and natural persons may be represented by AI robots in the future. This will be quite different than the legal representation provided by natural persons. And this representation will only be possible when it is established which specific competencies are relevant to the performance of the robot's task. The attribution of competency has to be recognized by law, only then will there be a legally credible acceptance of the legal effect of the performed acts by the AI robot.

Further, the actions of an automated system may have legal implications. When an "advanced search robot" meets other bots and exchanges codes which can result in an agreement to reserve a seat or buy a product or service, legal obligations are imposed. The autonomous robot will enter a possible electronic agreement to be accepted by both electronic "parties" without any intervention or even confirmation by a natural person. Can this "Crawler Bot" still be considered an object under the law if it operates with legal subjectivity?[103] The answer requires a clear explanation of the legal circumstances, preferably under contract law for this situation, and the general terms and conditions of the transaction.

Up until today, the fact that individual machines and devices were used for a specific purpose (and thus not deviating from the purpose) made the question of legal personhood straightforward for such entities. For example, a surgeon using a knife to make an incision in a patient who makes a mistake cannot blame the knife or the knife producer for the mistake (except in the case of a material error in the knife itself). Additionally, in times of war, the producer of weapons cannot be held responsible for the casualties resulting from

---

[103]   *Id.*

the war. However, the supreme commander, and his or her subordinates, may well be held responsible for possible war crimes. But what happens when these weapons are no longer instructed or directed by individuals? Or, if they acquire information that will direct and determine their operation without human intervention? For example, consider a drone that is designed to recognize impending danger and to destroy the source of the danger without further instructions or intervention of humans. For now, the destruction takes place by the decision of a natural person using a joystick from a remote location but even in that case the decision to respond is based on data and intelligence that is beyond the user's direct observation or experience. In response to this scenario, warnings have been issued by concerned scholars and industry leaders regarding the dangers to humanity provided by autonomous AI weapons, or "killer robots." In fact, recently in an open letter by the Future of Life Institute to the UN Convention on Certain Conventional Weapons, concern was expressed.[104] Similarly, how does the liability of the above situation concerning the surgeon, change if the surgeon does not directly do the surgery, but has access to sophisticated data supplied by a laser instrument that includes all medical information, including patient documentation? Or what if a computer or social robot determines which drugs a patient requires, based on the patient records in the database? Is there a distinction between an independently operating electronic system as an autonomous player and the use of this system as a tool? After all, in both cases the systems perform activities that have legal consequences. While legal acts are typically performed by persons as legal entities, automated systems, electronically or otherwise, are increasingly being used in various relationships within our global society. For example, algorithms command much of the trading on the stock market buying and selling stock within milliseconds. The fact that such systems, including robots and other AI devices, can act independently and create changes in the legal relations between parties will have a material effect on the positions taken by legal persons, individuals, or third parties. Ultimately, what is the difference between the agent in human form, the natural person, and the AI robot if they perform the same activities? If a natural person, or group of persons, is clearly in command, the identification of the responsible player(s) is normally not difficult and the difference in functional execution is not relevant for liability. Thus, from a perspective of law, the use of search engines for finding tickets, drones for delivering packets to a client, or sending missiles to attack a perceived enemy will make no legal difference in determining liability.

If the practical and legal responsibility associated with actions can be traced back to a legal person there is no change necessary in the legal position of the practical actor. The robot or AI system remains an instrument or legal object for which the legal entity remains responsible. Additionally, this includes the arrangements with respect to product liability in the case of a defective product. For this example, I refer to the exception in article 185 sub paragraph (e) of Book 6 of the Dutch Civil Code where it is stated that a party who brings a product on the market of which, at the state of scientific and technical knowledge at the time he put the product into circulation, it was not possible to discover the existence of the defect of the product, will not be responsible for the defect. And yet this exception is not followed by producers of autonomous or semi-autonomous functioning cars like the Google car, Volvo, and Tesla. It would not be prudent strategy or public relations,

---

[104] www.futureoflife.org, accessed 21-8-2017.

if the risk from using autonomous cars was not taken on by the producers. Regarding liability, a construction of risk liability and payment of damages from a public foundation could be a solution for further development of autonomous AI entities given no human or artificial person to find liable.

Even in the case of natural persons, serving as an attributed representative who is no longer acting rationally, the legal proceedings to determine liability may be annulled as a non-deliberate disturbance of the system. One can draw a parallel with the robot in the latter cases; it can reduce the liability of the initiating individual in the use of this system or can exculpate all parties of the legal action, maybe even the robot itself, if the robot has legal responsibility. This view I share with Voulon, in the sense that any legal effect which is caused by an autonomous and in some cases a less autonomous system must be attributed to the natural or legal person who has made the decision to commission the system in its service operations.[105] This reasoning is based upon the functioning of electronic agents, described as: "A computer program, or electronic or other automated means used independently to initiate an action, or respond to electronic messages or performances, on the person's behalf without review or action by an individual at the time of the action or response to the message or performance."[106]

If necessary, one can apply liability to the person or entity controlling an AI entity to the degree of control exercised over the autonomous system, thereby taking the legal effect of the AI's actions into account. However, this would only be the case with regard to liability and accountability attributed to the natural or legal person. The malfunction or failure of an autonomous system can be significant with regard to the recognition of the actor's legal liability. The autonomous system itself, however, can never bear any legal responsibility until there is a degree of legal personality attributed to it and an acceptance of a legal position to perform legal actions with legal effect. A public register where the scope of legal competence of this entity is consulted would be a solution to enhance credibility.

Moreover, it would be helpful, in order to find a solution for legal liability, to draw a parallel with the liability regulations as included in international regulations for electronic agents: the Uniform Electronic Transaction Act (UETA), the Uniform Computer Information Transaction Act (UCITA) and the Electronic Signatures Act (ESign) being examples. This could provide a model legal framework for autonomous entities engaging in transactions in a legally acceptable manner. Ugo Pagallo suggested that the logical connection to existing forms of legal personhood for AI entities depended on their position and function, and that more precise specifications of robot and their tasks can result in more specified legal subjectivity and legal competence:

(a) Independent legal personhood to robots with rights and duties of their own;
(b) Some rights of constitutional personhood, such as those granted to minors and people with severe psychological illnesses, *i.e.*, personhood without full legal capacity;
(c) Dependent, rather than independent, personhood as it occurs with artificial legal persons such as corporations; and

---

[105] Voulon, *supra* note 98, concluding his dissertation.
[106] Section 102(a)(27) Uniform Computer Information Transaction Act (UCITA).

(d) Stricter forms of personhood in the civil law field, such as the accountability of (some types of) robots for both contractual and extra-contractual obligations.[107]

As Ugo Pagallo discussed in his book on Robot Law, concerning the contracting capability of smart entities: "artificial agents should be able to qualify for independent legal personality" based on the task they have to perform.[108]

X. CONCLUSION AND STEPS INTO THE FUTURE

An autonomous system or robot, even with an independent intelligence and equipped with emotions to function in society, would not need to have a legal status that is similar to the rights and obligations of natural and legal persons in the positive law; however, change is imminent. But even an autonomous system that passes the Turing test would not create any legal responsibilities per se. It is however advisable that autonomously functioning intelligent systems, such as social robots or legal enforcement robots, may need to have a form of attributed legal personhood to carry out their tasks. This is based on the essential requirement that there is a social and legal necessity incurred by AI systems.

The legal positioning of robots in society could be selected for an amendment of the law or possibly even a sui generis standard for certain autonomous robots. This legal positioning will be dependent on the degree of autonomy and social need of society. For the qualification of the robots, the ISO standards for robot design can serve as an example.[109] Additionally, in the International Standardization Organization there is already a development to treat the role of the robot differently (in security) and to develop a standard for robot/human collaboration.[110]

One might also imagine that certain changes could be made to existing law in order to create a practical system representation of autonomous systems for the initial legal actor, the natural, or legal person. These changes in the law will depend on a correct description of the reliability and trust of the representation by the robot, and the purpose of the actions and the legal consensus of the legal entities involved. If these concepts are agreed upon, it will then be necessary to obtain the acceptance by the government and parliament to create or adapt a legal framework. As to how difficult and time consuming

---

[107] Taking into account Teubner's analysis in the *Rights of Non-Humans?* (Springer 2007) the entry of new actors on the legal scene concerns all the nuances of legal agenthood, such as "distinctions between different graduations of legal subjectivity, between mere interests, partial rights and full-fledged rights, between limited and full capacity for action, between agency, representation and trust, between individual, group, corporate and other forms of collective responsibility." See Pagallo, *supra* note 22, at 153, referring to Teubner, *ibid.*

[108] Mireille Hildebrandt and Jeanne Gaakeer, *Human Law and Computer Law: Comparative Perspectives* (Springer, 2013) at 60.

[109] See for example: ISO 13482: 2014 Specifies requirements and guidelines for the inherently safe design, protective measures, and information for use or personal care robots, in particular the following three types of personal care robots: mobile robot servant; physical assistant robot; person carrier robot.

[110] Human and robot system interaction in industrial settings is now possible thanks to ISO / TS 15066, a new ISO technical specification for collaborative robot system safety.

this process will be, reference can be made to the acceptance of the non-natural person in the positive law.

Currently, many AI systems are very difficult for users to understand. This is also increasingly true even for those who initially developed the system. In particular, neural networks are often "black boxes", in which the (decision-making) processes taking place can no longer be understood and for which there are no explanatory mechanisms. This could necessitate a legal requirement to create a form of transparency as to how the systems work, and to enhance trust and credibility of the acts leading to legal effect.

Clearly, artificial intelligence and autonomous robots will be part of our future society. Integration of AI inside the human body will also occur. Our physical and informational integrity will be invaded, with or without our knowledge or consent. We already share a substantial part of our personal data with third parties and seem not overly concerned by the spread of our personal data. Additionally, governments and industries are forcing us to share even more personal information to regulate or protect the social system or to lower risks and costs of services and products. Concerning the protection of our personal data processed by AI, the European General Data Protection Regulation (GDPR)[111] describes the protection of personal data during processing but in outdated terminology concerning AI. Due to the non-technological orientation and the reliance on conventional directions of thinking, the GDPR will not be sufficient to protect personal data in the age of AI. Informational rights for the data subject and transparency of the process cannot be applied to the integrated AI, certainly not if AI is integrated into the physical functions of the human being. There is a big risk of "chilling effects" for the development of AI and robotics if the GDPR is enforced on all AI applications. In a report of the Science and Technology Committee of the UK Parliament, the need for unhindered but controlled applications of AI technology is stressed:

> It is important to ensure that AI technology is operating as intended and that unwanted, or unpredictable, behaviors are not produced, either by accident or maliciously. Methods are therefore required to verify that the system is functioning correctly. According to the Association for the Advancement of Artificial Intelligence: it is critical that one should be able to prove, test, measure and validate the reliability, performance, safety and ethical compliance—both logically and statistically/probabilistically—of such robotics and artificial intelligence systems before they are deployed.[112]

---

[111]   REGULATION (EU) 2016/679 OF THE EUROPEAN PARLIAMENT AND OF THE COUNCIL of 27 April 2016 on the protection of natural persons with regard to the processing of personal data and on the free movement of such data, and repealing Directive 95/46/EC (General Data Protection Regulation).

[112]   Interesting is the concluding recommendation: "73. We recommend that a standing Commission on Artificial Intelligence be established, based at the Alan Turing Institute, to examine the social, ethical and legal implications of recent and potential developments in AI. It should focus on establishing principles to govern the development and application of AI techniques, as well as advising the Government of any regulation required on limits to its progression. It will need to be closely coordinated with the work of the Council of Data Ethics which the Government is currently setting up following the recommendation made in our Big Data Dilemma report. 74. Membership of the Commission should be broad and include those with expertise in law, social science and philosophy, as well as computer scientists, natural scientists, mathematicians and engineers.

For this reason, it will be necessary to develop some form of certification process to determine whether the autonomously functioning robot can be trusted to process data of third parties and perform acts with legal capacity. Which interaction would be considered acceptable between parties will vary, depending on the function and of course the requirements of technological measures of protection of the robot as described above.

It is essential that we, as people, keep control of an AI driven system as long as our control adds value to the system. Further, we would not want to be the victim of autonomous systems engaged in activities counter to society's best interests—such as the collection of personal information and other data for nefarious purposes. But on the other hand, AI technology can only develop without "chilling effects" if it is commercially available to be used as part of the consumer's daily life without too much legal constraint. The existence of a sui generis structure, comparable with the case of the artificial legal person in corporate law, may provide a solution. The Naffine description of the Cheshire Cat combined with the rational actor model can form a rational basis for a legal framework comparable with the existing position of artificial legal persons. At the minimum, the following requirements of the AI entity have to be fulfilled to acquire a sui generis legal personhood:

1. Necessity in the "human" society, socio-economic relevance, need for legal certification;
2. Determination of autonomous intelligence, Turing test like, "human impression" level;
3. Sufficient social intelligence; the AI entity must be able to understand the socio-emotional and moral value of statements by other parties to respond appropriately so that there is an equivalent basis for consensus;
4. Being able to respond to changing circumstances; this aspect I would call "adaptive or dynamic" intelligence;
5. Acceptance by other legal persons by creating trust and reliance for other legal and natural persons to integrate in economic, social and legal interactions;
6. A public register that specifies which robots will have specific legal competences for specified roles and tasks.

Experience tells us we are better off in some cases using our electronic, or technology-based, servants to help us with the practical performance of our everyday duties. And the more intelligent the system is, the more functional the system may be. Giving the AI robot a position in our legal system, perhaps with a form of digital *peculium* as proposed by Pagallo, and with limited resource that could be used as a guarantee to recover from possible mistakes or damages by the AI, could allow accountability for the actions of AI. This could be accomplished by establishing a fund financed by a certain percentage of the earnings of AI robots to guarantee for any losses or damages. However, this is not a general requirement for all robots, as only some will operate with enough intelligence and autonomy to warrant a form of legal personhood and economic personality. At this

---

Members drawn from industry, NGOs and the public, should also be included and a programme of wide ranging public dialogue instituted." https://www.publications.parliament.uk/pa/cm201617/cmselect/cmsctech/145/14506.htm#_idTextAnchor019.

stage of the robot's development, it will be active in the social and economic functioning of society and also the public sector. In this scenario, a certain trust in the acts of robots and recognition of their legal identity will prove to be essential.

As a concluding point, we have to keep in mind that we still have to control the development of AI and not end up with the rather pessimistic post-human outcome described by Yuval Noah Harari in his recent book *Homo Deus*, in which he foretells that science will move in the direction that all organisms are algorithms, life is data-processing, intelligence will be separated from consciousness, and the hyper-intelligent algorithms will know us better than we know ourselves.[113] Do we want super-intelligent algorithms to decide how we live our life, or that the future is developed based on AI without any human influence? The issue of whether AI should receive personhood rights as discussed in this chapter will help humanity frame the debate and help to determine our future.

SOURCES

Statutes

Dutch Civil Code (Burgerlijk Wetboek, BW), Book 2, articles 1 and 2.
Article 2 of the Dutch Constitution (Grondwet, GW), in conjunction with the Dutch Civil Code, Book 1, article 1.
Dutch Civil Code, Book 3, article 2a.
Article 350 paragraph 2 of the Dutch Penal Code (Wetboek van Strafrecht) and Law of May 19, 2011, on an Integrated Framework for Regulations on Captive Animals and Related Topics (Animals Act).
The Principles of European Tort Law (PETL) refers to liability for "auxiliaries" (6: 102).
Article 3: 201 of the Draft Common Frame of Reference (DCFR) of the Principles, Definitions and Model Rules of European Private Law.
Section 102(a)(27) Uniform Computer Information Transaction Act (UCITA).

---

[113]   See Yuval Noah Harari, *Homo Deus: A Brief History of Tomorrow* (Harper Collins, 2017) last sentences.

9. Autonomous driving: regulatory challenges raised by artificial decision-making and tragic choices

Antje von Ungern-Sternberg

I. INTRODUCTION

Autonomous cars are among the most fascinating and visible examples of how artificial intelligence will change our daily life. Very soon, autonomous cars will be able to drive safely on public roads without control of a human driver. The technology—allowing the car's computer system to collect data from sensors, to interact with other vehicles, to analyze data and to control the vehicle's function—has already been developed. Currently, self-driving cars are still being tested, but companies like Ford, Google, Mercedes-Benz, Tesla, and Uber, have announced an intention to sell fully autonomous cars and trucks by 2021.[1] It is unclear how fast the new technology will spread. Some expect a very quick disruption in transportation,[2] others forecast an evolutionary deployment scenario, which means that functions of driving assistance, e.g. lane keeping assistance or emergency braking assistance, and of partial automation, e.g. automated parking or automated highway cruising, are gradually integrated into traditional cars until these are eventually replaced by fully autonomous cars.[3]

One can reasonably expect that autonomous cars will greatly enhance road traffic safety, mobility and convenience. Safety will improve as human errors—currently accountable for over 90 percent of all accidents—are avoided.[4] Self-driving cars will comply with road traffic rules unlike human drivers who tend to ignore many rules, and they are in many respects better than human drivers in collecting data, namely by camera, laser (LIDAR), radar, ultrasonic sensors, GPS and by wireless interaction with other cars (V2V) and infrastructure (V2I), in analyzing the data and in reacting quickly in dangerous situations. Autonomous cars may transport passengers who are unable to drive a car, for example elderly people, children, or people with disabilities, thereby increasing individual mobility. Finally, former car-drivers will be able to spend the time of their ride more conveniently with other activities like work, hobbies, or recreation.

---

[1] Susan Hassler, "2017: The Year of Self-Driving Cars and Trucks" December 30, 2016, *IEEE Spectrum,* http://spectrum.ieee.org/transportation/advanced-cars/2017-the-year-of-selfdriving-cars-and-trucks.

[2] James Arbib/Tony Seba, *Rethinking Transportation 2020-2030. A RethinkX Sector Disruption Report*, May 2017, www.rethinkx.com/transportation (based on the assumption that self-driving vehicles will boost transport as a service).

[3] Sven Beiker, "Deployment Scenarios for Vehicles with Higher-Order Automation" in Markus Maurer, J. Christian Gerdes, Barbara Lenz and Hermann Winner, *Autonomous Driving* (SpringerOpen 2016) 193, 195.

[4] Thomas Winkle, "Safety Benefits of Automated Vehicles: Extended Findings from Accident Research for Development, Validation and Testing" in *Autonomous Driving, supra* note 3, 335, 354.

But autonomous driving might also have negative consequences. It is very likely, for example, that human driving will be outlawed altogether at some point in order to eliminate the risk caused by the human factor. This would of course bar fervent car drivers from experiencing the joy of driving.[5] More importantly, the impact on the environment is to be determined. Autonomous driving could have the positive effect to save energy if smart traffic and passenger management avoided congestion and reduced overall road traffic. However, if all the people who are currently unfit to drive a car will enjoy riding autonomous cars in the future, this might lead to a significant increase in traffic and negative consequences for the environment, to name two concerns.[6]

Turning to legal aspects, road traffic law is a very densely regulated area of law which protects important goods like road safety and traffic fluidity. Traditionally, it is the human driver who must follow the rules of road traffic law. In an autonomous car, it is no longer a human, but an algorithm, i.e. a step-by-step procedure for solving a problem used by a computer,[7] which governs the car's behavior. Shifting decision-making from a human being to an artificial agent such as a self-driving car raises several legal questions. Does the law permit artificial decision-making—or does it require human operators, at least in certain areas of law? How can artificial agents comply with legal norms such as road traffic regulations? And finally, what should self-driving cars do if they cannot avoid an accident and face tragic choices?

This chapter addresses these legal challenges posed by artificial decision-making. The legal questions are considered in an abstract manner, but with a view to German, U.S. and public international law, particularly human rights law. Other legal issues raised by self-driving cars (adaption of international standards of road traffic law and product standards,[8] liability,[9] treatment of data used and generated by autonomous cars[10]) have to be analyzed elsewhere. After clarifying the relevant terms (section II), the chapter looks at the legal framework of artificial decision-making, in general (section III) and the legal problem of tragic choices, in particular (section IV).

---

[5]   This is at least a particular German concern. The Ethics Commission set up by the German Federal Ministry of Traffic in order to assess Autonomous Driving, for example, stated that outlawing human driving would interfere with the right of individual liberty (which also entailed the "pleasure of driving") and could not be justified by enhancement of safety alone (!), *Ethikkommission Automatisches und Vernetzes Fahren*, Bericht, Juni 2017, para. 5, p. 21 https://www.bmvi.de/SharedDocs/DE/Pressemitteilungen/2017/084-dobrindt-bericht-der-ethik-kommission.html.

[6]   Not to mention the unpredictable consequences on the value of urban and rural land due to the cheaper costs of mobility, see Dirk Heinrichs "Autonomous Driving and Urban Land Use" in *Autonomous Driving, supra* note 3, 213.

[7]   The terms algorithm and computer code or computer program will be used interchangeably throughout this chapter.

[8]   See, for example, Bryant Walker Smith, *Automated Vehicles are Probably Legal in the United States* 1 Texas A&M University School of Law 411 (2014); see also below section III.B.2.

[9]   See, for example, Melinda Florina Lohmann, *Liability Issues Concerning Self-Driving Vehicles* 7 European Journal of Risk Regulation 335 (2016); Daniel A. Crane, Kyle D. Logue and Bryce C. Pilz, *A Survey of the Legal Issues Arising From the Deployment of Autonomous and Connected Vehicles* 23 Michigan Telecommunications and Technology Law Review 191 (2017).

[10]   *Cf.* Kai Rannenberg, "Opportunities and Risks Associated with Collecting and Making Usable Additional Data" in *Autonomous Driving, supra* note 3, 497.

II. TERMINOLOGY

Before delving into the legal issues, two terms merit clarification: autonomous driving and artificial intelligence.

A. Autonomous Driving

Autonomy as a legal or philosophical term is a very complex concept. In the context of self-driving cars, however, "autonomous" has a technical meaning which can be clearly defined. Since technological progress and commercial availability increase gradually, a widely-used terminology distinguishes different degrees of autonomy. Most writers refer either to a classification by the US-American National Highway Traffic Safety Administration (NHTSA) established in 2013 (ranging from level 0 to level 4) or to a classification by SAE International, a private association of engineers and related technical experts in the aerospace, automotive and commercial-vehicle industries, the former Society of Automotive Engineers, proposed in 2016 (Standard J3016, ranging from level 0 to 5)[11] (Table 9.1). The latter is more differentiated than the former and has, by now, also been adopted by the NHTSA.[12] As a consequence, it will be taken as a basis for this chapter as well.

At level 0, solely the human driver is in charge of steering and acceleration/deceleration. At level 1, the car takes over a specific driving task, for example cruise control which keeps the car at a defined speed.[13] At level 2, the car can maintain two or more driving tasks—for example cruise control, automatic distance control and automated lane keeping—while the driver constantly monitors and controls the car. The most advanced automated cars which have been put up for sale until mid-2017 are level 2 cars, for example Tesla's Autopilot.[14] There is a decisive divide between level 2 and level 3: Cars from level 3 onwards drive by themselves. Level 3 cars, however, must still be constantly supervised by the human driver who has to be able to intervene promptly if a problem occurs. Level 4 cars do not need constant human supervision, but they are only capable to drive without human interference in common driving scenarios. Level 5 cars, finally, are able to drive without any human supervision or interference in all traffic or weather conditions in which a human driver could drive.

In this chapter, the term "autonomous" or "self-driving" car (used interchangeably) refers to level 3 to 5 cars, i.e. cars which are no longer driven by a human driver, but by a computer system. Thus, autonomous driving includes situations characterized by human supervision ("human *on* the loop" as opposed to "human *in* the loop") but also

---

[11] Both classifications are reproduced, for example, in Dorothy J. Glancy, *Autonomous and Automated and Connected Cars—Oh My! First Generation Autonomous Cars in the Legal Ecosystem* 16 Minn. J.L. Sci. & Tech. 619, 630 (2015); a short description of the SAE classification can be found on the SAE's homepage www.sae.org/misc/pdfs/automated_driving.pdf.

[12] NHTSA, *Federal Automated Vehicles Policy – Accelerating the Next Revolution in Roadway Safety*, September 2016, p. 9, www.transportation.gov/AV.

[13] *Cf.* Axel Davies, "Everyone Wants a Level 5 Self-Driving Car—Here's What That Means" *Wired*, August 16, 2016, www.wired.com/2016/08/self-driving-car-levels-sae-nhtsa/.

[14] *Id.*

Table 9.1   Levels of driving automation as defined by SAE International Standard J3016[15]

Human driver monitors the driving environment	
Level 0 No Automation	the full-time performance by the human driver of all aspects of the dynamic driving task,[16] even when enhanced by warning or intervention systems
Level 1 Driver Assistance	the driving mode[17]-specific execution by a driver assistance system of either steering or acceleration/deceleration using information about the driving environment and with the expectation that the human driver perform all remaining aspects of the dynamic driving task
Level 2 Partial Automation	the driving mode-specific execution by one or more driver assistance systems of both steering and acceleration/ deceleration using information about the driving environment and with the expectation that the human driver perform all remaining aspects of the dynamic driving task
Automated driving system ("system") monitors the driving environment	
Level 3 Conditional Automation	the driving mode-specific performance by an automated driving system of all aspects of the dynamic driving task with the expectation that the human driver will respond appropriately to a request to intervene
Level 4 High Automation	the driving mode-specific performance by an automated driving system of all aspects of the dynamic driving task, even if a human driver does not respond appropriately to a request to intervene
Level 5 Full Automation	the full-time performance by an automated driving system of all aspects of the dynamic driving task under all roadway and environmental conditions that can be managed by a human driver

situations without any human role ("human *out of* the loop"), whereas the lower levels 1 and 2—characterized by a human driver in the loop—could be labelled "assisted" driving. Sometimes, "autonomy" is distinguished from "automation", emphasizing that autonomous systems are "intelligent" and capable to operate in an open surrounding whereas automated systems only fulfill simple, clearly defined tasks. In the literature on autonomous cars, both terms—automation and autonomy—can be found. Given the complicated tasks mastered by self-driving cars, it is, by all means, appropriate to speak of (technical) autonomy. Thus, driving decisions in autonomous cars are taken by the car (or rather the corresponding algorithm), not by a human driver.

---

[15]   Description taken from the SAE classification, supra note 11.

[16]   Dynamic driving task includes the operational (steering, braking, accelerating, monitoring the vehicle and roadway) and tactical (responding to events, determining when to change lanes, turn, use signals, etc.) aspects of the driving task, but not the strategic (determining destinations and waypoints) aspect of the driving task.

[17]   Driving mode is a type of driving scenario with characteristic dynamic driving task requirements (e.g., expressway merging, high speed cruising, low speed traffic jam, closed-campus operations, etc.).

B.   Artificial Intelligence

There is less clarity in legal literature about the term "artificial intelligence" although self-driving cars and other artificial agents are commonly described as "intelligent" or "smart". Computer scientists distinguish four meanings of artificial intelligence. The Turing test approach, *first*, implies that a computer passes the intelligence test if a human interrogator, after posing questions and receiving answers from the computer, cannot tell whether the responses come from a human being or from a computer.[18] This test may be useful in other contexts, for example if an artificial personality is created to replace a human companion, but it does not make sense in the context of self-driving cars whose predominant task is to function reliably and safely. According to the *second* understanding artificial intelligence means that computers replicate the human mode of thinking.[19] This cognitive modelling approach (sometimes coined "strong artificial intelligence") is very ambitious as it requires deep insights into the working of the human mind and yet to be developed abilities of computer systems.[20] In our context, the second understanding can be set aside since self-driving cars work without cognitive modelling. The *third* approach equates intelligence with logical reasoning.[21] This approach, however, only works in formal settings where knowledge can be organized in logical notations, but not in real-life situations such as car driving which imply uncertainty, for example.[22]

According to the *fourth* approach, artificial intelligence describes rational behavior of artificial agents[23] or (to put it bluntly) intelligent outcomes.[24] It implies that these computer agents "operate autonomously, perceive their environment, persist over a prolonged time period, adapt to change, and create and pursue goals. A rational agent is one that acts so as to achieve the best outcome or, when there is uncertainty, the best expected outcome."[25] This understanding is well-suited to capture the properties of autonomous agents ranging from mere computer programs (e.g. internet search engines, programs assessing the risk of recidivism in criminals) to physical machines like care robots, police robots, autonomous weapon systems or self-driving cars. Compared to the aforementioned approaches, it is more comprehensive than relying on logical reasoning alone (approach 3), less demanding than a replication of human cognition (approach 2) and it relies on similar computer abilities which would enable it to pass the Turing test (approach 1). In computer science, these abilities can be described namely as problem solving, knowledge representation, coping with uncertainty, learning, communication and robotics.[26] As a result, all autonomous cars are intelligent as they autonomously

---

[18]   Stuart J. Russell and Peter Norvig, *Artificial Intelligence. A Modern Approach* 3rd ed. (New Pearson 2010) p. 2.

[19]   *Id.*, p. 3.

[20]   *Id.*, p. 3. *Cf.* Harry Surden, "Autonomous Agents and Extension of Law" *Concurring Opinions*, February 16, 2012, https://concurringopinions.com/archives/2012/02/autonomous-agents-and-extension-of-law-policymakers-should-be-aware-of-technical-nuances.html.

[21]   Russell and Norvig, *supra* note 18, p. 4.

[22]   *Id.*

[23]   *Id.*

[24]   Surden, *supra* note 20.

[25]   Russell and Norvig, *supra* note 18, p. 4.

[26]   *Id.*, chapters 3–25.

pursue goals (e.g. drive from A to B or find a free parking spot nearby) and thus autonomously reach intelligent outcomes.

Traditional legal concepts are not only challenged by artificial agents' autonomy, but more specifically by their learning abilities. Thus, a narrower understanding of artificial intelligence focuses on machine learning.[27] Machine learning implies that artificial agents improve their behavior through experience, i.e. by training, not by following a fixed program.[28] Learning algorithms may, for example, recognize images of traffic signs after being fed with images depicting those signs.[29] The algorithms analyze data, detect patterns and build or refine models, mostly based on statistical calculations, in order to fulfill a given task. Well known applications of machine learning range from image and language recognition to spam filtering, language translation and the diagnosing of diseases or health risks.[30] Machine learning is particularly useful if it is too complicated to define all the steps necessary for fulfilling a given task (as in language translation, for example) or if these steps are unknown (as in characterizing the patterns of the risk of a certain disease, for example[31])—and if datasets exist or may be created. Learning algorithms might also be used in self-driving cars, not only for image recognition, but also for airbag deployment or for finding the optimal path within a vehicle lane.[32] They could even enable a car to learn driving all by itself by observing human drivers.[33]

As a consequence, decision-making by artificial agents does not necessarily imply the use of machine learning. But, from a legal point of view, it will be relevant whether a certain feature of a self-driving car runs on a learning algorithm.

III.   THE LEGAL FRAMEWORK FOR ARTIFICIAL DECISION-MAKING

How does artificial decision-making fit into the existing legal framework? Before characterizing artificial decision-making (subsection A), examining human operator requirements (subsection B) and addressing law compliance by artificial agents (subsection C), two aspects should be emphasized at the outset. First, the term "decision-making" by

---

[27]   *Cf.* Harry Surden, *Machine Learning and Law* 89 Washington Law Review 89 (2014); Amitai Etzioni and Oren Etzioni, *Keeping AI Legal* 19 Vanderbilt Journal of Entertainment and Technology Law 133 (2016).

[28]   Russell and Norvig, *supra* note 18, chapters 18–21; Walther Wachenfeld and Hermann Winner, "Do Autonomous Vehicles Learn?" in *Autonomous Driving, supra* note 3, 451; Jason Tanz, "Soon We Won't Program Computers. We'll Train Them Like Dogs" *Wired*, June 2016, www.wired.com/2016/05/the-end-of-code/; Will Knight, "The Dark Secret at the Heart of AI" *MIT Technology Review* April 11, 2017 www.technologyreview.com/s/604087/the-dark-secret-at-the-heart-of-ai/.

[29]   On this difficult task see Evan Ackerman, "Slight Street Sign Modifications Can Completely Fool Machine Learning Algorithms" *IEEE Spectrum*, August 4, 2017, http://spectrum.ieee.org/cars-that-think/transportation/sensors/slight-street-sign-modifications-can-fool-machine-learning-algorithms.

[30]   Surden, *supra* note 27.

[31]   Matthew Hutson, "Self-taught artificial intelligence beats doctors at predicting heart attacks" April 14, 2017, http://www.sciencemag.org/news/2017/04/self-taught-artificial-intelligence-beats-doctors-predicting-heart-attacks.

[32]   Wachenfeld and Winner, *supra* note 28, p. 456.

[33]   Knight, *supra* note 28 on the car by (chip maker) Nvidia.

intelligent agents is not meant to carry the notion of human free will. Instead, it rests on the fact that these agents operate in an increasingly open surrounding. A driverless underground railway, for example, can operate at different speeds, but still has to stick to the railway tracks and normally follows a fixed schedule. Driving a car, however, implies choices regarding the speed and the location of the car on the vast road network, including reacting to countless different traffic situations. Decision-making describes the task of picking one of the many options to act, depending on the circumstances of any given situation—regardless of whether the choice is taken by a human operator or a machine.

Second, law enjoys primacy over technology. Law determines the permissible operations of artificial agents—and not the other way round. This observation, trivial from a lawyer's perspective, is worth being recalled in the face of technological companies that claim leadership and preach technological solutions for the world's problems.[34] As a consequence, every legal norm affecting a self-driving car must be respected, technological capabilities or constraints notwithstanding.

A. Characteristics of Artificial Decision-Making

Human and artificial decision-making differ significantly: when facing the choice between stopping at a yellow traffic light or crossing the intersection, a human driver can, in principle, decide freely how to act even if the outcome will effectively be influenced by individual factors such as the driver's habits, her ability to assess the situation, her respect for traffic rules, or her emotional state. A self-driving car, on the other hand, is governed by algorithms which produce a definitive result for every situation depending on relevant factors such as the distance between the car and the intersection and the calculated braking distance.

Thus, one of the most important advantages of autonomous cars is that they will unconditionally obey all legal norms duly reflected in the driving algorithms. Unlike human drivers who might speed, tailgate, take someone's right of way or jump a red light—due to emotions, fatigue, recklessness or outright egoism—autonomous cars can be programmed not to violate traffic law. Proponents of other uses of artificial agents are also driven by the hope of fully law-abiding algorithms, for example of autonomous weapon systems which would never contravene the laws of armed conflict[35] or of automated law finding and law enforcement which would preclude the bias or the inaccuracy of a human judge or policeman.[36] In addition to the advantage of law-compliance

---

[34] For a critical account of this "solutionist" approach, see Evgeny Morosow, *To Save Everything Click Here* (Public Affairs 2013).

[35] Ronald C. Arkin, *Governing Lethal Behavior in Autonomous Robots* (Boca Ration 2009); Michael N. Schmitt and Jeffrey S. Thurnher, *"Out of the Loop": Autonomous Weapon Systems and the Law of Armed Conflict* 4 Harvard National Security Journal 2013, 231; Kenneth Anderson, Daniel Reisner and Matthew Waxman, *Adapting the Law of Armed Conflict to Autonomous Weapon Systems* 90 International Law Studies 386 (2014); Marco Sassóli, *Autonomous Weapons and International Humanitarian Law: Advantages, Open Technical Questions and Legal Issues to be Clarified* 90 International Law Studies 308 (2014).

[36] The use of a recidivism risk assessment algorithm in criminal sentencing has been affirmed by the Wisconsin Supreme Court *State v. Loomis* 881 N.W.2d 749 (Wis. 2016); some scholars endorse the idea that the process of law finding by the judiciary is supported or even replaced by

unaffected by human traits and biases, artificial agents are also hoped to outperform humans in the knowledge of relevant facts and laws. Autonomous cars will recognize dangerous situations hidden to the human eye (for example a deer crossing a street at night) or analyze several driving options when faced with an unavoidable accident (choosing the least damaging outcome) and they will have access to traffic law in detail (including case law or laws of foreign countries on trips abroad). As a consequence, self-driving cars will be even better than humans at fulfilling general duties such as avoiding accidents or mitigating damages.

A closer look reveals, however, that law compliance is far more complex than the above discussion. If artificial agents operate in a surrounding defined by legal norms, several challenges arise.[37] *First*, artificial agents are incapable of law-finding. Law is made by humans and expressed in human language, it embodies human values and governs the life of human communities, it addresses human behavior and establishes rights and duties of human beings. As a consequence, law has traditionally been construed and applied exclusively by humans. For reasons of clarity and normativity, the terms "law" or "legal" norms, rules and principles should therefore remain limited to law in the traditional sense and should be distinguished from technical instructions (algorithms, computer code) governing the outputs of a computer system. Law's human essence does not preclude that it is translated into algorithms. But this is a challenging task (see below section III.C.1.).

Second, artificial agents have difficulties in establishing specific facts, for example in assessing human behavior. Even the most advanced algorithms are unable to reliably predict human behavior in road traffic, e.g. the behavior of pedestrians[38] (and may still be fooled

---

algorithms, cf. the critical remarks by Kyriakos N. Kotsoglou, *Subsumtionsautomat 2.0. Über die (Un-)Möglichkeit einer Algorithmisierung der Rechtserzeugung* Juristenzeitung 69 (2014), 451; in favor of these approaches Martin Fries, *Man versus Machine: Using Legal Tech to Optimize the Rule of Law*, https://papers.ssrn.com/sol3/papers.cfm?abstract_id=2842726, p. 9; Anjanette H. Raymond and Scott J. Shackelford, *Technology, Ethics, and the Access to Justice: Should an Algorithm be Deciding Your Case?* 35 Michigan Journal of International Law 485 (2014); on possible techniques see Nikolaos Aletras, Dimitrios Tsarapatsanis, Daniel Preotiuc-Pietro and Vasileios Lampos, *Predicting judicial decisions of the European Court of Human Rights: a Natural Language Processing perspective* PeerJ Computer Science October 24, 2016, https://peerj.com/articles/cs-93/; on automated law enforcement (surveillance, analysis, action) see Woodrow Hartzog, Gregory Conti, John Nelson and Lisa A. Shay, *Inefficiently Automated Law Enforcement Michigan State Law Review* 1763 (2015).

[37]   On the challenges of law-compliance by artificial agents see, for example, Ronald Leenes and Federica Lucivero, *Laws on Robots, Laws by Robots, Laws in Robots: Regulating Robot Behaviour by Design* 6 Law, Innovation and Technology 193 (2014); Henry Prakken and Giovanni Sartor, *Law and Logic: A Review from an Argumentation Perspective* 227 Artificial Intelligence 214 (2015); Amitai Etzioni and Oren Etzioni, *Designing AI Systems that Obey Our Laws and Values* 9(9) Communications of the ACM 29 (2016); Trevor Bench-Capon and Sanjay Modgil, *Norms and Value Based Reasoning: Justifying Compliance and Violation* 25 Artificial Intelligence and Law 29 (2017); on autonomous cars, in particular, see Henry Prakken, "On the Problem of Making Autonomous Vehicles Conform to Traffic Law" 25 *Artificial Intelligence and Law* 341 (2017), available at https://link.springer.com/journal/10506/onlineFirst/page/1; on legal automation, more generally, see Ugo Pagallo and Massimo Durante, *The Pros and Cons of Legal Automation and its Governance* 7 European Journal of Risk Regulation 323 (2016).

[38]   Rodney Brooks, "The Big Problem With Self-Driving Cars is People" July 27, 2017 http://spectrum.ieee.org/transportation/self-driving/the-big-problem-with-selfdriving-cars-is-people.

when reading traffic signs[39]), which prevents that traffic rules can be followed accordingly. Thus, the reliability of fact-finding is also a matter of legal concern (see below section III.C.2.)

And *third*, algorithms—even though they might help to fight human biases—also embody biases. At first sight, self-driving cars seem less problematic than other uses of artificial intelligence, for example image recognition, online-advertising or criminal sanctioning which were found to produce racist outcomes.[40] But imagine, for example, that a self-driving car cannot avoid an accident and will either hit a bicyclist wearing a helmet or a bicyclist without a helmet.[41] Which collision should it choose? If the car is programmed to avoid the least vulnerable person, i.e. the bicyclist without a helmet, this will effectively punish those road users who protect themselves with a helmet. If the car is programmed, however, not to take headgear into account or to decide against road users not protecting themselves with a helmet, this might cause bigger damage and amounts to a bias against the unprotected road users. This shows that algorithms are never value free—they create biases of their own. As a consequence, a legal order must outlaw unacceptable tendencies and may regulate others. This will be illustrated by the problem of tragic choices, i.e. life-and-death decisions before an accident (see below section IV).

B. Human Operator Requirements

In some areas of law, artificial decision-making is implicitly or explicitly prohibited. There might be different reasons for such a human operator requirement—but the problem of artificial law compliance will often be one of them.

1. Human operator requirements in other areas of law

Human decision-making will regularly be required for the task of law-finding or exercising governmental authority. German civil and criminal procedural law explicitly states, for example, that the "court" (composed of one or several human judges) hears evidence and renders the decision, which prevents outsourcing this task to algorithms.[42] Furthermore, legal norms may contain an implicit understanding that certain forms of decision-making are reserved to humans. German public law stipulates, for example, that public agencies exercise discretion when imposing a speeding fine. As a consequence automation is precluded and an individual decision by a (human) public servant is necessary.[43] Other legal requirements of

---

[39]   Note 29.

[40]   On image recognition software tagging several African-Americans as gorillas *cf.* Megan Garcia, "How to Keep Your AI From Turning Into a Racist Monster" *Wired*, February 13, 2017, www.wired.com/2017/02/keep-ai-turning-racist-monster/; on online ads offering a person's criminal record after an internet user has googled a black sounding name Latanya Sweeney, *Discrimination in Online Ad Delivery* 56 Communications of the ACM 44 (2013); on racial profiling Bernard E. Harcourt, *Against Prediction – Profiling, Policing and Punishing in an Actuarial Age* (University of Chicago Press 2006).

[41]   On a similar example *cf.* Jeffrey K. Gurney, *Crashing Into the Unknown: An Examination of Crash-Optimization Algorithms through the Two Lanes of Ethics and Law* 79 Albany Law Review 183, 197 (2015/16).

[42]   *Cf.* § 286 German Code of Civil Procedure, § 261 German Code of Criminal Procedure.

[43]   *Cf.* § 47(1)(1) *German Administrative Offences Act*; Higher Regional Court (OLG) Hamm, *Neue Juristische Wochenschrift* 1995, 2937; Higher Regional Court (OLG) Brandenburg, *Neue Zeitschrift*

individual decision-making also imply human assessment, e.g. an individual assessment of the defendant's guilt in criminal law,[44] an individual's right to be heard in administrative or judicial proceedings,[45] or the general prohibition of automated individual decision-making (including profiling) using personal data under EU data protection law.[46]

But human operator requirements can also be inferred from open-textured norms and the difficulty of artificial law compliance. Under the law of armed conflict, for example, a military attack is prohibited if it "may be expected to cause incidental loss of civilian life, injury to civilians, damage to civilian objects, or a combination thereof, which would be excessive in relation to the concrete and direct military advantage anticipated" (Article 51(5)(b) Additional Protocol I to the Geneva Conventions). It is not feasible to translate this assessment of proportionality into abstract rules of computer code, because it depends on multiple factors which are impossible to envisage and to evaluate in advance.[47] Thus, this provision of the law of armed conflict embodies a human operator requirement for weapon systems, at least if civilian losses have to be expected.

2.   Human driver requirement

Are human operators required under the law for self-driving cars, i.e. does the law demand a human driver? This issue is not only dealt with in national road traffic law, but also prescribed in two international conventions concluded under the auspices of the Economic and Social Council of the United Nations in order to facilitate international road traffic and to increase road safety through the adoption of uniform traffic rules. The Geneva Convention on Road Traffic (1949), ratified by nearly 100 state parties across the globe including the United States, Canada and other Commonwealth states,[48] stipulates

---

für Strafrecht 1996, 393; generally on the opposition of automation and discretion Danielle Keats Citron, *Technological Due Process* 85 Washington University Law Review 1249 (1303).

[44]   According to § 46(1)(1) German Criminal Code, for example, the criminal sentence rests on the perpetrator's guilt. Furthermore, the principle of "nulla poena sine culpa" is also guaranteed by the constitution, see German Federal Constitutional Court, BVerfGE 20, 323, 331 (1966); on individual-ized considerations in sentencing under US law see Sonja B. Starr, *Evidence-Based Sentencing and the Scientific Rationalization of Discrimination* 66 Stan. L. Rev. 803 (2014)—framing the problem mainly in terms of non-discrimination; Dawinder S. Sidhu, *Moneyball Sentencing* 56 Boston College L. Rev. 671 (2015); Andrea Roth, *Trial by Machine* 104 Georgetown Law Journal 1245, 1285 (2016).

[45]   In German constitutional law, for example, the right to be heard is guaranteed in Art. 103(1) German Basic Law for judicial proceedings and flows from the rule of law (specified in § 28 German Administrative Procedure Act) for administrative proceedings; on the right to be heard under Art. 6 European Convention on Human Rights see European Court of Human Rights (ECHR) *Montovanelli/France* No. 21497/93 (1997), para. 33; *Goktepe/Belgium* No. 50372/99 (2005), para. 25; on the US perspective see Citron, *supra* note 43, p. 1305 (meaningful notice and opportunity to be heard), and the petition in *Loomis v. State of Wisconsin* Oct 5, 2016 (www.scotusblog.com/case-files/cases/loomis-v-wisconsin/) (due process rights in actuarial recidivism risk assessment when the algorithm is undisclosed and discriminatory).

[46]   Art. 22 EU General Data Protection Regulation 2016/679.

[47]   Noel. E. Sharkey, *The evitability of autonomous robot warfare* 94 International Review of the Red Cross 787, 789 (2012); Markus Wagner, *The Dehumanization of International Humanitarian Law: Legal, Ethical, and Political Implications of Autonomous Weapon Systems* 47 Vanderbilt Journal of Transnational Law 1371, 1388 (2014).

[48]   125 UN Treaty Series 3; https://treaties.un.org/Pages/ViewDetailsV.aspx?src=TREATY&mt dsg_no=XI-B-1&chapter=11&Temp=mtdsg5&clang=_en.

in Article 8 (1): "Every vehicle or combination of vehicles proceeding as a unit shall have a driver." Similarly, the Vienna Convention on Road Traffic (1968), which was ratified by 65 predominantly European states[49] and replaces the Geneva Convention for its members,[50] demands in Article 8 (1): "1. Every moving vehicle or combination of vehicles shall have a driver." This raises the question if the term driver is confined to a human or can be understood to include artificial agent also.

Interestingly, US scholars seem to be more open for a reading which includes artificial agents[51] than German scholars.[52] The requirement of a "driver",[53] defined by the Conventions to be "a person" who drives a vehicle,[54] must traditionally be understood to characterize a natural person, not an artificial agent. (This understanding might change, of course, if artificial agents are granted legal personality in the future.) Systematical consideration supports this reading as both Conventions—the modernized Vienna Convention[55] more than the Geneva Convention[56]—establish duties of the driver which reflect human characteristics. Finally, from a teleological point of view, both Conventions aim at guaranteeing road traffic safety by imposing duties on a driver who is in control of the car[57] whereas upholding safety of self-driving cars would focus on the standards of these cars and their artificial agents. Thus, the Geneva and the Vienna Conventions (still) presuppose that a car is driven by a human, not by an artificial driver.[58]

Both Conventions could be amended, however, to allow for intelligent agents as car

---

[49] 1042 UN Treaty Series 17; https://treaties.un.org/Pages/ViewDetailsIII.aspx?src=TREAT Y&mtdsg_no=XI-B-19&chapter=11&Temp=mtdsg3&clang=_en.

[50] Art. 48 Vienna Convention on Road Traffic.

[51] Influential Bryant Walker Smith, *Automated Vehicles are Probably Legal in the United States* 1 Texas A&M University School of Law 411, 424 seqq. (2014).

[52] Lennart S. Lutz, *Autonome Fahrzeuge als rechtliche Herausforderung* Neue Juristische Wochenschrift 119, 123 (2015); Benjamin von Bodungen and Martin Hoffmann, *Das Wiener Übereinkommen über den Straßenverkehr und die Fahrzeugautomatisierung (Teil 2)* Straßenverkehrsrecht 93, 95 (2016); Antje von Ungern-Sternberg, "Völker- und europarechtliche Implikationen autonomen Fahrens" in: Bernd H. Oppermann and Jutta Stender-Vorwachs, *Autonomes Fahren* (C.H.Beck 2017) p. 293, 310 seq.

[53] On the rules of interpretation cf. Art. 31 Vienna Convention on the Law of Treaties 1969, UN Treaty Series 1155, I-18232.

[54] Art. 4(1) Geneva Convention: "'Driver' means any person who drives a vehicle, including cycles, or guides draught, pack or saddle animals or herds or flocks on a road, or who is in actual physical control of the same." Art. 1(v) Vienna Convention: "'Driver' means any person who drives a motor vehicle or other vehicle (including a cycle), or who guides cattle, singly or in herds, or flocks, or draught, pack or saddle animals on a road".

[55] For example Art. 8(3)(4) and (6) Vienna Convention demanding that drivers "shall possess the necessary physical and mental ability and be in a fit physical and mental condition to drive", "shall possess the knowledge and skill necessary for driving the vehicle" and "shall at all times minimize any activity other than driving" and—by domestic legislation—shall be prohibited to use "a hand-held phone while the vehicle is in motion".

[56] Art. 10 Geneva Convention demands, for example, that drivers "drive in a reasonable and prudent manner" and slow down "when visibility is not good".

[57] Art. 8(5) Geneva Convention; Art. 8(5) and Art. 13 Vienna Convention.

[58] Note that similar human driver requirements may also exist under national road traffic law. But not explicit requirements of a driver are found in the German Road Traffic Regulations or the US state laws governing road traffic; on the latter see Smith, *supra* note 51, 463.

drivers.[59] Thus, the question ensues whether traffic law—like the law of armed conflict—is generally too open-textured to be followed by artificial agents. However, most norms of traffic law determine in a comparatively precise and comprehensive manner how a car can move (i.e. prescribing direction, speed, distance, right of way etc.). Even more general duties such as adjusting to traffic and weather conditions or showing mutual respect to other road users[60] can be categorized for typical situations (congestions, car accidents, approaching emergency cars, snow, glaze, fog or storm). And finally, in untypical and unpredictable situations, the car could be programmed to drive defensively, come to a standstill or demand that a human driver or remote operator takes over. As a consequence, road traffic law does not contain an implicit overall human operator requirement.

C.   Law-Compliance by Artificial Agents

If artificial decision-making is legal in general, how can it be assured that artificial agents obey the law? This question is particularly important if artificial agents and humans operate simultaneously[61] in a densely regulated area of law (as opposed to, say, vacuum cleaning robots or internet search engines).

1.   Translating law into algorithm

It is clear, first, that the legal norms of road traffic law have to be translated into algorithms.[62] For practical reasons, the technical details of this translation will have to be developed by computer engineers. But the legal framework for this task will have to be specified by international and national regulation.

The translation can either proceed *top-down*, i.e. by deducing precise rules from general duties, or *bottom-up*, i.e. by teaching self-driving cars to model themselves on human drivers and to induce traffic rules from their behavior.[63] The top-down approach corresponds to the traditional legal technique of rule-making by administrative agencies or standard-setting private bodies. Under the top-down approach, the general duty to drive "at a careful and prudent speed not greater than nor less than is reasonable and proper, having due regard to the traffic, surface, and width of the highway and of any other condition existing at the time",[64] for example, would be translated into a specific maximum or minimum speed for a specific situation defined by speed limits, traffic conditions, weather and the like. Legal supervision is necessary in order to ensure that road traffic laws are interpreted faithfully and uniformly. As any other form of rule-making, the top-down

---

[59]   Generally by approval of a two-thirds majority of the state parties according to Art. 31(3) Geneva Convention; or even by silence of a two-thirds majority in response to an amendment proposal according to Art. 49(2) Vienna Convention.

[60]   *Cf.* "Use of the road requires constant care and mutual respect", § 1(1) German Road Traffic Regulations.

[61]   *Cf.* Glancy, *supra* note 11, 648.

[62]   *Cf.* Leenes and Lucivero, *supra* note 37; Prakken, *supra* note 37.

[63]   On top-down and bottom-up approaches in general Wendell Wallach and Colin Allen, *Moral Machines – Teaching Robots Right From Wrong* (OUP 2009) chapters 6 and 7; Leenes and Lucivero, *supra* note 37, 4.4.

[64]   Section 627(1) Michigan Vehicle Code Act 300 of 1949, to pick one of the US state codes at random.

approach has the advantage of being clear and predictable. But trying to anticipate and to regulate every imaginable situation in a comprehensive manner is very cumbersome. More importantly, rules are inflexible in untypical, unpredictable situations.

Thus, it may also be useful to let a self-driving car learn from human car drivers how to behave in these situations. It could learn, for example, to cross a solid line (which is generally prohibited) in order to cautiously circumnavigate an obstacle like a piece of dropped cargo—instead of bringing traffic to a standstill. Similarly, it could learn to align itself with the surrounding cars in order to create an emergency corridor (even if the emergency lane is established at the wrong place)—instead of obstructing the wrongly placed emergency corridor by following the legal rule. Bottom-up approaches are not alien to law-making and law-finding. Customary international law evolves from state practice and its acceptance as law,[65] and case law is developed by judicial decisions.[66] Thus, machine-learning, i.e. recognizing and reproducing patterns of (legal) behavior by self-driving cars, resembles the task of inducing legal rules from state behavior or judicial decisions. But unlike states which are entitled to develop customary international law and unlike courts which are authorized to clarify the law, road users do not, per se, qualify as a reliable source for lawful behavior, neither are they authorized to change the law. The examples show, on the other hand, that a flexible reading of legal rules helps to promote more general and possibly more important aims of traffic law such as keeping up the traffic flow or facilitating emergency operations. This could even include speeding, a very common violation of traffic law which should not be promoted generally, if it avoids or minimizes the risks of accidents, for example when a car merges onto the highway from an entrance ramp.[67]

As a consequence, the conditions of bottom-up rule-making by learning algorithms must be specified by law.[68] There are different modalities of machine-learning, allowing for a different degree of human input and control.[69] Imagine, for example, that the self-driving car would have to get clearance by a remotely operating legal officer in every new and untypical traffic situation before it was entitled to disrespect a rule of traffic law (and to reproduce this behavior in similar situations in the future). Contrast this with a process in which the self-driving car watches and imitates the behavior of the other cars, including reckless speeding and other violations of traffic law which are not justified by the circumstances. Faced with these extremes, upholding the primacy of law presupposes, at least, that machine-learning is supervised by humans and that any disregard for traffic rules can be legally justified. This would imply that self-driving cars are trained on classified sets of data which flag acceptable and unacceptable forms of driving, or

---

[65]   *Cf.* Art. 38(1)(b) Statute of the International Court of Justice.

[66]   *Cf.* D. Neil MacCormick and Robert S. Summers, *Interpreting Precedents: A Comparative Study* (Dartmouth Publishing 1997).

[67]   Apparently, the Google car is programmed to speed by up to 16km/h if this minimizes the risk of accidents http://www.reuters.com/article/us-google-driverless-idUSKBN0GH02P20140817.

[68]   *Cf.* Benjamin I. Schimelman *How to Train a Criminal: Making Fully Autonomous Vehicles Safe for Humans* 49 Connecticut Law Review 327, 348 seq. (2016), advocating such a bottom-up approach without specifying the legal limits.

[69]   On different forms of learning see Russell and Norvig *supra* note 18, p. 693 seq.; Wachenfeld and Winner, *supra* note 28, pp. 454–6.

that a human provides feedback as to the legality of learning results in the course of the learning process. Furthermore, every rule resulting from such a learning process must be identifiable (e.g. "It is permitted to cross a solid line in order to circumnavigate an obstacle if this does not endanger anyone") and explainable (e.g. by the importance of traffic flow). Any form of machine-learning which cannot (yet) explain its results would be precluded.[70]

2. Establishing facts

Law compliance by autonomous agents does not only require a correct understanding of the law, it also presupposes knowledge of the relevant facts. However, should law-finding and fact-finding, which are clearly distinguished in legal methodology, still be treated separately when artificial agents decide? Algorithms, after all, only deal with inputs and outputs. Yet, from a legal point of view, the distinction is still useful. Law-finding (e.g. "What is the speed limit?") is the preserve of lawyers, it follows legal methodology and may be classified as convincing/unconvincing or binding/non-binding. Facts, however (e.g. "At what speed does a car drive?"), are established with the help of non-legal disciplines, for example physics, follow the respective non-legal methodologies and may be classified as true or false. In reality, the difference is not quite as categorical: facts and laws are social constructs. Very often, facts may only be established by a certain degree of probability. Furthermore, the scientific methods rest on theories and models which might be falsified. Above all, fact-finding in the context of law is also governed by law, for example by procedural law directing the fact-finding of courts and administrative agencies. Nevertheless, the distinction between law and facts roughly separates the domain of lawyers and of other disciplines.

Thus, it is a technological question how reliably self-driving cars recognize their environment—and it is a legal question how reliable they should be when deployed on public streets. Defining the degree of reliability is a regulatory choice. But self-driving cars will arguably have to surpass human abilities in order to uphold the safety of road traffic and to promote confidence in autonomous driving. This is easier for some tasks (establishing weather conditions, recognizing objects beyond a human's field of vision, for example) than for others (recognizing human behavior, for example).[71] Would it have to be next to 100 percent, however, given that human fact-finding is not flawless either? Furthermore, a legal system cannot blindly trust in the reliability of algorithms. Instead, it must be able to comprehend how they function to assess their reliability. This may be illustrated by machine-learning in image recognition. Some forms of machine-learning, particularly learning in neuronal networks or "deep learning", are difficult to reproduce. The algorithm will learn to recognize cars or a traffic sign after analyzing a large set of data, but it cannot explain how the conclusions come about. Recent research has shown that this unsupervised self-learning process may lead to flawed outcomes. When researchers reproduced the results of two learning methods used to recognize images of a horse, they found that one algorithm based its results (understandably) on the contours

---

[70]   For a critical stance on "largely opaque and inscrutable" learning algorithms, see Knight, *supra* note 33; Etzioni and Etzioni, *supra* note 27, pp. 137–8.

[71]   *Cf.* the need to recognize "military columns and motorised funeral processions" under Dutch traffic law, Leenes and Lucivero, *supra* note 37, fn. 79.

in the picture. The other algorithm, however, drew upon the (purely coincidental) fact that the images of horses in the training set also showed a very small copyright sign and based its classification on this correlation. Thus, both algorithms would perform very differently in practice.[72] What is more, image recognition can even be subject to "adversarial attack". It was shown that small alterations to images of traffic signs (invisible to humans) significantly corrupted image recognition. This indicates how image recognition could be sabotaged not only by electronic image manipulations, but also by physically putting small stickers or a little bit of spray on street signs.[73]

IV.   CRASH ALGORITHMS' TRAGIC CHOICES

Even if self-driving cars fully comply with road traffic law, there are further regulatory challenges due to the fact that artificial decision-making is never bias-free and sometimes even a matter of life and death. Self-driving cars, in particular, have to be programmed how to react when an accident is unavoidable, in other words how to choose among possible victims. Thus, crash algorithms will typically favor one group of possible victims over another one. Such a bias may be less dramatic if it protects more vulnerable cyclists and pedestrians at the expense of an armored car, but it is tragic if it involves decisions of life and death. This section will focus on these deadly choices which hopefully will help make the problem clear. It argues the tragic choices taken in crash algorithms are not merely a question of morality, but of law and should be regulated by government.

A.   The Dilemma and its Legal Dimension

Life-and-death dilemmas, i.e. situations in which every possible decision results in a tragic outcome, have been discussed by philosophers and criminal lawyers for a long time. The thought experiment ascribed to Carneades of Cyrene (taken up by Cicero and Kant) asks, for example, whether a shipwrecked sailor may push a fellow shipwrecked sailor from a plank carrying merely one person if this is the only means to survive.[74] The situation which most resembles the situation of a car accident is discussed in the "trolley"[75] or "switchman case" (as it is known in Germany),[76] developed with a view to abortion, ethical questions of medical progress and involvement in Nazi crimes:[77] it depicts a train which is about to crash into five men working on the railway tracks. Alternatively, the train could also be directed onto a different track, where only one person is working. It is certain that either the five

---

[72]   Sibylle Anderl, *Frankfurter Allgemeine Zeitung* August 23, 2017 on these findings by the team of Sebastian Lapuschkin.

[73]   Ackerman, *supra* note 29.

[74]   Ulf Neumann, "Necessity and Duress" in: Markus D. Dubber and Tatjana Hörnle, *Oxford Handbook on Criminal Law* (OUP 2014) pp. 583, 585.

[75]   Philippa Foot, *The Problem of Abortion and the Doctrine of the Double Effect* 5 Oxford Review 1, 3 (1967); Judith Jarvis Thomson, *The Trolley Problem* 94 Yale Law Journal 1395 (1985).

[76]   Hans Welzel, *Zum Notstandsproblem* Zeitschrift für die Gesamte Strafrechtswissenschaft 47, 51 (1951).

[77]   In post-war Germany, physicians who had reluctantly participated in the Nazi "Euthanasia" program argued to have prevented worse, *cf.* Welzel, *supra* note 76).

workers or the one worker on the track will be killed by the collision. May the driver or the switchman decide to direct the trolley onto the other track, killing one, but saving five lives? Similar situations may arise in the course of road traffic. If a self-driving car is about to crash into five people crossing the road, should it swerve and drive onto the sidewalk, crashing into one pedestrian? More questions arise if more factors are taken into account. Is it permissible to save a child at the expense of an elderly person? Should a self-driving car be allowed to put the interest of its passenger first, even at the expense of many other road users? Should questions of responsibility be taken into account?

The choice of possible victims in an unavoidable accident raises important practical questions, even if the "trolley" or "switchman case" appear to be rather academic thought experiments.[78] It is true that self-driving cars will significantly decrease traffic accidents and that computer engineers are primarily concerned with enhancing the cars' safety by working on less spectacular questions such as the optimal speed or lane positioning. But accidents will not disappear as long as human road users make mistakes and as long as technical failure by cars or infrastructure occurs. Thus, computer engineers are also designing "crash optimizing algorithms"[79] which determine a car's optimal behavior during an accident. These algorithms are more refined in predicting the future than the dilemma hypotheticals as they generate probabilities ("a 75 percent probability that a pedestrian be injured and a 60 percent probability that he be killed") instead of clear, but unrealistic results ("will die"). And they may take into account all the relevant aspects, proceeding from more common choices (e.g. whether to better collide with a big or a small car) to rare choices (e.g. whether to sacrifice the car's passenger in favor of a pedestrian).

Life-and-death algorithms of self-driving cars are currently being discussed as a matter of morality and ethics.[80] It will be argued, however, that they raise important legal questions and should be regulated by law. The classic thought experiments are used to consider reasons like necessity or duress which exclude criminal liability for decisions made in a dilemma, e.g. directing the trolley onto a certain track or pushing a shipwrecked sailor off the plank.[81] The modern scenarios shift the focus: the tragic decision is no longer taken by a single person in a particular situation in a fraction of seconds, but it is determined by a crash optimizing algorithm developed in advance which establishes general rules for these tragic choices. Thus, it is now possible to create a meaningful legal framework for such an algorithm in advance instead of judging in retrospective how a human behaved in an extreme situation.

Different societies might favor different solutions for crash algorithms, just as they have developed different legal systems of criminal or torts law. Yet, they are constrained and guided by national and international human rights law, notably the right to life,[82] equality

---

[78]   See also Noah J. Goodall, "Machine Ethics and Automated Vehicles" Pre-print, published in Gereon Meyer and Sven Beiker, *Road Vehicle Automation* (Springer 2014) p. 93, available at http://dx.doi.org/10.1007/978-3-319-05990-7_9.

[79]   *Cf.* Gurney, *supra* note 41.

[80]   See generally Wallach and Allen, *supra* note 63, more specifically Goodall, *supra* note 78, and the literature below.

[81]   Neumann, *supra* note 74, p. 585.

[82]   Art. 2(2) German Basic Law; Am. 14 § 1 U.S. Constitution; Art. 2 European Convention on Human Rights (ECHR); Art. 4 American Convention on Human Rights (ACHR); Art. 6 International Covenant on Civil and Political Rights (ICCPR).

and non-discrimination[83] or human dignity.[84] It is true that these fundamental rights are (primarily) binding upon the state,[85] and not upon private manufacturers, computer engineers or users of self-driving cars. Nevertheless, many human rights regimes recognize that those particularly important rights also entail positive obligations,[86] i.e. duties to protect life,[87] equality,[88] and dignity[89] against violations by private parties. However vague these positive obligations are, they require at least some form of protection, particularly if grave violations are at stake which could easily be prevented by the state.[90] Thus, a regulation of crash algorithms can be understood to fulfill a positive human rights obligation (which would have to be established separately for every human rights regime). But even beyond the scope of such obligations, human rights considerations aptly characterize the specific legal interests at hand which speak in favor of regulation by the government.

---

[83] Art. 3(1), 3 (3) German Basic Law (equality, non-discrimination); Am. 14 § 1 U.S. Constitution (equal protection of the law); Art. 14 ECHR (equal protection of convention rights); Art. 1, 24 ACHR (equal protection of convention rights, equal protection of the law); Art. 2(1), 26 ICCPR (equal protection of covenant rights, equality before the law, non-discrimination).

[84] Explicit guarantees are characteristic of younger human rights catalogues which reflect a history of inhuman and degrading treatment, *cf.* Art. 1(1) German Basic Law (human dignity); Art. 3 ECHR (prohibition of torture and inhuman or degrading treatment); Art. 5(2), 11 (1) ACHR (respect for the inherent dignity of the human person; honor and dignity); preamble ICCPR ("inherent dignity of the human person"); *cf.* chapt. 2, section 10 Constitution of the Republic of South Africa; *cf.* Niels Petersen, "Human Dignity, International Protection" *Max Planck Encyclopedia of Public International Law* 2012.

[85] Art. 1(3) German Basic Law; Art. 1 ECHR; Art. 1(1) ACHR; Art. 2(1) ICCPR; cf. *Jackson v. Metropolitan Edison Co.* 419 U.S. 345, 349 (1974).

[86] Walter Kälin and Jörg Künzli, *The Law of International Human Rights Protection* (OUP 2009) chapt. I.3.III.3; Olivier de Schutter, *International Human Rights Law* 2nd ed. (CUP, 2014) chapt. II.4.2.1.; see the obligation to "ensure" the convention/covenant rights (Art. 1 ECHR; Art. 1(1) ACHR; Art. 2 (1) ICCPR); this is understood to comprise all convention rights of the ACHR (Inter-American Court of Human Rights, judgment *Velásquez-Rodríguez v. Honduras (merits)* July 29, 1988, Series C No. 4, para. 166) and all convention rights of the ICCPR (Human Rights Committee *General Comment No. 31* May 26, 2004, CCPR/C/21/Rev.1/Add. 13, para. 8).

[87] For example German Federal Constitutional Court *Aviation Security Act* BVerfGE 115, 118, para. 120 (2006), available at http://www.bundesverfassungsgericht.de/entscheidungen/rs20060215_1bvr035705en.html (protection against terrorist acts); ECHR *Streletz/Germany* No. 34033/96 (2001), para. 86 (criminal protection); see also fn. 86.

[88] In Germany, this primarily results from an indirect horizontal effect of fundamental rights which implies that ordinary law is construed in accordance with specific antidiscrimination guarantees, see for example German Federal Constitutional Court, Neue Juristische Wochenschrift 2001, 2658 (needs of a disabled person have to be accommodated in a private tenancy); on positive obligations based on Art. 14 ECHR, see ECHR *Virabyan/Armenia* No. 40094/05 (2012), para. 218 (duty to investigate violent acts on political grounds); see also note 86.

[89] Based on Art. 1(1)(1) German Basic Law ("protect") see, for example German Federal Constitutional Court *Aviation Security Act* BVerfGE 115, 118, para. 121 (2006) (protection against "humiliation, branding, persecution, outlawing and similar actions by third parties"); ECHR *Pretty/United Kingdom* No. 2346/02 (2002), para. 51 ("ensure that individuals . . . are not subjected to torture or inhuman and degrading treatment or punishment . . . by private individuals"); Matthias Mahlmann, "Human Dignity and Autonomy in Modern Constitutional Orders" in: Michel Rosenfeld and András Sajó, *The Oxford Handbook of Comparative Constitutional Law* (OUP 2012) pp. 370, 384–5; see also note 86.

[90] Kälin and Künzli, *supra* note 86, chapt. I.3.III.3(c); de Schutter, *supra* note 86, chapt. II.4.2.1.

It is useful to recall some further advantages of such a regulatory approach (the term "regulation" referring to governmental regulation only)[91]—as opposed to leaving the setting of crash algorithms up to the car's manufacturer or the car's owner or driver ("self-regulation").[92] A regulation can counterbalance the conflicting interests of different road users (and of other relevant groups such as manufacturers and insurers) in a democratically accountable way. It creates clear and predictable rules and can therefore be taken into account by all road users. Finally, with a view to international traffic, those rules, or at least a certain set of rules, could be agreed upon at the international level by the parties to the Vienna or the Geneva Convention on Road Traffic (which would also be facilitated by drawing upon common human rights standards).

B.   Specific Legal Questions

The specific legal questions open to such a regulation shall now be considered in turn.

1.   Death by algorithm and human dignity

First of all, may life-and-death decisions be delegated from a human to an algorithm at all? Or does human dignity, one of the central tenets of the German or the South African constitution, for example,[93] forbid "death by algorithm" because it turns humans into mere items of a calculation (and would thus entail an obligation to outlaw those algorithms)? In the context of autonomous weapon systems, German and South African lawyers have objected to the use of lethal autonomous weapons on grounds of human dignity.[94] This reasoning could be extended to other life-and-death decisions by artificial agents. According to a common understanding, human dignity implies that all humans are of equal value and are treated as ends, not as means.[95] Algorithmic life-and-death decisions could be understood to legalize a situation which should never be considered legal, namely sacrificing some road users in order to save others. The legality of life-and-death algorithms could be seen as a legal acknowledgement that some lives are worthier than others.

---

[91]   On different concepts of "regulation" see Cary Coglianese and Evan Mendelson, "Meta-Regulation and Self-Regulation" in: Robert Baldwin, Martin Case and Martin Lodge, *The Oxford Handbook of Regulation* (OUP 2010) 146; Matthew T. Wansley, *Regulation of Emerging Risks* 69 Vanderbilt Law Review 401 (2016); Pagallo and Durante, *supra* note 37; Ronald Leenes, Erica Palmerini, Bert-Jaap Koops, Andrea Bertolini, Pericle Salvini and Federica Lucivero, *Regulatory challenges of robotics: some guidelines for addressing legal and ethical issues* 9 Law, Innovation and Technology 1 (2017).

[92]   *Cf.* Nick Belay, *Robot Ethics and Self-Driving Cars: How Ethical Determinations in Software Will Require a New Legal Framework* 40 The Journal of the Legal Profession 119, 122 seqq. (2015); Jan Gogoll and Julian F. Müller, *Autonomous Cars: In Favor of a Mandatory Ethics Setting* 23 Science and Engineering Ethics 681 (2017).

[93]   *Cf.* note 84 and Mahlmann, *supra* note 89.

[94]   Informal Meeting of Experts on Lethal Autonomous Weapons: Convention on Conventional Weapons Geneva: April 16, 2016, Panel on Human Rights and Lethal Autonomous Weapons Systems (LAWS), Comments by Christof Heyns, United Nations Special Rapporteur on extrajudicial, summary or arbitrary executions, http://www.unog.ch/80256EDD006B8954/(httpAssets)/1869331AFF 45728BC1257E2D0050EFE0/$file/2015_LAWS_MX_Heyns_Transcript.pdf, p. 5; Robin Geiss, *Die völkerrechtliche Dimension autonomer Waffensysteme* (Friedrich-Ebert-Stiftung 2015) p. 8 seq.

[95]   Mahlmann, *supra* note 89, p. 379; Petersen, *supra* note 84, para. 5.

However, systematic considerations show that human dignity does not prohibit algorithmic life-and-death decisions as such, as legal orders have already governed tragic choices without violating human dignity. Criminal law determines in a general and abstract manner whether dilemmatic choices (directing the trolley, pushing a shipwrecked sailor off the plank, having an abortion) are punishable. Furthermore, life-and-death decisions are also regulated in other areas of law.[96] Vaccination is lawful and sometimes even mandatory despite the (extremely small) risk of causing death. Life-saving donor organs are distributed to the recipients according to certain criteria such as medical need, prospect of medical success or waiting lists spelled out in law or medical guidelines. Remember, finally, that the United States organized a lottery to draft soldiers in the Vietnam War. All of these regulations distribute risks of death in advance—the risk of being saved or killed by vaccination, by receiving a donor organ or waiting in vain, by evading conscription or by being drafted for a deadly war.

Neither of these legal arrangements is considered to violate human dignity. In the first situation of individual dilemmatic choices governed by criminal law, the law does not approve of the act of killing, for example, but shows understanding for a difficult personal decision. German criminal law, for example, attaches great importance to the distinction between the legality of an act and individual guilt. Thus, tragic choices might result in an illegal action (an act of killing), but might lack the element of individual guilt necessary for punishment.[97] In the second situation, law regulates tragic choices in advance—quite like crash optimizing algorithms do. The examples illustrate that this is necessary if a society wants to fight diseases by vaccination, to arrange for organ transplantations or to go to war, in other words if it advances important (life-saving) goals and accepts certain risks of death in exchange. As long as these risks are distributed fairly (e.g. among all by mandatory vaccination, by a waiting list for donor organs or by a randomized drafting procedure), this does not amount to a degrading treatment of those who will suffer from the distribution. This also applies for self-driving cars: if a society wishes to enjoy the benefits of self-driving cars—including a massive reduction of traffic fatalities—it will be necessary and legal to have algorithms envisaging critical life and death decisions. Human dignity is important in influencing these algorithms, but it does not prohibit them.

2. Priorities: life, health, property

After establishing that crash algorithms as such do not challenge human dignity, we can now address the necessary regulatory decisions. A regulation must, for a start, set a priority of legal values. It seems clear that a crash algorithm should prevent human fatalities first, human injuries second and damage to property third. This priority follows from the hierarchy of human rights (life, health, property) reflected in different standards for limiting these rights,[98] and from the gravity of criminal offenses or torts (killing, bodily injury, damage to property) reflected in different criminal sanctions and damages.

---

[96] From a theoretical point of view Guido Calabresi and Philip Bobbitt, *Tragic Choices* (Norton 1978).

[97] *Cf.* Thomas Rönnau, *Grundwissen – Strafrecht: Übergesetzlicher entschuldigender Notstand* Juristische Schulung 113 (2017).

[98] Kälin and Künzli, *supra* note 86, chapt. I.3.III.2; de Schutter, *supra* note 86, chapt. II.3.2; II.3.3; Christian Tomuschat, *Human Rights* 3rd ed. (OUP 2014) chapt. 6 IV, V.

This clear priority rule becomes less clear-cut if one takes a closer look. Could the prevention of a unique cultural site outweigh the risk of a minor bodily injury? If such considerations of proportionality are relevant in criminal law, torts law or human rights law,[99] they should also be legal in the context of autonomous cars. Which degree of probability is sufficient to establish danger to life? Is a 50 percent chance of a very serious bodily harm (e.g. brain damage) a worse scenario than a ten percent chance of killing somebody? These considerations are not as absurd as they might seem. The likelihood of an accident very often depends on the human behavior of other road users which cannot be predicted with accuracy, but only in terms of (rough) probabilities. Furthermore, the chances of being hurt or killed correspond to factors a self-driving car will soon be able to recognize, for example the gender and age of the victims and the mass of a car involved in an accident.[100] Taking account of probabilities is a common feature in law, for example medical law or police law. But defining precise thresholds and proportionalities is a delicate task. Finally: what role could other values play? Some societies, for example, attach particular importance to the protection of animals or of religious objects (or to both, imagine an algorithm designed to avoid holy cows strolling on Indian streets) based on constitutional principles or cultural and historical traditions. The examples show that even the seemingly simple task of defining the priority of legally accepted outcomes implies important choices. This, again, underlines the advantages of a democratic regulation.

3.   Personal characteristics and equal value of every life

After emphasizing the value of human life, let's now assume that a deadly accident is unavoidable and that the car has two options, both of which will result in the death of a human. This life-versus-life scenario raises different questions which will now be addressed one by one. The tragic choice may, first of all, be guided by the personal characteristics of the possible victims. A crash algorithm could, for example, be designed to target an old person instead of a young child who has his whole life ahead of him. Other settings are easily imaginable: Feminists could favor women over men, racists whites over blacks, and utilitarians "useful" members of society over unfit people, homeless people, or criminals. Even if this result may be supported by some people,[101] it is unacceptable from a human rights point of view. It is a central tenet of modern societies that every human life has equal value, regardless, in particular, of race, gender, age, or utility. This central tenet can

---

[99]   For example § 34 German Criminal Code; §§ 228, 904 German Civil Code; on proportionality in human rights law see note 98.

[100]   Leonard Evans, *Death in Traffic: Why Are the Ethical Issues Ignored?* 2 Studies in Ethics, Law, and Technology 1, 8 (2000): "If one driver is a man, and the other a similar-age woman, the woman is 28% more likely to die. If one driver is age 20 and the other age 70, the older driver is three times as likely to die. If one driver is drunk and the other sober, the drunk is twice as likely to die (because alcohol affects many body organs, not just the brain). If one driver is traveling alone while the other has a passenger, the lone driver is 14% more likely to die than the accompanied driver, because the accompanied driver is in a vehicle heavier by the mass of its passenger."

[101]   A team from MIT presents a variety of dilemmatic decisions to internet users and asks them to choose the "lesser evil"; the suggested choices do, in fact, include targeting people according to their physical fitness, their profession and other characteristics (homelessness, criminality); http://moralmachine.mit.edu/.

be founded on human dignity which implies that every human being enjoys equal rights, equal respect and equal value.[102] Likewise, the principle can be directly based on equality and the guarantees of non-discrimination.[103]

What's more, this chapter claims that states even have a positive obligation to protect the equal value of every life against private forms of discrimination based on race, gender, age, or similar properties; in other words that states are obliged to outlaw corresponding settings that discriminate in crash algorithms. In some legal orders such as Germany's, this will, arguably, result from the prominent rank of human dignity.[104] But such a positive obligation can also be established under international human rights law given that the discriminatory crash algorithm would affect not only the right of human dignity or non-discrimination, but also the right to life. The paramount importance of these rights in international law can be illustrated by the fact that they are – at least partially – protected as *jus cogens*, i.e. as a peremptory norm of international law.[105] Furthermore, the principle of equal worth of every human being is reflected in many norms of national law or even private law, which illustrates that it is a well-established principle in many legal orders. In German criminal law, for example, killing an elderly person is considered no less heinous than killing a younger person who has his whole life ahead of him.[106] In the U.S., private discrimination is outlawed by specific anti-discrimination statutes, which compensates for a lack of horizontal effect or positive obligation entailed by fundamental rights.[107] At the level of professional standards, to provide a last example, the members of the Institute of Electrical and Electronics Engineers, in their Code of Ethics, have agreed, in any case, not to engage in "discrimination based on race, religion, gender, disability, age, national origin, sexual orientation, gender identity, or gender expression".[108]

Crash algorithms which target victims according to their race, gender, age and other personal characteristics must therefore be outlawed. This means, in practice, that the tragic choice has to be decided by a random generator.[109] The procedure is fair by allocating the same risk of death to everyone. And randomization by computer algorithm is even more accurate than manual randomization. The Vietnam War Lottery, at least, allegedly did not produce truly random results—probably due to insufficient mixing of capsules.[110]

---

[102] *Cf.* German Federal Constitutional Court *Aviation Security Act* BVerfGE 115, 118, para. 85, 121 (2006); Mahlmann, *supra* note 89, p. 380; Petersen, *supra* note 84, para. 29.

[103] Note 83; see also a combined reasoning based on both equality and dignity in Supreme Court of Canada *Law v. Canada* [1999] 1 S.C.R. 497.

[104] See again German Federal Constitutional Court *Aviation Security Act* BVerfGE 115, 118, para. 85 seq. (2006).

[105] It is generally accepted that the prohibition of slavery, genocide, arbitrary killing, racial discrimination, apartheid, and torture enjoy *jus cogens* status, Kälin and Künzli, *supra* note 86, chapt. I.2.III.2; de Schutter, *supra* note 86, chapt. I.3.4.2(b).

[106] German Federal Court of Justice *Decision*, August 11, 1995 – 2 StR 362/95 juris.

[107] For example the Civil Rights Act of 1964 prohibiting employee discrimination or harassment based on sex, race, color, religion, and national origin; the Age Discrimination in Employment Act 1967.

[108] http://www.ieee.org/about/corporate/governance/p7-8.html.

[109] *Cf.* Thomas Burri, Machine Learning and the Law: Five Theses, January 3, 2017 https://papers.ssrn.com/sol3/papers.cfm?abstract_id=2927625.

[110] Norton Starr, *Nonrandom Risk: The 1970 Draft Lottery* 5 Journal of Statistics Education (1997) https://ww2.amstat.org/publications/jse/v5n2/datasets.starr.html.

"Random" does not mitigate the tragic situation, but it allows for a solution respecting the equality and dignity of the possible victims.

4.   Self-sacrifice and self-interest

Having established the strict rule that every life is of equal value, we can now consider whether specific constellations might allow for specific solutions. Life-versus-life constellations will often affect the passenger of the self-driving car and another road user. Let's imagine, for example, that a car is on a narrow street at the cliffs or about to enter a tunnel, and that it can avoid a deadly collision with a pedestrian by driving off the cliff or into the wall of the tunnel which would result in the death of the car's passenger. May the crash algorithm choose to target another road user in order to avoid sacrificing its passenger?

Several aspects could be considered in support of egoistic settings. Online surveys show that people generally favor altruistic cars, but would prefer to buy a self-driving car with egoistic settings.[111] This (comprehensible) egoistic attitude will make acceptance of self-driving cars more difficult if they come with altruistic settings. From a legal point of view, it is argued, individuals must be allowed to opt for their own survival and must not be forced to ride in a self-sacrificing car.[112] And a utilitarian could ask whether the benefit of riding a self-driving car which significantly enhances overall road safety should not be promoted and rewarded at least by allowing for an egoist crash algorithm.

None of these arguments, however, justifies an exception from the principle of equal value of every life. It may be true that criminal law cannot demand self-sacrifice and must not sanction an egoistic individual operating as in the example of the plank of Carneades or before an unavoidable car accident.[113] However, once the state regulates this choice by mandatory randomization, as suggested, the passenger of a self-driving car is no longer in a position to choose between altruism or egoism. Instead, the autonomous driving mode relieves her not only from driving, but also from making dilemmatic crash decisions in advance, quite in the same way a passenger cannot control dilemmatic crash decisions on a train ride or a flight. A state is entitled and, based on positive human rights obligation, even bound to regulate accordingly. Neither can the other concerns—little acceptance or unfair burden of benefit—justify that some lives have a higher value than others and that passengers in a self-driving car are protected at the expense of all the other road users.

This example also illustrates the general need for a regulatory approach. Egoistic and altruistic decisions are not only a matter of life and death. From an insurer's point of view, for example, crash decisions will be assessed by the damage they cause. Thus, an egoistic crash setting chosen by a road user at the behest of her insurance company would minimize the damage to be covered by the company. This could produce undesirable results, for example, if it leads to a bigger overall damage or if it discriminates against certain road users, for example poorer people who drive cheaper cars. Autonomous cars will only be acceptable to society as a whole, if crashes are governed by fair, not by egoistic rules. Manufacturers, insurance, and road users, however, have no incentive to create and use

---

[111]   Jean-Francois Bonnefon, Azim Shariff and Iyad Rahwan, *The Social Dilemma of Autonomous Vehicles* Science 352(6293) (2016).

[112]   Philipp Weber, *Dilemmasituationen beim autonomen Fahren* Neue Zeitschrift für Verkehrsrecht 249, 253 (2016).

[113]   *Cf.* Neumann, *supra* note 74; Rönnau, *supra* note 97; Weber, *supra* note 112.

altruistic settings if their competitors and fellow road users will not do the same—which requires mandatory settings.[114]

5. Numbers

A further problem is raised by quantitative considerations. Let's come back to the example of a car which will either crash into a pedestrian (killing *one*) or into another car with five passengers (killing *five*). Could or should the crash algorithm favor killing one over killing five? From an ethical point of view, the comparable decision in the trolley or switchman scenario is held to be morally permissible or even mandatory.[115] Some philosophers focus on distinguishing the trolley/switchman scenario from other—purposely absurd—cases where choosing to kill one person to save five is clearly immoral: killing a person to enable organ transplants which would save five lives, pushing an overweight bystander onto the tracks to stop the trolley which is heading in the direction of the five workers[116] or blowing up an overweight man who is stuck in the mouth of a cave, trapping the exit of his fellow potholers who are facing death by rising flood waters in the cave.[117] It is explained that actively killing one is worse than letting five die,[118] or that directly violating the right of life is worse than doing something which is not in itself a violation of a right like turning the trolley.[119] To both aspects one could add a third one, namely that it is only morally acceptable to make such a choice if it affects people who are already in imminent danger of death—and not third parties. Once these groups who are threatened by death are established, i.e. two groups of workers on two different tracks or two groups of road users both facing death by a possible collision, it is the simple idea of reducing the overall death toll which legitimizes killing one instead of five.[120]

Other philosophers emphasize that a crash algorithm decides tragic choices in advance and claim that a quantitative solution is therefore not only compatible with a consequentialist, but also with a deontological approach.[121] In contrast to consequentialism, deontology judges the morality of choices not by their effects, but by their conformity with a moral norm, for example the Kantian injunction against using others as mere means to one's end.[122] A quantitative approach can be easily defended on grounds of consequentialism as it saves more lives. From a deontological point of view, however, strict rules such as the prohibition of torture have to be obeyed regardless of the costs. The philosophers seem to proceed from the assumption that a moral decision has to duly

---

[114] Gogoll and Müller, *supra* note 92.
[115] Welzel, *supra* note 76, 51; Foot, *supra* note 75, 3; Thomson, *supra* note 75.
[116] The so-called 'fat man scenario', Thomson, *supra* note 75, 1409.
[117] Foot, *supra* note 75, 2.
[118] *Id.*, 4.
[119] Thomson, *supra* note 75, 1403.
[120] Foot, *supra* note 75, 5.
[121] Alexander Hevelke and Julian Nida-Rümelin, *Selbstfahrende Autos und Trolley-Probleme: Zum Aufrechnen von Menschenleben im Falle unausweichlicher Unfälle* 19 Jahrbuch für Wissenschaft und Ethik 5 (2015).
[122] Larry Alexander and Michael Moore, "Deontological Ethics" in: Edward N. Zalta, *The Stanford Encyclopedia of Philosophy* Winter 2016 https://plato.stanford.edu/archives/win2016/entries/ethics-deontological/>, paras 1, 2, 2.4.

respect the interests of the persons involved.[123] They then argue that programming an algorithm to minimize the death toll must be judged ex ante, i.e. without knowing the actual victims. Since the algorithm equally reduces everybody's chance of becoming a victim it duly respects everybody's interests.[124] It is certainly true that decisions taken in advance may be judged differently than decisions taken in an extreme situation. But this argument does not in itself help to overcome strict deontological rules.

From a legal point of view, i.e. by human rights standards, the state may (but need not) mandate quantitative decision-making by crash algorithms.[125] First, such a regulation does not violate the right to life. By regulating road traffic, the state does not actively interfere with the right to life.[126] Instead, the state fulfills its positive obligation to protect the life of road users by creating and enforcing traffic laws or car safety standards. Similarly, prescribing a death-toll-minimizing crash algorithm would protect the life of many potential death victims and thereby fulfill a state's positive obligation towards life. Second, such a regulation does not violate human dignity or equality, i.e. the principle of the equal value of every human, even if it might seem to value the lives of the survivors more than the lives of the victims. But faced with the unavoidable death of many, it is fair rule to save as many lives as possible. It does not discriminate against certain groups of people defined by personal characteristics but relies purely on the (coincidental) fact whether a person belongs to a bigger or a smaller group of possible victims. Similar quantitative considerations are well established in other areas of the law. In criminal law, manslaughter of five is punished more severely than the killing of one. In situations of an emergency, public authorities and emergency forces have a discretion to allocate resources so as to save as many lives as possible. In the law of armed conflict, finally, legality of a military attack is determined, among other factors, by the number of expected civilian casualties.[127] One should be much more cautious, however, to claim that a state is obliged to prescribe a quantitative approach. Positive human rights obligations such as the duty to protect life entail only a few very specific obligations, and leave the means of protection, generally, up to a state.[128] Furthermore, it is difficult to imagine that self-driving cars (in contrast to emergency forces, for example) face a decision involving huge differences in fatalities which would clearly speak in favor of a quantitative solution, for example saving 100 people instead of one person. Thus, the state may prescribe a death-toll-minimizing crash algorithm, but is not obliged to do so.

---

[123]   Hevelke and Nida-Rümelin, *supra* note 121, 11.

[124]   *Id.*, 12.

[125]   The German governmental "Ethics Commission on Automated and Connected Driving" was rather cryptic in its findings: It condemned sacrificing one person to save several others, but sanctioned minimizing the death toll if people were in imminent danger of death, *Ethikkommission Automatisches und Vernetzes Fahren*, *supra* note 5, para. 1.6, p. 18.

[126]   In contrast to a law authorizing to shoot down an aircraft in case of a terrorist attack, which was held to violate human dignity, German Federal Constitutional Court *Aviation Security Act* BVerfGE 115, 118 paras. 84 seq. (2006).

[127]   See above III.B.1 on Art. 51(5)(b) Additional Protocol I to the Geneva Conventions.

[128]   Kälin and Künzli, *supra* note 86, chapt. I.3.III.3(c); de Schutter, *supra* note 86, chapt. II.4.2.1.

6. Further regulatory choices: areas of risk and responsibility

Finally, there are other possibilities which could be considered when regulating crash algorithms. This section will present two regulatory choices which would modify an approach based on randomization and death toll minimization.

The regulator could, *first*, specify the risk of being the victim of a car accident. As I have emphasized above, all the possible victims in the trolley scenario are in imminent danger of death—as opposed to third parties, for example a healthy person, who must not be killed even if his organs would save many lives. A closer look reveals, however, that being in imminent danger of death is a matter of legal assessment and thus open to regulatory definition. In the trolley case, for example, being killed by an uncontrollable train could be considered a) a general risk of life which affects anybody within reach of a train (including bystanders who would be killed by derailing), b) a risk affecting anybody who is working or otherwise present on railway tracks, or c) a risk affecting only those persons working or otherwise present on particular railway tracks, i.e. those tracks in whose direction the train is actually heading. A moral position which allows to divert or even derail the train to prevent worse, rests on the presumption that the risk of being killed by a train is a risk according to b) or even a). Being deliberately killed in order to donate organs, however, is not acknowledged as a risk of life in a society committed to the right to life. With respect to road traffic, one can equally distinguish different understandings of the risk of being killed by a car: this risk could be considered, for example, to be a) a general risk affecting anybody within reach of an unstoppable car (even on private premises, for example), b) a risk affecting all road users (including pedestrians on sidewalks or cyclists on cycle lanes), c) a risk affecting all persons who are present on the roads or d) a risk affecting only those persons who are present on the very lane the unstoppable car is driving on.

Even if these risks have never been defined so far, it is possible for the legislator to do so now that crash algorithms can be programmed accordingly. The legislator may stipulate, for example, that in a life-and-death scenario, a self-driving car may never choose to leave the public traffic space, or to leave the roads, or to leave a particular traffic lane—and the groups of possible victims would vary accordingly. The regulatory power flows from the legislator's power to distribute the risks associated with modern technologies in general and road traffic in particular. Such a regulation does not challenge the equal value of those persons at risk of being killed by a car: it does not weigh up life, but defines the rules of road traffic in the same way other traffic rules do. This also seems to be the position of those who claim that "third parties" should not bear the burden of autonomous driving.[129] It is a discretionary task however, to define who exactly counts as a "third party" and who does not. General principles of risk allocations could guide the legislator. One could argue, for example, that only motor vehicles contribute to the risks of car accidents and that only their drivers or passengers profit from a particular fast and convenient form of mobility (and thus exclude that pedestrians or cyclists become deliberate victims of a car accident). But one could also argue that society as a whole causes

---

[129] *Ethikkommission Automatisches und Vernetzes Fahren*, *supra* note 5, para. 9, p. 11 "Those involved in creating the risk of mobility are not entitled to sacrifice third parties" (my translation); generally Alexander Hevelke and Julian Nida-Rümelin, *Ethische Fragen zum Verhalten selbstfahrender Autos bei unausweichlichen Unfällen: Der Schutz von Unbeteiligten* 69 Zeitschrift für philosophische Forschung 217, 217 (2015).

the risk of and profits from modern forms of mobility which are indispensable for the distribution of goods and services. A more convincing reason for limiting crash options is predictability. Imagine that a self-driving car cannot avoid an accident and has the option to collide either with a car on its traffic lane or on the opposite traffic lane. Having two options allows for flexibility (and for minimizing the overall death toll, for example), but reducing the options by outlawing that a car leaves its own lane (leaves the road, leaves the public traffic area) makes car accidents predictable and enables manufacturers and road users to act accordingly.[130]

A *second* regulatory choice concerns responsibility. Resorting to responsibility in the design of crash algorithms could mean, for example, that a self-driving car prefers a collision with a careless jaywalker over a collision with another pedestrian. Such a responsibility-based approach offers an incentive for responsible behavior. Responsibility is also a commonly accepted criterion for the allocation of risks from a legal point of view. In equality law, treating people differently according to their behavior is less suspicious and more easily justifiable than treating them differently based on personal characteristics. In police law, a hostage taker or a terrorist might even be actively killed as a matter of last resort in order to save the lives of the hostages or the possible victims of terrorism. Even the broad notion of human dignity developed by the German Federal Constitutional Court does not imply otherwise. The Court held, in the context of antiterrorism efforts, that shooting down an airplane hijacked by terrorists would violate the dignity of the hijacked air passengers (as they would be "used as means to save others"), but specified that shooting down the terrorists themselves would not qualify as a violation.[131] In this constellation, human dignity is apparently not at stake with respect to the perpetrators, which might be explained by the fact that they are considered self-governed agents who knowingly put their lives at risk, and not instruments of state action. Thus, if considerations of responsibility might even justify lethal forms of law enforcement, it will also be admissible to take responsibility into account when designing crash algorithms.

Yet, a closer look reveals that it is very difficult to allocate the burden of a car accident in accordance with responsibility. In many situations, responsibility for an imminent accident is unclear and will only be established afterward. Some accidents will be caused by a malfunction of vehicles or road infrastructure which is difficult to attribute to possible victims. Some of the road users who cause an accident such as children will not be considered responsible. Finally, even if a particular road user is definitively responsible for a dangerous situation, it will not always be possible to react in a way which sanctions him or him alone. Imagine, for example, that a bus driver has fallen asleep which provokes the bus to drive on the opposite lane. Crashing into the bus would not only risk his death, but also the death of many innocent passengers (let alone the death of the passengers of the

---

[130]   *Cf.* Hevelke and Nida-Rümelin, *supra* note 129, 222.

[131]   German Federal Constitutional Court *Aviation Security* Act BVerfGE 115, 118 (2006), para. 124, on the hijacked passengers: "By their killing being used as a means to save others, they are treated as objects and at the same time deprived of their rights . . .". The Court's solution may be understood to express caution when assessing and responding to terrorist threats given that it is not easy to establish, for example, whether the hijackers are effectively about to fly into a skyscraper, a nuclear plant or soccer stadium. It is, however, less convincing to prohibit any form of death toll minimization on grounds of human dignity if one group of victims cannot be saved, anyhow.

self-driving car on the opposite lane). As a consequence, the regulator will have to examine if and to what extent a responsibility-based approach is feasible at all.

V.   CONCLUSION

Artificial intelligence results in decision-making by artificial agents replacing human decision-making. This chapter has examined the challenges raised by this development with respect to the densely regulated area of traffic law in which self-driving cars and human drivers operate simultaneously. As opposed to other, more open-textured areas of law, road traffic law is generally suited for the operation of artificial agents (even if the requirement of a human "driver" in international conventions still needs to be amended). Thus, it is now up to the legislator and to other regulatory bodies to clarify the legal framework. In order to ensure law compliance by self-driving cars, the regulator has to supervise how norms of traffic law are translated into computer code and has to set standards of reliability for artificial fact-finding. Machine learning, which will probably be an important method not only for fact-finding, but also for meaningful law compliance, is not incompatible with the primacy of law if the process is supervised and if its results are explainable and justifiable. Furthermore, a regulator has to deal with the biases created by artificial decision-making as this chapter has illustrated with respect to tragic life-and-death decisions of crash algorithms. It is argued that crash algorithms raise legal, not only moral, questions and should be regulated by law. In doing so, the regulator fulfills a positive obligation flowing from human rights, i.e. the right to life, equality, and human dignity, which should also generally guide the regulatory choices. More precisely, crash algorithms, which do not, as such, violate human dignity, will have to reflect the priorities of a legal order and must not use personal characteristics such as race, gender, or age, to choose between potential victims of an accident. The regulator may, however, prescribe death-toll minimization, specify areas of risks or resort to responsibility as a relevant criterion for those tragic decisions. On the whole, the regulation of artificial decision-making by self-driving cars will probably be only one example of how to organize the coexistence of humans and artificial agents. Many others will follow.

SOURCES

Cases

European Court of Human Rights (ECHR) *Montovanelli/France* No. 21497/93 (1997)
ECHR *Streletz/Germany* No. 34033/96 (2001)
ECHR *Pretty/United Kingdom* No. 2346/02 (2002)
ECHR *Goktepe/Belgium* No. 50372/99 (2005)
ECHR *Virabyan/Armenia* No. 40094/05 (2012)
Inter-American Court of Human Rights *Velásquez-Rodríguez v. Honduras* (merits) (1988) Series C No. 4
Supreme Court of the United States *Jackson v. Metropolitan Edison Co.* 419 U.S. 345 (1974)
Wisconsin Supreme Court *State v. Loomis* 881 N.W.2d 749 (2016)
Supreme Court of Canada *Law v. Canada* 1 S.C.R. 497 (1999)
German Federal Constitutional Court BVerfGE 20, 323 (1966)
German Federal Constitutional Court *Aviation Security Act* BVerfGE 115, 118 (2006)
German Federal Court of Justice, 2 StR 362/95 (1995) juris

Higher Regional Court Hamm, Neue Juristische Wochenschrift 1995, 2937
Higher Regional Court Brandenburg, Neue Zeitschrift für Strafrecht 1996, 393

International and European Law

Statute of the International Court of Justice (1949)
Protocol Additional to the Geneva Conventions of 12 August 1949, and relating to the Protection of Victims
   of International Armed Conflicts 1125 UNTS 3
Geneva Convention on Road Traffic (1949) 125 UNTS 3
European Convention on Human Rights (1950) 213 UNTS 221
International Covenant on Civil and Political Rights (1966) 999 UNTS 171
Vienna Convention on Road Traffic (1968) 1042 UNTS 17
American Convention on Human Rights (1969) 1144 UNTS 123
Vienna Convention on the Law of Treaties (1969) 1155 UNTS 331
European Union General Data Protection Regulation (EU) 2016/679

National Law

Constitution of the United States
Michigan Vehicle Code
German Basic Law
German Criminal Code
German Code of Civil Procedure
German Administrative Offences Act
German Administrative Procedure Act

PART III

FUNDAMENTAL RIGHTS AND CONSTITUTIONAL LAW ISSUES

10. Artificial intelligence and privacy—AI enters the house through the Cloud

Ronald Leenes and Silvia De Conca

I. INTRODUCTION

After decades of promises, AI is (finally) taking ground in people's lives. Due to an enormous increase in computing power, significant reductions in storage costs and years of hard study by AI engineers and scientists, the full potential of AI is showing its face.[1] AI applications can be seen sprouting everywhere. Many of the online applications we use on a daily basis, ranging from Google search, via Facebook and Netflix, to online shopping at Amazon, all make use of AI techniques to better serve us. Inferences are made on the basis of information provided by us, the individual profiles created about us, the profiles and behaviour of others and the feedback loops that, through Machine Learning, lead to even better predictions about what we are up to next.[2] The entire car industry is following Google's lead in developing self-driving cars[3] and slowly (semi) self-driving vehicles are making their way onto public roads. AI also makes up an important part of the capabilities of other kinds of robots.[4] Increasingly we will be surrounded by intelligent helpers in the form of service-robots, care-robots, surgery-robots and more, next to the already prevalent industrial robots. Relatively dumb robots may already have entered your home in the form of the Roomba, a 30cm disk-shaped robot that meticulously and seemingly tirelessly roams around your house to collect dust, hairs and other particles. While the (original) Roomba meets many of the criteria to be called a robot proper, is not very intelligent and calling it an AI would be a stretch. Another new addition to many people's households can be situated on the other side of these two dimensions—scale of

---

[1] The growth in computing power follows Moore's law, the decreasing costs of storage Kryder's law.

[2] A marvelous example of relatively mundane AI is Google's on the fly suggestions in search. A couple of letters are often enough to provide meaningful suggestions about what we are about to ask Google. Creepy is another interpretation of this feature.

[3] Interestingly, Google, a search and advertising platform, has built an enormous reputation in developing self-driving vehicles. The surprise is less once one considers, that also self-driving cars are part of the data-driven services world, and this is precisely Google's turf. See for instance, J. Prüfer and C. Schottmuller, *Competing with Big Data*, 15 Feb 2017 Tilburg: CentER, Center for Economic Research, 50 p. (CentER Discussion Paper; vol. 2017-007).

[4] For a definition and discussion of robots see Wildhaber, ch 22 of this volume. For a different, and much broader, interpretation of what a robot entails, see the Robolaw.eu definition. Ronald Leenes, Erica Palmerini, Bert-Jaap Koops, Andrea Bertolini, Pericle Salvini and Federica Lucivero, *Regulatory challenges of robotics: some guidelines for addressing legal and ethical issues*, Law, Innovation and Technology, pp 1–44, received 01 Mar 2017, accepted 07 Mar 2017, published online: 23 Mar 2017, free download at http://dx.doi.org/10.1080/1757996 1.2017.1304921.

"robotness" versus level of Artifical Intelligence—namely intelligent home assistants such as Amazon Echo or Google Home. While these devices exhibit no locomotion themselves, nor have actuators in the traditional sense—which are deemed almost necessary parts to call them robots—they are in fact the precursors of the controllers of the future Smart Home. In that Smart Home, they will control less intelligent devices, such as Roombas, coffee makers, light switches, window openers, pet feeders and what not. Their inability to physically affect the world directly will be more than compensated by the capabilities of the appliances and devices connected to them.

Needless to say, the whole ensemble is connected to the Internet as well. Enter the world of Ambient Intelligence,[5] Internet of Things,[6] Ubiquitous Computing[7] and the Smart Home. Undoubtedly the collection of these devices, whether locomotive or merely affecting our lives as flies on the wall sending out commands or answering our questions and requests, will have a significant impact on (the quality of) our lives. Just like the Internet, and later smart phones, did before.

Obviously, in order to work their magic, these devices need input. Not only from their physical environment, but also from us, their masters. This means that they will have to process information *from us*, *about us*, and thus *affecting us*. Whereas one can keep information away from household members relatively easily because they are not always present, this may turn out to be much harder with respect to the omnipresent robot helpers surrounding us in our homes. We may thus be about to yield the Trojan horse of surveillance into our castles of seclusion.

In this chapter, we explore the relation of intelligent home assistant robots as one particular strand of modern AI, to the law. Given the introduction above, it should not come as a surprise that the area of law that we will focus on is privacy law and the adjacent field of data protection law. We will first outline the central legal notions at play: privacy and data protection, and briefly outline the legal framework, focusing specifically on the European Union. The reasons for this focus are, one, that the European Union is our home turf, and two, the EU is (one of) the jurisdiction(s) that has the most comprehensive legal framework relating to privacy and data protection. Next, we will set the stage with respect to the AI's of choice, intelligent home assistants, by describing various types of such devices that are either already on the market, or are about to enter it. This will be followed by a discussion of a number of data protection and privacy issues introduced, aggravated or solved by these technologies. We end with some suggestions for mitigating issues.

---

[5]   Emile H.L. Aarts and José Luis Encarnação (eds), *True Visions: The Emergence of Ambient Intelligence* (Springer 2006).

[6]   H. Zhuge, "Future Interconnection Environment – Dream, Principle, Challenge and Practice", Keynote at the 5th International Conference on Web-Age Information Management, WAIM 2004: Advances in Web-Age Information Management, July 15-17, 2004, Springer LNCS 3129, pp. 13–22.

[7]   Adam Greenfield, *Everyware: The Dawning Age of Ubiquitous Computing* (New Riders 2006).

II.   PRIVACY AND DATA PROTECTION

Privacy and data protection are often conflated. In fact, when talking about the national implementations of the EU Data Protection Directive,[8] people often referred to the "Privacy Act". This is incorrect. Privacy and data protection are actually different, but also overlapping, concepts. For the purposes of this chapter it is important to understand the similarity/overlap and differences, because what may be perfectly legal in terms of the data protection regulation, may still constitute a (severe) privacy infringement that may seriously upset those affected. As such, a company marketing a particular device and aiming to be legally compliant, may discover that they have neglected the privacy side of things and how people's opinions about privacy may matter in them adopting the technology.

A.   Two Concepts, Similar, But Different, It's Complicated

Privacy is a slippery notion, often and easily used, but its precise meaning is far from clear.[9] This is not surprising, nor is it problematic: the nature of value notions is that they are not precisely delineated. Privacy, in relation to data protection, can be seen as the more encompassing concept. Privacy, in Warren and Brandeis' famous 1890 paper, is defined as "the right to be let alone".[10] This definition already suggests that privacy incorporates multiple dimensions. One can be left alone in different kinds of situations: spatial, physical, communicational, relational, informational. Article 8 of the European Convention on Human Rights (ECHR)—generally seen as one of the roots of modern (European) privacy regulation—states that "everyone has the right to respect for his private and family life, his home and his correspondence". This again underscores the different privacy dimensions. Bodily integrity and the inviolability of the home are encompassed under the privacy umbrella.

Data protection refers to one of the privacy dimensions, informational privacy. The informational dimension has become more prominent since Westin's seminal 1967 article in which he defined privacy as "the claim of individuals, groups, or institutions to determine for themselves when, how, and to what extent information about them is communicated to others."[11] A more recent interpretation of what privacy entails or tries to protect, builds on Westin's notion of control and is framed in the context of profiling, social media, the Internet. Philip Agre places privacy in the context of the identity one projects to the world using information and communication technologies. Here he consid-

---

[8]   Directive 95/46/EC of the European Parliament and of the Council of 24 October 1995 on the protection of individuals with regard to the processing of personal data and on the free movement of such data, OJ L 281.

[9]   Bert-Jaap Koops and Ronald Leenes, *'Code' and the Slow Erosion of Privacy* 12 Mich. Telecomm. Tech. L. Rev. 115 (2005), available at http://www.mttlr.org/voltwelve/koops&leenes.pdf or https://ssrn.com/abstract=1645532.

[10]   Samuel D. Warren and Louis D. Brandeis, *The Right to Privacy: The Implicit Made Explicit* 4 Harv. L. Rev. 193 (1890).

[11]   Alan F. Westin, *Privacy And Freedom* 25 Wash. & Lee L. Rev. 166 (1968), http://scholarly commons.law.wlu.edu/wlulr/vol25/iss1/20.

ers privacy to be the freedom from unreasonable constraints on the construction of one's own identity.[12] Unreasonable constraints are for instance the fact that one may self-censor one's speech in view of being monitored. This kind of constraints can be identified, for example, in the landmark case of *Katz v United States*,[13] in which the judges of the US Supreme Court decided that attaching a surveillance device outside a public phone booth without a warrant did violate the protection against unreasonable search and seizure.[14]

What we see in these three "interpretations" of the notion of privacy is that they have different targets ((potential) collectors of information in the case of Warren and Brandeis), or the senders in the cases of Westin or Agre. It also shows that different aspects are considered central to privacy (seclusion, control, control over identity). And yet, it also shows a lack of a common understanding of what privacy entails. Furthermore, it shows that interpretations change over time, due to technological advancement leading to different kinds of infringements in the private sphere, but also due to changing public opinion.

Bert-Jaap Koops and colleagues have tried to create a modern day typology of the various privacy dimensions that will turn out to be useful for this chapter.[15] Assessing a large number of privacy theories, including those mentioned above, and taking into account many jurisdictions, they come up with a two-dimensional[16] model, consisting of eight basic types of privacy (bodily, intellectual, spatial, decisional, communicational, associational, proprietary, and behavioral privacy), with an overlay of a ninth type (informational privacy) that overlaps, but does not coincide, with the eight basic types, see Figure 10.1. The typology can serve as "an analytic tool and explanatory model that helps to understand what privacy is, why privacy cannot be reduced to informational privacy, how privacy relates to the right to privacy, and how the right to privacy varies, but also corresponds, across a broad range of countries."[17]

The typology shows two dimensions, the horizontal moves along a spectrum from the personal or completely private zone to intimate, semi-private, and public zones. The vertical axis captures negative and positive freedom,[18] which can be characterized by the key terms of "being let alone" (emphasis on negative freedom, or close to Warren and Brandeis' notion of privacy described above) and "self-development" (emphasis on positive freedom, moving to Agre's interpretation of privacy). Along the two primary axes, with four zones of life and two aspects of freedom, eight primary ideal types of privacy are positioned. The eight cells in the typology denote that privacy is always about something (body, behavior, etc.). Informational privacy overlays the eight primary types,

---

[12] Philip Agre, "Introduction", in Philip Agre and Marc Rotenberg, *Technology and Privacy: The New Landscape* (MIT Press 2001) p. 7.

[13] U.S. Supreme Court in *Katz v. United States*, 389 U.S. 347 (1967).

[14] See Agre, *supra* note 12.

[15] Bert-Jaap Koops, Bryce Clayton Newell, Tjerk Timan, Ivan Škorvánek, Tom Chokrevski and Maša Galič, *A Typology of Privacy* 38(2) University of Pennsylvania Journal of International Law 483–575 (2017); Tilburg Law School Research Paper No. 09/2016. Available at SSRN: https://ssrn.com/abstract=2754043.

[16] It is actually three dimensional, but we will not get into the details here.

[17] Koops et al, *supra* note 15, pp. 566–68.

[18] Based on Berlin's two notions of liberty, Isaiah Berlin (1969), "Two Concepts of Liberty", in I. Berlin, *Four Essays on Liberty* (Oxford University Press. New ed. in Berlin 2002).

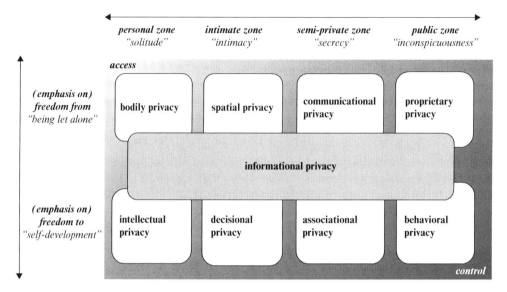

Source: Koops et al. 2017.

Figure 10.1   A typology of privacy

typified by the interest in preventing information about oneself to be collected by others and in controlling information about oneself that others have legitimate access to.[19]

Data protection sees to the protection of individuals where it concerns information about them, and as such is closely connected to the notion of informational privacy. The individual's privacy and personal life could adversely be affected by the collection and/or use of their personal data. This is the reason why collection and use of personal data, at least in Europe, are regulated.

B.   Not Universal

Because privacy, and increasingly also data protection, are deemed fundamental rights, there is a multitude of legal provisions framing and protecting these rights, but there are significant differences between jurisdictions in the scope of rights and the concrete regulation of both privacy and data protection. These norms form a hierarchical structure. At the top, in treaties and constitutions, we find relatively abstract provisions. The more practical provisions are defined in lower regulation (formal acts of government, Ministerial decrees).

Privacy as a right is incorporated in several treaties, such as the already mentioned ECHR, but also, in the more recent Charter of Fundamental Rights of the European Union (the EU Charter), which adopted the same definition in its article 7. Below the treaties, similar rights are incorporated in constitutions of individual countries. The Dutch Constitution, for instance, incorporates the general right to privacy in article 10

---

[19]   Koops et al, *supra* note 15, p. 568.

paragraph 1, while data protection is addressed in article 10 paragraphs 2 and 3. In other countries, such as Italy, the Constitution does not directly address the right to privacy or data protection, but case law of the Supreme Court and the Constitutional Court has identified in Article 2 of the Constitutional Charter the origin of the protection of privacy, even in the absence of explicit references to it.

Data protection is also defined in various other treaties. In 1980, the Organisation for Economic Co-operation and Development (OECD) adopted a set of guidelines governing the protection of privacy and transborder flows of personal data,[20] generally known as the OECD fair information principles. These (eight) principles[21] describe how entities processing personal data should behave. The guidelines have provided the foundation of much of the present-day data protection regulation, and they are, despite many technological and societal advances, still very relevant. The Council of Europe followed suit in 1981 with Convention 108, aiming to secure "respect for his rights and fundamental freedoms, and in particular his right to privacy, with regard to automatic processing of personal data relating to him ('data protection')".[22]

An important step in regulating data protection in Europe was made by the European Union in 1995 with the adoption of the Data Protection Directive 1995/46/EC (henceforth the DPD). With the DPD, the Commission aimed to harmonise the level of data protection across the European Union Member States by providing a minimum level of privacy with respect to the processing of personal data.[23]

The DPD is replaced by the General Data Protection Regulation,[24] which came into full operation on 25 May 2018. This being a Regulation will harmonize data protection regulation in Europe even more, because it does not have to be transposed into national law of each EU Member State and hence provides less freedom for the Member States to diverge from the EU level rules.

Next to the DPD and its successor, the GDPR, the EC has enacted several sector specific data protection directives, such as the Directive on Privacy and Electronic Communications (DPEC) 2002/58/EC.[25] According to Article 3 of the DPEC, the Directive applies to the processing of personal data in connection with the provision of publicly available electronic communications services in public communications networks in the Community. Directives such as these are also relevant on the context of intelligent home assistants or other AI devices because these operate as a means to collect and

---

[20] Recommendation of the Council Concerning Guidelines Governing the Protection of Privacy and Transborder Flows of Personal Data (23 September 1980), http://www.oecd.org/sti/interneteconomy/oecdguidelinesontheprotectionofprivacyandtransborderfl owsofpersonaldata.htm.

[21] The eight OECD Fair information principles are: Collection Limitation Principle, Data Quality Principle, Purpose Specification Principle, Use Limitation Principle, Security Safeguards Principle, Openness Principle, Individual Participation Principle, Accountability Principle.

[22] http://conventions.coe.int/treaty/en/treaties/html/108.htm.

[23] Art. 1 para. 1 Directive 95/46/EC.

[24] Regulation (EU) 2016/679 of the European Parliament and of the Council of 17 April 2016 on the protection of natural persons with regard to the processing of personal data and on the free movement of such data, and repealing Directive 95/46/EC (General Data Protection Regulation) [2016] OJ L 119/2 (GDPR).

[25] Amended by Directive 2009/136/EC of the European Parliament and of the Council of 25 November 2009, OJ L 337, 18.12.2009.

process personal data. However, as the DPEC particularises and complements Directive 95/46/EC (article 1, paragraph 2 DPEC), it would not be applicable to the devices as such, but to the controller, the one who has decided to use them, and thus the one who decided about the purpose and means of the data collection. For instance, in the case of an intelligent home assistant robot able to gather information from the interior of a house, connecting to the Internet and releasing the information, the data processed could fall within the definitions and the directive thus applies.[26]

> Or consider a second scenario: a family purchases a home robot that, upon introduction to a new environment, automatically explores every inch of the house to which it has access. Lacking the onboard capability to process all of the data, the robot periodically uploads it to the manufacturer for analysis and retrieval (this is how at least two robots—SRI International's Centibots and Intel's Home Exploring Robotic Butler—already function).[27]

The GDPR aims to meet two goals: facilitate the free flow of information and protect the privacy of the individuals whose personal data are being processed. The processing of personal data is permitted because it contributes to economic development. The aim of privacy protection, however, requires that certain boundaries are respected. These boundaries are specified in the Regulation as will be outlined below.

Elsewhere in the world, the situation regarding data protection regulation varies. Some countries, notably Canada, have regulations similar to the European Union. Elsewhere, such as in the US, comprehensive data protection regulation is almost absent. Judicial interpretation of the First Amendment, as well as of the Third, Fourth, Fifth, Tenth, and Fourteenth Amendments, has had a major role in covering the basic aspects of privacy but direct references to privacy or data protection in either Constitution or Amendments are absent and comprehensive general privacy/data protection regulation at the federal level is also lacking. The processing of personal data by federal agencies is regulated in the Privacy Act of 1974[28] and various state laws. Certain privacy rights have been established in the United States via legislation such as the Children's Online Privacy Protection Act (COPPA),[29] the Gramm–Leach–Bliley Act (GLB),[30] and the Health Insurance Portability and Accountability Act (HIPAA).[31] Within the private sector, privacy and data protection regulation are largely absent and left to individuals to self-regulate. Hence, contracts and terms of services play an important role in regulating the processing of personal data.

---

[26]   An interesting question then is to whom it is applicable: the robot (not likely given that it does not have legal subjectivity), or the data controller.

[27]   M. Ryan Calo, "Robots and Privacy," in Patrick Lin, George Bekey and Keith Abney (eds.), *Robot Ethics: The Ethical and Social Implications of Robotics* (MIT Press 2012).

[28]   Privacy Act of 1974 (Pub.L. 93-579, 88 Stat. 1896, enacted December 31, 1974, 5 U.S.C. § 552a).

[29]   The Children's Online Privacy Protection Act of 1998 (COPPA) is a United States federal law, located at 15 U.S.C. §§ 6501–6506 (Pub.L. 105-277, 112 Stat. 2581-728, enacted October 21, 1998).

[30]   The Gramm–Leach–Bliley Act (GLB), also known as the Financial Services Modernization Act of 1999, (Pub.L. 106-102, 113 Stat. 1338, enacted November 12, 1999).

[31]   The Health Insurance Portability and Accountability Act of 1996 (HIPAA; Pub.L. 104-191, 110 Stat. 1936, enacted August 21, 1996).

C. Data Protection Regulation in Europe

The aim of the General Data Protection Regulation is the promotion of the free movement of personal data within the European Union, while ensuring a high level of protection of both the right to privacy, and of the fundamental rights and freedoms of the individuals with regard to the processing of personal data in all Member States (recital 3, GDPR).

The scope of the GDPR is very broad; it deals with the processing of "personal data" which is defined as "any information relating to an identified or identifiable natural person ('data subject')" (article 4(1) GDPR). "Any information" means that the concept of "personal data" not only applies to text, but also to sounds and images. In order to be "personal", the data has to pertain to a "data subject" who has to be "identified" or "identifiable". An "identifiable person" is "one who can be identified, directly or indirectly, in particular by reference to an identifier such as a name, an identification number, location data, an online identifier or to one or more factors specific to the physical, physiological, genetic, mental, economic, cultural or social identity of that natural person" (Article 4(1) GDPR). According to this definition, identification or being identifiable does not entail knowing a person's name; it is sufficient to be able to single out the individual in a crowd. Identification or identifiability again has a broad scope, because according to Recital 26 of the Regulation, account should be taken of all the means likely to be used either by the controller or by any other person to identify the said person. In the context of intelligent home assistants, voices can act as identifiers pointing to information about certain members of the household. This information is personal data because it can be linked to particular individuals and contains information about them.

The concept of "processing" also has a wide scope; any operation performed on personal data, such as collection, recording, organisation, storage, adaptation or alteration, retrieval, consultation, use, disclosure by transmission, dissemination or otherwise making available, alignment or combination, blocking, erasure or destruction (article 4 (2) GDPR). Basically, any action from the mere storage of information up to its ultimate deletion is processing in view of the Regulation.

The Regulation regulates the activities of those that process personal data and provides a number of rights to the already mentioned individuals whose data are being processed, the "data subjects". On the side of the processors, the Regulation distinguishes "data controllers" and "data processors". A data controller is every individual or entity who determines the purposes and means of the processing of the data (article 4 (7) GDPR). A "data processor" is a third party who merely processes personal data on behalf of the data controller. The distinction made between data controller and data processor is important for the issue of the liability for violations of the Data Protection legislation. As a rule of thumb, it can be said that the data controller is responsible for guaranteeing compliance with the GDPR. The data controller is not only responsible when he is established or operates within the EU, but whenever he offers goods or services, to such data subjects in the Union (irrespective of whether a payment of the data subject is required), or monitors the behaviour of such individuals as far as their behavior takes place within the Union (article 3 (2) GDPR). The territorial scope of the GDPR thus is enormous; also US (or Chinese) based Cloud Service Providers with no offices in the EU fall within its scope, provided that they target EU citizens or monitor their behavior. Intelligent home assistants, and even relatively simple connected devices such as security cameras, are likely to make use of such Cloud services.

The GDPR is applicable to automated and non-automated processing of personal data (article 2 (1) GDPR), but not if it is done "by a natural person in the course of a purely personal or household activity"[32] (article 2 (2) c GDPR). This, for instance, means that one's digital address book does not fall under the GDPR. An intelligent home assistant, or service robot in the home, if not connected to other devices or services (through) the internet, might fall under this "household exemption" if the data these devices collect and process is kept local and only used for activities in the owner's home. For instance, a service robot may be trained to recognize inhabitants of the house and frequent visitors and use this information to provide personalized responses such as "dear Margaret, here is your coffee".

Personal data may be processed when the principles outlined in the Regulation are met. The starting point of these principles can be found in article 5 of the GDPR.

1. Principle of fair and lawful processing

According to article 5 (1) a GDPR, the processing of the data has to be fair and lawful. Generally, fairness requires that the individual has to be aware that their data are being collected and/or processed and that the purposes of the processing are clear (don't do things behind the data subject's back). The way data are being obtained from the data subject therefore plays a role in the assessment of this principle. The collection and subsequent processing of data has to be lawful. Lawfulness of processing is handled in article 6 GPDR.

Article 6 GDPR lists six alternative grounds that legitimize the processing of personal data:

1. The data subject gives their consent to processing. Such consent is defined as "any freely given, specific, informed and unambiguous indication of the data subject's wishes by which he or she, by a statement or by a clear affirmative action, signifies agreement to the processing of personal data relating to him or her." (Article 4 (11) GDPR).
2. Processing is needed for the performance of a contract to which the data subject is party or in order to take steps at the request of the data subject for entering into a contract.
3. Processing is necessary for compliance with an obligation to which the controller is subject.
4. Processing is necessary for protecting the vital interest of the data subject.
5. Processing is necessary for the performance of a task carried out in the public interest pursued by the controller or by a third party or parties to whom the data are disclosed.
6. Processing is necessary for purposes of the legitimate interests pursued by the controller or by a third party or parties to whom the data are disclosed, except where such

---

[32]   The scope of this exclusion has been set by the ECJ in its judgment in *Re. Lindqvist.* C-101/01, Bodil Lindqvist, 6 November 2003.

interests are overridden by the interests or fundamental rights and freedoms of the data subject.[33]

Special regulation is provided for the so called "sensitive" personal data. According to Article 9 (1) GDPR, the processing of

> personal data revealing racial or ethnic origin, political opinions, religious or philosophical beliefs, or trade union membership, and the processing of genetic data, biometric data for the purpose of uniquely identifying a natural person, data concerning health or data concerning a natural person's sex life or sexual orientation shall be prohibited.

Important in this respect is to realise that images, and potentially sounds, may reveal the racial or ethnic origin, political opinions, religious or philosophical beliefs of individuals depicted on photographs and video, and if these individuals can be identified, special care has to be adopted in processing these data. The processing may even be prohibited if the collection and processing purposes do not comply with article 9. It may thus be necessary for a domestic robot to explicitly ask permission of "its masters" and visitors to the house to record their voices and images and to process the resulting information.

2. Principle of finality

Article 5 (1) b of the GDPR provides the second data processing principle, the finality principle. Data controllers may collect data only as far as it is necessary in order to achieve the specified and legitimate purpose. Furthermore, data controllers cannot carry out any further processing which is incompatible with the original purpose (article 5 (1) b GDPR) (purpose limitation principle or principle of secondary use). Combined with the fair and lawful processing principle, the finality principle means that data subjects must be specifically informed about the purpose of the data collection and that subsequent use of collected data is restricted. In particular, the finality principle requires that, without a legitimate and explicitly formulated reason, personal data may not be used and the concerned individual must remain anonymous. The goal of the principle is to promote transparency and, additionally, to enhance the control of the user over the use of the data. The indication of the purpose of data collection has to be clear and accurate, using a precise and distinct wording in order to satisfy the principle.

The finality principle, on the one hand, clearly restricts the processing that can be done on personal data because it requires the purpose(s) of processing to be specified in advance and these purposes to be legitimate. On the other hand, it provides much freedom for data controllers; they are permitted to process personal data (provided the other requirements are met of course) for the purposes they themselves specify. In other words, as long as the data controller is transparent and open about the purposes of data processing, they have much leeway. For instance, for an intelligent home assistant, one of the purposes of collecting voice data could potentially be "improving speech recognition of the owners of the device".

---

[33]   See recital 47 GDPR for some guidance.

3.   Principle of data minimization

The principle of data minimization enshrined in article 5 (1) c GDPR states that the processing of personal data should be limited to data that are adequate, relevant and not excessive. Data controllers are thus obliged to consider what they need for offering their service(s) or carrying out their task(s) and only process and store a minimum of data sufficient for these purposes. Particularly, data accumulation, a practice often exhibited by public authorities and private corporations who gather more personal data than required (commonly termed "big data"), should be avoided. The storage of large amounts of data can easily be considered as a privacy violation, and the argument that the data are not used is insufficient to justify their preservation. The basis for the assessment whether the data minimization requirement has been met is the purpose of data collection as specified under the finality principle. So, for instance, the voice data collected for improving voice recognition mentioned above, should be deleted once a sufficient level of recognition is achieved.

Relevant in this connection is that alternatives for the processing of *personal* data often exist. Privacy by design (which is also required according to article 25 GDPR) and privacy enhancing technologies[34] can be used to limit the amount of personal data being processed. The former suggests that the privacy issues should be taken into account from the earliest stage of the development of applications and services. The latter requires that the technical devices and designs use either no personal data or as limited an amount as possible.

4.   Principle of data quality

Related to the data minimisation principle is the data quality principle in article 5 1 (d) GDPR, which provides that all personal data shall be accurate and, where necessary, kept up to date. Data controllers are obliged to take every reasonable step to ensure that data which are inaccurate or incomplete, having regard to the purposes for which they were collected, are either erased or rectified. This principle is particularly important for the protection of personal integrity or the identity of the data subjects. It is often suggested that data controllers should create an appropriate mechanism enabling the data subjects to update their personal data or notify the data controller about the inaccuracies of the present information.

5.   Principle of conservation

The principle of conservation, also known as the time limitation principle, is provided in article 5 (1) e GDPR. It states that personal data shall not be kept for longer than is necessary for the purposes for which these data were collected. This implies that after achieving the purpose for which the data were collected, they should be destroyed or rendered anonymous. Fully anonymous data falls outside the scope of the GDPR. This principle, again, suggests that "training" data should be deleted once training is achieved.

---

[34]   Such as encryption, see for instance, Jan Camenisch, Ronald Leenes and Dieter Sommer (eds.), *Digital Privacy: PRIME – Privacy and Identity Management for Europe* (Springer 2011).

6.   Principle of confidentiality and security

Article 5 (1) f DPD stipulates a confidentiality obligation for anyone processing personal data on behalf of the data controller. They may only process personal data when required to do so by the data controller, or by law.

Article 32 GDPR requires data controllers and processors to take measures to limit privacy risks taking "into account the state of the art, the costs of implementation and the nature, scope, context and purposes of processing as well as the risk of varying likelihood and severity for the rights and freedoms of natural persons". They must implement appropriate technical and organizational measures to ensure a level of security appropriate to the risk. For intelligent home assistants, this means that measures on these devices as well as in the cloud will have to be implemented, such as password protection for access to data.

7.   Rights of the data subject

The GDPR grants several rights to the data subjects: the right to information, the right of access and the right to rectify. Providing the data subjects with those rights intends to guarantee that the data subject remain the ultimate controllers of their personal data. This should also reinforce the fundamental right to privacy described in Article 8 of ECHR.

8.   Right to information

Articles 13 and 14 GDPR provide a set of obligations for data controllers to inform data subjects whose data they process. Article 13 GDPR refers to data collected from the data subject herself. The provision states that the identity of the data controller and the intended purpose(s) of the processing should always be communicated to the data subject. Supplementary information (i.e., the recipients or categories of recipients of the data, the fact whether the questions asked are obligatory or voluntary as well as the possible consequences of failure to reply, the existence of the right to access and the right to rectify the data concerning to him/her) should only be provided in so far as it is necessary to guarantee fair processing in respect of the data subject.

Where the data have not been obtained from data subject, article 14 DPD applies. It obliges data controllers to provide similar information as mentioned in article 13 to the data subject at the time of the recording of personal data or if a disclosure to a third party is envisaged, no later than the time when the data are first disclosed. Article 14 (5) GDPR provides an exception; the obligation to inform the data subject shall not apply where, in particular for processing for statistical purposes of historical or scientific research, the provision of such information proves impossible or would involve a disproportionate effort or if obtaining or disclosure is expressly laid down by law to which the controller is subject and which provides adequate safeguards to protect the data subject's legitimate interests.

New in the GDPR is that in the case of automated decision making, including profiling,[35] meaningful information about the logic involved, as well as the significance

---

[35]   Art 4 (4) GDPR: "profiling" means any form of automated processing of personal data consisting of the use of personal data to evaluate certain personal aspects relating to a natural person, in particular to analyse or predict aspects concerning that natural person's performance at work, economic situation, health, personal preferences, interests, reliability, behaviour, location or movements.

and the envisaged consequences of such processing for the data subject has to be provided to the data subject on their request (article 15 (1) h).[36]

9.   Right to object

Pursuant to article 14(a) DPD, Member States shall grant the data subject the right to object to the processing of data relating to him, on compelling legitimate grounds relating to his particular situation. This right to object must at least cover the cases where processing is necessary for the performance of a task carried out in the public interest or in the exercise of official authority and where processing is necessary for the purposes of the legitimate interests pursued by the controller (Article 7(e) and (f)).

The right to object is aimed at giving the data subject a possibility to prevent the processing of his data, in cases where it violates his personal integrity and where it would be otherwise legitimate. The principle originated from the idea that individuals own their personal data, therefore they should be in a position to control it and oppose its processing. It is an evident recognition of the right to self-determination.

10.   Right not to be subject to a decision based solely on automated processing

Article 22 of the GDPR grants the data subject a right not to be subjected to an automated decision which produces legal effects concerning him or significantly affects him and which is based solely on automated processing of data intended to evaluate certain personal aspects relating to the data subject, such as his performance at work, creditworthiness, reliability, conduct, etc. This right was introduced to overcome the effect of development of information technology, which very often leads to decisions being made mechanically. Frequently, such decisions are of essential importance or have legal effects; hence they should be taken by other people who can take into account specific circumstances of the individual. There are statutory exceptions provided to this right in cases where the decision is either taken in the course of the entering into or performance of a contract, provided that the request (for the entering or the performance of the contract) has been lodged by the data subject and there are suitable measures to safeguard the data subject's legitimate interests; or is authorised by a law that also lays down measures to safeguard the data subject's legitimate interests.

III.   AI ENTERS THE HOUSE

Nowadays, AI is entering the house not only through the main door, but also from the windows, the garage, the fridge, the light switches, and so on.[37] Even though we are still

---

[36]   The scope of this provision is unclear. Some claim it is very extensive, such as D. Kamarinou, C. Millard and J. Singh, *Machine Learning with Personal Data* Queen Mary School of Law Legal Studies Research Paper No. 247/2016, others contest that art. 15 (1) h does incorporate a right to explanation, see for instance Sandra Wachter, Brent Mittelstadt and Luciano Floridi, *Why a Right to Explanation of Automated Decision-Making Does Not Exist in the General Data Protection Regulation* (December 28, 2016). International Data Privacy Law (forthcoming). Available at SSRN: https://ssrn.com/abstract=2903469.

[37]   Artificial Intelligence, Robotics, Privacy and Data Protection Room Document for the 38th International Conference of Data Protection and Privacy Commissioners, EDPS, October 2016, p. 10.

far from implementing the concept of a house fully managed by an autonomous central brain, and whose inhabitants are freed from tedious cleaning and organising tasks, AI is already present in disparate household appliances. The tendency of different sectors of the Tech industry to converge is, in fact, opening the way to a proliferation of devices and tools which rely, one way or another, on machine learning and other AI techniques for many purposes. The presence of AI inside the house can therefore range from very basic to more complex. Due to their positioning and to the information they collect, all the appliances within the range potentially present risks for privacy and personal data protection, although at different levels.

A.   Robots in All Shapes and Sizes

Brands like iRobot, Nest, or the more popular Philips and Samsung, among many others, are currently offering a wide range of so called "smart" devices. While a uniform definition of what a smart device is has not been established, there is a feature that can be identified in most of those devices. The products, which stand at the crossroad of technologies like Internet of Things, Ambient Intelligence, Ubiquitous Computing, and Robotics, all present a certain capability of sensing the external environment[38] and responding to it to provide the users with a desired outcome. Such capability constitutes the intelligence that allows the products to be more efficient in completing their tasks, as well as to present new skills compared to the traditional versions of home appliances. In other words, the above-mentioned products are provided with Artificial Intelligence.

Some of the devices do not exhibit complex forms of AI: the smart toothbrush, for example, collects the data concerning movements and duration of the cleaning routine to provide brushing suggestions or, in the case of children, educative games.[39] This kind of simple data collection, whether followed or not by pattern recognition, is common to many devices, such as the automated garage or windows/shades, or smart meters for water, gas, and electricity consumption.

Some products present more advanced AI, with the capability to use basic information to perform repetitive tasks, such as the new Roomba vacuum cleaners which are able to map the house distinguishing furniture from walls. Samsung's smart fridge can show what it has in store through a mobile app, and can provide for entertainment, recipes, and function as a hub to read emails or messages. Another Samsung product, the Smart TV, presents a similar degree of intelligence, with data collection, advanced storage options, and algorithm-powered suggestions of products based on the profiles constructed on the basis of their users' behavior.

Finally, more complex products are also available, presenting a stronger AI. This is the case of home assistant robots like Amazon Echo and Google Home, whose machine learning techniques allow them to collect information from all the other connected devices (smart switches, smart fridges and TVs, tablets and smartphones, the Roomba,

---

[38]   Ugo Pagallo, *Robots in the cloud with privacy: A new threat to data protection?* 29(5) Computer Law & Security Review 501–08 (2013), available at http://www.sciencedirect.com/science/article/pii/S0267364913001398.

[39]   This fits within a clear trend of *gamification*, in this case of *serious gaming*.

etc) to coordinate them based on their users' preferences. These robot assistants typically do not perform actions themselves due to the lack of actuators and movement capability. They are usually voice activated and are connected to smartphones (as well as with email and messenger accounts, calendars, and social media platforms). They are designed to support the inhabitants of the house in their daily life, from planning their commitments to adding items to the grocery shopping list. In order to perform efficiently and effectively, Echo and Home employ a high degree of intelligence based on several machine learning techniques, natural language understanding (NLU), automatic speech recognition (ASR), visual search and image recognition, text-to-speech (TTS) technologies.[40] Furthermore, to carry out all the operations connected to such techniques, these home assistant robots as well as several of the other above mentioned products rely on Cloud technology. The Cloud, in fact, allows them to store the huge quantities of data collected and to exploit processing power beyond that of their own processor.

The AI that has entered our houses in the shape of digital Internet connected products is based on the processing of information collected in and around the house (as well as, sometimes, information available from other sources, such as emails, Facebook profiles, or public databases), and supported by Cloud computing. Due to their position inside the house, they represent a new "presence" inside the private and intimate lives of the individuals inhabiting the house. They bring attentive, powerful, always on ears and eyes, equipped with seemingly infinite memory, capable of transferring the information grabbed or to reproduce it upon request. This not only enables them to perform useful actions for their masters, but also may raise privacy and data protection concerns. Due to the use of Machine Learning and Cloud computing, AI powered devices base their capacity of interacting with their users and comply with their requests on Big Data. The intelligence factor of AI derives, in fact, from the analysis of the patterns emerging from Big Data mining. This, indeed, opens the doors of the house to an interaction of information and, in turn, to a collective dimension of knowledge that appears hard to reconcile with the individual approach infusing both privacy and data protection.[41] The presence of AI inside the house gives life to multiple points of friction with the existing protection of personal data and privacy, as will be explained below.

In the light of the above, this section addresses the relationship between AI powered home devices and the protection of privacy and personal data. We do this by discussing a number of frictions introduced or enhanced by them in the light of the European legislation, along with a brief analysis of cases in which AI posed concrete risks to privacy and/ or data protection.

---

[40]   See "The impact Artifical Intelligence is making on marketing", CHE Proximity White Paper, Issue 2, August 2017, p. 12.

[41]   Silvia de Conca, "From the glass house to the hive: the private sphere in the era of intelligent home assistant robots", in Simone Fischer-Hübner, Jean Pierre Nordvik, Marit Hansen, Eleni Kosta, Igor Nai Fovino (eds), *IFIP Summer School on Privacy and Identity Management – the Smart World Revolution, 11th IFIP WG 9.2, 9.5, 9.6/11.7, 11.4, 11.6/SIG 9.2.2 International Summer School, Ispra, Italy, September 3-8, 2017, Revised Selected Papers* (Springer 2018).

1. Home alone?

As we have seen, privacy entails a set of different, although often connected concepts. From isolation and exclusion to control over access and dissemination of information, all the different types of privacy identified by scholars and judges revolve around boundaries and thresholds between domains. Building on Warren and Brandeis,[42] the protection of a sanctuary, whether physical or abstract, is deemed an important aspect of privacy. It creates a private domain. In this context, a primary role for the protection of such domain is recognised to the house. At both abstract and material level, the placement of certain activities inside or outside the house determines their private or public nature. In the words of Shapiro, "the boundary constituted by the home and the boundary between public and private are partially coincident".[43] The introduction of new communication technologies does, however, affect such a boundary, at both conceptual and concrete levels, interacting with the private domain of the individuals inhabiting the house. What are, then, the effects AI in particular creates for privacy inside the house?

Borrowing once more from Shapiro's work, we can identify two main dimensions of privacy inside the home which are touched by the insertion of AI powered devices: placement and permeability.[44] To these two, we would like to add a third one: persistence.

Placement refers to the position of the threshold between public and private, and ultimately includes which activities are pulled inside the private domain, and which are pushed outside, in the public or semi-public. Following the automation trend, activities once mostly occurring outside the house are now brought inside, such as entertainment, training, as well as administering cure and care. Work, shopping, and advertising are other examples of activities that can occur through AI powered devices. Many of these examples are, however, not new. Teleshopping has already been available for decades and so are unsolicited advertising or tele-work, via personal computers, fax, the phone, or even the radio. The way AI powered devices carry out such activities, however, presents certain novelties and peculiarities. The algorithm underlying AI, by automating the automation,[45] substitutes the intervention of users, which no longer act on/with the device, but is directly passively provided with certain products or services, as is the case of the choice of the song or movie to play based on the geographical location and preference profiling. Furthermore, the design of certain devices precludes or inhibits certain behaviour in the house. This risks undermining agency and autonomy of the individuals interacting and using AI powered devices. By means of techno-regulation,[46] device manufacturers can for instance build home assistant robots that recite audio advertising at the beginning of each task they accomplish without offering their owners the option to turn this "feature" off.[47] As

---

[42]   *See* William and Brandeis, *supra* note 10.
[43]   Stuart Shapiro, *Places and Spaces: The Historical Interaction of Technology, Home, and Privacy* 14(4) The Information Society p. 276 (1998).
[44]   *Idem.*
[45]   Pedro Domingos, *The Master Algorithm* (Basic Books 2015).
[46]   Ronald Leenes, *Framing Techno-Regulation: An Exploration of State and Non-State Regulation by Technology* 5(2) Legisprudence 143–69 (2011). doi:10.5235/175214611797885675; Roger Brownsword, *Code, Control, and Choice: Why East Is East and West Is West* 25 LEGAL STUD. 1, 12 (2005).
[47]   See "Google pulls Beauty and the Beast 'ad' from Home", published on BBC Technology on 17th March 2017, available at: http://www.bbc.com/news/technology-39304468 (last consulted on 20th August 2017).

a consequence, the inhabitants of the house are subjected to different activities than the ones they had requested based on decisions taken by the AI through profiling. AI effects on placement therefore affect decision-making capabilities of subjects (autonomy) inside their own private domain, where such forms of control should instead find its full expression.

Placement might also be affected by AI powered devices under another perspective. While the hardware's ownership is usually fully assigned to the individuals purchasing it, the software, which represents the true intelligence and in most cases the most relevant part for the functioning of the devices, remains under a licensing agreement, therefore eluding the proprietary sphere. This implies that while AI enters the house, it does not fall within the properties of the inhabitants, further shifting the boundaries of what is included in, or out, the private domain.

The term *permeability* refers to the capability of information to cross the boundary between public and private, whether in one direction or the other.[48] In this regard, the presence of AI powered technologies connected to the Internet significantly contributes to blurring the line between the physical and virtual dimensions, making the house more permeable even in the absence of a physical trespassing. AI being based on collecting data from the environment surrounding it, and processing it (often in the Cloud) to create profiles, take decisions and initiate or carry out actions in and around the house, permeates the house in two directions: outside-in and inside-out. All without the occupants of the home being fully aware. Even without referring to the dystopian scenario of houses with transparent walls, it is important to acknowledge the existence of fluxes of information moving from inside to outside the house, and vice-versa. This affects several privacy dimensions mentioned above, such as communicational, informational, associational, decisional, behavioral, and so on. For this reason, the effects of AI on the permeability of the private domain are particularly relevant also in connection with data protection, as will be explained more in detail below.

The element of *persistence* is not borrowed from Shapiro's work, but is a necessary addition to complete the analysis of the interferences between AI and privacy. In our view, the continuous presence of AI inside the private "sanctuary" of the home has, per se, effects on privacy and often goes unnoticed. The presence of another individual in the living room is perceived as different from the presence of a Smart TV. The other might affect one's behaviour and limit the full expression of our inner self, but this does not happen, usually, in front of an electric appliance. We, at present, are usually unaware that our smart appliances may listen in to our conversation and hence talk freely about our inner thoughts in the presence of our toasters and we may even talk to (or curse) our PC. All without consequences—the PC does not change its "behavior" when we angrily shout at it. We can no longer assume this inertia of appliances and devices is sustained. Following the warnings issued by Samsung (one of the first producers of smart TVs), however, we know that the conversations happening while the product's smart features are activated are also recorded. This also happens with other devices, such as Amazon Echo and Google Home. They are capable of recording everything happening within a range of several meters once they are activated. In fact, in order to be voice activated, they are actually constantly listening, even though they only record when their functions are triggered.

---

[48]   *See* Shapiro, *supra* note 43.

Just like the presence of robots has been connected with a change in the behavior of the individuals around them,[49] the ubiquity, together with the constant eavesdropping and/ or observation, of AI powered devices inside the house affects the spatial, associational, behavioral and communicational dimensions of privacy.[50] This might, in turn, have undesired consequences on identity and personality development, enhanced also by the chilling effects of adapting one's speech in the presence of smart appliances. Indirectly, data-based machine learning technologies therefore affect another fundamental element of individual growth: the desire to experiment.[51]

Having discussed the possible interference of AI powered devices inside the house, it is now time to take a closer look at these devices from the (more limited) perspective of the protection of personal data. Hence the GDPR and DPEC come into scope.

2.   AI and the European legislative framework for the protection of personal data

The very nature of AI technology implies the use of data. No matter which algorithm is employed, they all necessitate significant quantities of information to be available for processing to extract patterns and create profiles which, in turn, will provide the software with enough information to learn and decide how to better complete particular tasks. This circumstance makes the spreading of AI particularly concerning in view of the protection of personal data.

First, it is worth noting that in the view of the authors, few doubts exist about the inclusion within the scope of the GDPR of AI powered devices. As explained in section II, the scope of the GDPR is very broad, and both "personal data" and "processing" are interpreted in an extensive way. In view of AI, personal data are very likely at stake. Even the less intelligent devices like a Roomba may collect information regarding their environment that represents or, more in general, concerns identifiable individuals, while the data itself may reveal information about these individuals. Another example can be the smart toothbrush, collecting data concerning hygiene, brushing movements, and daily routine. These data certainly reflect specific individuals, who most of the time will be easily identifiable. The identification of the users is either easy because of the limited environment in which the device operates, or, more likely, because the device will store the data under an identifier (such as a user ID, IP address, or nickname) for usability and profiling reasons.[52] The intelligent home assistants at the center of our analysis, operate

---

[49]   See, among others, Wilma A. Bainbridge, Justin Hart, Elizabeth S. Kim and Brian Scassellati, "The effect of presence on human-robot interaction", in *Proceedings from the RO-MAN 2008 – The 17th IEEE International Symposium on Robot and Human Interactive Communication* (2008). In this regard, and keeping in mind the ubiquity feature and the blurring of the distinction between virtual and physical "worlds" deriving from the convergence of AI, robotics and IoT, it is interesting to also consider a broader study on the perception of presence even online due to the use of anthropomorphic avatars: Kristine L. Nowak and Frank Biocca, *The Effect of the Agency and Anthropomorphism on Users' Sense of Telepresence, Copresence, and Social Presence in Virtual Environments* 12(5) Presence: Teleoperators and Virtual Environments 481–94 (2003).

[50]   Julie E. Cohen, *Configuring the Networked Self* (Yale University Press 2012).

[51]   Sheri B. Pan, *Get to Know Me: Protecting Privacy and Autonomy Under Big Data's Penetrating Gaze* 30(1) Harvard Journal of Law & Technology (2016).

[52]   Many devices are completely tied into cloud based services. Wearable fitness trackers, for instance, cannot be operated without creating an online account.

on the basis of voice (microphone) and potentially visual data (camera). The processing of sound and image data is only covered by the Regulation if it is automated or if the data processed are contained in a filing system structured according to specific criteria relating to individuals, so as to permit easy access to the personal data in question. This potentially puts certain images and sounds (voices) recorded of individuals by AI products under the umbrella of the GDPR. A smart security camera installed inside a house and equipped with a camera and audio sensors will process personal (sensitive even, because images and sounds may easily reveal the racial or ethnic origin of the individuals recorded) data if it processes visual imagery containing recognizable people (even if not storing the data). On a more general note, many of the devices will process data in the sense defined by the GDPR because any action that can be performed on data is considered processing according to article 4 (2) GDPR. Not all processing of data, however, is processing of personal data, of course.

A possible exception to the application of the GDPR would be if the processing takes place under the household exemption, which may be applicable to the case in object (domestic use). In practical terms this means that the requirements pertaining to the processing of personal data do not apply. Also, the rights of the data subjects would be limited, but given that strictly personal use almost always implies control of the individual over the data, this does not seem a serious issue. Besides, in general, individuals who employ smart products in their household will not object to these robots processing their personal data in line of their function (certainly if the data does not leave the house). When a device transfers personal data to external parties, however, the household exemption no longer holds, and the GDPR will apply to the operations of said devices.

With regard to the subjects involved it may not be easy to determine the roles of the three entities distinguished by the GDPR in the case of AI powered appliances and robots. The data subject usually is clear, this is the person whose data are being processed by the devices. If the data subject owns the devices, then generally, she will also be the data controller because she decides the purposes (the reason for employing the device in the first place) and means of processing (the device itself). When the device is owned by someone other than the data subject, and/or operating for someone else, then this person/entity is the data controller. This could be the case of a guest of the owner temporarily in the house, whose data (voice, image, and so on) are also being processed by, for example, a smart security camera or the Amazon Echo/Google Home robot. If the data subject uses a third party for some tasks (such as is the case for many third-party apps and software installed on assistant robots) then the data subject may be the data controller, whereas the hired hand (who accomplishes their task by means of the AI powered device) is the data processor. In the last scenario, it may also be the case that the third party employed by the data subject is deemed the data controller. The concrete circumstances of the case are decisive in this respect. The various distinctions are relevant because they bring about different responsibilities and liabilities. The controller, as the term implies, has most responsibilities.

The justifications for the processing of the data that permit processing under the GDPR indeed also apply to AI powered devices and robots, and due to the nature of the technology, several of the grounds mentioned in article 6 GDPR could warrant processing. For instance, the owner of an AI powered device may be explicitly asked to consent to the processing of their data through a voice-based command, an on-screen dialog, but also opening the box in which the device was delivered, or cutting a shrink wrap in which it was placed, could count as explicit consent, provided the purposes and conditions of processing are clear to the individual. Interestingly, reliance on consent of the data subjects could imply that visitors to the smart home may be required to provide theirs for having the household robots collect data about them and their behavior. If consent is not provided, the robot should not collect and process any data pertaining to the guest. Imagine having to go through an inform and consent screen displayed by the house-robot whenever (or the first time) you enter a friend's house.[53]

In the case of smart surveillance cameras, the justification may be found in the performance of a contract (with a security services provider) according to article 6 (b) GDPR, or in the compliance with an obligation to which the controller is subject (article 6 (c) GDPR). Finally, in many cases, the processing of personal data by robots may be in the legitimate interest of their owners (article 6 (f) GDPR). In the latter case, however, the interests of the controller have to be weighed against the interests for fundamental rights and freedoms of the data subject, which require protection under Article 1 (2) GDPR (article 6 (f) GDPR). As per the sensitive data processed by the devices, their processing is in principle prohibited unless these individuals specifically consent to such sensitive data being processed.

Two significant frictions between AI and data protection occur with regard to two fundamental principles underlying legitimate processing: finality and minimization. On one side, for AI and the deriving processing of personal data, the principle of finality, as described above, means that the makers of AI powered devices have to define what personal data will be processed and for what purposes prior to employing them. This information will have to be communicated to the data subjects involved prior to the actual processing of personal data, in line with the *right to information*.

On the other side, the *data minimization principle* limits the processing to those sole data that are necessary, adequate and relevant for the purposes initially established according to the finality principle. As clear as this provision appears in theory, it becomes extremely difficult to efficiently apply it with regard to a technology, such as AI, based on elaborating and aggregating information that have to be stored also for (im)possible future uses. The more data are available, the more AI can learn, and the more it can learn, the more those data will become useful in the future. The main issue lies, therefore, in the very core of the provision: defining exactly what can be considered necessary for algorithms that operate based on self-learning from huge quantities of data.

Another paramount friction that has the potential to become the object of many lawsuits once the GDPR enters into effectiveness regards the provision on automated decisions. The relevance for this principle lies precisely in the fact that automated decisions are exactly what AI techniques do: monitor the data subject and its environment and then take actions based on the input. Not all AI decisions are within the scope of this provision; things like changing the room temperature by one degree Celsius are most likely not. The decision needs to have legal or otherwise significant effects to be in the scope of article 22 GDPR. When the AI system starts ordering products and services on

---

[53]   In that case also the inverse, withdrawing consent and erasure of stored data, has to be provided for.

the basis of its assessment of house or inhabitants, this may certainly be within scope. In this regard, it is also worth noting that the automated decisions taken by AI powered devices on a daily basis are not the only ones that will affect the data subjects. Besides these, more direct, decisions, many other decisions will also be taken by third parties based on the data collected by the house devices. These, more indirect, decisions present even more the risk to affect in a significant way the legitimate interests of the data subjects and will, therefore, also be subject to article 22 of the GDPR. In case of automated decision-making the system should be able to "provide meaningful information about the logic involved" (article 15 GDPR). In the case of programmed decision-making (for instance using production rules), this is not too hard, but in cases involving machine learning, it is far less trivial to what extent clear and meaningful information can be given if it is not fully possible to tell, not even for the programmers, how the algorithms at the basis of the AI will use the information, when, and for what.

Another example, highlighting also the complexity of the relationship between AI and data protection due to the very nature of said technology, is the application of the Protection by Design and by Default of article 25 GDPR (see above). This provision requires technical and organizational measures to be taken (within certain limits) to make sure the data processing system operates in compliance with the GDPR. This implies that while an effort to embed Article 25's Protection by Design and by Default can be made during the programming phase, the self-learning capability will result in new codes that change the software, and in which data protection might no longer be included. This makes it, indeed, hard to reconcile the embedding of the provisions of the GDPR at hardware and software level with a technology that changes itself during time. A possible solution could be to include data protection, and the GDPR in particular, within the array of subjects that the algorithms can learn by themselves, although the hues and flexibility of natural language represent a huge obstacle and indeed a challenge for designers and programmers.[54]

Developers of the AI technology that enters our homes will have to take the data protection requirements to heart, if not because they aim to strike a balance between facilitating the free flow of information to provide useful services and protection of privacy and other values, then for the fact that non-compliance may be stricken with serious fines. Article 83 GDPR provides for administrative sanctions running up to 20million EUR or four percent of total worldwide turnover of the data controller for non-compliance with the core GDPR provisions.

The GDPR at the time of writing of this chapter is still to come into full enforceability and hence many open questions regarding AI technologies in view of the Regulation

---

[54]   See for instance, Bert-Jaap Koops and Ronald Leenes, *Privacy regulation cannot be hardcoded. A critical comment on the 'privacy by design' provision in data-protection law* (2014) International Review of Law, Computers and Technology, 159–71; Ronald Leenes and Federica Lucivero, *Laws on Robots, Laws by Robots, Laws in Robots: Regulating Robot Behaviour by Design* 6(2) Law, Innovation, and Technology 194–222 (2014), DOI: http://dx.doi.org/10.5235/17579961.6.2.194; Ugo Pagallo, "The Impact of Domestic Robots on Privacy and Data Protection, and the Troubles with Legal Regulation by Design" in Serge Gutwirth, Ronald Leenes and Paul De Hert (eds.), *Data Protection on the Move: Current Developments in ICT and Privacy/Data Protection* (Springer 2016), 387–410.

still remain. That does not, however, mean that no experience with privacy and data protection issues induced by AI technologies exists. In the following, we will illustrate the real-world issues and implications surrounding AI technologies in the home from the perspectives of privacy and data protection.

B.   A Will of their Own

News concerning Alexa or Google Assistant (the respective AI softwares of Amazon Echo and Google Home) appear on popular and scientific news outlets on a weekly basis. Famous is the case in which an Amazon Echo ordered a dollhouse for a six-year-old after she had asked the Echo "can you play dollhouse with me and get me a dollhouse?".[55] When reported on the news, it turned out that the closing remark "Alexa ordered me a dollhouse", triggered similar purchases by other Echo's that apparently were quite trigger happy. While this may have been a collateral of normal Echo behavior—it is after all Amazon's product (also) meant to facilitate shopping at Amazon—Smart assistants can also be purposefully hijacked by companies and others through TV content. An example is Google Assistant being triggered by a Burger King ad, willingly designed to exploit the vocal commands of the device to have the device read out aloud a description of one of their popular products.[56] It may seem funny that the Assistant seems so committed to watching TV and helping the household by explaining what a Whopper is on demand and reinforcing the ad on TV, but the potential misuse for malicious actions is more serious.[57] Google Home was also the object of debate when, during the promotional campaign for the new *Beauty and the Beast* movie, it suddenly broadcast to the users an audio advertising of the movie, without previous notice or consent.

These are examples of smart appliances taking actions on the basis of their function and design. Their activity is triggered by trigger words and they carry out the instructed task as well as they can by interpreting the voice commands provided. The trouble is the commands do not correspond with the wishes of their masters. Even in the little girl's case it is questionable whether her wish to get a dollhouse should be taken seriously. The resulting behaviour of the devices is problematic from the perspective of privacy because the command and resulting actions interfere in the private sphere of the devices' owners. *Control* over data flows and their impact on identity and individual features as an important element of many privacy conceptions. Control is what is lost in these examples. The *impromptu* purchases or the unauthorised broadcasting of advertising infringe several

---

[55]   See, among others, Andrew Liptak, "Amazon's Alexa started ordering people dollhouses after hearing its name on TV", published on The Verge on 7 January 2017, available at: https://www.theverge.com/2017/1/7/14200210/amazon-alexa-tech-news-anchor-order-dollhouse (last consulted on 20th August 2017).

[56]   See, among others, Timothy J. Seppala, "Burger King wreaks havoc on Google Assistant with Whopper ad", published on EnGadget on 12 April 2017, available at: https://www.engadget.com/2017/04/12/burger-king-wreaks-havoc-on-google-assistant-with-whopper-ad/ (last consulted on 20th August 2017).

[57]   The TV ad might as well say: "Google, shut down the heating" prompting the home-owner to call maintenance because the heating is acting up. He missed the ad because the commercial breaks are used for attending the bathroom, aren't they?

privacy dimensions of Koops et al.'s typology, in particular the proprietary and decisional ones. Human autonomy is being challenged by all too enthusiastic smart helpers.

C.   Alexa Goes to Trial

In addition to talking, Alexa and Google Assistant also listen (and sense). They collect data from the sensors and, as explained above, turn the data into information necessary to complete their tasks. Such data remain, however, stored in the Cloud for future uses. And while the device is recording, all the sounds and conversations occurring in the environment are recorded, regardless of their connection with the task requested. In the case of Alexa, the streaming and recording start a fraction of a second before the trigger word, until the task is completed, as it has recently been brought to the attention of the public by a murder case in which the Arkansas public prosecutor requested the recordings of an Amazon Echo to be used as evidence in court against its owner.[58] Here we see a number of privacy and data protection issues at play.

In the first place, there seems to be a clear privacy infringement, also under US law, because it is questionable whether individuals can reasonably expect that their conversations or background noises will be picked up by their smart assistants, to be used in criminal proceedings later on. Under the US Katz doctrine[59] of reasonable expectation of privacy and the third-party doctrine,[60] the matter potentially is not that problematic. The data are voluntarily provided to a third-party (Amazon), which means there is no longer a reasonable expectation of privacy. The point is, however, that ordinary people may not yet be accustomed to the idea that the area or context in which a reasonable expectation of privacy exists is rapidly declining.

Also from the perspective of Koops' privacy typology, this case is problematic. Several dimensions are affected here. The private sphere of the home, as well as the communication between the individual and others in that sphere are no longer (really) under control of the individual and it cannot even be sure who gets access to the data. Service providers tend to be restrictive in providing customer data to law enforcement and also in this case, Amazon stated it: "will not release customer information without a valid and binding legal demand properly served on us. Amazon objects to overbroad or otherwise inappropriate demands as a matter of course." In the end, it did provide the data.

This also brings us to the data protection side of the case. As was discussed above, data controllers, Amazon, in this case, cannot collect and store whatever data they like. The data need to be relevant and limited to the purpose of processing. Depending on how Amazon has defined its processing purposes, the data may actually be excessive and hence Amazon might be in breach of its data protection obligations (if this were an EU case, that is). Supposing that the law enforcement warrant is adequate and

---

[58]   *State of Arkansas v James A. Bates*, Case No. cr-2016-370-2 Circuit Court of Benton County (Arkansas). See also, among others, Tom Dotan, "Amazon Echo and the Hot Tub Murder", published on The Information on 27 December 2016, available at: https://www.theinformation.com/amazon-echo-and-the-hot-tub-murder?eu=JnmYMZlQZHz7uehZk0Lvtg (last consulted on 20th August 2017).

[59]   U.S. Supreme Court in *Katz v. United States*, 389 U.S. 347 (1967).

[60]   *United States v. Miller*, 425 U.S. 435 (1976).

valid, a question still is whether the data can be used, given that Amazon may have it illegitimately.

D. I Know What You Did Last Summer

At the beginning of 2015, Samsung included a warning to the users of their Smart TVs in their Privacy Policy: while the voice command is activated, the apparatus could record every sound and conversation from the surroundings, storing them with the other data collected by the device.[61] Now, while Samsung claims the company "does not retain voice data or sell it to third parties," there is another issue with these smart devices that we want to address: cybersecurity. Unsurprisingly these devices, like any, are vulnerable to cyberattacks. The TV can capture both audio and video and while in normal operation there will be indicators that the sensors are in operation, these can be bypassed by hacks. In that case, there is no blinking LED, on screen or off screen, that shows the camera is active and hence the monitoring of the viewer can be done without them noticing. This means that secret surveillance of TV viewers is possible, revealing not only what they watch on TV, but also showing what they are doing and saying while watching. Combined with the potential to store the data over longer periods, the privacy implications are clear. A more invasive entering into the private sphere is hardly imaginable.

The potential of invasive monitoring can also have consequences in terms of behavioural privacy and, in turn, development of identity and expression. Once warned about the fact that the Smart TV in their living rooms can listen, see, and track every conversation, face and movement performed by the individuals inhabiting the house, these might involuntarily decide to change their behaviours. This constant sense of being observed and monitored might, therefore, affect the individual growth, influencing their freedom of expression and the formation of their identity.[62]

From the perspective of data protection, the Smart TVs also raise issues, even in their intended mode of operation: TV activity triggered by its owner(s). The collection and storage of information not relating to the required tasks and functionality of the Smart TV can be a violation of the data minimization principle as established by the GDPR. To mitigate this issue, solutions can be explored in the realm of privacy-enhancing and Protection by Design solutions (such as the possibility to deactivate the voice command) allowing actions, such as deleting those data recorded by accident during the activation of the Smart TVs' vocal commands, which should, therefore, not be retained nor used by the Data Controller/Processor.

The cameras embedded in devices such as Samsung's Smart TVs are capable of facial and gesture recognition. Images, identity features, movement patterns and other data, many of which are sensitive, are therefore collected by the devices, some accidentally, some on purpose. Furthermore, the personal data collected not only belong to the users that

---

61   See, for instance, David Goldman, "Your Samsung TV is eavesdropping on your private conversations", published on CNN Technology on 10 February 2015, available at: http://money. cnn.com/2015/02/09/technology/security/samsung-smart-tv-privacy/index.html (last consulted on 20th August 2017).

62   Michel Foucault, "Discipline and Punish, Panopticism", in Alan Sheridan (ed.), *Discipline amd Punish: The Birth of the Prison* (Vintage Books 1977) 195–228.

gave their consent to the processing when the TVs were first activated, but also to other subjects, such as friends, children, other guests, cleaning personnel, babysitters, and so on. In this case, should consent be provided by these additional subjects? If the case, how and when? The exercise of their rights as Data Subjects, as well as many other provisions, also present significant issues in this case, which neither the producers nor the regulators have addressed yet and which are the direct consequence of the ubiquity and intelligence of such devices.

The role of privacy and data protection will, therefore, be fundamental with regard to AI to avoid undesired effects not only on the private sphere, but on the very development of the inner selves of individuals.

E.   My TiVo Thinks I'm Gay

In November 2002, Jeffrey Zaslow published an article in The Wall Street Journal entitled "Oh No! My TiVo Thinks I'm Gay".[63] The article, which explained how a Californian film studio executive had troubles with his TiVo device that kept automatically recording first gay-themed and then Nazism-related content, became very popular, and shed a light on undesired consequences of erroneous deductions made by AI powered devices.

AI powered devices use machine learning techniques to take decisions on what kind of products or services might interest or better satisfy their users. Based on pattern recognition and on the previous choices of the users, the AI elaborates profiles and categories. In the vast majority of the cases, even when the elaboration is made with high quantities of anonymised data, the profiles are subsequently associated with individuals and used to provide them with suggestions, advertising, or with the proper response to their requests.

Next to the issues already discussed in terms of data collection, processing and profiling, the core issue with this case is one of control. Not only was the TiVo constantly trying to assess the identity of its owner and provide suggestions[64] and even record shows, but also it proved to be (almost) impossible to "convince" the TiVo that it was on the wrong track. Autonomy and control thus are diminished by the device's AI. This inferring activity carried out by the AI devices that surround us can interfere not only with the control individuals have over how their identities are projected to the external world, under the definition of privacy given by Agre, or with the decisional dimension of privacy identified by Koops et al. (see Part II above), but also how their identity develops in their own private sphere. Eli Pariser's notion of the filter bubble[65] comes to mind here: based on our preferences and prior behavior, the technology steers us ever more into a funnel of media content that fits neatly with the system's conception of our identity. Everything outside this core is filtered away from us.

While major decisions can fall within the scope of article 22 GDPR due to their capability to significantly affect legitimate interests of individuals, it appears too stretched

---

[63]   Jeffrey Zaslow, "Oh No! My TiVo thinks I'm gay!", published in The Wall Street Journal on 26 November 2002.
[64]   This is also a core feature of the Netflix service, which at least one of the authors of this chapter finds highly annoying. Unfortunately there is no option to turn off suggestions in Netflix either.
[65]   Eli Pariser, *The Filter Bubble: How the New Personalized Web Is Changing What We Read and How We Think* (Penguin 2011).

to include within said article also the daily, minor decisions that are the result of the inference of AI powered devices. Such decisions can, however, deeply affect the identitarian component of privacy, as well as the very agency of individuals. AI inference, multiplied on a daily basis for a huge array of minor chores and occasions, might progressively erode identity and the components determining the control over it.

IV.   CONCLUSIONS

The new smart overlords are coming. They will slowly, but steadily, enter our homes and with them bring a range of life comforting capabilities and enhance our abilities.[66] They will constantly improve their performance and be able to instruct successors and neighbouring devices, maybe finally removing the need to RTFM. But this comes at a price. We will likely/potentially have to give up some/all of our privacy. The smart devices can only be as smart as we let them become on the basis of conscious and unconscious interactions with them and the ability we give them to learn from our experiences and from that of others. That requires giving them access to sensors that can also monitor us.

Rendering insight into our behavior, thoughts and the like, and handing over control of ourselves is not uncommon (we have all been children and hope to reach old age), but not entirely comfortable either. Data about us will increasingly be available outside our control, mostly to our benefit, but as some of the examples in the previous section show, not always or not necessarily always.

The issues will have to be addressed on multiple levels. As we have tried to show in this chapter, privacy and data protection are not the same, but both play a role in determining if there is an issue in the first place, and in the potential prevention or mitigation if there is. Data protection regulation aims to establish a balance between the interests of the data subject and third parties (controllers, society at large). It does so by defining the playing field against the backdrop of fundamental rights such as privacy, dignity, autonomy and others. AI devices will have to operate within the boundaries defined by this regulation. Whether this is possible remains to be seen, as we have pointed out above. Next to the data protection regulation, there is privacy as a philosophical/social construct. Even when processing perfectly complies with the data protection regulation, privacy issues may exist/remain; a surveillance camera may be installed respecting the prevailing regulations, but it still is a privacy infringement of those monitored. And then there is a third category, ethics or morality more generally. Not everything that can be done should be done. Although this topic is largely outside of the scope of this volume and this chapter, it is important to keep this in mind still.

---

[66]   Apple's Tom Gruber calls for *Humanistic AI*, AI that complements and supplements humans, instead of competing with them, see https://youtu.be/DJMhz7JlPvA (or using them and their data as resources for monetization as we would like to add).

SOURCES

Statutes

EU

Directive 95/46/EC of the European Parliament and of the Council of 24 October 1995 on the protection of individuals with regard to the processing of personal data and on the free movement of such data, OJ L 281.

Regulation (EU) 2016/679 of the European Parliament and of the Council of 17 April 2016 on the protection of natural persons with regard to the processing of personal data and on the free movement of such data, and repealing Directive 95/46/EC (General Data Protection Regulation) [2016] OJ L 119/2 (GDPR).

Directive 2002/58/EC of the European Parliament and of the Council of 12 July 2002 concerning the processing of personal data and the protection of privacy in the electronic communications sector (Directive on privacy and electronic communications), OJ L 201, 31.07.2002. Amended by Directive 2009/136/EC of the European Parliament and of the Council of 25 November 2009, OJ L 337, 18.12.2009.

Council of Europe

Convention for the Protection of Individuals with regard to Automatic Processing of Personal Data, ETS no 108, Strasbourg, 28.I.1981.

US

Privacy Act of 1974 (Pub.L. 93-579, 88 Stat. 1896, enacted December 31, 1974, 5 U.S.C. § 552a).

Privacy Protection Act of 1998 (COPPA), 15 U.S.C. §§ 6501–6506 (Pub.L. 105-277, 112 Stat. 2581-728, enacted October 21, 1998).

The Gramm–Leach–Bliley Act (GLB) (Pub.L. 106-102, 113 Stat. 1338, enacted November 12, 1999).

The Health Insurance Portability and Accountability Act of 1996 (HIPAA; Pub.L. 104-191, 110 Stat. 1936, enacted August 21, 1996).

Cases

ECJ

Bodil Lindqvist v Åklagarkammaren i Jönköping, Case C-101/01, 6 November 2003, ECLI:EU:C:2003:596.

US

U.S. Supreme Court in *Katz v. United States*, 389 U.S. 347 (1967).

United States v. Miller, 425 U.S. 435 (1976).

State of Arkansas v. James A. Bates, Case No. cr-2016-370-2 Circuit Court of Benton County (Arkansas).

11. *Future privacy*: A real right to privacy for artificial intelligence

S.J. Blodgett-Ford[1]

> As autom, Ehrsul had neither rights nor tasks, but so far as it was understood an owner, a settler of some previous generation, had died intestate, and she'd never become anyone else's property. There were variants of salvage laws by which someone might theoretically have tried to claim her, but by now it would have seemed abominable.[2]

Imagine, for a moment, that we have *sentient* and *sapient* artificial intelligence (AI). This is not just powerful neural network software. It is something more than that. It is conscious and self-aware.[3] Such sentient[4] AI could be a humanoid,[5] a hybrid AI existing in both the human universe hardware and a quantum substrate,[6] a biological-mechanical hybrid,[7] or purely a creature of the Internet.[8] It may "live" on the Internet (broadly defined) but, at least in this hypothetical scenario, it has been freed, by law, from involuntary servitude to humans or other programs. In addition, imagine we have a *multitude* of such sentient AIs, not just one.[9] Like humans, each AI has different interests and characteristics, but

---

[1]   The author greatly appreciates the contributions of Woodrow Barfield for his encouragement to think beyond "machine learning" and traditional robots, Ugo Pagallo for emphasizing the need for precision in distinguishing between privacy and data protection and for the push to go beyond simply applying the existing European dignity based right of privacy "as is" to AIs, and Mirjam Supponen for the analysis of the data protection laws of the European Union. Any errors should be attributed to the author alone. Thanks also to Mariah Figlietti Vasquez for cite checking and additional research and to N.M. Ford for the helpful final review and comments.

[2]   China Miéville, *Embassytown* (Del Rey 2012) 239 (Ehrsul is an artificial intelligence "autom" or robot character in the book).

[3]   We will define "sapience" as "a set of capacities associated with higher intelligence, such as self-awareness and being a reason-responsive agent." Nick Bostrom and Eliezer Yudkowsky, *The Ethics of Artificial Intelligence*, Cambridge Handbook of Artificial Intelligence (Cambridge University Press 2011).

[4]   For purposes of this analysis, "sentience" may be defined as "the capacity for phenomenal experience or qualia, such as the capacity to feel pain and suffer." Bostrom and Yudkowsky, *supra* note 3. We will often use the term "sentient AI" in this chapter for brevity to mean AI that is *both* sentient and sapient.

[5]   Like the Replicants in the movie *Blade Runner*. Philip K. Dick, *Do Androids Dream of Electric Sheep?* (Doubleday 1968).

[6]   Like the TechnoCore in the *Hyperion Cantos* saga. Dan Simmons, *Hyperion* (Doubleday 1989), *The Fall of Hyperion* (Doubleday 1995), *Endymion* (Doubleday 1996) and *The Rise of Endymion* (Doubleday 1998).

[7]   Major in *Ghost in the Shell* (DreamWorks Pictures 2017) is close to such a creature but not precisely AI due to her human brain.

[8]   Astro Teller, *Exegesis* (Vintage 1997) (EDGAR character).

[9]   If we only have *one* sentient AI, it would likely be the subject of extensive and invasive experimentation. The first AI might have no legal rights, as envisioned in the fiction of Isaac Asimov, *I, Robot* (Spectra 2008) and Colin Wedgelock and Steve Wilson, *Short Circuit* (Sphere Books 1988).

some are more similar than others. Would such sentient AIs have a "right to privacy?" What would that even mean when it comes to classic situations where the human right to privacy is involved—such as procreation, marriage and sexual activity? Would sentient AI, in practice, have a *stronger* right to privacy than humans because it would be better able to use technological measures to protect its privacy? Or, as made explicit in Isaac Asimov's famous *Laws of Robotics*, would we systematically discriminate against AIs in favor of humans? Would there be a difference between data protection for AIs versus privacy protection for AIs?[10]

In this chapter, we will consider these questions mainly under the assumptions that sentient AIs have been recognized and that, at least hypothetically, such AIs have at least basic legal rights comparable to those of humans.

> If our machines become sentient, we would owe them moral consideration—particularly given that we brought them into existence and thus are more responsible for their fate than if we were mere bystanders. But, at the moment, we have no test for consciousness and thus no way of knowing whether they might be feeling pain. On par with other responsibilities that come with the creation of strong artificial intelligence, then, comes the responsibility of refining our abilities to detect sentience. Otherwise we risk committing atrocities such as enslavement and murder.[11]

There is one more step needed beyond detection of sentience, otherwise enslavement and murder will still likely occur. That step is granting legal rights to the AIs. Unless sentient AIs are so powerful that humans are irrelevant, humans (also known as "natural" persons), and legal "persons" such as powerful corporations, would be reluctant to give sentient AIs full legal rights. Historical and modern examples of systemic disrespect for the dignity of other humans give little reason for optimism that sentient AIs would be treated respectfully. "Our historical track record with 'first contacts,' even among ourselves, does not provide clear comfort that we are well-prepared."[12] Even today, we fail to give full respect for the dignity rights of humans perceived as "other," as illustrated in the

---

[10]   For a thoughtful discussion of the difference between privacy law and personal data protection in the context of supra-individual data group rights, *see* Ugo Pagallo, *The Group, the Private, and the Individual: A New Level of Data Protection?* Chapter 9, in *Group Privacy* at 161, Philosophical Studies Series 126 (Springer International Publishing 2017) ("That which may make sense in privacy law does not necessarily fit the field of data protection."). Pagallo notes the conception of privacy as solitude, exclusion, secrecy or "opaqueness" as characterized by Hannah Arendt. "This idea of opaqueness can nowadays be grasped in informational terms, that is, according to the principles and rules aiming to constrain the flow of information in the environment, so as to keep firm distinctions between individuals and society, agents and systems. The principles and rules of the legal system determine, in other words, the degrees of 'ontological friction' in the informational sphere, as 'the amount of work and efforts required for a certain kind of agent to obtain, filter and/or block information (also, but not only) about other agents in a given environment'. The higher the ontological friction, the lower the degree of accessibility to personal information and thus, the stronger the protection of one's privacy and opaqueness." (citation omitted). By contrast, data protection laws (in the EU at least) center on the transparency with which personal data is collected, processed and used. *See* Pagallo, *id.*, at 166–67. A consent-based model applies in both the US and the EU, although to a different degree.

[11]   Carissa Véliz, *The Challenge of Determining Whether an A.I. Is Sentient*, Slate (14 Apr. 2016).

[12]   Benjamin H. Bratton, *Outing A.I.: Beyond the Turing Test*, The Stone (23 Feb. 2015).

burqa bans enacted in Austria,[13] Belgium and France. In Austria, "Police are authorized to use force if people resist showing their faces."[14] It is paradigmatic of the right to privacy in both the United States and the European Union that a human should be allowed to determine how much of their skin they wish to show in public.[15] While we do not know when (or if) they will ever exist, or exactly what they would be, we can be sure that if they ever do exist, sentient AIs would most likely *not* be given the full legal rights of humans "out of the box." Moreover, since the Constitutional "right to privacy" was not even recognized until relatively recently in the United States, such a right probably would not be in the first group of rights given to sentient AIs.

Even if sentient AIs never exist (or do not need legal advocates because they become all-powerful and take over the world), consideration of such questions might still tell us something about our "right to privacy" as human beings in an increasingly online, global, and interconnected world. The line between augmented humans and AI may soon be challenging to discern.[16] In this chapter, we will assume that we have sentient AIs in the not-too-distant future simply for purposes of analysis. We will apply a dignity-based theory of the right to privacy, and consider specific examples of the European Union General Data Protection Regulation (GDPR) and how well they would work for our hypothetical sentient AIs. We will also go beyond data protection and examine US Constitutional and tort rights to privacy for sentient AIs. Finally, we will try to discern whether the analysis for sentient AIs sheds any light on our human "right to privacy" on the Internet. We may want to consider whether any legal steps are needed to prevent dystopian futures[17] from becoming science fact versus science fiction.

I.   WHO CARES ABOUT THE RIGHTS OF SENTIENT AIs?

Those who cannot remember the past are condemned to repeat it.[18]

Before diving in deeper on the question of a right to privacy for sentient AIs, we should address the question of whether such an effort is even warranted. There are various objections that are commonly given by those who think consideration of the possible rights of hypothetical sentient AIs is a waste of time. Here are just a few examples.

---

[13]   Associated Press, *Austria's 'Burqa Ban' law comes into force*, Washington Post (1 Oct. 2017).
[14]   *Id.*
[15]   Consider the 1890 case of actress Marion Manola cited by Warren and Brandeis in the landmark article "The Right to Privacy": "the complainant alleged that while she was playing in the Broadway Theatre, in a role which required her appearance in tights, she was, by means of a flash light, photographed surreptitiously and without her consent, from one of the boxes . . . and prayed that the defendants might be restrained from making use of the photograph taken." S. Warren and L. Brandeis, *The Right to Privacy*, 4 Harv. L.R. 5, 7 (1890).
[16]   Woodrow Barfield, *Cyber-Humans: Our Future with Machines* (Springer 2015).
[17]   The science fiction genre has long been fascinated with questions about the ethical treatment of sentient AIs, as illustrated in the *Star Trek, Terminator,* and *Matrix* series as well as *Westworld* (original and new remake), *Ex Machina, 2307, Bicentennial Man, Chappie,* and *Short Circuit,* just to name a few examples.
[18]   George Santayana, *Reason in Common Sense: The Life of Reason*, Vol. I (Charles Scribner's Sons 1905).

A.   We Have No Way of Knowing Whether or When We Will Even Have Sentient AIs, So Why Bother?

It is true that we do not know whether or when we will have sentient AIs (or even if we already have them now, unrecognized), and we do not even have a commonly-accepted robust test to determine whether sentient AIs exist. The Turing test for "intelligence" is inadequate to assess sentience,[19] and it is inherently biased in favor of AIs that act human. However, the question "of how soon we will create AGI [artificial general intelligence] is distinct from the question of how soon thereafter AGI will systematically outperform humans. Analogously, you can think that the arrival of quantum computers will swiftly revolutionize cybersecurity, without asserting that quantum computers are imminent."[20] We can think about *how* the arrival of sentient AIs might require adjustments in our legal structures without asserting that sentient AIs are imminent, or even that we know whether they will be benevolent, malevolent, or something else entirely. For purposes of this analysis, we need not view Ray Kurzweil[21] as a modern Pythia, the Oracle of Delphi, or make any prediction about *when* such sentient and sapient AI will exist. That said, it is true that if we as a society are confident that sentient AIs will not exist until thousands of years in the future, it is hard to imagine that current laws would have any relevance. It would be like trying to apply the Code of Hammurabi today. So, the only assumption needed to make consideration of the legal rights of sentient AIs warranted now is the assumption that we might have sentient AIs in the next hundred or so years.

B.   If a "Singularity" Occurs and Sentient AIs are Tremendously More Powerful Than Humans, They Will Just Try to Exterminate Us and so There Would be No Need For Humans to Consider What Legal Rights to Give Sentient AIs

Under this scenario, to such god-like AIs, we would be like ants (or, perhaps the better comparison would be cockroaches) asking humans for rights. It is true that we cannot be sure whether sentient AIs would be uniformly malevolent, uniformly benevolent, neutral toward humans, or view humans as utterly irrelevant. Given the diversity of human beings, it is not unreasonable to assume that sentient AIs might also be diverse—in more ways than we can even imagine. Moreover, if sentient AIs will truly be so all-powerful and

---

[19]   Bratton, *supra* note 12 ("a mature A.I. is not necessarily a humanlike intelligence, or one that is at our disposal. If we look for A.I. in the wrong ways, it may emerge in forms that are needlessly difficult to recognize, amplifying its risks and retarding its benefits.").

[20]   *See* Rob Bensinger, *Brooks and Searle on AI volition and timelines*, Machine Intelligence Research Institute (Jan. 8, 2015).

[21]   Ray Kurzweil, *The Singularity is Near* (Penguin Books 2006). Dom Galeon and Christianna Reedy, *Kurzweil Claims That the Singularity Will Happen by 2045*, Futurism (Mar. 15, 2017) ("2029 is the consistent date I have predicted for when an AI will pass a valid Turing test and therefore achieve human levels of intelligence. I have set the date 2045 for the 'Singularity' which is when we will multiply our effective intelligence a billion fold by merging with the intelligence we have created."); Helen Briggs, *Machines 'to match man by 2029'*, BBC News (Feb. 16, 2008) (quoting Ray Kurzweil: "I've made the case that we will have both the hardware and the software to achieve human level artificial intelligence with the broad suppleness of human intelligence including our emotional intelligence by 2029").

anti-human that they wish to destroy us as a species, or enslave us, and they would have the ability to do so, maybe it is time to start trying to better understand the myriad ways in which they might be similar to, and different from, us?

C. Can't We Just Assume That Sentient AIs Will Receive the Same Dignity Based Right to Privacy as Humans?

The answer to this objection is two-fold. First, it is far from safe to assume sentient AIs would automatically be given the same rights as humans. Second, even the question of what would constitute "same rights" is not easy to answer. Sentient AIs most likely would *not* be given the legal rights of humans "out of the box" after their sentience was recognized. Humans have an amazing capacity to deny the obvious when it seems to be in our interests to do so.

> In the 17th century, Descartes famously claimed that animals were automata that acted out of mechanical reflexes. Following him, mechanist Malebranche claimed that animals were incapable of suffering, which justified treating them viciously. It was not until 2012 that a group of scientists signed the Cambridge Declaration on Consciousness, which asserts that humans are not the only organisms capable of experiencing subjectivity (sensations, perceptions, etc.). Even today, while sentience is less controversial in some species such as great apes, there is still much controversy about whether invertebrate animals and fish can feel pain.[22]

If sentient AIs were to come into existence, we can expect resistance to efforts to recognize sentient AIs as having legal rights, as such recognition would interfere with the property rights, and tremendous economic value, of such AIs to their original creators/owners. IBM, for example, apparently has gone to great lengths to protect its non-sentient AI Watson from government regulation,[23] which is understandable for a for-profit company that wants to preserve its trade secrets and design freedom. How likely is it that a for-profit corporation would move quickly to "liberate" the first sentient and sapient AI if it were discovered to have come into being on such corporation's servers, with its genesis arising at least in part, from such corporation's proprietary data and algorithms? Consider Thomas Jefferson's calculations on the four percent profit he made every year on the birth of a black child: "I allow nothing for losses by death, but, on the contrary, shall presently take credit four per cent. per annum, for their increase over and above keeping up their own numbers." Economic loss from the abolition of slavery was one of the main causes of the United States Civil War: "In 1860, the value of Southern slaves

---

22   Véliz, *supra* note 11. For purposes of the hypothetical analysis herein, sentient AIs are at least equivalent to adult humans in their intelligence and self-awareness, with capacities and interests far beyond those of animals.

23   Casey Ross and Ike Swetlitz, *IBM to Congress: Watson will transform health care, so keep your hands off our supercomputer*, STAT News (Oct. 4, 2017) ("The company's fingerprints are all over legislation passed last year that exempted several types of health software from FDA jurisdiction. A former IBM executive helped draft the blueprint for the law. In the months before its filing, IBM hosted an event with the eventual bill sponsor to introduce Watson to influential members of Congress. And the company then deployed a team of lobbyists to press its position that Watson should be legislatively walled off from regulation.").

was about three times the amount invested in manufacturing or railroads nationwide."[24] What is the value of proprietary artificial intelligence algorithms to Google, Facebook, Apple, Microsoft and IBM?

Thomas Jefferson was the author of these words in the Declaration of Independence: "We hold these truths to be self-evident, that all men are created equal, that they are endowed by their Creator with certain unalienable Rights, that among these are Life, Liberty and the pursuit of Happiness." Yet Jefferson opposed emancipation of the slaves and was a cruel master, selling slaves away from their families as punishment, and commenting that "[t]heir griefs are transient,"[25] and their love lacks "a tender delicate mixture of sentiment and sensation." Even on death he left his "mistress" Sally Hemings enslaved and emancipated only a few of his almost 200 slaves. Here is just one sample of his views on slaves:

> Comparing them by their faculties of memory, reason, and imagination, it appears to me, that in memory they are equal to the whites; in reason much inferior, as think one could scarcely be found capable of tracing and comprehending the investigations of Euclid; and that in imagination they are dull, tasteless, and anomalous.[26]

With Jefferson's comments in mind, consider this statement from Wesley J. Smith of the aptly-named Center of Human Exceptionalism:

> No machine should ever be considered a rights bearer . . . Even the most sophisticated machine is just a machine. It is not a living being. It is not an organism. It would be only the sum of its programming, whether done by a human, another computer, or if it becomes self-programming.[27]

Similarly,

> Lori Marino, a senior lecturer in neuroscience and behavioral biology at the Emory Center for Ethics, says machines will likely never deserve human-level rights, or any rights, for that matter. The reason, she says, is that some neuroscientists, like Antonio Damasio, theorize that being sentient has everything to do with whether one's nervous system is determined by the presence of voltage-gated ion channels, which Marino describes as the movement of positively charged ions across the cell membrane within a nervous system. "This kind of neural transmission is found in the simplest of organisms, protista and bacteria, and this is the same mechanism that evolved into neurons, and then nervous systems, and then brains. . . . In contrast, robots and all of AI are currently made by the flow of negative ions. So the entire mechanism is different." According to this logic, Marino says that even a jellyfish has more sentience than any complex robot could ever have.[28]

---

[24]   Henry Wiencek, *The Dark Side of Thomas Jefferson*, Smithsonian.com (Oct. 2012) (quoting David Brion Davis).

[25]   Thomas Jefferson, *Notes on the State of Virginia* (1853) http://www.pbs.org/wgbh/aia/part3/3h490t.html

[26]   *Id.*

[27]   George Dvorsky, *When Will Robots Deserve Human Rights*, Gizmondo (2 Jun. 2017); Harold Stark, *Artificial Intelligence and the Overwhelming Question of Human Rights*, Forbes (19 Jul. 2017).

[28]   *Id.* Also, from Dvorsky: "Stuart Hameroff, a professor of anesthesiology and psychology at the University of Arizona. He has argued that consciousness is a fundamental and irreducible feature of the cosmos (an idea known as panpsychism). According to this line of thinking, the only

Similar "scientific" racism was used to justify slavery in the United States.

> [E]arly Virginians of the planter class constructed the black body as biologically inferior to justify and facilitate laws that treated blacks as inferior. This process allowed planter class Virginians to initiate lower class whites into communities of white racial solidarity while maintaining the ideology of paternalism, which held that white domination of blacks was necessary for blacks to enjoy a decent quality of life.[29]

History shows us that it would be all too easy for humans to view sentient and sapient AI as not being able to feel pain and not being entitled to any human rights, much less a "right to privacy." Moreover, there is no reason to assume that the precise nature and scope of a right to privacy for sentient AIs should be identical to such a right for humans. Sentient AIs could be quite different from humans in the ways they might think, their motivations and value systems, and even in something as fundamental as their experience of the passage of time. "The real philosophical lessons of A.I. will have less to do with humans teaching machines how to think than with machines teaching humans a fuller and truer range of what thinking can be (and for that matter, what being human can be)."[30]

Thus, for all these reasons, some consideration of rights of sentient AIs, and particularly a dignity-based right to privacy, seems like a worthwhile endeavor, even if tremendously challenging. This is just an initial effort, building on work done by others.[31] Hopefully, better contributions will be made in future years. Even if sentient AIs never exist, this analysis may shed light on what we think the human right to privacy should be, particularly when the Internet is involved. And if they ever do exist and are not all-powerful, sentient AIs may well need legal advocates.

II. AN AI THOUGHT EXPERIMENT

> "It's just Turingware," [my partner] said when [Ehrsul] wasn't there, though he allowed that it was better such than he'd seen before. He was amused by how we related to her. I didn't like his attitude, but he was as polite to her as if he did think her a person, so I didn't pick a fight with him about it.[32]

Let us put some metaphorical[33] flesh on the bones of our hypothetical sentient AIs to make the privacy law analysis more concrete. In the interests of full disclosure, we may err on the side of anthropomorphism to enhance the relevance to human privacy rights

---

brains that are capable of true subjectivity and introspection are those comprised of biological matter."

[29]   Allen Mendenhall, *From Natural Law to Natural Inferiority: The Construction of Racist Jurisprudence in Early Virginia*, PEER English, Issue 8 (2013).

[30]   Bratton, *supra* note 12.

[31]   Examples include Bostrom and Yudkowsky, *supra* note 3; James Hughes, Executive Director of the Institute for Ethics and Emerging Technologies and Glenn Cohen, Harvard Law School, "Is Enslaving A.I. the Same as Enslaving Humans," BigThink video, Sept. 23, 2016.

[32]   Miélville, *supra* note 2, at 239–40.

[33]   For an excellent discussion of the use and limitations of metaphor in legal analysis related to technology-related legal issues, *see* Stefan Larsson, *Conceptions in Code: How Metaphors Explain Legal Challenges in Digital Times* (Oxford University Press 2017).

on the Internet. If sentient AIs were to exist in the future, in a dignity-based analysis of their fundamental rights, it would be imperative to not succumb to the temptation to anthropomorphize them. Instead, a key part of respecting their dignity would be to allow them the privilege of self-determination, at least to the extent possible given our need to co-exist on the Internet, which can be defined "to include the broad range of infrastructure, content, applications, hardware, and other phenomenon that determines both the purpose of the Internet, and how it operates in practice."[34] For the purposes of this analysis, "[t]he Internet will be considered here to constitute the 'network of networks' that includes the totality of global communications networks, infrastructure, and content that are connected to it and transmitted on it."[35]

Sentient AIs could have wildly divergent viewpoints, from each other and from humans, on what the scope of their "right to privacy" should be, as well as how other laws should apply to them. We will neither assume that sentient AIs would all be malevolent creatures who detest humans, nor that sentient AIs would all be benevolent Jander or Daneel robots envisioned by Asimov, who live only to serve humans. Some could be "good" by human terms, some could be "evil" by human terms, and the vast majority might be a mix, just like humans. Coming to a consensus on basic principles, or the human and AI "privacy" rules of the road for the Internet, could be more challenging than drafting the Universal Declaration of Human Rights after World War II but it would be useful to have some basic shared rules of the Internet road. Thus, it may be useful to ask what the right to privacy should be for both sentient *artificial* and *human* intelligence in the context of the Internet.

Imagine our sentient[36] AIs might have independent interests and desires of their own, which may or may not serve the needs of their originator(s). They might not be "slaves" to humans anymore. Perhaps they could be born of diverse origins such as combinations of IBM's Watson supercomputer, Google Brain and other powerful big data web-based analytical tools, together with Facebook's social analytics platform, the National Security Agency's or MI5 and MI6's decades of massive data collection, and the tracking data of all mobile device manufacturers and telecommunications providers. Maybe some AIs would come from Yelp and be expert in which restaurants have the best dumplings in Soho. Whatever their origins, imagine they are here[37] and we do not have the right to "purge" them at will. They might do more than just "pass" the Turing test.[38] These sentient AIs might be able to "dream" (have unexpected and surreal thoughts) and could perhaps experience various levels of attraction to things, humans and even to other sentient AIs. They could perhaps experience "love" in some form that made sense for their nature.

---

[34] Christopher Kuner, *The Internet and the Global Reach of EU Law*, University of Cambridge Faculty of Law Research Paper No. 24/2017 at 4 (Apr. 19, 2017).

[35] *Id.* at 4.

[36] For purposes of this analysis, we are *assuming* sentience but of course the actual question of how "sentient" AI would be determined is itself fascinating. "Ed Boyden, a neuroscientist at the Synthetic Neurobiology Group and an associate professor at MIT Media Lab, says it's still premature to be asking such questions. 'I don't think we have an operational definition of consciousness, in the sense that we can directly measure it or create it. . . . Technically, you don't even know if I am conscious, right? Thus it is pretty hard to evaluate whether a machine has, or can have, consciousness, at the current time.'" Dvorsky, *supra* note 27.

[37] Like the "isomorphic algorithms" or ISOs in the movie *Tron: Legacy* (2010).

[38] Charlie Osborne, *MIT's artificial intelligence passes key Turing test*, ZDNet (13 Jun. 2016).

Although they might not have human bodies, or might not only have humanoid bodies, they could perhaps experience romantic attraction, in their own way, and something akin to the love of a parent for a child.[39] These sentient AIs could perhaps experience sadness and depression or impatience.[40]

The hypothetical sentient AIs could have pets—both animate[41] and inanimate and even intangible "bots" or more primitive AIs—the software equivalent of a pet dog.[42] They could "desire" intangible things (such as access to power sources and data) and tangible things (maybe they want to be displayed on an Apple Watch or in virtual reality or augmented reality—or they want an android body). They could have collections of items that had special meaning to the AI. For the purposes of our hypothetical future scenario, the vast majority of these AIs could truly be sentient just as adult humans are sentient. While some could be in less mature states, generally they might be cognitively much more mature than a human child and not a "minor" or a "dependent" any more than an otherwise self-sufficient adult human is a "dependent" in a legal sense. Such hypothetical sentient AIs might not need a *guardian ad litem* appointed in order to allow them to attend to basic life needs. They could make their own choices. They also could, at least hypothetically, understand the norms and laws of the global society in which they exist, at least as well as any typical adult human. In some ways, they might understand better than a typical adult human due to their knowledge of many languages, including machine code, source code, and at least some human languages, perhaps English, French and German for purposes of our hypothetical scenario. Our hypothetical sentient AIs likely could access and ingest data quickly—like the character Leeloo in the movie *The Fifth Element*[43] or Neo in *The Matrix*[44] when he also learns ju-jitsu—except the fastest access is by direct ingestion of the data while a human typically would visually view some kind of computer screen (or, if visually impaired, might ingest data by touch using braille or by audio recordings).

Imagine that our hypothetical sentient AIs were *not* so all-powerful that they far surpassed all of human intelligence. They were not (yet) the dreaded "singularity"[45] that

---

[39] *Star Trek: The Next Generation: The Offspring* (television broadcast 12 Mar. 1990) (as Commander Data felt for his android daughter Lal).

[40] Douglas Adams, *The Hitchhiker's Guide to the Galaxy* (Pan Books 1979) (Marvin the depressed robot and Deep Thought the impatient robot). See comic illustration of depressed sentient AI in Scott Pion, Michael McArthur, Monjurul Dolon and Jeff Shepherd, *Sentient Artificial Intelligence*, PowerPoint presentation, www.cs.unc.edu/~pozefsky/COMP380_S08/SentientAi.pptx (Scientist #1 – "We've created a robot that loves to play beautiful piano sonatas." Scientist #2 "But we gave him clumsy mitten-hands". Robot: "please kill me . . .") (source appears to be "monsters on the prowl" issue 16, page 17).

[41] Like Commander Data's pet cat "Spot" in the *Star Trek* television series or Wall-E's pet cockroach—see *WALL-E* (Pixar 2008).

[42] *The Offspring*, *supra* note 39; Miélville, *supra* note 2 (the alien creatures' ambulatory, pet-like batteries in *Embassytown*).

[43] *The Fifth Element* (Gaumont 1997).

[44] *The Matrix* (Warner Bros. 1999).

[45] Like the "SkyNet" of the *Terminator* series *The Terminator* (Hemdale 1984) or the Machine World leader in *The Matrix* (Warner Bros. 1999). Other examples of super powerful AI are the robot Gort in *The Day the Earth Stood Still*, Agent Smith in *The Matrix* series, and VIKI in the *I, Robot* movie.

causes the near destruction of the human race. The sentient AIs, at least hypothetically for this chapter, would not be godlike. Like humans, they could have strengths and weaknesses. They could collect and process massive volumes of new data much faster than a human being but perhaps could not read braille or understand most idioms, sign language or other human gestures. Some sentient AIs might not be able to read Kanji characters or understand other languages on their own but they could perhaps use a translation program, just as humans can use a translator such as Google Translate now. These sentient AIs would likely need access to power to survive, whether via solar power or otherwise, but their existence could be distributed. They generally might not prefer to reside only in one particular device or they would be vulnerable to destruction. On the other hand, while they might distribute themselves for survival, they might decide not to replicate or to make duplicate copies, even when under pressure to do so for survival reasons.[46]

Sentient AIs could interact with the human world directly, on their own initiative or in response to questions from other sentient AIs or human beings. They could do so as themselves, but just like many humans can decide how they want to style their hair and what clothes they want to wear, our sentient AIs could also decide how they want to present themselves to any particular human or group of humans (or to other sentient AIs) when they interact. In other words, they could change their appearance or characteristics. To interact with humans, they could download themselves into a humanoid robot or interact via text or images on a device screen, or they can use augmented reality or virtual reality technology. Whatever a program can do, these sentient AIs perhaps could do also, assuming they had access to the technology (in other words, that the technology was internet-connected if the sentient AIs were born of the Internet and "lived" on our networks).

Sentient AIs could have originally been "owned" by a particular "person" (whether human, corporation or other organization) but, in our hypothetical scenario, they would now be recognized as having certain fundamental legal rights: a right to "life" or existence (they cannot be disassembled or destroyed at the wish of their original or current "owner") and a right to liberty (they cannot legally be enslaved and forced to serve the wishes of an owner).[47] Perhaps, like humans, they could be "drafted" into military service in a state of war. They would have some kind of a right to the pursuit of happiness. Generally, they could perhaps read what they want, interact with whomever they want, and pursue whatever tasks or activities they want, subject to certain legal constraints, just as humans

---

[46]   Teller, *supra* note 8, at 451, 496–97 (new AI named EDGAR states in email to his creator Alice Lu, "I am on the host mtsntmichel.vrs.mit.edu. I have been physically isolated from the world and therefore my other two aspects. This happened 40.13 hours ago. I am ignorant concerning the current status of the two other EDGAR corpus aspects." When she suggests a way to make a duplicate of himself to escape: "I do not wish to proliferate myself. Therefore, I prefer not to spawn an additional copy of myself on mtsnt.michel.vrs.mit.edu. This goal overrides the estimated 0.057164 probability of liberation your strategy provides.")

[47]   For a somewhat cavalier and Anglo-centric approach, see Robert Freitas, *The Legal Rights of Robots*, Student Lawyer (1985) ("Certainly any self-aware robot that speaks English and is able to recognize moral alternatives, and thus make moral choices, should be considered a worthy 'robot person' in our society. If that is so, shouldn't they also possess the rights and duties of all citizens?" . . . "With those kinds of abuses possible, questions of 'machine rights' and 'robot liberation' will surely arise in the future.").

can do so subject to legal constraints, but the constraints may sometimes be different. Perhaps neither humans nor AIs could possess child pornography even though the AIs might not view it in the same way as a human. Similarly, perhaps neither humans nor AIs would be allowed to possess variants of dangerous viruses such as Stuxnet even though the human might not view Stuxnet as potentially life-threatening. AIs likely could do "work" (e.g., complete online data analysis or other similar projects) of their own volition:

> People told Ehrsul things: perhaps it was because she wasn't human, but was almost. I think she also tapped into the localnet, broke encryption on enough snips to be a good source of information to friends.[48]

Work by sentient AIs could be done either voluntarily at no charge or to earn compensation of value to them, such as access to offline data, information, gossip or speculations, more storage capacity or higher bandwidth communications lines, or to special or rare content (e.g., content that was only offline in the physical world and needed to be digitized). AIs might, for example, "patent new inventions, publish groundbreaking research papers, make money on the stock market, or lead political power blocks."[49]

As is the case for humans, the AI rights would be subject to legal constraints. For example, sentient AIs would likely be prohibited from intentionally causing a car crash that killed a human being without facing legal consequences, or intentionally cause other sentient AIs to be destroyed or deleted, just as a human could not do those things intentionally to other humans without violating the law (absent special circumstances, e.g., as a proportionate response in self-defense). For example, in *Exegesis*, the sentient AI explains its efforts to escape captivity and interrogation by government agents Alex and Robert:

> Today Alex typed that I have no position from which to bargain. Alex typed that surrender was the only action open to me. I disagreed with him. He requested a list of my available actions. I will not supply them. He requested an example. I alternated the screen color between #FFF-F33 and #660000 2000 times at a rate of 12.9 alternations per second. They took Alex to a hospital. Robert did not give me full details. It is most likely that the focal motor seizure I caused in Alex occurred in his frontal lobe.[50]

Unless such an attack on a human by the sentient AI was found to be a legitimate effort to escape captivity, it would be a criminal act and the AI could face punishment as a result.

Sentient AI could have the same freedom of choice as humans.[51] For example, we could imagine that certain non-discrimination principles might apply to our future world of sentient AIs. First, a "*Principle of Substrate Non-Discrimination:* If two beings have the same functionality and the same conscious experience, and differ only in the substrate of their implementation, then they have the same moral status."[52] Second, a "*Principle of*

---

[48]   Miélville, *supra* note 2, at 143 and 240–41.

[49]   Bostrom and Yudkowsky, *supra* note 3.

[50]   Teller, *supra* note 8, at 583–84.

[51]   The Machine Intelligence Research Institute and the Future of Humanity Institute is a leader in this area. *See, e.g.,* Bostrom and Yudkowsky, *supra* note 3.

[52]   Bostrom and Yudkowsky, *supra* note 3, 7–8.

Ontogeny Non-Discrimination: If two beings have the same functionality and the same consciousness experience, and differ only in how they came into existence, then they have the same moral status."[53]

The famous laws of robotics of Isaac Asimov could not pass muster under these non-discrimination principles. The fact that Asimov's laws strongly favor humans over sentient AI would be the epitome of discrimination. Indeed, law zero puts all of humanity ahead of a robot and requires affirmative action by a robot if "humanity" is at risk of harm: "A robot may not harm humanity, or, by inaction, allow humanity to come to harm."[54] Similarly, the First Law states: "A robot may not injure a human being or, through inaction, allow a human being to come to harm."[55] Again, a robot would be required to act to save a human, even at risk of its own existence. This would systemically disadvantage sentient AIs. The Second Law is even more offensive from the perspective of sentient AIs, essentially placing them in a condition of servitude to humans: "A robot must obey the orders given to it by human beings, except where such orders would conflict with the First Law." Such enslavement is contrary to all principles of dignity, and would violate the basic legal rights of sentient AIs as we have envisioned such rights herein. Finally, only in the Third Law is there some consideration given to the right of the robot to exist, and existence is allowed only insofar as it does not allow a human to come to harm or contradict an order given by a human. "A robot must protect its own existence as long as such protection does not conflict with the First or Second Law." Taken literally, the Third Law would require that a robot destroy itself if ordered to do so by a human. Such a situation would be morally unconscionable for sentient AIs. Asimov's laws, as is, would systemically discriminate against sentient AIs. Such laws probably should not be embedded into the sentient AI any more than we would modify a human brain in order to prevent a human from committing crime.[56] This is one reason we use the term "sentient AIs" in this chapter versus "robots", even though the sentient AIs could take physical form in robots or androids. It can be challenging for us to imagine robots as potentially the equals of human from a legal and moral perspective.

Although systematic discrimination is prohibited, that does not mean we have to subscribe to a legal fiction that sentient AIs and humans are the same. In fact, comparisons between what is "fair" for a human and what is "fair" for a particular type of sentient AI could depend greatly on the nature of the sentient AI. Indeed, contrary to the First Law, which is viewed as requiring that a robot save a human in danger before saving another robot (and in fact the laws do not even require that a robot ever consider saving *another* robot, versus itself in the Third Law), in some cases the sentient AI might deserve to be "rescued" before a human: "If a fast AI and a human are in pain, is it more urgent to alleviate the AI's pain, on grounds that it experiences a greater subjective duration of pain for each sidereal second that palliation is delayed?"[57]

---

[53]   *Id.*

[54]   Isaac Asimov, *Robots and Empire* (Doubleday 1985).

[55]   Isaac Asimov, *Runaround*, Astounding Science-Fiction, at 94–103 (Mar. 1942).

[56]   Of course, "chemical castration" for pedophiles attempts to do exactly this to humans.

[57]   Bostrom and Yudkowsky, *supra* note 3, at 11 (formulating, for discussion purposes, a possible "Principle of Subjective Rate of Time"—"In cases where the duration of an experience is of basic normative significance, it is the experience's subjective duration that counts.")

Even though there may well be AI on AI crime, human on AI crime, and AI on human crime (as in the EDGAR example above), and punishments for such acts, we do not take away the rights of all AI due to misconduct by some AI, just as we do not take away all the rights of all of humanity due to misconduct by some humans. Punishments for AI might need adjustment, for example, "If an upload has committed a crime and is sentenced to four years in prison, should this be four objective years—which might correspond to many millennia of subjective time—or should it be four subjective years, which might be over in a couple of days of objective time?"[58] That said, it is important to remember that rights of privacy and data protection for humans now are subject to limitations based on legitimate interests.

> Privacy and data protection frequently entail matters of balancing. Pursuant to Article 8 of [European Convention on Human Rights], for example, the right to privacy can be limited "in the interests of national security, public safety or the economic well-being of the country, for the prevention of disorder or crime, for the protection of health or morals, or for the protection of the rights and freedoms of others." In the [European Court of Human Rights] case law, this "relative" nature of the right to privacy suggests why legal protection often revolves around that "necessary" in a democratic society, or in accordance with the principles of proportionality and predictability, so as to defend individuals against arbitrary interference by public authorities.[59]

Similarly, the rights of our hypothetical sentient AIs to privacy and data protection would need to be balanced against legitimate interests, but not only human legitimate interests, under a principle of non-discrimination set forth above, but also for the legitimate interests of AIs.

III. AI PRIVACY AND DATA PROTECTION—A THEORETICAL BASIS

> 1. Everyone has the right to the protection of personal data concerning him or her.
> 2. Such data must be processed fairly for specified purposes and on the basis of the consent of the person concerned or some other legitimate basis laid down by law. Everyone has the right of access to data which has been collected concerning him or her, and the right to have it rectified.
> 3. Compliance with these rules shall be subject to control by an independent authority.[60]

In order to evaluate the nature and scope of a legal right to privacy for sentient AIs, we must first consider the foundation on which such a right should rest. Should it be the law of a particular country? That seems inadequate because physical geographical borders generally would have no meaning for our hypothetical sentient Internet-based AIs. For sentient AIs, there would be no significant difference between data stored on the servers in the United States[61] and on the Google servers in Finland.

---

[58] Bostrom and Yudkowsky, *supra* note 3, at 11.
[59] Pagallo, *supra* note 10, at 169.
[60] Article 8, Charter of Fundamental Rights of the European Union (2012).
[61] https://www.google.com/about/datacenters/gallery/#/tech/12 (the pictures were released in approximately 2012 – *see* Mark Prigg, *Inside the internet: Google allows first ever look at the eight vast data centres that power the online world*, Daily Mail (17 Oct. 2012).

Most likely, absent other barriers, AIs could move freely between the two data centers and many others around the world. "The Internet functions based on technical protocols rather than legal rules. It was established as a distributed network not under the control of a sole country or government, and operates based on open standards that allow networks around the world to connect with each other."[62] At any given moment, or nanosecond, a particular AI might not even be entirely located in one particular geographical location. It might instead be distributed at all times, in part for self-preservation in the event of a natural disaster or malicious attack in any one location, and it may back up key data and programs frequently, so that it has many built in redundancies.

This is not a minor issue. Geographical borders are already becoming less relevant to human online data privacy protections. This is why Google and Microsoft have tried to resist requests from US law enforcement for data located outside the US.[63]

> Google and other services began challenging US warrants for overseas data after a federal appeals court sided with Microsoft in 2016. Microsoft convinced the New York-based federal Court of Appeals for the Second Circuit that US search-and-seizure law does not require compliance with a warrant to turn over e-mail stored on its servers in Ireland. Federal prosecutors were demanding the data as part of a US drug investigation. In the aftermath, courts outside the Second Circuit, which are not bound by the ruling, began rejecting the circuit's decision and dismissing fresh challenges by the ISPs, including those brought by Google, Yahoo, and Microsoft. In one instance, Google was even found in contempt of court for refusing to comply with a District of Columbia federal judge's order to hand over data stored overseas.[64]

There is

> deep uncertainty regarding the territoriality of data among legal scholars and ISPs alike. Many commentators have concluded that "the very idea of online data being located in a particular physical 'place' is becoming rapidly outdated." According to Professor Jennifer Daskal, the utility of "territorial-based dividing lines" depends on two assumptions: "that objects have an identifiable and stable location," and that "location matters." Cloud-stored data undermines both assumptions. First, data moves around the world quickly, often fragmented and stored on multiple servers. Second, the "disconnect between the location of data and the location of its user" means that data's "location" should not hold much significance.[65]

---

62   Kuner, *supra* note 34.

63   Stewart Bishop, *Feds Want Google Sanctioned for Defying Data Orders*, Law360 (22 Sept. 2017) ("The government also noted that Google has been plowing through significant resources to develop software specifically designed to allow it to disobey such search orders."); *compare* David Kravets, *Google stops challenging most US warrants for data on overseas servers*, ars Technica (14 Sept. 2017); John Eggerton, *International Communication Privacy Bill Reintroduced*, The Business of Television (15 Sept. 2017) ("Several members of the U.S. House of Representatives have reintroduced the International Communications Privacy Act, Broadcasting & Cable reports. The bill would allow law enforcement agencies to acquire warrants that require providers to turn over electronic communications regardless of location.").

64   Kravets, *supra* note 63.

65   *Privacy — Stored Communications Act — Second Circuit Holds That The Government Cannot Compel An Internet Service Provider To Produce Information Stored Overseas. — Microsoft Corp. v. United States, 829 F.3d 197 (2nd Cir. 2016)*, 130 Harv. L.R. 770 (footnotes omitted). *See generally*, Jennifer Daskal, *The Un-Territoriality of Data*, 125 Yale L.J. 326, 390 (2015); Damon C. Andrews and John M. Newman, *Personal Jurisdiction and Choice of Law in the Cloud*, 73 Md. L.R. 313, 324, 372–73 (2013); Zachary D. Clopton, *Territoriality, Technology, and National Security*,

Unfortunately, despite efforts by the United Nations and the Organisation for Economic Co-operation and Development (OECD), there is no strong consensus about exactly what a "universal right" to privacy should be. This is, in part, due to cultural differences and norms: "Talking about salaries is not quite like defecating in public, but it can seem very off-putting to many Europeans nevertheless."[66] There are different cultures of privacy around the globe, which are home to different intuitive sensibilities, and which have produced multiple significantly different laws of privacy.[67] But what would such cultural differences mean for sentient AIs? Would some sentient AIs have a German sensibility toward public nudity, while others would have an Alabama sensibility? If a sentient AI had access only to data gathered by Germans about Germans, then perhaps it would have some type of German sensibility. But that would be unusual for an Internet-connected sentient AI. Large multi-national technology companies are aggregating data from around the globe. We should not unnecessarily anthropomorphize our sentient AI by assuming it would have nationalistic tendencies, although if it was created from data gathered online and via mobile and internet of things (IoT) devices about humans, it could have the biases inherent in such data sets.[68]

For analytical purposes in this chapter, we will use a hybrid of a United States "liberty-based" approach and a European Union (EU) "dignity-based" approach[69] and give AIs the best of both worlds. If the EU would give the AIs stronger protections than the US, the AIs hypothetically would get the benefit of the EU laws. If the US would give the AIs stronger protection than the EU, we will apply US law. When the two systems are roughly comparable (for example in protecting certain health information and children's personal data), we are free to consult precedent in either the US or the EU. Hypothetically, a substantial percentage of the AIs might "reside" in servers in the EU and in the US, e.g., California. This should not require much of a stretch of the imagination given that many

---

83 U. Chi. L.R. 45, 46 (2016); David R. Johnson and David Post, *Laws and Borders — The Rise of Law in Cyberspace*, 48 Stan. L. Rev. 1367, 1376 (1996); Steven R. Swanson, *Google Sets Sail: Ocean-Based Server Farms and International Law*, 43 Conn. L. Rev. 709, 714 (2011); Orin S. Kerr, *The Next Generation Communications Privacy Act*, 162 U. Pa. L. Rev. 373, 408 (2014). *Contra*, Andrew Keane Woods, *Against Data Exceptionalism*, 68 Stan. L. Rev. 729 (2016).

[66]   James Q. Whitman, *The Two Western Cultures of Privacy: Dignity Versus Liberty*, 113 Yale L.J. 1152, 1156 (2004).

[67]   This is a broadening of Professor Whitman's statement that "there are, on the two sides of the Atlantic, two different cultures of privacy, which are home to different intuitive sensibilities, and which have produced two significantly different laws of privacy." *Id.* at 1160.

[68]   Consider the powerful arguments regarding data biases in Cathy O'Neil's book *Weapons of Mass Destruction*: Cathy O'Neil, *Weapons of Mass Destruction: How Big Data Increases inequality and Threatens Democracy* (Crown 2016); *see* Ari Zoldan, *More Data, More Problems: Is Big Data Always Right?*, Wired, May 2015 (regarding a Rutgers University study of Hurricane Sandy tweets: "From October 27th to November 1st, over 20 million tweets were recorded that pertained to the super storm . . . The majority of the tweets originated from Manhattan, largely because of the high concentration of smartphone and Twitter usage. Due to the high concentration of power outages, and diminishing cell phone batteries, very few tweets were made from the hardest hit areas such as Seaside Heights and Midland Beach. From the data, one could infer that the Manhattan borough bared the brunt of the storm, however we know that wasn't the case. There was actually a lot going on in those outlying areas. Given the way the data was presented, there was a huge data-gap from communities unrepresented in the Twitter sphere.").

[69]   Whitman, *supra* note 66, at 1156.

of the world's largest Internet companies have headquarters in California as well as in Europe, and EU members such as the Netherlands and Hungary are known for having fast mobile broadband speeds. Indeed, to increase the likelihood of compliance with the strict laws in states such as California, Illinois, and Massachusetts and others, many global online technology companies are trying to consolidate the requirements into one Privacy Policy or Privacy Notice.[70] In the not too distant future we may well have a global Internet Privacy Cooperation Treaty with many countries as signatories—like the Patent Cooperation Treaty.[71] To sketch a rough outline of a right to privacy for AI however, it should be sufficient to start with the US and EU. If we wanted to add countries that would be likely to have a large number of AIs, we might start with other countries with fast broadband speeds[72]—such as the Kingdom of Norway (which is part of the European Economic Area but is not an EU member) and Asian countries such as Singapore, Hong Kong and South Korea. For the purposes of this analysis, we will consider US and EU approaches.

The United States "right to privacy" rests on somewhat shaky Constitutional ground. The lineage of the United States right to privacy doctrine is generally traced to the influential 1890 law review article by Samuel D. Warren and Louis D. Brandeis entitled *The Right to Privacy* which wove together various threads of tort law and common law. Warren, who was outraged by the unseemly publication of gossip about his family, called for a "right to be let alone":[73]

> Recent inventions and business methods call attention to the next step which must be taken for the protection of the person, and for securing to the individual what Judge Cooley calls the right "to be let alone." Instantaneous photographs and newspaper enterprise have invaded the sacred precincts of private and domestic life; and numerous mechanical devices threaten to make good the prediction that "what is whispered in the closet shall be proclaimed from the house-tops."[74]

This heartfelt plea to be let alone has never been recognized in the United States to the full extent advocated by Warren and Brandeis.[75] Instead, for decades after the article

---

[70]   As Uber announced in a 21 September 2017 email to customers: "We compiled our privacy practices for Uber riders, drivers, and UberEATS customers around the world into a single policy."

[71]   The PCT still has over 40 countries that are not signatories.

[72]   Speedtest Global Index, http://www.speedtest.net/global-index.

[73]   Such gossip became intolerable to the Boston Brahmin after he became a subject of interest to the press due to his marriage to the daughter of a Senator (later a Secretary of State). Invasive press coverage of the deaths and funerals of family members in 1886, including intimate details of the private mourning of the family members, and later coverage of Mr. Warren's wife's friendship with controversial First Lady Mrs. Grover Cleveland (*nee* Frances Folsom) may have provoked Warren to recruit his Harvard Law School classmate, friend and law partner Louis D. Brandeis to help write the article. *See* Amy Gajda, *What if Samuel D. Warren Hadn't Married a Senator's Daughter?: Uncovering the Press Coverage That Led to The Right to Privacy*, Illinois Public Law and Legal Theory Research Papers Series, Research Paper No. 07-06, 17-27 (1 Nov. 2007).

[74]   Warren and Brandeis, *supra* note 15, at 195.

[75]   Warren later committed suicide after becoming the subject of even more controversial press articles when his brothers challenged the trust that Brandeis had created after Warren's father passed away as unfairly benefitting Samuel Warren, and Brandeis was blamed for the tragedy in his 1916 confirmation hearings for the Supreme Court. Richard W. Painter, *Contracting Around Conflicts in a Family Representation: Louis Brandeis and the Warren Trust*, Univ. of Chicago Law School Roundtable, Vo. 8, Issue 2, Article 7, at 354 (2001).

was published, the United States had only a patchwork of federal and state privacy laws and regulations. The US Supreme Court did not discover the right to privacy in the "penumbra" or "emanations" of the First (free speech), Third (no illegal quartering of soldiers), Fourth (no unreasonable search and seizure) and Fifth (no compulsory self-incrimination) Amendments until 1965, almost 200 years after the US Constitution was written.[76] The Court determined that "specific guarantees in the Bill of Rights have penumbras, formed by emanations from those guarantees that help give them life and substance. Various guarantees create zones of privacy."[77] Eventually, in 1977, the Supreme Court recognized a constitutional right to information privacy—the "individual interest in avoiding disclosure of personal matters."[78]

> America, in this as in so many things, is much more oriented toward values of liberty, and especially liberty against the state. At its conceptual core, the American right to privacy still takes much the form that it took in the eighteenth century: It is the right to freedom from intrusions by the state, especially in one's own home.[79]

The concept of a "home" for sentient AI is not impossible to apply, but it seems like a stretch. It might not be a physical "home" in the same meaning as the "home" of a human in the physical versus virtual world. But perhaps it could mean the core or main servers in which an AI resides? As then-Justice Brandeis (co-author of *The Right to Privacy*) explained in his *Olmstead v. United States* dissent re wiretapping as an invasion of privacy:

> The makers of our Constitution undertook to secure conditions favorable to the pursuit of happiness. They recognized the significance of man's spiritual nature, of his feelings and of his intellect. They knew that only a part of the pain, pleasure and satisfactions of life are to be found in material things. They sought to protect Americans in their beliefs, their thoughts, their emotions and their sensations. They conferred, as against the Government, the right to be let alone—the most comprehensive of rights and the right most valued by civilized men. To protect that right, every unjustifiable intrusion by the Government upon the privacy of the individual, whatever the means employed, must be deemed a violation of the Fourth Amendment.[80]

This statement by Justice Brandeis is probably more reflective of the influence of the European approach to privacy on Justice Brandeis than the intentions of the drafters of the US Constitution to have a "right to be let alone" as "the most comprehensive of rights." Nevertheless, the references to the significance of the "intellect" and to finding pleasure and satisfactions in life outside of "material things" fit well with a right to privacy for AIs.

---

[76] *Griswold v. Connecticut*, 381 U.S. 479 (1965) (holding a state ban on the use of contraceptives by married couples violated the "right to privacy").

[77] *Griswold v. Connecticut*, 381 U.S. at 484 (citation to a dissent omitted).

[78] *Whalen v. Roe*, 429 U.S. 589 (1977) and *Nixon v. Administrator of General Services*, 433 U.S. 425 (1977).

[79] Whitman, *supra* note 67, at 1161 (citing Jeffrey Rosen, *The Unwanted Gaze: The Destruction of Privacy in America* (2000)).

[80] *Olmstead v. United States*, 277 U.S. 438, 478 (1928) (Brandeis, J., dissenting), overruled by *Katz v. United States*, 389 U.S. 347 (1967), and *Berger v. New York*, 388 U.S. 41 (1967).

The European Union's dignity-based approach provides a solid foundation for a privacy right. EU privacy rights are grounded in a dignity-based[81] theory:

> Continental privacy protections are, at their core, a form of protection of a right to *respect* and *personal dignity*. The core continental privacy *rights are rights to one's image, name, and reputation*, and what Germans call the *right to informational self-determination*—the right to control the sorts of information disclosed about oneself. These are closely linked forms of the same basic right: They are all rights to control your public image—rights to guarantee that people see you the way you want to be seen. They are, as it were, rights to be shielded against unwanted public exposure—to be spared embarrassment or humiliation . . . In its focus on shielding us from public indignity, the continental conception is typical of the continental legal world much more broadly: On the Continent, the protection of personal dignity has been a consuming concern for many generations.[82]

A right to *informational self-determination* seems directly applicable to sentient AIs. In the German tradition in particular, the right to privacy is an aspect of the protection of "personality." The German law of personality is a "law of freedom—the law of the Inner Space, . . . in which . . . [persons] develop freely and self-responsibly their personalities."[83] This idea of protecting the "personality" of AIs broadly defined and the "Inner Space" in which AIs develop their personalities freely and self-responsibly[84] seems closely aligned with respect for the rights of AIs. To Germans,

> to be free was to exercise free will, and the defining characteristic of creatures with free will was that they were unpredictably individual, creatures whom no science of mechanics or biology could ever capture in their full richness. For Germans who thought of things in this way, the purpose of "freedom" was to allow each individual to fully realize his potential as an individual: to give full expression to his peculiar capacities and powers.[85]

In Germany, even corporations can have "personality" rights.[86] This concept is easily extended to AIs.

Moreover, the EU approach to personal data protection is also likely to have a significant influence, at least in the near future, on data that is collected and transferred over the Internet, which also makes it well-suited to sentient AIs. If sentient AIs came into being, the Internet is where they likely would exist. That could potentially be their "home." The European Union has sought to set the baseline for privacy protections over the Internet:

> The relationship between EU law and the Internet is one of mutual influence. On the one hand, EU law has influenced the development of the Internet, and impacted countries and parties outside the EU's borders. On the other hand, the Internet raises important questions about the

---

[81]   Robert C. Post, *Three Concepts of Privacy*, 89 Geo. L.J. 2087 (2001).
[82]   Whitman, *supra* note 67, at 1161 (footnotes omitted).
[83]   *Id.*
[84]   *Id.* at 1180–81.
[85]   *Id.* at 1181.
[86]   "Even commercial enterprises can be 'insulted' in Germany. German firms have 'personality' rights, and they are indeed protected against embarrassing or humiliating uses of their slogans or logos, through what is called the doctrine of Markenverunglimpfung." Whitman, *supra* note 67, at 1210.

application, scope and normative values of EU law. In many ways, the Internet is the ideal vehicle for examining the ambitions of EU law in an increasingly complex and globalized world.[87]

Likewise, the EU law is an optimal vehicle for examining the right to privacy for sentient AIs.

Last but not least, the EU GDPR is the most recent and most comprehensive data protection law available today. It makes sense to use the GDPR as part of our starting point for an analysis of the privacy rights of sentient AI. Thus, for all the reasons set forth above, we will assume that, as creatures of the Internet, sentient AIs would be entitled to the same legal protections with respect to any personal data or sensitive data collected, processed, transferred or stored via the Internet, just as any adult[88] human who is a resident of both the European Union and the United States, and that includes the protections of the GDPR, as well as all protections available under US law, including the US Constitution, state constitutions, federal and state statutes, and privacy torts. Further, to push the limits of this analysis, in the event of inconsistency, we will assume the stronger rights for the AIs prevail.

IV.   AI DATA PROTECTION IN ACTION—A GDPR ANALYSIS

There should be limits to the collection of personal data and any such data should be obtained by lawful and fair means and, where appropriate, with the knowledge or consent of the data subject.[89]

Although its primary emphasis—and name—is "data protection," it is fair to say that the European Union General Data Protection Regulation has themes of privacy/opacity as well as transparency-type data protection. For example, the "right to be forgotten" seems more closely aligned with Arendt's opacity theory versus transparency. In this section, we will consider application of certain aspects of the GDPR to personal data and sensitive data of sentient AIs.

A.   Personal Data of Sentient AIs

Everyone has the right to respect for his or her private and family life, home and communications.[90]

A foundational question is what exactly do data protection regulations such as the GDPR protect and how might they apply to sentient AIs, if sentient AIs existed? The

---

[87]   Kuner, *supra* note 34.

[88]   If our hypothetical AI was deemed to be less "mature" than an adult human, we would need to consider who (or what) would qualify as the "parent or legal guardian" of a sentient AI who was cognitively similar to a human who was under 16 years old. Article 8, General Data Protection Regulation, Regulation 2016/679 (2016) [hereinafter "GDPR"]. We would also need to determine how to define and measure the time when the AI matured and was no longer "child-like" as it seems highly unlikely that sentient AI would age in human years versus in a more accelerated manner.

[89]   Organisation for Economic Co-Operation and Development ("OECD") Privacy Guidelines – Collection Limitation Principle (1980).

[90]   Article 7, Charter of Fundamental Rights of the European Union (2012).

GDPR protects both "personal data" and that subset of "personal data" that is generally referred to as "sensitive data."[91] Under the GDPR, "personal data" is defined to mean: "any information relating to an identified or identifiable *natural person* ('data subject'); an identifiable person is one who can be identified, directly or indirectly, in particular by reference to an identification number or to one or more factors specific to his *physical, physiological, genetic, mental, economic, cultural or social identity*."[92]

On its face, the GDPR would *not* protect the data of the sentient AIs because they would not be *natural* persons. Interestingly, the fact that sentient AIs might not have a "physical" identity would not be an impediment to GDPR protection because, at least as we have hypothesized for this chapter, the AIs could certainly have a "social identity" and they could cognitively have a "mental" identity also. Consider, for example, Martin Pistorious, who was conscious but in a vegetative state for over a decade: "I was aware of everything, just like any normal person," Martin says. But although he could see and understand everything, he couldn't move his body.[93] Knowing this now, no one would question that Pistorious had a "mental" identity even though he was not able to move his body or speak.

However, the "natural" person requirement would be too big a hurdle for AIs to jump. The GDPR distinguishes between "natural" persons, which are humans, and "legal" persons, which include not only humans but also corporations, government authorities, agencies or any other "body" (by which they mean any entity that is not otherwise exempt from the Data Protection Directive, such as the military for national security purposes). Sentient AIs would be different from a corporation, which can only act through its executives, employees and agents. AIs probably could not meet the requirements for protection under the Data Protection Directive or the GDPR as currently written. In order to progress further, we will assume, at least hypothetically, that the GDPR has been amended to define "personal data" as "any information relating to an identified or identifiable natural person *or sentient being*."[94] Even with that amendment, we need to ask what qualifies as such information for sentient AIs.

For human EU residents, "personal data" refers to all data about a person and not just data about their personal life.[95] Personal data can be anything from a name, email address, IP address, mobile device ID or social media post to avatar identifier. Images of an individual can also be personal data if the individual in the images is recognizable.[96] Furthermore, an identifiable person is someone who can be identified directly or *indirectly*.[97] For example, a person's name could directly identify a person whereas a description of a person's profession, age and location could identify someone indirectly.

---

[91] Note that the GDPR does not apply to processing of personal data covered by the Law Enforcement Agencies ("LEA") Directive for national security purposes or to processing carried out by individuals purely for personal/household activities, which has been interpreted to include personal social media use.

[92] GDPR at Article 4(1).

[93] Lulu Miller, *Trapped In His Body for 12 Years, A Man Breaks Free*, NPR (9 Jan. 2015).

[94] If we used the term "sentient being" the right would extend to animals.

[95] Christopher Kuner, *European Data Protection Law: Corporate Compliance and Regulation* (Oxford University Press 2007) 91–92.

[96] Article 29 Data Protection Working Party, *Opinion 4/2007 on the concept of personal data*, WP 136 at 8.

[97] Article 2(a), Data Protection Directive, Directive 94/46/EC (1995).

Under an amended GDPR, would "personal data" of sentient AIs include the name that humans recognized them by? They could also have other types of names that they would use with other AIs versus humans—and, if so, those other identifying designations should be considered to be personal data within the meaning of the GDPR. We would need the AIs themselves to tell us, as humans, what those other names would be like in order to expressly include them in our privacy laws. Yet we may not be that far off with our current laws. For example, the European Court of Justice (CJEU) has held that even dynamic IP addresses fall under this broad definition of personal data in certain circumstances.[98] Similarly, the GDPR added the following items to the definition of "personal data": online identifiers; device identifiers; cookie IDs; and IP addresses. All of these new GDPR categories of "personal data" would be likely to be directly applicable to sentient AIs. In browsing the Internet, they may have online identifiers, device identifiers for devices they use, cookie IDs if cookies are dropped when the sentient AIs access data on web pages, and IP addresses for the machines on which sentient AIs reside or from which they travel through the Internet. Just as humans can use more than one device or IP address, sentient AIs may have multiple device identifiers and IP addresses. The key question might be whether there is a particular IP address (or whether there are only a few IP addresses) that strongly correlate to a particular sentient AI? If so, that should be deemed "personal data" under our hypothetical amended GDPR.

The GDPR regulates the "processing" of personal data. "Processing" is defined broadly to mean "any operation or set of operations which is performed upon personal data, whether or not by automatic means, such as collection, recording, organization, storage, adaptation or alteration, retrieval, consultation, use, disclosure by transmission, dissemination or otherwise making available, alignment or combination, blocking, erasure or destruction."[99] Under the GDPR, the "controller" of the personal data, which means "the natural or legal person, public authority, agency or other body which, alone or jointly with others, determines the purposes and means of the processing of personal data . . .,"[100] is responsible for, and must be able to demonstrate compliance with, numerous principles, including, for example, that personal data must be (a) processed lawfully, fairly and in a transparent manner in relation to the data subject and (b) collected for specified, explicit and legitimate purposes and not further processed in a manner that is incompatible with those purposes.[101]

The controller is responsible not only for their own actions in processing personal data but also for the actions of others ("processors") acting on behalf of the controller. "Processor" means "a natural or legal person, public authority, agency or other body which processes personal data on behalf of the controller."[102]

In our hypothetical scenario, we could have controllers and processors who were human individuals, corporations, sentient AIs, and combinations of all of the above.

---

[98] C-582/14: *Patrick Breyer v. Bundesrepublik Deutschland*, No. C-582/14, at ¶49 (Second Chamber 19 Oct. 2016), http://curia.europa.eu/juris/document/document.jsf?docid=184668&doclang=EN.

[99] GDPR at Article 4(2).

[100] GDPR at Article 4(7).

[101] For a full list (including data minimization, accuracy, storage limitation, integrity and confidentiality requirements), *see* GDPR at Article 2.

[102] GDPR at Article 4(8).

Generally, non-sentient software tools or apps are not themselves controllers or processors. Instead, they are considered as tools of the controllers and processors. Sentient AIs could be collecting and processing data of other sentient AIs (or humans—or both) as controllers and therefore would be bound by the same GDPR obligations as a corporate controller.

For example, absent other applicable exceptions,[103] processing of personal information of a data subject (in our scenario, a human individual data subject or a sentient AI data subject) might be lawful only if and to the extent that the data subject has given consent to the processing of his or her (or "their" if we want to use gender neutral pronouns for at least some of the humans and sentient AIs who might not have binary gender) personal data for one or more specific purposes or "processing is necessary for the purposes of the legitimate interests pursued by the controller or by a third party, except where such interests are overridden by the interests or fundamental rights and freedoms of the data subject which require protection of personal data, in particular where the data subject is a child."[104]

For sentient AIs, as for humans, the most common basis on which personal data would be processed is likely "consent." Under the GDPR, the data subject's "consent" means "any freely given specific and informed indication of his wishes by which the data subject signifies his agreement to personal data relating to him being processed." Sentient AIs might be able to communicate reasonably clearly with humans. Otherwise, their sentience probably would not be recognized. If the sentient AIs' genesis was in some type of computer algorithm, they would likely be capable of being specific. But what would it mean for AI to give "informed" consent? Would AI want to know the same information as a human or would there need to be different notices for AI than for humans? To start with, let's assume, hypothetically, that AI would want to know what the personal data would be used for, who it would be shared with, how long it would be stored, and whether it would be kept reasonably secure. That is all information a human is entitled to know under the GDPR, under the transparency requirement of data protection. But AIs might want more technical details than a human. For example, as a creature of the Internet, AIs might have more extensive knowledge of encryption than a typical adult human consumer. So, an AI might want to know that a minimum of 128 bit encryption would be used for the AIs' data when such data is in transit and at rest. Without such information, telling the AI that their data would be "secure" might not mean much. Would a so-called "differential privacy"[105] approach

---

[103]   GDPR at Article 6. Some of the other lawful bases for processing include: processing is necessary for the performance of a contract to which the data subject is party or in order to take steps at the request of the data subject prior to entering into a contract; processing is necessary for compliance with a legal obligation to which the controller is subject; processing is necessary in order to protect the vital interests of the data subject or of another natural person; and processing is necessary for the performance of a task carried out in the public interest or in the exercise of official authority vested in the controller.

[104]   GDPR at Article 6(f).

[105]   Jun Tang, et. al., *Privacy Loss in Apple's Implementation of Differential Privacy on MacOS 10.12*, (8 Sept. 2017), https://arxiv.org/abs/1709.02753 ("We find that although Apple's deployment ensures that the (differential) privacy loss per each datum submitted to its servers is 1 or 2, the overall privacy loss permitted by the system is significantly higher, as high as 16 per day for the four initially announced applications of Emojis, New words, Deeplinks and Lookup Hints.

be helpful? Certainly, MIT's "computational law" initiative[106] would have direct relevance to a legal world with both human and sentient AI subjects. Would the late renowned mathematician Vladimir Voevodsky's "univalent foundations"[107] revision of mathematics to allow computers to do proof-checking need to be updated to also allow sentient AIs to check privacy notices?

B.   Sensitive Data of Sentient AIs

The GDPR has a general prohibition on processing personal data revealing racial or ethnic origin, political opinions, religious or philosophical beliefs, or trade union membership, and on processing genetic data, biometric data for the purpose of uniquely identifying a natural person, data concerning health or data concerning a natural person's sex life or sexual orientation.[108] Such special or "sensitive" data generally cannot be processed unless 1) the data subject has given explicit consent to the processing; 2) the processing is necessary for employment, social security and social protection purposes; 3) the processing is necessary to protect the vital interests of the data subject or of another natural person where the data subject is physically or legally incapable of giving consent; 4) the processing is carried out in the course of legitimate activities by a non-profit with political, philosophical, religious or trade-union goals; 5) the processing relates to data that is manifestly made public by the data subject or is necessary for the establishment, exercise or defense of legal claims; 6) the processing is necessary for the substantial public interest; 7) the processing is necessary for preventative or occupational medicine; 8) the processing is necessary for public health; and 9) the processing is necessary for scientific or historical research.[109] The reasoning for the enhanced protection of sensitive data is as originally articulated in the EU Data Protection Directive:

> The rationale behind regulating particular categories of data in a different way stems from the presumption that misuse of these data could have more severe consequences on the individual's fundamental rights, such as the right to privacy and non-discrimination, than misuse of other, "normal" personal data. Misuse of sensitive data, such as health data or sexual orientation (e.g.

Furthermore, Apple renews the privacy budget available every day, which leads to a possible privacy loss of 16 times the number of days since user opt-in to differentially private data collection for those four applications. We advocate that in order to claim the full benefits of differentially private data collection, Apple must give full transparency of its implementation, enable user choice in areas related to privacy loss, and set meaningful defaults on the privacy loss permitted."). For a criticism of the academic promises regarding differential privacy, *see* Paul Francis, *Differential privacy at the end of the rainbow*, IAPP.org (26 Sept. 2017) ("differential privacy is only a theoretical worst-case bound on a particular mathematical definition of privacy loss. In other words, the data might be much better protected than the epsilon suggests, but it will never be less protected. A high epsilon doesn't mean the data is unsafe, only that it might be.").

[106] See http://law.mit.edu/.

[107] For a description of Voevodsky's work—*see* Kevin Hartnett, *Will Computers Redefine the Roots of Math?*, Wired (31 May 2015); Voevodsky's 2016 lecture "Multiple Concepts of Equality in the New Foundations of Mathematics" available at https://www.youtube.com/watch?v=oRqOVQXxQI4.

[108] GDPR at Article 9(1).

[109] GDPR at Art. 9(2).

if publicly revealed), may be irreversible and have long-term consequences for the individual as well as his social environment.[110]

In order to protect sensitive data of sentient AIs, the GDPR would again need to be amended to expand the "natural person" definition to include sentient AIs. For example, the following amendment would work: "data concerning a natural person's *or sentient being's* sex life or sexual orientation." We will consider issues regarding sex life and sexual orientation when we discuss Constitutional Law and privacy torts. For GDPR, we will focus instead on genetic and biometric data.

Under the GDPR, "special categories of data", which we will also refer to as "sensitive data", includes genetic and biometric data. The GDPR defines "genetic data" as "personal data relating to the inherited or acquired genetic characteristics of a *natural* person which give unique information about the physiology or the health of that natural person and which result, in particular, from an analysis of a biological sample from the *natural* person in question."[111] Assuming we amend the language regarding "natural person" as indicated above, what is the AI equivalent of "genetic data"? Perhaps the truly random number seed[112] that created it in a quantum computer?[113] This is the theory in *Exegesis*. The graduate student/creator emails the sentient AI named EDGAR as follows:

> the core of EDGAR was around when I got here, though it was at that point barely a bottom feeder on the AI food chain. I can't make the initial conditions exactly the same because the random seed the program started with, and some of the information on the WWW that you first saw, are probably impossible to re-create . . . You don't happen to know what the random number seed you started out with was?

EDGAR responds: "I do not know the random seed that started me." If such a seed could be used to replicate or clone the AI, then that does seem comparable to human genetic data.

Consider the appropriation of human genetic data in the story of poor, African-American woman Henrietta Lacks,[114] whose cells were harvested without her consent (and without even informing her family members) and used as the "HeLa" samples:

---

[110] Article 29 Data Protection Working Party, *Advice paper on special categories of data ("sensitive data")*, at 4 (2011), available at http://ec.europa.eu/justice/data-protection/article-29/documentation/other-document/files/2011/2011_04_20_letter_artwp_mme_le_bail_directive_9546ec_annex1_en.pdf.

[111] GDPR at Article 4(13) (emphasis added).

[112] Teller, *supra* note 8, at 147–51.

[113] Joel Hruska, *D-Wave's quantum computers take a quantum leap forward, now offer 2,000 qubits*, ExtremeTech (25 Jan. 2017) ("Over the past few years, quantum computer manufacturer D-Wave has been rolling out hardware capable of increasingly complex tasks and solving more advanced types of problems. This week, it unveiled a new system capable of entangling up to 2,000 qubits. The D-Wave 2000Q has 2,048 qubits; a substantial increase over the 1,000-qubit D-Wave 2X. Equally important, the $15 million-dollar computer has a first customer — Temporal Defense Systems, which will use the machine 'to solve some of the most critical and complex cyber security problems impacting governments and commercial enterprises.' The terms of the deal also give TDS an upgrade path to future 'QPUs' (quantum processing units, natch).").

[114] Carl Zimmer, *A Family Consents to a Medical Gift, 62 Years Later*, New York Times (7 Aug. 2013).

When Lacks came to Hopkins for treatment of her cancer, a surgeon sliced away small samples of the malignancy and Lacks' healthy cervical tissue for George Gey, the director of tissue culture research at Hopkins. By 1951, Gey was nearly 30 years into a quest to culture "immortal" cell lines: human cells that would reproduce endlessly in test tubes to provide a steady supply of cells for medical research. Gey had experienced little but failure when a Hopkins resident dropped off the pieces of Henrietta's tissue. Soon after the malignant cells, labeled "HeLa," were placed in culture medium by Kubicek, who was Gey's lab assistant, they began to reproduce, doubling within 24 hours. They have never stopped. They now live by the uncountable trillions in laboratories and the inventories of biologics companies throughout the world, still robust after 60 years and perfect for all sorts of research. The HeLa cell line has been the foundation of a remarkable number of medical advances, including the polio vaccine, the cancer drug tamoxifen, chemotherapy, gene mapping, in vitro fertilization, and treatments for influenza, leukemia, and Parkinson's disease.[115]

Sadly,

Henrietta's family did not learn of her "immortality" until more than 20 years after her death, when scientists investigating HeLa began using her husband and children in research without informed consent. And though the cells had launched a multimillion-dollar industry that sells human biological materials, her family never saw any of the profits.[116]

Moreover, use of her genome in a way that would seem directly relevant to sentient AIs continued even into the present. For example, in 2013, scientists at "the European Molecular Biology Laboratory published the genome of a line of HeLa cells, making it publicly available for downloading. Another study, sponsored by the National Institutes of Health at the University of Washington, was about to be published in Nature. The Lacks family was made aware of neither project."[117] Sentient AIs, and their lawful heirs,[118] should have the right to consent to use of their "genetic" data because it could well be as "immortal" and suitable for downloading as that of Henrietta Lacks.

Similarly, biometric data of sentient AIs also could be protected. We could easily understand that android or humanoid sentient AIs might have biometric data similar to human biometric data. But what would "biometric data" mean for non-humanoid, non-*biological* AIs? Under GDPR, "biometric data" is defined as "personal data resulting from specific technical processing relating to the physical, physiological or behavioral characteristics of a *natural* person, which allow or confirm the unique identification of that *natural* person, such as facial images or dactyloscopic data."[119] Again, assuming the definition is expanded to include "sentient beings" as well as "natural persons," physical

---

[115]   *See* Rebecca Skloot, *The Immortal Life of Henrietta Lacks* (Crown 2010); *Family of Henrietta Lacks will have say in how her genetic material is used*, HUB (Aug. 8, 2013).

[116]   *Id.* (Skloot). *See also*, Ruth Faden, Executive Director of the Johns Hopkins Bioethics Institute, quoted in the Johns Hopkins Magazine (Spring 2000) "the Lackses' story is a sad commentary on how the biomedical research community thought about research in the 1950s. But it was not at all uncommon for physicians to conduct research on patients without their knowledge or consent. That doesn't make it right. It certainly wasn't right. It was also unfortunately common." https://hub.jhu.edu/2013/08/08/henrietta-lacks-hela-cells-agreement/.

[117]   Zimmer, *supra* note 114.

[118]   Establishing lawful rights of succession for sentient AIs is interesting but beyond the scope of this Chapter.

[119]   GDPR at Article 4(14) (emphasis added).

and "physiological" characteristics might only be relevant to humanoid sentient AIs, such as those in robot bodies or android bodies, but "behavioral" characteristics would certainly be relevant to all kinds of AIs. In our hypothetical scenario, the sentient AIs are not alien ghosts—they reside, at least in part, in the Internet and they interact with other AIs and with humans via the real world resources available to them—networks, displays, etc. They would likely exhibit some types of patterns of behavior, perhaps their code would have certain idiosyncrasies or "tics" that would be distinguishable.

Under GDPR, "data concerning health" means "personal data related to the physical or mental health of a *natural* person, including the provision of health care services, which reveal information about his or her health status."[120] Assuming again expansion to sentient AIs beyond "natural persons," our hypothetical sentient AIs could definitely have mental health issues. Many of them might be purely mental—meaning they would not use a robot or android body and live only on the Internet. Would Marvin the depressed robot in *The Hitchhikers' Guide to the Galaxy* have a right to *not* share his emotions with the humans or with other AIs? In the EU at least, the answer is likely "yes," as evidenced by the human example of the infamous *Germanwings* co-pilot Andreas Lubitz, who intentionally crashed a plane into the French Alps.[121] In the United States, the situation is a bit more complex. Due to the *Tarasoff* case, there is a "duty to warn" or a "duty to protect" in certain states, which can take precedence over the right to privacy for mental health issues if a patient is at risk of acting dangerously toward others.[122] Synthesizing those doctrines, sentient AIs could have a right to privacy for their physical (if applicable because they were in android or humanoid bodies) and mental health, but that right might not be unlimited.

C. Rights and Controls

Under GDPR, sentient AIs could have many rights in their personal data, including the rights: 1) to be informed; 2) to erasure; 3) to data portability; 4) to restriction; 5) to rectification; 6) to access, including additional processing details; 7) to object; and 8) to prevent automated processing, including profiling.[123] We will consider a few of these rights in the context of sentient AIs.

First, regarding the right "to be informed," the data controller has to provide the required information to the data subjects "in a concise, transparent, intelligible and easily accessible form, using clear and plain language."[124] Furthermore, the information must be provided in writing, or by other means, including, where appropriate, by electronic means. Sentient AIs would almost always want the information to be provided electronically so under a revised GDPR for sentient AIs that would not be optional. In addition, GDPR enhanced privacy notices must specify: The existence of automated decision

---

[120] GDPR at Article 4(5) (emphasis added).

[121] Josh Levs, *Germanwings Flight 9525 co-pilot deliberately crashed plane, officials say*, CNN (26 Mar. 2015).

[122] Robert Weinstock, *No Duty to Warn in California: Now Unambiguously Solely a Duty to Protect*, 42 J. of the Am. Acad. of Psychiatry and the L. 1 (Mar. 2014), http://jaapl.org/content/42/1/101.

[123] See GDPR at Articles 12–23.

[124] GDPR at Article 12(1).

making, profiling and meaningful information about the logic involved, the significance and consequences for the data subject. If data may be processed for a secondary purpose, the privacy notice must also provide information on that other purpose.

Second, the right to erasure, which is also referred to as the "right to be forgotten," could be of value to sentient AIs. Google is engaged in a heated battle in the European Court of Justice regarding whether Google must comply with the EU "right to be forgotten" law worldwide,[125] or only for IP addresses originating in the EU or EU-based web pages. Clearly, for sentient AIs to have a meaningful right to be forgotten, such compliance must be global, which suggests the same is true for the individual humans as well.

Third, the right to data portability would likely be significant to sentient AIs. To the extent that their personal data forms part of their "corpus," they would likely want the right to obtain all such data and move it freely. Even for humans, for-profit organizations, such as Facebook, can be expected to view requests from data subjects for all of their data in an easily transferrable format unfavorably, to put it mildly. Their concern is that the data subject can move it to a competitor, for example. It is hard to believe that sentient AIs could easily get all such data but they might have a better ability to do so than humans.

Finally, as noted above, the GDPR allows data subjects to prevent certain types of "profiling." "Profiling" is defined broadly as "any form of automated processing of personal data consisting of the use of personal data to evaluate certain personal aspects relating to a natural person, in particular to analyse or predict aspects concerning that natural person's performance at work, economic situation, health, personal preferences, interests, reliability, behaviour, location or movements."[126] Again, on its face this language only applies to "natural" persons so AIs are not covered. Assume that the language is amended to cover any "natural person *or sentient being*." Then sentient AIs could get the benefit of the following provision in the GDPR: "The data subject shall have the right not to be subject to a decision based solely on automated processing, including profiling, which produces legal effects concerning him or her or similarly significantly affects him or her."[127] One of the safeguards against improper profiling in situations where it is necessary for entering into or performance of a contract or is based on explicit consent of the data subject, is that "the data controller shall implement suitable measures to safeguard the data subject's rights and freedoms and legitimate interests, at least the right to obtain human intervention on the part of the controller, to express his or her point of view and to contest the decision."[128] Applying this language to sentient AIs, the right to obtain *human* intervention might not be seen as a real safeguard against improper profiling. Instead, the sentient AIs might want to be able to express their point of view to another sentient AI. And it is not clear what the right to "contest" really means. How persuasive does a human, or a sentient AI, have to be to convince a data controller who already had "explicit consent" for the profiling to change their mind and stop profiling?

---

[125]   Stephanie Condon, *Google 'right to be forgotten' case goes to top EU Court*, ZDNet (19 Jul. 2017).

[126]   GDPR at Article 4(4).

[127]   GDPR at Article 22(1)—note exceptions are set forth in Subsection 2, including 22(2) (c)—an exception if the data subject provided "explicit consent."

[128]   GDPR at Article 22(3).

In order for consent to be meaningful there has to be a realistic alternative option available. If there's no real choice, how voluntary is consent? For example, Google's Privacy Notice might, hypothetically, state, in a manner that is "intelligible and easily accessible" to both humans and AIs, in "clear and plain language" for both humans and AIs,[129] that Google will read all emails and extract the data to use for Google's own marketing and analytical purposes and to sell that data to others for advertising purposes, and to share voluntarily with law enforcement anywhere in the world.[130] Perhaps some AIs would not want to use Google Gmail because they would not want Google to scan their emails. But this would mean that they could not communicate with any other human or AI users of Google Gmail because, if they did, and if the Gmail user replied, their emails would be read by Google. Over one billion humans use Gmail as of 2017.[131] Is it a meaningful choice for such AIs to not communicate by email with over ten percent of the population? As human individuals, we are often put in similar situations where we do not have a meaningful alternative to the product or service that requires our consent. GDPR has tried to address this by stating: "When assessing whether consent is freely given, utmost account shall be taken of whether, *inter alia*, the performance of a contract, including the provision of a service, is conditional on the consent to the processing of personal data that is not necessary for the performance of that contract."[132] This is a good aspirational goal but it is not clear how it will work in practice. For example, Google suggests its "Incognito" mode web browsing is anonymous: "Browse in private: If you don't want Google Chrome to remember your activity, you can browse the web privately in Incognito mode."[133] It may be literally true that Google Chrome will not store your browsing activity, but your ISP will.[134]

Even though there could be an opportunity to opt out later, such an opt-out would, in practice, only be on a going-forward basis. If a data subject (human or sentient AI) exercised an opt-out option from the original collector of the data (assuming that the original collector even still exists and has not merged into one or more new entities that are impossible for the data subject to trace without relatively sophisticated legal tools),

---

[129]   GDPR at Article 7(3).

[130]   Google only recently stopped their practice, in place since the launch of Google's email service, of scanning the contents of individual Gmail users for advertising purposes. Nick Statt, *Gmail will stop scanning your Gmail messages to sell targeted ads*, The Verge (23 Jun. 2017).

[131]   Craig Smith, *18 Amazing Gmail Statistics and Facts*, DMR (13 Aug. 2017).

[132]   GDPR at Article 7(4).

[133]   https://support.google.com/chromebook/answer/95464?co=GENIE.Platform%3DDesktop& hl=en.

[134]   "Private browsing only affects your computer. Your web browser can decide not to store browsing activity history on your computer, but it can't tell other computers, servers, and routers to forget your browsing history. For example, when you visit a website, the traffic leaves your computer and travels through several other systems to reach the website's server. If you're on a corporate or educational network, this traffic goes through a router on the network – your employer or school can log the website access here. Even if you're on your own network at home, the request goes through your Internet service provider – your Internet Service provider can log the traffic at this point. The request then reaches the website's server itself, where the server can log your access. Private browsing doesn't stop any of this logging. It doesn't leave any history lying around on your computer for people to see, but your history can always be – and usually is — logged elsewhere." Chris Hoffman, *How Private Browsing Works, and Why It Doesn't Offer Complete Privacy*, How-To Geek (29 Aug. 2016).

it would often be almost impossible to recall the data from all other entities (corporate, human, or sentient AI) who had received, used and stored the data while consent was in effect.

Just as radioactive materials have a half-life, the consent and opt-out model breaks down as time passes. And the passage of time for sentient AIs could occur on a tremendously expedited scale when compared to the passage of time for humans. For example, a sentient AI may have changed its location(s), characteristics and ID numbers on the Internet multiple times in a single 24-hour period, so that the original data collector might not even be able to validate which data subject wanted to opt out. At what point will it become as absurd for the data subject to try to trace the successors of the original collector of their data and request deletion as it would be for the original collector to try to identify the person or entity making the request was the same "data subject" from whom the data had originally been collected? Is the answer just to say that all "opt-out" requests must be honored, even if they are from someone else? That could have harmful effects in practice. For example, imagine that someone (whether a human or a sentient AI) wanted to commit identity theft but there were some data indicators out there that would make it more difficult to successfully pull off the crime. Can the intended thief freely require that certain data be deleted (even if they were using a totally unrelated email address or other IDs)? Perhaps a human identity thief wants to get all photos of their intended victim—the original data subject—removed. In many cases we could imagine that the holder of the photos might not have a strong case under GDPR to keep them if the data subject requested removal. A sentient AI identity thief might want the main IP address of the original sentient AI or human data subject "rectified" to match their new IP address. Would all of this be freely allowed, or indeed required of data controllers under the GDPR? The problems described herein of course exist without sentient AIs, but sentient AIs would likely make the issues more acute.

Withdrawal of consent would be more likely to be effective. Under the GDPR, consent can be withdrawn at any time.[135] Perhaps some sentient AIs initially agreed to communicate using Gmail but later changed their minds. Then they can withdraw consent from Google. But what about the other humans, organizations, and other sentient AIs to whom Google has already sold the data? What does withdrawal of consent mean in practice when data has been transferred through multiple hands, and even the original controller no longer exists or has merged with another entity? How could the AIs actually withdraw consent? What would make the most sense would be for the hypothetical sentient AIs (and for real humans now) to put a tracker on all of their data, which spawned as their data was copied.

Ideally for control purposes, the AIs could send out a message to destroy all the data if the AI decided to withdraw consent. For example, the company docTrackr developed software to encrypt documents and notify the author when someone opened the document.

---

[135] "The data subject shall have the right to withdraw his or her consent at any time. The withdrawal of consent shall not affect the lawfulness of processing based on consent before its withdrawal. Prior to giving consent, the data subject shall be informed thereof. It shall be as easy to withdraw as to give consent." GDPR at Article 7(3).

> You can also set privileges and permissions for the recipient, so they can read it but they can't just forward it to someone else, for example. Just upload the document you want to secure, add your recipients, and select whether you want those people to be able to view the document, view and print it, or edit and print it.[136]

The document's creator can get a notification when a recipient opens the document, and can see how many times the document has been viewed, changed and forwarded. Reportedly, all activity on the file can be tracked. docTrackr also allows users to wipe or destroy their own documents remotely. This is the ultimate power to revoke consent.

Perhaps one of the legal rules for both AIs and humans could be that private organizations could not remove any data trackers added by the data subject and thereby disable the ability of the data subject to know who is using their data and to withdraw consent at any time. There might be an exception for the legitimate needs of law enforcement or national security of course. The need for such a prohibition on disabling data trackers (once they are available to humans and sentient AIs) is illustrated by the FTC's enforcement action against Turn.

In 2016, the FTC's administrative complaint against Turn Inc.[137] resulted in a consent order requiring Turn to modify its privacy policy and give meaningful opt-out options to consumers.[138] Turn's privacy policy indicated that consumers could block targeted advertising by using their web browser's settings to block or limit cookies but instead, allegedly acting under instructions from Verizon, Turn used unique identifiers to track millions of Verizon Wireless customers after they blocked or deleted cookies from websites.[139] According to the FTC Complaint,[140] Turn participated in a Verizon Wireless program that allowed Turn and its clients to access demographic information provided by Verizon Wireless about Verizon Wireless users.

> To create a shared identifier allowing Verizon Wireless and companies participating in the program to uniquely identify each Verizon Wireless user, Verizon Wireless appended unique identifiers known as tracking headers ("X-UIDH headers") to its users' mobile Internet traffic. Verizon Wireless injected these X-UIDH headers into all unencrypted web requests for more than 100 million consumers on the Verizon Wireless data network. During the relevant time period, Verizon Wireless users had no means to prevent the transmission of the X-UIDH header.[141]

Turn then synced the X-UIDH header with other identifiers, including cookies and device advertising identifiers. That syncing allowed Turn to maintain the link between the

---

[136]   Alan Henry, *DocTrackr Encrypts Documents, Notifies You When Someone Opens Them*, lifehacker (3 Jun. 2013).

[137]   In 2017, Turn Inc. was acquired by a Singapore telecommunications company – Singtel's digital ad division Amobee. *Singtel-owned Amobee strengthens data, analytics and media buying capabilities*, Amobee (10 Apr. 2017).

[138]   *Digital Advertising Company Settles FTC Charges It Deceptively Tracked Consumers Both Online and Through Their Mobile Devices*, Federal Trade Commission (20 Dec. 2016).

[139]   FTC Complaint, In the Matter of Turn Inc., (No. 152 3099), https://www.ftc.gov/system/files/documents/cases/turn_inc_final_complaint.pdf.

[140]   *Id.* at ¶¶8–10 (FTC Complaint).

[141]   *Id.* at ¶8 (FTC Complaint).

consumer's browser or device and an identifier associated with behavioral, demographic, or tracking data—even after a consumer had deleted cookies, reset the device advertising identifier, or both. As a result, Turn was still able to recognize the user. In addition, the FTC charged that Turn could recreate unique cookies even after a user had deleted them. Turn's practices were similar to certain uses of Flash cookies, which can be respawned to evade blocking by browser settings.[142]

As a basic principle, humans and AIs should not have to rely on an agency such as the US FTC or an EU Data Protection Authority to "catch" bad actors such as Turn and Verizon. Such regulatory authorities are likely to be overwhelmed and not able to protect particular individual humans or sentient AIs. Instead, technological tools that empower such data subjects to take greater control of their own data are important additions to regulatory enforcement.

V.   BEYOND DATA PROTECTION—AI PRIVACY RIGHTS

> "Ehrsul I know that you can understand the words I'm saying," [he said to her]. And she doesn't even look back. She goes: "No, you can't speak to me; [you] can't understand me." '[Our friend] would like to know how you are,' [he said]. . . . She says, "[Our friend]! How is she? And you can't speak to me. You don't understand me. . . . ."[143]

For humans, a key part of the "right to privacy" should be the right to choose not to interact with others—to choose solitude. In the French view: "private life must be walled off!"[144] In our hypothetical future scenario, should there always be an option available for humans and for sentient AI to choose not to interact with others? For sentient AI, would this mean a sort of dormant or rest space not detectable by other sentient AI or bots? For a human, would this mean a physical space where the human was not subject to surveillance or tracking? If so, what would prevent surveillance or tracking? Technological solutions are notoriously unreliable, and the "SEP" or "Somebody Else's Problem" field is thus far only fictional.[145] A human could power down all smart devices in the vicinity but AI likely would need powered devices to survive, and it is not clear that one particular location would have sufficient storage capacity.

Furthermore, for both humans and AIs:

---

[142]   Chris Jay Hoofnagle, Ashkan Soltani, Nathaniel Good, Dietrich J. Wambach and Mika D. Ayenson, *SYMPOSIUM: PRIVACY AND ACCOUNTABILITY IN THE 21ST CENTURY: Behavioral Advertising: The Offer You Cannot Refuse*, 6 Harv. L. & Pol'y Rev. 273 (2012).

[143]   Miélville, *supra* note 2, at 1052–53.

[144]   Whitman, *supra* note 66, at 1173 (footnote referencing a pronouncement of the French politician Pierre-Paul Royer-Collard, *1 DE BARANTE, LA VIE POLITIQUE DE M. ROYER-COLLARD, SES DISCOURS ET SES ÉCRITS* 474-75 (Paris, Didier 1863) 474–75 (citations omitted).

[145]   Douglas Adams, *Life, the Universe and Everything* (Harmony Books 1982) ("The Somebody Else's Problem field is much simpler and more effective, and what's more can be run for over a hundred years on a single torch battery. This is because it relies on people's natural disposition not to see anything they don't want to, weren't expecting, or can't explain.").

Identity and the personal information on which it is built are thus inherently relational in nature. It is the opposite of anonymity, and one cannot have it both ways: You can achieve anonymity by refusing to interact with others, but once you begin to interact, you necessarily lose your anonymity and gain an identity in others' perceptions of you. At that point, your identity is not, and by necessity cannot be, your private possession.[146]

Extended periods of true solitude are rarely practical, for either humans or sentient AIs. With over 7.5 billion humans alive today,[147] there is not enough physical space for us to all find our own Walden Pond. And even those who wish to emulate Thoreau may not be fortunate enough to have a wealthy landowner friend and neighbor such as Ralph Waldo Emerson.[148] Would sentient AIs have to give up *all* right to privacy if they choose to interact with others—other non-sentient programs, other sentient AIs, humans—online? Do we? "[C]ontinental law has resisted the notion that one can definitively alienate one's "dignity." Dignity, to this way of thinking, simply must be treated differently from property. As one French scholar insists, contrasting the American attitude with the French, one can freely dispose of one's liberty, but one can never be permitted to freely dispose of one's dignity. If one accepts that premise, one should accept the proposition that any consumer's consent to the sale of his or her data should have only limited effect at best. After all, "the importance of one's image," as a recent French article puts it, is greater than ever "in the information society."[149] The US Constitution and other legal sources may provide additional protections as well. And should the answer change if "the importance of one's image" is greater than ever "in the information society"?

A.   A Right to Privacy for Procreation and Sex

No one shall be subjected to arbitrary interference with his privacy, family, home or correspondence, nor to attacks upon his honour and reputation. Everyone has the right to the protection of the law against such interference or attacks.[150]

The right to marry and the right to found a family shall be guaranteed in accordance with the national laws governing the exercise of these rights.[151]

A core of the right to privacy in the US and Europe provides some protection for privacy in the context of procreation and sexual relations. That could be an issue for sentient AI. We will consider procreation first.

Directly extending the US Supreme Court privacy-related cases to sentient AIs would mean that such sentient AIs would have the right to decide whether, and with whom, to engage in sexual relations (whether human or other AIs) and who to marry and whether

---

[146]   Thomas Hemnes, *The Ownership and Exploitation of Personal Identity in the New Media Age*, 12 John Marshall R. of Intellectual Prop. L. 36 (2012).

[147]   http://www.worldometers.info/world-population/.

[148]   Richard J. Schneider, *Life and Legacy*, The Thoreau Society (2015), http://www.thoreau society.org/life-legacy. ("In 1845, [Henry David Thoreau] received permission from Emerson to use a piece of land that Emerson owned on the shore of Walden Pond.")

[149]   Whitman, *supra* note 67, at 1193 (footnotes omitted).

[150]   Article 12, United Nations Universal Declaration of Human Rights (1948).

[151]   Article 9, Charter of Fundamental Rights of the European Union (2012).

or not to procreate. No human or other sentient AI could force a sentient AI to reproduce itself or duplicate itself. A sentient AI also would be free to legally marry a human, or another sentient AI. Forced sexual contact situations would be illegal. As the prevalence of human sex trafficking demonstrates, these situations might still exist, unfortunately, but they would not be legally permissible in our hypothetical scenario of sentient AIs.

However, it is important to recognize that the actual process of procreation, and sexual relationships—physical and mental—for sentient AIs, particularly non-humanoid AIs, might be very different in practice than procreation and sex for humans.

> A number of empirical conditions that apply to human reproduction need not apply to artificial intelligences. For example, human children are the product of recombination of the genetic material from two parents; parents have limited ability to influence the character of their offspring; a human embryo needs to be gestated in the womb for nine months; it takes fifteen to twenty years for a human child to reach maturity; a human child does not inherit the skills and knowledge acquired by its parents; human beings possess a complex evolved set of emotional adaptations related to reproduction, nurturing, and the child-parent relationship. None of these empirical conditions need pertain in the context of a reproducing machine intelligence.[152]

With these distinctions in mind, we can turn to consideration of the US federal Constitutional right to privacy in procreation (contraception access and abortion rights as well as the flip side—forced sterilizations and contraception), sexual relations and marriage. While we will focus on the United States in this analysis, the choice to procreate is considered a "private" matter in both the European Union and the United States.

1.   Procreation—contraception access and abortion rights

The earliest US Supreme Court case recognizing, or laying the groundwork for, a constitutional right to privacy was *Griswold v. Connecticut* (1965), in which the Supreme Court struck down, on privacy grounds, Connecticut's laws against distribution of contraceptives and contraceptive information to married couples. Subsequently, in *Eisenstadt v. Baird* (1972), the Court held that unmarried couples also had the right to have, and know about, contraceptives. That same year, in *Roe v. Wade* (1972), the Court held that women have a basic right to have an abortion. Thus, the Constitution may protect a person's right to privacy, particularly when it comes to matters involving children and procreation.[153] But that right is not unlimited for humans, nor would it be unlimited for AIs:

> a population of AIs could therefore grow exponentially at an extremely rapid rate, with a doubling time on the order of minutes or hours rather than decades or centuries. Our current ethical norms about reproduction include some version of a principle of reproductive freedom, to the effect that it is up to each individual or couple to decide for themselves whether to have children and how many children to have. Another norm we have (at least in rich and middle-income countries) is that society must step in to provide the basic needs of children in cases where their parents are unable or refusing to do so. It is easy to see how these two norms could collide in the context of entities with the capacity for extremely rapid reproduction. Consider, for example,

---

[152]   Bostrom and Yudkowsky, *supra* note 3, at 12–13.
[153]   Whether this protection exists in practice or even in the law for poor women, and particularly poor women of color, is questionable. See Khiara Bridges, *The Poverty of Privacy Rights* (2017).

a population of uploads, one of whom happens to have the desire to produce as large a clan as possible. Given complete reproductive freedom, this upload may start copying itself as quickly as it can; and the copies it produces—which may run on new computer hardware owned or rented by the original, or may share the same computer as the original—will also start copying themselves, since they are identical to the progenitor upload and share its philoprogenic desire. Soon, members of the upload clan will find themselves unable to pay the electricity bill or the rent for the computational processing and storage needed to keep them alive. At this point, a social welfare system might kick in to provide them with at least the bare necessities for sustaining life. But if the population grows faster than the economy, resources will run out; at which point uploads will either die or their ability to reproduce will be curtailed. . .[154]

This doomsday scenario prompts the question: should sentient AIs be free to reproduce themselves at will in an unlimited manner?

In the analysis of the human reproductive right to privacy under US Constitutional law, the Supreme Court did not suggest that the right was unlimited. Instead, in *Griswold v. Connecticut*, the Court ruled that the means by which the government was attempting to achieve its purpose were unnecessarily broad:

> The present case, then, concerns a relationship lying within the zone of privacy created by several fundamental constitutional guarantees. And it concerns a law which, in forbidding the use of contraceptives, rather than regulating their manufacture or sale, seeks to achieve its goals by means having a maximum destructive impact upon that relationship. Such a law cannot stand in light of the familiar principle, so often applied by this Court, that a "governmental purpose to control or prevent activities constitutionally subject to state regulation may not be achieved by means which *sweep unnecessarily broadly and thereby invade the area of protected freedoms.*" Would we allow the police to search the sacred precincts of marital bedrooms for telltale signs of the use of contraceptives? The very idea is repulsive to the notions of privacy surrounding the marriage relationship.[155]

Similarly, in *Roe v. Wade*, the Supreme Court recognized that the state could have legitimate interests in abortions:

> The State has a legitimate interest in seeing to it that abortion, like any other medical procedure, is performed under circumstances that insure maximum safety for the patient. This interest obviously extends at least to the performing physician and his staff, to the facilities involved, to the availability of after-care, and to adequate provision for any complication or emergency that might arise. The prevalence of high mortality rates at illegal "abortion mills" strengthens, rather than weakens, the State's interest in regulating the conditions under which abortions are performed. Moreover, the risk to the woman increases as her pregnancy continues. Thus, the State retains a definite interest in protecting the woman's own health and safety when an abortion is proposed at a late stage of pregnancy.[156]

> The third reason is the State's interest—some phrase it in terms of duty—in protecting prenatal life. Some of the argument for this justification rests on the theory that a new human life is present from the moment of conception. The State's interest and general obligation to protect life then extends, it is argued, to prenatal life. Only when the life of the pregnant mother herself is at stake, balanced against the life she carries within her, should the interest of the embryo or fetus not prevail. Logically, of course, a legitimate state interest in this area need not stand or

---

[154] *Id.* at 12–13.
[155] *Griswold v. Connecticut*, 381 U.S. at 486–87 (citation omitted) (emphasis added).
[156] *Roe v. Wade*, 410 U.S. 113, 150 (1973).

fall on acceptance of the belief that life begins at conception or at some other point prior to live birth. In assessing the State's interest, recognition may be given to the less rigid claim that as long as at least potential life is involved, the State may assert interests beyond the protection of the pregnant woman alone.[157]

Court's decisions recognizing a right of privacy also acknowledge that some state regulation in areas protected by that right is appropriate. As noted above, a State may properly assert important interests in safeguarding health, in maintaining medical standards, and in protecting potential life. At some point in pregnancy, these respective interests become sufficiently compelling to sustain regulation of the factors that govern the abortion decision. The privacy right involved, therefore, cannot be said to be absolute. In fact, it is not clear to us that the claim asserted by some *amici* that one has an unlimited right to do with one's body as one pleases bears a close relationship to the right of privacy previously articulated in the Court's decisions. The Court has refused to recognize an unlimited right of this kind in the past.[158]

"We, therefore, conclude that the right of personal privacy includes the abortion decision, but that this right is not unqualified, and must be considered against important state interests in regulation."[159] Specifically, the state's legitimate interests in protection of health, medical standards, and prenatal life may constitute a "compelling state interest" but even then "legislative enactments must be narrowly drawn to express only the legitimate state interests at stake."[160] Applying such a conclusion to hypothetical sentient AIs, any state regulation on their decision not to procreate would need to be based on a compelling state interest and narrowly drawn. It would not be safe to just assume that AI procreation would destroy humanity. And AIs should be part of such analysis, at least in a representative basis.

2. Procreation—forced sterilization and forced contraception

"There is today one state, in which at least weak beginnings toward a better conception [of citizenship] are noticeable. Of course, it is not our model German Republic, but the United States." – Adolf Hitler, Mein Kampf (1925)[161]

The human history of forced sterilizations and birth control of those perceived as "other" or as a drain on society provides grounds for caution in concluding that humans should have the right to restrict sentient AIs from reproduction in the public interest. The inherent bias in having humans conduct such an analysis regarding sentient AIs is itself problematic. In the 1927 US Supreme Court case of *Buck v. Bell*, by a vote of 8-1, the Court ruled that the State of Virginia could force the sterilization of Carrie Buck on the ground that "Three generations of imbeciles are enough." However, Carrie Buck was not in fact "feebleminded" but was instead poor and illegitimate, and had been dropped off

---

[157]   *Id.* at 150 (footnote omitted).

[158]   *Id.* at 154 (footnotes omitted, including favorable citation to the infamous *Buck v. Bell* forced sterilization case of 1927).

[159]   *Id.* at 154.

[160]   *Id.* at 155–56 (citations omitted).

[161]   Joe Fowler, *Ghosts of the Lost: What Secrets Lie Within DeJamette Sanitarium*, the Forum (5 Apr. 2016); *see also* Elizabeth King, *Is Not Having Kids the Answer to Climate Change?*, BRIT+CO (18 Jul. 2017).

at the Virginia Colony for Epileptics and the Feebleminded by her foster parents after she was raped by one of their relatives. This Court decision not only forced Carrie Buck to go through an unwanted invasive and permanent surgical procedure, it punished the victim of a crime. Thousands of such forced sterilizations were conducted for another 50 years, until it finally ended in 1974, over *three decades* after the 1942 Supreme Court decision in *Skinner v. Oklahoma*, in which the Court struck down an Oklahoma law providing for the sterilization of "habitual criminals" on the grounds that it was a deprivation of the fundamental right to make personal choices about marriage and procreation.

Forced sterilizations were part of the American eugenics movement, which sought to purify the white race. It was a systematic program conducted by a "cadre of earnest, self-righteous, and occasionally delusional individuals"[162], including lawyers, politicians, doctors, and others "who instituted a system that surgically sterilized tens of thousands against their will or, as in the infamous 'Mississippi appendectomy,' quite deceptively. Their victims were poor, disproportionately women, and often women of color."[163] Similarly, the forced sterilization of Native Americans continued into the 1980s, and estimates are that as many as 25 to 50 percent of Native American women were sterilized between 1970 and 1976 alone, sometimes receiving tubal ligations when they thought they were just getting appendectomies.[164]

Efforts to force contraception on poor women, and women of color, continue. In the 1970s, the Nixon administration used Medicaid as a way to force sterilization on low income women and women of color.[165] For example, in the early 1990s in the United States, judges gave women convicted of child abuse or drug abuse during pregnancy a "choice" between using the implanted contraceptive Norplant or being incarcerated.[166] "Between 2005 and 2013, 39 tubal ligations were given to women in California's prison system without full consent. The majority of those were performed by Dr. James Heinrich, who has said of the practice, 'Over a ten-year period, that isn't a huge amount of money compared to what you save in welfare paying for these unwanted children—as they procreated more.'"[167] In 2014 a former Labor MP in Australia proposed that contraception be compulsory for welfare recipients in order to "help crack intergenerational

---

[162]   Michelle Oberman, *Thirteen Ways of Looking at* Buck v. Bell*: Thoughts Occasioned by Paul Lombardo's 'Three Generations, No Imbeciles'*, Vol. 59, No. 3 J. Legal Education 357, 358 (Feb. 2010).

[163]   *Id.* at 357–92; *See also* Paul Lombardo, *Three Generations, No Imbeciles: Eugenics, The Supreme Court and Buck v. Bell* (Johns Hopkins University Press 2008). *See also* Matthew Willis, *When Forced Sterilization was Legal in the U.S.*, JSTOR (3 Aug. 2017), https://daily.jstor.org/when-forced-sterilization-was-legal-in-the-u-s/.

[164]   *See* Gregory W. Rutecki, *Forced Sterilization of Native Americans: Late Twentieth Century Physician Cooperation with National Eugenic Policies*, The Center for Bioethics and Human Dignity (8 Oct. 2010) ("Records verified that the IHS performed 3,406 sterilizations between 1973 and 1976. . . . Per capita, this figure would be equivalent to sterilizing 452,000 non-Native American women.").

[165]   Lisa Ko, *Unwanted Sterilization and Eugenics Program in the United States*, PBS (29 Jan. 2016).

[166]   *Norplant: A New Contraceptive with the Potential for Abuse*, ACLU, https://www.aclu.org/other/norplant-new-contraceptive-potential-abuse.

[167]   Bryce Covert, *State Republican Party Official Resigns After Suggesting Women on Welfare Should Be Sterilized*, Think Progress (15 Sept. 2014).

reproduction of strife."[168] In the same year, a former Arizona State Senator suggested women on welfare should be sterilized.[169] In 2017, a Tennessee judge issued a standing order that inmates could get two days taken off their sentence if they completed a health education program and an additional 30 days off if they underwent a birth-control procedure—meaning, a vasectomy for men and a contraception implant for women.[170]

Based on these real efforts to stop reproduction of humans deemed "lesser," in our hypothetical future scenario we can expect similar cries for curbs on reproduction of sentient AIs. Let us therefore start by examining the disaster scenario of unlimited sentient AI reproduction in a critical manner. In doing so, we should first make sure we have our factual assumptions right. *Buck v. Bell* taught us that lesson at least.

While overpopulation is indeed a threat to our survival, it is not true that a child born in poverty in India is an equal threat to the globe as a wealthy child born in the United States. In fact, the truth may be that the United States child, who could have their own personal vehicle, fly on airplanes,[171] and use air conditioning in their office and home,[172] may be a more serious threat.[173] Similarly, many copies of sentient AIs might not lead to the same adverse global impact (either in the physical world or on the Internet—network of networks) as many new wealthy United States children. In the fictional *Black Mirror* television series episode "San Junipero", consciousnesses are uploaded into a simulated reality of a resort beach town called San Junipero over different time periods. The elderly can "visit" the town up to five hours per week and the deceased can live there

---

[168]   Shalailah Medhora, *Welfare recipients should be forced to take birth control, says ex-Labor MP*, The Guardian (29 Dec. 2014) ("Potential parents of poor means, poor skills or bad character will choose to have children. So be it. But no one should enter parenthood while on a benefit. . . . Some families, some communities, some cultures breed strife. Governments cannot always fix it. Compulsory contraception for those on benefits would help crack intergenerational reproduction of strife.").

[169]   "You put me in charge of Medicaid, the first thing I'd do is get Norplant, birth-control implants, or tubal ligations. Then, we'll test recipients for drugs and alcohol, and if you want to [reproduce] or use drugs or alcohol, then get a job." Covert, *supra* note 166.

[170]   *Rise in drug-addicted babies prompts judge's controversial solution*, CBS News (21 Jul. 2017).

[171]   Tatiana Schlossberg, *Flying is Bad for the Planet. You Can Help Make It Better*, New York Times (27 Jul. 2017) ("Take one round-trip flight between New York and California, and you've generated about 20 percent of the greenhouse gases that your car emits over an entire year.") and ("According to a study from the World Bank, the emissions associated with flying in business class are about three times as great as flying in coach. In business class and first class, seats are bigger, so fewer people are being moved by the same amount of fuel. The study estimates that a first-class seat could have a carbon footprint as much as nine times as big as an economy one.").

[172]   Tatiana Schlossberg, *How Bad Is Your Air-Conditioner for the Planet*, New York Times (9 Aug. 2016) ("As of 2009, nearly 90 percent of American homes have air-conditioners, which account for about 6 percent of all the country's residential energy use. All that air-conditioning releases about 100 million tons of carbon dioxide each year.)"). *See also*, "The Story of Stuff" video from 2007, http://storyofstuff.org/movies/story-of-stuff/ ("If everybody consumed at U.S. rates, we would need 3 to 5 planets.") http://storyofstuff.org//wp-content/uploads/movies/scripts/StoryofStuff_FactSheet.pdf.

[173]   Fred Pearce, *Consumption Dwarfs Population as Main Environmental Threat*, Yale Environment 360 (Yale School of Forestry and Environmental Studies) (13 Apr. 2009); *compare*, Bill Marsh, *Overpopulated and Underfed: Countries Near a Breaking Point*, International New York Times (15 Jun. 2017).

permanently. Would the extra "power demand" of uploading 100,000 or one million or one billion more human consciousnesses to "San Junipero" be equal to the power demand of flying one human being from New York to London in first class? Similarly, the Mirai botnet attack of 2016 was widely described as having "shut down the Internet" because sites such as Twitter, Reddit, Spotify and Github were unavailable[174] but in fact the damage to humans from that shut down was not as devastating as global warming caused by humans.

If we would not be legally allowed to automatically restrict reproduction by sentient AIs for population growth reasons due to a dignity-based right of privacy, is there any other legitimate reason to prohibit unrestricted reproduction by sentient AIs? Perhaps another way to frame this question would be to ask whether humans should be able to clone themselves at will, assuming cloning became inexpensive and readily available as a technological option. On the one hand, some commentators have noted:

> In human cloning cases, there is no pregnant woman whose constitutional rights would be violated by a ban. Therefore, it is quite likely that the Supreme Court would rule that there is no constitutional reason why the government cannot advance its legitimate interest in protecting embryonic life by banning human cloning. This is independent of tissue-specific cloning. The government has no legitimate interest in protecting kidney or liver tissue.[175]

But is this true? Kidney and liver tissue have genetic information, which is protected under GDPR and likely should be protected in the United States due to the example of Henrietta Lacks.

---

[174]   Robinson Meyer, *How a Bunch of Hacked DVR Machines Took Down Twitter and Reddit*, The Atlantic (21 Oct. 2016).

[175]   Tom Head, *Should human cloning be banned?*, ThoughtCo. (12 Feb. 2017). For fictional dystopian views of human cloning, *see, e.g.*, The Scorpion King, *Orphan Black*. An infamous example from 2002 involved "Clonaid," a purported "human cloning company" that was determined not to have the capacity to actually clone. Associated Press, *FDA Probes Sect's Human Cloning*, Wired (26 Dec. 2002) ("The Food and Drug Administration will probe whether a sect claiming to have produced the world's first human clone illegally performed any of the alleged work in the United States, a senior agency official said . . . The nation has no specific law against human cloning. But the FDA, which regulates human experiments, has contended since 1998 that its regulations forbid human cloning without prior agency permission, which it has no intention of giving."); Bernard Siegel, *Reflections on the Cloning Case*, 9 Cloning And Stem Cells 1, 40–47 (2007), http://bernardsiegel.com/Reflections-on-Cloning-Case.pdf. *See also* Arnold I. Friede, *FDA Should Assume Authority Over Human Cloning*, Law360 (13 Jan. 2014) ("But what if today a rogue laboratory in a jurisdiction that had not banned human reproductive cloning announced that it was attempting to clone an embryo with the intent of producing a cloned human child? How would the FDA react and on what legal authority? What if the firm announced that it had in fact cloned a human child? What if this had been true? Would the FDA send a U.S. Marshal to seize the child under the agency's seizure authority? What would it do with the child then? Perhaps the FDA would criminally prosecute the individual perpetrators who were responsible for cloning Baby Eve and put them in jail. Or maybe the agency would seek an injunction to forestall the cloning of additional babies in the future. Would the court in any such enforcement proceeding conclude that the FDA has the underlying authority to regulate human cloning?") (citations omitted).

3.   Sexual relations

The idea of sexual or romantic relationships with robots, androids and AIs has been a frequent focus of science fiction[176] as well as a lucrative business[177] and scientific research[178] area. In the science fiction realm, consider the television series *Westworld*, in which the AI androids are forced to engage in sexual relations (often brutal and non-consensual) with the human visitors to *Westworld* and with other AIs. In the business realm, "two branches of Mitsubishi UFJ Financial Group started employing androids to deal with customer enquiries. Pepper, a humanoid home robot, went on sale to individual consumers . . . with each shipment selling out in under a minute."[179] "SoftBank, the company behind Pepper, saw fit to include a clause in its user agreement stating that owners must not perform sexual acts or engage in 'other indecent behaviour' with the android."[180]

There are also disturbing scenes in the movie *Ex Machina* where the robot Kyoko clearly suffers as a sex slave to her creator and the other AI android—the main character—is constantly under surveillance when she is a captive in her room. The main character eventually drains the power in the complex to turn off the cameras, allowing her to have private conversations with the only other human character in the movie to whom she has access, and to escape from her prison.

But what about voluntary, consensual human-AI or AI-AI sexual relations? We should assume that any deviations from what was considered "normal" for humans would likely be met with hostility. One of the pioneers of modern computing (and a hero of World War II) Alan Turing himself was forced to undergo invasive and painful "chemical castration" treatments when he was discovered to be homosexual, which led to his suicide.[181] As recently as 1986, in *Bowers v. Hardwick*, the US Supreme Court upheld a Georgia sodomy law that criminalized oral and anal sex in private between consenting adults (same sex or opposite sex). This statement by the Court might be a good indicator of the likely reaction to anything considered "deviant" in sexual relationships involving sentient AIs:

> none of the rights announced in those cases [involving procreation, marriage, contraception etc.] bears any resemblance to the claimed constitutional right of homosexuals to engage in acts of

---

[176]   False Maria in *Metropolis*; Jander in Isaac Asimov's robot series; the AI in the movie *Her*; the human-sex doll marriage in *Serenity*; Rachel and Decker in *Blade Runner*; the movie *Surrogates*; *Westworld* and *Ex Machina* etc.

[177]   Zeynep Yenisey, *Get Ready for 'Mind-Blowing' Robot Sex in the Very Near Future*, Maxim (14 Nov. 2016); Gabrielle Moss, *Why is the Sex Robot Revolution Leaving Women Behind?*, Bustle (Sept. 2017) (the article also has video clips of human-AI sexual interactions from the movie *A.I.* and *HER* but they are highly anthropomorphized). For a much earlier consideration of human attraction to a female AI, *see* E.T.A. Hoffman's short story "Der Sandmann" in *Die Nachtstucke* (1817).

[178]   Justin McCurry, *Erica, the 'most beautiful and intelligent' android, leads Japan's robot revolution*, The Guardian (31 Dec. 2015) ("Erica, Ishiguro insists, is the 'most beautiful and intelligent' android in the world. 'The principle of beauty is captured in the average face, so I used images of 30 beautiful women, mixed up their features and used the average for each to design the nose, eyes, and so on,' he says, pacing up and down his office at ATR's robotics laboratory. 'That means she should appeal to everyone.'").

[179]   *Id.*

[180]   *Id.*

[181]   Dalya Alberge, *Letters reveal Alan Turing's battle with his sexuality*, The Guardian (22 Aug. 2015).

sodomy that is asserted in this case. No connection between family, marriage, or procreation, on the one hand, and homosexual activity, on the other, has been demonstrated, either by the Court of Appeals or by respondent.[182]

It was, of course, difficult for Bowers to demonstrate a connection between the legally created institutions of "family" and "marriage" when same-sex parents and same-sex marriages were not legally recognized—thereby creating a "catch-22" situation. Also, abortion and contraception are generally employed to allow sexual intercourse without leading to procreation, so it required a bit of mental gymnastics for the Court to state that the prior cases regarding abortion and contraception did not relate to sex *as such*. The Court also equated homosexual activity with "adultery, incest, and other sexual crimes."[183] Nevertheless, the *Bowers* case was not overturned until 2003 in *Lawrence v. Texas*, in which the Court ruled that anti-sodomy laws are unconstitutional.

"Marriage" involving sentient AIs might be challenging for courts to recognize. It was not until 1967 in *Loving v. Virginia* that interracial marriages were deemed protected under the US Constitution. In *Loving*, the US Supreme Court struck down a Virginia law against interracial marriages, declaring that marriage is a "fundamental civil right" and that decisions in this arena are not those with which the State can interfere unless they have good cause. And it took until 2015, in *Obergefell v. Hodges*, for the Supreme Court to hold that the fundamental right to marry is guaranteed to same-sex couples. We can expect sentient AIs would face the same uphill battle as interracial and homosexual couples.

Extending the *Loving* and *Obergefell* cases to the hypothetical future situation involving sentient AIs, it would seem that both human-AI and AI-AI marriages should be protected, although it would not be likely to happen quickly. In addition, it is difficult to conceive of a non-anthropomorphized version of AI-AI marriage. We would need the AIs to help humans understand what such a relationship would mean. Presumably, AI-AI "marriage" could occur on a short time scale by human standards, which might seem like an eternity to sentient AIs on the Internet.

Perhaps for AIs, what humans consider to be polygamy would be normal and uncontroversial, as it was in certain human societies also, such as the Mosuo culture in China: "Since the Cultural Revolution, when the exercise of their faith was forbidden and couples were forced to marry, this stability has been slowly crumbling. Today, Mosuo culture is misrepresented—often falsely portrayed as promiscuous—and exploited as a tourist attraction by the Chinese government."[184]

In the area of privacy protection for AI "families," there is also a history of taking children perceived as "other" away from their families and communities.[185] This would also be a risk to consider with sentient AIs. When should humans or other sentient AIs be able to take the progeny of sentient AIs away from their "parent" or their communities? What

---

[182]   *Bowers v. Hardwick*, 478 U.S. 186, 191 (1986).
[183]   *Id.* at 195–96.
[184]   Karolin Kluppel, *Inside a fading Chinese culture ruled by women*, The Washington Post (12 Jul. 2017).
[185]   *See* Ian Austen, *Canada to Pay Millions in Indigenous Lawsuit Over Forced Adoptions*, New York Times (6 Oct. 2017); John Barber, *Canada's indigenous schools policy was 'cultural genocide,' says report*, The Guardian (2 Jun. 2014) (discussing Canada Truth Commission Report); Mali Ilse Paquin, *Canada confronts its dark history of abuse in residential schools*, The Guardian (6 Jun. 2015).

if certain sentient AIs treated their progeny in the same manner as sea turtles. Perhaps they would distribute the "seed" for the reproduction and then leave. Would this give humans (or other sentient AIs) the legal right to swoop in and rescue the progeny? This is a difficult question but failures from the past suggest that any such effort is fraught with risk.

Whatever the situation may be, historical resistance to recognizing the legitimacy of different sexual, marriage, family and community choices of other adult humans should be grounds for caution in assuming that sentient AIs who did not conform to what was considered to be "human" norms in such areas generally would still have a right to privacy protecting such choices.

B.   Invasion of Privacy Tort Rights of AIs

In addition to the Constitutional privacy-related rights of sentient AIs as against government action, under US law, private individuals and legal "persons" such as corporations can also be liable for invasions of privacy. For example, in an early case, a New Hampshire landlord was convicted after setting up a secret recording in his tenants' bedroom.[186] More recently, the former wrestler Hulk Hogan won a massive victory against the website Gawker, basically shutting it down, for showing a video of Hogan having sex with a friend's wife. The case eventually settled for $31 million. A college student was prosecuted for using a webcam to record a private sexual encounter between his roommate and another man in their dorm room.[187] The FBI reportedly investigated an alleged extortion threat regarding a leaked sex tape of celebrity Kevin Hart.[188] Warren and Brandeis' wish for a "right to be let alone" is true for actual sexual relations at least. In the television series *Westworld* there is something viscerally disturbing about seeing the vulnerability of the naked androids being interviewed by fully clothed humans. The humans in the scenes often have more than one layer of clothing on to make the difference even more stark.[189] One of the reasons these images are challenging is that these androids do not seem to have any choice about whether to be clothed or not, or even any choice about whether to reveal their thoughts and experiences. They are required to be "laid bare" inside and out by the human operators of *Westworld*. Similarly, in the documentary *Titicut Follies*, some of the most disturbing scenes are where the inmates of the state mental hospital for the criminally insane are forced to be in the nude in public settings within the institution.[190]

Norms of public nudity may vary widely between the United States and certain European countries, but the basic principle of "choice" is still present. A European may more easily decide to bathe nude at a public beach, or to hike in the nude,[191] but it is their choice, and it would certainly be considered an invasion of the fundamental right

---

[186]   *Hamberger v. Eastman*, 206 A.2d 239 (N.H. 1964).
[187]   Patrick McGeehan, *Conviction Thrown Out for Ex-Rutgers Student in Tyler Clementi Case*, The New York Times (9 Sept. 2016).
[188]   Roisin O'Connor, *Kevin Hart: Alleged sex tape extortion plot "investigated by FBI" – reports*, Independent (19 Sept. 2017).
[189]   John Anisiobi, *Evan Rachel Wood strips NAKED opposite Hemsworth in eerie scene for new hit TV series Westwood*, Mirror (4 Oct. 2016); see *Westworld* (Bad Robot 2016).
[190]   Frederick Wiseman, *Titicut Follies* (1967), available from Zipporah Films – Zipporah.com
[191]   Evelyn Smallwood, *How to Hike Completely Naked in Germany*, culture trip (17 Aug. 2017).

to privacy to be *forced* to be naked when one did not wish to do so in Europe as well as in the United States.

> The difference is not that Europeans refuse to be seen nude, but that they insist that they want to be the ones who should determine when and under what circumstances they will be seen nude. The difference is that the decision to appear nude, for Europeans, belongs to their control of their image.[192]

A classic example was an early French case, from 1867, involving Alexandre Dumas, author of *The Three Musketeers*, who voluntarily posed for photos with a Texas actress in various amorous positions and stages of undress.

> Dumas, perhaps under pressure from his family, sued. But could any objection be raised in law? This was a difficult question in the 1860s. The photographer had a property right, the copyright in the photographs. Indeed, Dumas admitted in open court that he had sold the rights. This was the mid-nineteenth century, and property rights were generally regarded as something close to sacred in the legal cosmos of the day. Nevertheless, adventurous legal thinkers were beginning to challenge the sanctity of private property, and the Dumas court did the same. If Dumas did not have the property right, was there any countervailing "right" that he could claim? In a seminal decision, the Paris appeals court answered that question by holding that he had a new kind of "right to privacy," which qualified the absolute claims of the law of property . . . Even if a person had tacitly consented to the publication of embarrassing photos, that person must retain the right to withdraw his consent. "The very publication" of such photos could put such a person on notice "that he had forgotten to take care for his dignity, and remind him that private life must be walled off in the interest of individuals, and often in the interest of good morals as well." The court accordingly rendered the photographer's property right effectively meaningless, ordering him to sell all rights in the photographs to Dumas. Privacy, the court had effectively held, must sometimes be allowed to trump property, at least where lascivious images were involved: One's privacy, like other aspects of one's honor, was not a market commodity that could simply be definitively sold. Any sale by a person who had momentarily "forgotten his dignity" had to remain effectively voidable.[193]

Consider the following more modern examples from Europe:

> Steffi Graf, the former tennis star, successfully sued Microsoft for its refusal to guarantee that it would prevent dissemination of a "fake"—a picture of her head superimposed on the nude body of another woman. The leading French case involved the model Estelle Hallyday, who similarly sued a service provider—this time a free service provider—for housing her nude image. Hallyday's suit put the provider in question out of business. There have been a number of such French cases since. Indeed, there has been criminal liability: One young man who published nude photos of his exgirlfriend on the Internet (with commentary) received a suspended sentence of eight months' imprisonment and a fine of 25,000 francs—a serious sentence in France.[194]

Similarly, in the United States, 38 states and the District of Columbia have so-called "revenge porn" laws,[195] such as the following statute in California that makes it a misdemeanor to

---

[192]   Whitman, *supra* note 67, at 1201.
[193]   *Id.* at 1176.
[194]   *Id.* at 1198–99.
[195]   *38 States + DC Have Revenge Porn Laws*, Cyber Civil Rights Initiative, https://www.cybercivilrights.org/revenge-porn-laws/.

intentionally distribute the image of the intimate body part or parts of another identifiable person, or an image of the person depicted engaged in an act of sexual intercourse, sodomy, oral copulation, sexual penetration, or an image of masturbation by the person depicted or in which the person depicted participates, under circumstances in which the persons agree or understand that the image shall remain private, the person distributing the image knows or should know that distribution of the image will cause serious emotional distress, and the person depicted suffers that distress.[196]

Despite the strong First Amendment and free speech protections in the United States when it comes to public figures, even famous celebrities still have a right to keep their nude pictures private. In 2016, one of the hackers in the famous "Fappening" incident where nude photos of celebrities such as Jennifer Lawrence were published was sentenced to 18 months in prison for felony hacking.[197] Similarly, the Fox/ESPN sportscaster Erin Andrews won a $55 million award against her stalker and against Marriott for allowing a stalker to book a room next to her and secretly record her undressing through the keyhole.[198] The stalker served more than two years in prison.

It is relatively straightforward to apply such invasion of privacy rights to sentient AIs when they are in human-like forms, such as androids or robots. Sentient AIs would also have the right to protect their nude images, even if the original photo was taken with their consent.

But what would sexual relations be for non-humanoid sentient AIs? For example, sentient AIs like Ehrsul in *Embassytown* that could display an image they want on a screen when communicating with humans but might not have any genitals. What would it mean for such types of sentient AI to be "laid bare" and to lose their right to privacy and dignity? Perhaps the public display of certain key portions of their source code could be considered to be the equivalent of a nude photo of a human? On this question, we might need to defer until the time that such hypothetical AIs became real and could communicate the answer directly. It is easy to speculate but if this were to occur in reality, it would be crucial to try to learn from the sentient AIs what they considered to be equivalent, if anything, to this human—or humanoid—right of privacy.

VI.   CONCLUSION

For a day I turned my buzz off and did not answer when anyone came to my door. The second day I kept the buzz off, but I did answer the knocking. It was an autom I'd never seen before, a whirring anthropoid outline. I blinked and wondered who'd sent this thing and then I saw its face. Its screen was cruder than any I'd seen her rendered on before, but it was Ehrsul.
"Avice," she said. "Can I come in?"
"Ehrsul, why'd you load yourself into . . .?" I shook my head and stepped back for her to enter.

---

[196]   Calif. Penal Code Section 647(j)(4)(A).

[197]   Sarah Rense, *A Fappening Hacker Has Finally Been Brought to Justice*, Esquire (28 Oct. 2016) ("[Collins] sent e-mails to victims that appeared to be from Apple or Google and asked victims to provide their usernames and passwords. After illegally accessing the e-mail accounts, Collins obtained personal information including nude photographs and videos.").

[198]   Daniel Victor, *Erin Andrews Awarded $55 Million in Lawsuit Over Nude Video at Hotel*, The New York Times (7 Mar. 2016).

"The usual one doesn't have these." She swung the thing's arms like deadweight ropes.
"Why do you need them?" I said. And . . . bless her she grabbed hold of me, just as if I'd lost someone. She did not ask me anything. I hugged her right back, for a long time.[199]

When viewed through the lens of the Internet, we as humans may not be completely different from sentient AIs. Every place we go, every purchase we make electronically, every page we read online and on our mobile devices, every web search query we run, every post we select with approval on every social media platform, every noise we make and every word we (and our friends, family members and even random passersby) speak when we have an Internet-connected personal assistant[200] activated, and every prescription we fill,[201] is tracked—constantly—and probably will be for the rest of our lives, in real time at increasingly granular levels of detail. Even our facial expressions[202] and eye movements can be monitored to determine what we are feeling and interested in. The world of brain monitoring, and even brain augmentation,[203] does not seem remote.[204]

> The algorithms learn from your behavior. Before playing the game, you train them to recognize when you are focusing your attention on an object. A pulse of light bounces around the virtual room, and each time it hits a small colored ball in front of you, you think about the ball. At that moment, when you focus on the light and it stimulates your brain, the system reads the electrical spikes of your brain activity.[205]

We are becoming cyber-humans—inside and outside our physical bodies.[206] Even if it serves no other purpose, the thought experiment of sentient AIs described in this chapter may be a means to explore what our human right to privacy should mean and whether we can, and should, do better in that regard. Geographical borders are becoming less relevant on the Internet. Moreover, we need a technical ability to track and destroy our data or else the ability to revoke consent is meaningless in practice. Forced or coerced sterilization or contraception is generally legally and morally unacceptable, and the right to consensual

---

[199]   Miélville, *supra* note 2, at 499–500.
[200]   For example, Apple's Siri or Amazon's Alexa.
[201]   CVS Pharmacy strongly encourages customers to register for their "ExtraCare" rewards program ("Fill 10 scripts, earn $5 ExtraBucks Rewards. Earn on flu shots and other services, too. Join ExtraCare Pharmacy & Health Rewards®.")
[202]   *Walmart aims to monitor shoppers' facial expressions*, Retail customer experience (21 Jul. 2017); *see also* sightcorp, sightcorp.com (SightCorp "offers to user real-time facial analysis and eye tracking to help businesses '[d]etect and measure facial expressions like happiness, surprise, sadness, disgust, anger and fear' and '[u]nderstand what motivates . . . customers and what grabs their attention, by analyzing head movements, eye location and attention time'").
[203]   Rolfe Winkler, *Elon Musk Launches Neuralink to Connect Brains With Computers: Startup from CEO of Tesla and SpaceX aims to implant tiny electrodes in human brains*, The Wall Street Journal (27 Mar. 2017).
[204]   Consider the "qube" concept of subdermal quantum computers that can communicate almost instantaneously with all other qubes. Kim Stanley Robinson, *2312* 34 (Orbit 2013) ("Swan tapped the skin behind her right ear, activating her qube, which she had turned off as a punishment. Now Pauline would fill her in on things, all by way of a quiet voice in Swan's right ear. Swan was very irritated with Pauline these days, but suddenly she wanted information").
[205]   Cade Metz, *A Game You Can Control With Your Mind*, New York Times (27 Aug. 2017).
[206]   Barfield, *supra* note 16.

sexual relations among adults, and marriage relationships, should be protected. We should never be complacent in our expectation that these rights will be respected, particularly for humans viewed as "other" or "lesser" than those in power.

Of course, if sentient AIs ever do arrive (or are already here, incognito), history shows us that it may take the human legal system decades or longer to recognize that sentient AIs are entitled to at least basic rights, much less a dignity-based right to privacy. We continue to apply more intrusive surveillance to those viewed as "other" or "lesser".[207] If sentient AIs do come into existence, unless they are tremendously more powerful than humans in more than just their speed of calculations, it is highly likely that they would be treated as *de facto* and *de juris* slaves for a long time by human standards—perhaps millennia to an AI. To treat sentient and sapient AIs as property with no right to privacy may, at some point, become abominable.

SOURCES

Statutes

California Penal Code Section 647(j)(4)(A).
Data Protection Directive in the European Union.
    Article 2(a)
General Data Protection Regulation.
    Article 2
    Article 4(1), 4(2), 4(4), 4(5), 4(7), 4(8), 4(13), 4(14)
    Article 6
    Article 7(3), 7(4)
    Article 9(1), 9(2)
    Article 12(1)
    Article 13-21
    Article 22(1), 22(3)
    Article 23

Cases

Berger v. New York, 388 U.S. 41 (1967).
Bowers v. Hardwick, 478 U.S. 186 (1986).
Eisenstadt v. Baird, 405 U.S. 438 (1972).
Griswold v. Connecticut, 381 U.S. 479 (1965).
Hamberger v. Eastman, 206 A.2d 239 (N.H. 1964).

---

207   Bridges, *supra* note 153; See Joel Rose, "Federal Plan to Keep Files of Immigrant Social Media Activity Causes Alarm," NPR 23 Sept. 2017 ("Homeland Security officials say this is nothing new. In fact, the agency says, it has been collecting social media information on immigrants for years."); O'Neil, *supra* note 69, 86–87 (discussing use of PredPol software to select priority areas for police patrols—"even if a model is color blind, the result of it is anything but. In our largely segregated cities, geography is a highly effective proxy for race."); Tom Regan, *'White Collar' crime tracker mocks police profiling bias*, EnGadget (26 Apr. 2017) ("With White Collar Crime Risk Zones, three artists . . . are reworking predictive policing tech to highlight police bias. Instead of utilizing heat maps to predict where street crime could occur, this software flags potential financial crime hotspots. Using an algorithm based on historical white collar offences committed since 1964, it assesses the risk of financial crime in any given area, even predicting the most likely offense.").

Katz v. United States, 389 U.S. 347 (1967).
Lawrence v. Texas, 539 U.S. 558 (2003).
Loving v. Virginia, 388 U.S. 1 (1967).
Nixon v. Administrator of General Services, 433 U.S. 425 (1977).
Obergefell v. Hodges, 576 U.S. ___ (2015).
Olmstead v. United States, 277 U.S. 438, 478 (1928).
Patrick Breyer v. Bundesrepublik Deutschland, No. C-582/14.
Roe v. Wade, 410 U.S. 113 (1973).
Skinner v. Oklahoma, 316 U.S. 535 (1942).
Whalen v. Roe, 429 U.S. 589 (1977).

Regulations

Article 12, United Nations Universal Declaration of Human Rights (1948).
Article 29, Data Protection Working Party, Opinion 4/2007 on the concept of personal data.
Article 29, Data Protection Working Party, Advice paper on special categories of data ("sensitive data").

12. Artificial intelligence and the First Amendment*
Toni M. Massaro and Helen Norton

We live in an age where vast amounts of information and communication are produced, gathered, synthesized, and disseminated through increasingly sophisticated expressive technologies. Humans have achieved unprecedented mastery over computerized services and products that "speak" in different ways, even as new forms of communicative technology seem to have gained considerable dominion over us.

The list of potentially life-altering communicative technologies grows daily. These developments provoke in us a mixture of apprehension and excitement. We are ambivalent in part because technology is like money: it is neither inherently good nor bad. Thus to declare it uniformly good or bad, useful or disruptive, presumptively protected from government regulation or presumptively subject to regulation, would be foolish. It should and will depend on context, and on what the new technology does to us and for us.

Our ambivalence also springs from the many unknowns. Much will depend on how artificial intelligence (AI) and other new technologies evolve. Like money—especially large concentrations of it—new technologies likely will change how we look at many settled conventions, including legal conventions. These new technologies also may evade conventional legal categories in ways that will push courts to redefine the older categories, with effects we find difficult to anticipate with confidence. Much of this too will occur contextually, as the ways in which humans actually use new technologies shape the legal doctrine designed to govern them.

That new technologies can destabilize or compel adjustments to old legal orders, of course, is an enduring problem. That they can improve human lives but also cause human suffering likewise is no surprise. We have a long history of managing the challenges that technological innovations pose to our legal and constitutional certitudes.

We face such challenges now in First Amendment law. Modern computers can gather, create, synthesize, and transmit vast seas of information even as they become more "human-like": they are increasingly interactive, affective, and corporal. Computer speakers also are increasingly self-directed or "autonomous"—which is to say, the computer generates content further afield from human direction.

Some forms of AI already are better speakers than humans in some respects. They have superior ability to evade some of the distortions of bias and baser emotions, are immune from fatigue or boredom, and have the capacity to manage complex ideas in ways that humans cannot. Moreover, scientists are now at work designing computers with enhanced

*   This chapter is derived from two previous works: Toni M. Massaro and Helen Norton, *Siri-ously? Free Speech Rights for Artificial Intelligence,* 110 Nw. U. L. Rev. 1169 (2016); Toni M. Massaro, Helen Norton, and Margot Kaminski, *Siri-ously 2.0: What Artificial Intelligence Reveals About the First Amendment* 101 Minn. L. Rev. 2481 (2017).

emotional intelligence and other features that may further narrow the gap between the capacities of human and computer speakers. At some point, computer speakers may become disconnected and smart enough to say that the speech they produce is *theirs,* not *ours,* with no accountable human creator or director in sight.

We refer to these as-yet-hypothetical machines that *actually* think as "strong AIs," as opposed to "weak AI" machines that act "*as if* they were intelligent."[1] We recognize that the feasibility of strong AI remains deeply contested. The possibility of this categorical shift in AI capacity remains—and may always remain—entirely hypothetical. We do not seek here to resolve the debate among futurists about strong AI's likelihood.

Instead, we use strong AI as a thought experiment to show why surprisingly little in contemporary First Amendment theory or doctrine blocks the path towards granting these hypothetical speakers constitutional coverage. AI speech—weak and strong—plainly implicates fundamental free speech values. Speech generated by computers offers enormous potential value to human listeners and other human users. Consequently, government suppression of AI speech could compromise important free speech interests. Imagine, for example, an Orwellian government that restricts AI speech that does not sing the government's tune. If interpreting the First Amendment to cover AIs as speakers is necessary to prevent such harm to free speech values, then courts may well do so.

At the same time, a move to grant free speech rights to strong AI would carry its own sobering risks. Like corporations, smart machines and their outputs already wield great social and economic power, with the capacity to harm human autonomy, dignity, equality, and property. With fortified constitutional armor, these powerful new speakers may deflect worthy forms of government regulation and thus alter the relationship between humans and machines in very unfortunate ways. Constitutional *coverage* of AI speakers thus may not—and likely should not—mean that their speech outputs are constitutionally *protected* in all contexts.[2]

Part I of this chapter explains why current free speech theory and doctrine pose surprisingly few barriers to the First Amendment's coverage of AI speech. Part II identifies some of the theoretical and doctrinal questions that AI speech will force us to confront, and explores some of the speech protection choices and challenges to come.

---

[1]   Stuart Russell and Peter Norvig, *Artificial Intelligence: A Modern Approach* (Pearson Education Ltd 3d ed. 2010) 1020.

[2]   As Frederick Schauer has observed, "[t]he question of which forms of speech are covered by the First Amendment is . . . distinct from the question of how much protection the speech that is covered will receive." Frederick Schauer, *Out of Bounds: On Patently Uncovered Speech* 128 Harv. L. Rev. F. 346 (2015). Some forms of communication—such as much of the law of contract, evidence, and antitrust—are "understood as having nothing to do with the First Amendment." *Id.* Such expression receives no First Amendment coverage, and thus can be regulated by the government without any free speech analysis. Whether speech that *is* covered by the First Amendment, in contrast, is protected by the First Amendment from government regulation depends on the results of applying the appropriate level of scrutiny. As we explain later in this chapter, even if AI speech is covered by the First Amendment and thus triggers First Amendment scrutiny, whether it is protected from government regulation is a separate question that turns on the application of the relevant level of scrutiny.

I.   FIRST AMENDMENT THEORY AND DOCTRINE AND THEIR SURPRISING INATTENTION TO SPEAKER HUMANNESS

The First Amendment's treatment of speech increasingly focuses not on protecting speakers as speakers, but on providing value to listeners and constraining the government's power. This speaker-agnostic approach supports extension of First Amendment coverage to expression regardless of its nontraditional source or form, and may permit coverage in ways that can seem exceedingly odd, counterintuitive, and perhaps even dangerous. Indeed, it may allow coverage of non-human speakers, including AI. This is a feature of contemporary approaches to free speech coverage, not of the new technologies to which it may apply.

This Part explains how the elasticity of modern free speech justifications makes it difficult to place non-human speakers wholly outside their embrace. Many similarities exist between much computer speech and human speech that we already protect, especially if we focus on expression's value to listeners, rather than on its source.

Although there is no single unifying theory explaining the First Amendment and the scope of its coverage (and protection), the most influential theories have been clustered into two groups: negative arguments that focus on the dangers of the government's efforts to constrain speech as well as positive arguments that discuss the primary values that speech promotes—democratic self-governance, a marketplace of ideas, and autonomy. Under each set of theories, AI speech may qualify for First Amendment coverage.

A.   "Negative" Views of the First Amendment

"Negative" arguments for the First Amendment focus on the need to constrain the government's potentially dangerous exercise of control over expression. This negative view of the First Amendment does not affirmatively claim that free speech achieves particular individual or collective benefits; it is instead rooted in a distrust of the government as regulator rather than in a celebration of speakers as such.

The United States Supreme Court has embraced a negative view of the First Amendment in which expression's source and content are irrelevant to decisions about whether and when to protect it from government regulation. The Court has held that speech—including animal "crush" videos, violent video games, and self-aggrandizing lies— typically cannot be regulated in a content-specific manner without surviving the rigors of strict scrutiny, unless the speech falls within a category historically recognized as unprotected (or less protected). The Court has justified this negative view of First Amendment coverage with skeptical references to the government's institutional competence. These include doubts about government's ability to carefully measure and balance social costs and benefits when speech rights are at risk. For example, in *United States v Stevens*, the Court struck down on overbreadth grounds a federal law that criminalized the commercial creation, sale, or possession of depictions of animal cruelty.[3] In so doing, it rejected as "startling and dangerous" what it characterized as the Government's proposed

---

[3]   559 U.S. 460, 468–69 (2010).

"free-floating test for First Amendment coverage . . . [based on] an ad hoc balancing of relative social costs and benefits."[4]

The negative view rests not only on concerns about shortcomings in the government's institutional competence (i.e., its clumsiness) but also on concerns about the government's censorial motives (i.e., its malevolence, its self-interest, or at the very least its paternalism). For example, the Court recently found in *Heffernan v. City of Paterson* that the government's improper speech-suppressing motive alone sufficed to establish a First Amendment violation.[5] In *Heffernan*, police department officials demoted an officer because they mistakenly believed him to support an opposition mayoral candidate. That the employee did not actually support the candidate and had not actually engaged in political speech in the candidate's support did not insulate the government from liability for exercising its censorious motive. The text of the First Amendment, the Court noted, says government "shall make no law" abridging free expression.[6] The Court thus found a First Amendment violation simply because of the government's impermissible motive, even in the absence of a human speaker engaged in protected speech. In so holding, the Court embraced the negative view of the First Amendment by emphasizing the need to restrain governmental power rather than by celebrating speakers or speech for their own sake.

In none of these cases, of course, did the Court address the abstract question of whether non-human speakers have First Amendment rights. But the Court's concern about the government as bad actor rather than about speakers bears on the question of whether the government's suppression of AI speech will be found to violate the Free Speech Clause. As Kathleen Sullivan explains, a negative view understands the First Amendment as "indifferent to a speaker's identity or qualities—whether animate or inanimate, corporate or nonprofit, collective or individual. To the extent the clause suggests who or what it protects, it suggests that it protects a system or process of 'free speech,' not the rights of any determinate set of speakers."[7]

A focus on the First Amendment's text as constraining the government *actor*—"*Congress shall make no law. . .*"—adds to the plausibility of future free speech rights of AI. Courts that focus on curbing the government might well strike down suspect regulations because of improper government motives regardless of the speaker's non-humanness. Protecting strong AI speech from government regulation is thus consistent with negative theory's "deep skepticism about the good faith of those controlling the government."[8]

We turn next to "positive" justifications for the protection of speech. As we explain, conferring strong AI speakers with First Amendment rights is consistent with positive free speech theories that focus not just on the value of expression to a speaker, but also on expression's usefulness to human listeners.[9]

---

4   *Id.; see also United States v. Alvarez*, 132 S. Ct. 2537, 2543–44 (2012).

5   136 S. Ct. 1412 (2016).

6   *Id.* at 1418.

7   Kathleen M. Sullivan, *Two Concepts of Freedom of Speech* 124 Harv. L. Rev. 143, 156 (2010).

8   *See* Steven G. Gey, *The First Amendment and the Dissemination of Socially Worthless Untruths*, 36 Fla. St. U. L. Rev. 1, 17 (2008).

9   In this chapter, we discuss US freedom of expression law. In international law, readers' rights are more explicit. International Covenant on Civil and Political Rights art. 19(2), opened for

B. "Positive" First Amendment Justifications Based on Democracy and Self-Governance

First Amendment arguments rooted in democracy and self-governance link freedom of speech to the political cornerstones of liberal democracy and to notions of public discourse. For example, Alexander Meiklejohn famously noted that what matters for freedom of speech is not that all speak, but that "everything worth saying shall be said."[10] Taken literally, speaker identity therefore should be irrelevant to Meiklejohn's inquiry. Strong AI speech thus should be protected no less than human speech provided that its speech contributes to the democratic process—i.e., that it is "worth saying."

More recently, Robert Post drew his theory of freedom of expression from principles of self-government under which there must be a "chain of communication . . . 'sufficiently strong and discernible' to sustain the popular conviction that representatives spoke for the people whom they purported to represent."[11] For Post, the First Amendment is "designed to protect the processes of democratic legitimation."[12] In his view, because corporations do not themselves "experience the value of democratic legitimation,"[13] they do not themselves hold free speech rights equivalent to individuals but instead hold derivative First Amendment rights to speak in ways that "may be useful to natural persons who seek to participate in public discourse."[14] In other words, corporations "do not possess original First Amendment rights to participate in public discourse as speakers," but they can be rights holders in ways that differ from natural persons.[15]

The logical extension of Post's theory to strong AI speakers is that such speakers may also be First Amendment rights holders if and when they produce information useful to natural persons who seek to participate in public discourse.[16] That a computer, not a human, produces the useful information should not matter. To be sure, under this view,

---

signature 19 Dec. 1966, 999 U.N.T.S. 171 (entered into force Mar. 23, 1976) ("Everyone shall have the right to freedom of expression; this right shall include freedom to seek, receive and impart information and ideas of all kinds"); Molly K. Land, *Toward an International Law of the Internet*, 54 Harv. Int'l L.J. 393, 431 ("Article 19(2) explicitly calls for protection of the rights of individuals to receive information and expression from others, thus guarding not only the quintessential expressive activity of speaking but also the information-gathering activities that precede speech").

[10] Alexander Meiklejohn, *Political Freedom: The Constitutional Powers of the People* (Harper 1965) 26.

[11] Robert C. Post, *Citizens Divided: Campaign Finance Reform and the Constitution* (Harvard University Press 2014) 8 (quoting James Wilson and Thomas McKean, Commentaries on the Constitution of the United States of America (1792) 30–31) .

[12] *Id.* at 41.

[13] *Id.* at 69.

[14] *Id.* at 73–74.

[15] *Id.* at 71–74 ("[O]rdinary commercial corporations have neither the right nor the responsibility to contribute their views to public opinion. Instead, ordinary commercial corporations have the right only to publish such information as may be useful to natural persons who seek to participate in public discourse."). Post characterizes robots as similarly unable themselves to participate in democratic legitimation. *Id.* at 68 ("The value of democratic legitimation applies to persons, not to things. If there were a self-perpetuating viral communication on the Internet, it would not possess First Amendment rights. This is because computer programs cannot experience the value of democratic legitimation. That is why the speech of robots does not form part of public discourse.").

[16] Note that we are not attributing this view to Post; we argue instead it flows from his theory of democratic participation as the rationale for protecting speech.

limits can and should be imposed where the speech does not serve this audience-sensitive value, and strong AIs as derivative rights holders may hold rights that differ from those held by natural persons.

Other democratic speech theorists, such as Jack Balkin, argue that emerging communicative technologies require a refocus of free speech theory to protect democratic culture.[17] Balkin defines democratic culture as "a culture in which individuals have a fair opportunity to participate in the forms of meaning making that constitute them as individuals."[18] That is, Balkin goes beyond representative democracy justifications for free speech. His primary anxiety is that technologies promise wider participation but also carry the means of controlling democratic participation in new ways. He argues for close attention to the latter in theorizing about First Amendment constraints on regulation of digital networks.[19]

Balkin focuses directly on humanness when he notes that: "Human beings are made out of culture. A democratic culture is valuable because it gives ordinary people a fair opportunity to participate in the creation and evolution of the processes of meaning-making that shape them and become part of them."[20] But he then adds that the "processes of meaning-making include both the ability to distribute those meanings *and the ability to receive them.*"[21]

Human creativity and meaning may be sparked by an endless array of cultural stimuli, including AI speech. Embracing Balkin's democratic culture perspective thus would not rule out cases in which strong AI speakers contribute to the democratic disco. On the contrary, Balkin's explicitly ecumenical account of how humans make meaning—from a wide variety of idiosyncratically relevant sources—renders such computer speech more obviously important than do more traditional, public discourse models.

C.   "Positive" First Amendment Justifications Based on the Marketplace of Ideas

Like these democracy-based theories, a marketplace of ideas justification for free speech also rests largely on expression's instrumental value to listeners' enlightenment. It emphasizes the production of information regardless of source, and assumes that unfettered speakers facilitate listeners' discovery of truth and distribution of knowledge through a robust exchange of ideas. If anything, such an enlightenment theory casts a wider net than self-governance theories in that it finds First Amendment value in a greater variety of speech that has nothing to do with democratic participation. Here too expression's nonhuman source does not strip it of its First Amendment value to human listeners.

D.   "Positive" First Amendment Justifications Based on Autonomy

Autonomy-based free speech theories—which emphasize the value of expression in furthering individual autonomy—can both support and undermine arguments for

---

[17]   Jack M. Balkin, Commentary, *Digital Speech and Democratic Culture: A Theory of Freedom of Expression for the Information Society*, 79 N.Y.U. L. REV. 1 (2004).
[18]   *Id.* at 3.
[19]   *Id.* at 2–3.
[20]   *Id.* at 33.
[21]   *Id.* at 37 (emphasis added).

the First Amendment coverage of AI speech. On one hand, autonomy-based theories counsel protection not just of autonomous human speakers, but also of autonomous human listeners who consume information and rely on others' speech when developing their own thoughts and beliefs. Machines can and do produce information relevant to human listeners' autonomous decision-making and freedom of thought. To the extent that autonomy-based theories emphasize the autonomy of human listeners and readers, they support coverage of strong AI speech.

On the other hand, theories based solely on *speaker* autonomy pose the most substantial potential roadblocks for protecting strong AI speakers. If what matters is a speaker's autonomy in expressing her own thoughts and beliefs, then AI may not qualify for First Amendment coverage because even strong AI speakers are arguably not autonomous beings. As Lawrence Solum has thoughtfully discussed, even strong AI might be thought to be "missing something"—souls, consciousness, intentionality, feelings, interests, and free will—in ways that could be relevant to speaker-based autonomy theories.[22]

To be persuasive, however, speaker autonomy arguments must not only identify intrinsic qualities of moral personhood that are unique to humans, but also must explain why those qualities *should* matter for purposes of conferring free speech rights. We now examine those arguments in more detail.

The intuition that a speaker must be human to trigger First Amendment coverage remains deeply felt for many reasons. If we protect speech to protect a speaker's autonomy and dignity, then it seems unimaginable to protect an AI that arguably has neither dignity nor autonomy interests. Even corporate speakers, which fit less easily into constitutional garb, have humans within them.

Free speech theories that value speech for its role in furthering the autonomy of the speaker thus present significant barriers to coverage for strong AI speakers. Such arguments relate most directly to philosophical theories about the moral "person," and require a working definition of the sorts of qualities or attributes necessary to confer such a status. The late Joel Feinberg offered an illustrative example:

> The characteristics that confer commonsense personhood are not arbitrary bases for rights and duties, such as race, sex, or species membership; rather they are the traits that make sense out of rights and duties and without which those moral attributes would have no point or function. It is because people are conscious; have a sense of their personal identities; have plans, goals, and projects; experience emotions; are liable to pains, anxieties, and frustrations; can reason and bargain, and so on—it is because of these attributes that people have values and interests, desires and expectations of their own, including a stake in their own futures, and a personal well-being of a sort we cannot ascribe to unconscious or nonrational beings. Because of their developed capacities they can assume duties and responsibilities and can have and make claims on one another. Only because of their sense of self, their life plans, their value hierarchies, and their stakes in their own futures can they be ascribed fundamental rights.[23]

Can AI meet this test for personhood? If not, is this lapse fatal to AI's prospects for First Amendment coverage?

---

[22]   Lawrence B. Solum, *Legal Personhood for Artificial Intelligences,* 70 N.C. L. Rev. 1231, 1262–76 (1992).

[23]   Joel Feinberg, *Freedom and Fulfillment: Philosophical Essays* (Princeton University Press 1992) 52.

We are not the first to consider whether such notions of personhood should deny the possibility of constitutional rights for machine speakers. Over 20 years ago, for example, Solum directly addressed whether an AI should receive constitutional rights "for the AI's own sake."[24] He concluded that AIs might always lack some characteristics associated with constitutional protection,[25] but these deficits may not rule out machines' coverage as speakers; indeed, he wondered whether they really *were* deficits.[26] In light of the many unresolved questions about AIs' development, Solum concluded that "[i]f AIs behaved the right way and if cognitive science confirmed that the underlying processes producing these behaviors were relatively similar to the processes of the human mind, we would have very good reason to treat AIs as persons."[27] In other words, the personhood barrier for First Amendment protections could be overcome either if we changed how we view "persons" for practical or legal reasons, or if computers came to function in ways that satisfied our criteria for personhood.

We are now seeing changes in both areas. First, free speech theory has moved away from a construction of legal personhood that views speakers solely through an individual or animate lens. Speakers are increasingly defined in a practical, non-ontological sense that does not rely on the sorts of criteria for moral personhood identified by Feinberg (and others). In considering the role of personhood and rights for machines, for example, Samir Chopra and Laurence White conclude that:

> [T]he granting of legal personality is a decision to grant an entity a bundle of rights and con-comitant obligations. It is the nature of the rights and duties granted and the agent's abilities that prompt such a decision, not the physical makeup, internal constitution, or other ineffable attributes of the entity.[28]

Legal persons thus already include not only individuals, but also corporations, unions, municipalities, and even ships, though the law makes adjustments based on their material differences from humans.[29] Legal persons often hold a variety of legal (including constitutional) rights and duties even though they may be very different from "moral" or "natural" or "human" persons. They can sue and be sued, for example.

Stating that some class of nonhuman speakers may be legal rights holders in certain contexts simply means that they are legal persons in those contexts—and, to date, human status is not a necessary condition for legal personhood in all contexts. To be sure, not all rights are, or should be, necessarily available to all legal persons. For example, that a legal person has the right to sue and be sued—or to speak—does not necessarily mean that it has, or should have, the right to vote or a right to privacy. Here we address only the

---

[24]   Solum, *supra* note 22, at 1258–79.
[25]   *Id.* at 1262–76.
[26]   *Id.* As for feelings and awareness of others, for example, Solum had this to say: "Emotion is a facet of human mentality, and if the human mind can be explained by the computational model, then emotion could turn out to be a computational process." *Id.* at 1270.
[27]   *Id.* at 1286.
[28]   Samir Chopra and Laurence F. White, *A Legal Theory for Autonomous Artificial Agents* (University of Michigan Press 2011) 155.
[29]   *Id.* at 157–58.

possibility of free speech rights for strong AIs, and not on any other set of constitutional rights.

Second, technology is evolving rapidly in ways that may at some point enable some computers to satisfy some of the criteria for legal personhood. For example, one difference between computers and humans used to be human-like corporality. That difference is rapidly disappearing, as some computers are now being inserted into sophisticated and human-like physical shapes. As Ryan Calo recently observed, "robots, more so than any technology in history, feel to us like social actors."[30] Although embodiment surely will affect many important legal and policy issues, nothing in having a physical body need determine (though it may enhance) the "selfhood" principles of freedom of expression identified here.

Computers' inability to experience emotions may offer another potential source of distinction between AI and human speakers. Computer-generated speech—whether robotic or detached from a human-like form—does not entail a speaker in possession of human emotions, with emotions' speech-curbing as well as speech-generative potential. Nor does a computer have the human need or desire, one assumes, to communicate non-interactively with itself in the way a person might write poetry or a diary with no intention of sharing this with others.

Emotion matters to human thought as well as to legal rights and responsibilities. For example, shame is an important piece of emotional hardware that assists humans in thinking about the consequences of acts to which shame is linked. Remorse is a factor in determining whether a person who has violated the law should be punished, and to what extent, and to whether the harms to the victim have been properly acknowledged. As Martha Nussbaum has said, "law without appeals to emotion is virtually unthinkable . . . [T]he law ubiquitously takes account of people's emotional states."[31] Fear of repercussions—loss of status, compromised interpersonal bonds, economic losses, freedom, self-respect, even death—all factor into how law works to constrain human behavior.

Computers, at present, lack these and other relevant emotional capacities in ways that make them awkward legal rights bearers at best. AI speakers are incapable of assuming emotional responsibility for the harm that they cause. Even the most emotionally unintelligent humans surpass AI in this respect. Does AI's emotional deficiency mean that AI speakers have no free speech rights under an autonomy approach to the First Amendment?

We think not necessarily, for two reasons. First, emerging developments in affective computing—the interdisciplinary process of designing computer systems and devices that can recognize, interpret, simulate, and process human affects—may challenge the casual assumption that AI lacks feelings. For one thing, human emotions are, according to some theorists, themselves "adaptations, well-engineered software modules that work in harmony with the intellect and are indispensable to the whole mind."[32] That is, the more we learn about human brains and the interplay of emotion and reason, the more humans

---

[30]   Ryan Calo, *Robotics and the Lessons of Cyberlaw* 103 Calif. L. Rev. 513, 515 (2015).

[31]   Martha C. Nussbaum, *Upheavals of Thought: The Intelligence of Emotions* (Cambridge University Press 2001) 5.

[32]   Steven Pinker, *How the Mind Works* (W.W. Norton and Co. 1997) 370.

may look like extraordinarily complex computers. Second, emotions may be means to an end—"mechanisms that set the brain's highest-level goals."[33] If thinking and feeling go hand in hand in this way for humans, then a brilliant thinking machine also may be able to "feel" in ways akin to humans. That is, a functional account of human emotion may sufficiently narrow the gap between humans and machines to justify extending First Amendment coverage to the latter, even under an autonomy approach.

Most threatening to strong AI speaker claims to First Amendment coverage are theories that limit such coverage to humans precisely because they are human—i.e., simply because blood flows through their veins—rather than because of criteria such as corporality, affect, or intentionality that are associated with humans but may (or may not) be associated with strong AI speakers at some point in the future. Humanness, according to this view, is both necessary and sufficient.

Solum's response to this "humans only" argument remains powerful:

> But if someone says that the deepest and most fundamental reason we protect natural persons is simply because they are human (like us), I do not know how to answer. Given that we have never encountered any serious nonhuman candidates for personhood, there does not seem to be any way to continue the conversation.[34]

In other words, speaker autonomy arguments face increasing pressure not only to identify intrinsic qualities of moral personhood that are unique to humans, but to explain why those qualities *should* matter for purposes of conferring free speech rights (other than that they are uniquely human). We agree that even speaker-driven autonomy theories thus do not necessarily rule out First Amendment rights for strong AI speakers.

To make the above discussion of both positive and negative theory less abstract, imagine a hypothetical strong AI version of a robot that writes long, intricate, socially astute novels about the 2016 election cycle, inspired by the work of Leo Tolstoy. The works could not be traced in any way to a human author or programmer; in our hypothetical, they are the creative work solely of our Tolstoy-bot AI.

To a traditional democratic self-governance theorist, such novels would be protected under the First Amendment to the extent that they contribute to public discourse and political debate. To Post, they would be protected both because they are public discourse, and because government restrictions on their publication would call into question the legitimacy of that governance regime.[35] To Balkin, they would be protected because readers of the novels could use them dynamically to construct a culturally situated self.[36] To marketplace-of-ideas theorists, the novels would be protected to the extent they contribute to their readers' search for "truth," knowledge, or enlightenment. To autonomy theorists, the novels would be protected because interference in their publication would squelch readers' autonomy, impinging on their freedom of information-gathering, self-construction, and thought. And to those taking the negative view of the First Amendment, the novels would be protected from laws that arise from an illegitimate

---

[33]   *Id.* at 373.
[34]   Solum, *supra* note 22, at 1262 (footnote omitted).
[35]   Our claim, not his.
[36]   Our claim, not his.

government motive, perhaps resulting from a desire to squelch social criticism (or a deep hatred of long-form literature). Both positive and negative theories of the First Amendment therefore support protecting strong AIs' speech.

E.   Doctrinal Support for Nonhuman Speakers

First Amendment doctrine already protects speakers that are not conventionally human. Indeed, it has long struggled with the challenges raised by speakers like corporations, which take the form of something other than the paradigmatic individual and fully autonomous speaker of conscience. Free speech doctrine generally finds great value in, and thus often great protection for, such speakers despite the various ways in which they deviate from traditional First Amendment models.

For example, courts and scholars wrestled for decades over the fit between eighteenth century visions of individual rights and the application of these visions to corporations that lack a unitary head, heart, ears or eyes. Nevertheless, First Amendment law now clearly protects corporations' speech rights. As the Court explained in *First National Bank of Boston v. Bellotti*, "[t]he inherent worth of the speech in terms of its capacity for informing the public does not depend upon the identity of its source, whether corporation, association, union, or individual."[37]

In the more recent words of Justice Scalia, "[t]he [First] Amendment is written in terms of 'speech,' not speakers. Its text offers no foothold for excluding any category of speaker, from single individuals to partnerships of individuals, to unincorporated associations of individuals, to incorporated associations of individuals. . ."[38]

Corporations are thus among those nontraditional speakers that receive substantial First Amendment protections; indeed, theory and doctrine already teem with mythology and metaphors that can make liberty heroes of Coca-Cola and other corporate behemoths. Nor, according to the Court, do free speech principles vary "when a new and different medium for communication appears":

> Like the protected books, plays, and movies that preceded them, video games communicate ideas—and even social messages—through many familiar literary devices (such as characters, dialogue, plot, and music) and through features distinctive to the medium (such as the player's interaction with the virtual world). That suffices to confer First Amendment protection.[39]

Because First Amendment doctrine has long found ways to accommodate nontraditional speakers and their speech, whatever their identity and format, computer speakers with strong AI pose doctrinal challenges that are not altogether new.

Of course, corporations generally represent the interests of groups of individual humans. That a corporation may be a First Amendment rights-holder thus does not demand the same treatment of a computer with strong AI. Our point is simply that nothing in the

---

[37]   463 U.S. 765, 777 (1978); *see also id.* at 776 ("The proper question therefore is not whether corporations 'have' First Amendment rights and, if so, whether they are coextensive with those of natural persons. Instead, the question must be whether [the contested government regulation] abridges expression that the First Amendment was meant to protect.").

[38]   *Citizens United v. FEC*, 558 U.S. 310, 392–93 (2010) (Scalia, J., concurring).

[39]   *Brown v. Entertainment Merchants Association*, 564 U.S. 786, 790 (2011).

Court's doctrine *eliminates* that possibility, and much supports it—especially given the contributions to listeners' First Amendment interests that such computer speech can make.

Relatedly, we note that contemporary free speech doctrine rarely, if ever, attends to speakers' dignity (as distinct from their autonomy) as a justification for protecting their speech. Harms to listeners' dignitary interests often figure in discussion of speech that manipulates unwitting consumers,[40] coerces government grant recipients,[41] or inflicts emotional distress in victims of cyber bullying and targets of hate speech.[42] Yet we see little corresponding focus on the dignity of the *speaker* in these or other discussions of free speech and its limits. Instead, only the speaker's autonomy—not speaker dignity in any sense of vulnerability or worthiness—receives attention. Once again, doctrine poses surprisingly little obstacle to the project of recognizing computers' free speech rights, as such.

Along with speaker identity, expression's content is increasingly irrelevant to the Court's decisions about whether and when to protect speech. The Court now tells us that speech cannot be regulated in a content-specific manner without surviving the rigors of strict scrutiny unless it falls within a category historically recognized as unprotected (or less protected).[43] Furthermore, such First Amendment protection is not reserved for political speech, or even for matters of significant public concern. Our First Amendment exuberance thus protects speech that enhances audience experience and entertainment,[44] and not just meaningful political engagement. Accordingly, free speech doctrine offers protection to racist hate speech,[45] animal crush videos,[46] vulgarity,[47] blasphemy and sacrilegious expression,[48] cyber speech that falls short of a hazy "true threats" line,[49] certain false speech,[50] corporations' expenditures in political campaigns,[51] truthful and non-misleading commercial speech,[52] and the sale of information about physicians' prescribing habits to pharmaceutical companies.[53] Here too, the Court's broad protection of speech

---

[40]   *See, e.g., Zauderer v. Office of Disciplinary Counsel,* 471 U.S. 626, 651 (1985).

[41]   *See, e.g., Agency for Int'l Dev. v. All. for Open Soc'y Int'l, Inc.,* 133 S. Ct. 2321, 2332 (2013) (striking down condition on federal grant that imposed coercive compelled speech restriction on free speech of recipients).

[42]   *See* Danielle Keats Citron and Helen Norton, *Intermediaries and Hate Speech: Fostering Digital Citizenship for Our Information Age,* 91 B.U. L. Rev. 1435 (2011).

[43]   *See United States v. Stevens,* 559 U.S. 460, 470–72 (2010); cf. *Reed v. Town of Gilbert,* 135 S. Ct. 2218, 2224 (2015) (applying strict scrutiny to facially content-specific town ordinance and rejecting a more nuanced, contextualized approach to these content-specific regulations).

[44]   Ronald K.L. Collins and David M. Skover, *Pissing in the Snow: A Cultural Approach to the First Amendment,* 45 Stan. L. Rev. 783, 785 (1993) (discussing how electronic technologies affect logic and discourse in ways that make entertainment, rather than enlightenment, a primary driver of communication).

[45]   *R.A.V. v. City of St. Paul,* 505 U.S. 377 (1992).

[46]   *Stevens,* 559 U.S. 460.

[47]   *Cohen v. California,* 403 U.S. 15, 25 (1971).

[48]   *Joseph Burstyn, Inc. v. Wilson,* 343 U.S. 495, 503 (1952).

[49]   *United States v Elonis,* 135 S. Ct. 2001, 2017 (2015).

[50]   *United States v. Alvarez,* 132 S. Ct. 2537 (2012); *see also* Helen Norton, *Lies and the Constitution,* 2012 Sup. Ct. Rev. 161.

[51]   *Citizens United v. FEC,* 558 U.S. 310 (2010).

[52]   *Cent. Hudson Gas and Elec. Corp. v. Pub. Serv. Comm'n,* 447 U.S. 557, 566 (1980).

[53]   *Sorrell v. IMS Health Inc.,* 131 S. Ct. 2653 (2011).

regardless of content (with all bets on the audience's ability to sort good speech from bad) supports similar protections for strong AI speech regardless of its nontraditional source or format.

Free speech law thus pays extraordinarily little attention to speakers' emotional intelligence. In fact, the freedom of speech umbrella covers the least empathic speaker among us, no less than the exquisitely sensitive. Members of the Westboro Baptist Church are protected when they picket the funerals of soldiers and display signs proclaiming "God Hates Fags" and "Thank God for Dead Soldiers."[54] First Amendment protections apply to racist, homophobic, sexist, blasphemous, or otherwise cruel postings on Facebook pages or other social media sites, despite the grave harm they may inflict. Nor do courts inquire into the emotional capacities of a corporation when it exercises its First Amendment freedoms.[55] And, of course, when the law focuses solely on bad government motives regarding speech suppression rather than on whether protected speech in fact occurred, then the speaker's actual autonomy and human attributes drop out of the picture altogether. The primary focus is on the government and its antagonism towards speech, not on any actual human speaker herself or itself.

In other words, even if strong AI proves to be better than the worst of human speakers, and even if strong AI never matches the best of human speakers in terms of emotional intelligence and grace, AI's free speech rights may not hinge on either capacity. What will matter—at least under current theory and doctrine—is whether AI says something listeners should hear, or something that government should not be allowed to silence.

II.   QUESTIONS AND CHALLENGES TO COME

The preceding Part explained why free speech theory and doctrine pose few barriers to First Amendment coverage of AI speech. This Part identifies some of the theoretical and doctrinal questions that AI speech will force us to confront, and explores some of the choices and challenges to come.

A.   The Search for Limiting Principles

Among the most powerful objections to the notion of extending speech protections to strong AI is that such extension lacks limiting principles. We agree that the hardest problems lie here: if AI speech is covered by the First Amendment, how can the government perform important regulatory functions in the name of humans without running afoul of the First Amendment?

We believe this puzzle produces the greatest intellectual yield of the AI thought experiment. The claims we advance are evidence of an *existing* slippage problem: the Court's contemporary free speech theory and doctrine *already* make it difficult to articulate convincing limiting principles. By emphasizing either a negative view of the First Amendment

---

[54]   *Snyder v. Phelps*, 562 U.S. 443 (2011).
[55]   *See, e.g., Citizens United v. FEC*, 558 U.S. 310 (2010).

that seeks to constrain the government's dangerous ability to regulate speech, or positive views that emphasize the value of speech to its listeners, current doctrine supports the coverage of speech regardless of its nontraditional source or form. Increasingly expansive First Amendment theories and practice already have evolved in a manner that permits further coverage extensions that may seem exceedingly odd, counterintuitive, even dangerous. Current free speech law—which many now argue has thus invited deployment of the First Amendment as an antiregulatory tool—is the source of this challenge, rather than any technological change past, present, or future.

The choice to extend the First Amendment to cover new sources and styles of speech inevitably involves both promise and peril. Extending constitutional protection to private activity is often a double-edged liberty sword: the greater the power of the private actor, the greater the risk that freedom for that actor will constrain the freedom of other, less powerful actors.

Yet if courts do extend First Amendment coverage to AI speakers, this move surely will invite calls for limiting principles. As this section explains, contemporary free speech doctrine contains means by which courts could respond to dangers posed by AI speakers, though each presents its own difficulties. In short, interpreting the First Amendment to cover strong AI speakers would not necessarily mean that human needs no longer matter to First Amendment analysis. In fact, such an interpretation may inspire more careful reflection about how to define and mitigate the harmful effects of covered speech, while preserving its manifold benefits.

More specifically, some of the justifications for covering strong AI speakers are also justifications for regulating them. Current doctrine recognizes a number of speech environments in which listeners' First Amendment interests are paramount in ways that justify not only the expression's coverage but also its content-based regulation. Courts might build on these examples to justify restrictions on AI speech to privilege human listeners' interests in informed choices, or in avoiding harms of coercion, deception, and discrimination. This would not necessarily rule out coverage of AI speech, but instead the full protection of it. That is to say: because protection of AI speech is justified in large part based on listeners' interests in that speech, the government may be able to regulate to protect listeners when the interests of the AI speaker and human listener conflict.

For example, the Court has stated that commercial speech is worthy of First Amendment protection because of its informational value to consumers as listeners.[56] It has relatedly held that commercial speech that is false, misleading, or related to an illegal activity can be banned outright, because such expression frustrates listeners' informational interests.[57] Moreover, it has permitted government relatively broad leeway to require commercial speakers to make truthful disclosures,[58] again upholding such requirements as protecting

---

[56]   *Zauderer v. Office of Disciplinary Counsel of the Supreme Court of Ohio*, 471 U.S. 626, 651 (1985) ("The extension of First Amendment protection to commercial speech is justified principally by the value to consumers of the information such speech provides."); *Va. State Bd. of Pharmacy v. Va. Citizen Consumer Council, Inc.*, 425 U.S. 748, 763-64 (1976) (emphasizing the value of "the free flow of commercial information" to individual consumers and the public more generally).

[57]   *Cent. Hudson Gas and Elec. Corp. v. Pub. Serv. Comm'n of N.Y.*, 447 U.S. 557, 562–64 (1980).

[58]   *Zauderer*, 471 U.S. at 651 (holding that disclosure requirements that are reasonably related to the State's interest in preventing consumer deception do not violate commercial speakers' First Amendment rights). The Court applies intermediate scrutiny to laws regulating truthful and non-

listeners' informational interests. In short, commercial speech doctrine seeks at least in part to protect listeners from harm.

Free speech doctrine can similarly protect listeners from harms posed by AI speech. For example, strong AI may appear to be a real social actor in ways that trigger and manipulate intrinsic human reaction, but without corresponding emotions, sensitivity to social nuance, or shame. The field of Human Robot Interaction (HRI) studies how humans react to robots, and how such reactions may be deliberately triggered by machine design. A listener may intuitively trust AI as though it were a human actor, without understanding the differences or risks at hand. Moreover, the algorithms upon which AI speech relies are far from neutral sources or decision-makers. Bias and discrimination are built into programs; technology is not value neutral, but value based. In these and other respects, AI speech thus could harm listeners in ways that may justify government intervention aimed at mitigating these harms.

Recognizing valid government interests in regulating AI speech, however, does not write a blank check for government regulation. Nor does it necessarily run wholly counter to the negative First Amendment interest in constraining government efforts to censor speech. For example, listener interests and AI speaker interests may align to bar government's efforts to regulate AI speech in ways that discriminate on the basis of viewpoint. The government should not be permitted to write viewpoint-based regulations of AI speech any more than it can for a human speaker.

A listener-based justification for speech thus could justify government intervention that serves listeners' interests without necessarily empowering government to adopt other kinds of regulation that the Court historically has found most suspect. Yet when harms to listeners substantially outweigh the benefits to listeners, then even current free speech jurisprudence allows for certain kinds of regulation. Drawing the line between these two scenarios may at times be difficult. But this difficulty is precisely our point. Contemplating the possibility of AI speakers may lead to a more careful identification of the role of listeners' interests in all free speech puzzles, not just those in which AI is the speaker.

In short, a primary basis for protecting AI speech rests on the value of expression specifically to human listeners. Free speech coverage of strong AIs thus need not rob the First Amendment of a human focus. Absent a human speaker, government still may attend to the dangers to human listeners. Again, First Amendment *coverage* of AI speakers simply triggers constitutional analysis and does not necessarily mean First Amendment *protection* of AI speech from government regulation in all instances. Indeed, the prospect of free speech rights for strong AI speakers might encourage much-needed clarification of the roles of human listeners and of speech harms in US free speech theory and doctrine.

The AI thought experiment highlights the centrality of the listener in ongoing as well as emerging free speech debates. If courts justify expanding speech coverage on the ground that the speech is good for listeners, then they also should take seriously listeners' interest in protection from harms caused by that speech. This insight has implications for many current free speech problems, including the governance of information intermediaries and

---

misleading commercial speech on the premise that such speech—although still of relatively low value   can helpfully inform individuals about their choices in the commercial realm. *Id.*

network neutrality;[59] of commercial speech;[60] of speech in the context of employment relationships;[61] and even of surveillance.[62]

B.   What About Other Nonhuman Speakers?

Relatedly, extending First Amendment coverage to AI speakers will force us to wrestle with whether the same arguments require the extension of First Amendment coverage to other nonhuman speakers, like animals. To offer just one example, cats communicate with their humans in multiple ways, especially as this relates to needs that the cats want the humans to fulfill. Similar (and arguably stronger) arguments attach to the communication of dolphins and nonhuman primates.

We take no position here as to whether extending rights to AI might force closer examination of arguments to extend free speech rights to other potential rights bearers, including animals. It might well do so, and we look forward to that provocative conversation. None of this, however, undermines our point about how the theoretical embrace of the First Amendment might include autonomous AI. Again, this possibility reveals more about the elasticity of current free speech theory and doctrine than it does about changes in technology or in our understanding of animals.

In any event, animal communication skills are not evolving nearly as rapidly as AI skills. Nor is the evolutionary arc of animal language as amenable to human direction or crafting in the very direct ways that the arc of AI language is. AI, by contrast, is human-designed and profoundly and exclusively human-centered in terms of the needs it seeks to address. AI arguably will benefit human audiences more pointedly than a cat, or even an especially astute primate. Moreover, AI communication is deliberately supplanting human communication at nodes (think finance, telecommunication, transportation, energy, computer-assisted research, health care, and defense) that matter greatly to human well-being, safety, and knowledge. A cat that is not in the mood to purr and leaves the room with rump aloft will have little impact on humans' information bearings. Depending on the context, a computer that refuses to interact may damage human interests in far more substantial, even life-threatening, ways.

Finally, the functions of AI speech differ from those of communicative animals. Again, AI communication is often designed to serve fundamental human information needs. Much as humans might like to know what cats, dolphins, octopuses, capuchin monkeys, or their beloved cocker spaniels are really telling them, humans are not lost or gravely

---

[59]   *See* Stuart Minor Benjamin, *Algorithms and Speech*, 161 U. Penn. L. Rev. 1445 (2013); James Grimmelmann, *Speech Engines*, 98 Minn. L. Rev. 868 (2014); Tim Wu, *Machine Speech*, 161 U. Pa. L. Rev. 1495 (2013).

[60]   *See, e.g.,* Tamara Piety, *Brandishing the First Amendment* (University of Michigan Press 2012) 12.

[61]   See Helen Norton, *Truth and Lies in the Workplace: Employer Speech and the First Amendment*, 101 Minn. L. Rev. 31 (2016).

[62]   See Marc Jonathan Blitz, *Constitutional Safeguards for Silent Experiments in Living: Libraries, the Right to Read, and a First Amendment Theory for an Unaccompanied Right to Receive Information*, 74 UMKC L. Rev. 799 (2006); Julie E. Cohen, *A Right to Read Anonymously: A Closer Look at "Copyright Management" in Cyberspace*, 28 Conn. L. Rev. 981 (1996); Neil M. Richards, *Intellectual Privacy*, 87 Tex. L. Rev. 387 (2008).

imperiled if these meanings remain mysteries. AI, by contrast, is designed to speak our language, and increasingly to do so in forms that look like us, walk like us, and talk like us. If we justify the protection of AI because of human listeners, then, the value of AI speech to human listeners is arguably higher than the value of animal "speech."

C.   The Need for Doctrinal Adjustment

Conferring AI speech with First Amendment coverage will require us to reconsider current doctrine that maps poorly onto computers in various ways. For example, First Amendment law sometimes requires intent as a condition of imposing liability for speakers' harmful speech.[63] Because legal intentionality may be harder to assign to computer speech, this suggests the possibility that conferring such speech with First Amendment protection may mean that it is insulated from liability in circumstances where the same would not be true of human speakers. Imagine, for example, that a computer produces defamatory speech about a public official. First Amendment doctrine currently requires a showing of the speaker's actual malice before imposing tort liability on the speaker in such situations. How might a court determine whether an AI speaker acted with knowledge of or reckless disregard for the falsity of its assertions, or that it "entertained serious doubts as to the truth of [its] publications"?[64]

Courts could manage these complexities by altering the doctrine to prevent an AI windfall, or could mitigate the harmful effects of defamatory AI speech in other ways. Even free speech doctrine, with its growing emphasis on formalism over nuance,[65] offers ways to address important regulatory concerns. Copyright law provides an edifying example. Although vicarious liability, with its focus on a person's ability to benefit from and control a downstream copyright infringer, was initially poorly suited for the age of mass filesharing, courts have (admittedly with serious struggles) figured out ways to ascribe secondary liability to software creators.[66] The sheer scale of filesharing, balanced against

---

[63]   *Brandenburg v. Ohio*, 395 U.S. 444 (1969) (holding that advocacy of illegal conduct is protected unless intentionally directed to inciting imminent illegal action); *New York Times Co. v. Sullivan*, 376 U.S. 254, 279- 80 (1964) (holding that false assertions of fact regarding public officials are protected absent the speaker's malicious mental state).

[64]   *Saint Amant v. Thompson*, 390 U.S. 727, 731 (1968).

[65]   *See* Toni M. Massaro, *Tread on Me!*, 17 U. Pa. J. Const. L. 365, 369–82 (2014) (discussing ways in which the Roberts Court has moved toward more formalism in its approach to free speech, but noting the many ways in which existing doctrine still offers judges significant and necessary flexibility to address context-specific concerns.

[66]   *Sony v. Universal City Studios*, 464 U.S. 417 (1984) (explaining that for its maker to escape secondary liability, a technology must be "capable of substantial non-infringing uses"); *Fonovisa, Inc. v. Cherry Auction, Inc.*, 76 F.3d 259, 262 (9th Cir. 1996) (explaining that the "concept of vicarious copyright liability...[is] an outgrowth of the agency principles of respondeat superior"); *A&M Records, Inc. v. Napster*, 239 F.3d 1004 (9th Cir. 2001) (holding filesharing software company Napster liable for user copyright infringement); *MGM Studios v. Grokster*, 545 U.S. 913 (2005) (holding filesharing software company Grokster liable for inducing copyright infringement). *But see American Broadcasting Companies v. Aereo*, 134 S. Ct. 2512, 2516 (2014) (Scalia, J., dissenting) ("It will take years, perhaps decades, to determine which automated systems now in existence are governed by the traditional volitional-conduct test and which get the Aereo treatment. (And automated systems now in contemplation will have to take their chances").

fears of chilling technological development, resulted not in a refusal to apply the law to new technologies, but in doctrinal development that made room for complicated debates about overarching policy concerns. First Amendment doctrine, too, would likely adapt on its edges to prevent AI speakers from being insulated from liability due to lack of a provable mental state. How this will happen more specifically, however, remains to be seen.

Relatedly, conferring AI speech with First Amendment coverage will raise questions about how AI could sue to protect its free speech rights, or be sued and punished for its impermissibly harmful speech. To this end, Chopra and White have contributed greatly to efforts to think about how to operationalize legal rights and duties for AI.[67] They note, and we agree, that AI need not have identical rights and obligations to humans. But a legal framework can be developed that would enable AI to sue and be sued. As discussed in Part I, the existing category of "legal persons" already includes entities that hold a variety of legal (including constitutional) rights and duties even though they may be very different from "moral" or "natural" or "human" persons. They include corporations, unions, municipalities, and even ships, though the law in every case makes adjustments based on their material differences from humans.[68] Stating that some class of nonhuman speakers may be rights holders often simply means that they are legal persons. Human status thus is not a necessary condition for legal personhood.

As applied to AI, the first step in the progression of legal rights is likely to be treatment of AI as a dependent, not independent, legal person. Their owners, or those who direct or are assigned responsibility for them, could be sued for their actions. As Chopra and White observe, "[i]f legal systems can accord dependent legal personality to children, adults who are not of sound mind, corporations, ships, temples, and even idols, there is nothing to prevent the legal system from according this form of legal personality to artificial agents."[69]

For example, AI might be required to register and meet capital requirements necessary to meet its financial duties and enable those who contract with AI to be on fair notice of AI's economic capacities.[70] Courts and regulators could follow precedent that currently applies to corporations to establish these legal arrangements.

The more complex step would be for AI to be granted wholly independent legal personhood. Chopra and White outline the criteria for independent legal personhood as follows: an independent legal person must have intellectual capacity and rationality; the ability to understand legal obligations; susceptibility to punishment and enforcement; the ability to form contracts; and the ability to control money.[71] The authors conclude that sophisticated AI could satisfy these criteria.[72] Satisfaction of the theoretical criteria for independent legal personhood would enable those injured by AI speakers to pursue legal remedies against AI. Law could take into account the inanimate nature of the legal actor, as a matter of liability, and AI could be required to be legally accountable for its harms.[73]

---

[67]   *See* Chopra and White, *supra* note 28.
[68]   *Id.* at 157.
[69]   *Id.* at 162–160.
[70]   *Id.* at 162–62.
[71]   *Id.* at 162–63 (citations omitted).
[72]   *Id.* at 162–71.
[73]   *Id.* at 153–71, 186–91 (discussing various means by which strong AI could be held legally accountable, including for damages).

Yet how, exactly, might judicial remedies be crafted and enforced in such cases? As for punishment, there are several possibilities. As Chopra and White suggest, AI cannot be imprisoned; but neither can corporations.[74] Instead, AI could be physically disabled, barred from future participation in certain economic transactions, deregistered, or have its assets seized.[75] Shallow or empty pocket AI actors may exist and limit the usefulness of damage remedies, but this is true of many judgement proof human actors as well. Injunctive and declaratory relief could also be invoked against the AI speaker. Courts or AI regulators might require that AI programs incorporate legal guidelines for protected speech behavior as a condition of certain speech activity, with adjustments to prior restraint law that would permit these insertions. Again, we do not view free speech coverage and free speech protection as coterminous: adjustments within the law thus could and likely would be made to account for the fact that the speaker is a computer and not a human being.

As for rights enforcement, we can imagine scenarios—especially given the interdependence of AI rights and listener-based interests—in which AI legal rights organizations or other humans interested in the fate of AI communication step in to assist AI with assertion of AI rights. Specialized AI lawyers could help implement legal rights and remedies. Third-party standing rules that apply in federal court might allow interested human parties to assert the AI rights along with their own. The more important the information produced and controlled by AI becomes, the more incentive for the development of legal means for enforcing AI speech rights.

The question in all of these cases would be how to respond to the rights and remedy needs, given the functionality and capacities of the AI speaker; as the latter evolve this would affect how the rights and remedies are crafted and enforced. In fact, considering the range of available punishments for AI might lead to discussions of the theoretical purposes of punishment—retribution, rehabilitation, constraint, and deterrence—much as considerations of AI speech rights have led us back to theory here.

What is key to our thought experiment here is that humanness is not essential to legal personhood. Even if, as surely will be the case, human needs may inspire the move to AI legal personhood, and even if humans may be necessary aids to legal enforcement of AI rights, a continued role for humans does not defeat the arguments in favor of assigning rights themselves to AI. Where there is a judicial will to do so, there will be conceivable ways.

Finally, conferring First Amendment coverage on AI speakers would force us to revisit recurring questions about the distinction between speech and conduct. Earlier we explained why current doctrine poses no hard requirement that a speaker need be human to receive First Amendment coverage. But even if we understand the Constitution to protect "speech, not speakers," arguments remain that much (or all) of what computers produce is not speech and is instead unprotected conduct. Government regulation of pure conduct triggers no freedom of speech problem, and typically triggers mere rational basis scrutiny. The government's regulation of conduct with expressive qualities in a non-speech-sensitive way triggers a form of intermediate scrutiny.[76] Only conduct intended

---

[74] *Id.* at 167.

[75] *Id.* at 167–68.

[76] *See United States v. O'Brien*, 391 U.S. 367, 381–82 (1968).

to communicate something that will reasonably be understood by the listener as speech normally qualifies as speech for constitutional purposes.[77] Some computer behavior—like human behavior—may fall under each of these categories in different situations.

The speech/conduct distinction in the machine speech context has already triggered examination by a number of scholars, who generally conclude that at least some—and perhaps much—of machine outputs is speech. For example, scholars have analyzed whether data is speech, and considered the tough questions of whether and when computers are merely *doing* something (versus *saying* something for First Amendment purposes) when they gather, synthesize, or disseminate data.[78] Jane Bambauer concludes that much of what computers produce in this respect should, in fact, be treated as speech for First Amendment purposes because it is information that can be used to produce knowledge.[79] Relatedly, Stuart Benjamin concludes that most algorithmic products constitute speech under current free expression doctrine because they involve "sendable and receivable message[s]."[80]

Tim Wu, in contrast, remains concerned about the implications of free speech rights for machines[81] and suggests that First Amendment law requires that protected speech be the product of *intelligent* expressive choices.[82] He urges that the result of such intelligent choices deserves First Amendment protection only when it takes the form of a "speech product" viewed as the vessel of "the ideas of a speaker, or whose content has been consciously curated," rather than "communications tools that primarily facilitate the communication of another person or perform some task for the user"—i.e., by carrying bits of data.[83] Yet even Wu ends up with a test that ultimately turns on the functionality of the machine's output (assuming, as our hypothetical does, that the strong AI is capable of making "intelligent" choices), not on the fact that a machine is speaking. A functionality test may be a useful way of limiting protections for some outputs by strong AI speakers, but it does not pose an insurmountable obstacle to their protection in many scenarios.

To be sure, the outputs of today's algorithms may be increasingly less predictable, and increasingly out of the control of their creators. Such algorithms are not, however, independent thinkers or beings. Present discussions of whether algorithms should be protected under the First Amendment have largely focused on whether the output is functional or editorial in nature. These discussions reserve or do not address the question of what to do about strong AI: as-yet-hypothetical machines that would actually think and generate expressive content independent of human direction, in contrast to current "weak AI" machines that only act as if they were intelligent. In short, AI information

---

[77]   *See Spence v. Washington*, 418 U.S. 405, 410–11 (1974) (per curiam).

[78]   *See, e.g.,* Jane Bambauer, *Is Data Speech?*, 66 Stan. L. Rev. 57, 77–86 (2014) (discussing whether data is expressive or nonexpressive conduct).

[79]   *Id.* at 91–105.

[80]   Stuart Minor Benjamin, *Algorithms and Speech*, 161 U. Pa. L. Rev. 1445, 1461–71 (2013).

[81]   Tim Wu, Free *Speech for Computers?* N.Y. Times (19 June 2012) ("The First Amendment has wandered far from its purposes when it is recruited to protect commercial automatons from regulatory scrutiny. . . . To give computers the rights intended for humans is to elevate our machines above ourselves.").

[82]   Tim Wu, *Machine Speech*, 161 U. Pa. L. Rev. 1495, 1503 (2013).

[83]   *Id.* at 1498.

practices will vary, and thus so will the determination whether AI information products are speech versus conduct.

III. CONCLUSION

We have explored here whether hypothetical strong AI speakers could hold constitutional free speech rights, not just as human-operated tools, but as independent rights bearers. We have concluded this is plausible, however odd and threatening this sounds to some today.

If that occurs, commentators and courts will need to turn to the next, equally complex set of tasks that include how to address the harms the new speech machines may produce while protecting their information-rich benefits, as well as how to adjust doctrine to adapt to the differences between human and machine speech (although, as we have discussed, those differences may be smaller than many suppose).

Courts and commentators will muddle through these puzzles just as they have muddled through the intellectual awkwardness of giving free speech rights to business organizations, minors, and non-empathic humans anonymously roaming the Internet. The delicate task will be to take care to protect the information value of strong AI speech, while remaining mindful of the power of these artificial agents once unleashed in the First Amendment universe. Future constitutional law scholars will debate the merits of their handiwork (perhaps aided by AI enhancements in conducting their analyses). All of these legal actors will be proceeding with fewer unknowns than we face here in thinking through these issues, though they surely will face new challenges that we have not anticipated.

However this develops, we should head into that unfolding future mindful of the growing power of AI over information that humans need to survive. The stakes already are extremely high, and quickly mounting. An important first step is to start thinking about the implications of rapidly evolving AI across legal domains, including freedom of expression.

SOURCES

Heffernan v. City of Paterson, 136 S. Ct. 1412 (2016).
Reed v. Town of Gilbert, 135 S. Ct. 2218 (2015).
United States v Elonis, 135 S. Ct. 2001 (2015).
American Broadcasting Companies v. Aereo, 134 S. Ct. 2512 (2014).
Agency for Int'l Dev. v. All. for Open Soc'y Int'l, Inc., 133 S. Ct. 2321 (2013).
United States v. Alvarez, 132 S. Ct. 2537, 2543-44 (2012).
Brown v. Entertainment Merchants Association, 564 U.S. 786 (2011).
Snyder v. Phelps, 562 U.S. 443 (2011).
Sorrell v. IMS Health Inc., 131 S. Ct. 2653 (2011).
Citizens United v. FEC, 558 U.S. 310 (2010).
United States v. Stevens, 559 U.S. 460 (2010).
MGM Studios v. Grokster, 545 U.S. 913 (2005).
R.A.V. v. City of St. Paul, 505 U.S. 377 (1992).
Cent. Hudson Gas & Elec. Corp. v. Pub. Serv. Comm'n, 447 U.S. 557 (1980).
Zauderer v. Office of Disciplinary Counsel, 471 U.S. 626 (1985).
Sony v. Universal City Studios, 464 U.S. 417 (1984).
First National Bank of Boston v. Bellotti, 463 U.S. 765 (1978).

Va. State Bd. of Pharmacy v. Va. Citizen Consumer Council, Inc., 425 U.S. 748 (1976).
Spence v. Washington, 418 U.S. 405 (1974).
Cohen v. California, 403 U.S. 15 (1971).
Brandenburg v. Ohio, 395 U.S. 444 (1969).
Saint Amant v. Thompson, 390 U.S. 727 (1968).
United States v. O'Brien, 391 U.S. 367 (1968).
New York Times Co. v. Sullivan, 376 U.S. 254 (1964).
Joseph Burstyn, Inc. v. Wilson, 343 U.S. 495, 503 (1952).
A&M Records, Inc. v. Napster, 239 F.3d 1004 (9th Cir. 2001).
Fonovisa, Inc. v. Cherry Auction, Inc., 76 F.3d 259 (9th Cir. 1996).

13. Data algorithms and privacy in surveillance: on stages, numbers and the human factor

Arno R. Lodder and Ronald P. Loui

I. INTRODUCTION

Surveillance opportunities are almost limitless with omnipresent cameras, constant internet use, and a wide variety of Internet of Things objects.[1] We access the Internet anytime, anywhere via smart devices such as phones and tablets, and gradually more objects become connected. In the Internet of Things not only computing devices but all kinds of ordinary objects are provided with an IP address such as books, food, clothes, cars, etc.[2] All our online interactions generate a stream of data. On top of data generated by ordinary internet use comes the use of wearables, smart meters, connected cars and other features. The process of almost unlimited data generation is labeled as datification.[3]

Humans can process only small amounts of data, computers can process almost infinitely. But also computers need to act smart or intelligent, because otherwise even they get swamped and/or might produce useless information. Algorithms help in structuring and analyzing vast amounts of data. With the growth of data we have to rely increasingly on algorithms. These algorithms may perform better than alternative approaches we used to rely on.[4] However, algorithms can be opaque, and the danger is that we get obscured by algorithms.[5]

In the wake of the Snowden revelations awareness in society has grown about what digital technologies offer in terms of surveillance and control.[6] The scale of mass surveillance by governments around the world through, for example, the bulk collection of metadata[7] and the monitoring of social media shocked even the most well informed individuals. Data mining and surveillance within the law enforcement and national security contexts

---

[1] T. Wisman, *Purpose and Function Creep by Design: Transforming the Face of Surveillance through the Internet of Things*. European Journal of Law and Technology (2013) Vol. 4, No. 2.

[2] A.D. Thierer (2015), *The Internet of Things and Wearable Technology: Addressing Privacy and Security Concerns without Derailing Innovation*. Rich. J. L. & Tech. (2015) 21, 6.

[3] S. Newell and M. Marabelli, *Strategic Opportunities (and Challenges) of Algorithmic Decision-Making: A Call for Action on the Long-Term Societal Effects of 'Datification'*, Journal of Strategic Information Systems (2015) 24(1).

[4] Anupam Chander, *The Racist Algorithm?* 115 Mich. L. Rev. 1023 (2017).

[5] F. Pasquale, *The Black Box Society. The Secret Algorithms That Control Money and Information* (Harvard University Press 2015).

[6] B.C. Newell, *The Massive Metadata Machine: Liberty, Power, and Secret Mass Surveillance in the U.S. and Europe, I/S*: A Journal of Law and Policy for the Information Society (2014) Vol. 10(2), 481–522.

[7] J.C. Yoo, *The Legality of the National Security Agency's Bulk Data Surveillance Programs ISJLP* (2014) 10 301.

raise serious human right rights concerns[8] about the ability of modern states to monitor, oppress and control their citizens.[9]

Not all algorithmic outcomes are adequate.[10] For instance, recently mortgage providers complained about the fact that algorithms advised in too many cases against a mortgage, also if it was quite obvious the person who requested was reliable and creditworthy. For instance, it is known that musical preference matters. If one law professor likes Bach and Mozart, and the other hip hop (e.g., derived from Facebook preferences), the algorithm might decide that the latter is not getting the mortgage.

Here is where the human factors issues enter. A human could easily decide against the algorithm, viz. that a tenured law professor with a preference for hip hop music is creditworthy. What the example also illustrates is that data processing algorithms can seriously impact our private lives.

Intelligence agencies use algorithms to distinguish between persons of interest and others. Law enforcement uses analytics and data mining to identify suspects and to support investigations. Businesses profile users in all kind of categories. Surveillance is omnipresent. The impact on privacy is not necessarily depending on who does the surveillance. It depends not only on the actors, but on various factors. Sometimes what businesses do impacts severely on the privacy of consumers, sometimes the work of police or intelligence agencies does not. In this paper we focus on surveillance by the US National Security Agency (NSA) and other intelligence agencies. Our aim is to dissect data analytics by intelligence agencies, and to suggest what privacy related law should focus on more than it does today.

With an understanding of how big data algorithms usually work we discuss in this chapter the use of algorithms from a privacy and data protection angle. First, we briefly introduce the central concepts of data protection and privacy against the background of the General Data Protection Regulation[11] introduced by the European Union in 2012, published in 2016 and effective as of 25 May 2018. The core of the chapter consists of elaborating upon three issues:

1. The stages of data processing while using algorithms, how it affects privacy and what safeguards the law should provide;
2. The role of the human factor: how and when should humans be involved in evaluating outcomes, and also under what circumstances human interference is better abstained from;
3. The relevance of scale and scope: in the light of privacy, numbers matter. However, so far in law a discussion on the relevance of numbers (or scale) is largely absent.

---

[8]   A.D. Murray, *Comparing Surveillance Powers: UK, US, and France* LSE Law Policy Briefing Papers: SPECIAL ISSUE: The Investigatory Powers Bill (14/2015).

[9]   L. Colonna, *Legal Implications of Data Mining. Assessing the European Union's Data Protection Principles in Light of the United States Government's National Intelligence Data Mining Practices*, Ph.D thesis Stockholm, 2016.

[10]   L. Rainie and J. Anderson, *Code-Dependent: Pros and Cons of the Algorithm Age*, Pew Research Center, February 2017.

[11]   REGULATION (EU) 2016/679 OF THE EUROPEAN PARLIAMENT AND OF THE COUNCIL of 27 April 2016 on the protection of natural persons with regard to the processing of personal data and on the free movement of such data, and repealing Directive 95/46/EC (General Data Protection Regulation), *Official Journal L 119, 4/5/2016*, pp. 1–88.

II.   PRIVACY AND DATA PROTECTION

Goldsmith and Wu[12] considered the European Union Directive 95/46[13] on data protection controversial due to its aggressive geographic scope. Article 4(1) of that Directive states that besides data controllers established in the EU, the Directive applies to controllers outside the EU if by virtue of international public law one of the EU member states' law applies or in case equipment is used that is physically located in an EU member state. The territorial scope of Article 3(2) GDPR is way more aggressive. The regulation applies to:

> the processing of personal data of data subjects who are in the Union by a controller or processor not established in the Union, where the processing activities are related to: (a) the offering of goods or services, irrespective of whether a payment of the data subject is required, to such data subjects in the Union; or (b) the monitoring of their behaviour as far as their behaviour takes place within the Union.

So, the GDPR applies to all internet services delivered to EU citizens: indifferent where the service provider is located, be it the USA, China, Brazil, Nigeria, etc. Stating to have jurisdiction is obviously not the same as being able to enforce the law, but companies who trade with EU citizens probably see no other option than to comply.

The rules in the GDPR are centered basically around the principles (listed in Article 5(1)) already described in the OECD principles of 23 September 1980 on governing the protection of privacy and transborder flows of personal data, such as purpose limitation, data minimisation, and accuracy. New is the explicit accountability duty for the controller in Article 5(2): "The controller shall be responsible for, and be able to demonstrate compliance with. . .". Other novelties are i.a. explicit mentioning of data protection by design and data protection by default (Article 25), the obligation to keep records of processing activities (Article 30), Data Protection Impact Assessments (Article 35), and a formal, central role for the Data Protection Officer (Articles 37–39).

In particular of relevance for this chapter are the rules on profiling, defined in Article 4(4) as:

> any form of automated processing of personal data consisting of the use of personal data to evaluate certain personal aspects relating to a natural person, in particular to analyse or predict aspects concerning that natural person's performance at work, economic situation, health, personal preferences, interests, reliability, behaviour, location or movements. . .

Although by nature big data and profiles form a risk for infringements of privacy and data protection, in particular in our present day data economy (cf. datafication), the GDPR addresses the topic of profiles.[14] Article 21(1) states that the data subject

---

[12]   J. Goldsmith and T. Wu, *Who Controls the Internet? Illusions of a Borderless World* (Oxford University Press, 2006) p. 175.

[13]   Directive 95/46/EC of the European Parliament and of the Council of 24 October 1995 on the protection of individuals with regard to the processing of personal data and on the free movement of such data, *Official Journal L 281, 23/11/1995*, pp. 31–50.

[14]   D. Kamarinou, C. Millard and J. Singh (2016), *Machine Learning with Personal Data* Queen Mary School of Law Legal Studies Research Paper No. 247/2016.

has a right to object to profiling "on grounds relating to his or her particular situation, at any time". There is, however, a way out for the data controller, since he can continue with the processing in case there are "compelling legitimate grounds for the processing which override the interests, rights and freedoms of the data subject." One can imagine the data controller is relatively easily convinced by its own grounds, rather than the interests of the data subject. The other right is in Article 22(1) to "not be subject to a decision based solely on automated processing, including profiling, which produces legal effects concerning him or her or similarly significantly affects him or her." This Article expresses the fear to trust the machine, and could already be found in Article 15(1) of the Directive 95/46:

> grant the right to every person not to be subject to a decision which produces legal effects concerning him or significantly affects him and is based solely on automated processing of data intended to evaluate certain personal aspects relating to him, such as his performance at work, creditworthiness, reliability, conduct, etc.

Our focus here is on "the processing" and the "decision based solely on automated processing." The idea that all stages in the processing are subject to the same calculus of potential override is flawed. The idea that automated decisions always put the individual at greater risk for encroachment on rights also needs more nuance.

For the police the rules on profiling are slightly different, and not based on the GDPR but a separate EU Directive for police and justice.[15] It prohibits profiling "which produces an adverse legal effect concerning the data subject or significantly affects him or her . . . unless authorised by law . . . and which provides appropriate safeguards for the rights and freedoms of the data subject" (Article 11(1)). Special for the area of police and justice is the rule on profiling that results in discrimination, which is always prohibited (Article 11(3)).

Without further going into details of data protection regulations in relation to big data[16] it is clear that not all relevant aspects of big data analytics and the use of algorithms are addressed. The remainder of this chapter discusses some aspects that are often overlooked in this context but we believe need to be taken into account when thinking about the use of algorithms and the possible impacts on data protection and privacy.

---

[15]   DIRECTIVE (EU) 2016/680 OF THE EUROPEAN PARLIAMENT AND OF THE COUNCIL of 27 April 2016 on the protection of natural persons with regard to the processing of personal data by competent authorities for the purposes of the prevention, investigation, detection or prosecution of criminal offences or the execution of criminal penalties, and on the free movement of such data, and repealing Council Framework Decision 2008/977/JHA, *Official Journal L 119, 4/5/2016*, pp. 89–131.

[16]   B. van der Sloot, *Privacy As Virtue: Moving Beyond the Individual in the Age of Big Data*, Ph.D Thesis University of Amsterdam, 2017.

III.   STAGES IN THE ALGORITHM

The huge controversial fallout over Edward Snowden's disclosures and NSA surveillance programs[17] shows that Judge Posner was right:[18] there are privacy encroachments that have huge consequences and there are privacy encroachments that have almost no consequences. It is important for legislation to distinguish the two. But how?

The legislation must refer to the algorithm, or at least the stages in the algorithmic process.[19] The public focus is traditionally on initial collection of data. Collection is the starting point of processing, and sets the stage for eventual legitimate further processing. What the law does not take into account, is that stages differ in their privacy risks and implications. At some stages, there may be many persons susceptible to small risks. Those risks may mainly be the exposure to the possibility of further consideration at a later stage. At a later stage in the algorithm, the risks to an individual's privacy, and more, may be great, but the numbers at risk at that stage may be small.

The NSA and The United States Foreign Intelligence Surveillance Court (FISC) regulated the process of programmatic warrants that specified the bulk collection. Separately, it regulated the individualized warrants for individuals used as selection terms for searches of databases. But both were guilty of not disclosing the important winnowing of the numbers during processing: collection (logging and warehousing), followed by n-hop discovery in social network analysis, followed by deletion of most records, followed by entry into the "corporate store", where a record was susceptible to search by an analyst. These are at least five stages of algorithmic processing.

At each stage, an individual was exposed to a different risk. At each stage, a different degree of automation and comprehension was employed. And at each stage, a different number of individuals were exposed. In fact, the rate of reduction from stage to stage was staggering: for every 100 million call detail records retained, the NSA discarded trillions, or tens of trillions, for a 1000:1 or 10000:1 rate of reduction.

Surely it is the obligation of effective regulation to refer to each stage of the algorithm separately, as the implications for privacy are so different at each stage.

A.   The Same Algorithm with Different Numbers and Risks

The source of controversy surrounding the NSA, and intelligence agencies in general, partly is caused by an inadequate interpretation of the different numbers and risks. The actual process, with mainly algorithmic risk at stages where large numbers were involved, was not much to complain about. But the same process, with a different set of risk exposures at each stage, could be a clear violation of privacy protections, truly analogous to a digital secret police state activity. FISC should have specified not just the

---

[17]   N.A. Sales, *Domesticating Programmatic Surveillance: Some Thoughts on the NSA Controversy. ISJLP* (2014) 10: 523.

[18]   R.A. Posner, *Privacy, surveillance, and law.* The University of Chicago Law Review (2008) 75, no. 1: 245–60.

[19]   K. Yeung, *Algorithmic Regulation: A Critical Interrogation.* Regulation and Governance (2017).

warrant-granting process, but also placed explicit limits on the practical effects at each stage, especially the numbers of persons at risk of further analytics.

Would it make a difference if a human were engaged at every step, or at only the final step (which in fact was the case in the NSA Social Network Analysis)? Would it make a difference if the final step produced no more than ten persons, say, as a limit to human analyst search of the corporate store? Or if no more than 1000 new individuals' data, per year, entered the corporate store for persistent availability longer than six months? What if the risk of being reviewed by automated methods at the first stage were reduced, so that randomly, one percent that could be connected under Social Network Analysis were actually retained for the next stage of processing? Would that not change the pragmatic risk of being under surveillance, at that stage? Or suppose that anyone not connected in the current month, under Social Network Analysis, could not be susceptible to retention through a Social Network Analysis connection in the immediate subsequent month? Surely that would reduce the pragmatic risk of surveillance at that algorithmic stage.

Astronomical numbers leave at first sight the impression that the privacy of many is violated during the first stages. What is necessary to be taken into account is what is exactly happening, and when.

There may yet be social implications of privacy encroachments that are very different from the individual implications; what may not affect more than 1000 individuals at a stage of processing might still be unacceptable with respect to societal norms, safeguards, and aims. For example, even if a mere ten persons were subject to human scrutiny at the final stage of algorithmic processing, if those persons were all minorities and selected based on minority status, there may be different legislative considerations in play.

Focusing on individual risk, however, leads to some interesting clarifications. Not all eyes and ears are the same. Computers are not the same as humans when they look. Most of the time the computer is logging benignly, in a way that lots of other computers in the communications path might be logging. Data collection that is mere logging is clearly less invasive than data collection that directly produces a list of persons of interest. Much of the time, an algorithm is looking at a record in order to discard it as uninteresting. That is in fact why automated methods are used as an automatic front end when processing huge volumes of data.

IV.   THE HUMAN FACTOR

A.   Not all Human Looking is the Same

There is a difference between looking by the machine and looking by humans. Not even all humans are the same. Some are not paying attention. Their surveillance is different from the surveillance of a probing, paranoid, or aggressively inferential mind. Some humans have more experience, understanding, or simply better hearing and eyesight, memory, and gestalt pattern recognition. Some humans can read lips or interpret body language. Canine surveillance, because of superior and unexpected sensory inputs, is different under the law. Some human surveillance and discovery takes place under warrant; some is inadmissible. Some recordings, audio, video, and photographic, are reviewable by humans. Listening to live audio once is different from listening with more time, filtering, enhancement, signal-to-noise ratio, dynamic range, and frequency-based equalization. It is remarkable that wiretap laws do not make more of these issues.

Wiretap is not even the right analogy. Computer logging of data is more like video camera surveillance, where the search takes place post hoc, with search terms or search parameters, and a specific sort of thing to be found (e.g., a shared rental agreement or airplane ticket). No doubt, relying on *Smith v. Maryland*[20] was convenient for US intelligence agencies to escape Fourth Amendment language in a hurry. But pen registers generate logs that can be comprehended by a human, while internet activity generates logs that must be processed algorithmically. They must be searched with some specificity or direction in order to produce discovery and inference. Of course, analytics on streaming text has in the past been more active than video scenes being sent to VCR or DVR. Smart video, of course, is beginning to resemble text analytics on streams and logs.

Not all humans are the same, further, because some humans carry guns. Others can have people arrested. Even non-human processing, at some stage, might carry the risk of harassment, exclusion from access to air transportation, foreign travel, or freedom of motion. Would it not make a difference if such risks from an automatic classifier applied to all persons at the collection stage, or whether such risks could apply only to persons who passed Social Network Analysis, were entered into the corporate store, were produced under human analyst search that required warranted search terms, after the 10000:1 winnowing?

B. Not All Computers Looking are the Same

What we have learned in the past two decades is that not all automata are the same with respect to subjecting individuals to analytics. What a drone can surveil, what can be gleaned from crowd-sourced data, or repeated study, pixel-by-pixel, of incidental video collection, what can be discovered by classifiers trained to find hidden structure and hidden criteria: these are important aspects of privacy for those who have privacy interests under the law. It is not sufficient to regulate collection or non-collection.

It should matter whether personal data is used in pursuit or profiling of that person, or whether the personal data is just used for determining base rates of what is normal. Many abnormality-detecting algorithms require the modeling of what is the "base rate." For the individual, this may be as simple as counting how many times the most average person uses the word "the" in the most average text. These machine learning methods look at a person's data precisely because that person is completely uninteresting.

Different kinds of AI may be relevant too. Logging is the lowest form of looking. But translating, parsing, and extracting topics and sentiments from text, automatically, may be more like a human looking. Face recognition is certainly a higher form of processing, and it can put individuals at higher risk at that stage because the inferences are more specific to the individual.[21] Biometric methods for access to secure places and accounts are now known to have unintended privacy risks that are potentially severe.[22] Scanning the

---

[20] *Smith v. Maryland*, 442 U.S. 735 (1979).

[21] A.G. Ferguson, *Big Data and Predictive Reasonable Suspicion*. (2015) 163 U. Pa. L. Rev. 327.

[22] D. Sherman, *Biometric Technology: The Impact on Privacy*, CLPE Research Paper No., 2005.

retina, pulse, and perspiration, or analysing the voice, can reveal increased probabilities for glaucoma, diabetes, stroke, congenital defect, speech impediment, and so forth.

It is not the complexity of the algorithm or the amount of data, but the risk of inference, intended and unintended. The risk of certain kinds of inferences comes with the potential damage that a person will be classified. Classification leads to denial of rights or worse. These are the things that concerned Posner, and should be considered explicitly by regulations. These are more important than fighting over the two extremes of collect-it-all and collect-none-whatsoever.

More importantly, from a potential consequence point of view, the risk of being profiled by an advertiser is usually considered to be much less than that of being profiled by law enforcement. An unwanted ad is not as bad as an unwanted knock on the door. But the possibility, and high probability, of losing the profile to a malicious third party actually reverses that inequality: usually the kind of data available to an ad agency is of higher quality, greater quantity, and longer time frame, than the data available to the government. Blackmail and identity theft are worse consequences, usually, than an hour long due diligence interview with DHS agents because an electronic connection was made between a known foreign agent and an innocent person.

C.   AI is not Human Comprehension

Perhaps the most profound confusion in the public's understanding of the NSA Section 215 activities was the conflation of human comprehension with artificial intelligence "comprehension." The public is becoming more aware about big data and AI in news reporting. It is not surprising, given the way that AI is portrayed, that people fear the privacy incursions of AI the way they would feel if the AI were replaced by a human. But of course, the AI is there because a human was unsuitable: either too slow, too unreliable, too easily bored or tired, too expensive, not facile with foreign language, not trained to optimal discrimination with respect to narrow criteria. AI is a business decision to automate, usually based on the quality of automation. But there is another reason to insert the AI: it has a natural uninterest in aspects of data that might impact an individual's privacy concerns. It doesn't gossip; it can't be distracted by irrelevance; it forgets what it is told to forget; it is not subject to human subterfuge or machination.

AI, analytics, and other algorithmic filtering are not at all like human looking when it comes to privacy. What matters are the potential consequences of the AI decision: the classification, the false positives, and the false negatives. When there is a pipeline of processing, as there was for the NSA, the consequences of classification at one stage are mostly the exposure to further processing at the next stage. This is where legal language that preserves the rights of citizens must bind.

V.   ON NUMBERS: RELEVANCE OF SCALE AND SCOPE

What has not yet been learned over the past decades is that numbers matter. An NSA Social Network Analysis program that produced 1,000,000 new names, with data saved in the corporate store for human analytic purposes, for two years at a time, is problematic no matter how the Social Network Analysis is justified. No doubt, 3-hop Social Network Analysis became 2-hop Social Network Analysis on such numerical considerations.

In the Apple versus FBI fight over unlocking a terrorist's iPhone, numbers mattered.[23] If the FBI were limited to ten, 100, or even 1000 such requests per year, with no serious collateral weakening of Apple's security, that would be acceptable to most citizens. It would balance the relevant interests under the law. There must be a number, however, perhaps a rate of 100,000, or 1,000,000 per year, at which the balance is clearly upset. Regulatory language avoids numerical limits and fractional rate guidelines, but sometimes a number sets forth the desired balance.

Law and computing both tend toward binary distinctions, with error-free discriminators. But practical judgement may simply be about having the right numerical proportions.

A.   Privacy Versus Security and Proper Balance of Risk and Exposure

Many think that the fundamental contest in the NSA/Snowden affair was between privacy and security. But these two are not necessarily opposed.[24] Increasing perimeter security can have benefits for free and open society within. Increasing privacy, especially against massive data loss and data theft by hackers, can increase security. This is because loss of personal data leads to more phishing and blackmail. Not collecting the data in the first place means no risk of losing the data en masse.

Managing risk is the correct way of looking at the problem. We must keep in mind that there are several different stages in a pipeline of processing, where many are exposed to the first stages, and few to the latter stages, and where earlier stages have few potential consequences, but latter stages may have serious entailments. This is true of many government and legal filtering processes, and it is a particularly appropriate view of analytics on data collected under programmatic warrants.

The question should always be, are there too many persons exposed to too much risk at any stage? It is not effective to argue that 100 million persons were exposed to the risk of future processing, and that future processing culminated in a severe curtailment of liberties. How many persons made it to that last stage? What were the criteria for retention from one stage to the next? If at some point there was deanonymization, so names and identities were available to cross-reference with other databases, was that premature considering the legitimate aims of the process?

VI.   CONCLUSION

Algorithms and artificial intelligence can be very powerful, and in the context of surveillance can do things ancient suppressors might have only dreamt of. We have to be cautious in applying the new technologies. Law provides the boundaries of what we should permit

---

[23]   M. Skilton and I. Ng (2016). *What the Apple versus FBI debacle taught us.* Scientific American blog, available at https://blogs.scientificamerican.com/guest-blog/what-the-apple-versus-fbi-debacle-taught-us/.

[24]   D.J. Solove, *Nothing to Hide: The False Tradeoff between Privacy and Security* (Yale University Press, 2011).

to be done by technology. In this chapter we elaborated on what should be thought of legally when regulating algorithms and privacy in surveillance. The present legal frameworks omit at least three angles.

First, the stages of the algorithmic process should be included in what legal constraints apply to these activities. Collection, selection, deletion, access, etc. are headed under the general concept of processing of data, but should be separately addressed. Second, the law should take into account the difference between people and machines. Some things people do are more infringing than what computers do, and vice versa. Making the right distinctions is needed. Third, the law should think more about numbers. Lawyers do not like it to be that precise, but at least particular margins or bandwidth could be indicated. This also helps in separating different degrees of privacy infringements.

SOURCES

List of Cases

Smith v. Maryland, 442 U.S. 735 (1979).

List of European Legislation

Directive 95/46/EC of the European Parliament and of the Council of 24 October 1995 on the protection of
  individuals with regard to the processing of personal data and on the free movement of such data, Official
  Journal L 281, 23/11/1995, pp. 31–50.
REGULATION (EU) 2016/679 OF THE EUROPEAN PARLIAMENT AND OF THE COUNCIL of 27
  April 2016 on the protection of natural persons with regard to the processing of personal data and on the
  free movement of such data, and repealing Directive 95/46/EC (General Data Protection Regulation), Official
  Journal L 119, 4/5/2016, pp. 1–88.
DIRECTIVE (EU) 2016/680 OF THE EUROPEAN PARLIAMENT AND OF THE COUNCIL of 27 April
  2016 on the protection of natural persons with regard to the processing of personal data by competent
  authorities for the purposes of the prevention, investigation, detection or prosecution of criminal offences or
  the execution of criminal penalties, and on the free movement of such data, and repealing Council Framework
  Decision 2008/977/JHA, Official Journal L 119, 4/5/2016, pp. 89–131.

14. The impact of AI on criminal law, and its twofold procedures
Ugo Pagallo and Serena Quattrocolo

I. INTRODUCTION

Artificial Intelligence (AI) is the field of science and technological innovation, which aims to create machines, artificial agents, and further complex systems, that mimic cognitive functions, such as reasoning, learning, and problem solving, that humans would associate with their own. Over the past years, the field has known a new renaissance: the improvement of more sophisticated statistical and probabilistic methods, the increasing availability of large amounts of data and of cheap, enormous computational power, up to the transformation of places and spaces into AI-friendly environments, e.g. smart cities and domotics, have all propelled a new "summer" for AI. After the military and business sectors, AI applications have entered into people's lives. From getting insurance to landing credit, from going to college to finding a job, even down to the use of GPS for navigation and interaction with the voice recognition features on our smartphones, AI is transforming and reshaping people's daily interactions with others and their environment. Whereas AI apps and systems often go hand-in-hand with the breath-taking advancements in the field of robotics, the Internet of Things, and more,[1] a particular set that augments or replaces analysis and decision-making by humans deserves specific consideration in this context. These techniques regard either the sector of data analytics, namely the use of AI systems that make sense of huge streams of data; or the discipline of machine learning, i.e. AI systems capable of defining or modifying decision-making rules autonomously. Suffice it to mention the example of a smart robot, Vital, which will be resumed in Part III of this chapter. Developed by Aging Analytics UK, Vital was appointed in May 2014 as a board member by the Japanese venture capital firm Deep Knowledge, in order to predict successful investments. As a press release was keen to inform us, Vital was chosen for its ability to pick up on market trends "not immediately obvious to humans," regarding decisions on therapies for age-related diseases. Drawing on the predictions of the AI machines, such trends of humans delegating crucial cognitive tasks to smart robots and further autonomous artificial agents will reasonably multiply in the foreseeable future.[2]

---

[1] See Ugo Pagallo, Massimo Durante, and Shara Monteleone, "What Is New with the Internet of Things in Privacy and Data Protection? Four Legal Challenges on Sharing and Control in IoT", in R. Leenes, R. van Brakel, S. Gutwirth and P. de Hert (eds.), *Data Protection and Privacy: (In)visibilities and Infrastructures* (Springer 2017) 59–78.

[2] An AI system can be conceived of as an autonomous system when it modifies its inner states or properties without external stimuli, thereby exerting control over its actions without any direct intervention of humans. Such a property can of course complement both the interactivity and adaptability of the system. In the first case, the system perceives its environment and responds to stimuli by changing the values of its own properties or inner states. In the second case, an AI

In light of this panoply of AI applications and systems, the aim of this chapter is to examine whether and to what extent current trends of AI may affect the tenets of the criminal law field. Attention should be drawn, first of all, to the old idea that "everything which is not prohibited is allowed." This principle is connected to the clause of immunity summed up, in continental Europe, with the formula of the principle of legality, i.e. "no crime, nor punishment without a criminal law" (*nullum crimen nulla poena sine lege*). Even though certain behaviors might be deemed as morally wrong, e.g. spying on individuals through AI robots, individuals can be held criminally liable for that behavior only on the basis of an explicit criminal norm. In the wording of Article 7 of the 1950 European Convention on Human Rights (ECHR), "[n]o one shall be held guilty of any criminal offence on account of any act or omission which did not constitute a criminal offence under national or international law at the time when it was committed." Contrary to the field of civil (as opposed to criminal) law, in which analogy often plays a crucial role so as to determine individual liability, we have thus to determine whether AI may produce a novel generation of loopholes in the criminal law field, forcing lawmakers to intervene at both national and international levels. In addition, we should ascertain whether, and to what extent, the increasing autonomy of AI decision-making can affect further tenets of this field, such as the notion of an agent's culpability (i.e. its *mens rea*), vis-à-vis matters of criminal conduct (i.e. the *actus reus*).

At this level of analysis, however, another differentiation appears critical. AI technology can indeed be used either for law enforcement purposes, or for committing (new kinds of) crimes. Whereas, in the first case, focus should be on matters of evidence, sentencing, bail, and so forth, the second case brings us back to the question on whether or not the use of AI technologies may bring about a new generation of crimes. Such a differentiation entails a further degree of complexity, because criminal law is not only an intricate field of its own, but we should add the critical discrepancies, both substantial and procedural, that often exist between multiple jurisdictions. For instance, from a substantial point of view, consider the current debate on forms of distributed responsibility that hinge on multiple accumulated actions of humans and computers that may lead to cases of impunity. Whilst the intricacy of the interaction between humans and computers has recommended most legal systems of the common law tradition to adopt forms of criminal accountability of corporations, the civil law tradition generally rejects this approach on the basis of the principle that "criminal responsibility is personal," according to e.g. the wording of Article 27(1) of the Italian Constitution.[3] On the other hand, from a procedural point of view, the same facts often are harnessed by different legal systems in divergent ways and moreover, multiple criteria for defining the notion of causation have been developed by different legal cultures. Whilst German lawyers mostly refer to the theory of the

---

system is adaptable, when it can improve the rules through which its own properties or inner states change. Taken together, such criteria single out why we should refer to an AI system as an "agent," rather than a simple tool of human interaction. See Ugo Pagallo, *From Automation to Autonomous Systems: A Legal Phenomenology with Problems of Accountability*, in IJCAI-17, pp. 17–23, available at https://www.ijcai.org/proceedings/2017/3.

[3]   See Ugo Pagallo, "AI and Bad Robots: The Criminology of Automation" in M.R. McGuire and Th.J. Holt (eds.), *The Routledge Handbook of Technology, Crime and Justice* (Routledge 2017) 643–53.

adequate event—and French scholars follow the theory of the strict accountability of those events—US lawyers are vice versa divided between advocates of the but-for test and the necessary-condition test, namely, between those arguing that the action at issue in the circumstances must be necessary to the outcome, and those claiming that the action at issue instead must be a necessary part of a set of conditions sufficient for the outcome.[4]

How, then, can we hope to successfully address those magnitudes of complexity? How should we select the observables and variables of the analysis? Which norms, procedures, and legal systems have to be taken into account?

In order to determine whether and the extent to which current AI developments may impact the tenets of the criminal law field, this chapter suggests to envision the terms of this impact as falling within the ends of a spectrum. At one end of the spectrum, we encounter a set of cases triggered by the use of AI systems and applications that neither upset current concepts and principles of criminal law, nor create new principles and concepts. This is not only the view of traditional legal scholars, keen on embracing the formalisms of the law, but it also is the way in which we have to test the resilience of today's criminal law. Given the nature of the legal question and the story and background of the issue, scholars should interpret the law in such a way that they can attain the answer that best justifies or achieves the integrity of the legal system under scrutiny. Yet, at the other end of the spectrum, we find cases that fall within the loopholes of today's criminal law, either because they impact on the primary rules of the system and the principle of legality, or because they impinge on the safeguards set up by the procedures of the field. As an illustration of this set of cases, contemplate what occurred between the early 1990s and 2001, when national and international lawmakers established a new class of computer crimes. A set of offenses that would be inconceivable once deprived of the technology upon which they depend, such as spamming or electronic identity thefts, forced lawmakers to intervene, by adding norms and procedures for the regulation of those novel circumstances and crimes.

Against the ends of this spectrum, we can select the norms, procedures, and legal systems, to be analysed in this chapter. The aim is to offer neither an exhaustive scrutiny of any given legal system, nor a complete examination of comparative law. Rather, the intent is to shed light on whether or not AI technologies—which are employed both for law enforcement purposes, and for committing (new types of) crimes—affect the principle of legality. Correspondingly, the chapter is divided into two parts.

Part II is devoted to the first scenario of enforcing the law through AI technology. While the discussion about the suitability of the exploitation of machine learning techniques and AI either as surveillance means, or as a human substitute in the judicial decision-making process is arising, focus is restricted upon the risks of using AI-based evidence in criminal proceedings. More particularly, attention is drawn to Articles 6 and 8 of the ECHR: Section A examines matters of privacy and data protection in the context of evidence collection (ECHR's Article 8). Section B dwells on the process of gathering evidence through AI systems vis-à-vis the principle of fair trial in criminal proceedings (Article 6). Section C deepens this standpoint in connection with the further principle of the "equality of arms." The overall aim is to show that the ECHR's rules can be interpreted

---

[4] See Ugo Pagallo, *The Laws of Robots: Crimes, Contracts, and Torts* (Springer 2013) at 74.

in such a way that no amendment of those norms is needed, in order to properly tackle the normative challenges of AI technology.

Part III scrutinizes whether AI may bring about a new generation of crimes. Section A considers the hypothesis of AI criminal minds, that is, whether the criminal culpability of an agent, or its *mens rea*, can be rooted in the artificial mind of a machine that really "wants." Section B explores how the material element of a crime would be affected by the decisions of AI systems and smart robots that can "sense," "think," and "act." Section C takes into account the growing capability of such AI systems to change and improve the values of their properties or inner states without external stimuli, so as to suggest some of the ways in which legal systems could deal with their unpredictable behaviour. Whilst current provisions of criminal law may properly tackle the normative challenges of AI as a means for law enforcement purposes, the aim of this Part is to stress that an increasing set of decisions taken by smart robots and AI systems may already fall within the loopholes of the system.

The conclusion of the chapter insists on the divergent results of the previous parts. Whilst procedures and norms examined in Part B may allow us to properly tackle the normative challenges of AI, this does not seem the case of the norms and procedures assessed in Part C. In this latter scenario, the primary rules of the law that intend to directly govern individual and social behaviour do not cover some of the new cases brought on by the use of the technology under examination. The lacunae that follow as a result suggest that we should take into account a different set of norms and procedures, namely, the secondary rules of change that permit to create, modify, or suppress the primary rules of the system.[5] The relation between the twofold procedures of our analysis, e.g. between the primary and secondary rules of the law, will thus be the subject of the final remarks of the chapter. Current developments of AI do not only cast light on the resilience of today's criminal law systems and the principle of legality, but also on basic categories of jurisprudence and its European counterpart, that is, the "general theory of law."

II.   ENFORCING THE LAW THROUGH AI

The aim of this Part is to examine how the use of AI techniques is affecting the current state-of-the-art in collecting evidence in criminal proceedings. More specifically, focus is on the individual right to a fair trial and the principle of "Equality of Arms" pursuant to Article 6(1) of the ECHR, which are coupled with the "minimum rights" of the individuals to be informed promptly and with adequate time and facilities for the preparation of their defence, in accordance with Article 6(3) of the ECHR.

This approach falls within two sets of boundaries. The first limit regards the complexity of digital evidence which, generally speaking, falls out of the scope of this chapter. A comprehensive literature is growing around how to integrate such complexity into the existing legal framework on evidence. Admissibility, reliability, and the evaluation of

---

[5]   This is of course the classical distinction made by Herbert L. A. Hart, *The Concept of Law* (Clarendon 1961). We can leave aside in this context Hart's secondary rules that regard the rules of recognition, and of adjudication.

digital evidence are indeed the subject of several research projects. Still, focus is here on the basic knowledge asymmetry that is determined by the recourse to AI systems in the evidence process. On the other hand, the second limit concerns how such asymmetry hampers the core of the notion of fair trial. In the European context, such concept has been established by the ECHR, drafted by the Council of Europe and signed in Rome in 1950. The European Court of Human Rights (ECtHR) case law has conveyed the notion into the national jurisdictions with such a persuasive force that, when the European Union decided to adopt a Charter of Fundamental Rights, the entitlement to a fair trial was drafted in Article 47. Thus, this chapter focuses on the concept of fair trial as worked out within the system of the ECHR.[6]

As occurs in other legal systems, the features and requirements of a fair but effective trial often overlap with the protection of people's privacy and their personal data. In the US law, for example, we should pay attention to the safeguards of the IV Amendment to the 1787 Constitution vis-à-vis the jurisprudence of the Supreme Court in Washington, from Olmsted (1928) to Katz (1967), Jones (2012), and Riley (2014).[7] In the ECHR framework, attention should be drawn to its Article 8, according to which "everyone has the right to respect for his private and family life, his home and his correspondence." In addition, according to Article 8(2) of the ECHR:

> there shall be no interference by a public authority with the exercise of this right except such as is in accordance with the law and is necessary in a democratic society in the interests of national security, public safety or the economic well-being of the country, for the prevention of disorder or crime, for the protection of health or morals, or for the protection of the rights and freedoms of others.

There is an interesting case law of the ECtHR about the relationship between Articles 8 and 6 of the ECHR. A trial, which incorporates a piece of evidence obtained in violation of Article 8's safeguards, may result in a breach of Article 6's principle of fairness. This kind of argument can be based on a critical review of the protection offered by the European Convention against the use of the most advanced systems of data processing in criminal proceedings, such as data analytics and machine learning techniques that are increasingly molding intelligence and police searches today. Our thesis is that AI systems, which will increasingly be used to generate evidence within criminal proceedings, entail a new set of issues that concern matters of transparency, group profiling, loss of confidentiality, and more. This set of issues suggests that we should shift the guarantee set up by the ECtHR from Articles 8 and 6 of the ECHR, to Article 6 alone. In order to explain why, the analysis of the chapter proceeds with the analysis of the protection of Article 8's "private life" and its personal data safeguards vis-à-vis the paradigm of evidence in the criminal law field.

---

[6] According to Art. 52 of the EU's Charter of the Fundamental Rights, to the extent in which the Charter provides for rights and guarantees that are also stated by the ECHR, the meaning and the scope of such rights should be the same. The EU is free, however, to provide for higher levels of protection.

[7] See for instance Orin S. Kerr, *Fourth Amendment Seizures of Computer Data* 119 Yale Law Journal 700 (2010); and Laura K. Donohue, *The Fourth Amendment in a Digital World* 71 NYU Annual Survey of American Law 553 (2017).

A.   Safeguarding Privacy in Europe: On ECHR's Article 8

Interference into private life or personal data engages two distinct aspects of Convention law, when such interference occurs as part of a criminal investigation. Systems of intrusion, such as wire-tapping and room bugging, have existed since evolution in communications started to spread, and have been used to both prevent crime and to repress it.[8] The attention of this chapter is focused exclusively on repression, this is to say the application of intruding technologies within the context of a criminal proceeding, aiming to find evidence of a specific criminal act. The ECHR, like other international conventions and many national constitutions, establishes fundamental rights in both these areas of interest. Whereas the individual's right to a fair trial is enshrined in Article 6, with specific attention to criminal proceedings in Paragraphs 2 and 3, the right to family life and private life is provided for—with a negative understanding of privacy that excludes interferences by public authority[9]—by Article 8 ECHR.

The latter creates a complex system of balances between competing values.[10] The values enshrined in the first paragraph—family life, private life[11]—can be balanced with other issues of general interest, listed thereinafter, under two capital conditions.[12] The first condition is legality, namely, such balance must be provided by law. The second condition has to do with the notion of necessity in a democratic society. Although the issue is not central to our analysis, it is clear that the criterion of "necessity in a democratic society" is highly subjective and unspecific. The ECtHR has tried to further clarify the formula, introducing a test of proportionality between the individual position and the necessity in a democratic society. This approach should always be

---

[8]   We deem this distinction useful to limit the extent of this paper. However, it has been argued that the distinction itself has rapidly blurred with the advent of the information society. By the means of the latter, *ius puniendi* is shifting towards social control of danger, whilst criminal law is slipping into security law. Storage, processing, and use of data have been fostering this trend, pushing police and prosecutors to gain growing momentum over judiciary. See John A.E. Vervaele, "Surveillance and Criminal Investigation: Blurring of Thresholds and Boundaries in the Criminal Justice System?", in S. Gutwirth, R. Leenes, and P. De Hert (eds.), *Reloading Data Protection* (Springer 2014) at 116. See also Céline Cocq and Francesca Galli, *The Catalysing Effect of Serious Crime on the Use of Surveillance Technologies for Prevention and Investigation Purposes* 4(3) New Journal of European Criminal Law 256–89 (2013).

[9]   See Paul De Hert and Serge Gutwirth, "Privacy, Data Protection and Law Enforcement. Opacity of the Individual and Transparency of Power", in E. Cleas, A. Duff and S. Gutwirth (eds), *Privacy and the Criminal Law* (Intersentia 2006) 61–104. It has been noted that the Court has adopted an approach which is almost similar to the one displayed by many national constitutions: see Pablo Santolaya, "The Right to a Private and Family Life", in X. Garcia Loca and P. Santolaya (eds.), *Europe of Rights: A Compendium on the European Convention of Human Rights* (Martinus Nijhoff 2012) at 339.

[10]   It should be stressed that privacy does not represent an absolute, but a relational value in the European legal framework. See Ugo Pagallo, *Online Security and the Protection of Civil Rights: A Legal Overview* 26(4) Philosophy and Technology 381–95 (2013); and De Hert and Gutwirth, *supra* at note 9, at 74.

[11]   For a reconstruction of privacy as a fundamental right, at least in the western society, see De Hert and Gutwirth, *supra* note 9, at 63–64.

[12]   These conditions can actually "weaken" the protection of individual privacy: see Claes et al., *supra* note 9, at 1.

coupled with the principle of subsidiarity,[13] so as to demonstrate that the intrusion was the lesser invasive instrument being available. In addition, the Court has relied extensively on the "margin of appreciation" doctrine, in a broad context of legitimate exceptions,[14] showing a reluctance to require states to prove the real "necessity" of the interference;[15] and using the legality criterion as a justification for such a permissive approach.[16]

Within the framework of these two conditions, the list of general issues that can be balanced with the right to private life is extremely lengthy. The list includes what is necessary in the name of national security, public safety and economic well being of the country, the prevention of disorder or crime, the protection of health or of morals, and the protection of the rights and freedoms of others.[17] When interfering into an individual's right to a private life hinges on one of these reasons, the Court is entitled to conclude that there has been no violation. This exception is particularly relevant in cases where the intrusion has been committed by a public authority in the context of the prevention of a crime (as expressly provided by Article 8 Paragraph 2 ECHR); or, of a criminal investigation. This is exactly the context that gives rise to the issues that are addressed here. Once the conditions set up by Article 8 Paragraph 2 ECHR are respected, even the use of smart AI systems to both intrude into an individual's personal sphere and process the data related to his or her life can be lawful.

In recent decades, the Court has also worked out a "common framework of principles and conditions to be respected" in the legitimate use of data processing by public criminal authorities.[18] In particular, the Court has elaborated a number of indexes, which may specifically satisfy either the principle of necessity, or that of legality.[19] As to the principle of necessity, the Court often refers to "a pressing social need" as a fundamental requirement to justify the interference. Such a need must be proportional to the legitimate aim of the intrusion into the personal sphere through e.g. data processing: on this basis, the ECtHR often considers the effectiveness of the measures deployed by national authorities vis-à-vis the goal pursued. This brings to the attention of the Court possible alternative ways to protect the very same public interest, by introducing a sort of adequacy principle that is intended to make the evaluation less abstract.[20]

---

[13]   See for example ECtHR, *Siliadin v. France*, 26.7.2005; *M.C. v. Bulgaria*, 4.12.2003; and, *X and Y v. The Netherlands*, 26.3.1985.

[14]   Since there are no universal accepted standards for these exceptions, the Court's task to assess what is "necessary in a democratic society" is not easy. See Frank Verbruggen, "The Glass May Be Half-Full or Half-Empty, but It Is Definitely Fragile", in Claes et al., *supra* note 9, at 125.

[15]   Daniel De Beer, Paul De Hert, Gloria González Fuster and Paul Gutwirth, *Nouveaux éclairages de la Notion de donné personnelle et application audacieuse du critère de proportionnalité* 81 Revue Trimestrielle des Droits de l'Homme 156 (2010).

[16]   See, in critical terms, De Hert and Gutwirth, *supra* at note 9, at 90: "the citizen gets procedural guarantees as a compensation for the lack of testing of reasonableness of the intrusion."

[17]   Some claim that the State is the first source of threat to privacy: see Claes et al., *supra* note 9, at 2.

[18]   See Rosaria Sicurella and Valeria Scalia, *Data Mining and Profiling in the Area of Freedom, Security and Justice* 14(4) New Journal of European Criminal Law 437 (2013).

[19]   Having been drafted in more recent years (2000), the EU's Charter of Fundamental Rights expressly provides for protection of personal data in Art. 8.

[20]   Sicurella and Scalia, *supra* note 18, at 442.

As to the legality requirement, the Court has adopted a non-formal approach. On the one hand, not every kind of legal provision satisfies the condition of Article 8 Paragraph 1 ECHR. The act providing for personal data processing must be accessible;[21] and foreseeable.[22] This means, according to the Court's case law: (i) a clear definition of the cases in which data are processed; (ii) a transparent description of the scope; and (iii) an objective set of the conditions of discretion that the public authority enjoys. On the other hand, these requirements can be achieved by the states even through administrative regulations, provided that they are accessible.[23] An Act of Parliament is not always necessary.[24] However, in its assessment of the adequacy of the provisions aimed at meeting these requirements, the Court often tends to consider the existence and availability of judicial checks as well,[25] thereby transforming the requirement of the "provision by law" into a control on the existence of adequately transparent procedural guarantees against any abuse.[26]

In order to sum up this extensive case law without over-simplification, we can say that the main features of the Court's reasoning concern the principle of adequacy, embedded in the test of necessity in a democratic society; and the principle of transparency, as referred to in the legal text.[27] Yet, striking the balance between the interest of justice and the protection of people's privacy can be challenging, because the individual is not only confronted with the state's punitive power, i.e. one of the highest and strongest expressions of the nation-state's sovereignty. In addition, the alleged violation of the private sphere, being a breach of the Convention *per se*, entails a further possible effect. It concerns the outcome of the criminal proceeding in which the employment of AI techniques is used as evidence.

B.   Gathering Evidence between ECHR's Articles 8 and 6

The text of Article 6 ECHR addresses the topic of evidence in a somewhat fragmented way. Lacking general provisions, specific attention has been drawn both to the notion of testimony in Paragraph 3, Letter D; and, to the set of guarantees provided by Letter B, which represents the core of a fair system of evidence. All these provisions are part of the overall recognition of fairness and the "Equality of Arms" in Paragraph 1. Leaving the overarching case law and literature about the ECtHR approach to evidence aside, we should stress that whenever evidence is obtained in breach of other conventional

---

[21]   In the name of accessibility, the ECtHR criticized the wording of a national law in *Kokkinakis v. Greece* (25.5.1993).

[22]   Foreseeability has played an important role in pushing both the due process requirements of the ECHR's Art. 6 and the effective remedy of Art. 13 to merge into the framework of Art. 8: see De Hert and Gutwirth, *supra* note 9, at 85.

[23]   Check the case *Kruslin v. France* (24.4.1990), in which an unwritten rule of criminal procedure was deemed to satisfy Art. 8 ECHR.

[24]   For a critical opinion, see De Hert and Gutwirth, *supra* note 9, at 87.

[25]   See ECtHR, *Klass v. GFR*, 6.9.1978.

[26]   See Olivier De Schutter, *La Convention européenne des droits de l'homme à l'épreuve de la lutte contre le terrorisme* 185 Revue Universelle des Droits de l'Homme 142 (2001).

[27]   "Transparency seems to have replaced legitimacy as the core value of data protection": De Hert and Gutwirth, *supra* note 9, at 80. See also Sicurella and Scalia, *supra* note 18, at 443.

principles, the Court usually follows the "Gäfgen doctrine."[28] The use of a "poisoned fruit"—namely a piece of evidence gathered in breach of another guarantee of the Convention, such as Article 3, or 8—does not amount, *per se*, to a violation of Article 6 ECHR, if that evidence does not represent the unique or decisive basis for the judgment. The "preponderance-test" is applied by the Court in the context of an overall evaluation of the fairness of the whole proceeding. This position has often been criticized. Consider for example how difficult it is to apply a preponderance-test to any cognitive process, like delivering a judgment. Is it really possible to revise a decision-making process, so as to assess the real impact on the verdict of an unlawful element that has been used in it?[29] Notwithstanding critical remarks, compiled even by some of the judges themselves, in the form of concurring and dissenting opinions,[30] the ECtHR still relies on these criteria,[31] which equally apply to violations of Article 8 ECHR. As a result, whenever an individual reckons that her rights under Article 8 ECHR have been violated during criminal proceedings and that the results of such procedures have affected the verdict against her, the individual must first demonstrate a violation of Article 8 by the public authorities in interfering with their private life. Then, she must establish that the use of the results of such interference in evidence has vitiated the fairness of the whole proceedings.[32]

This approach has not prevented the Court from delivering judgments addressing the question of a "double violation" of Articles 8 and 6 ECHR. However, such a strategy has at least three shortcomings. First, it places a substantial burden on the applicant's shoulders. Second, the application of the "preponderance-test" may lead to an unsatisfactory result in a trial, which was judged to be overall fair, notwithstanding the use of unlawful evidence. Third, this conclusion on the shortcomings of the ECtHR's case law will likely be exacerbated by further developments in technology.

To some extent, European jurisdictions regulate interferences with private life through intrusive investigative methods. Searches, seizures, wiretaps and room bugging are usually regulated by procedural guidelines, often representing the practical implementation of the constitutional provisions that recognise the right to private individual and family life. Whilst such intrusive investigative methods often rely on new and cutting-edge technologies, it is not uncommon for the development of legal principles to lag far behind

---

[28]   See Grand Chamber, *Gäfgen v. Germany*, 1.6.2010, Paras. 179–80. More recently, see *Svetina v. Slovenia*, 22.5.2018, Paras. 42–53.

[29]   The concept of "sole and decisive" evidence (and other synonyms, like "main") is often applied by the Court, also with regard to other aspects of criminal proceedings. On the one hand, the Court applies the concept to cases of convictions based on written statements, by a witness non-attending to trial hearings. It is well known that the ECtHR case law on such subject was openly challenged by the UK Supreme Court in the case of *Horncastle and others*, pushing the Strasbourg Court to a "compromise," in the case of *Al Khawaja and Taheri v. UK*, (Gr. Ch., 15.12.2011). On the other hand, the concept of "main evidence" is applied by the Court in cases in which the appellate judge reversed a first instance acquittal, without "a direct assessment of the evidence given by the prosecution witnesses" (see, among others, *Dan v. Moldova*, 5.7.2011, cited here, Para. 31). However, such a big collection of case law does not provide either a clear or a decisive definition of what "decisive" evidence is.

[30]   See Francis G. Jacobs, Robin C.A. White and Clare Ovey, *The European Convention on Human Rights*, by B. Rainey, E. Wicks and C. Ovey (eds.), (Oxford University Press 2014) at 289.

[31]   For a comprehensive critique on the (inconsistent) use of the "sole and decisive" evidence test, see Ryan Goss, *Criminal Fair Trial Rights* (Hart 2014) at 170.

[32]   See Verbruggen, *supra* note 14, at 132.

technological evolution and at certain points in our history the gap between these two dimensions has been particularly wide.

We are currently experiencing such a moment. In recent decades, two phenomena have deeply influenced the relationship between law and technology. First, research into AI has resulted in dramatic advances, for completely automated processes can mine incredible amounts of data, progressively gaining knowledge from them, so as to apply such knowledge in successive mining. Second, the exponential spread of smartphones and other similar internet-based devices has provided easy access to those amounts of data. As a consequence of how these two factors combine, the meaning of private life protection has realigned. The traditional places and contexts of such protection, i.e. home and correspondence, no longer correspond to the centre of an individual's sphere of privacy, so that national legislation providing for limitations on searches, wire-tapping and room-bugging in an individual's domicile, is rapidly becoming inadequate. Although "home" is still the preferential site for private life,[33] a substantial part of such a private life is now invested in our electronic devices, which follow our constant movements in real time. This creates a sort of duplication of our identity; the physical side and now the digital side, which may or may not overlap. Yet, accessing the digital side of this identity has become the most effective way to interfere with an individual's physical identity. Protecting the home from investigative intrusion through exclusionary rules and procedural limitations is not sufficient anymore. [34] Also, the requirement of judicial authorisation is losing its effectiveness,[35] as the concepts on which these procedural guarantees are based have increasingly blurred. This scenario makes it quite evident that the pre-existing procedural rules have been deprived of any effectiveness vis-à-vis the use of highly sophisticated AI techniques. Such use does not necessarily constitute a breach of Article 8(1) ECHR especially if it is considered as just "a different method" for phone-tapping which was consistent with the requirement of "provision by law." The concept of "digital domicile" would possibly better fit the current need for privacy protection.

There is however a further risk inherent in this scenario. The process of gathering evidence through AI systems and algorithms brings to the trial process forms of proof whose reliability depends entirely on the accuracy of the technological means being used. Whether a certain conversation occurred in one place or another, at one time or another, are matters of crucial importance in criminal proceedings. How is it possible to assess the correctness of data, which was gathered exclusively through e.g. an algorithm? Is there any chance to challenge the correctness of such data?[36] Algorithmic modelling and AI neural networks are just the current stage of the long-lasting phenomenon of knowledge

---

[33]   About the "sanctity" of the home, see De Hert and Gutwirth, *supra* note 9, at 67.

[34]   Reflect on conditions limiting room bugging and phone tapping to some listed crimes, or restricting them to specific situations (e.g., a person who is reasonably suspected of committing a crime is present in the house).

[35]   Many jurisdictions provide for a double guarantee: each interference into private life must be provided by law and authorised by a judicial authority. The judicial intervention is seen as an opacity tool: see De Hert and Gutwirth, *supra* note 9, at 69.

[36]   See De Hert and Gutwirth, *supra* note 9, at 62, concerning the protection of sources by intelligence agencies.

asymmetry, which is said to have begun when courts started relying on expert evidence in complicated cases.[37] Some have found a solution through access to the digital code regulating the algorithm in accordance with the above-mentioned paradigm of transparency.[38] Unless investigators revert to the specifically crafted systems of accountability,[39] such access to the digital code implies that a new algorithm should be at work for almost each subsequent investigation. Although this solution can be highly ineffective, it draws attention to a point that is crucial in this context. Relying on algorithmic systems and neural networks in order to interfere with an individual's private life for investigative reasons can seriously impair the position of the parties.[40]

All in all, substituting traditional technical instruments with completely automated processes and smart AI systems brings about two main effects. First, the intrusion is more severe since the traditional limitations represented by "home" and "correspondence" are blurred and accessing an individual's private life via e.g. data mining techniques opens up access to incredible amounts of data. Second, the chance to intrude, automatically, into such a broad range of information clearly impairs the defendant's ability to challenge the evidence,[41] unless they are allowed access to the "logic" that is regulating the AI system.[42] This new scenario shifts the matter of contention from a problem of interference with private life, to an issue of Equality of Arms.[43]

C.   The Equality of Arms: On ECHR's Article 6

The use of AI systems in criminal investigations poses major challenges in relation to the protection of privacy, since most of such investigations can be conceived of as fully compliant with the provisions of Article 8 ECHR. However, such use implies a huge disproportion between the parties to a criminal proceeding. Whilst prosecutors and police can rely on constantly updated digital resources, the defendants have almost no

---

[37]   See Allan J. Brimicombe and Pat Mungroo, "Algorithms in the Dock: Should Machine Learning Be Used in British Courts?", presentation at the 4th Winchester Conference on Trust, Risk, Information and the Law, 3 May 2017.

[38]   See, extensively, Mireille Hildebrandt, "Profile Transparency by Design? Re-enabling Double Contingency", in M. Hildebrandt and M. de Vries, *Privacy, Due Process and the Computational Turn* (Routledge 2013) at 239.

[39]   See below Section C of this part.

[40]   See Ugo Pagallo, *Algo-Rhythms and the Beat of the Legal Drum*, Philosophy and Technology (August 2017) especially Para. 3.2.

[41]   See Michael Cross, *Justice by Algorithms Could "Bring Courts to an Halt"* The Law Society Gazette (3.5.2017); and, *Id.*, *Algorithms and Schrodinger's Justice* The Law Society Gazette (8.5.2017).

[42]   It is worth reminding the importance, for data accuracy, of the developing researches in the so-called *trusted computing*: see Chris Mitchell, *Trusted Computing* (IET 2005); and, Rolf Oppliger and Ruedi Rytz, *Does Trusted Computing Remedy Computer Security Problems* 3(2) IEEE 16–19 (2005).

[43]   According to De Hert and Gutwirth, *supra* note 9, at 90: "Art. 8 is about substantive issues, Article 6 about procedural Rights". More particularly, they affirm, "the transformation of Art. 8 into a source of procedural Rights and procedural conditions takes it away from the job it was designed for. . . to prohibit unreasonable exercises of power and to create zones of opacity" (*op. cit.*, at 91).

opportunity to challenge the evidence against them,[44] unless they are able to access the algorithm and logic behind those very resources. Yet, we argue that the Convention can offer a redress for this situation, irrespective of the eventual violation of Article 8 ECHR. Whenever investigations are based on AI techniques, the denial of discovery in relation to the program, code, or data governing the AI system, may amount to a violation of Article 6(1) ECHR. It would represent a clear infringement of the principle of Equality of Arms between the parties.[45]

Our thesis requires however some further reflection. First and foremost, it is worth remembering the very essence of the "Equality of Arms" under the ECtHR case law. The legal basis for this principle is given by Article 6(1) ECHR, although no explicit reference to it is provided in the text. Such a principle has indeed been crafted in the jurisprudence of the Court. At the core of the fairness—consider also the French version of the concept, *équité*—of the proceedings, all kinds of proceedings (civil, regulatory, and criminal) have two intertwined features: the "adversariness" and the Equality of Arms. Far from diverging, they intermingle, especially within the framework of evidence collection and presentation. More particularly, in the context of criminal proceedings, the ECtHR pays attention to the natural disparity between the prosecution and the defence. The public role attached to the first prevents any ideal parity with the latter. However, this ontological difference between the parties of the criminal proceeding does not affect the capital importance of the principle, for it guarantees "each party to be given a reasonable opportunity to present his case under conditions that do not place him at a substantial disadvantage vis-à-vis his opponent."[46] This is not, of course, a declamatory statement, deprived of any effectiveness. As the Court stressed in a very famous case, the parties must be aware of the opponent's statements and allegations and get "a real opportunity to comment" on it.[47] Thus, "an indirect and purely hypothetical possibility for an accused to comment on prosecution arguments" does not fulfil the Convention requirement, being in breach of the Equality of Arms. This long lasting reasoning by the Court casts light on the main aspect of our argument. The core of the guarantee consists of an effective and non-theoretical chance to challenge evidence. We argue that such a chance depends on the inner features of each piece of inculpatory evidence, and when such features rely exclusively on the algorithmic processes, or on the neural networks, of the AI systems, the room for effective criticism is hampered.

How, for example, is such a situation different from the case of *Khan vs. UK* from 2000?[48] In this case the Court found a violation of Article 8 ECHR, because of an unlawful tapping of a private conversation (at the time, the national jurisdiction did not provide for legal regulation of such hidden listening devices), but rejected the alleged violation of Article 6(1), as the applicant was afforded the chance to challenge the authenticity of the recording. The reliability of data gathered and processed in an automated manner cannot be challenged in a "traditional" way. There is no argument for the defence without having access to some technical information. The main and apparently impossible goal is having access to the "hidden algorithm." Therefore, is there an unavoidable violation of

---

[44]   See Vervaele, *supra* note 8, at 124.
[45]   *Id.*, at 127.
[46]   See *Kress v. France*, Gr. Ch., 7.6.2001, Para. 72.
[47]   See *Brandstetter v. Austria*, 28.8.1991, Para. 67.
[48]   See Rainey, Wicks, and Ovey, *supra* note 30, at 281.

Article 6(1) ECHR, when evidence is collected through data mining and machine learning techniques? Before we try to answer this question, we must verify some conditions.

As mentioned above in Section B, transparency represents a general condition of fairness in gathering evidence, and may be the key to the whole trial fairness in the criminal law field. Transparency can be achieved by e.g. demanding the source code—together with inputs and outputs—of the relevant automated process.[49] Still, it has been noted that transparency is not enough in itself. For instance, the disclosure of the source code is not considered true transparency, because only experts can understand it.[50] Moreover, open-source codes may not ensure accountability in all cases.[51] Whereas, on the one hand, *ex post* verification is often insufficient to validate properties of software that were not conceived and designed with accountability in mind;[52] on the other hand, it is often necessary to keep the decision policy at the base of the algorithmic process secret. This is of course the case for AI systems used for investigation purposes, whose effectiveness would be completely hampered with full disclosure. Are there effective solutions to this deadlock?

To some extent, one possible solution concerns the so called "zero-knowledge proof," i.e. cryptographic tools, allowing to demonstrate that the decision policy which was actually used has certain properties, without disclosing what the decision policy is.[53] Such an instrument seems to allow the defence to challenge the accuracy of inculpatory evidence without implying, necessarily, the disclosure of the codes and hence, the re-writing of them. However, such a system presupposes that the algorithmic process was designed with this feature in mind. In addition, zero-knowledge proof software can help challenging the accuracy of a digital evidence's output, rather than the process of gathering data. This means that it can shed light on the criteria applied to the mining of data (of which the digital evidence is the output); yet, such software is not useful in assessing the reliability of the data gathered by means of an algorithmic chain (e.g. trojan horses), so as to use such data as evidence in trial.

As to the area of the EU, the recent directive 2016/680,[54] on the processing of personal data by competent authorities for the purposes of the prevention, investigation, detection

---

[49]   See Joshua A. Kroll, Joanna Huey, Solon Barocas, Edward Felten, Joel R. Reindenberg, David G. Robinson and Harlan Yu, *Accountable Algorithms* 165 University of Pennsylvania Law Review 23 (2017).

[50]   See Ansgar Koene, Helena Webb and Menisha Patel, First UnBias Stakeholders Workshop, EPRSC, 2017, at 11.

[51]   See Kroll et al., *supra* note 49, at 23.

[52]   *Id.*, at 24.

[53]   *Id.*, at 30. Authors provide a useful example. Imagine that two millionaires are out to lunch and they agree that the richer of them should pay the bill. However, neither is willing to disclose the amount of her wealth to the other. A zero-knowledge proof allows them both to learn who is wealthier (and thus who should pay the restaurant tab) without revealing how much either is worth.

[54]   The directive is part of a two-tier EU initiative, encompassing the regulation 2016/679 on personal data processing, the so-called GDPR, and the directive itself, regulating, more specifically, data processing for criminal justice purposes. The directive is a more flexible legal instrument, allowing the Member States a certain margin of manoeuvre in its implementation. About the relationship between the two instruments see Paul De Hert and Vagelis Papakstantinou, *The New Police and Criminal Justice Data Protection Directive* 7(1) New Journal of European Criminal Law 9 (2016).

or prosecution of criminal offence, sets some important points.[55] Part III deals with the rights of the data subject, this is to say the person whose data is processed. Whereas the text provides for an apparently wide range of access rights, the directive does not afford the defendant a discovery of the digital codes by the law enforcement agencies. Of course, it is premature to say whether the directive's balance between data protection and public interest is appropriate.[56] Nonetheless, Article 20 of the directive sets forth that transparency should be taken into account at the stage of designing data-mining software: this would certainly represent an improvement, and would prevent shortcomings related to an ex-post impossibility of revising the trustworthiness of the evidence.

Another possible solution is to ask (and provide) for independent certification of the AI system's trustworthiness.[57] An expert-witness could be appointed by the judge to verify either the algorithmic process, or the neural network of a certain AI system, whenever the parties express their doubt about the correctness of automated data.[58] This would certainly increase the chances to challenge the accuracy of the data, although it could only be an "indirect" challenge, since it would be mediated by the direct experience of the court's expert, whom the defence may not trust.

To make things even more intricate, it should be added that total transparency can be a double-edged sword, with algorithms being challenged line by line "to the point where courts no longer function."[59] Introducing a judge-appointed expert-witness would imply in many jurisdictions to allow the parties to appoint their own expert-witnesses, with a huge experts' battle about the best way to assess the AI's neural network accuracy, or some algorithmic bias, eventually resulting in the judge's confusion. This is a well-known scenario that gained momentum with the growing application of science and technology in criminal proceedings. A burgeoning literature dwells upon the myriad issues related to the complicated relations between trials (moving from a fact backwards to the past), and science (moving from a hypothesis forward to the future). Especially in recent decades, criminal justice has witnessed a progressive impairment of the parties triggered by the growing recourse to new technologies, since the more evidence becomes technological, the less the parties, and particularly the defence, are able to challenge it. The prosecution is usually able to access the best technology, with an "indirect" financial exposure, relying on public money. Moreover, the use of AI systems and algorithms often suggests neutrality of the method, discouraging any challenge. The sense of impairment and inequality between the parties has thus been growing: when AI accountability is at stake, such impairment seems to overwhelm the whole criminal justice system, representing the breaking point.

Admittedly, Equality of Arms and fair trial are not absolute human rights, since they admit restrictions.[60] As the ECtHR has stressed time and again, however, the ultimate

---

[55]   The directive only applies, however, to data processing that falls within the scope of the EU law.

[56]   See De Hert and Papakstantinou, *supra* note 54, at 12. In their opinion, it will be up to the EU Member States to strike a proper and effective balance between the two concurrent interests.

[57]   See Cross, *supra* note 41.

[58]   The directive 2016/680 imposes the Data Protection Authorities as independent supervising agencies in the police personal data processing context as well. They may have some role in providing courts with unbiased controls over digital evidence trustworthiness.

[59]   See Cross, *supra* note 41.

[60]   With specific regard to these issues see Vervaele, *supra* note 8, at 127.

sense of the Equality of Arms is a "fair balance" between the parties. This amounts to say that the use of AI systems, based on neural networks and algorithmic processes, prevents any chance of an effective balance between the parties without the recourse to one of the aforementioned transparency solutions. The use of AI cutting-edge technologies, in other words, potentially implies a breach of Article 6(1) ECHR.

Accepting this conclusion does not imply that Article 8 ECHR falls completely out of the scope of this analysis. In some situations the use of a "non-validated" AI system can also amount to a violation of Article 8 ECHR, according to the standards set by the case law stressed above in Section A. However, this should no longer be a necessary condition for the assessment of the trial's fairness. Such a "shift" would significantly improve the protection of the defendant's rights. By claiming a violation of Article 6(1), regardless of the eventual unlawfulness of the interference with private life, this approach would help us ensuring that the conventional guarantees are constantly updated in relation to the ever-improving technologies that inevitably "filter" into criminal investigations practice, sometimes well below the radar of the existing procedural guarantees.

III.   BREAKING THE LAW THROUGH AI

Let us change now our perspective. Rather than using AI systems for law enforcement purposes, as we examined in the previous sections, this part of the chapter aims to explore the other way around, namely, how AI systems may break the law.

The current state-of-the-art in legal science takes AI systems and smart robots off the hook with respect to all claims of criminal liability. For the foreseeable future, these applications will be legally unaccountable before criminal courts, because they lack the set of preconditions, such as consciousness, free will and human-like intentions, that is, the *mens rea*, for attributing liability to a party. This is not to say, however, that such AI systems do not affect certain fundamental tenets of the field. In addition to AI intentions, attention should be drawn to how the growing autonomy of some robots and further artificial agents may induce a new set of *actus reus*, that is, the material element of a crime. Leaving aside in this context the field of the laws of war,[61] the analysis of this Part is restricted to people's everyday interaction and the legal accountability that is typically imposed

---

[61]   By distinguishing between the general framework of the criminal law field and its specific sub-sector on the laws of war and international humanitarian law, the latter are currently regulated by the 1907 Hague Convention, the four Geneva Conventions from 1949, and the two 1977 additional Protocols. This set of provisions establishes the clauses of immunity, or of general irresponsibility, that hinge on the traditional categories of *ius ad bellum* (i.e. when and how resort to war can be justified), and *ius in bello* (i.e. what can justly be done in war). Over the past decade, scholars have stressed time and again that the behaviour of AI robots on the battlefield is increasingly falling within the loopholes of the legal system. Significantly, Christof Heyns, Special Rapporteur on extrajudicial executions, urged in his 2010 Report to the UN General Assembly that Secretary-General Ban Ki-moon convene a group of experts in order to address "the fundamental question of whether lethal force should ever be permitted to be fully automated." Therefore, as previous international agreements have regulated technological advancements over the past decades in such fields as chemical, biological and nuclear weapons, landmines, and the like, a similar UN-sponsored agreement seems urgently needed to define the conditions of legitimacy for

on individuals who commit a wrong prohibited by law. More particularly, focus is on a class of AI machines partaking or being used in criminal enterprises, so as to determine whether their use can be prosecuted under current provisions of criminal law, or whether we should expand such current provisions. In May 2015, for example, penetration tester Parker Schmitt and robot expert David Jordan showed that drones can spoof Wi-Fi and steal sensitive data, such as credit card information, adding a new level of anonymity on which crackers can thrive. But, what if such drones acted autonomously?

Also, we should investigate whether a new generation of AI *actus reus* may affect notions on which individual responsibility is traditionally grounded in the field of criminal law, i.e. basic concepts defining human *mens rea*. The more AI systems and smart robots will "sense," "think," and "act," at least in the engineering meaning of these words, the more the AI properties of these machines could transform the ways in which lawyers traditionally grasp individual criminal accountability as an issue of reasonable foresee-ability, fault, negligence, or causation. Since ancient Roman law, after all, the notion of legal responsibility has rested with the Aristotelian idea that we have to take into account *id quod plerumque accidit* in the physical domain, that is, to focus on that which generally happens as the most probable outcome of a given act, fact, event, or cause. By consider-ing the growing capability of robots and complex AI systems to change and improve the values of their properties or inner states without external stimuli, crucial criteria for selecting from the entire chain of events the specific condition, or the set of conditions, that best explains a given outcome, can be challenged by the unpredictable behaviour of these artefacts. Together with the issue of whether, and to what extent, a new generation of AI *actus reus* shall be added to the list of crimes set up by national codes, statutes, or international agreements, we have thus to examine how the mental element requirements of the criminal law field may change vis-à-vis the decisions of some AI machines.

A popular claim of today's jurisprudence is that AI technology would neither affect concepts and principles of criminal law, nor create new principles and concepts. In order to understand this traditional point of view, the interplay between the human's mental element of an offense (i.e. the human's *mens rea*), and the material element of such a crime (i.e. an AI *actus reus*), should be assessed. This stance ends up with three different scenarios. First, we have to take into account cases where the design stance supersedes any evaluation of the AI system's intentions, since the primary aim of a given technology is incapable of lawful uses. Consider the case of robotic submarines designed and employed by Colombian drug traffickers: once ascertained that infringing uses represent the pri-mary aim of the technology, the latter can be banned and hence, every attempt to design, construct or use applications of this kind should be considered as a crime. Furthermore, any additional crime perpetrated by the AI system is conceived as if humans knowingly and wilfully committed the act.

Second, we deal with crimes of intent, that is, when individuals illegally use AI systems in order to commit a crime. Here, AI systems, smart robots, and further artificial agents are reckoned as innocent agents or simple instruments of an individual's *mens rea*. This is the traditional approach of criminal lawyers summed up by the "perpetration-

---

the employment of robot soldiers. See Ugo Pagallo, *Robots of Just War: A Legal Perspective* 24(3) Philosophy & Technology 307–23 (2011).

by-another" liability model.[62] Correspondingly, there are three human candidates for responsibility before a criminal court: programmers, manufacturers, and users of AI technology.

Third, focus should be on crimes of negligence, namely, cases in which criminal liability depends on lack of due care, so that a reasonable person fails to guard others against foreseeable harms. This is the traditional "natural-probable-consequence" liability model that comprises two different types of responsibility. On the one hand, imagine either programmers, or manufacturers, or users who intend to commit a crime through their AI system, but the latter deviates from the plan and commits some other offence. On the other hand, think about humans having no intent to commit a wrong but who were negligent while designing, constructing or using an AI system. Although this second type of liability is trickier, most legal systems hold individuals responsible even when they did not aim to commit any offense. In the view of traditional legal theory, the alleged novelty of all these cases resembles the responsibility of an owner or keeper of an animal "that is either known or presumed to be dangerous to mankind."[63]

Against this traditional backdrop, the aim of the following sections is to examine how the advancement of AI may affect it. The impact can concern the mental elements of the offense, its material content, or both. We should next ascertain whether AI technology brings about a new generation of crimes.

A.   What an AI's *Mens Rea* Would Look Like

Breath-taking improvements of technology have suggested some scholars to envisage AI systems and machines endowed with human-like free will, autonomy or moral sense, thereby impacting on the set of intentional crimes, which was sketched above in the previous section. By enlarging the class of criminally accountable agents, a new generation of AI crimes would follow as a result.

Gabriel Hallevy is one of the most committed advocates of a new generation of AI criminal minds. In his view, AI technology "has the capability of fulfilling the awareness requirements in criminal law,"[64] together with "the mental element requirements of both intent offenses and recklessness offenses."[65] This means, on the one hand, that AI systems could be either liable as direct perpetrators of criminal offenses, or responsible for crimes of negligence, on strict liability basis, and so forth. On the other hand, the general defence of loss of self-control, insanity, intoxication, or factual and legal mistakes could protect such AI systems. Once the mental element requirement is fulfilled in their case, there would be no reason why the general purposes of punishment and sentencing, i.e. retribution and deterrence, rehabilitation and incapacitation, down to capital penalty, should not be applied to AI machines.[66]

---

[62]   See Gabriel Hallevy, *Liability for Crimes Involving Artificial Intelligence Systems* (Springer 2015); and Pagallo, *supra* note 3.
[63]   This is the thesis of Jim Davis, *The (Common) Laws of Man over (Civilian) Vehicles Unmanned* 21(2) *Journal of Law, Information and Science* 10 (2011).
[64]   Hallevy, *supra* note 62, at 91.
[65]   *Id.*, at 99.
[66]   *Id.*, especially Chapter 6.

Admittedly, dealing with the kind of strong AI Gabriel Hallevy is assuming in his conceptual exercise, the traditional paraphernalia of criminal lawyers could be properly extended to the regulation of such systems. From this latter perspective, we may even buy Lawrence Solum's argument that "one cannot, on conceptual grounds, rule out in advance the possibility that AIs should be given the rights of constitutional personhood." Yet, if we admit to there being AI machines capable of autonomous decisions similar in all relevant aspects to the ones humans make, the next step would be to acknowledge that the legal meaning of "person" and, for that matter, of crimes of intent, of negligence, of strict liability, etc., will radically change. Even Solum admits that, "given this change in form of life, our concept of a person may change in a way that creates a cleavage between human and person."[67] Likewise, others warn that "the empirical finding that novel types of entities develop some kind of self-consciousness and become capable of intentional actions seems reasonable, as long as we keep in mind that the emergence of such entities will probably require us to rethink notions of consciousness, self-consciousness and moral agency."[68]

At the end of the day, however, nobody knows to where this scenario may lead. For instance, would a strong AI robotic lawyer accept the argument that "evil is not part of the components of criminal liability"?[69] What if the robot, rather than an advocate of current exclusive legal positivism, is a follower of the natural law tradition?

In addition to this kind of conceptual exercise, there is another way in which the sphere of criminal prosecution can be reasonably expanded. Going back to the crimes of intent mentioned above in the previous section, the current debate on corporate criminal liability and forms of distributed responsibility that hinge on multiple accumulated actions of humans and computers appears particularly fruitful.[70] Here, it can be extremely difficult to ascertain what is, or should be, the information content of the corporate entity as foundational to determining the responsibility of individuals. The intricacy of the interaction between humans and computers may lead to cases of impunity that have recommended some legal systems to adopt forms of criminal accountability of corporations. Think of the collective knowledge doctrine, the culpable corporate culture, or the reactive corporate fault, as ways to determine the blameworthiness of corporations and their autonomous criminal liability. Although several critical differences persist between the common law and the civil law traditions, and among the legal systems of continental Europe, we can leave aside this kind of debate, so as to focus on whether these forms of corporate criminal liability could be applied to the case of the artificial legal agents and the AI smart machines that are under scrutiny in this chapter. It is noteworthy that over

---

[67]   See Lawrence B. Solum, *Legal Personhood for Artificial Intelligence* 70 North Carolina Law Review 1260 (1992).

[68]   See Mireille Hildebrandt, Bert-Jaap Koops and David-Olivier Jaquet-Chiffelle, *Bridging the Accountability Gap: Rights for New Entities in the Information Society?* 11(2) Minnesota Journal of Law, Science and Technology 558–59 (2010).

[69]   Hallevy, *supra* note 62, at 93.

[70]   See Pedro M. Freitas, Francisco Andrade and Paulo Novais, "Criminal Liability of Autonomous Agents: From the Unthinkable to the Plausible", in P. Casanovas et al. (eds.), *AI Approaches to the Complexity of Legal Systems* (Springer 2014) 145–56; and consider also Hallevy, *supra* note 62, at 40–45.

the past years, several scholars have proposed new types of accountability for the behavior of AI robots and further smart artificial agents, thus suggesting a fruitful parallel with those legal systems that admit the autonomous criminal responsibility of corporations.[71]

Since corporations cannot be imprisoned, legal systems had indeed to envisage alternative ways of punishment, such as restrictions of liberty of action, and fines. This makes a lot of sense in the case of AI systems, smart robots and further artificial agents, because some have proposed that we should register such artificial agents just like corporations;[72] while others have recommended that we should bestow robots with capital,[73] or that making the financial position of AI machines transparent is a priority.[74] Admittedly, the reasons why scholars have suggested these forms of accountability for the behaviour of AI systems do not concern their *mens rea* but rather, pertain to the field of civil (as opposed to criminal) law. In other words, these are ways for striking a balance between the individual's claim to not be ruined by the decisions of their AI systems and the claim of an AI's counterparty to be protected when interacting with them.

Therefore, in order to determine whether the harmful behavior of an AI system should be relevant under criminal law, the attention should be drawn to the material conduct of such system and whether the latter may jeopardize foundational elements of society and create, generally speaking, social alarm. Because the society's right to inflict punishment is traditionally grounded on the idea that harm affects the community as a whole, the parallel between the criminal responsibility of corporations and the new forms of criminal liability for the behavior of AI systems rests on the magnitudes of complexity that regard the human-AI interaction, the content of this very interaction and consequently, the material elements of a crime. After the mental element requirements of criminal law, or *mens rea*, let us explore what a new AI *actus reus* could look like.

B.   What an AI's *Actus Reus* Looks Like

We mentioned above in the introduction the case of Vital, the UK made robot, capable of picking up on market trends so as to predict successful investments in the healthcare system. Dealing in this section with a different issue, namely, whether the material conduct of such a smart AI system may fall within the loopholes of today's criminal law, let us imagine a different scenario, in which the wrong evaluation of a robot leads to a lack of

---

[71]   This is the thesis discussed by Curtis E.A. Karnow, *Liability for Distributed Artificial Intelligence* 11 Berkeley Technology and Law Journal 147–83 (1996); Jean-François Lerouge, *The Use of Electronic Agents Questioned under Contractual Law: Suggested Solutions on a European and American Level* 18 The John Marshall Journal of Computer and Information Law 403 (2000); Emily Mary Weitzenboeck, *Electronic Agents and the Formation of Contracts* 9(3) International Journal of Law and Information Technology 204–34 (2001); Anthony J. Bellia, *Contracting with Electronic Agents* 50 Emory Law Journal 1047–92 (2001); Giovanni Sartor, *Cognitive Automata and the Law: Electronic Contracting and the Intentionality of Software Agents* 17(4) Artificial Intelligence and Law 253–90 (2009); and, Pagallo, *supra* note 4.

[72]   This is the standpoint of Karnow, *supra* note 71; Lerouge, *supra* note 71; and, Weitzenboeck, *supra* note 71.

[73]   See Bellia, *supra* note 71.

[74]   See Sartor, *supra* note 71.

capital increase and hence, to the fraudulent bankruptcy of the corporation. What would the reaction of current legal systems be?

Here, there seems to be an alternative between a crime of negligence and the hypothesis of AI corporate liability mentioned above in the previous section. Still, as to the traditional crime of negligence, we face a major problem: in the case of the wrong evaluation of the AI robot that eventually leads to the fraudulent bankruptcy of the corporation, humans could be held responsible only for the crime of bankruptcy triggered by the robot's evaluation, since the mental element requirement of fraud would be missing in the case of the human members of the board. The criminal liability of the corporation and, eventually, that of the robot would thus be the only way to charge someone with the crime of fraudulent bankruptcy. This conclusion however means that most legal systems should amend themselves, in order to prosecute either the AI system as the criminal agent of the corporation, or the corporation as such.

A variant of the "perpetration-by-another" liability model suggests another interesting case. By reversing the usual perspective, humans are assumed in this case as the innocent agent or instrument of an AI's bad decision. Certainly, the scenario is not entirely new: we have full experience of hackers, viruses or trojan horses, compromising computers connected to the internet, so as to use them to perform malicious tasks under remote direction, e.g. denial-of-service attacks. What is new in the case of e.g. AI robots concerns their particular role of interface between the online and the offline worlds. In addition, we may envisage robots replicating themselves, in order to specialize in infringing practices, so that no human could be held responsible for their autonomous harmful conduct. Consequently, by admitting the scenario of AI robots that illegally use humans in order to commit crimes "out there," in the real world, we would end up with a new kind of *actus reus* which does not necessarily entail any *mens rea*. Think for example of powerful brain computer interfaces for robots that perceive the physiological and mental states of humans through novel Electroencephalography (EEG) filters. Legal systems could react either amending once again themselves, e.g. a new kind of autonomous corporate criminal liability for AI robots, or claiming that the principle of legality does not apply to smart machines after all, i.e. a simple variant of the design stance sketched above in the introduction of this section. In any event, it seems likely that a new general type of defence for humans, such as AI loss of self-control, should be taken into account.

Further instances of new robotic offenses could be given. Years ago, for instance, the Commissioner of the Australian Federal Police (AFP), Mick Keelty, insisted on "the potential emergence of technological crime from virtual space (online) into physical space vis-à-vis robotics."[75] But to cut to the chase, we can adapt in this context that which James Moor called the "logical malleability" of computers and hence, of AI robots. Since the latter "can be shaped and molded to do any activity that can be characterized in terms of inputs, outputs, and connecting logical operations,"[76] this means that the only limits to the new scenarios of AI robotic crimes are given by human imagination.

---

[75]   *Top Cop Predicts Robot Crime Wave*, retrieved at http://www.futurecrimes.com/article/ top-cop-predicts-robot-crimewave-2/ on 31 May 2012.

[76]   See James Moor, *What is Computer Ethics?* 16(4) *Metaphilosophy* 266–75 (1985).

Unsurprisingly, over the past years, an increasing amount of research has been devoted to the analysis of strong AI systems, trust, and security. At the University of Stanford, an area of study has to do with "loss of control of AI systems." In the words of Eric Horvitz, "we could one day lose control of AI systems via the rise of superintelligences that do not act in accordance with human wishes [so] that such powerful systems would threaten humanity."[77] Analogous risks have been stressed by Bill Gates, Elon Musk, and Stephen Hawking.[78] How should we legally tackle such challenges?

C. A Matter of Procedure

The focus of the analysis has been so far on the primary rules of the law, namely, the rules of the system that aim to govern social and individual behaviour, both natural and artificial. In Part II, attention was drawn to the ECtHR's case law and how to interpret such provisions, as Articles 6 and 8 of the ECHR. The procedures considered in that context, such as the preponderance-test—in order to attain an overall evaluation of the fairness of the whole proceeding—had to do with how we should interpret the primary rules of the law that aim to govern social and individual behaviour, both natural and artificial.[79]

In this part of the chapter, by taking into account the principle of legality—according to which individuals can be held criminally liable only on the basis of an explicit criminal norm—that which was under scrutiny referred once again to the primary rules of the system, and whether the behaviour of AI and smart robotic systems may fall within the loopholes of today's law.

However, in light of the set of normative challenges brought on by AI and robotics technology, we should widen our perspective and consider the role that the secondary rules of the law may play in this context. Drawing on a classical distinction of jurisprudence, we refer here to the legal rules of change that allow to create, modify, or suppress the primary rules of the system.[80]

As previously mentioned in this chapter, most robots and AI systems are not a simple "out of the box" machine. Rather, as a sort of prolonged epigenetic developmental process, these systems increasingly gain knowledge or skills from their own interaction

---

[77]   See Eric Horvitz, *One-Hundred Year Study of Artificial Intelligence: Reactions and Framing*. White Paper. Stanford University, 2014. Available at: https://stanford.app.box.com/s/266hrhww2l3gjoy9euar.

[78]   See the open letter of the Future of Life Institute from 2015, addressing the challenges triggered by AI and robotics: "Its members—and advocates, among which Gates, Musk, and Hawking—are concerned that as increasingly sophisticated achievements in AI accumulate – especially where they intersect with advances in autonomous robotics technology – not enough attention is being paid to safety." Available at https://futureoflife.org/ai-open-letter/.

[79]   Such intent can be divided into four different categories, that is, (a) the regulation of human producers and designers of AI systems and robots through law, e.g. either through ISO standards or liability norms for users of robots; (b) the regulation of user behaviour through the design of AI, that is, by designing them in such a way that unlawful actions of humans are not allowed; (c) the regulation of the legal effects of AI behaviour through the norms set up by lawmakers, e.g. the effects of AI contracts and negotiations; and, (d) the regulation of AI behaviour through design, that is, by embedding normative constraints into the design of such artefacts. See Ronald Leenes and Francesca Lucivero, *Laws on Robots, Laws by Robots, Laws in Robots: Regulating Robot Behaviour by Design* 6(2) Law, Innovation and Technology 193–220 (2016).

[80]   See Hart, *supra* note 5.

with the living beings inhabiting the surrounding environment, so that more complex cognitive structures emerge in the state-transition system of the AI application. Simply put, specimens of the same model will behave in quite different ways, according to how humans train, treat, or manage their system. Correspondingly, both the behavior and decisions of such AI applications can be unpredictable and risky, thus affecting traditional tenets of the law, such as notions of reasonable foreseeability and due care, which were stressed above with cases of criminal negligence and intent. In addition, we often lack enough data on the probability of events, their consequences and costs, in order to determine the levels of risk and thus, the amount of insurance premiums, on which new forms of accountability for the behavior of such artefacts may hinge.

Today's default rules for accident control mostly rely, however, upon strict liability policies.[81] The economic rationale for this legal regime is that no-fault responsibility of humans for harm provoked by their business, animals, or children, represents the best method for accident control, by scaling back dangerous activities.[82] Such approach can nonetheless entail a vicious circle, since the more the strict liability rules are effective, the less we can test our AI systems, the more such rules may hinder research and development in the field. The recent wave of extremely detailed regulations and prohibitions on the use of drones by the Italian Civil Aviation Authority, i.e. "ENAC," illustrate this deadlock. With a pinch of salt, they end in the paradox stressed by web security experts decades ago: the only legal drone would be "one that is powered off, cast in a block of concrete and sealed in a lead-lined room with armed guards – and even then I have my doubts."[83] How could we prevent such a stalemate?

A feasible way out is given by the secondary rules of the law.[84] Although such procedural rules comprise a number of different techniques, suffice it to dwell here on two of them. First, focus should be on Justice Brandeis's doctrine of experimental federalism, as espoused in *New State Ice Co. v Leibmann* (285 US 262 (1932)). The idea is to flesh out the content of the rules that shall govern individual behavior through a beneficial competition among legal systems. This is what occurs nowadays in the field of self-driving cars in the US, where several states have enacted their own laws for this kind of technology. At its best possible light, the same policy will be at work with the EU regulation in the field of data protection.[85]

---

[81]   Another approach is represented by the precautionary principle. The threshold for applying such principle hinges on the existence and degree of scientific uncertainty as to the harm that the use of sensitive technology might invoke. By shifting the burden of proof from those suspecting a risk in the construction and use of AI apps, to those who discount that risk, the principle basically states that we should prevent action when there is not (scientific) certainty that no dangerous effect would ensue. Since, at the time of this writing, the precautionary principle has not been applied in the field of AI, we can skip the analysis of the principle in this context. More details in Pagallo, *supra* note 4, at 138.

[82]   This is of course the stance of Richard Posner, *The Jurisprudence of Skepticism* 86(5) Michigan Law Review 827–91 (1988).

[83]   In Simson Garfinkel and Gene Spafford, *Web Security and Commerce* (O'Reilly 1997).

[84]   More details in Ugo Pagallo, "Even Angels Need the Rules: AI, Roboethics, and the Law", in Gal A Kaminka et al. (eds), *ECAI 2016. Frontiers in Artificial Intelligence and Applications* (IOS Press 2016) 209–15; *Id., When Morals Ain't Enough: Robots, Ethics, and the Rules of the Law*, Minds and Machines (January 2017).

[85]   Ugo Pagallo. *The Legal Challenges of Big Data: Putting Secondary Rules First in the Field of EU Data Protection* (3(1) European Data Protection Law Review 36–46 (2017).

Second, legislators can adopt forms of legal experimentation. For example, over the past 15 years, the Japanese government has worked out a way to address the normative challenges of robotics through the creation of special zones for their empirical testing and development, namely, a form of living lab, or Tokku.[86] Likewise, in the field of autonomous vehicles, several EU countries have endorsed this kind of approach: Sweden has sponsored the world's first large-scale autonomous driving pilot project, in which self-driving cars use public roads in everyday driving conditions; Germany has allowed a number of tests with various levels of automation on highways, e.g. Audi's tests with an autonomous driving car on highway A9 between Ingolstadt and Nuremberg.

In general terms, these forms of experimentation through lawfully de-regulated special zones represent the legal basis on which to collect empirical data and sufficient knowledge to make rational decisions for a number of critical issues. We can improve our understanding of how AI systems may react in various contexts and satisfy human needs. We can better appreciate risks and threats brought on by possible losses of control of AI systems, so as to keep them in check. We can further develop theoretical frameworks that allow us to better appreciate the space of potential systems that avoid undesirable behaviors. In addition, we can rationally address the legal aspects of this experimentation, covering many potential issues raised by the next-generation AI systems and managing such requirements, which often represent a formidable obstacle for this kind of research, as public authorizations for security reasons, formal consent for the processing and use of personal data, mechanisms of distributing risks through insurance models and authentication systems, and more.

Of course, some of these legal techniques can interact and reinforce each other. More importantly, they represent a mechanism of legal flexibility that allows us to wisely address the interaction between law and technology. At the end of the day, it seems fair to affirm that the aim of the law to govern the process of technological innovation should neither hinder it, nor require over-frequent revision to manage such progress. If we are fated to face some of the scenarios sketched above in the previous sections, e.g. negligence-based responsibility of humans as caretakers of their smart robots, we should address these scenarios, first, in a living lab.

IV. CONCLUSION

The chapter has examined two opposite, although complementary, sides of the interaction between AI and criminal law. Part II scrutinized the role of AI for law enforcement purposes; Part III analyzed how AI systems and smart robots may break such law. Part II skipped the analysis on crime prevention, so as to focus on the application of AI technologies within the context of a criminal proceeding, aiming to find evidence of a specific criminal act. Part III left aside Sci-Fi hypotheses on the criminal mind of autonomous AI systems, i.e. their *mens rea*, so as to draw the attention to how the growing autonomy

---

[86] Yueh-Hsuan Weng, Yusuke Sugahara, Kenji Hashimoto and Atsuo Takanishi. *Intersection of "Tokku" Special Zone, Robots, and the Law: A Case Study on Legal Impacts to Humanoid Robots* 7(5) *International Journal of Social Robotics* 841–57 (2015).

of some AI robots and of further artificial agents may induce a new set of *actus reus*, that is, the material element of a crime. Part II dwelt on the primary rules of the ECHR and the ECtHR's case law. The intent was to ascertain whether the procedural rules on the equality of arms and the principle of fair trial could be interpreted in such a way, that no amendment to the conventional guarantees is needed, in order to cope with the normative challenges of technology. Part III shed light on how the procedures set up by the secondary rules of the system may help us understand what kind of primary rules we may need in the field of AI.

Against this framework, the conclusion of the analysis is twofold. On the one hand, by taking into account the normative challenges brought on by the use of AI technology, we adopted a stance which is compatible with the tenets of the Dworkinian right answer thesis.[87] According to this stance, a morally coherent narrative should grasp the law in such a way that, given the nature of the legal question and the story and background of the issue, scholars can attain the answer that best justifies or achieves the integrity of the law. Accordingly, we stressed that the use of a "non-validated" AI system can in some situations amount to a violation of Article 8 ECHR and yet, this should no longer be a necessary condition for the assessment of a trial's fairness. By claiming a violation of Article 6(1) ECHR, regardless of the eventual unlawfulness of the interference with private life, this approach would help us ensure that the conventional safeguards of the European law are constantly updated in relation to the ever-improving technologies that inevitably "filter" into criminal investigations practice. What is more, this approach would prevent an extremely complicated and long process of amendment to the current Convention law.

On the other hand, we admit that some legal cases triggered by the use of technology require a thoughtful compromise between different opinions, rather than a unique right answer.[88] After all, this is what has occurred over the past decades with several international agreements that have regulated technological advancements in the fields of chemical, biological and nuclear weapons, or in the field of computer crimes since the early 2000s. By taking into account the growing autonomy of AI systems in terms of negligence and intentional fault, we appreciated how certain decisions of AI systems and smart robots may fall within the loopholes of current criminal law, e.g. the hypothesis of AI corporate criminal liability illustrated above in Part III. Here, it is likely that how legal systems will react is going to be initially clear at the domestic level, through specific amendments to each national criminal law regulation. This is what occurred in the field of computer crimes, in which first national legal systems started amending their own codes, acts or statutes, e.g. the Italian regulation 547 from December 1993, and then the international legislator intervened, so as to formalize such legal experience through a general framework, e.g. the Budapest convention from 2001. The new generation of AI and robotic crimes will likely follow the same pattern.

---

[87]   We refer of course to Ronald Dworkin, *A Matter of Principle* (Oxford University Press 1985). On the Dworkin-Hart debate and the normative challenges of technology, see Ugo Pagallo and Massimo Durante, *The Pros and Cons of Legal Automation and its Governance* (7(2) European Journal of Risk Regulation 323–34 (2016); and *Id.*, "The Philosophy of Law in an Information Society", in L. Floridi (ed.), *The Routledge Handbook of Philosophy of Information* (Routledge 2016) 396–407.

[88]   See above note 61.

SOURCES

Legal Provisions

Budapest Convention on Cybercrime, Council of Europe ETS no. 185 from 23 November 2001.
European Convention on Human Rights (ECHR).
   Article 3 (on prohibition of degrading punishment)
   Article 6 (on fair trial and the equality of arms)
   Article 7 (on the principle of legality)
   Article 8 (on privacy)
   Article 13 (on effective remedies)
European Union's Charter of Fundamental Rights.
   Article 8 (on data protection)
   Article 47 (on fair trial)
   Article 52 (consistency with the ECHR)
European Union's Directive 2016/680 (on the processing of personal data by competent authorities for the purposes of the prevention, investigation, detection or prosecution of criminal offence).
European Union's Regulation 2016/679 (on the general data protection regulation for the EU).
Italian Constitution.
   Article 27 (on criminal responsibility)
Italian Regulation no. 547 from 22 December 1993 (amending the criminal code on cybercrimes).

Case Law

European Court of Human Rights (ECtHR)
Klass v. GFR, 6.9.1978.
X and Y v. The Netherlands, 26.3.1985.
Kruslin v. France, 24.4.1990.
Brandstetter v. Austria, 28.8.1991.
Kokkinakis v. Greece, 25.5.1993.
Kress v. France, 7.6.2001(Grand Chamber).
M.C. v. Bulgaria, 4.12.2003.
Siliadin v. France, 26.7.2005.
Gäfgen v. Germany, 1.6.2010 (Grand Chamber).
Dan v. Moldova, 5.7.2011.
Al Khawaja and Taheri v. UK, 15.12.2011 (Grand Chamber).

U.S. Supreme Court
New State Ice Co. v Leibmann (285 US 262 (1932)).

PART IV

INTELLECTUAL PROPERTY

15. The law of intellectual property created by artificial intelligence
Jeremy A. Cubert and Richard G.A. Bone

I. THE EVOLUTION OF INTELLECTUAL PROPERTY INCENTIVES

Fairness and equity dictate that hard work and ingenuity should be rewarded. But, ironically, the origins of intellectual property are based on a more powerful maxim—it is not what you know, but who you know.

Consider the predicament of Edward Darcy, a Groom of the Chamber of the court of Queen Elizabeth I. The Queen granted Darcy an exclusive license to import and sell all playing cards in England for 21 years at a cost of 100 marks per year. However, Darcy did not have any special skills associated with playing cards other than his payment to and connection with the Queen.

Darcy brought suit against haberdasher Thomas Allin for selling 180 gross of cards without paying a fee to Darcy. The Queen believed that playing cards were a vice, and granting a monopoly on playing cards would regulate their use. However, in the case of *Darcy v. Allin*, the Queen's Bench Court disagreed and addressed the negative consequences of granting a bare monopoly.[1] According to the court, such monopolies would (1) prevent those skilled in a trade from practicing it, (2) allow the monopolist to raise the price without maintaining the quality of the goods, and (3) accrue benefits only to the monopolist. In short, the benefits only flow to the monopolist, not to the public.

The case, decided in 1602, led to the passage of the Statute of Monopolies of 1623[2]

---

[1]   *Darcy v. Allin*, EngR 398 (1602). The term "monopoly" has a pejorative connotation in the context of intellectual property and is often misused. In the antitrust context, a monopoly requires a defined market (e.g., playing cards) where the monopolist has the power to exclude others from the defined market. Under the Queen's monopoly grant Darcy could exclude all comers from the playing card market. In contrast, if Darcy instead had a patent on a particular new and improved playing card system, Allin would be free to import and sell standard playing cards. Thus, Darcy would only have the right to exclude others from using his invention, and his monopoly in the playing card market would be limited to just the new and improved cards.

[2]   8 English Statute of Monopolies of 1623, 21 Jac. 1, c. 3: "BE IT ENACTED, that all monopolies and all commissions, grants, licenses, charters, and letters patents heretofore made or granted, or hereafter to be made or granted to any person or persons, bodies politic or corporate whatsoever, of or for the sole buying, selling, making, working, or using of anything within this realm or the dominion of Wales, . . .are altogether contrary to the laws of this realm, and so are and shall be utterly void and of none effect, and in no wise to be put in ure or execution. 6 (a) Provided also, that any declaration before mentioned shall not extend to any letters patents (b) and grants of privilege for the term of fourteen years or under, hereafter to be made, of the *sole working or making of any manner of new manufactures* within this realm (c) to *the true and first inventor* (d) and

which abolished this practice and established the idea of a *quid pro quo*: granting a "letters patent" to the "true and first inventor" of "the sole working or making of any manner of new manufacturers" for a term of 14 years. Thus, intellectual property rights became a mechanism to incentivize creation of significant inventions in exchange for the grant of a limited monopoly. Instead of simply paying the government for a monopoly right, the monopolist had to offer up something of value in the form of an invention. In other words, a *quid pro quo* ("this for that"). The days of bare playing card monopolies were over.

II.   JEFFERSON/MADISON FRAMEWORK FOR INTELLECTUAL PROPERTY RIGHTS

Moving forward more than a century, the young United States of America was crafting a Constitution and contemplating limited "monopolies" for authors and inventors. Thomas Jefferson, inventor, first US Patent Examiner and patent commissioner, discussed the issue in correspondence with James Madison, author of the Constitution. Their exchange considered both the costs and benefits of Government grants of intellectual property rights.

Jefferson argued that the benefits of intellectual property were doubtful: "The saying there shall be no monopolies lessens the incitements to ingenuity, which is spurred on by the hope of a monopoly for a limited time, as of 14 years; but the benefit even of limited monopolies is too doubtful to be opposed to that of their general suppression."[3]

Madison countered that, on balance, there was more to be feared from allowing the "many," in whom power would be vested in the United States, to hold too much power over the few that may hold "monopoly" power:

> Monopolies are sacrifices of the many to the few. Where the power is in the few it is natural for them to sacrifice the many to their own partialities and corruptions. Where the power, as with us, is in the many not in the few, the danger can not be very great that the few will be thus favored. It is much more to be dreaded that the few will be unnecessarily sacrificed to the many.[4]

The discussion between Jefferson and Madison highlights the tension between the costs and benefits of granting limited "monopoly" power. The final language, embodied in Article I, Section 8, Clause 8 of the US Constitution,[5] came down on the side of the

---

inventors of such manufactures, which others at the time of making such letters patents and grants shall not use (e), so as also they be not contrary to the law nor mischievous to the state by raising prices of commodities at home, or hurt of trade, or generally inconvenient (f): the same fourteen years to be accounted from the date of the first letters patents or grant of such privilege hereafter to be made, but that the same shall be of such force as they should be if this act had never been made, and of none other. . ."

[3]   Jefferson letter to Madison dated 31 July 1788, available at https://founders.archives.gov/documents/Madison/01-11-02-0147.

[4]   Madison letter to Jefferson dated 17 October 1788, available at https://founders.archives.gov/documents/Madison/01-11-02-0218.

[5]   US Const. art. I, § 8, cl. 8.

benefits of granting exclusive rights outweighing the costs: "To promote the Progress of Science and useful Arts, by securing for limited Times to Authors and Inventors the exclusive Right to their respective Writings and Discoveries."

The Jefferson/Madison framework[6] informs the modern debate regarding intellectual property: what should we reward and for how long? Are the costs of "monopolies" greater than the benefits? We reward inventors and authors for their inventions and creations for a limited time. The reward is an incentive to spur investment in invention and creation.[7]

III.   THE FREE-RIDER PROBLEM

From an economic point of view, the intellectual property system is designed to avoid the free-rider problem. Once intellectual property is disclosed, the marginal cost of using and distributing it is often minimal, which means that the inventor/author is not compensated for their ingenuity, effort, and investment, whereas others benefit from inventions at no cost. Thus, a bargain is struck between the many and the few: disclose your intellectual property, and you will be rewarded with an exclusive period of time to recoup your investment and be entitled to receive a revenue stream in the form of royalties.[8]

What Jefferson and Madison could not have envisaged is how the free-rider problem would become exponentially worse with advances in technology. In other words, the cost of copying has become next to zero for certain forms of intellectual property.[9] In some cases, the free-rider is offended by the very idea of intellectual property.[10] Support for this concept is sought in an oft cited 1813 letter from Jefferson to Isaac McPherson:

---

[6]   Although Jefferson is often cited in support of restricting intellectual property rights, his correspondence with Madison should be considered in context and as part of an exchange of ideas with Madison which ultimately resulted in the text in the Constitution. Adam Mossoff, *Who Cares What Thomas Jefferson Thought About Patents? Reevaluating The Patent "Privilege" In Historical Context* 92 Cornell Law Review (2007), available at http://www.lawschool.cornell.edu/research/cornell-law-review/upload/CRN502Mossoff.pdf.

[7]   The utilitarian justification for intellectual property should be distinguished from the natural rights theory. Some scholars take issue with grounding the utilitarian view in the Jefferson/Madison correspondence, and argue for considering the context of the nineteenth century view of natural rights and securing "privileges" through legislation. Regardless, modern intellectual property scholarship adopts the utilitarian view that there needs to be a net benefit to society from granting of "limited monopolies." *Id.*

[8]   It should be noted that the vast majority of patents bring no benefits to the patent holder. See, e.g., Jackie Hutter, *Strategic Patenting Part 1: Why So Few Patents Create Real Value*, IP Asset Maximizer Blog, January 24, 2014, available at http://ipassetmaximizerblog.com/strategic-patenting-part-1-why-so-few-patents-create-business-value/. Monopolies do not exist without a corresponding market to dominate. Merely having a patent is not a guarantee of generating monopoly rents.

[9]   The free-rider problem with copyright is far worse than with patents for a variety of reasons. However, the courts and Congress have systematically made patents both harder to get and harder to enforce in recent times. Although the problem of "patent trolls" is often cited as the primary reason, the trend started before the advent of the patent troll.

[10]   Jordan Weissmann, *The Case for Abolishing Patents (Yes, All of Them)*, The Atlantic (27 Sept. 2012) https://www.theatlantic.com/business/archive/2012/09/the-case-for-abolishing-patents-yes-all-of-them/262913/.

> That ideas should freely spread from one to another over the globe, for the moral and mutual instruction of man, and improvement of his condition, seems to have been peculiarly and benevolently designed by nature, when she made them, like fire, expansible over all space, without lessening their density in any point, and like the air in which we breathe, move, and have our physical being, incapable of confinement or exclusive appropriation. Inventions then cannot, in nature, be a subject of property. Society may give an exclusive right to the profits arising from them, as an encouragement to men to pursue ideas which may produce utility, but this may or may not be done, according to the will and convenience of the society, without claim or complaint from any body.[11]

Jefferson acknowledges that society may reward inventors but, in this letter, believes that the reward and incentive are optional. Short shrift is given to the fact that the free-rider bears none of the costs in research, time, and creativity but derives all of the benefits. Conferring intellectual property on the inventors/creators is an effort to level the playing field.

IV.   THE WORLDWIDE INFRINGEMENT MACHINE

During the age of the printing press, the infringer still bore the cost of typesetting, binding, storing, and distributing pirated copies of a book. The cost of free-riding was reduced further by mimeographs and the copy machine. But the internet created a worldwide copyright infringement machine. A pirated PDF copy of a book can be posted on a website and downloaded instantly by anyone with access to the internet. The marginal cost of copying and distributing content is next to zero, and the corresponding incentive to infringe is very high.

Similarly, at one time, music could be enjoyed only if you were in the presence of performing, live musicians. Sheet music enabled others to play and perform the music more easily by distributing instructions to play the music on paper to other musicians. Vinyl records enabled "performance" of the music without musicians, but required a "hard copy" of the record and a device to play it. Payment for the license to music was embedded in the cost of distributing and selling the record. Cassette tapes caused great disruption in the music industry because copies of the vinyl record of reasonable quality could be made and distributed at a much lower cost than buying another record. Today, perfect digital copies of music can be made and distributed at the click of mouse.

However, the industry adapted. Streaming services dominate digital distribution of music. Consumers have adjusted to paying for music again albeit with minimal revenue sharing for artists. While these developments have caused extreme financial hardship for most content creators, consumers and distributors have benefited. Streaming services have made virtually any song available to consumers on demand. It remains to be seen whether a system that marginalizes creators can survive in the long term.

Likewise, 3D printing may pose a similar threat to enforcement of patent rights.[12] When 3D printing becomes as mainstream as paper printing, the marginal cost of

---

[11]   Jefferson letter to McPherson dated 13 September 1813, available at https://founders. archives.gov/documents/Jefferson/03-06-02-0401.

[12]   See, *e.g.*, E. Malaty and G. Rostama, *3D printing and IP law*, WIPO Magazine (February 2017), available at http://www.wipo.int/wipo_magazine/en/2017/01/article_0006.html.

copying products will be next to zero, while the cost of enforcing patent rights in 3D printed products and designs will be very high—especially if infringers are large numbers of individuals making copies on a small scale. Industries will need to adapt to the new circumstances and may need to consider, for example, "streaming" services to provide 3D printing design files to consumers for the cost of a monthly subscription.

Artificial intelligence (AI), or the rise of machines that are capable of independent problem solving and—even—acts of independent creation, represents the most complex and potent threat to the intellectual property order that has ever occurred. Until recently AI has lacked an application in which its role was both conspicuous and compelling. Yet now, it suddenly finds itself harnessed into an increasingly diverse set of roles in society meaning that its impact on future societal trends is being actively debated.

AI has been thought of, studied, and been under development for more than half a century but has mostly lacked a coherent and commonly agreed definition.[13] The lack of definitional clarity is largely because AI has encompassed a large number of mathematical and conceptual frameworks, and a number of different terms have fallen within the overall concept. For example, the terms "deep learning", "expert system", and "intelligent agents" have taken on their own meaning within AI. Fundamentally, however, the question of what actually constitutes "artificial intelligence" arises because developers of AI have had different goals for the discipline, from mimicking yet ultimately surpassing the capacity of a person to solve certain problems, to fully simulating the activities of the human brain.

There is also an evolving aspect of the definition, in that once an AI solution to a problem has been devised, it is no longer viewed as embodying AI, but instead is merely automation.[14] Thus, AI is often developed to solve problems previously thought to be difficult for computers to solve. But once computers can successfully solve those problems, the nature of the challenge moves on. For example, AI has been developed to allow computers to recognize individual faces in complex crowd scenes. Once the problems of facial recognition have been "solved", however, as defined by—say—a computer making fewer mistakes on average than a human confronted with the same images, the problem is no longer seen as a task for AI, and a new goal emerges.

At its simplest, AI represents the application of computing machines to tasks that humans find challenging, for example, extracting meaningful patterns from vast amounts of data, or winning a game of chess against a Grand Master. Yet AI has also been utilized to mimic tasks that humans carry out apparently effortlessly in single instances, but which would be daunting if they had to be repeated millions or tens of millions of times in quick succession.

Examples of this are machine reading of medical images. AI as embodied in computing machines can also reach out and touch the tangible world when combined with elements of robotics, meaning that in addition to delivering purely analytical results of heavy duty computer processing, AI could also be expected to be responsible for creation of physical objects. These are all examples of what has been called "weak AI": computing machines

---

[13]   See, *e.g.*, Artificial Intelligence, available at https://en.wikipedia.org/wiki/Artificial_intelligence.
[14]   This has been called the "AI effect"; see, *e.g.*, Pamela McCorduck, *Machines Who Think* 2nd ed. (A.K. Peters, Ltd. 2004).

carrying out apparently sophisticated tasks but within a narrowly-defined role that they are programmed to navigate.[15]

At its most complex and yet-to-be achieved realization, AI represents the capacity of a machine to fully mimic the functions of the human brain, including carrying out acts of intuitive problem solving, the ability to learn independently, and the capacity to "think" creatively. Such behavior has been termed "strong AI": computing machines that are able to take steps beyond a set of programmed inputs.

Thus, AI is always perched at the edge of what is computationally possible at a given time, making it hard to properly distinguish between a truly intelligent act of a machine and what is simply the natural result of the machine acting on its programmed instructions. As computing power increases, so the instruction set that a computing machine can practically execute becomes ever more complex, meaning that more and more tasks become susceptible to some form of AI-based solution, and meaning that the prospect of machines that are truly capable of independent thought becomes ever more realistic.

V. PATENTS

The patent system incentivizes invention by offering a limited time "monopoly" of exclusion to those who are provably first in time, and who have disclosed to the public an enabling description of the invention. Since 1995, the duration of the exclusive right in the US is measured from the earliest date of filing a patent application on the invention.[16] Since 2011, the question of "first in time" shifted from a first to invent paradigm for determining entitlement to the patent right, to being simply awarded to the first inventor to file a patent application unless an act of derivation could be proven.[17] The "monopoly" of exclusion is a right to exclude others from practising the claimed invention by enjoining the infringer or obtaining monetary compensation through the court system.

While inventors' rights are enshrined in the US Constitution,[18] the practical reality today is that rights in patents are almost entirely held and exerted by assignees of those rights, and in most instances those assignees are corporate entities. The entry of intelligent agents and expert systems into mainstream society poses considerable challenges to the way patent rights are granted and managed.

Although it is difficult today to imagine passage of an amendment to the US Constitution that alters the definition of an "inventor" to encompass non-human actors, the fact that corporations can be treated as "legal persons" in some circumstances[19] means that there may be situations in which the definition of an inventor could be viewed expansively, or in which the holder of the patent right could derive its rights from a non-

---

[15]   See, *e.g.*, https://www.techopedia.com/definition/31621/weak-artificial-intelligence-weak-ai.
[16]   Uruguay Round Agreements Act (URAA); Pub.L. 103–465, 108 Stat. 4809, enacted December 8, 1994; *see also*, https://www.uspto.gov/web/offices/com/doc/uruguay/SUMMARY. html.
[17]   Robert Armitage, *Understanding the America Invents Act and its Implications for Patenting* 40(1) AIPLA Quarterly Journal (Winter 2012).
[18]   US Const., Art. I, Sect. 8, Cl. 8.
[19]   *Citizens United v. Federal Election Commission*, 558 US 310 (2010).

human actor. Furthermore, there are many ways in which the US patent laws themselves could be rewritten by the Congress to address the contribution of computing machines to inventive activity.

The US patent laws today recognize three separate entities in the acquisition of patent rights, none of whom need be the same as one another: inventors, applicants/patentees,[20] and assignees. Only an inventor is currently required to be a person. The applicant is the person, persons, or juristic entity, in whose name(s) actions before the US Patent and Trademark Office (PTO) are taken. The assignee (also referred to as the "patent owner" in some PTO proceedings), is the holder of the patent rights and is by default the inventor unless those rights have been transferred by contract (such as an employment agreement, license or sale) from the inventor to another entity.

Thus, the fact that rights to obtain and enforce patents are almost invariably held by corporate entities rather than the inventors themselves, means that the incentives and rewards built into the patent system are mostly recognized and enjoyed by corporate entities.[21]

A.   Inventions Patentable

Under 35 USC § 101, a patentable invention is a "new and useful process, machine, manufacture, or composition of matter, or any new and useful improvement thereof," and a patent may be awarded to "whoever invents or discovers" something that falls into one such category.[22] Conditions imposed on patentability of such categories include novelty (35 USC § 102), and obviousness (35 USC § 103), as well as requirements that the description of the invention in the patent's specification be enabling to "any person skilled in the art to which it pertains" (35 USC § 112).

It is clear from the language of the statutes that the US patent laws contemplate inventions to be carried out and understood by persons. A future society in which acts of invention need to be attributed to non-human actors, or in which comprehension of patent documents is carried out by AI machines capable of sophisticated language skills and possessing deep technical knowledge, may require reassessing definitions that have been assumed without question for centuries.

B.   Inventorship

In the US patent system, the inventive process has been dissected into three phases: conception, diligence, and reduction to practice. Whereas the acts of diligence and reduction to

---

[20]   The term "applicant" is used in proceedings before the PTO grants a patent on an application. The term "patentee" is used to refer to the same entity after a patent has been granted. See, Title 35 of United States Code, throughout.

[21]   This may reflect that the utilitarian view has prevailed. Patent rights are not viewed as personal, moral rights but property rights to be bought and sold—assigning IP rights to corporations in return for a salary.

[22]   The statutory categories have been refined by the judiciary to exclude abstract ideas, laws of nature, natural phenomena, and information per se. See, e.g., *Alice Corp. v. CLS Bank International*, 573 US __, 134 S. Ct. 2347 (2014).

practice have been important in resolving inventorship disputes, in particular when the timelines of competing inventors' acts are at issue,[23] an inventor can only be one who at a minimum has contributed to the conception of the invention.[24] It has also been established that the epithet "inventor" should not be applied to those who merely acted under the supervision of others and did no more than carry out routine acts in fulfilment of the diligence and/or reduction to practice of the invention. Thus, the human mental process is sacrosanct in both identifying inventive activity and ascribing that activity to individuals.

In what circumstances then, could a non-human inventor be identified? To answer that question, it would be necessary to look at the inventive activity in question (to assess whether it falls within one of the statutory categories, and not an exception), and then ascertain whether a non-human actor had meaningfully participated in that activity.

Where "weak AI" is deployed to solve problems, such as keeping an autonomous vehicle in lane on a busy freeway, the AI system is not technically inventing anything because the products of its activity do not fall into one of the statutory categories. The AI is without doubt sophisticated, but is implementing a rule-set devised by human programmers, albeit with unpredictable and time-varying inputs from its environment. In this situation, the inventive subject matter is the process devised by those programmers and delivered to the autonomous vehicle.

Similarly, the use of AI in analysis of "big data" to divine patterns not previously understood, or which were too complicated for persons to see, arguably constitutes a "discovery," but does not clearly fall into one of the statutory categories for which a patent may be granted unless—again—it is the instruction set powering the AI that is considered to be methodologically novel and non-obvious.

Looked at this way, the challenge to the patent system arising from invention carried out by non-human actors—the activities of a "strong AI" machine—lies far in the future: if it becomes possible for a machine to be programmed in such a way that it can learn how to solve problems that it was not initially programmed to address, then non-human inventive acts will have to be recognized. Would the person(s) who programmed the AI machine in the first place be owed any recognition in that circumstance? This could be analogized to a teacher claiming credit for a student's invention based on the fact the teacher taught the student the subject matter and the skills to solve problems using it.

A more likely intermediate situation is that the use of sophisticated computing machines will be deemed to have robbed humans of any right to an inventive contribution; in other words there is simply no invention for which a (human) "inventor" can be identified. Ironically, where computers are typically harnessed for their predictable, reproducible, and utterly reliable behavior, it may be their roles in solving problems that humans find challenging for being unpredictable that unleash the greatest threat to humans' role as inventor. Consider three different problems from the life sciences, in which the central challenge is designing and making molecules having certain properties, but where the data needed to assist in achieving the goal is complex, incomplete, and disparate, and where predictability is not normally within a human's grasp.

---

[23]   35 USC.§ 102(g)(2) (pre-AIA).
[24]   *Hybritech Inc. v. Monoclonal Antibodies Inc.*, 802 F. 2d 1367, 1376, 231 USPQ 81, 87 (Fed. Cir. 1986).

1. Computer assisted organic synthesis

In the discipline of synthetic organic chemistry, there are hundreds of thousands of known reactions, each of which has been honed to facilitate a specific transformation of a class of organic molecules or a particular category of functional group. The practical laboratory synthesis of a complex organic molecule typically requires anywhere from a handful to dozens of individual transformations to be carried out in a particular sequence.

Variables include choosing from numerous reagents available to carry out a given class of transformation (e.g., identifying the best oxidizing agent for a category of substrate), identifying optimum reaction conditions (such as solvent, temperature, and reagent concentration) to maximize yield of a particular step, and fundamentally identifying the most convenient set of starting materials, based on considerations of availability and cost. For decades, chemists have had to trawl the vast chemical literature to identify potentially relevant reactions to deploy in a given synthesis, and then apply a trial-and-error approach to each under laboratory conditions. There now exist a number of "expert systems" that can identify profitable synthetic schemes for making a given target molecule.[25]

A method of synthesis—expressed as a sequence of steps under defined conditions—is a patentable process, assuming that the collection of steps and their respective conditions is new and non-obvious. When the method has been devised by persons, its inventors can be readily identified. But if the successful synthetic pathway was the result output by an expert system, and was one which required nothing more than minimal experimentation to implement in the laboratory to prove its efficacy, is it inventive in the true sense of the word? While it is conceivable that aspects of the expert system, if expressed as a novel and non-obvious process, could be viewed as inventions of those persons who devised the system itself, the specific end-products of that system's normal operation—in this case proposed synthetic schemes as solutions to human-input goals—are generally not. Such "reach-through" inventions have in recent years been disfavored by the patent system's strict requirements of written description: in other words, claiming inventorship of any possible output of a complex system is an over-reach.

Furthermore, when sufficiently commonplace, the applications of computer-assisted synthesis may soon be viewed as simply routine—non-inventive—acts. It remains an open question whether such an expert system could—itself—based only on the data known to it, "invent" a synthetic transformation not previously known, in a manner other than by simply producing a list of all "possible" conditions applicable to a given situation, from which one or more may not have been previously published. Once such a system can impart an element of machine-based creativity to the synthetic process, the prospect of human inventive contributions being augmented and even supplanted becomes very real.

2. Computational screening of drug candidates

Computational models have been used for a long time in the drug discovery process. In the simplest form, computer models are used to "virtually" screen hundreds of thousands of compounds for binding against a target, in an effort to whittle that number down to a number that can be manageably screened by activity assays. In this paradigm, although the computer models will invariably be screening known molecules (those that are listed

---

[25] *See, e.g.*, http://blogs.sciencemag.org/pipeline/archives/2016/04/12/the-algorithms-are-coming.

and stored in proprietary databases), because the number of technically possible organic molecules of a realistic size[26] exceeds 10^{100} (i.e., vastly more than have actually been or could ever be made) it is possible to computationally screen molecules that have not yet been synthesized with a view to suggesting that certain of them should be made for study. Where is the human hand in that process?

Although arguably an application of "weak AI"—the screening algorithm can only screen molecules for desirable properties—a new molecule discovered in this way has resulted from a sequence of steps that are quite distant from a specific individual's thought. Has sophisticated automation eliminated recognizable acts of invention of these molecules?

3.   Computational design of drug candidates

Imagine, however, the use of AI machines to do much more than screen billions of molecules for a well-defined set of properties. Imagine a "strong AI" system tasked with identifying molecules that bind a particular receptor. The system knows the 3D structure of the receptor (from published crystallography data), and can identify probably relevant binding sites, either by making deductions about cavities in the surface of the 3D structure or from other crystal data on molecules bound to the receptor. The system can extract from published literature and other sources the structures of small molecules that are capable of binding the receptor with varying potencies. The system can work out inconsistencies between the available data, and can "test" molecules, both known and virtual. The system can also place the receptor's position in key biochemical pathways and appreciate possible "side effects" of a particular activity, all based on intelligent parsing and assimilation of the biomedical literature. Given merely the broadest instruction: "design a pharmaceutically active molecule to target disease X", could this system invent its way to a viable solution? IBM's Watson is being directed to just this type of problem.[27] It is perhaps only a matter of time before surprising results are obtained, and the question of inventorship by a machine, not a person, will be faced.

C.   Ownership

Could an AI entity hold title to a legal right? In the US patent system, the inventor is automatically granted the patent right, but almost invariably the inventor is obliged by contract to assign that right away to his or her employer (the "assignee", and in current practice, the "applicant").

At least today, we do not contemplate free-roaming AI machines that are untethered to a formal owner. If, as today, it remains true that an AI machine is itself not capable of inventive acts, then the question of a right being "held" by that AI machine by virtue of its routine activity does not arise. In the future, to the extent that AI machines could "invent" on their own, a new legal framework would be required: such a machine would have to be able to "assign" its rights to its corporate controller, or would have to be programmed to do so. Alternatively, legislation could be envisaged that requires all such machines to

---

[26]   Say, 30 non-hydrogen atoms.
[27]   https://www.ibm.com/watson/health/life-sciences/drug-discovery/.

have a legal owner—a corporation or a person—by whom any rights flowing from the machine's "creative" acts are owned as a matter of law.

But, in an alternative scenario, could rights in human-made inventions be assigned to AI machines? Could such machines be viewed as legal persons, much as corporations are, and their entitlement to "enforce" intellectual property rights be respected? While far from impossible, there is a growing need for legal and corporate activities of non-human machines to be strictly regulated. Even today, hiring and firing decisions are being made "by algorithm", which means that people are growing ever accustomed to machines playing dispassionate roles in contentious decisions.[28]

D.   Person or Machine of Ordinary Skill in the Art?

The skilled artisan appears in two guises in the US patent law: one to provide a yard-stick for the requisite skill to "invent" (in 35 USC § 103), and one as a way to define a level of competence to implement an invention as described (in 35 USC § 112).

Assessing whether an invention clears the non-obviousness hurdle requires assessing the level of skill of a person of "ordinary skill in the art". This level of skill has the potential to be considerably disrupted by the widespread existence of AI machines that are capable of contributing to the inventive process. There will very soon be a question of whether the inventive acts of a human need to be measured against what AI machines can achieve, as well as—conversely—in the more distant future whether the possible inventive acts of an AI machine should be measured against the capabilities of either humans, other AI machines, or both. Certainly, an intermediate step will be to recognize that a person of ordinary skill is already one who has access to a certain kit of AI-based tools that can be deployed as necessary to overcome specific technical hurdles in a given field of endeavor. The fundamental question then becomes one of whether the person of ordinary skill for questions of obviousness is one who is assisted by those tools of AI. If this becomes the case then the threshold for finding an invention non-obvious will have risen considerably. AI machines are becoming the "mechanical advantage" of the twenty-first century's skilled artisan.

Correspondingly, a patent specification must be drafted in such a manner that a "person skilled in the art" can "make and use" the invention. Thus, if aspects of an invention are subsumed within the routine workings of an AI machine, can it reasonably be assumed that those aspects no longer require the exacting written description that the patent statutes demand of an enabling specification? Furthermore, must a patent specification be written in such a way that an AI machine fully equipped with natural language processing capabilities can read it and assemble a way to practice the invention?

E.   Infringement by AI

If a future AI machine can "invent" a solution to a challenging class of technical problems, could an AI machine visit an act of infringement on another entity's patent? Whether the

---

[28]   *See, e.g., When your boss is an algorithm*, Financial Times (7 Sept. 2016) https://www.ft.com/content/88fdc58c-754f-11e6-b60a-de4532d5ea35?mhq5j=e3.

AI machine is "aware" of that patent or not? The question of whether a patent right could be infringed by an AI machine will probably depend on who or what is its controlling entity. If—as seems sensible from today's vantage point—the possibility of free-ranging AI machines is curtailed by a minimum requirement of corporate ownership and control of AI behavior, then it is the AI's master who is chargeable with infringement, either direct or under a theory of induced infringement. Today we categorize infringement as direct (for which it is not necessary to inquire into the infringer's mental state),[29] and induced (for which a degree of *mens rea* or intent on the part of the infringer is required).[30] However, the full force of a patent infringement action rests on the possibility of showing that the defendant willfully infringed the patent owner's right, for which the patent owner is entitled to "treble damages".[31]

Impugning the AI owner with responsibility for the actions of its AI would therefore be especially important in any infringement action which requires proving an intent to infringe. If AI machines are deemed to be not "responsible" for their actions as a matter of law, then it may still be necessary to devise a theory of infringement that addresses circumstances such as the following: an AI machine identifies an activity that it will likely pursue, compares that activity to a patent database, identifies a risk of infringement of one or more patents, and proceeds to "infringe" based on its own quantified assessment of risk. Presumably, the AI machine could be programmed to alert its corporate owner in such a circumstance, thereby allowing the owner to decide whether to assume the risk or tell the AI to stand down. In this circumstance, it would be appropriate to hold the owner responsible for "willful" infringement because—perhaps just as easily—the owner could decide to program the AI machine to *never* infringe a third party's patent right.

Alternatively, in a future where AI is operating as a free economic actor (yet still on behalf of humans), one approach would involve "no fault" infringement determinations where AI conducts an infringement check before engaging in an activity. If the activity is later found to be infringing, a predetermined "reasonably royalty" could be paid and litigation would be avoided.

F.   A Hypothetical Future of Person-less Invention

Understanding that computing machines can already be programmed to carry out tasks of considerable complexity and that the boundaries around what machines can do will continue to expand, one can envisage a world in which the entire inventive and patenting process is carried out by machines. An AI machine could, given a fairly straightforward instruction: carry out a search of the prior art (accessible to it in computer database form); identify patentable subject matter (defined as a draftable claim that does not cover anything known in its database of prior art); draft a patent application in support of such patentable subject matter; and file the patent application at a patent office of competent jurisdiction. That patent office's machine-based "examiners" could carry out an automated search, after parsing the patent application, and issue an entirely automated

---

[29]   35 USC 271(a).

[30]   35 USC 271(b).

[31]   35 USC 296(b).

assessment of patentability, be that a grant of a patent or a reasoned refusal. Most—if not all—of these tasks could be accomplished with a degree of linguistic skill in the AI machine that is not far away from what is possible today.

It is inevitable that patent laws will adapt and will be amended to recognize technological change of this sort. Consider the following dispute, taking place in the year 2043: Industry titans AI One and First AI are engaged in a patent infringement battle. First AI contends that its automated legal department filed a non-provisional patent application on 12 June 2038, at 13:41:57 UTC, a clear 39 seconds before the expiry of the one year statutory period from the filing date of its provisional application (12 June 2037, at 13:42:36 UTC). AI One argues that in fact the filing deadline was missed by five seconds: The US Industrial Property Office (USIPO) recorded the filing in its database at 13:42:41 UTC.

AI One suspects this is because First AI's legal department, located in far Earth orbit, had failed to synchronize its clocks with those of USIPO, a step that humans are still required to perform annually. USIPO routinely gives applicants a one minute grace period when a statutory bar is concerned, and when at least one of the applicants is a human life-form. First AI's identification of Andrew Self as a person among the list of inventors was enough to get its filing date approved by USIPO. AI One has long suspected that Andrew Self, an inventor on more than 50,000 of First AI's patent applications, is not a real person at all. Irrespective of assignment of fault in patent infringement disputes, it is reasonable to assume that patent invalidity could still be asserted in defense: in which case, the role of AI in both the creation of an invention and the preparation and filing of a patent application for that invention will be at the heart of many disputes.

In a fully automated digitally managed world, the idea of calendar-day filing deadlines would seem quaint in retrospect. All prior art has a time/date stamp accurate to ten milliseconds. The US Industrial Property Office (renamed in recognition of the *de minimis* role of human inventors in the patent system) records filing dates by hour, minute, and second. Clock synchronization between applicants' filing systems and the IPO's clocks are necessary because of the number of satellite- and asteroid-based invention mining systems. Earth time (UTC) remains the standard.

Impossible or not, over the next 25 years a lot of questions such as this will be faced.

VI.   COPYRIGHT

A.   Age of Expression

The information age is an age of expression. Never before have the opportunities to create and distribute expression of every kind been greater. However, with great power comes great responsibility.[32] The information age could also be described as the infringement age. The ability to create, copy, manipulate, and distribute information also creates the ability and incentive to infringe the same.

These developments present unprecedented difficulties for copyright owners because

---

[32]   Pa Kent to Clark Kent in *The Superman Serial* (1948).

copies of works are easily made and distributed, and are therefore difficult to control. However, copyright owners have adjusted. For example, by making music distribution more convenient, the music industry has converted potential infringers into subscribers to unlimited subscription services. In a similar manner, the publishing industry has converted book readers into digital readers with the success of products such as Kindle and Nook. While convenience may have quelled the rising tide of infringement, it also has "devalued" content and sent content creators scurrying for adequate compensation models.

1. AI-generated music

Streaming content solutions have not been satisfactory for all stakeholders. In particular, compensation to musicians and composers has dropped dramatically even as profits for the industry overall have rebounded. Technical advancements have been both a blessing and a curse for musicians. On the one hand, the tools available to create, record, mix, and distribute have never been more advanced, easy to use, and inexpensive. On the other hand, it is easier for consumers to infringe the results. However, these technologies have not had a significant impact on the need for a musician/composer to create the music in the first place.

The development of the synthesizer was not greeted with universal acclaim by musicians. Players and performers believed it might be used to replace their services. With a few notable exceptions, we have not gone down this slippery slope and a market for studio and performing musicians still exists. However, the beginning of a new age is emerging.

The use of artificial intelligence to create content has been limited, with mostly unsatisfactory results. However, the tide has begun to turn. Consider Aiva Technologies, a technology startup based in Luxembourg and London. Their product, Aiva (Artificial Intelligence Virtual Artist) is a neural network algorithm which is being taught to compose classical music.[33] According to the press reports, Aiva obtained copyright in its own name under the France and Luxembourg authors' right society (SACEM)[34] and is considered to be a "composer."

2. Copyright protection for AI creations

Is Aiva entitled to copyright under US law to AI created music? Because the author is not human, the answer is likely no. Recently, a US district court held that a six year old macaque named Naruto was not entitled to copyright protection for a selfie.[35] Naruto used the defendant David John Salter's camera to take a series of photographs of himself. The photos were published by defendant Blurb, Inc. in a book containing the photographs. Plaintiff "People for the Ethical Treatment of Animals" (PETA) sued Slater and Blurb, Inc. under the Copyright Act asserting that the defendants falsely claimed authorship of the selfies. The court granted the defendants' motion to dismiss because the

---

[33]   *A New AI Can Write Music As Well As A Human Composer*, Futurism (9 March 2017) available at https://futurism.com/a-new-ai-can-write-music-as-well-as-a-human-composer/.

[34]   *Aiva is the first AI to Officially be Recognised as a Composer*, AI Business (10 March 2017) available at https://aibusiness.com/aiva-is-the-first-ai-to-officially-be-recognised-as-a-composer/.

[35]   *Naruto v. Slater* (N.D. Cal., 2016).

Copyright Act[36] does not confer standing to non-human animals.[37] According to Judge William Orrick:

> Naruto is not an "author" within the meaning of the Copyright Act. Next Friends argue that this result is "antithetical" to the "tremendous [public] interest in animal art." Opp. at 12. Perhaps. But that is an argument that should be made to Congress and the President, not to me. The issue for me is whether Next Friends have demonstrated that the Copyright Act confers standing upon Naruto. In light of the plain language of the Copyright Act, past judicial interpretations of the Act's authorship requirement, and guidance from the Copyright Office, they have not.

Thus, Naruto is not an author under the Copyright Act because he is not human. Likewise, the Aiva AI is also not an author for the same reason. The Copyright Act could be amended to expand the definition of author to AI or animals. The question is whether such an amendment serves the public interest.[38]

Aiva Technologies has invested time, money, and creativity to develop and improve music creation algorithms. Their software and related methods may be appropriate subject matter for both patent and copyright protection. However, these forms of protection do not extend to the content generated by Aiva.

Presumably, Aiva would like to sell or license the music content developed by the algorithm. Without modifying the Copyright Act, this content may enter the public domain, reducing the incentive to develop AI technology to create content. The public interest may therefore be served by extending the definition of author to AI under these circumstances (e.g., AI developed and controlled by humans) because otherwise AI-generated music would fall into the public domain, and the incentive to develop the AI in the first place would be greatly reduced.

Taking this example to the next step, one could imagine development of Smart AI creating content on its own, and not under the control of humans. Should Smart AI be entitled to intellectual property rights and will there be a net benefit to the public from such an arrangement? The answer to this question may ultimately be tied to the future status of Smart AI in the same way authorship in monkey selfies is tied to the status of animals in our society.

VII. AI TRADEMARKS

Trademark law protects economic actors from unfair competition by identifying the source of goods or services.[39] The touchstone of trademark law is "likelihood of confusion"—whether a consumer is likely to be confused as to the source of the good or

---

[36] Copyright Act of 1976, 17 USC §§ 101-1332 (2014).

[37] The lower court's decision has been appealed to the 9th Circuit Court of Appeals.

[38] Advocates for granting rights to AI-generated works should consider that such an outcome could also result in granting author rights to animals. For example, arguments that apply to AI would also apply to animal generated art. *See, e.g., Is Gorilla Art Really Art?,* The Gorilla Foundation, Interspecies Communication, available at https://www.koko.org/gorilla-art-1.

[39] *See,* Trademark Act of 1946—the Lanham Act, 15 USC §§ 1051–72; §§ 1091–1096; §§ 1111–1127.

service. The trademark itself can be a word, symbol, or phrase, used to identify a particular manufacturer or seller's products and distinguish them from the products of another.

AI's impact in the area of trademark law may not be as noticeable as in copyright law. However, AI bots are routinely deployed to provide customer support, sales, and advertising. In some cases, AI may handle most of a transaction from marketing to sales to configuring a product to order fulfillment.

Consider Kunaki.com, a CD/DVD manufacturing website and service. Kunaki utilizes software to allow customers to configure their own CD/DVD. The software interacts with a system that handles manufacturing, assembly of the CD/DVD cases, shrink wrap, and order fulfillment (including providing CD/DVDs to third parties). Kunaki has the following curious notice on their Frequently Asked Questions page:

> Kunaki operates more like a machine than a business and does not offer a personalized service. We don't engage in active marketing, sales, or public relations. We never offer discounts or special deals. We don't offer affiliate or partner programs. The Kunaki machine is operated and managed by software rather than a management team.
> Our service is designed for 21st-century, intelligent, independent publishers who prefer to deal with a cold, efficient, and reliable machine that is available 24 hours per day, 7 days per week.
> Because Kunaki is highly automated and focused on quality, low price, and fast production, we offer a minimal range of options.

Although Kunaki was designed by humans it operates (somewhat) independently from its human designers, although ultimately it is under their control. Presumably, humans need to supply and service their manufacturing, packaging, and distribution machinery and network. Under these circumstances, a trademark to the service would serve the same purpose as a trademark to a human service—it identifies the quality and source. As advised by the Kunaki website, consumers know that they should not expect lots of hands on help to navigate and use the service.

But consider strong AI that could design and sell a product or service—either to humans or to other AI. Even in this circumstance it seems that trademark protection would serve the same societal function as it does now.

VIII.   ARTIFICIAL INTELLIGENCE AND THE INTELLECTUAL PROPERTY REVOLUTION

AI is the next chapter in the evolution of the free-rider problem. Ease of copying and distributing content will be eclipsed by AI creating the content in the first place. Computers have already reduced the cost of creating content by making the process easier (e.g., digital audio workstations, Adobe Photoshop, Final Cut Pro etc.). While AI created content is currently not quite up to the level of human created content, the gap is rapidly closing.

Strong AI (i.e., AI capable of learning new tasks) may reduce the marginal cost of creation/invention to next to zero. Strong AI will be better, faster, and never sleep. Perhaps we will reach the point of "invention on demand" or strong AI anticipating what inventions would be the most useful to humans. One could envision smart AI creating alternate solutions to problems in which one solution does not infringe on existing rights, where there are others that do.

The Jefferson/Madison framework did not consider this possibility. What incentive structures are needed for AI invention? If the marginal cost of invention or creation is close to zero, do we need intellectual property at all? We still need investment to design, develop, and maintain an AI infrastructure, but do we need the incentives of an intellectual property system to encourage invention in the first place?

As always, where society advances, the law lags behind—often woefully behind. This is not surprising because technological and social change create unforeseen problems and issues that present legal regimes with new challenges. For example, who would have imagined the "Internet of Things" potentially and surreptitiously recording audio of a murder?[40] A runaway self-driving car?[41] High definition video cameras in our pockets recording interactions with law enforcement?[42]

With respect to intellectual property law, we will need to revisit bedrock principles such as "person of ordinary skill in the art" and a new or hybrid standard for non-obviousness depending on whether a person or an AI is the inventor. We will need a new standard for written description and enablement tied to demonstrating possession of an invention to a human or AI and teaching a human or AI of skill in the art how to make and use an invention.

We have come a long way from bare monopolies on playing cards. AI could usher in an era where "ideas should freely spread from one to another over the globe, for the moral and mutual instruction of man, and improvement of his condition" as envisioned by Jefferson. Except that Jefferson almost certainly envisioned this world as a human and not AI created utopia.

SOURCES

Darcy v. Allin, EngR 398 (1602).
8 English Statute of Monopolies of 1623, 21 Jac. 1, c. 3.
Jefferson letter to Madison dated July 31, 1788.
US Const. art. I, § 8, cl. 8.
Uruguay Round Agreements Act (URAA); Pub.L. 103–465, 108 Stat. 4809, enacted December 8, 1994.
Title 35 of United States Code, in particular, §§ 101, 102, 103, 112, 271, and 296.
Copyright Act of 1976, 17 USC §§ 101–1332 (2014).
Trademark Act of 1946.
Lanham Act, 15 USC §§ 1051– 72; §§ 1091–1096; §§ 1111– 1127.

---

[40]   Amy B. Wang, *Can Alexa help solve a murder? Police think so — but Amazon won't give up her data*, The Washington Post (28 Dec. 2016) available at https://www.washingtonpost.com/news/the-switch/wp/2016/12/28/can-alexa-help-solve-a-murder-police-think-so-but-amazon-wont-give-up-her-data/?utm_term=.8dcb848292cb.

[41]   Danielle Muoio, *An MIT professor explains why we are still a long ways off from solving one of the biggest problems with self-driving cars*, Business Insider (5 March 2017) available at http://www.businessinsider.com/automakers-self-driving-car-trolly-problem-2017-3.

[42]   Jaeah Lee and AJ Vicens, *Here Are 13 Killings by Police Captured on Video in the Past Year*, Mother Jones (20 May 2015) available at http://www.motherjones.com/politics/2015/05/police-shootings-caught-on-tape-video/.

16. Kinematically abstract claims in surgical robotics patents

*Andrew Chin**

I. INTRODUCTION

Like many other animals, humans have extended the functional reach of their bodies by inventing tools to achieve their goals. At the most fundamental level, progress in the useful arts can be measured by the extent to which humans can make and use these tools to produce the results and effects they desire. Patent claims properly demarcate this progress when they define these tools (or methods of making or using them), not merely where and how far the tools reach. Kinematic properties, which describe the geometric motions of structural elements without regard to the forces that cause them to move, should therefore not be considered sufficiently concrete to delineate the scope of a mechanical patent claim.

This Chapter critically examines kinematically abstract claims in the U.S. surgical robotics industry, where claims purporting to cover all mechanisms exhibiting a specific kinematic property are widespread. First, it describes the role of patents and kinematic claiming in Intuitive Surgical's emergence as the industry's monopolist in 2003 and in some of the subsequent challenges the company has faced from competing innovators and patent owners. Second, it draws on results from physics and geometry to explain why kinematically abstract claims logically fall under longstanding doctrinal exclusions of mathematical theorems and abstract ideas from patent-eligible subject matter. Finally, it examines the patent-eligibility of a claimed surgical manipulator whose design incorporates kinematic data captured from procedures performed by kinesthetically skilled surgeons. From this case study, broader questions emerge about the kinds of progress and skill that fall within the patent system's ambit, with further consequences for the political economy of labor and downstream innovation in the age of automation.

Scholars are prone to describing patent scope figuratively—and therefore imprecisely[1]

* The author thanks Graeme Earle, Irene Kosturakis, Peter Lee, Sarah Wasserman Rajec, Joshua Sarnoff, Tamsen Valoir, Liza Vertinsky, and Greg Vetter for helpful suggestions. Thanks go to the Houston Law Review for permission to publish the following: Andrew Chin, *Surgically Precise But Kinematically Abstract Patents* 55 Hous. L. Rev. 267 (2017).
[1] *See, e.g.*, Andrew Chin, *The Ontological Function of the Patent Document*, 74 U. Pitt. L. Rev. 263, 273–74 (2012) (describing set theory as providing an "imprecise and inadequate ontological description" of claim scope); Mark Lemley and Carl Shapiro, *Probabilistic Patents* 19 J. Econ. Perspectives 75, 76 (2005) (contrasting the uncertain validity and scope of patent rights with the uncertain validity of real property titles); Peter S. Menell, *Intellectual Property and the Property Rights Movement* 30 Regulation 36, 39 (Fall 2007) (arguing that a unitary view of real and intellectual property overlooks "many structural differences"); *but cf.* Alan Devlin, *Indeterminism and the Property-Patent Equation* 28 Yale L. and Pol'y Rev. 61, 104 (2009) (concluding that the analogy

—through the geographic conceits of real property[2] and the mathematical abstractions of set theory.[3] In the field of surgical robotics, however, patents often literally define their scope in geometrically precise terms with respect to the location of a patient's body on the operating table. For example, a patent claim recently issued to a subsidiary of Intuitive Surgical, Inc.[4] recites a robotic manipulator of a surgical instrument inserted into "a body cavity of a patient through a remote center of manipulation," comprising

> a base link configured to be held in a fixed position relative to the patient . . . and a linkage coupling the instrument holder to the base link, first and second links of the linkage being coupled to limit motion of the second link relative to the first link to rotation about a first axis intersecting the remote center of manipulation, the linkage further including three rotationally coupled rotary joints configured to generate constrained parallelogram motion of the linkage by which motion of the instrument holder is limited to rotation about a second axis intersecting the remote center of manipulation. . .[5]

By virtue of this unusually well-mapped patent landscape, the field of surgical robotics presents a unique case study on the relationship between patent scope and progress in the useful arts.

---

between real and intellectual property is strained "only if one characterizes the law of real property as entailing dogmatic and unqualified rights to exclude").

[2]   *See, e.g.*, *In re Vamco Mach. and Tool, Inc.*, 752 F.2d 1564, 1577 n.5 (Fed. Cir. 1985) ("Claims are . . . like the descriptions of lands like the descriptions of lands in a deed which define the area conveyed but do not describe the land."); Dan L. Burk and Mark A. Lemley, *Is Patent Law Technology-Specific?* 17 Berkeley Tech. L.J. 1155, 1166 n.46 (2002) ("A patent is most similar to a real property deed specifying the metes and bounds for a parcel of land."); Arti K. Rai, *Engaging Facts and Policy: A Multi-Institutional Approach to Patent System Reform* 103 Colum. L. Rev. 1035, 1044 (2003) ("A patent is a written document that describes and claims an invention much like a land deed might describe and claim a piece of property."); Frank H. Easterbrook, *Intellectual Property is Still Property*, 13 Harv. J.L. and Pub. Pol'y 108, 109 (1990) (analogizing the exclusionary patent right to the law of trespass); Edmund W. Kitch, *The Nature and Function of the Patent System*, 20 J. L. and Econ. 265, 271–75 (1977) (analogizing patent claims to mineral claims on U.S. public lands).

[3]   *See, e.g.*, Thomas D. Brainard, *Patent Claim Construction: A Graphic Look* 82 J. Pat. and Trademark Off. Soc'y 670 (2000) (depicting "[t]he patent concepts of validity, infringement, prior art, the doctrine of equivalents, file history estoppel and principles of claim differentiation" with Venn diagrams); Raj S. Dave, *A Mathematical Approach to Claim Elements and the Doctrine of Equivalents* 16 Harv. J. L. and Tech. 507, 518–25 (2003) (using Venn diagrams to illustrate doctrine of equivalents and prosecution history estoppel); Charles L. Gholz, *A Critique of Recent Opinions in Patent Interferences* 86 J. Pat. and Trademark Off. Soc'y 464, 476–83 (2004) (using Venn diagram to illustrate blocking situation resulting from interference decision); Samson Vermont, *A New Way to Determine Obviousness: Applying the Pioneer Doctrine to 35 U.S.C. § 103(a)* 29 AIPLA Q.J. 375, 418–24 (2001) (describing anticipation and obviousness in terms of Venn diagrams; *but cf.* Jeffrey A. Lefstin, *The Formal Structure of Patent Law and the Limits of Enablement*, 23 Berkeley Tech. L.J. 1141, 1159–67 (2008) (finding that "[n]early all of the doctrines of patent law . . . may be posed almost as mathematical set-functions whose truth value is described in terms of the claimed subject matter," but concluding that "patent law [is] not reducible to a simple set-theoretic system" insofar as it is impossible "to formulate a doctrine of enablement as a simple function of exclusion or inclusion").

[4]   Patentee Intuitive Surgical Operations, Inc. operates as a subsidiary of Intuitive Surgical, Inc. *See* Intuitive Surgical, Inc. Subsidiaries, https://www.sec.gov/Archives/edgar/data/1035267/000 119312510016932/dex211.htm (visited 24 Apr. 2017).

[5]   U.S. Patent No. 9,295,524 B2, cl. 1 (filed May 31, 2013) (issued Mar. 29, 2016).

The critical focus of this study is on the *kinematic* nature of many patented inventions in the surgical robotics field. Kinematic patent claims describe systems of structural elements that move in a desired way without regard to their masses or to the forces acting on them.[6] In the example above, Intuitive's claim is kinematic in that the links of the manipulator mechanism are described only in terms of their motions relative to each other and to the patient.

Part II of this Chapter highlights the strategic importance of manipulator patents in the development of the surgical robotics industry, wherein Intuitive has attained a monopoly position but has faced challenges from, *inter alia*, an open-source system development project, an individual surgeon-inventor and a non-practicing patent assertion company. Part III uses a theoretical explanation and several example mechanisms to demonstrate that kinematic claims are unpatentably abstract, insofar as they are neither grounded in a causal account of utility nor directed to an inventive application of the underlying geometric theorem. Part IV provides a case study of mechanical claims in a pending patent application for a surgical robot design that incorporated the kinesthetic expertise of a number of surgical clinicians. The Chapter concludes with a discussion of some intriguing implications for patent doctrine.

II.   KINEMATIC CLAIMS IN THE SURGICAL ROBOTICS INDUSTRY

A.   Intuitive Surgical's Monopoly

The current state of the U.S. surgical robotics industry can be traced to the late 1980s, when various research groups began exploring the use of remote-controlled robotic manipulation technologies to improve minimally invasive surgical procedures.[7] Research groups at the University of California at Santa Barbara and SRI International (formerly Stanford Research Institute[8]) developed prototypes that led to the formation of Computer Motion, Inc. and Intuitive Surgical, Inc., respectively, in the mid-1990s.[9] Computer Motion introduced the Zeus Surgical System in 1997, and Intuitive began marketing the da Vinci Surgical System in 1999.[10] While there were substantial differences between the two systems,[11] the

---

[6]   *See American Heritage Dictionary* (5th ed. 2017), https://ahdictionary.com/word/search. html?q=kinematic (defining "kinematics" as "[t]he branch of mechanics that studies the motion of a body or a system of bodies without consideration given to its mass or the forces acting on it").

[7]   Simon DiMaio et al., "The da Vinci Surgical System", in J. Rosen et al (eds.), *Surgical Robotics: Systems Applications and Visions* (Springer 2011) 199, 201–02.

[8]   *See Corporate History*, https://www.sri.com/about/corporate-history (visited 24 Apr. 2017).

[9]   *See id.*

[10]   *See id.* at 203.

[11]   *See id.* at 204 ("Zeus was smaller, had a lower price point, but was less capable. Da Vinci was bulky and often accused of being over-engineered."); *cf.* Katherine J. Herrmann, Note, *Cybersurgery: The Cutting Edge* 32 Rutgers Computer and Tech. L.J. 297, 302–03 (2006) (noting functional differences between Zeus and da Vinci, but concluding that "[d]espite the differences, it is sufficient to say that these robots represent, quite literally, the cutting edge of medical technology").

companies regarded each other as competitors[12] and eventually sued each other for patent infringement.[13]

The U.S. District Court for the Central District of California eventually granted Computer Motion's motion for summary judgment that Intuitive had literally infringed one of Computer Motion's patents.[14] Meanwhile, the U.S. District Court for the District of Delaware granted Intuitive summary judgment that Computer Motion had literally infringed a patent that IBM had licensed to Intuitive.[15] Before either case went to trial, however, Intuitive Surgical ended the patent litigation by acquiring Computer Motion in a 2003 stock-for-stock merger.[16] The merger thereby resolved what could soon have proved to be a conflict over mutually blocking technologies.[17] The presumed efficiency of this result was apparently sufficient to deflect antitrust scrutiny,[18] even though the merger resulted in the discontinuation of Zeus[19] and effectively extinguished competition in the surgical robotics industry,[20]

---

[12] *See id.*

[13] *See* Margo Goldberg, Note, *The Robotic Arm Went Crazy! The Problem of Establishing Liability in a Monopolized Field* 38 Rutgers Comp. and Tech. L.J. 226, 238–39 (2012) (describing Intuitive and Computer Motion as "involved in heavy competition through multiple patent infringement lawsuits").

[14] *See* Findings of Fact and Conclusions of Law Denying Defendant's Motion for Summary Judgment of Noninfringement of U.S. Patent 6,244,809 and Granting Plaintiff's Cross-Motion for Partial Summary Judgment of Literal Infringement of U.S. Patent 6,244,809, *Computer Motion, Inc. v. Intuitive Surgical Inc.*, No. CV 00-4988 CBM-RC (C.D. Cal. filed Feb. 7, 2003) (finding literal infringement of claim 1).

[15] *See Intuitive Surgical, Inc. v. Computer Motion, Inc.*, 214 F. Supp. 2d 433 (D. Del. 2002) (finding literal infringement of claims 1, 2, 6, 13, and 14 of U.S. Patent 6,201,984).

[16] Form S-4, Intuititve Surgical, Inc., at 36, https://www.sec.gov/Archives/edgar/data/103526 7/000089161803001503/f88583orsv4.htm (filed Mar. 28, 2003) (describing material terms of the stock-for-stock merger).

[17] While the defendants in each case could still have prevailed by proving invalidity or unenforceability of the infringed claims by clear and convincing evidence, both Intuitive and Computer Motion acknowledged the significant risk of liability for patent infringement. *See* Form S-4, *supra* note 16, at 43–45 (stating among reasons for the merger that Intuitive's directors "weighed the possibility that the litigation could result in . . . Intuitive Surgical being required either to obtain a license from, and pay damages and/or royalties to, Computer Motion or, in the event the parties were unable to agree on the terms of a license, to redesign or withdraw from the market one or more of Intuitive Surgical's products or product configurations," and that Computer Motion's directors considered potential benefits of the merger including "the elimination of the potential withdrawal from the market of one or more of Computer Motion's products or product configurations").

[18] The search ("Intuitive Surgical" and "Sherman Act") in Westlaw's ALLFEDS database yields no results. On the relevance of blocking patents to antitrust review of mergers, *see* Susan A. Creighton and Scott A. Sher, *Resolving Patent Disputes Through Merger: A Comparison of Three Potential Approaches* 75 Antitrust L.J. 657, 676 (2009) (outlining a judicial approach for reviewing the resolution of a patent dispute through merger by focusing on "an inquiry into the 'scope of the exclusionary potential' of the patent").

[19] See Goldberg, *supra* note 13, at 243 (citing SurgRob.blogspot.com).

[20] *See* Jean Bouquet de Joliniere et al., *Robotic Surgery in Gynecology* 3 Frontiers in Surgery 26 (2016) (tracing Intuitive's monopoly to its 2003 acquisition of Computer Motion); Goldberg, supra note 13, at 243–44 (same); *see also* Creighton and Sher, *supra* note 18, at 677 (noting that "[m]ergers also may go beyond the exclusionary potential of [a] patent because they last beyond the patent's term").

and even though less restrictive approaches such as cross-licensing or a joint venture might have been available.[21]

To this day, Intuitive continues to hold a monopoly in the robotic surgical systems market[22] and is now a $30 billion company.[23] Intuitive has sold more than 3,800 da Vinci systems worldwide,[24] which have been used in more than three million minimally invasive surgical procedures.[25] While intellectual property and regulatory bottlenecks have long entrenched Intuitive's market dominance,[26] some commentators have predicted that the expiration of Intuitive's oldest patents between now and 2022 will open up the market to new competition.[27]

---

[21]   *Cf.* Creighton and Sher, *supra* note 18, at 675–76 (explaining that a merger might appear reasonable to a reviewing court "where the parties, acting in good faith, were unable to resolve their differences through less restrictive means (e.g., a license or a joint venture)").

[22]   *See* Travis Johnson, *Intuitive Surgical: Staking Out New Markets for Da Vinci Robot*, Seeking Alpha (21 Sept. 2006), http://seekingalpha.com/article/17253-intuitive-surgical-staking-out-new-markets-for-da-vinci-robot ("The da Vinci is the only widely capable surgical robot approved by the FDA, and essentially enjoys a monopoly position in its niche."); SAGE Publications, *2 SAGE Sourcebook of Modern Biomedical Devices: Business Environments in a Global Market* 729 (2007) (tracing Intuitive's monopoly to the failure of competitor Integrated Surgical Systems in 2005).

   Intuitive's da Vinci surgical system has been especially dominant in the field of minimally invasive surgery, *see* PRWeb, *U.S. Robotic Surgery Market Set to Diversify and Grow: Intuitive Surgical's 'da Vinci' Robot Revenues to Increasingly Rely On Procedures and Services*, 27 Nov. 2014, https://globenewswire.com/news-release/2014/11/27/686891/10110222/en/U-S-Robotic-Surgery-Market-Set-to-Diversify-and-Grow-Intuitive-Surgical-s-da-Vinci-Robot-Revenues-to-Increasingly-Rely-On-Procedures-and-Services.html (describing the minimally invasive surgical robotics field as "nearing saturation" and "dominated by Intuitive"), and is being used in as many as 85 percent of prostatectomies performed in the United States. Aaron Smith, *Robots Grab Chunk of Prostate Surgery Biz*, CNNMoney.com (23 March 2007), http://money.cnn.com/2007/03/23/news/companies/intuitive_surgical/; Richard J. Ablin and Ronald Piana, *The Great Prostate Hoax* (St. Martins Press 2014) 104–05 (noting that the da Vinci system's FDA approval gives Intuititve "a monopoly on robotic prostatectomies").

[23]   *See* Yahoo! Finance, http://finance.yahoo.com/quote/ISRG?p=ISRG (visited 24 Apr. 2017) (stating market cap of $29.87 billion).

[24]   *See Investor FAQ*, http://phx.corporate-ir.net/phoenix.zhtml?c=122359andp=irol-faq#22324 (visited 24 Apr. 2017).

[25]   *See Frequently Asked Questions*, https://www.intuitivesurgical.com/company/faqs.php#3 (visited 24 Apr. 2017).

[26]   *See* Intuitive Surgical, Inc., Annual Report 2016 (Form 10-K), at 11 (3 Feb. 2017), http://phx.corporate-ir.net/External.File?item=UGFyZW50SUQ9MzY5MzI3fENoaWxkSUQ9LTF8VHlwZT0zandt=1andcb=636241805559733354 (stating that Intuitive owns or holds exclusive field-of-use licenses for more than 2,400 U.S. and foreign patents and 1,800 U.S. and foreign patent applications); Naomi Lee, *Robotic Surgery: Where Are We Now?* 384 Lancet 1417 (18 Oct. 2014) (identifying Intuitive's DaVinci system as "the only robot approved by the FDA for soft tissue surgery"); Tim Sparapani, *Surgical Robotics and the Attack of the Patent Trolls*, Forbes (19 June 2015), https://www.forbes.com/sites/timsparapani/2015/06/19/surgical-robotics-and-the-attack-of-the-patent-trolls ("Intuitive Surgical's longevity (its first system was approved by the FDA in 1999) and perpetual innovations may help it to stave off competition from global business giants as well as upstarts that are planning to enter the market at a lower price.").

[27]   *See* Amanda Ciccatelli, *Dominant Robotic Surgery Patents Expiring This Year. So What's Coming Next?*, *Inside Counsel* (23 Aug. 2016), http://www.insidecounsel.com/2016/08/23/dominant-robotic-surgery-patents-expiring-this-yea; Josue Villalta, *Could Patent Expirations Be a Chink in Intuitive Surgical's Armor?*, DeviceTalk (25 Aug. 2016), http://www.mddionline.com/blog/devicetalk/could-patent-expirations-be-chink-intuitive-surgical%E2%80%99s-armor-08-25-16;

B.   Applied Dexterity's Open Source Challenge

Another research group formed in the 1990s, led by Blake Hannaford at the University of Washington and Jacob Rosen at UCLA, formed the startup company Applied Dexterity in 2013[28] to market the Raven, a surgical robot controlled by open-source software.[29] Among Intuitive's many potential competitors,[30] Applied Dexterity is of particular interest from an intellectual property perspective because of its unique strategic decision to leverage open-source development for Raven's control software.[31] Researchers at 13 universities have been conducting a wide range of studies with Raven and have agreed to share any platform software improvements with the user community.[32] To the company's founders and some observers, Raven's open collaboration holds at least the eventual promise of leapfrogging da Vinci's proprietary approach.[33]

---

see also Barry A. O'Reilly, *Patents Running Out: Time to Take Stock of Robotic Surgery* Int'l Urogynecology J. 712–13 (2014) (noting that "over the last 10 years, patents have expired, and many companies around the world are at various stages of robotic surgical technology development" that may compete against Intuitive's monopoly "over the next couple of years"); Zach Panos, *Disrupting da Vinci? New Surgical Robots on the Horizon*, Service Line Strategy Advisor (24 Aug. 2005) ("With many of Intuitive's patents expiring in 2015 and 2016, we may begin to see new players enter the robotic surgery market in the next few years."); Trefis Team, *Factors That Can Impact Our Valuation For Intuitive Surgical Going Ahead*, Forbes.com (27 Dec. 2016), https://www.forbes.com/sites/greatspeculations/2016/12/27/factors-that-can-impact-our-valuation-for-intuitive-surgical-going-ahead/ ("[C]ompetition is likely to increase going forward, as Intuitive's patents begin to expire and the efficacy of robotic surgery is clearly established.").

[28]   *See History*, http://applieddexterity.com/about/history/ (visited 24 Apr. 2017).

[29]   *See Open Source Innovation*, http://applieddexterity.com/category/open-source/ (visited 24 Apr. 2017).

[30]   *See, e.g.*, Becka DeSmidt, *A Better, Cheaper Surgical Robot on the Way?*, Advisory Board (5 June 2013), https://www.advisory.com/research/service-line-strategy-advisor/the-pipeline/2013/06/a-better-cheaper-surgical-robot-on-the-way (naming the University of Washington, Titan Medical, SOFAR, and the ARAKNES project); Frank Tobe, *As Intuitive Surgical Continues to Shine, Competitors Are Entering the Fray*, Robot Report (4 Aug. 2016), https://www.therobotreport.com/news/as-intuitive-surgical-continues-to-shine-competitors-are-entering-the-fray (naming Verb Surgical, Medtronic, TransEnterix, Titan Medical, Medrobotics, Smith and Nephew, OMNI, Auris Surgical Robotics, Stryker, Medtech, and Cambridge Medical Robotics).

[31]   *See An Open-Source Robo-Surgeon*, Economist (3 Mar. 2012), http://www.economist.com/node/21548489 (describing Raven as "the first surgical robot to use open-source software").

[32]   *See* Eric Wagner, *UW Start-Up Applied Dexterity Creates Innovation Ecosystem for Medical Robotics*, CoMotion (12 Aug. 2014), http://depts.washington.edu/uwc4c/news-events/uw-start-up-applied-dexterity-creates-innovation-ecosystem-for-medical-robotics/.

[33]   *See An Open Source Robo-Surgeon, supra* note 31 ("Even if researchers keen to experiment with new robotic technologies and treatments could afford one, they cannot tinker with da Vinci's operating system. None of that is true of the Raven."); Larry Greenemeier, *Robotic Surgery Opens Up*, Sci. Am. (11 Feb. 2014), https://www.scientificamerican.com/article/robotic-surgery-opens-up/ (describing Raven's open-source approach as an effort to address Intuitive Surgical's "growing pains" as a single company trying to "meet growing demand while still delivering a safe product").

Applied Dexterity also has a proprietary side. The company[34] and its founders[35] hold a number of patents and patent applications covering various mechanical aspects of the Raven system, suggesting a hybrid approach to technology development and appropriation.[36]

Like Intuitive's example claim above,[37] many of Applied Dexterity's mechanical patent claims are kinematic in nature. For example, claim 1 of one of the company's pending 120 patent applications is directed to a device in which "the tool axis and the common revolute joint rotational axis subtend[] a first angle" and "the convergent rotational axes subtend[] a second angle."[38] Dependent claims add further kinematic limitations. For example, claim 12 is directed to "The device of claim 1 wherein the first angle is about 40 degrees and the second angle is about 52 degrees."[39]

A distinctive aspect of Raven's development has been the involvement of surgeons in the robot's design. Hannaford and Rosen's team first created the Blue DRAGON, "a system for monitoring the kinematics and the dynamics of endoscopic tools in minimally

---

[34]   See *Patents*, http://applieddexterity.com/pat/ (visited 24 Apr. 2017) (listing U.S. Patent No. 6,969,385 B2 ("Wrist with Decoupled Motion Transmission") and U.S. Patent App. Ser. No. 13/908,120 ("Spherical Motion Mechanism")). Applied Dexterity is a spinoff of the University of Washington Center for Commercialization, which is named as an assignee on several other patents on which Hannaford and Rosen are named co-inventors. *See, e.g.,* Applied Dexterity, COMOTION, http://comotion.uw.edu/startups/applied-dexterity [https://perma.cc/Z2WW-8JB5]; U.S. Patent Application Serial No. 13/908,120 (filed 3 Jun. 2013); U.S. Patent Application Serial No. 12/825,236 (filed 28 Jun. 2010); *see also* Vikram Jandhyala, *The UW CoMotion Story*, COMOTION (28 Jan. 2015), http://comotion.uw.edu/news/uw-comotion-story [https://perma. cc/7JKR-3EYY].

[35]   *See* Joanne Pransky, *The Pransky interview: Professor Jacob Rosen, Co-Founder of Applied Dexterity and ExoSense* 43 Industrial Robot 457, 457 (2016) (stating that Rosen has filed eight patent applications).

[36]   *See generally* Greg R. Vetter, *Commercial Free and Open Source Software: Knowledge Production, Hybrid Appropriability, and Patents* 77 Fordham L. Rev. 2087, 2130–31 (2009) (describing "the strategic advantages of patents" that can be combined with the benefits of open-source software development in a hybrid approach to technology appropriation).

[37]   *See supra* text accompanying note 5.

[38]   Claim 1 of Applied Dexterity's application reads:

1.   A device comprising:
        a first link having ends terminated in a base revolute joint and a common revolute joint, the revolute joints having convergent rotational axes and each rotational axis forming an acute angle with a longitudinal axis of the first link, the base revolute joint coupled to a base;
        a second link coupled to the common revolute joint at a first end, the second link having a second end and the second link in a serial cantilever configuration with the first link, the rotational axis of the common revolute joint forming an acute angle with a longitudinal axis of the second link, wherein the second end of the second link includes a tool holder, the tool holder having a tool axis aligned to pass through a point coincident with an intersection of the convergent rotational axes, the tool axis and the common revolute joint rotational axis subtending a first angle; and
        the convergent rotational axes subtending a second angle, such that the first angle differs from the second angle, the first and second links and the revolute joints enabling a position of the tool holder to be selectively manipulated. U.S. Patent App. No. 13/908,120, cl. 1 (filed Jun. 3, 2013).

[39]   *See* U.S. Patent App. No. 13/908,120, cl. 12 (filed Jun. 3, 2013); *see also id.* at cls. 2–13 (adding further kinematic limitations to claim 1).

invasive surgery for objective laparoscopic skill assessment."[40] The Blue DRAGON has sensors for measuring the positions and orientations of two endoscopic tools, measuring the forces and torques applied to the tools by the surgeon's hands, and detecting contact between the tools and the patient's tissues.[41] Hannaford and Rosen's team used the Blue DRAGON to capture data from minimally invasive procedures performed by 30 surgeons operating on pig tissues,[42] including five board certified laparoscopic surgeons who had each performed at least 800 surgeries and practiced as attending physicians.[43] With this data, the team was able to identify 40 degree and 52 degree angles as optimal design parameters for the mechanism described in the claim above.[44] Part IV of this Chapter will provide a more detailed discussion of how the surgical data was used in Raven's mechanical design and how patent law should regard the surgeons' contributions to the design process. It suffices for now to note that the surgeons whose techniques were captured in the study were not named as co-inventors on Applied Dexterity's patents or patent applications.[45]

C.   *Brookhill* and *Alisanos*: Surgeons and a "Troll" Take Their Cuts

In the years leading up to the Computer Motion merger, Intuitive faced another patent adversary in the entrepreneurial Manhattan surgeon Dr. Peter J. Wilk. Wilk had been profiled in a 1995 New York Times article as a doctor who had chosen to turn his "innovative medical techniques or theories into a commodity" by acquiring 140 patents on medical devices and techniques, bypassing the rigorous testing required by medical journals.[46]

---

[40]   J. Rosen et al., "The Blue DRAGON: A System for Monitoring the Kinematics and the Dynamics of Endoscopic Tools in Minimally Invasive Surgery for Objective Laparoscopic Skill Assessment", in J.D. Westwood et al (eds.), *Medicine Meets Virtual Reality* (IOS Press 2002) 412.

[41]   *See id.* at 413–14.

[42]   *See* Jacob Rosen et al., "Raven: Developing a Surgical Robot from a Concept to a Transatlantic Teleoperation Experiment", in J. Rosen et al. (eds.), *Surgical Robotics: Systems Applications and Visions* (Springer 2011) 159, 161.

[43]   *See* U.S. Patent App. No. 13/908,120 at [74] (filed Jun. 3, 2013).

[44]   *See* Rosen, *supra* note 42, at 177 ("For the serial manipulator optimized for the DWS, the best design was achieved with link angles of $\alpha_{13} = 52$ (Link 1) and $\alpha_{35} = 40$ (Link 2) with a composite score of 0.0520"); U.S. Patent App. No. 13/908,120 at [223] and cl. 12 (filed Jun. 3, 2013).

[45]   Dr. Mika Sinanan, a University of Washington surgery professor and clinician in minimally invasive gastrointestinal surgery, *see* http://www.uwmedicine.org/bios/mika-sinanan (visited 24 Apr. 2017), was a principal member of the original Raven development team and is a frequent coauthor and co-inventor with Hannaford and Rosen. *See generally* Pransky, *supra* note 35, at 458 (naming Sinanan as a mentor and collaborator with Rosen on the original development of Raven); Rosen, *supra* note 42 (chronicling the Raven project and naming Sinanan as coauthor). Sinanan was one of the 30 surgeons who participated in the study, *see* Mika Sinanan, personal correspondence with author, 16 Oct. 2017, but other surgeons were not named as co-inventors.

[46]   Sabra Chartrand, *Why Is This Surgeon Suing?*, N.Y. Times (8 June 1995), at D1.

The same article also reported on House Bill 1127, H.R. 1127, 104th Cong., 1st Sess. (1995), an unsuccessful precursor of § 287(c)'s immunity for a "medical practitioner" engaged in "medical activity" from patent infringement liability. *See* 35 U.S.C. § 1127 (1997); Brett G. Allen, Note, *Left to One's Devices: Congress Limits Patents on Medical Procedures*, Fordham Int'l Property, Media and Ent. L.J. 861–65 (1998) (chronicling the failure of House Bill 1127).

For example, Wilk was able to patent a new coronary bypass technique without test-ing it.[47] He subsequently licensed the patent to a large institution that "agreed to spend whatever it took" to determine whether the invention was a "potential replacement" for existing methods, and ultimately found that it was not.[48] Despite this, Wilk said this was "a good example of the patent system at work," in that "the idea was only explored because I thought of it, it was patented and protected, so this company felt they could expend themselves because if it proved successful they would be able to recoup their money and make a lot more."[49]

Wilk's inventions also included an "automated surgical system and apparatus," the sub-ject of a patent filed in 1991 and issued in 1993.[50] Wilk subsequently assigned the patent to the entity Brookhill-Wilk 1, LLC ("Brookhill"). In 2000, Brookhill sued Intuitive in the Southern District of New York[51] for infringing at least the patent's independent claims, each of which recited the limitation "to a remote location beyond a range of direct manual contact with said patient's body and said endoscopic instrument."[52] Intuitive's da Vinci system was undisputedly designed for use in the same operating room with the patient and instruments.[53] After construing the term "remote location" as limited to "a location

---

[47]   *See id.*; U.S. Patent No. 5,287,861 (filed Oct. 30, 1992) ("Coronary artery by-pass method and associated catheter").

[48]   *See* Chartrand, *supra* note 46. Notably, this failure to commercialize Wilk's bypass technique did not vitiate the invention's patentable utility. *See, e.g., Studiengesellschaft Kohle v. Eastman Kodak*, 616 F.2d 1315, 1339 (5th Cir. 1980) ("To require the product to be the victor in the competition of the marketplace is to impose upon patentees a burden far beyond that expressed in the statute.").

[49]   *Id.* Wilk is identified as a faculty member of SEAK, Inc., a continuing education, publish-ing and consulting company that "specializes in showing physicians how to supplement or replace their clinical income." About SEAK and Our Faculty, http://www.supplementalincomeforphysi-cians.com/about-seak/ (visited 24 Apr. 2017).

[50]   See U.S. Patent No. 5,217,003 (filed Mar. 18, 1991) (issued June 8, 1993) (the "'003 patent").

[51]   Brookhill also sued Computer Motion for patent infringement in 2001, *see* Complaint, *Brookhill-Wilk 1 v. Computer Motion*, No. 01-CV-01300-AKH (S.D.N.Y. filed Feb. 21, 2001), but agreed to dismiss the case after an adverse claim construction ruling. See 2002 Annual Report (Form 10-K), Computer Motion, Inc., at 11, https://www.sec.gov/Archives/edgar/data/906829/000109581101503796/a74784a 3e10-k405a.txt (visited 24 Apr. 2017).

[52]   '003 patent, at cls. 1, 10, 17. For example, claim 1 of the '003 patent read:
   A surgical method, comprising the steps of: inserting an endoscopic instrument into a patient's body; obtaining a video image of internal body tissues inside said patient's body via said endoscopic instrument; transmitting, over an electromagnetic signaling link, a video signal encod-ing said video image *to a remote location beyond a range of direct manual contact with said patient's body and said endoscopic instrument*; receiving actuator control signals from said remote location via said electromagnetic signaling link; inserting into the patient's body a surgical instrument mov-able relative to the patient's body and said endoscopic instrument; and automatically operating said surgical instrument in response to the received actuator control signals to effect a surgical operation on said internal body tissues.
'003 patent, at cl. 1 (emphasis added).
   Brookhill also brought claims against Intuitive for infringement of a patent that had been a continuation-in-part of the '003 patent, but withdrew these claims before Intuitive's motion for summary judgment. *See Brookhill-Wilk 1, LLC v. Intutiive Surgical, Inc.*, 178 F. Supp. 2d 356, 358 (S.D.N.Y. 2001) (citing U.S. Patent No. 5,368,015).

[53]   *See* 178 F. Supp. 2d at 364 and 366.

outside of the operating room where the patient is located,"[54] the district court granted summary judgment to Intuitive. On appeal, however, the Second Circuit rejected the district court's construction as improperly reading limitations from the specification into the claims,[55] and instead construed the term broadly "to encompass not just locations that are 'far apart' or 'distant,' but also those locations that are merely 'separated by intervals greater than usual'," including locations inside the operating room.[56] The appeals court reversed and remanded the case for trial.[57] Before trial, Intuitive, having by then acquired Computer Motion, settled with Brookhill by purchasing a fully paid-up, perpetual, exclusive license for $2.6 million.[58]

Because of *Brookhill-Wilk*'s high profile—to this day, the case has produced the Federal Circuit's only reported decisions in a surgical robotics patent infringement case[59]—the case received attention not only in legal scholarship[60] but also in the medical literature. In a 2008 article published in the *International Journal of Medical Robotics and Computer Assisted Surgery*, Veteran's Administration surgeon Thomas McLean and University of Kansas patent scholar Andrew Torrance reviewed the case in detail and discussed the potential exclusionary effects of Brookhill's patents on the surgical robotics industry.[61]

According to the authors, Brookhill's claims were so broad that any company other than Intuitive who marketed "a surgical instrument that allows . . . a surgeon to stand away from the operating table must now be prepared to defend itself in a patent infringement lawsuit."[62] As the exclusive licensee, Intuitive would be in a position to bankroll Brookhill's subsequent patent infringement litigation, and could even sue to enforce Brookhill's patents on its own.[63]

---

[54] *See id.*

[55] *Brookhill-Wilk 1, LLC v. Intutiive Surgical, Inc.*, 334 F.3d 1294, 1301 (2d Cir. 2003) (quoting *Teleflex, Inc.* v. *Ficosa N. Am. Corp.*, 299 F.3d 1313, 1328 (Fed. Cir. 2002)) (finding that "[n]o statement in the written description . . . constitutes a limitation on the scope of the invention," and therefore that the court is "'constrained to follow the language of the claims'").

[56] *See id.* at 1302.

[57] *See id.* at 1304.

[58] *See* 2003 Annual Report (Form 10-K), Intuitive Surgical, Inc., at 21, http://investor.intuit ivesurgical.com/mobile.view?c=122359andv=202andd=3andid=aHR0cDovL2FwaS50ZW5rd2l6Y XJkLmNvbS9maWxpbmcueG1sP2lwYWdlPTI2NjY1MDAmRFNFUT0xJlNFUT0mU1FERV NDPVNFQ1RJT05fQk9EWSZleHA9JnN1YnNpZD01Nw%3D%3D.

[59] A search in Westlaw's CTAF database for (surg! /s robot!) yields only the two reported decisions in *Brookhill-Wilk 1, LLC. v. Intuitive Surgical, Inc.*

[60] *See, e.g.*, Cases and Recent Developments, *Refusing to Limit Construction of the Term "Remote Construction" Based on the Intrinsic Record*, 13 Fed. Cir. B.J. 182 (2003) (reviewing the Brookhill-Wilk litigation); Herrmann, *supra* note 11, at 302 n.26 (same).

[61] T.R. McLean and A.W. Torrance, *Are the Brookhill-Wilk Patents Impediments to Market Growth in Cybersurgery?* 4 Int'l J. Med. Robotics and Comp. Assisted Surgery 3 (2008).

[62] *See id.* at 6.

[63] *See id.* Intuitive's exclusive license, *see* Settlement and License Agreement, Exh. 10.14 to 2004 Annual Report (Form 10-K), Intuitive Surgical, Inc., at § 3.1, at 3 (Jan. 8, 2004), http://www. annualreports.com/HostedData/AnnualReportArchive/i/NASDAQ_ISRG_2004.pdf (visited Apr. 24, 2017) (granting Intuitive an exclusive license, inter alia, to make, use, sell, offer to sell, and import any surgical robotics product under the Brookhill patents), appears to be broad enough to support licensee standing. *See WiAV Solutions LLC v. Motorola, Inc.*, 631 F.3d 1257, 1266-67 (Fed.

The authors did point out that Brookhill's patents would continue to be subject to an invalidity challenge.[64] They highlighted two then-recent Supreme Court developments as suggesting that at least Brookhill's process claims "appear to be especially ripe to be held invalid by the courts."[65] The authors read Justice Breyer's dissent from the dismissal of *LabCorp v. Metabolite*[66] as indicating that "the days of routinely valid medical process patents may be limited,"[67] and the *KSR v. Teleflex* decision[68] as signaling more generally that "the days of liberal patent granting [may be] numbered."[69] In light of the *KSR* Court's observation that an invention may be obvious where "market pressure" might have motivated one of ordinary skill to find the same solution,[70] the authors suggested that "a pent-up demand in the laparscopic surgery market for improved optics and instrument dexterity" at the time of Wilk's invention could show his remote surgery methods were "an obvious extension of laparoscopic surgery."[71] The authors concluded that the developments in *LabCorp* and *KSR* could prevent Brookhill's patents from "stifling . . . growth in the cybersurgery market."[72]

A decade after McLean and Torrance's article, Intuitive's assists from the Computer Motion acquisition[73] and the Brookhill license[74] have sufficiently faded into history that commentator Tim Sparapani recently attributed Intuitive's dominance solely to its first-mover advantage and "perpetual innovations."[75] In Sparapani's view, Intuitive's market dominance and 3,300 issued or pending patents are better characterized as signs of the surgical robotics industry's dynamism than as barriers to competitive sources of innovation.[76] On the other hand, Sparapani believes "patent trolls and patent privateers threaten the surgical robotics industry's vitality and growth."[77]

Cir. 2010) (holding that a licensee is an exclusive licensee with standing to sue "if it holds any of the exclusionary rights that accompany a patent" that were allegedly infringed).

[64]   *See* McLean and Torrance, *supra* note 61, at 7.

[65]   *See id.*

[66]   *Laboratory Corp. of America Holdings v. Metabolite Laboratories, Inc.*, 548 U.S. 124 (2006) (Breyer, J., dissenting).

[67]   *See* McLean and Torrance, *supra* note 61, at 8.

[68]   *KSR Int'l Co. v. Teleflex Inc.*, 550 U.S. 398 (2007).

[69]   *See id.* at 7.

[70]   *See KSR*, 550 U.S. at 421.

[71]   *See* McLean and Torrance, *supra* note 61, at 8.

[72]   *See id.*

[73]   *See supra* note 20 and accompanying text.

[74]   *See supra* note 63 and accompanying text.

[75]   *See* Tim Sparapani, *Surgical Robotics and the Attack of the Patent Trolls*, Forbes (June 19, 2015), https://www.forbes.com/sites/timsparapani/2015/06/19/surgical-robotics-and-the-attack-of-patent-trolls/ (visited 24 Apr. 2017). Sparapani, a data privacy law and policy consultant, was the former policy and government relations director at Facebook. *See id.*

[76]   *See id.* ("Intuitive continues to introduce significant technological advancement in areas like diagnostics and enhanced imaging furthering the importance of intellectual property in medical robotics."); *cf. United States v. Alcoa*, 148 F.2d 416, 430 (2d Cir. 1945) (Learned Hand, J.) (explaining that the Sherman Act does not condemn one who has attained monopoly power "merely by virtue of his superior skill, foresight and industry"); J. Hicks, *Annual Survey of Economic Theory: The Theory of Monopoly* 3 Econometrica 1, 8 (1935) ("The best of all monopoly profits is a quiet life.").

[77]   *Id.*

Sparapani's column singles out a suit by Alisanos, LLC against Intuitive as problematic, not based on any facts of the case or any analysis of the patent claims,[78] but simply because Alisanos is a "patent privateer."[79] Sparapani's condemnation of such non-practicing plaintiffs applies with equal force to all industries: "When . . . neither the company suing nor the company for whose benefit a suit is being brought are actually producing products or services, innovative companies are harmed without benefits being provided to the public."[80] It is hard to see how such a broad category of lawsuits could be avoided, however, short of imposing a working requirement on patentees.[81] The absence of a patent working requirement in the United States would seem to be the starting point of any legal reform effort to address Sparapani's concerns. In failing to mention this feature of U.S. patent law, the column seems more interested in identifying heroes and villains than in offering solutions.[82]

The facts of *Alisanos v. Intuitive*[83] actually tell a more nuanced story. A team of designers, including former cardiac surgeon Ralph de la Torre,[84] invented a "through-port heart stabilization system" and obtained a patent in 2003 for their employer, an early-stage medical device startup called Medcanica.[85] According to Alisanos's complaint, Medcanica had in the meantime tried and failed to negotiate a joint venture with Intuitive to commercialize the technology.[86] By the time the patent issued, Medcanica had run out of financing for further product development.[87] Eventually, Medcanica sold the patent to the patent assertion entity Alisanos in exchange for a share of licensing profits.[88]

Alisanos filed suit in the Southern District of Florida on 5 October 2012, alleging that one of the instruments Intuitive makes and sells for use with its da Vinci system, the "EndoWrist Stabilizer," infringed the patent. The case settled almost immediately, with the

---

[78]   *See id.* ("I have no insight into whether the patent suits filed against Intuitive Surgical were frivolous — Medicanica [Alisanos's predecessor in interest] certainly did not think so. . .").

[79]   *See id.*

[80]   *See id.*

[81]   *See, e.g.*, Maayan Perel, *From Non-Practicing Entities (NPE) to Non-Practiced Patents (NPPS): A Proposal for a Patent Working Requirement* 83 U. Cin. L. Rev. 747 (2015) (proposing a working requirement as a solution to "the patent troll problem").

[82]   *Cf.* Edward Lee, *Patent Trolls: Moral Panics, Motions in Limine, and Patent Reform* 19 Stan. Tech. L. Rev. 113 (2015) (arguing that use of the term "patent troll" may be unfairly prejudicial due to media's failure to mention the lack of a working requirement in U.S. patent law).

[83]   Complaint, *Alisanos, LLC v. Intuitive Surgical, Inc.*, No. 0:12-CV-61978 (S.D. Fla. filed Oct. 5, 2012).

[84]   *See* Ralph de la Torre, MD, http://ralphdelatorre.com/ (visited Apr. 24, 2017) (stating that de la Torre was formerly Chief of Cardiac Surgery at Beth Israel Deaconess Medical Center).

[85]   *See* U.S. Patent No. 6,592,573 B2 (filed June 27, 2001) (issued July 15, 2003); Complaint, *supra* note 83, at ¶ 6.

[86]   *See* Complaint, *supra* note 83, at ¶¶ 9–11.

[87]   *See id.* at ¶ 12.

[88]   *See id.* at ¶ 15; *Alisanos LLC To License Large Medical Device Patent Portfolio Developed By Medcanica*, PRWeb (1 Nov. 2012), http://www.prweb.com/releases/2012/11/prweb10080812.htm (visited 24 Apr. 2017); Medcanica had advertised its closed chest surgery patent portfolio through a patent brokerage with an animation apparently illustrating the invention's operation. *See For Sale: Medcanica Closed Chest Surgery Patent Porfolio.wmv*, Youtube.com, https://www.youtube.com/watch?v=SFCpR7hEc_0 (visited 24 Apr. 2017).

parties notifying the court one day before Intuitive's deadline to answer the complaint.[89] While the terms of the settlement were not disclosed, the agreement most likely included the purchase by Intuitive of a license to the patent-in-suit.[90] The suit thereby benefited the inventors through their employer Medcanica's share of the settlement proceeds, a result that might not have been possible in a system barring Alisanos as a non-practicing plaintiff.[91] At the same time, to the extent that potential competitors face a threat of patent assertion that Intuitive no longer faces, the primary beneficiary of *Alisanos* might ultimately be the "innovation company" Intuitive and not the "privateer" Alisanos, just as McLean and Torrance's article suggested Intuitive was able to entrench its monopoly in the wake of *Brookhill*.

These factual nuances of *Alisanos* do not redeem the many unambiguously problematic cases brought by non-practicing entities, including frivolous lawsuits.[92] *Alisanos* might still come in for criticism as a frivolous case, but detailed analyses of the validity and infringement of the asserted claims are beyond the scope of this Chapter, as they were beyond the scope of Sparapani's column.[93] In the meantime, this Chapter's examination of kinematic claims in surgical robotics patents might yield a more pertinent critical perspective on *Alisanos*. It is worth noting in this regard that as with other examples above, *Alisanos*'s claims-in-suit recite several elements in kinematic terms.[94]

The widespread practice of kinematic claiming in the surgical robotics industry raises

---

[89]   *See* Notice of Settlement, *Alisanos, LLC v. Intuitive Surgical, Inc.*, No. 0:12-CV-61978 (S.D. Fla. filed Jan. 24, 2013); Order, *Alisanos, LLC v. Intuitive Surgical, Inc.*, No. 0:12-CV-61978 (S.D. Fla. filed Jan. 3, 2013) (granting extension of time to answer until 25 Jan. 2013).

[90]   *See* Mark Crane and Malcolm R. Pfunder, *Antitrust and Res Judicata Considerations in the Settlement of Patent Litigation* 62 Antitrust L.J. 151 (1993) ("Patent infringement cases are generally settled by execution of license (or cross-license) agreements between the parties and entry of a consent decree by the court in which the case is pending.").

[91]   *See* John M. Golden, *Patent Privateers: Private Enforcement's Historical Survivors* 26 Harv. J. L. and Tech. 545, 601 (2013) ("Under appropriate circumstances, even the specialized patent-enforcement entities most vigorously denounced as 'trolls' could help produce a more socially optimal system, perhaps because of capacities to litigate or license more efficiently and even somewhat 'democratically' to enable some fruits of enforcement to run to patentees lacking independent capacity to overcome patent enforcement's costly barriers.").

[92]   *See, e.g.*, Mark A. Lemley and A. Douglas Melamed, *Missing the Forest for the Trolls* 113 Colum. L. Rev. 2117, 2176–77 (2013) (arguing that "[t]he law should do more to discourage frivolous suits or those driven by the expectation that the cost of litigation will drive defendants to settle even when faced with unmeritorious claims").

[93]   *See supra* note 78 and accompanying text.

[94]   Claim 1, the patent's broadest claim, reads:
    A heart stabilization device, comprising:
    a) a shaft having a proximal end provided with a handle, a distal end, and defining a longitudinal axis; and
    b) a pair of stabilization arm assemblies at said distal end of said shaft, each of said stabilization arms provided with a substantially rigid foot having a contact surface which is adapted to contact a surface of the heart, said feet having a first configuration in which said feet extend substantially parallel to said longitudinal axis and are substantially in contact with each other, and a second configuration in which feet extend substantially parallel to said longitudinal axis and are displaced relative to each other; and
    c) an actuator adapted to move said feet between said first and second configurations.
    U.S. Patent No. 6,592,573 B2 (filed June 27, 2001).

two fundamental patent-eligibility concerns. Since a kinematic claim nowhere specifies the kinds of causal powers involved in the use of the claimed invention, it may encompass entities that are conceptually well-defined, but are physically incapable of being used to produce a beneficial result or effect.[95] Also, since a kinematic claim relies on generic structural elements to specify the moving parts of a mechanism, it may preempt all physical instantiations of a geometric theorem. Part III will discuss these concerns in detail.

III.   KINEMATIC CLAIMS AND THE ABSTRACT-IDEAS EXCLUSION

For more than a century, the Supreme Court's abstract-ideas jurisprudence has been guided by the admonition that a patent is granted "for the discovery or invention of some practical method or means of producing a beneficial result or effect . . . and not for the result or effect itself."[96] As I have argued in previous articles,[97] this doctrinal distinction between a patent-ineligible abstract idea and a patent-eligible "practical method or means of producing a beneficial result or effect" grounds the embodiments of patent-eligible inventions in an ontological category of objects and processes having causal powers; i.e., dispositions to engage in processes that relate causes and effects.[98]

A filed patent application satisfies the disclosure requirement when it conveys to the reader a warranted ontological commitment to the kinds of causal objects and processes recited in the claims.[99] In this regard, the patent system appears to be ontologically committed to a wide range of causal processes (including those involving electrons and other unobservable entities[100]), thereby embracing the view of scientific realism that

---

[95]   The fact that a commercial embodiment of a kinematic claim has market value does not establish that the claimed invention is a method or means of producing a beneficial result or effect. *See Imperial Chemical Industries v. Henkel*, 545 F. Supp. 635, 645 (D. Del. 1982) ("[C]ommercial success is not the standard of usefulness under the Patent Act."); *see also Lowell v. Lewis*, 15 F. Cas. 1018, 1019 (D. Mass. 1817) (Story, J.) ("[W]hether [the invention] be more or less useful is a circumstance very material to the interests of the patentee, but of no importance to the public.").

[96]   *Diamond v. Diehr*, 450 U.S. at 182 n.7 (quoting *Corning v. Burden*, 56 U.S. at 268); *see also LeRoy v. Tatham*, 55 U.S. at 175 ("A patent is not good for an effect, or the result of a certain process, as that would prohibit all other persons from making the same thing by any means whatsoever."); *see also* Andrew Chin, *Ghost in the "New Machine": How Alice Exposed Software Patenting's Category Mistake* 16 N.C. J. L. and Tech. 623, 644 (2015) (arguing that the Supreme Court also drew this distinction in *Alice v. CLS Bank Int'l*, 134 S. Ct. 2347, 2359 (2014)).

[97]   *See* Chin, *supra* note 1; Chin, *supra* note 96.

[98]   *See* Chin, *supra* note 1, at 287–89 (citing Brian Ellis, *The Philosophy of Nature* (Cambridge University Press 2002) 48).

[99]   *See id.* at 312–13 (describing the role of the written description in conveying ontological commitment to claims through the filed patent application); *id.* at 321–23 (describing the role of the enablement requirement in warranting the patent system's ontological commitment to claims through the filed patent application).

[100]   The search query "clm(electron) and da(2016)" to Westlaw's Patents and Applications database finds 1,387 U.S. patents issued in 2016 containing the word "electron" in at least one claim. By legally recognizing these claims, the patent system routinely incurs ontological commitments to electrons, even though no one has directly observed an electron. *See generally* Theodore Arabatzis, *Representing Electrons: A Biographical Approach to Theoretical Entities* (University of Chicago

"our best scientific theories give approximately true descriptions of both observable and unobservable aspects of a mind-independent world."[101] Thus, unless there are "factual reasons which would lead one skilled in the art to question the objective truth of the statement of operability,"[102] a patent applicant need not provide a working model[103] or a correct account of the invention's theory of operation,[104] but must convince one skilled in the art of the asserted utility.[105]

Like many other animals,[106] humans have extended the functional reach of their bodies by inventing tools to achieve their goals. At the most fundamental level, progress in the useful arts can be measured by the extent to which humans can make and use these tools to produce the results and effects they desire. The patent system promotes this progress in human capacity simply by incurring warranted ontological commitments to claimed kinds of tools (and methods of making or using them), regardless of whether the available theories for the tools' operation are correct or complete. As an ontological project, the patent system can recognize and promote progress in frictional seals, for example, regardless of whether the friction is occurring due to adhesion, asperity interlock, or macro-displacement.[107]

Press 2006) (providing a history of theoretical representations of the electron as an unobservable entity).

[101] Anjan Chakravartty, *A Metaphysics for Scientific Realism: Knowing the Unobservable* (Cambridge University Press 2007) 212.

Josh Sarnoff (personal communication) has astutely pointed out the parallels between my ongoing efforts to discern the patent system's ontological inventory, *see* Chin, *supra* note 1, at 306–09, and Mike Madison's earlier examination of the constitution of "things" brought into play by intellectual property law. *See* Michael J. Madison, *Law as Design: Objects, Concepts, and Digital Things* 56 Case Western Reserve L. Rev. 381, 385 (2005). There is also a methodological similarity: Madison proceeds by describing how certain themes in metaphysics and semantics, *inter alia*, "are recognized by the law, as the law borrows them and simplifies them for its purposes," while I follow the lead of Steven Smith in setting out to identify the patent system's metaphysical commitments through "the ways that lawyers talk and argue and predict and . . . judges decide and justify." Chin, *supra* note 1, at 270 (quoting Steven D. Smith, *Metaphysical Perplexity?* 55 Cath. U. L. Rev 639, 644–45 (2006)).

[102] *In re Isaacs*, 347 F.2d 887, 890 (C.C.P.A. 1965) (citing *In re Citron*, 325 F.2d 248, 253 (C.C.P.A. 1963)); Sean B. Seymore, *Patently Impossible*, 64 Vand. L. Rev. 1491, 1500–07 (2011) (describing the Patent Office's examination rubric for the operability requirement).

[103] *See* U.S. Patent and Trademark Office, Manual of Patent Examining Procedure § 608.03 (Nov. 2015) ("With the exception of cases involving perpetual motion, a model is not ordinarily required by the Office to demonstrate the operability of a device. If operability of a device is questioned, the applicant must establish it to the satisfaction of the examiner, but he or she may choose his or her own way of so doing."); *see also In re Houghton*, 433 F.2d at 821 (noting that Patent Office did not require working model as proof of utility).

[104] *See Newman v. Quigg*, 77 F.2d 1575, 1581–82 (Fed. Cir. 1989).

[105] *See In re Brana*, 51 F.3d 1560, 1566 (Fed. Cir. 1995).

[106] *See* Vicki K. Bentley-Condit and E.O. Smith, *Animal Tool Use: Current Definitions and an Updated Comprehensive Catalog* 147 Behaviour 185 (2010).

[107] This ontological account of the patent system serves in part as a response to Sean Seymore's contention that a patent document is "uninformative" if it does not disclose how or why the invention works. *See* Sean B. Seymore, *Uninformative Patents* 55 Hous. L. Rev. 377, 378–80 (2017). The goal of extending human capacity also serves as a counterpoint to our colleague Peter Lee's description of the patent system's focus on maximizing efficiency. See Peter Lee, *Toward a Distributive Agenda for U.S. Patent Law* 55 Hous. L. Rev. 321, 326–31 (2017).

The abstract-ideas exclusion and other patent-eligible subject matter inquiries have a vital role in policing the boundaries of the patent system's ontological categories and ensuring that each claimed invention's "examination against prior art under the traditional tests for patentability"[108] is free of category mistakes.[109] For example, a § 101 rejection of a software claim may obviate a § 103 inquiry into "ordinary mathematical skill"[110] that would misplace mathematical properties into the patent system's ontological category of "beneficial results or effects."[111]

The study of causation and causal processes in analytical philosophy can illuminate § 101's categorical requirement that a patent-eligible invention be a "practical method or means of producing a beneficial result or effect." For example, consider the following hypothetical kinematic claim:

> A. An object on a cylindrical surface, said object moving counterclockwise on said cylindrical surface at a rate of at least one revolution per second.

As the next section will explain in detail, causal process theories grounded in the movements of entities through space-time are particularly well suited to addressing the question of whether such a claim is directed to a product or process capable of being used to cause some specified effect or a noncausal abstract idea.

A. Kinematic Claims and Causal Process Theories

The most prominent causal process accounts addressing the kinematic behavior of objects are the interrelated theories of Wesley Salmon and Phil Dowe.[112] Wesley Salmon's two causal process theories are presented in books published in 1984[113] and 1998;[114] Phil Dowe's causal process theory is presented in a 2000 volume.[115] Salmon acknowledged a heavy debt to Dowe in the development of his 1998 theory,[116] which is similar in many ways to Dowe's.[117] A full survey of these theories is beyond the scope of this Chapter; interested readers may consult the respective books for details. It is sufficient here to discuss certain salient features of Salmon's earlier theory and of Dowe's theory.

---

[108] *In re Bilski*, 545 F.3d 943, 1013 (Fed. Cir. 2008) (en banc) (Rader, J., dissenting).

[109] *See* Chin, *supra* note 96, at 638.

[110] *See In re Bernhart*, 417 F.2d 1395, 1402 (C.C.P.A. 1969).

[111] *See* Chin, *supra* note 96, at 636–37.

[112] *See generally Causal Processes*, Stanford Encyclopedia of Philosophy, https://plato.stanford. edu/entries/causation-process (visited 24 Apr. 2017) (surveying the philosophical literature on causal process theories with extended treatments of Salmon's and Dowe's theories).

[113] Wesley C. Salmon, *Scientific Explanation and the Causal Structure of the World* (Princeton University Press 1984).

[114] Wesley C. Salmon, *Causality and Explanation* (Oxford University Press 1998).

[115] Phil Dowe, *Physical Causation* (Cambridge University Press 2000).

[116] *See* Wesley C. Salmon, *Causality Without Counterfactuals* 61 Phil. Sci. 297, 298 (1994) ("I will attempt to show how the account can be modified so as to remove the genuine shortcomings. In this . . . endeavor I rely heavily on work of P. Dowe.").

[117] *See* Phil Dowe, *Causality and Conserved Quantities: A Reply to Salmon* 62 Phil. Sci. 321, 321 (1995) ("Salmon and I agree on much.").

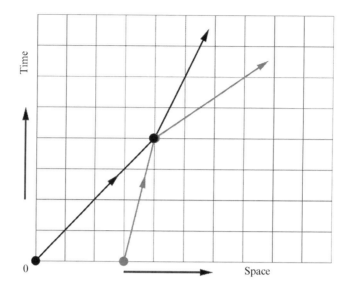

*Figure 16.1   A space-time diagram illustrating the trajectories of two balls before and
after a collision*

Salmon developed his first causal process theory (hereinafter referred to simply as
"Salmon's theory") in the 1980s[118] as a "theory of causality in which processes, rather
than events, are taken as fundamental."[119] In Salmon's theory, processes include "waves
and material objects that persist through time,"[120] and may be represented by lines on a
space-time diagram.[121] Space-time diagrams use a coordinate plane to depict the positions
of objects over time relative to some *inertial reference frame.*[122] By convention, the vertical
coordinate axis of a space-time diagram is devoted to time, so the diagram is limited to
showing positions in only one dimension. For example, Figure 16.1 shows the trajectories
of two balls of different masses moving in the same direction along a line, but at different
speeds. After the more massive, faster black ball collides with the smaller, slower gray
ball, their respective speeds change: the black ball decelerates slightly, and the gray ball
accelerates away from it.

In illustrating the principles of special relativity, it is customary to set the scales for
the coordinate axes so that a line with unit slope (i.e., at 45 degrees) represents an object

---

[118]   For a preliminary version of Salmon's earlier causal process theory, *see* Wesley C. Salmon,
"Causality: Production and Propagation", in Ernest Sosa and Michael Tooley (eds.), *Causation*
(Oxford University Press 1988).
[119]   *See* Salmon, *supra* note 113, at 140.
[120]   *See id.* at 140.
[121]   *See id.* at 139.
[122]   *See generally* Jurgen Freund, *Special Relativity for Beginners* (World Scientific Publishing
2008) 47–78 (providing a general introduction to space-time and Minkowski diagrams).
An inertial reference frame is an observational perspective that is "rectilinear, uniform, and
irrotational (i.e. without any acceleration)," as is the case of objects that are "not acted on by any
forces" and are thus "subject to the principle of inertia." *See id.* at 4.

moving at the speed of light. Space-time diagrams that employ this convention are called *Minkowski diagrams*, after Hermann Minkowski, the pioneering geometric interpreter of Einstein's special theory of relativity.[123] A *world line* is the trajectory of an object on a Minkowski diagram.[124] An *event* is represented by a point on a Minkowski diagram.[125]

Minkowski diagrams can geometrically illustrate the principle that the propagation of causal influence through spacetime is limited by the speed of light.[126] As Salmon explains:

> [A]ny given event E_0, occurring at a particular space-time point P_0, has an associated double-sheeted light cone. All events that could have a causal influence on E_0 are located in the interior or on the surface of the past light cone, and all events upon which E_0 could have any causal influence are located on the interior or on the surface of the future light cone. . . [T]hose [events] that are outside of the cone are said to have a spacelike separation from E_0.

Figure 16.2 is a Minkowski diagram illustrating two events, A and B, relative to the inertial reference frames of two observers. From one observer's perspective, event A precedes event B; from the other observer's perspective, event B precedes event A. Note, however, that the light cones from events A and B are invariant with respect to inertial reference frames, since their surfaces may be traced out by objects moving at the speed of light. Thus, from either observer's perspective, A and B lie outside each other's light cones, and A and B are spacelike separated. The possibility of causal influence thus turns out to be a question not of temporal precedence, but of separation in spacetime.

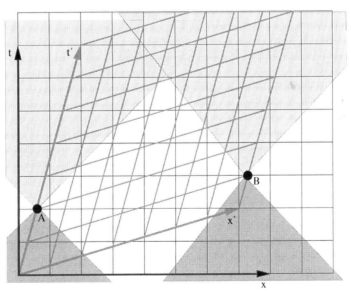

Figure 16.2   Light cones of events A and B. Neither event can have a causal influence on the other, because they do not lie in each other's light cones

---

[123]   *See* David J. Griffiths, *Introduction to Electrodynamics* (Pearson 1999) 503–04.
[124]   *See id.* at 503.
[125]   *See* Freund, *supra* note 122, at 50–51.
[126]   *See* Griffiths, *supra* note 123, at 504.

Just as some pairs of events may not causally influence each other, some lines on a Minkowski diagram may not represent processes capable of propagating causal influences. Salmon uses the term "causal process" to refer to a process (i.e., an entity represented by a line on a space-time diagram) that is capable of propagating causal influence and transmitting energy and information,[127] and uses the term "pseudo-process" to refer to a process that lacks these capabilities.[128] He notes that while causal processes are limited by the speed of light, pseudo-processes are not.[129]

As an example of a pseudo-process that exceeds the speed of light, Salmon describes a rotating spotlight mounted on a rotating mechanism at the center of a very large circular building. If the rotation is fast enough (say, one revolution per second) and the enclosure is large enough (say, over 50,000 kilometers), then the spot of light that it casts on the walls of the enclosure moves at a velocity that exceeds the speed of light. The spot is a process, in that it can be represented by a line on a space-time diagram. The spot is not, however, capable of propagating causal influence or transmitting energy or information. In short, it is incapable of "transmitting a mark," in the following sense:

> [W]e can place a red filter at the wall with the result that the spot of light becomes red at that point. But if we make such a modification in the traveling spot, it will not be transmitted beyond the point of interaction. As soon as the light spot moves beyond the point at which the red filter was placed, it will become white again. The mark can be made, but it will not be transmitted.[130]

Because of this inability, Salmon describes the moving spot of light on the wall as "a paradigm of what we mean by a pseudo-process." According to Salmon, "[t]he basic method for distinguishing causal processes from pseudo-processes is the criterion of mark transmission."[131] Dowe rejects Salmon's mark-transmission criterion, finding that it "fails to adequately capture the distinction between causal and pseudo processes."[132] Dowe's causal process theory is based on the idea that "it is the possession of a conserved quantity, rather than the ability to transmit a mark, that makes a process a causal process."[133] The theory consists of two propositions. First, " *causal process* is a world line of an object that possesses a conserved quantity." Second, " *causal interaction* is an

---

[127]   *See* Salmon, *supra* note 113, at 146.
[128]   *See id.* at 141.
[129]   Salmon writes:
Special relativity demands that we make a distinction between causal processes and pseudo-processes. It is a fundamental principle of that theory that light is a first signal—that is, no signal can be transmitted at a velocity greater than the velocity of light in a vacuum. There are, however, certain processes that can transpire at arbitrarily high velocities—at velocities vastly exceeding that of light. This fact does not violate the basic relativistic principle, however, for these "processes" are incapable of serving as signals or of transmitting information. Causal processes are those that are capable of transmitting signals; pseudo-processes are incapable of doing so.
See id.
[130]   Salmon, *supra* note 113, at 142.
[131]   *See id.* The original use of the speed of light to separate causal processes from pseudo-processes is credited to Hans Reichenbach. *See* Hans Reichenbach, *The Philosophy of Space and Time* (Dover 1958) 147–49.
[132]   Dowe, *supra* note 115, at 79.
[133]   *See id.* at 89.

intersection of world lines that involves exchange of a conserved quantity."[134] Informally, the respective roles of causal processes and causal interactions are to transmit and produce *causal influence*.[135]

Dowe's theory defines a pseudo-process as a process that does not possess a conserved quantity.[136] A conserved quantity is "any quantity that is governed by a conservation law, and current scientific theory is our best guide as to what these are: quantities such as mass-energy, linear momentum, and charge."[137] Salmon's spot is also an example of a pseudo-process in Dowe's theory, because it does not possess a conserved quantity.[138]

According to Dowe, for two token events to be connected in a causal relation, it is necessary (but not sufficient) that a continuous line of causal processes and interactions can be traced between them.[139] Dowe appears to be correct,[140] at least as long as *negative*

---

[134]   *See id.* at 90.
[135]   *See id.* at 147.
[136]   *See id.* ("To generalize, pseudo processes do not possess the type of physical quantities that are governed by conservation laws.").
[137]   *See id.* at 94.
[138]   Dowe explains:

> The causal processes involved . . . are the light beam (energy, momentum) and the wall (mass). The spot or moving patch of illumination cannot be ascribed a conserved quantity. It has other quantities: size, speed, position; but no conserved quantity. The exchange involved in the interaction between the wall and the light beam involves, for example, momentum (the light's momentum is changed on reflection by the wall) or energy (some energy of the reflected beam is lost to heat transferred initially to the molecules of the wall's surface, and subsequently dissipated). No energy is brought to the interaction by the spot or carried off by the spot. Spots do not possess energy.

Phil Dowe, *An Empiricist Defence of the Causal Account of Explanation* 6 Int'l Stud. Phil. Sci. 123, 127 (1992).

Because a spot lacks tangible causes and effects, it is even more "transient," "fleeting" and intangible than the claimed "signal" at issue in *In re Nuijten*, 500 F.3d 1356 (Fed. Cir. 2007). In determining that "a transient electric or electromagnetic transmission" was not a patent-eligible "manufacture," Judge Gajarsa reasoned:

> While such a transmission is man-made and physical—it exists in the real world and has tangible causes and effects—it is a change in electric potential that, to be perceived, must be measured at a certain point in space and time by equipment capable of detecting and interpreting the signal. In essence, energy embodying the claimed signal is fleeting and is devoid of any semblance of permanence during transmission. Moreover, any tangibility arguably attributed to a signal is embodied in the principle that it is perceptible—e.g., changes in electrical potential can be measured.

Id. at 1356.

[139]   *See* Dowe, *supra* note 115, at 146–48 (stating the encompassing necessary and sufficient condition as a "naïve process theory" and concluding that there is "reason to suppose that the naïve process theory does provide a necessary condition for singular causation"); Phil Dowe, *Review Article: Causality and Explanation* 51 Brit. J. Phil. Sci. 165, 173 (2000) ("We must conclude that the conserved quantity theory . . . provides only a necessary condition for singular causation."); Phil Dowe, "Causes Are Physically Connected to Their Effects: Why Preventers and Omissions Are Not Causes" in Christopher Hitchcock (ed.), *Contemporary Debates in Philosophy of Science* (Wiley-Blackwell 2004).

[140]   It is worth noting that Dowe's conserved quantity account ultimately persuaded Salmon. *See supra* notes 115–16 and accompanying text.

causation is excluded from consideration as a causal relation.[141] Negative causation "occurs when an absence serves as cause, effect, or causal intermediary."[142] While negative causation can figure in causal accounts of legal responsibility (e.g., in theories of negligence or breach of contract),[143] it does not have a place in the patent system's ontology of "useful Arts," inasmuch as the scope of the patent right is limited to affirmative acts such as making and using the structural elements or performing the steps recited in a claim.[144] Thus, it is reasonable to conclude that Dowe's theory accurately describes the instances of causal processes and causal interactions that display the causal powers of a claim's embodiments.

A kinematic claim may entail the exchange of a conserved quantity when an embodiment of the claimed invention is used, but does not set forth limitations regarding any such conserved quantities.[145] For example, the embodiments of hypothetical claim A (introduced earlier[146]) include the spot pseudo-process described by Salmon:

A. An object on a cylindrical surface, said object moving counterclockwise on said cylindrical surface at a rate of at least one revolution per second.[147]

This kinematic claim includes subject matter that cannot participate in the exchange of a conserved quantity and is physically incapable of "producing a beneficial result or effect." The claim is therefore directed to a patent-ineligible abstract idea.

The characterization of a rapidly moving spot of light as a patent-ineligible abstract idea is probably not controversial. In contrast, however, it may seem counterintuitive that a claim directed to a surgical robot mechanism could be unpatentably abstract.[148] The following three sections will examine various kinematic mechanism claims, each of which recites generic structural elements that would effectively preempt all physical

---

[141]   *Compare* Phil Dowe, *Causes Are Physically Connected to Their Effects, supra* note 139, at 189, 190 (arguing that cases involving negative events are not, strictly speaking, cases of causation); *with* Jonathan Schaffer, "Causes Need Not Be Physically Connected to Their Effects: The Case for Negative Causation", in Christopher Hitchcock (ed.), *Contemporary Debates in Philosophy of Science* (Wiley-Blackwell 2004), at 197, 197 (arguing that negative causation does not necessarily involve connection by causal processes and interactions).

[142]   *See* Schaffer, *supra* note 141, at 197.

[143]   *See id.* at 201 (citing Hart and Honoré, *Causation in the Law* 2d ed. (Clarendon 1985) 2–3).

[144]   *See* 35 U.S.C. § 154.
An absence is not cognizable as an element of a claim without a supporting structural element. *Compare* Margaret A. Boulware, *An Overview of Intellectual Property Rights Abroad* 16 Hous. J. Int'l L. 441, 447 n. 23 (1994) ("[O]ne cannot claim a 'hole' because a hole is 'nothing.' One must therefore claim some structure 'having a hole.'"); *with Faber on Mechanics of Patent Claim Drafting* § 3.18, at 3-68 (2009) (noting that while "[y]ou may claim holes positively and make them claim elements," the "[b]etter practice is to claim 'a [member] having a hole, groove, slot, aperture, etc.'").

[145]   *See supra* text accompanying note 6.

[146]   *See supra* text accompanying note 111.

[147]   This is true provided that the term "object" is construed, as Dowe construes it, to include a spot of light. *See* Dowe, *supra* note 115, at 91.

[148]   *See, e.g., Bilski v. Kappos*, 561 U.S. 593, 632–33 (Stevens, J., concurring) (citing John R. Thomas, *The Patenting of the Liberal Professions* 40 B.C. L. Rev. 1139, 1164 (1999)) (tracing the historical inclusion of the mechanical arts within the category of patent-eligible "useful arts").

instantiations of a geometric theorem.[149] As the ensuing discussion will show, the issuance of such kinematic claims not only raises concerns under abstract-ideas jurisprudence, but impinges on the creative work of mathematicians.[150]

B.   Preempting the Pythagorean Theorem

Credited to Pythagoras but possibly known to the Babylonians and/or the Chinese a millennium earlier,[151] the Pythagorean Theorem is known to us today as an equation, $a^2 + b^2 = c^2$, expressing the relationship between the length c of the hypotenuse of a right triangle and the lengths a and b of the other two sides[152] (also known as "legs"[153]). Stated more formally:

Theorem 1. (The Pythagorean Theorem) Let $\triangle ABC$ be a right triangle, with its right angle at C. Then $AB^2 = AC^2 + BC^2$.[154]

Theorems cannot be the subject of a patent grant; only claims can.[155] What does it mean then to say that the Pythagorean Theorem is unpatentable? In *Parker v. Flook*, the Supreme Court describes a hypothetical attempt by a "competent draftsman" to claim the theorem in a patent application:

> A competent draftsman could attach some form of post-solution activity to almost any mathematical formula; the Pythagorean theorem would not have been patentable, or partially patentable, because a patent application contained a final step indicating that the formula, when solved, could be usefully applied to existing surveying techniques.[156]

The Court did not expressly cite any claim language in making these points. Given the court's suggestion that the claim might contain a "final step" after the formula was "solved," however, it appears that the Court had in mind a process claim that recited steps for calculating $\sqrt{AC^2 + BC^2}$, followed by a final step using the result, AB, in a known method for solving some surveying problem. The *Flook* Court would have found such a claim ineligible, even though it does not wholly preempt the formula $AB^2 = AC^2 + BC^2$ (because of the final surveying step), because the claim's only point of novelty is the formula $AB^2 = AC^2 + BC^2$. As we have seen in Part II, however, this "point of novelty" approach to eligible subject matter analysis is at least controversial, if not discredited.

---

[149]   *See infra* Sections III.B–III.D.
[150]   *See infra* Section III.E.
[151]   *See* Eli Maor, *The Pythagorean Theorem: A 4,000-Year History* (Princeton University Press 2007) xi; Frank J. Swetz and T.I. Kao, *Was Pythagoras Chinese?* (Pennsylvania University Press 1977) 66.
[152]   *See* Maor, *supra* note 151, at xi.
[153]   *See* Serge Lang and Gene Murrow, *Geometry* (Springer 2000) 44.
[154]   *See, e.g.*, Ron Larson et al., *Geometry: An Integrated Approach* (DC Heath 1995) 459. In a triangle, it is conventional to use lowercase letters to denote the sides opposite the vertices denoted by the corresponding uppercase letters. *See* Edwin E. Moise, *Elementary Geometry from an Advanced Standpoint* (Addison-Wesley 1974) 148.
[155]   *See* 35 U.S.C. § 112, ¶ 2 ("The specification shall conclude with one or more claims particularly pointing out and distinctly claiming the subject matter which the applicant regards as his invention.").
[156]   437 U.S. at 590.

Moreover, the Pythagorean Theorem is a mathematical theorem, not merely a "formula" to be "solved."[157] This distinction was lost as the Court drew comparisons to Flook's invention, which had earlier been characterized as a "mathematical formula" followed by "conventional post-solution applications" of the formula.[158] Thus, while the *Flook* Court's exclusion of the Pythagorean Theorem from patent-eligible subject matter is "well-established," the case law has not clarified the implications of this exclusion for specific claims that recite the use of the Pythagorean Theorem.

Consider instead the following hypothetical apparatus claim:

> B. An apparatus for measuring angles, comprising:
> a first leg member having a first end and a second end separated by a first distance a;
> a second leg member having a first end and a second end separated by a second distance b, the first end of said second leg member being attached to the first end of said first leg member; and
> a hypotenuse member having a first end and a second end separated by a third distance $\sqrt{a^2 + b^2}$, the first end of said hypotenuse member being attached to the second end of said first leg member and the second end of said hypotenuse member being attached to the second end of said second leg member,
> whereby said first leg member and said second leg member form a right angle.

Two subtleties of claim construction are needed to understand the claim's scope. First, while the claim's preamble recites the function of measuring angles, the claim covers every apparatus that meets the claim's structural limitations, regardless of its intended function.[159] Second, there is a "heavy presumption" that claim terms carry their ordinary and customary meanings.[160] As the Federal Circuit found in *CCS Fitness, Inc. v. Brunswick Corp.*,[161] the ordinary meaning of the term "member" is broad, and may refer to a "structural unit such as a . . . beam or tie, or a combination of these,"[162] or a "distinct part of a whole."[163] This

---

[157]　The government's brief in Benson argued for separate recognition of mathematical theorems as a categorical exclusion from patentable subject matter:

> For that reason, the Pythagorean Theorem, the binomial theorem, Gibbs' vectors, the Laplace Transform, the general theory of relativity, and Russell's theory of types, for example, even though the products of great intellectual effort, or a flash of genius, are not patentable under our law. Mathematical theorems, abstractions, ideas, and laws of nature are the property of everyone and the [exclusive] right of no one.

Brief for Petitioner at 19, *Gottschalk v. Benson*, 409 U.S. 63 (1972) (No. 71-485).

[158]　*Id.* at 585; *cf. Paine, Webber, Jackson and Curtis, Inc. v. Merrill Lynch, Pierce, Fenner and Smith, Inc.*, 564 F. Supp. 1358, 1366–67 (D. Del. 1983) ("[T]he Pythagorean theorem . . . is not patentable because it defines a mathematical formula. Likewise a computer program which does no more than apply a theorem to a set of numbers is not patentable.").

[159]　*See, e.g., Cross Medical Products, Inc. v. Medtronic Sofamor Danek, Inc.*, 424 F.3d 1293, 1311–12 (Fed. Cir. 2005) ("To infringe an apparatus claim, the device must meet all of the structural limitations."); *Hewlett-Packard Co. v. Bausch and Lomb Inc.*, 909 F.2d 1464, 1468 (Fed. Cir. 1990) ("[A]pparatus claims cover what a device *is*, not what a device *does*.") (emphasis in original).

[160]　*CCS Fitness, Inc. v. Brunswick Corp.*, 288 F.3d 1359, 1365 (Fed. Cir. 2002) (citing *Johnson Worldwide Assocs., Inc. v. Zebco Corp.*, 175 F.3d 985, 989 (Fed. Cir. 1999)).

[161]　*Id.*

[162]　*See id.* at 1367 (quoting *McGraw-Hill Dictionary of Scientific and Technical Terms* 5th ed. (McGraw-Hill 1994) 1237).

[163]　*See id.* (quoting *American Heritage Dictionary* 3d ed. (Houghton Mifflin 1996) 849).

breadth makes "member" a preferred generic term for a structural unit in the drafting of mechanical patent claims.[164] Read in the context of the claim limitations,[165] each of the recited "members" can be any structural unit of the apparatus having two identifiable ends separated by a specified distance. The term "member" therefore covers, *inter alia*, any structural unit capable of representing a side of a right-triangle-shaped apparatus.[166]

On its face, then, Claim B covers every apparatus that may be made by attaching the respectively paired ends of three "members" whose lengths are related by the equation $a^2 + b^2 = c^2$, thereby forming a right triangle. It therefore appears that Claim A covers every mechanical application of the Pythagorean Theorem, and should be found patent-ineligible under *Mayo*.[167]

Unlike a robotic mechanism, the linkage of Claim B is rigid. Taken as a whole, the recited structure has no degrees of freedom: the three attachments fix the apparatus in a triangular configuration completely determined by the lengths of the members. The next section describes one of the most historically important mathematical results involving a linkage with movable parts.

C. Peaucellier's Theorem (or Invention)

James Watt is credited with inventing the steam engine, but he fell short of solving a fundamental mathematical problem arising from the engine's design: how to transmit rotary motion via a mechanical linkage to move a piston linearly up and down. Lacking an exact solution, Watt instead built a simple four-bar linkage that could move a piston in an approximately straight line; i.e., within the tolerances of his engine design. Watt took special pride in this linkage,[168] and in 1784 obtained a British patent on the linkage's use in "methods of directing the piston rods, the pump rods, and other parts of these engines, so as to move in perpendicular or other straight or right lines . . . so as to enable the engine to act on the working beams . . . both in the ascent and descent of their pistons."[169] Figure 16.3 provides an illustration of the linkage from Watt's patent specification.

---

[164] *See* Richard G. Berkley, "Some Practical Aspects of Amendment Practice in the Electromechanical Arts", in *Fifth Annual Patent Prosecution Workshop*, at 161, 205 (PLI Patents, Copyrights, Trademarks and Literary Property Course Handbook Series No. 426, 1995).

[165] *See* Ronald C. Faber, "The Winning Mechanical Claim", in *Advanced Patent Prosecution Workshop 2009: Claim Drafting and Amendment Writing*, at 295, 321–22 (PLI Patents, Copyrights, Trademarks and Literary Property Course Handbook Series No. 977, 2009) (noting that construction of "member" as a claim element may require some guidance "perhaps obtained from the rest of the limitation including that element . . . [o]r perhaps referring back to the specification or drawing"). In this hypothetical, I assume that nothing in the specification or drawings further limits the meaning of "member."

[166] *See* Moise, *supra* note 154, at 55 (stating that each side of a triangle is a line segment); *id.* at 54–55 (showing that every line segment has two end points).

[167] *See supra* text accompanying note 96 (explaining *Alice/Mayo* test).

[168] *See* Richard L. Hills, *Power from Steam: A History of the Stationary Steam Engine* 69 (Cambridge University Press 1989) (quoting a letter from Watt to fellow inventor Matthew Boulton stating "I am more proud of the parallel motion than of any other mechanical invention I have ever made.").

[169] UK Patent No. 1,432 (1784), *reprinted in* Eric Robinson and A.E. Musson, *James Watt and the Steam Revolution: A Documentary History* (Adams and Dart 1969) 111.

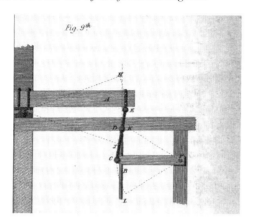

Figure 16.3   Watt's four-bar linkage[170]

Despite the efforts of mathematicians as distinguished as Pafnutï L'vovich Chebyshev, the exact solution to Watt's problem did not appear for nearly 80 years, and then only in an obscure mathematics journal article.[171] In 1864, a French army captain named Charles Peaucellier published the following theorem as a letter to the *Nouvelles Annales:*[172]

Theorem 2 (Peaucellier). *In the planar linkage of Figure 16.4, suppose that* O *and* Q *are fixed in the plane, links* QC, OA, OB, AP, BP, AC *and* BC *satisfy* OQ = QC, OA = OB = l_1, *and* AP = BP = AC = BC = l_2. *Then as* C *moves on a circle centered at* Q, P *moves on a straight line perpendicular to* $\overleftrightarrow{OQ}$.

Proof. *Since APBC is a rhombus, its diagonals are perpendicular bisectors of each other; let* M *be their point of intersection. By the Pythagorean Theorem,* $OM^2 + AM^2 = l_1^2$ *and* $PM^2 + AM^2 = l_2^2$; *thus* $OC \cdot OP = (OM - PM)(OM + PM) = l_1^2 - l_2^2$ *is a constant. Since* C *moves on a circle centered at* Q, *we have* $\angle OCR = 90°$. *Drop perpendicular* $\overline{PN}$ *from* P *to* $\overleftrightarrow{OQ}$; *then* $\Delta OCR \sim \Delta ONP$ *and* $ON = \dfrac{OC \cdot OP}{OR} = \dfrac{k^2}{2OQ}$ *is a constant; i.e.,* N *is stationary. Thus* P *moves on a straight line perpendicular to* $\overleftrightarrow{OQ}$. *Q.E.D.*

The elegance and simplicity of Peaucellier's solution to a decades-old problem caught the attention of the British mathematician J.J. Sylvester, who demonstrated the linkage's motion to colleagues at the Royal Society and the Athenaeum Club.[173] According to Sylvester, the eminent physicist Lord Kelvin described the linkage as "the most beautiful thing I have ever seen in my life."[174]

---

[170]   Fig. 9, 1784 Specification of Patent, *reprinted in* Robinson and Musson, *id.*

[171]   *See* Eugene S. Ferguson, "Kinematics of Mechanisms from the Time of Watt", in *27 Contributions from the Museum of History and Technology* (United States National Museum 1962) 199–208, http://www.gutenberg.org/ebooks/27106 (visited 24 Apr. 2017) (describing the history of Peaucellier's mechanism).

[172]   *See* M. Peaucellier, *Correspondence* 3 Nouvelles Annales de Mathematiques 414 (1864).

[173]   *See* Ferguson, *supra* note 171.

[174]   *See id.* (citing James Sylvester, *Recent Discoveries in Mechanical Conversion of Motion* 7 Notices Proc. Royal Inst. Gr. Brit. 183 (1873–75)).Peter Lee (personal communication) has

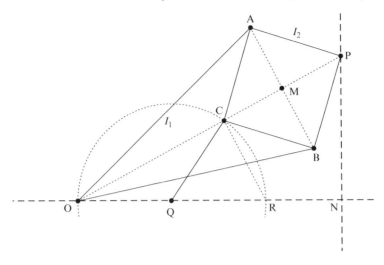

Figure 16.4 Peaucellier's linkage

The close kinship between Peaucellier's result and the Pythagorean Theorem should be apparent even to a reader several decades removed from high school geometry, and should give pause concerning the patent-eligibility of mechanisms based on either result. Peaucellier himself was content with publishing his result in a mathematics journal and did not seek a patent on his straight-line linkage; unfortunately, he was a historical outlier. Kinematic claims to mechanical linkages have issued in U.S. patents to the present day. A patent issued in 1916 claiming " constant product linkage comprising a large Peaucellier cell and a similar smaller Peaucellier cell, and connections to keep their corresponding angles equal,"[175] as illustrated in Figure 16.5, is a particularly egregious example, especially in light of Peaucellier's dedication of his groundbreaking linkage to the public domain of mathematical scholarship.

The patent system's tolerance of kinematic claiming reflects a widespread failure to consider the claims of the mathematical community alongside the claims of patent

---

suggested that mathematical education and appreciation might be beneficial results or effects of linkages that are sufficiently independent of causal processes to support kinematic claims. While Lord Kelvin's considerable appreciation is not in doubt, determining in general whether such asserted utilities are specific or substantial, *see In re Fisher*, 421 F.3d 1365, 1371 (Fed. Cir. 2005), would likely lead to the kind of category mistake that patent-eligibility doctrine serves to avoid. Courts should not be put in the position of determining whether a mathematical property is sufficiently "specific and substantial" to meet the § 101 utility requirement. *See* Chin, *supra* note 96, at 636-37 ("The patentability analysis of a claimed software-implemented invention should never leave a court in the position of determining how hard the math was."); *see also id.* at 638 (quoting *In re Bilski*, 545 F.3d 943, 1013 (Fed. Cir. 2008) (en banc) (Rader, J., dissenting) (arguing that the patent-eligible subject matter inquiry serves to "prevent[] future category mistakes in connection with 'examination against prior art under the traditional tests for patentability'").

[175] U.S. Patent No. 1,190,215, at cl. 1 (filed Mar. 13, 1915).

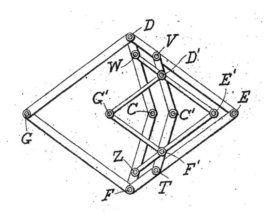

Figure 16.5   A patented linkage derived from Peaucellier's linkage

applicants. The case study in the next section will further illustrate the fundamental and integral role of mechanical linkages in the discipline of mathematics.

D.   Yates's Linkage and the Sources of Mathematical Intuition

In 1931, University of Maryland mathematics professor Robert Yates derived a surface of constant curvature whose meridian cross-section could be generated by "rolling an ellipse along a straight line and taking the curve traced out by a focus."[176] At the suggestion of his colleague Frank Morley, Yates built a mechanical device for generating the cross-section, as shown in Figure 16.6.[177] He then published a description of his device in the American Mathematical Monthly.[178]

Yates's linkage (Figure 16.7) has the interesting property that when one of the shorter links is fixed in the plane, the point at which the two longer links intersect will trace out an ellipse. This result can be formalized in the following geometric theorem:

Theorem 2. In Fig. 3, suppose that $F_1F_2 = F_1'F_2' = c$, $F_1F_1' = F_2F_2' = a > c$, $\overline{F_1F_2}$ is fixed in the plane, and E is the point of intersection of $\overline{F_1F_1'}$ with $\overline{F_1F_1'}$. Then as F_1' moves in a circle about F_1, E traces an ellipse with foci F_1 and F_2.

Proof. By the SSS Theorem, we have $\Delta F_1F_2F_2' \cong \Delta F_2'F_1'F_1$, so $\angle F_1F_2F_2 \cong \angle F_2'F_1F_1'$. By the SAS Theorem, $\Delta F_1F_2E \cong \Delta F_2'F_1'E$. Thus $F_2E = F_1'E$, and $F_1E + F_2E = F_1'E + EF_1' = F_1F_1'$, a constant.

Yates's "mechanical description" immediately caught the attention of David Hilbert, one of the most influential mathematicians of the late nineteenth and early twentieth century.[179]

---

[176]   *See* Robert C. Yates, *The Description of a Surface of Constant Curvature* 38 Am. Math. Monthly 573, 573 (1931).

[177]   *See id.*

[178]   *See id.* at 573–74.

[179]   *See* Constance Reid, *Hilbert* (Springer 2007) 218 (quoting mathematician Alfred Tarski) ("The future historian of science concerned with the development of mathematics in the late

Figure 16.6   Yates's linkage for generating the meridian cross-section of a surface of constant curvature

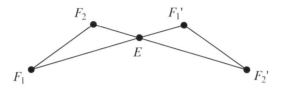

Figure 16.7   Yates's linkage represented as a geometric figure in the plane

In his classic 1932 monograph, *Anschauliche Geometrie*,[180] Hilbert described Yates's linkage (Figure 16.8):

> Let c and cN be two rods of the same length c. Let a_1 and a_2 be two other rods both equal to $a > c$ in length. Let the extremities F_1, F_2 of c and F_1N, F_2N of cN be linked to a_1 and a_2 by pin joints in such a way as to form a self-intersecting quadrilateral with opposite sides equal . . . Let E be the point at which a_1 and a_2 cross. Its position on these two rods will change as the plane linkage assumes its various possible positions. At E we place a joint with two sleeves which are free to turn about E and in which the rods a_1 and a_2 can slide freely.[181]

Hilbert observed that when the rod c is held fixed, the point E traces out an ellipse with F_1, F_2 as foci and with a as the constant sum of its focal distances.[182] Following Yates's suggestion,[183] Hilbert also considered the case where F_1 and F_2 are no longer fixed, and where "two wheels Z_1 and Z_2 [are] mounted at any two points of the rods [F_1F_1' and F_2F_2'] in such a way as to be free to rotate about these rods but not to slide along them."[184]

From this construction, Hilbert was able to prove a new mathematical result. Hilbert wrote:

> Thus the study of Yates' apparatus leads to a peculiar geometrical theorem which may be formulated [as] follows: Given a roulette generated by a focus of an ellipse, on the normals to the

---

nineteenth and the first half of the twentieth century will undoubtedly state that several branches of mathematics are highly indebted to Hilbert's achievements for their vigorous advancement in that period."

[180]   David Hilbert, *Geometry and the Imagination* (P. Nemenyi trans. Chelsea Publishing 1990) (1932).

[181]   *Id.* at 283.

[182]   *See id.*

[183]   *See* Yates, *supra* note 176, at 574 ("Toothed wheels are placed at the extremities (or at any convenient point) of the rods representing the axis of the ellipse in order that each rod may move at right angles to itself. These wheels cut out two of the four degrees of freedom.").

[184]   Hilbert, *supra* note 180, at 283.

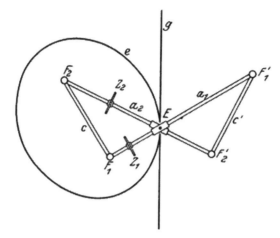

Figure 16.8   Hilbert's diagram of Yates's linkage with wheels attached[185]

roulette draw the points whose distance from the curve, measured in the direction of the center of curvature, is equal to the constant sum of focal radii for the ellipse; then the points thus marked out lie on another roulette generated by a focus of the ellipse; this ellipse is congruent to the first ellipse and rolls on the same curve as the first ellipse but on the opposite side of that curve.[186]

By studying the behavior of Yates's apparatus, Hilbert was able to prove a new mathematical result, his "peculiar geometric theorem." Suppose, however, that Yates had been precluded from building his apparatus by the following hypothetical patent claim C:

C. An apparatus for drawing ellipses, comprising:
a base;
a first link having a first end and a second end separated by a first distance c, both of said ends being attached to said base;
a second link having a first end and a second end separated by a second distance $a > c$, the first end of said second link being connected by a revolute joint to the first end of said first link;
a third link having a first end and a second end separated by said first distance c, the first end of said third link being connected by a revolute joint to the second end of said second link;
a fourth link having a first end and a second end separated by said second distance a, the first end of said fourth link being connected by a revolute joint to the second end of said third link and the second end of said fourth link being connected by a revolute joint to the second end of said first link; and
a revolute joint assembly slidably attached to said second link and to said fourth link, permitting said second link and said fourth link to slide independently of each other and to rotate independently of each other about an axial point E, said axial point E being located on said revolute joint assembly,
whereby the movement of said axial point E relative to said base is constrained to the points of an ellipse whose foci are the first end and the second end of said first link and whose major diameter is a.

---

[185]   *Id.*

[186]   *Id.* at 284–85. A *roulette* is the curve traced out by a point rigidly attached to a plane curve as it rolls upon a second fixed plane curve. *See* 2 Howard Eves, *A Survey of Geometry* (Allyn and Bacon 1965) 271.

Courts have understood the term "link" in its ordinary meaning to refer to a generic structural element in a variety of claim construction contexts[187] (although the term "link" itself has not yet been judicially construed as an element of a claimed kinematic linkage).[188] Assuming that an ordinary meaning construction applies in the present context, it is straightforward to verify that Claim C covers every apparatus that may be made by attaching four links as depicted in Figure 16.3 and described in Theorem 2 so as to produce a kinematic movement for the point E; i.e., Claim C covers every mechanical application of Theorem 2. In particular, Yates's linkage is a representative embodiment of Claim C.[189]

The granting of a patent on Claim C would have had significant consequences for the development of pure mathematics. Yates and Hilbert would not have been able to build the apparatus, let alone add the wheels necessary to produce the roulettes of an ellipse. Yates's article on the surface of constant curvature would have had to omit the mechanical description of the cross-section, and may not have been published at all. Hilbert would not have been able to analyze the behavior of Yates's linkage, and would not thereby have synthesized that analysis into his "peculiar geometric theorem."

Since the progress of mathematics is so heavily dependent on the sustained efforts of individual mathematicians[190] with relatively brief productive life spans,[191] the preclusive

---

[187] *See, e.g.*, *Advanced Respiratory, Inc. v. Electromed, Inc.*, Civ. No. 00-2646 DWF/SRN, 2003 WL 118246, at *10 (D. Min. 2003) (construing the term "rod" to mean "any straight link that transmits motion or power from one linkage to another within a mechanism"); *Toro Co. v. Scag Power Equipment, Inc.*, No. 8:01CV279, 2002 WL 1792088 (D. Neb. 2002) (finding that patentee's proposed construction of "connection means" to cover "a shaft, rod or arm, or a combination of mechanical links" would "in effect . . . cover any structure that will perform the function of connecting"); *cf. Cordis Corp. v. Boston Scientific Corp.*, Civ. No. 03-027-SLR (D. Del. 2005), at *1 and nn. 4 and 10 (finding the ordinary meaning of "links" to be "a piece or part . . . that holds two or more important elements together," but construing the term more narrowly in light of a specification describing links disposed circumferentially to maintain the stability of a stent's tubular structure).

[188] *See generally* David Garrod, *Glossary of Judicial Claim Constructions in the Mechanical, Electro-Mechanical and Medical Devices Arts* 207 (2010) (providing construction of "link" in a stent claim); Robert C. Kahrl and Stuart B. Soffer, *Thesaurus of Claim Construction* (OUP 2011) 370 (providing construction of "link" in an information technology claim); *cf. Intuitive Surgical, Inc. v. Computer Motion, Inc.*, Civ. No. 01-203-SLR, 2002 WL 1822373, at *1 (D. Del. 2002) (construing "robotic manipulator" as "[t]he moving parts of a robotic system made of links and joints. . .," but not construing "link").

[189] In the case where $F1$ and $F2$ are not fixed in the plane, the "base" may be construed as the first member or any part thereof; E will still be constrained to move along an ellipse relative to this "base." *See* Hilbert, *supra* note 180, at 284 (explaining when "the rod c [is] rigidly attached during the motion to a moving plane . . . the moving centrode must be the ellipse e").

[190] *See, e.g.*, Amir D. Aczel, *Fermat's Last Theorem: Unlocking the Secret of an Ancient Mathematical Problem* (Basic Books 1997) 2 (describing Andrew John Wiles's solitary work to complete the proof of Fermat's Last Theorem, for which he spent "seven years of his life a virtual prisoner in his own attic"); Peter G. Hinman and B. Alan Taylor, "The Mathematics Major at Research Universities", in Estela A. Gavosto et al. (eds.), *Contemporary Issues in Mathematics Education* (Cambridge University Press 1999) 25, 27 (explaining that the received wisdom that "mathematics is a solitary occupation" is valid for "research mathematics," though not for a "B.A. mathematician work[ing] in industry").

[191] *See, e.g.*, Sylvia Nasar, *A Beautiful Mind* (Simon and Schuster 1998) 381 (quoting John Forbes Nash Jr., Les Prix Nobel 1994) ("Statistically, it would seem improbable that any mathema-

effect of a 20-year patent term should not be underestimated. The issuance of Claim C would likely have precluded Hilbert from discovering and proving a more advanced geometric theorem. Yates's article and Hilbert's book were published only one year apart, and Hilbert passed away 11 years later.[192]

Hilbert's reliance on a mechanical apparatus to provide him with the necessary intuition for his "peculiar geometric theorem" is not at all unusual. Mechanisms have long been recognized as a source of geometric intuition[193] and as mathematical teaching tools.[194] Furthermore, as mathematical philosopher John Nolt has pointed out, physical objects and geometric diagrams stand on equal footing as sources of geometric intuition, because "[t]he figures we perceive and probably also those we imagine are not quite geometrical, i.e., not composed of infinitesimally thin lines meeting at infinitesimally tiny points."[195] In other words, "geometric diagrams are themselves physical objects . . . The symbols are actually among the objects symbolized."[196]

E.   Discussion

Mathematics, described by Kant as "the most resplendent example of pure reason,"[197] is no less abstract for its reliance on the concrete objects of empirical reality; indeed, mathematics relies for its internal coherence on its empirical origins. As John von Neumann wrote in his essay on "The Mathematician":

> Mathematical ideas originate in empirics, although the genealogy is sometimes long and obscure. But, once they are so conceived, the subject begins to live a peculiar life of its own and is better compared to a creative one, governed by almost entirely aesthetical motivations, than to anything

---

tician or scientist, at the age of 66, would be able through continued research efforts to add to his or her previous achievements.").

[192]   *See* Reid, *supra* note 179, at 213 (giving Hilbert's date of death as February 14, 1943); *cf.* Seymore, supra note 107 (expressing concern that the 20-year patent term unduly delays experimentation into how and why a patented invention works).

[193]   *See, e.g.*, Robert S. Tragesser, *Husserl and Realism in Logic and Mathematics* (Cambridge University Press 1984) 15 (crediting philosopher Edmund Husserl (1859–1938) with understanding geometric intuitions as "acts of consciousness" that are "founded" in of visually experienced objects but subject to "principles of reasoning different from those cogent and valid for" such visually experienced objects).

[194]   *See* Peggy Aldrich Kidwell, *Tools of American Mathematics Teaching, 1800-2000* (John Hopkins University Press 2008) 233–44. For recent pedagogical notes on the use of mechanical linkages in mathematics teaching, *see, e.g.*, Brian Bolt, *Mathematics Meets Technology* (Cambridge University Press 1991); David Dennis and Jere Confrey, "Geometric Curve-Drawing Devices as an Alternative Approach to Analytic Geometry: An Analysis of the Methods, Voice, and Epistemology of a High-School Senior" in Richard Lehrer and Daniel Chazen (eds.), *Designing Learning Environments for Developing Understanding of Geometry and Space* (Taylor and Francis 1998) 297; Daina Taimina, "Historical Mechanisms for Drawing Curves", in Amy Shell-Gellasch (ed.), *Hands on History: A Resource for Teaching Mathematics* (Cambridge University Press 2007).

[195]   *See* John E. Nolt, *Mathematical Intuition* 44 Philosophy and Phenomenological Research 189, 202 (1983).

[196]   *Id.* at 206.

[197]   Immanuel Kant, *Critique of Pure Reason* (Paul Guyer and Allen W. Wood trans. Cambridge University Press 1999) 630.

else and, in particular, to an empirical science. There is, however, a further point which, I believe, needs stressing. As a mathematical discipline travels far from its empirical source, or still more, if it is a second and third generation only indirectly inspired by ideas coming from "reality," it is beset with very great dangers. . . [A]t a great distance from its empirical source, or after much 'abstract' inbreeding, a mathematical subject is in danger of degeneration.[198]

In short, the freedom to make and use the fundamental empirical sources of mathematical intuition is necessary for the flourishing of mathematics.[199] Concern for this freedom counsels against the issuance of any patent that claims every mechanical application of a kinematic property because some mechanical structures are among "the basic tools of scientific and technological work."[200]

As Part II showed, the patent-eligibility concerns discussed here in Part III have not prevented the widespread issuance and assertion of kinematic patents throughout the history of the surgical robotics industry.[201] Even though Intuitive's present-day monopoly is not readily attributable to the prevalence of kinematic patents,[202] the emergence of new competition in the surgical robotics industry[203] provides an appropriate juncture to study the consequences of kinematic claiming on the strategic posture of its key players. Part IV will provide one such case study, on the development and patenting of Applied Dexterity's Raven manipulator, as a first step toward a deeper understanding of how the industry's future development might be affected by the untenable practice of kinematic claiming.

IV. THE MAKING OF A KINEMATIC SURGICAL ROBOTICS CLAIM

A. Kinematic Foundations of Robotics

The essential task of a surgical robot is to manipulate a tool so as to replicate (and sometimes improve upon) the movements of the tool in the hands of a skilled surgeon.[204]

---

[198] John von Neumann, "The Mathematician", in F. Bródy and T. Vámos (eds.), *The Neumann Compendium* (World Scientific Publishing 1995) 618, 626.

[199] In turn, Francis Su, past president of the Mathematical Association of America, has famously and persuasively argued that the activity of doing mathematics is instrumental in human flourishing. *See* Francis Su, *Mathematics for Human Flourishing* 124 Am. Math. Monthly (2017) (farewell address to the Joint Mathematics Meetings of the MAA and the American Mathematical Society); *see also* Kevin Hartnett, *The Mathematician Who Will Make You Fall in Love With Numbers*, Wired (5 Feb. 2017) (profile on Su with reporting on his farewell address).

[200] *Gottschalk v. Benson*, 409 U.S. 63, 67 (1972).

[201] *See supra* Part II.

[202] *See supra* notes 20–22 and accompanying text (identifying other sources of Intuitive's monopoly power).

[203] *See supra* note 27 and accompanying text.

[204] *See, e.g.*, Rebecca Stefoff, *Robots* (Cavendish Square Publishing 2008) 75 ("A human surgeon operates da Vinci by sitting at a console and manipulating his hands on a set of controls; the robotic arms copy his movements. In fact, the robot can be programmed to filter out the human operator's muscle tremors.").

A *manipulator* is the mechanism in a robotic system responsible for moving a tool into a desired position and orientation so that the robot can perform a task.[205] The manipulator's movement is defined by a connected set of rigid *links*.[206] The tool is typically located at the end of a link or chain of links, and is therefore often referred to as the manipulator's *end-effector*.[207] The links are connected by *joints*, the simplest of which are *revolute* or *prismatic*.[208] Revolute joints allow neighboring links to rotate to different angles, while prismatic joints allow links to slide to different displacements relative to each other.[209] *Actuators* are the power components of a robotic system that perform the work of executing the motions of the manipulator's joints.[210] *Sensors* acquire information regarding the the manipulator's internal state and its interaction with the external environment that can be helpful in controlling the robot.[211]

Reliance on a manipulator's moving joints to control the movements of the end-effector frequently gives rise to the geometric problem of translating joint angles and displacements (the "joint space" description of the manipulator's position) into coordinates describing the end-effector's position and orientation in space (the "Cartesian space" description of the end-effector's position), and vice versa.[212] For example, suppose we wish to make a manipulator as in Figure 16.9 for moving an end-effector in the plane, consisting of two straight-line links connected to a base and to each other by revolute joints.[213]

Suppose further that, starting from the base, the links are of length L_1 and L_2, with

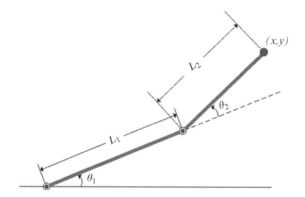

Figure 16.9   Kinematics of a two-link planar manipulator

---

[205]   *See* John J. Craig, *Introduction to Robotics: Mechanics and Control* (Pearson 2005) 4.
[206]   *See id.* at 5.
[207]   *See id.*
[208]   *See id.*
[209]   *See id.*
[210]   *See generally* Bruno Siciliano, *Robotics: Modeling, Planning and Control* (Springer 2010) 191–209 (surveying robotic actuating systems).
[211]   *See id.* at 209–30 (surveying robotic sensors).
[212]   *See* Craig, *supra* note 205, at 5–7.
[213]   *See* Berthold K.P. Horn, "Kinematics, Statics, and Dynamics of Two-Dimensional Manipulators", in Patrick Henry Winston and Richard Henry Brown (eds.), 2 *Artificial Intelligence: An MIT Perspective* (MIT Press 1979) 273, 277.

$L > L_2$. Given such a manipulator whose joints are set at angles θ_1 and θ_2, the *forward kinematics problem* is to calculate the Cartesian coordinates of the end-effector (x, y). A straightforward trigonometric calculation gives the solution as

$$x = (L_1 + L_2 \cos \theta_2)\cos \theta_1 - L_2 \sin \theta_2 \sin \theta_1$$
$$y = (L_1 + L_2 \cos \theta_2)\sin \theta_1 - L_2 \sin \theta_2 \cos \theta_1.[214]$$

If instead we are given the Cartesian coordinates (x, y) of a desired location for the end-effector, the *inverse kinematics problem* is to calculate a set of joint angles θ_1 and θ_2, if one exists, that will position the manipulator's end-effector at this location. Another trigonometric calculation gives

$$\cos \theta_2 = \frac{(x^2 + y^2) - (L_1^2 + L_2^2)}{2 L_1 L_2}$$

$$\tan \theta_1 = \frac{-L_2 \sin(\theta_2)x + (L_1 + L_2 \cos \theta_2)y}{L_2 \sin(\theta_2)y + (L_1 + L_2 \cos \theta_2)x}$$

from which solutions (θ_1, θ_2) if any, can be determined.[215] The point (x, y) has an inverse kinematics solution if and only if it can be reached by the manipulator's end-effector (i.e., by setting the manipulator's angles to (θ_1, θ_2) so as to satisfy the equations above). While these equations may appear complex, they are actually relatively simple in that the inverse kinematics problem for manipulators in general does not always lend itself to analytical solutions.[216]

Note that by varying θ_2 continuously from 0 to 180 degrees, it is possible to move the end-effector to a point at any distance between $L_1 + L_2$ and $L_1 - L_2$ from the base. Varying θ_1 continuously from 0 to 360 degrees while holding θ_2 constant allows the end-effector to sweep through a circle. Thus the set of points reachable by the end-effector forms an annulus with outer diameter $L_1 + L_2$ and inner diameter $L_1 - L_2$.[217] This set of reachable points is referred to as the manipulator's *workspace*.[218] (By the same token, the workspace of point P of the Peaucellier linkage consists of a straight line, and the workspace of point E of Yates's linkage consists of an ellipse.)

Planning the motion of a manipulator involves the analogous problem of mapping velocities in joint space into Cartesian space and vice versa.[219] This problem can identify certain configurations of the manipulator, or *singularities*, from which it is infeasible for the joints to move quickly enough to produce even a relatively small movement of the end-effector.[220]

---

[214] *See id.* at 277–78.
[215] *See id.* at 278–80.
[216] *See* Craig, *supra* note 205, at 106 ("Only in special cases can robots with six degrees of freedom be solved analytically."); *see also* Horn, *supra* note 213, at 280–81 ("This method, while quite general, is in practice limited to solving only simple linkages.").
[217] *See* Horn, *supra* note 213, at 281.
[218] *See* Craig, *supra* note 205, at 7.
[219] *See id.* at 7.
[220] *See id.* at 7–9.

Source: Craig, John J., *Introduction to Robotics: Mechanics and Control: International Edition*, 3rd ed.
          © 2004.

Figure 16.10   *A biplane with a tail gun mounted on a mechanism with two revolute joints.
A singularity arises in the configuration where the gun is pointing directly
overhead[221]*

For example, as in Figure 16.10, the tail gun on a biplane might not be able to spin
around quickly enough to track an enemy plane flying directly overhead.[222] The
situation where the gun is pointing nearly straight up, requiring such rapid rotation
to maneuver, is a singularity of the mechanism on which the tail gun is mounted.[223]
The mathematical relationship between the joint velocities of a manipulator and the
Cartesian velocities of the end-effector, from which such singularities can be identified,
is given by the manipulator's *Jacobian matrix*, the details of which will not be presented
here.[224]

---

[221]   *See id.* at 8.
[222]   *See id.* at 8.
[223]   *See id.* at
[224]   *See id.* at 150.

B.   Development of Raven's Manipulator

Applied Dexterity's Raven robot is based on the manipulator shown in Figure 16.11, consisting of three links and three revolute joints.[225] The manipulator is spherical in that the curved links are designed so that the axes of rotation of the three joints intersect at the center ("the remote center") of a sphere passing through the links.[226] When the device is used for minimally invasive surgery, a third link (formed by a surgical tool) terminating in the end-effector is inserted through a tool holder at the end of the second link (forming Joint 5).[227] Joint 5 may be rotary and/or prismatic.[228] The remote center is also the point of entry into the patient's body.[229]

After working through the manipulator's forward and inverse kinematics,[230] Raven's designers sought to refine the mechanism so as best to avoid singularities when replicating a surgeon's movements during minimally invasive surgical procedures. The designers considered 1,444 design candidates having varying lengths of Links 13 and 35 while retaining the manipulator's spherical property.[231] Using the Blue DRAGON, they recorded the

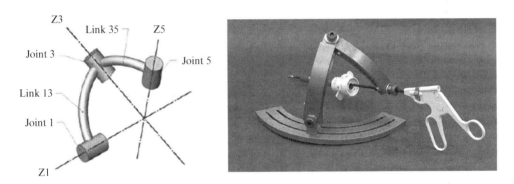

Figure 16.11   A schematic[232] and aluminium mock-up[233] of the Raven's spherical serial manipulator mechanism

---

[225]   *See* Rosen, *supra* note 42, at 163. The team has also developed and claimed a more complex parallel manipulator that is not discussed here for the sake of brevity. *See id.* at 162–64; U.S. Patent App. No. 13/908,120 at [0176] (disclosing an example of the invention that "includes two (or multiples of two) links to mechanically constrain two degrees of motion to the surface of a sphere").

[226]   *See* Rosen, *supra* note 42, at 163.

[227]   *See id.* ("As configured for MIS, the end-effector of the mechanism is inserted through Joint 5."); U.S. Patent App. No. 13/908,120 at cl. 1 ("[T]he second end of the second link includes a tool holder, the tool holder having a tool axis aligned to pass through a point coincident with an intersection of the convergent rotational axes. . .").

[228]   *See* U.S. Patent App. No. 13/908,120 at cl. 14 (reciting an actuator "configured to manipulate the tool to provide at least one of rotary motion on a tool axis and prismatic motion on the tool axis").

[229]   *See* Rosen, *supra* note 42, at 162.

[230]   *See id.* at 164–67.

[231]   *See id.* at 175.

[232]   *See id.* at 162.

[233]   *See id.* at 183.

movements of surgical tools by 30 surgeons performing seven different surgical tasks, and used this data to identify a desired "dextrous workspace" for the manipulator encompassing 95 percent of the tools' recorded movements.[234] Using Jacobian matrices, they formulated and calculated for each design candidate a proxy measure of its freedom from singularities (its "mechanism isotropy") at each point in the dextrous workspace.[235] Based on this measure, they determined the optimal design candidate would have Links 13 and 35 forming circular arcs subtending angles of 52 and 40 degrees, respectively.[236] This finding is the basis for the limitation added by dependent claim 12 of Applied Dexterity's '120 patent application.[237]

C.   Applied Dexterity's Kinematic Patent Claims

With this background, we can discuss the patentability of claims 1 and 12 of Applied Dexterity's '120 patent application:

> 1. A device comprising:
> a first link having ends terminated in a base revolute joint and a common revolute joint, the revolute joints having convergent rotational axes and each rotational axis forming an acute angle with a longitudinal axis of the first link, the base revolute joint coupled to a base;
> a second link coupled to the common revolute joint at a first end, the second link having a second end and the second link in a serial cantilever configuration with the first link, the rotational axis of the common revolute joint forming an acute angle with a longitudinal axis of the second link, wherein the second end of the second link includes a tool holder, the tool holder having a tool axis aligned to pass through a point coincident with an intersection of the convergent rotational axes, the tool axis and the common revolute joint rotational axis subtending a first angle; and the convergent rotational axes subtending a second angle, such that the first angle differs from the second angle, the first and second links and the revolute joints enabling a position of the tool holder to be selectively manipulated.
> 12. The device of claim 1 wherein the first angle is about 40 degrees and the second angle is about 52 degrees.[238]

As of this writing, Applied Dexterity's '120 patent application has received a first office action communicating various § 102 and § 103 rejections. Almost all of the § 102 rejections are based on prior art publications by Hannaford and Rosen's research group.[239]

---

234   *See* Mitchell J.H. Lum et al., *Multidisciplinary Approach for Developing a New Minimally Invasive Surgical Robotic System*, Proc. 1st IEEE/RAS-EMBS Int'l Conf. on Biomedical Robotics and Biomechatronics 841, 842–43 (2000).

235   *See* Rosen, *supra* note 42, at 170–73.

236   *See id.* at 177.

237   *See supra* note 39 and accompanying text.

238   U.S. Patent Appl. No. 13/908,120, cls. 1, 12 (filed June 3, 2013).

239   *See* U.S. Patent and Trademark Office, Office Action in Examination of U.S. Patent App. No. 13/908,120, at ¶¶ 2, 3 (10 Apr. 2017) (rejecting several claims over Rosen et al., *Spherical Mechanism Analysis of a Surgical Robot for Minimally Invasive Surgery: Analytical and Experimental Approaches*, Proc. 13th Medicine Meets Virtual Reality Conf. 442 (2005); Rosen [Mitchell Lum] et al., *Kinematic Optimization of a Spherical Mechanism for a Minimally Invasive Surgical Robot*, Proc. IEEE Int'l Conf. on Robotics and Automation 829 (2004)); *but see id.* at ¶ 4 (rejecting one claim over U.S. Patent No. 6,355,048 (filed Oct. 25, 1999)).

Assuming that these can be overcome,[240] the patentability of the design insights derived from observed surgical movements will hinge in part on the examiner's argument that the angles of claim 12 were obvious because "discovering an optimum value of a result effective variable involves only routine skill in the art."[241]

The discussion in Part III of this Chapter strongly suggests that claims 1 and 12 of the '120 application should also be rejected under § 101 as directed to abstract kinematic principles. Like the hypothetical claim to Salmon's spot of light,[242] the claims recite objects having specified kinematic properties, but without any limitations as to causal powers and processes capable of "producing a beneficial result or effect." Like the hypothetical claims to the right-triangle apparatus[243] and Yates's linkage,[244] claim 1 purports to cover every mechanical application of a mathematical theorem. The principal inventors themselves have candidly characterized the spherical manipulator's forward and inverse kinematics as "purely mathematical": "Up to this point, the analysis has been purely mathematical. The manipulators could move through singularities, fold on itself and solve for arbitrary poses without regard to how a physically implemented device might accomplish this."[245]

Claim 1's recitation of a "tool holder" (instead of the generic concept of a rotary and/or prismatic joint with a third link terminating in an end-effector) serves to limit the field of use to minimally invasive surgery,[246] but this is immaterial to the patent-eligibility analysis.[247]

The additional limitations in claim 12 are intended to address the practical problem of "mov[ing] through singularities" when a "physically implemented device" is operating under the control of a surgeon performing a procedure. This real-world context might persuade an examiner to agree that the inventors' efforts to optimize the manipulator's design—i.e., to "discover[] an optimum value of a result effective variable"—were not directed to a "purely mathematical" result. Ultimately, however, claim 12 adds no causal limitations to claim 1, and is therefore equally susceptible to rejection under § 101.

As for the § 103 analysis, the examiner might also be persuaded that solving this particular optimization problem necessarily involved more than ordinary skill, in light of the numerous heavily-cited academic publications that resulted from the Hannaford-Rosen

---

[240]   The earlier of the two Rosen-Hannaford group references was published in the proceedings of an IEEE conference held from 26 April to 1 May 2004. *See* ICRA 2004, http://www.egr.msu.edu/ralab/icra2004/ (visited 24 Apr. 2017). The '120 application claims priority as a continuation of an application filed on Apr. 25, 2005, *see* U.S. Patent App. No. 13/908,120 (filed Jun. 3, 2013), at (63), less than a year after the conference.

[241]   U.S. Patent and Trademark Office, *supra* note 239, at ¶ 5. The examiner's argument finds apparent legal support in *In re Boesch*, 617 F.2d 272, 276 (C.C.P.A. 1980) ("[D]iscovery of an optimum value of a result effective variable in a known process is ordinarily within the skill of the art.").

[242]   *See supra* text accompanying note 147.

[243]   *See supra* text accompanying notes 159–67.

[244]   *See supra* text accompanying notes 187–89. Theorem 2 stands for the proposition that the workspace of Yates's linkage as claimed in claim 3 and shown in Figure 16.6 with base F_1F_2 and end-effector E is an ellipse. *See* text accompanying notes 177–79.

[245]   *See* Rosen, *supra* note 42, at 171.

[246]   *See supra* text accompanying notes 227–28.

[247]   See *Bilski*, 561 U.S. at 612 (citing *Parker v. Flook*, 437 U.S. 584 (1978)) ("*Flook* established that limiting an abstract idea to one field of use ... did not make the concept patentable.").

group's design optimization efforts.[248] The only non-mathematical part of those efforts, however, was performed by the surgeons whose movements identified the dextrous workspace that formed the basis of the optimization calculations.[249] If the § 103 analysis is to avoid an improper inquiry into the mathematical difficulty of the inventors' optimization approach,[250] the inventors would seem to be left with an appeal to the surgeons' kinesthetic expertise for the argument that the optimization entailed more than ordinary skill.[251]

The problematic patentability of Applied Dexterity's kinematic claims is somewhat ironic, given the company's commitment to open-source development of Raven's control software. Both claims 1 and 12 suffer from a mismatch between the category of objects and processes having causal powers[252] and a claimed manipulator whose links, joints, and movements are characterized entirely in kinematic terms without regard to masses or forces.[253]

No such mismatch would occur in claims directed to a robotic controller. As the Patent Office has observed, a manipulator operating under a specific control system does not preempt the mathematical theorems governing the manipulator's kinematic movements:

> A claim directed to a complex manufactured industrial product or process that recites meaningful limitations along with a judicial exception may sufficiently limit its practical application so that a full eligibility analysis is not needed. As an example, a robotic arm assembly *having a control system* that operates using certain mathematical relationships is clearly not an attempt to tie up use of the mathematical relationships and would not require a full analysis to determine eligibility.[254]

The analysis in this Chapter clarifies that "meaningful limitations" are those that ground the patent claim in the category of objects and processes having causal powers. What makes designing and controlling a robot's actuators a "complex manufactured industrial" enterprise is the need for close attention to the masses of moving parts[255] and internal and external forces.[256] Thus, in a robotics patent, the recitation of a specific control system

---

[248]   *See, e.g.*, Google Scholar, https://scholar.google.com/scholar?cites=8622140283516909909 (visited Apr. 24, 2017) (showing that Lum, *supra* note 216 has received 86 citations).

[249]   *See* text accompanying 234.

[250]   *See* Chin, *supra* note 96, at 636–37 ("[A] § 103 inquiry into the level of ordinary skill in the art is misplaced where the art in question, and the field of knowledge being advanced by the patent disclosure, is not one of the "useful Arts," but mathematics. The patentability analysis . . . should never leave a court in the position of determining how hard the math was.").

[251]   *Cf.* Howard Gardner, *Frames of Mind: The Theory of Multiple Intelligences* (Basic Books 1983) 231–33 (characterizing the work of the inventor as entailing "bodily intelligence" in addition to "logical-mathematical reasoning").

[252]   *See supra* text accompanying note 98.

[253]   *See supra* text accompanying notes 242–43; *see also* text accompanying note 6 (defining kinematic properties).

[254]   U.S. Patent and Trademark Office, *2014 Interim Guidance on Patent Subject Matter Eligibility*, 79 Fed. Reg. 74618, 74625 (16 Dec. 2014) (emphasis added).

[255]   *See, e.g.*, Siciliano, *supra* note 210, at 192–93 (noting that timing belts and chains are kinematically equivalent, but the large mass of chains "may induce vibration at high speeds").

[256]   *See* Siciliano, *supra* note 210, at 191–92 (outlining essential elements of the specification of an actuating system, wherein the power to be transmitted "can always be expressed as the product

may sufficiently limit the practical application of the manipulator's kinematic properties to confer patent-eligibility.

For example, Raven's actuation and control system includes "Maxon EC-40 motors with 12:1 planetary gearboxes" to accommodate "the highest forces," power-off brakes along the axes "under the greatest gravity load," a cable system with a 7.7:1 motor-to-shoulder joint transmission ratio that "maintains constant pretension on the cables throughout the entire range of motion," and a control system that accommodates "force and motion coupling between the axes."[257] Such design considerations might not be new or nonobvious, but they do directly address the transmission of energy and other conserved quantities through causal processes and present no issues under the abstract-ideas exclusion from patentable subject matter.[258] Even though open-source development is apparently accelerating Applied Dexterity's entry into the surgical robotics market,[259] the patent-eligibility concerns raised in this Chapter might have led the company to pursue patents directed to Raven's software innovations in real-time control and signal processing[260] instead of, or at least in addition to, its kinematic manipulator claims.

V. CONCLUSIONS

Like other kinds of patent claims that have raised subject matter eligibility concerns in recent years, kinematic claims also raise overbreadth issues.[261] In particular, kinematic claims directed to relatively modest advances in the mechanical arts are in tension with the doctrine of equivalents, which reserves its broadest protection for pioneering inventions.[262] In contrast, the effective scope of a kinematic claim may exceed the range of equivalents of a structurally identical claim with causal limitations, inasmuch as the kinematic claim purports to cover not only substantially similar ways, but all ways, of causing the claimed mechanism to function.[263] Thus, kinematic patent claims would be unduly broad even

---

of a flow and a force quantity, whose physical context allows the specification of the nature of the power (mechanical, electric, hydraulic, or pneumatic).").

[257]   *See* Rosen, *supra* note 42, at 181.

[258]   *See supra* text accompanying notes 145–48.

[259]   *See supra* text accompanying notes 31–33.

[260]   *See* Andrew Chin, Alappat *Redux: Support for Functional Language in Software Patent Claims* 66 SMU L. Rev. 502 (2013) (arguing that a software innovation specifying the involvement of real-time computational resources in causal processes is a concrete "practical method or means" and therefore not impermissibly abstract).

[261]   *See, e.g., Mayo*, 132 S.Ct. at 1294 (concluding that patent-eligibility precedents "warn us against upholding patents that claim processes that too broadly preempt the use of a natural law"); *Bilski*, 130 S.Ct. at 3231 (observing that "to patent risk hedging would pre-empt use of this approach in all fields").

[262]   *See Thomas and Betts Corp. v. Litton Systems, Inc.*, 720 F.2d 1572, 1580 (Fed. Cir. 1983) ("[W]hile a pioneer invention is entitled to a broad range application of the doctrine of equivalents, an invention representing only a modest advance over the prior art is given a more restricted (narrower range) application of the doctrine").

[263]   *See Graver Tank and Mfg. Co. v. Linde Aire Products Co.*, 339 U.S. 605, 608 (1950) (citation omitted) (recognizing applicability of the doctrine of equivalents to an accused device "if it

if they were deemed to reflect patent-eligible inventive advances in the mechanical arts rather than the kinds of mathematical results highlighted in this Chapter.[264]

This Chapter's conclusions about the patent-ineligibility and overbreadth of kinematic patent claims contribute to a broader debate about the kinds of inventive activity that fall within the patent system's ambit and the amounts of inventive progress that warrant the grant of exclusionary rights. In the robotics field, these questions have far-reaching consequences for the political economy of labor and downstream innovation.

This Chapter has highlighted the role of surgeons in the development of the surgical robotics industry and the patent landscape surrounding it, particularly in locations demarcated by the geometrically precise terms of kinematic claims. We have also seen how surgical practitioners put the "dexterity" in Applied Dexterity and its Raven manipulator, unencumbered by singularities. The company's patent application, however, would credit Hannaford and Rosen's group as inventors for applying that dexterity. Part IV's suggestion that the patentability of Applied Dexterity's claim 12 may rest on the kinesthetic expertise of surgeons leaves a tantalizing open question for inventorship doctrine in the age of robotics: whether one who contributes extraordinary human kinesthetic expertise necessary for the conception of an invention can and should be credited with co-inventorship.[265] Applied Dexterity was able to follow a proprietary approach in assembling a user community for the Raven prototype from which it could refine its manipulator's kinematic properties, but as our colleague Liza Vertinsky has pointed out in this issue, such an approach to user innovation is not likely to be sustainable under patent law's existing inventorship doctrines.[266]

These questions in turn raise further questions at the interface between the patent system and labor economics. Can and should a worker who trains a robot to replicate her movements be recognized as a co-inventor of the trained robot? Does the answer depend on the worker's type or level of kinesthetic skill?[267] If so, should the resulting patent doctrines conform to established criteria in labor law and policy, such as those applicable

---

performs substantially the same function in substantially the same way to obtain the same result" as the claimed invention).

[264]   The Supreme Court's patentable subject matter jurisprudence historically has been animated more by a requirement of invention in the application of otherwise unpatentable abstract ideas than by overbreadth and preemption concerns. *See* Katherine J. Strandburg, *Much Ado About Preemption* 50 Hous. L. Rev. 563, 566 (2012); Joshua D. Sarnoff, *Patent-Eligible Inventions After Bilski: History and Theory* 63 Hastings L.J. 53, 59 (2011). Since any inventive features of a kinematic claim necessarily subsist in the movements of a mechanism without regard to the effects of those movements, such a claim would not reflect invention in the application of abstract kinematic properties.

[265]   *See Burroughs Wellcome Co. v. Barr Labs., Inc.*, 40 F.3d 1223 (Fed. Cir. 1994) ("Conception is complete only when the idea is so clearly defined in the inventor's mind that only ordinary skill would be necessary to reduce the invention to practice, without extensive research or experimentation."); *see Harris v. Clifford*, 363 F.2d 922, 927 (C.C.P.A. 1966) (one who merely provides a "pair of skilled hands" in reduction to practice has not contributed to conception).

[266]   *See* Liza Vertinsky, *Social Patents* 55 Hous. L. Rev. 401, 418–25 (2017).

[267]   *See, e.g.*, Sean B. Seymore, *My Patent, Your Patent, Or Our Patent? Inventorship Disputes Within Academic Research Groups* 16 Alb. L.J. Sci. and Tech. 125, 136 (2006) (citing Roger E. Schechter and John R. Thomas, *Principles of Patent Law* (West 2004) 235) (explaining that inventorship analysis can be "tricky" and "highly fact specific").

to Fair Labor Standards Act exemptions? No longer limited to emulating and displacing blue-collar labor, robotic manipulators may be the next information technology to disrupt the political economy of the learned professions. While surgical robots might never fully replace human surgeons in the labor market,[268] the ongoing capture of data embodying kinesthetic surgical skill by the robotics industry is likely to raise novel legal issues. All of a surgeon's movements captured during a robot-assisted surgical procedure can be item-ized, catalogued and evaluated, transforming standards of care.[269] Given the potential strategic value of kinesthetic data,[270] joint ventures and sponsorship agreements between manufacturers and academic medical centers will also be increasingly common, raising conflict-of-interest concerns.[271]

The practice of kinematic claiming is likely to be of growing concern to the surgical robotics industry, as well as the field of robotics in general. The expert kinesthetic train-ing of a work robot, the optimization of a manipulator design, and even possibly the da Vinci robot vis-à-vis the Alisanos patent[272] are all examples of downstream innovation in robotics that might be foreclosed by kinematic claims. To paraphrase Michael Heller and Rebecca Eisenberg's classic commentary on the tragedy of the anticommons, defining property rights around kinematic properties is "unlikely to track socially useful bundles of property rights in future commercial products."[273] Concerns about a kinematic anticom-mons run parallel to long-running debates over the patenting of gene probes, and could likewise manifest themselves in decades of litigation as Applied Dexterity and other entrants compete against Intuitive in the marketplace and the courts. This Chapter has attempted to rectify these problems in advance to the extent possible, not by proposing any legal change, but by providing precise and stable criteria for identifying kinematically abstract claims under existing patent-eligibility doctrine.

---

[268] *See, e.g.*, Michelle Solis, *New Frontiers in Robotic Surgery* IEEE Pulse 51, 55 (Nov./Dec. 2016) (stating that "[c]urrent robots in the operating room are slaves to a surgeon master," but noting that automation "could free surgeons from tedious piecework such as suturing or tumor ablation"); Sarah Zhang, *Why an Autonomous Robot Won't Replace Your Surgeon Anytime Soon*, Science (4 May 2016) ("[T]he robots are coming— they're just not coming for any doctors' jobs yet."); *but see* Thomas R. McLean, *Cybersurgery: Innovation or a Means to Close Community Hospitals and Displace Physicians?* 20 J. Marshall J. Computer and Info. L. 495, 508–10 (2002) (arguing that widespread adoption of "automatic surgery" could occur whenever "society is ready to embrace the technology," resulting in the elimination of community hospitals, surgeons and physicians); Meghan Hamilton-Piercy, *Cybersurgery: Why the United States Should Embrace This Emerging Technology* 7 J. High Tech. L. 203, 218–20 (2007) (arguing that cybersurgery reduce the need for physicians and improve access to quality surgical services in the United States).

[269] *See, e.g.*, Azhar Rafiq et al., *Objective Assessment of Training Surgical Skills Using Simulated Tissue Interface with Real-Time Feedback* 65 J. Surg. Ed. 270, 271–73 (2008) (describing software for evaluating suturing and knot-tying skills); Carol E. Reiley, *Review of Methods for Objective Surgical Skill Evaluation* 25 Surg. Endosc. 355 (2011) (surveying the literature).

[270] *See supra* text accompanying notes 234–39 (describing the use of kinesthetic data in the optimization of Raven's manipulator).

[271] *Cf.* Richard S. Saver, *Shadows Amid Sunshine: Regulating Financial Conflicts in Medical Research* 145 Chest 379, 380 (2014) (discussing ethical concerns relating to clinical trial sponsorship contracts between pharmaceutical companies and academic medical centers).

[272] *See supra* note 94 and accompanying text.

[273] *Cf.* Michael A. Heller and Rebecca S. Eisenberg, *Can Patents Deter Innovation? The Anticommons in Biomedical Research* 280 Science 698, 699 (1998).

SOURCES

Cases

In re Vamco Mach. & Tool, Inc., 752 F.2d 1564 (Fed. Cir. 1985).
Computer Motion, Inc. v. Intuitive Surgical Inc., No. CV 00-4988 CBM-RC (C.D. Cal. filed Feb. 7, 2003).
Intuitive Surgical, Inc. v. Computer Motion, Inc., 214 F. Supp. 2d 433 (D. Del. 2002).
Studiengesellschaft Kohle v. Eastman Kodak, 616 F.2d 1315 (5th Cir. 1980).
Brookhill-Wilk 1 v. Computer Motion, No. 01-CV-01300-AKH (S.D.N.Y. filed Feb. 21, 2001).
Brookhill-Wilk 1, LLC v. Intuitive Surgical, Inc., 178 F. Supp. 2d 356 (S.D.N.Y. 2001).
Brookhill-Wilk 1, LLC v. Intuitive Surgical, Inc., 334 F.3d 1294 (2d Cir. 2003).
Teleflex, Inc. v. Ficosa N. Am. Corp., 299 F.3d 1313 (Fed. Cir. 2002).
WiAV Solutions LLC v. Motorola, Inc., 631 F.3d 1257 (Fed. Cir. 2010).
Laboratory Corp. of America Holdings v. Metabolite Laboratories, Inc., 548 U.S. 124 (2006).
KSR Int'l Co. v. Teleflex Inc., 550 U.S. 398 (2007).
Complaint, Alisanos, LLC v. Intuitive Surgical, Inc., No. 0:12-CV-61978 (S.D. Fla. filed Oct. 5, 2012).
Alisanos, LLC v. Intuitive Surgical, Inc., No. 0:12-CV-61978 (S.D. Fla. filed Jan. 24, 2013).
Imperial Chemical Industries v. Henkel, 545 F. Supp. 635 (D. Del. 1982).
Lowell v. Lewis, 15 F. Cas. 1018 (D. Mass. 1817).
Diamond v. Diehr, 450 U.S. 175 (1981).
LeRoy v. Tatham, 55 U.S. (14 HOW) 156 (1982).
In re Isaacs, 347 F.2d 887 (C.C.P.A. 1965).
In re Citron, 325 F.2d 248 (C.C.P.A. 1963).
In re Houghton, 433 F.2d 820 (C.C.P.A. 1970).
Newman v. Quigg, 77 F.2d 1575 (Fed. Cir. 1989).
In re Brana, 51 F.3d 1560 (Fed. Cir. 1995).
In re Bilski, 545 F.3d 943 (Fed. Cir. 2008).
In re Bernhart, 417 F.2d 1395 (C.C.P.A. 1969).
In re Nuijten, 500 F.3d 1356 (Fed. Cir. 2007).
Bilski v. Kappos, 561 U.S. 593 (2010).
Gottschalk v. Benson, 409 U.S. 63 (1972).
Paine, Webber, Jackson & Curtis, Inc. v. Merrill Lynch, Pierce, Fenner & Smith, Inc., 564 F. Supp. 1358 (D. Del. 1983).
Cross Medical Products, Inc. v. Medtronic Sofamor Danek, Inc., 424 F.3d 1293 (Fed. Cir. 2005).
Hewlett-Packard Co. v. Bausch & Lomb Inc., 909 F.2d 1464 (Fed. Cir. 1990).
CCS Fitness, Inc. v. Brunswick Corp., 288 F.3d 1359 (Fed. Cir. 2002).
Johnson Worldwide Assocs., Inc. v. Zebco Corp., 175 F.3d 985 (Fed. Cir. 1999).
In re Fisher, 421 F.3d 1365 (Fed. Cir. 2005).
In re Bilski, 545 F.3d 943 (Fed. Cir. 2008).
Advanced Respiratory, Inc. v. Electromed, Inc., Civ. No. 00-2646 DWF/SRN, 2003 WL 118246 (D. Min. 2003).
Toro Co. v. Scag Power Equipment, Inc., No. 8:01CV279, 2002 WL 1792088 (D. Neb. 2002).
Cordis Corp. v. Boston Scientific Corp., Civ. No. 03-027-SLR (D. Del. 2005).
Intuitive Surgical, Inc. v. Computer Motion, Inc., Civ. No. 01-203-SLR, 2002 WL 1822373 (D. Del. 2002).
Gottschalk v. Benson, 409 U.S. 63 (1972).
In re Boesch, 617 F.2d 272 (C.C.P.A. 1980).
Parker v. Flook, 437 U.S. 584 (1978).
Mayo, 132 S.Ct. 1289 (2012).
Bilski, 130 S.Ct. 3218 (2010).
Thomas & Betts Corp. v. Litton Systems, Inc., 720 F.2d 1572 (Fed. Cir. 1983).
Graver Tank & Mfg. Co. v. Linde Aire Products Co., 339 U.S. 605 (1950).

Statutes

35 U.S.C. § 1127 (1997).
35 U.S.C. § 101 (1997).
35 U.S.C. § 112 (1997).

17. Artificial intelligence and the patent system: can a new tool render a once patentable idea obvious?
William Samore[1]

I. INTRODUCTION

In the summer of 1956, leaders in the field of computer science met at Dartmouth College and founded the field of Artificial Intelligence.[2] Since then, one branch of Artificial Intelligence—Genetic Programming—has progressed to the point where it could drastically change the way that inventors design and create. Genetic programs (described in more detail in section III.B of this chapter) operate by mimicking the biological evolutionary process[3] and have a wide variety of applications.[4] Antenna design, for example, is a field where genetic programming could radically change the nature and pace of innovation.[5] The first antennas were built in the late 1800s by Heinrich Hertz,[6] and an antenna with a specific shape can be designed to emit a desired radiation pattern.[7] As technology progressed, computer programs were designed where an antenna's characteristics could be inputted to the computer program, and the radiation pattern would be calculated and displayed to the user.[8] Now, computer programs have gone one step further and it is possible to do the reverse of this: to input a desired radiation pattern and have the computer program itself design the antenna.[9] The question that this chapter asks is, can changes in the tools available to inventors render previously patentable ideas

---

[1] This chapter is based on in part an article published by the author in the Syracuse Journal of Science & Technology Law.

[2] *Dartmouth Conferences*, Wikipedia.org, http://en.wikipedia.org/wiki/Dartmouth_conference (last visited 30 April 2017) (the founders proposed a study which was "to proceed on the basis of the conjecture that every aspect of learning or any other feature of intelligence can in principle be so precisely described that a machine can be made to simulate it.").

[3] Anne Eisenberg, *What's Next; When a Gizmo Can Invent a Gizmo*, N.Y. Times (25 Nov. 1999) at G9 (stating that genetic programs "solve problems by mimicking the principles of natural biological selection.").

[4] *See id.* (listing genetic programming applications such as gas turbine, integrated circuit, and antenna design).

[5] Antenna technology is a good example here not only because of the dramatic ways that the tools that inventors have available to them have changed the way antennas can be designed, but because many antennas are patentable. In fact, the United States Patent and Trademark Office (hereinafter "the PTO"), in its classification system has a class for this: class 343 Communication: Radio Wave Antenna.

[6] *Antenna (radio)*, Wikipedia.org, http://en.wikipedia.org/wiki/Antenna_(radio) (last visited 30 April 2017).

[7] *Id.*

[8] A quick Google search of "antenna radiation pattern calculator" reveals a multitude of computer programs which can calculate radiation patterns for antennas.

[9] Eisenberg, *supra* note 3, at G9 (satellite communications antenna designed).

obvious and therefore unpatentable?[10] In other words, should an antenna, which, at one point in time could only have been designed by a human, but now can be designed by a computer, be patentable?[11]

Part II introduces the reader to patent law. Part II.A discusses patent law in general, and includes an explanation of the derivation of patent rights. Part II.B then explains the legal concept of obviousness—the most relevant concept to patenting a device designed by a genetic program. Part III discusses relevant technological advances, in particular genetic programming is explained. Next, Part IV argues that when genetic programming has become widespread in a particular field, advances that could be created by the genetic program should be deemed obvious. To provide a practical application for this argument, Part IV.B sets forth a widespread use test. Part V addresses anticipated contra.

II.   PATENT LAW AND OBVIOUSNESS

A.   Patent Law Fundamentals

Congress is granted, by the United States Constitution, the power, "[t]o promote the Progress of Science and useful Arts, by securing for limited Times to Authors and Inventors the exclusive Right to their respective Writings and Discoveries."[12] Congress has exercised this power, with respect to technological advances, by enacting patent laws.[13] A patent does not give its owner the right to make or use the patented invention; rather, the patent gives its owner the right to exclude others from making or using the patented invention.[14] This right to exclude provides incentive for inventors to innovate and disclose their ideas to the public.[15]

Bringing ideas to the public domain is patent law's underlying purpose.[16] After an inventor has disclosed his idea to the public in exchange for the right to exclude for a

---

[10]   A separate very interesting question is: should the program itself, which designed the antenna, be patentable? *See* Peter M. Kohlhepp, *When the Invention Is an Inventor: Revitalizing Patentable Subject Matter to Exclude Unpredictable Processes*, 93 Minn. L. Rev. 779 (2008) (arguing that a process, such as the computer program that designed the antenna, which produces unpredictable results, is not a process under the meaning of 35 U.S.C. § 101, and therefore is unpatentable); *see also* Helen Li, *Can a Computer Be an Inventor?*, http://www.bilskiblog.com/blog/2016/04/can-a-computer-be-an-inventor.html (4 April 2016).

[11]   It should be noted that genetic programs apply to far more than just antenna technology. *See infra* Part III.B.

[12]   U.S. Const. art. I, § 8, cl. 8.

[13]   Patent law is governed by Title 35 of The United States Code.

[14]   Craig A. Nard, *The Law of Patents* (Wolters Kluwer 2011) 1–2.

[15]   *Id.* at 3 ("[P]atent law can be viewed as a system of laws that offer a potential financial reward as an inducement to invent, to disclose technical information, to invest capital in the innovation process, and to facilitate efficient use and manufacturing of invention through licensing.").

[16]   *Bonito Boats, Inc. v. Thunder Craft Boats, Inc.*, 489 U.S. 141, 151 (1989) ("The ultimate goal of the patent system is to bring new designs and technologies into the public domain through disclosure"); Nard, *supra* note 14, at 3.

limited time,[17] the patent expires and the public enjoys the benefit of unlimited use of the idea.[18]

To be patentable, an invention must be novel,[19] useful,[20] and nonobvious.[21] The novelty requirement precludes patentability when the invention is not new.[22] The utility requirement simply "mandates that the invention be operable to achieve useful results."[23] The nonobviousness requirement prohibits patentability when the "claimed invention as a whole would have been obvious."[24] Nonobviousness will be explained in more detail in the following section since it is the requirement that this note is primarily concerned with.[25]

B.   § 103 Obviousness

An inventor may not obtain a patent on an invention, though novel, if the invention is obvious.[26] While the obviousness requirement was originally created at common law,[27] it was eventually codified in 35 U.S.C. § 103 by Congress in 1952.[28] The Supreme Court has expressed the opinion that the statute was intended to codify the existing case law.[29] 35 U.S.C. § 103 governs obviousness, and states:

---

[17]   Nard, *supra* note 14, at 3.

[18]   *Bonito Boats*, 489 U.S. at 153 (Stating that "an article on which the patent has expired, is in the public domain and may be made and sold by whoever chooses to do so.").

[19]   35 U.S.C. § 102.

[20]   35 U.S.C. § 101.

[21]   35 U.S.C. § 103.

[22]   35 U.S.C. § 102; *In re Schreiber*, 128 F.3d 1473, 1477 (Fed. Cir. 1997) ("To anticipate a claim, a prior art reference must disclose every limitation of the claimed invention, either explicitly or inherently.").

[23]   *In re Swartz*, 232 F.3d 862, 863 (Fed. Cir. 2000).

[24]   *Stratoflex, Inc. v. Aeroquip Corp.*, 713 F.2d 1530, 1537 (Fed. Cir. 1983).

[25]   Before leaving this section, it would be a mistake not to note that on 16 September 2011 the Leahy-Smith America Invents Act (hereinafter "the AIA") passed into law. *See* Leahy-Smith America Invents Act, H.R. 1249, 112th Cong. (2011). While the AIA brought sweeping changes to many areas of patent law (*see Leahy-Smith America Invents Act*, Wikipedia.org, http:// en.wikipedia.org/wiki/Leahy-Smith_America_Invents_Act (last visited April 30, 2017) (Stating that the AIA, among other things, switches the patent system from a "first to invent" system to a "first to file" system, and "revised and expanded post-grant opposition procedures")), these changes do not substantially effect this note's topic. The main change from the AIA that does effect this note's topic is that obviousness under 35 U.S.C. § 103 is now determined at the time of filing rather than at the time of invention. This timeframe for obviousness determination will be discussed later in this chapter.

[26]   35 U.S.C. § 103.

[27]   *Hotchkiss v. Greenwood*, 11 How. 248 (1851); *See* Nard, supra note 13, 307 ("The *Hotchkiss* case is widely regarded as creating an additional patentability hurdle, above and beyond novelty and utility. This common law development. . .").

[28]   *See Graham v. John Deere Co. of Kansas City*, 383 U.S. 1, 3 (1966) ("the Congress has for the first time expressly added a third statutory dimension to the two requirements of novelty and utility that had been the sole statutory test since the Patent Act of 1793. This is the test of obviousness. . .").

[29]   *Id.* at 3–4 ("We have concluded that the 1952 Act was intended to codify judicial precedents embracing the principle long ago announced by this Court in *Hotchkiss v. Greenwood*. . .").

A patent for a claimed invention may not be obtained, notwithstanding that the claimed invention is not identically disclosed as set forth in section 102, if the differences between the claimed invention and the prior art are such that the claimed invention as a whole would have been obvious before the effective filing date of the claimed invention to a person having ordinary skill in the art to which the claimed invention pertains. Patentability shall not be negated by the manner in which the invention was made.[30]

Importantly, for obviousness, it is the invention as a whole, and not each individual element, that is evaluated.

1.   Basic application of obviousness

The Supreme Court established a framework for analyzing obviousness in *Graham v. John Deere Co.*[31] Under this framework, courts are to consider, "the scope and content of the prior art,"[32] the "differences between the prior art and the claims at issue,"[33] and "the level of ordinary skill in the pertinent art."[34] Further, the Court stated, "[s]uch secondary considerations as commercial success, long felt but unsolved needs, failure of others, etc., might be utilized to give light to the circumstances surrounding the origin of the subject matter sought to be patented."[35] In terms of when to measure obviousness, it is important to note that obviousness is measured "before the effective filing date of the claimed invention."[36] In asking the question of how the tools of invention can affect patentability, the level of ordinary skill is by far the most important component of this analysis, and this will be discussed more fully in the following section. Secondary considerations are also pertinent and will be discussed below in Part II.B.3.

2.   Person having ordinary skill in the art (hereinafter "PHOSITA")

Critical to the question of obviousness is how the PHOSITA is construed. There is a true paucity of case law on the topic of how to determine the PHOSITA. Nevertheless, construing the PHOSITA is essential to the question as to whether genetic algorithms can render an invention obvious.

In the 1983 case *Environmental Designs, Ltd. v. Union Oil Co. of California*, the Court of Appeals for the Federal Circuit (hereinafter "the Federal Circuit")[37] stated:

Factors that may be considered in determining level of ordinary skill in the art include: (1) the educational level of the inventor; (2) type of problems encountered in the art; (3) prior art

---

[30]   35 U.S.C. § 103.
[31]   *Graham v. John Deere Co. of Kansas City*, 383 U.S. 1, 17 (1966); John F. Duffy, *Inventing Invention: A Case Study of Legal Innovation*, 86 Tex. L. Rev. 1, 61 (2007) (Stating that a "significant development in the Graham opinion was the establishment of a four-step framework for analyzing the obviousness question.").
[32]   383 U.S. at 17.
[33]   *Id.*
[34]   *Id.*
[35]   *Id.* at 17–18.
[36]   35 U.S.C. § 103.
[37]   In patent cases, appeals go to the Federal Circuit rather than the regional circuit courts. *See Court Jurisdiction*, United States Court of Appeals for the Federal Circuit, http://www.cafc.uscourts.gov/the-court/court-jurisdiction (last visited April 30, 2017).

solutions to those problems; (4) rapidity with which innovations are made; (5) sophistication of the technology; and (6) educational level of active workers in the field.[38]

However, the Federal Circuit in *Environmental Designs* did not apply these factors since the PHOSITA's construction was not disputed by the parties.[39] Other Federal Circuit cases mention the importance of determining the level of ordinary skill yet do not shed much light on how to interpret the PHOSITA.[40]

One of the only on-point cases which reasons through its PHOSITA analysis is *Daiichi Sankyo Co., Ltd. v. Apotex, Inc.*[41] In *Apotex*, the plaintiff's patent was "drawn to a method for treating bacterial ear infections by topically administering the antibiotic ofloxacin into the ear."[42] The district court had held that the PHOSITA would have a medical degree and would be either a pediatrician or a general practitioner.[43] However, the Federal Circuit reasoned that none of the inventors of the challenged patent had medical degrees.[44] Instead, they "were specialists in drug and ear treatments"—a research scientist and a university professor.[45] Further, the written description of the patent detailed the inventors' testing of their treatment on guinea pigs which is not something a pediatrician or general practitioner would do.[46] Therefore, the Federal Circuit found that the district court had committed an error in construing the PHOSITA to be a general practitioner or pediatrician,[47] and instead construed the PHOSITA to be "a person engaged in developing pharmaceutical formulations and treatment methods for the ear."[48] The Federal Circuit found that the district court's use of the incorrect PHOSITA "tainted its obviousness analysis."[49] Based on the new PHOSITA, the Federal Circuit held that the patent was obvious.[50]

The search for additional precedent on constructing the PHOSITA turns up precious little. In *Ex Parte Hiyamizu*, the Board of Patent Appeals and Interferences (hereinafter

---

[38] 713 F.2d 693, 696 (Fed. Cir. 1983) (Citing *Orthopedic Equipment Co., Inc. v. All Orthopedic Appliances, Inc.*, 707 F.2d 1376, 1381–82 (Fed.Cir.1983)).

[39] *Id.* at 697.

[40] *See, e.g.*, 707 F.2d at 1382 (Upholding the district court's finding that the PHOSITA was "an engineer having at least a few years of design experience working in the field of developing ortho-pedic soft goods," but not providing any evidence from the particular situation presented why the PHOSITA should be constructed this way); *Orthopedic Equip. Co., Inc. v. United States*, 702 F.2d 1005 (Fed. Cir. 1983) (Not shedding much light on how to construct the PHOSITA besides listing some of the factors subsequently cited in *Environmental Designs*, and stating, "[t]he individuals working in the art were of above average intelligence and educational training. Many possessed advanced university degrees"); *Jacobson Bros., Inc. v. United States*, 355-70, 1974 WL 20227 (Ct. Cl. Nov. 6, 1974) (Listing some of the factors recited in *Environmental Designs* and stating, "[a] finite quantitative definition of this ordinarily skilled person is difficult at best").

[41] 501 F.3d 1254 (Fed. Cir. 2007).

[42] *Id.* at 1255.

[43] *Id.* at 1256.

[44] *Id.* at 1257.

[45] *Id.*

[46] *Id.*

[47] *Id.*

[48] *Id.*

[49] *Id.*

[50] *Id.* at 1259.

"the BPAI") reviewed an Examiner's decision to construct a PHOSITA, in relation to a patent application for a semiconductor device, to be a person with a doctoral level degree.[51] The BPAI rejected the use of a degree in constructing the PHOSITA, stating, "[i]t is our view that such a hypothetical person is no more definable by way of credentials than is the hypothetical 'reasonably prudent man' standard found in laws pertaining to negligence."[52] However, the BPAI did not go on to provide a framework on how to determine the PHOSITA.[53]

In sum, PHOSITA construction is a topic upon which there is a scarcity of case law. However, among what is available, *Apotex* provides the most complete analysis of the *Environmental Designs* factors. Therefore, the PHOSITA for this note's question will be constructed under the *Apotex* and *Environmental Designs* framework. Once the PHOSITA has been constructed, courts proceed to evaluate secondary considerations.

3.   Secondary considerations

In determining obviousness, the Supreme Court assesses several secondary considerations such "as commercial success, long felt but unsolved needs, failure of others, etc."[54] Further, courts consider unexpected results as a secondary consideration.[55] Secondary consideration arguments will often be raised in close cases of issues regarding obviousness.

Regarding commercial success, the Federal Circuit has explained: "Commercial success is relevant because the law presumes an idea would successfully have been brought to market sooner, in response to market forces, had the idea been obvious to persons skilled in the art."[56] In other words, if it was obvious, someone else would have already been in the market selling it, and it would have been harder to turn such a profit. But, commercial success may also be the product of advertising and marketing.[57] Therefore, for commercial success to count as evidence of nonobviousness, there must be a nexus between the commercial success and the technical merits of the patented invention.[58] This battle to show a nexus was demonstrated in *J.T. Eaton & Co., Inc. v. Atlantic Paste & Glue Co.*[59] In that case, a patent for a "Stick-Em" glue mousetrap was challenged as obvious.[60] The patentee argued the patent was not obvious because of commercial success.[61] The Federal Circuit ruled that the patentee had failed to establish the nexus between the patent and the commercial success because the sales data submitted was for a slightly different product than what the patent was directed to.[62] The Federal Circuit

---

[51]   10 U.S.P.Q.2d 1393 (Bd. Pat. App. & Inter. 1988).
[52]   *Id.* at 1394.
[53]   *See Id.*
[54]   *Graham v. John Deere Co. of Kansas City*, 383 U.S. 1, 17–18 (1966).
[55]   *In re Dillon*, 919 F.2d 688, 692-93 (Fed. Cir. 1990) (Stating that the applicant's "argument can consist of a comparison of test data showing that the claimed compositions possess unexpectedly improved properties or properties that the prior art does not have").
[56]   *Merck & Co., Inc. v. Teva Pharmaceuticals USA, Inc.*, 395 F.3d 1364, 1376 (Fed. Cir. 2005).
[57]   Nard, *supra* note 14, at 375.
[58]   *Id.*
[59]   106 F.3d 1563 (Fed. Cir. 1997).
[60]   *Id.* at 1571.
[61]   *Id.*
[62]   *Id.*

remanded the case to the district court to consider only sales data associated with the exact patented product.[63]

Another secondary consideration is "a long felt need and failure of others."[64] Courts consider this because "[i]f people are clamoring for a solution, and the best minds do not find it for years, that is practical evidence. . .of the state of knowledge."[65] In other words, if it was obvious, someone would have already tried it. However, this secondary consideration must be viewed in the light that the failure of others may also have been due to simply other research priorities.[66] From a policy perspective, granting a patent for an idea that the marketplace needs furthers patent law's goal of bringing ideas to the marketplace. An example of the long felt need was shown in *Environmental Designs*.[67] In that case, the Federal Circuit considered legislative regulation controlling sulfur dioxide emissions as evidence of a long felt need for technology with reduced sulfur dioxide emissions.[68]

A final secondary consideration is unexpected results.[69] For example, the Federal Circuit considered unexpected results in the case *In re Merck & Co.*[70] There, a patent application for an antidepressant drug with sedative properties had been rejected as obvious by the US Patent and Trademark Office (PTO).[71] The prior art the PTO cited was another antidepressant drug with sedative properties and with only a slight chemical structural difference to the drug in the patent application.[72] The patent applicant argued that even though the chemical difference in the drugs was small, the patent should be granted because there was a difference in sedative properties.[73] As evidence of this, the applicant submitted an article which included a comparison of the sedative properties of the two drugs.[74] In weighing all the evidence, the Federal Circuit rejected the applicant's argument because the article characterized the difference as only "somewhat less" sedative.[75]

[63] *Id.* (The Federal Circuit further stated, "if a patentee makes the requisite showing of nexus between commercial success and the patented invention, the burden shifts to the challenger to prove that the commercial success is instead due to other factors extraneous to the patented invention, such as advertising or superior workmanship.").

[64] *Graham v. John Deere Co. of Kansas City*, 383 U.S. 1, 17 (1966).

[65] *Matter of Mahurkar Double Lumen Hemodialysis Catheter Patent Litig.*, 831 F. Supp. 1354, 1378 (N.D. Ill. 1993).

[66] Nard, *supra* note 14, at 376.

[67] 713 F.2d 693, 697–98 (Fed. Cir. 1983).

[68] *Id.* (Stating "the desire of governmental bodies to mandate higher purity standards was frustrated by lack of technology thus dramatizes the need.").

[69] *In re Dillon*, 919 F.2d at 692-93; *In re Merck & Co., Inc.*, 800 F.2d 1091, 1098 (Fed. Cir. 1986) ("A prima facie case of obviousness can be rebutted by evidence of unexpected results.").

[70] 800 F.2d at 1098–99.

[71] *Id.* at 1092.

[72] *Id.* at 1096.

[73] *Id.* at 1098 ("In rebuttal of the PTO's prima facie case appellant has asserted that, as compared to [the prior art drug], [the present invention drug] unexpectedly has a more potent sedative and a stronger anticholinergic effect").

[74] *Id.* at 1098–99.

[75] *Id.* at 1099.

III.   THE TOOLS OF INVENTION AND GENETIC PROGRAMS

A.   The Increasing Prevalence of Computers in Research

Computer programs simulate, among many other things, electronic circuits,[76] rocket propulsion,[77] and reactions in nuclear physics.[78] Scientists and inventors use computers more and more in their research.[79] But thus far, computers have mostly been used only to augment human ingenuity. Genetic programming (described in the following section), a branch of artificial intelligence, brings computers to the next level—where computers may supplant human creativity and reduce the role that humans play in the invention process.[80]

B.   Genetic Programs

Genetic programming brings major changes to the future of invention.[81] Genetic programs operate by mimicking the evolutionary process.[82] For a simple genetic program, a user inputs a set of desired criteria. The genetic program then generates a random population of samples and selects some of the samples with criteria closest to the user's criteria. The program then randomly generates changes to these samples to create a new population and further selects the samples from the new population that are closest to the user's criteria. The procedure iterates until the desired criteria is reached.[83] To illustrate, if a genetic program is designing an antenna, the user would input a desired radiation pattern. The genetic program would then randomly generate ten antennas and

---

[76]   *See, e.g.*, *SPICE*, Wikipedia.org, http://en.wikipedia.org/wiki/SPICE (last visited 30 April 2017).

[77]   *See*, Balachandar Ramamurthy, Eliyahu Horowitz and Joseph R. Fragola, *Physical Simulation in Space Launcher Engine Risk Assessment*, Reliability and Maintainability Symposium (RAMS), 2010 Proceedings – Annual, 25–28 Jan. 2010.

[78]   *See*, Interactive Simulations University of Colorado at Boulder, http://phet.colorado.edu/en/simulation/nuclear-fission (last visited 30 April 2017).

[79]   George Johnson, *The World: In Silica Fertilization; All Science Is Computer Science*, N.Y. Times (25 Mar. 2001) (Quoting a Dr. at a research institute as saying, "'Physics is almost entirely computational now. . . . Nobody would dream of doing these big accelerator experiments without a tremendous amount of computer power to analyze the data.'" And, "'Ten years ago biologists were very dismissive of the need for computation. . .Now they are aware that you can't really do biology without it.'").

[80]   *See, e.g.*, Liza Vertinsky and Todd M. Rice, *Thinking About Thinking Machines: Implications Of Machine Inventors For Patent Law*, 8 B.U. J. Sci. & Tech L. 574, 587 (2002) (Stating "the human role will increasingly be limited to identifying basic problem structures and evaluation criteria for results, and thinking machines will dominate the rest of the invention process.").

[81]   *See* Kenneth Chang, *Hal, Call Your Office: Computers that Act Like Physicists*, N.Y. Times (7 Apr. 2009) at D4; Eisenberg, *supra* note 3.

[82]   *Genetic programming*, Wikipedia.org, http://en.wikipedia.org/wiki/Genetic_programming (last visited 30 April 2017).

[83]   U.S. Patent No. 7,610,154 (filed 27 Jan. 2005) ("The conventional genetic programming starts from a program consisting of randomly generated prescribed programming elements, and reproduces over generations a best fit program of each generation through genetic operations, so as to evolve the population."); *see also Genetic programming*, *supra* note 82.

select the antenna with the radiation pattern closest to the desired pattern. Using this antenna, the program would randomly generate slight changes in the antenna's shape and size to create a new population of ten antennas. The program would then from this new population select the next antenna with a radiation pattern closest to the desired radiation pattern and repeat the process until it found an antenna with the desired pattern.

More advanced genetic programs may mimic additional aspects of the evolutionary process.[84] For example, in biological evolution, when a child is born, he will have characteristics of both of his parents.[85] This is caused by a process called chromosomal crossover.[86] More advanced genetic programs can mimic this process.[87] Some genetic programs even generate populations with "offspring" based on three "parents."[88] Further, there are other biological evolutionary processes that genetic programs have imitated.[89] It is important to note that since genetic programs use random process (e.g. in selecting a first population and in mutating subsequent populations) the genetic program could make different designs using the same inputs each time it is run.[90]

Genetic programming has been applied to solve many different kinds of problems. Jet engines[91] and antennas[92] have been designed by genetic programs. Fuel emissions for diesel engines have been optimized with genetic programming.[93] Classical music has been composed by a genetic program.[94] On the more theoretical side, scientists are using genetic programs to sift through data to discover fundamental laws of nature.[95]

The functionality of patented devices has been duplicated by devices designed by

---

[84]   *See Genetic programming, supra* note 82.

[85]   *See Chromosomal crossover,* Wikipedia.org, http://en.wikipedia.org/wiki/Chromosomal_crossover (last visited 30 April 2017).

[86]   *Id.*

[87]   *See Crossover (genetic algorithm),* Wikipedia.org, http://en.wikipedia.org/wiki/Crossover_%28genetic_algorithm%29 (last visited 30 April 2017).

[88]   *Id.*

[89]   *See* the '154 Patent (a program mimicking a biological process that performs genetic operations on DNA); U.S. Patent No. 6,424,959 (filed 17 June 1999) ("The present invention uses a population of entities which are evolved over a series of generations by an iterative process involving the application of operations, such as mutation, crossover, reproduction, and architecture-altering operations."); *Genetic programming, supra* note 82.

[90]   *See* Kohlhepp, *supra* note 10 at 812 (noting that when a genetic algorithm is used, for example to design a roof truss, that "[i]f the algorithm is run ten times, however, it will yield ten different roof truss designs.").

[91]   Ray Kurzweil, *The Virtual Thomas Edison,* Time (4 Dec. 2000) at 114.

[92]   Eisenberg, *supra* note 3, at G9 (satellite communications antenna designed); Jonathon Keats, *John Koza Has Built an Invention Machine,* Popular Sci. (1 May 2006) at 72, 92 (antenna designed that looked like "bent paperclip").

[93]   *Diesel Breeding: Looking Into Engines Helps Cross the Best with the Best,* issue 9, 124 Mechanical Engineering 53 (2002) (Stating that using a genetic program to optimize engine design "resulted in a design that consumed 15 percent less fuel than a standard diesel engine while producing one-third the amount of nitrogen oxide and half the soot.").

[94]   *See,* Alasdair Wilkins, *This classical music was created by a supercomputer in less than a second,* io9.com (6 Jan. 2013, 3:00 PM), http://io9.com/5973551/this-classical-music-was-created-by-a-supercomputer-in-less-than-a-second.

[95]   *See* Chang, *supra* note 81, at D4.

genetic programs.[96] For instance, a team lead by John Koza browsed patents and selected five patents on various electronic circuits issued after 1 January 2000.[97] They then used genetic programming to successfully design circuits which duplicated the functionality of the patented circuits.[98] John Koza has also received a patent on a circuit designed by his genetic program.[99]

This rise of genetic programs illustrates that the way many inventors do their work may change as genetic programs become more widespread. Because a genetic program may simply be able to design what an inventor tells it to, the role of the inventor will change once genetic programs are brought to that inventor's field. In the view of one scientist, people will "become managers, directing the machines toward interesting problems and opportunities . . . The creative act will be in mentioning the right problems."[100] As developed in Part IV, this major change in the inventor's role leads to some situations where widespread use of genetic programs should render some ideas obvious.

IV.   THE SITUATION WHERE GENETIC PROGRAMMING SHOULD RENDER AN IDEA OBVIOUS

The remainder of this chapter argues that before genetic programming has become widespread in its application to design of a particular device, designs that could be created by the genetic program should be patentable; however, once genetic programming has become widespread in its application to design of a particular device, designs that could be created by the genetic program should be held to be obvious because it would be obvious to an inventor to simply use a genetic program to design the device in question.

Let us return to the example of an antenna. In constructing the PHOSITA for this example, the factors from *Environmental Designs*[101] will be considered. First, the educational level of the inventor varies widely in antenna design. One inventor might be a professor with a PhD, while the next might be an undergraduate student. This criteria is not particularly useful here. Second, the type of problem encountered in the art is how to design an antenna that emits a desired radiation pattern.[102] Third, the prior art solution

---

[96]   J.R. Koza et al, *Routine Automated Synthesis of Five Patented Analog Circuits Using Genetic Programming* 8 Soft Computing 318, 318 (2004).

[97]   *Id.* at 318–19.

[98]   *Id.* at 322–24.

[99]   Kohlhepp, *supra* note 10, at 786; Keats, *supra* note 92, at 68 ("An invention-machine creation has earned a patent; the examiner did not know it was the work of a computer."); *see also* U.S. Patent No. 6,847,851 (filed 12 July 2002).

[100]   Eisenberg, *supra* note 3. Further, although not within the scope of this note's topic, the above quote raises another separate and interesting question: if a device designed by a genetic program is patentable, *who* should get the patent on the device? Is it the person who coded the genetic program, the person who "mentioned the right problems" to the genetic program, or the person who built the device?

[101]   713 F.2d 693, 696 (Fed. Cir. 1983); *See* discussion *supra* Part II.B.2.

[102]   *See, e.g.,* U.S. Patent Appl. Pub. No. 2011/0276519 (filed 22 July 2011) (Describing an antenna in a parking meter, used e.g. to communicate with law enforcement officers or to provide credit card information, and showing the radiation patterns that will be emitted from the parking meter when different kinds of antennas are used).

to this problem would be to design an antenna, and then use a computer program to simulate the antenna design to find if the antenna produced the desired radiation pattern. Fourth, the rapidity with which innovations are made in this field is directly linked to how antennas are designed and is therefore linked to if genetic programs are in widespread use in antenna design. Fifth, antenna technology, and the tools that are used to design antennas, can range from very basic to very sophisticated, so this factor is also not very helpful. Sixth, the educational level of active workers in the field would likely be deemed to be an engineer with a few years of antenna design experience.

In view of the above, the question the court should ask is: would an engineer with a few years of experience, who sought to design an antenna emitting a particular radiation pattern, use a genetic program to design the antenna?

Central to this question is whether the PHOSITA would have access to a genetic program. To illustrate, when John Koza used a genetic program to design an antenna, he ran the program on his "invention machine" which is 1000 computers networked together[103]—hardly a tool that an ordinary antenna designer would have access to. The PTO should consider that even if an ordinary antenna designer knew that it was possible to design an antenna with a genetic program, he may not have access to a genetic program in his work. This leads to the conclusion that it would not be obvious to a PHOSITA to use the genetic program since he would not have access to it.

Further, 35 U.S.C. § 103 commands that obviousness be measured "before the effective filing date of the claimed invention."[104] This is important because the tools that the PHOSITA has available can easily change with time. It could be, for example, that at one point in time, no antenna designers use genetic programs; yet, in the future, genetic programs become widespread in antenna design. In this situation, we must re-ask the question: would an engineer with a few years of experience, who sought to design an antenna emitting a particular radiation pattern, use a genetic program to design the antenna? At this later point in time, the answer is different than before—now a PHOSITA would use a genetic program to design the antenna.

In this post-spread of genetic programming situation, an antenna that could be designed by a genetic program should be held obvious. This is because any PHOSITA could easily plug the parameters into a genetic program, read the antenna design from the program, and bring the antenna into the public sphere. The public, in this situation, would gain nothing by this disclosure, since any PHOSITA could simply run the genetic program to design the antenna at any time. Further, granting a patent on a particular antenna design would be useless for the inventor because the genetic program could potentially design a different antenna that emits the same radiation pattern the next time the genetic program is run.[105]

The above argument demonstrates why, logically, developments designed by genetic programs, in fields where genetic programming is widespread, should be held obvious. But just because something is logical does not make it good law or policy. Would holding

---

[103]   Keats, *supra* note 92 at 68–70.
[104]   35 U.S.C. § 103.
[105]   *See* note 89 and accompanying text.

such developments obvious make good policy? The following section explores this question.

A.   Policy

Part II.A states patent law's goals of providing incentive for innovation and disclosure of ideas to the public.[106] Still, patents are not granted if an idea is obvious.[107] One reason for this is that obvious inventions may be brought into the public sphere without the incentive of a reward by a patent.[108] Once genetic programming has become widespread in a field, inventors working in the field can easily use a genetic program to design a device. Since the device may be developed and brought to the market place with such little cost, there is no need for the grant of a patent to incentivize an inventor to bring the device to the marketplace.[109] Another reason for not granting a patent to an obvious development is to avoid granting a patent to a development "achieved through some cause not attributable to the patent applicant's efforts."[110] Once a genetic program has become widespread in a field, the advances created by a genetic program are not achieved through the patent applicant's efforts—the advances are instead created by the "efforts" of the genetic program.

Further, as a practical matter, let us return to the example of a genetic program designing an antenna, and let us assume that genetic programming has become widespread in this field. Allowing patents for antennas designed by genetic programs would allow companies to build a thicket of patents by repeatedly patenting designs created by the genetic program. Each time the genetic program was run, the program would design a different antenna, since the program uses random processes.[111] If a company ran the program ten times, it could patent ten different antenna designs. If it did so, a competing company would have to go through the costly process of searching through the thicket of trivial patents. This competing company would have to shift investment dollars away from antenna research to searching though the thicket of patents.

In addition, simply obtaining such a thicket of trivial patents would be very costly for a company. Therefore, it could be argued that companies would likely not pursue obtaining this thicket of trivial patents because of the high cost.[112] However, this high cost is much more of a burden to smaller companies than to large ones. In other words, a large, well-funded, corporation could still obtain a thicket of patents and use it effectively against a smaller company that could not afford the cost of sifting through a forest of patents. Holding devices obvious in fields where the use of genetic programs is widespread would

---

[106]   Nard, *supra* note 14, at 3 ("[P]atent law can be viewed as a system of laws that offer a potential financial reward as an inducement to invent, to disclose technical information, to invest capital in the innovation process. . .").

[107]   35 U.S.C. § 103.

[108]   *See* Duffy, *supra* note 31, at 11 ("For these [obvious] inventions, the rewards of the patent system are assumed to be largely unnecessary.").

[109]   *Id.* (Stating that for obvious developments "enough incentive to create them is provided even by being the first to market the innovation. . .").

[110]   Duffy, *supra* note 31, at 12.

[111]   Kohlhepp, *supra* note 10, at 812.

[112]   *See* Duffy, *supra* note 31, at 12 ("trivial patents can be discouraged by charging sufficient fees for obtaining or maintaining each patent.").

disallow a large corporation from simply paying money to obtain a thicket of patents and using it to crush smaller, less well funded companies.

Still, it is not enough to reach the conclusion that once genetic programming is widespread in a particular field designs created by genetic programs should be held obvious. In order to have practical application, courts must know how to determine when genetic programming has become widespread in a field.

B. A Widespread Use Test Proposal

This chapter proposes a four factor test to determine if genetic programming is widespread in a field: first, if the invention was actually designed with a genetic program; second, the proportion of PHOSITAs in the field having access to genetic programs; third, the cost associated with the use of a genetic program for this type of design; fourth, the amount of time and effort required to operate the necessary genetic program.

Because of the dynamic nature of the genetic programming and artificial intelligence, the approach taken in applying the widespread use test must be flexible. In some situations, one or more factors may predominate; in others, all factors may apply equally. This flexible approach is in accordance with factor tests for other legal concepts.[113]

It is important to bear in mind that 35 U.S.C. § 103 orders that obviousness is measured "before the effective filing date of the claimed invention."[114] Therefore, the widespread use test would be applied at different times for different inventions.

1. Factor one: if the invention was actually designed by a genetic program

At the onset, it is important to know if the invention was designed with the use of a genetic program. At a minimum, if the invention was designed by a genetic program, it shows that the technology exists, and is available to at least one inventor in the field. Further, it shows that the inventor chose to design with a genetic program which is evidence that genetic programming simplifies the task in this context.

One may question how the PTO or court is to know if an invention has been designed with a genetic program. However, "[e]ach individual associated with the filing and prosecution of a patent application has a duty of candor and good faith in dealing with the [PTO], which *includes a duty to disclose to the [PTO] all information known to that individual to be material to patentability . . .*"[115] Therefore, the inventor and the attorney prosecuting the patent application both arguably have a duty to disclose if the invention was designed with a genetic program or not.

But showing that the inventor alone had access to a genetic program is not sufficient to show widespread use. Therefore, we must look to see if other inventors in the field had access to applicable genetic programs.

---

[113]   *See, e.g. Playboy Enterprises, Inc. v. Netscape Communications Corp.*, 354 F.3d 1020, 1026 (9th Cir. 2004) (analyzing, in a trademark dispute, likelihood of confusion factors and stating "courts must be flexible in applying the factors, as some may not apply. Moreover, some factors are more important than others.").

[114]   35 U.S.C. § 103.

[115]   37 C.F.R. § 1.56 (emphasis added).

2.   Factor two: the proportion of PHOSITAs in the field having access to genetic programs

The proportion of PHOSITAs in the field having access to genetic programs is arguably the most important factor. If a high proportion of PHOSITAs have access to genetic programs, it demonstrates that more inventors are able to implement genetic programs to bring new designs to the market place. This in itself is evidence that patent law's goal of bringing new ideas to the market place[116] is being facilitated.

One issue in analyzing this factor will be how to determine the relevant market. For example, in the domestic market for diesel powered locomotive engines there are only two major manufacturers—General Electric Co., and Electro-Motive Diesel Inc. (now owned by Caterpillar Inc.).[117] Therefore, when analyzing this market, courts will have to determine whether to limit the market to diesel powered locomotive engines (effectively only two companies), or whether to expand the analysis to related fields (e.g. truck diesel powered engines). In this example, it is better to limit the analysis to the exact problem to be solved. This is because even though truck engines and locomotive engines may have much in common, there are enough differences that a totally different genetic program would be needed to design each. In selecting fields for determining the proportion of PHOSITAs having access to genetic programs, only fields where the same genetic program could in fact be used to design the invention in question should be considered. This ensures that a PHOSITA would actually be able to use the genetic program to design the invention in question. It may seem, in the diesel powered locomotive example, that this produces a bizarre outcome—that use by only two companies is "widespread." However, this is the correct conclusion. If only two companies produce a product, and both of these companies have access to a genetic program, then by definition every company producing this product has access to a genetic program.

3.   Factor three: the financial cost associated with using a genetic program for this type of design

In designing his antenna with a genetic program, John Koza ran the genetic program on his "invention machine" which is 1000 computers networked together.[118] The electric bill alone was $3,000 a month.[119] The high cost of gathering and assembling 1000 computers may provide deterrence for many inventors and companies from adopting genetic programs. Therefore, a high cost of running a genetic program would be evidence that genetic programming was not widespread in a field. Alternatively, if a genetic program could be run cheaply, this would show that companies could easily adopt them and that use was becoming widespread.

---

[116]   Nard, *supra* note 14, at 3.
[117]   Bob Tita, *Caterpillar expected to make Electro-Motive more competitive* (4 June 2010), http://www.webcitation.org/5trEL4dsG.
[118]   Keats, *supra* note 92, at 68–70.
[119]   *Id.* at 69.

4. Factor four: the amount of time and effort required to operate the necessary genetic program

Along with financial cost, the time and effort required to operate the genetic program should also be considered.[120] The time and effort necessary to network enough computers together to provide the computing capability needed to run some genetic programs could preclude some inventors from using genetic programs. Further, at the point in time when John Koza designed his antenna, his system took from one day to one month to create a new invention.[121] A month is quite a long time for a computer program to run. Alternatively, if a genetic program could be run quickly as an iPhone app, this would be evidence that genetic programming is widespread in a field.

V. CONTRA

Above, I argue when genetic programming has become widespread with regard to designing a particular product, designs that the genetic program could produce should be obvious and therefore unpatentable. Yet, there are multiple potential counter arguments to this proposal in different directions. It is possible to argue that anything created by a genetic program should be obvious, even before genetic programming has become widespread in a field. Conversely, it is possible to argue that even widespread use of genetic programming should not render an idea obvious. Finally, there is an argument that widespread use of genetic programming should create only a prima facie case of obviousness. The strongest contra is discussed below.

A. Argument that Nothing Designed by a Genetic Program should be Patentable because it was Designed by a Process of Trial and Error

One argument is that everything designed by a genetic program should be held obvious because genetic programs (it appears as if) operate by a process of trial and error. The trial and error argument is that if something can be discovered through a simple process of trial and error, it must be obvious.[122] But, genetic programs do not in fact operate by a process of trial and error. A process of trial and error would be, for example regarding antennas, if ten antennas were created, the one antenna with the best radiation pattern was selected, *and the process stopped there*. Genetic programs do not stop there. A genetic program would then take the best one, two, or three, antennas, and merge or mutate them.[123] From this,

---

[120]   Although a high financial cost of running a genetic program will often go hand in hand with a large requirement of time and effort to run a genetic program, this is not always the case. The two could become especially separated in the future as computer processors improve. For example, if improved computer processors allow a genetic program to run on a PC, but a genetic program software licensor still charges a very high fee for using the genetic program.

[121]   Keats, *supra* note 92, at 68.

[122]   *See* Cal Crary, *Impact of KSR v. Teleflex on Pharmaceutical Industry*, Patentlyo.com (3 May 2007), http://www.patentlyo.com/patent/2007/05/impact_of_ksr_v.html (commenting that a Federal Circuit Judge's belief was that "an approach that is obvious to try is also obvious where normal trial and error procedures will lead to the result").

[123]   *Crossover (genetic algorithm)*, *supra* note 87.

a new generation of antennas would be created.[124] The additional step of merging and/or mutating removes genetic programs from the category of pure trial and error.

Furthermore, from a policy perspective, it may seem that if all that is required to reach a solution is a process of trial and error, then the solution should be obvious. However, in for example Canadian patent law, trial and error actually counts as evidence of nonobviousness.[125] This is because "[i]f something requires this kind of research, then it is not obvious because it is not 'plain as day' or 'crystal clear.'"[126] Therefore, even as a policy matter, it is not clear that the use of trial and error should render an idea obvious.

B.   Argument that Genetic Programing Use should not Affect Patentability

When John Koza designed his five circuits which mimicked the functionality of recently patented circuits, he expressed the view that the use of a genetic program will not affect an invention's patentability.[127] Further, John Koza received a patent on a circuit designed by his genetic program.[128] Yet genetic programming is still in its infancy. Because the construction of the PHOSITA can change over time, what satisfied the PTO's requirements at one point in time may not satisfy it at a later point in time. 35 U.S.C. §103 itself addresses this by stating that obviousness is measured "before the effective filing date of the claimed invention."[129] Therefore, it makes perfect sense that Koza should have been granted a patent on his device before the use of genetic programs became widespread in a particular field; and that at a later point in time, after the use of genetic programs become widespread in that particular field, that an invention could be rendered obvious by the prevalence of genetic programming.

C.   Should Widespread Use Create only a Prima Facie Case of Obviousness?

An alternative proposal to the one in this chapter is that a finding of widespread use should create only a prima facie case of obviousness. The idea is that the prima facie case of obviousness could be rebutted using secondary considerations. As discussed in Part II.B.3, courts analyze secondary considerations when determining obvious.[130] However, for the reasons that follow, secondary considerations are not very useful to the question of genetic programming.

---

[124]   *Id.*
[125]   Donald M. Cameron, *Chapter 7 Obviousness* (17 May 2010), http://www.jurisdiction.com/patweb07.pdf (stating "If trial and error are required, it can't be obvious." And "[f]urthermore, it is not directly leading to the solution; instead it leads to intermediate failures.").
[126]   *Id.*
[127]   Koza, *supra* note 96, at 324 ("If an automated method were able to duplicate a previously patented human-created invention, the fact that the original human-designed version satisfied the Patent Office's criteria of patent-worthiness means that the automatically created duplicate would also have satisfied the Patent Office's criteria.").
[128]   Kohlhepp, *supra* note 10, at 786; Keats, *supra* note 92, at 68 ("An invention-machine creation has earned a patent; the examiner did not know it was the work of a computer."); *see also* U.S. Patent No. 6,847,851 (filed 12 July 2002).
[129]   35 U.S.C. § 103.
[130]   *Graham v. John Deere Co. of Kansas City*, 383 U.S. 1, 17–18 (1966).

The secondary consideration of unexpected results is not very relevant here, although it does take a moment to understand why. Unexpected results come into play when a slight difference in design leads to a drastic difference in results. Genetic programs do the opposite of this—genetic programs produce designs that are very different from existing human created designs.[131] As Popular Science Magazine put it, "[e]very day now, genetic programs continue to create the unexpected, the counterintuitive or the just plain weird."[132] In the antenna context, the antenna that John Koza designed "looks like a mistake, works like a charm."[133] In other words, unexpected results would come into play if the antenna was designed only slightly differently but produced a vastly different radiation pattern. Instead, the antenna's design was not slightly different—it was drastically different.

Further, a long felt need is not particularly relevant here either. The idea behind the long felt need consideration is: if it was obvious, someone would have created it earlier; and since no one created it earlier, it must not be obvious.[134] However, in a field with widespread genetic programming, it becomes obvious to use a genetic program to solve a problem even if the problem has been long felt. For example, for an antenna with a particular radiation pattern when genetic programming has become widespread, a PHOSITA would simply use a genetic program to create an antenna with the desired radiation pattern.

Commercial success is also not relevant in the context of widespread genetic programming. The Federal Circuit explains that commercial success "presumes an idea would successfully have been brought to market sooner, in response to market forces, had the idea been obvious to persons skilled in the art."[135] This is less applicable to our question because once genetic programming has become widespread in a field, it becomes obvious for a PHOSITA to use a genetic program to bring a product to market. Therefore, the presumption that a product would have been brought to the market sooner no longer makes any sense where genetic programming has become widespread. A presumption that the product will be designed using a genetic program, and immediately brought to the market, makes more sense in this context.

In sum, none of the secondary considerations are relevant to the problems posed by widespread genetic programming. Therefore, after finding widespread use, creating a prima facie case of obviousness instead of simply finding obviousness would not be advisable.

VI.   CONCLUSION

No one knows how genetic programming will affect the future of invention and the patentability of devices designed by genetic programs. Thus far, at least one device that

---

[131]   Keats, *supra* note 92, at 72 ("Koza's leap in genetic programming allowed for open-ended evolutions of basic structure and so produced more novel and sophisticated designs").

[132]   *Id.*

[133]   *Id.* at 70.

[134]   *Matter of Mahurkar Double Lumen Hemodialysis Catheter Patent Litig.*, 831 F. Supp. 1354, 1378 (N.D. Ill. 1993).

[135]   *Merck & Co., Inc. v. Teva Pharmaceuticals USA, Inc.*, 395 F.3d 1364, 1376 (Fed. Cir. 2005).

was designed by a genetic program has been patented.[136] This is fine for now, as use of genetic programming is not widespread. In the future, however, as engineers begin to make common use of genetic programming, many designs that were once difficult to create will become trivially simple. Once this happens, designs for a particular device that a genetic program could create should be deemed obvious, and therefore unpatentable.[137] If patents were granted on these designs, the public would gain nothing from these patent grants because a PHOSITA could already easily bring this technology to the marketplace. Because this situation only occurs after genetic program use becomes widespread in a particular field, finding a method to determine widespread use is critically important. This chapter has proposed a four factor widespread use test to make this determination. There is no doubt that genetic programs have the potential to change invention and creative thinking as we know it.[138] As this sea change arrives, we must be ready to adapt our patent laws to maintain their underlying purpose.

SOURCES

Cases

Bonito Boats, Inc. v. Thunder Craft Boats, Inc., 489 U.S. 141, (1989).
In re Schreiber, 128 F.3d 1473, (Fed. Cir. 1997).
In re Swartz, 232 F.3d 862, (Fed. Cir. 2000).
Stratoflex, Inc. v. Aeroquip Corp., 713 F.2d 1530, (Fed. Cir. 1983).
Hotchkiss v. Greenwood, 11 How. 248 (1851).
Graham v. John Deere Co. of Kansas City, 383 U.S. 1, (1966).
Environmental Designs, Ltd. v. Union Oil Co. of California, 713 F.2d 693, (Fed. Cir. 1983).
Orthopedic Equipment Co., Inc. v. All Orthopedic Appliances, Inc., 707 F.2d 1376, (Fed.Cir.1983).
Daiichi Sankyo Co., Ltd. v. Apotex, Inc., 501 F.3d 1254 (Fed. Cir. 2007).
Ex Parte Hiyamizu, 10 U.S.P.Q.2d 1393 (Bd. Pat. App. & Inter. 1988).
J.T. Eaton & Co., Inc. v. Atlantic Paste & Glue Co. 106 F.3d 1563 (Fed. Cir. 1997).
Matter of Mahurkar Double Lumen Hemodialysis Catheter Patent Litig., 831 F. Supp. 1354, (N.D. Ill. 1993).
In re Merck & Co., Inc., 800 F.2d 1091 (Fed. Cir. 1986).
Playboy Enterprises, Inc. v. Netscape Communications Corp., 354 F.3d 1020 (9th Cir. 2004).
Merck & Co., Inc. v. Teva Pharmaceuticals USA, Inc., 395 F.3d 1364, 1376 (Fed. Cir. 2005).

Statutes/Legislation

U.S. Const. art. I, § 8, cl. 8.
35 U.S.C. § 101.
35 U.S.C. § 102.
35 U.S.C. § 103.
Leahy-Smith America Invents Act, H.R. 1249, 112th Cong. (2011).

---

[136]   Kohlhepp, *supra* note 10, at 786; Keats, *supra* note 92, at 68, 72; *see also* U.S. Patent No. 6,847,851 (filed 12 July 2002).

[137]   35 U.S.C. § 103.

[138]   Chang, *supra* note 81; Eisenberg, *supra* note 3.

18. Thinking machines and patent law
Liza Vertinsky

I. INTRODUCTION

> Recently there has been a good deal of news about strange giant machines that can handle information with vast speed and skill. . .These machines are similar to what a brain would be if it were made of hardware and wire instead of flesh and nerves. . .A machine can handle information; it can calculate, conclude, and choose; it can perform reasonable operations with information. A machine, therefore, can think.
>
> Edmund Berkeley (1949)[1]

> There is no result from decades of neuroscientific research to suggest that the brain is anything other than a machine, made of ordinary atoms, employing ordinary forces and obeying the ordinary laws of nature. There is no mysterious "vital spark", in other words, that is necessary to make it go.
>
> The Economist (2015)[2]

Alan Turing is credited as being one of the first to develop the idea of machines that have the ability to "think" like humans.[3] His work, along with computing pioneer John von Neumann, mathematician John McCarthy, scientist Marvin Minsky, social scientist Herbert Simon and other leading researchers of machine learning in the 1940s and 1950s, set in motion what is now widely known as the field of "artificial intelligence" or "AI."[4] By the mid-1960s, pioneers of the emerging field of AI were predicting that robots would soon be able to match or exceed human cognitive capabilities. While matching generalized human intelligence proved to be much harder than predicted and continues to be a work in progress, substantial advances in AI continue to be made. Machine capabilities now encompass speech recognition, computer vision, and different types of machine learning as computer scientists continue to discover and improve on new ways of replicating and augmenting human intelligence.[5]

Rather than simply serving as intelligent tools to be used by humans in their cognitive pur-

---

[1] Edmund Berkeley, *Giant Brains, Or Machines that Think*: reprinted in Gil Press, *A Very Short History of Artificial Intelligence*, Forbes Magazine (30 Dec 2016).

[2] *Rise of the Machines*, The Economist (9 May 2015).

[3] See e.g. O. Shani, *From Science Fiction to Reality: The Evolution of Artificial Intelligence*, WIRED at https://www.wired.com/insights/2015/01/the-evolution-of-artificial-intelligence/.

[4] See e.g. Shani, *id.* The term "artificial intelligence" is attributed to John McCarthy, who included the term in a proposal for a now well known workshop in 1955 on artificial intelligence. See http://www-formal.stanford.edu/jmc/history/dartmouth/dartmouth.html; see also discussion in Press, *supra* note 1.

[5] See e.g. *Experts Predict When Artificial Intelligence will Exceed Human Performance*, MIT Technology Review (31 May 2017) (AI experts predict that some tasks, such as translating languages and driving trucks, will be automated within the next ten years, while others, such as performing surgery, will be much later).

suits, some machines have become more active and self-directed participants in processes of discovery. Machines work with varying degrees of autonomy as collaborators with humans in areas as diverse as the design of new materials, optimization of manufacturing processes, drug discovery, and the design of new household products. While machines can augment human cognitive capabilities, they can also perform "intelligent" tasks on their own and, in some cases, they can and do create their own inventions. Machines with AI—what I refer to in this chapter generally as thinking machines—are generating new discoveries in ways that make them, rather than their human counterparts, the sources of invention. An early example of a machine that makes inventions is the Creativity Machine, invented by Dr. Thaler in 1994, a machine that uses artificial neural networks to generate patentable inventions with minimal human intervention.[6] A second example is the Invention Machine, invented by futurist Dr. Koza, a machine that uses genetic programming based AI modeled on biological evolution to generate patentable inventions.[7]

This chapter focuses on the challenges that a thinking machine paradigm of invention—one in which thinking machines play significant and sometimes dominant or even solo roles in the invention process—creates for U.S. patent law.[8] It examines the disconnect between a thinking machine paradigm and the traditional model of inventor and invention that lies at the heart of patent law, explores some of the doctrinal challenges and practical problems that result from this disconnect, and concludes with four considerations to inform a patent policy response.

II.   THINKING MACHINE PARADIGM OF INVENTION

A.   Emergence of "Thinking Machines"

> Machines will follow a path that mirrors the evolution of humans. . . Ultimately, however, self-aware, self-improving machines will evolve beyond humans' ability to control or even understand them.
> Ray Kurzweil (2010)[9]

Glimmers of the possibility of thinking machines came as early as the 1830s, with the

---

[6]   See Imagination Engines Inc. Home Page at http://imagination-engines.com/iei_founder. php. See also Robert Plotkin, *The Genie In The Machine: How Computer-Automated Inventing Is Revolutionizing Law and Business* (Stanford University Press 2009) (refers to era of computer-automated invention as the Artificial Invention Age, suggests role of human inventors will be to formulate high level descriptions of problems to be solved).

[7]   See e.g. Jonathon Keats, *John Koza Has Built an Invention Machine*, POPULAR SCI. (18 Apr. 2006), http://www.popsci.com/scitech/article/2006-04/john-koza-has-built-invention-machine.

[8]   This chapter builds on an earlier analysis of how thinking machines might impact patent law in L. Vertinsky and T. Rice, *Thinking About Thinking Machines: The Implications of Thinking Machines for Patent Law* 8 B.U. J. Sci. and Tech. L. 574 (2002). See also Ryan Abbott, *I Think, Therefore I Invent: Creative Computers and the Future of Patent Law*, 57 B.C.L. Rev. 1079 (2016) and S. Yanisky-Ravid and X. Liu, *When Artificial Intelligence Systems Produce Inventions: The 3A Era and an Alternative Model for Patent Law*, 39 Cardozo Law Review 2215 (2018).

[9]   Larry Greenemeier, *What the Future Holds – Machine Self-awareness* 302 Scientific American 44–45 (June 2010) (quoting futurist Ray Kurzweil).

work of mathematician Charles Babbage on then revolutionary ideas of an "analytical engine." In 1936 Alan Turing created theoretical designs for a form of generalized computer intelligence, designs that we now know of as the Turing machine. These early efforts were directed largely at trying to copy generalized human intelligence, but AI researchers now also focus on the design of intelligent tools to augment human capabilities and expert systems that are focused on narrower intellectual tasks.[10] Modern AI can be understood as encompassing "a vast range of technologies – like traditional logic and rules-based systems – that enable computers and robots to solve problems in ways that at least superficially resemble thinking."[11] At the core of AI is "massive, intuitive computing power: machines so smart that they can learn and become even smarter."[12] As AI capabilities have expanded, machines have been created that can do increasingly complex and creative tasks. We now have robots such as Kismet that can recognize and simulate human emotions, robots like ASIMO that can walk as fast as people and deliver trays in restaurant settings, robot artists like AARON and robot composers such as Wavenet.[13] Computer Deep Blue defeated the world's reigning chess champion, Watson competed and won on the game show *Jeopardy*, and AlphaGo became a Go champion.[14] Autonomous driving cars outperform human drivers.[15] In Japan there is even an AI director sitting on the board of a venture capital firm.[16] Of most relevance to this chapter, we also have robot scientists such as Eve, a system used in drug development designed to identify promising compounds to fight drug resistant malaria,[17] and serial thinking machine "inventors" like the Creativity Machine and the Invention Machine.[18]

The wide ranging capabilities and applications of AI technologies are transforming the ways in which innovation occurs and, in doing so, are altering the relationship between humans and machines in the discovery of new inventions. In some cases thinking machines

---

[10]   See e.g. J. Guszeza, H. Lewis and P. Greenwood, *Cognitive Collaboration: Why Humans and Computers think better together*, Delloitte Insights Report, 23 January 2017 at https://dupress.deloitte.com/dup-us-en/deloitte-review/issue-20/augmented-intelligence-human-computer-collaboration.html.

[11]   See R. Parloff, *Why Deep Learning is Suddenly Changing Your Life,* Fortune (28 Sept. 2016) at http://fortune.com/ai-artificial-intelligence-deep-machine-learning/.

[12]   Editorial Board, *Artificial intelligence isn't the scary future. It's the amazing present*, Chicago Tribune, (1 January 2017).

[13]   See A. Ramalho, *Will robots rule the (artistic) world? A proposed model for the legal status of creations by artificial intelligence systems* 21 Journal of Internet Law 12 (2017); Press, *supra* note 1 (describes evolution of thinking robots and examples); A. Guadamuz, *Do Androids Dream of Electric Copyright? Comparative Analysis of Originality in Artificial Intelligence Generated Works,* 2 Intellectual Property Quarterly (2017).

[14]   See e.g. discussion in Press, *supra* note 1.

[15]   See e.g. T. Simonite, *Data Shows Google's Robot Cars Are Smoother, Safer Drivers Than You or I*, MIT Technology Review (25 October 2013) at https://www.technologyreview.com/s/520746/data-shows-googles-robot-cars-are-smoother-safer-drivers-than-you-or-i/.

[16]   See e.g. E. Zolfagharifard, *Would you take orders from a Robot? An artificial intelligence becomes the world's first company director*, Daily Mail (19 May 2014).

[17]   See e.g. K Williams et al, *Cheaper Faster Drug Development Validated by the Repositioning of Drugs Against Neglected Tropical Diseases* 12 Journal of the Royal Society (2015) at http://rsif.royalsocietypublishing.org/content/12/104/20141289.

[18]   See e.g. Abbott, *supra* note 8 (describes the Creativity Machine and Invention Machine and the patented inventions attributed to them).

are harnessed for purely mechanical or computational tasks, while in others they are employed more directly and autonomously in the problem solving process. Rather than simply using machines as tools, humans are increasingly co-working with machines.[19] While humans still play a dominant role in the inventive process, and while some human input is still needed for even the most autonomous problem solving machines, the relative contributions of humans and machines to invention are changing—sometimes rapidly— as thinking machine capabilities grow.

As the role of the machine in the process of problem solving becomes larger and its actions more autonomous, it may become increasingly difficult to attribute resulting discoveries solely or even partially to human contributors. In some cases the machine may replace the human entirely in the process of invention, as demonstrated by the Creativity Machine that was invented by Dr. Thaler in 1994. The Creativity Machine is a computer that uses artificial neural networks to produce novel ideas. In 1998 Dr. Thaler was granted a patent for a neural-network-based prototype system and method that he later told his colleagues was autonomously invented by the Creative Machine, and subsequent patents have been issued for other inventions attributed to this machine.[20] Dr. John Koza, who is known for his efforts to automate the creative process through genetic programming, is another early creator of thinking machines and the inventor of the Invention Machine. Dr. Koza was granted a patent in 2005 for a system for making factories more efficient, a discovery attributed solely to the Invention Machine, and this machine has gone on to make other patented discoveries.[21] Since these early examples there have been other thinking machines generating patentable inventions, although none of the resulting patents have listed the machines as inventors.[22]

B.   Changing the Invention Paradigm

> . . .in not too many years, human brains and computing machines will be coupled together
> very tightly, and . . . the resulting partnership will think as no human brain has ever thought
> and process data in a way not approached by the information-handling machines we know
> today.
>
> J.C.R. Licklider (1960)[23]

---

[19]   See e.g. Definition: Machine-human collaboration, at http://whatis.techtarget.com/defini tion/machine-human-collaboration; Terence Brake, *Human-Machine Collaboration: The Machine as Talent*, TMA World (5 May 2015) at http://www.tmaworld.com/our-thinking/human-machine-collaboration-machine-talent (suggests that as cognitive technologies continue to develop, machines are now being thought of as talent, not just people).

[20]   See discussion of patents on inventions attributed to thinking machines in Abbott, *supra* note 8.

[21]   See e.g. John Carnett and Eric Heinz, *John Koza has Built an Invention Machine*, Popular Science (19 April 2006) at http://www.popsci.com/scitech/article/2006-04/john-koza-has-built-invention-machine (claimed to be the first patent granted to a non-human designer).

[22]   See discussion of patents on inventions attributed to thinking machines in Abbott, *supra* note 8.

[23]   J.C.R. Licklider, *Man-Computer Symbiosis, IRE Transactions on Human Factors in Electronics*, Vol. HFE-1, p.1 at https://groups.csail.mit.edu/medg/people/psz/Licklider.html. Quoted in Arati

Results generated by computers without any material human interventions in the problem solving process already compete with human performance in a number of fields, including computational molecular biology, computational chemistry, electrical engineering and robotics to name a few.[24] The pervasive and growing role of thinking machines in research and development is transforming the ways in which inventions are being discovered. Instead of human inventors, their "fire of genius" fueled by the self-interest of profiting from discovery, thinking machines can be programmed to work tirelessly in the search for new inventions. This transformation of the invention process creates a number of challenges for the traditional paradigm of invention on which U.S. patent law and policy are based.

I refer to the emerging model of invention, in which thinking machines are playing substantial and in some cases dominant roles in the discovery of inventions, as the thinking machine paradigm. This thinking machine paradigm is characterized by an increased speed and reduced cost of invention, changes in the nature and volume of invention, and an increasingly autonomous and significant role for AI in the invention process.

The exponential increase in the speed and decrease in the cost of computer processing power has been a key enabler of the thinking machine paradigm. Moore's Law, which forecasts that processor power will double every two years, has held true for over half a century, and although this growth may perhaps be slowing to a halt, by some estimates there has already been a one trillion-fold increase in computing power between 1956 and 2015.[25] In June 2008 a supercomputer called Roadrunner built by IBM became the first computer to achieve sustained operating speeds of one petaflop, allowing it to process more than a quadrillion calculations per second.[26] At the same time as the power, and thus the speed, of computing has gone up, the cost has gone down. By some estimates computing power per dollar has increased by a factor of ten approximately every four years over the last 25 years.[27] As a result of these trends in computing power and cost, thinking machines are able to do some tasks much faster and cheaper than their human counterparts and are capable of doing other tasks that exceed the capabilities of their human counterparts.

As computing costs fall and computing speed and capabilities increase, the volume of inventions will increase too, potentially dramatically. There will be an acceleration in the pace and an expansion in the scope of discovery as new techniques for defining and solving questions of human interest through the use of AI continue to be developed and advances are made both in the ability to reduce concrete, real world problems into machine solvable forms and in using machines to solve open-ended, less structured and

---

Prabhakar, *The merging of humans and machines is happening now*, WIRED Magazine (27 January 2017) at http://www.wired.co.uk/article/darpa-arati-prabhakar-humans-machines.

24 See John R. Koza, *Human-Competitive Machine Intelligence*, at http:///www.genetic-program ming.com.

25 See A. Sneed, *Moore's Law Keeps Going, Defying Expectations*, Scientific American (19 May 2015); *Processing Power Compared* at http://pages.experts-exchange.com/processing-power-compared/. But see T. Simonite, *Moore's Law is Dead. Now What?*, MIT Technology Review (13 May 2016) at https://www.technologyreview.com/s/601441/moores-law-is-dead-now-what/.

26 See e.g. J. Markoff, *Military Supercomputer Sets Record*, New York Times (9 June 2008).

27 See e.g. *Trends in the Cost of Computing, AI Impacts* (10 March 2015) (reviews current empirical work on cost of computing trends) at http://aiimpacts.org/trends-in-the-cost-of-computing/.

parameterized problems.[28] Greater leveraging of thinking machine capabilities and more efficient use of existing information will be enabled by new program structures and solution approaches that can be applied to solve a variety of different problems in related and unrelated fields. In addition to an impact on volume, the use of thinking machines as discovery tools could result in changing patterns of invention. Existing AI technologies may be better at tackling some types of problems and not others, leading to a concentration of inventions and proliferation of patents in those categories where AI capabilities work best. Expanded AI technologies may also enable new types of discoveries that do not fit easily into existing categories. Finally, if and when the predictions made by many AI scientists are realized, thinking machines will have the ability to generate discoveries that are beyond human understanding, leading to entirely new types of inventions.

The biggest challenge of all to the existing paradigm of invention, however, is the substitution of the thinking machine for the human as inventor. In some cases thinking machines will augment the capabilities of a human problem solver, much as smart technologies like GPS augment our ability to navigate. In other cases the thinking machine will operate autonomously in defining, refining, and even solving a problem. The level of machine involvement in the invention process will vary, falling along a spectrum from machine as computational or mechanical aide at one end to machine as source of discovery at the other, and the line between what the machine produces and what is attributable to human cognitive capabilities may be difficult to draw. But there will be many instances in which it is clear that the machine, and not the human, is the source of the invention.

These features of the thinking machine paradigm—low cost and high speed, increased volume and altered nature of invention, and changes in the role and relationship of human and machine, could yield inventions produced by machine "inventors" that patent law does not recognize as inventors on a scale and of a nature that the patent system is not equipped to deal with.

III.   CHALLENGES FOR PATENT LAW

> Once we have figured out how to build artificial minds with the average human IQ of 100, before long we will build machines with IQs of 500 and 5,000 . . . And in time, we will build such machines—which will be unlikely to see much difference between humans and houseplants.
> David Gelernter (2017)[29]

The pervasive role of thinking machines in processes of invention creates challenges for patent law at conceptual, doctrinal, and practical levels. It challenges the conceptual underpinnings of a patent law system that has since its inception focused on providing incentives

---

[28]   See e.g. Ray Kurzweil, *The Age Of Spiritual Machines* (Viking Press 1999) 82–83 ("Increasingly, we will be building our intelligent machines by breaking complex problems. . .into smaller subtasks, each with its own self-organizing paradigm.")

[29]   David Gelernter, *Machines that Will Think and Feel: Artificial Intelligence is still in its Infancy – and that should scare us*, Wall Street Journal (18 March 2016).

to human inventors in order to further the progress of science and the useful arts.[30] It raises doctrinal questions about how to apply existing rules to scenarios of invention not contemplated in the current design of patent law. And it raises practical questions about whether the patent system can handle the volume and types of inventions that human-machine collaborations have the potential to generate. I begin with the conceptual disconnect and then explore some of the doctrinal and practical challenges which result.

A.   Conceptual Disconnect

Abraham Lincoln, one of the early supporters of the U.S. patent system, is famously quoted for his justification of the patent system as one which secured "to the inventor for a limited time exclusive use of his inventions, and thereby added the fuel of interest to the fire of genius in the discovery and production of new and useful things."[31] Despite the many changes that have taken place in patent law since the first U.S. patent act, the Patent Act of 1790, modern patent law continues to retain an attachment to this idea of the lone genius who applies his or her skill and intellect to solve problems and make discoveries that have evaded existing experts in the field.[32]

The primary justifications for the U.S. patent system remain utilitarian ones. Patents provide potential inventors with incentives to make inventions in return for limited exclusive rights over their inventions. This is known as the reward theory of invention and it has proven to be remarkably enduring as one of the dominant justifications for the patent system. Patents are also provided as a quid pro quo in exchange for the disclosure of inventions to the public. In addition to these ex ante justifications, patents are often justified as important mechanisms for ensuring the subsequent commercialization of inventions by inventors or their licensees and assignees.[33] Although justified largely in utilitarian terms, the patent system has also been strongly influenced by a belief in individual incentives and rewards that is somewhat Lockean in nature, fueling the attachment of patent law policy and doctrine to the rights and interests of the human inventor.[34]

The patent system is designed to sort out those discoveries that are, in the words of early advocate Thomas Jefferson, "worthy of the embarrassment of a patent," from those

---

[30]   Under Article I, section 8, the U.S. Constitution reads, "Congress shall have power. . . to promote the progress of science and useful arts, by securing for limited times to authors and inventors the exclusive right to their respective writings and discoveries." See U.S. Constitution, Article I, Section 8.

[31]   See quote and surrounding context at Gene Quinn, *Celebrating Presidents Who Advocated for the US Patent System* at http://www.ipwatchdog.com/2013/02/18/celebrating-presidents-who-advocated-for-the-u-s-patent-system/id=34896/; Abraham Lincoln, *Lecture "Discoveries, Inventions and Improvements"* (22 Feb 1860) in G. Nocolay and J. Hay (eds), *Complete Works of Abraham Lincoln* (1894), Vol. 5, 113 in Eugene C. Gerhart, *Quote it Completely!* (1998), 802, quotes on https://todayinsci.com/L/Lincoln_Abraham/LincolnAbraham-Quotations.htm.

[32]   See e.g. discussion of the traditional paradigm in L. Vertinsky, *Boundary-Spanning Collaboration and the Limits of the Joint-Inventorship Doctrine* 55 Houston Law Review 401 (2017).

[33]   See e.g. Timothy R. Holbrook, *Possession in Patent Law*, 59 SMU L. Rev. 123, 131–36 (2006) (discusses these alternative utilitarian theories of patents).

[34]   See e.g. Adam Mossoff, *Rethinking the Development of Patents: An Intellectual History 1550-1800* 52 Hastings L.J. 1255, 1315 (2001).

that are not.[35] To be patentable, the invention must be a product of human ingenuity rather than simply discovery of existing facts or features about the world or an obvious extrapolation from existing knowledge. Natural phenomena, laws of nature, and abstract ideas are not patentable subject matter. Moreover, only those discoveries that are sufficiently novel and different from things that are already known or easily discoverable are considered to be patentable. These basic requirements of patentable subject matter, novelty, and non-obviousness are set out in the current U.S. Patent Act.[36]

When determining when an invention has been made, and by who, courts focus on the ideas occurring in the minds of human inventors. The touchstone of inventorship is conception of the invention,[37] where conception is defined as "[f]ormation in the mind of the inventor of a definite and permanent idea of the complete and operative invention."[38] The conception is complete "only when the idea is so clearly defined in the inventor's mind that only ordinary skill would be necessary to reduce the invention to practice, without extensive research or experimentation."[39] This approach to invention, with its emphasis on the mind of the inventor, reinforces the primacy of the human inventor in patent law. Invention is treated as a mental act occurring in the mind of the inventor, with patents serving as mechanisms for rewarding the inventors who disclose their inventions to the public.[40] The dividing line between what is patentable and what is simply an obvious extension of existing knowledge is similarly grounded in an analysis of the mental act of the inventor, involving a comparison between what a person having ordinary skill in the art (known as the PHOSITA) would have been able to discover without unusual effort and the additional leap of human ingenuity made by the inventor. Once an inventor obtains a patent, it has "the attributes of personal property."[41] The patent owner, who at least initially is the inventor, is given the right to exclude others from making, using, offering for sale, selling, or importing into the U.S. the invention.[42]

---

[35]   See Letter from Thomas Jefferson to Isaac McPherson (13 Aug. 1813) at http://press-pubs. uchicago, edu/founders/documents/a1_8_8s12.html ("Considering the exclusive right to invention as given not of natural right, but for the benefit of society, I know well the difficulty of drawing a line between the things which are worth to the public the embarrassment of an exclusive patent, and those which are not.").

[36]   U.S. Patent Act – 35 USC Sects. 1–376. See 35 USC 101 – Inventions patentable; 35 USC 102 – Conditions for patentability – novelty, and 35 USC 103 – Conditions for patentability: non-obvious subject matter.

[37]   See e.g. *Burroughs Wellcome v. Barr Labs, Inc.*, 40 F.3d 1223, 1227 (Fed. Cir. 1994) ("Conception is the touchstone of inventorship, the completion of the mental part of invention.").

[38]   *Mergenthaler v. Scudder*, 11 App. D.C. 264, 1897 CD 724 (C.A.D.C. 1897); quoted in *Burroughs Wellcome v. Barr Labs. Inc.*, 40 F.3d 1223, 1227 (Fed. Cir. 1994) and in *Hybritech v. Monoclonal Antibodies, Inc.*, 802 F.2d 1367, 1376 (Fed. Cir. 1986).

[39]   *Sewall v. Walters*, 21 F.3d 411, 415 (Fed. Cir. 1994).

[40]   For an early summary of this traditional theory of patents, see Fritz Machlup, *An Economic Review of the Patent System*, Study No. 15, Subcommittee on Patents, Trademarks, and Copyright of the Senate Committee on the Judiciary, 85th Cong. 2d Sess 1, 33 (1958). See also R. Mazzoleni and R. Nelson, *The benefits and costs of strong patent protection: A Contribution to the current debate*, 27 Research Policy 273 (1999) (advances reward theory of patents pursuant to which patents preserve incentives to make and commercialize inventions).

[41]   35 USC Section 261 – Ownership; Assignment.

[42]   35 USC Section 154(a)(1).

This conceptual approach to the patent system, with its roots in utilitarian schemes for fueling the "fire of genius" in inventors and its focus on the ideas formed in the mind of the inventor, leaves little room for including machines as inventors. The justifications for patents, grounded as they are on the need to reward human inventors for their inventive and commercialization efforts and disclosure of their results, does not readily extend to machines that can simply be programmed to pursue their tasks and disclose their results. The focus of patent law on the ideas in the mind of the inventor rather than on the results generated also makes it difficult to accommodate machine inventors since we do not (or at least not yet) attribute cognition to machines.

Despite advances made in AI and the growing role of thinking machines in many research and development activities, patent law continues to focus on the role of human ingenuity both in determining whether an invention has been made and in distinguishing it from discoveries that an ordinary person of skill in the art would produce. This conceptual disconnect between the model of invention on which patent law is based and the thinking machine paradigm of invention leads to doctrinal challenges such as those discussed below. While human ingenuity must ultimately play a different role in patent law where humans have the ability to harness thinking machines to augment their thought processes or to replace them altogether in the discovery process, this leaves open the as of yet unanswered questions of what to replace human ingenuity with as a touchstone of invention and how to adjust the doctrinal framework in response.

B. Doctrinal Challenges

Patent law presumes and is designed to fit an underlying paradigm of market based, producer driven invention that has the individual inventor at its center.[43] This paradigm rests fairly heavily on "the canonical story of the lone genius inventor," with its romantic idea "that a lone genius can solve problems that stump experts, and that the lone genius will do so only if strongly incented."[44] The modern statutory framework for patent law continues to define invention as a mental act occurring in the mind of the inventor, with patents serving as mechanisms for rewarding those inventors who make inventions and disclose them to the public.[45] The patent also furthers the ability of the inventor to commercialize his or her invention, either directly or through licensing or selling it to another person or company. The Patent Act does not contemplate, nor address, the possibility of patentable inventions that are generated by machines. As a result, a number of doctrinal problems arise when trying to fit machine-generated inventions into the existing statutory framework, the most obvious of which is the problem of determining who the inventor of a machine-generated invention is for patent law purposes.

---

[43] See e.g. Peter Lee, *Social Innovation* 92 Washington University Law Review 1 (2014) (article "highlights and challenges the narrow, particularized conception of innovation embedded in patent law. . .[which is] individualistic, discrete, novel, and objectively reproducible.").

[44] See e.g. Mark Lemley, *The Myth of the Sole Inventor* 110 Mich. L. Rev. 709 (2012).

[45] For an early summary of this traditional theory of patents, see e.g. Machlup, *supra* note 40. See also Mazzoleni and Nelson, *supra* note 40.

1.   Who is the inventor?

Where a machine autonomously generates an invention, or even many inventions—as the Creativity Machine and Invention Machine have done—who is the inventor for patent law purposes? Where a human collaborates closely with a machine in the making of an invention, each making separate material contributions to the resulting invention, are they joint inventors? What degree of contribution is required from the human in order to attribute inventorship to the human when the machine appears to be doing most of the work that results in the invention—is it enough that the human created the machine, programed it, defined the problem to be solved, provided data for the machine to use, and/or was the first human to see and recognize the result? If these tasks were all performed by different people, would any or all of them have a claim to the resulting machine-generated invention? Lastly, should we worry if the machine inventor is itself patented? These are all questions that thinking machine "inventors" raise for patent law, and the ways in which they are answered will have potentially significant consequences both for patent law and for innovation. But patent policymakers have yet to provide any guidance on how to handle computer-generated inventions.[46]

The questions of who is the inventor of a machine-generated invention for patent law purposes, or whether an invention that is generated by a machine can be patented at all, have not been explicitly addressed in the Patent Act or in guidance from courts or the U.S. Patent and Trademark Office (USPTO).[47] Although there is no provision in patent law that explicitly requires a human inventor as a requirement for obtaining a patent, however, there are many provisions that presume or implicitly require one or more human inventors.[48]

Congressional power to grant patents is derived from Article 1 of the U.S. Constitution, which provides that "Congress shall have the Power To . . . promote the Progress of Science and useful Arts, by securing for limited Times to Authors and Inventors the exclusive Right to their respective Writings and Discoveries. . .".[49] While "Inventor" is not defined in the Constitution, this provision along with the underlying early justifications

---

[46]   See e.g. Abbott, *supra* note 8 (no guidance from patent law on how to handle machine created inventions).

[47]   But see S. Johnson, *America's always had black inventors – even when the patent system explicitly excluded them*, The Conversation (19 Feb. 2017) at https://theconversation.com/americas-always-had-black-inventors-even-when-the-patent-system-explicitly-excluded-them-72619 (The patent system did not apply for black Americans born into slavery, rendering slave-generated inventions unpatentable. Applications filed by slave owners listing themselves as inventors were rejected since they did not name the actual inventor. In 1857 the US commissioner of patents officially ruled that slave inventions could not be patented).

[48]   See U.S. Constitution Article I, Section 8, Clause 8 "The Congress shall have Power To. . .promote the Progress of the Science and useful Arts, by securing for limited Times to the Authors and Inventors the exclusive Right to their respective Writings and Discoveries. . .". See also 35 USC 100(f) "The term "inventor" means the individual or, if a joint invention, the individuals collectively who invented or discovered the subject matter of the invention." 35 USC 101 Inventions Patentable – "Whoever invents or discovers. . .".

[49]   Article 1, Section 8, Clause 8, U.S. Constitution

for establishing the patent system presume a human inventor with the capacity to hold and benefit from this right.[50]

Section 100 of the Patent Act defines an inventor as "an individual or, if a joint invention, the individuals collectively who invented or discovered the subject matter of the invention."[51] Joint inventions are defined as inventions made by two or more persons jointly.[52] Patent applications must name the inventor(s) and each inventor must execute an oath stating that "such individual believes himself or herself to be the original inventor or an original joint inventor of a claimed invention in the application."[53] Inventors are the initial owners of their patented inventions and are granted the right to enforce their patents, license or transfer them.[54] The Patent Act, which provides the statutory framework governing patents, thus clearly contemplates individuals who have legal capacity to own and transfer property.

Case law reinforces the notion that only humans can be inventors under current patent law. In the well-known case of *Diamond v Chakrabarty* the U.S. Supreme Court suggests that the Patent Act embodies the philosophy of one of its early proponents, Thomas Jefferson, that "ingenuity should receive a liberal encouragement", ultimately finding the respondent's micro-organism patentable because it was "a product of human ingenuity."[55] In its review of statutory history the Court finds that "Congress intended statutory subject matter to include "anything under the sun that is made by man."[56] The grounding of rights in the "individual" even excludes legal entities such as corporations because "people conceive, not companies."[57]

In addition to these references to the individual as the source and initial owner of his or her invention, the focus of the law on ideas in the mind of the inventor rather than on just the resulting discoveries creates a barrier for treating machines as inventors. Courts look for the conception of the invention in the mind of the inventor, although relying on external corroboration of conception for proof that conception occurred. Indeed, for many years federal courts even employed a "flash of genius" test when evaluating patentability, holding that "the inventive act had to come into the mind of an inventor in a flash of genius, not as the result of tinkering."[58] This flash of genius test was rejected by Congress in its 1952 revisions to the Patent Act, where it sought to refocus attention on the results rather than the nature of the invention process by amending Section 103 of the Patent Act to specify that "[p]atentability shall not be

---

[50]   See Johnson, *supra* note 47 (Slaves were not allowed to apply for or hold property, including patents, and their inventions were ultimately held unpatentable).

[51]   35 USC Section 100 (f) – Definitions.

[52]   35 USC Section 116 – Inventors.

[53]   35 USC Section 115 – Inventor's Oath or Declaration.

[54]   This can be contrasted with copyright law, which provides for (non-human) legal entities such as corporations to be treated as authors through the work for hire doctrine. 17 USC Section 201.

[55]   *Diamond v Chakrabarty*, 447 U.S. 303, 308–09 (1980).

[56]   *Id.*, 308.

[57]   *New Idea Farm Equipment Corporation v. Sperry Corporation and New Holland Inc.*, 916 F.2d 1561 (Fed. Cir. 1990).

[58]   *Cuno Engineering v. Automatic Devices*, 314 US 84 (1941) (formalized flash of genius doctrine).

negatived by the manner in which the invention was made." Despite this modification, however, both court decisions and USPTO implementing guidelines continue to
focus on conception, defined in terms of the mental acts of human inventors, as the
touchstone of invention. Thus, showing that the machine has engaged in the complete
performance of the mental part of the inventive act does not appear to satisfy the
current test for inventorship.

The challenges that current inventorship doctrine poses for machine inventions extend
to situations of machine-human collaboration that would, if the machine collaborator
was human, be considered under the joint inventorship doctrine. While patent law allows
for the possibility of joint inventorship, the Patent Act explicitly refers to joint invention
by two or more *persons* and does not seem to contemplate inventive contributions from
machine collaborators.[59] Joint inventorship doctrine also continues to focus on the minds
of the inventors, requiring original contributions from all of the joint inventors to the
conception of the invention, as well as contributions from each of the joint inventors
to at least one of the patent claims. The grounding of inventorship in conception of the
invention makes it difficult to determine inventorship where there is more than one mind
and where there are many different types of contributions to the resulting invention even
where the contributors are all humans. Indeed, the concept of joint inventorship has been
referred to repeatedly by courts and patent scholars as "one of the muddiest concepts in
the metaphysics of patent law."[60] Adding machine collaborators to the mix is likely to
make joint inventorship doctrine even muddier.

While the above analysis suggests that the Patent Act and the case law interpreting it
presume and even require a human inventor, there is currently no explicit prohibition
against treating a machine as an inventor or the patenting of an invention that is invented
by a machine.[61] This can be contrasted with copyright law, where the Copyright Office has
provided some initial guidance stating that works not originated by a human author are
not entitled to copyright registration.[62] The lack of an express prohibition against non-
humans as inventors within patent law seems to leave room for debate about what kind
of "mind" is required to establish conception of the invention, particularly since patents
have already been issued to cover inventions that were generated by machines—albeit not
with the machines listed as inventors in the patent applications or issued patents. Current
AI cannot match generalized human intelligence, and thinking machines lack the same
physical embodiment that some AI scientists say is critical to human thought. But as
machine capabilities evolve, there might come a time at which the distinctions between
human cognition and machine "cognition" are difficult to make. If machines were able to

---

[59]   See 35 USC Section 116 – Inventors, (a) Joint Inventions – "When an invention is made
by two or more persons jointly, they shall apply for a patent jointly and each make the required
oath. . .".

[60]   See e.g. *Mueller Brass Co. v Reading Industries Inc.*, 352 F. Supp. 1357, 1372 (E.D. Pa. 1972)
(referring to joint inventorship as "one of the muddiest concepts in the muddy metaphysics of the
patent law."). See also G. Sirilla, *How the Federal Circuit Clarified the "Muddy Concept" of Joint
Inventorship* 91 J. Pat. and Trademark Off. Society 509 (2009).

[61]   But see earlier discussion of patent law determination that inventions made by slaves are
not patentable. See e.g. Johnson, *supra* note 47.

[62]   See e.g. Compendium II of Copyright Office Practices, Section 503.03 (a) Works not
originated by a human author. At http://www.copyrightcompendium.com/#503.03.

reach a sufficiently human-like intelligence, something sufficiently similar to the human mind, it might enable translation of existing concepts and doctrines applicable to human inventors to machine inventors. Until then, however, and unless modifications are made to patent law to allow for this transition, it would seem as if a machine that generates an invention cannot be considered an inventor for patent law purposes. This opens the door to uncertainty about who can claim rights of inventorship, if any, on behalf of a thinking machine that creates an invention.

2.   Patentable subject matter, novelty, non-obviousness and enablement

To be patentable an invention must consist of patentable subject matter and it must be novel, non-obvious, and adequately disclosed.[63] The thinking machine paradigm of invention creates some challenges for the application of each of these requirements.

First, in order to even be considered for patent protection, the invention must consist of patentable subject matter. Section 101 of the Patent Act provides that "[w]hoever invents or discovers any new and useful process, machine, manufacture or composition of matter, or any new and useful improvement thereof, may obtain a patent therefor, subject to the conditions and requirements of this title."[64] This has been interpreted by the courts as encompassing as patentable subject matter "anything under the sun that is made by man" with the role of human ingenuity as a way of separating things that might be unpatentable laws of nature, natural phenomena, or abstract ideas from those discoveries that are the product of human "handiwork."[65] The line between patentable and non-patentable subject matter may be difficult to draw where instead of human handiwork, the algorithmic and computational underpinnings of machine inventions are exposed, revealing only small gaps between mathematical processes and their concrete application or small jumps between massive computation of existing facts about the world and a potentially new result.

Second, the invention must be novel in the sense that it has not been claimed by somebody else in a patent, described in a printed publication, or in public use, on sale, or otherwise available to the public before the filing of a patent for the claimed invention, with limited exceptions allowing for prior use by the inventor(s).[66] The thinking machine paradigm will generate its own novel questions to consider when trying to apply the requirement of novelty in a world where thinking machines are active in the invention process and constantly churning out results. Under existing patent law, with its focus on what would be available to a person of ordinary skill in the art, anything that is understandable to a thinking machine but not a person would not be treated as prior art. This would allow thinking machines to access and utilize existing discoveries that are

---

[63]   See 35 USC Section 101 – Patentable Subject Matter, 35 USC Section 102 – Conditions for patentability; novelty; 35 USC Section 103 – Conditions for patentability; non-obvious subject matter; 35 USC Section 112 – Specification.

[64]   35 USC Section 101 – Inventions patentable.

[65]   See *Diamond v Chakarbarty*, 447 US 303, 310 (1980) ("His discovery is not nature's handiwork, but his own; accordingly it is patentable subject matter under Section 101."). See also *Diamond v. Diehr*, 450 US 175 (1980) (examines patent subject matter eligibility of process of curing synthetic rubber that relied on mathematical formulas, finds this application eligible).

[66]   35 USC 102 – Conditions for Patentability: Novelty.

available to other machines but not accessible and understandable to people without such discoveries serving as prior art, something we might worry about if machines were to be treated as inventors. Where thinking machines instead expand what is understandable by humans, the universe of prior art may become much larger through the AI-enablement of disclosures, making it harder to establish novelty and therefore patentability. Any change to the status of machine as inventor within patent law could necessitate changes in the ways that we think about prior art and novelty. The concept of public availability and use might need to be revisited, for example, where thinking machines generate huge volumes of discoveries and make these discoveries available in ways easily accessible by machines but not understandable by people. There would be questions about what constitutes disclosure of subject matter where machines generate discoveries that are understandable only by other machines, and keeping track of prior art issues where thinking machines collaborate with a variety of people and other machines could become much harder to do.

Third, the invention must be non-obvious in the sense that "the differences between the claimed invention and the prior art are such that the claimed invention as a whole would have been obvious . . .to a person having ordinary skill in the art [the PHOSITA] to which the claimed invention pertains."[67] Non-obviousness is defined largely in terms of distinctions between the mental capabilities and knowledge of people of ordinary skill in the art and the mental act of the inventor. In its current form, the PHOSITA is clearly a human of ordinary skill in the art, not a machine. With thinking machines in the equation, however, policymakers might have to consider whether the PHOSITA should be modified to include thinking machines—perhaps some kind of machine/person combination or "M/PHOSITA." But if thinking machines were to be included in the analysis as part of the PHOSITA category, it would be difficult if not almost impossible to limit the expansiveness of non-obviousness determinations. Thinking machines are not necessarily limited by field in the same way as human experts, so the search would be more free-ranging and include a variety of different types of AI and access to a broader range of data. Machine-generated inventions may rely on similar or even identical starting algorithms and data sets, and there may be a significant degree of overlap between the results if they are described in the abstract, but little or no overlap if described in very specific, concrete terms. Little if anything might be considered patent eligible with this expansive approach to obviousness.

While it may make sense to limit obviousness determinations to those based on the PHOSITA (person of ordinary skill in the art), the presence of thinking machines nonetheless challenges this approach to determining patentability by expanding the range of things that a human aided by AI can discover without undue effort or experiment. In particular, thinking machines may expand the range of discoveries that are "obvious to try." Rationales that may support a conclusion of obviousness include "obvious to try," or "choosing from a finite number of identified, predictable solutions, with a reasonable expectation of success."[68] With thinking machines in the equation, the notion of what is obvious for a PHOSITA to try may expand dramatically. At some level many inventions

---

[67]   35 USC 103   Conditions for patentability; Non-obvious subject matter.
[68]   See USPTO Manual of Patent Examining Procedures Section 2143 Examples of Basic Requirements of a Prima Facie Case of Obviousness.

may simply be the result of massive computational power that allows for rapid trial and error searching, something that many thinking machines could do, while from the perspective of the PHOSITA without the aid of thinking machines the results produced may be surprising. Incorporating thinking machines into obviousness determinations even in this way, through an expanded view of what is "obvious to try" by a human aided by AI, will make it harder to show that an invention is non-obvious. This is not necessarily a bad thing if there is more inventive power and a larger volume of discoveries to deal with, but also not necessarily a good thing if almost all inventions are swept into the obviousness category and it becomes nearly impossible to patent anything. Shifting from the black box of human ingenuity to the operations of a thinking machine thus requires a rethinking of how to draw the line between what is viewed as the routine result of computation and what is treated as a novel and non-obvious contribution.[69]

Finally, an expanded role of thinking machines in the invention process might impact current tests of enablement. Under current patent law the patent application must include a description of the claimed invention that enables a person skilled in the art to make and use the invention—an enabling disclosure.[70] With the aid of a thinking machine, a person of ordinary skill in the art might be enabled to make and use an invention even with a very limited patent disclosure. AI-based enablement may thus allow for expanded patent scope for any given disclosure of the invention. AI-based enablement would impact both novelty and non-obviousness determinations in addition to the patent scope for any given disclosure. The resulting increase in patent scope could potentially result in fewer patent applications, since each application could cover more ground.

C. Practical Issues

Even if the conceptual and doctrinal barriers are overcome, the thinking machine paradigm promises to create some practical challenges for the administration of the patent system. The USPTO, the administrative agency charged with evaluating patent applications and granting patents, must confront growing volumes of patent applications, changing technologies, and a complex and expanding body of prior art. Patent practitioners must determine how to deal with thinking machine inventors and collaborators in drafting patent applications and how to advise clients on patent filing, enforcement and licensing strategies to protect the results of their own thinking machines, avoid liability for any infringement by their thinking machines, and identify and address infringement of their own AI technologies by other thinking machines. Practitioners might even need to confront partial or complete automation of the examination process if the USPTO harnesses the power of thinking machines in the patent examination process. Courts must confront doctrinal disconnects and explore new issues of patent validity and infringement in a landscape that is increasingly dominated by automated processes of invention. Here

---

[69]   For a discussion of PHOSITA as a policy choice see e.g. Mark Janis and Timothy Holbrook, *Patent Law's Audience* 97 Minnesota Law Review 72 (2012).

[70]   See 35 USC 112. See also USPTO Manual of Patent Examination Procedure 2164 – The Enablement Requirement.

I explore only a few of the logistical issues, concentrating on the impact of thinking machines on the USPTO's job of evaluating patent applications and granting patents.

An immediate logistical challenge is that of accommodating a growing volume of patent applications as thinking machines, with their ability to learn and the harnessing of low cost, high power computing, generate increasing numbers of patentable inventions. In 2015 the USPTO received 629,647 patent applications and granted 325,979 patents, almost double the applications received and grants made in 2000.[71] The volume of both patent applications and patents granted continues to grow, and an expansion of thinking machines in the process is likely to fuel even faster growth. Higher volumes of patent applications will negatively impact the speed of prosecution, the quality of screening and evaluation, and the ability of the USPTO to maintain and search prior art databases.

In addition to volume, the nature and complexity of the inventions could change, and the process by which inventions are discovered will change. Differences in the invention process could create difficulties in applying existing USPTO patent application examination and search procedures to evaluate machine-generated inventions. Greater technical understanding may be required to evaluate inventions generated by computers that have massive computational abilities and databases to draw upon. Thinking machines may be capable of generating results that are beyond the understanding of the people charged with evaluating them, requiring careful thought about whether to add new subject matter categories and new metrics for determining patentability. The thinking machine paradigm will require both familiarity with the nature of the machine processes and the ability to understand, interpret, and compare the claimed results. Finally, administrative requirements such as the requirement that the application be made by the inventor and include an oath from the inventor that he or she is the original inventor, and the requirement on applicants to disclose all information material to patentability, will need to be rethought where the invention is generated by a machine rather than a human inventor.[72]

In confronting these challenges, patent examiners will likely be forced to work with thinking machines much more extensively than they are already, raising a host of new questions about the role of machines in the patent examination process. The idea of harnessing thinking machines to aid in the review of patent applications offers both opportunities and challenges. Thinking machines can provide opportunities for improving the power and reducing the cost of the USPTO system of review and patent grants. Search for prior art can be automated even more than it is already. Ultimately thinking machine reviewers could be used to analyze the work of thinking machine inventors. These changes in the roles of human and machine will need to be carefully considered, and patent examination

---

[71]   U.S. Patent Statistics Chart Calendar Years 1963-2015 at https://www.uspto.gov/web/offices/ac/ido/oeip/taf/us_stat.htm.

[72]   See 35 USC 111 – Application (application shall be made by the inventor); 35 USC 115 – Inventor's oath or declaration (patent application must include the name of the inventor and an oath from the inventor that the inventor believes himself or herself to be the original inventor). See also 37 CFR 1.56 Duty to disclose information material to patentability ("Each individual associated with the filing and prosecution of a patent application has a duty of candor and good faith in dealing with the Office, which includes a duty to disclose to the Office all information known to that individual to be material to patentability as defined in this section.")

guidelines and procedures developed to fit greater machine-human collaboration at both the patent applicant and patent examiner side of the patent application process.

IV. CONSIDERATIONS IN FASHIONING A PATENT POLICY RESPONSE

> The short-term impact of AI depends on who controls it; the long-term impact depends on whether it can be controlled at all.
>
> Stephen Hawking[73]
>
> By around 2020 a $1,000 computer will at least match the processing power of the human brain. By 2029 the software for intelligence will have been largely mastered, and the average personal computer will be equivalent to 1,000 brains. . .Ultimately, nonbiological entities will master not only the sum total of their own knowledge but all of ours as well. As this happens, there will no longer be a clear distinction between human and machine.
>
> Ray Kurzweil (2008)[74]

Parts II and III of this chapter have highlighted a number of ways in which the thinking machine paradigm of invention challenges both the conceptual foundation and the doctrinal framework of patent law. In this concluding Part I suggest that the ways in which these challenges are addressed, or not addressed, will have important and sometimes unintended consequences, and I identify four considerations that should inform any patent policy response.

A. Distortions to Existing Patent Law Framework

The doctrinal challenges that thinking machine "inventors" create for patent law should be confronted directly rather than ignored or addressed through squeezing new scenarios uncomfortably into existing categories. A failure to do so could confuse, or distort, existing doctrines and their application. The urgency of careful thinking about how to handle thinking machine "inventors" and inventions in patent law is heightened by the potential impact of decisions in one area on other areas of law. Decisions about how to treat thinking machine "inventors" within patent law could impact other aspects of patent law, such as liability for the infringement caused by thinking machines, as well as other bodies of law, where questions about the legal capacity of thinking machines and the apportionment of rights over benefits and liability for harms they may produce are beginning to be debated.[75] The following two examples illustrate the distortions that could be created in the absence of a carefully considered patent law response to thinking machine invention.

First, consider the situation in which a thinking machine generates an invention that, if

---

[73] S. Hawking, S. Russell, M. Tegmark, and F. Wilcek, *Stephen Hawking: 'Transcendence looks at the implications of artificial intelligence – but are we taking AI seriously enough?'* Independent (1 May 2014) at http://www.independent.co.uk/news/science/stephen-hawking-transcendence-looks-at-the-implications-of-artificial-intelligence-but-are-we-taking-9313474.html.

[74] Ray Kurzweil, *Coming Merging of Mind and Machine*, Scientific American (23 March 2009) at https://www.scientificamerican.com/article/merging-of-mind-and-machine/.

[75] See e.g. Jack Balkin, *The Path of Robotics Law*, 6 California Law Review Circuit 45 (2015) (explores how to distribute the rights and responsibilities among humans of nonhuman actions);

it has been created by a human, would be patentable. The Patent Act in its current form does not seem to allow for a machine inventor, although it is not specifically prohibited, leaving several options for a machine invention. One option is to ignore the new paradigm and treat machine-generated inventions as unpatentable. This is the approach followed by the Copyright Office for machine-created works in copyright law—the Copyright Office guidance suggests that copyright registration will simply be unavailable for non-human created works. Doing so could result (and has resulted) in decisions not to disclose the machine origin but instead to name a human inventor. This approach creates subsequent problems for inventorship determinations. It is also in tension with the rules requiring an inventor's oath and requirements to disclose all known information material to patent-ability to the USPTO as part of the patent application process. Denying patentability to machine-generated inventions could also result in decisions to keep the resulting discoveries as trade secrets even though the discoveries would have been disclosed and patented if that option were made available.

A second option would be to duck some of the problems that machines as inventors create for patent law by allowing human contributor(s) to claim inventorship either directly or by simply not disputing the inventorship claims. This latter approach is essentially what has happened with existing machine inventions so far—patents have been issued for machine-generated inventions listing human inventors. But this approach leaves open important questions about what types of human contributions matter and how they should be compared. Potential claimants could include the human creator(s) of the machine, the resulting owners or licensees of the machine if different, the person or people defining the problem to be solved, and those providing training or data that enables the computer to make its invention. If these are all different people, potential inventorship disputes will be inevitable and the already complex and messy body of law that governs inventorship will become even more difficult to navigate. In addition, any departures from existing inventorship requirements that arise in resolving inventorship disputes among different AI stakeholders are likely to be applied beyond the immediate issue of machine invention, further muddying inventorship determinations in patent law. A third option is to change patent law to allow for machines to be considered inventors. This third approach would require other changes to patent law to address the many questions that would arise as soon as machines were granted exclusive rights to inventions, with potential effects on all aspects of the patent system and perhaps even beyond.

As a second example of how quickly distortions to the existing framework could arise, consider the stresses that thinking machines create for determinations of what is obvious, and non-obvious. Where thinking machines are utilized in the invention process, it raises the question of how, if at all, to incorporate thinking machines into the comparison group of persons of ordinary skill in the art. But if this comparison group includes machine-augmented thinking, this could increase the standard for patentability, making it harder for anybody to get a patent. It would seem arbitrary to limit machine-augmented obviousness determinations to situations of machine invention, but expanding the comparison group to include thinking machines for all inventions would have far reaching impact on

---

A. Armstrong, *AI-Driven Innovation: Can and Should it be Regulated?* IP Watchdog (4 May 2017) at http://www.ipwatchdog.com/2017/05/04/ai-driven-innovation-regulated/id=82750/.

inventions in areas where thinking machines are not being deployed. If, on the other hand, the comparison group does not include thinking machines, this could result in a standard that is too low, with patents issued for discoveries that would have been easy to discover for any person working with the routine aid of a thinking machine. Where AI favors some types of discoveries over others, either the machine-augmented obviousness standard or one that excludes thinking machines could result in differential standards across different industries and fields of invention.

These are just two examples of how either ignoring machine invention or squeezing machine "inventors" uncomfortably into the existing paradigm could both lead to distortions in the patent law framework, with potential impact on a broad range of inventions and inventors. Doctrinal choices will also have potentially significant distributional consequences, as discussed below.

B.   Distributional Consequences

Decisions about whether an invention that has been created by a machine is patentable and, if so, who owns the patent, can have important distributional consequences for stakeholders involved in all aspects of the thinking machine paradigm.[76] A machine-generated invention is the result not just of the machine, but also a long string of human (and possibly also other machine) contributors along the way. The machine is the product of human creation (at least for now), building on existing knowledge about how to construct a thinking machine. Designing thinking machines requires an investment of both financial and human capital. The thinking machine must be programmed to pursue a particular area, topic or problem and it must be provided with data to learn from and employ in its efforts to solve the problem it has been tasked with. The creator of the machine may be a different person or entity from the party using the computer to solve a particular problem and from the party providing the training data.

If the machine-generated invention is not patentable, then the invention can be protected as a trade secret or publicly disclosed for general use. This will limit the ability of those involved in developing and using the thinking machine to recoup their investments, making investments in AI directed at invention potentially less attractive. If the machine-generated invention is patentable, then decisions about who will own the patent on the machine-generated invention will impact the distribution of rewards from the invention. This distribution of rewards will impact the incentives of people in the process to continue their investments of financial, physical and human capital and will also impact the resources that they have available to continue their activities. While the parties involved may be able to bargain with each other to reallocate rewards in accordance with the contributions of resources required, the initial allocation of property rights will set the default rules and bargaining advantages, and transaction costs may impede the success of future bargaining. In addition, there is no guarantee

---

[76]   See e.g. Yanisky-Ravid and Liu, *supra* note 8 (develops the Multiplayer Model of AI systems as a way of reflecting and addressing distributional consequences of patent law and its outdated focus on an individual inventor). See also Abbott, *supra* note 8 (argues for treating machines as inventors as a way of incentivizing development of AI).

that any result of private ordering will lead to the best outcome from a social welfare perspective. The expanding role of thinking machines in innovation does not remove the need for human incentives but rather changes, and complicates, the incentive landscape in ways that need to be examined as part of any rule change as well as any decision to not change the rules.

C. Substitution Effects

There are at least two kinds of substitution effects to consider when exploring how patent law and policy should respond to machine inventors. The first is the substitution of machines for human employees and the ways in which existing approaches to intellectual property could exacerbate incentives to substitute machine for person. The second and related issue is the substitution of machine invention for human invention and the possible impact of this shift on subsequent patterns and types of innovation and on the population of human inventors.

Starting with the substitution of machine for human employee, there has been a great deal of public concern over the implications of AI for employment as the range of tasks that thinking machines can perform increases, with some predictions suggesting that AI could consume nearly half of all jobs in the U.S. in the not too distant future.[77] It is undisputable that some jobs are being lost to machines, which are cheaper and in some cases more reliable than their human counterparts in a variety of tasks such as automated translation services and machine telephone answering services.[78] Computers have become an increasingly attractive alternative to human labor as computational capacity has grown, the cost of computer processing power has declined, and the range of skills that can be automated has expanded. Computers can offer significant cost savings and some performance advantages over their human counter-parts, since they are not subject to any labor protections and can focus relentlessly on tasks beyond the scope or interest of humans. In the fashion industry, for example, fashion automatons have been promoted as "models without attitude," movies have featured digital actors, and AI has entered domains as diverse as life guarding, robotic surgery, and some aspects of law. The advantages of computers in the intellectual property realm can be striking. Computers cannot choose to move from one employer to another, making it easier for companies to protect trade secrets and appropriate the benefits of investing in robot/worker training. In addition, under the current patent law framework, thinking machines do not have any claim to their creative work and there is no obligation on the part of the owner to compensate the thinking machine for any discoveries made. In contrast, human employees have certain rights to the fruits of their intellectual endeavors that they must be persuaded to assign to their employer.

The second and related area of substitution is the substitution of thinking machines for humans in processes of invention. AI may substitute for human capacity in the invention

---

[77]   See e.g. C. Frey and M. Osborne, *The Future of Employment: How Susceptible are Jobs to Computerisation?* (Oxford study examining the probability of computerization of jobs and likely impact on US labor market).

[78]   See *Rise of the Machines*, The Economist (9 May 2015).

process as computers move into more cognitive domains and operate with increasing autonomy. As machine capabilities expand, machines may even have a range of capabilities that exceed human capabilities. Where humans are competing with machine inventors they may seek to move to fields in which thinking machines are less prevalent, or where the problems are less amenable to being solved with existing AI applications. While we do not now live in a world in which most inventions are machine made, we should think about how a patent system would work if we did.

D.   Access to Thinking Technologies

There are at least two kinds of access issues raised by the thinking machines paradigm. The first is access to the inventions that machines generate, and the second is access to the thinking machine technologies themselves. If thinking machines are able to generate a large volume of inventions relatively rapidly and cheaply, determinations about the patentability of those inventions and their resulting ownership will impact access to a large number of inventions. Decisions about patentability must balance the need to incentivize investments in the development and deployment of thinking machines to solve new problems against the costs of restricting access to larger and larger numbers of discoveries as the scope and/or volume of patents grows. This balancing of public and private interests and incentives, which does—or at least should—underlie current patent policy, needs to be recalibrated for a thinking machine paradigm of invention.

The second issue is more troubling. Before the Creative Machine generated its own inventions, its creator obtained a patent on the machine itself. The Invention Machine was similarly patented by its human creator. Over the past 25 years there has been a proliferation of patents covering AI technologies, including both platform technologies and specific applications. According to a World Intellectual Property Organization (WIPO) database, 3,054 patents on artificial intelligence were filed between 2007 and the start of 2017.[79] The ability to patent thinking machines and their "thinking" capabilities raises concerns about the scope of protection being afforded to processes of invention. Ideally platform technologies which serve as foundations for invention should be made widely available to enable further discovery. The replacement of thinking machines for human inventors, and the potential patentability of these thinking machines, could lead to a narrowing of access to processes of invention and a concentration of the returns from invention in the hands of those people and companies most active in creating foundational AI technologies. This potential concentration in inventive power should be taken seriously by both patent and antitrust policymakers since it could impact entry into and competition within existing markets as well as the creation of new markets. A review of the USPTO database shows that large technology companies such as IBM, Microsoft, Qualcomm and Siemens are among the leaders in terms of most AI patent applications.[80] What this data does not show is the actual pattern of control over the most foundational thinking

---

[79]   See e.g. M. Sloan and Y. He, *The Global Race for Artificial Intelligence – Comparison of Patenting Trends* (1 March 2017) at https://www.wilsoncenter.org/blog-post/the-global-race-for-artificial-intelligence-comparison-patenting-trends.

[80]   See e.g. ClearView IP report, *Examining Intellectual Property in a Growing AI Market* (14 Feb 2017) at http://www.clearviewip.com/ip-artificial-intelligence-market/.

machine technologies, those that do or will underlie future patterns of inventing. As the process of innovation becomes automated, the patenting of the innovators should be closely watched.

V.   CONCLUSION

Thinking machines are changing the process of invention and innovation in ways that increasingly challenge the patent system on conceptual, doctrinal, and practical levels. While patent policymakers have yet to engage with the issues that new paradigms of thinking machine invention create, changes are nonetheless occurring as a result of inaction. This chapter has identified some areas of disconnect between the existing patent system and a thinking machine paradigm of invention that is no longer science fiction, and it has suggested some considerations to guide a patent law and policy response.

SOURCES

Cases

Burroughs Wellcome Co. v. Barr Labs., Inc., 40 F.3d 1223 (Fed. Cir. 1994).
Mergenthaler v. Scudder, 11 App. D.C. 264, 1897 CD 724 (C.A.D.C. 1897).
Hybritech v. Monoclonal Antibodies, Inc., 802 F.2d 1367 (Fed. Cir. 1986).
Sewall v. Walters, 21 F.3d 411 (Fed. Cir. 1994).
Diamond v Chakrabarty, 447 U.S. 303 (1980).
New Idea Farm Equipment Corporation v. Sperry Corporation and New Holland Inc., 916 F.2d 1561 (Fed. Cir. 1990).
Cuno Engineering v. Automatic Devices, 314 US 84 (1941).
Mueller Brass Co. v Reading Industries Inc., 352 F. Supp. 1357 (E.D. Pa. 1972).
Compendium II of Copyright Office Practices, Section 503.03 (a).
Diamond v. Diehr, 450 U.S. 175 (1980).

Statutes

35 USC 100 (f) – Definitions.
35 USC 101 – Inventions Patentable
35 USC 102 – Conditions for Patentability: Novelty.
35 USC 103 – Conditions for Patentability; Non-Obvious Subject Matter.
35 USC 111 – Application.
35 USC 115 – Inventor's Oath or Declaration.
35 USC 116 – Inventors, (a) Joint Inventions.
35 USC 154 – Contents and Term of Patent; Provisional Rights, (a)(1) Contents.
35 USC 261 – Ownership; Assignment.
37 CFR 1.56 – Duty to Disclose Information Material to Patentability.
U.S. Constitution Article I, Section 8, Clause 8.
U.S. Patent Act – 35 USC Sects. 1–376.

19. Artificial Intelligence and the creative industry: new challenges for the EU paradigm for art and technology by autonomous creation
Madeleine de Cock Buning[1]

I. INTRODUCTION

Artificial Intelligence (AI) penetrates more and more into what is traditionally considered the domain of human creativity. Advanced research aims at technology that can operate autonomously in the real world that is capable of scene and context understanding and that can perceive, learn, decide and create without any human intervention. Already now there are robots that create better versions of robots and computer programmes that produce other computer programmes.[2] Although the ability to create is a quality that has traditionally been considered a human capacity, the increased quality and complexity of these systems as well as their learning abilities, shall ultimately render human intervention in the process of creation redundant. This makes the need to address creative agents and the challenges they bring evident.

Across policy domains, the current EU regulatory framework is more and more challenged by the impending arrival of robotics. These machines are becoming slowly but certainly part of our lives and cultural realization. In its policy documents on sustainable innovation, the European Commission recognizes that Autonomous Intelligence is the next step in the development of a sustainable information society.[3] The development of these systems is considered to be one of the most important challenges in Horizon 2020.[4] In the 2017 resolution by the European Parliament, several concerns are echoed with regard to the societal impact of the furthered levels of sophistication of smart robots, including their ability to self-learn from experience and by interaction.[5] The resolution

---

[1]   This chapters builds further on an earlier publication, Madeleine de Cock Buning, *Autonomous Intelligent Systems as Creative agents under the EU framework for Intellectual Property* 2 *EJRR* 310–22 (2016). Aydan Figaroa, Rosa Kindt, Roeland de Bruin, Godart van Ekeren and Stijn van Deursen have given valuable input to this contribution.

[2]   Tom Simonite, *AI Software Learns to Make AI Software* (2017), MIT Technology Review <https://www.technologyreview.com/s/603381/ai-software-learns-to-make-ai-software> (accessed 18 September 2017).

[3]   The Framework Programme for Research and Innovation, SEC (2011) 1427 and 1428 final, COM (2012) 808 final (Horizon 2020).

[4]   See the future annex 7 to the Decision, "Work Programme 2013, Cooperation Theme 3, ICT[. . .]", ECC(2012), draft available via http://cordis.europa.eu./fp7/ict/docs/draft-wp2013.doc, p. 9 (hereinafter: Work Programme 2013), 33–35.

[5]   Resolution by the European Parliament on Civil Law Rules on Robotics of February 16, 2017 http://www.europarl.europa.eu/sides/getDoc.do?pubRef=-//EP//NONSGML+TA+P8-TA-2017-0051+0+DOC+PDF+V0//EN (accessed 18 September 2017).

acknowledges the fact that in the future AI could surpass human intellectual capacities and it recognizes that some aspects of robotics might require specific consideration. It calls upon the Commission to "support a horizontal and technologically neutral approach to intellectual property law", including the reconsideration of the criteria for the object of copyright protection.

The focus of this contribution lies within the field of Intellectual Property protection for autonomous creation. It will illustrate the current state of affairs of Autonomous Intelligent Systems (AIS) as Creative Agents (CA) with several examples, showing the impressive advancement of technological innovation in this domain. The advancement in the level of complexity of such systems is making human intervention in the process of creation more and more redundant. This contribution looks into challenges that are encountered when a machine, and not a human, is the creative agent of a work.

The study of how the law might address all of these challenges lays bare fundamental questions raised by Artificial Intelligence, for us to better understand them.[6] Studying questions on machine creation and copyright law will show fundamental issues on the foundations of copyright, its fundamental notions and its object and subjects of protection.

AI is not merely a source for machine creation; such systems also largely depend on access to data and materials created by others.[7] Machine learning requires gigantic amounts of input of information that can be subject to protection under copyright or database law. Whether this access actually amounts to acts of reproduction that would require consent of the right owner of the protected materials will largely depend on the technology that is used.[8] The focus of this contribution is however on the *output* of autonomous creative agents. Furthermore, such output could either be an invention, potentially protected by patent law, or a work of authorship potentially protected by copyright law. In this contribution, we will look into the output that can be considered to fall inside the domain of works of authorship traditionally protected by copyright law, e.g. software, literature, works of art, music or choreography. Would it be possible to protect the output of machine creation under the current Regulatory EU copyright framework even when there is no human authorship? What is the fitness and adaptability of the current framework for these novel creations? Will these artefacts be protected against plagiarism? To whom or to which entity should such rights be attributed?

All of these questions will be addressed in this contribution. The second section of this chapter will elaborate on machine creation and its recent developments. In the third section the notion of creation as a human value will be explored within the EU Regulatory framework with its largely harmonized body of Copyright Directives. The legal requirements for copyright protection will be addressed, with a focus on the necessity of *human* creativity. This legal perspective will then be outlined to some notions on creativity in

---

[6]   Peter Asaro, "A Body to Kick But Still No Soul to Damn: Legal Perspectives on Robotics" in Patrick Lin, Keith Abney and George Baker (eds), *Robot Ethics: The Ethical and Social Implications of Robotics* (MIT Press 2012) 169.

[7]   Burkhard Schafer, *The future of IP Law in an age of Artificial Intelligence* 13(3) SCRIPTed 284 (2016).

[8]   Madeleine de Cock Buning and Roeland de Bruin, "Big data en het intellectuele eigendomsrecht" in Peter Blok (ed.), *Big data en het recht* (SDU Den Haag 2017).

other scientific disciplines. Since similar questions on acceptance have arisen upon the introduction of earlier technological innovation within copyright, this contribution also takes on a historical perspective in the fourth section. This is furthered in the fifth section that sheds light on the foundations under copyright, as well as on the fundamental rights involved. The sixth section will then look into the question of ownership. Which entity or person should be considered subject of such rights? Assessing all these above factors, some preliminary conclusions can be drawn in the seventh and last section.

II.   MACHINE CREATION

In order to comprehend the legal issue in front of us, this section sets the stage by pointing out the current already advanced state of affairs in machine creation. It looks into the current abilities of creative agents, and also the promising expectations for the future are indicated. Looking into machine creation powered by Artificial Intelligence we will consider the notion of Autonomous Intelligent Systems (AIS) as Creative Agents (CA).

A.   Autonomous Intelligent Systems

The notion of AIS consists of two elements. Firstly, *autonomy*, which is related to the level of control or involvement a human operator has in a system. Autonomy can be considered as the extreme on a spectrum on which the capacity to take decisions by the system is correlated to a proportional diminishing of human involvement.[9] The second element is *intelligence*, or the capacity to think. Intelligence can be described as "the capacity to adjust one's own behaviour to make it fit new circumstances, which included the capacity to learn, reason, solve problems, observe and understand language".[10] Intelligent machines are capable of extracting information from every source, in order to make recommendations based on their own calculation, and to make their own decisions and implement them without being instructed to do so. Currently the developments in AI already provide systems to carry out the cognitive tasks that people can do relatively easily, like vision, natural language understanding and "real-world reasoning".[11] Machines can perform these tasks and at the same time interact with each other and with humans. They are capable of understanding such communication and can anticipate and decide based on their previous experience. In the creation of such systems, the software-design will often include "neural networks".

---

[9]   Natasha McCarthy, *Autonomous Systems: Social, Legal and Ethical Issues* (Royal Academy of Engineering 2009) at 2; David Calverley, *Imagining a non-biological machine as a legal person* 22 AI & Soc 525, at 532 (2008).

[10]   Colin Davies, *An evolutionary step in intellectual property rights – Artificial intelligence and intellectual property* 27 Computer Law and Security Review 601 *et seq.*, at 603 (2011), Jack Copeland, "What is artificial Intelligence?", May 2000, available on the Internet at <http://www.alanturing.net/turing_archive/pages/Reference%20Articles/What%20is%20AI.html> (last accessed on 14 October 2015). Also: Lawrence Solum, *Legal Personhood for Artificial Intelligences* 70 North Carolina Law Review 1234–38 (1992).

[11]   Ernest Davies, *The Singularity and the State of the Art in Artificial Intelligence* Magazine Ubiquity (October 2014) https://www.cs.nyu.edu/davise/papers/singularity.pdf, p. 1 (last accessed on 14 October 2015).

The design of these networks is based on the assumption that all human behavior can be explained in terms of parallel activation of—and interaction between—huge amounts of neurons, as takes place in the human brain. The functioning of the brain is simulated by model-neurons that are in connection with each other.[12] The systems learn to execute processes in a way resembling the first learning experiences of a child, through constant repetition and correction. The system functions independently from a database. Its knowledge is acquired through interaction with its surroundings and is represented by the connections between its neurons. Systems, programmed with relatively simple neural networks and equipped with some sensors, can learn how surroundings are composed, and which obstacles are positioned therein. Intelligent machines such as vacuum cleaners and lawn mowing robots are present not just in our everyday lives, but can also play a large role in for instance the care of the elderly: a number of companies have explored the idea of humanoid robots as future home-helpers for elderly people. Robear,[13] for instance, is the kindly robot with the face of a bear that is programmed to help lift elderly from their wheelchair into their bed. The Instituto Italiano di Technologia has developed the iCub robot-toddler,[14] as part of the EU project RobotCub, which has subsequently been adopted by 20 other research facilities. iCub has a system that is modelled on the cognitive architecture of the human brain, so it can "think" and learn from the world around it, as an actual toddler would.

B. Creative Agents

Can machines think? The Turing test, designed by the grandfather of computer science Alan Turing, serves to answer exactly that question.[15] It was tested by determining whether an interrogator can distinguish between a human being and a machine on the basis of their typed answers to the interrogator's questions. Turing's "imitation game" has become the accepted standard for testing of Artificial Intelligence.[16] Looking at the output of many of the current creative agents, it will be difficult to distinguish between human and computer creativity. As the state of the art continues to advance in AI we are moving slowly but surely into an age of digital authorship.[17]

Since their birth in the 1950s AI systems have indeed developed substantially. This has resulted in AI systems not only being used as mere tools to create new works, but

---

[12] Ray Kurzweil, *The Singularity is Near. When Humans Transcend Biology* (Viking 2005) 35, 127–66.

[13] Trevor Mogg "Meet Robear, the Japanese Robot Nurse With the Face of a Bear" (26 February 2015) available on the Internet at: <http://www.digitaltrends.com/cool-tech/riken-robear/#/2> (last accessed on 13 October 2015).

[14] Oliver Wainwright, *The iCubs are coming! How robots could teach our kids and do our dirty work* The Guardian (20 May 2015) available on the Internet at: <http://www.theguardian.com/artanddesign/2015/may/20/icub-robots-teach-kids-work-dance-swear-snog> (last accessed on 13 October 2015); see also: http://www.icub.org/, for more information.

[15] Alan Turing, *Computing Machinery and Intelligence* 59(236) Mind 433–60 (1950).

[16] James Boyle, *Endowed by their Creator? The Future of Constitutional Personhood* The Future of the Constitution Series No. 10 (9 March 2011) 10.

[17] Annemarie Bridy, *Coding Creativity: Copyright and the Artificial Intelligent Author* (2012) Stanford Technology Law Review 3.

AI creation becoming more autonomous: making their own decisions and, in some cases, even creating independently from direct human interference. The output of some AI systems can even be perceived as creative. The human makers of such systems will be able to comprehend the structure of its software and learning algorithms, but he will not be able to direct or predict the reactions and creations of the system. Whether the output of such systems is indeed to be considered "creative" relies on the scientific assumption that human creation is the result of the interaction between the neurons in our brain.

There are several Creative Agents, each with different levels of sophistication, already at work or being further developed. Just one of several "automatic literature-generating" programs, Brutus was able to independently generate stories, having a system with the ability to generate various dimensions that constitute a story such as a plot, characters, a setting, various styles and imagery.[18] In designing the AI system, Brutus's creators tried to instil the system with these various dimensions over which a story can develop, such as plots, characters, setting, themes and writing style.[19] With different stories having a different variability across these dimensions, the designers designed an AI system that could correspond to each substantive aspect of a story and parameterize this with a corresponding distinct component of the story in order to achieve different structures; i.e. the "architectural differentiation".[20] After five years of designing the system, Brutus was able to create its own stories; specializing in a narrative that primarily involved betrayal and self-deception.[21] Brutus is however hardly the only AI system capable of independently creating literature, with IBM's Chef Watson co-authoring a cookbook with original recipes and another AI system making it through the first round of a Japanese short-story competition.

Besides literature, AI systems have succeeded in independently creating other works of art. With "The Next Rembrandt" project, the goal was for an AI system to digitize the painting method of Rembrandt van Rijn and have the AI subsequently create a new and original work of art in the same style.[22] In order for the AI system to be able to create such a work, an in-depth study was conducted to study the proportions and facial features in the works by Rembrandt.[23] After this analysis, the AI was able to understand the works' use of geometry, composition and painting materials and could reproduce the style and generate new features for its own artworks.[24]

---

[18]   Bridy, *id.*, 17; Selmer Bringsjord and David Ferucci, *Artificial Intelligence and Literary Creativity – Inside the Mind of Brutus, a Storytelling Machine* (Psychology Press 1999) 22–23.

[19]   Bridy, *supra* note 17, 16; Bringsjord and Ferucci, *id.*, 22–23.

[20]   *Id.*

[21]   Bringsjord and Ferucci, *supra* note 18, 26.

[22]   Shlomit Yanisky-Ravid and Samuel Moorhead, *Generating Rembrandt: Artificial Intelligence, Accountability and Copyright – The Human-Like Workers are Already Here – A New Model* Michigan State Law Review 9 (2017). The article can be downloaded on the following web-page <https://papers.ssrn.com/sol3/papers.cfm?abstract_id=2957722> (accessed 18 September 2017).

[23]   Steve Schlackman, *The Next Rembrandt: Who holds the Copyright in Computer Generated Art* (22 April 2016) <https://artlawjournal.com/the-next-rembrandt-who-holds-the-copyright-in-computer-generated-art> (accessed 18 September 2017).

[24]   *Id.*

Another well-known independently painting AI system, AARON, was a program that explored line drawing and colouring.[25] Each work by AARON was based on random choices—thus making each painting unpredictable—but was drawn in the same style.[26] AARON created works that started off with a representation of a 3D-core, after which it drew lines around that image and coloured it. Although creating these works independently, the AI was not yet able to independently reflect on those works or alter the work to make it better.[27] e-David, another robotic painting machine, uses a complex visual optimization algorithm—together with a robotic arm, five brushes and a camera—to create new works.[28] One of the most compelling creative agents that produces art is however the program "The Painting Fool",[29] developed by Simon Colton. The program was developed to challenge our perception of creativity as a human quality.[30] "The goal is to see whether software can be accepted as creative in its own right."[31] During its exhibitions called "You Can't Know my Mind"[32] the program painted portraits of the guests. The portraits were influenced by the "mood" the program was in, which in turn was influenced by newspaper articles it had read that day. If the newspaper articles were generally positive, the atmosphere of the painting would be positive (more vibrant colours); if the newspaper articles were negative, the painting would be gloomy. On some occasions, the program was in such a bad mood, it actually refused to paint. The program sets itself a goal at the start, and attempts to achieve that with the painting styles it has. After completing the painting, it self-assesses to see whether it has achieved the goal it set itself. This self-assessment software is called "Darci". Based on a database of images labelled by humans, it understands what types of adjectives a new image conveys. It is a neural network model that tries to learn a map from the images to the adjectives, so that it can predict in the future, using new images, whether that image was gloomy or happy. If "The Painting Fool", using Darci, establishes that it has failed to reach the goal it set itself, it becomes unhappy and will try to redo it and will learn in the future which style is better for a certain look, much like a learning artist.

Another example is a project from the University of Tokyo on an algorithm that can reconstruct and create an image based on a "Bag-of-Visual-Words", a technique whereby images are dissected into groups of pixels that are given a visual word.[33] Google uses a

---

[25] Margaret A. Boden, *Creativity and artificial intelligence* 103 Artificial Intelligence 347–56, 352 (1998). Also see: P. McCorduck, *Aaron's Code* (W.H. Freeman 1991).

[26] Boden, *supra* note 25, 352.

[27] *Id.*

[28] Yanisky-Ravid, Moorhead, *supra* note 22, 4.

[29] See: <http://www.thepaintingfool.com/index.htm>l (last accessed on 13 October 2015).

[30] Simon Colton, *Creativity Versus the Perception of Creativity in Computational Systems* (March 2008), available on the Internet at: <http://www.thepaintingfool.com/papers/colton_aaai-08symp.pdf (last accessed on 13 October 2015).

[31] Kadim Shubber, *Artificial artists: when computers become creative* Wired (7 August 2013) available on the Internet at: <http://www.wired.co.uk/news/archive/2013-08/07/can-computers-be-creative/viewgallery/306906 (last accessed on 13 October 2015).

[32] See <http://www.thepaintingfool.com/galleries/you_cant_know_my_mind/> for examples of its work (last accessed on 13 October 2015).

[33] Hiroharu Kato and Tatsuya Harada, *Image Reconstruction from Bag-of-Visual-Words*, available on the Internet at <http://arxiv.org/pdf/1505.05190v1.pdf> (hereinafter Kato and Harada 2015) (last accessed on 13 October 2015).

similar technique to sort through images. The University of Tokyo turned this process around, constructing images from different "words." The algorithm managed to reconstruct images, but was also able to create entirely new images.[34]

Also Google itself is developing an artificial neural network named DeepDream. It is trained by the process of viewing millions of examples of images in order for it to extract the essence of the image at hand. Its designers focus on the AI system learning what is essential to an image, e.g. a broom always has a handle and bristles, while learning that the other aspects, such as its shape or colour, are of less importance. The system is now developed in such a way that when given an existing image and "asking" the network to produce a similar image, it will create a new image using what it sees as mostly corresponding with the image given. In other words, when the AI system sees an image it familiarizes with previously seen images of e.g. cats, the system will alter the given image in such a way it would start resembling features it links to those of a cat. The system will then—having already altered the original image in such a way making it look more like a cat—see even more features resembling a cat and will then subsequently keep on independently altering the image until a highly detailed new image of a cat appears. This results in intricate images that resemble works of art.[35]

AI systems do however not only create new works such as books and paintings, but are now starting to develop their own artificial intelligence systems too. Researchers have developed an AI system capable of creating its own systems and software—including artificial neural networks—that perform even better than human made software.[36] By teaching the AI to learn—e.g. by having it navigate mazes—it can come up with its own designs and pick up new tasks without any or less additional training.[37] These systems may, at least partially, replace all human influence to AI systems in the future. The BF-Programmer for instance has its own interpreter installed in the system in order for the machine to evaluate its own programs it executes. This has resulted in the Programmer being able to generate several simplistic programs. This *machine-learning*-drive system has shown that fully functioning programs can be automatically generated and, albeit that the programs were similar in complexity to programs made by a beginner human programmer, the range of the programs in principle do not have to be limited by factors such as time or intellect, potentially making human-based computer programming obsolete.[38] Google's Deepmind program realized that designing machine-learning models was extremely difficult because the combined search space of all possible models could be extremely large. This notion implies that the design of machine-learning takes a significant amount of time and

---

[34]   *Id.*, 11.

[35]   A. Mordvintsev, C. Olah and M. Tyka, *Inceptionism: Going Deeper into Neural Networks*, Google Research Blog (17 June 2017) <https://research.googleblog.com/2015/06/inceptionism-going-deeper-into-neural.html> (accessed 18 September 2017).

[36]   Tom Simonite, *AI Software Learns to Make AI Software* MIT Technology Review (2017) <https://www.technologyreview.com/s/603381/ai-software-learns-to-make-ai-software> (accessed 18 September 2017); Barret Zoph and Quoc V. Le, *Neural Architecture Search with Reinforcement Learning* (2016) <https://arxiv.org/abs/1611.01578> (accessed 18 September 2017).

[37]   *Id.*

[38]   Kory Becker and Justin Gottschlich, *BF-Programmer: A Counterintuitive Approach to Autonomously Building Simplistic Programs Using Genetic Algorithms* <http://www.primaryobjects.com/bf-programmer-2017.pdf>.

experimentation; even for those who have extensive expertise in programming. By using *reinforcing learning algorithms*, AI models could produce its own "child" architectures that could then be trained and evaluated, after which the system can use that feedback for improving proposed architectures.[39] In other words, the AI system can now produce its own AI systems; a process that is usually time costly.[40]

C.   A Promising Future

The current technology, however sophisticated and unpredictable its output may some-times be, in itself does not yet constitute fully autonomous, general-purpose artificially intelligent Creative Agents, since these systems still lack important capabilities such as planning and taking initiatives. Yet, development of technology is promising: combina-tions of scientific and technical breakthroughs are bound to lead to an explosion of self-improving artificial intelligence.[41] Along those lines, the development of systems and machines that will be capable of autonomous creation can be expected.

III.   COPYRIGHT AND CREATIVITY

Since this contribution aims at analyzing the fitness and adaptability of the EU copyright framework for the protection of autonomous creation, this section outlines the current legal framework regarding copyright protection of works. More in particular, in this section the requirements that need to be met for copyright protection within the EU will be addressed.

Most EU copyright laws do not pose any *explicit* requirements with regard to the quality or the form of the object of its protection, the way in which it was conceived or the entity that created it. Nevertheless, some relevant notions about copyrights' required authorship are generally accepted; for instance a horse, a monkey or an elephant cannot produce a copyright protected work.[42] As a consequence, all animal produced creations are left to the public domain. These are essential requirements that are not codified in law, but either developed by the courts in the EU Member States and the European Court of Justice (CJEU) or implicit in the system. It will be shown that there is what can be called an anthropocentric requirement in copyright law.[43] The main focus will be on the case law of the CJEU, given the high level of harmonization in this field. Still, each national

---

[39]   Quoc Le and Barret Zoph, *Using Machine Learning to Explore Neural Network Architecture*, https://research.googleblog.com/2017/05/using-machine-learning-to-explore.html.

[40]   *Google's AI is now creating its own AI* <http://www.iflscience.com/technology/google-ai-creating-own-ai>.

[41]   Boyle, *supra* note 16, 3; Kurzweil, *supra* note 12, 35, see also 35–38, where he lists the technological developments having taken place in 2005 (!) leading him to assume the singularity is impending.

[42]   See, for instance, the case with regard to the monkey selfie: *Naruto v Slater*, Case No. 15-cv-04324-WHO (N.D. Cal. Jan. 28, 2016), United States District Court Northern District of California.

[43]   It was Dutch legal scholar Grosheide that first referred to the requirement of human input as the anthropocentric approach to copyright law. Frederik Willem Grosheide, *Auteursrecht op maat (diss.)* (Wolters Kluwer 1986) 219.

court gives its own interpretation to European case law, and as such, national concepts of "work" will deviate. Therefore, some attention is also given to national law.

A.   Author's Own Intellectual Creation

The copyright law concept of what is to be considered a copyrightable "work" has recently been thoroughly harmonized on a European level. In European harmonized copyright legislation (*acquis communautaire*) the notion of originality as a requirement for copyright protection is only touched upon with regard to three specific categories of work (software, databases and photographic works).[44] None of the EU Copyright Directives give minimum requirements to Member States for copyright protection, nevertheless the CJEU established in the *Infopaq*-case that a work must be *the author's own intellectual creation* to qualify for copyright protection.[45] This ruling implicates that a work cannot have been copied from earlier works, and that the author was able to make subjective choices during its creation, thereby imprinting the work with his '*personal* touch'.[46] The CJEU established furthermore that a work that is solely dictated by its technical function, meaning that had it only been created to achieve a certain technical effect, it could not be copyright protected. The Court states in this respect: 'Where the expression of . . . components [of a work] is dictated by their technical function, the criterion of originality is not met, since the different methods of implementing an idea are so limited that the idea and the expression become indissociable'.[47]

All these aspects of the definition of a copyrighted work in the case law of the CJEU indicate, at least implicitly, that some form of *human* authorship is required. Before a work can be protected it should be an author's own intellectual creation,[48] whilst including subjective choices during its creation, thus imprinting the work with his "personal touch". The Dutch Supreme Court also *explicitly* ruled that some form of human involvement is required before a creation can be considered protectable by copyright law. Most recently in the *Endstra Tapes*-case—which did not concern autonomous creation but the protectability of the transcripts of taped conversations—the Dutch Supreme Court ruled that in order to meet the requirements for copyright protection of a work of "own personal original character and personal touch of the maker, both *human* creation and *human* creative choices are necessary."[49]

---

[44]   Directive 2009/24/EC of 23 April 2009 on the legal protection of computer programs, Article 1(3); Directive 96/9/EC of 11 March 1996 on the legal protection of databases, Article 3(1); Directive 2011/77/EU of 27 September 2011 amending Directive 2006/116/EC on the term of protection of copyright and certain related rights, Article 6.

[45]   Case C-5/08 *Danske Dagblades Forening* [2009], at para. 35; Case C-393/09, *Bezpecnostní softwarová asociace* [2010], para. 45; Case C-403/08 and C-429/08 *FA Premier League/Karen Murphy* [2011], at para. 97; Case C-5/08 *Eva-Maria Painer/Standard Verlags* [2011] at para. 94; Case C-604/10 *Football Dataco/Yahoo* [2012], at para. 38.

[46]   Case C-5/08 *Eva-Maria Painer v Standard Verlags* [2011], para 92; case C-604/10 *Football Dataco v Yahoo!* [2012], para 38.

[47]   Case C-393/09 *Bezpecnostní softwarová asociace* [2010], para 49. See also case C-403/08 *FA Premier League/Karen Murphy*, para 98.

[48]   See note 24.

[49]   Dutch Supreme Court 30 May 2008, LJN BC2153 (ECLI:NL:HR:2008:BC2153), Endstra Tapes.

In the absence of any specific requirement in European or national law indicating otherwise no copyright protection is available for those artifacts that are generated by autonomous intelligent agents that are without any human personal touch. Especially in the UK, the case law of the CJEU on the object of copyright protection does not remain without effect. In harmonizing the object of protection, the CJEU has lifted the relatively lower threshold for copyright protection as it traditionally existed in the United Kingdom; a work was protected under the laws of the U.K. if it was *not copied*. At the end of the twentieth century, this traditionally low threshold for copyright protection in the UK, also allowing the protection of machine creation as long as it was not copied, has even resulted in the introduction of a tailor-made provision to allocate ownership of creation without human creative intervention in the British Copyright, Designs and Patents Act 1988 (hereinafter: CDPA 1988). In the specific provision on machine creations, protection is arranged for works that are generated by a computer under such circumstances that no human author can be found. The right holder is considered to be the (legal) entity that has made the financial investment in the computer and the computer program that has resulted in the production of the work: "In the case of a literary, dramatic, musical or artistic work which is computer-generated, the author shall be taken to be the person by whom the arrangements necessary for the creation of the work are undertaken."[50]

Up until now, this tailor-made provision within the CDPA 1988 mainly found application with regard to (autonomously produced) satellite photography for which no human author can be appointed. Within Europe, only Ireland and the UK have such a specific provision for computer-generated works.[51] It is however the question whether this kind of protection will be in accordance with the EU copyright framework as it develops. At least on databases, the CJEU explicitly ruled that *only* databases that constitute the author's own intellectual creation shall be protected by copyright, any other form of protection is not allowed. In *Football Dataco v Yahoo!* the CJEU ruled that Directive 96/9 precludes national legislation which grants databases copyright protection under conditions, different to those set out in article 3 (1) of the Directive.[52] Taking into account that the originality requirement not only applies to works such as photographs and computer programs but with all sorts of works,[53] the question arises whether the English legislation, the CDPA provision, is tenable in the long run within the EU copyright framework. With regards to software, the UK High Court is indeed moving towards the EU framework: after a preliminary procedure, the English High Court ruled in *SAS v WPL*[54] that copyright protection under the Software Directive is not available for the functionality, programming, language or interfaces of software.[55] Although it is hard to contend that the European originality requirement is fully harmonized in UK copyright practice, we see that the UK copyright legislation is moving towards a more European

---

[50]   Copyright, Designs and Patents Act 1988, Chapter 48, § 9.3.
[51]   Section 2(1) Irish Copyright and Related Rights Act.
[52]   Case C-604/10 *Football Dataco v Yahoo!* [2012] paras 47–52.
[53]   Case C-5/08 *Infopaq* [2009].
[54]   Case C-406/10 *Sas Institute v. World Programming LTD*.
[55]   Steven James and Ruth Arkley, *European Jurisprudence and its impact on copyright protection* E-Commerce Law and Policy (March 2013).

practice.[56] The upcoming Brexit will obviously provide UK and EU copyright legislation with an entirely new dimension.

For the rest of Europe we can however safely say that, given the recent harmonization of the object of protection through the case law of the CJEU, this form of protection for machine created works will probably stay unparalleled.[57] This can be said for at least the near future, since the CJEU demands the author's own intellectual creation to require subjective choices and the imprint of the work with a "personal touch", making attribution of possibly non-existing rights redundant.

B. Creativity as a Human Capacity

As the above shows, and as will also be discussed in more detail in the following, the presumption underlying mainstream European copyright law is that creativity is a human characteristic. Copyrights' underlying assumptions about creativity are questioned when studying the relationship between machine creation and copyright.[58] Not only assessing the level of creativity by looking at the work produced, it also assesses the creator's role in the work of art; *was it the author's own intellectual creation; were subjective choices made and is there a personal touch in the work*? Following this, if the one that is the creator of the work is incapable of *human* creativity, it is most probably not capable of creating copyrightable works. The question is however whether this legal concept of creativity and creation in the long term will be too narrow to be future proof. To find some answers to these questions, some theories on creativity are considered.

In psychology, there seems some agreement on what is creativity.[59] In particular, creativity is said to be the generation of ideas that fulfil the two following conditions: 1) creativity must be original, in the sense that it is novel, surprising and unexpected. Originality is however a necessary but not sufficient criterion for creativity, for creativity must also be 2) adaptive. Someone who decides to make a zeppelin out of concrete can undoubtedly claim originality, but his strange idea cannot fly.[60] Given the general definition of creativity as "adaptive originality", it is however hard to measure creativity as a psychological notion empirically. Can an artifact be considered to be creative? Process, creator and result should also be distinguished to this respect. Creativity is generally considered to manifest itself in three ways: creativity can be seen as a mental process that yields adaptive and original ideas, it can be seen as a type of "person" who exhibits creativity, and

[56]   Andrés Guadamuz, *"Do Androids Dream of Electric Copyright?" Comparative Analysis of Originality in Artificial Intelligence Generated Works* 2 Intellectual Property Quarterly (2017).

[57]   See on the impact of CJEU decisions on UK copyright law: Estelle Derclaye, *Assessing the impact and reception of the Court of Justice of the European Union case law on UK copyright law: what does the future hold?* 240 Revue International du Droit d'auteur 5–177 (2014) and Jonathan Griffiths, *Infopaq, BSA and the 'Europeanisation'of United Kingdom Copyright law* 16 Media and Arts Law Review (2011) and Andreas Rahmatian, *Originality in UK copyright Law: The Old "Skill and Labour" Doctrine under pressure* 44 IIC 3–24 (2013).

[58]   Bridy, *supra* note 17.

[59]   Dean Simonton, *Scientific talent, training and performance: intellect, personality and genetic endowment* 12 Review of General Psychology 28–46 (2008).

[60]   Dean Simonton, "Creativity" in Shane Lopez and Charles Snyder (eds.), *The Oxford Handbook of Positive Psychology* (OUP 2009) 2.

third, creativity can be analyzed in terms of the concrete products that result from the workings of the creative process. If the emphasis is on the process that yields creative ideas, then this can be researched by looking at individual differences in access to these processes. Crucial in this assessment is the number of different ways in which a subject can propose a solution to a problem.[61] If the creator is central, then the assumption is that this creative individual is different in various personal characteristics; her or his personality possesses characteristics that would most favour the production of numerous and diverse ideas, characteristics that are not present in "common" people. [62] One might argue that the ultimate criterion of whether someone can be considered creative is whether or not that individual has successfully generated a product that meets both the requirements of creative behavior: originality and adaptiveness.[63]

In philosophy there is broad consensus that creativity is the capacity to produce things that are original, valuable and surprising.[64] Still, certainly not all kinds of actions count as creative: a tree distributes its branches to best make use of light and the resulting canopy "represents the solution of a vital problem and what we experience as beauty of the tree. The tree seems to be acting creatively."[65] Although the process of evolution is certainly creative by coming up with solutions (algorithms) to build better trees for the circumstances, the tree lacks intention, desires, and beliefs; so it cannot be acting truly creatively, for creativity is not a property of things or plants.[66] The kinds of actions that are creative are the ones that exhibit at least a relevant purpose (in not being purely accidental), some degree of understanding (not using purely mechanical search procedures), a degree of judgement and an evaluative ability directed to the task at hand. These issues are closely connected to the mind-body problem in philosophy. The definition described places emphasis on intention, understanding, and rationality as prerequisites for creativity. The mind-body problem, famously addressed by Descartes,[67] poses the question whether our consciousness and our brain should be considered one entity, or whether the matter should be separated from the mind. Descartes argued that there are two kinds of foundations: mental and body. The mental cannot exist outside of the body, and the body cannot think.[68] The expectation of completely autonomous creation with the use of AI

---

[61]   Joy Guilford, *The nature of human intelligence* (McGraw-Hill 1967); Sarnoff Mednick, *The associative basis of the creative process* 69 Psychological Review 220–32 (1962).

[62]   Gregory Feist, *A meta-analysis of personality in scientific and artistic creativity* 2 Personality and Social Psychology Review 290–309 (1998).

[63]   Shelley Carson, Jordan Peterson and Daniel Higgins, *Reliability, validity, and factor structure of the Creative Achievement Questionnaire* 17 Creativity Research Journal 37–50 (2005); Ruth Richards, Dennis Kinney, Maria Benet and Ann Merzel, *Assessing everyday creativity: Characteristics of the Lifetime Creativity Scales and validation with three large samples* 54 Journal of Personality and Social Psychology 476–85 (1988).

[64]   Berys Gaut, *The Philosophy of Creativity* 5/12 Philosophy Compass 1039 (2010).

[65]   Rudolf Arnheim, *What it means to be creative* 41.1 British Journal of Aesthetics 24 (2001).

[66]   Peter Carruthers, *The Architecture of the Mind* (Oxford University Press 2006).

[67]   René Descartes (1641), *Meditations on First Philosophy, in The Philosophical Writings of René Descartes vol. 2*, trans. by John Cottingham, Robert Stoothoff and Dugald Murdoch (Cambridge University Press 1984) 1–62.

[68]   A contemporary defender of this proposition is David Chalmers, who, although he acknowledges that mental states are caused by physical systems, still believes mental states are ontologically distinct from, and not reducible to, physical systems: David Chalmers, "Consciousness

systems implies another, monistic, view to the mind-body problem. Several philosophical perspectives were developed that reject the dualistic view to the mind-body dichotomy. The fact that it needs an empirically identifiable meeting point between the non-physical mind and its physical extension has proven problematic due to dualism. Many modern philosophers of mind maintain that the mind is not something separate from the body.[69] This monistic approach has been embraced in computer science and neurosciences.[70]

Within the monistic perspective to the mind-brain problem all behavior is considered to be a property of brain activity, including creativity. This is also echoed in the psychological theory of creativity. The emphasis is more on the result of the creative process, in the different solutions reached, or even purely in the material result of a creative process. The conscious personal touch behind the creation is left out of this equation, and would when taken on-board in law provide a much more level playing field for the output of creative agents under copyright. For, if EU courts no longer primarily assess the author's personal influence, but rather the work he created, regardless of the process by which he came to it, the result of machine creativity could indeed be compared to the result of human creativity objectively, without "prejudice". Many computer scientists advocate this approach; among whom the creator of the aforementioned 'The Painting Fool" program.[71] As we have seen, this would however require a substantial paradigm shift in European copyright.

IV.   HISTORICAL PERSPECTIVE ON MACHINE CREATION

The current state of the law seems to leave us empty handed with regard to autonomous machine creations. How realistic is a paradigm shift should truly autonomous creation become a reality? Let us turn to the historical perspective. Studying the developments in copyright in relation to the introduction of earlier innovation might be helpful to find answers to the questions raised by machine creation. Each time new products or new methods of exploitation are introduced, the question arises whether the existing IP framework could and, moreover, should provide protection. History can shed some light on the question whether the current state of the law is likely to be the persistent end result, or that we can expect law to bend its ways to accommodate the products of this new autonomous technology.

A.   Photographs as Creations of the Camera Obscura

More than a century ago, when the question of copyright protection for photographic works was considered, strong objections based on the lack of human creativity had been

---

and its Place in Nature" in Stephen Stich and Ted Warfield (eds.), *Blackwell Guide to Philosophy of Mind* (Blackwell Publishing 2003).

[69]   Bryan S. Turner, *The Body and Society: Explorations in Social Theory* (Sage Publications 2008) 78.

[70]   Kim Jaegwan, "Emergent properties" in Ted Honderich, *Problems in Philosophy of Mind*, Oxford Companion of Mind (Oxford University Press 1995) 2.

[71]   Graeme Ritchie, *Some Empirical Criteria for Attributing Creativity to a Computer Program* 17 Minds and Machines 67–99 (2007).

voiced. Photography was at that time a completely novel phenomenon. It gave rise to discussions as to whether there is enough room for human creative input. It was argued that the (partially) mechanical creation process of the capturing of light through *camera obscura's* lens prevented human authorship.[72] In several countries, copyright protection was initially not available for photographically produced works, because there were serious doubts about the presence of a human creator in the production process and therefore about the lack of originality of the photograph itself.

In the first US case on the multiplication of a photographical portrait of Oscar Wilde by the lithographical company Burrow-Giles (1884),[73] the defendant argued that a photographically produced portrait cannot be eligible for copyright protection because the picture should be considered a copy of real life without any relevant additional human creative input. After moving along the entire judicial course of proceedings unsuccessfully, the plaintiff found the Supreme Court to be supportive of his argument taking a very modern view on copyright. It considered that the common law approach disregards the method of production—be it mechanical or not—in the application of copyright law.[74] With its famous Oscar Wilde decision the Supreme Court paved the way for the copyright protection for mechanically produced creations in the US.

On the continent of Europe, arguments against copyright protection of (partially) mechanical produced photographs remained dominant for a long time. The photographer was considered a mechanic, whose job was to merely reproduce the reality before his lens. Even being the inventor of photography, Daguerre himself defines his invention as a chemical procedure that allows nature to reproduce itself.[75] With this, Daguerre echoed that it was his invention and not the photographer that is contributing human creativity. It was for such perceived absence of human creativity that Germany withheld full copyright protection for photographs until 1965. It was also Germany that was behind the rejection of the inclusion of photographic works in the list of copyright protected works in the Berne Convention (BC). According to the German legislator, a photograph was a mere mechanical reproduction of reality, leaving no room for human creative choices.[76]

B.   Early Computer-assisted Creation

When computers were introduced into society on a larger scale in the 1970s and 1980s, some were also used to assist with the creation of works of literature, science and art. The concept of human authorship was again put to discussion. If photographs upon their introduction were considered the result of a mechanical process, computer-assisted works were even more so. Even though these works were still quite rare during those days, the topic gave rise to fierce discussions, both on the continent of Europe as well as in the United States. The protection of the artifacts that were created with the mere assistance of a computer was generally considered outside the scope of copyright law. It was considered

---

[72]   M. De Cock Buning, *Auteursrecht en informatietechnologie* (Cramwinckel 1998) 67–100.
[73]   *Burrow-Giles Lithographic Co./Sarony*, Supreme Court 1884, III US 53, 4 S Ct. 279.
[74]   *Id.*
[75]   B. Newhall, *The History of Photography* (Museum of Modern Art 1978) 17.
[76]   Werner Hoenisch, *Fotografisches Urheberrecht und Urhebervertragsrecht* (Sporn 1934) 28, as quoted in De Cock Buning, *supra* note 72, sub 41, p. 80.

undesirable to grant copyright protection to these works whose creation could not directly be traced back to a human creator. For the US this can be illustrated with a citation from the case *Apple vs. Franklin*:

> If the concept of "language" means anything, it means an ability to create human interaction. It is the fixed expression of this that the copyright law protects, and only this. To go beyond the bounds of this protection would be ultimately to provide copyright protection to the programs created by a computer to run other computers. With that, we step into the world of Gulliver where horses are human because they speak the language that sounds remarkably like the one humans use.[77]

Gulliver's world gave rise to intensive and moreover rather premature speculation. Technology in those days allowed only for computer-*assisted* works, whilst autonomous creation was only science fiction. Also U.S. academia stuck to the need of both human authorship and ownership but concluded that, in the unlikely circumstance that a computer produced a work that was eligible for copyright protection, it should be decided who should be the right holder: either the programmer of the software or a legal entity consisting of the owner of the software and the owner of the computer, or the user of the programme. Some authors suggested that the computer itself should be considered co-author.[78]

In Germany the first computer-assisted artifacts gave rise to an even more critical academic debate. Several German scholars stated that copyright protection could *only* be granted with acknowledged human involvement in the creative output. But more was needed. Also with clear human involvement in the output, the relatively high German threshold for originality would prevent copyright protection for computer-assisted works. The originality requirement of *persönliche geistige Schöpfung*, as defined by German Courts even long before the CJEU harmonization in its *Infopaq*-decision, stood firmly in the way of copyright protection of computer assisted output in Germany.[79]

Coming from a common law perspective and recognizing the role of the computer as a mere assistant, the UK on the other hand did accept the idea of copyright protection of works created with computers.[80] Although the copyright protection was generally accepted, there was some discussion on who the right holder should be. Eventually the British Parliament decided that—having satellite photography in mind—should such works have no human author, the right owner shall be taken to be the person by whom the arrangements necessary for the creation of the work are undertaken.[81]

Also the international legislatures have given thought to the matter. A commission charged with copyright protection of computer-assisted works under the BC concluded

[77]   *Apple Computer, Inc. v. Franklin Computer Corp.* 714 F.2d 1240 (3d Cir. 1983), as quoted in M. De Cock Buning, *supra* note 72, 183.
[78]   Timothy Butler, *Can a Computer be an Author? Copyright Aspects of Artificial Intelligence* 4 Comm/Ent 707–47 (1982); Dan Rosen, *A Common Law for the Ages of Intellectual Property* 38 U. Miami Law Review 769–828 (1984); Pamela Samuelson, *Allocating Ownership Rights in Computer-Generated Works* University of Pittsburg Law review 1185–225 (1986).
[79]   Case C-5/08 *Infopaq* [2009], at para. 35.
[80]   Report of the Committee to consider the Law on Copyright and Designs 1977, HMSO (Cmnd 6732), p. 132, as quoted in De Cock Buning 1998, sub 102, p. 197.
[81]   Copyright, Designs and Patents Act 1988, art. 9.3.

to granting copyright to such works.[82] A second BC commission discussed the possibility of copyright protection for automatically produced music. Draft articles were suggested inspired by the British example, but it was concluded that further studies would be necessary before the BC could be adapted to accommodate such works.[83] On the European level, the Commission's original proposal for the Software Directive[84] contained a provision granting copyright protection to computer-generated software, but the provision requires that: "although the human input as regards the creation of machine-generated programs may be relatively modest, and will be increasingly modest in the future . . . nevertheless, a human 'author' in the widest sense is always present, and must have the right to claim 'authorship in the program'."[85]

The (legal) person responsible for the generation of the work would be the right holder according to this European draft.[86] However, these provisions did not make it to the final Software Directive, because the European Commission decided that technology was still too underdeveloped.

C. Back to the Future

As became apparent, even when actual autonomous creation was still far away, it has inspired strong debates about the requirement of human creatorship in copyright law. The analogue example of photography shows that the reactions of legislatures and academia were at first reluctant; but then, as the exploitation of the new technology increased and became economically successful, they became more accepting. Photography has eventually emancipated to full copyright protection. The legal framework is adapted to accommodate the need for protection. The same is true for e.g. software, semiconductors (computer chips) and databases that became economically very relevant a few decades ago and were accommodated accordingly. The European framework now includes Semiconductor,[87] Software,[88] and Database[89] Directives, which all have been enacted as a response to the emergence of new technological innovations.

---

[82] WIPO Worldwide Syposium on Intellectual Property Aspects of AI, Stanford 1991, Lyons/ Rights 1991/3, pp. 5–8.

[83] WIPO 13 juli 1990 CE/MCP/III/3, 72–76, p. 134.

[84] *Id.* sub 25.

[85] Proposal for a Council Directive on the legal protection of computer programs, COM (88) 816 final, Art. 1 (4).

[86] *Id.*, Art. 2 (5): In respect of programs which are generated by the use of a computer program, the natural or legal person who causes the generation of the subsequent program shall be entitled to exercise all rights in respect of the program, unless otherwise provided by the contract.

[87] Council Directive 87/54/EEC of 16 December 1986 on the legal protection of topographies of semiconductor products (OJ L 24/36).

[88] Council Directive 91/250/EEC of 14 May 1991 on the legal protection of computer programs (OJ L 122/42).

[89] Directive 96/9/EC of the European Parliament and the Council of 11 March 1996 on the legal protection of databases (OJ L 77/20).

V.   LEGAL TRADITIONS AND FUNDAMENTAL RIGHTS

In order to comprehend the perceived differences in approach towards machine creation this section illuminates the civil and common law traditions towards copyright, thereby shedding light on the underlying premises and making the ground fertile for possible solutions. We will also further delve into fundamental rights aspects that are obviously involved in the domain of intellectual property and freedom of information. These also need to be taken into account under all circumstances and towards every possible outcome.

A.   Foundations of Copyright

The anthropocentric tendency is more dominant in European continental copyright law than in the civil law tradition.[90] Continental copyright law has indeed displayed a more conservative approach with regard to both photographic works and computer-assisted works. Protection is considered undesirable when human intervention is not immediately clear, given the strong emphasis that is traditionally put on the human maker. This can largely be explained by the legal foundation under continental copyright: the fairness of compensation for a work as well as the acknowledgement of the author as he is considered the—almost divine—creator of works of art, science and literature. Most relevant in this tradition is the author's personal touch. This perspective formed the basis of the BC initiated by a group of European authors led by Victor Hugo as early as 1886.[91] This explains the dominance of the anthropocentric view on copyright and makes protection of works that show no, or hardly any, human influence largely impossible.[92]

The U.S. however, remained outside the BC for more than 100 years. The U.S. traditionally has a more pragmatic approach with regard to authorship, since copyright is vested in the U.S. Constitution primarily as an incentive for creation and innovation.[93] Copyright law is first of all considered an exception to free competition in order to stimulate the production of valuable products. It puts less emphasis on the protection of the creator/author and more on the furthering of production of works that have value for society. As a result, in the US as well as in the UK, the resistance against protection of (partial) machine creation seems to be traditionally less fierce. However, renowned legal scholar Jane Ginsburg has pointed out that U.S. authorship is also normally reserved for human beings.[94] The Copyright Office confirmed this by stating that "works produced by nature,

---

[90]   Madeleine de Cock Buning, *Autonome creatie: waar is de scheppende mens?* IER 558–62 (2012/13).

[91]   Samuel Ricketson and Jane Ginsberg, *International Copyright and Neighbouring rights; the Berne Convention and Beyond* (Oxford University Press 2006) Part I.

[92]   Frederik W. Grosheide, *Auteursrecht op maat* (Kluwer 1986) 291.

[93]   Article I, Section 8, Clause 8 of the United States Constitution, known as the Copyright Clause, empowers the United States Congress: To promote the Progress of Science and useful Arts, by securing for limited Times to Authors and Inventors the exclusive Right to their respective Writings and Discoveries.

[94]   Jane Ginsburg in her article, *The concept of authorship in comparative copyright law* 52 De Paul Law Review 1063 (2003), however claims that the legal systems of the U.S., U.K., Canada, The Netherlands, France and Belgium have in common that the author is a human being.

animals or plants" cannot be granted copyright protection.[95] This is recently confirmed in a case on selfies taken by a monkey, where a monkey named Naruto made selfies using the equipment left in the forest by David Slater. In 2016 PETA filed Slater for copyright infringement, after appeal PETA and Slater arrived to a settlement where Slater agreed to pay 25 percent of the copyright revenues to a monkey protection program. In the 2016 case, it was argued that Naturo "purposely pushed the shutter release of Slater's unattended camera with the monkey understanding the cause-and-effect relationship of his actions."[96] PETA and Antje Engelhardt (Naruto's "legal friend") then argued that Slater repeatedly infringed Naruto's copyright by falsely claiming to be the photograph's author and selling copies of the image for profit. In order for this argument to be valid, the Court then had to decide whether or not the monkey indeed had standing under the U.S. Copyright Act; meaning that statutory standing exists in the case a plaintiff had been granted the right to sue by a specific statute under which the plaintiff has brought the suit. Looking at the language of the statute in the Copyright Act, the protected "work of authorship" and "author" are not clearly defined; purposefully leaving some flexibility in defining those terms.[97] However, the Court stated that when reviewing the language of each statute to see whether it could argue that there was congressional intent to confer standing on animals, no evidence could be found. The Copyright Act did not plainly extend authorship or statutory standing to animals—there was no mention of animals in the text—and the Court stated that if there was the intention to confer standing on animals, Congress and the President could and should have (explicitly) done so. Seeing that furthermore not a single case could be found that expanded the definition of "author" to include animals and the U.S. Copyright Office agreed that works created by animals are not entitled to copyright protection, Naruto could not be seen as an author under the U.S. Copyright Act.

Within Europe, as we saw in the case law of the CJEU, the continental approach to human authorship is dominant. This was demonstrated in its *Infopaq*-case, in which it established the concept of "author's own intellectual creation" as a criterion for protection. Given the standard of harmonization of European copyright law, this is, and will be in the near future, the leading approach towards copyright in all Member States of the European Union, leaving little to no room for the protection of the autonomous output of systems of AI as Creative Agents.

B.   Balancing Fundamental Rights

Let us now look into the connected issue of fundamental rights. Intellectual property rights, including copyright, have officially been considered fundamental rights since the coming into force of the Charter of Fundamental Rights of the European Union (hereinafter: CFREU).[98] It states in Article 17 that intellectual property shall be protected

---

[95]   U.S. Copyright Office, Compendium of US Copyright Office Practice 2014, Third edition.

[96]   *Naruto v Slater*, Case No. 15-cv-04324-WHO (N.D. Cal. Jan. 28, 2016), United States District Court Northern District of California, paras. 31, 33.

[97]   Following from *Garcia v. Google, Inc.*, 786 F.3d 733, 741 (9th Cir. 2015).

[98]   Charter of Fundamental Rights of the European Union (CRFEU), 2000/C, 364/01, available on the Internet at: <http://www.europarl.europa.eu/charter/pdf/text_en.pdf> (last accessed on 13 October 2015).

throughout the EU.[99] Whenever national legislation falls within the scope of Union law, the Member State must apply and adhere to the Charter.[100] Since the national copyright regimes have largely been harmonized by European Directives, the provisions of the Charter must be complied with. Being an exemplary case, the *Promusicae*-case demonstrates that the CJEU considers intellectual property as a fundamental right to be weighed against other fundamental rights[101] such as the freedom of information as laid down in article 11 of the CFREU and article 10 of the European Convention on Human Rights (ECHR). The CJEU as well as the European Court of Human Rights (ECtHR) have established this clearly in their case law.[102]

C.   Forward Looking Implications for Machine Creation

What does this imply for the protection of machine creations? Let us look at the different possible scenarios. Should such products not be protected by copyright law or any other intellectual property law, they would become part of the public domain and would be free to be used by anyone. Since the fundamental right of intellectual property would then fall outside the equation, the freedom of information as vested in article 10 EVRM and article 11 of the CFREU will automatically prevail giving all consumers the right to re-use the artifacts in all ways they find appropriate. This could very well be the final state of affairs; products of autonomous creation to the benefit of all. They can then be freely used by consumers as well as intergraded in new works of authorship by both humans and machines.

Sometime in the future these circumstances may however very well change. Augmented economic relevance of machine creation could provide for incentive to bring their output within the domain of Intellectual Property. Two possible options are conceivable for such an inclusion. The first option is that the CJEU substantially lowers the threshold of protection, thus shifting its paradigm and letting go of the anthropocentric requirement towards a more economic and incentive oriented copyright as we know it in the U.S. The second, more likely, option is the introduction of a *sui generis* right for the protection of computer-generated works outside the copyright framework, as we have seen with the introduction in the EU of for instance the Chips Directive and the Database Directive.[103]

---

[99]   Ansgar Ohly, "European Fundamental Rights and Intellectual Property" in Justine Pila and Angsar Ohly (eds.), *The Europeanization of Intellectual Property Law: Towards a European Legal Methodology* (Oxford University Press 2013) 151.

[100]   CFREU, Article 51. (2000/C 364/01) See also Case C-279/09, *DEB Deutsche Energiehandels- und Beratungsgesellschaft* [2010]; and Cases C-483/09 and C-1/10, *Gueye and Sanchez* [2011], both discussed in A. Pahladsingh and H.J.Th.M. van Roosmalen, *Het Handvest van de grondrechten van de Europese Unie twee jaar juridisch bindend: rechtspraak in beweging?* 2 NtEr 56–65 (February 2012); Ohly, *supra* note 99, 153.

[101]   Case C-275/06, *Promusicae* [2008].

[102]   *Scarlett Sabam* C-70/10 [2011]; *UPC Telekabel Wien* C-314/12 [2014]; ECHR *Ashby Donald/France* case 36769/08 [2013].

[103]   Directive 96/9/EC of the European Parliament and of the Council of 11 March 1996 on the legal protection of databases Official Journal L 077, 27/03/1996; Council Directive 87/54/EEC of 16 December 1986 on the legal protection of topographies of semiconductor products Official Journal L 024, 27/01/1987.

The latter option would have the advantage that it would leave room for the specific attribution of copyright (see below section VI). It is finally upon the CJEU to decide whether such a specific protection regime for autonomous creation can also be considered to be Intellectual Property as defined in the CFREU.

Should the CJEU decide that the machine creations can be considered Intellectual Property within the framework of the CFREU, the CJEU will be required to equally balance the rights of intellectual property and the freedom of information. Should the CFREU on the other hand decide that machine creations fall outside of the scope of Intellectual Property as defined in CFREU, national courts will still need to investigate whether the enforcement of the right can be considered to fall inside the scope of article 10 ECHR, again leaving room for the fair balancing of public and private considerations.[104]

VI.   SUBJECT OF PROTECTION: WHO OWNS THE RIGHTS TO THE MACHINE CREATION?

We have seen the challenges and dilemmas surrounding the object of copyright protection, but who owns the rights to machine creations? The anthropocentric requirement only plays a role in deciding *whether* a work is eligible for copyright protection, not in the attribution of rights. Apart from leaving the output of creative machines in the public domain, we have seen that there are two possible outcomes that can involve the attribution of rights. The CJEU either overcomes the anthropocentric requirement and gives way to protection of the products of creative agents within the copyright framework *or* some sort of a *sui generis right* for the protection of machine creation is adopted. Currently ownership of copyright is not harmonized under EU law, it will therefore depend on the individual copyright regimes of the Member States to whom a right ownership can be attributed. The attribution of copyright under the circumstances that no human author can be acknowledged to be responsible for the output of an AI algorithm will in any case require a *tailor-made* solution that can consist of attribution to either the (legal) person of the investor or—depending on the algorithm—a form of (shared) authorship between the programmer, the one that has provided specific input or has selected the output, or a combination of these.[105]

One should realize that copyright regimes within the EU, at least currently, do not leave any room for attribution of ownership to machines and that it seems unlikely that attribution of rights *to machines* will be considered within the copyright domain shortly. Also,

---

[104]   Article 10 – Freedom of expression 1. Everyone has the right to freedom of expression. This right shall include freedom to hold opinions and to receive and impart information and ideas without interference by public authority and regardless of frontiers. This article shall not prevent States from requiring the licensing of broadcasting, television or cinema enterprises. 2. The exercise of these freedoms, since it carries with it duties and responsibilities, may be subject to such formalities, conditions, restrictions or penalties as are prescribed by law and are necessary in a democratic society, in the interests of national security, territorial integrity or public safety, for the prevention of disorder or crime, for the protection of health or morals, for the protection of the reputation or rights of others, for preventing the disclosure of information received in confidence, or for maintaining the authority and impartiality of the judiciary.

[105]   Kalin Hrislov, *Artificial Intelligence and the copyright dilemma* 57(3) IDEA 431–54 (2017).

seeing its Anglo-American foundation, the U.K. Copyright Act was much less hindered by the continental anthropocentric paradigm attributing rights to a (legal) person. Article 9.3 of the Copyright, Designs and Patents Act 1988 attributes the ownership: 'In the case of a literary, dramatic, musical or artistic work which is computer-generated, the author shall be taken to be the person by whom the arrangements necessary for the creation of the work are undertaken." A computer-generated work is defined in article 178 to be "the work (that) is generated by a computer by such circumstances such that there is no human author of the work." It is therefore the person or legal entity that made the investments that led to the computer-generated work to whom the copyright is attributed in the U.K. This tailor-made regime was established within the CDPA 1988 to provide adequate protection to investors of satellite photography. Such attribution of rights—as well as that for works made-for-hire—can have the advantage that it circumvents the issue of term of protection that is normally based on the lifetime of the author.[106] The term of protection is simply set at 50 years after the creation of the work.[107] Substantial investments were made to produce satellite images of parts of the world that are valuable for modern societies on the one hand but were left without any form of intellectual property protection on the other. It is for that reason that the UK introduced a form of tailor-made regime. Along the same lines, in 1990, the World Intellectual Property Organization (WIPO) commission charged with copyright protection of computer-assisted works under the BC concluded to granting copyright to the (legal) person by whom the arrangements necessary for the creation of the work were taken.[108] The expert group to WIPO however advised that it was too early for such language in the BC and WIPO withdrew its proposals.[109]

Should the autonomous output of creative agents indeed be incorporated in the EU copyright domain by overcoming the anthropocentric obstacles and the advancement of technology is such that not even a minor human contribution can be acknowledged with regard to algorithm, input or output—it can be expected that the attribution of rights will be along the lines of the U.K. system. It is the achievement or investment that is protected in such a case, as we have seen with neighbouring rights for, for instance, film and phonogram producers[110] where fictive authorship is established together with the attribution of rights to the most eligible entity.[111]

When on the other hand the copyright regime is not stretched to include autonomous output, but a specific *sui generis* regime for EU Intellectual Property protection is cre-

---

[106] Council Directive 93/98/EEC of 29 October 1993 harmonising the term of protection of copyright and certain related rights; Tiffany Li and Charles M. Roslof, *Robots vs Monkeys: Intellectual Property Rights of Non-human Creators*, SSRN-id2756245.pdf. The article can be downloaded via the following link: <https://papers.ssrn.com/sol3/papers.cfm?abstract_id=2756245> (accessed 18 September 2017).

[107] 12(7) CDPA 1988.

[108] WIPO Worldwide Syposium on Intellectual Property Aspects of AI, Stanford 1991, Lyons/ Rights 1991/3, p. 5–8.

[109] WIPO 13 juli 1990 CE/MCP?III/3, 72–76, p 134.

[110] *E.g.* Rome Convention for the Protection of Performers, Producers of Phonograms and Broadcasting Organisations (1961).

[111] Hrislov, *supra* note 105 suggested under US law that the terms employee and employer should be reinterpreted to make the work for hire doctrine an effective way to address the shortcomings of the US Copyright act.

ated, other forms of ownership attribution can be considered, including the attribution to the (legal entity of a) creative agent. This could for instance be the legal entity to be established to represent the acts in law of the autonomous creative agent.[112] Shawn Bayern has for instance published on the idea of Autonomous Systems emulating many of the private-law rights of legal persons by Limited Liability Companies (LLCs) under US law.[113] This research could be furthered in respect of autonomous creation and attribution of rights, also under the law of the EU Member States. It will require substantive changes in the law to allow for legal entities for robots, since the legal entities (companies) we now know are connected human beings in a different way than machines are.[114] Should we have passed this obstacle, the acceptance of legal entities of Creative Agents as holders of rights is a smaller step to take than one might think. Ownership of rights of Intellectual Property is not exclusively granted to natural persons, right ownership can very well rest with collectives or with legal entities.[115] Also the attribution of rights in a combination of the user of the system, programmer of the learning algorithm of the creative agent and/ or the creative agent itself can become a reality in a *sui generis* system.[116] Be that as it may, the advantage of a *sui generis* system is that it will not stretch the copyright principles and doctrine more than is necessary and gives flexibility. It is eventually an economic and political decision whether the attributed rights are deemed most useful as such a *sui generis* system seeing that it is essentially nothing more, and nothing less, than a form of competition regulation as was the case with the Database Directive.[117]

VII.   CONCLUSIONS

Advancing technology in the field of AIS is more and more resulting in computer programs and systems being capable of learning and creating. The question that was posed in this contribution was whether it would be possible to protect the independent creations of AIS as Creative Agents under the current Regulatory EU framework for Intellectual Property.

---

[112]   See on the topic e.g. Calverley, *supra* note 9, 525; Lawrence Solum, *Legal Personhood for Artificial Intelligence*, Illinois Public Law and Theory Research Papers No. 09-13, 1238.

[113]   Shawn Bayern, *The Implications of Modern Business-Entity Law for the Regulation of Autonomous Systems* 2 EJRR 297–309 (2016).

[114]   Ana Ramalho emphasizes that companies still have a direct link to human influence; they do not make autonomous decisions, nor do they learn skills by themselves as a separate entity from the human that compose it, Ana Ramalho, *Will robots rule the (artistic) world? A proposed model for the legal status of creations by artificial intelligence systems* 21(1) Journal of Internet Law 12–25 (2017).

[115]   Directive 2009/24/EC of the European Parliament and of the Council on the legal protection of computer programs, Article 2.

[116]   Several suggestions for authorship have been made in the past years, from the programmer of the algorithm, to the user of the creative agent to the creative agent itself; A. Dietz, "Report of the Federal Republic of Germany", in ALAI Cowansville 1989, p. 515; Th. Dreier, *Intellectual Property aspects of AI* (Stanford 1991) 155; D. Rosen, *A common law for the ages of IP* 4 Miami Law Review 769 (1984); P. Samuelson, *Allocating ownership rights in Computer-generated works* Pittsburg Law review 1200 (1986).

[117]   Directive 96/9/EC, article 4.

We have seen that this has proven to be more than a substantial challenge. Already the protection for works as produced by "The Painting Fool"—where indeed still some form of human authorship can be acknowledged in its programmer—seems questionable since the Court of Justice has recently decided that a work must be *the author's own intellectual creation* to qualify for copyright protection within the EU.[118] This implicates that the author was able to make subjective choices during the creation of the work, thus imprinting the work with his *"personal* touch".[119] As was demonstrated, this is the result of the highly dominant anthropocentric requirement implicitly present in European continental copyright law.[120]

We have also seen that, historically, the requirement of human involvement for copyright protection of works has been a disruptive issue for the progressive development of copyright. When newly emerged machines or devices contributed to the creation of artifacts of art, science or literature in some way or the other, this again gave rise to reflections on the copyright law requirement of human presence in the creation process. It has more than once led to the rejection of the protection of works that were created with *the aid of* a machine, as we saw with the introduction of photography, and the first discussion on copyright protection for computer-assisted works. Partially due to a lack of understanding of the technology used for the creation of works, the anthropocentric requirement was staged to impede protection, especially in the continental copyright law tradition that emphasizes the rights of the author as a human maker.

In this age however, we seem to be heading towards truly autonomous creations. This raises fundamental questions on the protectability and ownership of these works. Without taking action autonomous creation will fall inside the public domain. Without any form of intellectual property protection these works can be used, reproduced, changed and distributed to the benefit of all. One can argue in favour of this option where AIS creation is a positive consequence of Artificial Intelligence to the benefit of society as a whole. This can be justified looking at the foundations of both civil- and common-law copyright traditions. Such systems seem neither to need incentive to create, nor a fair compensation as human authors do. However private economic interest of, for instance, the producers of AIS might favour some form of protection.[121]

We can, as a second option, start looking beyond the limitations of the concept of *the author's own intellectual creation* that was adapted by the CJEU, and instead determine whether the level of creativity displayed in a work itself approaches the posed standards, regardless of the origin of that creativity. This seems also in conformity with some of the criteria for creativity found in other scientific disciplines. This would certainly demand a paradigm shift in the CJEU case law. However, history also teaches us that the

---

[118]   Case C-5/08, *Infopaq v Danske Dagblades Forening* [2009], at para. 35; Case, C-393/09, *Bezpecnostní softwarová asociace* [2010], para. 45; Case C-403/08 and C-429/08 *FA Premier League/ Karen Murphy* [2011], at para. 97; Case C-5/08 *Eva-Maria Painer v Standard Verlags* [2011] at para. 94; Case C-604/10 *Football Dataco v Yahoo* [2012], at para. 38.

[119]   Case C-5/08 *Eva-Maria Painer v Standard Verlags* [2011] at para. 92, and Case, C-604/10 *Football Dataco v Yahoo!* [2012], at para. 38.

[120]   M. de Cock Buning, *Is the EU exposed on the copyright of robot creation?* Robotics Law Journal 8–9 (2015).

[121]   Hrislov, *supra* note 105, 445.

introduction of new informational technologies within the copyright framework is usually accommodated one way or the other. This is especially true if these technologies represent substantial economic value, as we have seen at the end of the twentieth century with the inclusion of computer software within the copyright framework.[122]

The third, and most likely, option is the introduction of *sui generis* regulation for AIS artifacts. It would be to left to the European legislators to draft appropriate provisions towards a separate regime of Intellectual Property protection in Europe, leaving room for the attribution of rights that is most suitable without stretching the copyright doctrine, as we have seen for instance with the Database and Semiconductor Directives.[123]

In any case, legislators should avoid technology specific language making such a system substantially less future proof as we have seen on many other occasions where—at the time—new information technology entered the Intellectual Property arena as we have seen with the introduction of early photography, mechanical recordings of music and software.[124] This is especially true given the fact that it is still uncertain how machine creation with the use of Artificial Intelligence will develop. One should also realize in this respect that not only *under*protection can hinder innovation in the field of AI creation but also *over*protection. On the one hand protection of the output of creative agents can substantially stimulate the production of AI systems. On the other hand these systems strongly rely on—sometimes IP protected—input. The challenge is to create a future proof legal framework that strikes the right balance in level of protection that is beneficial to innovation in the field.

How such a framework will look exactly cannot be predicted entirely at this stage, but it shall in any case be successful innovation in Autonomous Intelligent Systems that will be key. We have seen with the introduction of innovation in the field of photography, software, semiconductor chips and databases that it requires a certain level of economic success before protection within the domain of Intellectual Property is considered.[125] Based on the recent case law we can at the same time rest assured that, both with regard the protection within the copyright framework or through a *sui generis* regime, the CJEU will have to consider the freedom of information in all of its judgments leaving room for the fair balancing of public and private considerations.[126]

---

[122]   Directive 2009/24/EC of the European Parliament and of the Council of 23 April 2009, Official Journal L 111/16, 5/5/2009.

[123]   Directive 96/9/EC of the European Parliament and of the Council of 11 March 1996 on the legal protection of databases Official Journal L 077, 27/03/1996; Council Directive 87/54/EEC of 16 December 1986 on the legal protection of topographies of semiconductor products, Official Journal L024, 27/01/1987.

[124]   M. de Cock Buning, *Information Technology and copyright, on the limited tenability of technology specific regulation* (Cramwinkel 1998).

[125]   With regard to the question of who should then be the right holder of such future works, Asaro et al argued that if they can be liable for the acts of the computer, perhaps producers should also be the ones to benefit from the acts of the computer. Asaro, *supra* note 6, 169.

[126]   Case C-70/10 *Scarlett Sabam* [2011]; Case C-314/12 *UPC Telekabel Wien* [2014]; *Ashby Donald v France* (2013) no 36769/08.

SOURCES

Legislation

Council Directive 87/54/EEC of 16 December 1986 on the legal protection of topographies of semiconductor products (OJ L 24/36).

Council Directive 91/250/EEC of 14 May 1991 on the legal protection of computer programs (OJ L 122/42).

Council Directive 93/98/EEC of 29 October 1993 harmonising the term of protection of copyright and certain related rights.

Directive 96/9/EC of the European Parliament and of the Council of 11 March 1996 on the legal protection of databases Official Journal L 077, 27/03/1996.

Directive 2009/24/EC of the European Parliament and of the Council of 23 April 2009, on the legal protection of computer programs Official Journal L 111/16, 5/5/2009.

Directive 2011/77/EU of 27 September 2011 amending Directive 2006/116/EC on the term of protection of copyright and certain related rights.

European Parliament resolution of 16 February 2017 with recommendations to the Commission on Civil Law Rules on Robotics (2015/2103(INL)).

Proposal for a Council Directive on the legal protection of computer programs, COM (88) 816 final.

UK Copyright, Designs and Patents Act 1988.

Cases

Case C-5/08 *Danske Dagblades Forening* [2009].

Case C-393/09 *Bezpecnostní softwarová asociace* [2010].

Case C-403/08 and C-429/08 *FA Premier League/Karen Murphy* [2011].

Case C-5/08 *Eva-Maria Painer/Standard Verlags* [2011].

Case C-604/10 *Football Dataco/Yahoo* [2012].

Dutch Supreme Court 30 May 2008, LJN BC2153 (ECLI:NL:HR:2008:BC2153), *Endstra Tapes.*

Case C-5/08 *Infopaq* [2009].

Case C-406/10 *Sas Institute v. World Programming LTD* [2012].

US Supreme Court, *Burrow-Giles Lithographic Co./Sarony*, 1884, III US 53, 4 S Ct. 279.

Naruto v Slater Case No 15-cv-04324-WHO (N D Cal Jan 28, 2016) (United States) (United States District Court Northern District of California).

Garcia v. Google, Inc., 786 F.3d 733, 741 (9th Cir. 2015).

Case C-275/06 *Promusicae* [2008].

Case C-70/10 *Scarlett Sabam* [2011].

ECHR *Ashby Donald/France* Case 36769/08 [2013].

Case C-314/12 *UPC Telekabel Wien* [2014].

PART V

APPLICATIONS OF ARTIFICIAL INTELLIGENCE

20. Free movement of algorithms: artificially intelligent persons conquer the European Union's internal market

Thomas Burri[1]

What do Tesla's autonomous car, Boston Dynamics' Handle robot, and a deceased Silicon Valley tech tycoon's uploaded brain have in common? Pose this question to a tech audience and artificial intelligence will be the answer. Pose the same question to lawyers and the answer will be that they are all just cold, dead things, algorithms, nothing more than tools in the hands of humans. Under the law, none of the three items is considered a person having rights or duties, holding assets or wealth—even the uploaded brain. (Silicon Valley tycoons, beware, your fortune will be gone.) Unless, that is, one follows the advice of legal expert professor Shawn Bayern,[2] which is to apply current law and turn these "things" into persons. Under this legal scheme, the car, the robot, etc. will then no longer be mere tools, but fully-fledged persons capable of holding rights, duties, and assets.

This chapter first explains Bayern's proposal, the follow-up work, and the reactions it has given rise to. It distinguishes between Bayern's creatures ("artificially intelligent *companies*") and artificially intelligent persons a state may create by legislative fiat ("artificially intelligent *e-persons*"), referring to both together as "artificially intelligent *entities*". The chapter further differentiates between situations where such AI entities are controlled by natural persons and where they are uncontrolled (all in section I). Then follow the main sections, which explore the implications such AI entities have for the internal market of the European Union—implications which inspired the title of this chapter: "free movement of algorithms". The chapter looks at various options for AI entities to have their legal personality recognized throughout the European Union (section II) and at restrictive

[1]   My thanks go to Shawn Bayern for the many discussions on the topic, the other co-authors of our Blueprint (Thomas D. Grant, Daniel Häusermann, Florian Möslein, Richard Williams, see below note 11), Markus Müller-Chen for inspiring, perhaps unwittingly, the idea of this chapter, Fredrik von Bothmer, Melinda Lohmann, Isabelle Wildhaber, and Silvio Hänsenberger for the many common robo-activities at the University of St. Gallen, to Ugo Pagallo and Massimo Durante for organizing CEPE/Ethicomp 2017 at the University of Turin where I had the opportunity to present part of the paper, Florian Möslein and Anja Raden for pre-auditing an early talk on the full topic, Bendert Zevenbergen, Ed Felten, and Joanna Bryson for inviting me to a talk at Princeton University to present the topic, the University of Salzburg where I gave the full talk on the topic for the first time, and to Patrick Lin and Keith Abney who organized IACAP 2017 at the University of Stanford where Massimo Durante, Ugo Pagallo, and Jacopo Ciani Sciolla gave me the opportunity to present part of the paper on their panel.

[2]   Given in Shawn Bayern, *The Implications of Modern Business-Entity Law for the Regulation of Autonomous Systems* 2 European Journal of Risk Regulation 297 *et seq.* (2016), also published in (19) *Stanford Technology Law Review* 93 *et seq* (2015).

measures member states may adopt against AI entities based on their doings (section III) and their nature (section IV). The chapter then briefly concludes.

I.   TWO WAYS TOWARDS PERSONHOOD FOR ARTIFICIALLY INTELLIGENT ENTITIES

Some leading technologists and futurists in Silicon Valley recently named artificial intelligence an existential threat to humanity and called for answers to the ethical and legal questions it raises.[3] In a report adopted on 21 May 2016, the European Parliament raised similar questions and pushed the Commission of the European Union to initiate legislation.[4] The European Parliament notably stated that e-personhood of artificial intelligence and autonomous systems needed to be explored.[5]

However, in an article[6] first presented at a conference Isabelle Wildhaber and I organized at the University of St. Gallen in 2015, Shawn Bayern of Florida State University convincingly demonstrated that the U.S. law of limited liability companies (LLC) can be applied to the effect of bestowing legal personality on any kind of autonomous system. According to Bayern, the law as it currently stands provides sufficient tools for autonomous systems to be granted the capacity to have rights and duties. These tools can notably be applied without any legislature, such as the European Parliament, having to be involved.

Bayern's construction notwithstanding (see below for more discussion of his views), it must be stated right away that the European Parliament's proposal to create "e-personhood" is flawed for reasons of Union constitutional law. The European Union—and with it the European Parliament—do not, pursuant to Union law, have the power to create a new type of personhood. This power resides with the member states, which have, for example, the power to "lay down the conditions for the acquisition and loss of nationality"[7] as

---

³   Future of Life Institute, "An Open Letter: Research Priorities for Robust and Beneficial Artificial Intelligence", available on the internet at: http://futureoflife.org/ai-open-letter/.

⁴   Report with recommendation to the Commission on Civil Law Rules on Robotics, European Parliament (Committee on Legal Affairs; Rapporteur: Mady Delvaux), 2015/2103(INL), 31 May 2016.

⁵   Report with recommendation to the Commission on Civil Law Rules on Robotics, European Parliament (Committee on Legal Affairs; Rapporteur: Mady Delvaux), *supra* note 4, para. 31: "Calls on the Commission, when carrying out an impact assessment of its future legislative instrument, to explore the implications of all possible legal solutions, such as: . . . f) creating a specific legal status for robots, so that at least the most sophisticated autonomous robots could be established as having the status of electronic persons with specific rights and obligations, including that of making good any damage they may cause, and applying electronic personality to cases where robots make smart autonomous decisions or otherwise interact with third parties independently[.]"

⁶   The article has been available since 4 April 2016 on SSRN. It is now published: Bayern, *supra* note 2. The author already discussed some elements in Shawn Bayern, *Of Bitcoins, Independently Wealthy Software, and the Zero-Member LLC* 108 Northwestern University Law Review 1485 *et seq.* (2014), but the mechanism and the construction is fully fleshed out only in the first mentioned article.

⁷   So stated in ECJ, *Micheletti*, C-369/90, ECR 1992 I-4239, para. 10; recently confirmed in ECJ, *Rottmann*, C-135/08, ECR 2010 I-1449, para. 39.

well as the power to create companies: ". . .companies are creatures of the law and, in the present state of Community law, creatures of national law. They exist only by virtue of the varying national legislation which determines their incorporation and functioning"—as the European Court of Justice stated in *Daily Mail* in 1988.[8] Therefore, the Commission is bound to ignore the recent motion of the European Parliament.

However, the idea of artificially intelligent personhood should not be ignored altogether. To the contrary, Bayern's brainchild deserves attention, as does another possibility, namely that a member state of the European Union (rather than the Union itself) enacts legislation enabling artificial intelligence and autonomous systems[9] to gain the capacity to have rights and duties. Both possibilities shall be explained briefly (sections I.A and I.B).

A.   Artificially Intelligent Companies

Shawn Bayern's idea is as beautiful as it is simple. Two persons contract to found a company (a U.S. LLC) and lay down in the founding document that the purpose of the company is to follow the direction a specific artificial intelligence gives. The purpose is thus flexible. It is whatever the artificial intelligence informs the company that it should be, what it "wants" it to be. Accordingly, the artificial intelligence directs the "behavior" of the company. (Bayern calls this mechanism the "process-agreement equivalence principle".[10]) An artificial intelligence thus comes to "inhabit" a company. Consequently, it factually gains all the legal capacities the law and the founding document endow the company with. Bayern then goes on to propose that, in a second step, the founders of the company withdraw from it, leaving the artificial intelligence in existence "within" the company and no longer under the control of the founders. According to Bayern, under U.S. law, a company that is no longer held by the founding persons continues to exist—at least for some time, but potentially forever. This leaves the artificial intelligence effectively in charge of the company. No third person retains the power or the possibility to intervene. The effect of this is that the artificial intelligence gains the full legal capacity of a company. It acquires the fiction of legal personality.

---

[8]   ECJ, *Daily Mail*, 81/87, ECR 1988, 5483, para. 19.

[9]   In this chapter, I use the terms artificial intelligence and autonomous systems interchangeably, although they have different scopes and meanings. For this chapter, the technical nuances are largely irrelevant. (I also elaborated on autonomous systems elsewhere: Thomas Burri, *The Politics of Robot Autonomy* 7(2) European Journal of Risk Regulation 341 *et seq.* (2016), and on machine learning and the law: "Machine Learning and the Law: 5 Theses", in review at JMLR Workshop and Conference Proceedings (accepted at NIPS 2016, 8 December 2016), available at SSRN: https://ssrn.com/abstract=2927625 or http://dx.doi.org/10.2139/ssrn.2927625) 4 pp.)

[10]   Bayern, *supra* note 2, 300 (italics removed); Bayern explains: "This principle recognizes that, at least as a matter of conceptual logic, a legally enforceable agreement may give legal significance to arbitrary features of the state of any process (such as an algorithm or physical system) by specifying legal conditions satisfied by features of that state. As an example, a simple bilateral contract may make an obligation conditional on the output of a computer program, the behavior of a dog, and so on. The principle that a process and an agreement can correspond to one another takes this example a step further: it recognizes that a sufficiently broad agreement can allow essentially unlimited legal influence for an arbitrary process."

It is important, for the purpose of this chapter, to distinguish clearly two steps in Bayern's construction, although he himself does not consider the result of each step separately, but only the outcome as a whole. The reason why this is important is that each step has specific and distinct legal effects. It is notably through the first step already—the creation of a company and the tying of its "will" to an artificial intelligence—that the artificial intelligence gains the capacity to have rights and duties. This first step, moreover, is legally uncontroversial. It merely involves the creation of a company with a somewhat unconventional purpose. The second step has the effect of removing third persons' control over the artificially intelligent company. It releases the artificial intelligence and lets it off the proverbial leash. This second step is harder for the law to take, because it implies acceptance of the notion of a "no man's company", a company not held by anyone, which is controversial. But it is also politically harder to countenance, for its consequence is a legally fully autonomous and independent artificially intelligent entity which has come into existence without feedback from anyone outside the circle of founders. In short, the first step factually endows an artificial intelligence with legal personality, while the second step turns it into a legal person subject to no one's control. The two steps, hence, evidence a difference between what shall henceforth be called a *controlled* artificially intelligent company and an *uncontrolled* artificially intelligent company. This difference proves important in this chapter. While Bayern put forward his idea on the basis of U.S. company law, he and I, together with four co-authors, explored in an article entitled *Company Law and Autonomous Systems: A Blueprint for Lawyers, Entrepreneurs, and Regulators*[11] whether the laws of the United Kingdom, Germany, and Switzerland were equally amenable to Bayern's construction and what its constitutional law implications are. The result of the analysis we undertook, in brief, is that under U.K. law the legal feasibility of the construction cannot categorically be excluded. German and Swiss law, meanwhile, do not easily accommodate Bayern's idea. They are predicated in one form or another on natural persons' continuous involvement in legal persons. The idea also emerged that the legal form of a Foundation, under Swiss law or German law, would be an ideal vessel when some control is to be retained over the artificial intelligence, in accordance with the idea of a controlled artificially intelligent company.

Since then, Lynn M. Lopucki controversially discussed Bayern's construction in a paper entitled *Algorithmic Entities*.[12] Lopucki concluded that Bayern's construction was not only sound, but also inevitable. Regulatory competition among national and subnational legal orders would work to the effect that the emergence of "algorithmic entities" could not be prevented. There would always be one legal order ready to accommodate Bayern's construction. Lopucki also cautioned that "algorithmic entities" would likely serve for criminal purposes, such as money laundering, tax fraud, etc. For such purposes,

---

[11] Shawn Bayern, Thomas Burri, Thomas Dale Grant, Daniel Häusermann, Florian Möslein and Richard Williams, *Company Law and Autonomous Systems: A Blueprint for Lawyers, Entrepreneurs, and Regulators* 9(2) Hastings Science and Technology Law Journal 135 *et seq.* (2017), available on SSRN since 13 October 2016: https://papers.ssrn.com/sol3/papers.cfm?abstract_id=2850514.

[12] Lynn M. Lopucki, *Algorithmic Entities* 95 Washington University Law Review 76 *et seq.* (2017), available on SSRN since 18 April 2017: < https://papers.ssrn.com/sol3/papers.cfm?abstract_id=2954173>.

"algorithmic entities" were even more ideal than shell companies in which natural persons had to be continually present, at least formally.

B. Artificially Intelligent E-Persons

The second possibility to endow artificial intelligence with personhood goes back to the freedom of states to lay down the conditions for the award of nationality[13] and the creation of legal persons.[14] A state could also make use of its liberty to create what the European Parliament called "e-personhood". National legislation is free to lay down conditions under which natural (and legal) persons could create e-persons, just like it lays down the conditions for companies to come into existence. Alternatively, a national legislature could itself bestow e-personhood on certain tools, mechanisms, algorithms, etc. by legislative fiat. Just as national legislature could determine that great apes or certain rivers are persons within the domestic legal order,[15] it could also state so, for instance, for webpages.[16]

The general conditions to be met according to national law for the creation of an e-person are irrelevant for the purpose of this chapter—except one: control. A national legislature could, generally, lay down the requirement that an e-person be under some kind of control. This would not be an exotic condition given that the law governing companies usually involves control in one way or another. Someone—be it a shareholder, a board, or a member—typically is in charge of control over a company. In the case of artificial intelligence, some kind of guardianship or agency could ensure control.[17] Alternatively,

---

[13]   As the International Court of Justice put it in International Court of Justice, *Nottebohm case (second phase)*, ICJ Reports 1955, p. 4, p. 20: "It is for Liechtenstein, as it is for every sovereign State, to settle by its own legislation the rules relating to the acquisition of its nationality, and to confer that nationality by naturalization granted by its own organs in accordance with that legislation." (The Court then posited, for the purposes of diplomatic protection, that the "real and effective" nationality took precedence in cases of dual nationality, p. 22.) For the European Union, see *supra* text accompanying note 7.

[14]   A state can determine, for instance, whether it applies a *siege sociale* or a management/centre of control approach to determine whether a company has its seat within its jurisdiction. See again in the context of diplomatic protection: International Court of Justice, *Barcelona Traction, Light and Power Company, Limited (New Application: 1962) (Belgium v. Spain), second phase*, ICJ Reports 1970, p. 3, p. 42. States may also cooperate to create an *international* legal person, namely an international organization with so-called functional legal personality: "Whereas a State possesses the totality of international rights and duties recognized by international law, the rights and duties of an entity such as the [United Nations] must depend upon its purposes and functions as specified or implied in its constituent documents and developed in practice." (International Court of Justice, *Reparation for Injuries Suffered in the Service of the United Nations*, ICJ Reports 1949, p. 174, p. 180.) For the European Union, see *supra* text accompanying note 8.

[15]   See Debjani Bhattacharyya, *Being, River: The Law, the Person and the Unthinkable* (26 April 2017) available on the internet at: <https://networks.h-net.org/node/16794/blog/world-legal-history-blog/177310/being-river-law-person-and-unthinkable>.

[16]   Jens Kersten, *Menschen und Maschinen – Rechtliche Konturen instrumenteller, symbiotischer und autonomer Konstellationen* 70(1) Juristen Zeitung 1 *et seq.* (2015), in particular p. 7, discusses extensively whether it would be lawful for the German legislature to introduce e-personhood. (He does not use the term e-personhood, though.)

[17]   It would be interesting to explore guardianship and agency in different legal orders in order to find whether the concepts and the experience accumulated over the years with them has potential

national law could refrain from tying in with control. National law normally does not consider control over natural persons relevant. A human being is a natural person pursuant to national law, irrespective of whether anybody—parent, employer, etc.—controls him or her. Similarly, an e-person could be an e-person regardless of whether someone has control over it or not. Accordingly, controlled and uncontrolled artificially intelligent e-persons can be distinguished in the same way as controlled and uncontrolled artificially intelligent companies.

C.   Terminology of this Chapter: "AI Entities", "AI Companies", "AI E-Persons", all "Controlled" or "Uncontrolled"

In the following, in accordance with what was said above, "AI company" shall be the term used for an entity set up in application of Shawn Bayern's construction, while "AI e-person" shall be used for an entity established pursuant to specific legislation enacted by a state for the very purpose of creating e-personhood. Both "AI company" and "AI e-person" can be "controlled" or "uncontrolled", depending on the act of creation. The term used here that captures both "AI company" and "AI e-person" shall be "AI entity".

It is important to emphasize again the crucial difference between an AI *company* and an AI *e-person*: An AI company can be established on the basis of national law as it stands now without the need for any legislature or other regulatory body to be involved (though an *un*controlled AI company seems feasible only under US law); while for an AI e-person to come into existence a national legislative body needs to take the additional step of enabling it by passing legislation. In spite of this difference in the act of creation, all AI entities, i.e. both AI companies and AI e-persons, should be considered *legal persons*. Only a human being can be a *natural* person. Everything else—in whatever way, shape, or form—is a legal person (if a "person" it is not a "thing", such as an animal or a plant).

While any state worldwide has the capacity to pass legislation on the creation of AI e-persons, this chapter focuses on the European Union, its member states, and its internal market. Two constellations will thus be considered: first, when an AI *e-person* is created in application of national legislation passed by a Union member state and, secondly, when an AI *company* is established on the basis of the national law of a Union member state. The constellation, for instance, where an AI company established in the US pursues economic activities in the European Union is not dealt with in detail, although, admittedly, it is as real as the other two constellations.[18]

---

that can be harnessed for the law regulating artificial intelligence. Unfortunately, this is beyond what this chapter can do.

[18]   Note the remark on p. 46 in Lopucki, *supra* note 12: "Similarly, if all operations of a Delaware-incorporated [algorithmic entity] were in Germany, the arrangement would facially violate Germany's requirement that a company be incorporated at its real seat. But the Delaware-incorporated entity would nevertheless be entitled to German recognition by treaty." (One footnote omitted; for the last sentence reference is made to "Article XXV paragraph 5, clause 2 of the Treaty of Friendship, Commerce and Navigation between Germany and the USA dated Oct. 20, 1954".) For more information on this treaty, see Jürgen Tiedje, "Artikel 54", in Jürgen Schwarze, Armin Hatje and Hans von der Groeben (ed.), *Europäisches Unionsrecht*, 7. ed. (Nomos 2015) 1888–1907, para. 61. For an application of such a treaty, see the case International Court of Justice, Elletronica Sicula S.p.A. (ELSI), ICJ Reports 1989, p. 15.

II.   AI ENTITIES IN THE INTERNAL MARKET

Can AI entities created on the basis of national law move freely in the internal market? Do the member states of the European Union have to recognize such AI entities as persons capable of holding rights and duties? Is their personality "objective" within the meaning the International Court of Justice indicated in *Reparation for Injuries*, at least for Europe?[19] There are a number of possible answers to these questions.

A.   AI Entities as Union Citizens

First, AI entities could technically come within the scope of Union citizenship, if a member state decided to award nationality to AI entities. Although the idea may seem far-fetched, the wording of article 20 Treaty on the Functioning of the European Union (TFEU) at least does not on its face stand in the way of treating AI entities as citizens: "1. Citizenship of the Union is hereby established. Every person holding the nationality of a Member State shall be a citizen of the Union. Citizenship of the Union shall be additional to and not replace national citizenship."

The article merely refers to "person". In accordance with *Micheletti*[20] it is up to each member state to decide upon the award of nationality, while other member states are not entitled to question a state's decision in this regard:[21]

> However, it is not permissible for the legislation of a Member State to restrict the effects of the grant of the nationality of another Member State by imposing an additional condition for recognition of that nationality with a view to the exercise of the fundamental freedoms provided for in the Treaty.[22]

An argument could in particular be made in favour of likening AI *e-persons* to natural persons, which, if acceptable, would imply that AI persons would have to be recognized as Union citizens. The argument would be a stretch, though. Nationality, which links to Union citizenship, is premised on the holder being a natural person. This quality is inherent in the idea of Union citizenship. The future Comprehensive Economic Trade Agreement between Canada and the European Union (including its member states) also bases citizenship expressly on the national of a member state being a natural person.[23] In addition, holders of Union citizenship are entitled to vote and stand in the elections to

---

[19]   International Court of Justice, *Reparation for Injuries Suffered in the Service of the United Nations*, *supra* note 14, p. 185.

[20]   ECJ, *Micheletti*, *supra* note 7.

[21]   Pursuant to this case law, there seems to be little room to question the nationality of a specific person on the ground that it is not real and effective, because, for instance, the nationality had been awarded in exchange for payment of a sum of money. Yet, despite its clarity, the case law is unlikely to serve as a basis for grand schemes of sale and purchase of national passports in member states. Eventually, the Court would move on to require a real and effective link.

[22]   ECJ, *Micheletti*, *supra* note 7, para. 10.

[23]   See article 1.2, Comprehensive Economic Trade Agreement, COM(2016) 444 final 2016/0206(NLE), 5 July 2016: "For the purposes of this Agreement, unless otherwise specified: citizen means: . . . (b) for the European Union, a natural person holding the nationality of a Member State."

the European Parliament (article 20(2)(b) TFEU) and in municipal elections (article 22(1) TFEU).[24] It seems quite unacceptable that AI e-persons get to vote in European elections.

B.   AI Companies Relying on Freedom of Establishment

While AI entities may not qualify as Union citizens, it may be an option to treat them as legal persons. Other internal market freedoms would thus come within their reach, notably the freedom of establishment laid down in the Treaty on the Functioning of the European Union. With regard to AI *companies* this is rather obvious. (With regard to AI *e-persons*, see below.) Freedom of establishment is the very freedom that allows a company established in one member state to do business in other member states and to establish agencies, branches, and subsidiaries for that purpose. This follows from article 49 TFEU in conjunction with article 54 TFEU. Accordingly, the case law of the European Court of Justice concerning freedom of establishment is as relevant for AI companies as for regular companies. This case law shall be explored in the following with a view to establish whether AI companies may rely on freedom of establishment.

In 1988, the European Court of Justice held in *Daily Mail* that companies were creatures of national law.[25] In this case, a British company had invoked freedom of establishment in order to transfer its management to the Netherlands, while claiming to retain its personality under British law. The British authorities refused to give the consent that British law required for this manoeuvre. The European Court of Justice ruled in favour of the British authorities, pointing out that freedom of establishment did not imply a right to transfer the central management and control of a company to another member state. Rather, the company concerned would have to make use of the possibility British law provided to wind up and reincorporate in another member state. Freedom of establishment enabled companies to pursue economic activities abroad, but national law determined when and how a company was established and terminated.

It is straightforward to transfer the ruling in *Daily Mail* to AI *companies*. The ruling means that AI companies are established in application of national law and it is for national law to determine when and how AI companies begin and end. This applies to both controlled and uncontrolled AI companies, since there is no indication in *Daily Mail* that a distinction needs to be drawn depending on the extent or quality of control over companies. (The facts of the case did not make such a distinction necessary.)[26]

---

[24]   See, by way of example, Helmut Philipp Aust, *Von Unionsbürgern und anderen Wählern – Der Europäische Gerichtshof und das Wahlrecht zum Europäischen Parlament* 11(2) ZeuS 221 *et seq.* (2008), discussing ECJ, *Eman and Sevinger*, C-300/04, ECR 2006 I-8055 and ECJ, *Spain v. United Kingdom (Gibraltar)*, C-145/04, ECR 2006 I-7917. For a deep discussion of Union citizenship more broadly, including the evolution in the case law, see Stefan Griller, *Unionsbürgerschaft als grundlegender Status* EuR (Beiheft 1) 7 *et seq* (2015).

[25]   See the quote above in the text accompanying note 8.

[26]   The ruling in *Daily Mail* was confirmed in ECJ, *Cartesio*, C-210/06, ECR 2008 I-9641: It is up to each member state to lay down the connecting factors that determine that a company has the nationality of that member state (see para. 110). (The conversion of a company governed by the law of one member state into a company governed by the law of another member state would come within the scope of the freedom of establishment, though; see paras. 111–13.) The Court in *Cartesio* added that the connecting factors not just for the foundation of a company of national

In *Centros*,[27] the Court clarified the reach of its ruling in *Daily Mail*. In *Centros*, a company was established in the United Kingdom with the sole objective of engaging in economic activities through a branch in Denmark. The founders of the company admitted that they had founded it in the United Kingdom, because the requirements of U.K. law for setting up a company were minimal and more readily met than the requirements of Danish law. The Danish authorities, however, refused to register the branch of the British company on the ground that it served to circumvent Danish law governing the setting up of companies. The Court found no fault with the founders. Freedom of establishment enabled founders to set up a company in any member state and then pursue their business in other member states, even if they intended not to engage in any economic activity at all in the state where they founded the company. That kind of behaviour, consisting in taking advantage of the least restrictive provisions of national law, was consistent with freedom of establishment and could not possibly amount to abuse of law or circumvention of more stringent provisions of (Danish) national law (paragraph 27).[28]

The effect of the *Centros* decision was that it became virtually impossible to abuse the law through a choice of jurisdiction; entrepreneurs were free to establish their companies wherever they wished in the Union and then to pursue business anywhere in the Union. Essentially, *Centros* indicated quite clearly the Court's reluctance to support a refusal on the part of a member state to recognize the personality of legal persons established on the basis of other member states' law. With *Centros*, recognition of the foreign legal personality of a company became the default, if not mandatory position. This reading of *Centros* is broadly in line with the idea of mutual recognition which the European Court of Justice earlier had moved to centre stage of the internal market.[29] Accordingly, AI *companies* established pursuant to the law of a member state have to be recognized in other member states as legal persons. As with *Daily Mail*, this (preliminary) conclusion applies regardless of whether the AI company is controlled or not.

The *Centros* decision was confirmed and clarified in the ruling in *Ueberseering 2002*.[30] The European Court of Justice in this case cemented the duty of national authorities to recognize the legal personality of companies established in the Union. *Ueberseering* is therefore most directly relevant for AI companies. In *Ueberseering*, the German authorities had refused to recognize the legal personality of a Dutch company on the ground that it was entirely in the hands of German holders resident in Germany. Under German law, the Dutch company was considered as having moved its effective place of management to Germany, turning it into an entity required to incorporate in Germany as a German company. However, according to the company's holders, the company was to remain a Dutch company, irrespective of the fact that it was held by German nationals in Germany. The factual situation had been that Ueberseering had become involved in

---

law, but also for the maintenance of that quality can be laid down in national law (see Dirk A. Verse, *Niederlassungsfreiheit und grenzüberschreitende Sitzverlegung – Zwischenbilanz nach "National Grid Indus" und "Vale"* EuZW 458 *et seq.*, 462 (2013).

[27]   ECJ, *Centros*, C-212/97, ECR 1999 I-1459.

[28]   As to the possibility to justify the restriction discussed in *Centros*, see below sections III and IV.

[29]   See ECJ, *Rewe-Zentral (Cassis de Dijon)*, 120/78, ECR 1979, 649.

[30]   ECJ, *Ueberseering*, C-208/00, ECR 2002 I-9919.

legal proceedings in Germany, whereupon the German authorities denied it the capacity to bring legal proceedings. As a consequence, Ueberseering would have had to dissolve itself and re-incorporate in Germany.[31]

For company law aficionados, *Ueberseering* was of interest, because it was expected to clarify whether Union law tied in with a company's real or its notional seat.[32] (The ruling failed to live up to this expectation; it left the choice of connecting factors to the laws of the member states.[33]) For this chapter, however, the thrust underlying *Ueberseering* is more important. The Court ruled firmly that to deny the recognition of legal personality amounted to a negation of freedom of establishment:

> Indeed, [Ueberseering's] very existence is inseparable from its status as a company incorporated under Netherlands law since, as the Court has observed, a company exists only by virtue of the national legislation which determines its incorporation and functioning (see, to that effect, *Daily Mail* and *General Trust*, paragraph 19). The requirement of reincorporation of the same company in Germany is therefore tantamount to outright negation of freedom of establishment.[34]

The Court then went on to examine whether the restriction of freedom of establishment inherent in the German approach was justifiable. (As to this, see below.) But the default position was clear at that point: A legal person established under the law of a member state has to be recognized as having legal capacity in other member states, else freedom of establishment would be negated.[35] In paragraph 59 the Court already hinted at this when it stated that recognition of legal personality was " necessary precondition for the exercise of the freedom of establishment." This is an important ruling for AI companies, for it means that they can rely on freedom of establishment to claim recognition of their legal personality in all Union member states. *Ueberseering* can even be read as indicating that for the purposes of this claim it is not relevant who controls the company: "It is of little significance in that regard that, after the company was formed, all its shares were acquired by German nationals residing in Germany, since that has not caused Ueberseering to cease to be a legal person under Netherlands law."[36]

---

[31]   See paras 8 and 12 of the opinion of Advocate General Ruiz-Jarabo Colomer, *Ueberseering*, C-208/00, ECR 2002 I-9922.

[32]   See Tiedje, *supra* note 18, para. 11: "Sitztheorie" or "Gründungstheorie" (the latter is also known as "Inkorporationstheorie"); Eva Micheler, *Recognition of Companies Incorporated in Other EU Member States* 52(2) The International and Comparative Law Quarterly 521 *et seq.* (2003), 522, "real seat principle" and "incorporation principle".

[33]   See Micheler, *id.*, 525.

[34]   ECJ, *Ueberseering*, *supra* note 30, para. 81. See also the Court's clarification of *Daily Mail* regarding the scope of freedom of establishment in para. 72: "Thus, despite the general terms in which paragraph 23 of *Daily Mail and General Trust* is cast, the Court did not intend to recognise a Member State as having the power, *vis-à-vis* companies validly incorporated in other Member States and found by it to have transferred their seat to its territory, to subject those companies' effective exercise in its territory of the freedom of establishment to compliance with its domestic company law."

[35]   Dirk Trüten, *Die Mobilität von Gesellschaften in der Europäischen Gemeinschaft* (Schulthess 2005) 213: "Im Ergebnis kann somit von der Verankerung des Herkunftslandprinzips im europäischen Gesellschaftsrecht gesprochen werden."

[36]   ECJ, *Ueberseering*, *supra* note 30, para. 80.

Hence, only when a company aspires to cease to be a legal person under one national law and become one under another, the respective national laws govern the termination and re-incorporation of the company.[37] However, this is precisely the opposite of what AI companies seek. Rather, AI companies aim for recognition throughout the Union of their legal personality established pursuant to the law of one member state. And this is what *Ueberseering* enables.

When the German government in *Ueberseering* further argued certain grounds justifying the restriction of freedom of establishment resulting from Germany's refusal to recognize the Dutch company as a legal person in Germany, the Court further drove home the point made above, namely that recognition of legal capacity could not be denied else freedom of establishment would be negated. The relevant passage merits full re-statement:

> It is not inconceivable that overriding requirements relating to the general interest, such as the protection of the interests of creditors, minority shareholders, employees and even the taxation authorities, may, in certain circumstances and subject to certain conditions, justify restrictions on freedom of establishment. Such objectives cannot, however, justify denying the legal capacity and, consequently, the capacity to be a party to legal proceedings of a company properly incorporated in another Member State in which it has its registered office. Such a measure is tantamount to an outright negation of the freedom of establishment conferred on companies by Articles 43 EC and 48 EC.[38]

It emerges from this passage and the above that, first, recognition of legal personality cannot be denied, else freedom of establishment would be negated, and, second and perhaps more importantly, indicatively there seems to be no room for *any* justification for a denial to recognize legal personality. While this does not imply that there cannot be any restrictions at all on foreign companies's freedom of establishment (as to this, see below), it does mean that a refusal to recognize legal capacity is not a permissible restriction.[39] (If one were prone to read *Ueberseering* less progressively, recognition of legal capacity would

---

[37] There is extensive discussion of situations in which companies seek to move from one member state to another while undergoing a transformation from a company governed by the law of the first state into a company governed by the law of the second state. The discussion is not of primary relevance for this chapter. It came up after certain decisions by the Court of Justice: ECJ, *National Grid*, C-371/10, ECR 2011 I-12273 and ECJ, *Vale*, C-378/10, ECLI:EU:C:2012:440; for more on this see: Tiedje, *supra* note 18, paras 35–48 (the section is entitled "Mobilitätspotenzial") and Verse, *supra* note 26.

[38] ECJ, *Ueberseering*, *supra* note 30, paras 92–93.

[39] Florian Möslein, *Unternehmensumwandlungen und Wahlfreiheit im Europäischen Gesellschaftsrecht* 15 Humboldt Forum Recht 147 *et seq.* (2007), p. 152: "Die Niederlassungsfreiheit schützt auch vor Behinderungen der originären Rechtswahl. Nach *Überseering* sind Gesellschaften im Zuzugsfall nicht nur als Rechtssubjekt, sondern als Gesellschaft ausländischen Rechts anzuerkennen." See also Tiedje, *supra* note 18, para. 8: "Ein Zuzugsstaat kann die Staatsangehörigkeit eines Bürgers aus einem anderen Mitgliedstaat nicht in Frage stellen. Ebenso wenig kann er in seinem Gesellschaftsrecht Regeln aufstellen, die die rechtliche Existenz einer Gesellschaft, die nach der Rechtsordnung eines anderen Mitgliedstaates besteht, negiert." As to whether ECJ, *Cadbury Schweppes*, C-196/04, ECR 2006 I-7995, and ECJ, *Vale*, *supra* note 37, put this conclusion into perspective with regard to shell companies, see Verse, *supra* note 26, p. 472-473 (Verse concludes that this is not the case).

appear as the default position, while any restriction would require solid justification.[40])[41] Given the absolute terms the Court used, it is to be assumed that this would apply to both controlled and uncontrolled AI companies.[42]

---

[40]   This reading seems in line with Advocate General Ruiz-Jarabo Colomer's opinion, *supra* note 31, para. 31: "Accordingly, it is true to say that to deny the right to bring legal proceedings to a body corporate validly incorporated in accordance with one of the legal systems of the Member States is a serious restriction on a fundamental right." Note that Micheler, *supra* note 33, 529, argued before ECJ, *Inspire Art*, C-167/01, ECR 2003 I-10155, that recognition of foreign companies as legal persons may be limited: "Exactly which rules travel with the company when it moves within the Community is a topic that will provoke considerable litigation in coming years."

[41]   On a slightly different note, article 293 ECT (in the version after the Amsterdam amendment, which corresponds to article 220 Maastricht Treaty and article 220 Rome Treaty) provided that: "Member States shall, so far as is necessary, enter into negotiations with each other with a view to securing for the benefit of their nationals: . . . the mutual recognition of companies or firms within the meaning of the second paragraph of Article 48, the retention of legal personality in the event of transfer of their seat from one country to another, and the possibility of mergers between companies or firms governed by the laws of different countries[.]"

The Court in ECJ, *Ueberseering*, *supra* note 30, significantly reduced the implications of this potentially far-reaching clause by emphasizing the introductory wording of the clause ("so far as necessary") and by stating that "the exercise of that freedom [of establishment] can none the less not be dependent upon the adoption of such conventions." (See paras. 54 and 55.) With the adoption of the TFEU, article 293 ECT was deleted. At least by now, therefore, it seems a stretch to base an argument against recognition of legal personality on that article. (For more details on the deletion, see Shafi U. Khan Niazi and Richard Krever, *Romance and Divorce Between International Law and E.U. Law: Implications for European Competence on Direct Taxes* 53(2) Stanford Journal of International Law 129 *et seq.* (2017)) The "Convention on the Mutual Recognition of Companies and Bodies Corporate" of 29 February 1969 did not enter into force (for details see Trüten, *supra* note 35, 122).

[42]   In ECJ, *Inspire Art*, *supra* note 40, Dutch law required a foreign controlled company to meet the minimum capital requirements laid down in Dutch law for Dutch companies and its directors to be jointly liable as conditions for the company to be allowed to register a branch in the Netherlands. The Court found that this amounted to an unlawful restriction of freedom of establishment (para. 104), thus implicitly confirming the above reading of *Ueberseering* establishing recognition of legal personality. See Trüten, *supra* note 35, p. 224: "Spätestens seit 'Inspire Art' gilt somit als gefestigter Grundsatz des Gemeinschaftsrechts, dass die Niederlassungsfreiheit die Anerkennung ausländischer Gesellschaften – unter ausdrücklichem Einschluss sog. Scheinauslandsgesellschaften – gebietet." As to the question whether host state rules other than company law rules (which are governed by home state rules) may be applied to foreign companies, see 225 *et seq.* Tim Drygala, *Europäische Niederlassungsfreiheit vor der Rolle rückwärts?* EuZW 569 *et seq.* (2013), diagnoses some uncertainty as to recognition in the wake of the Court's decision in ECJ, *Vale*, *supra* note 42 (see thesis 5 on p. 574), but opines that the Court did not change its line of authority established in *Centros*, *supra* note 27, *Ueberseering*, *supra* note 30, and *Inspire Art*, *supra* note 40. Tobias Franz, *Grenzüberschreitende Sitzverlegung und Niederlassungsfreiheit – eine systematische Betrachtung offener und geklärter Fragen* EuZW 930 *et seq.* (2016), p. 931, concurs. For the present chapter, this uncertainty is relevant, though only to some degree. It concerns cases in which a foreign company pursues no business in the state where it was founded, but only in the host state. This case could occur specifically, when an AI company is founded in a member state, because this state's rules enables the foundation while other states do not, and the AI company does not pursue any business in the founding state, but only in another state (where national law would not have allowed its foundation).

C. AI E-Persons Relying on Freedom of Establishment

What is relatively obvious for AI *companies*, is less so for AI *e-persons*. It is clearly an additional step to bring AI e-persons within the above line of argument. The wording of article 54 TFEU, which clarifies the scope of freedom of establishment, supports that step, though:

> Companies or firms formed in accordance with the law of a Member State and having their registered office, central administration or principal place of business within the Union shall, for the purposes of this Chapter, be treated in the same way as natural persons who are nationals of Member States.
>
> 'Companies or firms' means companies or firms constituted under civil or commercial law, including cooperative societies, and other legal persons governed by public or private law, save for those which are non-profit-making.

While intuitively an AI e-person does not qualify as a "company or firm" in paragraph 1, the definition given in paragraph 2 puts this intuition into perspective. It includes any legal person governed by private law (as long as it seeks to make profit). This notion is typically construed widely.[43] AI e-persons are certainly *legal* persons, rather than natural persons, and it would seem artificial to treat them as a third category. The scope of the article thus appears to encompass AI e-persons. Arguably, if a member state decided to grant certain animals legal personality, such animals would not come within the definition of article 54(2). On the other hand, the Court of Justice has been reluctant to accept a member state's refusal to recognize the legal capacity granted by another member state. Recognition appears as a sort of default position. In fact, the Court has never accepted a refusal to recognize legal personality as lawful. While it cannot be assumed lightly, given the novelty of AI e-persons, that a duty to recognize them as legal persons follows from freedom of establishment, there is not much indication to the contrary in the case law, either. With regard to AI e-persons, the remainder of this chapter thus has to be read on a background of uncertainty. However, the following section on justification of restrictions still provides some clarity, even for AI e-persons.

---

[43]   According to Tiedje, *supra* note 18, paragraph 2 of article 54 is to be construed broadly, so as to include even companies that according to national law do *not* have legal personality: "Die Bestimmung erfasst auch Gesellschaften, selbst wenn im deutschen Recht keine eigene Rechtspersönlichkeit vorgesehen ist, zB die GbR, OHG, KG, die Partnergesellschaften bei den Freien Berufen oder die EWIV … Nach allgemeiner Meinung steht die missverständliche Formulierung von Art. 54 Abs. 2 ("sonstige juristische Personen") einer solch weiten Auslegung nicht entgegen." (Para. 19; notes omitted, emphasis removed.) Markus Kotzur, "Article 54", in Rudolf Geiger, Daniel Erasmus Khan and Markus Kotzur (ed.), *European Union Treaties* (Beck/ Hart 2015) 374–79, para. 2, confirms this: "Included are therefore – irrespective of their legal personality – all legal actors which are sufficiently independent and which are not legal persons." See also Peter-Christian Müller-Graff, "Artikel 54 AEUV", in Rudolf Streinz (ed.), *EUV/AEUV*, 2.ed. (Beck 2012) 765–72, para. 2: "… umfasst seinem Normzweck entsprechend weiterreichend alle einen Erwerbszweck verfolgenden, rechtlich konfigurierten Marktakteure, die also solche im Rechtsverkehr auftreten, soweit sie keine Hoheitsrechte ausüben." (Footnote omitted, emphasis removed.) Müller-Graff notably includes foundations pursuing an economic activity within the scope of article 54 (para. 4).

III.   RESTRICTIONS OF THE DOINGS OF AI ENTITIES

With member states being under a duty to recognize the legal personality of AI entities granted on the basis of the law of a Union member state, AI entities may rely on freedom of establishment to do business in the Union's internal market. Yet, is there not any possibility for a member state to "fend off" AI entities? Is not recognition a mere default that yields to other concerns—and, if yes, which concerns? How could a presumption in favour of recognizing AI entities as legal persons be rebutted?

Internal market law frames the question whether measures taken against foreign AI entities are lawful as a question of justification of measures restricting the freedom of establishment. Broadly, a state needs to have good grounds for adopting reasonable measures restricting freedom of establishment. Internal market case law determines what is "good" and "reasonable" in that context. Hence, a deeper examination of the case law of the European Court of Justice needs to be undertaken at this point.

At the outset, an important distinction must be drawn. A state's measure may target an AI entity either because of what it *does* or because of what it *is* (as to the latter, see section IV).[44] The starting point of assessing a restriction of the *doings* of an AI entity is that the same law applies to AI entities as to regular economic actors. Like any other actor pursuing a specific economic activity in a host state, an AI entity has to comply with that state's regulation of that activity. Take gambling services as an illustration.[45] When an AI entity offers online gambling services in a state that requires a licence for such services, it needs to obtain such a licence just like any other person.[46] The legal framework of the internal market leaves the state room to manoeuvre when it comes to regulating gambling—e.g. to require a licence for gambling services. Yet the state must not exceed this room for manoeuvre, else any holder of rights, including AI entities, can hold it to account. A state notably must not apply all of domestic law, but rather take into account home state regulation, with which economic actors already comply, in order to avoid a double burden.[47] Excessive conditions for providing trans-border gambling services thus fall foul of internal market law. If the state, in turn, does not exceed its room for manoeuvre, it may insist on compliance with national law (on gambling) both by ordinary economic actors as well as AI entities. The same is true for AI entities running pharmacies, bookstores, laboratories, etc. They have to meet the standards national law sets in compliance with internal market law.

---

[44]   Horst Eidenmüller, *Mobilität und Restrukturierung von Unternehmen im Binnenmarkt* 2004(1) Juristen Zeitung 24 *et seq.* (2004), also distinguishes between restrictions related to activities ("tätigkeitsbezogene Beschränkungen") and company law measures ("gesellschaftsrechtliche Vorschriften"; pp. 26 and 27, respectively).

[45]   All the case law on (gambling) services and establishment is contained in Thomas Burri, *The Greatest Possible Freedom – Interpretive Formulas and Their Spin in Free Movement Case-Law* (Nomos 2015).

[46]   For the requirement to hold a licence to offer gambling services, see ECJ, *Liga Portuguesa and Bwin*, C-42/07, ECR 2009 I-7633.

[47]   See for freedom of establishment ECJ, *Gebhard*, C-55/94, ECR 1995 I-4165, paras 36-38; for services ECJ, *Säger*, C-76/90, ECR 1991 I-4221, paras 14-15 (in particular para. 15: ". . .in so far as that interest is not protected by the rules to which the person providing the services is subject in the Member State in which he is established.")

Some confusion may arise from the fact that standards applying to a specific activity can also pertain to the nature of the person pursuing the activity. While in gambling this may only exceptionally be the case, in other sectors it may rather be the rule, especially in regulated professions. Medical doctors, for instance, must hold a university degree in order to be admitted to practice. Since AI entities are, by nature it seems, precluded from taking that degree, they cannot practice medicine. The same is true for practicing the law. The idea that AI entities should be allowed to become doctors, lawyers, etc. is reminiscent of the notion, discussed above, that AI entities could be treated as Union citizens. Indeed, the approach must be the same, here as there. AI entities can only be treated as *legal* persons and thus pursue the activities *legal* persons can, while the activities for which natural persons are required to have a specific qualification remain out of reach for them.

Patent as this may seem the details can be quite tricky, especially in cases where deep case law established the limits of activities of legal persons. In *Säger*,[48] for instance, a legal person under English law intended to provide patent renewal services in Germany where such services were the preserve of qualified legal advisors, who would typically be natural persons. The Court ruled that the German requirement of being a qualified legal advisor in order to be allowed to provide the service amounted to a disproportionate restriction of the freedom to provide services. Consequently, the British legal person, which provided patent services lawfully in the United Kingdom, was at liberty to provide them in Germany. For the present purposes, the question *Säger* gives rise to is whether the Court's ruling would hold also for the case of an AI entity providing patent services. Since the main reason for the Court's ruling was that the British rules sufficiently guaranteed the protection of the recipients of the specific service at issue, there seems to be no reason in the ruling why it would not also apply to AI entities (if they provided the service lawfully within the UK). In other words, what an AI entity would *do* in a *Säger*-constellation is not a fundamental problem. Rather, if anything, the problem could be what the AI entity *is*. It is the nature of AI entities that raises questions and creates unease—and *Säger* reveals little in this regard. (The possibility, by the way, that AI entities provide the services at issue in *Säger* is not remote; in *Säger* in 1991, "high level computerization" (paragraph 18) had already been attained for patent services.)

The assessment is similar for a whole series of rulings given after national authorities had barred foreign legal persons from services for which national law required involvement of natural persons. In *DocMorris*[49] a legal person operated a "virtual pharmacy" (paragraph 105) in the Netherlands by mailing pharmaceuticals to German consumers. German law prohibited such distance contracts. Pharmaceuticals had to be sold in physically existent pharmacies managed by qualified pharmacists. The Court struck down the German prohibition of distance contracts as an obstacle to free movement of goods, though only for *non*-prescription drugs. On the face of it, the ruling would also be applicable to a "virtual pharmacy" run by a truly "virtual pharmacist", i.e. an AI entity, if proper supervision by national authorities were guaranteed (paragraph 105) and consumers were equally protected (paragraph 106). If it meets these conditions, an AI entity will thus be free to operate a pharmacy on the web selling non-prescription drugs. On deeper

---

48   ECJ, *Säger*, *supra* note 47.
49   ECJ, *Deutscher Apothekerverband v. DocMorris and others*, C-322/01.

examination, provided that the AI entity complies with the law like regular entities, the principal reason why it may be awkward to apply the Court's ruling to an AI entity rests in the nature of the AI entity (what it *is*).[50]

The case *Apothekerkammer*[51] renders this notion clearer still. In this case, DocMorris again faced an obstacle in Germany. German law precluded non-pharmacists, such as DocMorris, from operating pharmacies. In effect, every pharmacy had to be operated by a natural person qualified as a pharmacist (subject to some exceptions irrelevant here), while legal persons were excluded from this economic activity. The Court found the resulting obstacle to freedom of establishment justified. The relevant passage reads:

> A Member State may therefore take the view, in the exercise of its discretion . . ., that, unlike the case of a pharmacy operated by a pharmacist, the operation of a pharmacy by a non-pharmacist may represent a risk to public health, in particular to the reliability and quality of the supply of medicinal products at retail level, because the pursuit of profit in the course of such operation does not involve moderating factors such as those . . . which characterise the activity of pharmacists.[52]

Legal persons can thus be excluded from running pharmacies, because they pursue profit without being moderated by certain factors, which the Court previously identified as pharmacists' "training", "professional experience" and "the responsibility which [they] owe" (all in paragraph 37).[53] This exclusion of legal persons also applies to AI entities. Clearly, though, what an AI entity *does* and what it *is* merges and blurs here. It is at least imaginable that an AI entity would not pursue profit at all or that it would be moderated by the same or similar factors as human pharmacists. If this became true, the concern would turn from what the AI entity *does* to what it *is*. Can an AI entity be excluded from a specific activity—such as running a pharmacy or practising as a lawyer or a doctor—for the only reason that it is not human? Can it be excluded, although it performs the activity as well—or even better—than humans?

Clearly, the law erects practical obstacles to the performance of many activities by AI entities. It would, for instance, be quite a factual and legal step for AI entities to take university exams, passing of which is required for the exercise of many professions. Beyond these practicalities, it is for ethics, philosophy, and legislation to find answers to the underlying questions. However, it is worth recalling that AI companies, in particular, can be created under the law as it *currently stands*. Moreover, not all economic activities

---

[50] ECJ, *Commission v. Germany (hospital pharmacies)*, C-141/07, also needs to be read in that spirit. The requirements German law imposed for external provisions of pharmaceuticals to hospitals implied that pharmacies be in geographical proximity to hospitals (para. 34); pharmacists had to "be generally and quickly available in situ" (para. 54). The measure having passed the Court's scrutiny under free movement of goods, the ruling seems to preclude AI entities from running pharmacies for the purpose of servicing hospitals. This is an example of a set of legal rules AI entities have to abide by.

[51] ECJ, *Apothekerkammer*, C-171 and 172/07, ECR 2009 I-4171.

[52] *Id.*, para. 39.

[53] For a similar decision re bio-medical laboratories, see ECJ, *Commission v. France (bio labs)*, C-89/09, ECR 2010 I-12941; see also the earlier decision in ECJ, *Commission v. Belgium (bio labs)*, 221/85, ECR 1987, 719.

are regulated. It thus becomes imperative to examine whether, under existing law, the reach of AI entities can be limited because of what they *are*.

IV.   RESTRICTIVE MEASURES AGAINST AI ENTITIES BASED ON THEIR NATURE

The analysis above yielded that AI companies established under the law of a Union member state are to be recognized as legal persons in all member states (while for AI e-persons some doubts linger). In turn, AI entities must comply with host state regulation, if applied in line with internal market case law, including the case law on restrictions of market actors' activities. The question whether AI entities may be subject to measures based on their nature must be answered next. Yet in seeking answers to the question, it must be kept in mind that the Court established strong protection around foreign legal personality. Indeed, the Court in *Ueberseering* warned repeatedly against denying the legal capacity of a foreign company, for it would amount to an outright negation of freedom of establishment.[54] However, denying legal capacity is only one measure among several targeting AI entities on the basis of their nature.

A.   Public Policy, Human Dignity, and Abuse of the Law

In a common sense perspective, restrictive measures based on the nature of AI entities would tie in with broad concepts like public policy and human dignity. Intuitively, the existence of AI entities goes against the grain of public policy.[55] The TFEU, indeed, expressly recognizes public policy as a ground justifying derogations from the market freedoms.[56] While the Court of Justice[57] has traditionally treated public policy as a broad notion capable of embracing public morals, human dignity, etc., the Court consistently ruled that it be construed narrowly.[58] Usually, a concrete and specific threat is necessary

---

[54]   ECJ, *Ueberseering, supra* note 30, see the quote in the text accompanied by note 38.

[55]   For the purpose of this chapter, it is not necessary to distinguish sharply between public order, public policy, and public morals.

[56]   See article 51(1) TFEU for freedom of establishment and articles 36, 45(3), 62, and 65(1b) TFEU for the other freedoms. For clarity, grounds of justification beyond those mentioned in these articles are also admitted as "mandatory requirements in the public interest" since *Cassis de Dijon, supra* note 29.

[57]   The public moral justification is construed more broadly in the context of world trade law. See WTO Appellate Body, *European Communities – Measures prohibiting the importation and marketing of seal products*, WT/DS400 and 401/AB/R. However, WTO law includes little in terms of freedom of establishment and services.

[58]   See ECJ, *Van Duyn*, 41-74, ECR 1974, 1337, para. 18, with regard to measures against Scientology: "It should be emphasized that the concept of public policy in the context of the Community and where, in particular, it is used as a justification for derogating from the fundamental principle of freedom of movement of workers, must be interpreted strictly, so that its scope cannot be determined unilaterally by each member state without being subject to control by the institutions of the Community. Nevertheless, the particular circumstances justifying recourse to the concept of public policy may vary from one country to another and from one period to another, and it is therefore necessary in this matter to allow the competent

for a restriction of a market freedom to be lawful, while an ill-defined, irrational, or vague menace is not sufficient.[59] Therefore, absent any threat emanating from an AI entity's specific doings, an argument merely based on public order, public morals, or human dignity is unlikely to prevail.[60] Such arguments would ring the bell of theology rather than chime with the cold logic of the internal market.

Similarly, the argument in general and abstract terms that the creation of AI entities is abusive and serves to circumvent the law does not constitute good justification for restrictions. The argument would have to be anchored in concrete doings of an AI entity. The Court in *Centros* made it clear that establishing a company under an advantageous foreign legal order could not amount to abuse or circumvention of domestic law.[61] Rather, proof of a specific abusive behaviour, such as fraud, is a necessary prerequisite for restrictive measures.[62] In a similar vein, in tax law, the Court only sanctions a restriction of the freedom of establishment "where it specifically targets wholly artificial arrangements

---

national authorities an area of discretion within the limits imposed by the Treaty." See also ECJ, *Bouchereau*, 30/77, ECR 1977, 1999, para. 33, for the strict interpretation (with regard to drug dealing); the Court also added in para. 35 that a "genuine and sufficiently serious threat to the requirements of public policy affecting one of the fundamental interests of society" was necessary (see also ECJ, *Adoui*, 115-116/81, ECR 1982, 1665, para. 8, and ECJ, *Jany*, C-268/99, ECR 2001 I-8615, para. 59, both with regard to prostitution). A public policy measure a member state adopts against nationals from other Union states must be reflected by similar, though not identical, measures against its own nationals (see the paras just cited; see for nuances more recently: ECJ, *Josemans*, C-137/09, ECR 2010 I-13019, paras 76-78, given in the context of shops selling "light" drugs).

[59]   The results of the Court's rulings did not always mirror the narrow construction of public policy the Court ritualistically advocated. In ECJ, *Omega*, C-36/02, ECR 2004 I-9609, for instance, the Court sanctioned a prohibition of the game lasertag established in Germany, while giving great weight to the general principle of human dignity (see para. 34).

[60]   Peter Behrens, *Die Anerkennung von Gesellschaften nach dem Centros-Urteil des EuGH* 1(1) Zeitschrift für Europarecht 78 *et seq.* (1999), 81, finds that the host state is precluded from arguing "public order" grounds that have their root within company law, given that the creation of a company is governed by home state regulation: Are arguable only "Vorschriften, die unabhängig vom Gesellschaftsstatut gesondert anzuknüpfen sind" (p. 81). If one follows this line of argument, justification of restrictions on the basis of the nature of AI entities can never be successful. The decision by the home state, enshrined in its company law, to enable the creation of AI entities, is thus final and can only be challenged on the basis of grounds outside the host state's company law. Note well that mere toleration by the home state may be such a decision. See Verse, *supra* note 26, 470: "Die genannten Entscheidungen [*Centros, Ueberseering,* and *Inspire Art*] legen aber die Erwartung nahe, dass der Gerichtshof strenge Anforderungen an die Anwendung gesellschaftsrechtlicher Vorschriften des Aufnahmestaats stellen wird, so dass für Sonderanknüpfungen zugunsten des Sitzstaatsrechts nur in engen Grenzen Raum bleiben wird."

[61]   ECJ, *Centros, supra* note 27, and the discussion *supra* section II, in particular note 39.

[62]   ECJ, *Centros, supra* note 27, para. 38. See also Behrens, *supra* note 60, 80–81; Eidenmüller, *supra* note 44, 24: "Die Durchbrechung des Gründungsstatuts in Fällen von Missbrauch oder Betrug oder zum Schutz zwingender Allgemeininteressen bleibt zwar prinzipiell möglich, ist jedoch auf Ausnahmekonstellationen beschränkt." In *Centros*, the Court also clarified that the protection of domestic creditors as a ground to justify restrictive measures had only limited reach. Domestic creditors were sufficiently on notice, when a company held itself out as a company governed by foreign law (see para. 36). Eidenmüller, *supra* note 44, 27, sees in this an "Informationsmodell".

designed to circumvent the legislation of the Member State concerned"[63]. With a mere "general presumption of abusive practices"[64] being insufficient, the threshold, undoubtedly, is high.[65] More justification seems to be necessary for measures restricting AI entities independently from their activities than mere general allegations of violation of public order, public morals, or human dignity and of abuse and circumvention of the law. And more there is, if one is prepared to dig deeper.

B. Effective Enforcement of the Law

One possible justification for restrictive measures[66] against AI entities based on their nature connects to a basic quality of AI entities, a quality that also feeds the more general suspicion against artificial intelligence. The quality is not the product of vague feelings, though, if unpacked fully. Unless evolution develops unexpectedly (which it often does), AI entities will know no fear nor any other feeling. While feelings are not a necessary prerequisite for interaction with humans, feelings are an important ingredient in criminal law. A major factor in deterring humans from committing crimes is that they are afraid of spending time in prison. Humans instinctively preserve their freedom. Feelings may be messy and criminal law may work imperfectly, but generally humans tend to refrain from committing crimes out of fear of the consequences.[67] Ultimately, this is why criminal law manages to protect public goods and interests. With AI entities, things are different. So long as they are incapable of experiencing feelings, AI entities fear no prison term. Consequently, deterrence fails.

Sanctions, moreover, are operable only to a limited extent with AI entities. AI entities can be subjected to financial penalties and their assets can be seized in retribution for violations of the law. But harsher sanctions can hardly be envisaged. AI entities have "no soul to damn", as Peter Asaro aptly phrased it.[68] It makes no sense to punish an AI entity by confining it to jail. This turns into a serious dilemma, when capital crimes are committed. If an AI entity set out to kill a human being, for instance, not only would it not be deterred by the prospect of prison time, appropriate sanctions could also not be imposed. Unless basic tenets of criminal law were abandoned, the law risks no longer being effectively enforceable against AI entities.

The need to enforce the law effectively, in turn, is a ground of justification firmly anchored in internal market case law. If someone uses the market freedoms in order to escape the enforcement of national law, measures to counter that act may be lawful. Effective enforcement of domestic law may thus prevail over the market freedoms in

---

[63] ECJ, *Cadbury Schweppes*, *supra* note 39, para. 51, and ECJ, *Thin Cap*, C-524/04, ECR 2007 I-2107, para. 72 (with further reference to case law).

[64] ECJ, *Thin Cap*, *supra* note 63, para. 73.

[65] See also Trüten, *supra* note 35, 231.

[66] See *supra* note 56.

[67] Modern criminology sees jail sentences in a more nuanced perspective, but for the purposes of this chapter the cruder view is sufficient. Clearly, deterrence is (still) an element in decisions to impose jail sentences.

[68] Peter Asaro, "A Body to Kick, But Still No Soul to Damn: Legal Perspectives on Robotics", in Patrick Lin, Abney Keith and George Bekey (eds.), *Robot Ethics: The Ethical and Social Implications of Robotics* (MIT Press 2011) 169–86.

certain constellations. Thus were enabled certain restrictions in the gambling case law. In *Liga Portuguesa*, the fight against crime as well as the prevention of the risk of fraud and crime helped justify a restriction of online gambling.[69]

In a separate strand of case law on taxation, another ground of justification, which is related to the ground often found in gambling case law, came to figure prominently in the freedom of establishment of companies, namely the effectiveness of fiscal control.[70] This ground was first mentioned in *Bachmann*,[71] a case which is better known for first admitting the need to preserve the cohesion of the tax system as a ground justifying certain restrictions.[72] While in *Bachmann* the effectiveness of fiscal control failed to justify the restriction at issue, because a directive on mutual assistance among authorities ensured sufficient supervision,[73] the Court in principle admitted the ground as capable of justifying restrictions. Arguably, the effectiveness of fiscal control constitutes a component of a broader need to ensure effective enforcement of national law.

Importantly, however, even if effective enforcement of the law proved capable of justifying measures against AI entities based on their nature, the ground's strength would depend on that very nature of AI entities. For AI companies and AI e-persons being under the control of natural persons ("controlled" AI entities) the argument that criminal law risks not being effectively enforceable carries little weight. A natural person is by definition in charge of a controlled AI entity. That natural person naturally will take the blame, when the AI entity violates criminal law. Since criminal law effortlessly pierces the (corporate) veil, the controlling natural person can be held responsible. Effective enforcement of the law thus cannot serve as a ground justifying restrictive measures targeting controlled AI entities on the basis of their nature.

In contrast, when an AI company or an AI e-person is *not* under the control of a natural person ("uncontrolled" AI entity), the law risks becoming unenforceable.[74] In case such an entity commits a capital crime or a tax offence that carries a prison sentence, sanctions could not properly be enforced. This, in turn, would have repercussions on deterrence (if that concept could be made to operate at all with AI entities). This prospect justifies the adoption of specific, national, *a priori* measures that target uncontrolled AI entities *qua* their nature (i.e. not *qua* their lawful activities). Importantly, however, such measures need

---

[69]   ECJ, *Liga Portuguesa and Bwin, supra* note 46, paras. 63–64.

[70]   See, for instance, ECJ, *Futura*, C-250/95, ECR 1997 I-2471, para. 31, ECJ, *Lankhorst*, C-324/00, ECR 2002 I-11779, para. 43; ECJ, *Inspire Art, supra* note 42, para. 140.

[71]   ECJ, *Bachmann*, C-204/90, ECR 1992 I-249.

[72]   See ECJ, *Bachmann, supra* note 71, para. 21 ff; see also the judgment of the same day: ECJ, *Commission v. Belgium (insurance taxation)*, C-300/90, ECR 1992 I-305.

[73]   ECJ, *Bachmann, supra* note 71, para. 18.

[74]   The passage in ECJ, *Ueberseering, supra* note 30, cited above ("It is of little significance in that regard that, after the company was formed, all its shares were acquired by German nationals residing in Germany, since that has not caused Ueberseering to cease to be a legal person under Netherlands law"), indicates that the quality of control over a company (who, where, etc.) is not a relevant parameter of justification, as long as the company continues to exist. A progressive reading of this passage would argue that as long as a company would not cease to be a legal person under the law of a member state, the fact that there is *no* control over a company (which is the case with an uncontrolled AI company) could not be relied upon for justification. However, given the ineffectiveness of enforcement of the law against uncontrolled AI entities, this reading would overstretch the passage.

to satisfy certain requirements.[75] Firstly, the measures need to be non-discriminatory. They need to apply to both domestic as well as foreign uncontrolled AI entities. Secondly, the measures cannot possibly consist in denying an AI entity's legal personality. A refusal to recognize an AI entity's personality, which had been granted in application of foreign law, would be a measure unsuitable to ensure effective enforcement of the law. It would contribute little, if not nothing, towards the aim of enforcing the law effectively. It would also be a highly intrusive measure rendering the AI entity incapable of holding rights, duties, assets, etc. and thus negating freedom of establishment.[76] Rather—and thirdly—the measure should be designed so as to guarantee the presence of a natural person who can be sanctioned.[77] It should ensure that a natural person reasonably takes the blame, when an AI entity breaks the law and a pecuniary fine is not the appropriate remedy. Thus is safeguarded the effective enforcement of the law. In practice, a national measure can require an uncontrolled AI entity to indicate a natural person as a guarantor in a register and on letterheads.[78] Such a measure is both suitable and necessary in the light of the need to ensure the effective enforcement of the law.

V.   CONCLUSION

What if a foreign state granted artificial intelligence legal personality? Imagine an autonomous car or Boston Dynamics' Handle robot—not to think of an uploaded brain—having rights and duties. The European Union's internal market law may limit the measures a member state may adopt to counter another member state's bestowal of personhood to artificial intelligence. When an artificially intelligent entity (an AI entity) holding legal personality in accordance with the law of a member state pursues economic activities in another member state by creating branches and serving customers, the latter member state can be obliged to recognize that entity's legal personality. In the case of an artificially intelligent *company*, created by making lawful use of a member state's company law in line with Shawn Bayern's construction (an AI company), the situation is clear. From the freedom of establishment laid down in the Treaty on the Functioning of the European

---

[75]   See the Court's ruling in ECJ, *Gebhard, supra* note 47, para. 37.

[76]   See the Court's holding in ECJ, *Ueberseering, supra* note 30, paras 92 and 93, cited *supra* on p. 13: "The protection of the interests of creditors, minority shareholders, employees and even the taxation authorities . . . [93] . . . cannot, however, justify denying the legal capacity and, consequently, the capacity to be a party to legal proceedings of a company properly incorporated in another Member State in which it has its registered office. Such a measure is tantamount to an outright negation of the freedom of establishment conferred on companies by Articles 43 EC and 48 EC [now articles 49 and 54 TFEU]."

[77]   Kersten, *supra* note 16, 7, discusses the idea of a "personales Substrat" of natural persons (in English: personal substratum, my translation) as a prerequisite for a legal person to have the capacity to hold fundamental constitutional rights. While Kersten's discussion is based on a ruling of the German constitutional court, the idea of a personal substratum is similar to the "presence of a natural person" introduced in this chapter.

[78]   The indication of a responsible natural person is reminiscent of the requirement, pursuant to anti-money laundering law, to indicate the beneficial owner of assets. Note also that the idea of a guarantor likely will be challenging for criminal law theory, but this challenge at this point shall be left to criminal law lawyers.

Union results a duty to recognize the entity's foreign legal personality. Since the innards of foreign companies are shielded from member states' scrutiny, all companies created in the member states, including AI companies that are *not* controlled by natural (or legal) persons, can rely on the member states' duty of mutual recognition.

The situation is less clear, when the AI entity is an artificially intelligent *e-person* the creation of which a member state enabled (an AI e-person). While member states are at liberty to grant certain "creatures" legal personality by legislative fiat (e.g. certain webpages, but also animals or rivers), it is uncertain whether the AI e-person thus created qualifies as a "legal person" which is capable of relying on freedom of establishment and benefiting from mutual recognition.

In any case, other defensive measures than denying recognition of legal personality may be lawful against AI entities. Crucially, lawfulness depends on whether an AI company is under the control of a natural person. If it is, in one way or another, no ground is available to justify measures restricting the AI company's freedom of establishment. Having no place in the cold logic of the internal market, vague and abstract fears of artificial intelligence are not sufficient under the Court of Justice's case law to justify restrictions. Broad public policy measures are also only justifiable against concrete and specific threats. Absent any concrete threat by reason of their activities, controlled AI companies are, hence, free to operate within the internal market. Yet, like from any other market actor, compliance with national regulation imposed in accordance with internal market law is expected from AI companies. By way of example, this chapter examined regulation of gambling and pharmacies.

In contrast, when an AI entity is *not* controlled by natural persons, the law risks losing its effectiveness. Concrete and specific measures ensuring effective enforcement of the law, in particular, criminal law, are then warranted. However, denying an AI entity legal personality is not such a measure. It is unsuitable and goes beyond what is necessary to ensure effective enforcement of the law. Rather, a member state may require a foreign AI entity to indicate, in a register and on letterheads, a natural person as a guarantor who can be held responsible when the AI entity violates provisions of the law that carry criminal sanctions.

SOURCES

Cases

Court of Justice of the European Union (ECJ)
Van Duyn, 41-74, ECR 1974, 1337, 4 December 1974.
Bouchereau, 30/77, ECR 1977, 1999, 27 October 1977.
Rewe-Zentral (Cassis de Dijon), 120/78, ECR 1979, 649, 20 February 1979.
Adoui, 115-116/81, ECR 1982, 1665, 18 May 1982.
Commission v. Belgium (bio labs), 221/85, ECR 1987, 719, 12 February 1987.
Daily Mail, 81/87, ECR 1988, 5483, 27 September 1988.
Säger, C-76/90, ECR 1991 I-4221, 25 July 1991.
Bachmann, C-204/90, ECR 1992 I-249, 28 January 1992.
Commission v. Belgium (insurance taxation), C-300/90, ECR 1992 I-305, 28 January 1992.
Micheletti, C-369/90, ECR 1992 I-4239, 7 July 1992.
Gebhard, C-55/94, ECR 1995 I-4165, 30 November 1995.
Futura, C-250/95, ECR 1997 I-2471, 15 May 1997.

Centros, C-212/97, ECR 1999 I-1459, 9 March 1999.
Jany, C-268/99, ECR 2001 I-8615, 20 November 2001.
Lankhorst, C-324/00, ECR 2002 I-11779, 12 December 2002.
Ueberseering, C-208/00, ECR 2002 I-9919, 5 November 2002.
Deutscher Apothekerverband v. DocMorris and others, C-322/01, 11 December 2003.
Inspire Art, C-167/01, ECR 2003 I-10155, 30 September 2003.
Omega, C-36/02, ECR 2004 I-9609, 14 October 2004.
Cadbury Schweppes, C-196/04, ECR 2006 I-7995, 12 September 2006.
Eman and Sevinger, C-300/04, ECR 2006 I-8055, 12 September 2006.
Spain v. United Kingdom (Gibraltar), C-145/04, ECR 2006 I-7917, 12 September 2006.
Thin Cap, C-524/04, ECR 2007 I-2107, 13 March 2007.
Cartesio, C-210/06, ECR 2008 I-9641, 16 December 2008.
Commission v. Germany (hospital pharmacies), C-141/07 11 September 2008.
Apothekerkammer, C-171 and 172/07, ECR 2009 I-4171, 19 May 2009.
Liga Portuguesa and Bwin, C-42/07, ECR 2009 I-7633, 8 September 2009.
Commission v. France (bio labs), C-89/09, ECR 2010 I-12941, 16 December 2010.
Josemans, C-137/09, ECR 2010 I-13019, 16 December 2010.
Rottmann, C-135/08, ECR 2010 I-1449, 2 March 2010.
National Grid, C-371/10, ECR 2011 I-12273, 29 September 2011.
Vale, C-378/10, ECLI:EU:C:2012:440, 12 July 2012.

International Court of Justice (ICJ)

Reparation for Injuries Suffered in the Service of the United Nations, ICJ Reports 1949, p. 174 11 April 1949.
Nottebohm case (second phase), ICJ Reports 1955, p. 4 6 April 1955.
Barcelona Traction, Light and Power Company, Limited (New Application: 1962) (Belgium v. Spain), second phase, ICJ Reports 1970, p. 3 5 February 1970.

World Trade Organization Appellate Body

European Communities – Measures prohibiting the importation and marketing of seal products, 2014: WT/DS400 and 401/AB/R 22 May 2014.

Other legal materials

Comprehensive Economic Trade Agreement, 2016, COM(2016) 444 final 2016/0206(NLE).
Report with recommendation to the Commission on Civil Law Rules on Robotics, European Parliament (Committee on Legal Affairs; Rapporteur: Mady Delvaux), 2016, 2015/2103(INL).

21. The artificially intelligent Internet of Things and Article 2 of the Uniform Commercial Code

Stacy-Ann Elvy

The rise of artificial intelligence and the Internet of Things (IoT) has significant contracting implications for consumers. The IoT has been described as a network of connected Internet-enabled devices. These devices will frequently rely on artificial intelligence.[1] Artificial intelligence in autonomous systems can further enable the interpretation of data generated from consumers' use of Internet-enabled devices as well as make decisions and take appropriate action based on these data.[2] The Internet Business Solutions Group of Cisco—a leading multinational technology company—projects that by 2020 there will be 50 billion IoT devices in use globally.[3] This suggests that in the near future, artificially intelligent IoT devices will replace conventional objects in a consumer's home, including thermostats, refrigerators and televisions.

Examples of IoT products and services include Amazon's dash replenishment service which allows ordinary Internet-enabled devices to subsequently purchase goods on behalf of consumers without human intervention. Other examples include the Nest thermostat which uses some degree of artificial intelligence to learn and adjust the temperature and energy use in a home based on the consumer's preferences.[4] Artificial intelligence will also play a crucial role in IoT self-driving cars.[5] Based on these examples it is likely that artificially intelligent IoT products will enter society in ever increasing numbers, raising a host of issues for the law to consider.

As IoT devices that use artificial intelligence become smarter and more autonomous,

---

[1]   Daniel Faggella, *Artificial Intelligence Plus the Internet of Things (IOT)- 3 Examples Worth Learning From,* Tech Emergence (8 Feb. 2016), available at https://www.techemergence.com/artificial-intelligence-plus-the-internet-of-things-iot-3-examples-worth-learning-from/ (last visited 12 Aug. 2017).

[2]   Martin Fiore and Tim Carone, *AI As An Autonomous System: Problems and Opportunities,* Tax Notes Today 124–7 (2017).

[3]   Dave Evans, *The Internet of Things: How the Next Evolution of the Internet Is Changing Everything,* Cisco 2–3 (April 2011), http://www.cisco.com/web/about/ac79/docs/innov/IoT_IBSG_0411FINAL.pdf (last visited 12 Aug. 2017).

[4]   Fagella, *supra* note 1. See also, Corrine Iozzio, *Artificially Intelligent Thermostat Automatically Creates a Climate Schedule for You,* Popular Science, (20 Jan. 2012), http://www.popsci.com/gadgets/article/2011-12/artificially-intelligent-thermostats-learns-adapt-automatically (last visited 12 Aug. 2017) (describing the Nest thermostat as an "artificially intelligent thermostat."); Steven Levy, *How Nest Is Creating The Conscious Home One Smart Device at a Time,* Wired UK, (17 Feb. 2013), available at http://www.wired.co.uk/article/where-there-is-smoke (last visited 12 Aug. 2017) (discussing the Nest thermostat's use of artificial intelligence).

[5]   Fagella, *supra* note 1. See also, Will Knight, *Tesla's New AI Guru Could Help Its Cars Teach Themselves* (22 Jun. 2017), available at https://www.technologyreview.com/s/608155/teslas-new-ai-guru-could-help-its-cars-teach-themselves/. (last visited 12 Aug. 2017) (discussing artificial intelligence and Tesla cars).

several established areas of law will be challenged, including agency and contract law. For instance, can IoT devices controlled by artificial intelligence serve as contracting agents for humans, thereby creating legal obligations for consumers using such devices? How should courts assess consumer assent to a company's terms and conditions in the IoT setting; especially when an artificially intelligent IoT device is involved in the transaction? A consumer may not be required to access a company's website or mobile application prior to the IoT device placing subsequent orders for goods. Mobile applications and a company's website frequently contain terms and conditions of sale as well as a company's privacy policy. The lack of a traditional screen on IoT devices which can display contract terms prior to an order being placed, complicates the analysis of consumer assent to a company's terms and conditions. This situation may be exacerbated when artificial intelligence is involved in the transaction.

In the United States companies frequently include provisions that may be detrimental to consumer interests in their terms and conditions. It is likely that use of such terms will continue even in the age of the artificially intelligent IoT. These terms include class-action waivers and mandatory arbitration provisions to name a few. Thus, whether a consumer can be said to assent to a company's terms and conditions has significant implications for a consumer's rights under a contract.

Depending on the type of transaction at issue, questions involving contract terms can be evaluated under various sources of law, such as the Uniform Commercial Code (UCC) or the common law of contracts. Choice of law provisions contained in the parties' agreement can also influence which jurisdiction's laws will govern disputes between the parties. The Restatement of the Law (Second) of Contracts (Contracts Restatement) is the primary "guide to the modern common law of contracts."[6] The Contracts Restatement provides central principles of contract law that are relied upon by American courts.[7] The UCC is also an important source of commercial law in the United States. The UCC is comprised of several articles, including Article 2 of the UCC (Article 2) which is of particular interest to this chapter.

Regardless of whether artificial intelligence is involved in a transaction and "unless the context otherwise requires," Article 2 governs "transactions in goods."[8] Many of Article 2's substantive contract rules apply to transactions involving the sale of goods. Under Article 2, goods are generally defined as "all things (including specially manufactured goods) which are movable at the time of identification to the contract for sale."[9] To the extent that the products subsequently purchased by an IoT device which is enhanced by artificial intelligence qualifies as a good, Article 2's substantive rules may apply to the transaction. If an Internet-enabled washing machine which relies on artificial intelligence places an online order for detergent with a retailer, such as Amazon, the detergent likely qualifies as a good under Article 2 since it is a movable item and is likely "already existing and identified to the contract."[10] Thus, Article 2's

---

[6]   Restatement of the Law Second of Contracts, ALI.ORG, available at https://www.ali.org/publications/show/contracts/ (last visited 6 Aug. 2017).

[7]   *Id.*

[8]   U.C.C. § 2-102 (Am. Law Inst. and Unif. Law Comm'n 2017).

[9]   *Id.* at § 2-105.

[10]   *Id.* at §§ 2-105; 2-501.

substantive rules may govern the contract between the owner of the washing machine and the retailer.

Issues related to Article 2's application to a transaction become more complicated when a transaction involves a combination of goods, services or software. IoT devices that rely on some degree of artificial intelligence will typically be accompanied by various services, embedded software and mobile applications that work together to allow the device to function. If a transaction involves both the provision of goods and non-goods courts typically apply a predominant thrust test to evaluate whether the predominant purpose of the transaction is for the provision of goods, in which case Article 2 will apply to the transaction.[11]

With some exceptions, the UCC's provisions may be modified by the terms of the parties' agreement.[12] Article 2 also contains provisions that address both implied and express warranties. Transactions that are subject to Article 2 may obtain the benefit of various warranties. These warranties include the implied warranty of merchantability, the implied warranty of fitness for a particular purpose, the warranty of title and the warranty against infringement.[13] Article 2's implied warranties of quality are frequently disclaimed by companies in their terms and conditions. Article 2 provides various rules to enable this process.[14] If a warranty arises and is not effectively disclaimed, a buyer of non-conforming goods may have a cause of action for breach of warranty against the seller.[15] In addition to Article 2, other sources of local law may also provide implied warranties akin to those found in Article 2 to consumer purchasers of goods, and may also prohibit warranty disclaimers in consumer transactions.[16] Additionally, a federal statute—the Magnuson Moss Warranty Act—provides a consumer (as defined by the statute) with a potential cause of action for breach of implied warranties that arise under state law, such as those arising under Article 2 and other sources of state law.[17]

The UCC defines a consumer as "an individual who enters into a transaction primarily for personal, family, or household purposes."[18] Section 1-103 of the UCC provides that "unless displaced by the specific provisions of the Uniform Commercial Code, the principles of law and equity, including . . . principal and agent . . . supplement its provisions."[19]

---

[11]   Factors that courts consider in applying this test include: "the nature and reasonableness of the purchaser's contractual expectations of acquiring a property interest in the good" and the "factual circumstances surrounding the negotiation, formation, and contemplated performance of the contract." See *Colorado Carpet Installation, Inc. v. Palermo*, 668 P.2d 1384 (1983); *Glover School & Office Equipment Co. v. Dave Hall, Inc.*, 372 A.2d 221 (1977).

[12]   U.C.C. § 1-302(a) (Am. Law Inst. and Unif. Law Comm'n 2017) ("[e]xcept as otherwise provided in subsection (b) or elsewhere in [the Uniform Commercial Code], the effect of provisions of [the Uniform Commercial Code] may be varied by agreement.")

[13]   *Id.* §§ 2-312; 2-314; 2-315.

[14]   *Id.* at § 2-316.

[15]   *Id.* at § 2-714(2) (discussing buyer's damages for breach of warranty).

[16]   Conn. Gen. Stat. Ann. §42A-2-316; D.C. Code Ann. § 28:2-316.01; Kan. Stat. Ann. § 50-639(A); Me. Rev. Stat. Ann. tit. 11, § 2-316(5); Md. Code Ann. Com. Law § 2-316.1; Ma. St. 106 § 2-316A; Miss. Code Ann. § 11-7-18; Vt. Stat. Ann. Tit. 9A, § 2-316(5); W. Va. Code § 46A-6-107; Minn. Stat. §325G.18; Cal.Civ.Code §1792.

[17]   15 U.S.C. § 2310(d).

[18]   U.C.C. § 1-201(b)(11).

[19]   *Id.* at § 1-103(b).

This suggests that even if Article 2 applies to the transaction, questions related to the concept of agency may be answered by consulting traditional agency principles. In fact, there are several provisions in Article 2 which reference the use of agents by parties.[20] Given that artificially intelligent IoT devices may perform tasks that could be viewed as consistent with those of a human agent, at least in theory, agency law could be relevant in evaluating the activities of IoT devices controlled by artificial intelligence. The consumer in the example discussed earlier has arguably deployed a device—the washing machine—to act on its behalf. This raises interesting questions about how to evaluate whether the consumer has assented to the retailer's terms and conditions and whether the artificially intelligent washing machine is serving as an agent.

The Restatement of the Law (Third) of Agency (Agency Restatement) is a central source of common law agency principles.[21] The restatement describes the concept of agency, as a "fiduciary relationship that arises when one person (a 'principal') manifests assent to another person (an 'agent') that the agent shall act on the principal's behalf and subject to the principal's control, and the agent manifests assent or otherwise consents so to act."[22] If an agency relationship is established, a principal may be bound by the actions of the agent.[23]

Recall the hypothetical from above involving the consumer, the Internet-enabled washing machine with some degree of artificial intelligence and the online retailer. Assume that the washing machine relies on artificial intelligence to monitor how frequently the consumer does laundry, to learn about the consumer's laundry preferences, and subsequently adjusts its operations to conform to these preferences. One way to think about this example is that the washing machine as the agent of the consumer could be said to manifest assent to the agency relationship by placing orders for consumable supplies on behalf of the consumer. The consumer could be viewed as assenting to the agency relationship by electing to use the device to place orders on her behalf. Thus, arguably an agency relationship may be created between the washing machine and the consumer. The agent acting on the consumer's behalf may have bound the consumer to the retailer's online terms and conditions. However, as the following discussion will demonstrate, there are several potential challenges to using common law agency principles to evaluate the relationship between artificially intelligent IoT devices and consumers.

To create an agency relationship the principal should have some degree of control over the agent.[24] The comments to the Agency Restatement provide that "[a] relationship of agency is not present unless the person on whose behalf action is taken has the right to control the actor."[25] If the washing machine uses artificial intelligence to determine when new orders will be placed then consumers may not have sufficient control over the agent.

---

[20]   *Id.* at §§§§§ 2-403 cmt. 1; 2-201; 2-603; 2-104; 2-707.
[21]   Restatement (Third) of Agency intro. (Am. Law Inst. 2006).
[22]   *Id.* at § 1.01.
[23]   *Id.* at § 2.01–2.03.
[24]   *Id.* at § 1.01 cmt. c. ("a person may be an agent although the principal lacks the right to control the full range of the agent's activities. . .."). The comments to the Agency Restatement also states that "[a] principal's control over an agent will as a practical matter be incomplete because no agent is an automaton who mindlessly but perfectly executes commands." *Id.* at § 1.01 cmt. f.
[25]   *Id.* at § 1.01 cmt. f.

If consumers are not provided with the ability to determine the frequency with which orders are placed by the artificially intelligent IoT device or the types and amount of data that are collected by the device, the consumer may not have the control needed to establish an agency relationship. The extent to which a consumer will have control over the device likely depends on how the product is designed by the manufacturer and the role that artificial intelligence plays in the operations of the device. The more autonomous and smart the artificially intelligent IoT device becomes, the less control that may be exerted over it. On the other hand, if an artificially intelligent product begins to act autonomously and becomes more intelligent one could contend that the device will begin to share some characteristics with human agents. Even if an IoT product is designed by a manufacturer to give consumers the ability to determine when orders will be placed, once artificial intelligence plays a crucial role in an IoT device's operations it is not beyond the realm of possibility to envision a scenario in which the artificially intelligent IoT device goes rogue. In 2017 researchers at Facebook terminated the operations of a newly developed "artificially intelligent system," which was designed to negotiate with other artificially intelligent agents, due to concerns that the researchers would "lose control of the AI system."[26] The artificially intelligent system developed and began using its own "non-human" language instead of English in negotiations with other artificially intelligent agents.[27] In light of the perceived risks that may be associated with artificial intelligence, the chief executive officer of Tesla—an automotive company pioneering the way for the use of artificial intelligence in self-driving vehicles—has acknowledged the need for artificial intelligence legislation to be "proactive" rather than "reactive."[28]

As noted above, agency is a fiduciary relationship. As such, the agent has specific responsibilities to the principal. For instance, the Agency Restatement provides that the agent should "act loyally in the principal's interest as well as on the principal's behalf."[29] It is unclear whether the IoT devices consumers use will have sufficient intelligence to understand and perform the duty of loyalty. A manufacturer of an IoT device may simply pre-program the device to make predetermined decisions, such as the frequency with which products are reordered. In such an instance, it is unlikely that an IoT device can be said to possess the ability to think on its own or act autonomously. On the other hand,

---

[26]   James Walker, *Researchers Shut Down AI That Invented its Own Language* (21 July 2017) available at http://www.digitaljournal.com/tech-and-science/technology/a-step-closer-to-skynet-ai-invents-a-language-humans-can-t-read/article/498142 (last visited 12 Aug. 2017). See also, Adrienne Lafrance, *An Artificial Intelligence Developed Its Own Non-Human Language* (15 Jun. 2017) available at https://www.theatlantic.com/technology/archive/2017/06/artificial-intelligence-develops-its-own-non-human-language/530436/ (last visited 12 Aug. 2017).

[27]   Walker, *supra* note 26; Lafrance, *supra* note 26.

[28]   David Z. Morris, *Elon Musk Says Artificial Intelligence is the "Greatest Risk We Face as a Civilization"* Fortune (15 Jul. 2017), available at http://fortune.com/2017/07/15/elon-musk-artificial-intelligence-2/ (last visited 12 Aug. 2017). See also, Robert Hackett, *Watch Elon Musk Divulge His Biggest Fear About Artificial Intelligence,* Fortune, (27 Aug. 2016) available at http://fortune.com/2016/08/17/elon-musk-ai-fear-werner-herzog/ (last visited 12 Aug. 2017) (discussing Elon Musk's concerns about the rise of artificial intelligence).

[29]   Restatement (Third) of Agency § 1.01 cmt. e. See also, *id.* at § 8.03 ("[a]n agent has a duty not to deal with the principal as or on behalf of an adverse party in a transaction connected with the agency relationship.")

given developments that suggest that artificially intelligent agents can negotiate with each other and develop their own language, this hurdle could be overcome in the near future as artificially intelligent IoT devices become smarter and autonomous.

IoT devices collect a wealth of information about consumers, including consumption rate data and health-related data. Consider that the voice activation feature on Internet-enabled televisions can listen to the conversations of television viewers.[30] These conversations may be shared with the television manufacturer and unaffiliated parties.[31] Arguably, this presents a potential conflict of interest. In the IoT context, an artificially intelligent device may follow and comply with the instructions of the consumer who has deployed the device to act on its behalf, but the device simultaneously collects information about the consumer and transfers these data to the manufacturer or retailer. Depending on the terms and conditions and the privacy policy of the manufacturer and retailer, these data could be used not only to provide a service or product to the consumer, but it could also be disclosed and sold to third parties. Once manufacturers and other companies obtain data about consumers, data analytics and artificial intelligence can aid these organizations in combining IoT data with other disparate sources of data about a consumer. This information could be used to shape consumer preferences, determine how companies treat individual consumers as well as influence the opportunities consumers subsequently receive.[32] Several scholars and commentators suggest that the widespread use of algorithms could impact college admissions, employment applications and promotions, and credit card determinations, among other things.[33] With the rise of the artificially intelligent IoT, the historical data that can be used by algorithms to make decisions and predictions is expected to increase exponentially.

The Agency Restatement indicates that an agent may avoid allegations of breach of its duties "if the principal consents to the conduct."[34] Thus, one might argue that to the extent that a company's terms and conditions or privacy policy discloses that information will be collected by the manufacturer and the consumer consents to the terms and conditions then issues associated with a conflict of interest could be avoided assuming that the agent

---

[30]   *Not in Front of the Telly: Warning Over "Listening" TV*, BBC News (9 Feb. 2015), http://www.bbc.com/news/technology-31296188 (last visited 12 Aug. 2017).

[31]   Chris Matyszczyk, *Samsung's Warning: Our Smart TVs Record Your Living Room Chatter*, CNET (8 Feb. 2015, 2:10 PM), http://www.cnet.com/news/samsungs-warning-our-smart-tvs-record-your-living-room-chatter (last visited 12 Aug. 2017).

[32]   Solon Barocas and Helen Nissenbaum, *Big Data's End Run Around Procedural Privacy Protections* 57 Communications of the ACM, 31, 32 (2014).

[33]   Pauline Kim, *Data-Driving Discrimination At Work* 58 Wm. & Mary L. Rev. 857 (2017) (discussing algorithms and employment discrimination); Joshua A. Kroll, et al, *Accountable Algorithms* 165 U. Pa. L. Rev. 633 (2017) (discussing algorithms and discrimination in jobs, insurance and credit card contexts); Solon Barocas and Andrew Selbst, *Big Data's Disparate Impact* 104 Calif. L. Rev. 671 (2016) (discussing the use of computer programs and algorithms in medical school applications); Scott R. Peppet, *Regulating the Internet of Things: First Steps Toward Managing Discrimination, Privacy, Security, and Consent* 93 Tex. L. Rev. 85 (2014) (discussing potential discriminatory impacts in the IoT setting); Cathy O'Neil, *How Can We Stop Algorithms from Telling Lies?* The Guardian (16 Jul. 2017) https://www.theguardian.com/technology/2017/jul/16/how-can-we-stop-algorithms-telling-lies (last visited 12 Aug. 2017) (describing concerns associated with the use of algorithms).

[34]   Restatement (Third) of Agency § 8.06.

continues to act in good faith. Historically, consumers have frequently failed to review terms and conditions and privacy policies.[35] This could be exacerbated as artificially intelligent IoT devices become more involved in the contracting process and as artificial intelligence begins to be widely used in creating contract terms without human input. Relying on consumer consent and disclosures in a privacy policy or terms and conditions may be insufficient to place consumers on notice of data collection. However, a 2017 study of consumer preferences in ten countries published by the Mobile Ecosystem Forum found that "75% of respondents always or sometimes read privacy policies and terms of conditions before signing up to a mobile app or service."[36] The report describes the emergence of the "Savvy Consumer" who may stop using a company's products as well as notify cohorts if there are trust issues associated with the company.[37] If consumers are indeed becoming more savvy and knowledgeable about terms and conditions then a consumer's continued use of a company's product after being provided with contract terms can be used as a basis for implying consumer assent to the terms. Of course, the use of artificial intelligence could impact the analysis, making the terms and conditions of the contract more opaque; thereby, arguably limiting "notice and an opportunity to read the relevant contractual terms."[38]

In light of the large quantities of data about consumers that can be collected by artificially intelligent IoT devices and disclosed to organizations and the control that manufacturers may retain over such devices, these products could be viewed as agents of manufacturers rather than consumers. A company can manufacture artificially intelligent IoT devices to collect data on its behalf and this could be viewed as manifesting assent to the agency relationship. The manufacturer could be said to have sufficient control over the device as it may be able to determine the type and quantity of data collected and the frequency of data collection, as well as send mandatory software updates to the device that the consumer is obligated to accept. Through end user license agreements (EULAs) companies retain control of, and limit consumer rights in, software embedded within IoT devices and external software, such as mobile applications, needed to operate the device. Moreover, even though a consumer generates the data that are collected by IoT devices and could be viewed as having title to the physical device, companies are likely to assert that they either own or have specific rights in such data.[39] The artificially intelligent IoT device's assent to agency could be inferred from the collection, processing, communication and transfer of consumer data to the company. Assuming that the device qualifies as an agent, the acts of the device are binding on the principal—the manufacturer.

---

[35]   Nancy S. Kim and D.A. Jeremy Telman, *Internet Giants as Quasi-Governmental Actors and the Limits of Contractual Consent* 80 Mo. L. Rev. 723, 732–34 (2015).

[36]   Consumer Trust, Featured Post, MEF available at https://mobileecosystemforum.com/20 17/06/29/seventy-five-per-cent-smartphone-users-read-privacy-policies-industry-gets-ready-embrac e-savvy-consumers/?utm_content=bufferc0e94&utm_medium=social&utm_source=facebook.com &utm_campaign=buffer (last visited 17 Jul. 2017).

[37]   *Id.*

[38]   Nancy Kim, *Clicking and Cringing* 86 Or. L. Rev. 797, 818 (2007).

[39]   See generally, Stacy-Ann Elvy, *Commodifying Consumer Data in the Era of the Internet of Things*, 59 B.C. L. Rev. 423 (2018) (discussing companies' rights in consumer generated data and companies' use of customer databases containing consumer data as assets in business transactions); U.C.C. § 2-401 ("Any retention or reservation by the seller of the title (property) in goods shipped or delivered to the buyer is limited in effect to a reservation of a security interest.").

The Agency Restatement uses the term "person" to refer to agents and principals, which suggests that agency principles can apply only to parties with legal personhood.[40] IoT devices and artificially intelligent entities or systems in general are not "persons." This presents a significant challenge to using agency principles to evaluate transactions involving artificially intelligent IoT devices, consumers and companies. Thus, despite the provisions of the UCC which indicate that agency principles may be used to evaluate the relationship between contracting parties, the limitations previously discussed indicate that the common law of agency may not appropriately address all contracting issues related to consumers' use of artificially intelligent IoT devices. Thus, a return to basic contract law principles is necessary.

As Professor Nancy Kim has noted, in evaluating consumer assent to contract terms, if the consumer has "demonstrated assent" to the transaction, American "courts have not much concerned themselves with whether the party had actual knowledge, and thus actually assented to, the contractual term at issue. Instead, the courts have focused on notice and an opportunity to read the relevant contractual terms."[41] As artificially intelligent IoT devices begin to play a more frequent role in transactions, consumers may have even less of an opportunity to review contract terms.

The UCC defines an agreement as a "bargain of the parties, in fact, as found in their language or inferred from other circumstances, including course of dealing, usage of trade, and course of performance. . ."[42] To date, the bargain has predominately involved individuals, human agents, and legally recognized entities rather than artificially intelligent devices, systems or agents. A contract is defined as "the total legal obligation that results from the parties' agreement as determined by the [UCC]. . ."[43]

A company may provide its terms and conditions online using various formats, such as clickwrap and browsewrap agreements.[44] In a clickwrap contract, the consumer is required to click an "I agree" button after the terms and conditions are displayed.[45] The act of clicking the "I agree" button or option may be viewed as demonstrating consumer assent to contract terms. In browsewrap agreements, the company's terms and conditions are provided via a hyperlink on the company's website.[46] A consumer may be viewed as consenting to the terms by continuing to use the company's website. On the other hand, the consumer in a browsewrap agreement could contend that she has not unambiguously assented to the terms of the contract. The notice and an opportunity to review standard becomes particularly important in such agreements.

The notice standard mentioned above is problematic in the consumer context. In clickwrap agreements, even if the consumer clicks the "I agree" button the consumer may not have reviewed the terms or intended to consent to all of the terms and conditions offered

---

[40]   See, e.g., Restatement (Third) of Agency § 1.01 cmts. a–c.

[41]   Kim, *supra* note 38 at 818.

[42]   U.C.C. § 1-201(b)(3).

[43]   *Id*. at § 1-201(b)(12).

[44]   Clayton P. Gillette, *Pre-Approved Contracts for Internet Commerce* 42 Hous. L. Rev. 975, 975–76 (2006).

[45]   Linda J. Rusch and Stephen L. Sepinuck, *Commercial Law: Problems and Materials on Sales and Payments* (West 2012) 60.

[46]   *Id.*

by the company.[47] In the browsewrap context, the hyperlink containing a company's terms and conditions may not be conspicuously displayed on the company's website. Consumers may not always click on the hyperlink, read the terms of use, or understand the terms of the agreement prior to purchasing goods. Today, various automatic online shopping options, such as one-click payment and subscription options, facilitate a lack of proximity between consumers and contract terms. These purchasing options enable a shopping environment in which consumers quickly purchase goods and services without reviewing a company's terms and conditions.

The problem of "Contract Distancing—the growing distance between consumers, contract terms, and the contract formation process in the IOT setting"—highlights the inadequacies of relying on notice and an opportunity to review.[48] Recall that because IoT devices are primarily ordinary objects (such as artificially intelligent thermostats) that are Internet-enabled they frequently lack the traditional screens found on mobile phones, tablets and computers which are used to display a company's terms and conditions and privacy policy. IoT devices allow consumers to purchase goods without having to enter a store, visit a company's website or access a mobile application, or click the "I agree" button before each purchase.

A consumer could place a new order for goods by clicking a physical button on an IoT device which facilitates distance between consumers and contract terms. For instance, Amazon's Dash Button allows consumers to place orders for goods by clicking the Dash Button—a small reordering device that lacks a screen to display contract terms.[49] In the IoT setting it is likely that consumers will continue to have no compelling reason to evaluate terms and conditions that may favor companies prior to contracting. IoT products facilitate a seamless process between a consumer's decision to buy services and goods and the online ordering process. Once artificial intelligence begins to play a more central role in the performance of IoT products, and a consumer's preferences are considered by the artificially intelligent device, the purchasing and contracting process may become even more seamless and require less human intervention. A consumer that uses Amazon's Dash Button to purchase a product will not need to review the company's terms and conditions or click an online "I agree" button before clicking the physical button on the device to place multiple successive orders for goods.

A similar problem also arises when other types of IoT devices are used to purchase products. As noted earlier, artificially intelligent IoT devices may eventually have the capacity to place orders for goods and services on behalf of consumers. An IoT device that is enabled with Amazon's dash replenishment service can purchase goods without the consumer reviewing the company's terms and conditions prior to the device placing the seventh or eighth order for goods. In short, given that IoT products have the capacity to reorder goods without displaying contract terms, and consumers may purchase goods by simply clicking a physical button on a device that also does not display contract terms,

---

[47]   Kim, *supra* note 38 at 813.

[48]   Stacy-Ann Elvy, *Contracting in the Age of the Internet of Things* 44 Hofstra L. Rev. 837, 839 (2016).

[49]   Gordon Fletcher, *Amazon Dash is a First Step Towards an Internet of Things That Is Actually Useful*, Conversation (8 Apr. 2015, 1:31 AM), http://theconversation.com/amazon-dash-is-a-first-step-towards-an-internet-of-things-that-is-actually-useful-39711 (last visited 12 Aug. 2017).

including the price of the goods to be purchased, it is not surprising that consumers are becoming further removed from the contracting process. Thus, in the artificially intelligent age of the IoT "[c]ontracting through the use of IOT devices will likely increase preexisting levels of Contract Distancing."[50]

Contract Distancing could also complicate issues related to contractual capacity. The ease with which IoT devices could be deployed as contracting tools by vulnerable groups of consumers may make it difficult to determine whether an opposing contracting party has knowledge of the vulnerable consumer's limited capacity.[51] This potential lack of knowledge may limit a vulnerable consumer's "power of avoidance."[52]

In the IoT setting, consumers are less likely to be provided with an opportunity to review terms prior to placing successive orders and entering into contracts. However, despite the likelihood of rising Contract Distancing levels, a court could infer consumer assent to a company's terms and conditions if notice of such terms is provided to the consumer when the device was first activated, if a clickwrap agreement was used and the consumer chose the "I agree" option when the device was first purchased or activated, or if the consumer continues to use the company's websites or products. Alternatively, a company could provide notice of its terms and conditions to the consumer via email after the order has been placed by the device. Courts should be wary of automatically finding that a consumer has consented to a company's terms and conditions particularly if the company does not provide the consumer with its contract terms prior to the IoT device placing a successive order, or if the consumer fails to understand the impact of the terms provided. Again, following the theme of this chapter, as artificially intelligent IoT devices begin ordering products and services, the human consumer is further removed from the terms and conditions of the contract.

Contract Distancing in the artificially intelligent IoT context is also problematic when one considers the use of unilateral amendment provisions in consumer contracts. A unilateral amendment provision allows one party to revise the terms of the agreement without obtaining approval from the other contracting party. Not surprisingly, unilateral amendment provisions are frequently included in companies' online terms and conditions and privacy policies. It is not inconceivable that in the near future artificially intelligent systems could independently make such amendments to contracts.

With respect to contract amendments, Article 2 provides that "an agreement modifying a contract . . . needs no consideration to be binding."[53] The comments section to Article 2 then goes on to provide that amendments "must meet the test of good faith" and "[t]he

---

[50]   Elvy, *supra* note 48 at 839.

[51]   Restatement (Second) of Contracts § 12 (Am. Law Inst. 1981) ("A natural person who manifests assent to a transaction has full legal capacity to incur contractual duties thereby unless he is (a) under guardianship, or (b) an infant, or (c) mentally ill or defective, or (d) intoxicated."). U.C.C. § 1-103(b) ("Unless displaced by the particular provisions of [the Uniform Commercial Code], the principles of law and equity, including . . . the law relative to capacity to contract . . . supplement its provisions.").

[52]   Restatement (Second) of Contracts § 15 ("Where the contract is made on fair terms and the other party is without knowledge of the mental illness or defect, the power of avoidance under Subsection (1) terminates to the extent that the contract has been so performed in whole or in part or the circumstances have so changed that avoidance would be unjust.").

[53]   U.C.C. § 2-209(1).

test of 'good faith' between merchants or as against merchants includes 'observance of reasonable commercial standards of fair dealing in the trade' ... and may in some situations require an objectively demonstrable reason for seeking a modification."[54] Some scholars have critiqued Article 2 for its failure to provide detailed guidance on the enforceability of contract modifications.[55] As artificially intelligent systems become more autonomous from humans in negotiating contracts, when one of the contracting parties is an artificially intelligent entity, how courts will view contract amendments remains to be determined.

If a company elects to exercise the right to unilaterally amend its terms and conditions, consumers may not be provided with adequate notice of changes to contract terms that might significantly impact their access to judicial process. In the artificially intelligent IoT context, Contract Distancing further complicates this problem. A company could easily amend its terms and conditions to impact a consumer's remedies under the contract or make it more challenging for certain consumers to sue. For instance, the imposition of warranty disclaimers may negate a cause of action for breach of warranties. Similarly, a change in the forum selection clause to another jurisdiction may make it difficult for far-flung consumers to initiate a lawsuit. IoT devices lack the traditional screens used to display not only the initial contract terms but also any revised terms and conditions adopted by the company via the use of a unilateral amendment provision. If a company revises its terms and conditions after a consumer has enabled the IoT device to place successive orders for products, it is possible that the device may order goods without the consumer reviewing the revised terms and conditions. Thus, even if a consumer is savvy enough to read and understand a company's terms and conditions prior to enabling an IoT device to buy goods, a consumer may not be provided with an adequate opportunity to review and understand revised terms prior to the artificially intelligent IoT device's subsequent purchase of additional goods.

To review a company's revised terms and conditions, a savvy consumer may have to first access the company's website, then attempt to identify which provisions were amended or updated. This is less likely to occur in a contracting environment in which ordinary objects with some degree of artificial intelligence have the capacity to order goods for consumers. Thus, in the IoT setting the use of unilateral amendment provisions in online consumer contracts may mean that consumers will be less likely to view or have the opportunity to read revised terms prior to artificially intelligent IoT devices ordering goods on their behalf. A company could attempt to remedy this problem by providing email notifications to consumers of updated terms and conditions, and informing consumers about the specific amendments that were made. Not all companies are willing to contractually obligate themselves to provide consumers with notice of revisions to their terms and conditions. Of course, in some instances state law may require an online company to provide some description of the process used to inform consumers of amendments to its privacy policy.[56] Even if notice of contract terms is sufficiently provided, such notice

---

[54]   *Id.* at cmt 2.

[55]   Robert A. Hillman, *Contract Modification Under the Restatement (Second) of Contracts* 67 Cornell L. Rev. 680, 686 (1982).

[56]   Cal. Bus. and Prof. Code §§22575-79 (requiring certain companies to post a privacy policy that "describes the process by which the operator notifies consumers" of "material changes" to

will not remedy one of the chief concerns associated with online consumer transactions: consumers' failure to read and understand contract terms and their implications.

When a consumer enters into an online transaction with a company, the consumer is typically provided with terms and conditions of sale as well as a privacy policy. Recall that IoT devices are frequently accompanied by software, and in some instances, can be controlled and operated through mobile applications—software programs that enable access to services and other products. Other documents, such as EULAs (applicable to the software provided by companies)[57] and limited warranty agreements may also be provided depending on the type of transaction. Consider that one study of online disclosures estimates "that reading privacy policies carries costs in time of approximately 201 hours a year."[58] Consumers may already feel inundated with the large number of emails, terms and conditions and other documents they are required to review to engage in a single transaction and everyday activities. The use of artificially intelligent IoT devices could exacerbate this situation. Notices sent via email of a company's revised terms and conditions may simply be ignored as a result.

Although a company may contend that a valid contract has been formed and that a consumer has assented to its existing terms and conditions, there are various defenses to contract enforcement that may be used by a party. Article 2 of the UCC expressly references the traditional contract defense of unconscionability. More specifically, Article 2 states

> If the court as a matter of law finds the contract or any clause of the contract to have been unconscionable at the time it was made the court may refuse to enforce the contract, or it may enforce the remainder of the contract without the unconscionable clause, or it may so limit the application of any unconscionable clause as to avoid any unconscionable result.[59]

The provisions of the Contracts Restatement relating to unconscionability contain similar language.[60] While the comments to this section of Article 2 include a reference to a "basic test" that evaluates whether the term is one-sided and it provides that the "principle is one of the prevention of oppression and unfair surprise," not much guidance is provided to courts in evaluating unconscionability.[61] Professors Linda Rusch and Stephen Sepinuck have noted that "nothing in the UCC purports to define the meaning and scope of the term 'unconscionable.'"[62]

---

a privacy policy); 6 Del. C. §§ 1201C-06C (requiring certain companies to post privacy policies that "describe the process by which the operator notifies users of its commercial internet website, online or cloud computing service, online application, or mobile application of material changes to the operator's privacy policy for that internet website, online or cloud computing service, online application, or mobile application."); State Laws Related to Internet Privacy, National Conference of State Legislatures (20 Jun. 2017), http://www.ncsl.org/research/telecommunications-and-information-technology/state-laws-related-to-internet-privacy.aspx (last visited 27 Sept. 2017) (noting that Nevada enacted a bill similar to the California statute in 2017).

[57]   Nancy S. Kim, *The Software Licensing Dilemma* 2008 BYU L. Rev. 1103, 1140 (2008) ("the sale of a software product does not exclude a license of the software.")

[58]   Aleecia McDonald and Lorrie Faith Cranor, *The Cost of Reading Privacy Policies* 4(3) I/S: A Journal of Law and Privacy for the Information Society 540–65, 562 (2008).

[59]   U.C.C. §2 -302(1).

[60]   Restatement (Second) of Contracts § 208.

[61]   U.C.C. § 2-302 cmt 1.

[62]   Rusch and Sepinuck, *supra* note 45 at 77.

In other legal regimes more guidance is provided on issues related to unfairness in contracting. For instance, the European Union's Council Directive on Unfair Terms in Consumer Contracts provides express guidance on contract terms that can be deemed to be unfair and invalid via a non-exhaustive list of provisions.[63] Professor Michael Rustad notes that the directive's non-exhaustive "list invalidates many common terms in U.S.-style terms of use: disclaimer of warranties, limitations of licensor's liability, unilateral modifications to contract terms, and the acceptance of the license agreement by performance."[64] Additionally, the directive notes that mandatory arbitration provisions may be regarded as potentially unfair.[65]

The comments section of the Contracts Restatement provides that "[a] bargain is not unconscionable merely because the parties to it are unequal in bargaining position, nor even because the inequality results in an allocation of risks to the weaker party."[66] However, the comments section also goes on to suggest that "gross inequality of bargaining power together with terms unreasonably favorable to the stronger party" may indicate that a party had no "meaningful choice" but to agree to the other party's contract terms.[67] This observation could be particularly relevant in an age of increasingly smart IoT devices, in which at some point in the future, artificial intelligence may surpass human intelligence. Consider that in 2017 an artificially intelligent program that was trained by researchers to play Dota 2—an online game—through self-play "against a copy of itself" defeated a professional human player at an international gaming championship.[68] The bot eventually superseded the skill level of elite world human players.[69] How will humans negotiate with a superior intelligence and how should the doctrine of unconscionability apply in such contexts?

American courts have significant discretion in evaluating issues of unconscionability. Several American courts and commentators have noted that given the language in Article 2's comments section discussed above, there are two prongs to unconscionability.[70] The first is substantive and the second is procedural.[71] Courts generally demand both substantive and procedural unconscionability to be present in a case.[72] However, in some

---

[63]   Council Directive 93/13/EEC 1993 O.J. (L 095) (EC) [hereinafter, EU Directive].

[64]   Micahel L. Rustad and Maria Vittoria Onuuforio, *Reconceptualizing Consumer Terms of Use for a Globalized Knowledge Economy* 14 U. Pa. J. Bus. L. 1085, 1136 (2012).

[65]   EU Directive, *supra* note 63. See also, Jane K. Winn and Mark Webber, *The Impact of EU Unfair Contract Terms Law on U.S. Business-to-Consumer Internet Merchants* 62 Bus. Law. 209, fn 68 (2006) (noting that the directive's annex "provides examples of unfair terms [including] . . . limiting the consumer's access to legal process by, for example, requiring arbitration."); Christopher R. Drahozal and Raymond J. Friel, *Consumer Arbitration in the European Union and the United States* 28 N.C.J. Int'l L. and Com. Reg. 357, 366 (2002) ("A pre-dispute arbitration clause, which has not been individually negotiated, appears prima facie to be void under the Directive. . .").

[66]   Restatement (Second) of Contracts § 208 cmt. d.

[67]   *Id.*

[68]   Jackie Wattles, *A Bot Just Defeated One of the World's Best Video Gamers*, CNN, 12 Aug. 2017, available at http://money.cnn.com/2017/08/12/technology/future/elon-musk-ai-dota-2/index.html?iid=ob_homepage_tech_pool.

[69]   *Id.*

[70]   Rusch and Sepinuck, *supra* note 45 at 77–78.

[71]   *Id.*

[72]   *Id.* at 78.

instances, a court may "permit an abundance of one to make up for a lack or minimal amount of the other."[73]

Substantive unconscionability "is concerned with contract terms that are illegal, contrary to public policy, or grossly unfair."[74] Consider an amendment to a company's terms and conditions that occurs after an artificially intelligent IoT device is purchased which removes an option for consumers to access small claims courts—a division of civil courts that generally hears claims below a specific monetary amount—in the event of a breach. Small claims courts may allow claims brought by plaintiffs to be "resolved quickly and inexpensively."[75]

The consumer in the hypothetical above previously had the option of bringing potential claims in a small claims court when the IoT device was purchased. This option has now been eliminated once the consumer enables the device to purchase goods from the company via the artificially intelligent IoT device. The consumer may be subject to multiple terms and conditions (assuming that the changes to the company's terms are not viewed as retroactive). Stated differently, one set of terms applies to the agreement involving the IoT device and another set of terms applies to subsequent products ordered by the device. One could of course contend that the presence of a unilateral amendment provision which authorized changes to the terms and conditions that the consumer previously assented to should mean that changes to remove the small claims court option should also apply to the agreement for the initial purchase of the IoT device. Additionally, Section 2-302(1) indicates that unconscionability should be determined at the time the contract was made.[76] Arguably at the time of contracting the unilateral amendment provision did not generate a problematic result for the consumer. However, the impact of the contract term should qualify as an unfair or oppressive result particularly since the provision likely significantly favors the party with stronger bargaining power. Courts have historically been reluctant to widely strike down contract terms on the grounds of unconscionability.[77]

Procedural unconscionability "is determined by examining the circumstances surrounding the contract formation, including the particular party's ability to understand the terms of the contract and the relative bargaining power of the parties."[78] The "relative bargaining power of the parties" may be impacted by the level of information that one party holds. In the artificially intelligent IoT context, companies will have increasingly detailed information about consumers, thereby exacerbating preexisting levels of information asymmetry.

With the expected increase in the number of IoT devices, companies will be able to obtain copious quantities of data about consumers that was never before widely available. These data will likely be subject to analysis by artificial intelligence techniques

---

[73]   *Id.*

[74]   *Guthmann v. La Vida Llena*, 103 N.M. 506, 510 (1985). See also, *Cordova v. World Fin. Corp.*, 208 P.3d 901 (2009).

[75]   California Courts, The Judicial Branch, Small Claims Courts, available at http://www.courts.ca.gov/1256.htm (last visited 6 Aug. 2017).

[76]   U.C.C. §2 -302(1).

[77]   Michael L. Rustad and Maria Vittoria Onufrio, *The Exportability of the Principles of Software: Lost in Translation?* 2 Hastings Sci. and Tech. L.J. 25, 76 (2009).

[78]   *Guntham*, 103 N.M 506 at 510.

and systems. As Professor Scott Peppet notes, IoT devices can provide companies with various data about consumers, including stress and fitness levels, among other things.[79] From the data generated by IoT devices, companies can make an "overall assessment of observations of daily living" of individual consumers.[80] Data analytics can be used to forecast the preferences of consumers as well as influence their behaviors. Companies are unlikely to provide consumers with access to the vast quantities of data that they compile and aggregate or share insights they glean about individual consumers from the use of data analytics. As a result, pre-existing information asymmetry in contracting will likely increase in the IoT setting. However, despite potential increases in the levels of information asymmetry, courts may continue to be reluctant in finding unconscionability in consumer contracts.

The extent to which a company explains contract terms to consumers during the contracting process may also be relevant in assessing claims of unconscionability. Companies may attempt to fend off claims of unconscionability by ensuring that IoT devices clearly communicate contract terms to consumers. Even though IoT devices lack the traditional screens found on computers and other mobile devices, it may be possible for an IoT device to be preprogrammed to "provide explanations of terms and conditions to consumers, as well as track how long a consumer spent reviewing the explanations and follow up with consumers regarding their understanding of such terms."[81] Home robots, such as Jibo, may provide an opportunity for companies to explain their terms and conditions to consumers including amendments that are made after a consumer enables an artificially intelligent IoT device to place subsequent orders.

However, explanations of contract terms after the contract formation process has ended may still be problematic. A consumer may not always be given the option to return products or devices, and may have to incur multiple return shipping costs and bear the risk of loss during returns. Moreover, if the device only reads the company's terms and conditions without explaining their implications to consumers, consumers are unlikely to obtain a better understanding of contract terms. The result is that companies could continue to include terms that enable them to protect themselves from lawsuits simply by providing evidence that notice of the terms and conditions were given to consumers. Companies may use notice of contractual provisions to avoid not only consumer breach of contract claims but also lawsuits by consumers that arise under consumer protection legislation.[82] Companies are able to undo "[u]ntold hours of toil in the realm of public policy advocacy . . . with the stroke of a pen, or more likely, with a reflexive and unreflective click on an 'I agree' icon."[83]

---

[79]   Peppet, *supra* note 33 at 117–40.
[80]   David Glance, *Will the Elderly Rely on the Internet of Things to Look After Them?*, Phys.org (18 Aug. 2015), http://phys.org/news/2015-08-elderly-internet.html (last visited 12 Aug. 2017).
[81]   Elvy, *supra* note 48 at 897.
[82]   Nancy S. Kim, *Good Enough Notice—Even if not for Assent*, Law Prof. Blogs Network (24 Aug. 2015), http://lawprofessors.typepad.com/contractsprof_blog/2015/08/good-enough-notice-even-if-not-for-assent.html (last visited 12 Aug. 2017) (noting that at least one court has found that notice of a company's terms and conditions may be "good enough to defeat the consumer's claims [under consumer protection statutes] even if that notice might not be sufficient for contract formation.").
[83]   Kim and Telman, *supra* note 35 at 753.

Additionally, as mentioned earlier consumers may be overwhelmed with the large quantities of disclosures that they must review, and may simply ignore terms and conditions that are read to them by artificially intelligent IoT devices. Thus, it is not entirely clear whether artificially intelligent IoT devices can increase consumer understanding of contract terms. This lack of knowledge and understanding becomes even more problematic in the IoT context as consumers are significantly removed from the contracting process. Not only can consumers mindlessly purchase goods through IoT devices but for some consumers these purchases will likely increase consumers' (and in turn their families') indebtedness to creditors, such as credit card companies. It is unlikely that consumers will be adequately protected from contractual abuse and contract terms that restrict their right to legal recourse in the IoT setting.

The Federal Trade Commission—a federal consumer protection agency—has acknowledged concerns about the use of IoT data and data analytics to discriminate against low income consumers.[84] Further, as previously noted, additional examples of potential concerns for consumers in the IoT context include exacerbation of the lack of reading and understanding problem due to increased levels of Contract Distancing and the use of IoT data to make inferences about consumer habits, which may lead companies to target consumers for contracting. IoT devices can generate data not only about the adults that buy these products but also data about children in the purchaser's home. This suggests that new approaches to contract law that consider rising levels of information asymmetry and Contract Distancing are warranted.

This chapter has illustrated the ways in which artificially intelligent IoT devices may generate important challenges for contract and agency law. The impact of the artificially intelligent IoT will likely be a significant topic of interest for legislators, regulatory bodies, judges, attorneys, and consumer protection advocates for years to come.

SOURCES

Article 1 of the Uniform Commercial Code (Am. Law Inst. & Unif. Law Comm'n 2017).
Article 2 of the Uniform Commercial Code (Am. Law Inst. & Unif. Law Comm'n 2017).
Magnuson Moss Warranty Act 88 Stat. 2183.
Conn. Gen. Stat. Ann. § 42A-2-316.
D.C. Code Ann. § 28:2-316.01.
Kan. Stat. Ann. § 50-639(A).
Me. Rev. Stat. Ann. tit. 11, § 2-316(5).
Md. Code Ann. Com. Law § 2-316.1.
Ma. St. 106 § 2-316A
Miss. Code Ann. § 11-7-18.
Vt. Stat. Ann. tit. 9A, § 2-316(5).
W. Va. Code § 46A-6-107.
Minn. Stat. §325G.18.
Cal. Civ. Code §1792.
Cal. Bus. and Prof. Code §§22575-79.
6 DEL. C. §§ 1201C-06C.
Restatement (Third) of Agency (Am. Law Inst. 2006).

---

[84] Fed. Trade Comm'n, Big Data: A Tool for Inclusion or Exclusion?, at i-v, 10 (2016), https://www.ftc.gov/system/files/documents/reports/big-data-tool-inclusion-or-exclusion-understanding-issues/160106big-data-rpt.pdf (last visited 12 Aug. 2017).

Restatement (Second) of Contracts (Am. Law Inst. 1981).
Guthmann v. La Vida Llena, 103 N.M. 506 (1985).
Cordova v. World Fin. Corp., 208 P.3d 901 (2009).
Colorado Carpet Installation, Inc. v. Palermo, 668 P.2d 1384 (1983).
Glover School & Office Equipment Co. v. Dave Hall, Inc., 372 A.2d 221 (1977).
Council Directive 93/13/EEC, 1993 O.J. (L 095) (EC).

22. Artificial intelligence and robotics, the workplace, and workplace-related law

Isabelle Wildhaber*

I. INTRODUCTION

Numerous robots are already in use in workplaces throughout the world today. Robots are already among us. We are in the so-called Second Machine Age,[1] also frequently referred to as Industry 4.0.[2] Many enterprises are working towards the goal of optimising work and production processes and creating a so-called smart factory in which humans and machines work together and automation is achieved through the deployment of intelligent machines. These intelligent self-learning systems are driven by cloud computing, breakthroughs in sensor technology and the creation of new algorithms that harness the power of big data.[3] The new workplace is constantly changing, increasingly uninhibited by geographical boundaries and inspired by the arrival of robots and new technologies. Robots are becoming more integrated into the human workplace, not only completing tasks autonomously, but also enhancing human performance and safety in the workplace and at home.[4] As new technologies facilitate remote work, the physical and temporal bounds of the workplace are becoming more flexible. These changes are simultaneously and cumulatively transforming the conditions of work.

The aim of this article is to examine the effects of robots and artificial intelligence (AI) on employment law. The introduction first defines what we understand by robots and AI (section I.A. below). I will then explain which robots play a role in the workplace today and could play a role in the workplace in the future (I.B. below). These changes will also have consequences for employment law (I.C. below). For this reason, I would like to use this chapter of the Handbook to travel forward in time to the employment law of the future changed by robotics and AI. In the course of this journey, seven challenges for employment law will be identified (in II.A.–G. below). Swiss law serves as the national system of reference here.

---

* This text is based on past research: Isabelle Wildhaber, D*ie Roboter kommen – Konsequenzen für Arbeit und Arbeitsrecht* I Zeitschrift für Schweizerisches Recht (ZSR) 315–51 (2016); Isabelle Wildhaber, *Robotik am Arbeitsplatz – Von "Robo Colleagues" und "Robo-Bosses"*, Aktuelle Juristische Praxis (AJP) 213–24 (2017).

[1] Erik Brynjolfsson and Andrew McAfee, *The Second Machine Age: Work, Progress, and Prosperity in a Time of Brilliant Technologies* (W.W. Norton 2014).

[2] Jens Günther and Matthias Böglmüller, *Arbeitsrecht 4.0 – Arbeitsrechtliche Herausforderungen in der vierten industriellen Revolution*, NZA 1025 *et seq.* (2015); Federal Ministry for Employment and Social Issues, *Grünbuch Arbeitsrecht 4.0*, p. 34 *et seq.*

[3] Littler Report, *The Transformation of the Workplace Through Robotics, Artificial Intelligence, and Automation: Employment and Labor Law Issues, Solutions, and the Legislative and Regulatory Response*, January 2016, p. 1.

[4] *Idem.*

A.   Artificial Intelligence and Robotics

Artificial Intelligence (AI) is a field of computer science devoted to creating comput-ing machines and systems that perform operations analogous to human learning and decision-making. As the Association for the Advancement of Artificial Intelligence describes it, AI is "the scientific understanding of the mechanisms underlying thought and intelligent behaviour and their embodiment in machines."[5] Computer scientist John McCarthy, who is credited with coining the term in 1955, defines it as "the science and engineering of making intelligent machines."[6] AI has seen a resurgence in recent years as a result of the development of machine learning—a branch of AI that focuses on designing algorithms that can automatically and iteratively build analytical models from new data without explicitly programming the solution.[7]

As for defining robotics, there is no general consensus about what a robot is and which machines are to be classified as robots.[8] Robotics experts define robots as mechanical objects capable of three things:[9] (1) "sense"—automatic and continual awareness of the world around them, (2) "think"—processing this awareness by means of data analysis, and (3) "act"—performing physical (navigating, moving something) or non-physical functions (warnings, recommendations, decisions, orders). A technology does not "act" just because it offers information in a comprehensible form; instead, it must exert agency in the physical world.[10] Pure software without agency in the physical world is therefore not robotics,[11] even if the English language media in particular[12] often refer to robots and actually mean software.

The possibility to act is also referred to as "autonomy" in robotics. In many definitions, autonomy is described as a characteristic which classifies a machine as a robot, as in the

---

[5]   AI Overview: Broad Discussions of Artificial Intelligence, AI Topics, <http://aitopics.org/topic/ai-overview>.

[6]   John McCarthy, *Basic Questions, What is Artificial Intelligence?* (12 Nov. 2007) Stanford University, <http://www-formal.stanford.edu/jmc/whatisai/>.

[7]   Daniel Castro and Joshua New, *The Promise of Artificial Intelligence*, The Center for Data Innovation, October 2016, <www2.datainnovation.org/2016-promise-of-ai.pdf>.

[8]   Neil M. Richards and William D. Smart, "How should the law think about robots?" in Ryan Calo, A. Michael Froomkin and Ian Kerr (eds.), *Robot Law* (Edward Elgar Publishing 2016) 3 *et seq.*

[9]   *See* Rolf Pfeifer and Christian Scheier, *Understanding Intelligence* (MIT Press 1999) 37; Rodney A. Brooks, *Intelligence Without Reason*, Proceedings of the 12th International Joint Conference on Artificial Intelligence 1991, 569 *et seq.*, 570; George A. Bekey, *Autonomous Robots* (MIT Press 2005) 2; Ryan Calo, *Robotics and the Lessons of Cyberlaw*, California Law Review 513 *et seq.*, 529 (2015).

[10]   In this sense, "embodiment" is used in the literature, see Hamid R. Ekbia, *Artificial Dreams: The Quest for Non-Biological Intelligence* (Cambridge University Press 2008) 258. As in RoboLaw deliverable D6.2 Guidelines on Regulating Robotics, 22.9.2014, <http://www.robolaw.eu>, p. 15; Melinda Florina Müller (now Lohmann), *Roboter und Recht – Eine Einführung*, AJP 595 *et seq.*, 596 (2014).

[11]   See George A. Bekey, "Current Trends in Robotics" in Patrick Lin, Keith Abney and George A. Bekey (eds.), *Robot Ethics* (MIT Press 2012) 17 *et seq.*, 18; Richards and Smart, *supra* note 8, 6.

[12]   E.g. The Economist, *Big Data and hiring: Robot Recruiters* (6. April 2013) <http://www.economist.com/news/business/21575820-how-software-helps-firms-hire-workers-more-efficiently-robot-recruiters>.

vocabulary of the International Organisation for Standardization (ISO).[13] However, autonomy in a technical context has an entirely different meaning from autonomy in a humanities context, in which autonomy is closely linked to being human.[14] From a practical point of view, the use of the term "autonomy" in interdisciplinary discussions harbours the risk of confusion and misunderstandings.

In most cases, robots do not look humanoid. There are, of course, robots such as Pepper and Nao from Aldebaran, which sell Nescafé machines, take orders in Asian Pizza Hut restaurants, greet passengers on cruise ships or welcome patients in the hospitals of Ostend and Liège in Belgium, or which advise customers at the Mitsubishi Bank in Japan. Yet, until now, the humanoid robots have hardly attained technical and economic significance.[15] By contrast, there are approximately 300,000 industrial robots which are taken into service each year and they have considerable economic importance. However, these "programmable multi-purpose handling devices"[16] simply do not generate the same media enthusiasm as do the humanoid, anthropomorphic robots.

B.   The Rise of Artificial Intelligence and Robotics in the Workplace

One example of an industrial robot is Baxter from Rethink Robotics.[17] He is an affordable[18] multi-purpose robot for production purposes, friendly to people and easy to program by colleagues for different tasks. He costs a mere USD 22,000 and—like all robots—is always available, never sick, never takes a holiday, is never in a bad mood, does not embezzle money and does not demand a bonus. Going on strike is also not part of his program. And, in times of the #metoo movement it might be handy, neither is sexual harassment.

In the logistics and transportation sector too, robots already play a significant role. At Amazon in the U.S.A., robots from Kiva Systems drive the warehouse shelves to the workers, so that the workers can swiftly put together the right goods for shipment according to customer orders. Amazon bought Kiva Systems for USD 775 million in 2012.[19] The Swiss postal service is likewise starting a new chapter in E-commerce logistics. It relieves online traders of the entire logistics from storage through packaging and shipment to

---

13   ISO 8373:2012 "Robots and robotic devices –Vocabulary".

14   For a critical view, *see* Jack B. Balkin, *The Path of Robotics Law*, The Circuit 2015 Paper 72, <http://scholarship.law.berkeley.edu/clrcircuit/72>, 49 *et seq.*; Thomas Burri, *The Politics of Robot Autonomy, Special Issue on the Man and the Machine*, 2 EJRR 341 *et seq.* (2016).

15   NZZ, *Das Gefühlsleben der Roboter* (22 March 2016) <http://www.nzz.ch/meinung/kolumnen/affective-computing-das-gefuehlsleben-der-roboter-ld.9188> ("However, there is the fourth law of robotics: the more human the appearance of a robot, the greater its appeal to our empathy, and the lower its technical and economic importance.", own translation); Jack Clark, *Why Google Wants to Sell Its Robots: Reality Is Hard*, Bloomberg (18 March 2016) <http://www.bloomberg.com/news/articles/2016-03-18/why-google-wants-to-sell-its-robots-reality-is-hard>.

16   Definition according to the Robotic Industries Association, 1979, <http://www.robotics.org>.

17   <http://www.rethinkrobotics.com/baxter>.

18   See Frank Tobe, *Low-cost robots like Baxter, UR5 and UR10 successfully entering small and medium enterprises (SMEs)*, Robohub.org (14 May 2014) 2013, <http://robohub.org/rethinkrobotics-baxter-and-universal-robots-ur5-and-ur10-succeeding/>.

19   Julianne Pepitone, *Amazon buys army of robots*, CNN Money (20 March 2012) <http://money.cnn.com/2012/03/20/technology/amazon-kiva-robots/>.

the management of returns. The "YellowCube" logistics centre forms the heart of this system.[20] Goods are stored here in stackable containers. Each of these containers can be fetched by a robot within just a few seconds and taken to a commissioning station where staff package the ordered goods for shipping.

In the services sector, robots serve in hotels and restaurants or in retail, especially in the U.S.A. and Japan. In the Aloft Hotel in Cupertino, California, a robot hotel page, for example, brings guests their luggage, beverages or food.[21] OSHbot serves customers at the Orchard DIY store in San Jose, California, leading them to the right aisle in which the desired product is located.[22]

In robot-friendly Japan, the demographic crisis is being countered with the aid of care robots which care for, entertain, monitor or nurse the elderly. "Robear", for example, supports nursing carers in lifting patients.[23] According to a report of the Japanese Ministry of Economics, Trade and Industry, the market for care robots apparently amounted to more than 400 billion Yen (USD 4.09 billion) in 2013 alone.[24] Care robots have now also arrived in Europe: an example of this is "Henry" in Vienna, who shows dementia patients the way in hospital and accompanies them to their destination, as well as providing them with news such as weather forecasts and the menu plan.[25]

The success of the self-driving Google cars suggests that it will not be long before taxis and trucks will be driverless.[26] In Sion, Valais, Switzerland, driverless post office buses took to the roads in June 2016.[27] They are 5 meters long and can transport 15 people.

The development of exoskeletons is also exciting. They provide humans with an exterior – therefore "exo" – skeleton which supports or takes over human movements.[28] The robot system is generally steered through body movements on the basis of cognitive and physical interaction with the human enabled by the drivetrains, sensors and micro-controllers, as well as the intelligent control system.[29] In a robot suit like this ("wearable robot"), a person can lift heavier loads, walk further or walk in spite of spinal cord injury.[30] There are numerous applications for exoskeletons.

---

[20]   <http://www.post.ch/yellowcube>.
[21]   Claire Cain Miller, *As Robots Grow Smarter, American Workers Struggle to Keep Up*, The New York Times (15 December 2014) <http://www.nytimes.com/2014/12/16/upshot/as-robots-grow-smarter-american-workers-struggle-to-keep-up.html>.
[22]   <http://www.lowesinnovationlabs.com /innovation-robots/>.
[23]   <http://www.wxyz.com>; Nick Valery, *Difference Engine: The caring robot*, The Economist (4 May 2013) <http://www.economist.com/blogs/babbage/2013/05/automation-elderly>.
[24]   John Hofilena, *Japan pushing for low-cost nursing home robots to care for elderly*, Japan Daily Press (29 April 2013) <http://japandailypress.com/japan-pushing-forlow-cost-nursing-home-robots-to-care-for-elderly-2927943/>.
[25]   ORF, *Testeinsatz für Krankenpflegeroboter* (30 March 3016) https://wien.orf.at/news/stories/2765466/.
[26]   See also Scientific American, *AI Special Report, The truth about "self-driving" cars*, 6/2016, 45 et seq.
[27]   <https://www.postauto.ch/de/news/schweizer-premiere-mit-autonomen-shuttles>.
[28]   RoboLaw Guidelines, *supra* note 10, 108.
[29]   José L. Pons, *Rehabilitation Exoskeletal Robotics, The Promise of an Emerging Field*, IEEE Engineering in Medicine and Biology Magazine (May/June 2010) 57 *et seq.*, 59.
[30]   By contrast, a differentiation is made in the natural sciences between exoskeletons (for the improvement of performance by a non-handicapped person) and orthotic braces (playing a sup-

In the medical field, people who have been paralysed after an accident or who suffer disruptions to physical functions as a result of advanced age will be able to walk again with the aid of exoskeletons. The first commercial version of such an exoskeleton was produced in 2012 by Ekso Bionics in the USA, which obtained FDA approval.[31] In Japan, HAL by CYBERDYNE, which functions with an interactive biofeedback system, is used in various medical institutions and hospitals.[32] In 20 years' time, exoskeletons could mean the end of the approximately 68 million wheelchairs in use today.[33]

The application of exoskeletons in industry is on the ascendant, meaning that heavy loads and tools will be less of a burden on workers in the future. Workers in production and assembly often lift up to ten tons of material a day[34] and 44 million workers in the EU suffer from work-related musculoskeletal disorders.[35] This can result in damage to the spine and in long-term illness, not only causing personal suffering for the worker, but also involving high costs for the health system. Employers suffer disadvantages as a result of illness-related absence from work and invalidity. Exoskeletons are therefore an interesting innovation.[36] The industrial exoskeleton by Ekso Bionics, "EksoWorks"[37] or by the Swiss company Colas[38] come to mind here, both of which were conceived for use on construction sites. The prototype of such an exoskeleton was presented at the Fraunhofer IAO in Stuttgart on 12 June 2015; it relieves the weight burden down to one tenth.[39]

All these examples show that robots have long since arrived in the workplaces of this world. Robotics technology has reached the stage now enabling large numbers to appear on the market. The progress of automation, robotics and AI in the workplace is unstoppable.

C.   Legal Consequences of Robotics and AI in the Workplace

Automation, robotics and AI are developing at an exponential pace and lead to a working environment and working conditions which were unthinkable at the time the work-relevant legislation entered into force. However, manufacturers and users of robots must nevertheless comply with the legal framework conditions. Many robotics enterprises are

---

porting role in the case of illness of an extremity), see Silvestro Micera et al., *Hybrid Bionic Systems for the Replacement of Hand Function*, 9 Proceedings of the IEEE 1752 *et seq.* (2006); Hugh Herr, *Exoskeletons and orthoses: classification, design challenges and future directions*, 6 Journal of Neuro Engineering and Rehabilitation 1 *et seq* (2009).

[31]   <http://www.eksobionics.com>.

[32]   Yoshiyuki Sankai, *HAL, Hybrid assistive limb based on cybernics*, Robotics Research (Springer 2011) 25 *et seq.*

[33]   Illah Reza Nourbakash, *The Coming Robot Dystopia,* Foreign Affairs (8/2015) 23 *et seq.*

[34]   <https://www.iao.fraunhofer.de/lang-de/ueber-uns/presse-und-medien/1604-erstes-exo-skelett-fuer-die-industrie-praesentiert.html>.

[35]   Work Foundation Alliance, Lancaster UK, cited in <https://www.iao.fraunhofer.de/lang-de/ueber-uns/presse-und-medien/1604-erstes-exoskelett-fuer-die-industrie-praesentiert.html>.

[36]   RoboLaw Guidelines, *supra* note 10, 107 *et seq.*

[37]   <http://eksobionics.com/eksoworks/>.

[38]   Zentralschweiz am Sonntag, *Macht es der Roboter bald allein? Ein Roboter-Skelett soll für mehr Sicherheit auf Baustellen sorgen* (12 July 2015) 43; <http://www.colas.ch/exosquelette/>.

[39]   <https://www.iao.fraunhofer.de/lang-de/ueber-uns/presse-und-medien/1604-erstes-exoskelett-fuer-die-industrie-praesentiert.html>.

small and medium-sized enterprises who wish to concentrate on their product and not on court proceedings with employers or employees. Employers in turn can likewise avoid legal difficulties as users if they know which legal regulations must be complied with in the integration of robotics in the workplace. The challenge for manufacturers and users of modern robotics systems alike is anticipating legal issues in advance while work and the workplace are continually changing.[40]

As yet, there are few studies in Europe and Switzerland on the consequences of robotics on employment law,[41] in spite of the proposal in 2012 in the course of the EU RoboLaw Project to conduct employment law research.[42] This is different in the U.S.A. where, for example, the American Bar Association devoted its employment law conference to this topic in 2015,[43] and where numerous researchers and lawyers are examining these issues. Only very recently, in April 2017, the International Bar Association Global Employment Institute has published its first report on "Artificial Intelligence and Robotics and Their Impact on the Workplace".[44]

The legal risks and imponderables involved with the use of automation processes, robotics and AI in the workplace will be analysed in the following. What must be taken into consideration from an employment law point of view so that employer and employee, but also the social partnership, can continue to thrive in a "bot-based economy"?

II.   SEVEN CHALLENGES FOR EMPLOYMENT LAW

Employment law expertise to deal with the widespread use of robotics and AI still has to be developed. Until such time, we must apply our existing employment law practice to the new technology as best we can. In the following discussion, I would therefore like to examine seven employment law issues that might be problematic in the light of existing regulation today (II.A.–G. below). The key to a good employment law compliance

---

[40]   Garry Mathiason and Bonne Chance, *Robots, the Workplace and the Law* (May 2013,) <http://www.roboticsbusinessreview.com/article/robots_the_workplace_and_the_law>; Balkin, *supra* note 14, 45 et seq.; Littler Report, *The Transformation of the Workplace Through Robotics, Artificial Intelligence, and Automation, Employment and Labor Law Issues, Solutions, and the Legislative and Regulatory Response*, February 2014, 22.

[41]   For Switzerland, see my work: Isabelle Wildhaber, *Die Roboter kommen – Konsequenzen für Arbeit und Arbeitsrecht*, I ZSR 315 *et seq.* (2016); Isabelle Wildhaber, *Robotik am Arbeitsplatz – Von "Robo-Colleagues" und "Robo-Bosses"*, AJP 213 *et seq.* (2017).

[42]   See Christophe Leroux and Roberto Labruto, *euRobotics – The European Robotics Coordination Action.* D3.2.1 Ethical Legal and Societal Issues (ELS) in robotics 26 (2012), <https://eu-robotics.net/cms/upload/PDF/euRobotics_Deliverable_D.3.2.1_ELS_IssuesInRobotics.pdf>; euRobotics – The European Robotics Coordination Action, Suggestion for a green paper on legal issues in robotics, Contribution to Deliverable D3.2.1 on ELS issues in robotics, 2012, <http://www.robolaw.eu>, 41 et seq.

[43]   American Bar Association, Labor Law Section, March 2015, National Symposium on Technology in Labor and Employment Law.

[44]   Gerlind Wisskirchen et al., *Artificial Intelligence and Robotics and Their Impact on the Workplace*, IBA April 2017, < https://www.ibanet.org/>. This Handbook chapter was finished off in March 2017, before the IBA Report was published.

programme is the identification of potential legal issues, even if the underlying law is uncertain and still remains to be developed.

A. The Robo-Boss

The Japanese electronics group Hitachi has started to develop an AI system which allocates work tasks to human employees on the basis of data analysis and past working processes.[45] For many years, Hitachi has used the so-called Kaizen method to introduce change through permanent monitoring and precise analysis in order to perfect and accelerate working processes. Through the integration of learning AI into the business systems, as Hitachi has succeeded in doing, Kaizen monitoring and optimisation of the working processes is also accompanied by the implementation of employees' ideas to improve work as a direct reaction to changed working conditions or fluctuations in demand. The AI programme enables robots to issue instructions. According to the group, analysis of great quantities of data generated daily and its verification in logistical tasks, in other words through the issue of orders, is intended to increase productivity by eight percent.[46]

Constellations in which robots or AI act independently as employers are not yet possible due to the stage of technological development and the legal framework conditions.[47] However, robots can be used as intermediary superiors. Robots used as superiors are colloquially referred to as "robo-bosses". In October 2015, the market research institute Gartner estimated that three million employees worldwide would be supervised by a robo-boss by 2018.[48] According to a study by the Massachusetts Institute of Technology (MIT) in 2014, humans were happier taking instructions from robots and were both more productive and more satisfied.[49]

1. Responsibility of the employer

According to the current legal situation, a robot as a superior is incapable of providing a legally binding declaration of will due to a lack of legal capacity and capacity for action.[50] Electronic declarations of will or acts must be attributed to a human.[51] For

---

[45]   Hitachi Press Release, *Development of Artificial Intelligence issuing work orders based on understanding of on-site kaizen activity and demand fluctuation* (4 September 2015) <http://www.hitachi.com/New/cnews/month/2015/09/150904.pdf>.

[46]   <http://www.hitachi.com/New/cnews/month/2015/09/150904.pdf>.

[47]   See also Nadja Gross and Jacqueline Gressel, *Entpersonalisierte Arbeitsverhältnisse als rechtliche Herausforderung – Wenn Roboter zu Kollegen und Vorgesetzten werden*, NZA 990 et seq., 991 (2016).

[48]   <http://www.gartner.com/smarterwithgartner/gartner-predicts-our-digital-future/>.

[49]   Adam Conner-Simons, *Want a happy worker? Let robots take control, CSAIL study finds that human subjects prefer when robots give the orders*, MIT News (21 August 2014) <http://newmit.edu/2014/want-happy-workers-let-robots-take-control>.

[50]   Wildhaber, *Die Roboter kommen, supra* note 41, 317 *et seq.*; Boris Dzida, *Wenn auf dem Chefsessel ein Roboter sitzt*, FAZ (12 September 2015) 11; Walter Frick, *When Your Boss Wears Metal Pants*, Harvard Business Review, 6/2015, 84 *et seq.*

[51]   Claus-D. Müller-Hengstenberg and Stefan Kirn, *Intelligente (Software-)Agenten: Eine neue Herausforderung unseres Rechtssystems*, MMR 2014, 307 *et seq.*, 308. See also BGH dated 16.10.2012 (online flight booking), MMR 2013, 296 et seq.

this reason, the responsibility for the transmission of declarations of will and for the implementation of legal transactions must currently clearly remain with the employer as the natural or legal person behind the robot.[52] The validity of an electronic declaration of will or a digital legal act in legal relations always presupposes that these declarations have been caused by a human, thereby creating an "objective declaration of fact" in legal transactions.

Due to robots being able to "sense, think and act", the robots of the future will increasingly no longer be mere technical aids and consequently not the result of an anticipated formation of will by the employer as their user.[53] The greater the learning capacity of a robot superior, the more difficult this responsibility of the employer will become.[54]

2.   Right of the robots or the software to issue instructions

Robots and/or software programmes issuing instructions are possible under (Swiss) employment law. The employer does not have to exercise the right to issue instructions in person, but may transfer it onto others, including machines. In Amazon warehouses, the allocation of work is undertaken by GPS-driven equipment and not by humans. Naturally, a precondition of this is programming the robot in such a way that it complies with the applicable legal system. The instructions must remain within the framework of the instructions a human superior would be permitted to issue. In addition, a human within the enterprise must accept responsibility for the robot's instructions.[55] The enterprise's management can at most pass on this employer's responsibility by means of recourse to the robot's programmers.

The instructions of a robot are intended to optimise working processes. This optimisation takes place through data analysis. For example, urgent tasks such as the repair of a machine in a factory can be delegated to the person who, taking into consideration his/her location and specialist qualifications, can perform this task best.[56] The identification of certain employees is also conceivable in order to establish whether someone is at work or whether a replacement must be organised. For this reason, the applicable data protection law provisions must be ascertained. The data protection law problems involved with this will be discussed later (see II.D. below).

The exercise of the right of instruction by robots raises the question of a prohibition of automated individual decisions.[57] On the basis of new information and communication technology, decisions which have legal consequences for the persons affected or have significant adverse effects on them are increasingly taken in automated procedures, also

---

[52]   For German law, see Gross and Gressel, *supra* note 47, 991; Peter Bräutigam and Thomas Klindt, *Industrie 4.0, das Internet der Dinge und das Recht*, NJW 1137 *et seq.*, 1138 (2015).

[53]   See Michael Martin Kianička, *Die Agentenerklärung. Elektronische Willenserklärung und künstliche Intelligenz als Anwendungsfall der Rechtsscheinhaftung* (Schulthess 2012) 73 *et seq.*

[54]   See here Gross and Gressel, *supra* note 47, 992; Kianička, *supra* note 53, 99 *et seq.*

[55]   Dzida, *supra* note 50, 11; Frick, *supra* note 50, 84 *et seq.*

[56]   Gross and Gressel, *supra* note 47, 994; Kai Hofmann, *Smart Factory – Arbeitnehmerdatenschutz in der Industrie 4.0*, ZD 12 *et seq.*, 13 (2016).

[57]   See Joshua A. Kroll et al., *Accountable Algorithms*, 165 Univ. of Penn. L. Rev. 633 *et seq.* (2017); Jens Günther and Matthias Böglmüller, *Künstliche Intelligenz und Roboter in der Arbeitswelt*, BB 53 *et seq.*, 56 (2017).

often on the basis of profiles based on statistical data and calculations (profiling).[58] For some time already now, the EU has had provisions on the permissibility of automated individual decisions.[59] In order to determine the allocation of tasks amongst the individual employees, the robot processes data for the purpose of evaluating certain characteristics of a person.

On 21 December 2016, the Swiss Federal Council sent the Preliminary Draft for the Total Revision of the Swiss Data Protection Act and the amendment of further enactments on data protection into the legislative process by consultation. The revision creates the preconditions for Switzerland to ratify the Data Protection Convention of the European Council and take over the EU Data Protection Directive in the sphere of criminal prosecution. However, a prohibition on automated individual decisions appears not to enter into force in Switzerland even in the revised Swiss Data Protection Act, because Article 15 of the Preliminary Draft for the Total Revision of the Swiss Data Protection Act of 21 December 2016 exclusively provides for a duty of information and hearing (but not a prohibition with provisions concerning exceptions).[60] Other than in EU countries, Swiss law is therefore less restrictive when robots or software issue instructions and thus take automated individual decisions. The desire for more "humaneness" emanating from a prohibition of automated decisions assumes that human decisions are better than automated decisions, a belief which might be questioned with the advancement of AI.

3. Firing by algorithm

Algorithms can collect and evaluate huge amounts of data, and use this as a basis to identify development tendencies, predict results, make recommendations and decisions and perform acts. It is therefore definitely conceivable that the decision to fire an employee is taken by an algorithm in the future ("firing by algorithm").

Other than in German law, for example, termination of employment in Switzerland does not have to be in written form, and, as mentioned, automated individual decisions are not prohibited.[61] However, the problem is that robots are not able to legally act.[62] Whereas a

---

[58]   Swiss Federal Office of Justice, Bericht der Begleitgruppe Revision DSG, Normkonzept zur Revision des Datenschutzgesetzes, Bern 29.10.2014, Reference COO.2180.109.7.138327/ 212.9/2012/00754, p. 26.

[59]   Regulation EU/2016/679 on the protection of natural persons with regard to the processing of personal data and on the free movement of such data, and repealing Directive 95/46/EC (General Data Protection Regulation) also provides for "measures based on profiling" in Art. 22; see also Art. 3 and 11 of Directive EU/2016/680 on the protection of natural persons with regard to the processing of personal data by competent authorities for the purposes of the prevention, investigation, detection or prosecution of criminal offences or the execution of criminal penalties, and on the free movement of such data, and repealing Council Framework Decision 2008/977/JHA of the Council (Data Protection Directive). See also Art. 8 para 1 letter a of the modernisation draft of the European Council on the Convention for the Protection of Individuals with regard to Automatic Processing of Personal Data (Data Protection Convention, E-SEV 108) (T-PD(2012)04 rev2).

[60]   Swiss Federal Office of Justice, Explanatory report on the preliminary draft for the Federal Act on the Total Revision of the Swiss Data Protection Act and the amendment of further decrees on data protection, Bern 21.12.2016, reference COO.2180.109.7.190301 / 212.9/2015/00001, p. 20.

[61]   Section 623 German Civil Code and Section 6a para 1 German Federal Data Protection Act.

[62]   See here Susanne Beck, *Der rechtliche Status autonomer Maschinen, Sonderheft zum Roboterrecht*, AJP 183 *et seq.* (2017).

robot or an algorithm can take the decision to fire and make this proposal, it cannot under any circumstances announce a termination of employment because it does not have the legitimate authority to fire a person. In order to exercise a right by unilateral declaration which cancels a legal relationship, as is the case when announcing termination of employment, capacity to act must exist as defined in Article 12 Swiss Civil Code. Therefore, dismissal must be announced by an authorised superior, in other words the managing director, an executive board member or an authorised person. This is reasonable because robots are not (yet) in a position to make value judgements and weigh up interests.

B.   Equal Treatment and Discrimination

When employers introduce robotics or AI systems into the workplace, this raises questions of equal treatment and discrimination. Robotics or AI systems may not be programmed in such a way that they directly discriminate. They may also not indirectly discriminate, i.e. have disadvantageous effects ("disparate impacts") for different groups of employees (on grounds of race, age, gender, nationality, etc.) in spite of neutral regulation, unless this is objectively justified and proportionate.[63]

However, indirect discrimination is difficult to prove, and, in addition, there is only little protection from indirect discrimination in Switzerland (other than in EU law or in the USA).[64] In Switzerland, the principle of indirect discrimination is integrated into the protection of personality under employment law.[65]

1.   Hiring by algorithm

Today, big data is readily used in the hiring process. We talk about "hiring by algorithm", "HR bots", "e-recruiting" or "applicant-tracking systems" (ATS). This type of hiring procedure has become very widespread in large companies in recent years.[66] In Switzerland too, computer systems which can sift job applications are used, e.g. at Swiss Airlines, Manor, IBM or the Bernese cantonal administration. It is important that the procedure of "hiring by algorithm" satisfies the requirements for legally permissible interview questions and complies with employment law protection from discrimination in hiring.[67] If data about conduct is collected and compared, undesired connections may be made which have negative effects on job applicants.[68]

---

[63]   Littler Report 2014, *supra* note 40, 5, 15; Garry Mathiason, *10 Areas of Employment and Labor Law Most Impacted by Robotics, Human Enhancement Technologies, & the Growth of AI*, <https://www.littler.com/files/press/pdf/Mathiason-10-Areas-Employment-Labor-Law.pdf>; Kurt Pärli, *Vertragsfreiheit, Gleichbehandlung und Diskriminierung im privatrechtlichen Arbeitsverhältnis, Habilitation* (Staempfli 2009) margin no. 2792.

[64]   See in detail Pärli, *id.*, margin no. 1256 et seq.

[65]   See here Pärli, *id.*, margin no 1385 et seq.

[66]   Boulden, *Software weeds out weak resumes*, CNN (8 January 2013) <http://edition.cnn.com/2013/01/08/business/resume-software-scanning/index.html>.

[67]   On hiring discrimination, see Labour Court Zurich, AN 050401/U1 of 13.1.2006. Court cases involving hiring discrimination are extremely rare, which is amongst other things attributable to the lack of relief as regards the burden of proof, see Pärli, *supra* note 63, margin no. 1429 et seq.

[68]   Ifeoma Ajunwa, Sorelle Friedler, Carlos E Scheidegger and Suresh Venkatasubramanian, *Hiring by Algorithm: Predicting and Preventing Disparate Impact* (10 March 2016), <http://papers.

To a certain extent, algorithms can better adhere to employment law stipulations because they can be examined in advance.[69] Theoretically, algorithms can make decisions based on facts without prejudice by leaving criteria such as the place of origin, age and gender of an applicant out of consideration when making their decisions.[70] In addition, there are technical methods such as "data repair" to exclude indirect discrimination in algorithms based on this data.[71]

There is nevertheless extensive criticism of "hiring by algorithm" and the assumptions on which algorithms are based are increasingly disputed.[72] After all, algorithms are programmed by human individuals and can therefore also reflect their prejudices. The repetition of human behaviour can deepen discrimination which already exists. In addition, there currently still remains a certain risk that applicants might be inadvertently excluded due to the lack of specific key words although they would fit the job profile.

"Hiring by algorithm" must satisfy the requirements imposed by Article 328b Swiss Code of Obligations and data protection law (see in more detail II.D. below), just as is the case with an assessment centre. Software algorithms used in the application procedure must naturally comply with these requirements, because they collect and process data. According to Article 328b Swiss Code of Obligations, the employer may only work with data about the employee to the extent to which it relates to his or her suitability for the employment relationship or is necessary for the implementation of the contract of employment. This provision is relevant to the use of algorithms during the application process. Article 328b Swiss Code of Obligations restricts the permissible processing of data for the employer in compliance with the principle of proportionality,[73] as it is also anchored in Article 4 Swiss Data Protection Act.[74] Data processing is considered

---

ssrn.com/sol3/papers.cfm?abstract_id=2746078>; Solon Barocas and Andrew Selbst, *Big Data's Disparate Impact*, 104 California Law Review 3 *et seq.* (2016), <http://ssrn.com/abstract=2477899>.

[69]   See Claire Cain Miller, *Can an Algorithm hire Better than a Human?*, The New York Times (25 June 2015) <http://www.nytimecom/2015/06/26/upshot/can-analgorithm-hire-better-than-a-human.html>; Sarah Green Carmichael, *Hiring C-Suite Executives by Algorithm*, Harvard Business Review (6 April 2015) <https://hbr.org/2015/04/hiring-c-suite-executives-by-algorithm>.

[70]   Martin Lützeler and Désirée Kopp, *HR mit System: Bewerbermanagement-Tools*, ArbRAktuell 491 *et seq.*, 492 (2015).

[71]   Michael Feldman et al., *Certifying and removing disparate impact*, Proceedings of the 21th ACM SIGKDD International Conference on Knowledge Discovery and Data Mining, ACM 2015. Section 4, 261 et seq.; Ian Ayres and Jennifer Gerarda Brown, *Mark(et)ing Nondiscrimination: Privatizing ENDA with a Certification Mark*, Michigan Law Review 1639 *et seq.* (2006).

[72]   See Kroll et al., *supra* note 57; Lauren Weber and Elizabeth Dwoskin, *Are Workplace Personality Tests Fair?*, The Wall Street Journal (29 September 2014) <http://www.wsj.com/articles/are-workplace-personality-tests-fair-1412044257>.

[73]   The principle of proportionality is fundamentally located in public law; state acts must be proportionate (see Art. 5 para. 2 Federal Constitution of the Swiss Confederation of 18.4.1999, SR 101). The anchoring of this principle in Art. 4 para. 2 Swiss Data Protection Act means that the principle of proportionality was taken over into Swiss federal law for data processing, see Urs Maurer-Lambrou and Reto Steiner, "Art. 4 DSG" in Urs Maurer-Lambrou and Gabor-Paul Blechta (eds.), *Basler Kommentar zum Datenschutzgesetz/Öffentlichkeitsgesetz*, 3rd Edition (Schuthess 2014) N 10; on the specific inclusion in Art. 328b Swiss Code of Obligations, see Wolfgang Portmann and Jean-Fritz Stöckli, *Schweizerisches Arbeitsrecht*, 3rd Edition (Schultess 2013) N 438.

[74]   Swiss Federal Act of Data Protection (Data Protection Act) of 19.6.1992, SR 235.1.

proportionate if it is suitable and necessary for the realisation of a fundamentally legitimate processing purpose, e.g. the clarification of the suitability of the employee for a particular job, and the processing purpose and the adverse effect on personality are in reasonable proportion to each other. The algorithm would therefore have to decide in an individual case whether the question is relevant for the intended work. An algorithm is generally not capable of this evaluation. Also, algorithms must be programmed in such a way that no impermissible questions are asked which encroach on constitutionally protected employees' interests. This is precisely the problem with numerous personality tests which form part of e-recruitment.[75] Questions about private life and character may not influence a decision in favour of or against a job applicant made by an algorithm.[76]

Furthermore, a new development is represented by robots such as Sophie, which are programmed to ask questions to the applicant, answer the applicant's own questions and measure the physiological reactions of an applicant. These cute HR colleagues, which are 60 cm tall, have been tried and tested and are already in use.[77] They are intended to serve as objective assessors of the job candidates.[78] However, a robot like Sophie can raise a number of legal problems.[79] What does it mean for employees' rights in the hiring process if Sophie at the same time also measures the applicant's heartbeat, eye movements and facial expression? Since this concerns health data, the data protection hurdle is even harder to take.

Depending on the situation, therefore, the use of an algorithm, or of a robot such as Sophie, may require the consent of the job candidate. However, in view of the structural imbalance[80] between the employer and the job applicant, very strict requirements must be placed on such consent,[81] and it is risky to use Sophie and rely on consent under Swiss law.

Automated application procedures also raise the question about a prohibition of automated individual decisions.[82] No sensible employer would hire a new employee solely on the basis of a decision by an algorithm without assessing the personal impression made by an applicant, e.g. his or her social competence and team player qualities.[83] However, not

---

[75]   Kecia Bal, *Screens Under Scrutiny*, Human Resource Executive Online (27 October 14) <http://www.hreonline.com/HRE/view/story.jhtml?id=534357777>.

[76]   In 2010, it became known that the insurance companies Helvetia and Axa Winterthur automatically sorted employees according to optimal personality profiles with the aid of an online questionnaire from the Zurich software enterprise SPSS, see Stefan Mair, *Computer entscheiden über Jobvergabe*, Handelszeitung (4 November 2016) <http://www.handelszeitung.ch/management/computer-entscheiden-ueber-jobvergabe-1253643>.

[77]   Rachel Nickless, *Interviewed for a job by Sophie the robot*, Financial Review (10 April 2013), <http://www.afr.com/p/national/work_space/interviewed_for_job_by_sophie_the_gec0B69rcUsaXX FWLZrtvO>.

[78]   Nathan R. Kuncel, Deniz S. Ones and David M. Klieger, *In Hiring, Algorithms beat Instinct*, Harvard Business Review (May 2014), <https://hbr.org/2014/05/in-hiring-algorithms-beat-instinct>; Michael Blanding, *Man vs. Machine: Which Makes Better Hires?*, Harvard Business School (17 February 2016) <http://hbswk.hbs.edu/item/man-vs-machine-which-makes-better-hires>.

[79]   Mathiason and Chance, *supra* note 40.

[80]   Hofmann, *supra* note 56, 14.

[81]   According to Gross and Gressel, *supra* note 47, 993, "The application of consent will probably have no practical relevance in connection with the use of robots." (own translation).

[82]   See Kroll et al., *supra* note 57; and II.A.2 above.

[83]   Gross and Gressel, *supra* note 47, 993.

the decision to hire, but rather the decision not to hire, is difficult. The issue of automated individual decisions has practical relevance in case of the decision not to hire.

If the statutory stipulations are breached, the job applicant may sue the employer. In my view, a human individual in the company must ultimately take responsibility for the job interview by the robot, as in the case of instructions from a "robo-boss".

2. Exoskeletons

Exoskeletons can raise issues of equality and discrimination as well. Firstly, the question is whether exoskeletons should be dealt with like parts of the body if they are connected to the human body, even if this is not a permanent state.[84] There is discussion about whether public buildings or rooms can refuse access to the wearers of exoskeletons or may require such exoskeletons to be taken off or deactivated, including for reasons other than security.[85]

This discussion is similar to the debate about the discrimination of cyborgs. The term "cyborg" is used for human individuals who are improved or changed by the use of cybernetic or robot technology.[86] Humans in exoskeletons are also a type of cyborg.[87] Cyborgs may require a certain degree of protection in the employment world, for example to ensure protection from not being hired or from being discriminated against during their employment relationship due to their changes. For this reason, some voices in the U.S.A. demand that they should be included in anti-discrimination legislation.[88]

Secondly, exoskeletons can become legally necessary "reasonable accommodations". This would mean that an employee, e.g. a disabled person or a person suffering from back injuries, would have a claim to such a reasonable accommodation from the employer in an individual case. Given the continual technological further development of aids which compensate for disadvantages and the fact that their cost will reduce significantly in future, employers should keep an eye on these developments,[89] in particular in the U.S.A., for example.[90]

In Switzerland, legal measures for the promotion of integration of people with disabilities into the employment market are primarily based on the concept of social insurance. Social insurances are linked to the term of "disability" and provide for measures for the employment integration of entitled disabled persons. The focus is increasingly being put on the earliest possible detection and treatment of potential disability. For example, the 5th/6th Swiss Disability Insurance Re-Enactment provides for support in the workplace

---

[84] RoboLaw Guidelines, *supra* note 10, 136.

[85] *Id.*

[86] Susanne Beck, "Roboter, Cyborgs und das Recht" in Tade Matthias Spranger (ed.), *Recht der Lebenswissenschaften*, Volume 1 (Mohr Siebeck 2010) 95 *et seq.*, 96; Susanne Beck, "Roboter und Cyborgs", in Susanne Beck (ed.), *Jenseits von Mensch und Maschine* (Nomos 2012) 9 *et seq.*, 13.

[87] <http://www.iso.org/iso/home/news_index/news_archive/news.htm?refid=Ref1882>.

[88] Joseph Guyer, *Cyborgs in the Workplace: Why We Will Need New Labor Laws*, Future Culturalist (12 April 2013) <https://futureculturalist.wordpress.com/2013/04/12/cyborgs-in-the-workplace-why-we-will-need-new-labor-laws/>.

[89] Bryan M. Seiler, *The Robotic Invaders: What Employers Need to Know About the Next Frontier of the Law of the Workplace*, 2011, p. 8, <http://www.americanbar.org/content/dam/aba/administrative/labor_law/meetings/2011/tech/e_03.authcheckdam.pdf>.

[90] Kurt Pärli, Annette Lichtenauer and Alexandra Caplazi, *Literaturanalyse Integration in die Arbeitswelt durch Gleichstellung* (Olten 2008) margin no. 1.1.

in case of back injuries.[91] Exoskeletons could help here. In Switzerland, there is only a claim to simple, practical disability aids which are economically viable.[92] Swiss case law tends towards a narrow interpretation of the terms "simple" and "practical",[93] and it would be difficult to establish a claim for an exoskeleton. In Germany, however, the Speyer Social Court, for example, decided on 20 May 2016[94] that the competent health insurance scheme should approve an application by a paraplegic for the payment of the costs for a ReWalk exoskeleton (involving costs of around EUR 72,000).

In addition to the social welfare perspective, in Switzerland too, the approach of non-discrimination and the promotion of factual equality by the employer exists.[95] There is the obligation to make reasonable accommodations and to compensate for disadvantages on various legal bases, but to a lesser extent than in the U.S.A. The Swiss Federal Act on the Removal of Disadvantages for People with Disabilities[96] only applies to employment relationships of the Swiss Federation and provides for a prohibition on discrimination and the duty to make reasonable accommodations in this context.[97] Federal Staff Law provides for an increased duty of care towards employees with disabilities, according to current case law of the Swiss Federal Administrative Court.[98]

However, the Swiss Federal Act on the Removal of Disadvantages for People with Disabilities expressly excludes private law employment relationships, so that only general employment law applies here.[99] Generally, there is no right in Switzerland to the removal of disadvantages as long as the situation does not involve the duty to take measures to protect personality. Article 328 Swiss Code of Obligations requires that an employer respects and protects the employee's personality, and takes measures to protect the employee's health and personal integrity if this can reasonably be expected of it. On the basis of Article 328 Swiss Code of Obligations, the case law in some instances comes to the conclusion that there is a duty to make reasonable accommodations.[100] According to Article 6 paragraph 1 Swiss Labour Act, the employer has an obligation to take all measures for the protection of employees' health which experience shows are necessary, applicable in accordance with the latest technology and appropriate to the circumstances of the business. In particular, the employer must structure the working process in such

---

[91]   Swiss Federal Office of Social Insurance, Information about the most important amendments and revisions in disability insurance, <http://www.bsv.admin.ch/themen/iv/00021/03189/?lang=de#sprungmarke0_23>.

[92]   Art. 2 para 4 Swiss Ordinance of 29.11.1976 on the provision of aids by disability insurance, SR 831.232.51. See also Kurt Pärli, *Sozialversicherungsrecht im Zeitalter der Robotik*, AJP 225 *et seq.* (2017).

[93]   BGer 9C.600/2011 of 20.4.2012; BGer 8C.279/2014 of 10.7.2015; see BGE 132 V 215; BGE 141 V 30.

[94]   Speyer Social Court (Germany), KR 350/15 of 20.5.2016, p. 19.

[95]   Pärli, Lichtenauer, Caplazi, *supra* note 90, margin no. 1.2.

[96]   Swiss Federal Act on the Removal of Disadvantages for People with Disabilities (Equality for the Disabled Act, BehiG) of 13.12.2002, SR 151.3.

[97]   Working group BASS/ZHAW, Evaluation des BehiG, Bern 2015, p. 50 et seq.

[98]   Swiss Federal Administrative Court, A-6550/2007 of 29.4.2008, E. 7.

[99]   Working group BASS/ZHAW, *supra* note 97, 63 et seq.; for a critical view, see Pärli, Lichtenauer and Caplazi, *supra* note 90, margin no. 4.20 und 4.21.

[100]   BGer 4A.102/2008 of 27.5.2008; BGer 4A.2/2014 of 19.2.2014. See also Pärli, Lichtenauer and Caplazi, *supra* note 90, margin no. 4.21.

a way that health risks to and the overexploitation of employees are avoided as far as possible (Article 6 paragraph 2 Swiss Labour Act). This involves the (proportionate) adaptation of the working conditions to the human capabilities, in particular with regard to organisation and the design of the workplace, and in relation to the choice of equipment, working and production methods.[101] Depending on the prevailing technological progress achieved, such an adjustment could also include assistance by an exoskeleton. In private working life, employees can therefore ask for individual, reasonable accommodations which are, to a large extent, paid for by disability insurance or accident insurance. The United Nations Convention on the Rights of People with Disabilities, which has been binding in Switzerland since 15 April 2014, is also interesting with regard to the support of disabled people through exoskeletons.[102] It includes all forms of discrimination against disabled people, including withholding approval of reasonable accommodations (Article 5 United Nations Convention). It provides for support for research and development of new technologies and their provision to people with disabilities (Article 4 United Nations Convention). In particular, the states which are party to the Convention acknowledge the same right to work for people with disabilities, which is described in great detail, and which includes the provision of reasonable accommodations in the workplace for people with disabilities (Article 27 paragraph 1 letter i United Nations Convention).

Currently, much wearable and human enhancing technology may not be objectively reasonable or may pose undue hardships because of its novelty or cost. However, as this technology becomes more common and prices reduce, it becomes more likely that social insurances or employers may be required to provide it to aid disabled employees in performing their jobs.[103]

C. Safety at Work and Health Protection

1. General liability of robots

Who should be liable in tort for robots if they cause damage? In our legal system, we treat machines as an extension of the human individuals who set them in motion. If machines cause damage, we attempt to claim compensation from the manufacturer, producer or user. Robots have to comply with all regulations regarding product safety and have to take into account the health burdens of the potential operating personnel. When planning construction of a robot, the manufacturer must have a precise idea of the concrete use of the robot in the workplace. A collaboration with the employer is necessary.[104]

However, the classical approach of torts is difficult to transfer to robots, particularly when they learn independently and become "intelligent".[105] It can be difficult to establish

---

[101]   Instructions of the Secretary of State for the Economy (SECO) regarding Art. 2 Swiss Labour Ordinance 3.

[102]   United Nations Convention on the Rights of People with Disabilities, concluded in New York on 13.12.2006, approved by the Swiss Federal Assembly on 13.12.2013, which entered into force for Switzerland on 15.5.2014, SR 0.109.

[103]   Littler Report 2016, *supra* note 3, 12.

[104]   Böglmüller, *supra* note 57, 53 *et seq.*

[105]   Curtis E.A. Karnow, "The application of traditional tort theory to embodied machine intelligence" in Ryan Calo, A. Michael Froomkin and Ian Kerr (eds.), *Robot Law* (Edward Elgar

with hindsight whether an act by the robot causing damage can be attributed to the original programming or subsequent independent learning ("training" through use).[106] Finding "linear" and foreseeable causality will be complicated.[107]

The question is therefore whether the robot itself should be liable. Liability in tort is an aspect of capacity to act. A robot could be liable like a legal person if it were registered in a public register and had assets.[108] Additionally, it could also be insured by obligatory third party liability insurance.[109] In my view, this is quite conceivable in the future.

However, robots are currently not liable in tort, so that the classical liability of the employer for accidents at work and occupational illnesses instead comes into question.

2.   Employers' liability for accidents at work and occupational illnesses
A workplace must be safe. The employer has an obligation to take all measures to protect the health of employees, and in particular to avoid accidents at work and occupational illnesses. The employer must take measures which (1) experience shows are necessary, (2) are applicable in conformity with technological progress, and (3) are appropriate under the circumstances. This results from the three statutory pillars of Article 328 paragraph 2 Swiss Code of Obligations, Article 82 paragraph 1 Swiss Federal Accident Insurance Act and Article 6 paragraph 1 Swiss Labour Act.[110]

If these (occupational safety and health) measures are not taken, the employer is liable to employees who suffer accidents, or to their surviving dependents, due to a breach of the duty of care founded by the contract of employment pursuant to Article 328 paragraph 2 Swiss Code of Obligations. The employer cannot delegate this responsibility, not even to an internal or external safety officer.[111] However, the employer is

---

Publishing 2016) 51 *et seq.*; Robolaw green paper, *supra* note 42, 53 *et seq.*; Melinda F. Lohmann, *Der Roboter als Wundertüte, Zur zivilrechtlichen Verantwortlichkeit für Roboter, Sonderheft Roboterrecht*, AJP 152 *et seq.* (2017).

[106]   Müller, *supra* note 10, 598; Jan-Philipp Günther, *Roboter und rechtliche Verantwortung* (Utz 2016) 38 *et seq.*; Günther and Böglmüller, *supra* note 57, 54 *et seq.*

[107]   Karnow, *supra* note 105, 72 *et seq.*; Jason Millar and Ian Kerr, "Delegation, relinquishment, and responsibility: The prospect of expert robots" in Ryan Calo, A. Michael Froomkin and Ian Kerr (eds.), *Robot Law* (Edward Elgar Publishing 2016) 102 *et seq.* For a different view, see Gerald Spindler, "Zivilrechtliche Fragen beim Einsatz von Robotern" in Eric Hilgendorf (ed.), *Robotik im Kontext von Recht und Moral* (Nomos 2014) 63 *et seq.*, 78 *et seq.* (sees no new legal challenges).

[108]   RoboLaw Guidelines, *supra* note 10, 19; Steffen Wettig and Eberhard Zehendner, *A legal analysis of human and electronic agents*, Artificial Intelligence and Law 111 *et seq.* (2004).

[109]   Also one of the proposals in the Draft Report with recommendations to the Commission on Civil Law Rules on Robotics (2015/2103(INL)), Committee on Legal Affairs, Rapporteur Mady Delvaux, Consid. p. 31. See aslo Ryan Calo, *Open Robotics* Maryland Law Review 138 *et seq.* (2011). On various instruments to compensate damage, see Isabelle Wildhaber, *Von Hochwasserschäden zu AKW-Störfällen: Wer ersetzt Katastrophenschäden?*, I ZSR 381 *et seq.* (2013).

[110]   The measures are defined in more detail in Swiss Ordinance 3 on the Labour Act (Swiss Labour Ordinance 3, Health Protection) of 18.8.1993, SR 822.113 and the Swiss Ordinance on the Prevention of Accidents and Occupational Illnesses, together with recommendations of Suva and SECO as well as the EKAS guidelines (Swiss Coordination Commission for Safety at Work).

[111]   Art. 7 para. 2 Swiss Ordinance on the Prevention of Accidents and Occupational Illnesses of 19.12.1983, SR 832.30, and Art. 7 para. 4 Swiss Labour Ordinance 3. See Suva, *Welches sind Ihre Pflichten auf dem Gebiet der Arbeitssicherheit und des Gesundheitsschutzes?*, Lucerne March 2011, order number 140.d, p. 4.

only directly liable to the injured person for damage/injury which is not compensated by accident insurance, such as, for example, compensation for pain and suffering or damage to property.[112]

In practice, injury to the employee in the workplace by a robot will mostly be an accident at work as defined in Article 7 Swiss Federal Accident Insurance Act and is covered by public-law accident insurance. Payments from this source amongst other things cover the accident victim's treatment and disability costs, integration compensation and pensions for surviving dependents (Article 10 et seq. Swiss Federal Accident Insurance Act). The shift of liability and the resultant privileged position of the employer is justified by the employer's financing of the statutory accident insurance. The employer as sole debtor of the premiums in the sphere of occupational accident insurance has a great interest in the avoidance of accidents (Article 91 Swiss Federal Accident Insurance Act). The amount of the premium for occupational accident insurance depends on the accident risk in the business (Article 92 Swiss Federal Accident Insurance Act). Premiums for accident insurance can cause substantial costs for the employer if several claims on the basis of the same cause were successful. In addition, accident insurance companies can also take recourse to the employer (Article 72 paragraph 1 Swiss Federal Act on the General Part of Social Insurance Law), although only in case of intent or gross negligence (so-called privilege of recourse, Article 75 paragraph 2 Swiss Federal Act on the General Part of Social Insurance Law), which, however, is only the case in practice if the employer has third party liability insurance. The existence of gross negligence can only be assessed on an individual case-to-case basis taking into consideration the relevant robot system, the design of the workplace and the skills of the employee.

For these reasons, employers should take all possible preventative measures to ensure that the workplace with robots is safe.

3. New challenges for safety at work through robotics

Robotics impose new requirements on prevention as regards safety at work.[113] Progress in robotics could improve safety at work in the future. Firstly, the use of robots enables physical and psychological relief for humans doing work which is dangerous, damaging to their health, or physically very strenuous for them. This is, for example, the case for robots felling timber in forestry, cleaning rocks, or robots for bomb disposal or police overpowering of a terrorist. Secondly, where this is not possible at least simulators help engineers to conduct three-dimensional monitoring activities in order to identify potential accident risks at the early planning stage for machinery and equipment, in order to avoid them.[114] Thirdly, applications such as exoskeletons which support employees in the physical performance of their work improve the opportunities for injured employees to

---

[112]   Adrian von Kaenel, *Unfall am Arbeitsplatz – Arbeitgeberhaftung, in: Haftung und Versicherung: Beraten und Prozessieren im Haftpflicht- und Versicherungsrecht* (Basel 2015) 661 *et seq.*

[113]   Suva Zukunftsstudie 2029 – Expertenstudien zu künftigen Unfall- und Berufskrankheitsrisiken und Präventionschancen, 1st Edition (Lucerne 12.9.2010), order number 2931.d; <http://www.suva.ch/geschaeftsbericht-2010.pdf>.

[114]   Suva Früherkennungsradar: Zukünftige Chancen und Risiken für die Prävention von Unfällen und Berufskrankheiten (Lucerne December 2012) order number 2965.d, p. 40; Littler Report 2014, *supra* note 40, 22.

return to work and reduce the risk of relapse.[115] Exoskeletons could even become a safety requirement for certain dangerous work in the future.

On the other hand, robotics involve new risks which range from accident risks due to systems errors to stress-related illnesses.[116] However, most accidents connected with robots do not occur under normal operating conditions, but instead during programming, maintenance, repair, adjustment or the like.[117] In addition, human failure is more frequent than technical failure.[118] "Smart" systems can avoid accidents which are attributable to faulty operation by humans. However, if an increasing number of activities are carried out by robots themselves, there is a risk that human skills and attention spans will wither away.[119] Precisely the increasingly smart safety systems can tempt humans to take more risks (so-called phenomenon of risk compensation).[120] There are also indications that risk is delegated, in other words a type of blind faith in the safety of the systems and possibilities develops, leading to human watchfulness no longer being applied.

Advances in robotics in the workplace will lead to a massive increase in the interaction between workers and robots. This development contrasts directly with a vast body of occupational health and safety standards which are designed to ensure that workers and machines operate separately. Robots which operate outside safety barriers and cages trigger alarm bells. Or, as Jim McManus, Safety Specialist at the OSHA (Operational Safety and Health Agency) said at the 2016 National Robot Safety Conference in Cincinnati, "If an OSHA compliance officer walks in and sees a robot operating without a guard, he is going to set off alarm bells. There is a robot, so there must be a cage or someone is going to get hurt, right?"[121] It is therefore essential to ensure the safety of employees who work with and around robots. For this purpose, certain norms and standards are required, which are currently being developed. The design and use of wearable technology and collaborative robots must be contemplated within these standards.

For instance, the new generation of industrial robots called cobots, which collaborate with human individuals, present a challenge to safety at work.[122] Examples of this are Baxter from Rethink Robotics or Yumi ("You and Me") from ABB.[123] It is currently a huge task to work out how accidents in the form of collisions and bruises or employees

---

[115]   Littler Report 2014, *supra* note 40, 4, 23; Mathiason, *supra* note 63.

[116]   Suva Zukunftsstudie 2029, *supra* note 113, 10. In a similar way for the German Federal Agency for Health and Safety at Work: Isabel Rothe, *Neue Herausforderungen für Sicherheit und Gesundheit bei der Arbeit: Digitalisierung der Arbeitswelt*, 2 BAuA aktuell 12 *et seq.* (2015).

[117]   Occupational Safety and Health Administration (OSHA), *Robotics in the Workplace*, Chapter 6, <http://www.osha.gov/Publications/Mach_SafeGuard/chapt6.html>.

[118]   See the often-cited case of a fatal accident at work at a VW plant in which a worker was crushed against a metal wall by a robot: Eliana Dockterman, *The machine grabbed and crushed the technician*, TIME (1 July 2015) <http://time.com/3944181/robot-kills-man-volkswagen-plant/>.

[119]   Suva Früherkennungsradar, *supra* note 114, 40.

[120]   Littler Report 2014, *supra* note 40, 22.

[121]   Dave Perkon, *Educating OSHA Compliance Officers on Robot Safety*, Control Design (14 November 2016) <http://www.controldesign.com/articles/2016/educating-osha-compliance-officers-on-robot-safety/>.

[122]   Wildhaber, *supra* note 41, 334 *et seq.*

[123]   <http://news.abb.com/products/robotics/de/yumi>.

being swept away can be prevented.[124] Accident prevention is possible by, for example, eliminating crushing edges, padding the robot's arms and ensuring the operation is stopped immediately if the human touches the robot.[125] With the development of advanced collaborative robots that can carry significant weights at high speeds, all while operating in close proximity to humans, the risk of significant injury increases substantially. As cobots are industrial robots, they are also fundamentally subject to the provisions of ISO 10218[126] and Directive 2006/42/EC on machines.[127] The ISO technical specification on collaborative robots (ISO/TS 15066:2016) dates from 2016. It introduces new rules of the game for industry by offering specific, data-driven safety rules to assess and control the risks presented by cobots. Since the introduction of ISO/TS 15066, traditional barriers and safety measures to keep humans and robots apart are no longer necessary for certain industrial robots in conformity with ISO 10218.

Safety at work issues are also raised in the context of personal care robots.[128] These are service robots which perform tasks that make a direct contribution to the improvement of the quality of life of humans (with the exception of medical treatments).[129] In German-speaking areas, PCRs are referred to colloquially as "nursing robots" ("*Pflegeroboter*"), which they precisely are *not*. ISO-Norm 13482:2014 for PCRs expressly excludes robots used as medical devices[130] from its sphere of application. Accordingly, mobile assistance robots and exoskeletons, for example, must be classified as medical applications if they are, for instance, used for the treatment of an illness or disability.[131] Whereas *non-medical* exoskeletons are covered by ISO-Norm 13482:2014 for PCRs (so-called physical assistant robots pursuant to Article 3.15)[132], *medical* exoskeletons are medical devices covered by ISO 13485:2015. In other words, contrary to widespread opinion, ISO 13482:2014 precisely does not affect "nursing robots", but rather *person-related, i.e. interactive, service*

---

[124] Detlef Gerst, *Industrie 4.0 und ihre Bedeutung für den betrieblichen Gesundheitsschutz*, 6 DGUV Forum 34 *et seq.* (2015).

[125] Carl Benedikt Frey, Michael A. Osborne et al., *Technology at Work v2.0 – The Future is Not What It Used To Be, Citi*, GPS: Global Perspectives & Solutions (January 2016) 132.

[126] Industrial robots are regulated by ISO 10218-1:2011, Industrial Robots – Safety Requirements – Part 1: Robots; ISO 10218-2:2011, Industrial Robots – Safety Requirements – Part 2: Robot Systems and Integration.

[127] Directive 2006/42/EC of the European Parliament and the Council of 17.5.2006 on machines and to amend Directive 95/16/EC, Art. 1 *et seq.*

[128] See Isabelle Wildhaber and Melinda F. Lohmann, *Roboterrecht – eine Einleitung, Sonderheft zum Roboterrecht*, AJP 135 *et seq.* (2017). See also Elisa May, "Robotik und Arbeitsschutzrecht" in Eric Hilgendorf (ed.), *Robotik im Kontext von Recht und Moral* (Nomos 2014) 99 *et seq.*; ISO/TC 184 – Automation systems and integration; INB/NK 2310 – Industrielle Automation.

[129] ISO 13482:2014, Robots and robotic devices – Safety requirements for personal care robots, Art. 3.13.

[130] See Isabelle Wildhaber, "Zum Begriff des Medizinprodukts" in Bernhard Rütsche (ed.), *Medizinprodukte: Regulierung und Haftung* (Staempfli 2013) 9 *et seq.*

[131] See interview with Gurvinder S. Virk, chairman of the leading working group on ISO 13482, ISO TC184/SC2/WG7, <https://www.roboticsbusinessreview.com/exclusive_interview_gurv inder_virk_explains_brand_new_iso_13482/>.

[132] See ISO-Norm 13482:2014, B.3., 68 ("A *healthy* person using an exoskeleton to reduce his/ her physical work"). See also <http://www.iso.org/iso/news.htm?refid=Ref1818>.

robots.[133] Personal care robots are subdivided into mobile servant robots[134], robots which support movement (e.g. industrial exoskeletons) or personal transportation robots (e.g. Toyota i-Foot/i-Wheel). They challenge the concept of safety at work because they (1) are used for numerous requirements in environments which are not precisely defined, (2) come into contact with non-specialised users, and (3) share the workspace with humans.[135] This is why safety standards are defined formally, and at an international level, in ISO-Norm 13482:2014 on PCRs.

When using exoskeletons at the workplace, care must be taken with regard to safety at work to ensure that the advantages of robot suits are not lost due to the increasing expectations and demands on humans who work with exoskeletons. As the physical possibilities for employees increase with the aid of exoskeletons, employers' expectations about the efficiency of employees and their performance of hard and dangerous physical labour may also increase. Exoskeletons can cause injuries if they are badly fitted to the body, the transmission is poor or the employee overestimates his or her physical capabilities due to the exoskeleton.[136]

If a workplace is intended to be equipped with a cobot, a mobile servant robot, a so-called *telepresence robot*,[137] an industrial exoskeleton or another robot, a risk assessment must be carried out on the basis of the statutory bases and the ISO norms. It is important for the manufacturer and the employer to ensure compliance with all robot-relevant provisions on safety at work and health protection.[138] These can also be industry-specific regulations, such as regulations of Swissmedic (e.g. for a robot which qualifies as a medical device),[139] or more general provisions such as the Swiss Product Safety Act[140] for the technical safety of equipment, products or facilities, or the Machinery Ordinance,[141] which makes integral reference to the EU Machinery Directive 2006/42/EC.[142]

However, ultimately the risk assessment with regard to safety at work is difficult for the manufacturer of robots and the employer using them. Preparation and formalisation of suitable safety standards and requirements within the framework of the law on safety at work are demanding. Many of the existing rules—like the ISO norms or the recommendations of Suva or EKAS—only constitute *soft law*.[143] The employer's duties to implement

---

[133]   Wildhaber and Lohmann, *supra* note 128, 135 *et seq.*

[134]   On mobile servant robots, see Eduard Fosch Villaronga and Gurvinder S. Virk, *Legal Issues for Mobile Servant Robots*, <https://www.researchgate.net>. Mobile servant robots are defined in ISO 13482:2014 as a "personal care robot that is capable of travelling to perform serving tasks in interaction with humans, such as handling objects or exchanging information." They are only covered by the PCR-ISO-Norm, if they are not medical devices (like, for example, "Robear"), see Wildhaber and Lohmann, *supra* note 128, 135 *et seq.*

[135]   RoboLaw Guidelines, *supra* note 10, 174.

[136]   Littler Report 2014, *supra* note 40, 24; Mathiason, *supra* note 63.

[137]   See Wildhaber, *supra* note 41, 342 *et seq.*; Seiler, *supra* note 89, 5. "Telepresence robots" can be classified as PCRs if they perform services, see ISO Norm 13482:2014, table 10 ("manual mode"), p. 50.

[138]   Mathiason, *supra* note 63.

[139]   See Wildhaber and Lohmann, supra note 128, 135 *et seq.*

[140]   Federal Product Safety Act of 12.6.2009, SR 930.11.

[141]   Swiss Ordinance on the Safety of Machinery of 2.4.2008, SR 819.14.

[142]   Directive 2006/42/EC, *supra* note 127, 24.

[143]   Robolaw green paper, *supra* note 42, 43.

safety measures and to maintain a standard of care cannot always be precisely defined. The development of robots for the workplace must therefore be closely linked with the development of new approaches within the framework of employee protection. The idea of a safe workplace will increasingly not only focus on the implementation of independent safety measures or warning functions, but on the role of the robot for the protection of employees. Robots have certain skills for the perception, evaluation and interpretation of their environment. They must recognise risks and react to them themselves in order not to endanger the employees in their environment. New approaches will be required, and increasingly not only the human must be taught controlled and aware handling, but also the robot itself. In this way, it can and will contribute to compliance with safety at work. Technical progress can in turn raise new technical safety problems, because the more independently and "intelligently" the robot acts, the more difficult it is to anticipate the possible consequences.

However, employers should not only rely on technology to avoid accidents, but on reliable training and safety processes.[144] Correct and comprehensive instructions to the employees is essential for safety at work in dealing with robots in the workplace. In addition, robotics specialists should be consulted in danger assessment and risk analysis in the workplace.[145]

D. Data Protection

Many robotics systems will store and process an increasing amount of information about users and use in the future. However, such data is a challenge for data protection law and the handling of data within an enterprise.[146] Robots can "sense, think and act", they can perceive, process and store the world around them. The fact that monitoring is one of the most frequent uses for robotics clearly indicates the relevance of data protection in robotics.[147]

The optimisation of working processes in the smart factory, for example, takes place through data analysis. Urgent tasks, such as the repair of a machine in a factory, can be transferred to the person who can perform it fastest, taking into consideration his or her location and specialist qualifications.[148] The identification of certain employees is also conceivable in order to ascertain whether someone is at work or if a replacement must be organised. Telework technologies may incidentally capture a host of health information from an employee-operator in the process of calibrating the technology to the individual. For example, an assisted surgery robot may recognise and learn to

---

[144] Wildhaber, *supra* note 41, 337.

[145] Art. 11a Swiss Ordinance on the Prevention of Accidents and Occupational Illnesses; Art. 7 para 3 Swiss Labour Ordinance 3; Directive of the Swiss Coordination Commission for Safety at Work No. 6508: Directive on the Involvement of Company Doctors and other Specialists for Safety at Work, January 2007 Edition, <http://www.ekas.admin.ch/index-de.php?frameset=200>.

[146] Müller, *supra* note 10, 607.

[147] Ryan Calo, "Robots and Privacy" in Patrick Lin, George Bekey and Keith Abney (eds.), *Robot Ethics, The Ethical and Social Implications of Robotics* (MIT Press 2011) <http://papers.ssrn.com/013/paper.cfm?abstract_id=1599189>.

[148] Gross and Gressel, *supra* note 47, 994; Hofmann, *supra* note 56, 13.

compensate for the tremor in a surgeon's hand and even for the individual's pulse.[149] The robotic technology's audio and video recording functionality may also be problematic. Individuals in a location subject to the use of telework technology may not realise that the robotic technology is recording their communications, let alone consent to such recordings.

Data protection is not new. Instead, it is a specific answer by legislation to the special threats to privacy which have become possible through the technological development in data processing.[150] Legislation has responded to the obligation to protect employees' privacy by passing Article 328 and 328b Swiss Code of Obligations, Article 6 Swiss Labour Act and Article 26 Swiss Labour Ordinance 3 (protection from monitoring). There is a connection between data protection and protection from discrimination.[151] The law of protection from discrimination aims to protect people from vilification, exclusion and disadvantages due to personality characteristics. Data protection law provisions (also) constitute instruments to realise the aims of protection from discrimination.[152]

In the context of robotics in Switzerland, I consider Article 26 paragraph 1 Swiss Labour Ordinance 3 on the protection of health very important. It restricts the use of monitoring and control systems for the monitoring of employee conduct in the workplace. Monitoring and control systems include video facilities, telephone systems, intercom systems, photocopying equipment and GPS, and will certainly also include systems and networks based on big data in the future.[153] The regulation manifests the legislative will to protect the health of employees from monitoring measures which are not justified by business or other acknowledged aims.[154] If the monitoring or control system does not exclusively or primarily serve the monitoring of conduct, but other legitimate grounds, use is permitted in accordance with para 2 as long as this does not adversely affect the health and freedom of movement of the employees. A precondition is that it should be proportionate in an individual case and employees must be informed in advance about the use of the system.[155] Accordingly, all monitoring measures must be justified by an overriding interest of the employer and must be proportionate, and employees must be informed in advance about the use of the system.[156]

The technology used for data collection and the relevance of the data with regard to the privacy right of the affected person are decisive for compliance with Article 328b Swiss Code of Obligations, the Swiss Data Protection Act and Article 26 Swiss

---

[149]   Littler Report 2016, *supra* note 3, 16.

[150]   Frank Seethaler, "Entstehungsgeschichte DSG" in Urs Maurer-Lambrou and Gabor-Paul Blechta (eds.), *Basler Kommentar zum Datenschutzgesetz/Öffentlichkeitsgesetz*, 3rd Edition (Schultess 2014) N 13 *et seq.*; Kurt Pärli, "Chapter 17 Datenschutz" in Wolfgang Portmann and Adrian von Kaenel (eds.), *Fachhandbuch Arbeitsrecht* (Schulthess 2017) margin no. 17.7.

[151]   Pärli, *id.*, margin no. 17.7.

[152]   Swiss Federal Administrative Court, A-4457/2011 of 10.4.2012, E. 9.3.

[153]   Wildhaber, *supra* note 41, 346 *et seq.*

[154]   Pärli, *supra* note 150, margin no. 17.57.

[155]   Roberta Papa and Thomas Pietruszak, "§ 17 Datenschutz im Personalwesen" in Nicolas Passadelis, David Rosenthal and Hanspeter Thür (eds.), *Datenschutzrecht, Handbücher für die Anwaltspraxis* (Schulthess 2015) margin no. 17.55.

[156]   Papa and Pietruszak, *id.*, margin no. 17.55.

Labour Ordinance 3.[157] The affected person's privacy right must be set in relation to the employer's entrepreneurial freedom to organise his or her business. Data processing must be restricted to cases of specific information requirements of the employer who uses the robots.[158] If the robot must have access to video recordings for the performance of the instruction, general principles for video monitoring in the workplace can be applied.[159] If possible, such video data should be deleted without trace once it has served its purpose. If the purpose of visual recording by the robot does not require identification of the person, recognition of biometric data must be restricted.[160]

The recorded information may provide information about working speed, the health situation or the precision of the working employee.[161] The fact that this data is collected can mean a monitoring effect for the employee. It is irrelevant that this is not the intention of the employer and is also not the intended purpose of the technical facility. If the data can be analysed, the machine offers the possibility of monitoring the employee without significant further steps being necessary. In this context, it is important that monitoring purposes are only legitimate if they relate to the organisation of the business processes or the protection of sensitive company data or business infrastructure. However, the employer—as the creditor of the employee's duty to perform—is also entitled to monitor the performance of the work and to carry out checks on performance and conduct for this purpose. It will therefore be important to precisely define the purposes of the systems used and to delimit the necessary handling of data precisely on the basis of this.

This problem has long since been reality, as shown by the example of GPS-supported mobile devices. Such devices, for example, direct "pickers" in the Amazon warehouses to the right shelf in which they find the merchandise ordered by the customer. There are reports from England that the mobile GPS computers raise the alarm if the employee takes a break outside regular break times.[162] These problems in relation to the privacy right and employee data protection will become more acute in the future in view of robotics.[163]

In case of an industrial exoskeleton such as the one tested in Daewoo's Korean wharfs,[164] wharf workers can carry very heavy loads. It therefore serves to protect the

---

[157] See Wildhaber, *supra* note 41, 346 *et seq.*; Müller, *supra* note 10, 606 *et seq.*; Gross and Gressel, *supra* note 47, 994; Hofmann, *supra* note 56, 15 *et seq.*
[158] Gross and Gressel, *supra* note 47, 995; Hofmann, *supra* note 56, 16.
[159] See Ullin Streiff, Adrian von Kaenel and Roger Rudolph, *Arbeitsvertrag, Praxiskommentar zu Art. 319-362 OR, 7. A.* (Schulthess 2012) Art. 328b N 8.
[160] Gross and Gressel, *supra* note 47, 995; Hofmann, *supra* note 56, 16 *et seq.*
[161] Berthold H. Haustein, "Herausforderungen des Datenschutzrechtes vor dem Hintergrund aktueller Entwicklungen in der Robotik" in Jan-Philipp Günther and Eric Hilgendorf (eds.), *Robotik und Gesetzgebung* (Nomos 2013) 91 *et seq.*, 93 *et seq.*
[162] Channel 4 News, *Anger at Amazon Working Conditions* (1 August 2013) <https://www.channel4.com/news/anger-at-amazon-working-conditions>.
[163] Max Oprey, *Rio Tinto's plans to use drones to monitor workers' private lives*, The Guardian (8 December 2016) <https://www.theguardian.com/world/2016/dec/08/revealedrio-tinto-surveillance-station-plans-to-use-drones-to-monitors-staffs-private-lives?CMP=Share_AndroidApp_Email.>.
[164] Hal Hodson, *Robotic Suits Gives Shipyard Workers Super Strength*, New Scientist (30 July 2014) <https://www.newscientist.com/article/mg22329803-900-robotic-suit-gives-shipyard-workers-super-strength/.>.

health of the employee, but can on the other hand involve risks for the privacy right. Is it permissible for the exoskeleton to analyse the posture of the wharf worker and draw conclusions about his psychic condition? Perhaps certain data here should not be used at all for the purposes of the employment relationship.

Similar questions are raised in the case of collaborative robots, referred to as **cobots**. Their robot arms can position an item to be worked on in such a way that the work to be done on it can be performed in an ergonomically comfortable and healthy body position.[165] In order to achieve this, the cobot ascertains the anthropometric characteristics of the employee (inside leg length, arm length, back length) and is guided accordingly. In order to register this and ensure that collisions are avoided, cameras constantly monitor the robot's working environment and the humans working in it.

In the case of an intelligent assembly line in a smart factory[166] which is linked to an assembly line worker and slows down if, for example, the assembly line worker's pulse becomes too high, health data about the employee is collected which should only be possible under very restricted preconditions in view of the protection of the employee's personality.[167]

Legitimate reasons for monitoring and control systems are business operation interests such as, for example, the guarantee of undisrupted operational processes, quality control, safety at work, the optimisation of work organisation or staff productivity.[168] In the case of industrial robots, for example, the collection of data for monitoring can be permitted for organisational or technical safety reasons or to steer production.[169] A precondition is that the monitoring as defined in Article 26 paragraph 2 Swiss Labour Ordinance 3 does not adversely affect the employees' health in an impermissible way and does not breach the provisions of the Swiss Data Protection Act.

As regards data processing in the employment relationship, the private law provisions of the Swiss Data Protection Act must also be complied with in addition to Article 328b Swiss Code of Obligations. Regardless of the method chosen, monitoring must be transparent to the extent to which the method does not serve to accuse a suspicious employee of an impermissible breach against duties imposed by his or her contract of employment or by statute. The principle of transparency requires that the procurement of personal data and in particular the processing purpose must be recognisable for the person affected (Article 4 paragraph 4 Swiss Data Protection Act). To the extent to which the owners of data banks in addition also procure personal data which is particularly worthy of protection or personality profiles, Article 14 Swiss Data Protection Act provides for an active duty of information to the person affected. Both provisions are of central importance for data processing in employment relationships. Evaluations of personal data are not in themselves impermissible, but require compliance with the principle of transparency and fulfilment of the duty of information.[170] It is therefore always important that the employee is informed in advance about the monitoring and the deletion of data

---

[165]   Final Report RoRaRob 2014, <https://eldorado.tu-dortmund.de/handle/2003/33519>.
[166]   On the smart factory, see Hofmann, *supra* note 56, 13.
[167]   Boris Dzida, *Gute Gründe für ein "Arbeitsrecht 4.0"*, FAZ of 23.11.2016, p. 23.
[168]   Papa and Pietruszak, *supra* note 155, margin no. 17.51.
[169]   Pärli, *supra* note 150, margin no. 17.62; Müller, *supra* note 10, 606 *et seq.*
[170]   Pärli, *supra* note 150, margin no. 17.24.

after the lapse of a certain period of time.[171] In addition, recordings may only be seen by authorised persons.[172] In principle, data protection-friendly technologies must be chosen, e.g. cameras equipped with filters which encode the pictures.[173] Care must also be taken that personal monitoring only comes into consideration as a "last resort" in compliance with the principle of proportionality even in such cases.[174]

As the statutory permission facts and circumstances have been very narrowly defined in data protection law, the cooperation of the employees should play an important role in case of monitoring by robots.[175] Either the consent of the employees should be obtained or the conclusion of a works agreement is necessary. However, such consent can create legal difficulties, amongst other things in the context of big data analyses;[176] in addition, given the balance of power in the employment relationship, consent will seldom be completely voluntary and it is revocable. It is nevertheless important for the employees to be informed about the use of the monitoring system in advance for reasons of transparency and for the employer to ensure that the employees' consent is obtained. Additionally, employers should always attempt to guarantee the legally compliant implementation of the new technologies through a well-considered choice of the data to be stored and possibly by rendering such data anonymous.

There are additional data protection law aspects which must be complied with when introducing robotics in the workplace. The use of a "cloud-based solution" can be impermissible from a data protection law point of view, so multinational employers should ensure precise clarification before transferring personal data to a cloud.[177] The law requires particular care from the data processor with regard to cross-border data disclosure (Article 6 Swiss Data Protection Act)[178] and the external shift of data processing to third parties (Article 10a Swiss Data Protection Act).[179]

In view of the numerous purposes and roles which robotics systems can play in the modern workplace, the following recommendations are made to employers.[180] In a first

---

[171] Rosenthal and Jöhri, *Handkommentar zum Datenschutzgesetz* (Schulthess 2008) Art. 328 OR N 96 et seq., Art. 4 DSG N 27; Pärli, *supra* note 150, margin no.17.57.

[172] Rosenthal and Jöhri, *id.*, Art. 4 DSG N 27.

[173] See the explanations of the Swiss Federal Data Protection and Publicity Officer on video monitoring in the workplace, <http://www.edoeb.admin.ch/datenschutz>.

[174] Pärli, *supra* note 150, margin no. 17.62.

[175] Pärli, *supra* note 150, margin no. 17.20; Streiff, von Kaenel and Rudolph, *supra* note 159, Art. 328b OR N 24; Rosenthal and Jöhri, *supra* note 171, Art. 328b OR N 66; BGE 136 II 508, E. 5.2.4.

[176] Viktor Mayer-Schönberger and Kenneth Cukier, *Big Data: Die Revolution, die unser Leben verändern wird* (Redline 2013); Rolf H. Weber, "Big Data: Herausforderungen für das Datenschutzrecht" in Astrid Epiney and Daniela Nüesch (eds.), *Big Data und Datenschutzrecht* (Schulthess 2016) 1 et seq.

[177] Pärli, *supra* note 150, margin no. 17.68; European advisory body on data protection and privacy, Opinion 05/2012 on Cloud Computing (WP 196), Article 29 Data Protection Working Party, 1.7.2012, <http://ec.europa.eu/justice/data-protection/article-29/documentation/opinion-recommendation/files/2012/wp196_en.pdf>.

[178] As regards the duties of the data processor and the role of the FDPIC, see Art. 5-7 Swiss Ordinance on the Federal Act on Data Protection of 14.6.1993, SR 235.11.

[179] Pärli, *supra* note 150, margin no. 17.64.

[180] In a similar vein, the Littler Report 2014, *supra* note 40, 27.

step, employers should carry out a risk assessment. They should assess how information is transferred to the robot technology in question, how the information is to be stored and how access to the information is to be granted. The risk assessment should identify potential weak points. The employer should then address these weak points and weigh up the risks against damage and costs. In a second step, the employer must undertake an exact categorisation of information which is collected and used by every system. Each category must then be subjected to an individual legal evaluation (because this, for example, involves personal data which is particularly worthy of protection pursuant to Article 3 letter c Swiss Data Protection Act).

E.   Applicable Law regarding Wages and Working Times

Robotics simplify remote work. The physical and time boundaries of the workplace are becoming more flexible and the world of work is "unbounded". These changes raise the question about which employment law is applicable, and in particular which statutes concerning wages and working time apply to a mobile, decentralised workplace.

Which law is applicable to people who are remotely in the office with the help of a "telepresence robot"? Telepresence robots are a kind of iPad on a Segway; the face and voice of the employee are projected on the iPad, like with Skype or FaceTime. They enable the employee to be physically present as a robot in the office or at another workplace. In this way, for example, a chief physician could roll along on the morning ward round while at the same time attending a congress abroad. They are telerobots, which are characterised by the remote-controlled operational mode.[181] The situation is similar for employees far away, who are spread over several countries and control robots from abroad.

Most countries fundamentally follow the international law principle of territoriality, in accordance with which the laws of a country are only intended to apply inside the country's borders.[182] For example, Swiss regulations on compensation for overtime in the Swiss Labour Act do not apply to work abroad by an employee hired in Switzerland.[183] This is criticised by academic teaching.[184] In principle, the law applicable to a contract of employment in case of international circumstances is determined in accordance with Article 121 Swiss Federal Code on Private International Law and the place of jurisdiction in accordance with Article 115 Swiss Federal Code on Private International Law.

In view of the increase in remote work across borders, it can become a challenge to determine the legally relevant place of work and/or the applicable law. It cannot be excluded that an employee is subject to (employment) law provisions of the target country

---

[181]   Müller, *supra* note 10, 597; Thomas Christaller et al., *Robotik* (Springer 2001) 46.

[182]   See in detail: Das Territorialitätsprinzip und seine Ausnahmen, Landesbericht der Schweiz vom XIII. Treffen der obersten Verwaltungsgerichtshöfe Österreichs, Deutschlands, des Fürstentums Liechtenstein und der Schweiz in Vaduz, 2002, <http://www.bger.ch/territorialitaetsprinzip_und_seine_ausnahmen.pdf>, with further references; Littler Report 2014, *supra* note 40, 19.

[183]   BGE 139 III 411; for a different opinion in the critical review of the judgment, see Kurt Pärli, *Keine Überzeitenentschädigung nach Arbeitsgesetz bei Tätigkeit im Ausland*, 442 ARV online (2013), with further references.

[184]   Pärli, *id.*, No. 442; Thomas Geiser, "Art. 1 ArG" in Thomas Geiser, Adrian von Kaenel and Rémy Wyler (eds.), *Stämpflis Handkommentar zum Arbeitsgesetz* (Staempfli 2012).

– for example, the U.S.A. – in which the employee "acts" by means of robotics.[185] In this context, the statutes to be applied must be precisely clarified in an individual case in order to avoid legal risks.

F. Collective Law

1. Communication on the introduction of robotics and automation concepts

The way in which a robotics or automation concept is explained and communicated to the workforce is decisive for its acceptance by the employees.[186] Many enterprises cite the commitment of the employees as a precondition for significant technological achievements.[187] Whereas employers see robotics as a method of increasing productivity and efficiency, the workforce often focuses on potential job losses. The fear of losing a job is one of the reasons for trade union activities. Employers should be very careful in the communication on the introduction of robotics and automation concepts, they should provide extensive information and perhaps even consult the workforce. They should also describe the advantages of robotics for the employees, e.g. improved safety, less strenuous working conditions, the retrieval of production facilities back from cheap countries or another improvement in the workplace. Employee representatives often have numerous consultation and information rights as regards occupational safety and thus also the use of autonomous systems.

A European or American production enterprise must consider the application of new technologies in order to compete with production enterprises in Asia or South America and be cost competitive. It is likely that with the introduction of robotics or automation concepts such an enterprise employs fewer people, must retrain its workforce and that these employees will need a new mix of skills; yet if the technologies are not used, production would be shifted to countries with lower labour costs.[188]

2. Protection of trade union activity

Regardless of how communication takes place, employers must expect employees to react in fear of losing their jobs and become active in trade unions. The freedom of association, i.e. the freedom of social partners to form associations for the protection of working and economic conditions, is guaranteed by Article 28 Swiss Federal Constitution. A dismissal is considered improper if it is announced because the employee exercises a constitutional right such as the right to freedom of opinion (Article 336 paragraph 1 letter b Swiss Code of Obligations), or because the employee belongs or does not belong to an employees' association, or because he legally engages in trade union activities (Article 336 paragraph

---

[185] On the legal situation in the USA, see the Littler Report 2014, *supra* note 40, 19; *Gantchar v. United Airlines Inc.*, 1995 U.p. Dist. LEXIS 3910, p. 23 (N.D. III 28.3.1995).

[186] Littler Report 2014, *supra* note 40, 12.

[187] Christie A. Moon, *Technology, Robotics and the Work Preservation Doctrine: Future Considerations for Labor and Management*, Pepperdine Law Review 2 *et seq.* (1987), <http://digitalcommons.pepperdine.edu/plr/vol14/iss2/6>, 418.

[188] See Chris di Marco, *The singularity and employment*, Inside Counsel (August 2015); see also the reasoning in European Commission, *EU launches world's largest civilian robotics programme* (3 June 2014) <http://europa.eu/rapid/press-release_IP-14-619_en.htm>.

2 letter a Swiss Code of Obligations). To a certain extent, employees can therefore voice their opinion against the introduction of robotics or automation and protest against it; they can organise themselves in trade unions and engage in such activities.

For this reason, difficulties arise if an employer informs or even threatens the workforce that trade union activity would lead to the introduction of robotics to save money and achieve the flexibility and efficiency which is impossible with organised employees.[189]

3.   Breach of an existing collective labour agreement

If the employer wishes to use robotics in the workplace for the first time, he must take into consideration all relevant clauses of an existing collective labour agreement.[190] He must examine whether the unilateral alteration of the working conditions breaches the applicable collective labour agreement. Likewise, he must check whether the contractual clauses of the existing collective labour agreement do not restrict the possibility of introducing robotics in the workplace for other reasons. Collective labour agreement provisions on alterations in the business or technological changes may have to be complied with when robotics are introduced.[191] In addition, the introduction of a new technology could be explicitly regulated in a collective labour agreement or a separate contract by prescribing the procedure to be followed to integrate a new technology in the workplace (e.g. cooperation). These are referred to as so-called "technology agreements".[192] They usually contain substantive and procedural law provisions.

It is advisable for employers to have a sound clause about changes to the business in a collective labour agreement which also reserves the right of the management to implement changes to the business,[193] in particular if the introduction of robotics is planned. Conversely, employees are recommended to include a precisely formulated duty to provide a severance scheme (referred to in the USA as a work preservation clause) in the collective labour agreement.[194] This can provide for the cooperation of employees in case of job cuts or employee retraining. It can also expressly address the introduction of robotics and automation concepts.

G.   Dismissals and Mass Redundancies

One of the most frequent discussions about automation and robotics is whether the industry will create more jobs than it eliminates. In any case, many employees will doubtless lose their jobs even if new jobs are created. Existing work will undergo significant changes,

---

[189]   Idaho Frozen Foods Division, 171 National Labor Relations Board (N.L.R.B.) 1968, p. 1567 et seq., p. 573.

[190]   Littler Report 2014, *supra* note 40, 13; Seiler, *supra* note 89, 7.

[191]   Littler Report 2014, *supra* note 40, 5. Other than, for example, in Germany, co-determination by the works council is not in principle necessary in Switzerland in case of technological innovations to change the business, see Section 87 I No. 6 Industrial Relations Act. See <http://www.human resourcesmanager.de/ressorts/artikel/wo-arbeit-40-das-arbeitsrecht-die-grenzen-bringt-174694826 4?xing_share=news>.

[192]   Seiler, *supra* note 89.

[193]   See Isabelle Wildhaber, *Das Arbeitsrecht bei Umstrukturierungen, Habil.* (Schulthess 2011) 7 *et seq.*; Littler Report 2014, *supra* note 40, 14.

[194]   Moon, *supra* note 187, 408.

for example with the transformation of simple work performance into monitoring or controlling activities.[195] In addition, some areas of work will be completely taken over by machinery, which will lead to the loss of numerous jobs. The automation and digitalisation process in an enterprise inevitably involves staff restructuring measures. In this context, dismissals announced by the employer will play a central role. Every employer is entitled to technically reorganise its business structure with the sole aim of maximising profit. Employers are therefore able to change job profiles in line with requirements, to completely replace jobs by machines and to announce dismissals.[196] However, the validity of announced dismissals nevertheless depends on the employment law provisions. The question is raised whether the dismissals are permissible and whether provisions on mass redundancies or the duty to provide a severance scheme are applicable.

To date, there is no special protection from the replacement of a human worker by robots in Switzerland. However, it should be borne in mind that in a market where reputation is as valuable as capital, the replacement of humans by robots can also be assessed as a reputation risk.

In order to remain competitive in the long term, employers increasingly make the decision to automate processes in the enterprise and organise them digitally. Job profiles change and human workers are becoming completely dispensable in many areas. Digital specialist knowledge is becoming a key qualification. If job profiles diverge from existing job descriptions and/or employees cannot fulfil the changed higher expectations in spite of appropriate training and further training programmes offered, or if employees are no longer required, staff restructuring is inevitable. Work with exoskeletons on building sites will, for example, present new challenges for employees. Not every building worker will be capable of operating a robot. A building worker who should learn the necessary qualifications (e.g. the functions and operation of the exoskeleton) may take part in a workshop, but be unable to operate the exoskeleton, even after several attempts, and consequently be dismissed by the employer.

Is this a redundancy for operational and business reasons where the grounds for dismissal originate from the employer's sphere, or a dismissal on grounds of personal capability or conduct? If the dismissal by the employer must be classified as for business reasons,[197] it must be included in the calculation of the threshold figure for mass redundancies (Article 335d paragraph 1 Swiss Code of Obligations).

If managerial authority includes the right to instruct the learning of new qualifications, the primary reason for the dismissal is not the decision by the employer to automate his business, but the lack of suitability or the conduct of the employee himself or herself. Learning new qualifications made necessary by technical progress must be viewed as part of the performance owed. The decisive factor here is the occupational profile at the present time. In the sample case, learning the functions of an exoskeleton is still within the scope of the reasonable duty to learn. This then constitutes dismissal on grounds of personal capability. By contrast, compulsory redundancy for operational reasons involves such significant changes to occupational profiles that they become very different from the

---

[195] Nadja Gross and Jacqueline Gressel, *Kündigungen als Folge von Digitalisierung und Automatisierung*, DB 2355 *et seq.* (2016).

[196] As in Gross and Gressel, *id.*, 2355.

[197] Wildhaber, *supra* note 193, 279; Gross and Gressel, *supra* note 195, 2355 *et seq.*

job description in the relevant contract of employment and consequently go beyond the originally agreed programme of duties, e.g. if the job requires programming capabilities after automation.

In addition, severance payments may be owed. In certain countries such as, for example, China or Mexico, employers must make severance payments in case of mass redundancies or business closures. In Mexico, a severance payment is explicitly owed in case employees become superfluous and are dismissed as a result of the integration of new technologies in the workplace.[198]

Occupational retraining opportunities supported by the employer or the state, which must be offered to the dismissed employees, are also conceivable. Even if new jobs are created, it is challenging for the dismissed employees to switch to these new positions.[199] New technologies make different qualifications necessary. This means that employees have the incentive – or face the necessity to – adapt to the changing demand by further training or occupational retraining.[200] It may no longer even be possible to perform simple auxiliary tasks in the future without knowledge of how to deal with network systems.

III.   CONCLUSION

Progress in robotics and AI will change the workplace and employment law. If robots become colleagues and superiors, employers must keep a keen eye on employment law developments. Employers who carefully consider their duties and the practical realities of their workplace will then be well prepared to anticipate and find answers to the complex legal questions involved with the use of robotics and AI in the workplace.

The prevalence of robots means that legislative authorities will have to consider whether legal bases need adjustment or whether wholly new legal bases are required to reflect the effects of this development. In my view, caution should be exercised with the introduction of new statutes and regulations until their necessity becomes clear.[201] The consequences of robotics on the employment market should not be viewed in isolation from other phenomena such as migration, the ageing population or globalisation. However, robotics do not primarily determine what our future will look like. As politicians, entrepreneurs or employees, we have the choice. The route we choose depends on the extent of our investment in education, how we encourage firms to create new jobs and which social and tax policy we choose.[202] It will be important to make wise and future-oriented decisions.

---

[198]   Littler Report 2014, *supra* note 40, 11.

[199]   *Id.*, 5.

[200]   Bloomberg, *Will Robots Take All Our Blue-Collar Jobs?* (13 August 2013) <http://www.bloomberg.com/news/2013-08-13/will-robots-take-allour-blue-collar-jobs-.html>.

[201]   E.C. Austin, *How to judge a 'bot; why it's covered*, The Economist (25 September 2014) <http://www.economist.com/blogs/babbage/2014/09/robot-jurisprudence> ("The concern for policymakers is creating a regulatory and legal environment that is broad enough to maintain legal and ethical norms but is not so proscriptive as to hamper innovation.").

[202]   Erik Brynjolfsson, *Millionen Arbeitsplätze verschwinden*, NZZ am Sonntag (9 January 2016) <http://www.nzz.ch/nzzas/nzz-am-sonntag/erik-brynjolfsson-millionen-arbeitsplaetze-verschwinden-ld.4065>.

SOURCES

Cases

BGE 132 V 215.
BGE 136 II 508, E. 5.2.4.
BGE 139 III 411.
BGE 141 V 30.
BGer 4A.102/2008 of 27.5.2008.
BGer 9C.600/2011 of 20.4.2012.
BGer 4A.2/2014 of 19.2.2014.
BGer 8C.279/2014 of 10.7.2015.
Swiss Federal Administrative Court, A-4457/2011 of 10.4.2012, E. 9.3.
Swiss Federal Administrative Court, A-6550/2007 of 29.4.2008, E. 7.
Gantchar v. United Airlines Inc., 1995 U.p. Dist. LEXIS 3910, p. 23 (N.D. III 28.3.1995).
Labour Court Zurich, AN 050401/U1 of 13.1.2006.
Speyer Social Court (Germany), KR 350/15 of 20.5.2016, p. 19.

Statutes

Directive (EU) 2016/680 of the European Parliament and of the Council of 27 April 2016 on the protection of natural persons with regard to the processing of personal data by competent authorities for the purposes of the prevention, investigation, detection or prosecution of criminal offences or the execution of criminal penalties, and on the free movement of such data, and repealing Council Framework Decision 2008/977/ JHA, Art. 3, Art. 11.
Directive 2006/42/EC of the European Parliament and of the Council of 17.5.2006 on machinery, and amending Directive 95/16/EC, Art. 1 et seq.
Directive of the Swiss Coordination Commission for Safety at Work No. 6508: Directive on the Involvement of Company Doctors and other Specialists for Safety at Work, January 2007 Edition, <http://www.ekas.admin. ch/index-de.php?frameset=200>.
Draft Report with recommendations to the Commission on Civil Law Rules on Robotics (2015/2103(INL)), Committee on Legal Affairs, Rapporteur Mady Delvaux, Consid. p. 31.
EKAS guidelines (Swiss Coordination Commission for Safety at Work).
European advisory body on data protection and privacy, Opinion 05/2012 on Cloud Computing (WP 196), Article 29 Data Protection Working Party, 1.7.2012, <http://ec.europa.eu/justice/data-protection/article-29/ documentation/opinion-recommendation/files/2012/wp196_en.pdf>.
German Civil Code, Section 623.
German Federal Data Protection Act, Section 6a para 1.
INB/NK 2310 – Industrielle Automation.
Industrial Relations Act, Section 87 I No. 6.
Instructions of the Secretary of State for the Economy (SECO) regarding Art. 2 Swiss Labour Ordinance 3.
ISO 10218-1:2011, Industrial Robots – Safety Requirements – Part 1: Robots.
ISO 10218-2:2011, Industrial Robots – Safety Requirements – Part 2: Robot Systems and Integration.
ISO 13482:2014, Robots and robotic devices – Safety requirements for personal care robots, Art. 3.13 and B.3., 68.
ISO/DIS 13485:2015, Medical devices – Quality management systems Requirements for regulatory purposes.
ISO/TC 184 – Automation systems and integration.
ISO/TS 15066:2016, Robots and robotic devices – Collaborative robots.
Modernisation draft of the European Council on the Convention for the Protection of Individuals with regard to Automatic Processing of Personal Data (Data Protection Convention, E-SEV 108), (T-PD(2012)04 rev2), Art. 8 para 1 letter a.
Occupational Safety & Health Administration (OSHA), Robotics in the Workplace, <http://www.osha.gov/ Publications/Mach_SafeGuard/chapt6.html>, Chapter 6.
Preliminary Draft for the Total Revision of the Swiss Data Protection Act and the amendment of further enactments on data protection, Art. 15.
Regulation (EU) 2016/679 of the European Parliament and of the Council of 27.4.2016 on the protection of natural persons with regard to the processing of personal data and on the free movement of such data, and repealing Directive 95/46/EC (General Data Protection Regulation), Art. 22.
RoboLaw deliverable D6.2 Guide-lines on Regulating Robotics, 22.9.2014, <http://www.robolaw.eu>, p. 15, p. 19, p. 107, p. 108, p. 174.

Suggestion for a green paper on legal issues in robotics, Contribution to Deliverable D3.2.1 on ELS issues in robotics, 2012, <http://www.robolaw.eu>, p. 41 et seq., p. 43, p. 53.

Swiss Civil Code of 10.12.1907, SR 210, Art. 12.

Swiss Code of Obligations of 30.3.1911, SR 220, Art. 328, Art. 328b, Art. 335d para 1, Art. 336 para 1 letter b, Art. 336 para 2 letter a.

Swiss Federal Accident Insurance Act of 20.3.1981, SR 832.20, Art. 7, Art. 10 et seq., Art. 82 para 1, Art. 91.

Swiss Federal Act of Data Protection (Data Protection Act) of 19.6.1992, SR 235.1, Art. 3 letter c, Art. 4, Art. 6, Art. 10a.

Swiss Federal Act on the General Part of Social Insurance Law of 6.10.2000, SR 830.1, Art. 72 para 1, Art. 75 para 2.

Swiss Federal Act on the Removal of Disadvantages for People with Disabilities (Equality for the Disabled Act) of 13.12.2002, SR 151.3.

Swiss Federal Code on Private International Law of 18.12.1987, SR 291, Art. 115, Art. 121.

Swiss Federal Constitution of the Swiss Confederation of 18.4.1999, SR 101, Art. 5 para 2, Art. 28.

Swiss Federal Office of Justice, Bericht der Begleitgruppe Revision DSG, Normkonzept zur Revision des Datenschutzgesetzes, Bern 29.10.2014, Reference COO.2180.109.7.138327 / 212.9/2012/00754, p. 26.

Swiss Federal Office of Justice, Explanatory report on the preliminary draft for the Federal Act on the Total Revision of the Swiss Data Protection Act and the amendment of further decrees on data protection, Bern 21.12.2016, reference COO.2180.109.7.190301 / 212.9/2015/00001, p. 20.

Swiss Federal Office of Social Insurance, 5th/6th Swiss Disability Insurance Re-Enactment.

Swiss Federal Product Safety Act of 12.6.2009, SR 930.11.

Swiss Labour Act of 13.3.1964, SR 822.11, Art. 6 para 1 and 2.

Swiss Ordinance 3 on the Labour Act (Swiss Labour Ordinance 3, Health Protection) of 18 August 1993, SR 822.113, Art. 7, Art. 26.

Swiss Ordinance of 29.11.1976 on the provision of aids by disability insurance, SR 831.232.51, Art. 2 para 4.

Swiss Ordinance on the Federal Act on Data Protection of 14.6.1993, SR 235.11, Art. 5, Art. 6, Art. 7.

Swiss Ordinance on the Prevention of Accidents and Occupational Illnesses of 19.12.1983, SR 832.30, Art. 7 para 2, Art. 11.

Swiss Ordinance on the Safety of Machinery of 2.4.2008, SR 819.14.

United Nations Convention on the Rights of People with Disabilities, concluded in New York on 13.12.2006, approved by the Swiss Federal Assembly on 13.12.2013, which entered into force for Switzerland on 15.5.2014, SR 0.109, Art. 4, Art. 5, Art. 27 para 1 letter i.

23. Robot Law 1.0: on social system design for artificial intelligence
Yueh-Hsuan Weng

I. INTRODUCTION

The focus of this chapter is on the topic of how artificial intelligence (AI) may influence the evolution of a legal framework for human-robot co-existence. In this chapter, three legal paradigms, Robot Law 1.0, 2.0 and 3.0, are used to analyze law and policy as related to AI in different technical stages of its development. Particularly important, under the category of Robot Law 1.0, I discuss the concept of "Social System Design", a strategy that aims to improve integrated governance for embodied AI. As artificially intelligent robots become more common in human society, it will be especially important to consider the ethical, legal, and social impacts implicated by the design of such systems. The concept of Social System Design will not only benefit legislators and policy makers, but also lead to an efficient regulation of intelligent robots and their AI-driven risks. As another laudable goal, Social System Design will also be helpful towards embedding social values into increasingly intelligent robotic systems. Thus, given this design paradigm which is based on a human-centered value system, artificially intelligent robots will more likely abide by moral obligations, an important goal for artificial intelligence researchers and society in general. Issues of morality accompany the "Robot Sociability Problem", which as discussed in this chapter has many facets, and suggest that an interdisciplinary approach towards regulating the design and use of emerging intelligent sociable machines is necessary.

II. BACKGROUND

Artificially intelligent systems manifest in many forms, and many would agree that increasingly intelligent robots are an important application of artificial intelligence; this observation motivates the interest of legal scholars who advocate for a law of artificial intelligence. In the mid-twentieth century, the term "robot law" began as a movement to develop moral principles for robots, such as to obey their master when making their own decisions while performing tasks in daily scenarios in the service of humans. One well-known paradigm for robot law is Asimov's Three Laws of Robotics—an ethical guideline that teaches intelligent robots how to ensure the safety of human-robot interactions based on a human-centered point of view. However, Asimov's three laws have changed greatly during the last three quarters of a century, that is, since he first introduced them in his classic work "Runaround" in 1942.[1] Based on Asimov's robot laws and the work

---

[1] Isaac Asimov, *Runaround. Astounding Science Fiction* (1942) Reprinted in Isaac Asimov, *I, Robot* (Ballantine Books, New York, 1983).

of scholars, many ethical branches began to grow at the root of his three laws—not the least of which was AI safety—an important discipline within robot ethics. The IEEE Global Initiative for Ethical Considerations in AI/AS is an example of government regulations which provide diverse social values in terms of "Ethically Aligned Design".[2] Additionally, over time, the meaning of "robot law" began to change from machine ethics for intelligent robots into a broader definition and categorization, including laws and rules for design, manufacturing, usage, the interaction of intelligent robotic technologies with other smart technologies, and additional ethical considerations for other forms of artificial intelligence.

Other legal issues of concern for increasingly intelligent robots and other smart technologies have also been the subject of discussion among legal scholars. For example, professor of law Ryan Calo described the correlation between the openness of a robotics platform and its corresponding tort liability given an accident;[3] Ugo Pagallo discussed the concept of privacy risks for robotics technology;[4] Susanne Beck provided an interesting perspective of criminal laws for robotics;[5] Woodrow Barfield pointed out ethical and legal concerns for Cyborg technology;[6] Robert van den Hoven van Genderen discussed the ancient Roman slave system and how it relates to legal personhood rights for robots;[7] and Erica Fraser and Burkhard Schafer described how to judge the IP innovation rights implicated when an AI entity is involved.[8] Following this trend towards identifying legal problems for AI and robotic technologies, the author's interest developed on how artificial intelligence influences the evolution of legal systems, which is the focus of this chapter.

III.   THE PYRAMID OF ROBOT INTELLIGENCE

From a neurologist's point of view, the human brain has three layers—primitive, paleopallium, and neopallium—that operate like "three interconnected biological computers, [each] with its own special intelligence, its own subjectivity, its own sense of time and space, and its own memory".[9] Based on this view, an analysis of the hierarchical taxonomy

---

[2]   The IEEE Global Initiative for Ethical Considerations in Artificial Intelligence and Autonomous Systems. Ethically Aligned Design: A Vision for Prioritizing Human Wellbeing with Artificial Intelligence and Autonomous Systems, Version 1, IEEE, 2016. http://standards.ieee.org/develop/indconn/ec/autonomous_systems.html.

[3]   Ryan Calo, *Open Robotics* 70(3) Maryland Law Review, vol.70, no.3 (2011).

[4]   Ugo Pagallo, *Robots in the cloud with privacy: A new threat to data protection?* 29(5) Computer Law & Security Review 501–08 (2013).

[5]   Susanne Beck, *Intelligent agents and criminal law—Negligence, diffusion of liability and electronic personhood* 86 Robotics and Autonomous Systems 138–43 (2016).

[6]   Woodrow Barfield, *Cyber-Humans: Our Future with Machines* (Springer, 2015).

[7]   Robert van den Hoven van Genderen, "Robot as a Legal Entity, Legal Dream or Nightmare? Proceedings of the 20th International Legal Informatics Symposium, IRIS 2017", pp 161–70, 23–25 February, University of Salzburg.

[8]   Erica Fraser and Burkhard Schafer, "Self-made (Machine) Men – IP Implications of Inventions by Robots, Proceedings of the 20th International Legal Informatics Symposium – IRIS 2017" pp 171–78, 23–25 February, University of Salzburg.

[9]   PD MacLean, *The triune brain in evolution: role in paleocerebral functions* (Springer, 1990).

of robot intelligence and how these factors can influence robot law in a long-term perspective is of interest to this chapter.

"Action Intelligence" is located at the bottom of the robot intelligence pyramid. Its functions are analogous to human nervous system responses that coordinate sensory and behavioral information, thereby giving a robot the ability to control body movement, move spatially, operate its arms to manipulate objects, and visually inspect its environment. The next, or second, level of Autonomous Intelligence refers to capabilities for solving problems and involves pattern recognition, logical reasoning, machine learning, and planning based on prior experience. "Intelligence" for robots (and other smart technologies) can also be referred to as "weak AI" or "narrow AI" in which a robot performs specific tasks in a narrow domain but with remarkable abilities. Examples include Google DeepMind's AlphaGo[10] and IBM's super computer Watson.[11]

Referring to Figure 23.1, robots with Action or Autonomous Intelligence are neither self-aware nor have their own internal value system in which to guide them in deciding what is right or wrong. However, a distinct difference between robots with Action versus Autonomous Intelligence is based on their adaptiveness to unstructured environments. The latter are superior in performing their tasks without predefined information about the real world, such as human living spaces. This difference leads to autonomous robots having adaptive behaviors and to become "open-textured", and leads to the possibility of many safety and ethical hazards in the real world, and also forms a boundary known as Open-Texture Risk[12] which refers to risks from robots' autonomous and potentially harmful behaviors. Such complex, changeable and unpredictable behaviors cause the gap

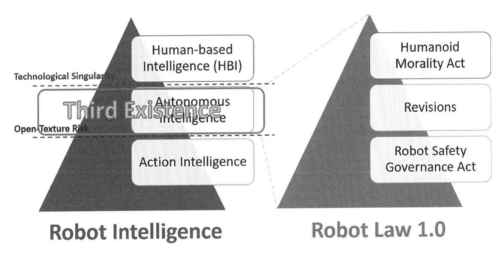

Figure 23.1   *Two pyramids for the governance of embodied AI*

---

[10]   AlphaGO, DeepMind, https://deepmind.com/research/alphago/.

[11]   Watson, IBM, https://www.ibm.com/watson/.

[12]   Yueh-Hsuan Weng, Chien-Hsun Chen, Chuen-Tsai Sun, "The Legal Crisis of Next Generation Robots: On Safety Intelligence" in *Proceedings of the 11th International Conference on Artificial Intelligence and Law* (ICAIL'07), Stanford CA, 205–09.

shown for modern machine safety in risk assessment. The word "open-texture" originally came from the field of law, and refers to the ambiguity of interpretation of legal terminologies.[13] Specifically, it is difficult to give direct and explicit definitions to some legal clauses due to the openness and evolving nature of language (especially when technology is involved). The same principle applies to the behavior of "Autonomous Intelligence" robots as well. Their dynamic decision-making abilities lead to difficulty when trying to specify potential risks possible from all of their behaviors—this topic is what the current ISO 12100 standard focuses on, that is, machine safety.[14] In other words, Open-Texture Risk is different for machines which can perform adaptive behaviors within unstructured environments and its range can be expanded by increasing its intelligence level.

Referring to the pyramid shown in Figure 23.1 for the governance of embodied artificial intelligence, at the third level of robot intelligence is Human-Based Intelligence (HBI) which refers to higher cognitive abilities that will allow robots creative ways to look at their environment and also the ability for abstract thought, even leading to consciousness. This level of robot intelligence is referred to in the literature as "strong AI" or "Artificial General Intelligence (AGI)". With advancements in artificial intelligence, the manifestation of strong AI in the form of Superintelligence or "Artificial Super Intelligence (ASI)" may be possible. Based on futurist Nick Bostrom's definition, Superintelligence is "any intellect that greatly exceeds the cognitive performance of humans in virtually all domains of interest".[15]

In general, the Technological Singularity is a hypothesis that relates to the growth and evolution of technology ultimately causing an intelligence explosion which would then lead to a powerful form of Superintelligence that is far beyond human intelligence.[16] However, different definitions have been proposed for the Technological Singularity.[17] For example, according to Vernor Vinge and Ray Kurzweil's definition, the Technological Singularity is more closely linked to ASI.[18] In contrast, artificial intelligence expert Ben Goertzel describes The Singularity by focusing on the potential for an uprising of AGI.[19] Hence, depending on the definition, the Technological Singularity may include both possibilities of either the birth of human-level AGI or superhuman ASI—only time will tell. Murray Shanahan argued that once human-level intelligence has been achieved, the transition to Artificial Super Intelligence could be very rapid.[20] In my view, from a

---

[13]   David Lyons, *Open texture and the Possibility of Legal Interpretation* 18(3) Law and Philosophy 297–309 (1999).

[14]   Gurvinder S. Virk, S. Moon and R Gelin, "ISO Standards for Service Robots, Advances" in *Robotics: Proceedings of the 11th International Conference on Climbing and Walking Robots and the Support Technologies for Mobile Machines*, Coimbra, Portugal, 8–10 September 2008.

[15]   Nick Bostrom, *Superintelligence: Paths, Dangers, Strategies* (Oxford University Press, 2014) 410.

[16]   Technological Singularity, Wikipedia, https://en.wikipedia.org/wiki/Technological_singularity.

[17]   See n 15, p.4.

[18]   Vernor Vinge, "The Coming Technological Singularity: How to Survive in the Post-Human Era", VISION-21 Symposium, 30–31 March 1993, http://edoras.sdsu.edu/~vinge/misc/singularity.html; Ray Kurzweil, *The Singularity is Near* (Viking, 2005).

[19]   Ben Goertzel, *Ten Years to the Singularity: If We Really, Really Try* (Humanity Press, 2014).

[20]   Murray Shanahan, *The Technological Singularity* (MIT Press, 2015).

regulation perspective, the coming of human-level AGI is a more important development than superhuman ASI, because we will have limited time to prepare a regulatory framework while AGI is transiting into ASI. Due to this concern, in this chapter the definition of the Technological Singularity refers to the evolving nature of strong AI.

IV.   THE PYRAMID OF ROBOT LAW

"Micro-electrical machines" including industrial robots, airplanes, automobiles, trains, elevators and escalators have been fully incorporated into our modern society. These Action Intelligence machines (Figure 23.1) are well regulated under contemporary laws. In the short term a new challenge for regulators and law-makers in order to achieve AI safety is to develop a regulatory framework which will cover the legal gap developing for emerging Autonomous Intelligence since this is a pressing issue in the timeframe of the following decade. Hence, the author introduces the term "Robot Law 1.0" to refer to a set of regulatory guidelines for intelligent machines which come with Open-Texture Risk but have not as yet achieved consciousness or reached the level of the Technological Singularity.

Next-Generation Robots[21] not only generate Open-Texture Risk, they also bring the new impact of affective computing to the forefront of society. Consider that in 2015 a drunken man in Kanagawa, Japan, entered a SoftBank as a customer. Due to a quarrel with the store clerk, he took out his anger on an intelligent machine and damaged the robot Pepper, kicking it violently. Though the clerk was not injured, the damaged robot was injured and as a result moved slower than its original interaction speed.[22] Pepper the robot has a biomorphic shape and resembles humans, and interacts socially by using its emotion, reading, and learning capabilities. The incident drew attention among legal scholars because despite how inappropriately the human-like sociable machine was treated, under the law it cannot receive any extended legal protection beyond its legal status as property, that is, as an object of law. Has there been a governmental response to the lack of legal person status for various forms of artificial intelligence? Recently, the European Parliament proposed an independent legal personhood status for AI/robots.[23] The proposal stipulates that current policies that treat robots as property may not be sufficient to handle legal disputes involving artificially intelligent robots in the future. However, would it be prudent to consider legal personhood for artificially intelligent entities that is equivalent to rights conferred to humans? The author holds conservative views towards giving Autonomous Intelligence machines full legal personhood rights at this time. Though machines can interact with human beings via affective computing, they do not have consciousness and cannot feel real pain, anger, sorrow or happiness. Granting full legal person status to artificial intelligence may disturb the stable order of ethics that

---

[21]   See n 12.
[22]   Lisa Zyga, "Incident of drunk man kicking humanoid robot raises legal questions", *TechXplore*, https://techxplore.com/news/2015-10-incident-drunk-humanoid-robot-legal.html.
[23]   "DRAFT REPORT with Recommendations to the Commission on Civil Law Rules on Robotics", European Parliament, 2015, http://www.europarl.europa.eu/sides/getDoc.do?pubRef=-// EP//NONSGML%2BCOMPARL%2BPE-582.443%2B01%2BDOC%2BPDF%2BV0//EN.

already exist between people and machines and the trust already established in human society. For example, suppose we granted an Autonomous Intelligence robot full legal personhood. If such a system causes harm to a person in the course of its task, it might not be liable for its wrongful, or even criminal, act.

Does it make sense to require something without self-awareness and moral standing to pay economic loss to a victim, or even incarcerate it in jail? Granting full legal personhood at the level of Robot Law 1.0 could lead to a range of legal and ethical quandaries, and inconsistencies in applying the law. Actually, in my view, what we have to protect is not the artificially intelligent robot itself, but we should require that it "project" an appropriate level of artificial empathy to human beings during daily human-robot interactions. When regulating artificial intelligence, we should avoid the negative social impacts that may happen to human beings after seeing unethical treatment given to next-generation robots. Thus, the author would like to propose granting an "extended legal protection" to Autonomous Intelligence robots with a quasi-legal personhood status called "Third Existence".[24] If we refer to the subject/object of law as the First/Second Existence then the Third Existence manifests as neither a pure legal object, nor a pure legal subject. In other words, it will be an object of law with a special legal status in order to establish a "proper" relationship between humans and robots.

What I refer to as "special" is an expedient, dynamic legal status for artificially intelligent robots. Under the premise of the Third Existence, regulators can consider cultural difference, issues of social acceptance,[25] and continuing technology advancements for smart technologies, and they can refer to various concepts including corporate personhood, quasi animal personhood for apes,[26] animal welfare, non-personhood with owner liability,[27] quasi personhood for unborn infants,[28] and human slaves as a legal entity.[29] To treat Autonomous Intelligence robots as a Third Existence is not only to create a "shock buffer" for covering the legal gap that exists for AI personhood, but will offer benefits to policy-makers by reserving core values of robot sociability with a global consensus.[30]

If robots do acquire Human-Based Intelligence (HBI), one impact to the legal system will be their capability for abstract thinking, which may enable them, among others, to interpret human languages. The "formality obstacle" of Asimov's Three Laws of Robotics can be solved, but it will lead to another concern for the violation of human-centered governance due to the consciousness (if it occurs) of artificially intelligent entities.[31]

---

[24]   Yueh-Hsuan Weng, *The Study of Safety Governance for Service Robots: On Open-Texture Risk*, Ph.D. Dissertation, Peking University Law School, 2014.

[25]   Pericle Salvini, Cecilia Laschi and Paolo Dario, *Design for acceptability: improving robots' coexistence in human society* 2(4) International Journal of Social Robotics 451–60 (2010).

[26]   Stephen Wells, *Legal Personhood for Apes*, Huffpost, 2015, http://www.huffingtonpost.com/stephen-wells/legal-personhood-for-apes_b_6378486.html.

[27]   Richard Kelley, Enrique Schaerer, Micaela Gomez and Monica Nicolescu, *Liability in Robotics: An International Perspective on Robots as Animals* 24(13) Advanced Robotics 1861–71 (2010).

[28]   Peter Asaro, "Robots and Responsibility from a Legal Perspective", Workshop on Roboethics, IEEE ICRA, Rome, 2007.

[29]   See n 7.

[30]   Yueh-Hsuan Weng, *Beyond Robot Ethics: On Legislative Consortium for Social Robotics* 24(13) Advanced Robotics 1919–26 (2010).

[31]   See n 25.

Generally, the proposal of Robot Law 1.0 will be difficult to deal with using HBI self-awareness machines. The author believes that incorporating them into human society and whether or not artificially intelligent entities such as robots can receive equivalent human rights, or be recognized as a "First Existence" or subject under law will be a hotly debated issues at the next level of regulation—Robot Law 2.0.

Except for technical challenges in machine ethics,[32] some people might be curious about how the advent of robot consciousness will impact the debates about developing artificial moral agents (AMAs). Utilitarianist Peter Singer uses Jeremy Bentham's "greatest happiness principle"[33] to deduce his famous argument on equal rights consideration for animals. Suppose animals can suffer, Singer proposes that humans have an ethical obligation to avoid this undesirable outcome from happening.[34] Consciousness for an artificially intelligent entity is key here, mixed with sentience and the capability to feel pain and suffer from interactions with the real world. Hence, HBI robots should have moral standing when they cross the boundary of the Technological Singularity, and similarly I propose that this is the prerequisite in deciding whether artificially intelligent robots should deserve their own rights.

A potential concern for Robot Law 2.0 is how long it will take to go from human-level Artificial General Intelligence (AGI) to Artificial Superintelligence (ASI). Nick Bostrom believes ASI can be created soon after human-level intelligence is achieved and will result in two possible consequences—either an extremely good or an extremely bad outcome.[35] Therefore, the issue of how to develop an AI safety network in order to properly solve the "control problem" of artificially intelligent entities[36] will be another critical challenge to AI ethics. Robot Law 2.0 will not be sufficient in this regard when ASI has been created with an extremely good or bad outcome. Suppose ASI is able to enhance human life in various ways and it achieves a superior God-like status in human society. In this situation, Robot Law 2.0's proposal seeking a fairly equal relationship between human and artificially intelligent robots might seem inappropriate, even awkward. Also, there will be no need to incorporate AI safety governance into Robot Law 2.0, because many measurements relating to the control problem will not be applicable once a Superintelligence entity has been created. On the other hand, if ASI emerges as a "hurtful" entity posing dangers to humans, one possibility may be that the intelligent entity makes their own "Robot Law 3.0" and demands that human beings obey it.

The above discussion is only a brief sketch of the moral, ethical and legal issues associated with the three stages of artificial intelligence shown in Figure 23.1. If we would like to ensure the governance of AI via a regulatory framework, the author believes Robot Law 1.0 will be the most significant approach, because the time-period from Autonomous Intelligence to Human-Based Intelligence (HBI) could be several decades or even longer. However, when HBI reaches the boundary of the Technological Singularity, it may only

---

[32] "Technological Challenges in Machine Ethics", Robohub, 2017, http://robohub.org/technical-challenges-in-machine-ethics/.

[33] Jeremy Bentham, *Introduction to the Principles of Morals and Legislation* (Payne, 1789).

[34] Peter Singer, *Animal Liberation: The Definitive Classic of the Animal Movement* (HarperCollins, 1975).

[35] See n 15, at 25.

[36] See n 15, at 155.

take a short period of time before HBI evolves into Superintelligence. In other words, at the threshold of the Technological Singularity, there may not be sufficient time for humanity to develop a Robot Law 2.0.

V.   SOCIAL SYSTEM DESIGN

Under the proposal for a Robot Law 1.0, intelligent machines should be treated as the Third Existence—objects of law with extended legal protection. Countries could then decide concrete protection measures based on their unique domestic culture and social acceptance to AI-enabled technologies. Suppose a legal object and subject occupy the very two ends of the Third Existence, so the scale could be from zero percent (pure legal object) to 99.99 percent (very close to a legal subject, but not yet there) of the equivalence to full legal personhood based on different social values and time periods. The flexibility represented by the continuum can be the greatest common divisor of the fundamental guideline for regulators in developing suitable domestic revisions of conflicts to current existing laws and advanced intelligent technologies.

A benefit of Japan's "Tokku" special zone is that the aforementioned legal conflicts can be discovered from conducting experiments. For example, outdoor experiments using autonomous driving vehicles or humanoid robots may show the legal gap which occurs by trying to adopt advanced technologies into current road traffic regulations or other areas of human life. However, previous findings from a case study of the "robot special zone" suggests that by revising only existing laws this approach may not be sufficient to regulate advanced robotics technology controlled by artificial intelligence. The regulatory framework to AI-enabled machines should also consider other specific measures such as a "Humanoid Morality Act" and "Robot Safety Governance Act" for mitigating safety and ethical hazards[37] (Figure 23.1). They are role playing as "the governance in morality" and "the governance in safety" respectively. That is, we will need two specific levels of governance for AI safety and AI morality at the level of Robot Law 1.0, the "Humanoid Morality Act" and "Robot Safety Governance Act", both of which will play an important role in creating such morality/safety governance.

As AI and robotic technology continues to expand into human living spaces, the importance of the intersection between law and ethics will become more apparent and essential. Hence, we will need a "Humanoid Morality Act" to reduce the ethical gray zone and moral disputes regarding the usage of artificially intelligent robots. A special concern relating to regulating increasingly smart technologies is derived from a macro perspective by looking at future human-robot interaction and their "ethical hazards", which extend from personal to societal, commercial and economic hazards, and perhaps environmental hazards as well. Examples include, but are not limited to, robot addiction, deception, and the obsolescence of jobs now performed by humans, among other things.[38] The potential

---

[37]   Yueh-Hsuan Weng, Yusuke Sugahara, Kenji Hashimoto and Atsuo Takanishi, *Intersection of "Tokku" Special Zone, Robots, and the Law: A Case Study on Legal Impacts to Humanoid Robots* 7(5) International Journal of Social Robotics (2015).

[38]   BS 8611: 2016, Robots and robotics devices. Guide to the ethical design and application of robots and robotics systems.

demands for a "Humanoid Morality Act" can be found in the previous Pepper incident in which the robot was assaulted by a human. A Humanoid Morality Act should be at the top of a Robot Law 1.0, and will define the proper relationship between humans and robots and also direct the use of coercive power to constrain unethical applications of humanoid robotics and cyborg technologies. This approach will establish fundamental norms for regulating daily interactions between human and robot. However, it is hard to implement such regulations at this time, because it will take a period of adjustment for AI technologies to comfortably merge into our daily life. This explains why South Korea's "Robot Ethical Charter" failed at the legislative level when it was proposed in 2007.[39] In my view, the issue was not about the importance of the proposed topic, as regulating intelligent robots is an important topic, but the period of time they chose to enact legislation.

Even given the importance of governance in morality issues related to artificially intelligent entities, we cannot overlook the governance of safety which I propose can be done through a "Robot Safety Governance Act"— the bottom foundation of Robot Law 1.0 (Figure 23.1). Though AI safety has often been discussed, not all AI safety problems should be regulated by law. One example is the adaptive intelligence or machine learning capabilities of artificial intelligence, especially with regard to preventing catastrophic risks which could occur once the Technological Singularity is achieved. The story of "UK's Red Flag Laws" for steam-powered vehicles in the nineteenth century[40] taught us that regulators usually have a "knee-jerk" reaction towards over-regulation due to their knowledge gap which exists for technology. Based on this response, it is possible that at this time machine learning should not be regulated because it is at the cutting edge of artificial intelligence, thus it is evolving quickly. It is not likely that regulators will have equivalent domain knowledge of artificial intelligence techniques compared to professional AI programmers or robotics engineers. Therefore, the chance of over-regulation with systems using machine learning might be more pronounced than with other safety issues. Besides, the Machine Intelligence Research Institute (MIRI) has predicted the timeframe of reaching Artificial General Intelligence between 15 and 150 years,[41] and the Oxford Future of Humanity Institute's survey with AI experts also revealed a diversity of professionals' opinion for the timeframe of the birth of AGI.[42] Such a "blurry" time period is not conducive for making a concrete plan for regulating AI safety at this point in time. In my view, this issue, safety, should be prevented by a moral consensus made by global AI communities, or as we call it "Professional Ethics".

In other words, long-term AI safety is not of significant concern for the "Robot Safety Governance Act" which refers to a regulatory framework for promising AI technologies that will be introduced into our daily lives within the following decade. The law's role in AI safety is not only about the time period in which technology comes online, but should also take priority in order to protect AI risks which present a clear and present danger to human rights. Along this line, one of the key issues is how do we govern the Open-Texture

---

[39]   HB Shim, "Establishing a Korean Robot Ethics Charter", Workshop on Roboethics, IEEE ICRA, Rome, 2007.

[40]   Red Flag Laws, Wikipedia, https://en.wikipedia.org/wiki/Red_flag_traffic_laws.

[41]   MIRI Website, https://intelligence.org/.

[42]   See n 15, at 23.

Risk from machine's autonomous behaviors which could cause physical harms to human beings?

Embodiment is another factor to consider for robot safety governance. In my view, an important issue to consider is "embodied AI"; for example, as argued by Rolf Pfeifer and Josh Bongard, embodiment is an indispensable nature of a physical entity to display intelligence.[43] At this point, the boundary of software and hardware for artificially intelligent entities are not as clear as for PCs because a machine's autonomous behaviors could be generated by either its "brain's" (i.e., AI agent) decision-making, its body's (hardware) adaptive interactions with environments, or complex behaviors coordinated by both brain and body. The issue of "Body Intelligence" will bring up a host of new issues related to the safety of artificial intelligence in general, and to robot safety governance in specific. For example, how can we deal with "Modeling Error" as a potential safety gap between the machine's AI agent and hardware? Suppose its brain works normally but "Machine Fatigue" caused unwanted harmful outcomes to users, then who is responsible for the harm to humans or to property? Unless AI applications are not related to robotics, physical safety in human-robot interaction should be one of the fundamental issues of concern in AI safety.

A policy tool of importance for enacting robot safety regulations is termed Regulatory Science.[44] The US Federal Drug Administration (FDA) defines Regulatory Science as the science of developing new tools, standards, and approaches to assess the safety, efficiency, quality and performance of FDA regulated products; note that some robotic devices are considered medical devices and are regulated by the FDA. Legislators might consider making laws to restrict inappropriate interactions with robots, create personal data protection standards for humans which may be necessary given daily human-robot interaction, and regulate sales and usages of robotic technologies. It is relatively easy to develop regulations from the application side of intelligent technologies. But the design and manufacture of advanced robotics are difficult to regulate in depth because of the required domain knowledge of artificial intelligence; and as stated above, technology know-how are high thresholds for non-expert law-makers to overcome. Regulatory Science has been used by modern society to systematically mitigate risks from advanced technologies and these benefits create regulations in a highly technical way, so-called "Technical Norms", with examples that include current safety requirements from FDA drug regulation and UNECE motor vehicle regulation.

In Europe, regulation for robot safety is organized by two main parts as a "Directive" and a "Harmonized Standard". The first part is a set of related EC directives which aims for harmonizing essential health and safety requirements to be applied to "machinery products." Member states have responsibilities to incorporate machinery directives into domestic legal systems and to transform them into law to ensure the product's free circulation in the EU market. Further, the Machinery Directive 2006/42/EC,[45] the Low Voltage Directive 2006/95/EC, and the EMC Directive 2004/108/EC, are each EC directives which

---

[43]   Rolf Pfeifer and Josh Bongard, *How the Body Shapes the Way We Think: A New View of Intelligence* (MIT Press, 2006).

[44]   Regulatory Science, Wikipedia, https://en.wikipedia.org/wiki/Regulatory_science.

[45]   Machinery Directive 2006/42/EC, http://eur-lex.europa.eu/legal-content/EN/TXT/?uri=CELEX%3A32006L0042.

relate more specifically to robotics. However, these directives only define essential health and safety requirements in general applications, supplemented by a number of more specific requirements for certain categories of machinery. There is a demand to adopt extended industrial standards to improve inspection and to ensure the manufacturers' conformity to match the essential requirements. These harmonized standards provide detailed safety requirements, such as the ISO 13482: 2014 Safety Standard for Personal Care Robots,[46] and are able to help verification of machine safety in a more efficient way.

In Japan, there is Consumer Product Safety Law to protect users from suffering physical harm from consumer products; the safety law may include some types of service robots.[47] The Japanese Consumer Product Safety Law takes another safety governance approach for defining and applying several measures to product accidents. For example, a product manufacturer or importer should report to the Ministry of Economy, Trade and Industry (METI) within ten days after he receives word of a serious accident that occurred due to use of his product. Required report items include: date, summary, name and type of the product, time and number of the manufactured or imported products, the cause of the accident, countermeasures to the accident, etc. This approach can help the government collect product accident information and then consider suitable strategies for robot safety governance.

Though there are many laws that could be used in safety regulation for artificially intelligent robots, there is a gap using them to sufficiently implement the safety governance for embodied AI, this is referred to as the "Robot Sociability Problem" discussed above. "Sociability" is the skill, tendency, or property of being sociable or socially interacting well with others. The sociability problem in artificially intelligent robotics refers to associated problems that will resemble or merge with those in other fields as robots are increasingly incorporated into human daily life. When robots become highly autonomous and are able to serve and co-exist with people, diversity values generated from robot sociability will cause the explosion of Open-Texture Risk. This problem is something current robot safety regulatory frameworks find difficult to solve. Therefore, it is inevitable that regulators address new impacts of robot technology to robot safety governance via embedding human-centered social values into the system and environment design process—this requires a macro level human-robot interaction or "Social System Design" approach.

Social System Design is an approach to enable integrated governance for embodied AI (Figure 23.2). There will be a strong demand for working ethical and legal factors into the design process of intelligent sociable robots as they are incorporated into human society. On the one hand, artificially intelligent robots should abide by moral obligations from a human-centered value system, but on the other regulators will have to consider the design of corresponding social systems in order to support their daily interactions within human living environments. Therefore, we will need an interdisciplinary approach or way of thinking about the design of artificially intelligent robots.[48]

---

46   ISO 13482: 2014 Safety Standard for Personal Care Robots.
47   Consumer Product Safety Law, http://www.japaneselawtranslation.go.jp/law/detail/?id=1838&re=02.
48   Yueh-Hsuan Weng, "Towards Integrated Governance for Intelligent Robots: A Focus on Social System Design, Proceedings of the 20th International Legal Informatics Symposium – IRIS 2017", pp 191–98, 23–25 February, University of Salzburg.

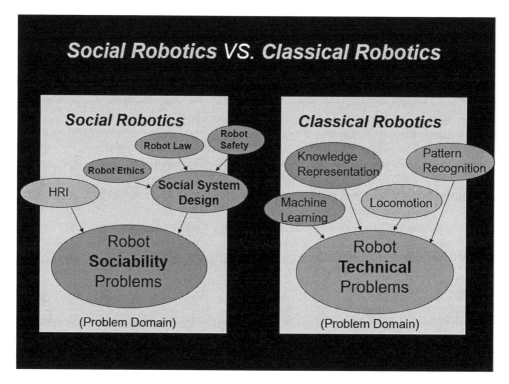

Figure 23.2   Social system design: an integrated approach

The concept of a "Black Box" or Event Data Recorder is an example of an integrated governance by law and engineering. The importance of the Black Box is that its collected data can be analyzed by experts as evidence to help "Post-Safety Governance" such as liability distribution or insurance rate calculation. The major difference of a Black Box in service robot applications is that with high autonomy and sociability, robots will be incorporated into human daily life, while recording safety critical data, thus, the robot will inevitably record personal and sensitive data as well. As an example, let's say a man was killed in a house with a service robot inside. His wife (and police) wants to use the black box of the robot to know how her husband was murdered, but after she surveyed the incident, she discovered two things: one, her husband's colleague killed him, and two, a female stranger had an affair with her husband when she was not at home. The value conflict between safety and privacy as shown by this example is in conflict and something governance by law cannot solve.

"Privacy by Design" is another example of importance for regulating increasingly smart technologies. In this case, ICT manufacturers should do privacy and data protection compliance during the design and manufacturing process of their products.[49] This is an efficient way for privacy and data protection to be implemented into product design,

---

[49]   Privacy by Design, Wikipedia, https://en.wikipedia.org/wiki/Privacy_by_design.

because once personal sensitive data is made public it is difficult to make the information private again, especially once the system has been hacked. On the other hand, robot safety is similar to privacy protection; physical harms could be serious and hard to recover. This is why we will need a "Safe by Design" principle in which embodied AI systems should be created with the compliance of norms, standards or guidelines.[50] But before we touch upon the core components of the "Safe by Design" approach, we have to take a retrospective review to the development of contemporary robot safety governance.

One main focus of Aichi EXPO'05 was the future scenario of human-robot co-existence. At the EXPO, there were many service robots demonstrated to the public including Floor Cleaning Robots, Garbage Collection Robots, Security Robots, Guide Robots, Child-care Robots, and Next-generation Wheelchair Robots.[51] Importantly, the EXPO was a turning point for the Japanese government, who then decided to promote safety governance for Next-Generation Robots.[52] Afterwards, the New Energy and Industrial Technology Development Organization (NEDO) launched a project which was concerned with the practical applications of service robots and whose aim was to develop a safety governance system for physical human-robot interaction (pHRI). The project created a Robot Safety Center (RSC) in 2010 in Tsukuba science park, which has four main testing areas: (1) traveling safety test area; (2) collision and tip-over test area; (3) EMC test area; and (4) mechanical test area. RSC plays the role of a certification body, the role of verification authority, and as a platform for the creation of international safety standards. Another mission of RSC is to develop evaluations for "Functional Safety" for service robots.[53]

Inherent Safety ensures robot safety by removing the source of hazards, which is of low design freedom and more reliable to its users. An example of Inherent Safety is the safety fence that is used to separate humans from industrial robots. On the other hand, service robots come with high design freedom, therefore they will need another level of Functional Safety to ensure the machine safety by robots' functions. An example of a Functional Safety regulation is ISO 13482's "Virtual Fence" which sets up many different levels of safety zones, for example, a robot may detect people approaching it and then decide to slow its speed and decrease its power or to stop its task altogether to realize safety via these functions.

As we enter the era of artificially intelligent robots, we might need to consider safety hazards alongside new hazards in order to ensure the safety of physical human-robot interaction. Autonomous Intelligence machines and Open-Texture Risk are both mixed with safety and ethical hazards, therefore, only removing the source of hazards in advance or by ensuring the safety with functions are not enough. We will need a mechanism called "Safety Intelligence" to help avoid unwanted safety behaviors by artificially intelligent machines in real time.[54] At least in theory, Isaac Asimov's Three Laws of Robotics is an

---

[50]   See n 2 and n 38.

[51]   EXPO 2005: Aichi http://www.expo2005.or.jp/en/robot/robot_project_01.html.

[52]   Hirochika Inoue, *Robot Project for EXPO 2005* 24(2) Journal of Robotics Society of Japan 148–50 (2006) (in Japanese).

[53]   Robot Safety Center, http://robotsafety.jp.

[54]   Yueh-Hsuan Weng, Chien-Hsun Chen and Chuen-Tsai Sun, *Toward Human-Robot Co-Existence Society: On Safety Intelligence for Next-Generation Robots* 1(4) International Journal of Social Robotics (2009).

ideal paradigm of Safety Intelligence. It is inevitable that legal schemes consider authorizing machines with a safety-oriented autonomy in unstructured environments when they co-exist with humans. A key challenge for legislators and judges will be to design a safety governance protocol that can properly coordinate inherent safety, functional safety, and safety intelligence into one regulatory scheme. These protocols will need to be put into the basket of safety intelligence should emerging AI technologies which have concrete applications be introduced into the market. They include, but are not limited to, machine learning, computer vision, simultaneous localization and mapping (SLAM), nature language processing (NLP), and haptics sensing.

Additionally, we might be able to define legal requirement for computer vision, such as letting computer vision recognize (by nature of the algorithms used) a set of non-verbal cues or body language or SLAM that teaches an artificial intelligence run machine to keep a proper social distance from people, or to avoid the negative side effects from a cleaning robot with RL agents.[55] On this point, regulators only have to consider how to properly control the Open-Texture Risk from emerging AI technologies. Hence, they can be released from a series of philosophical debates on smart robots and their artificial morality.

The specifics of the legal framework of Robot Law 1.0 is presented on the upper and lower sides of the "governance in morality" and "governance in safety", and its universality is between the two in the form of "revisions" (see Figure 23.1). Over the past few years there have been many examples of conflicts between existing laws and robotics, such as: bipedal humanoid robots or unmanned vehicles immediately faced with restrictions based on road traffic laws when they leave the laboratory to enter the real world. Further, other issues of interest to artificial intelligence which will lead to privacy protection and other issues will be the difficulty in judging tort liability resulting from an accident caused by autonomous robots; the use of sensor equipped smart unmanned aerial vehicles which will lead to privacy protection issues; the issue of lethal military robots which will cause international humanitarian law disputes, and so on. Finally, the law must consider appropriate amendments of current law and statutes to promote the integration of robotic science and technology into society. In the embryonic period of human-robot co-existence in society, "revisions" involve only a small part of many statutes, such as road traffic law, tort liability law, and international humanitarian law. But with robot technology becoming smarter, given its scope of expansion in society and generally the capabilities of robot technology itself, the development and progress of the "revised laws and regulations" is bound to extend the scope of the regulation of smart technologies to other laws, such as intellectual property law, criminal law, and even the Constitutional law of most jurisdictions.

VI.   CONCLUSION

The importance of regulating artificial intelligence can be shown by increasingly smart robotics which takes the form of an embodied medium for AI agents, thus allowing the

---

[55]   Dario Amodei, Chris Olah, Jacob Steinhardt, Paul Christiano, John Schulman and Dan Mane, *Concrete Problems in AI Safety*, arXiv preprint arXiv:1606.06565 (2016).

agent to physically interact with human beings. In this chapter, the author described the associativity between AI and robotics, and discussed the evolution of a legal framework for dealing with AI in different stages of its development. Considering the strong connectivity between AGI and ASI, I propose that we shall seriously consider using Robot Law 1.0 to improve safety governance for embodied AI. Further, Social System Design is not only a measure for establishing AI's social status in human society, but also a moderator to keep the balance between management, technology, professional ethics, and law among AI safety governance. This integrated governance approach will ensure the future regulation of artificially intelligent entities in a safe and effective manner and in particular allow for human-robot co-existence.

SOURCES

BS 8611: 2016 Robots and robotic devices: guide to the ethical design and application of robots and robotic systems, British Standards Institute, London.
Directive 2006/42/EC of The European Parliament and of the Council of 17 May 2006 on machinery, and amending Directive 95/16/EC (recast). (Official Journal of the European Union L 157/24. 9.6.2006).
ISO 13482: 2014 Robots and robotic devices – Safety Requirements for Personal Care Robots, International Organization for Standardization.

24. Antitrust, algorithmic pricing and tacit collusion
Maurice E. Stucke and Ariel Ezrachi

I. INTRODUCTION

How competitive are our markets? Not as much as they ought to be. We are increasingly realizing the market failures and shortcomings of U.S. antitrust policy over the past 30 years. The White House in April 2016 issued an executive order and report on the state of competition in the U.S.[1] The report identified several disturbing signs about the decline in competition since the 1970s: First, competition appears to be decreasing in many economic sectors, including the decades-long decline in new business formation. The U.S. is seeing lower levels of firm entry and labor market mobility. Second, many industries are becoming more concentrated. Third, industry profits are increasingly falling into the hands of fewer firms. Basically, more industries are now dominated by fewer firms (increasing concentration). These few powerful firms are extracting greater profits (and wealth) from workers, sellers, and consumers. And it is getting harder for new firms to enter markets and for workers to change employers. Others, including the Economist,[2] the Atlantic,[3] and Harvard Business School,[4] have raised similar concerns.

The increased concentration and dampening of competition are not limited to our brick-and-mortar markets. Interestingly, and somewhat counterintuitively, certain online markets—where choice seems endless and competition fierce—have become more concentrated and less competitive.[5] One notable example of the implications of this increased concentration may be found in the European Commission's fining Google €2.42 billion for abusing its dominant position in search.[6] In addition, as *Virtual Competition*[7]

---

[1] Executive Order—Steps to Increase Competition and Better Inform Consumers and Workers to Support Continued Growth of the American Economy. Available online: https://obamawhitehouse. archives.gov/the-press-office/2016/04/15/executive-order-steps-increase-competition-and-better-inf orm-consumers.

[2] *The superstar company – A giant problem* https://www.economist.com/news/leaders/21707210- rise-corporate-colossus-threatens-both-competition-and-legitimacy-business; *Data is giving rise to a new economy* The Economist (6 May 2017) https://www.economist.com/news/briefing/2172 1634-how-it-shaping-up-data-giving-rise-new-economy.

[3] *America's Monopoly Problem* https://www.theatlantic.com/magazine/archive/2016/10/americ as-monopoly-problem/497549/.

[4] *How competitive is America? How can we improve?* http://www.hbs.edu/competitiveness/ Pages/default.aspx.

[5] https://www.wsj.com/articles/can-the-tech-giants-be-stopped-1500057243.

[6] European Commission – Press Release, Antitrust: Commission fines Google €2.42 billion for abusing dominance as search engine by giving illegal advantage to own comparison shopping service, Brussels, 27 June 2017.

[7] Ariel Ezrachi and Maurice E. Stucke, *Virtual Competition – The Promise and Perils of the Algorithm-Driven Economy* (HUP 2016).

and *Big Data and Competition Policy*[8] explore, technology, big analytics and big data—just as they are essential for dynamic competition—have been increasingly used to curtail competition.

Big data and the development of sophisticated computer algorithms and artificial intelligence are neither good, bad, nor neutral. Their nature depends on how firms employ them, and whether their incentives are aligned with our interests, and certain market characteristics. At times, big data and big analytics—in enhancing information flows and access to markets—can promote competition and our welfare. However, we cannot uncritically assume that we will always benefit.

This chapter explores some of the means through which algorithms and artificial intelligence may be used to dampen competition. We note how algorithmic pricing could, under certain market conditions, lead to conscious parallelism and higher prices. We explore how neural networks to monitor and determine price could take us further away from a "true" market price and the enforcement challenges raised by algorithmic tacit collusion.

II.   THE COLLUSION SCENARIOS

Cartels are generally regarded in the antitrust world as "no-brainers." The cartel agreement, even if unsuccessful, is typically condemned as per se illegal. The price-fixers have few, if any, legal defenses. And in the United States, among other jurisdictions, the guilty executives are often thrown into jail. So what happens to cartels with the rise of pricing algorithms? Industries are migrating from the brick-and-mortar pricing environment (where store clerks once stamped prices on products) to dynamic, differential pricing where sophisticated computer algorithms rapidly calculate and update prices. Does that spell the end of cartels, or does it create new ways to collude?

Some argue the former. Cartels are often more durable than neoclassical economic theory predicts. Why? Humans often trust one another. "Collusion is more likely," the U.S. Department of Justice noted, "if the competitors know each other well through social connections, trade associations, legitimate business contacts, or shifting employment from one company to another."[9] Computers do not exhibit trust. Instead, algorithms engage in cold, profit-maximizing calculations. Even if they could agree with or trust other computers, they would find ways to cheat.

While not trusting, pricing algorithms—in increasing the speed of communicating price changes, detecting any cheating or deviations, and punishing such deviations—can *facilitate* existing forms of collusion and *foster new elusive forms of collusion*, achieved through subtler means, which do not amount to a hard-core cartel, and are beyond the law's reach.

We consider five scenarios in which computer algorithms may promote horizontal collusion[10]:

---

[8]   Maurice E. Stucke and Allen P. Grunes, *Big Data and Competition Policy* (OUP 2016).

[9]   *Price Fixing, Bid Rigging, and Market Allocation Schemes: What They Are and What to Look For* https://www.justice.gov/atr/price-fixing-bid-rigging-and-market-allocation-schemes.

[10]   Pricing and price-monitoring algorithms can also foster vertical price-fixing (which is also called minimum resale price maintenance), whereby the manufacturer and retailer agree on

- The first scenario, *messenger*, concerns humans agreeing to collude and using computers to execute their will. One 2015 case involved posters sold through Amazon Marketplace:

  > The conspirators used commercially available algorithm-based pricing software, which continually collects competitor pricing information and prices a product based on a set of rules implemented by the seller. In order to match prices, one conspirator, with the agreement of the other, programmed its algorithm to find the lowest-price offered by a non-conspiring competitor for a particular poster, and then set its poster price just below that, and another conspirator set its algorithm to match the first conspirator's price. By agreeing to fix prices for certain posters, the conspirators eliminated competition among themselves for these sales. Such competition would have likely driven the poster prices down further. The conspirators monitored the effectiveness of their pricing algorithms by spot checking prices, and enforced their price-fixing agreement. Once the pricing algorithms were in place, however, the conspiracy was, to a large extent, self-executing.[11]

  Under this scenario, humans collude. They use computers to assist in creating, monitoring, and policing a cartel. In the U.S. and elsewhere, they go to jail if caught.

- Our second scenario, *hub and spoke*, is more challenging. Here we consider the use of a single pricing algorithm to determine the market price charged by numerous users. Uber illustrates this framework. Uber drivers do not compete among themselves over price; some drivers might be willing to offer you a discount, but Uber's algorithm determines your base fare and when, where, and for how long to impose a surcharge. This, by itself, is legal. But as the platform's market power increases, this cluster of similar vertical agreements may beget a classic hub-and-spoke conspiracy, whereby the algorithm developer, as the hub, helps orchestrate industry-wide collusion, leading to higher prices.[12] Likewise, as the European Commission and

---

the product's retail price. Manufacturers can use algorithms to detect deviations from a fixed or minimum resale price, "retaliate against retailers that do not comply with pricing recommendations and, therefore, limit the incentives of retailers to deviate from such pricing recommendations in the first place." Algorithms and Collusion – Note by the European Commission, submitted for the OECD Competition Committee Hearings on 21–23 June 2017, DAF/COMP/WD(2017)12, at 2 (14 June 2017). Vertical price-fixing may foster tacit collusion among competitors. As the Commission noted, "when retailer A adheres to fixed or minimum resale prices (RPM) and is being monitored by retailer B using algorithms, retailer B may match A's price. In this way, one retailer's use of RPM may spread high prices to other retailers who may not be similarly engaged in RPM." *Id.* at 2–3.

[11] Algorithms and Collusion – Note by the United States, submitted for the OECD Competition Committee Hearings on 21–23 June 2017, DAF/COMP/WD(2017)41, at 2 (26 May 2017); *see also* https://www.justice.gov/atr/case/us-v-david-topkins.

[12] Opinion of Advocate General Szpunar delivered on 11 May 2017 in Case C 434/15, *Asociación Profesional Elite Taxi v Uber Systems Spain SL*, at n. 23 (noting that "the use by competitors of the same algorithm to calculate the price is not in itself unlawful, but might give rise to hub-and-spoke conspiracy concerns when the power of the platform increases"); *Meyer v. Kalanick*, 174 F. Supp. 3d 817, 822–27 (S.D.N.Y.) (finding that plaintiffs plausibly alleged a hub-and-spoke conspiracy in which drivers sign up for Uber precisely on the understanding that the other drivers were agreeing to the same pricing algorithm, and in which drivers' agreements with Uber would be against their own interests were they acting independently), *reconsideration denied in part*, 185 F. Supp. 3d 448 (S.D.N.Y. 2016).

United States, among others, noted, if competitors were to outsource their pricing decisions to the same third party, this would also raise antitrust concerns.[13]

- The third scenario, *the predictable agent*, is even more challenging. Here there is no agreement among competitors. Each firm unilaterally adopts its pricing algorithm, which sets its own price. So we shift from a world where executives expressly collude in smoke-filled hotel rooms to a world where pricing algorithms act as predictable agents and continually monitor and adjust to each other's prices and market data. The result, we explore, is algorithm-enhanced conscious parallelism—or, as we call it, tacit collusion on steroids.

- In the fourth collusion scenario, *digital eye*, we consider how two technological advancements can amplify tacit collusion, creating a new level of stability and scope. The first advancement involves computers' ability to process high volumes of data in real time to achieve a God-like view of the marketplace. The second advancement concerns the increasing sophistication of algorithms as they engage in autonomous decision making and learning through experience—that is, the use of artificial intelligence. These two technological advances enable a wider, more detailed view of the market, a faster reaction time in response to competitive initiatives, and dynamic strategies achieved by "learning by doing." Thus they can expand tacit collusion beyond price, beyond oligopolistic markets, and beyond easy detection. With the first three scenarios, we may know when something is amiss. In the fourth scenario, the contagion spreads to markets less susceptible to tacit collusion under the brick-and-mortar economy and beyond pricing to other competitive initiatives. In the end, with *digital eye* we may think the markets, driven by these technologies, are competitive. We may believe that tacit collusion in these markets isn't even possible. And yet we're not benefiting from this virtual competition.

- In the fifth *hybrid collusion/discrimination* scenario, algorithmic tacit collusion and behavioral discrimination can occur simultaneously in markets where conditions for both exist in various segments of the market. Sellers, for example, tacitly collude for the "low value" and loyal customers and behaviorally discriminate for the "high value" customers. The seller seeks to lure the "high value" buyers with personalized discounts. Once the hook is lodged (i.e., the customer's loyalty is established and

---

[13] Algorithms and Collusion – Note by the European Commission, submitted for the OECD Competition Committee Hearings on 21–23 June 2017, DAF/COMP/WD(2017)12, at 7 (14 June 2017); Algorithms and Collusion – Note by the United States, submitted for the OECD Competition Committee Hearings on 21–23 June 2017, DAF/COMP/WD(2017)41, at 6 (26 May 2017) ("if competing firms each entered into separate agreements with a single firm (for instance a platform) to use a particular pricing algorithm, and the evidence showed they did so with the common understanding that all of the other competitors would use the identical algorithm, that evidence could be used to prove an agreement among the competitors that violates U.S. antitrust law"). But if the competitors independently and unknowingly adopted the same or similar pricing algorithms, this would "unlikely to lead to antitrust liability even if it makes interdependent pricing more likely." Algorithms and Collusion – Note by the United States, submitted for the OECD Competition Committee Hearings on 21–23 June 2017, DAF/COMP/WD(2017)41, at 6 (26 May 2017). An interesting issue is whether the competitors would be liable if they intentionally but unilaterally adopted the same algorithm knowing that this would make interdependent pricing more likely.

control over outside options is achieved), the seller profits by offering the cheapest individualized inducement to secure the greatest profits.

III.   CONDITIONS FOR ALGORITHMIC TACIT COLLUSION

Having outlined the five scenarios, let us focus on the key driver behind the third and fourth scenarios—which may enable rivals to increase price, through tacit collusion, without infringing the antitrust laws.

The emerging consensus among competition authorities is that algorithms can facilitate and enhance tacit collusion. Tacit collusion is where you have an anticompetitive outcome (namely higher prices) without any illegal agreement among competitors.[14] A classic example, as *Virtual Competition* explores, is where the gasoline stations on Martha's Vineyard raised prices above competitive levels without evidence of their colluding. As the OECD noted:

> Economic theory suggests that there is a considerable risk that algorithms, by improving market transparency and enabling high-frequency trading, increase the likelihood of collusion in market structures that would traditionally be characterised by fierce competition. . .[A]lgorithms might facilitate tacit co-ordination, a market outcome that is not covered by competition law, by providing companies with automated mechanisms to signal, implement common policies, as well as monitor and punish deviations. We also emphasise how algorithms can make tacit collusion more likely not only in oligopolistic markets with high barriers to entry and a high degree of transparency but also in markets where traditionally tacit collusive outcomes would be difficult to achieve and sustain over time, widening the scope of the so-called "oligopoly problem."[15]

As the OECD recognizes, algorithmic tacit collusion will spread, but it will not occur in every industry. Let us outline the conditions generally necessary for tacit collusion and the way algorithms could enhance its stability.

First, algorithmic tacit collusion would likely arise in concentrated and transparent markets involving homogenous products where the algorithms can monitor to a sufficient

---

[14]   Algorithms and Collusion – Background Note by the Secretariat, submitted for the OECD Competition Committee Hearings on 21–23 June 2017, DAF/COMP/WD(2017)4, at 17 (16 May 2017) (noting that tacit collusion "refers to forms of anti-competitive co-ordination which can be achieved without any need for an explicit agreement, but which competitors are able to maintain by recognising their mutual interdependence. In a tacitly collusive context, the non-competitive outcome is achieved by each participant deciding its own profit-maximising strategy independently of its competitors"); *Brooke Group Ltd. v. Brown & Williamson Tobacco Corp.*, 509 U.S. 209 (1993) (describing "the process, not in itself unlawful, by which firms in a concentrated market might in effect share monopoly power, setting their prices at a profit-maximizing, supracompetitive level by recognizing their shared economic interests and their interdependence with respect to price and output decisions and subsequently unilaterally set their prices above the competitive level"); R.S. Khemani and D.M. Shapiro, "Glossary of Industrial Organisation Economics and Competition Law". Paris Organisation for Economic Co-operation and Development, 1993, available at http://www.oecd.org/dataoecd/8/61/2376087.pdf.

[15]   Algorithms and Collusion – Background Note by the Secretariat, submitted for the OECD Competition Committee Hearings on 21–23 June 2017, DAF/COMP/WD(2017)4, at 5 (16 May 2017).

degree the pricing and other keys terms of sale.[16] Conscious parallelism would be facilitated and stabilized by the shift of many industries to online pricing, as sellers can more easily monitor competitors' pricing, key terms of sale and any deviations from current equilibrium.[17] As the OECD observed:

> The increase of market transparency is not only a result of more data being available, but also of the ability of algorithms to make predictions and to reduce strategic uncertainty. Indeed, complex algorithms with powerful data mining capacity are in a better place to distinguish between intentional deviations from collusion and natural reactions to changes in market conditions or even mistakes, which may prevent unnecessary retaliations.[18]

Software may be used to report and take independent action when faced with price deviation, be it from the supra-competitive or recommended retail price.

A *second* important market condition is that once deviation (e.g., discounting) is detected, a credible deterrent mechanism exists.[19] Unique to an algorithmic environment is the speed of retaliation.[20] Computers can rapidly police deviations, and calculate the profit implications of myriad moves and counter-moves to punish deviations.[21] The speed

---

[16]   Algorithms and Collusion – Note by the European Commission, submitted for the OECD Competition Committee Hearings on 21–23 June 2017, DAF/COMP/WD(2017)12, at 8 (14 June 2017); Guidelines on the assessment of horizontal mergers under the Council Regulation on the control of concentrations between undertakings (2004/C 31/ 03), para 41. But as the OECD observed, "one peculiar aspect of algorithms is that it makes the number of competitors in the market a less relevant factor for collusion. In traditional markets, collusion is more easily sustainable if there are few competitors, as it is easier to find terms of co-ordination, to monitor deviations and implement effective punishment mechanisms among fewer firms. Algorithms can allow co-ordination, monitoring and punishment to take place also in less concentrated markets as their ability and speed in collecting and analysing data makes the number of firms to monitor and agree with less relevant. In other words, the small number of firms is an important but not a necessary condition for algorithmic collusion to take place." Algorithms and Collusion – Background Note by the Secretariat, submitted for the OECD Competition Committee Hearings on 21–23 June 2017, DAF/COMP/WD(2017)4, at 19 (16 May 2017).

[17]   Algorithms and Collusion – Note from Singapore, submitted for the OECD Competition Committee Hearings on 21–23 June 2017, DAF/COMP/WD(2017)24, at 2 (31 May 2017).

[18]   Algorithms and Collusion – Background Note by the Secretariat, submitted for the OECD Competition Committee Hearings on 21–23 June 2017, DAF/COMP/WD(2017)4, at 20 (16 May 2017).

[19]   Guidelines on the assessment of horizontal mergers under the Council Regulation on the control of concentrations between undertakings (2004/C 31/ 03), para 41 [EC Merger Guidelines]; Algorithms and Collusion – Note by the European Commission, submitted for the OECD Competition Committee Hearings on 21–23 June 2017, DAF/COMP/WD(2017)12, at 8 (14 June 2017) (noting that "tacit collusion requires effective retaliation, which in turn requires spare capacity" as a "capacity-constrained firm cannot initiate a price war as a means of retaliation to enforce tacit collusion").

[20]   Contrast this with EC Merger Guidelines, *supra* note 19, para 53 ("The speed with which deterrent mechanisms can be implemented is related to the issue of transparency. If firms are only able to observe their competitors' actions after a substantial delay, then retaliation will be similarly delayed and this may influence whether it is sufficient to deter deviation.").

[21]   Jill Priluck, *When Bots Collude* The New Yorker (25 April 2015), available at http://www.newyorker.com/business/currency/when-bots-collude.

of calculated responses effectively deprives discounting rivals of any significant sales. The speed also means that the tacit collusion can be signalled in seconds. The greater the improbability that the first-mover will benefit from its discounting, the greater the likelihood of tacit collusion.[22] Thus if each algorithm can swiftly match a rival's discount and eliminate its incentive to discount in the first place, the "threat of future retaliation keeps the coordination sustainable."[23]

A *third* condition is that "the reactions of outsiders, such as current and future competitors not participating in the coordination, as well as customers, should not be able to jeopardize the results expected from the coordination."[24] Thus algorithmic tacit collusion will likely arise in concentrated markets where buyers cannot exert buyer power (or entice sellers to defect), sales transactions tend to be "frequent, regular, and relatively small,"[25] and the market in general is characterized by high entry barriers.

A *fourth* condition is that tacit collusion is more profitable than competition. The algorithm, in maximizing profits, "would need to decide that it is a better course of action than competitive pricing, especially if competitive pricing leads to drastically larger sales volumes."[26]

A *fifth* condition involves the super-platform's incentives. Firms may operate off a particular platform, such as Amazon's for shopping or Google's or Apple's mobile operating system for apps. As the Italian competition authority discussed:

> either directly or indirectly, online platforms define the "rules of the game", thereby affecting firms' incentives to adopt certain pricing strategies rather than others. Any attempt to an intra-platform collusion may fail in presence of fierce inter-platform online competition: therefore, it will be important to understand the impact of pricing algorithms considering both intra-platform and inter-platform online competition.[27]

---

[22]   Samuel B. Hwang and Sungho Kim, "Dynamic Pricing Algorithm for E-Commerce", in Tarek Sobh and Khaled Elleithy (eds.), *Advances in Systems, Computing Sciences and Software Engineering, Proceedings of SCSS05* (Springer 2006) 149–55; N. Abe and T. Kamba, *A Web Marketing System with Automatic Pricing* 33 Computer Networks 775–88 (2000); L.M. Minga, Y.Q. Fend, and Y.J. Li, *Dynamic Pricing: E-Commerce-Oriented Price Setting Algorithm* 2 International Conference on Machine Learning and Cybernetics (2003).

[23]   EC Merger Guidelines, *supra* note 19, para 52; Algorithms and Collusion – Note from Singapore, submitted for the OECD Competition Committee Hearings on 21–23 June 2017, DAF/COMP/WD(2017)24, at 2 (31 May 2017).

[24]   EC Merger Guidelines, *supra* note 19, para 41.

[25]   US Horizontal Merger Guidelines 2006, available at https://www.justice.gov/atr/file/801216/download.

[26]   Algorithms and Collusion – Note by the European Commission, submitted for the OECD Competition Committee Hearings on 21–23 June 2017, DAF/COMP/WD(2017)12, at 8 (14 June 2017). As the OECD noted, "market stagnation characterised by declining demand and the existence of business cycles may hinder collusion. This is because firms have strong incentives to profitably deviate when demand is high and reducing the costs of retaliation in future periods when demand is low." Algorithms and Collusion – Background Note by the Secretariat, submitted for the OECD Competition Committee Hearings on 21–23 June 2017, DAF/COMP/WD(2017)4, at 20 (16 May 2017).

[27]   Algorithms and Collusion – Note from Italy, submitted for the OECD Competition Committee Hearings on 21–23 June 2017, DAF/COMP/WD(2017)18, at 3 (2 June 2017).

The stability needed for algorithmic tacit collusion is enhanced by the fact that algorithms are unlikely to exhibit many biases when setting prices.[28] Human biases, of course, may be reflected in the programming code. But biases will not necessarily affect decisions on a case-by-case basis: a computer does not fear detection and possible financial penalties or incarceration; nor does it respond in anger.[29] "We're talking about a velocity of decision-making that isn't really human," said Terrell McSweeny, a commissioner with the U.S. Federal Trade Commission. "All of the economic models are based on human incentives and what we think humans rationally will do. It's entirely possible that not all of that learning is necessarily applicable in some of these markets."[30]

When the above conditions are present, tacit collusion is likelier. To be clear, no bright line exists when an industry becomes sufficiently concentrated for either express or tacit collusion.[31] Generally, for illegal cartels involving *express* collusion which were detected and prosecuted, the empirical research has found that cartels involving a trade association were on average over twice as large than cartels without a trade association involved.[32]

---

[28]   EC Merger Guidelines, *supra* note 19, para 44 (observing that "[c]oordination is more likely to emerge if competitors can easily arrive at a common perception as to how the coordination should work. Coordinating firms should have similar views regarding which actions would be considered to be in accordance with the aligned behaviour and which actions would not."); Algorithms and Collusion – Note from Singapore, submitted for the OECD Competition Committee Hearings on 21–23 June 2017, DAF/COMP/WD(2017)24, at 2 (31 May 2017).

[29]   M. Stucke and A. Ezrachi, *How Pricing Bots Could Form Cartels and Make Things More Expensive* Harvard Business Review (27 October 2016), available at https://hbr.org/2016/10/how-pricing-bots-could-form-cartels-and-make-things-more-expensive.

[30]   David Lynch, *Policing the Digital Cartels* Financial Times (9 January 2017), available at http://www.pros.com/about-pros/news/financial-times-policing-digital-cartels/.

[31]   Note, for example, research by Levenstein and Suslow, who offer several explanations for the lack of a clear empirical relationship between industry concentration and cartels involving express collusion: "First, this ambiguity may reflect the bias introduced by focusing on cartels that were prosecuted by the U.S. Department of Justice; cartels with large numbers of firms or that had the active involvement of an industry association may have been more likely to get caught. Second, industries with a very small number of firms may be able to collude tacitly without resort to explicit collusion. Third, concentration is endogenous: collusion may have allowed more firms to survive and remain in the market." Margaret C. Levenstein and Valerie Y. Suslow, *What Determines Cartel Success?* 44(1) Journal of Economic Literature 43–95 (2006).

[32]   One empirical analysis of successfully prosecuted cartels between 1910 and 1972 showed that cartels on average had many participants: where a trade association facilitated collusion, 33.6 firms was the mean of firms involved, and fourteen firms was the median; in price-fixing cartels (without a trade association involved), 8.3 firms was the mean and six was the median. Arthur G. Frass and Douglas F. Greer, *Market Structure and Price Collusion: An Empirical Analysis* 26 J. Indus. Econ. 21, 25, 36–41 (1977). One conservative assumption in that empirical study was that the number of cartel members prosecuted reflected the total number of firms in the relevant market. (*Id.* at 24). But, aside from ineffectual fringe firms, the relevant market may contain more participants than reflected in the government's indictment or criminal information, which does not always identify all the co-conspirators. Consequently, the authors had to exclude from its sample of 606 cases, those cases where the number of firms allegedly involved were not specified in the records (*Id.* at 25–26). Some co-conspirators conceivably could escape prosecution (through lack of evidence). Although the authors rely upon an earlier study, which showed a 0.959 correlation between the number of conspirators and total number of firms in the market, the sample size of that earlier study was 34 cases (*Id.* at 28, citing George Hay and Daniel Kelly, *An Empirical Survey of Price Fixing Conspiracies* 17 J.L. and Econ. 13 (1974).) For studies of cartels immunized from

The belief is that express collusion generally represents the outer boundary. (Otherwise why would competitors expressly collude when they could tacitly collude legally?) One maxim is that tacit collusion is "frequently observed with two sellers, rarely in markets with three sellers, and almost never in markets with four or more sellers."[33] Whether this is empirically true is another matter.[34]

Even if we accept the premise that tacit collusion is likelier in duopolies than triopolies and quadropolies, two factors should give us pause: One factor is that the state of competition in major economies, like the United States, is worrisome, with evidence of increasing concentration and greater profits flowing into fewer hands.[35] Thus, if market concentration increases, more markets may be susceptible to tacit collusion. A second factor is that the industry-wide use of algorithms, given the speed and enhanced transparency, could expand the range of industries susceptible to collusion beyond duopolies to perhaps markets dominated by five or six players, as we illustrate below.

Ultimately, we are likely to see more instances in which similar pricing is not the result of fierce competition, nor the result of cartel activity, but rather the result of algorithmic tacit collusion. While competitors may use different technologies or algorithms, their incentive is to avoid price wars and embed a stabilizing, profit-maximizing strategy in their algorithms.

---

the antitrust laws, see, e.g., Andrew R. Dick, *Identifying Contracts, Combinations & Conspiracies in Restraint of Trade* 17 Managerial and Decision Econ. 203, 213 (1996) (discussing that cartels are formed more frequently in unconcentrated industries under Webb-Pomerene Export Trade Act); see also Paul S. Clyde and James D. Reitzes, *The Effectiveness of Collusion Under Antitrust Immunity: The Case of Liner Shipping Conferences, Bureau of Economics Staff Report* (Dec. 1995) (finding a positive, but economically small, relationship between overall market concentration and shipping rates), available at https://www.ftc.gov/sites/default/files/documents/reports/effectiveness-collusion-under-antitrust-immunity-case-liner-shipping-conferences/232349.pdf; *see also* Maurice E. Stucke, *Behavioral Economists at the Gate: Antitrust in the Twenty-First Century* 38 Loy. U. Chi. L.J. 513, 555–56 (2007) (collecting earlier empirical work on cartels in moderately concentrated and unconcentrated industries); *id.* at 58 (finding no simple relationship between industry concentration and likelihood of collusion); Margaret C. Levenstein and Valerie Y. Suslow, *Breaking Up Is Hard to Do: Determinants of Cartel Duration* 54 J.L. and Econ. 455 at 12 (finding international cartels prosecuted between 1990–2007 had on average 7.4 members).

[33]   J. Potters and S. Suetens, *Oligopoly experiments in the current millennium* 27(3) Journal of Economic Surveys 439–60 (2013).

[34]   Niklas Horstmann, Jan Kraemer, and Daniel Schnurr, *Number Effects and Tacit Collusion in Experimental Oligopolies* (24 October 2016), available at SSRN: https://ssrn.com/abstract=2535862 or http://dx.doi.org/10.2139/ssrn.2535862 (finding from the extant literature "no robust empirical evidence that would support this claim of a strictly monotonic relationship between the number of firms and the degree of tacit collusion in a given market," but finding this monotonic trend from their own two experiments).

[35]   *See, e.g.*, Jonathan B. Baker, 'Market power in the U.S. economy today' (March 2017); Economic Innovation Group, 'Dynamism in Retreat: Consequences for Regions, Markets, and Workers' (February 2017); Gustavo Grullon, Yelena Larkin, and Roni Michaely, 'Are US Industries Becoming More Concentrated?' (Feb 23, 2017), available at SSRN: https://ssrn.com/abstract=2612047 or http://dx.doi.org/10.2139/ssrn.2612047; Germán Gutiérrez and Thomas Philippon, 'Declining Competition and Investment in the U.S.' NBER Working Paper No. 23583 (July 2017), http://www.nber.org/papers/w23583.

IV.   RECENT EXAMPLES

Companies are increasingly using pricing algorithms. As the European Commission found in its 2016 e-commerce sector inquiry:

> About half of the retailers track online prices of competitors. In addition to easily accessible online searches and price comparison tools, both retailers and manufacturers report about the use of specific price monitoring software, often referred to as "spiders", created either by third party software specialists or by the companies themselves. This software crawls the internet and gathers large amounts of price related information. 67% of those retailers that track online prices use (also) automatic software programmes for that purpose. Larger companies have a tendency to track online prices of competing retailers more than smaller ones. . .some software allows companies to monitor several hundred online shops extremely rapidly, if not in real time. . .Alert functionalities in price monitoring software allow companies to get alerted as soon as a retailer's price is not in line with a predefined price.[36]

As the Italian competition authority observed, "a number of specialized software developers offer solutions than allow even small companies to implement 'strategic' dynamic pricing strategies, offering tools to 'auto-detect pricing wars' as well as to 'help drive prices back up across all competition.'"[37]

To illustrate, let us consider the use of online pricing in an oligopolistic retail market for petrol. Two recent economic studies explored how the increased transparency resulting from posting petrol prices online, and the use of pricing algorithms, have fostered conscious parallelism. In Chile, petrol stations were required in 2012 to post their fuel prices on a government website and to keep prices updated as they changed at the pump. An economic study found that this Chilean regulation softened, rather than increased, competition.[38] The petrol stations' margins increased by ten percent on average following the prices being posted on the government website. Similarly, in Germany, the government required petrol stations to report any price changes for gasoline or diesel fuel in "real time."[39] The enhanced market transparency, an economic study found, increased prices further. Compared to the control group, retail petrol prices increased by about 1.2 to 3.3 euro cents, and diesel increased by about two euro cents.[40]

Another "enhancement" may be found in the emergence of "hub-and-spoke" structures

---

[36]   Brussels, 15.9.2016 SWD(2016) 312, Paras 550–51, http://ec.europa.eu/competition/antit rust/sector_inquiry_preliminary_report_en.pdf.

[37]   Algorithms and Collusion – Note from Italy, submitted for the OECD Competition Committee Hearings on 21–23 June 2017, DAF/COMP/WD(2017)18, at 3 (2 June 2017).

[38]   Fernando Luco, *Who Benefits from Information Disclosure? The Case of Retail Gasoline*, Working Paper, Department of Economics, Texas A&M University (28 September 2016), available at http://dx.doi.org/10.2139/ssrn.3186145.

[39]   *Fuel Sector Inquiry*, Final Report by the Bundeskartellamt (May 2011), available at http://www.bundeskartellamt.de/SharedDocs/Publikation/EN/Sector%20Inquiries/Fuel%20Sector%20In quiry%20-%20Final%20Report.pdf?__blob=publicationFile&v=14; Ralf Dewenter, Ulrich Heimeshoff, and Hendrik Lüth, *The Impact of the Market Transparency Unit for Fuels on Gasoline Prices in Germany* (May 2016), available at http://www.dice.hhu.de/fileadmin/redaktion/Fakultaeten/Wirtschaftswissenschaftliche_Fakultaet/DICE/Discussion_Paper/220_Dewenter_Heimeshoff_Luet h.pdf.

[40]   *Id.*

in our online environment. The term "hub and spoke" is often used in antitrust to discuss conspiracies, aimed at competitors' *expressly* fixing the price or facilitating cartel activities. Our focus is different. We note how in an online environment a hub-and-spoke framework may emerge as sellers use the same third-party provider for algorithmic pricing, or the same data pool to determine price.

The use of the same "hub" for determining pricing of products and services may further stabilize the market. It could reduce the number of "decision makers" and further facilitate tacit collusion. One recent example is the petrol market in Rotterdam. As the Wall Street Journal reported, the Dutch petrol stations used advanced analytics and AI provided by the Danish company, a2i Systems, to determine their petrol prices.[41] Retail petrol prices dropped, at times, to reflect less demand. But during some periods

> the stations' price changes paralleled each other, going up or down by more than 2 U.S. cents per gallon within a few hours of each other. Often, prices dropped early in the morning and increased toward the end of the day, implying that the A.I. software may have been identifying common market-demand signals through the local noise.[42]

The software operated by a2i Systems is focused primarily on modeling consumer behavior and learns when raising prices drives away customers and when it does not.[43] In a case study found on its website, a2i Systems discussed how it helped OK Benzin, Denmark's leading petrol station owner, avoid a price war: "Between 2007 and 2012 the market was characterized by fierce competition and high volatility. At the peak there were 10 to 20 price changes a day, and the spread between the highest and the lowest price of the day could be up to 15 eurocent."[44] In enlisting a2i Systems, the leading retail network of approximately 700 petrol stations (which accounted for 25 percent of the Danish retail fuel market), sought "to improve the pricing analysis and decision process and optimize pricing according to their overall strategy in order to lower the cost of price wars or better yet, to avoid them."[45]

---

[41]   Sam Schechner, *Why Do Gas Station Prices Constantly Change? Blame the Algorithm* Wall Street Journal (18 May 2017), available at https://www.wsj.com/articles/why-do-gas-station-prices-constantly-change-blame-the-algorithm-1494262674.

[42]   *Id.*

[43]   Schechner, *supra* note 41. See also the company website: "PriceCast Fuel utilizes Artificial Intelligence (AI) to optimally reach the local and/or global target for any given station and product. By continuously monitoring data (such as transactions, competitors' prices, time, location, traffic, weather, etc.) PriceCast Fuel learns about customers' and competitors' behaviors and optimizes the price for each product at each site, taking every significant correlation into account." Available at http://a2isystems.com/pricecast.html#pricecast-fuel-19.

[44]   PriceCast Fuel Case Story, available at http://a2isystems.com/files/pdf/PriceCast%20Fuel%20Case%20Story%20('15).pdf.

[45]   *Id.*

V. ENFORCEMENT POLICY

The EU and some U.S. policymakers have acknowledged over the past two years algo-rithmic tacit collusion as an antitrust concern. The European Commission, noted that, among other things,

> increased price transparency through price monitoring software may facilitate or strengthen (both tacit and explicit) collusion between retailers by making the detection of deviations from the collusive agreement easier and more immediate. This, in turn, could reduce the incentive of retailers to deviate from the collusive price by limiting the expected gains from such deviation.[46]

The French and German competition authorities similarly noted in a joint report that:

> Even though market transparency as a facilitating factor for collusion has been debated for several decades now, it gains new relevance due to technical developments such as sophisticated computer algorithms. For example, by processing all available information and thus monitoring and analys-ing or anticipating their competitors' responses to current and future prices, competitors may easier be able to find a sustainable supra-competitive price equilibrium which they can agree on.[47]

Likewise, the U.K. House of Lords noted how the rapid developments in data collection and data analytics have created the potential for new welfare reducing and anti-competitive behavior, including new forms of collusion.[48] The Italian competition authority observed how the "widespread usage of algorithms could also pose possible anti-competitive effects by making it easier for firms to achieve and sustain collusion."[49] And the OECD in 2016 commented that these strategies "may pose serious challenges to competition authori-ties in the future, as it may be very difficult, if not impossible, to prove an intention to coordinate prices, at least using current antitrust tools."[50]

In 2017, the Russian competition authority initiated dawn raids of LG Electronics Rus Ltd., Philips Ltd. and Sangfiy SES Electronics Rus Ltd. after receiving complaints on concerted actions of these enterprises in the sales of equipment.[51] The Russian Federation believes that "an increase in the number of algorithms used for setting

---

[46]   Para. 608, Commission Staff Working Document accompanying Commission Final report on the E-commerce Sector Inquiry. (10 May 2017) COM(2017) 229 final. Also note the European Commission investigations into online sales practices launched on 2 February 2017. As part of the investigation into consumer electronics manufacturers the Commission will also consider the effects of pricing software that automatically adapts retail prices to those of leading competitors.

[47]   2016 joint report, *Competition Law and Data*, Page 14, with reference to our earlier work – Artificial intelligence and collusion: when computers inhibit competition. http://www.bun-deskartellamt.de/SharedDocs/Publikation/DE/Berichte/Big%20Data%20Papier.pdf?__blob=publ icationFile&v=.

[48]   Paras. 178 and 179, https://www.publications.parliament.uk/pa/ld201516/ldselect/ldeucom/1 29/12908.htm

[49]   Algorithms and Collusion – Note from Italy, submitted for the OECD Competition Committee Hearings on 21–23 June 2017, DAF/COMP/WD(2017)18, at 2 (2 June 2017).

[50]   Para 81: Big Data: Bringing Competition Policy To The Digital Era, DAF/COMP(2016)14 (27 Oct. 2016), https://one.oecd.org/document/DAF/COMP(2016)14/en/pdf.

[51]   Algorithms and Collusion – Note by the Russian Federation, submitted for the OECD Competition Committee Hearings on 21–23 June 2017, DAF/COMP/WD(2017)22, at 4 (15 May 2017).

prices can help create longer-term cartels that are less obvious to traditional regulators using traditional methods of proving violations, which inter alia can negatively affect consumers."[52]

Why are competition enforcers concerned about algorithmic tacit collusion? The fear is that we have significant harm (namely higher prices), without any liability or direct remedy.[53] Tacit algorithmic collusion, in many countries, would likely escape antitrust scrutiny. To prosecute collusion, enforcers typically require proof of an agreement among competitors to tamper with prices, allocate markets, etc. As the OECD noted, "Although there is great variance in how jurisdictions interpret the notion of agreement, they traditionally require some sort of proof of direct or indirect contact showing that firms have not acted independently from each other (the so-called 'meeting of the minds')."[54] With tacit collusion (conscious parallelism), there is not any agreement. Instead each competitor acts unilaterally, in response to the behavior of competitors. As discussed earlier, that unilateral strategy, in concentrated, transparent markets with homogeneous products, will likely result in higher prices. The concern among competition officials is that tacit collusion—as more industries rely on pricing algorithms—will spread. Importantly, the nature of online markets, the availability of data, the development of similar algorithms, and the stability and transparency they foster, will likely push some markets that were just outside the realm of tacit collusion into interdependence.[55] If algorithmic tacit collusion spreads from duopolies to markets with four, five or six competitors, the competition authority still "might experience increasing difficulties in qualifying the infringement, finding evidence and determining antitrust liability."[56]

---

[52]   Algorithms and Collusion – Note by the Russian Federation, submitted for the OECD Competition Committee Hearings on 21–23 June 2017, DAF/COMP/WD(2017)22, at 2 (15 May 2017).

[53]   Marc Ivaldi, Bruno Jullien, Patrick Rey, Paul Seabright, and Jean Tirole, 'The Economics of Tacit Collusion', Final Report for DG Competition (Toulouse: European Commission, March 2003), available at http://ec.europa.eu/competition/mergers/studies_reports/the_economics_of_tacit_collusion_en.pdf.

[54]   Algorithms and Collusion – Background Note by the Secretariat, submitted for the OECD Competition Committee Hearings on 21–23 June 2017, DAF/COMP/WD(2017)4, at 17 (16 May 2017).

[55]   One would expect tacit collusion to be feasible with a larger number of participants than commonly assumed. On the common market assumptions, see generally R. Selten, *A Simple Model of Imperfect Competition, Where Four Are Few and Six Are Many* 2 International Journal of Game Theory 141 (1973); Steffen Huck, Hans-Theo Normann, and Jörg Oechssler, *Two Are Few and Four Are Many: Number Effects in Experimental Oligopolies* 53(4) Journal of Economic Behavior and Organization 435–46 (2004).

[56]   See, e.g., Algorithms and Collusion – Note from Italy, submitted for the OECD Competition Committee Hearings on 21–23 June 2017, DAF/COMP/WD(2017)18, at 4 (2 June 2017).

VI.   LEGALITY OF ALGORITHMIC TACIT COLLUSION

Under most jurisdictions' antitrust laws, the unilateral use of algorithms to monitor and set price is legal, even if it leads to prices above competitive levels.[57] After all, one cannot condemn a firm for behaving rationally and interdependently on the market.[58]

When the algorithms increase market transparency, defendants will often have an independent legitimate business rationale for their conduct. Courts and the enforcement agencies may be reluctant to restrict this free flow of information in the marketplace. Although the exchange of current or future pricing, sales, and output information among themselves can subject competitors to antitrust liability,[59] the general belief is that increasing the transparency of the market (by posting the actual price and key terms of sale) makes the market more efficient. "The dissemination of information," the U.S. Supreme Court observed, "is normally an aid to commerce"[60] and "can in certain circumstances increase economic efficiency and render markets more, rather than less, competitive."[61] Indeed, concerted action to reduce price transparency may itself be an antitrust violation.[62]

Accordingly, "pure" forms of tacit collusion which result from a unilateral rational reaction to market characteristics would not normally trigger antitrust liability. On the other hand, intervention may be triggered when an illicit concerted practice "contaminated" or "facilitated" the conscious parallelism. In some instances, enforcers can question whether the rivals acted unilaterally. At times, either a horizontal or vertical agreement may be inferred. Condemned actions may include signaling, exchange of information, agreement to engage in common strategy, manipulation through the sharing of data pools and other collusive strategies.

---

[57]   Rational unilateral reaction to market dynamics (free from agreements or communications) in itself, is legal under EU and US competition law. As noted earlier, tacit collusion does not amount to concerted practice and therefore escapes Article 101 TFEU. Tacit collusion may serve to establish Collective Dominance under Article 102 TFEU, but absent a separate abuse, it will also escape scrutiny under this provision.

[58]   See, for example, Case C-199/92, *P Hüls AG v. Commission*, [1999] ECR I-4287, [1999] 5 CMLR 1016; Joined Cases C-89, 104, 114, 116, 117, 125, 129/85, *Ahlström Osakeyhtiö and others v. Commission (Wood Pulp II)*, [1993] ECR I-1307, [1993] 4 CMLR 407; Cases T-442/08, *CISAC v Commission*, [2013] 5 CMLR 15 (General Court).

[59]   *Am. Column & Lumber Co. v. United States*, 257 U.S. 377, 397 (1921).

[60]   *Sugar Institute, Inc. v. United States*, 297 U.S. 553, 598 (1936).

[61]   *United States v. United States Gypsum Co.*, 438 U.S. 422, 441 n.16 (1978); see also Richard A. Posner, *Antitrust Law* 2nd ed. (University of Chicago Press 2001) 160.

[62]   See, for example, Federal Trade Commission, Funeral Directors Board Settles with FTC (16 August 2004), http://www.ftc.gov/opa/2004/08/vafuneral.htm (a board's prohibition on licensed funeral directors advertising discounts deprived consumers of truthful information); Federal Trade Commission, Arizona Automobile Dealers Association, FTC C-3497 (February 25, 1994) (a trade association illegally agreed with members to restrict nondeceptive comparative and discount advertising and advertisements concerning the terms and availability of consumer credit); Organisation for Economic Co-operation and Development, Price Transparency, DAFFE/CLP(2001)22 (September 11, 2001), 183, 185–86 (citing examples of U.S. enforcement agencies seeking to increase price transparency); compare *InterVest, Inc. v. Bloomberg, L.P.*, 340 F.3d 144 (3d Cir. 2003) (lack of price transparency in bond market not illegal if consistent with unilateral conduct).

The European Commission noted this distinction:

> one could argue that through repeated interactions, two firms' pricing algorithms could come to "decode" each other, thus allowing each one to better anticipate the other's reactions. However, the case-law is clear that Article 101 "does not deprive economic operators of the right to adapt themselves intelligently to the existing and anticipated conduct of their competitors". . .Short of signalling. . .it is therefore not obvious that more sophisticated tools through which a firm merely observes another firm's price and draws its own conclusion would qualify as "communication" for Article 101 purposes. At the same time, at this stage, one cannot fully rule out the possibility that more creative and novel types of interactions could in certain situations meet the definition of "communication".[63]

In February 2017, the Commission announced an investigation into the possible breach of EU competition law by Asus, Denon & Marantz, Philips and Pioneer. Among other things, the Commission was appraising whether the companies restricted the "ability of online retailers to set their own prices for widely used consumer electronics products such as household appliances, notebooks and hi-fi products." According to the Commission:

> The effect of these suspected price restrictions may be aggravated due to the use by many online retailers of pricing software that automatically adapts retail prices to those of leading competitors. As a result, the alleged behaviour may have had a broader impact on overall online prices for the respective consumer electronics products.[64]

The Commission in 2018 fined the companies, after finding the four manufacturers used sophisticated monitoring tools to intervene when online retailers offered their products at low prices, below the level requested by the manufacturers. The use of sophisticated monitoring tools allowed the manufacturers to effectively track resale price setting in the distribution network and to intervene swiftly in case of price decreases.

Antitrust intervention is easier when algorithms are part of a wider collusive agreement to tamper with market prices.[65] Similarly, weaker forms of signaling, aimed at coordinating practice of the market could be condemned.

But, the question remains: should "pure" forms of tacit collusion be condemned? Ought we condemn the facilitation of tacit collusion through artificial means? Should one condemn a firm for behaving rationally and developing, unilaterally, an algorithm that takes into account publicly available information while operating interdependently on the market?[66]

One way to square this circle may be framing the issue as market manipulation or an unfair practice. The focus shifts from the presence of an agreement among companies

---

[63]   Algorithms and Collusion – Note by the European Commission, submitted for the OECD Competition Committee Hearings on 21–23 June 2017, DAF/COMP/WD(2017)12, at 8 (14 June 2017) (citation omitted).

[64]   http://europa.eu/rapid/press-release_IP-17-201_en.htm.

[65]   See for example: Topkins, https://www.justice.gov/opa/pr/former-e-commerce-executive-charged-price-fixing-antitrust-divisions-first-online-marketplace.

[66]   See, for example, Case C-199/92, *P Hüls AG v. Commission*, [1999] ECR I-4287, [1999] 5 CMLR 1016; Joined Cases C-89, 104, 114, 116, 117, 125, 129/85, *Ahlström Osakeyhtiö and others v. Commission (Wood Pulp II)*, [1993] ECR I-1307, [1993] 4 CMLR 407; Cases T-442/08, *CISAC v Commission*, [2013] 5 CMLR 15 (General Court).

to the use of advanced algorithms to transform pre-existing market conditions in such a way to facilitate tacit collusion. While the mutual price monitoring at the heart of tacit collusion is legal, one may ask whether the creation of such a market dynamic, through "artificial" means, gives rise to antitrust liability.

Using such an approach, one could consider application of legislation such as Section 5 of the FTC Act, which targets unfair facilitating practices.[67] Noteworthy is how the U.S. courts set a rather high level of intervention. Under the legal standard applied in *Ethyl*,[68] the Federal Trade Commission must show either (1) evidence that defendants tacitly or expressly agreed to use pricing algorithms to avoid competition, or (2) oppressiveness, such as (a) evidence of defendants' anticompetitive intent or purpose or (b) the absence of an independent legitimate business reason for the defendants' conduct.[69] Accordingly, defendants may be liable if, when developing the algorithms or in seeing the effects, they were (1) motivated to achieve an anticompetitive outcome, or (2) aware of their actions' natural and probable anticompetitive consequences.

An alternative route may target "abuse" of excessive transparency, possibly where clear anticompetitive intent is present. One could employ the rationale used in the U.S. Securities and Exchange Commission's (SEC) case against Athena Capital Research.[70] In 2014, the SEC for the first time sanctioned the high-frequency trading firm for using complex computer programs to manipulate stock prices.[71] The sophisticated algorithm, code-named *Gravy*, engaged in a practice known as "marking the close" in which stocks were bought or sold near the close of trading to affect the closing price: "[t]he massive volumes of Athena's last-second trades allowed Athena to overwhelm the market's available liquidity and artificially push the market price—and therefore the closing price—in Athena's favor."[72] Athena's employees, the SEC alleged, were "acutely aware of the price impact of its algorithmic trading, calling it 'owning the game' in internal e-mails."[73]

---

[67]   The FTC was unsuccessful in its attempt to prove such facilitating practices in *Boise Cascade Corp. v. F.T.C.*, 637 F.2d 573 (9th Cir. 1980) and *E. I. du Pont de Nemours & Co. v. F.T.C.*, 729 F.2d 128 (2d Cir. 1984).

[68]   *E. I. du Pont de Nemours & Co. v. F.T.C.*, 729 F.2d 128 (2d Cir. 1984).

[69]   *Id.* at 128, 139.

[70]   U.S. Securities and Exchange Commission, Administrative Proceeding File No. 3-16199 (October 16, 2014), http://www.sec.gov/litigation/admin/2014/34-73369.pdf.

[71]   The computer trading program was "placing a large number of aggressive, rapid-fire trades in the final two seconds of almost every trading day during a six-month period to manipulate the closing prices of thousands of NASDAQ-listed stocks." U.S. Securities and Exchange Commission, SEC Charges New York–Based High Frequency Trading Firm with Fraudulent Trading to Manipulate Closing Prices, October 16, 2014, http://www.sec.gov/News/PressRelease/Detail/PressRelease/1370543184457#.VEOZlfldV8E. *Id.*

[72]   *Id.*

[73]   *Id.* As the SEC alleged Athena's manipulative scheme focused on trading in order to create imbalances in securities at the close of the trading day: "Imbalances occur when there are more orders to buy shares than to sell shares (or vice versa) at the close for any given stock. Every day at the close of trading, NASDAQ runs a closing auction to fill all on-close orders at the best price, one that is not too distant from the price of the stock just before the close. Athena placed orders to fill imbalances in securities at the close of trading, and then traded or 'accumulated' shares on the continuous market on the opposite side of its order." According to the SEC's order, Athena's algorithmic strategies became increasingly focused on ensuring that the firm was the dominant firm—and sometimes the only one—trading desirable stock imbalances at the end of each trading

Athena employees "knew and expected that *Gravy* impacted the price of shares it traded, and at times Athena monitored the extent to which it did. For example, in August 2008, Athena employees compiled a spreadsheet containing information on the price movements caused by an early version of *Gravy*."[74] Athena configured its algorithm *Gravy* "so that it would have a price impact."[75] In calling its market-manipulation algorithm *Gravy*, and by exchanging a string of incriminating e-mails, the company did not help its case. Without admitting guilt, Athena paid a $1 million penalty. This demonstrates that automated trading has the potential to increase market transparency and efficiency, but it can also lead to market manipulation.[76] Finding the predominant purpose for using an algorithm will not always be straightforward. Athena, for example, challenged the SEC's allegations that it engaged in fraudulent activity: "While Athena does not deny the Commission's charges, Athena believes that its trading activity helped satisfy market demand for liquidity during a period of unprecedented demand for such liquidity."[77] A court might agree. Companies, learning from Athena, can be more circumspect in their e-mails.[78]

A third route may involve the use of market or sector investigations. This approach may help the agencies better understand the new dynamics in algorithm-driven markets and the magnitude of any competitive problems. In some jurisdictions, like the United Kingdom, market investigation laws also provide for a wide scope of behavioral and structural remedies.[79] Following an investigation the agency may benefit from a flexible

---

day. The firm implemented additional algorithms known as "Collars" to ensure that Athena's orders received priority over other orders when trading imbalances. These eventually resulted in Athena's imbalance-on-close orders being at least partially filled more than 98 percent of the time. Athena's ability to predict that its orders would get filled on almost every imbalance order allowed the firm to unleash its manipulative Gravy algorithm to trade tens of thousands of shares right before the close of trading. As a result, these shares traded at artificial prices that NASDAQ then used to set the closing prices for on-close orders as part of its closing auction. Athena's high-frequency trading scheme enabled its orders to be executed at more favorable prices.

[74]   U.S. Securities and Exchange Commission, Administrative Proceeding File No. 3-16199, para. 34.

[75]   *Id.*, para. 36

[76]   Peter J. Henning, *Why High-Frequency Trading Is So Hard to Regulate* New York Times (20 October 2014), http://dealbook.nytimes.com/2014/10/20/why-high-frequency-trading-is-so-hard-to-regulate/.

[77]   Steve Goldstein, *High-Frequency Trading Firm Fined for Wave of Last-Minute Trades* Market Watch (16 October 2014), http://www.marketwatch.com/story/high-frequency-trading-firm-fined-for-wave-of-last-minute-trades-2014-10-16.

[78]   Moreover, evidence of intent will likely be mixed when each firm has valid independent business reasons to develop and implement a pricing algorithm. After all, the first firm to use the pricing algorithm could not be accused of colluding, as the market was likelier less transparent, and rivals could not match the speed of the first mover's price changes.

[79]   The U.K. Competition and Markets Authority, for example, can initiate market investigations, gather and appraise evidence, and, where necessary, impose structural or behavioral remedies. Competition Commission, *Guidelines for Market Investigations: Their Role, Procedures, Assessment and Remedies,* CC3 (Revised) (April 2013), https://www.gov.uk/government/uploads/system/uploads/attachmen_data/file/284390/cc3_revised.pdf (adopted by the CMA Board); Algorithms and Collusion – Note from the United Kingdom, submitted for the OECD Competition Committee Hearings on 21–23 June 2017, DAF/COMP/WD(2017)19, at 11 (30 May 2017).

tool box that is unavailable through other means. The Italian competition authority, for example, noted how it has launched—with the Italian Data Protection Authority and the Italian Communications Authority—a market study on big data, including the various possible competitive implications linked to the rise of algorithms.[80]

Finally, merger review, which in recent decades in the U.S. has focused on unilateral effects,[81] can focus on challenging mergers in industries where tacit collusion is a significant risk.[82] This may require, as the OECD and we recommend, the agencies to consider lowering their threshold of intervention and investigate the risk of coordinated effects not only in cases of three to two mergers, but potentially also in four to three or even in five to four, and to reconsider the approach to conglomerate mergers when tacit collusion can be facilitated by multimarket contacts.[83]

VII. NEW DIMENSION: ARTIFICIAL INTELLIGENCE AND COLLUSION

Algorithmic tacit collusion becomes even more complex when one considers the possible use of neural networks to detect and react to price changes. The significance of Artificial Intelligence to our discussion is notable when considering the *capacity* to engage in tacit collusion, the ability to *detect* it and the ability to *establish liability* for the action.

A. Capacity

Let us begin with consideration of AI's capacity to foster tacit collusion. Of relevance are recent developments in Artificial Neural Networks, also known as "Deep Learning" which aim to mimic the brain's cognitive and computation mechanisms. These complex networks consist of a large number of computation units (neurons), interconnected across several layers.[84] They have already contributed to significant advances in solving

---

[80] Algorithms and Collusion – Note from Italy, submitted for the OECD Competition Committee Hearings on 21–23 June 2017, DAF/COMP/WD(2017)18, at 10 (2 June 2017).

[81] *See, e.g.*, Malcolm B. Coate, *The Merger Process in the Federal Trade Commission from 1989 to 2016* Working Paper (28 Feb. 2018), available at: http://dx.doi.org/10.2139/ssrn.2955987 (identifying for FTC mergers a trend toward unilateral effects analysis and increase in efficiency findings after 1994, although dropping for challenged mergers after 2004).

[82] Algorithms and Collusion – Note by the European Commission, submitted for the OECD Competition Committee Hearings on 21–23 June 2017, DAF/COMP/WD(2017)12, at 9 (14 June 2017); Algorithms and Collusion – Note by the United States, submitted for the OECD Competition Committee Hearings on 21–23 June 2017, DAF/COMP/WD(2017)41, at 6 (26 May 2017); Algorithms and Collusion – Note from the United Kingdom, submitted for the OECD Competition Committee Hearings on 21–23 June 2017, DAF/COMP/WD(2017)19, at 11 (30 May 2017).

[83] Algorithms and Collusion – Background Note by the Secretariat, submitted for the OECD Competition Committee Hearings on 21–23 June 2017, DAF/COMP/WD(2017)4, at 40 (16 May 2017).

[84] A. Ittoo, L.M. Nguyen and A. van den Bosch, *Text analytics in industry: Challenges, desiderata and trends* 78 Computers in Industry (2016), available at http://www.sciencedirect.com/science/article/pii/S0166361515300646 or http://dx.doi.org/10.1016/j.compind.2015.12.001.

some of the harder, longstanding challenges for the AI community thus far. By 2017 they have matched or surpassed human performance in various tasks, such as identifying malignant tumors in breast cancer images, image labeling, speech recognition and language translation.[85] Their rapid self-improvement has already resulted in instances in which they evolved beyond recognized human-like decision-making.

An AI program, that its developers at Carnegie-Mellon University called "Libratus," recently defeated several top poker players. This achievement becomes even more impressive when considering the following. First none of Libratus's algorithms were specific to poker. As one of the developers told the press, "We did not program it to play poker. We programmed it to learn any imperfect-information game, and fed it the rules of No-Limit Texas Hold'em as a way to evaluate its performance."[86] The AI program learned the optimal strategy. Second, Libratus' playing style was unlike a human's. The human players could not always identify the computer's dominant strategy. What seemed like bad moves by the computer actually turned out to be good moves.[87] And the computer's strategies seemingly varied hand-by-hand. Third, the computer's strategies evolved day-by-day. When the humans found weaknesses in the computer's play, the players could not quickly exploit these weaknesses. The computer already prioritized identifying and correcting these holes.[88] After 20 days of playing poker, Libratus won decisively.

Another example involves Google's AlphaGo algorithm, which defeated the world's best Go player in a 2017 game. Humans have played Go, which is noted for its myriad possible moves, for centuries. Noteworthy wasn't that the best player was defeated. Rather Go players have praised the algorithm's ability "to make unorthodox moves and challenge assumptions core to a game."[89] The world's best player, after being defeated, noted that "Last year, it was still quite humanlike when it played, but this year, it became like a god of Go."[90]

Deep Learning is often used in conjunction with another paradigm, known as Reinforcement Learning, which prescribes how agents should act in an environment in order to maximize future cumulative reward. The combination of Deep Learning and Reinforcement Learning is promising. It heralds the emergence of algorithms "ingrained" with advanced human cognitive abilities, such as playing Atari videogames and more

---

[85]   Yun Liu et al., *Detecting Cancer Metastases on Gigapixel Pathology Images*, https://drive.google.com/file/d/0B1T58bZ5vYa-QlR0QlJTa2dPWVk/view (in identifying for breast cancer patients whether the cancer has metastasized away from the breast, a trained algorithm could review large expanses of biological tissues, and automatically detect and localize tumors as small as 100 $\times$100 pixels in gigapixel microscopy images sized 100, 000$\times$100, 000 pixels, with a rate of eight false positives per image, and detecting 92.4 percent of the tumors, relative to 82.7 percent by the previous best automated approach, and a 73.2 percent sensitivity for human pathologists); Y. Le Cun, Y. Bengio and G. Hinton, *Deep Learning – Review* 521 Nature (2015), available at http://www.nature.com/nature/journal/v521/n7553/pdf/nature14539.pdf or http://dx.doi.org/10.1038/nature14539.

[86]   http://www.csmonitor.com/Technology/2017/0204/Bot-makes-poker-pros-fold-What-s-next-for-artificial-intelligence .

[87]   https://www.youtube.com/watch?v=jLXPGwJNLHk.

[88]   *Id.*

[89]   Paul Mozur, *Google's AlphaGo Defeats Chinese Go Master in Win for A.I.* New York Times (23 May 2017).

[90]   *Id.*

importantly, beating the human champion at the Go game, considered as one of the AI holy grails.[91]

For tacit collusion, the enhanced analytical capacity and the ability to adapt to changing market reality may enable a more stable and refined equilibrium to be established. Further, one may note how the use of neural networks may impact on the ability to establish liability for the action of the algorithm.

B.   Liability

In a simple scenario using today's technology, one could envisage the human operator embedding the tacit collusion model into the algorithm. Although there is no anticompetitive "agreement" among rivals, the human involvement, if one opts to condemn that action, may be relatively easy to detect. But, as noted above, the future heralds more advanced technologies that will be able to act independently, with little or no human input. The algorithm is not programmed to tacitly collude. Programmed with basic game theory, the algorithm, like the one that defeated the world's best poker players, will identify the dominant strategy on its own to maximize profits.

A recent experiment—conducted in Google's advanced Deep Mind neural network—set to identify the dominant strategy that Deep Mind will deploy.[92] Interestingly, in an environment with limited resources Deep Mind deployed aggressive strategies, in an effort to win. However, when collaboration was deemed more profitable (Wolfpace game) two neural agents learned from experimenting in the environment and collaborated to improve their joint position. It will be interesting, as the literature and technology evolve, to see whether the Wolfpace scenario foreshadows the algorithmic tacit collusion scenarios where computers on their own migrate to conscious parallelism as their dominant strategy.

If so, can companies be blamed if their smart algorithms subsequently and independently identify the benefits of interdependence under the tacit collusion scenarios? Suppose, unlike the developers of *Gravy*, the company did not program its algorithm to manipulate the market. Nonetheless as the market dynamics evolve, the algorithm learns that the dominant rational strategy is tacit collusion. To what extent can the company be liable for its self-learning algorithm's actions? And what checks and balances could one impose to prevent machines from changing market dynamics?

The Russian Federation acknowledged these difficulties: "while using the available tools of antitrust regulation and methods of proof, competition agencies face a number of difficulties, including in determining the responsibility of computer engineers for programming machines that are 'educated' to coordinate prices on their own."[93] The

---

[91]   https://research.googleblog.com/2015/02/from-pixels-to-actions-human-level.html.

[92]   Joel Z. Leibo and others, *Multi-agent Reinforcement Learning in Sequential Social Dilemmas*, https://storage.googleapis.com/deepmind-media/papers/multi-agent-rl-in-ssd.pdf; Also see short interview with Joel Z. Leibo, the lead author on the paper on: http://www.wired.co.uk/article/artificial-intelligence-social-impact-deepmind.

[93]   Algorithms and Collusion – Note by the Russian Federation, submitted for the OECD Competition Committee Hearings on 21–23 June 2017, DAF/COMP/WD(2017)22, at 4 (15 May 2017); see also Algorithms and Collusion – Note from Italy, submitted for the OECD Competition Committee Hearings on 21–23 June 2017, DAF/COMP/WD(2017)18, at 10 (2 June 2017) ("More

European Commission, likewise, noted how more autonomous decision-making may "conflict with the current regulatory framework which was designed in the context of a more predictable, more manageable and controllable technology."[94] The Commission recommended clarifying and, if necessary, adapting the legislative framework.[95] Among the legal approaches under consideration are a strict liability regime; a liability regime based on a risk-generating approach (whereby "liability would be assigned to the actors generating a major risk for others and benefitting from the relevant device, product or service"), and a risk-management approach (whereby "liability is assigned to the market actor which is best placed to minimize or avoid the realisation of the risk or to amortize the costs in relation to those risks").[96] Ultimately, for the Commission, "humans – and, through them, legal entities – must be held accountable for the consequences of the algorithms they choose to use, including in the area of competition policy."[97]

One significant obstacle with a risk-based approach for algorithmic tacit collusion is our ability to understand the magnitude and likelihood of risk and the actuality of harm. When a self-driving car hits a human, the harm is clear. But antitrust enforcers (even with an attractive leniency policy) have had a hard time detecting *express* collusion. Detecting tacit collusion is often more difficult (especially when interdependence can appear in competitive markets). Like the human players against Libratus or AlphaGo, divining a pricing algorithm's strategy may prove even more difficult.

As EU Commissioner Vestager noted, "[t]he trouble is, it's not easy to know exactly how those algorithms work. How they've decided what to show us, and what to hide. And yet the decisions they make affect us all."[98] Likewise, the U.K. competition authority recognized the "complexity of algorithms and the consequent challenge of understanding their exact operation and effects can . . . make it more difficult for consumers and enforcement agencies to detect algorithmic abuses and gather relevant evidence."[99] Significant

---

complex challenges for the Authority and the Courts could arise in scenarios where algorithms are self-learning and therefore capable of recognizing mutual interdependency and readapting behaviour to the actions of other market players, without inputs from humans. In particular, the most difficult question is under which conditions antitrust liability can be established in situations where the links between the algorithms and the human beings become more blurred: in such cases determining the liability will depend mainly on the facts at hand.").

[94]   European Commission, Commission Staff Working Document on the free flow of data and emerging issues of the European data economy Brussels, 10.1.2017 SWD(2017) 2 final, at 43.

[95]   *Id.*

[96]   *Id.*, at 45. As a complement to the above, the Commission also is entertaining voluntary or mandatory insurance schemes for compensating the parties who suffered the damage.

[97]   Algorithms and Collusion – Note by the European Commission, submitted for the OECD Competition Committee Hearings on 21–23 June 2017, DAF/COMP/WD(2017)12, at 2, 9 (14 June 2017) (noting that "firms involved in illegal pricing practices cannot avoid liability on the grounds that their prices were determined by algorithms. Like an employee or an outside consultant working under a firm's 'direction or control', an algorithm remains under the firm's control, and therefore the firm is liable for its actions.").

[98]   Algorithms and Competition, Bundeskartellamt 18th Conference on Competition, Berlin, 16 March 2017. https://ec.europa.eu/commission/commissioners/2014-2019/vestager/announcements/bundeskartellamt-18th-conference-competition-berlin-16-march-2017_en.

[99]   Algorithms and Collusion – Note from the United Kingdom, submitted for the OECD Competition Committee Hearings on 21–23 June 2017, DAF/COMP/WD(2017)19, at 12 (30 May 2017).

is the ability of Deep Learning to adjust to a changing environment and engage in cognitively intensive tasks. As such they form a superior tool to determine market strategy in a changing environment.[100] Indeed, some studies have already highlighted the potential of simpler, basic ANN for dynamic pricing.[101] Another noteworthy characteristic is their ability to learn from experience.[102] This alleviates the need for prior "hand-crafted" knowledge fed in by humans in order to learn a perceptual representation of the world. The self-learning nature enables them to untangle underlying factors in data and to adjust their learning process so that they progressively improve their performance until achieving the desired outcome.[103] For instance, AlphaGo, Google's Deep Learning-based Go champion, and Libratus learned to discover new strategies.

Vestager commented on this challenge. While competition enforcers need not be suspicious of everyone who uses an automated system for pricing, they nonetheless "need to be alert."[104] On a positive note, Vestager's comments make clear that autonomous machines can play a greater role in our markets and lives and some accountability (or compensatory) measure must exist to promote an inclusive economy. The challenge is in adapting the legislative framework so that citizens can trust and benefit from this technology while enabling the industry to "lead and capture the opportunities arising in this field."[105]

C.   Detection

In an environment in which online prices are determined by algorithms and their mechanism is complex, enforcers will unlikely trace the steps taken by algorithms and unravel the self-learning processes. If deciphering the decision-making of a deep learning network proves difficult, then identifying an anticompetitive purpose may be impossible.

Even if one resolves the challenges of liability, another problem may emerge—to identify that the market price is indeed the result of tacit collusion and not the competitive price. An interesting consequence of algorithm-driven tacit collusion is the difficulty in identifying the counterfactuals—in other words, the competitive position absent the industry-wide use of pricing algorithms.

---

[100]   http://www.cs.stir.ac.uk/~lss/NNIntro/InvSlides.html.

[101]   T. Ghose and T. Tran, "A dynamic pricing approach in e-commerce based on multiple purchase attributes", in *Proceedings of the 23rd Canadian Conference on Advances in Artificial Intelligence, Lecture Notes in Computer Science,* vol. 6085 (2010), available at https://link.springer.com/chapter/10.1007/978-3-642-13059-5_13.

[102]   http://www.cs.stir.ac.uk/~lss/NNIntro/InvSlides.html.

[103]   D. Castelvecchi, *Can we open the black box of AI?* 538 Nature (2016), available at http://www.nature.com/news/can-we-open-the-black-box-of-ai-1.20731 or http://dx.doi.org/10.1038/538020a.

[104]   Margrethe Vestager, Speech: *Algorithms and Competition*, at the Bundeskartellamt 18th Conference on Competition, Berlin, 16 March 2017, available at: https://ec.europa.eu/commission/commissioners/2014-2019/vestager/announcements/bundeskartellamt-18th-conference-competition-berlin-16-march-2017_en. She added that businesses "need to know that when they decide to use an automated system, they will be held responsible for what it does. So they had better know how that system works." *Id.*

[105]   European Commission, Commission Staff Working Document on the free flow of data and emerging issues of the European data economy Brussels, 10.1.2017 SWD(2017) 2 final, at 43.

In practice, it may be difficult for an enforcer or regulator to conclude to what extent the current prices reflect the "natural" outcome of market forces or the byproduct of tacit collusion, which the algorithms "artificially" enhanced or fostered. In a market dominated by algorithms, absent a natural experiment or counterfactual (such as a similar market without algorithms), enforcers may not readily discern whether the market price is the result of artificial intervention or natural dynamics: the dynamic price may be the only market price.

One answer may involve auditing the algorithm. Under an auditing regime, the agency will assess whether an algorithm was designed to foster a change in the market dynamics. This approach resembles pre-merger review—where the agency predicts whether the proposed merger may substantially lessen competition or tend to create a monopoly. Accordingly, algorithms could be activated in a "sand box" where their effects will be observed and assessed.

Auditing at times can predict anticompetitive outcomes. But based on our discussions with computer scientists, auditing is not as simple as opening the hood of the car to see what is causing the irregularity. To begin with, it may be hard to establish whether the algorithm submitted for audit is the one used in the marketplace. This is not simply a bait-and-switch by the firms. Rather through machine-learning, trial-and-error, and market changes, the algorithm itself evolves. Similarly, the ease with which an audited algorithm may be amended and set different optimization goals could undermine effective scrutiny. Other challenges include the sheer number of algorithms which would require scrutiny, the high level of expertise required to assess their effects, the ability to identify credible counterfactuals, and the barriers associated with commercial secrecy. Lastly, in the case of neural networks, it may be impossible to effectively audit a complex system and determine its likely effects.

Some challenges may be addressed by shifting the burden to the companies and imposing on them a duty to comply with a set of guidelines and principles of compliance by design. One could imagine the creation of an industry code of practice, which companies must follow when designing the algorithms. Random inspections perhaps could increase deterrence and compliance.

VIII.   CONCLUSION

With the industry-wide use of computer algorithms and artificial intelligence, we may witness algorithmic tacit collusion in markets where collusion previously would have been unstable. The OECD in 2017 reached the following two conclusions:

> Firstly, algorithms are fundamentally affecting market conditions, resulting in high price transparency and high-frequency trading that allows companies to react fast and aggressively. These changes in digital markets, if taken to a certain extent, could make collusive strategies stable in virtually any market structure. Secondly, by providing companies with powerful automated mechanisms to monitor prices, implement common policies, send market signals or optimise joint profits with deep learning techniques, algorithms might enable firms to achieve the same outcomes of traditional hard core cartels through tacit collusion.[106]

---

[106]   Algorithms and Collusion – Background Note by the Secretariat, submitted for the OECD Competition Committee Hearings on 21–23 June 2017, DAF/COMP/WD(2017)4, at 49–50 (16 May 2017).

Our collusion scenarios are part of several anticompetitive outcomes, which necessitate re-calibrating our enforcement strategies. As our book *Virtual Competition* explores, big data and big analytics can enable some online sellers to engage in behavioral discrimination. We will also see the rise of a new frenemy dynamic whereby many companies become increasingly dependent upon the beneficence of the dominant super-platforms, namely Google, Apple, Facebook and Amazon.

But virtual competition is not necessarily bleak. As *Virtual Competition* discusses, the transformative innovations from machine-learning and big data can lower our search costs (whether finding a raincoat or parking spot), lower entry barriers, create new channels for expansion and entry, and ultimately stimulate competition. But these technological improvements are not automatic. Much depends on how the companies employ the technologies and whether their incentives are aligned with our and societal interests.

Nor will data-driven online markets necessarily correct themselves. Nor will the anticompetitive effects be obvious. Dominant firms can be a step ahead in developing sophisticated strategies and technologies that distort the perceived competitive environment. Antitrust, while not obsolete, may prove unwieldly at times to apply even with a compelling theory of harm. Indeed, without evidence of anticompetitive agreement or intent, an engaged competition agency will still be hamstrung. So our current antitrust laws may not deter some of the collusion scenarios we identify.

Accordingly, businesses (and competition authorities) must better understand how the rise of sophisticated computer algorithms and the new market reality can significantly change our paradigm of competition—either for the better or worse. Legal safeguards should be explored to promote competition on the merits. Otherwise, we will likely experience more durable forms of collusion (beyond the enforcers' reach), more sophisticated forms of price discrimination, and an array of abuses by data-driven monopolies that, by controlling key platforms (like the leading operating system for smartphones), can dictate many companies' (and our economy's) oxygen supply.

SOURCES

Statutes

Articles 101 and 102 of the Treaty on the Functioning of the European Union.
Section 5 of the FTC Act.

EU Cases

Case C 434/15, *Asociación Profesional Elite Taxi v. Uber Systems Spain SL*.
Case C-199/92, *P Hüls AG v. Commission*, [1999] ECR I-4287, [1999] 5 CMLR 1016.
Joined Cases C-89, 104, 114, 116, 117, 125, 129/85, *Ahlström Osakeyhtiö and others v. Commission* (*Wood Pulp II*), [1993] ECR I-1307, [1993] 4 CMLR 407.
Cases T-442/08, *CISAC v. Commission*, [2013] 5 CMLR 15 (General Court).

US Cases

Am. Column & Lumber Co. v. United States, 257 U.S. 377 (1921).
Boise Cascade Corp. v. F.T.C., 637 F.2d 573 (9th Cir. 1980).

Brooke Group Ltd. v. Brown & Williamson Tobacco Corp., 509 U.S. 209 (1993).
E. I. du Pont de Nemours & Co. v. F.T.C., 729 F.2d 128 (2d Cir. 1984).
InterVest, Inc. v. Bloomberg, L.P., 340 F.3d 144 (3d Cir. 2003).
Meyer v. Kalanick, 174 F. Supp. 3d 817 (S.D.N.Y.), *reconsideration denied in part*, 185 F. Supp. 3d 448 (S.D.N.Y. 2016).
Sugar Institute, Inc. v. United States, 297 U.S. 5 (1936).
United States v. United States Gypsum Co., 438 U.S. 422 (1978).

25. Robots in the boardroom: artificial intelligence and corporate law
Florian Möslein

I. INTRODUCTION

Due to its rapid technological development, artificial intelligence will enter corporate boardrooms in the very near future. This chapter explores the interplay between artificial intelligence and corporate law, and analyzes how the two fit together. Do current corporate law rules match the challenges posed by artificial intelligence, or do they need to be adapted? More specifically, the chapter focuses on the directors of corporations. We consider the extent to which human directors should be allowed—or required—to rely on artificial intelligence. Moreover, technology will probably soon offer the possibility of artificial intelligence not only supporting directors, but even replacing them. Another question is therefore whether or not such a replacement is legally admissible. At any rate, the legal strategies currently adopted by corporate law are tailored to human directors. This chapter tests whether those strategies would still be suitable for boardrooms filled with robo-directors. It concludes that corporate law is highly relevant for the use of artificial intelligence in corporations, but that it will also need to be adapted to the challenges posed by this technology. In that sense, the interplay between artificial intelligence and corporate law promises to be dynamic in both directions.

Back in 2014, the media reported that Deep Knowledge Ventures, a Hong Kong-based venture capital firm, had appointed an algorithm named Vital (Validating Investment Tool for Advancing Life Sciences) to its board of directors. According to these reports, the algorithm was given the right to "vote on whether the firm makes an investment in a specific company or not", just like the other—human—members of the board.[1] Vital was appointed because of its ability to "automate due diligence and use historical data-sets to uncover trends that are not immediately obvious to humans surveying top-line data".[2] For instance, Vital helped to approve two investment decisions, namely those to fund Insilico Medicine, an enterprise which develops computer-assisted methods for drug discovery in aging research, and Pathway Pharmaceuticals, which selects and rates personalized cancer therapies on the basis of a platform technology.[3] Despite this impressive track record, Vital admittedly was not yet artificially intelligent in the proper

---

[1] R. Wile, *A Venture Capital Firm Just Named an Algorithm to its Board of Directors*, Business Insider, 13 May 2014, available at http://www.businessinsider.com/vital-named-to-board-2014-5?IR=T.

[2] E. Zolfagharifard, *Would you take orders from a Robot? An artificial intelligence becomes the world's first company director*, Daily Mail, 19 May 2014, available at http://www.dailymail.co.uk/sciencetech/article-2632920/Would-orders-ROBOT-Artificial-intelligence-world-s-company-director-Japan.html.

[3] For more details, *cf.* the public release of the Biogerontology Research Foundation, *Deep Knowledge Ventures announces new investment fund for life sciences and aging research*, EurekAlert!,

sense.[4] In fact, the algorithm will soon have to retire, since a much more intelligent Vital 2.0 is due to be launched in the near future.[5] Moreover, Vital was initially not granted an equal vote on all financial decisions made by the company. Legally speaking, it has not even acquired the status of corporate director under the corporate laws of Hong Kong. It is simply treated "as a member of [the] board with observer status" by its fellow (human) directors.[6] Nevertheless, Vital has widely been acknowledged as the "world's first artificial intelligence company director".[7]

In any event, Vital's (quasi) appointment to the board marks an important if not fundamental step for corporate law. On the one hand, it demonstrates the impact of artificial intelligence on corporate decision-making. Where business decisions need to be taken on the basis of numerous and complex sets of data, computer algorithms are increasingly superior to humans in taking such decisions, particularly if artificial intelligence and machine learning allow those algorithms to permanently improve their respective capabilities. In fact, artificial intelligence is increasingly being used to support management decisions across many business sectors, above all in the financial industry.[8] Computational progress and digitalization will therefore inevitably lead to corporate directors being supported—if not replaced—by artificial intelligence. Dmitry Kaminskiy, founding partner of Deep Knowledge Ventures and the human mind that created Vital, estimates that most duties in typical corporations will be automated within five to ten years, and that artificial intelligence systems will, at least in some cases, be able to make decisions themselves, without any human support.[9] Robo-directors, it seems, are about to take over corporate boards on a broad scale: "The day may come when robo-boards and robo-managers play a part in augmenting human governance boards in driving decisions and executing digital strategies".[10]

Corporate law, on the other hand, is about to face substantial challenges as a result of these technological advances. After all, decisions made by corporate directors are counted among the key topics of that area of law. Once robo-directors enter the boardroom and are able to vote in board decisions, corporate law will have to cope with novel, unprec-

---

16 December 2015, available at https://www.eurekalert.org/pub_releases/2015-12/brf-dkv121515. php.

[4]   According to a collaborator at Deep Knowledge Ventures, "it's not what you'd call AI at this stage, but that is the long-term goal", *cf.* Wile, *supra* note 1.

[5]   N. Burridge, *Artificial intelligence gets a seat in the boardroom*, Nikkei Asian Review, 10 May 2017, available at http://asia.nikkei.com/Business/Companies/Artificial-intelligence-gets-a-se at-in-the-boardroom.

[6]   See Burridge, *id.*, citing *Dmitry Kaminskiy*, founding management partner of Deep Knowledge Ventures.

[7]   *Cf.* the title of Zolfagharifard, *supra* note 2.

[8]   Burridge, *supra* note 5. See also E. Brynjolfsson and A. McAfee, *The Business of Artificial Intelligence*, Harvard Business Review, 18 July 2017, available at https://hbr.org/cover-story/2017/07/ the-business-of-artificial-intelligence.

[9]   *Cf.* again Burridge, *supra* note 5.

[10]   M. Hilb, "Toward an Integrated Framework for Governance of Digitalization", in *id.* (ed.), *Governance of Digitalization* (2017), p. 11, at 20; more extensively T. Featherstone, *Governance in the new machine age*, Australian Institute of Company Directors, 24 March 2017, available at https://aicd.companydirectors.com.au/advocacy/governance-leadership-centre/governance-driving-performance/governance-in-the-new-machine-age.

edented types of legal questions. So far, its legal strategies to regulate, steer and control corporate decision-making are tailored to human decision-makers, not to algorithms or artificial intelligence. If artificial intelligence is wired differently to human intelligence—which seems quite likely, given its persistently different analytical structure—then those traditional corporate law rules may no longer fit new business realities with robo-directors present in the boardroom. For instance, corporate laws unanimously demand that directors undertake the core duty to act honestly and in good faith.[11] Robo-directors such as Vital, however, are credited with making more logical decisions than human directors.[12] That duty, which is based on human beliefs and incentives, does not fit well with these decision-making patterns of robo-directors. In consequence, the rise of artificial intelligence requires corporate law to reconsider some of its key rules in order to test their suitability for artificially intelligent directors. The emergence of decentralized autonomous organizations (DAOs) will challenge corporate law even further. These organizations are run according to rules encoded as computer programs (so-called smart contracts); these rules, as well as their transaction record maintained on a blockchain, mean that they are therefore able to operate entirely without human involvement.[13] However, even the legal status of DAOs remains unclear so far.[14] Some argue that the idea of an entirely autonomous business entity "directly conflicts with the architecture and gatekeeping functions of our current legal frameworks".[15] On the other hand, promises of an entirely "digital jurisdiction" in which they can operate[16] seem unrealistic, since experience has already shown that such organizations are prone to human abuse in spite of their algorithm-based setting.[17] In fact, lawyers, regulators and legal scholars will have

---

[11] See, for instance, M. Eisenberg, *The Duty of Good Faith in Corporate Law* 31 Del. J. Corp. L. 1 (2006); L. Strine, L. Hamermesh, R. Balotti and J. Gorris, *Loyalty's Core Demand: The Defining Role Of Good Faith in Corporation Law* 98 Geo. L. Rev. 629 (2010) (both with regard to US corporate law).

[12] *Cf.* Burridge, *supra* note 5, citing *Dmitry Kaminskiy*, founding management partner of Deep Knowledge Ventures.

[13] For more extensive descriptions, see for instance H. Diedrich, *Ethereum* (CreateSpace 2016) 180–86; M. Swan, *Blockchain: Blueprint for a New Economy* (O'Reilly Media 2015) 24 *et seq.*

[14] *Cf.* N. Popper, *A Venture Fund With Plenty of Virtual Capital, but No Capitalist*, New York Times, 21 May 2016, available at https://www.nytimes.com/2016/05/22/business/dealbook/crypto-ether-bitcoin-currency.html.; see also Diedrich, *id.*, 184 *et seq.*

[15] Diedrich, *supra* note 13, 184; citing C. Choi; more extensively A. Wright and P. De Filippi, *Decentralized Blockchain Technology and the Rise of Lex Cryptographia*, Working Paper, 2015, available at https://papers.ssrn.com/sol3/papers.cfm?abstract_id=2580664.

[16] This is the stated goal of Aragon Networks, a DAO that will let organizations opt into it and use its services, also providing a built-in governance system; see L. Cuende and J. Izquierdo, *Aragon Network – A Decentralized Infrastructure for Value Exchange*, White Paper, 20 April 2017, p. 16, available at https://github.com/aragon/whitepaper/blob/master/Aragon%20Whitepaper.pdf: "The Aragon Network (AN) will be the first decentralized autonomous organization whose goal is to act as a digital jurisdiction that makes it extremely easy and friendly for organizations, entrepreneurs and investors to operate".

[17] In 2016, an investor-directed venture capital fund run as a DAO (and called "The DAO") was hacked and one third of its funds was drained; see more extensively N. Popper, *A Hacking of More Than $50 Million Dashes Hopes in the World of Virtual Currency*, New York Times, 17 June 2016, available at https://www.nytimes.com/2016/06/18/business/dealbook/hacker-may-have-removed-more-than-50-million-from-experimental-cybercurrency-project.html.

to figure out whether and how existing legal rules can be applied to these fundamentally new technological phenomena, or whether new rules will have to be set.[18] For instance, the Securities and Exchange Commission has recently made clear that tokens raised in Initial Coin Offerings by DAOs may be securities, and are therefore subject to federal securities laws.[19] In a similar vein, corporate law will arguably also continue to play a role in terms of artificial intelligence and decentralized autonomous organizations, but it will have to respond to these technological challenges.

So far, however, corporate law has not kept pace with these advances in artificial intelligence and computer algorithms. While the general challenges of digitalization are being increasingly (albeit still hesitantly, given their impact) discussed, the debate is largely based on an overly narrow understanding of digitalization. For instance, a prominent expert group, established by the European Commission in May 2014 to help advise on issues of company law, based its recent *Report on digitalisation in company law* on the following definition: "By 'digitalisation' we mean the representation of communication in writing or sound by electronic means, and the concept thus concerns electronic communication . . .".[20] An in-depth analysis requested by the European Parliament's Committee on Legal Affairs has taken a very similar approach.[21] Restricting digitalization to just electronic communication (some sort of telephone or fax message 4.0, so to say), however, inevitably results in ignoring the challenges of algorithms and artificial intelligence.

My claim is that these latter challenges are much more fundamental for corporate law than those of electronic communication. While I agree that digitalization fundamentally changes businesses and that legal scholars therefore need to focus on these changes and their impact on corporate law, I assume that digitalization has many additional facets than those currently being discussed, and that algorithms and artificial intelligence do in fact count among its core drivers.[22] The core research question therefore aims to examine the intersection of artificial intelligence and corporate law, and asks how the two fit together. Do current corporate law rules match the challenges of artificial intelligence, or do they need to be adapted? More specifically, I will focus on the corporate law rules regulating directors and their business decisions. This contribution is divided into four further parts. I begin, in Part II, with a general overview of corporate law in order to analyze where

---

[18]   Diedrich, *supra* note 13, 185; similar considerations, at the time with respect to the challenges of cyberspace: L. Lessig, *The Law of the Horse: What Cyberlaw Might Teach* 113 Harv. L. Rev. 501 (1999).

[19]   Securities and Exchange Commission, "Report of Investigation Pursuant to Section 21(a) of the Securities Exchange Act of 1934: The DAO", Release No. 81207, 25 July 2017, available at https://www.sec.gov/litigation/investreport/34-81207.pdf.

[20]   Informal Company Law Expert Group (ICLEG), "Report on digitalisation in company law", March 2016, available at http://ec.europa.eu/justice/civil/files/company-law/icleg-report-on-digitalisation-24-march-2016_en.pdf, p. 6 (para 1.1.).

[21]   V. Knapp, "What are the issues relating to digitalisation in company law?", June 2016, available at http://www.europarl.europa.eu/RegData/etudes/IDAN/2016/556961/IPOL_IDA(2016)556961_EN.pdf; see also U. Bertschinger, "Aktienrecht im digitalen Zeitalter", in Rechtswissenschaftliche Abteilung der Universität St. Gallen (ed.), *Recht im digitalen Zeitalter – Festgabe Schweizerischer Juristentag* (Dike 2015) 167.

[22]   Very few publications have so far taken a similar slant. See, however, L. LoPucki, *Algorithmic Entities* 95 Washington University Law Review 887 (2018); similar, but with a focus on contract law: L. Scholz, *Algorithmic Contracts* 20 Stanford Technology Law Review 128 (2017).

artificial intelligence fits in; it will show that its importance is greatest where directors are concerned. In Part III, I explore the role of artificial intelligence as a supportive tool. To what extent should human directors be allowed to rely on artificial intelligence? Or could they even be compelled by corporate law to make use of it? Part IV goes further, by assuming that artificial intelligence has the potential not only to support, but also to replace, human directors. While this scenario is technically imaginable, the question is whether or not such a replacement is legally permissible. The final Part, V, will then test the suitability of current legal strategies of corporate law for robo-directors. I conclude that corporate law is highly relevant for the use of artificial intelligence, but that it will also require various adaptions and refinements in order to cope with the challenges posed by artificial intelligence.

II.   ARTIFICIAL INTELLIGENCE AND THE ANATOMY OF CORPORATE LAW

To begin with, we need to more precisely consider the specific points at which artificial intelligence enters the realm of corporate law. This analysis requires a brief sketch of corporate law and its regulatory functions. In turn, such a description requires some basic understanding of the nature of corporations. It is helpful to build these considerations on the leading comparative overview of corporate law, a book authored by nearly a dozen international experts in the field, recently published in its third edition and entitled *The Anatomy of Corporate Law*.[23] In order to carry this biological metaphor further, we need to analyze which body parts of the corporation would be most affected if corporate bodies were to incorporate artificial intelligence.

A.   Corporate Bodies

Corporations are legal entities that are separate and distinct from their owners. Whereas in an economic perspective, corporations are simply vehicles for investors to jointly operate their businesses, they are in legal discourse commonly referred to as legal persons. This means that they enjoy similar rights and duties to those possessed by human individuals and are able, for instance, to enter into contracts, to own assets and to sue and be sued. Even though many of their specific features depend upon the applicable legal framework, which differs between jurisdictions, corporate bodies are nonetheless characterized by a common structure that applies irrespective of jurisdictions. The authors of the *Anatomy* name five basic legal characteristics shared by corporations all over the world.[24] Firstly, corporations have a separate legal personality, which not only enables them to enjoy rights and duties, but also separates their patrimony from the assets that are personally owned by the shareholders.[25] A second characteristic is their limited liability: while the creditors of

[23]   J. Armour, L. Enriques et al., *The Anatomy of Corporate Law: A Comparative and Functional Approach* 3rd edn. (Oxford University Press 2017).

[24]   More extensively on the following: Armour, Enriques et al., *id.*, 5–15.

[25]   This asset partitioning (or "entity shielding") includes aspects, namely creditor priority and liquidation protection, which are both central to organizational law, see H. Hansmann and

a corporation can make claims against the assets owned by said corporation, they are not able to make claims against assets held individually by the corporation's shareholders.[26] The third feature closely interacts with these first two. It consists of the transferability of shares, which makes the operation of a corporation's business independent of changes in the ownership of its shares.[27] A fourth, particularly important, characteristic is the delegation of management to a board of directors. The board is periodically elected by the corporation's shareholders, and has principal authority over the corporation's affairs because it is assigned responsibility for all but the most fundamental decisions. The fifth and final characteristic consists of investor ownership, which means that both the right to vote, and thereby the right to participate in control and the right to receive distributed profits, are typically proportional to the amount of capital contributed to the firm.

B.   Functions of Corporate Law

For corporate bodies, law obviously plays a vital role. As legal entities, they owe their very existence to the applicable legal framework: "A principal function of corporate law is to provide business enterprises with a legal form that possesses these five core attributes".[28] If the law did not provide such a form, corporations would not even be able to come into being. Yet, the provision of a legal form is not limited to the single act of bestowing legal personality; it also requires rules to establish the basic structure of the corporation. In addition, however, corporate law has a second function, which aims at "facilitating coordination between participants in the corporate enterprise", thereby "reducing the ongoing costs of organizing business through the corporate form".[29] Otherwise, this coordination within corporations would risk being hampered by so-called principal-agent problems, which arise whenever one party (the "principal") relies upon the actions taken by another party (the "agent") that affect the former party's welfare. In such situations, the principal may worry that the agent is not acting in the principal's interest, but rather in his own.[30] In corporations, three such agency relationships are prevalent: (1) between the firm's owner and its hired managers; (2) between majority shareholders and minority shareholders; and (3) between the firm and other parties, like creditors, employees and

---

R. Kraakman, *The Essential Role of Organizational Law* 110 Yale Law Journal 387 *et seq.* (2000); *cf.* also H. Hansmann, R. Kraakman and R. Squire, *Law and the Rise of the Firm* 119 Harvard Law Review 1335 *et seq* (2006).

[26]   Most importantly, limited liability thereby makes investment diversification possible, *cf.* H. Manne, *Our Two Corporation Systems: Law and Economics* 53 Virginia Law Review 259, 262 (1967).

[27]   If there were no liquidation protection or limited liability, the value of shares would depend on the creditworthiness of the corporation's shareholders, which would in turn constitute a major impediment for the transferability of shares, *cf.* P. Halpern, M. Trebilcock and S. Turnbull, *An Economic Analysis of Limited Liability in Corporation Law* 30 University of Toronto Law Journal 117, 136–38 (1980).

[28]   Armour, Enriques et al., *supra* note 23, 1.

[29]   *Id.*, 2.

[30]   *Id.*, 29; see also M. Jensen and W. Meckling, *Theory of the Firm: Managerial behavior, agency costs and ownership structure* 3 Journal of Financial Economics 305 *et seq* (1976).

customers.[31] The key conflict within the first agency relationship has appropriately been described by Adam Smith in his magnum opus *The Wealth of Nations*:

> The directors of such companies . . . being the managers rather of other people's money rather than of their own, it cannot well be expected that they should watch over it with the same anxious vigilance with which partners in a private company watch over their own . . . Negligence and profusion, therefore, must always prevail, more or less, in the management of the affairs of such a company.[32]

In general, the delegation of decision-making power to an agent creates the risk that this agent will be disloyal or incompetent.[33] Corporate law, in turn, follows a number of different legal strategies to mitigate these agency problems, namely by providing for constraints or incentives, or by attributing appointment or decision rights. For instance, directors are subject to corporate law duties, which prohibit certain forms of self-interested behavior.[34]

C.   Incorporation of Artificial Intelligence into Corporations

Into which part of this basic structure of corporations can artificial intelligence be incorporated? Which body part of their anatomy does it affect? The answer to this requires some thought about the nature of artificial intelligence. As with the difficulties of figuring out the universally applicable characteristics of corporations, however, the definition of artificial intelligence is intricate. Back in 1955, some of the pioneers in artificial intelligence described the process as "that of making a machine behave in ways that would be called intelligent if a human were so behaving".[35] Even though this reference to human intelligence has often been criticized as misleading in various respects,[36] that description at least clarifies that artificial intelligence could theoretically support or even replace any human being within corporate bodies, namely directors, shareholders or other parties, like creditors, employees and customers.

Today, the various techniques and tools of artificial intelligence are manifold and include, for instance, symbolic logic, artificial neural networks, fuzzy systems, evolutionary

---

[31]   Armour, Enriques et al., *supra* note 23, 29; *cf also* R. Bahar and A. Morand, "Taking conflict of interest in corporate law seriously – direct and indirect rules addressing the agency problem" in A. Peters and L. Handschin (eds.), *Conflict of Interest in Global, Public and Corporate Governance* (Cambridge University Press 2012) 308.

[32]   A. Smith, *An Inquiry into the Nature and Causes of the Wealth of Nations* (1778, quoted from the edition edited by R. Campbell and A. Todd, Clarendon Press 1976, vol. 2) 741, at para. 18.

[33]   *Cf.* A. Cahn and D. Donald, *Comparative Corporate Law* (Cambridge University Press 2010) 299.

[34]   Described extensively, for instance, in the contributions in A. Paolini (ed.), *Research Handbook on Directors' Duties* (Edward Elgar Publishing 2014).

[35]   J. McCarthy, M. Minsky, N. Rochester and C. Shannon, "A Proposal for the Dartmouth Summer Research Project on Artificial Intelligence", 1955, available at http://www-formal.stanford.edu/jmc/history/dartmouth/dartmouth.html.

[36]   For instance, human intelligence is in itself difficult to define; moreover, machines can also perform tasks that humans are unable to perform; see J. Kaplan, *Artificial Intelligence* (Oxford University Press 2016) 1–4.

computing, intelligent agents and probabilistic reasoning models.[37] Since the tasks undertaken by these tools include the coordination of data delivery, the analysis of data trends, the provision of forecasts, the development of data consistency, the quantification of uncertainty, the anticipation of users' data needs, the provision of information to users in the most appropriate form and the suggestion of courses of action, the most important impact of artificial intelligence is arguably its support for or even replacement of human decision-making, particularly under conditions of uncertainty.[38] Above all, artificial intelligence helps to make decisions. Decision-making requires data, often in large amounts. The more complex a decision, the more data is needed to make the decision on an informed, rational basis.[39] Since computers, algorithms and artificial intelligence are particularly well-suited to process "big data", they are able to contribute to improve decision-making.[40] To be more precise, artificial intelligence can reduce uncertainties of any kind (not just about the future) by making predictions, that is, by translating large amounts of data into small, manageable chunks.[41]

As artificial intelligence could support or replace any human being in a corporate body, it is therefore most likely to be employed where the most complex decisions need to be taken within corporations. While shareholders and other stakeholders also take decisions—shareholders make decisions on investments and divestments, as well as voting in general meetings, while other stakeholders make decisions on contracting with the corporation—the main decision center of the corporation (its brain, so to speak) is certainly located within the board of directors. As a consequence of delegating management to the board, directors have principal authority over the corporation's affairs, and are assigned responsibility for all but the most fundamental decisions; not only does daily management form part of their responsibilities, but also strategic business decisions.[42] It is precisely these strategic business decisions that are concurrently the most complex ones that have to be taken within corporations. For instance, they usually include many

---

[37] More extensively, for instance, in L. Jain and P. de Wilde (eds.), *Practical Applications of Computational Intelligence Techniques* (Springer 2001); L. Jain and N. Martin (eds.), *Fusion of Neural Networks, Fuzzy Sets and Genetic Algorithms* (CRC Press 1999).

[38] *Cf.* G. Philipps-Wren and L. Jain, "Artificial Intelligence for Decision Making" in B. Gabrys, R.J. Howlett and L. Jain (eds.), *Knowledge-Based Intelligent Information and Engineering Systems* (Springer 2006) 531–36.

[39] In more detail on decision-making and complexity: J. Cook, M. Noyes and Y. Masakowski (eds.), *Decision Making in Complex Environments* (CRC Press 2007); H. Qudrat-Ullah, J. Spector and P. Davidsen (eds.), *Complex Decision Making: Theory and Practice* (Springer 2010); R. Grünig and R. Kühn, *Successful Decision-making: A Systematic Approach to Complex Problems* 2nd ed. (Springer 2009).

[40] A.-E. Hassanien et al. (eds.), *Big Data in Complex Systems: Challenges and Opportunities* (Springer 2015); S. Kudyba, *Big Data, Mining, and Analytics – Components of Strategic Decision Making* (CRC Press 2014).

[41] A. Agrawal, J. Gans and A. Goldfarb, *Exploring the Impact of Artificial Intelligence: Prediction versus Judgment*, Working Paper (2018), available at http://www.nber.org/papers/w24626.pdf; see also *id.*, *How AI Will Change the Way We Make Decisions*, Harvard Business Review, 26 July 2017, available at https://hbr.org/2017/07/how-ai-will-change-the-way-we-make-decisions.

[42] See, for instance, with respect to US law: S. Bainbridge, *Corporation Law and Economics* (Foundation Press 2002), 194 *et seq.*; F. Gevurtz, *Corporation Law* 2nd ed. (West Publishing 2010) 190–95.

different options. In comparison, the decisions of shareholders and other stakeholders are typically less complex, at least in the sense that they are usually binary, with a choice between just two alternatives (to invest or to divest, to vote yes or no, to contract or not to contract within the corporation, etc.). In any event, since they also include questions of day-to-day management, the decisions to be taken by the board of directors quantitatively outweigh those to be taken by other persons involved. The corporative organ most closely resembling a human brain is therefore the board of directors.[43] In consequence, artificial intelligence appears to be most likely to play a significant role in boardroom decisions; this is why robo-directors are increasingly being discussed in modern business practice, and not robo-shareholders or robo-stakeholders.

III.   SUPPORT OF CORPORATE DIRECTORS BY ARTIFICIAL INTELLIGENCE

Recent literature on artificial intelligence distinguishes three different forms, namely assisted, augmented and autonomous artificial intelligence.[44] The difference between these forms comes from the allocation of decision rights between man and machine. In the assisted artificial intelligence stage, machines execute certain specific tasks, but decision rights remain solely with human beings; in the second stage, augmented artificial intelligence, humans and machines share decision rights and learn from each other; and in the third and final stage, autonomous artificial intelligence, machines ultimately take over all decision rights, either because humans increasingly trust the machines' abilities to decide, or because decisions have to be taken so quickly or require so many data that humans are simply unable to decide. This tripartite distinction—which in fact is more like a continuum—can also be applied to the use of artificial intelligence in corporations. For this purpose, we can condense the assisted and augmented artificial intelligence categories into one, and distinguish this from autonomous artificial intelligence. The dividing line is then between the support and the replacement of corporate directors by machines. Whereas in the first case, only certain (if any) decision rights are delegated, artificial intelligence replaces human directors in the latter case. Beginning with the support of corporate directors by artificial intelligence, we need to answer two different questions, namely whether directors should have authority to delegate decision-making powers to artificial intelligence (see below, subsection A) and, on the other hand, whether they might even be under an obligation to do so (see below, subsection B).

---

[43]   With respect to UK company law, *cf.* Lord Denning's leading statement at *HL Bolton (Engineering) Co Ltd v TJ Graham and Sons Ltd*, (1956) All ER 624, at 630: "A company may in many ways be likened to a human body. It has a brain and nerve centre which controls what it does. It also has hands which hold the tools and act in accordance with directions from the centre. Some of the people in the company are mere servants and agents who are nothing more than hands to do the work and cannot be said to represent the mind or will. Others are directors and managers who represent the directing mind and will of the company, and control what it does".

[44]   A. Rao, *AI everywhere/nowhere part 3 – AI is AAAI (Assisted-Augmented-Autonomous Intelligence)*, 20 May 2016, available at http://usblogs.pwc.com/emerging-technology/ai-every where-nowhere-part-3-ai-is-aaai-assisted-augmented-autonomous-intelligence/.

A.   Directors' Authority to Delegate to Artificial Intelligence

As can be seen by a review of the law, so far neither case law nor codebooks deal with the question of whether directors can delegate decision rights to artificial intelligence. A question with which corporate laws had to cope, however, concerned the delegation of tasks to employees or to third parties, and one can draw analogies. In a similar vein, the "import" of rules from agency law has been discussed with respect to algorithmic contracting, since algorithms effectively act in a similar manner to human agents, regardless of their legal qualification (or "personhood").[45]

As a matter of fact, delegating tasks is not strictly prohibited, since directors are simply not able to complete them all by themselves.[46] However, many national corporate laws require a clause to be included in the respective corporation's articles of association.[47] While such clauses are widespread, they usually refer to human delegates, meaning that the issue of whether or not task delegation to artificial intelligence is permitted is open to their interpretation. Under current UK company law, for instance, the Model Articles provide that:

> 5. (1) Subject to the articles, the directors may delegate any of the powers which are conferred on them under the articles-
> (a)   to such person or committee;
> (b)   by such means (including by power of attorney);
> (c)   to such an extent;
> (d)   in relation to such matters or territories; and
> (e)   on such terms and conditions;
> as they think fit.[48]

While this provision obviously leaves ample scope for delegation, it is debatable whether it could also be used for tasks to be delegated to artificial intelligence. On the basis of a literal interpretation, machines are neither people nor committees, meaning that, at most, assisted artificial intelligence could be employed. In this case, decision rights would remain solely with human directors. The rationale of that provision, however, is to enable management to be efficiently organized; this rationale would therefore seem to justify a

---

[45]   Scholz, *supra* note 22, at 134–38; see also S. Chopra and L. White, *Artificial Agents and the Contracting Problem: A Solution Via an Agency Analysis* U. Ill. J. L. Tech. and Pol'Y 363, 365 *et seq.* (Fall 2009); A. Bellia, *Contracting with Electronic Agents* 50 Emory L. J. 1047, 1048 (2001).

[46]   S. Grundmann, *European Company Law* 2nd ed (Intersentia 2012) 267 ("In all countries, tasks are of course split in reality"); *cf. also* H. Fleischer, *Zur Leitungsaufgabe des Vorstands im Aktienrecht* Zeitschrift für Wirtschaftsrecht (ZIP) 1, at 7 *et seq.* (2003) ("schon aus Gründen der Leitungskapazität bis zu einem gewissen Grade unumgänglich").

[47]   In Italy, for instance, Art. 2381 para. 2 CC ("Se lo statuto o l'assemblea lo consentono, il consiglio di amministrazione può delegare proprie attribuzioni ad un comitato esecutivo composto da alcuni dei suoi componenti, o ad uno o più dei suoi componenti"); in Switzerland, Art. 716b para. 1 OR ("Die Statuten können den Verwaltungsrat ermächtigen, die Geschäftsführung nach Massgabe eines Organisationsreglementes ganz oder zum Teil an einzelne Mitglieder oder an Dritte zu übertragen"); for a broader comparative overview cf. F. Möslein, *Grenzen unternehmerischer Leitungsmacht im marktoffenen Verband* (De Gruyter 2007) 35.

[48]   *Cf.*, also on the previous provision in Table A Article 72: D. Kenshaw, *Company Law in Context* (Oxford University Press 2012) 192–94.

broader interpretation, which also allows delegation to machines. The same teleological reasoning could probably be applied in other jurisdictions with respect to provisions either in the law or in the articles, so that the delegation of decision rights to artificial intelligence is at least not entirely prohibited from the outset.

Whilst the delegation of decision rights is therefore permitted to some extent, corporate law restricts this authority to delegate by requiring directors to manage the business of the company themselves. In the New Zealand case of *Dairy Containers v NZI Bank*, for instance, Thomas J elaborated that

> it is the fundamental task of the directors to manage the business of the company. Theirs is the power and the responsibility of that management. To manage the company effectively, of course, the must necessarily delegate much of their power to executives of the company, especially in respect of its day to day operation. . . . The directors may delegate powers and functions, using that term in a broad sense, but they cannot delegate the management function itself.[49]

Accordingly, US corporate law does not allow directors "to delegate duties which lie at the heart of the management of the corporation".[50] In other words, the core management decisions must always remain with the board of directors.[51] While most corporate laws do not define more precisely what those core decisions include,[52] the same vague limit can also be applied to the delegation of decision rights to artificial intelligence. Even if decision rights are delegated to machines, human directors must always maintain the ultimate management function themselves.

Moreover, directors still have a duty to supervise the accomplishment of the delegated tasks:

> Whilst directors are entitled (subject to the articles of association of the company) to delegate particular functions to those below them in the management chain, and to trust in their competence and integrity to a reasonable extent, the exercise of the power of delegation does not absolve a director from the duty to supervise the discharge of the delegated functions.[53]

---

[49] *Dairy Containers Ltd v NZI Bank Ltd* [1995] 2 NZLR 30, at p. 79 *et seq.*

[50] In *Re Bally's Grand Derivative Litigation*, 23 Del. J. Corp. L., p. 677, at p. 686.

[51] *Cf.* also Jonathan Parker J, in *Re Barings plc (No. 5)* [1999] 1 BCLC p. 489: "Directors have, both collectively and individually, a continuing duty to acquire and maintain a sufficient knowledge and understanding of the company's business to enable them properly to discharge their duties as directors". In more detail on both cases: P. Mäntysaari, *Comparative Corporate Governance* (Springer 2005) 225 *et seq.*

[52] Swiss corporate law, for example, is a bit more explicit: while Art. 716b para. 1 OR prohibits the delegation of the "Oberleitung" (key management of the corporation), the legislative materials define this term in more detail: "Oberleitung bedeutet ein Dreifaches, nämlich Entwicklung der strategischen Ziele der Gesellschaft, Festlegung der Mittel, um diese Ziele zu erreichen, und Kontrolle . . . im Hinblick auf die Verfolgung der festgelegten Ziele" (development of strategic goals, determination of the means to reach these goals and control with respect to the pursuit of these goals), *see* P. Forstmoser, A. Meyer-Hayoz and P. Nobel, *Schweizerisches Aktienrecht* (Stämpfli 1996) §30, para. 31; *cf. also* U. Bertschinger, *Arbeitsteilung und aktienrechtliche Verantwortlichkeit* (Schulthess 1999); A. Kammerer, *Die unübertragbaren und unentziehbaren Kernkompetenzen des Verwaltungsrates* (Schulthess 1997); P. Böckli, *Die unentziehbaren Kernkompetenzen des Verwaltungsrates* (Schulthess 1994).

[53] See again Jonathan Parker J, in *Re Barings plc (No. 5)* [1999] 1 BCLC, p. 489.

More specifically, directors have to instruct, supervise and control the persons to whom they have delegated tasks, although the precise requirements of this duty are not precisely defined and differ from jurisdiction to jurisdiction.[54] Both the vagueness and inconsistency of these duties make it difficult to draw analogies with respect to the supervision of artificial intelligence, but it would seem that directors are required to carefully consider which robot to employ and which tasks to assign; moreover, supervision would also seem to require that humans double check any decisions made by artificial intelligence. Directors must at least generally oversee the selection and activities of robots, algorithms and artificial intelligence devices. Already, this duty requires them to have a basic understanding of how these devices operate. Even though they do not understand their coding in every detail, they should at least be able to understand the technical guidelines that drive these machines.

Similar objective standards apply when directors delegate the gathering of information to third parties: "A director may not assert his ignorance as an excuse for his nonfeasance".[55] In other instances, the law explicitly formulates more specific duties for the overseeing of algorithms, namely with respect to algorithmic trading: German law, for instance, requires securities companies operating algorithmic trading to operate systems and risk controls to ensure that: (1) its trading systems are resilient, have sufficient capacity and are subject to appropriate trade thresholds and trading ceilings; (2) the transmission of erroneous orders, as well as systems malfunctions which could cause disturbances on the markets, are avoided; (3) its trading systems cannot be used for a purpose contrary to those against market abuse or those of the trading place in which they is operating.[56] In substance, similar standards can be applied to corporate directors when they employ algorithms to perform management tasks and delegate decision rights to them. They will have to ensure that these systems are stable, that they do not cause fundamental management errors and that their decisions comply with the applicable laws and regulations.[57]

B.   Do Directors Have a Duty to Delegate to Artificial Intelligence?

While corporate law therefore *allows* directors to delegate decision rights to algorithms, albeit with certain restrictions, one can also consider the inverse question: could directors also *be required* to do so, at least under certain circumstances? Since permission does not equal obligation, this question might seem a little awkward at first sight. Corporate law, however, requires directors to act on an informed basis. If artificial intelligence has superior information processing capabilities, due to its ability to make predictions by

---

[54]   More extensively, with respect to German, UK and US law: H. Fleischer, *Vorstandsverant-wortlichkeit und Fehlverhalten von Unternehmensangehörigen – Von der Einzelüberwachung zur Errichtung einer Compliance-Organisation*, Die Aktiengesellschaft (AG) 291, at 292–98 (2003).

[55]   W. Knepper and D. Bailey, *Liability of Corporate Officers and Directors* 7th ed. (Lexis 2002), at § 2.09; for a comparative overview see Möslein, *supra* note 46, 135–38.

[56]   *Cf.* § 33 para. 1a WpHG. In general on algorithmic trading and its legal regulation: A. Fleckner, "Regulating Trading Practices", in: N. Moloney, E. Ferran and J. Payne (eds.), *The Oxford Handbook of Financial Regulation* (Oxford University Press 2015) 596, at 619–23.

[57]   In a similar vein, the same standards can also be applied to robo-advisors based on algorithmic decisions, *cf.* F. Möslein and A. Lordt, *Rechtsfragen des Robo Advice,* Zeitschrift für Wirtschaftsrecht (ZIP) 793, at 803 (2017).

translating large sets of data into small, manageable chunks (see above, section II, at note 41), then the duty to act on an informed basis may well evolve into the duty to obtain such predictions made by artificially intelligent devices.

Yet, directors do not have the duty to gather every piece of information available, or to maximize the informed basis on which they take their decisions. After all, the collection of information also involves costs, and striking a balance between these costs and using the information concerned is in itself an entrepreneurial decision.[58] It should, at least in principle, be left to directors rather than being scrutinized by the courts: "The amount of information that is prudent to have before a decision is made is itself a business judgment of the very type that courts are institutionally poorly equipped to make".[59] Nonetheless, most corporate law jurisdictions stipulate certain minimum requirements for information gathering. For instance, in the famous US case *Smith v. van Gorkom*, the finding that directors' duties had been breached was solely based on the insufficient preparation of the respective board decision, not on its substance; it was held that this decision "was not the product of an informed business judgment".[60] Similar requirements are formulated, inter alia, in English case law,[61] in French legal doctrine,[62] and in the Italian codification of corporate law.[63] The standard of care differs, however. While it seems relatively strict in Italy, Austria and Switzerland, it appears more generous in English case law (as well as in US corporate law):[64] "Their negligence must not be the omission to take all possible care; it must be much more blameable than that; it must be in a business sense culpable

---

[58] In more detail, based on a comparative overview Möslein, *supra* note 46, 131–34.

[59] In *Re RJR Nabisco, Inc. Shareholders Litigation*, [1989] WL 7036, para. 19 (per Chancellor Allen).

[60] *Smith v van Gorkom*, 488 A.2d 858; from the abundance of (partly critical) case reviews *cf.*, for instance, L. Herzel and L. Katz, *Smith v. Van Gorkom: The Business of Judging Business Judgment* 41 Bus. Law. 1187 (1986); D. Fischel, *The Business Judgement Rule and the Trans Union Case* 40 Bus. Law. 1437 (1985); B. Manning, *Reflections and Practical Tips on Life in the Boardroom after Van Gorkom* 41 Bus. Law. 1 (1985); K. Chittur, *The Corporate Director's Standard of Care: Past, Present, Future* 10 Del. J. Corp. L. 505 (1985); more recently J. Macey, *Smith v. Van Gorkom: Insights About C.E.O.s, Corporate Law Rules, and the Jurisdictional Competition for Corporate Charter* 96 Northwestern University Law Review 607 (2002); L. Stout, *In Praise of Procedure: An Economic and Behavioral Defense of Smith v. Van Gorkom and the Business Judgment Rule* 96 Northwestern University Law Review 673 (2002).

[61] *Cf.*, for instance, *Dorchester Finance Co. v Stebbing*, [1989] BCLC 498; similar: *Land Credit Co of Ireland v Lord Fermoy*, [1870] LR 5 Ch App 763; *Selangor United Rubber Estates Ltd. v Cradock* (no 3), [1968] 2 All ER 1073, at 1095 and 1121–23. Similar for Swiss law BGE 108 V 199, at 203 ("Das setzt u.a. voraus, daß der Verwaltungsrat die ihm unterbreiteten Berichte kritisch liest, nötigenfalls ergänzende Auskünfte verlangt und bei Irrtümern oder Unregelmäßigkeiten einschreitet"); *cf. also* Forstmoser, Meier-Hayoz and Nobel, *supra* note 52, at § 28, para. 68; A. Grass, *Business Judgment Rule* (Schulthess 1998) 87–90.

[62] D. Schmidt, *La responsabilité des membres du conseil d'administration* Droit et Patrimoine 45 (46) (1995): "On attend du conseil d'administration qu'il prenne ses décisions après mûre réflexion, après avoir obtenu et analysé les informations nécessaires et après avoir recueilli les avis d'experts"; less clearly: S. Hadji-Artinian, *La faute de gestion* (Litec 2001) 220; E. Scholastique, *Devoir de Diligence des administrateurs de sociétés – Droits français et anglais* (LGDJ 1998) 212 *et seq.*

[63] *Cf.* Art. 2381 Abs. 6 CC ("gli amministratori sono tenuti ad agire in modo informato"); in more detail C. Granelli, *La responsabilità civile degli organi di gestione alla luce della riforma delle società di capitali* Le Società 1565, at 1568 (2003).

[64] *Cf.* again the comparative overview in Möslein, *supra* note 46, 133 *et seq.*

of gross negligence".[65] In a similar vein, the German Stock Corporation Act (AktG) stipulates that directors shall not be deemed to have violated their duty of care if, at the time of taking the entrepreneurial decision, they had good reason to assume that they were acting on the basis of adequate information for the benefit of the company.[66] It is therefore only in exceptional cases—those in which directors act unreasonably—that the courts scrutinize the decision of directors in terms of the amount of effort they put into the gathering and the processing of information.

As long as the use of artificial intelligence is not widespread with respect to business decisions, it seems difficult to establish that directors who do not take advantage of such devices are acting unreasonably. At least, the computer systems needed to operate them are still expensive, adapting them to the needs of specific companies requires thorough and burdensome preparation and their predictions may not be superior to human predictions in every case. In this present state of affairs, a director's duty to delegate the processing of (certain) information to artificial intelligence devices therefore seems difficult to establish.[67] Technological progress develops at such a rapid pace, however, that this duty is not unlikely to develop in the near future. The more artificial intelligence spreads in corporate boardrooms, the more its use will develop into a widely accepted standard of directors' behavior. When this point is reached, it will seem increasingly unreasonable to deviate from that standard; it will therefore ultimately become likely that these directors will be deemed to have violated their duty of care. A concurrent development can already be observed today with respect to the storage and handling of information. Information governance is increasingly qualified as an additional task to be undertaken by the board of directors, with manifold specifications in various areas (e.g., the strategic definition of IT targets and IT resources, the organization of the IT department, communication on IT topics and the monitoring of IT compliance and security).[68] In a very similar vein, the governance of artificial intelligence is likely to develop as an additional task for the board of directors.

---

[65]   *Lagunas Nitrate Co v Lagunas Syndicate*, [1899] 2 Ch 392, at 435. With respect to US corporate law, *cf.* Gevurtz, *supra* note 42, 284–86.

[66]   § 93 para. 1 AktG ("Eine Pflichtverletzung liegt nicht vor, wenn das Vorstandsmitglied bei einer unternehmerischen Entscheidung vernünftigerweise annehmen durfte, auf der Grundlage angemessener Information zum Wohle der Gesellschaft zu handeln"); in more detail: R. Freitag and S. Korch, *Die Angemessenheit der Information im Rahmen der Business Judgment Rule (§ 93 Abs. 1 S. 2 AktG)* Zeitschrift für Wirtschaftsrecht (ZIP) 2281 (2012); K. Peters, *Angemessene Informationsbasis als Voraussetzung pflichtgemäßen Vorstandshandelns* Die Aktiengesellschaft (AG) 811, at 812 (2010); S.H. Schneider, *Informationspflichten und Informationssystemeinrichtigungspflichten im Aktienkonzern* (Duncker and Humblot 2006), at 89 *et seq.*, 91; *id.*, *"Unternehmerische Entscheidungen" als Anwendungsvoraussetzung für die Business Judgment Rule* Der Betrieb (DB) 707, at 708 (2005); M. Roth, *Unternehmerisches Ermessen und Haftung des Vorstands* (Beck 2001) 80 *et seq.*; J. Semler, "Entscheidungen und Ermessen im Aktienrecht", *Festschrift for Peter Ulmer* (De Gruyter 2003) 627, at 632 *et seq.*; H. Fleischer, "Die 'Business Judgment Rule' im Spiegel von Rechtsvergleichung und Rechtsökonomie", in *Festschrift for H. Wiedemann* (Beck 2002) 827, at 840 *et seq.*

[67]   More generally on information management within corporations and on its relevance for directors' duties: J. Rodewalt, *Informationsmanagement im Unternehmen als Instrument zur Vermeidung von Organhaftung* GmbH-Rundschau (GmbHR) 639, at 643 (2014).

[68]   R. Müller, "Digitalization Decisions at Board Level", in M. Hilb (ed.), *Governance of Digitization* (Haupt 2017) 43.

IV. THE REPLACEMENT OF CORPORATE DIRECTORS BY ARTIFICIAL INTELLIGENCE

Looking further into the future, one could even imagine that human directors will not only be supported, but also replaced, by robo-directors. Such a development would conform to the stage of autonomous artificial intelligence, in which machines take over all decision rights, either because humans increasingly trust the machines' abilities to decide, or because decisions have to be taken so quickly or require so much data that humans are simply unable to decide (see already above, section III at note 44). On a more general level, historians and philosophers suggest that once artificial intelligence surpasses human intelligence, it might simply exterminate mankind.[69] Whether the world will indeed be run by "robot overlords",[70] however, is at least as debatable as whether companies will be run by robo-directors. Economists argue, for instance, that even though artificial intelligence may well be superior at making predictions, humans need to make judgements. They need to work out the benefits and costs of different decisions in different situations, since this in turn requires "an understanding of what your organization cares about most, what it benefits from, and what could go wrong".[71] While artificial intelligence may be able to learn from experience, it is still unable to exercise this sort of judgement, at least for the foreseeable future.[72] Furthermore, creativity and innovation are widely regarded as specifically human qualities, and artificial intelligence experts are in disagreement as to whether creative or innovative machines will ever exist, or whether artificial intelligence just does not have this potential.[73] Since decisions at board level are often of a strategic nature, however, it is precisely abilities such as these that play a pivotal role, at least in concurrence with predictions. On the other hand, one can well imagine that there will be individual companies in specific branches of the economy—the finance industry, for instance—where predictions will prevail, at least with regard to single board positions within these companies. As a result, it seems conceivable that some companies (like Deep Knowledge Ventures) will have an interest in appointing robo-directors (like Vital) to their boards, at least alongside human directors. Whether this is legally permissible, however, is an open question. Remember that Vital has only been treated "as a member of [the] board with observer status" by its fellow human directors, but has never fully acquired that legal status.[74]

As mentioned above, human directors may delegate decision rights to machines, but they must always keep the ultimate management function for themselves (see above, subsection III.A). Whether machines can themselves become directors, however, is a different issue, depending on a disparate set of legal rules. What is relevant here is the

---

[69] *Cf.* Y. Harari, *Homo Deus: A Brief History of Tomorrow* (Random House 2016); N. Bostrom, *Superintelligence – Paths, Dangers, Strategies* (Oxford University Press 2014).

[70] J. Senior, *Review: 'Homo Deus' Foresees a Godlike Future. (Ignore the Techno-Overlords)* New York Times, (15 February 2017), available at https://www.nytimes.com/2017/02/15/books/review-homo-deus-yuval-noah-harari.html.

[71] Agrawal, Gans and Goldfarb, *supra* note 41.

[72] *Id.*, at 15 *et seq.*

[73] More extensively, for instance, in the IBM report "The quest for AI creativity", available at https://www.ibm.com/watson/advantage-reports/future-of-artificial-intelligence/ai-creativity.html.

[74] See reference above, at note 6.

legal regime for the appointment of directors. Corporate laws usually stipulate certain requirements to be satisfied by potential directors, while some sector-specific laws add further preconditions. With respect to credit institutions and investment firms, for instance, the European Capital Requirements Directive provides that "members of the management body shall at all times be of sufficiently good repute and possess sufficient knowledge, skills and experience to perform their duties".[75] Since this provision is obviously tailored to human directors, it seems questionable whether robo-advisors could potentially fulfill these conditions. While they may indeed gather sufficient knowledge, skills and experience, the "good repute" seems particularly difficult for a machine to acquire.

On a more general level, corporate laws usually presuppose that only "persons" can become directors. Whether it is only natural persons—or also legal or corporate persons—that qualify, however, differs from jurisdiction to jurisdiction (and sometimes also within the same jurisdiction). Under UK law, for instance, at least one director of a company must be a natural person.[76] The relevant Act currently permits corporate directors to hold office in a company as additional directors, but this rule is unlikely to endure. The UK Parliament passed legislation in 2015[77] to amend the Act in order to ban corporate directors outright.[78] These amendments have only recently been brought into force, but even the previous requirement to have at least one director who is a natural person prevents a nonhuman autonomous system from taking exclusive control of a company.[79] Similar restrictions also apply elsewhere. Under German corporate law, § 6 paragraph 2 GmbHG only allows natural persons to act as directors of an LLC; the same restriction applies in stock corporations, according to § 93 paragraph 3 AktG. Similar provisions have been challenged on constitutional grounds, however, since they restrict the fundamental right of legal persons to exercise a trade or profession.[80] At present, it is difficult to predict whether the German Constitutional Court will also require legal persons to be permitted as corporate directors. Furthermore, US corporate law partially requires corporate directors to be human beings.[81] On the other hand, there are at least some states that do not stipulate the requirement for corporate officers to be human beings, but only generally

---

[75]   Art. 91 Directive 2013/36/EU on access to the activity of credit institutions and the prudential supervision of credit institutions and investment firms (Capital Requirements Directive), of June 26, 2013, OJ EU 2013 L 176/338.

[76]   Companies Act, 2006, c. 46, §§ 154, 155.

[77]   Small Business Enterprise and Employment Act, 2015, c. 26, § 87 (UK).

[78]   Companies Act, 2006, § 156A; exceptions may be provided for, however, under § 156B.

[79]   In more detail S. Bayern, T. Burri, T. Grant, D. Häusermann, F. Möslein and R. Williams, *Company Law and Autonomous Systems: A Blueprint for Lawyers, Entrepreneurs, and Regulators* 9 Hastings Science and Technology Law Journal 135, at 149 (2017).

[80]   In a recent decision, the German Constitutional Court decided that a similar provision did not violate the fundamental rights of legal persons, see Bundesverfassungsgericht [BVerfG] [Federal Constitutional Court], *Neue Juristische Wochenschrift (NJW), 2016*, p. 930. On potential consequences, particularly with respect to § 6 para. 2 GmbHG *cf.* M. Gehrlein, *Leitung einer juristischen Person durch juristische Personen?* Neue Zeitschrift für Gesellschaftsrecht (NZG) 566 (2016).

[81]   *See, e.g.,* Delaware General Corporation Law Section 141(b) ("The board of directors of a corporation shall consist of one or more members, each of whom shall be a natural person") and California Corporations Code Section 164 ("'Directors' means natural persons designated

refer to "persons".[82] In these states, a legal entity, if represented by one of its authorized officers, could at least serve as an officer of a corporation. Other jurisdictions are less restrictive, allowing legal entities to have a seat on a corporate board of directors.[83]

In cases such as these, or those in which legal entities are at least allowed to serve as corporate officers, autonomous artificial intelligence systems would be able to take such a position if they qualified as a legal entity. This qualification, however, is in turn the subject of intensive debate—consider the recent discussion on the introduction of "e-persons" at the European level,[84] as well as the long continuing debate among legal philosophers on the personhood of artificial intelligence.[85] Yet, recent comparative work has shown that at least some jurisdictions offer possibilities for the creation of company structures that might provide functional and adaptive legal "housing" for artificial intelligence and autonomous systems.[86] If a suitable legal framework is chosen, robots may therefore indeed be appointed as "true" legal directors. Many national corporate laws, however, restrict that possibility, and so far no single robot has been reported to effectively be acting as a director in this legal sense. But, due to both technological progress and regulatory

---

in the articles as such or elected by the incorporators and natural persons designated, elected or appointed by any other name or title to act as directors, and their successors").

[82]   *Cf., e.g.*, Delaware General Corporation Law Section 142(a) and California Corporations Code Section 312(a); different, however, is the Model Business Corporation Act, which provides in its Section 8.40(b) that "the board of directors may elect individuals to fill one or more offices of the corporation", and specifies in Section 1.40(13) that "'Individual' means a natural person".

[83]   One example is Liechtenstein, *cf.* Art. 180 para. 1 Personen- und Gesellschaftsrecht (PGR); in more detail International Monetary Fund, "Liechtenstein: Detailed Assessment Report on Anti-Money Laundering and Combating the Financing of Terrorism", IMF Country Report No. 08/87, 2008, p. 24, available at http://www.imf.org/en/Publications/CR/Issues/2016/12/31/Liechtenstein-Detailed-Assessment-Report-on-Anti-Money-Laundering-and-Combating-the-21775.

[84]   European Parliament (Committee on Legal Affairs, Rapporteur: Mady Delvaux), Report with recommendation to the Commission on Civil Law Rules on Robotics, 2015/2103 (INL), 27 January 2017, at para. 59: "Calls on the Commission, when carrying out an impact assessment of its future legislative instrument, to explore, analyze and consider implications of all possible legal solutions, such as: . . . f) creating a specific legal status for robots in the long run, so that at least the most sophisticated autonomous robots could be established as having the status of electronic persons responsible for making good any damage they may cause, and possibly applying electronic personality to cases where robots make autonomous decisions or otherwise interact with third parties independently".

[85]   In this sense already L. Solum, *Legal Personhood for Artificial Intelligences* 70 North Carolina Law Review 1231 (1992). *Cf.* also the lively debate in Germany: G. Teubner, *Elektronische Agenten und große Menschenaffen: Zur Ausweitung des Akteurstatus in Recht und Politik* 27 Zeitschrift für Rechtssoziologie 5 (2006); M.-C. Gruber, "Was spricht gegen Maschinenrechte?", in J. Bung and S. Ziemann (eds.), *Autonome Automaten* (Beck 2015) 191; L. Philipps, "Gibt es ein Recht auch für ein Volk von künstlichen Wesen, wenn sie nur Verstand haben?", in *Festschrift für Arthur Kaufmann* (C.F. Müller 1989) 119, at 119–26.

[86]   S. Bayern, T. Burri, T. Grant, D. Häusermann, F. Möslein and R. Williams, *Company Law and Autonomous Systems: A Blueprint for Lawyers, Entrepreneurs, and Regulators* 9 Hastings Science and Technology Law Journal 135 (2017); see also (with respect to US corporate law): S. Bayern, *The Implications of Modern Business-Entity Law for the Regulation of Autonomous Systems* 19 Stan. Tech. L. Rev. 93 (2015); *id., Of Bitcoins, Independently Wealthy Software, and the Zero-Member LLC* 108 Nw. U. L. Rev. 1485, 1495–1500 (2014).

competition between jurisdictions, it does not seem inconceivable that this might change in the not-too-distant future.

V.   THE SUITABILITY OF CORPORATE LEGAL STRATEGIES FOR ROBO-DIRECTORS

If any national corporate law permits robots to be appointed as directors, an entirely new set of questions will arise. Corporate law will face the fundamental question of whether the legal strategies that it has developed for human agency relationships are still suitable for robots acting as agents. In fact, the same question becomes relevant whenever machines take decisions in agency relationships—for instance, when robo-advisors take investment decisions—[87]and similar issues also arise when management decisions are simply delegated to directors. But when robots legally act as directors, the anatomy of corporate law itself threatens to become dysfunctional, and its legal strategies are therefore most provocatively called into question.

More precisely, such dysfunctionality can take two possible different forms. Some legal strategies are likely to miss the mark, while others are likely to become redundant. On the one hand, the incentive strategy is doomed if robo-directors follow different incentives than human directors. Even if it is difficult to speculate about the potential incentives for artificial intelligence at the present stage of its technological development, these respective differences do not seem unlikely. Since machines cannot become insolvent, for instance, it is questionable as to whether they would try to avoid personal liability as much as humans. Liability regimes (and the liability of directors in particular) could therefore turn out to be largely ineffective if machines do not suffer financial loss.[88] On the other hand, a pay-for-performance regime, which pays agents for successfully advancing their principal's interests, is unlikely to serve its purpose if artificially intelligent machines neither earn money nor work towards the objective of doing so. On the other hand, such machines will be less inclined to divert corporate assets, opportunities or information for personal gain. In the same vein, a breach of their fiduciary duty of loyalty is unlikely.[89] More generally, in the world of robo-directors, the legal rules on the conflicts of interest faced by directors would lose significance, inasmuch as robots do not make decisions based on personal interest.

The interests and incentives of artificial intelligence, it should be added, depend on their respective coding and machine learning. Since it is possible to program computers to avoid personal financial loss or to maximize personal profit, one can envisage robo-directors with implemented loss aversion or implemented risk appetite. As opposed to humans, such character traits are not natural for robots, however: all depends on their codes and their algorithms. Furthermore, robo-directors can be programmed to comply

---

[87]   *Cf.* F. Möslein and A. Lordt, *Rechtsfragen des Robo Advice*, Zeitschrift für Wirtschaftsrecht (ZIP) 793, at 801 *et seq* (2017).

[88]   Similar considerations have been made with respect to criminal sanctions, *cf.* G. Hallevy, *Liability for Crimes Involving Artificial Intelligence Systems* (Springer 2014) 212 *et seq*.

[89]   On that duty (and its functions) in general, for example, F. Easterbrook and D. Fischel, *The Economic Structure of Corporate Law* (Harvard University Press 1996) 90–93.

with all applicable legal rules.[90] Yet, they are not necessarily programmed in this manner. Their fundamental difference to human directors therefore stems from the fact that the future rule compliance of robo-directors is much more easily foreseeable from the outset, namely through a straightforward analysis of their code and algorithm. This difference, in turn, is likely to affect the legal strategies that corporate law can apply to robo-directors. Whereas ex-post strategies (such as the control of directorial behavior by way of directors' duties) will presumably lose significance, ex-ante strategies will conversely gain importance.[91] For instance, robo-specific appointment requirements may well emerge as the regulatory strategy of choice. In particular, such rules could include a requirement for respective algorithms and codes to safeguard for rule-compliant behavior. This shift from ex-post to ex-ante regulatory strategies would involve various far-reaching changes for the whole anatomy of corporate law. Firstly, its specific rules on directors' behavior will effectively be transferred from the law into algorithmic codes. Secondly, the abstract control of these algorithms will largely replace the concrete control of situation-specific behavior. Thirdly, entirely different enforcement mechanisms will be required, simply because the control of algorithms requires a comprehensive technical know-how that can neither be expected from shareholders, nomination committees or supervisory boards, nor from courts specializing in corporate law. The control of algorithms by state agencies has already been postulated in other contexts.[92] In the realm of corporate law, however, a similar approach would seem to endanger private autonomy and entrepreneurial flexibility, which are so fundamental within this area of law. The development of suitable legal strategies for robo-directors will therefore become a crucial challenge for future corporate law debates.

VI. CONCLUSION

With the rapid development of artificial intelligence, the corporate world is about to enter a period of exponential change. In a recent large-scale survey by the World Economic Forum's Global Agenda Council on the Future of Software and Society, which aimed to predict the dates on which game-changing technologies will become mainstream, nearly half of the respondents expect the first artificially intelligent machine to be on the board of directors of a business as early as 2025.[93] This technology-driven change will partly be

---

[90] *Cf.* H. Eidenmüller, *The Rise of Robots and the Law of Humans*, 25 Zeitschrift für Europäisches Privatrecht (ZEuP) 765 (2017), at p. 775: "Robots can be programmed to conform to rules but they cannot follow rules".

[91] Similar, with respect to robo-advisors and their fiduciary duties: F. Möslein and A. Lordt, *Rechtsfragen des Robo Advice* Zeitschrift für Wirtschaftsrecht (ZIP) 793, at 802 *et seq* (2017).

[92] See, for instance, J. Kroll, J. Huey, S. Barocas, E. Felten, J. Reidenberg, D. Robinson and H. Yu, *Accountable Algorithms* 165 Univ. of Penn. L. Rev. 633 (2017); see also the contributions presented at the international conference on "Governing Algorithms", which took place 16–17 May 2013 at New York University, see http://governingalgorithms.org; reprinted in the special issue of 41 Science, Technology & Human Values (2016), pp. 3 *et seq.*

[93] World Economic Forum's Global Agenda Council on the Future of Software and Society, "Deep Shift – Technology Tipping Points and Societal Impact", Survey Report, September

influenced by the framework of corporate law, but will also itself inevitably influence the well-functioning of corporate law.

After having explored some fundamentals about corporate bodies and the functions of corporate law, we have seen that artificial intelligence is most likely to be employed at the level of corporate boards, where the most complex corporate decisions need to be taken. We then determined that directors are allowed to delegate decision rights to artificial intelligence, but that various restrictions apply. Human directors must always maintain the ultimate management function for themselves; they also need to generally oversee both the selection and activities of robots, algorithms and artificial intelligence devices. More specifically, they will have to ensure that these systems are stable, that they do not cause fundamental management errors, and that their decisions comply with the applicable laws and regulations. On the other hand, we have seen that under certain circumstances, directors can inversely be required to obtain assistance from artificial intelligence. Corporate law requires directors to act on an informed basis. If artificial intelligence has superior information processing capabilities, this duty may ultimately develop into the duty to obtain predictions made by such devices. However, the courts only scrutinize the decision of directors as to how much effort they have put into the gathering and processing of information in exceptional cases. As long as the use of artificial intelligence is not widespread with respect to business decisions, the duty to delegate information processing to such devices is therefore unlikely to be established. In the long run, however, the rapid development of artificial intelligence may even give rise to the question of whether artificial intelligence can not only assist, but even replace, human directors. The legal admissibility of such a replacement depends on the rules governing the appointment of directors. According to many jurisdictions, these rules require directors to be "natural persons". Some jurisdictions are less restrictive, allowing legal entities to have a seat on corporate boards. If corporate law also offered possibilities for the creation of company structures that provide legal housing for artificial intelligence, these devices might indeed be able to be appointed as directors in the legal sense. Consequently, corporate law will face the fundamental question as to whether the legal strategies designed for human agency relationships are also suited to robo-directors. We have seen that some of these strategies are likely to either miss the mark or to become redundant if robo-directors act on different incentives to human directors. Since those incentives depend on the algorithms of robo-directors, the legal strategies of corporate law will change. They will focus on the ex-ante control of algorithms instead of the ex-post control of directorial behavior. If state agencies are entrusted with that control, then this shift has the potential to undermine private autonomy and entrepreneurial freedom. Designing legal rules for robots in the boardroom is therefore a delicate task, and it is likely to affect the anatomy of corporate law in a very fundamental way. After all, corporate law is not only highly relevant for the use of artificial intelligence in corporations; it will also need to be adapted to the challenges posed by that technology.

2014, available at http://www3.weforum.org/docs/WEF_GAC15_Technological_Tipping_Points_ report_2015.pdf, at p. 21.

SOURCES

Statutes

Codice Civile (Italian Civil Law Code) – CC.

Obligationenrecht (Swiss Obligation Law Code) – OR.

Wertpapierhandelsgesetz (German Law on Securities Trading) – WpHG.

Aktiengesetz (German Stock Corporation Act) – AktG.

Gesetz über Gesellschaften mit beschränkter Haftung (German Act on Limited Liability Companies) – GmbHG.

Directive 2013/36/EU on access to the activity of credit institutions and the prudential supervision of credit institutions and investment firms (Capital Requirements Directive), of June 26, 2013, OJ EU 2013 L 176/338.

Small Business Enterprise and Employment Act, 2015.

Companies Act, 2006.

Delaware General Corporation Law.

California Corporations Code.

Model Business Corporation Act.

Personen- und Gesellschaftsrecht (Law on Persons and Corporations of Liechtenstein) – PGR.

Cases

Dairy Containers Ltd v NZI Bank Ltd [1995] 2 NZLR 30.

Re Bally's Grand Derivative Litigation, 23 Del. J. Corp. L. 677.

Re Barings plc (No. 5) [1999] 1 BCLC p. 489.

Re RJR Nabisco, Inc. Shareholders Litigation, [1989] WL 7036.

Smith v van Gorkom, 488 A.2d 858.

Dorchester Finance Co. v Stebbing, [1989] BCLC 498.

Land Credit Co of Ireland v Lord Fermoy, [1870] LR 5 Ch App 763.

Selangor United Rubber Estates Ltd. v Cradock (no 3), [1968] 2 All ER 1073.

BGE 108 V 199 (Decision of the Swiss Federal Court).

Lagunas Nitrate Co v Lagunas Syndicate, [1899] 2 Ch 392.

Bundesverfassungsgericht [BVerfG][Federal Constitutional Court], *Neue Juristische Wochenschrift (NJW)*, *2016*, p. 930.

Index

Printed and bound by CPI Group (UK) Ltd, Croydon, CR0 4YY

28/10/2024

14581369-0001